Get Instant Access
to thousands of editors and agents @

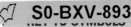

WRITERSMARKET.COM

Register now and save $10!

Sure, you already know **Novel & Short Story Writer's Market** is the essential tool for selling your fiction. And now, to complement your trusty "writer's bible," subscribe to WritersMarket.com (see back for more information) for **$10 off the regular price!**

WRITERSMARKET.COM

Your Writer's Market
Favorites Folders

Search Markets
Agent Q&A
Market Watch
Spotlight Market
Recent WM Changes
Submission Tracker

Encyclopedia
Web Resources
Free Newsletter
Expert Advice

Writersdigest.com
Writing Workshops

FAQs
Contact Us
Customer Help
Home

SEARCH WRITER'S MARKET

Choose a type of publication to narrow your search or use the form below to search all of WritersMarket.com.

BOOK PUBLISHERS
Large corporations to literary houses, industry-related publishers and more.

LITERARY AGENTS
Writers' business representatives, selling book outlines or manuscripts and negotiating deals.

CONSUMER MAGAZINES
Magazines for the general public or a specific niche.

TRADE MAGAZINES
Publications fostering professionals in a particular occupation or industry.

SCREENWRITING MARKETS
Scripts for TV, movies and business or educational purposes.

PLAYWRITING MARKETS
Stage plays and drama publishers.

CONTESTS & AWARDS
Competitions and awards for all types of writing.

GREETING CARDS & GIFT IDEAS
Includes greeting cards as well as gift items such as postcards and calendars.

SYNDICATES
Newspaper, magazine or radio syndicates distributing columns, articles, cartoons or other written material.

NEWSPAPERS
Local, regional and national newspapers.

ONLINE CONSUMER PUBLICATIONS
Online Publications for the general public or a specific niche of consumers.

ONLINE TRADE PUBLICATIONS
Online Publications intended only for professionals in a particular occupation or industry.

Search by Market Name: [ ]
Search by Market Location: [All]
Search by Area Code: [ ]
Search by Website URL: [ ]

updated DAILY

As a purchaser of **2007 Novel & Short Story Writer's Market**, get a $10 discount off the regular $29.99 subscription price for WritersMarket.com. Simply enter coupon code **WM07MB** on the subscription page at www.WritersMarket.com.

www.WritersMarket.com
The Ultimate Research Tool for Writers

Tear out your handy bookmark
for fast reference to symbols and abbreviations used in this book

---

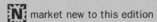
S0-BXV-893

KEY TO SYMBOLS

N market new to this edition

A publisher accepts agented submissions only

C publisher of graphic novels and comics

Ø market is closed to submissions

◐ actively seeking new writers

◑ seeks both new and established writers

◖ prefers working with established writers, mostly referrals

◉ only handles specific types of work

🏆 award-winning market

🍁 Canadian market

🌐 market is located outside of the U.S. and Canada

★ imprint, subsidiary or division of major book publishing house (in book publishers section)

$ market pays (in magazine sections)

● comment from the editor of *Novel & Short Story Writer's Market*

ms, mss manuscript(s)

SASE self-addressed, stamped envelope

SAE self-addressed envelope

IRC International Reply Coupon, for use in countries other than your own

(For definitions of words and expressions relating specifically to writing and publishing, see the Glossary in the back of this book.)

— TEAR ALONG PERFORATION —

2007 NOVEL & SHORT STORY WRITER'S MARKET KEY TO SYMBOLS

 N market new to this edition

 A publisher accepts agented submissions only

 C publisher of graphic novels and comics

 market is closed to submissions

 actively seeking new writers

 seeks both new and established writers

 prefers working with established writers, mostly referrals

 only handles specific types of work

 award-winning market

 Canadian market

 market is located outside of the U.S. and Canada

imprint, subsidiary or division of major book publishing house (in book publishers section)

$ market pays (in magazine sections)

● comment from the editor of *Novel & Short Story Writer's Market*

ms, mss manuscript(s)

SASE self-addressed, stamped envelope

SAE self-addressed envelope

IRC International Reply Coupon, for use in countries other than your own

(For definitions of words and expressions relating specifically to writing and publishing, see the Glossary in the back of this book.)

TEAR ALONG PERFORATION

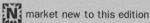
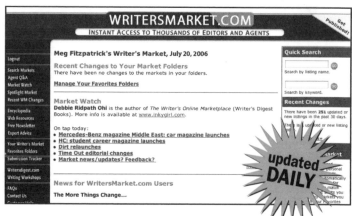

2007
Novel &
Short Story
Writer's
Market®

Lauren Mosko, Editor

Michael Schweer, Assistant Editor

WRITER'S DIGEST BOOKS
CINCINNATI, OH

Complaint Procedure

If you feel you have not been treated fairly by a listing in *Novel & Short Story Writer's Market*, we advise you to take the following steps:

- First try to contact the listing. Sometimes one phone call or a letter can quickly clear up the matter.

- Document all your correspondence with the listing. When you write to us with a complaint, provide the details of your submission, the date of your first contact with the listing, and the nature of your subsequent correspondence.

We will enter your letter into our files and attempt to contact the listing. The number and severity of complaints will be considered in our decision whether or not to delete the listing from the next edition.

If you are a publisher of fiction and would like to be considered for a listing in the next edition of *Novel & Short Story Writer's Market*, send a SASE (or SAE and IRC) with your request for a questionnaire to *Novel & Short Story Writer's Market*—QR, 4700 East Galbraith Road, Cincinnati OH 45236.

Editorial Director, Writer's Digest Books: Jane Friedman
Managing Editor, Writer's Digest Market Books: Alice Pope

Writer's Digest Books Web site: www.writersdigest.com.
Writer's Market Web site: www.writersmarket.com.

2007 Novel & Short Story Writer's Market. Copyright © 2006 by Writer's Digest Books. Published by F+W Publications, 4700 East Galbraith Road, Cincinnati, Ohio 45236. Printed and bound in the United States of America. All rights reserved. No part of this book may be reproduced in any form or by any electronic or mechanical means including information storage and retrieval systems without written permission from the publisher, except by reviewers who may quote brief passages to be printed in a magazine or newspaper.

Distributed in Canada by Fraser Direct
100 Armstrong Avenue
Georgetown, ON, Canada L7G 5S4
Tel: (905) 877-4411

Distributed in the U.K. and Europe by David & Charles
Brunel House, Newton Abbot, Devon, TQ12 4PU, England
Tel: (+44) 1626 323200, Fax: (+44) 1626 323319
E-mail: postmaster@davidandcharles.co.uk

Distributed in Australia by Capricorn Link
P.O. Box 704, Windsor, NSW 2756 Australia
Tel: (02) 4577-3555

ISSN: 0897-9812
ISBN-13: 978-1-58297-430-9
ISBN-10: 1-58297-430-6

Cover design by Kelly Kofron/Claudean Wheeler
Interior design by Clare Finney
Production coordinated by Robin Richie
Photographs © Frédéric Cirou/PhotoAlto

Attention Booksellers: This is an annual directory of F+W Publications. Return deadline for this edition is December 31, 2007.

Contents

CRAFT & TECHNIQUE

GETTING PUBLISHED

FOR MYSTERY WRITERS

FOR ROMANCE WRITERS

RESOURCES

From the Editor

© Donna Poehner

When I became editor of this book (with no small measure of wonder and glee), I set two immediate goals for myself:

I must summon some nerve, rework one of my half-baked stories, and submit it for publication. In order to be a credible fiction-publishing expert, I knew I needed to open myself to the same risks and heartbreaks you do. So I did it, just as I pledged in this very space a year ago. It was terrifying and, even after 10 + revisions, I'm still unsure of my story. (Is it skillfully crafted? Will it elicit emotion from readers? Have I totally embarrassed myself?) I'm now anxiously awaiting my first rejection, and I couldn't be more excited.

The satisfaction of laboring over art—sacrificing (desperately needed) sleep hours, handing your work to a friend who lovingly shreds it (more than once), experiencing an epiphany on the drive home from work, watching characters evolve and the story unfold just when you feel like giving up—makes fear of rejection seem inconsequential. Even if this story is never published, I learned so much about myself while creating it. (But if someone wants to publish it, no argument here.)

I must cultivate an understanding of and appreciation for the genres. Before I began putting this edition together, I was a monogamous reader: literary fiction was my one and only. I'd never curled up with a romance or fantasy novel. I'd never flirted with a SciFi magazine. I had a one-volume stand (okay, two volumes, I swear that was it) with a graphic novel. I hadn't been infatuated with a detective since Mssr. Poirot. It was downright prudish. I had to get busy.

I didn't consciously intend for this edition to focus on the genres, but I certainly wanted to expand our coverage of them. However, as I began receiving this year's interviews from my trusty freelance writers (thanks again, everyone), I was stunned by the genre bending and blending going on in almost all of the writers' work. The trend watchers at the conferences I attended this year also stressed that genre blending is hot. (Good news for those of you whose work has been criticized for not fitting neatly into a particular category.) Magical realism, paranormal romance, technothrillers, graphic novel memoirs . . . the possibility for hybrids is endless.

Editors are always looking for fresh ideas, so why not broaden the scope of fiction you read—and then try incorporating new styles or elements into your work? Be daring, but don't force anything you're not passionate about, since (as I learned) you have to live with your story for dozens of drafts.

Cheers to another writing year and to your dozens of drafts.

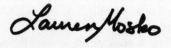

Lauren Mosko
lauren.mosko@fwpubs.com
Watch for www.nsswm.com.

You've Got a Story

So What Now?

To make the most of *Novel & Short Story Writer's Market*, you need to know how to use it. And with more than 600 pages of fiction publishing markets and resources, a writer could easily get lost amid the information. This quick-start guide will help you wind your way through the pages of *Novel & Short Story Writer's Market*, as well as the fiction publishing process, and emerge with your dream accomplished—to see your fiction in print.

1. Read, read, read. Read numerous magazines, fiction collections and novels to determine if your fiction compares favorably with work currently being published. If your fiction is at least the same caliber as what you're reading, then move on to step two. If not, postpone submitting your work and spend your time polishing your fiction. Writing and reading the work of others are the best ways to improve craft.

For help with craft and critique of your work:

- You'll find advice and inspiration from best-selling authors and top fiction editors in the The Writing Life section, beginning on page 5.
- You'll find articles on the craft and business aspects of writing fiction in the Craft & Technique section, beginning on page 47, and in the Getting Published section, beginning on page 59.
- If you're a genre writer, you will find information in For Mystery Writers, beginning on page 88; For Romance Writers, beginning on page 103; For Science Fiction/Fantasy & Horror Writers, beginning on page 117; and For Graphic Novel & Comics Writers, beginning on page 133.
- You'll find Contest listings beginning on page 470.
- You'll find Conference & Workshop listings beginning on page 506.

2. Analyze your fiction. Determine the type of fiction you write to best target markets most suitable for your work. Do you write literary, genre, mainstream or one of the many other categories of fiction? There are magazines and presses seeking specialized work in each of these areas as well as numerous others.

For editors and publishers with specialized interests, see the Category Index beginning on page 588.

3. Learn about the market. Read *Writer's Digest* magazine (F + W Publications, Inc.); *Publishers Weekly*, the trade magazine of the publishing industry; and *Independent Publisher*, which contains information about small- to medium-sized independent presses. And don't forget the Internet. The number of sites for writers seems to grow daily, and among them you'll find www.writersmarket.com and www.writersdigest.com.

4. Find markets for your work. There are a variety of ways to locate markets for fiction.

The periodicals sections of bookstores and libraries are great places to discover new journals and magazines that might be open to your type of short stories. Read writing-related magazines and newsletters for information about new markets and publications seeking fiction submissions. Also, frequently browse bookstore shelves to see what novels and short story collections are being published and by whom. Check acknowledgment pages for names of editors and agents, too. Online journals often have links to the Web sites of other journals that may publish fiction. And last but certainly not least, read the listings found here in *Novel & Short Story Writer's Market*.

Also, don't forget to utilize the Category Indexes at the back of this book to help you target the right market for your fiction.

5. Send for guidelines. In the listings in this book, we try to include as much submission information as we can get from editors and publishers. Over the course of the year, however, editors' expectations and needs may change. Therefore, it is best to request submission guidelines by sending a self-addressed stamped envelope (SASE). You can also check each magazine's and press' Web site, which usually contains a page with guideline information. And for an even more comprehensive and continually updated online markets list, you can obtain a subscription to www.writersmarket.com by visiting the site or calling 1-800-448-0915.

6. Begin your publishing efforts with journals and contests open to beginners. If this is your first attempt at publishing your work, your best bet is to begin with local publications or those you know are open to beginning writers. Then, after you have built a publication history, you can try the more prestigious and nationally distributed magazines. For markets open to beginners, look for the ❑ symbol preceding listing titles. Also, look for the ◉ symbol that identifies markets open to exceptional work from beginners as well as work from experienced, previously published writers.

7. Submit your fiction in a professional manner. Take the time to show editors that you care about your work and are serious about publishing. By following a publication's or book publisher's submission guidelines and practicing standard submission etiquette, you

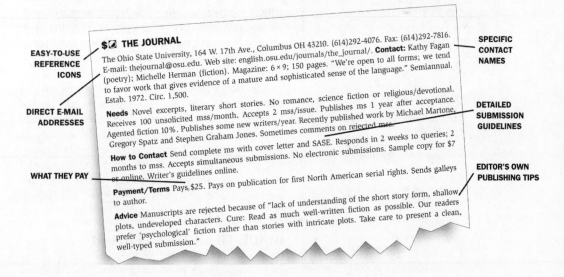

EASY-TO-USE REFERENCE ICONS

DIRECT E-MAIL ADDRESSES

WHAT THEY PAY

$☑ THE JOURNAL
The Ohio State University, 164 W. 17th Ave., Columbus OH 43210. (614)292-4076. Fax: (614)292-7816. E-mail: thejournal@osu.edu. Web site: english.osu.edu/journals/the_journal/. **Contact:** Kathy Fagan (poetry); Michelle Herman (fiction). Magazine: 6 × 9; 150 pages. "We're open to all forms; we tend to favor work that gives evidence of a mature and sophisticated sense of the language." Semiannual. Estab. 1972. Circ. 1,500.

Needs Novel excerpts, literary short stories. No romance, science fiction or religious/devotional. Receives 100 unsolicited mss/month. Accepts 2 mss/issue. Publishes ms 1 year after acceptance. Agented fiction 10%. Publishes some new writers/year. Recently published work by Michael Martone, Gregory Spatz and Stephen Graham Jones. Sometimes comments on rejected mss.

How to Contact Send complete ms with cover letter and SASE. Responds in 2 weeks to queries; 2 months to mss. Accepts simultaneous submissions. No electronic submissions. Sample copy for $7 or online. Writer's guidelines online.

Payment/Terms Pays $25. Pays on publication for first North American serial rights. Sends galleys to author.

Advice Manuscripts are rejected because of "lack of understanding of the short story form, shallow plots, undeveloped characters. Cure: Read as much well-written fiction as possible. Our readers prefer 'psychological' fiction rather than stories with intricate plots. Take care to present a clean, well-typed submission."

SPECIFIC CONTACT NAMES

DETAILED SUBMISSION GUIDELINES

EDITOR'S OWN PUBLISHING TIPS

2007 NOVEL & SHORT STORY WRITER'S MARKET KEY TO SYMBOLS

N   market new to this edition

A   publisher accepts agented submissions only

Ø   market is closed to submissions

◐   actively seeking new writers

◑   seeks both new and established writers

◉   prefers working with established writers, mostly referrals

◎   only handles specific types of work

🏆   award-winning market

🍁   Canadian market

🌐   market located outside of U.S. and Canada

★   imprint, subsidiary or division of larger book publishing house (in book publishers section)

C   publisher of graphic novels or comics

$ market pays (in magazine sections)

●   comment from the editor of *Novel & Short Story Writer's Market*

ms, mss manuscript(s)

SASE self-addressed, stamped envelope

SAE   self-addressed envelope

IRC   International Reply Coupon, for use in countries other than your own

(For definitions of words and expressions relating specifically to writing and publishing, see the Glossary in the back of this book.)

Find a handy pull-out bookmark, a quick reference to the icons used in this book, right inside the front cover.

can increase your chances that an editor will want to take the time to read your work and consider it for publication. Remember, first impressions last, and a carelessly assembled submission packet can jeopardize your chances before your story or novel manuscript has had a chance to speak for itself. For help with preparing submissions read "The Business of Fiction Writing," beginning on page 79.

8. Keep track of your submissions. Know when and where you have sent fiction and how long you need to wait before expecting a reply. If an editor does not respond by the time indicated in his market listing or guidelines, wait a few more weeks and then follow up with a letter (and SASE) asking when the editor anticipates making a decision. If you still do not receive a reply from the editor within a reasonable amount of time, send a letter withdrawing your work from consideration and move on to the next market on your list.

9. Learn from rejection. Rejection is the hardest part of the publication process, but it happens to every writer, and every writer needs to learn to deal with the negativity involved. On the other hand, rejection can be valuable when used as a teaching tool rather than a reason to doubt yourself and your work. If an editor offers suggestions with his or her rejection slip, take those comments into consideration. You don't have to automatically agree with an editor's opinion of your work. It may be that the editor has a different perspective on the piece than you do. But you may find that the editor's suggestions give you new insight into your work and help you improve your craft.

10. Don't give up. The best advice for you as you try to get published is be persistent and always believe in yourself and your work. By continually reading other writers' work, constantly working on the craft of fiction writing, and relentlessly submitting your work, you will eventually find that magazine or book publisher that's the perfect match for your fiction. *Novel & Short Story Writer's Market* will be here to help you every step of the way.

GUIDE TO LISTING FEATURES

On page 3 you will find an example of the market listings contained in *Novel & Short Story Writer's Market* with call-outs identifying the various format features of the listings. (For an explanation of the symbols used, see the sidebar on this page.)

Bret Lott

Spanning the Transom, from Jewel
to The Southern Review

© Rick Rhodes

by Kelcey Parker

When Bret Lott decided he "wanted to have a go" at a writing career, he bought a copy of *Writer's Market* and began to submit his fiction. He was rejected 597 times. But he was also accepted, publishing more than 60 stories and essays in literary journals. He has also written 11 books, including the novel *Jewel*, which was selected for Oprah's Book Club in 1999. Now Lott finds himself on the other side of the transom, as the editor of *The Southern Review*.

The secret to Lott's success as both the editor of a prestigious journal and best-selling Oprah Book Club author might be found in the following quotes from his memoir on the craft of writing, entitled *Before We Get Started* (Ballantine, 2005): "the word means everything" and "irony's necessary partners, then, are hope and love." Lott is as interested in issues of craft, in choosing the right word, as he is in addressing matters of the human heart.

Lott practices his philosophy in life as well. Shortly after he moved to Baton Rouge and took over at *The Southern Review*, Hurricane Katrina struck. He wanted to do something to help the victims, especially the displaced students, and he sent an e-mail "to about 50 friends" describing his idea. He was amazed by the response: "We ended up raising almost $54,000 for the Hurricane Katrina Student Relief Fund, mainly through $8 donations, in return for which we donated the summer issue. The offices here turned into a kind of assembly line for weeks. We ended up mailing out around 4,000 copies to people around the world—people from every state in the Union and 18 different countries. But it was quite gratifying to be a clearing house for so much generosity."

Even as things return to normal at the journal, Lott remains busy. A new novel, *Ancient Highway* (Random House), will be published later this year, coinciding with the paperback release of his recent collection, *The Difference Between Women and Men: Stories*. Here Lott talks about *The Southern Review*, the power of fiction, and the literary marketplace.

KELCEY PARKER is an assistant professor of English at Indiana University South Bend. She has a Ph.D. in Literature and Creative Writing from the University of Cincinnati. Her fiction has appeared in *Indiana Review, Image, Sycamore Review* and other journals. She studied with Bret Lott in the 2005 Prague Summer Program.

You recently took over the helm of a mighty literary ship. Why was it important to you—personally and professionally—to be the editor of *The Southern Review*?

There are plenty of reasons. Number one is the fact of this being, as you have said, "a mighty literary ship." *The Southern Review* was a journal I learned about when I was in undergrad classes way back in the '70s, and the notion of being handed the wheel of such an important journal proved too good of an opportunity to pass up. That may sound a bit self-serving, but my wife Melanie put it this way: "This is a once in a lifetime opportunity." Truer words were never spoken.

Next is that I wouldn't be here today without my life in the literary journals. My first publications, those short stories published so many years ago, were the beginning points of my career as an author, and so being able to help another generation with their own careers is my way of helping give back to the journals what was given to me so long ago.

Finally, I simply love literary journals. I subscribe to several, and when they arrive in my mailbox at home I feel a little like it's my birthday or Christmas, and here are these gifts of new stories and poems and essays I get to read. There's nothing like holding in your hand a new issue of a journal—and to be able to put one together, to send it out, to have others enjoy that feeling, is a grand part of why I do this.

You've already made noticeable changes to *The Southern Review*. What changes will you continue to make? What do you think is important to preserve?

Certainly it's important that we keep up the quality of the pieces we publish; that cannot and will not change. But adding the artwork and redesigning the pages doesn't make a

journal any better, just perhaps a little more readable, a little easier on the eye. The real changes we are making involve more space given to nonfiction. I am a huge fan of the essay and want more of that work given over to our pages. (Our spring 2006 was an all-nonfiction number.)

I also want to feature more reviews of books. I think a journal ought to be a place where books get more attention than they do in the media at large; to this end, I want to feature more smaller reviews than have been published here in the past. I also want to offer up a forum for readers—a place something akin to "Letters to the Editor"—so that we at the journal can hear from our readers, and readers of our journal can hear from each other. We are also beginning an award series that will feature the best poem, story and essay published in the prior volume year in our pages.

I know all of this sounds rather pedestrian, but I really don't want to change the fact that the important thing we are doing when reading a journal is *reading*; I don't want to head off into packaging CDs of new music with each issue, or jamming in too many graphics, or including rub-on tattoos of famous writers. A journal is a book of stories and poems and essays and artwork meant to allow a reader, in a world too full of itself—a world distracted to distraction, if I can paraphrase T.S. Eliot—to sit down and breathe deeply and appreciate the written word on the page.

What surprises—good or bad—have come your way since taking over the magazine?

Most surprising has been the quality of submissions. There are just too many good things we receive to allow me to publish them all. I don't mean to sound rosy and wild-eyed, but it's true: There's a lot of good writing out there.

Another thing that has surprised me is so very many people think *The Southern Review* is basically a regional publication, sort of like a literary *Arizona Highways* or *Yankee Magazine*. Wrong. The journal is an international compendium of the best writing happening out there, and so it's sort of my mission to make sure people understand that we are not looking for work that features what Mamaw said to Papaw inside the trailer just before he kilt the pig.

You have already published several first-time writers. What makes an unsolicited manuscript grab your attention?

The Southern Review has forever been committed to publishing new writers, and the works I am most proud of publishing aren't things from the known names of our day but those by brand new people. That's the most exciting stuff out there.

An unsolicited manuscript really makes me sit up and take notice when the writer has given me a fully formed voice and vision from the first sentence. This goes for poetry and stories and essays alike. There is no way for me to qualify or quantify this. It simply occurs, and my blood begins to run a little more quickly, and my heart beats a little more quickly because of that, and I find myself suddenly Elsewhere: I will be in a moment of recognition within a line of a poem, or a sentence of a story or essay; I will be taken Elsewhere, a moment that, in recognizing it, will make me recognize the next moment and the next, revealing to me that vision and voice I so strongly desire to experience.

The root of the word *authority* is *author*, and I want to find in the work I read an authority over the words the author chooses and the order in which he or she places them that gives me the confidence to trust we are going somewhere—somewhere meaningful—and going there now. Sorry not to be able to be more specific, but if I were to quote lines that do this, I would suddenly be derivative: It is up to each writer to discover his or her own authority. This is the one thing that cannot be taught: authority.

The title story of *The Difference Between Women and Men* ends with an image of a small woman holding a giant piece of furniture. The marital tension shifts to "this business of the armoire, and where to put it." This final, suspended moment seems to speak to the power of short fiction as a form, the way a story—like an impossibly heavy object we suddenly find ourselves holding—demands all of our attention.

I love the short story because of its ability to work under your skin in a way a novel can't. Novels are big hairy things that can kind of wander around a bit, that can park for a while and mosey and all kinds of things. But a story is a kind of pinprick, a kind of jewel outside of its setting, a kind of diamond in the palm of your hand that you can appreciate for its simplicity. I know I'm allowing my metaphors to run riot here, but it's difficult to say, save for the fact there is a purity to the short story form, a kind of guerilla tactic to it that makes it all the more surprising and memorable.

The Writing Life

In a *Washington Post* review of your latest story collection, Carolyn See asks, "If not for Bret Lott, who would tell us about the RC Cola salesman, the food brokers, the small-time insurance agents, the couples who are about six steps away from being homeless, if they stop to think about it, except that they don't have the time to stop and think about it?" She points to these class issues as the special value of your work. Do you agree?

I guess I do agree that these class issues are always present in my writing, though it's not anything I think about when I sit down and begin to see the world I am going to write about. Thinking about that sort of thing while you write would be like a jazz musician thinking about the scales while he reels out a beautiful line he hadn't ever played before.

As for the "special value" in my work, I would hope it's not so much the class issues that are indeed there, but that the stories I write make readers see the inherent value of these lives that so very often go unnoticed. The fact that Carolyn See, having read the stories, asks the question she does is the very essence of the "special value" I would hope my work has. I want readers to see the lives of other people as being valuable in and of themselves and to have to pause and think of RC salesmen and financially troubled couples as being people. An editor who rejected my first novel told me the most important thing she got out of reading *The Man Who Owned Vermont* was that she would never see the people who work in a grocery store—the salesmen and clerks and cashiers and stockers—the same way again. Although she didn't take the book, I still look back at that moment with the greatest sense of fulfillment. The story made someone see people around her, whom she had previously ignored, as being worthy of her attention; she was seeing them now with empathy.

NATIONAL BESTSELLER

A Song I Knew by Heart

"An affecting novel about the slow workings of forgiveness and redemption."
—MAUREEN CORRIGAN, National Public Radio

BRET LOTT
AUTHOR OF *Jewel* AND *The Difference Between Women and Men*

Your novel *A Song I Knew By Heart* (Random House, 2004) is a retelling of the biblical Book of Ruth, and your short story "Rose" offers an alternate perspective (and plot twist) on Faulkner's "A Rose For Emily." What drew you to do retellings—and to these stories in particular?

I chose to retell the story of Ruth because I have always loved that story and been intrigued by it. It's perhaps the most intimate portrait of love (beyond Song of Solomon and the story of Christ) to be found in the Bible, and it's about a mother-in-law and daughter-in-law, a relationship that, in our modern times, is rife with enmity and jokes. In the retelling of it, I really didn't give myself any ground rules; rather, I wanted to see what made these people tick and gave myself the license to go where the story wanted to go. As a result, the history of Naomi and of Ruth was, for me, the greatest discovery: I found out who they were and why they would act as they did. Anyone familiar with the Bible story (and it only takes about 10 or 15 minutes to read it) will see that there are plenty of changes: a streamlining of Naomi's children, the lack of Ruth's having a baby, etc. I simply wanted to find out what the nature of that love was, rather than re-enact it.

As for the story "Rose," I wrote that wanting to know the story from the point of view of Miss Emily. So the common denominator between these two efforts at retelling stories is a curiosity on my part: I want to *know* what makes people tick, and both the novel and that story were the results of that effort, of my trying to get into the heads of other people. A writer is only worth his curiosity, by the way. Unless you are trying to discover through your writing what you don't yet know, you will simply be rehashing what you already *do* know, which is boring and repetitive and doesn't make for much fun.

As someone who writes literary fiction, and as someone who has also been on *Oprah*, what is your understanding of the relationship between fiction and the marketplace?

There isn't one. John Grisham started by selling his first novel out of the trunk of his car; Tom Clancy's *The Hunt for Red October* was first published by the Naval Institute Press; Stephen King wrote his first works in the closet of his trailer. Even though we want to lump these people together as being writers whose writing lives are dictated by the marketplace, no one can doubt they were first writing what they wanted to write, and their hearts and minds were on fire with the stories they wanted to tell. The marketplace found *them*, because they wrote first—and kept writing.

Having said that, of course the marketplace matters, but I think it should matter only after you have written what it is your heart and mind have given you to write. No one should write a book because they want to be a famous writer and/or a best-selling author. No one. But a book has to be sold, and so writers need, once the book is written, to do the legwork of finding agents and editors who publish work that is simpatico with the work they have written. It's work we don't want to think about, but work we have to do—and hence a publication like the one you are holding in your hands right now, Dear Reader!

Related to questions of literary fiction and Oprah, Laura Miller said the following about Jonathan Franzen's snub of Oprah: "What makes Franzen's gaffe so unfortunate is that *The Corrections* is the kind of book that bridges the gap between high- and middlebrow readers, between people who like brainiac puzzle novels and those who want stories of family and emotional life." What is your take on the issue of highbrow and middlebrow fiction and its readers?

What I find puzzling about the comment is its entire omission of *lowbrow*. When I think highbrow versus middlebrow, I automatically think—I mean this—that I want to reach the lowbrow reader (whatever that is) *because he's the one pointedly left out of the equation*. Highbrow means smart to me, middlebrow means not so smart, and hence lowbrow means dumb. But I believe in my heart that we ought not see the world as being anything but *browed*. To think of the world as being split into certain groups of people who are more intelligent or sophisticated or experienced than another—that is, to decide one group is better

The Difference Between Women and Men

[STORIES]

AUTHOR OF A SONG I KNEW BY HEART AND JEWEL

BRET LOTT

The Writing Life

than another (which is, I think, what Franzen was at core saying about his own work, that it was for a certain group of people who were smarter than the rest of us)—is to think that one group of people is more valuable than another, and I do not for a moment believe that. I do not have a take on middle- versus highbrow readers, because I am too busy trying to tell the story of the one person about whom this novel I am writing is being written. I just want to tell that person's story; let the divisions between readers be damned.

You make similarly bold statements against irony and elitism in *Before We Get Started*, encouraging writers "to have hope, to look out at the world in love in order to discover it anew in whatever way you can, in whatever form you can . . . risking all the while cheese, corn, schmaltz." One risk you take in that book is revealing your own stumblings and failures—something many writers prefer to keep to themselves. Why did you choose this approach?
Because I think there are a lot of mystified people out there who think writing is some sort of romantic wizardry that has behind it a code of secrets that can be mastered. But it's simply not true, and having taught for 20 years students who, year in and year out, believe the hype about how drunk one has to be or what coffee house you have to be seen at or which clove cigarette you must smoke in order to be a writer, I decided I'd just tell the simple truth of the matter: In order to write, you have to be disciplined enough to do it. Creativity comes through discipline, I teach my students. That's it, and that message is what I wanted to get out through the book on writing.

Why does literature matter today?
Because we are in a world that is swamped with itself, and with words on itself, and with people whispering and shouting in our ears about what we should believe and why we should believe it. I am not talking here about religion, but about the media, those word traffickers who already know what they know and hence, as I said earlier, aren't about discovering anything at all, but only enjoying that shouting. Literature allows us time to think, to contemplate, to be quiet and, as I said, to breathe deeply. That's why it matters.

Other Works by Bret Lott

In addition to the books pictured in this article, Bret Lott has written:
- *A Dream of Old Leaves* (Viking, 1989)
- *Fathers, Sons and Brothers: The Men in My Family* (Harcourt, 1997)
- *How to Get Home* (John F. Blair, 1996)
- *The Hunt Club* (Villard, 1998)
- *Jewel* (Atria, 1991)
- *The Man Who Owned Vermont* (Viking, 1987)
- *Reed's Beach* (Atria, 1993)
- *A Stranger's House* (Viking, 1988)

Judy Budnitz

*The Fantastic, the Familiar and
the Funny Things that Happen Between*

by Joseph Bates

J udy Budnitz is a fantastic writer, for which she makes no apologies. Indeed, in *Flying Leap* (Picador, 1998) and *Nice Big American Baby* (Knopf, 2005), two highly praised collections, and in *If I Told You Once* (Picador, 1999), an elegiac debut novel that won the Edward Lewis Wallant Book Award and was short-listed for the UK's Orange Prize, Budnitz has created fiction which fits the very definition of the fantastic as offered by the theorist Tzvetan Todorov in *The Poetics of Prose*. It is a literature that creates for its reader a moment of "hesitation" when the extraordinary "occurs not in a marvelous world but in an everyday context, the one most familiar to us."

Budnitz's work is full of such moments, where the extraordinary and the everyday, the familiar and the unfamiliar, share the same space—to stunning, sometimes sidesplitting, and often startling effect. In "Dog Days," a family in a post-apocalyptic suburb finds that a man in a dog suit has taken up on their front stoop. In "Skin Care," a young woman goes off to college, contracts leprosy, and quickly begins to fall apart. And in "Where We Come From," an expectant mother from an unnamed country, having heard that children born in the United States are automatic citizens, tries to sneak across the border to give birth. The plan—and the pregnancy—ends up lasting four long years.

Budnitz's talents for blending, bending and subverting genre—from the speculative and the supernatural, from the gothic and the grotesque, all re-formed with a shrewd sense of humor—have naturally caused those critics trying to describe her work a moment of hesitation, too. She has been called a fabulist and a magical realist; an absurdist, satirist and dark humorist; a surrealist and a proponent of the "new unrealism"; a provocateur and an experimentalist. And then there was the *Newsweek* review of *Nice Big American Baby* in which the reviewer, praising the collection, warned those who might suggest Budnitz write realistic fiction: "She already does."

"I have a hard time classifying my own work," Budnitz admits, "so it's not surprising that other people have a hard time too. I don't think my work fits easily into a category. Maybe it has some aspects of magic realism, but that term has mystical and cultural connotations that I don't think my work shares. My work isn't exactly horror, or science fiction, but I certainly borrow from those genres. I like the fact that my writing isn't easily classified or described; it prevents people from forming preconceptions and expectations about it."

JOSEPH BATES is a recent graduate of the University of Cincinnati, where he earned a Ph.D. in Literature and Creative Writing. His short fiction has appeared in *The South Carolina Review*. He is currently at work on a collection and a novel.

Here Budnitz discusses the forms and functions of fantastic literature, the role of subjectivity in storytelling, and the writer's obligation to write the story that wants to be written.

It seems the fantastic is enjoying a resurgence given the success of such authors as yourself, George Saunders and Aimee Bender, to name a few. To what do you attribute this resurgence? Does the fantastic allow for examinations of the real world and its dilemmas that traditional realism doesn't?

Has there really been a resurgence? I feel like fantastic writing, in one form or another, has always had a presence. Everything from Joseph Heller to Louise Erdrich to Bret Easton Ellis to Haruki Murakami could fall into the category. Maybe particular styles have their moments of popularity, though.

And yes, I do think that writing in the fantastic realm does allow you to do things that you can't do when you confine yourself to reality. You're free to exaggerate, extrapolate, take things to their extremes. You can be allegorical or symbolic in a way that doesn't really work in realistic fiction.

Your short fiction has been honored in both *The O. Henry Awards* ("Flush") and *The Year's Best Fantasy and Horror* ("Hershel"). For you, is there a distinction to be made between literary fiction and what is generally considered genre fiction?

Nice Big American Baby

"These stories glow. Brilliant, unpretentious, and addictive . . . Budnitz is in a class by herself."
—Matthew Pearl, author of *The Dante Club*

Judy Budnitz

Reprinted with permission from Knopf.

I was at a panel discussion recently where a writer said that the main purpose of genres was to give bookstores a way to organize their shelves. I wish genre fiction and "literary" fiction weren't so distinctly divided, both on the shelves and in their packaging and design. It reinforces preconceptions and makes it easier for people to dismiss whole categories of books. I admit I do it myself: In a bookstore I'll walk right by the sci-fi and mystery and horror shelves, even though I know there's plenty of stuff there I'd like if I just gave it a chance.

In his review of *Nice Big American Baby* for *The New York Times*, Tom Perrotta makes the claim that you are, at heart, a "political writer." Do you feel the artist has a social or perhaps even a moral responsibility? How would you define your own ideas about the relationship between the social and the aesthetic?

I admit I was really surprised at the way nearly all reviews of *Nice Big American Baby* referred to it as "political." I guess I should have expected that response—the book has "American" in the title, after all—but I didn't. I don't think this book is so different from my others. I've always liked to write about basic social issues and moral questions. But I try to think about them on an intimate level, on the level of how one person treats another. The term "political," to me, implies something at once more specific (applying to specific regimes and historical events) and more general (doling out heavy-handed opinions about big overarching issues) than what I'm trying to do. I don't want to preach at readers. My goal is to present familiar situations in an unfamiliar way and allow readers to draw their own conclusions about what is right, what is wrong, what the reader himself would do in such a situation.

Of course, I can't deny that the book reflects a lot of what's been going on in our country and in the world during the past few years. And a lot of what I've absorbed I seem to have, consciously or unconsciously, worked into the stories.

I think an author's responsibility to a reader is simply to entertain and distract and transport. If, along the way, you can get a reader to mull over some moral questions, or see their world in a fresh way, then that's a bonus.

Is there a danger in writing the fantastic in that the reader naturally assumes allegory or satire? In other words, the reader looks for a way to "recuperate" a fantastic text by saying, "It's a story about blank, but it's *really* about . . ."?
Yes, that's certainly a consequence of writing the way I do—rather than simply accepting a story on face value, readers are quick to assign symbolic meaning. But I don't think that's a bad thing. I like the way readers tend to assign meaning to my stories. In a funny way, it makes my job easier. I don't really have to think about the "deeper meanings" myself. I can just write the story I want to write, and readers can project onto it as much or as little as they want to. Each reader's experience is unique, personal, depending upon the experiences and associations they bring to it.

You've described your writing process as similar to the one proposed by Flannery O'Connor in "Writing Short Stories," wherein you start with a first line or a conceit and then allow the story to naturally develop and even surprise you. Are there times when this approach takes you somewhere you didn't intend or perhaps even want to go? Does there come a point where you exercise authority over a story, or do you always trust the story to lead?
Whenever I've tried to seize the reins, the results always feel forced and artificial. Trusting my initial instincts invariably turns out to have been the right way to go. I remember writing one of my first stories, "Dog Days," and realizing, about halfway through, that the story was headed in a very bleak direction. At that moment, I hesitated and wondered if I should try to steer the story to a happier conclusion. But the dark ending, the one I stuck with, was the one that made sense, for every character and for the situation. It was the ending I'd been unconsciously writing towards all along.

If your writing process allows for happy accidents and surprise, how do you approach the more structured work of revision?
Revision used to be very hard for me. I did very minimal revisions on the stories in my first book, not because I was writing perfect first drafts, but because I tended to make stories worse the longer I picked at them. Over the years I think I've developed (slightly) better editing skills. I did extensive revisions on many of the stories in my latest book. In most cases, the revisions were less a matter of trying to fiddle around with what was there, and more about cutting, cutting, cutting, rethinking, rewriting, going in completely new directions. An important step for me was learning the patience to put a story aside for months, or even years, and then coming back to it with fresh eyes.

Did you find your approach to writing significantly changed when working on your first novel, *If I Told You Once*?
Writing my first novel was a big learning experience for me. Initially, the sheer length seemed really daunting, but as I was writing I began to realize all the ways in which novels are

actually more flexible, more forgiving than stories. Stories are all about tightness, efficiency. One weak spot or false moment in a story can ruin the whole thing. But with a novel you have more room, more time. You can slow down, go off on tangents. I think you can get away with some slow or shaky bits in a novel, as long as the overall structure is sound—as long as there's some sort of draw for the reader, whether it's an engaging character, a suspenseful plot, or simply an entertaining voice telling the story. Short stories are like a first date—you've got to impress right away, and if you blow it, you've failed and don't get a second chance. A novel is more like a marriage—the participants will forgive some bad moments because they're in it for the long haul.

At the end of _If I Told You Once_, Sashie believes she has discovered the "truth" of her mother's life: the documents that claim Ilana and Shmuel are brother and sister, the Fabergé egg and museum portrait that lead her to believe her family aristocracy. At every turn, the incontestable "proof" is misleading, thus showing the "fairy tales and magic" Ilana has spent the book spinning to be, if not the truth, at least _truer_. Is this, in a sense, a defense not only of the subjectivity of storytelling but of the fantastic—that the evidence of the physical world is often deceptive and that the unusual is more usual than one might think?

Yes, that's a valid interpretation. I remember when I was working on that novel I was thinking about Holocaust deniers, and how they insist that all evidence of the Holocaust (photographs, records) is forged. I was thinking about that and wondering what kind of evidence would be _more_ reliable than photographs and records. Perhaps the observations of a first-hand witness would be considered the most reliable evidence. And yet at the same time, one person's account of an event is the most subjective version possible.

I think when I wrote that novel I was also trying to illustrate how there's no way to know an absolute, absolutely objective reality. Everything we know is filtered through our point of view; there's no way to escape our own heads. Everything is subjective. So one person's version of the truth can be completely different from another person's version, and both can believe whole-heartedly in their own versions and stake their lives on them. That's what I was striving to illustrate with the different narrators and differing versions of the same events. And when truth becomes subjective, the distinction between reality and fantasy becomes meaningless; it all becomes the same subjective experience.

The subjectivities of storytelling are celebrated throughout your work, not only in those "modern fables" which seem to evoke the haunted forests of the Old World but in distinctly American terms. Your story "Yellville," for instance, seems very much a love letter to forms of the American fantastic, such as the tall tale and the yarn. How much of the fantastic is a matter of style, of _how_ the story is told, rather than subject?

I'm glad you noticed that about "Yellville." With that story I was definitely thinking about Mark Twain and the tall-tale form, and I thought it would be fun to couch a tall tale in the setting of an utterly conventional situation: bringing your boyfriend home to meet your parents for the first time.

Regarding style vs. subject—for me, it's hard to separate them. After I've finished a story, I can look back at it and say, "aha, I just wrote a contemporary story in a fairy-tale format" or "I just mixed sci-fi with suburban family drama" but when I'm in the process of writing I don't think in those terms. I just have an idea, an objective in mind, and write my way towards it, and a style and strategy sort of emerge without my consciously planning them.

***Flying Leap*, your first collection of stories, has much in common with *Nice Big American Baby*; both are full of wicked wit, striking conceits and sharp attention to language. In what ways, if any, do you see your practices, philosophies, or manners changed between the two?**

In some basic ways the two story collections seem quite similar to me. There are certain themes (birth, disease, apocalypse, the push and pull of families) that I repeatedly circle around. But my process, my approach, changed quite a bit from one book to the next. The stories in *Flying Leap* were all written in a spirit of playfulness, a kind of let's-see-what-I-can-get-away-with-*this*-time attitude. Can I write a convincing story about a man in a dog suit or a man donating his heart to his mother? It was like a game, to see how far I could push things and still keep the reader on board.

With *Nice Big American Baby*, I lost a bit of that playfulness. I felt an obligation to try to write stories that were more substantial—stories that delved deeper into a character or situation, stories that *said* something significant. I wanted to test myself by relying less on tricks and jokes and surprises. I do love those things, but I don't want them to become a crutch, an escape hatch.

if i told you once

judy budnitz

A NOVEL BY THE AUTHOR OF *FLYING LEAP*

Reprinted with permission from Picador.

Having seen two collections and a novel through to print, do you feel the publishing process has changed the way you approach your work in any sense? What have you learned from the experience that emerging writers would be wise to keep in mind?

I think the most important thing I've learned from being published is the importance of ignoring the whole publishing process when you're writing. I think it's impossible to write good fiction if you're worrying every minute "Will anyone want to publish this? Will people like it? Will they buy it? Is this story appropriate for this particular audience, or that particular market?" You have to just block all those thoughts out and concentrate on writing the story the way it demands to be written. You shouldn't think about pleasing anyone else; you should think only about doing justice to the story.

Sonny Brewer

The Importance of 'Place' and 'Home'

© David G. Spielman

by Brad Vice

Equal parts astute business man, literary guru and good-old-boy, Sonny Brewer—one of the South's most notable bookstore owners—is now one of the nation's most notable authors. For years Brewer ran Over the Transom, the premier book store in Fairhope, Alabama. Fairhope, as the name indicates, is one of the state's most serene pieces of coastal real estate.

Founded in the 19th century as a utopian colony, Fairhope today is the home of many bohemians and artists. Because of Brewer's contribution, including his bookstore's Southern Writers Reading series as well as his annual *Stories from the Blue Moon Café* anthology, Fairhope—like Oxford, Mississippi, or Chapel Hill, North Carolina—has become a town whose very name is synonymous with literature. This reputation is reinforced by the popularity of Brewer's best-selling novel, *The Poet of Tolstoy Park* (Ballantine, 2005), the story of a dying man's search for the right place to face his death. Like his protagonist, Brewer is a man whose greatest ambition is to build a home, brick by brick, word by word.

In this interview, Brewer discusses the three aspects of his literary life, as a writer, editor and bookseller.

Growing up in Alabama, were you always interested in literature?

I grew up in a house that did not have a bookshelf. There was a Bible on my daddy's bedside table to keep the devil away. Reading was at the schoolhouse and for homework. All of the stories came from somebody breathing them out into the air. Good tales were like songs that floated you up above the skinny pines and thick oak trees of Lamar County, Alabama. Got me the hell right out of there. When my feet were on the ground, they ran me through the woods and down the ravines, across pastures and down the road to Floyd McCullough's tin-roofed store, climbed me into barn lofts. Took me to the Luxapalila to go fishing for blue cats and goggle-eyed perch. My imagination was all about the outdoors.

Then my great-grandfather died, and somebody had to stay nights with my Granny. That would be me. Granny had a son, my great-uncle J—John William Estes—who'd gone off to Harvard to make a preacher man. He left behind in Granny's house books by the hundred. I had to walk the path to Granny's house before it got *good dark*, as she would say it. So, I found myself shut up inside with daylight just fading and not a damn thing to do. Of course I soon enough got into Uncle J's books. *Charlotte's Web* was the first book I read all the way

---

BRAD VICE has published fiction in *The Southern Review*, *The Georgia Review*, *The Atlantic Monthly*, *New Stories from the South*, *Best New American Voices* and other journals and anthologies.

through of my own choice. And my feet left the solid ground of those red clay hills west of Millport and I went higher and farther than I'd ever gone before. Does that make sense to you? Reading books, each time I closed one of the cursed things, I found myself dropped off at a place that was not quite back to where I'd started. Books took me away and never brought me back.

Why did you move to Fairhope, and what moved you to write about it?

I moved to Fairhope, a town, to get out of Mobile, a city. I had moved to the coast, following a woman I was married to at the time who was accepted to med school at the University of South Alabama in Mobile. Living there I felt like Bob Dylan's man: stuck. Don't get me wrong; nothing wrong with Mobile, nothing at all for the people who live there and love it. I know some who'd fight you to straighten out your thinking about their Azalea City. But I didn't feel in tune with the place. I'm going to sound like the old hippie I am when I say it's about harmony with the vibrations in a place. It was always interesting to me that both Jesus and Buddha left one place to go to another place to do their work.

Place matters a great deal to honest self-expression. And when you are in your right place, you are at home. For some people, it's where they were born and raised, the place where they spent their formative years. I think of William Faulkner in Oxford, Mississippi. For other people, that place we call home is a conscious choice. I was not at home until I came to Fairhope, Alabama. The Muse speaks to writers everywhere, but not just anywhere for every writer. It's a fact: In the meanest, most desolate and darkest corners of the shittiest places you can imagine, there's a poet and an author writing lines that are honest. They make the words ring, their characters dance, their stories live. But if I have a prayer of writing a page that's worth keeping, it's going to be set in and around Fairhope. The days are brighter and the nights are darker here. I hear the wind better here. I can see farther here. I was headed to this coastal town the first time my heart crossed the Lamar County line. I just didn't know back then where I was headed. Writers have to be in their right place to get the job done.

The Poet of Tolstoy Park is about finding a home. When did you start to work on it? How long did it take you to write?

Interesting you say that. Jinanne Verrill, the person who introduced me for my panel at last Fall's Southern Book Festival in Nashville, actually made bookmarks to hand out. She printed on the bookmarks this little poem from the novel: Down the hill the acorn rolled / until it struck a stone / stock-still it lay then / quite surprised / to find itself a home.

I began writing *The Poet of Tolstoy Park* about a month after finishing a novel called *Like Light Around a Bend in the River*, the first long work I ever completed. In drawers and boxes, in files on my computer, I had about a million unfinished things. If I thought about all the things I'd started and quit on, I'd get a headache. I wasn't really motivated to stay with a novel because I never thought I'd find a publisher. I knew the business. I knew the odds. I knew my level of skill and experience. I could write nonfiction well. Got paid by a Fortune 500 company as a writer-for-hire. I wrote press releases. I wrote speeches for vice presidents. I wrote ad copy. I wrote anything they asked me to write for $60 an hour. But fiction—that was another story, if you'll permit the pun.

Then it occurred to me to write a thinly disguised autobiographical novel, a *bildungsroman* with names of my Middle Alabama kinfolks changed to protect the guilty. My motivation to complete it was simple. I was writing it for my three children. I would tell them that if they ever became interested in the circumstances of their father's upbringing, then they could read their own copy of my novel. I'd bind one for each of them and a few more for posterity. I wrote that book over the course of about three years. When I finished it, I found I really

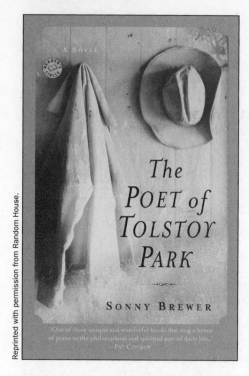

missed the late nights at the keyboard stringing scenes together into a book. It was fun to me. I don't experience the writerly angst I hear my writing friends complain about. If I did, I'd quit the game in a heartbeat.

So I got to work on something new, *Poet*. I'd written about 40 pages when my agent sold it to Ballantine Books at Random House. She called me to say she had good news and bad news. To the former: I had an offer on the table for my book, a preemptive offer of six figures. To the latter: the publisher wanted the completed manuscript by May 1. My agent was telling me this in mid-October. ''Can you write 300 more pages in nine months?'' Yes, I said, not adding that I wasn't sure the pages would be worth reading. We'd worry about that later. I finished the book in February. Let it cool for a month. Revised it in April. Turned it in on deadline. And 10 months later I held a hardcover book in my hand. The first printing sold out in 48 hours, and I found myself at age 55 a legitimate first-time novelist. The movie rights have been sold, Tom Epperson wrote the screenplay, and it really looks like filming could begin late this summer. It's all completely surreal to me.

When did you begin operating Over the Transom?

In 1997 as a used and rare bookstore with 3,000 used books that I bought for a dollar apiece with a cash advance from a MasterCard. The old man who sold me the books bought and sold used books out of his house in Fairhope. I asked him for advice. ''Two things,'' he said. ''Don't ever sell a Bible. Give them away. Don't worry about finding good books to sell. Your best books will find you.'' It was good advice that I followed faithfully, and he was right about the books coming to me. A man at a yard sale where I was buying books for 50 cents each said, ''Here, mister. Here's you another one.'' It was a first edition of *To Kill a Mocking-bird*, and I later sold the book for several thousand dollars.

Was it hard to be a businessman at the same time you were writing your book?

I couldn't make that work at all. I didn't even try for those short months I had to finish the novel under contract. I told my employee it was all his to keep afloat, that I had a book to write. On my Web site, overthetransom.com, there's an option on my home page called ''Where's the bookstore?'' The story about what happened since writing *The Poet of Tolstoy Park* is told there.

What's not told on my Web site is the very effort to get an agent and sell that first novel I spoke of writing was a last-ditch effort to save the bookstore from going bankrupt. It worked, though it wasn't *Light Around a Bend* that we sold. I'm not sure now that book will ever see the light of day. I believe it might have been a practice novel. But we'll see. It needs fixing. I can do it if I ever get jazzed to revise it. Another novel I wrote called *A Sound Like Thunder* was published by Ballantine, and I'm at work on a fourth novel, *The Tumble Inn and Sit Down Café*. My agent believes she will have an offer on that book soon.

What is your advice for aspiring writers?

I'd say there's really nothing new in this game. The shelves sag with books about how to get it done. It's all been said. I'll say it again: It's about doing the writing, endlessly, desperate to get the words right, and waiting for a shot at publication. I sat on a back porch with a buddy one time, a little after dark, on a warm, damp Alabama night. He'd just two days earlier finished tacking up new screen wire to enclose his fine porch. Had the ceiling fan turning at a lazy speed. Beers in the cooler. I sipped a Dewar's and soda. Talking was easy, our voices kind of low. All of a sudden, Paulie slaps his neck, spilling beer on his crotch. "Son of a bitch! How'd a damn mosquito get in here?" When I drew a breath and quit laughing, I told him it was easy, told him he left a hole someplace, told him Brother Skeeter spent the last two days with nothing else to do but find that one hole. Beginning writers have nothing else to do but find their hole in the publishing marketplace. You've got to be hungry for blood.

Where does your work as an editor fit into this?

My first gig as an editor was 30 years ago when I co-edited a college literary magazine, *The Southern Bard* at the University of South Alabama. The next year, I was founding associate editor of an Alabama weekly newspaper, *The Millport Gazette*, which is still in business. I'd studied journalism at the University of Alabama. Over the next several years, I was editor-in-chief of *Mobile Bay Monthly* magazine, editor and publisher of *Eastern Shore Quarterly*, editor of *Red Bluff Review*, and now I find myself working on the fifth volume of *Stories from the Blue Moon Café*.

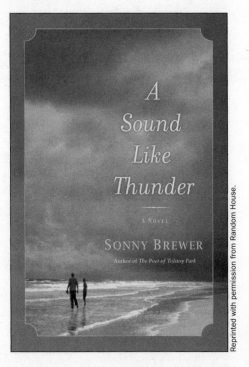

Reprinted with permission from Random House.

My position as editor of that anthology is about as crazy as the way the novel thing has worked out. While running the bookstore, I dreamed up the idea of bringing new Southern writers to Fairhope to read from their work. Just read. No panels, no workshops. I called it Southern Writers Reading. (Duh.) At the third annual such literary slugfest, it seemed like a good idea to put together a chapbook of the writers who'd participated. I asked aloud on stage if the writers in the room would throw in on such a project. Everyone said yes. There was a publisher in the audience, David Poindexter of MacAdam/Cage in San Francisco. He was in Fairhope to meet his new author Frank Turner Hollon, a local lawyer whose first book I'd published through my bookstore under an Over the Transom imprint. Frank's working on his sixth novel for MacAdam/Cage, and that half-baked notion of a chapbook turned into an on-the-spot offer from David Poindexter to publish in hardcover an anthology of Southern writing. We took him up on it, and *Stories from the Blue Moon Café* is still going strong. It's all so weird how these things have happened. That mosquito thing I talked about? It's like somebody keeps poking a hole in the screen and pointing for me to fly right on in. I mean, I've worked hard at writing all my life, and I love the work. And maybe that's it. Like Einstein said, the harder I work, the luckier I get.

Aimee Bender

The Art of Dreaming Outrageous Things

© David Bender

by Meg Leder

G rowing up with a father who was a psychologist and a mother who was a dancer, Aimee Bender witnessed and internalized the perfect balance of the fearsome and gorgeous energy that can come from bodies, as well as the lucid and logical way we make sense of and relate to that energy. The intersection of the beauty that comes from mess and the beauty that comes from order are at play in her work, which has been described as "daringly original" (*Publishers Weekly*) and "both ethereal and surprisingly weighty" (*Los Angeles Times*).

Bender is the author of two story collections, *The Girl in the Flammable Skirt* (Doubleday, 1998) and *Willful Creatures* (2005), and the novel *An Invisible Sign of My Own* (2000). Her stories have appeared in *Granta, GQ, Story, Harper's* and *The Antioch Review*, among others. Author Heidi Julavits observes, "Aimee Bender scrapes up the plain gunk of our world and transforms it into the menacing, hilarious, magical stuff of myths."

Here, Bender talks about her own blending of myth and realism, of making the abstract and dreamlike tangible.

How did you find your way to the world of magical realism? Was it a fascination with fairy tales when you were a child, a desire to work outside the limits of realism, something else?

I loved fairy tales as a kid, and it took me a while to be introduced to the magic realists, but when I did start reading [Italo] Calvino, and [Isabel] Allende, and [Gabriel] Garcia Marquez, I felt this amazing relief, that this beautiful, complex, enchanting work existed. That I did not have to give up that joy of reading as an adult. That I could try to write like that too.

In so many of your stories, the world of everyday objects becomes strange and human-like: a pumpkin-headed couple giving birth to an eyeless iron, a woman haunted by a group of baby-like potatoes. Where do these connections come from, that is, how does a writer start to think of a group of potatoes as surrogate children?

You know, I believe so strongly in dreamlike imagery, and it's all there to be used. We are all dreaming outrageous things each night. So for me, it's a matter of just putting in the time, and eventually I'll start making up stories, and some are very ordinary, and some are bizarre.

MEG LEDER is an editor in New York City. She is also the co-author of *Boys of a Feather: A Field Guide to North American Males* (Perigee).

Even though these stories deal with worlds very different from ours, the emotions are very intimate—heartbreaking even. Is there an advantage to exploring the mess of being human through these surreal images?

I find it easier to be honest, with images that are far from my actual life. Somehow, in that space, I find some kind of safety that lets me be darker, or more blunt, than I might be if I felt I had to portray a person exactly how they are, which feels too daunting.

You said at a reading recently that it's easier to sustain magic in the short story form than in novel form. Do you think this has to do with the reader's finite willingness to suspend disbelief? Or is something else at work?

I actually think that it's a point-of-view issue; for me, the magic often comes from a more distant third-person voice, a tale-teller's voice, and when I get closer to character, the third (or first) person changes the texture some-

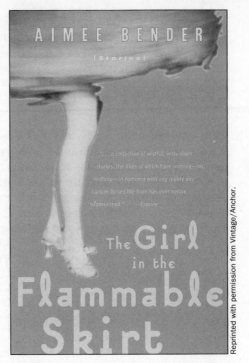

what, and then I lose my handle on that tale-telling feel. It's something I'd like to try again, and I admire [Garcia Marquez'] *100 Years of Solitude* or a book like Saramago's *Blindness* so much for precisely that reason—they sustain the tale-teller's voice and also get closer to characters and are able to build a long, sustaining narrative.

In an interview with N. M. Kelby, you said language comes "from two places— the mindful place (land of revision) and the soupy place (land of first draft)." In an interview with Ryan Boudinot, you said the more "you loosen the reins [when writing], the more resonant the work can be." How do you tap into that soupy place and loosen the reins? How do you maintain that writing state?

I fail a lot. I'm in my own way a lot. But I restrict my writing to two hours a day, and then I just try to keep myself interested, and often I don't. But with regular work, with putting in the time, eventually stuff starts to happen. I really believe that. I'm also a big believer, as a writing teacher, in writing exercises, because without the pressure of "story," students get looser and their sentences become more interesting, more vital.

How do you know it's time to move into that mindful place of revision?

Usually once something's down on the page, then I can work with that. But when I'm generating the material, I have to push it along, I can't stop and rethink each sentence.

Much of your writing philosophy seems to be built upon the importance of intuition, of trusting where the writing leads you and working until the story feels "right." How did you develop that intuition?

I'm not sure, but it's a good question. Lately I've been noticing how people ask, at readings: How do you know when a story's done? And I can't really answer them very well. I'm not sure how I know; sometimes I don't know. Usually I can tell when I'm picking at a story, like picking at a scab. Or, I can tell when it feels murky, or undercooked, like I'm not allowing the story itself to come forward. I'm not sure how I developed that, except creativity was really encouraged when I was a kid, so there was an underlying belief that I alone was the main authority about my drawing, or my song or my story, and I think it comes down to that, in many ways. Knowing, for yourself, what you think about your own work. Not to say that I'm never baffled. That happens too.

In *An Invisible Sign of My Own*, the heroine Mona's second grade students have a class segment called Numbers and Materials, for which they bring in everyday representations of numbers. In your short story "Fruits and Words," a woman sells words made out of their defining material. There seems to be something similar in the way numbers and words become tangible objects characters can hold. Is this what writing does? Puts a shape and texture and smell to things that are normally abstract?

Yes, I think words are at once abstract and tangible—the word *bird* is not a bird, but it evokes a bird, and it has a sound and shape all its own that is totally un-birdlike. But I rely on words, as objects. I like certain words and dislike others, and naming things, putting names (or numbers) to feelings, ideas, objects, is often deeply comforting to me.

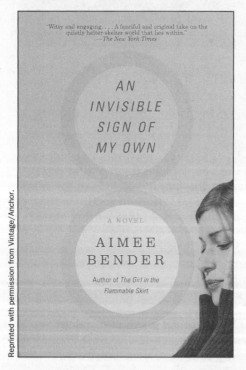

Your father was a psychiatrist and your mother was a dancer. It seems to me these two mindsets represent much of what's happening in your writing. That duality also seems to represent your ideas on writing—that fluid place of creativity and that mindful place of revision. Does this seem like a fair lens through which to view your work?

Thanks. I really think their careers influenced mine so much; I think it's a very fair lens. My father's work is highly verbal but also all about the workings of the unconscious, and my mother would talk about her dances in process as I was growing up and I always found that so interesting—how one day she'd have no idea where it was going, and the next day she'd come home and say, "we figured something out today. I turned out the lights and they danced in the dark and it was all new." That was thrilling to hear.

You have described the ability to make metaphors as a sixth sense in humans. Do you think any writer can be taught to hone that ability, or does it come more naturally to some?

I think it can be encouraged, that's for sure. But I do think some people will be wilder/more open with their ideas than others, and I don't know what that stems from. That said, I think a little encouragement goes a long way.

Describe your writing process. Do you have any writing rituals you ascribe to? Do you share your writing with any pre-publication readers?

I write two hours a day, six days a week. That routine has helped me immeasurably. I have tons of bad writing days, but with that system, they are just part of the whole. I have a few friends, writers and nonwriters, who I share work with, who are incredibly valuable to me as readers, and then my agent and editor will give me notes as the work becomes more of a full book.

What's the best piece of writing advice you've ever received?

Write what you're interested in.

Reprinted with permission from Random House.

The Invisible Hand of Art

What's Guiding Your Writing?

by Steve Almond

You've all heard of The Invisible Hand of the Market, the theory that unseen, and presumably benevolent, forces guide the free market and keep the great engine of capitalism running smoothly.

Somewhat less renowned is *The Invisible Hand of Art*, a theory of my own devising, which holds that an unseen (and often masochistic) force guides writers and keeps their creative energies from flagging.

I am not referring here to blind faith in one's own talent—this will bring you nothing but misery—but a sustained determination to convert the sorrow and beauty of the world into prose, to recognize where you have fallen short, and to do the dogged, unsung work of revision. The question is not one of execution (how we write), but of intention (why we write).

What I want to suggest in this essay is that those who wish to create must, to the greatest extent possible, allow themselves to follow The Invisible Hand of Art even—and especially—when The Invisible Hand of the Market bids otherwise.

I realize all this sounds annoyingly lofty, not to mention unpractical, so let me offer a few concrete examples.

Straight out of college, I took a job at a daily paper in El Paso, where I spent much of my time reviewing concerts. There were three essential genres of bands that passed through El Paso: heavy metal, country and Menudo. (Menudo was on a two-week loop.) To a 21-year-old itinerant narcissist, it all felt quite glamorous.

A month into my stay, an editor at *The Patriot Ledger* in Quincy called to tell me he had an opening for a town reporter. I had applied to *The Patriot Ledger* previously. The paper had been my top choice, because it was known as a feeder to the *Boston Globe* and the *Philadelphia Inquirer*. In the concentric world of daily journalism, it felt like a ticket to the Bigtime. So, after a few days of appropriately histrionic post-adolescent anguish, I took the job. But the decision didn't sit right.

A week later, I called the editor in Quincy and told him—to his amazement, to my own—that I was going to stay put.

I had no real idea why I'd made this decision at the time. I knew only that I felt a sense of dread about moving back East. But I can see, in retrospect, that The Invisible Hand of Art

---

STEVE ALMOND is the author of the story collections *My Life in Heavy Metal* (Grove Press, 2002) and *The Evil B.B. Chow* (Algonquin, 2005), the nonfiction book *Candyfreak* (Algonquin, 2004), and the novel *Which Brings Me to You*, co-authored with Julianna Baggott (Algonquin, 2006).

was guiding me, steering me away from the predictable path of daily journalism, toward the more extreme, idiosyncratic experience of living in El Paso.

A few years later, I got offered a job working at a free weekly paper in Miami. This was back in the early '90s. The notion that I would leave an established daily to join a weekly—particularly one that was given away for *free*—struck my editor as tragically misguided. She couldn't understand why I would throw my future away.

After all, I'd worked hard to distinguish myself in El Paso. My prose was the epitome of what passes for sparkling in the world of daily journalism: breezy, glib, laden with puns. It was only a matter of time until the *Dallas Morning News* came calling. Heck, the guy I replaced had moved on to *USA Today*, where he had interviewed Eric Clapton *on a private jet*.

The problem was this: I'd started to read fiction. It had begun to occur to me, however dimly, that a life spent in search of the perfect pun might not be my final ecstasy.

It took me another two years before I worked up the nerve to start writing short stories myself and another two after that before I decided to apply to MFA programs.

This decision was again met by general bewilderment. I can remember sitting at breakfast with the owner of the Miami paper and informing him, somewhat timidly, that I was leaving his employ to go back to school.

''What?'' he said. ''You want to write *books*?''

He uttered this question with a ferocious distaste, as if I had announced my desire to pursue a career involving rubber hoses and enema bags.

You can expect this sort of reaction when you heed The Invisible Hand of Art. Despite the tremendous freedoms Americans enjoy, we're a culture that prizes professional status, material comfort, and job security above all else. A career in the arts provides none of these things. It pretty much guarantees humiliation, if not poverty.

This would be a fair characterization of my MFA years.

It only got worse after graduation. I wrote scads of stories, most of which were actually (unbeknownst to me) outlines. I collected rejection slips. I joined the vast academic underclass known as adjunct professorship. Most nights, the menu board read: *cheap pasta*. It was a cold era, marked by calamitous affairs.

I wrote a story loosely based on one such affair, called ''The Body in Extremis,'' but the piece struck me as too much like a journal entry, so I put it in a drawer, where it remained for a year. I wound up sending the story to the editor of a small anthology about doomed love, who took it. Then, a few months later, I sent the story to an editor at *Playboy*. The fiction editor eventually wrote to accept the story, and I had to inform her (gulp!) that it had already been taken.

Why did I do this obviously very stupid thing?

Because some part of me knew the story was the most honest thing I'd written—and knew, more importantly, that the path to progress lay in pursuing this more pained, confessional style.

The key point to recognize here is that our

"I got a real sugar rush and cluster headache reading this bittersweet book by Steve Almond-joy, the sugar daddy himself. I won't sugar coat it—this book is one sweet treat."
—AMY SEDARIS

candy freak

A JOURNEY THROUGH THE CHOCOLATE UNDERBELLY OF AMERICA

"Steve Almond is the Dave Eggers of food writing."
— JOHN THORNE

by Steve Almond

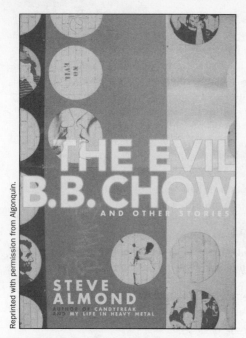

most profound resistance to The Invisible Hand of Art isn't external, but internal. Our best writing is often the stuff that causes us the most shame and anxiety, the stuff we're eager to avoid setting down on paper, or exposing.

Nonetheless, I eventually began writing more stories like "The Body in Extremis" and sold a first collection of stories. Like every other first-time author, I suffered the illusion that my life would suddenly be transformed. I was *someone* now. The roses would salute when I walked past. And so on.

Instead, I found myself reading to audiences of half a dozen and returning home to work on a novel that—a year and a half later—my agent politely declined to represent. So I'd been canned, essentially. I was a story writer who couldn't write novels. I was an unwanted commodity.

I fell into a serious funk. And, as invariably happens when I fall into a funk, I began eating candy by the pound. Almost as a lark, I set to work on a nonfiction book called *Candyfreak*. The first few chapters went out to four different agents, all of whom passed. The book seemed scattered. There were too many candy books on the market at the moment. And so on.

I considered dropping the project at this point. That was certainly the course recommended by The Invisible Hand of the Market. As nutty as it sounds, the only reason I kept going was because of this unseen force, The Invisible Hand of Art, which knew (even if I didn't yet) that the book was worth pursuing.

I wish I could report that the finished manuscript met with immediate acclaim. It did not. In fact, all five of the editors at the major houses I submitted to turned it down. They either didn't have time to read the book, or the marketing committee had concerns, or they worried about where Barnes & Noble would place such an odd book.

Once again, The Invisible Hand of the Market was giving me the finger.

I kept sending it out. And I did finally find an editor who got it—Kathy Pories at Algonquin.

When I mentioned the offer to one of the New York editors, he advised me not to go with a small press. "You'll ruin your career," he said, quite earnestly.

My point is this: Had I listened to any of the folks who doubted the book, I never would have finished *Candyfreak* or gotten it out into the world. And I would never have bothered to send out my second collection of stories, *The Evil B.B. Chow*, either. I would, in all likelihood, be sitting around trying to write that great big novel after which the market seems to pant so incessantly. And I would be miserable.

But, you see, good writing does not arise from focus groups. It is not produced to meet a particular economic demand. It arises from a single person who is able to document her deepest fears and wishes, whether in a fictive disguise or otherwise. It is a set of personal decisions, often wildly idiosyncratic, and necessarily organic.

And this is the reason that I've never hired another agent. I simply don't want the voice of commerce whispering, however sweetly, in my ear.

I am not suggesting that writers should live in some sort of anti-material haze, ignoring such pressing matters as their next meal and how it might get paid for. But I am suggesting that the only lasting salvation for a writer resides in the transmission of love, the evocation of mercy, the radical desire to make people feel more than they did before reading your words.

My advice to aspiring writers is not to fret over finding an agent, but to spend as much of your time as possible thinking about the characters in the books you're reading and in the stories you're writing. Place these emotional experiences at the center of your life. Trust The Invisible Hand of Art to do the rest.

This is the only way I know, really, to withstand the cycles of solitude and rejection that mark any worthwhile literary career.

Almondfreak

Like what you read? Want more?
- *My Life in Heavy Metal: Stories* (Grove, 2002)
- *Candyfreak: A Journey Through the Chocolate Underbelly of America* (Algonquin, 2004)
- *The Evil B.B. Chow and Other Stories* (Algonquin, 2005)
- *Which Brings Me to You: A Novel in Confessions,* co-authored with Julianna Baggott (Algonquin, 2006)

Still not satisfied? You'll find excerpts, candyfreak reader testimonies, a music zine, and updates from the book tour circuit at www.stevenalmond.com.

Darcy Cosper

*Countering Convention, or a Wolf
in Bridesmaid's Clothing*

© John Pilson

by Brad Vice

Darcy Cosper has everything most of us want. She writes book reviews for the notable publications DailyCandy.com and *Bookforum* and is the editor of the online edition of the literary journal *Swink*. Her debut novel, *Wedding Season* (Three Rivers Press, 2004)—in which a young woman "allergic to marriage" finds herself obligated to attend 17 weddings in six months and is forced to take a hard look at herself, her convictions and her own relationship—received more than a dollop of commercial and critical success, including a Paramount movie deal. How could one but envy Cosper, a "chick lit" darling with an Evelyn Waugh wit? Who could be unhappy with yet another hip-funny-sexy story of female empowerment in a subgenre at its peak?

Yet some readers and critics expressed confusion—some irritation, and some downright vitriol—about the novel's open suspicion of the book's very subject: marriage. Why the grumble? Aggrieved traditionalists wrote seething Amazon reviews clearly irked by the less-than-storybook ending. Others with more highbrow pretensions rolled their eyes at a chick lit novelist whose model was more Edith Wharton or Oscar Wilde than Helen Fielding.

Born in Los Angeles but raised in the mountains of Oregon in a community of "latter-day pioneer-gypsy-artisan types who lived off the grid," Cosper herself is a strange mix of winking fashion-conscious self-deprecation and tomboy rebel wit. Like her protagonist Joy Silverman, Cosper is a chic anti-heroine, or perhaps even a mustache-twirling villain in drag, who hopes that both literature and love can get at something deeper than the mere genre expectations demanded by most readers of romantic fiction.

When did you start writing? And when specifically did you start work on *Wedding Season*?

Apparently I started writing around the time I learned how to write—I wrote my first poem when I was five or six and didn't stop writing poetry until I was out of college and switched to journalism. Sadly, my poetry didn't seem to improve much from that first effort. I started writing fiction in the mid-'90s, I think. I was living in New York, and it was at the suggestion of Elizabeth Sheinkman, a friend of mine who was, at the time, an editorial assistant at Knopf and who would go on to become a literary agent and to represent me. We were out one night, we'd probably had too much to drink, and she told me that she liked the way I talked and I should try writing fiction. So I did. About a year later, when Elizabeth had started at

---

BRAD VICE has published fiction in *The Southern Review*, *The Georgia Review*, *The Atlantic Monthly*, *New Stories from the South*, *Best New American Voices* and other journals and anthologies.

the Elaine Markson Agency, I brought her several stories I'd written. She sent them around and I had the pleasure of being rejected by some of the most prestigious magazines in the country—but she was undeterred and suggested I write a novel.

Around that time chick lit was newly ascendant—Bridget Jones, *Sex and the City*—and I found its popularity completely baffling: How could young women of my generation, who came of age during feminism's Third Wave, want to write or read what seemed to me essentially romance novels, with contemporary outfits and faux-modern sensibilities, that seemed to adhere to very traditional narratives and reinforce very conventional values? Then writers like Melissa Bank and Lucinda Rosenfeld, quite literary authors who happened to be writing about young women and relationships, began to be marketed and responded to as chick lit, which in my opinion was wrong-headed and totally infuriating. So in this fit of absurd hubris I decided to write a novel that countered and subverted the genre. I began something in the fall of 1998 that was a false start, and about six months later started working on what would become *Wedding Season*. The original title was *Lies I Never Told You*; it was changed at the request of my market-savvy editor, who told me, "We want a title like *The Nanny Diaries*." It took me not quite three years to finish a first draft and another six months to revise.

The book is based on a near absurd premise: Joy Silverman is obliged to attend 17 weddings in six months. Most of us have a period in our 20s where it seems like all our friends are getting married at once. Did you have a similar experience?

It was originally 21 weddings. I cut it down because I couldn't stand the idea of writing that many wedding scenes. The book isn't at all autobiographical; or, rather, the milieu is mine and the narrator's voice, her tone and cadence are mine, because I wasn't an advanced enough writer to carry off a first-person voice very different from mine for the length of a novel. But the character is quite different from me, in background and in personality, and the events of the story are not at all autobiographical. I've been to perhaps 10 weddings in my entire life and was a bridesmaid only once. There was a stretch in my late 20s when I attended four weddings in 18 months, or something like that, but my inspiration came more from friends and acquaintances, a number of whom had gone to college in the South and seemed to spend every single summer weekend packing off to Virginia or Georgia with suitcases full of tulle and dyed-to-match shoes.

You have an epigraph from Jane Austen at the beginning of your book that attests, "I would have everyone married, as soon as they can do so to advantage." Why is marriage so important to the early novel? How do you see your novel being influenced by Austen?

I love that quotation. The social-climbing character whose line it is says it with such sincerity, but in context I think Austen is clearly questioning the notion of why we marry—or rather, why people of that era and class married—and the very circumscribed and problematic advantages to be gained from it. I'd be hard-pressed to say anything definitive about why marriage is important to the early novel; I've never made a formal study of 19th century literature. But Austen is among my favorite authors, and I see her as a very unconventional, very unromantic writer, a ferociously perceptive and insightful observer of society and, in particular, of power as it relates to gender and class. And of course she depicts all of this with such a light touch, such a subtle wicked sense of humor. As a woman of her time and social position, she was limited to depicting the dramas of drawing rooms, but she transformed them into social epics, showed them to be as significant, exciting and pitched as the adventures of any swashbuckling, continent-crossing hero. So her project as a whole inspires me—but she's also a master of plot, character, dialogue, the telling detail and practically the

The Writing Life

inventor of comedies of manners, so a number of times I went back to her novels, especially *Sense and Sensibility*, for advice. She's so good with revelations and reversals, with what each character knows that the others don't, with the results of wrong conclusions and misinformation, and what results from the actions people don't take out of propriety and fear of judgment. Just as a side note, I'm a slobbering fan of teen movies, and I think it's because high school is the only setting in contemporary American life where the social hierarchies and behavioral mandates are so rigid, and you can see character struggles akin to those in Austen (which is why *Clueless* worked so brilliantly).

You seem to have ambivalent feelings toward chick lit.

Ambivalent is not the word. I'm anti-chick lit. By which I *do not* mean that nobody should write it, or that nobody should read it, or that it can't be written intelligently and well—I know for a fact that it is. Jennifer Weiner, for example, is a proud practitioner who embraces and advocates for chick lit, and she's bright and hilarious and she's clearly doing something right because people love her books. Chick lit as I define it, contemporary romance novels, is genre fiction. And there's nothing wrong with genre fiction—it's formulaic, but that's part of the pleasure it affords, the pleasures of repetition and familiarity. I happen to love old crime fiction: Chandler, Highsmith, Hammett. But as a reader, the romance genre holds no interest for me personally, and as a writer I'm more interested in distorting and abusing genre than participating in it.

A Comedy of Manners, Matrimony & 17 Marriages in 6 Months

WEDDING
Season

DARCY COSPER

Reprinted with permission from Three Rivers Press.

My antipathy toward chick lit is not for the genre, but for the *label*, for what the label has come to signify, and for how writing that's been identified as such gets treated—both the books that fall under my definition of chick lit, and the books that don't but are labeled chick lit for marketing purposes.

In the case of the former, consider the fact that Stephen King and John le Carré are obviously, famously genre writers, but they aren't thought of, spoken of, with the sort of condescension directed at authors like Sophie Kinsella and Marian Keyes; 'thriller' is a neutral designation, but 'chick lit' implies judgment: It both denigrates and apologizes for itself. If a judgment is to be made about these books, it should be made on the basis of how well or poorly a particular book is written, how it succeeds or fails on the terms of the genre, the terms it sets out for itself, rather than damned in advance by a reductive term that demeans both the people who write it and the people who read it.

In the case of the latter—books that get positioned as chick lit but aren't, it's just a sales tool: A publishing company packages a book with, say, pastel bridesmaids' dresses on the cover, to announce that it features elements in common with the commercially successful contemporary romance genre—a young female main character, a romantic interest—and is therefore an addition to that genre. According to this criteria, they could put pink covers and girly typefaces on *Madame Bovary* and *Lady Chatterly's Lover*, too.

Either way, I think it's not-particularly-veiled sexism at work, a clinging to this antiquated but unfortunately very persistent notion that so-called women's concerns are inherently less worthy of attention, that they are of interest only to women and therefore of less value than men's stories which are, ostensibly, of interest to everyone.

Excuse me while I climb down from my soapbox.

Do you see your work as a literary subversion of the genre?

Wedding Season was an attempt to do so, as I mentioned earlier—a valiant one and perhaps a totally quixotic one, but ultimately I don't think I was successful. To subvert a genre, you have to use all of the genre's components—and I underestimated how powerful genre is, how clever and careful one has to be in order to avoid becoming the thing one is satirizing. I simply wasn't a good enough writer to pull it off completely.

What do you feel are the pros and cons of having a book marketed as chick lit?

The benefit of *Wedding Season* being marketed as chick lit was commercial success. It did quite well, and I'm sure it wouldn't have received the same media attention or gone into multiple printings if it had been published the way I'd pictured it, with the original title in some stern serif font and no irritating cover line and an Anselm Kiefer painting on the jacket. It probably would have sold a couple thousand copies and been remaindered in a matter of weeks.

The drawback, I think, is that the novel never had a chance to be taken seriously, to be read as literary fiction, which I believe it to be—whether good, bad or mediocre. I don't think it was a less literary effort than Dana Spiotta's *Lightning Field* or Stacy Richter's *My Date With Satan* or Matthew Klam's *Sam the Cat* or Jonathan Ames' *The Extra Man* (though unfortunately, it wasn't as well written). *Wedding Season* has themes, strategies, elements, character types in common with these books, but because of how it was marketed, very few critics or readers would ever consider it alongside such books.

In *The Washington Post*, the only venue considered 'major' by the publishing industry to review the novel, a critic wrote that the 17-weddings-in-six-months conceit "can't help smacking of marketing savvy (like the cover lines on women's magazines that promise '23 new looks for lips!')." To me this seems like a failure of imagination on the critic's part; it would have taken very little thought to identify my actual inspirations for the conceit, which included *The Odyssey*, the stations of the cross, and old European fairy tales in which a hero or heroine is required to perform a series of impossible tasks in return for freedom from a curse or the right to marry royal offspring. Perhaps this reviewer can't be blamed for not making the leap, though, or for treating the book with rather less gravity than its author had hoped for. One does, after all, judge a book by its cover, and nothing about *Wedding Season*'s packaging really says "serious literary endeavor herein."

Or, on the other hand, perhaps I'm mistaken, and despite my best efforts I really did write just a tarted-up and self-hating romance novel. In which case, better luck next time.

The other drawback with the chick lit marketing was that the book became something of a wolf in bridesmaid's clothing. From what I can tell, based on the Amazon reader responses, a fair number of chick lit fans were taken in by the book's appearance and weren't at all happy when they found themselves in the middle of a novel about a sanctimonious, self-consciously convention-flouting, pain-in-the-ass girl who disparages the values and goals that much mainstream chick lit elevates and enshrines. And let me tell you, hell hath no fury like a book club member scorned.

What are you working on now?

Another novel, a very stylized sort of black comedy about compulsion. It's inspired/influenced by Nicola Barker, A.L. Kennedy, Patrick McGrath and this great novel *Born Free*, by a

The Writing Life

Scottish novelist named Laura Hird. I'm also working on a screenplay—living in Los Angeles it's practically a residence requirement—an ensemble comedy I'm developing with the pair of young producers who originally optioned *Wedding Season* and got it set up at Paramount.

Do you have any fears about "wolf in bridesmaid's clothing" backlash affecting your second novel in the marketplace?

The public reception of *Wedding Season*—the negative aspects of it, because of course that's what cynical, hypersensitive ingrates like me focus on—definitely had a deleterious effect on my writing. I'd already started the second novel by the time my first one was published, but the negative responses really got to me, and I didn't write fiction for months. I wrote book reviews, I worked on a screenplay, but every time I pulled my new novel out, in my head I'd hear the harshest, most critical of the responses to the first one, and I'd be totally overcome with fear and doubt. And the new novel is completely different from the first—so of course I spent all sorts of time worrying about whether anyone would want to publish a novel like that by someone who was perceived as a chick lit writer, if I should publish under a pseudonym, ad infinitum, ad absurdum. I was doing much more agitating than writing, which was painful and totally ridiculous.

Then I did an interview with Sam Lipsyte, who'd had some ups and downs getting his second novel published, and he said, "It's idiotic for a literary artist to think he or she is owed something from a media conglomerate in a capitalist system. You just have to keep writing. If you get published by a big house, good for you, more people will come into contact with your work, but if you hitch your sense of validation to publishing, you're in trouble."

That was a wake-up call. And it reminded me of something William Monahan said to me in an interview, so I went into my files and pulled it out, and now that quote's on my desktop: "Novels are supposed to be entertainments worth your time and money. The artistry is extra, and if you have any, it takes care of itself. Art is involuntary; it has to do with what you are, and nothing to do with organized intention."

Basically, they're both saying: Shut up and write. That's the most important thing I learned from the publication of my first book. And now that's what I'm trying to do.

Mark Childress

Practice Makes Better,
or How to Avoid 'Honest Work'

© Daniel Rodrigez

by Will Allison

A year after the publication of his first novel, *A World Made of Fire* (Knopf, 1984), Mark Childress quit his 50-hours-a-week job as regional editor of *The Atlanta Journal-Constitution* to write fiction. He was 27 then, and he'd just spent two years working at the paper and trying to finish a novel in his spare time.

"I was frazzled," he says.

His bosses and parents thought he was making a mistake, but Childress was determined to give novel writing a go. "I figured I could always get another newspaper job if the fiction thing didn't pan out," he says.

That was 22 years ago, and thanks to a string of critically acclaimed novels, Childress has since managed to avoid what he calls "honest work." Best known for *Crazy in Alabama* (Putnam, 1993), a *New York Times* Notable Book of the Year, Childress also wrote the screenplay for the Columbia Pictures film adaptation, which was directed by Antonio Banderas and starred Melanie Griffith.

Childress' latest novel, *One Mississippi* (Little Brown, 2006), is the sharp-witted, softhearted story of Daniel Musgrove's junior year of high school. At the novel's center is a brilliant, hilarious premise of the sort that is a Childress trademark: What happens when the first-ever black prom queen of Minor High is struck by a car and wakes up from her coma thinking she's white?

The novel also affords Childress another opportunity to chronicle small-town life in the South, a milieu he evoked so memorably in *Crazy in Alabama*. Childress himself was born in Alabama and has lived in Ohio, Indiana, Mississippi, Louisiana, Georgia, California and Costa Rica. These days, he makes his home in New York and can be found online at www.mar kchildress.com.

Describe your novel-writing process.

I remember when the most important question in the world seemed to me to be: Pen, pencil or typewriter? Now all those technologies are nearly obsolete. I remember thinking that imitating a successful writer's process would make me a real writer—and, in a way, I was right. Practice doesn't make perfect, but it does make better. You don't become a pianist by starting off with a Tchaikovsky piano concerto. You start by playing scales.

You could do worse than taking [someone else's] short story you love and typing it up

---

Will Allison's (www.willallison.com) short stories have appeared in *Zoetrope: All Story, Glimmer Train, One Story, The Kenyon Review, Shenandoah, American Short Fiction, Atlanta* and other magazines.

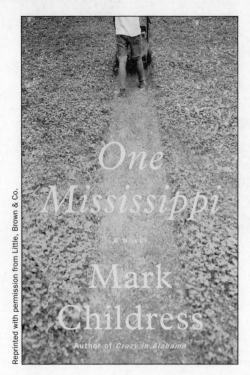

Reprinted with permission from Little, Brown & Co.

yourself, word for word, copying it over. I have done that with stretches of great prose when I wanted to see for myself how the master made it work. Let someone else's words come out through your fingers. That's the whole key to fiction writing, anyway.

I wrote my first novel on a Smith-Corona portable typewriter—11 drafts. I started at the beginning and wrote it until I was about half-way through. Suddenly the story stalled and all the characters threatened to wander off in different directions, so I wrote up an outline of the remainder, in an effort to convince them to get back in line. When the story was over, I went back to page one and began rewriting. Through each of those drafts the book got a little better, and my typing skills improved. I've written each of my novels following this general pattern, just because it's the way I taught myself to do it.

On a heavily researched novel like *Tender*, I'll do all the research before I start so I feel I have all the facts I need at my fingertips. Other-wise you can Google yourself out of house and home—you can waste all your time doing "re-search" of the most tenuous variety. Most of my books are more purely fiction [than *Tender*]. I start with a character, a scene, an image in my mind, and grow from there. That's why it takes me so long to write a book. I'm an obsessive rewriter and tend to move forward slowly.

What's your daily writing schedule?

After I've had the morning cup of joe and wasted as much time writing e-mails as I can possibly allow myself, I buckle down and work until I can't do it any more. Most days this is five or six hours. Sometimes less. Occasionally more. My rule is: When it's working, don't leave, and let the machine answer the phone. The best days are the ones, usually late in a novel, when I write four or five pages in an hour or two and give myself the rest of the day off.

Do you solicit feedback from readers as you're working on a novel? At what point do you begin sharing your work with others?

There are a couple of close friends, also writers, who do me the favor of reading along as I write. And my agents, who are also friends. They tend to be encouraging on the specific stuff, and a couple of times they've discouraged me just in the nick of time. Other than those folks, I keep it pretty close until I have at least one draft finished. If I solicit too many opinions or talk too much about the book, it dissipates the sense of urgency that led me to write it in the first place.

Every summer I participate in a writer's conference in California [the Community of Writers at Squaw Valley], and I love to read a chapter of new work there. There's nothing like a live audience to let you instantly know which sentence is working and which is not.

Who is your imagined reader/audience when you write?

I do have this person I imagine—or maybe it's just a part of me, the reader part—looking over my shoulder while I am writing. When I began writing novels, I loved to be obscure because I equated obscurity with cleverness, but the more I wrote, the more conscious I became of this person who is reading my book. For some reason I envision her as a woman—maybe because most readers are women and mostly women come to my book signings. This imaginary person is very bright, a close and exacting reader. I have learned not to try to impress her with empty pretty language or some tricky technical way of bringing a scene to a close before you've earned it. And whatever I do, I try not to confuse her, and I try to rein in my smart-aleck tendencies. I take her by the hand and show her the things I want her to see.

There's another voice in there too, a caustic voice. I think it's my own voice. Idiot! What does that mean? That's meaningless! Go back and take that out! Who are you trying to impress?

Every real writer I know has developed a thick skin about negative reviews, in part because we have hypercritical voices inside us, criticizing every sentence as it appears on the page. I have written terrible reviews, in my head, for each of my books-in-progress. These internal reviews are worse than the worst review I've ever actually gotten.

The only thing you can hope to do is to find as many examples of your fatal weaknesses as you can, and correct them, before the book gets loose in the world. For the beginning writer, this means never showing your work to anyone in the publishing business until you've made it as good as you can make it.

In a 1990 interview, you said you didn't want to be seen only as a Southern writer. What does the term "Southern writer" mean to you, and do you still feel that way?

Some bookstores used to segregate Southern books off to one side, as if to say, here we have American writers, and then over here we have Southern writers. But any ghetto that includes Flannery [O'Connor] and [William] Faulkner and Barry Hannah and Toni Morrison and Fannie Flagg and Robert Penn Warren and Walter Moseley and Clyde Edgerton and Jill McCorkle is pretty damn fabulous. Generally I find this kind of writer-labeling is really about marketing, which may be a necessity for the publishing industry but is no concern of the writer. Or shouldn't be, anyway.

A lot of fiction writers begin with short stories, then move on to novels. Have you ever written stories or considered writing a collection?

In high school and the undergraduate writing program at Alabama, the short story was the accepted form, so I wrote a lot of them. I'm not sure if they were any good. I'm fairly certain they weren't. Mostly I can't bear to look back at my old stuff.

Once I got out of school and began writing for myself, I wrote a few stories but soon found myself immersed in a novel and much more comfortable writing the longer form. It's the kind of book I love to read the most, so it's still the form I love to write. Occasionally I try my hand at a story, but it's either a novel compressed into 20 pages or it wanders off into nothingness after the initial energy has drained away. I would love to take a couple of years and read all the great stories and learn to write them again.

What unique challenges did your latest novel, *One Mississippi*, present?

The novel before was *Gone for Good*, which was a fairly ambitious book, the classic Greek hero myth told through the lens of magic realism and modern America's obsession with celebrity. After that, I thought I just wanted to write something simple and short. A book I could write in a year. That's what I always think in the beginning.

I'd been thinking a lot about high school, how much I thought I hated it at the time. What I hated, in fact, was my own adolescent self. To get all this in, I ended up writing for six years, almost 800 pages. I wound up with this great sprawling megalith of a manuscript. For

The Writing Life

some reason I always have this urge to put everything in there, everything I might possibly need. And then I cut, and cut, and cut more. It's hardly the most efficient way to write a novel, and I wish I could find some other way. Now I'm working on a new novel, and I'm thinking, short, sweet write it in a year, and I know even as I'm saying it that it's a lie. I'm lying to myself, to fool myself into doing the work.

You've lived all over the place. Has this been useful to you as a writer?

When I was a kid I thought it was an awful burden that we had to move every couple of years, because of my dad's job. (He was a traveling salesman for Ralston Purina.) I envied kids who got to grow up in one place, who got to go to school with the same set of friends, year after year. Now I look back and I'm glad we moved, and I find myself moving even more often, now that I'm on my own. Am I getting away from something or trying to find something? Probably both. All I know is, a new place brings new people and new thoughts and new discoveries and a fresh sense of myself, and I do think that helps a writer. I love learning about a place the way the natives know it. On the other hand, there's a lot of wasted motion in all that moving and traveling. Who knows? Emily Dickinson got a lot of work done by sticking close to home.

My parents used to laugh because I would get out of the car after a 600-mile drive and immediately ask one of them to take me somewhere. So I suppose I've been this way all along.

Your books are unusual in that they're considered "literary," but unlike most literary books, they've also found a popular audience. If you worked in a bookstore and were asked by a customer to characterize/classify Mark Childress' books, what would you say?

Probably I would be a lazy bookstore employee and just stick myself in with the other Southern writers. But my books actually have more in common with some of the Europeans and Latin Americans. I started writing fiction in the 1970s when the fiction scene in America was pretty inert. It was all later Vonnegut and Cheever and Gass, tired metafiction and leftover experimentalism from the '60s. I was a huge admirer of John Fowles and Anthony Burgess and William Styron, all of whose books seemed to me incredibly smart and also rich and big with these full-blooded, completely satisfying complex narratives. And I loved the work of Barry Hannah, a teacher of mine, because his raw humor seemed to me the only sane response to a very nutty time growing up in the South. And I wanted to be Gabriel Garcia Marquez and [Jorge Luis] Borges too. But I was from Alabama, and my family all came from there. I knew that was a place I could start that not everyone had already written about. I had to start somewhere close to myself, if the fiction would have any hope of being true.

I don't know what kind of writer I've become. I'm just an American trying to find new ways to write stories so that people don't want to put them down after 10 pages. We're battling the modern American attention span, and that ain't easy.

You left a job as regional editor of *The Atlanta Journal-Constitution* to write novels. Talk about that decision.

It was really scary, because although I was not making a huge amount of money—nobody at a newspaper makes lots of money except the publisher—it was a steady paycheck at the end of every week. And it was a great job, working with people I enjoyed and admired. But I had just spent two years trying to write a novel at night and on weekends while trying to perform well in a 50- to 60-hour job. I was frazzled. I'd managed to sell my second novel, and I had an offer to ghostwrite a book. That project would pay about half of my salary [at the newspaper], enough to last me for a year, I decided, and I could write fiction in all my free time. That was 1985. I was 27 years old. My bosses and my parents thought I was nuts. I figured I could always get another newspaper job if the fiction thing didn't pan out.

Every year around tax time, I see how much money is left and if it's enough to get me through another year. It's been 20 years now, and I've managed to avoid honest work. So far, so good.

In what ways has your journalism background served you as a novelist?

The newspaper taught me that there are lots of versions of the truth, but it's the writer's job to find and tell the most convincing version. Also I learned to write very fast, on deadline, with some eye to accuracy and at least a passing swipe at creativity. Having a city editor or a copy desk go over some lovely feature you've written with their axes and hatchets is a sobering experience, one I would recommend to every beginning writer. You quickly lose ego about your work. The story is the story; it's not you, but you have to fight to defend it and to make it better, even against your own instinct that it's fine the way it is. Practice, practice—I bet I wrote a million words for newspapers and magazines in the 10 years I was a full-time journalist. That got me warmed up and used to the process of sitting my restless self down in the chair and staying there until the damn thing was done.

What's your favorite writer joke?

"I never read reviews of my work."

Other Works by Mark Childress

In addition to his latest book *One Mississippi* (picture on page 34), Childress has published these novels:
- *V for Victor* (Knopf, 1988)
- *Tender* (Harmony, 1990)
- *Crazy in Alabama* (Putnam, 1993)
- *Gone for Good* (Knopf, 1998)

Also look for his children's books:
- *Henry Bobbity is Missing* (Crane Hill, 1996)
- *Joshua and Bigtooth* (Little, Brown, 1992)
- *Joshua and the Big Bad Blue Crabs* (Little, Brown, 1995)

The Writing Life

Premier Voices

Five Debut Writers Represent the Genres

by Lauren Mosko

Despite the amount of emphasis the publishing industry places on fiction labels, the truth is that they're merely a sales and marketing tool. While labels certainly help booksellers figure out where to shelve books and aid readers in finding books similar to what they already know they like, many people argue that they also contribute to narrow-minded writing, reading and purchasing because they don't encourage risk taking or boundary pushing.

Carrie Vaughn, whose debut novel, *Kitty and The Midnight Hour*, has been lauded for spanning the genres of fantasy and romance and who holds a master's degree in English literature, feels that labels often contribute to prejudice, not only in academia but also in general readership. "What I find bizarre is when a work of science fiction or fantasy becomes 'anointed' by the canon and suddenly it isn't genre anymore," she says. "I run into people who insist they hate science fiction, so I rattle off a list of titles—*Brave New World*, *The Handmaid's Tale*, *Fahrenheit 451*—and they tell me those aren't science fiction. I'm happy to be labeled a genre writer because I'm having fun, it's what I love, and my audience is able to find me there. But I can't tell you how many times I hear 'I don't normally read this sort of thing, but . . .' I had a friend tell me she liked my book even though she doesn't normally read fantasy—and I know for a fact she read the Harry Potter books, Philip Pullman, Robin McKinley, and so on. She just had an idea of what fantasy was and decided it didn't apply to her. I sometimes wish the labels would go away because I think they blind people to what the books are really about."

Even if you "don't normally read" one of the types of books featured in this series, you might be surprised to find that the differences between them—as well as their subtle similarities and overlap—spark your interest. After all, no matter what shelf it sits on at the bookstore, a good book is a good book.

Mystery
Donis Casey, *The Old Buzzard Had It Coming* (Poisoned Pen Press)

Alafair Tucker is a sharp, strong-willed farm wife and mother of nine children living in Oklahoma in 1912. Like other frontier women, her days are filled with cooking, cleaning, laundry and more cooking. Unlikely she'd have much time for sleuthing, even with a murder in her community. What would compel such a sedulous matron to spend her precious free moments questioning neighbors and traipsing through the woods by herself?

LAUREN MOSKO is the editor of *Novel & Short Story Writer's Market*. Of all the amazing things her job allows her to do, writing this feature is her favorite. If you would like to be considered for next year's "Premier Voices," please e-mail her at lauren.mosko@fwpubs.com.

Her tender and earnest 17-year-old daughter Phoebe is in love with the prime suspect.

It's the bond of family that motivates not only this daring protagonist but also her creator. Donis Casey, a former research librarian and small business owner, got the inspiration for her novel while researching her family's genealogy, a gift to her siblings for Christmas. "I kept coming up with these fabulous stories," she remembers. "I started talking to my mother about growing up on the farm and questioning all these older relatives of mine and my husband's. I put them all together, started writing these little books, and it didn't take me long to realize that I had something."

Donis Casey

© Poisoned Pen Press

Incorporating some of the "weirder" incidents in her family's history and her husband's "pretty wild sort of Oklahoma cowboy background" into the mystery she was already outlining, it took Casey only eight months to write *The Old Buzzard Had It Coming*, the first in her series of Alafair Tucker mysteries.

Working as a librarian, Casey had a strong foundation in academic writing, but she wrote fiction privately for fun. She'd really only been reading mysteries for four or five years prior to trying her hand at her own, but once she began, she felt as if she'd found her true voice. "I'd decided that, just for once, I wasn't going to be so damned sophisticated. I was going to write from the heart," she says. "I learned to be more authentic and not so intellectual. Like a lot of academics, you always want to write the Great American Novel, be like F. Scott Fitzgerald or James Joyce. Writing from the heart was an infinitely more satisfying experience."

In addition to the rich historical details mined from both her relatives and her regional libraries, Casey includes another element to authenticate the reading experience: recipes. "Alafair thought about food all the time; anybody with nine kids is thinking about food," laughs the author. "There's a scene early in the book where the family is sitting around the table eating cornbread and beans. I was writing about how everybody in the family has their own idea about how to eat the meal. But there's more to food than just recipes. I wanted to say a little bit about the lore of the food. I thought that might be something people could connect with."

Casey recalls the legend of her own grandmother's coffee, so strong it was "like amphetamines" to the sleepy members of her family. "It's your heritage," she says. "Not just recipes but the way it has to be eaten." With this in mind, her first book contains an appendix of "Alafair's Recipes," 10 in all, including three variations on cornbread and such down-home favorites as meatloaf, fried ham and gravy, peach cobbler and pecan pie.

It may take three tries to find the cornbread recipe that's right for you, but it only took Casey one try to find a home for her book.

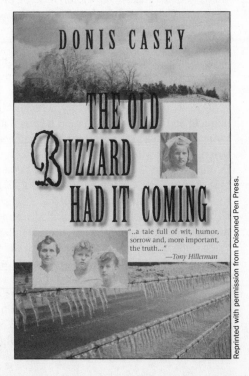

DONIS CASEY

THE OLD BUZZARD HAD IT COMING

"..a tale full of wit, humor, sorrow and, more important, the truth..."
—*Tony Hillerman*

Reprinted with permission from Poisoned Pen Press.

The Writing Life

From the beginning, she targeted Poisoned Pen Press in nearby Scottsdale, AZ. "I've lived in the Valley about 21 years, and I hung around Poisoned Pen Bookstore from its inception," she says. "I was aware when they started the press and I began reading the books they published. Then I began to read about them in publishers' magazines and newspapers, and I knew they had a good reputation. I studied their submission requirements and saw that they'd accepted unagented materials, and I thought before I go the whole route trying to find an agent, they might be intrigued by me because I'm local."

Poisoned Pen Press was indeed intrigued, and after the manuscript went through about 10 readers, it was accepted. "I was, let's say, thrilled to death," laughs Casey.

And Casey has had several reasons to stay thrilled. *The Old Buzzard* was one of the fiction finalists for the 16th Annual Oklahoma Book Award and was short-listed for the 2006 Oklahoma Reads Oklahoma project. Poisoned Pen Press released the second book *Hornswoggled* in fall of 2006. Just as the first book centers around Phoebe and her possible complicity in a crime, each successive book will concentrate on one of Alafair's other children. This time, Alice—Phoebe's fiery twin—sets her sights on a man whose wife was mysteriously murdered a year before. "He's been cleared, but Alafair is not so sure he's innocent. She's the only one in the whole town who doesn't like him," explains Casey. "We go from there."

Literary
Rebecca Meacham, *Let's Do*
(University of North Texas Press)

Rebecca Meacham likes to alarm her writing students at University of Wisconsin-Green Bay by telling them it took her almost 10 years to finish one story. Once class is dismissed, she'll admit that's not *entirely* true, since she put that story (now "Good Fences") away for nine of those years. Still, Meacham feels it's "a useful example of a writer having to wait until her life experiences and maturity matched up with a story's needs."

Rebecca Meacham

© University of North Texas Press

Meacham seems to be acutely aware of the needs of her stories and the characters within them. So much so, in fact, that they exert their wills even while she's creating them.

"I really thought my title story, which is the most depressing thing I've ever written, was going to end with a reconciliation between husband and wife. I was very excited to finally write a love story: Let's do something happy—hooray! Then, the voice of the obvious whispered, 'But the wife is sleeping with a stranger in the first sentence of the story. She's already in utter despair. Is joyful reunion really the natural path here?' Like my characters, I had the best of intentions. I wanted Estelle and Paul to reconnect and start fresh. Instead, she ends the story quite alone and near suicide," Meacham says. "Foiled again."

This dynamic between reality and idealism is at the heart of her collection *Let's Do*, winner of the 2004 Katherine Anne Porter Prize in Short Fiction from the University of North Texas Press. Among its tragic cast are a 70-year-old retired vacuum cleaner salesman and his alcoholic daughter ("Hold Fast"), a reluctant stalker ("The Assignment"), a high school art teacher impregnated and abandoned by the feckless ex-drama director ("Trim & Notions"), and a grief-stricken anorexic teen ("Weights and Measures").

"The turning point of each story arises from a character's intense desire, but utter failure, to act," explains Meacham. "These characters are idealists. In spirit, each really wants to act, to do—and to do good. They all begin with the best of intentions; they also begin flawed. So I can hear to varying degrees, and in some cases with biting sarcasm, each character in the collection saying, 'Let's do.' At the same time, I can also hear a number of these same characters, as the story unfolds, saying, 'On second thought, let's don't.' "

The author herself suffers from no such inability to act, as evidenced by the success of her collection and the 15 honors and awards it, and the stories within it, have received. Of course, before every great prize is a path marked by trial and error, obstacle and perseverance. Her first published story was rejected over 30 times before it was accepted. No wonder then that the search for a book publisher was daunting.

"I was terrified about publishing the collection," Meacham recalls. "I'm not particularly adept at, or interested in, networking, so I had no connections to pursue; the publishing industry seemed impenetrable, and I'd just begun a tenure-track assistant professorship, so I was pretty busy. What seemed most comfortable yet active was submitting the manuscript to short-story collection contests. I submitted the book to at least 20 contests over the next two years. The book was a finalist in two contests, and stories in it were getting accepted in various journals, so this was encouraging. At the same time, entering the book in the same contests year after year was becoming discouraging."

Finally the news arrived via e-mail. A phone call to UNTP was made and her award was confirmed. "Then I celebrated," she says, "which means I e-mailed everyone I knew and phoned my mom, dad and husband. There may have been some wine."

The next triumph came when Barnes & Noble chose the collection for its Discover Great New Writers program. "The impact was tremendous, both in visibility and sales," says Meacham. "You can win all kinds of accolades and literary awards, but to your family and friends, the real mark of success is when your book is displayed in the front rack of a national bookstore. When my family in Missouri sent me pictures of my book on the shelf in Springfield and my aunts in both California and Ohio could point out the book to friends while shopping, I understood how lucky I was to have been selected." (Because of the B&N promotion, *Let's Do* is now in its fourth printing.)

Despite her hard work and success, it's the thwarting of best laid plans—both for her characters and in her own writing process—that translates to the lesson Meacham feels is most valuable for her students to learn: "Get used to failure," she says. "Attempting to write fiction involves lots of revision and reconsidering, sometimes years later with fresh, adult eyes; attempting to publish your work involves lots of rejection." In order to stay focused, Meacham reads the works of her successful contemporaries. "I'm inspired by the chances other writers take, their audacity; reading their work makes me want to take risks in my own."

Romance
Kelley St. John, *Good Girls Don't* (Warner Forever)

It's a classic case of art imitating life. As Kelley St. John flipped through an issue of *TIME*, she found an article entitled "Alibis for Sale" (Oct. 29, 2001), which exposed the nefarious yet

WINNER, KATHERINE ANNE PORTER PRIZE IN SHORT FICTION
Jonis Agee, Judge

let's do

rebecca meacham

Reprinted with permission from University of North Texas Press.

wildly popular services of British and U.S. alibi agencies—companies that cover for cheating spouses by sending fictitious invitations to business conferences, fielding calls from home and forwarding them to "the hotel front desk," etc.

"I started pondering what kind of person would work at a place that helps spouses cheat. Then I asked myself what would happen if an alibi consultant ended up lying to a friend," says St. John. "That's when Colette came to life. She explained, *'I didn't plan to work here for long, only until I got my business going. And I never, ever planned to lie to Bill.'* "

Kelley St. John

Once St. John heard Colette's voice, she hopped into her car. "Almost all my plotting occurs on the interstate. Driving relaxes my mind, allows the characters to speak freely and jumpstarts my muse," she says. Colette's dilemma is the central plot of *Good Girls Don't*, a contemporary romance in which the heroine reconnects with her high school best friend (the now-gorgeous Bill Brannon) *after* her job has required her to lie to him about the whereabouts of the teenage niece of whom he has custody. As in life, one lie requires another and another—until it's clear she's put her chance for real love in jeopardy.

Although *Good Girls Don't* is St. John's first published book, she's completed 21 novels in a range of genres from mainstream action/suspense to steamy romance. She's received over 40 awards for her unpublished work, and she says these did much to boost her confidence and obtain useful critiques. As her writing improved, her goals became more ambitious. "I entered only the contests where the final judge was an agent or editor I was targeting. My goal was to be a finalist, to get my manuscript on the editor's or agent's desk and receive a request," she explains. As the awards and honors accumulated, it was clear St. John was attracting attention. But still no sale.

One day as St. John opened her e-mail inbox, her eyes immediately fell upon a friend's message with a subject line that read THE CALL. "I couldn't wait to read that author's story, and I realized that most authors have a sincere interest in learning the details regarding a fellow writer's first sale," she says. St. John thought a series of interviews with debut writers would be a nice addition to the Romance Writers Report, a publication of Romance Writers of America (RWA). (St. John is a long-time member of RWA and seven of its chapter organizations, as well as editor of two of their newsletters and a member of its Board of Directors.)

Just three weeks into her interview series (but over three years since joining RWA), St. John herself got The Call from her romance agent, Caren Johnson. (The details can be found on her Web site at www.kelleystjohn.com/TheCall.cfm, along with The Calls of nearly 150 other notable romance writers.) Warner had offered her a two-book deal.

"I had high expectations for Warner, and they didn't disappoint. The entire production staff is phenomenal. My editor never held back on her enthusiasm for the book, which really made the writing and revising process even more fun," St. John says.

The author admits that revision posed the biggest challenge for her, as her editor requested the removal of two supporting characters, Colette's mother and ex-boyfriend. St. John advises aspiring writers to "always keep an open mind regarding change. Getting too attached to a title, a prologue or even a secondary character (or two) isn't smart. Luckily, I realized my editor knew what she was talking about regarding her requested revisions. I wanted the best possible book, and I believe she helped me deliver my best."

For readers who can't get enough of Colette and Bill (or any of the other sexy couples in the book), St. John parlayed those edits into a promotional tool: a section of her Web site called Cutting Room Floor, which, much like a DVD, includes deleted scenes and alternate endings for *Good Girls Don't*.

Her Web site also hosts related contests that award trips to locations featured in her books. Readers have been flown to Tybee Island, Georgia, and Indian Rocks Beach, Florida. "I decided I should let my readers experience the beauty of the locales I selected for my novels," says St. John. These beaches are perfect places to experience not only romance but also St. John's second release, *Real Women Don't Wear Size 2*, another contemporary romance about a curvy woman whose 30th birthday inspires her to liberate and celebrate herself.

St. John is currently working on and shopping novels in several genres, including a romantic suspense that draws from her background as a writer for NASA. "Eventually, I'd love to be published in all of the genres," she says. "If I'm going to dream, I might as well dream big, right?"

Fantasy
Carrie Vaughn, *Kitty and The Midnight Hour* (Warner Aspect)

Carrie Vaughn

When Carrie Vaughn decided to write a story about a werewolf named Kitty who hosts a midnight call-in radio show that offers advice to vampires, lycanthropes and other woebegone supernaturals, she figured it was "too gimmicky" to support an entire novel. She hacked her original 10,000-word manuscript into a 4,000-word short story and sold it to *Weird Tales* as "Dr. Kitty Solves All Your Love Problems." But as soon as the story was printed, she knew she was wrong.

"I had Kitty's entire life basically mapped out, and I just kept thinking of more adventures she could have," Vaughn says. "The radio show format made it possible to discuss lots of ideas and introduce lots of characters and different stories, which was something I hadn't expected when I originally thought of it."

Wellspring of ideas aside, Vaughn knew that in order to allow Kitty her own novel, she had to find the arc. "Kitty was pretty static in the short stories. They were about ideas rather than the character. But the novel had to be about her. Once I decided on a 'coming of age' story, the pieces just fell into place." With the help of a critique group and many rounds of revisions, *Kitty and The Midnight Hour* took shape.

Thanks in part to Vaughn's impressive vitae of published stories, she found an agent who sold her book to Warner in just seven months. The editor anticipated the book's fantasy/romance crossover appeal, and Kitty has indeed been a genre-blending success. The splash page for Vaughn's Web site (www.carrievaughn.com) displays blurbs from both *Locus* and *The Romantic Times*.

"When I heard how much cross-promoting was happening and how much attention from the romance market the book was getting, I was surprised. There's not a whole lot of love going on in Kitty!" she says. "I've since revised my definition of romance and can understand why it's getting that kind of attention—the strong female protagonist, the sexual tension (even if it's not particularly positive or resolved). I think the very nature of having a story that places supernatural elements in the 'real' modern world is bound to give it a wide appeal. Any book like this necessarily draws from a lot of different areas to make it feel more complete."

Reprinted with permission from Warner Aspect.

Although Vaughn feels free to use elements from different types of fiction, she doesn't concern herself much with labels. Raised on a diet of science fiction, she feels it was her introduction to Ray Bradbury and his indefinable work that refocused the way she thinks about literature. "For me, it's the 'wow' factor. I want to be amazed; I want to see something I've never seen before or see the world in a new light. I want to see metaphors made real," she explains.

With the sequel, *Kitty Goes to Washington* released just seven months later and a contract for books three and four signed, Vaughn is now concentrating on what it takes to craft a series by studying other writers who both succeeded and fell short in their endeavor. While developing her own strategy, she's noted a few points she feels are particularly important.

"Each book should stand alone as much as possible and have enough of a satisfying story arc that readers aren't frustrated by too many loose ends," she offers. "And the character needs to end up in a different place at the end of the book than where she started. The corollary is that most successful series feature characters who, either by their personality or their positions, naturally end up in one spectacular life-altering situation after another. They should be the kind of people who need a whole series of books to tell their story."

She cites Lois McMaster Bujold's Vorkosigan saga as her own model for series writing. "She manages to do all these things, and as a result, even after reading a dozen or so books in her series, I'd follow her anywhere," Vaughn says. "That's the kind of series I want to write."

Vaughn also feels optimistic that the trend of genre-blending will continue. "I like to think that recognizing the appeal of works that cross genre boundaries will make it easier for writers whose work tends to be on the quirky side to find their audience. The flipside, though, is you have a lot of writers who want to break in *trying* to write these kinds of things and maybe not as successfully. It's important to strive for good books, so that the development doesn't get written off as a fad."

Graphic novel
Shane White, *North Country* (NBM)

Little did the young Shane White know that the solitary time he spent memorizing the *TV Guide* was research for his first book. Through this peculiar pastime, he learned to recognize a film and the year it was made just by observing the quality of a few frames. These picture memories—and the idea of linking time and the artistic elements of tone, texture and color—were the inspiration for the style of his graphic novel memoir, *North Country*.

Shane White

White narrates the story as he travels from Seattle to Albany via airplane to visit his parents. The prospect of returning home fills him with anxiety, and each action or encounter—from crouching to tie his shoelace to the smell of fried chicken—brings back waves of tormented memories. One of the most striking aspects of the book is the range of styles and color palettes White uses to differentiate between recollections. The vividness of each illustrated flashback is proportional to the vividness of his memory, and the colors are deliberately chosen to reflect time periods and moods rather than reality.

To achieve this effect, White scanned photos from the 1970s into his computer and examined their palettes. "There's hardly any color in some of those Polaroids or Kodachromes," he notes. True to his dated models, many sequences take sepia or monochromatic tones, with "worn" texturized backgrounds and blurry lines. Still others are surreal primary-colored caricatures, in the style of the 1930s or '40s children's books passed down to him by his parents. "I wanted the contrast of stark realism and this happy fun thing where something serious was still being conveyed. The play with imagination or that magical world of being a child is always being poked at, prodded, until the bubble bursts and you have to confront reality and adulthood."

Confrontation is exactly what White had in mind when he began the book. His manuscript started as a series of what he calls "greatest hits," a bulleted list of the most painful and resonant moments of his childhood that seemed to haunt him and constantly resurface in conversation. "I think the essential goal—the therapeutic goal—was to make room for new memories and stop carrying this luggage around," White says.

He'd relied on his sketchbooks to bear the brunt of his feelings all his life, but they didn't prepare him for the process of putting together a book.

"When I started having to write it, sit down and think, 'wow, I've got to make a story out of this material,' it just became a black hole. I'm pretty emotional I guess. I had to get through it.

"I really like the process of art and comics. I work in a variety of styles and I wanted to convey that first and foremost. But then when it came to writing, that was the hardest part because there's no interpretation. The word is the word. It's there, and I'm trying to convey this meaning or this emotion—this feeling."

It took him a few months to put together the first six pages of the book. Once they were completed, he showed them to editors at the Emerald City Comicon. He got a lot of positive feedback, but many thought the project was

NORTH COUNTRY
SHANE WHITE

NBM
ComicsLit

too ambitious for a first-time graphic novelist. White resigned himself to using the pages as a promotional tool on his Web site (www.shanewhite.com).

A friend saw the work and encouraged the creator not to give up. White had already submitted the pages to a few publishers and received no reply. He wasn't sure his manuscript was a good fit for NBM, but he thought his illustration style, which he describes as "old school—not stylized or artsy," might appeal to the editors. He sent the publisher the first six pages he'd created. Within four months, NBM responded and asked for a synopsis. White had no idea how to write a synopsis, and it took him three drafts (and some help from other writer friends) to get it right. A contract was offered, and he realized he now had the rest of the book to write.

"It would not be the way I'd work ever again," he says. "But I think, with this material, it's organic and emotional, and you have to allow that to breathe. It had to make sense to me. I'd have to believe in it before anybody else would."

Throughout the two-year publishing process, White worked closely with Terry Nantier and the production staff at NBM to make sure the story arc was effective and all the different styles and color palettes reproduced exactly during the transition from digital to print. It's this spirit of collaboration—and the unfailing support of his wife—that left the greatest impression on him.

"It's not a solo effort. I think any project takes more than the creator. You'd love to be a genius and go off and create on your own, but you need people," he says. "It's funny because a good part of my life I've just felt like this robot who does art because I just love working so much; I don't need people, I just need my imagination. That's really telling of my history and background, but in the end, I need to grow."

Courtesy of author

CRAFT & TECHNIQUE

Making Good Sense

Five Tips for Crafting Multisensory Worlds

by I.J. Schecter

No matter what other elements great stories may possess, they are made memorable through compelling characters, and characters are made compelling through the clarity of their experiences. Skilled writers let us experience the worlds of their characters through all five senses (or six, if you happen to be reading *The Dead Zone*), by allowing us not only to see the things their characters experience but also to hear, smell, taste and touch them. They create multisensory worlds that engage us on different levels and in different ways. Here are five tips for effectively integrating sensory description to make the world of your story, and your characters' experiences within it, as real as your readers' own.

1. Get real

The most powerful sensory moments are those that resonate within the context of readers' everyday lives. Rich sensory descriptions pack a punch not because they are elaborate or overly lyrical but because readers can relate to them. Observe the following use of touch (that is, the tactile sense—though the author displays a deft literary touch, too) from W.P. Kinsella's short story, "The Baseball Spur" (from *The Thrill of the Grass*, Penguin, 1985):

> I took the money and bought a box of baseballs, a whole dozen. I laid them out on my bed like a bagful of white oranges, and I smelled them, and touched them, and handled them like a miser fondling his money.

Anyone with even a slight affinity for baseball knows the thrill of this simple sensation. Instead of just telling us his character loves baseball, Kinsella places this knowledge, quite literally, in our hands.

Here's another example, from Barbara Kingsolver's *The Poisonwood Bible* (HarperCollins, 1998):

> I found a column of ants running up a tree trunk and picked a couple out of the lineup. Bad luck for those poor ants, singled out while minding their own business amongst their brethren.

We've all abused our human superiority in similar ways—with insects the usual victims—

I.J. SCHECTER (www.ijschecter.com) writes for leading magazines, newspapers and Web sites throughout the world, including *Condé Nast Brides*, *Golf Monthly*, *Men's Exercise*, *The Globe & Mail* and iParenting.com. He is also the author of two collections *The Bottom of the Mug* (Aegina Press Inc) and *Slices: Observations from the Wrong Side of the Fairway* (John Wiley & Sons).

and so we know exactly what it feels like to absently tweeze an ant between our fingers. Like Kinsella's character caressing the baseball, Kingsolver uses a universal sensory experience to draw us deeper into her story.

The use of sensory depiction is restricted neither to routine occurrence nor high drama. If the scene is germane to your story, it matters little whether that moment represents the mundane or the exceptional. Compare, for instance, the following two examples: the first from *A Fine Balance*, by Rohinton Mistry (Vintage, 2001)

> "Oh, to have young eyes again," she sighed, as he moistened the thread between his lips and passed it through the needle. Finding the holes in the button from the blind side took a bit of poking around with the needle. But he managed to finish in fair time, and snipped the threads, triumphant.

the second from John Irving's short story, "Trying to Save Piggy Sneed" (Ballantine, 1997)

> If you stood too close to the pig barn, the heat curled your eyelashes—the fluid under your eyelids felt searing hot. If you stood too far back, the chill of the winter night air, drawn toward the flames, would cut through you.

Threading a needle is a commonplace experience; watching a pig barn go up in flames, decidedly rare. Both experiences, however, are justified within the context of their stories, and both authors use deceptively simple writing to create a powerful sensory connection with the reader.

2. Use sense to develop character

Not only can sensory description be used to make a character's universe more real, it can also reveal important information about that character. In the story, "He's at the Office," (from *The Best American Short Stories 2000*, Houghton Mifflin) Allan Gurganus' narrator uses a short description to convey his father's regrettable priorities in life, as well as his own disappointment with them:

> He would then pull on his overcoat—bulky, war-efficient, strong-seamed, four buttons as big as silver dollars and carved from actual shell. He'd place the cake-sized hat in place, nod in our general direction, and set off hurrying.

Gurganus uses sensory integration to make his narrator's feelings about his father plain. By contrast, *Cry of the Peacock* (Crown, 1991) author Gina B. Nahai reveals just enough through the use of sensory description to intrigue us further:

> In 1937, electricity came to Peacock's street. One night, Blue-Eyed Lotfi came to her house and screwed a glass bulb into the ceiling of her room. Lotfi pulled at a string. Light burst into Peacock's eyes and blinded her.

In the above passage, full of vibrant sensory detail, Nahai communicates as much about Peacock's inexperience and wonder as the knowledge and wherewithal possessed by the mysterious Blue-Eyed Lotfi. In so doing, she helps demonstrate how sensory integration can be a subtle, but eloquent, tool for character development.

3. Describe variations on a sense

Like the fingers of your hand, our senses act as a collective antenna, each one working in concert with the other four. Yet each sense also functions as its own unique experiential interpreter. Rendering the experience of one sense on multiple levels can deepen a reader's involvement in your story.

Multilayered sensory description can come in different styles, from the ethereal illustration of hearing in *The Line of Beauty* (Bloomsbury, 2004), by Alan Hollinghurst . . .

> He lay awake listening to the silence, which was illusory, a cover to a register of other sounds . . . the sigh of a grey poplar, the late half-conscious toppings-up of the cistern overhead, and within his ears remote soft percussions, like doors closing in non-existent wings of the house.

. . . to John Irving's continued depiction of the pig barn's unfortunate end, this time with a focus on the olfactory sense . . .

> And what did we smell? That cooked-barnyard smell of mid-summer, the conflicting rankness of ashes in snow, the determined baking of manure—the imagination of bacon, or roast pork.

. . . to the urgent portrayal of libidinous floodgates crashing open, again courtesy of Hollinghurst . . .

> They kissed for a minute more—two minutes, Nick wasn't counting, half-hypnotized by the luscious rhythm, the generous softness of Leo's lips and the thick insistence of his tongue . . . . He felt the coaxing caress of Leo's hand at the back of his head, roaming through the curls there, and then lifted his other hand to stroke Leo's head, so beautifully alien in its hard stubbly angles and the dry dense firmness of his hair.

Each example above carries a different tone and rhythm, but each pulls the reader in by probing several layers of a single sense.

4. Use one sense to set up another

In real life, the experience of one sense can temporarily distract us from the presence of another. In writing, you can use this phenomenon to powerful effect by focusing a reader's attention on one type of sensation as a means to accentuate a second. In the story "The Fix" (from *Damned if I Do*, Graywolf Press, 2004), author Percival Everett lulls us with a prosaic aural description before shocking us with a disconcerting visual one:

> Douglas had been drawn outside from cleaning up in the storeroom by a rhythmic thumping sound, like someone dropping a telephone book onto a table over and over. He stepped out into the November chill and discovered that the sound was actually that of the larger man's fists finding again and again the belly of Sherman Olney, who was being kept on his feet by the second assailant.

At the beginning of this paragraph, we're slowly, innocuously taken in by the author's auditory metaphor. A few words later, he has us wondering who the heck Sherman Olney is— and what in God's name he did to deserve such treatment.

5. Combine senses

Though at a given moment we are always favoring one sense—whether awed by a flash of lightning, dipping a toe into the bath, or sniffing our morning coffee—this status is constantly shifting, with one sense frequently calling others to awareness. The most effective sensory descriptions often combine two senses or more, such as in the following from Robin Cook's *Contagion* (Putnam, 1995), containing elements of both touch and sound:

> Terese and Colleen greeted them with air kisses: the mere touching of cheeks accompanied by a smacking sound.

As the above example demonstrates, the exercise of combining multiple senses does not necessarily require the use of excessive words. Consider an additional example, from Louise Penny's *Still Life* (St. Martin's Minotaur, 2006):

> Gamache cupped his hands around the mug holding his hot, fragrant cider and waited.

Say this sentence had been written, "Gamache cupped his hands around the mug and waited." Comparatively ordinary, isn't it? Now read it again, and realize how the author finely employs two senses, touch and smell—not to mention the suggestion of taste—to make the description so forcefully evocative.

Sometimes it takes a while to figure out who your characters are or what they're supposed to be doing. But they do come with one built-in advantage: They have the same five senses you do. Incorporate those senses in your writing, let readers experience the same sights, sounds, smells, touches and tastes your characters do, and it's a good bet they'll remember your story long after they've turned the final page.

Does Size Matter?

*Four Editors Discuss the (Un)importance
of Story Length*

by Will Allison

What's the ideal length for a short story? Ask this question to any writer worth her salt and you'll likely get a blank stare, the answer's so obvious: A story should be as long as it needs to be, no more and no less.

But will any particular length give your story a better shot at being published? This is a trickier question. Of the more than 330 literary magazines whose listings appeared in the last edition of this book, roughly two-thirds specified no length limit. In other words, the editors don't care how long your story is as long as they like it.

However, the remaining third *did* indicate a maximum word count for submissions, and of the 120 or so magazines that cited an average length for the fiction they publish, more than 60% said their average piece of fiction was 3,000 or fewer words (about 10 double-spaced pages of 12-point Times New Roman text).

Given these figures, a story writer might reasonably conclude that the shorter her story is, the better chance it has of getting published. And it's no secret that—past a certain point—the longer a story is, the harder it is to find a home for it. There's even a literary magazine in Lawrence, Massachusetts, devoted solely to long stories. It is called, fittingly enough, *The Long Story*, and its editor, R.P. Burnham, characterizes long stories as "the most difficult literary form to publish in our country." (For the record, Burnham considers stories between 8,000 and 20,000 words.)

The reason long stories are difficult to publish—aside, perhaps, from the perceived shrinkage of the average American's attention span—involves space and budget constraints, which all print magazines (if not their online counterparts) must contend with. Given that space is limited, publishing an 8,000-word story can mean having to turn away two 4,000-word stories. Fortunately—for writers of longer stories, at least—length is only a secondary consideration (if it's a consideration at all) for the fiction editors in the following roundtable.

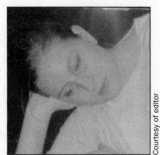

Courtesy of editor

Sarah Blackman

Sarah Blackman is an MFA student at the University of Alabama, where she serves as fiction editor for *The Black War-*

WILL ALLISON's (www.willallison.com) short stories have appeared in *Zoetrope: All-Story*, *Glimmer Train*, *Kenyon Review*, *One Story*, *Shenandoah*, *Atlanta* and other magazines and have been cited in *The Best American Short Stories* and *The Pushcart Prize XXX: Best of the Small Presses*. The shortest story of his collection-in-progress clocks in at 6,371 words; the longest, 8,746 words.

rior Review. Her most recent publications appear or are forthcoming in *The Roanoke Review*, *The Backwards City Review*, *The Bat City Review*, *Best New American Voices 2006* and *Here on the Chester*, an anthology of Chesapeake Bay area literature.

Howard Junker founded *ZYZZYVA*, a journal for West Coast writers and artists, in 1985. He has edited five antholog-ies of work from its pages, most recently, *AutoBioDiversity* (Heyday), as well as four *ZYZZYVA* first novels and three *ZYZZYVA* first collections of poems. He lives with his wife in San Francisco.

Courtesy of editor

Howard Junker

Andrew Tonkovich, editor of *Santa Monica Review*, has taught fiction and nonfiction writing workshops and has pub-lished short stories and essays. He is a graduate of UC Irvine's MFA writing program and recently started a book club in his community.

Nancy Zafris is the fiction editor of *The Kenyon Review.* She teaches at the Kenyon Review Writers Workshop each June. An excerpt from her latest novel, *Lucky Strike* (Unbridled Books), won a 2006 National Endowment for the Arts fellowship.

What's the average length of the fiction you publish?

Sarah Blackman (*Black Warrior Review*): *The Black Warrior Review* doesn't specify on either our submissions page or internally to our readers how long is too long for a short story, but generally we publish within the 6,000- to 7,500-word range. With that said, we always welcome and are frequently very excited by short-short stories (1,500 or fewer words). We have been known to publish substantially longer pieces, although this happens with less frequency.

Howard Junker (*ZYZZYVA*): Our stories have ranged from half a page to 30 pages (out of a total of 130 pages of text in each issue).

Andrew Tonkovich (*Santa Monica Review*): Twenty pages.

Nancy Zafris (*Kenyon Review*): Five thousand to 7,000 words.

In a fiction workshop I taught, we once decided that a story was officially "long" if the manuscript required two staples. In your mind, what constitutes a long story?

Blackman: I would say 10,000 words is definitely a long story. A story that has to be constrained with an industrial strength binder clip is a long story. A writer who feels the need to apologize for the length of her submission in the cover letter is quite possibly sending us too long a story.

Junker: A story gets longish around 15 pages.

Tonkovich: My mind, if engaged by a story or essay, often doesn't even register length except to hope that it doesn't stop, to root for the piece. If the terrific writing stops, I immedi-ately feel the story is too long.

Zafris: A long story for me is 8,000 words and above.

To what extent is length a factor as you're considering stories for publication?

Blackman: One of the things I really appreciate about *The Black Warrior Review* is that our only factor when considering submissions is the quality of the work. I think we have a reputation for publishing exciting, cutting-edge fiction and poetry, and the work that comes across my desk displays an incredible range of styles, focuses and authors—both nationally recognized and up-and-coming. With that said, the business of running the magazine de-mands that some editorial decisions be based on more boring practicalities. Our in-house screeners generally go through four to five stories every two weeks. If I get an unusually long story submission, I will frequently take that home to read myself, rather than making their load more difficult. In some ways this benefits the long short-story author, but in other ways it limits the potential audience the author will receive at our magazine. In such cases, the work is subjected to and evaluated based only on my opinion, rather than the myriad different viewpoints it may have been exposed to during our reading process.

Junker: Not at all, unless a deadline's near and I have a hole to fill.

Tonkovich: None.

Zafris: I tend to shy away from short shorts and stories under 3,000 words. I've noticed that more and more literary magazines are moving toward very short fiction and publishing fewer long stories. Even though I love short shorts and write them myself, I want to save space for those long stories whose depth and complexity demand length. Plus I just want to do my part not to cave in to the diminution of the American attention span.

Do you ever publish fiction that exceeds your stated limit? And, if so, what considerations come into play?

Blackman: We don't have a stated limit at our Web site—merely a suggestion of 7,500 words—but when we do publish substantially larger pieces, our decision is based first and foremost on the quality of the story—whether it excites interest and maintains that excitement—and secondarily on whether the length of the story is justified and utilized by its content.

Junker: We don't have a stated limit.

Tonkovich: I have published work that likely exceeds other magazines' stated limits, and I imagine that I have offered authors of longer stories or essays a place to send work for consideration. I have on three or four occasions published very, very long stories and twice published entire 75-page novellas.

© Roy Bauer

Andrew Tonkovich

Zafris: I don't actually know what our stated limit is. It might be 8,000 words. I know we just accepted a story by a new writer that weighs in at nearly 12,000 words (Rebecca Kanner's "Byblis"). This is her third publication, so it's not an exception we make for high-profile writers. It's an exception we make for stories that need to be that long. I didn't even realize it was that long while reading it. (It was an online submission.) For me, great stories always read too short.

Do you find any common weaknesses among the longer submissions you reject? For instance, do many of them strike you as being longer than necessary or, conversely, do many of them seem like they want to be novels?

Blackman: The most common weakness among rejected longer submissions is that their length doesn't seem to be justified by the story. Either the story seems like it would be more dynamic or contain more narrative tension if it were shorter, or the author is using the physical length of the piece to disguise a myopic conception of the story itself. Occasionally, we do see a long narrative that is rejected from the magazine because it hasn't had *enough* room to deal with its subject matter—I call them novelettes—but this is rarer.

Junker: All rejected stories are the same: I didn't feel like publishing them. In any case, I never worry about weaknesses; I'm interested only in strengths. A powerful story, an enchanting story—any kind of wonderful story may have all sorts of weaknesses, from bad spelling on up, but it doesn't matter, because I can fix (or disguise) weaknesses. Strengths, however, are a gift from the muse and cannot be produced by an editor.

Tonkovich: Common weaknesses: Too much of a not-so-good thing. The work must be engaging and terrific from word one to the end, which includes the middle. When the work starts to fail, the reader begins to feel a miserable obligation to see the writer redeemed somehow at the conclusion, which doesn't always make up for the unnecessary slowness or clumsiness of the getting there and causes the reader to feel guilt and self-hatred, obligation and impatience and resentment at going along for the ride in the first place. The editor has to protect the reader from having to enter this little Bermuda Triangle and must reject the work. Readers want pleasure, not to have started a checklist in their heads about the relative successes and failures of the writing as they are reading.

Zafris: Most stories have some fat on them. We often ask for tightening up, but I don't know if that's a matter of length. I think it's a matter of writers using a lot of expository back story that could be cut. It's a matter of generalizing when they should be dramatizing. It's a matter of starting the story at the top of page three without the first two pages of front matter. And so on. That happens no matter what the length. An 8,000-word story could probably be 7,000. A 7,000-word story could probably be 6,300. And a 3,500-word story that has all the problems I listed probably isn't a story yet. We asked Rebecca Kanner to cut her 40-page story by three or four pages. It's now 37 pages, and it makes a big difference.

© Jim Zafris

Nancy Zafris

A lot of literary magazines have length limits in the 5,000 word range, but a lot of first-rate stories exceed that length (see any recent edition of *The Best American Short Stories*), and at least one venerable story writer, Lee K. Abbott, has argued that it's unusual to see a successful story of fewer than 20 manuscript pages (~6,000 words). Do you think there's any merit to the idea that, when it comes to stories, perhaps longer equals better?

Blackman: I love a confident story. I want to be drawn into a world that knows its rules and boundaries—whatever those may be—and introduced to characters who will capture and hold my attention, sympathy or disgust, according to the aims of the author. Some people may be able to do that in 1,000 words, and some stories may need 10,000 words to fully explore the scope of their drama. So, I think when it comes to stories, better equals better, and that comes in all different packages.

Junker: I like both sprints and marathons.

Tonkovich: You can see that I have trouble quantifying all of this. I hope most editors don't quantify, frankly. Readers are smart, and they will recognize that work is defined by its content, so that a fragmented piece or an excerpt or a fully-developed traditional short story all carry a promise to the reader implicit in their voice and sentence strategy and, for instance, their reliance on dialogue. I don't publish much that's dialogue driven, for instance. There's a lot of white space on the page, which probably makes the story ''longer,'' right? But it's a quicker read. Perhaps development, intensity and engagement are what Abbott means by longer.

Zafris: I agree with Lee on this. When I teach writers who are fashioning stories between eight and 12 pages, the first thing I tell them is that no matter what, they have to push through and write a story of 17 to 18 pages. There is something ''chemically'' different about pushing through to 18 pages or so. The stories attain a complexity of layering and plot and resolution that most 12-page stories don't have. Many 12-page stories are simply laying out very interesting and fascinating premises and then calling it quits as soon as the premise (but not the plot, not the story) wears out. That is, just when things get complex—when the going gets rough, so to speak—the author seeks an arresting image and calls the story off. But, as always, there are exceptions to any rule.

From Trouble to Transformation

Character and the Dramatic Struggle

by W.E. Reinka

Anyone who has written a short story or a novel will vouch that it is not simple. Yet writing coach and seminar leader James N. Frey distills writing the dramatic story down to such simple terms that it almost seems easy, beginning with the simple definition that in a dramatic story the central character is transformed through a dramatic struggle. Think Samson and Delilah. Think Scrooge. Think *The Old Man and the Sea*.

Following his own advice, Frey has published nine novels including the Edgar-nominated *The Long Way to Die* (Pan Macmillan, 1989). But he's best known for the straight-forward primers on novel writing *How to Write a Damn Good Novel* (St. Martin's, 1987), *How to Write a Damn Good Novel II* (St. Martin's, 1994) and *The Key: How to Write Damn Good Fiction Using the Power of Myth* (St. Martin's, 2000). He conducts writing seminars that sell out quickly and critiques individual manuscripts.

"All the classic novels are dramatic," Frey says. "*War and Peace* is not an exercise in language. Dickens? Every page is dramatic. *The Brothers Karamazov* is a murder mystery. One hundred years from now *The Godfather* will be the literary novel of our time."

CHARACTERS DEFINE PLOT

Notice that his definition of a dramatic story mentions only character, not plot. Frey defines "plot" as a synopsis of who the character is, what the character's struggle is, and what transformation the character undergoes. "To me, plot means action and character transformation. Most people who say 'plot' mean action of the story. Whenever I hear a story idea, my first question is 'What's the hero like?,' " says Frey. "Any good story only works when the character changes. For example, in *The Godfather* Michael Corleone transforms from a college kid into a ruthless mobster. But there's always an underlying part where the character doesn't change. Michael Corleone's motivation stems from his love of family at the beginning of the novel and he loves his family at the end."

Frey's simple guidelines do have some parameters. For example, the dramatic struggle must have stakes, both in its nature and its results. The outcome must be in doubt. David must face Goliath, not a 90-pound weakling.

"The transformation must be dramatic and profound," Frey contends. "For example, a coward becomes brave. Or spirituality transforms a drunkard. A character has to be a certain type at the beginning so he can be a different character at the end." Case in point, after literally going blind, Samson is transformed when he figuratively sees the errors of his ways.

W.E. REINKA, who writes frequently about books and authors, contributes to magazines and newspapers nationwide.

Using a structure of character transformation through dramatic struggle not only produces entertaining reading but also publishing contracts. Frey challenges those who "yes but" his concepts to match his record of having 100 former students published by New York publishers. Humanity's innate love of a good story is on his side, and what makes a good story is character transformation.

CONFLICT EXPOSES CHARACTER

Frey shudders that students can go through creative writing programs without ever hearing the word conflict or understanding that conflict—a character's attempt or struggle to get out of trouble—is at the root of every good story, not only for the sake of action but also for pathos.

It's important for the reader to connect with some character in terms of pity right away. On his Web site (www.jamesnfrey.com) Frey posts an article entitled "Terrible Trouble and Other Important Stuff" where he warns against throat clearing, weather reports, and stage setting in favor of engaging the reader's sympathy by getting someone in trouble immediately. It doesn't even have to be the main character. Just as long as the reader can feel pity for someone and become emotionally involved in the tale.

"The best example is the Godfather," he tells us. "The Godfather has people killed, wrecks labor unions, bribes judges—the guy is not nice. But the author wants the reader to connect to this book emotionally so he starts out with this funeral director who's waiting for justice because his daughter was assaulted by two Anglos. He's in the Anglo court waiting for justice and what happens? The thugs get probation. So he turns to his wife and says, 'For justice we must go to the Godfather.' So the author takes this pitiful immigrant who trusted American justice and doesn't get it and uses him to connect us emotionally to the book. By the time we're introduced to the Godfather at his daughter's wedding, the FBI is writing down guests' license plates numbers and we're now completely in sympathy with the Godfather, who is basically a rat."

Story questions, not descriptions of the wallpaper in the protagonist's bedroom, grab the reader. In *How to Write a Damn Good Novel II*, Frey cites this opening from Kafka's *The Trial*: "Someone must have traduced Joseph K., for without having done anything wrong, he was arrested one fine morning."

Frey writes, "This opening sentence raises all kinds of story questions. Why was he arrested? What will happen to him? Who turned him in and why?"

OPPOSITES ON THE BELL CURVE

An effective device for introducing a dramatic struggle is to put characters, whether the hero or the antagonist or both, on a bell curve. Think what a different story *A Christmas Carol* would be if Scrooge feebly grumbled as he distributed Christmas bonuses or how ordinary Samson's transformation would seem if he didn't possess extraordinary strength. But every character doesn't need to be a Hannibal Lecter or Spider-Man. Seemingly ordinary characters can sit out on the bell curve—the insurance agent who's also a peeping tom or the Sunday school teacher who's an arsonist.

Character orchestration, which involves pairing opposites, also serves as catalyst for the tension that slowly builds to character transformation. So much the better if one or both pushes the edge of the bell curve. One of Frey's favorite examples of character orchestration is C.S. Forester's *The African Queen* in which missionary spinster Rose Sayer teams up in a trip down the river with drunkard Charlie Allnut. Opposites attract readers and make the job of sustaining conflict easier on the author. Had Allnut been another missionary, Forester might still have fashioned a love story but *The African Queen* would have been far less dramatic.

CHARTING RISING CONFLICT

Instead of a vertical outline, Frey uses what he calls a step sheet. The step sheet runs horizontally and serves as an outline, except it more graphically shows whether conflict is rising in each scene and in the novel as a whole. Each time conflict rises, Frey makes a little step up so that a well-structured book moves from the lower left to the upper right portion of the page. For example, a western may build on the basic conflict that "this town ain't big enough for the both of us." The conflict steps up as the antagonists strap on their guns and rises again as they face off for a gun fight in front of the saloon.

"Your step sheet should prove your premise for showing how this type of character is transformed in this sort of way through this form of struggle," Frey explains.

For example, in the film *High Noon*, the marshal's character transformation (and therefore the plot) is not complete after the marshal (played by Gary Cooper) shoots the villain (Frank Miller). The final step does not rise until the marshal exhibits transformation by throwing his badge in the dust and driving off in the buggy with his Quaker bride.

Ideally, conflict should rise slowly within the individual scenes as well as within the book as a whole. "Conflict can be subtle, soft or quiet and still be intense," says Frey. "One character wants something from another and is not getting it. As long as the conflict is continually rising, the reader is gripped. It's when conflict stops rising that we lose the reader."

COMMON FLAWS IN CONFLICT AND CHARACTERIZATION

Not all conflict is desirable; Frey cautions against static conflict and jumping conflict:

"Writers make the mistake of thinking that if they have intense conflict it can't be static. But static just means the characters aren't changing, like two boys out on the playground saying, 'My daddy can beat your daddy' back and forth, back and forth. Static conflict gets boring because it's the same.

"Jumping conflict is where you go from a situation of relative calm to one of tremendous conflict: BANG! The guy robs the bank in the Old West and the townspeople catch him right away and lynch him. The story shifts from no conflict to a lynching. The writer would make this dramatic with slowly rising conflict by introducing a character who says, 'Wait, let's talk about this first.' That makes it much more gripping than just stringing the guy up. Sometimes jumping conflict can't be avoided—a bomb goes off or a flying saucer appears—but normally the situation can be exploited for rising conflict. You want slowly rising conflict because it exposes the characters in their full range."

One reason writers often come up short on character transformation is they overly identify with their heroes. Frye laughingly recalls one time when a new novelist approached him about an individual critique and Frey had to beg off due to other commitments. He surprised the disappointed writer with some advice anyway.

"I said, 'I'll save you some time and money by telling you what's wrong with the book.'

"Conflict can be subtle, soft or quiet and still be intense," says Frey. "One character wants something from another and is not getting it. As long as the conflict is continually rising, the reader is gripped. It's when conflict stops rising that we lose the reader."

Craft & Technique

Of course, the fellow was astonished because I hadn't read his book. 'You have people who take actions and do dramatic things but they're not the protagonist. Your hero watches other people change and grow but your hero doesn't change and grow himself,' " says Frey. "Writers identify with their heroes, and writers tend not to do anything in their lives. They watch other people do things. And so the heroes of the stories don't tend to change."

Another common flaw Frey sees in his seminars is how both male and female writers get caught in gender roles they've learned from society. Men pack their pages with action but then come up short on how the characters react and feel about the action that bombards them. Women, on the other hand, avoid overt conflict and presume that their sensitive female readers will understand their characters' feelings, even when they're not shown. Either way makes for thin characters, and it's impossible to transform undeveloped characters.

Since plot is measured by character transformation, writers must know their characters as well as they know their best friends. Frey has his students write a third-person biography of each major character and follow that with a first-person essay in the character's voice. "This results in a sure-footed approach where the writer knows where and when characters are coming from and where they're going," he says.

Frey maintains that such a sure-footed approach serves the story better than delicate prose. "I think language is very important but it's not the focus. Language serves the story. One year I was teaching at Squaw Valley and a student who had published a literary novel came up to me and said of my lecture, 'It's very elegant. It's so simple.' And I said, yes, it's simple. You talk about all the great stories you've ever known and you'll find how a dramatic character through a dramatic struggle has a dramatic transformation. Just open your mind to it."

Making the Connection

What You Gain from Networking

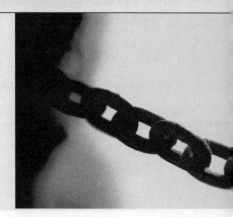

by Dena Harris

Mention the word "networking" and most writers wince. Just as the phrase "mud pies" conjures images of dark, squishy earth, "networking" brings to mind shallow interactions, insincere dialogue and a strong *ick* factor. But perhaps the term is misunderstood. Networking shouldn't function as an undeclared competition to see who can collect the most cards and build the biggest Rolodex. Real networking is about making connections—long term, reciprocal, expanding connections. And like it or not, it's a necessity for today's writer.

"I love to tell writers they're dividing their career into getting ready, getting read, and getting readers," says Katharine Sands of the Sarah Jane Freymann Literary Agency and editor of *Making the Perfect Pitch: How to Catch A Literary Agent's Eye* (Kalmbach Publications, 2004). "And getting ready means collecting names."

According to Sands, names are currency. An agent is likely to give your work more than a cursory read-through if you have been referred by one of that agent's current clients or someone the agent recognizes. Lynne Polvino, an associate editor at Clarion Books, notes that while she tries to look at every submission that comes across her desk, "those that come recommended by someone whose taste and opinions I respect usually get looked at a lot sooner."

WHERE TO START

Be where the action is:

- writers' conferences
- workshops
- book signings
- local and regional festivals where authors appear
- writers' groups (online and in person)
- continuing education classes
- book clubs
- libraries

There's no limit to the number of places you can find to network.

DENA HARRIS teaches public speaking and networking workshops at writers' conferences around the nation and is living proof an introverted writer can successfully network. Her humor/gift book on life with cats is available at *www.lessonsinstalking.com.*

"My best advice to writers is to be anywhere and everywhere you can connect with anyone who might read you, give you a blurb, or respond to what you're doing with your writing," says Sands.

But just showing up isn't enough. It's what you do with your time at these venues that counts.

Pamela Cable, a Southern fiction writer living in North Carolina, networked her way into a blurb from well-known Southern fiction author Cassandra King. "I met Cassandra at a book signing for her latest release, *The Same Sweet Girls*," says Cable. "I was able to spend a few minutes chatting with her and made sure to mention I'm a writer."

Cable sent King an e-mail thanking her for signing her book, and King e-mailed back. "Then, through a stroke of good fortune, she was a speaker at a literary league I belong to and I sat next to her at lunch," recalls Cable. "After a discussion about my upcoming collection of short stories, *Southern Fried Women*, she immediately offered to give me a blurb."

Cable admits she is an ardent networker, talking to everyone she meets. "Word of mouth is your best friend as an author," she declares.

Polvino agrees, adding, "Authors should put themselves wherever there are going to be people interested in the kind of writing they do—and just start talking."

QUID PRO QUO

But talking can be a challenge for the reserved writer. Many writers shy away from networking because they fear appearing insincere or overly aggressive with their intentions or they dislike the idea of asking for help.

Not asking for help is a common mistake of beginning novelists, according to Donald Maass of the Donald Maass Literary Agency and author of *Writing the Breakout Novel* (Writer's Digest Books, 2002). "Most writers work in isolation and as soon as they've accumulated enough pages, they go in search of an agent," says Maass. "Professional novelists belong to critique groups. At writers' conferences, the savvy newcomers have figured this out and are joining critique circles to connect with their peers."

The most successful networkers understand that networking is as much about giving as it is about taking—if not more so. The quickest way to advance your career is to always be looking for ways to help others. Why? The more people you help, the more people will be there for you when you need them.

Building a network is an ongoing process. It takes time to connect with people and effort to stay involved. But have you noticed how successful individuals in any field inevitably attribute large portions of their success to the many who helped them along the way? They're speaking of their network. Here are some ways to connect with your network:

Be prepared. You need to leave the house every day prepared to talk about yourself, your work, your accomplishments and any future projects in 15- to 60-second sound bites. Once you have your pitch down, it quickly becomes second nature and when someone asks what you do, you'll slide into pitch gear without even realizing it. Practice saying your pitch aloud, "I'm a historical romance writer and have completed my first manuscript called *Hearts Sheathed in Fire* about a late 18th-century Colonial woman locked in battle over her desire to see an America free from British rule and her love for the Commander of the English regiment she's fighting against. I'm also working on a series of short stories for *Of Ages Past*, an online magazine."

A pitch isn't meant to list all your talents and history. Rather, it whets the appetite of the listener and offers them tidbits to continue the conversation.

Know why you're there. Knowing your goals for a conference or workshop you attend will aid you in your networking. Are you looking for manuscript feedback, an agent to submit to, marketing ideas? Knowing what you want to accomplish will help determine who you need to speak to and what topics to concentrate on.

Make connections for others. Do you have a writer friend who needs to interview a cop for her next novel and a brother-in-law who happens to work in law enforcement? Offer to introduce them. Asking for help is challenging for most people, and they'll remember if you do the groundwork for them. This holds true even if the connection you make falls through. People will remember you tried to help—and they'll be willing to return the favor.

Listen. How do you determine the needs of other writers? *Listen.* Ask questions. Start conversations that don't just center around you and your work. Taking the focus off talking about you will also help you relax and be more natural when approaching others.

Cast a wide net. You might attend a conference hoping to find an agent, but don't limit yourself to speaking only to agents or to writers already represented by agencies. Talk to everyone. You don't know who will be the connection you need when you're ready to publish or promote your work. Your big break may come from an unexpected source, so stay in touch with writers, conference presenters, conference organizers, workshop teachers, local librarians, bookstore employees, former co-workers, neighbors and anyone else who crosses your path.

Consider this: Your publisher isn't going to spend time making sure your next Barnes & Noble signing is a success, but the local clerk whom you've been friendly with for years will almost certainly help you out.

Follow the 10-minutes-a-day rule. Spend 10 minutes each morning at your desk and network. Mail a clipping from yesterday's paper to a colleague you know would find it interesting. Make a quick phone call to a friend you haven't heard from in a while. Book your reservation at an upcoming writers' conference. Send follow-up notes, handwritten thank-you notes, or clippings to individuals to let them know you're thinking of them. A little old-world politeness makes an impression in today's fast-paced world.

WRITERS' CONFERENCES

Take advantage of writers' conferences, especially those offering access to agents and editors. You'll often find them more approachable than if you try to contact them at their office.

"Agents cannot be hired to give editorial opinions, and rarely do, but I'll offer substantive suggestions to conference attendees that I would never, ever do from my New York City office," says Sands. "Agents can't invest a lot of time focusing on the needs of writers they don't represent. But in the context of the conference, we're on hand to be helpful and to be involved in the writing process."

Sands goes on to state she'll offer a title idea for a work-in-progress or give a writer a clear sense of reasons she would decline their work despite liking its interesting elements. "Especially for new writers, conferences are the one sure place they'll find agents who are attentive and willing to give specific feedback," she concludes.

Master classes or workshops run by agents, editors or established writers also offer networking opportunities not usually available.

When Edmund Schubert first began writing science fiction, he attended a week-long boot camp hosted by the Hugo and Nebula Award-winning author Orson Scott Card. After attending camp, Schubert dropped by one of Card's book signings, mentioning he'd just finished a short story. Card gave Schubert his home number and within a couple of days Schubert was sitting in Card's home as Card reviewed his work. That meeting led to Schubert being published in the debut issue of *Orson Scott Card's Intergalactic Medicine Show*.

"I enrolled in Boot Camp because I wanted to learn more about writing," says Schubert. "But once there, I realized I would have access to Orson Scott Card in a way that I wouldn't have had otherwise. And that access has turned out to be a very valuable thing."

Getting Published

Professional or Pushy?

The stories of manuscripts slid under toilet stalls at conferences are, alas, true. Getting an agent's or editor's attention and getting *positive* attention are two different things. Follow the advice below to make sure you leave a good impression:

- **Be prepared.** Show up at a conference with your pitch, business cards, a one-page synopsis of your work, your confidence and your sense of humor.
- **Dress the part.** First impressions count. You may know you can knock 'em dead at a book signing tomorrow, but that's not the message those sweatpants are sending today.
- **Take advantage of circumstances.** If you don't typically have access to agents and editors, don't waste the opportunity. Gather your courage and approach them in the hall to say hello.
- **No stalking allowed.** Allow agents and editors a chance to eat breakfast or pee in peace.
- **Also, no hogging.** If a line has formed behind you and others are waiting their turn to talk to the agent or editor, be considerate and step aside. You're not winning brownie points by keeping them cornered.
- **Network with everyone.** The thrill of networking is never knowing where you'll hit pay dirt. The writer in line behind you or the conference organizer may have the connection you're seeking. It's fun to schoomze with the bigwigs but often it's your fellow writers who hold the key to your success. Don't snub them.
- **Courtesy counts.** Send thank-you notes to agents and editors, but also to other attendees who made the conference memorable for you.
- **Exercise common decency.** Treat others as you'd wish to be treated, listen more than you talk, ask questions, stay engaged. Editors and agents are people who, like us, respond to those who are genuine. Be yourself.

GAME ON

Not everyone arrives at a conference with a completed manuscript ready to pitch. What if you're not ready? Maass strongly recommends writers still introduce themselves to agents and editors. "I'm a repeat presenter at several conferences and I love meeting writers year after year and seeing their work progress," says Maass. "The people whose work I've read several times and with whom I've formed a relationship tend to be the writers I take on as clients."

As for an introduction, Maass recommends writers try this:

> Hi, I'm (name). I'm not ready to pitch to you yet, but I've (heard you speak/ know this client of yours/am aware of your reputation) and I just wanted to shake your hand and say I'm looking forward to sending you a query letter at some point in the future.

The agent or editor may then ask what you are working on and, if they like what they hear, may ask to see the work once it's ready. Here, Maass offers a caution to writers. "A frequent mistake of writers is cleaving to an artificial deadline of when they told the agent or editor they would have the work to them. Agents don't care about you getting the work to us by your deadline—we've got plenty to keep us busy. We care about receiving the work *when it's ready.*"

Maass emphasizes he'd rather wait years for a novel that has truly come into its own than be sent a partial, first-draft manuscript. Networking with other writers in your critique groups and at conferences will let you know when your work is ready to be sent.

WRITERS' COMMUNITIES

If traveling to conferences or attending master classes is outside your budget, opportunities for power networking may be blooming in your own backyard. Being involved in writers' communities—whether they are critique groups, online workshops, listservs or book clubs—can lead to connections, contacts, inspiration and knowledge.

Victor DiGenti self-published his first book, *Windrusher.* The book had been out less than a month when DiGenti met another local author who purchased two copies of *Windrusher* at a book signing. That author wrote a review in her online newspaper column, bringing DiGenti much attention, and she introduced him to her publisher.

From that introduction, the publisher asked to acquire the sequel, eventually acquiring the rights to *Windrusher* as well. "I encourage writers to put themselves out there, meet people and keep smiling," says DiGenti. "You never know when lightning will strike."

THE MOST COMMON NETWORKING MISTAKE

The most common networking mistake for writers is that they simply don't do it.

Naturally, writers like to focus on the writing. But, as Sands points out, "One of the big mistakes writers make is to put all of their energy, creative juices and passion into the one result: the Big Book. Succeeding as a writer in today's market is about creating a successful author platform, which may include all kinds of writing, publishing, blogging and networking."

However, stellar networking won't ever compensate for weak writing. "Writers like to indulge in 'magical thinking' such as 'it's only about who you know and not what you write' for getting published," says Maass. "That's not how it works. I might read a little further into a manuscript if I've had personal contact with the author, but that doesn't change the words on the page. It's either good writing or it's not."

While networking won't bring instant fame, it can make you a better writer as you interact and share your work with peers, and it can open doors in terms of who sees and has access to your work. So come out from behind the laptop, go to a book signing, attend a writers' conference, and find ways to start making connections today.

Getting Published

Sacred Texts

Christian Fiction Requires Strong Writing and Strong Values

by Rock Neelly

With the colossal success of Mel Gibson's movie *The Passion of the Christ*—its ticket receipts and sales approaching a half billion dollars—and the surge of buzz surrounding pastor Rick Warren's nonfiction self-help book *The Purpose Driven Life*—which sold 23 million copies—the eyes of booksellers at even the most mass-market of stores and of theater owners in every tiny rural town and booming metropolis were opened to a divine revelation: Christian consumers have major clout.

But it was co-authors Tim LaHaye and Jerry Jenkins and their Left Behind series that revolutionized the Christian fiction marketplace. The series about the "End Times" now numbers 13 books and has sold over 60 million copies.

Brandilyn Collins, an established Christian author with more than 10 novels in print and winner of an American Christian Fiction Writer's (ACFW) award in 2005, said of LaHaye and Jenkins: "They broke it wide open to the secular world of both readers and publishers by proving that a no-holds-barred Christian story can sell. After *Left Behind*, we saw more secular publishers wanting to jump on the bandwagon."

Brandilyn Collins

Courtesy of author

David Gregory, author of *Dinner with a Perfect Stranger* (WaterBrook Press, 2005) and its sequel, *A Day with a Perfect Stranger* (2006), concurs. "In one respect," says Gregory, "it's a good time to be a Christian author. The marketplace has certainly grown and there are many more potential readers. On the other hand, the ratio of people who want to get published to new authors that publishers are willing to take a risk on is probably shrinking. In that respect, it's a good time to be a Christian author who can write well and has some original ideas."

David Gregory

Courtesy of author

ROCK NEELLY is a writing instructor and contributing editor for *Wearables Business Magazine* and *Modern Uniforms*. He specializes in fashion features for apparel trade journals but has also written sports articles for a daily newspaper and feature articles for wire service distribution. He is currently at work on a novel.

What Would Jesus Write?

But both Gregory and Collins write outside what might be called traditional Christian fiction.

Gregory's *Dinner with a Perfect Stranger* places its protagonist, Nick, a present-day non-Christian, opposite Jesus Christ for dinner and conversation. The book has sold well, reaching the *New York Times* extended best-seller list, and is a favorite at Christian bookstores around the country. The novel, however, is hard to categorize.

"It's a 'tweener' book—not standard Christian fiction, not nonfiction apologetics," explains Gregory. "When I sent it to Waterbrook Press, however, they immediately saw the market potential for it and ran with it."

Collins, on the other hand, is best known for her suspense/thrillers with Christian themes. Her novel *Dead of Night* (Zondervan, 2005), a story of the power of prayer over evil, is the third in her Hidden Faces mystery series. The book won the ACFW award for Suspense in 2005. The finale to the series, *Web of Lies*, was released in 2006.

Collins says, "*Dead of Night* is on the far end of Christian suspense because of the amount of evil it presents (including the point of view of the serial killer). At the time I wrote it (spring of 2004), I thought it might be too much. My editor said to write it as I wanted, and if they needed to pull back a little, we'd do that in editing. Turned out we hardly pulled back at all. Now, just a year and a half later, I wouldn't even have qualms about writing a similar story. Christian suspense has changed dramatically in the last couple of years."

And certainly that is the case. The bookstore shelf space dedicated to Christian fiction is expanding, and the range of subject matter for faith-based fiction is widening as well. Linda Wichman is a great case in point. Wichman's first novel, *Legend of the Emerald Rose* (Kregel, 2005), is a story based upon Arthurian legend. In the novel, the son of the magician Merlin and the daughter of King Arthur and Lady Guenevere battle the forces of evil to save their kingdom.

"Since childhood, I've loved the legend of King Arthur," says Wichman. "I wanted to write a version in which the Arthur and Merlin legacies continued. When I became a Christian, I realized there were few Christian versions out there."

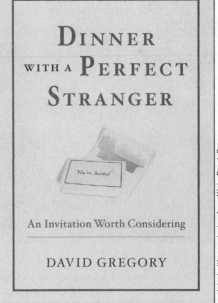

Reprinted with permission from Zondervan.

Reprinted with permission from WaterBrook Press.

Legend of the Emerald Rose found an ecstatic reading public, and the book won the ACFW award for Novel of the Year for General Fiction. However, the novel has been considered "pretty steamy" by some Christian standards.

Wichman acknowledges her publishers' reservations. "There was a lot of blushing on their end. For one, I write too sensually and gritty, thus there were editorial struggles on both ends. In fact, my publisher has [initially] turned down the second novel because it is too secularly geared.

"There's no denying I'm a maverick in the Christian terrain. I'm primarily called to write for seekers and nonbelievers, which leads me to write with a secular slant. That means I get my fingers slapped by a lot of the Christian editors."

Courtesy of author

Linda Wichman

Pushing boundaries, remaining faithful

With such a wide array of subjects and settings for Christian fiction, boundaries are constantly pushed, but the Christian message must be ever present.

Reprinted with permission from Kregel.

"Are lines being crossed? Oh, yes," says Joyce Livingston, well-known author of Christian romance novels and winner of the ACFW award in 2005 for the Short Contemporary Book of the Year for her novel *One Last Christmas* (Barbour, 2005). "That line," she notes, "seems to become grayer all the time. We see more books pushing the envelope every day, as writers want to write 'real.' Incest, child molestation, rape, drug use—all are taboo for many publishers of Christian fiction. If touched upon at all, it needs to be done tastefully.

"The protagonist has to be, or become, a Christian for my publishers, and I think for most of the others who publish the same type of book as I write. It's what our readers expect."

Livingston's new novel, *The Widow's Club*, is a departure for her. Where *One Last Christmas* was the tale of a middle-aged couple fighting to save their marriage, *The Widow's Club* is a sort of Christian version of television's "Desperate Housewives." In the book, Valentine Denay is the widow/heroine and the glue that holds together a group of neighborhood women. However, when her nemesis moves in next door, Valentine's world is turned upside down.

"*The Widow's Club* is quite different than anything I've written before, but I've had a blast writing it. I wanted this book to be light, fun, witty, sassy and entertaining, with frequent touches of humor."

Regardless, Livingston makes sure her writing stays within Christian norms throughout her new novel.

Collins and her suspense-themed novels allow more latitude. "Christian protagonist—no. Have to become a Christian—no. But I do think the protagonist needs to come closer to an understanding of God. In my Hidden Faces series featuring forensic artist Annie Kingston, in the first book, *Brink of Death*, she has little to no understanding of Christianity, and in fact was raised by a father who sneered at it. The book takes place over four days. That's not a lot of time for a 180-degree character arc change. By the end of the book, she's seeing some good things about Christianity and is willing to

Joyce Livingston

Courtesy of author

study more about it. Given her personality and the story's events, that is a believable arc for her."

Gregory agrees that Christian fiction is not restricted to Christian protagonists. "Neither of the protagonists in my first two novellas are Christians or become Christians, although both books end with them on that path. I didn't want to tie up the books in a nice little Christian knot. Life doesn't work that way."

Wichman believes there are "deal breakers," places where Christian fiction just can't go. "The Christian Booksellers Association (CBA) was and still is primarily geared toward edifying the church/Christian believers who demand and want books written with Christian moral values. They don't want to second-guess what they or their family read. As a Christian, I appreciate those high standards and, in fact, adhere to most of them in what I write."

Collins says, "We have to write by certain 'rules' such as no four-letter words, no sex on screen, careful attention to biblical principles. However, 'rules' sounds so negative. They actually are the 'expectations' of our target market. Therefore, to break them is to decrease possible readership of the story."

Wichman adds, "Most deal breakers remain a matter of no cursing, swearing, or sexually explicit scenes. While other [publishing] houses won't allow characters to mention body parts or natural body functions like burping or going to the bathroom. To me, that's

joyce livingston

THE *Widows' Club*

a novel

Reprinted with permission from Barbour Publishing.

totally unrealistic." She also notes the CBA's "reluctance to allow us to write true-life gritty situations with real characters who sin daily and make wrong choices and don't always come to faith in Jesus Christ at the end. That's real life."

Her resistance to this kind of restriction is not rooted in rebellion but in a careful consideration of the tenets of Christianity. "Jesus met sinners where they were and got to know them before He revealed who He was and why He'd entered their lives," she says. "The Christian authors called to write for those folks 'sitting on a fence' with their faith must always keep that in the forefront when we sit down to write a book."

Getting Published

Christian Editors Survey Trends

Trends are hard to predict—just ask Wall Street. The same is true in Christian fiction; nobody knows what's next after the unprecedented success of Tyndale House Publishers' Left Behind series.

"Trends are notoriously slippery phenomena to analyze," says **Paul Ingram**, associate editor for **Kregel Publications**. "Is something new and fantastic underway in the face of such amazing publishing and cinematic phenomena as *Passion, Purpose-Driven Life* and Left Behind? The most obvious effect of Left Behind at houses like Kregel is that apocalyptic demons and Antichrists suddenly hide behind every plot corner."

However Ingram acknowledges Kregel's faith-based catalog "has mysteries, novels exploring medical ethical issues, a courtroom thriller and stories of espionage, Columbian drug kingpins, and the plight of house churches in China. Soon we will have an excellent historical novel on the English Reformation, told largely from the viewpoint of Roman Catholic monks."

Despite the wide terrain, Ingram does offer this constant: "Kregel Publications very consciously follows a mission statement that our books will be biblically based and help individuals to know and serve Jesus Christ. We avoid plastic saints who have all of their halos in a row and stop the plot each Sunday to preach in a white clapboard chapel. But by the last page, we do hope they [our protagonists] have been confronted with the claims of Jesus Christ and authentic discipleship in a new way."

Rebecca Germany, senior editor of fiction for **Barbour Publishing**, considers Christian publishing's history. "It used to be that Christian fiction was primarily sweet romances, but now most every style of entertaining read can be found written from a Christian perspective. Romance and mysteries still sell the best."

Germany notes that Barbour is excited about a new historical novel about Caribbean pirates released in August 2006 from author M.L. Tyndall. "At first," she explains, "having a God-fearing hero in the role of violent, thieving pirate seems to go against Christian principles, but the characters and their motives are very well developed.

"A good story," she acknowledges, "need not contain graphic details of sex, violence and the like. We don't take the reader into a romantic couple's bedroom relations. A Christian novel should not use any descriptions or language just for shock or 'entertainment' value."

Dudley Delffs, editor-in-chief of **WaterBrook Press** (a division of Random House), is confident the market and genre will continue to grow. "I believe more Christian authors are selling in the general book market than ever before. Readers are intrigued by the way faith intersects with other areas of our lives—culture, politics, social issues, personal beliefs, etc."

When asked where Christian fiction is heading, Delffs says, "I believe the trends in Christian fiction will be for more blending of genres and subgenres—for example Christian chick-lit mysteries."

While he can't completely define what now identifies a work of fiction as Christian, he does know what each book must have. "Readers do expect to encounter a Christian worldview, including some of the harsh realities of life as well as redemptive hope and faith in the midst of it all."

The Christian in the marketplace

While Christian publishing houses may have different guidelines and standards than their secular counterparts, the process of finding a home for your work and submitting your manuscript is indistinguishable.

Livingston gives this tried and true advice: "Study the market. Learn your craft. Find a publishing house that accepts the type of books you want to write, then write exactly to their guidelines, which can usually be found on their Web site. Learn proper formatting, submission requirements, etc. Make your proposal and cover letter shine. No typos, please. A sloppy proposal will, quite often, get you a rejection letter without your manuscript even being read. Appear as professional and business-like as possible. Some authors submit years before selling. Some never sell, so make sure as many things are in your favor as possible."

Gregory offers, "Have fun with it. Don't take it too seriously, because no one may read it except you and your family members who can't escape you. Keep on hand a good guidebook to novel writing so you can constantly be honing your craft.

"Write what's on your heart, your passion," he adds. "It's for a reason that God has given you a passion for something. Pursue that, even if it may not have a wide market appeal. It's okay to aim at blessing a few. Enjoy the process. Whatever personal gain (financial or otherwise) you may realize from writing isn't worth it if you don't. Don't neglect loving God and loving others as you write. What does it profit a person if he gains the whole world, yet forfeits his soul?"

Take Control of Your Sales

Empower Yourself with a Marketing Plan

by Sonya Carmichael Jones

Regardless of your writing genre, marketing is the primary means by which your book sales are generated. This is true because marketing deals with every aspect that goes into the final sale of your book. Marketing determines:

- how your book is titled and designed
- how it's priced and distributed
- where it can be purchased
- where and how prominently your book is displayed at retailers

The terms *marketing* and *promotion* are often used interchangeably because both involve a series of activities where the end result is a book sale. More specifically, *promotions* refer to the communication elements of marketing that are usually executed right before and just after the book has been published. It is the way you announce to the world, "Hey, my book exists! This is why you can't live without it, and this is how you can buy it!" The most common promotions include media advertising, face-to-face selling at conferences or book fairs, book readings and radio interviews.

When you consider all the aspects of publishing that marketing affects, it's easier to understand why writers should be mindful of how their work is marketed. Still, if you're unfamiliar with the marketing process you might feel intimidated or confused about how to get involved. Successful marketing is as simple as striking a balance between your creative and business mind, the right combination you need to build your own marketing plan.

WHY MAKE A PLAN?

When you first began writing, you probably envisioned your book front and center on a table of best sellers at your local bookstore. That certainly is the "big picture," but it takes a lot of work to realize that dream. Think of your marketing plan like an album of individual snapshots, with each frame containing a smaller activity that will help you sell your book, bringing you closer to the bigger picture. Your marketing plan empowers you to have a direct impact on that big picture, so you don't have to rely solely on the marketing efforts of your publisher. Dr. Alma Bond, a retired psychoanalyst and author of 10 fiction and nonfiction books including *Tales of Psychology: Short Stories to Make You Wise* (Paragon, 2002) and

SONYA CARMICHAEL JONES is an independent marketing strategist, advertising copywriter and entrepreneurial success coach. She frequently writes for newspapers and business trade magazines. She also teaches marketing to writers through WritersWeekly.com and in learning centers throughout Seattle where she is currently based.

Who Killed Virginia Woolf? A Psychobiography (Human Sciences Press, 1989), relies on her own marketing plan because she believes without one, her books would be unknown. "Publishers are notoriously lax in promoting books unless you have written a best seller," she warns.

In addition to helping you reach your ultimate goal, creating and implementing a marketing plan is smart because:

• **It takes the guesswork out of what to do next and prevents you from wasting energy on meaningless tasks.** The plan lays out every activity you need to accomplish that leads to a book sale. All you have to do is follow the map you've created for yourself.

• **It lets you control your earning power.** You handle the what, when and where regarding promotional decisions.

• **It gives you the opportunity to track and measure your book sale results.** You will know when sales aren't increasing, and if you feel strategic changes are necessary, you can adjust your plan whenever you see fit until you get the results you want.

DEVELOPING YOUR PLAN

At what stage should authors develop a marketing plan? The short answer: Now. Pronto. Although a more definitive answer is when you begin to design the ideas for your book. A marketing plan enables you to clarify your career goals in terms of what you want to achieve with your book, whether it's $75,000 in sales, expanded readership, or a spot on a best-seller list. Regardless of your goal, when it's clear in your own mind, it's much easier for you to remain enthusiastic about your work and stick to a writing schedule. Developing a plan early in the writing process also encourages you to consider who your primary audience will be and to keep them in mind as you tell your story. A basic marketing plan essentially involves four steps: assessing your current writing situation, identifying your writing goals, designing a promotional strategy, and then measuring your results.

Step one: Assess your writing.

The first step is all about taking a close look at your writing skills. Taking stock of your current writing ability fully affirms your writing talents as well as gets you to fess up about those skills you need to work on. During the assessment phase, you safely place your ego aside while you honestly examine your writing strengths and weaknesses. Scrutinize your writing from a variety of angles. Consider things like your narrative style and how your writing stacks up against what's on the market with respect to dialogue, plotting, character development and description. When you know what your best-selling competition is doing, you become aware of what you need to do in order to make your book a best seller, too. Aside from those basic elements of fiction, try to isolate whatever you think makes your story particularly compelling, funny or inspirational. By determining what your greatest writing strengths are, you uncover unique characteristics that you can leverage as competitive selling advantages.

Consider this: Each genre places emphasis on certain elements of craft—for example, generally speaking, romances are heavy on dialogue and thrillers are plot-driven—so if one of your goals is to expand your audience by crossing over from contemporary romance to romantic suspense but you struggle with weaving together subplots or keeping the pacing of your plots up-tempo, you know you've got some serious plot practice to do before your marketing goal will be realistic. Conversely, if during your writing assessment you acknowledge you've got a knack for both crackling dialog and brisk plot but you hadn't considered trying your hand at a new genre or subgenre, you may have just discovered a new marketing goal for yourself. Your competitive selling advantage would be your potential to reach a crossover audience. And the ability to reach more than one audience is a huge advantage. If your goal is to enlist an agent or to attract a publisher, you'll increase your chances of doing so if publishers and agents believe your book already appeals to an easy-to-reach purchasing group (often called a "platform").

Step two: Identify your goals.

Make a chart with the following column headings: Strengths, Opportunities, Weaknesses and Threats. List at least five characteristics you consider to be your best writing assets. (Hint: Think about your writing strengths in terms of how a particular writing asset can influence a book purchase.) In the Opportunities column, list any nonwriting-related skills, knowledge or connections you have that might help your writing career. Under Weaknesses, list five areas that give you the greatest difficulty. These could be things like illustrating tension between characters, creating a love scene, or transitioning into a new chapter. In your Threats column, list five areas you view as obstacles that, if not acted upon, can prevent you from making a book sale. For example, you might be terrified of public speaking or have a hard time summing up your stories succinctly (called a "pitch") when conversing with other writers or with editors or agents at conferences. Resolving these issues before you're faced with an audience won't impact a sale.

The next phase of the marketing plan has to do with outlining your writing goals. Below your writing assessment, make a column with the following headings: Goals, Action Steps, Resources and Accomplish By Date. List five writing aims you would like to achieve. Then beside each goal list specific action steps you need to take in order to achieve a particular goal. Under the Resources column list items you will need to support your progress. These can be resources such as an encouraging friend, an updated Web site (with a free book chapter displayed), or a glossary of police terminology. Next put the date in which you plan to have all of the action steps completed.

Step three: Design a promotional strategy.

While writers usually have at least some promotional guidance from their publishing house, shrinking publicity budgets and a shortage of PR manpower across the industry encourage authors to provide not only promotional ideas but also a considerable amount of leg work. Because self-published authors are responsible for the entirety of designing and executing their promotional plan, it can be helpful to look at some of their creative (and even over-the-top) strategies to get ideas for your own plan.

Creating promotions can be the most exciting part of the marketing plan. Just ask Fran Capo, the only author on record to hold a book signing at both the top of Kilimanjaro. Capo and her son climbed to the top of the mountain to promote the release of her self-published book *Adrenaline Adventures: Dream It . . . Read It . . . Do It!* (Author House). "I guess you can say I'm into extreme book signings," says Capo. This motivational speaker and acclaimed stand-up comedienne (who happens to hold the Guinness Book record for fastest-talking woman) has made it a point to get involved with marketing her books.

"If you look at the simple numbers, publishers usually have a few dozen books they are promoting at any given time," she says. "It helps both the publisher and author to get the author's name out there as well as the name of the book. The more you are in the public eye, the better the sales."

Capo says she sustains readership interest by keeping herself in the press on a *weekly* basis using a combination of radio, TV, print and Web. Even if your marketing activities don't require quite the same level of adventure or intensity as Capo's, they can still create enough interest to inspire a reader to make a book purchase.

Self-published author Diane Craver developed an interesting promotional strategy around two of her best writing assets: her knowledge of downs syndrome and adult illiteracy. In her book *The Christmas of 1957* (Booklocker.com), Diane develops her story around the struggle of a family who deals with a special needs family member. Though Diane's book is a holiday story, she realized while building a marketing plan she could take advantage of subplots that provided additional two niche audiences.

"Promoting a book with a Christmas title can limit your selling time to just the holiday season," says Craver. But she certainly proves that when you think beyond the bookstore, you eliminate unnecessary selling limitations. "My book has a year-round message and I knew people would buy it if I could get media attention. I thought about what other times of the year might be good for me to get the media interested. Since my book is about a father-daughter relationship, I decided to promote it in conjunction with Father's Day. I e-mailed the morning host on a Findlay [Ohio] radio station and sent him a book copy. He loved the book and conducted a radio interview with me in June."

Craver's novel also dealt with the sensitive issue of adult illiteracy. "Here again, I didn't let the Christmas title limit me; I approached teachers and literacy groups to stimulate interest in my book for its educational aspects," she says. As interest in Craver's book grew, she received additional offers for radio interviews and speaking engagements—editors of local magazines and newspapers were calling *her*. Neither of these promotional activities cost her money but rather paid her in terms of producing more book sales.

As a rule of thumb, promotional strategies need not center on costly advertising. In fact, they can be more about creativity than spending money. The most important point to keep in mind is your promotional activities should build a connection between your book and your readership. Consider each aspect of your story and who might relate to it. Then spend some time thinking about how you might reach those people.

Here's another example: You're a mystery writer whose protagonists have all been males in the 30-something age bracket. You're kicking around the idea of creating a central character who's a retired but feisty night owl who appears at the scene of every murder with clues leading police to the real perpetrator. A character like this might appeal to mature readers who appreciate a classic whodunnit murder suspense told from the point of view of a sleepless but savvy eccentric. Your book will obviously be placed in the mystery section at your local bookstore, but readers of mystery aren't your only audience. Why not set up readings for yourself at local retirement communities or senior recreational centers? Inquire at specialty shops that cater to a senior demographic about selling your books at their stores. Submit an excerpt from your novel to magazines published for senior citizens. All of these ideas present better opportunities for your book to be noticed than just waiting for someone to pluck your novel from the rows and rows of books at the bookstore.

Lastly, incorporate materials that serve as gentle reminders into your promotions. Business cards, letterhead, taglines on your e-mail communications, and rubber stamped messages on all of your postal mail correspondence reinforce promotional messages.

Step four: Measure your results.

How do you know if your marketing plan is working? The simplest, most cost-effective way is to ask each reader you encounter at bookstores, conferences or through your Web site, "How did you hear about my book?" Chart the responses so you can keep track of which promotional activities are generating the most buzz. Dr. Bond says she consults Publishers Weekly online to get a daily reading of her book status on Amazon.com and Barnesandnoble.com.

You can also gauge the effectiveness of your marketing plan by the increase in your overall confidence about the marketing process. If you feel eager about trying new ideas, that's a sign you're fully engaged in the idea of self-promotion. Of course fan mail and the steady stream of income are obvious indicators, too.

If you're not happy with your progress, consider it an opportunity to pursue another marketing direction. Whether you view your changes as big or small, you won't have to reinvent the wheel. One of the best things about your marketing plan is that it gives you various check points where you can make adjustments. Just go back to your goal and writing assessment charts to locate any missed opportunities.

Sometimes revising your marketing plan is only a matter of increasing the intensity of a particular activity, for instance scheduling a reading in more than one library around your home town or making sure your local book store puts up signs a week or two before your upcoming book signing. Other times marketing blunders may result from reasons entirely beyond your control, such as e-mailed press releases that don't reach the intended recipient.

Still, if you're uncertain about a particular approach, seek help from writing colleagues whose opinions you trust. Peruse marketing Web sites that provide advice to small businesses; these often offer ideas you can adapt to your book marketing plan.

IF NOT YOU, WHO?

Perhaps you never thought much about marketing before. Maybe you assumed you didn't have the skills or underestimated the value marketing brings. By applying the same level of creativity to promoting your book as you do to developing your story, you create the best opportunity for sustaining your writing income. After all, when you consider how much of your heart and soul you contributed to the making of your book, who else would you entrust to ensure its success?

Success Story

Author Alan Neff Reflects on Late Nights,
Early Mornings and 2004 NSSWM

© Giau Truong

by Alan H. Neff

Through high school and college, I told everyone who'd listen that I wanted to write for a living. Instead, I went to law school, "to have," as my parents diplomatically suggested, "something to fall back on if writing didn't work out."

From the day I started working with my law degree, I supported myself in academic and research jobs by researching and writing books and articles about law, the courts and judges. Writing and selling legal nonfiction in various forms came easily to me. I didn't write any novels, though. After clearing away all the excuses, I have to say I wasn't disciplined enough then to apply myself.

After selling a nonfiction book to a major publisher for a small advance, I did quit the nine-to-five for a year to be a freelance writer-editor and to write a novel from start to finish. I finished a draft and persuaded my publisher to look at it. He liked it enough to agree to read a second draft. I wrote a second draft for him, but I lost interest in that book before he did. Writing it was more cathartic than creative. Then I received an offer to become an assistant professor, another career I'd coveted, so I gave up trying to write fiction.

While I worked as a professor for six years, I wrote and published more academic and technical articles. Eventually, I left academia to become a lawyer for the City of Chicago. Since then, I've added briefs and motions and memoranda to the pile of writing that's supported my family and me.

Eight years ago—two kids, two mortgages, one dog and three cats into the current job—I decided to try writing a novel again. The itch to realize a novel, the hunger, never had abated. I wrote the first line of the first draft of the first chapter on a yellow legal pad, in a U.S. District Judge's courtroom, during a break in a hearing. That line has never changed: "Milton leaned his fat little body into the lectern and sweated right through his suit."

I worked on Milton's story weeknights 'til 3 a.m., and even on weekend mornings, while cartoons exploded, buzzed and boinged in the background. Somehow, all that labor yielded *Blauser's Building*, a novel about lawyers—not a legal thriller, but a dark comedy about lawyers in love (but not, by and large, in love with Law).

When I finished a draft in 1998, I persuaded a friend who was a published novelist to read it. I also asked him to ask his agent to read it. My friend didn't want to do either, but he owed me $100 and showed no sign of ever paying it back. Even though he told me he didn't like the book, he knew it'd be bad form to decline a creditor's polite request. He passed it along to his agent. The agent thought *Blauser* was promising. Using his editorial suggestions, I wrote another draft. He pronounced it fit for circulation and agreed to try to place it.

After a year of waiting, calling, writing, waiting, writing and calling, he admitted to me that he'd done nothing with it. Nothing. I "fired" him—a good trick, since he'd never actually worked for me.

Next, I circulated it via queries to agents. I got one. I also persuaded a successful director in Hollywood (an old family friend) to look at it. His agency liked it and recommended the director consider it for development as a theatrical film or made-for-TV movie.

Consider! I thought I was going to be *rich*.

Another year of waiting, calling, writing, waiting, writing and calling. Unfortunately, Hollywood never returned my calls. Meanwhile, my second agent got nowhere with publishers, so I fired him, too. He didn't object.

BLAUSER'S BUILDING

A Novel
Alan H. Neff

another Denlinger book

© Giau Truong

Reluctant to give up, I sent the director's agency's comments to other writers I liked, seeking advice. They really didn't have any, other than, "Keep trying." One author whose work I admired, who seemed in interviews to be an amiable person, wrote me the rudest reply I've ever received from any person, in any context, for any purpose. I gave up then. I handed off *Blauser* to a few friends who read it and told me they liked it. I said thanks, but I shrugged off the praise as kind words from friends, the kind of noises I'd make in their place. Then I threw the manuscript on a shelf, figuring it was just toast, and got on to other things.

Still needing to scratch my creative itch, I started writing and performing poetry at open mics and slams in Chicago. I started a couple more novels, too, but they stalled, jammed up behind *Blauser*. Two years ago, I got a call from a friend of an old college girl-friend whom I hadn't seen in 30 years. "Lisa just had her novel published! She wants you to come to a reading."

I went. We talked about our literary paths: her success, my frustration. Lisa's story: "I wrote this about 10 years ago," she said. "I got an agent right away. But she couldn't sell it. So I threw it in the closet for eight years. Then I took it out. Circulated it again, unchanged. Got an agent who sold it in six months. *Six months*!"

Her story reminded me how difficult and random the walk to publishing a novel can be. Meanwhile, an English professor/friend read *Blauser*, liked it, and made some suggestions. I thought about them, and Lisa's slow-cooked success. I started work on my novel again. Using the professor's comments, I wrote some new material and decided to try to sell the book again. I purchased the 2004 *Novel & Short Story Writer's Market*.

First, I read the introductory material to orient myself to the current market. Next, I developed query letters for publishers and agents using the one-page model in the how-to section for first-time novelists. I wrote four different versions of the query, to account for varying e-mail and snail-mail submission guidelines. In the letters, I included favorable quotes from the film director's agency's comments. Also, I kept the letter to one page—a small but real demonstration of business-like concision, which I assumed the publishers expected.

While I revised the drafts of the queries, I crawled over the market listings for publishers and agents, looking for interest in my subject matter, which I could not easily characterize. Reluctantly, I settled on publishers who sought "mainstream" and "humor," not without misgivings. I identified about 60 publishers that might be interested in my subject matter and who accepted unagented material tossed over the transom in simultaneous submissions by e-mail or snail mail. For the e-mail queries, I included synopses, introductory chapters or both. I sent the other publishers snail packages with SASEs. Print, copy, staple, paperclip, sign, mail, repeat.

I argued with myself about whether to send query packages to agents. My prior agents had produced nothing. From researching agents, I knew that many of them are ex-editors, including my two former agents. If two ex-editors had liked it enough to take it on, I figured I'd market it directly to editors-in-place this time. But Lisa's experience told me not to shut any doors. I found agents whose entries in *NSSWM* suggested they might want to read it. I sent them e-mail or snail-mail queries, too. Mindful of my prior failures with agents, I viewed the agent circulations as prompted more by idle curiosity about their responses than any expectation that I'd find an agent willing to try to market it again.

In one respect, I took liberties with the publishers' and agents' guidelines. Generally, they asked for 1-3 chapters (usually the first, but occasionally including the last). I felt my first five chapters worked well as a group. They were short, too, only 12 pages altogether, so I sent them all rather than the fewer requested number.

I received a wave of quick rejections, mostly on forms, but a few were encouraging hand-written notes. One publisher *strongly* disliked the samples and told me so in a note that I might have found discouraging but for the positive feedback I'd gotten previously.

None of the agents bit, but I got requests from publishers for the entire manuscript. Four of them, all within six months of the first circulations.

When the fourth publisher requested the entire manuscript, I decided to see if I could leverage their requests into offers. I sent all four of them notes letting them know that four publishers had it and would let them know if I got any offers. (I named no names, of course.) I did this as a courtesy, but also to generate more interest, or at least provide the interested editors with enough validation of their editorial judgment to get them to ask for the whole manuscript.

Within two weeks of sending off that correspondence, I got an offer from Denlinger's Publishers, Ltd. in Edgewater, Florida. "Well," I thought, "maybe I can bootstrap that into a second offer." I let the other three know I had an offer. Two declined because of time constraints, and one answered ambiguously and then never answered any subsequent inquiries. But I didn't mind. I was satisfied with one offer. No, wait. I was *thrilled*. My initial feelings were of joy. Relief. Closure.

I wrote *Blauser's Building*, flogged it, and sold it. It took seven years from that first line written in court to the day I got the offer letter.

Just before it was released, my publisher placed a brief announcement in *Publishers Weekly*. A New York agent saw the notice and asked for my contact information. His inquiry was passed on to me, with the option to contact him or not. I researched the agent on the Web, learned he was prominent and successful, sent him my contact information, and got on with other things.

Soon enough, I got a note from the agent. He wrote that *Blauser* was a "terrific novel" and asked whether I had or wanted representation. I told him I was interested, but that my publisher held all of the rights to market *Blauser* further in other media, had first options on my next two novels, and had its own rights agent in New York. In short, I said I wasn't sure what he could do for me.

The agent's interest was exciting, so, after we spoke, I reviewed my contract with my publisher. I proposed to my publisher (via an e-mail) that we amend my contract by transferring to me both the right to market the motion picture rights and the costs of such marketing. I explained that this agent seemed to be a motivated seller with a record of substantial success selling motion picture rights, and that I would be willing to pay all costs of his agency, including his commission, which meant the publisher could enjoy the profits from any sales without bearing any of the costs. My publisher saw the sense in this win-win proposal, and I wrote the proposed amendments. In turn, I signed with the agent who is now marketing the movie rights and mass-market rights.

Now I have an enthusiastic, successful and well-connected agent working on my behalf. I'm not counting on his selling any rights to Hollywood, but it's pleasing to know I have someone else buying lottery tickets for me. I also learned three important lessons here.

First, modest beginnings can lead to big opportunities. My small/independent publisher's brief publication announcement in *PW* started a chain of events that might lead to a substantial second payday for my work.

Second, a scrupulous publisher is a valuable partner. My publisher could have ignored or discarded my agent's original inquiry. An agent can make a publishers' life more . . . challenging. After all, an agent's job on behalf of a writer-client is to extract as much as she can from a publisher. Regardless, my publisher let me know about the agent's inquiry and let me deal with it as I saw fit. I'm grateful for that.

Third, in negotiations over rights, it never hurts to ask for what you want. My amendments seemed perfectly sensible to me and a good deal for my publisher. So I asked for them, and my publisher agreed to them. After we executed the first amendment, I learned that it was the first time my publisher had ever been asked to modify one of its contracts as we had done. (Have a knowledgeable and competent agent or lawyer draft or, at least, review your agreements before you commit to them. Contract disputes can be stressful and costly, especially if they wind up in litigation.)

I know now I never really gave up on my fiction even during the three-year detour into performance poetry. I was recuperating from a fall, learning more about our language and how I could use it, recovering my focus and learning what I needed. Along the way, I realized I needed to sell *Blauser's Building*. And with the help of the 2004 *Novel & Short Story Writer's Market*, I did.

The Business of Fiction Writing

It's true there are no substitutes for talent and hard work. A writer's first concern must always be attention to craft. No matter how well presented, a poorly written story or novel has little chance of being published. On the other hand, a well-written piece may be equally hard to sell in today's competitive publishing market. Talent alone is just not enough.

To be successful, writers need to study the field and pay careful attention to finding the right market. While the hours spent perfecting your writing are usually hours spent alone, you're not alone when it comes to developing your marketing plan. *Novel & Short Story Writer's Market* provides you with detailed listings containing the essential information you'll need to locate and contact the markets most suitable for your work.

Once you've determined where to send your work, you must turn your attention to presentation. We can help here, too. We've included the basics of manuscript preparation, along with information on submission procedures and how to approach markets. We also include tips on promoting your work. No matter where you're from or what level of experience you have, you'll find useful information here on everything from presentation to mailing to selling rights to promoting your work—the "business" of fiction.

APPROACHING MAGAZINE MARKETS

While it is essential for nonfiction markets, a query letter by itself is usually not needed by most magazine fiction editors. If you are approaching a magazine to find out if fiction is accepted, a query is fine, but editors looking for short fiction want to see *how* you write. A cover letter can be useful as a letter of introduction, but it must be accompanied by the actual piece. The key here is brevity. A successful cover letter is no more than one page (20 lb. bond paper). It should be single spaced with a double space between paragraphs, proofread carefully and neatly typed in a standard typeface (not script or italic). The writer's name, address and phone number appear at the top, and the letter is addressed, ideally, to a specific editor. (If the editor's name is unavailable, address to "Fiction Editor.")

The body of a successful cover letter contains the name and word count of the story, a brief list of pevious publications if you have any, and the reason you are submitting to this particular publication. Mention that you have enclosed a self-addressed, stamped envelope or postcard for reply. Also let the editor know if you are sending a disposable manuscript that doesn't need to be returned. (More and more editors prefer disposable manuscripts that save them time and save you postage.) When sending a computer disk, identify the program you are using. Remember, however, that even editors who appreciate receiving your story on a disk usually also want a printed copy. Finally, don't forget to thank the editor for considering your story. See the sample short story cover letter on page 80.

Short Story Cover Letter

Lauren Mosko
4700 East Galbraith Rd.
Cincinnati, OH 45236
Phone (513) 531-2690
Fax (513) 531-2687
lauren.mosko@fwpubs.com

March 2, 2006

Toni Graham
Cimarron Review
Oklahoma State University
205 Morrill Hall
Stillwater, OK 74078-0135

Dear Toni Graham:

I am submitting my short story, "Things From Which You Can Never Recover" (6,475 words), for your consideration in *Cimarron Review*.

I am the editor of *Novel & Short Story Writer's Market* (F + W Publications) and my essays, interviews and reviews have been published in several other books in the Writer's Market series, as well as *The Writer's Digest Handbook of Magazine Article Writing* (2nd ed.), *I.D. Magazine*, and the alt weeklies *Louisville Eccentric Observer* and (Cincinnati's now-defunct) *Everybody's News.*

Enclosed you will also find an SASE for your response; you may recycle the manuscript. This is a simultaneous submission.

Your listing in *Novel & Short Story Writer's Market* said you are seeking work with "unusual perspective, language, imagery and character," and I think my story fits this description. I hope you enjoy it. Thank you in advance for your time and consideration.

Sincerely,

Lauren Mosko

Encl: Short story, "Things From Which You Can Never Recover"
       SASE

This sample cover letter is professional, brief and succinct so I don't waste a second of the editor's time and I allow my writing to speak for itself. The power is in the precise details: the name of the editor, the title of my story, the word count, my publishing history, and attention to their submission guidelines (noting that I've enclosed a SASE and that this is a simultaneous submission).

Query to Publisher: Novel

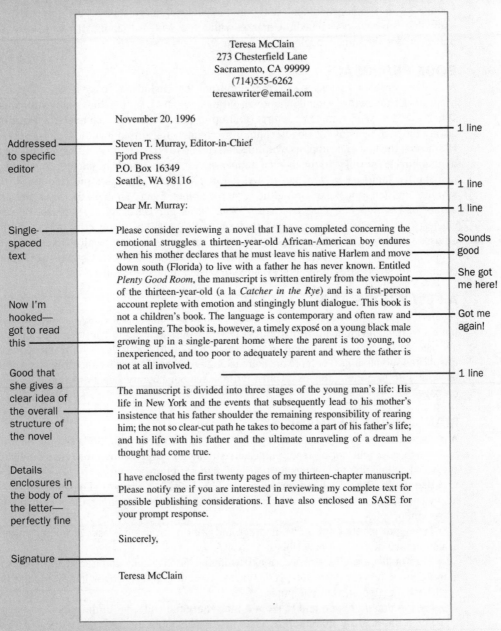

Teresa McClain
273 Chesterfield Lane
Sacramento, CA 99999
(714)555-6262
teresawriter@email.com

November 20, 1996 ─────────────────────── 1 line

Steven T. Murray, Editor-in-Chief
Fjord Press
P.O. Box 16349
Seattle, WA 98116 ───────────────── 1 line

Dear Mr. Murray: ─────────────── 1 line

Please consider reviewing a novel that I have completed concerning the emotional struggles a thirteen-year-old African-American boy endures when his mother declares that he must leave his native Harlem and move down south (Florida) to live with a father he has never known. Entitled *Plenty Good Room*, the manuscript is written entirely from the viewpoint of the thirteen-year-old (a la *Catcher in the Rye*) and is a first-person account replete with emotion and stingingly blunt dialogue. This book is not a children's book. The language is contemporary and often raw and unrelenting. The book is, however, a timely exposé on a young black male growing up in a single-parent home where the parent is too young, too inexperienced, and too poor to adequately parent and where the father is not at all involved.

The manuscript is divided into three stages of the young man's life: His life in New York and the events that subsequently lead to his mother's insistence that his father shoulder the remaining responsibility of rearing him; the not so clear-cut path he takes to become a part of his father's life; and his life with his father and the ultimate unraveling of a dream he thought had come true.

I have enclosed the first twenty pages of my thirteen-chapter manuscript. Please notify me if you are interested in reviewing my complete text for possible publishing considerations. I have also enclosed an SASE for your prompt response.

Sincerely,

Teresa McClain

Comments provided by Steven Murray of Fjord Press.

Annotations (left margin):
- Addressed to specific editor
- Single-spaced text
- Now I'm hooked—got to read this
- Good that she gives a clear idea of the overall structure of the novel
- Details enclosures in the body of the letter—perfectly fine
- Signature

Annotations (right margin):
- Sounds good
- She got me here!
- Got me again!
- 1 line

APPROACHING BOOK PUBLISHERS

Some book publishers do ask for queries first, but most want a query plus sample chapters or an outline or, occasionally, the complete manuscript. Again, make your letter brief. Include the essentials about yourself—name, address, phone number and publishing experience. Include a 3 or 4 sentence "pitch" and only the personal information related to your story. Show that you have researched the market with a few sentences about why you chose this publisher. See the sample book query on page 81.

BOOK PROPOSALS

A book proposal is a package sent to a publisher that includes a cover letter and one or more of the following: sample chapters, outline, synopsis, author bio, publications list. When asked to send sample chapters, send up to three *consecutive* chapters. **An outline** covers the highlights of your book chapter by chapter. Be sure to include details on main characters, the plot and subplots. Outlines can run up to 30 pages, depending on the length of your novel. The object is to tell what happens in a concise, but clear, manner. **A synopsis** is a shorter summary of your novel, written in a way that expresses the emotion of the story in addition to just explaining the essential points. Evan Marshall, literary agent and author of *The Marshall Plan for Getting Your Novel Published* (Writer's Digest Books), suggests you aim for a page of synopsis for every 25 pages of manuscript. Marshall also advises you write the synopsis as one unified narrative, without sections, subheads or chapters to break up the text. The terms synopsis and outline are sometimes used interchangeably, so be sure to find out exactly what each publisher wants.

A FEW WORDS ABOUT AGENTS

Agents are not usually needed for short fiction and most do not handle it unless they already have a working relationship with you. For novels, you may want to consider working with an agent, especially if you intend to market your book to publishers who do not look at unsolicited submissions. For more on approaching agents and to read listings of agents willing to work with beginning and established writers, see our Literary Agents section beginning on page 152.

MANUSCRIPT MECHANICS

A professionally presented manuscript will not guarantee publication. But a sloppy, hard-to-read manuscript will not be read; publishers simply do not have the time. Here's a list of suggested submission techniques for polished manuscript presentation.

 • **Use white, 8½ × 11 bond paper,** preferably 16 or 20 lb. weight. The paper should be heavy enough so it will not show pages underneath it and strong enough to take handling by several people.

 • **Type your manuscript** on a computer and print it out using a laser or ink jet printer, or use a typewriter with a new ribbon.

 • **Proofread carefully.** An occasional white-out is okay, but don't send a marked-up manuscript with many typos. Keep a dictionary, thesaurus and stylebook handy and use the spellcheck function on your computer.

 • **Always double space and leave a 1 inch margin** on all sides of the page.

 • **For a short story manuscript,** your first page should include your name, address, phone number and e-mail address (single spaced) in the upper left corner. In the upper right, indicate an approximate word count. Center the name of your story about one-third of the way down, skip a line and center your byline (byline is optional). Skip four lines and begin your story. On subsequent pages, put last name and page number in the upper right hand corner.

• **For book manuscripts,** use a separate title page. Put your name, address, phone number and e-mail address in the lower right corner and word count in the upper right. If you have representation, list your agent's name and address in the lower right. (This bumps your name and contact information to the upper left corner.) Center your title and byline about halfway down the page. Start your first chapter on the next page. Center the chapter number and title (if there is one) one-third of the way down the page. Include your last name and the novel's title in all caps in the upper left and put the page number in the upper right of this page and each page to follow. Start each chapter with a new page.

• **Include a word count.** If you work on a computer, chances are your word processing program can give you a word count. If you are using a typewriter, there are a number of ways to count the number of words in your piece. One way is to count the words in five lines and divide that number by five to find an average. Then count the number of lines and multiply to find the total words. For long pieces, you may want to count the words in the first three pages, divide by three and multiply by the number of pages you have.

• **Always keep a copy.** Manuscripts do get lost. To avoid expensive mailing costs, send only what is required. If you are including artwork or photos but you are not positive they will be used, send photocopies. Artwork is hard to replace.

• **Suggest art where applicable.** Most publishers do not expect you to provide artwork and some insist on selecting their own illustrators, but if you have suggestions, please let them know. Magazine publishers work in a very visual field and are usually open to ideas.

• **Enclose a self-addressed, stamped envelope (SASE)** if you want a reply or if you want your manuscript returned. For most letters, a business-size (#10) envelope will do. Avoid using any envelope too small for an $8\frac{1}{2} \times 11$ sheet of paper. For manuscripts, be sure to include enough postage and an envelope large enough to contain it. If you are requesting a sample copy of a magazine or a book publisher's catalog, send an envelope big enough to fit.

• **Consider sending a disposable manuscript** that saves editors time and saves you money.

• **When sending electronic (disk or e-mail) submissions,** check the publisher's Web site or contact them first for specific information and follow the directions carefully. Always include a printed copy with any disk submission.

• **Keep accurate records.** This can be done in a number of ways, but be sure to keep track of where your stories are and how long they have been "out." Write down submission dates. If you do not hear about your submission for a long time—about three weeks to one month longer than the reporting time stated in the listing—you may want to contact the publisher. When you do, you will need an accurate record for reference.

MAILING TIPS
When mailing short correspondence or short manuscripts:
• Fold manuscripts under five pages into thirds and send in a business-size (#10) envelope.
• Mail manuscripts five pages or more unfolded in a 9×12 or 10×13 envelope.
• Mark envelopes in all caps, FIRST CLASS MAIL or SPECIAL FOURTH CLASS MANU-SCRIPT RATE.
• For return envelope, fold it in half, address it to yourself and add a stamp or, if going to a foreign country, International Reply Coupons (available at the main branch of your local post office).
• Don't send by certified mail. This is a sign of an amateur, and publishers do not appreciate receiving unsolicited manuscripts this way.
• For the most current postage rates, visit the United States Postal Service online at www.usps.com.

Getting Published

When mailing book-length manuscripts:

First Class Mail over 11 ounces (about 65 8½×11 20 lb.-weight pages) automatically becomes **PRIORITY MAIL.**

Metered Mail may be dropped in any post office box, but meter strips on SASEs should not be dated.

The Postal Service provides, free of charge, tape, boxes and envelopes to hold up to two pounds for those using PRIORITY and EXPRESS MAIL. Requirements for mailing FOURTH CLASS and PARCEL POST have not changed.

Main branches of local banks will cash foreign checks, but keep in mind payment quoted in our listings by publishers in other countries is usually payment in their currency. Also note reporting time is longer in most overseas markets. To save time and money, you may want to include a return postcard (and IRC) with your submission and forgo asking for a manuscript to be returned. If you live in Canada, see Canadian Writers Take Note on page 549.

Important note about IRCs: Foreign editors sometimes find IRCs have been stamped incorrectly by the U.S. post office when purchased. This voids the IRCs and makes it impossible for foreign editors to exchange the coupons for return postage for your manuscript. When buying IRCs, make sure yours have been stamped correctly before you leave the counter. (Each IRC should be stamped on the bottom *left* side of the coupon, not the right.) More information about International Reply Coupons, including an image of a correctly stamped IRC, is available on the USPS Web site (www.usps.com).

RIGHTS

The Copyright Law states that writers are selling one-time rights (in almost all cases) unless they and the publisher have agreed otherwise. A list of various rights follows. Be sure you know exactly what rights you are selling before you agree to the sale.

• **Copyright** is the legal right to exclusive publication, sale or distribution of a literary work. As the writer or creator of a written work, you need simply to include your name, date and the copyright symbol © on your piece in order to copyright it. Be aware, however, that most editors today consider placing the copyright symbol on your work the sign of an amateur and many are even offended by it.

To get specific answers to questions about copyright (but not legal advice), you can call the Copyright Public Information Office at (202)707-3000 weekdays between 8:30 a.m. and 5 p.m. EST. Publications listed in *Novel & Short Story Writer's Market* are copyrighted *unless* otherwise stated. In the case of magazines that are not copyrighted, be sure to keep a copy of your manuscript with your notice printed on it. For more information on copyrighting your work, see *The Copyright Handbook: How to Protect & Use Written Works*, 8th edition, by Stephen Fishman (NOLO, 2005).

Some people are under the mistaken impression that copyright is something they have to send away for and that their writing is not properly protected until they have "received" their copyright from the government. The fact is, you don't have to register your work with the Copyright Office in order for your work to be copyrighted; any piece of writing is copyrighted the moment it is put to paper.

Although it is generally unnecessary, registration is a matter of filling out an application form (for writers, that's Form TX) and sending the completed form, a nonreturnable copy of the work in question and a check for $30 to the Library of Congress, Copyright Office, Register of Copyrights, 101 Independence Ave. SE, Washington DC 20559-6000. If the thought of paying $30 each to register every piece you write does not appeal to you, you can cut costs by registering a group of your works with one form, under one title for one $30 fee.

Most magazines are registered with the Copyright Office as single collective entities themselves; that is, the individual works that make up the magazine are *not* copyrighted individually in the names of the authors. You'll need to register your article yourself if you wish to have the additional protection of copyright registration.

For more information, visit the United States Copyright Office online at www.copyright.gov.

• **First Serial Rights**—This means the writer offers a newspaper or magazine the right to publish the article, story or poem for the first time in a particular periodical. All other rights to the material remain with the writer. The qualifier "North American" is often added to this phrase to specify a geographical limit to the license.

When material is excerpted from a book scheduled to be published and it appears in a magazine or newspaper prior to book publication, this is also called first serial rights.

• **One-time Rights**—A periodical that licenses one-time rights to a work (also known as simultaneous rights) buys the *nonexclusive* right to publish the work once. That is, there's nothing to stop the author from selling the work to other publications at the same time. Simultaneous sales would typically be to periodicals without overlapping audiences.

• **Second Serial (Reprint) Rights**—This gives a newspaper or magazine the opportunity to print an article, poem or story after it has already appeared in another newspaper or magazine. Second serial rights are nonexclusive; that is, they can be licensed to more than one market.

• **All Rights**—This is just what it sounds like. All rights means a publisher may use the manuscript anywhere and in any form, including movie and book club sales, without further payment to the writer (although such a transfer, or *assignment*, of rights will terminate after 35 years). If you think you'll want to use the material later, you must avoid submitting to such markets or refuse payment and withdraw your material. Ask the editor whether he is willing to buy first rights instead of all rights before you agree to an assignment or sale. Some editors will reassign rights to a writer after a given period, such as one year. It's worth an inquiry in writing.

• **Subsidiary Rights**—These are the rights, other than book publication rights, that should be covered in a book contract. These may include various serial rights; movie, television, audiotape and other electronic rights; translation rights, etc. The book contract should specify who controls these rights (author or publisher) and what percentage of sales from the licensing of these sub rights goes to the author.

• **Dramatic, Television and Motion Picture Rights**—This means the writer is selling his material for use on the stage, in television or in the movies. Often a one-year option to buy such rights is offered (generally for 10 percent of the total price). The interested party then tries to sell the idea to other people—actors, directors, studios or television networks, etc. Some properties are optioned over and over again, but most fail to become dramatic productions. In such cases, the writer can sell his rights again and again—as long as there is interest in the material. Though dramatic, television and motion picture rights are more important to the fiction writer than the nonfiction writer, producers today are increasingly interested in nonfiction material; many biographies, topical books and true stories are being dramatized.

• **Electronic Rights**—These rights cover usage in a broad range of electronic media, from online magazines and databases to CD-ROM magazine anthologies and interactive games. The editor should specify in writing if—and which—electronic rights are being requested. The presumption is that unspecified rights are kept by the writer.

Compensation for electronic rights is a major source of conflict between writers and publishers, as many book publishers seek control of them and many magazines routinely include electronic rights in the purchase of print rights, often with no additional payment. Alternative ways of handling this issue include an additional 15 percent added to the amount to purchase first rights and a royalty system based on the number of times an article is accessed from an electronic database.

MARKETING AND PROMOTION

Everyone agrees writing is hard work whether you are published or not. Yet once you achieve publication the work changes. Now, not only do you continue writing and revising your next project, you must also concern yourself with getting your book into the hands of readers. It becomes time to switch hats from artist to salesperson.

While even best-selling authors whose publishers have committed big bucks to marketing are asked to help promote their books, new authors may have to take it upon themselves to plan and initiate some of their own promotion, sometimes dipping into their own pockets.

About Our Policies

Important

We occasionally receive letters asking why a certain magazine, publisher or contest is not in the book. Sometimes when we contact listings, the editors do not want to be listed because they:

- do not use very much fiction.
- are overwhelmed with submissions.
- are having financial difficulty or have been recently sold.
- use only solicited material.
- accept work from a select group of writers only.
- do not have the staff or time for the many unsolicited submissions a listing may bring.

Some of the listings do not appear because we have chosen not to list them. We investigate complaints of unprofessional conduct in editors' dealings with writers and misrepresentation of information provided to us by editors and publishers. If we find these reports to be true, after a thorough investigation, we will delete the listing from future editions. See Important Listing Information on the copyright page for more about our listing policies.

There is no charge to the companies that list in this book. Listings appearing in *Novel & Short Story Writer's Market* are compiled from detailed questionnaires, phone interviews and information provided by editors, publishers, and awards and conference directors. The publishing industry is volatile and changes of address, editor, policies and needs happen frequently. To keep up with the changes between editions of the book, we suggest you check the market information on the *Writer's Market* Web site at www.writersmarket.com or on the *Writer's Digest* Web site at www.writersdigest.com. Many magazine and book publishers offer updated information for writers on their Web sites. Check individual listings for those Web site addresses.

Club newsletters and small magazines devoted to helping writers also list market information. For those writers with access to online services, several offer writers' bulletin boards, message centers and chat lines with up-to-the-minute changes and happenings in the writing community.

We rely on our readers, as well, for new markets and information about market conditions. Write us if you have any new information or if you have suggestions on how to improve our listings to better suit your writing needs.

While this does not mean that every author is expected to go on tour, sometimes at their own expense, it does mean authors should be prepared to offer suggestions for promoting their books.

Depending on the time, money and personal preferences of the author and publisher, a promotional campaign could mean anything from mailing out press releases to setting up book signings to hitting the talk-show circuit. Most writers can contribute to their own promotion by providing contact names—reviewers, hometown newspapers, civic groups, organizations—that might have a special interest in the book or the writer.

Above all, when it comes to promotion, be creative. What is your book about? Try to capitalize on it. Focus on your potential audiences and how you can help them to connect with your book. For more on marketing and promotion, see the article entitled ''Take Control Of Your Sales,'' by Sonya Carmichael Jones, on page 70.

Important Listing Information

- Listings are not advertisements. Although the information here is as accurate as possible, the listings are not endorsed or guaranteed by the editor of *Novel & Short Story Writer's Market*.

- *Novel & Short Story Writer's Market* reserves the right to exclude any listing that does not meet its requirements.

Mystery Roundtable

Four Writers on Living the Suspense

by I.J. Schecter

When Edgar Allan Poe gave readers a corpse's heart beating beneath the floorboards, they discovered two things: it scared them, and they liked it. Ever since, the mystery and suspense genres—and their more recent offspring, the thriller—have satisfied our relentless appetite for excitement and chills. Poe's tradition is carried on today by an array of talented authors who have, to the delight of readers, split these genres into further branches, from legal and political thrillers to modern whodunits.

In this article, four of today's leading mystery writers get together to discuss, among other topics, the relaxing effect of canines, the extent to which they identify with their bad guys, and why poison gas is sometimes just part of doing great research.

Grand Master of Mystery Writers of America and recipient of multiple Edgar and Shamus awards, **Lawrence Block** (www .lawrenceblock.com) was recently given a Lifetime Achievement Award from the Private Eye Writers of America and the Cartier Diamond Dagger for Life Achievement from the UK Crime Writers Association. His newest best sellers are *All the Flowers are Dying* (William Morrow, 2005) and *The Burglar on the Prowl* (William Morrow, 2004).

© Athena Gassoumis

Lawrence Block

Raelynn Hillhouse's (www.raelynnhillhouse.com) acclaimed first novel, *Rift Zone* (Forge, 2004), was informed by her previous experience running Cuban rum, smuggling jewels and slipping past some of the world's tightest security. Fortunately, Hillhouse has turned down recruitment offers from more than one hostile foreign government to continue writing books instead. Her new novel, *Outsourced* (Forge), will be released in early 2007.

A self-described "novelist with 37 dogs," **David Rosenfelt** (www.davidrosenfelt.com) was president of marketing for Tri-Star Pictures before deciding to try his hand at screenplays, and subsequently, fiction—a good decision, as it turns out. His previous book, *Bury the Lead* (Warner Books, 2005), was selected for the Today Show's Book of the Month Club, and his fourth novel, *Sudden Death* (Warner Books, 2006), is available now.

I.J. SCHECTER (www.ijschecter.com) writes for leading magazines, newspapers and Web sites throughout the world, including *Condé Nast Brides*, *Golf Monthly*, *Men's Exercise*, *The Globe & Mail* and iParenting.com. He is also the author of two collections *The Bottom of the Mug* (Aegina Press Inc.) and *Slices: Observations from the Wrong Side of the Fairway* (John Wiley & Sons).

New York Times best-selling author **Lisa Scottoline** (www.scottoline.com) is a former lawyer whose celebrated books are set in Philadelphia and feature memorably gutsy, resilient female characters. Her 13th novel, *Dirty Blonde* (HarperCollins, 2006), about a female judge leading a sexy double life, is in stores.

In the movie version of *Misery*, there's a moment where Paul Sheldon, trying to open a lock with a bobby pin, mutters, "Come on, you've written about this; now do it." Dropped into one of your own novels, how would you fare?

Lisa Scottoline: I drop myself into every one of my novels. For various books, I've taken boxing lessons, hung with ATF agents, gone to an internment camp for Italians in Montana, and subpoenaed files from the National Archives. In short, I don't write about it unless I've done it, or close to it.

Lawrence Block: I couldn't pick a lock, and I don't do a lot of street fighting. But I wouldn't do too badly.

David Rosenfelt: In terms of investigation, I'd be a disaster, especially the parts dealing with personal danger. When it comes to a lack of physical courage, I take a back seat to no one. But regarding legal strategy I'd do reasonably well, probably because, as my family and friends say, I'm "exasperatingly devoted to logic."

Raelynn Hillhouse: I was a smuggler behind the Iron Curtain and know the tricks of the trade intimately, but I still wouldn't last a heartbeat in my next novel, about a Pentagon spy who infiltrates a private military corporation suspected of selling arms to terrorists only to become a target. I've worked closely with all kinds of experts and have run through enough scenarios with an explosives-disposal guy that I'd have a decent chance at building or diffusing a bomb, but that's not something I want to test.

Raelynn Hillhouse

Courtesy of author

Name a mystery/suspense/thriller you wish you could have written.

Hillhouse: For the quality of work and its role in founding the modern espionage-thriller genre, *The Secret Agent* by Joseph Conrad. For the royalties, *The Da Vinci Code*.

Scottoline: I love so many authors, I can't name one. And I need friends, so I can't leave anyone out. Every time I read a new book, I see something I could be doing better, which simultaneously depresses and exhilarates me.

Block: There are any number of books I admire extravagantly, but that doesn't mean I wish I'd written them. It's been exhausting enough writing my own books.

Rosenfelt: I'd say pretty much any book written by Michael Connelly, Lee Child, Harlan Coben, Donald Westlake or Mr. Block, here.

Speaking generally, how much do you feel the mystery/suspense/thriller genre has evolved?

Block: The best of today's work is better than the best of yesterday, partly, I suppose, because we get to stand on the shoulders of giants, but also because we've got room; crime novels today can be as long as they want, can deal with whatever subjects they want, and aren't ghettoized to the extent they once were.

Scottoline: I teach a course on Justice and Fiction at the University of Pennsylvania Law School in which we try to answer that very question. I believe the characterizations are much more fleshed out and truer than they used to be. Relationships between characters are better and enrich the plot line, or even drive it forward. And girls get to play!

Hillhouse: Absolutely. Women are finally being published in what was long believed to be an area—criminal behaviour—only men could know and master. In 1996, the head of a major publishing company turned down Gayle Lynds' first spy thriller because she didn't believe a woman could write a book like *Masquerade*. The editor who acquired my first novel was shocked to learn I was a woman, and apologized by saying, "but you write like a guy." Now reviewers are recognizing that female writers can torture their characters with as much or more realism than any male author.

Can you remember the first moment you decided, "*This* is the kind of stuff I want to write?"

Scottoline: Yesterday. No joke, I have that feeling every day, either when I'm writing a sentence and it finally works or, often, when I'm reading other authors.

Block: I had a version of that when I read *The Jungle Kids*, a collection of Evan Hunter's stories. I had the sense that these stories were good, and yet that they were the sort of thing I *could* write.

Rosenfelt: I was motivated to write my first book after seeing "A Few Good Men."

Say I'm about to tackle my first mystery/suspense/thriller. What advice do you have?

Scottoline: Give yourself permission to write a stinky first draft. Don't massage each sentence until you know you have a story. Say it plain. Say each sentence aloud. If it's lousy, throw it out. Write something true. Tell on yourself.

Rosenfelt: Just sit down and do it. Remove from your mind the idea that writing has to be a painstaking process, and get your story down on paper. And don't be too harsh a critic of your own initial work.

Hillhouse: Study the genre, then do something fresh. Write about something you're an expert on—or become an expert. Most important, write about something you're passionate about.

David Rosenfelt

What's better, sex or nailing a sentence?

Rosenfelt: I don't think anyone would consider me an expert on either, but I don't know anyone who has a sentence drive.

Hillhouse: Compare the number of people writing books and the number having sex and you know which is more fun.

Block: I'd say it depends on your audience.

Besides writing, what activity most compels you?

Hillhouse: There is no greater joy for me than romping with my dogs. And snorkeling is like flying. Hanging onto a rope while being pulled behind a boat at high speeds is as good as it gets.

Rosenfelt: It's dogs for me, too. I've devoted much of the last 10 years to rescuing and caring for them.

Block: I got back into racewalking a little over a year ago and am absolutely obsessed. I've been in over 20 races, including a marathon and a 24-hour race in which I covered 63 miles. My wife says I'm trying to recapture my lost middle age.

Scottoline: I love reading. And talking, and listening. Eating, cooking. Walking dogs. Riding horses. Watching TV. The only thing I don't like is doing nothing.

Describe your ideal writing environment.

Block: To me, it matters little. It's the inner landscape that's most important.

Rosenfelt: My ideal writing environment is the one I write in every day: an office in my home, high up on a hill in the middle of nowhere. I'm surrounded by dogs—usually 15 or so at any one time. Generally they sleep peacefully, though when someone rings the doorbell, it sounds like there's a fox hunt taking place.

Scottoline: I can, and do, write anywhere, but most often in my office, with dogs sleeping underfoot or chewing socks, the TV on quietly, pistachios nearby.

Hillhouse: Most of my writing is done outside. I love sitting on my lanai with—like David and Lisa—my dogs snoozing around me. When I want to think, I look up and stare at the distant ocean or Mauna Loa volcano. I think we've hit upon the real secret to making it in this business: dogs. Truth is, they do all the work. We just channel.

© John Earle

Lisa Scottoline

What's the strangest piece of research you've done for a story?

Scottoline: For my new book, I went to Centralia, Pennsylvania, the site of an underground mine fire that has been burning continuously since the 1960s and can't be put out. Poison gases leak from huge rents in the earth and hot steam that melts the snow. I was woozy from carbon monoxide fumes and great research, but not in that order.

Hillhouse: I had to convince the Army to teach me how to hotwire, steal and then crash-land one of their Black Hawk helicopters. So if dropped into a book, I could probably hotwire one and get it in the air a few feet, but then I'd just keep spinning until it crashed.

To what extent do you live vicariously through your protagonists (or antagonists)? Are all mystery/suspense/thriller writers really just would-be corporate embezzlers, diamond thieves and hired assassins?

Block: Except for the handful of us who are psychopaths.

Hillhouse: Novels are about taking readers through an emotional journey, exploring places they would otherwise never go. I know of no other way to write than to live vicariously through the point-of-view characters—whether good, bad or one of the many dysfunctional

The Million-dollar Question

Complete the following sentence: **To make it in this business, you need . . .**

Scottoline: To work at it and never give up! I once received a letter from a New York agent that read, "We don't have time to take any more clients, but if we did, we wouldn't take you." You'll get plenty of these letters. Press on anyway.

Rosenfelt: Some talent and a great deal of luck. It is an absolute fact that there are worse writers than me on the best-seller list and far better writers than me who labor in obscurity.

Hillhouse: Drive, stamina, thick skin, discipline, sense of humor, business acumen, insatiable curiosity and, yes, luck.

Block: A trust fund wouldn't hurt.

shades of gray. I have to feel their pain, struggles and triumphs in order to chronicle them.

Rosenfelt: I think it's fair to say that I live somewhat vicariously through my protagonist. We are both sarcastic, argumentative people who have a tendency to badger others with logic. As a lawyer, I have put him in a position where he can be praised for these qualities. I can't think of a time where I've identified or lived vicariously through my antagonists.

Scottoline: I'm just a nice lady who loves books and likes to have fun. I wouldn't want to do any of the nasty things I write about.

What about everyone else? Do you think we're all suppressing the urge to lie, cheat, steal and murder, with some just better at it than others?

Scottoline: No. I believe in the goodness of all people, except my ex-husbands.

Hillhouse: I think we're all suppressing the urge to snack all the time, have sex nonstop, and sleep whenever we want. Lying, cheating, stealing and murdering take too much effort, and any rewards sure aren't that immediate or pleasurable. Human nature is more self-serving, hedonistic and lazy than it is evil.

Rosenfelt: In terms of lying and cheating, I don't detect too much suppressing going on. When it comes to stealing and murdering, I think most people are relatively free of those urges.

Psychologically speaking, what makes a professional thief, killer or other type of baddie?

Rosenfelt: I would imagine a lack of both conscience and fear would be helpful.

Block: An inability to perceive consequences seems to be part of the job description. That aside, you'll find the same sociopathic personality in corporate executive positions.

Hillhouse: It takes a very different psychology in real life than it does in a book. Talk to law enforcement professionals and social workers and you'll find that most real-life thugs are pretty dull, with low self-esteem and the IQ of a grape. This is generally too unattractive and too mundane to make someone read 500 pages. To make it in a novel, villains need an exaggerated sense of self and high intelligence—and some form of charisma helps.

Scottoline: I couldn't say, since I'm a writer and former lawyer—in other words, a goodie.

Are you better at handling criticism today than when you started writing?

Scottoline: Not in the least.

Block: Who, me? What are you implying?

Hillhouse: I'd say I've become much better at discerning what's useful and what's a bunch of crap.

Rosenfelt: I think I've always been pretty good at it. I see my manuscripts as works in progress, and I actually love receiving notes and suggestions. I only really resent when critics are obviously unfamiliar with the work itself, when they get the facts wrong. Those people deserve to spend a life of unending agony, writhing in pain and futilely begging for mercy.

What's your favorite moment in the manuscript process?

Scottoline: Finishing!

Block: No matter how much sense of the story I have going in, there's always something magical that happens spontaneously while I'm writing, some minor character who blossoms out of nowhere, some unanticipated bit of dialogue that sparkles on the page.

Hillhouse: For me, it's editing. The stress of completing the project is over and it's a true high to take the "finished" product to a new level.

Rosenfelt: Definitely a new plot twist crystallizing. I don't outline the story in advance, so I'm at the benevolent mercy of sudden crystallization. It's a great feeling; I just wish it happened more often.

Gregg Hurwitz

Raising the Bar on Crime Fiction

by W.E. Reinka

At 5 feet 2 inches tall and less than 100 pounds, Gregg Hurwitz decided to go out for high school track after being cut from freshman football the previous fall. Track didn't cut anybody. He remembers standing alongside the pole vault pit as seniors soared over the bar. At that time, Hurwitz was too puny to bend the pole, so it didn't look as if the pole vault offered any more of a future than football.

One day, a senior pointed a taunting finger at the scrawny freshman: "Why don't you just quit because you're never going to be any good at this."

Like the 90-pound weakling who turns into Charles Atlas after a beach bully kicks sand in his face, Hurwitz turned the remark into a defining moment in his life. "I made a silent vow that no matter how much work it was going to take, no matter how much time I had to put in, one day I was going to break the school pole vault record."

Come sophomore year, Hurwitz could finally bend the pole. By his junior year he was training year-round. As a senior, he owned the school record. College recruiters chased him. He chose Harvard over UCLA.

"People always ask me about being an English and psychology major at Harvard, but the discipline I learned from athletics is far more important to my writing. Pole vaulting is a great metaphor for writing. With pole vault, you train for months and months before you even get a pole in your hands. Only after a long learning curve and a lot of discipline can you step up and compete."

Hurwitz was only 19 years old and still at Harvard when he started his first novel, *The Tower* (Simon & Schuster, 1999). After he landed an agent and a book contract, he passed up lucrative job offers to concentrate on writing with the same intensity he had once devoted to pole vaulting. Now 32, he maintains that intensity. "After I sold *The Tower*, I told myself, 'This is what I do now, I'm doing it for a minimum of eight hours a day.' To be successful, new writers must declare that writing is their most important pursuit. If you don't make your writing schedule highest priority, it never will be because you always need to drop off your dry cleaning or pick up your kids or pay bills. Your writing schedule must be sacrosanct."

Another way Hurwitz sees that pole vaulting is like writing is that one learns by doing. "One of the most annoying meetings I ever had was with a screenwriter who wanted to talk about writing novels. He said, 'I don't do anything until I know exactly how to do it before I set out. Before I wrote for television I read all the books and figured out exactly how to

---

W.E. REINKA, who writes frequently about books and authors, contributes to magazines and newspapers nationwide.

write TV. It was the same thing with scripts; I figured out the formula. Now I want to write a novel and I want to know exactly what to do and how to do it.'

"I just looked at him and said, 'You're out of luck because there's no way to learn how to write a novel until you're writing it and messing it up. That's how you learn. You make all kinds of mistakes, figure out what's wrong and get your rhythm.' When I started *The Tower*, my learning curve was so steep that in the first draft the ends of the chapters actually were better than the beginnings of the chapters."

Just as Hurwitz stuck with pole vaulting with no guarantee of success, he stuck with *The Tower*. "A student at a writer's conference told me that she had written 12 unpublished novels. I suggested that may have been her problem—instead of writing 12 novels, maybe she should have written one novel 12 times."

Hurwitz had already been a professional writer for 10 years before he picked up Stephen King's *On Writing*, the first writing how-to book he had ever read. Though he heartily recommends King's book, he insists that reading about writing cannot substitute for actual writing, what he calls "in-chair time." Likewise, though he occasionally teaches at writer's conferences, he rolls his eyes at people who brag about attending their 15th writing conference. "I want to say, 'Well, after two you should have saved your money, stayed home and written.' People want to say that they're writing and to be the special writer in the family, but they're not serious about it unless they're willing to commit the time when no one else cares, when no one else is watching, when no one else is giving feedback."

"TERRIFYING." JONATHAN KELLERMAN

DO NO HARM

GREGG HURWITZ

BESTSELLING AUTHOR OF *THE KILL CLAUSE*

Reprinted with permission from HarperCollins.

Ask Hurwitz what he writes and he'll say "crime fiction." Pressed further, he might narrow that to "thrillers." Although the general reading public may lump thrillers with mysteries, they are structured differently. "In a thriller the audience is usually in a superior position. We're keeping up with the antagonist on some level. Typically the stakes are higher, there's media involvement and a ticking clock as a city or national security is threatened. Thrillers are weighted toward the end in terms of pacing and size of action, whereas mysteries are weighted toward the beginning when someone is killed. Thrillers often, but not always, involve more research, and the most exciting event is at the very end when someone gets hold of the nuke and diffuses it before it blows up Chicago." Hurwitz stops to chuckle. "By the way, these are crass generalizations."

Hurwitz remembers one day in high school when everything just came together at the pole vault pit and he soared to a new personal best. Likewise, he recently raised the bar for his writing with his latest novel, *Last Shot*. Its sophisticated design ambitiously blends those structural "crass generalizations" by opening a high-stakes thriller with a mystery-like "locked door" premise: A federal prisoner seemingly vanishes from a locked cell, and as U.S. Deputy Marshall Tim Rackley tracks the prisoner, he discovers the escapee is himself desperately unraveling a plot that threatens society.

After three stand-alone titles, Hurwitz first introduced Rackley in the highly praised novel

The Kill Clause (William Morrow, 2003). He hadn't planned to start a series but, after completing *The Kill Clause*, he found himself drawn to Tim Rackley's character and reprised him in *The Program* (2004) and *Troubleshooter* (2005). But Hurwitz expects to return to stand-alones with his next novel. "There's that great quote from Dennis Lehane about how no one ever says the 17th book in a series is their favorite."

Hurwitz will only return to the Tim Rackley series if he finds a way to continue the overall arc of the character that transcends the individual installments. Tim Rackley isn't a static character who finds himself in a new fix with each new installment but never grows personally. The books connect in a true tetralogy. "To me Tim is a living, breathing human being. I'm not interested in a series with a frozen-in-time action star like James Bond. I decided that if I was going to make a series, I needed something that would tie them together. Thematically, all of the books in the Rackley series have a different perspective. I call them 'an action meditation on vigilantism.'"

In *The Kill Clause*, Tim strays from his values after his daughter is viciously murdered and returns to them with conviction and weight of experience, knowing that they're correct. *The Program* follows up with Tim—an action-oriented former Army ranger—struggling to stay within ethical boundaries as he relies on psychological and legal tools, rather than arm twisting, against the wicked leader

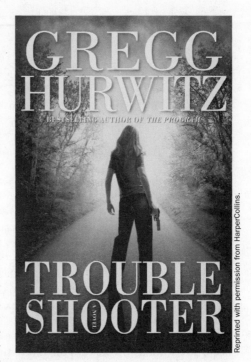

Reprinted with permission from HarperCollins.

of a mind-control cult. No easy task given that there's nothing illegal about mind control.

In *Troubleshooter*, Tim confronts sadistic motorcycle gangs competing in a drug war. Tim's pregnant wife Dray, who usually represents his voice of reason, is off scene in this installment. "It's about how, absent his voice of reason coupled with compelling reasons to go outside the law, he needs to internalize the values of his ethics. How if something happens to you personally, it doesn't give you license to move outside the law."

Hurwitz often uses the word "ethics" when describing his books. In *Do No Harm* (William Morrow, 2002), an emergency room doctor faces the uneasy challenge of whether to protect a deranged acid thrower from police vengeance. In *Minutes to Burn* (William Morrow, 2001), an eco-thriller set in the Galapagos, tough Navy SEALS balance environmental preservation against self-preservation when threatened by mutated monsters.

Sometimes his "living, breathing" characters become so human that they seemingly provide their own dialogue to match their motivations. Those are days that Hurwitz says "you're channeling and in the groove. A writer gets in a groove just like an athlete." It comes with hours of practice every day, even on terrible days where nothing seems right. Hurwitz became a pole vault champion by working out every day, whether or not he felt like it, whether his buddies suggested more fun things to do. "I don't have the luxury of sitting around waiting for a muse. I have to get myself in a place where I get something done every day."

Reed Farrel Coleman

Finding His Audience

by Michael Schweer

I t's about the writing, not about the money. It has to be," says novelist Reed Farrel Coleman. It's a principle most writers live by. Coleman, author of seven detective novels, is quick to point out the difference between making a "real" living and that of a writer. His "real" jobs have included baby food salesman, air freight manager, car leasing agent, restaurant trainer, cab driver and truck driver. The experiences he encounters from his "real" jobs give him an abundance of story ideas. "I could not live long enough to write the books I get ideas for in a single day," Coleman often says.

While financial success has been hard to come by, Coleman has faired well in creating a loyal fan base for his work. His latest book in the Moe Prager mystery series, *The James Deans,* was nominated for an Edgar Award. Coleman began his writing career publishing the Dylan Klein detective books in 1991 with Permanent Press, a reputable small publisher. His major step towards becoming a full-time writer came in 2001 when Plume Publishing purchased the paperback rights to his fourth novel, *Walking the Perfect Square.* Since then, Coleman has moved forward, writing three books for the Moe Prager mystery series and working on a new detective series under the pseudonym Tony Spinosa.

Here, Coleman discusses series mystery, the publishing game, and the liberating effects of writing under a pen name.

On your Web site you have a campaign running to save Moe Prager, the main character of your latest detective series. Could you tell me a little about this?
Well, my Moe Prager series has been your basic blessing and curse. Generally, critics have loved it. Fans of the series are devoted to it and the characters, but the sales have never met expectations. If I didn't sell the hell out of the book, there was a good chance Moe Prager would fade into that netherworld of finely written private eyes who always found their man but not their audience. So when *The James Deans*, the most recent Moe book, came out, I decided to try to boost sales by enlisting fans and creating a buzz to "Save Moe." Moe is on the verge of being saved by another house (Bleak House), but I don't want to jinx it until I've signed the contract. I am working on the next Moe book, however, entitled *Soul Patch*.

MICHAEL SCHWEER is the assistant editor of *Novel & Short Story Writer's Market* and *Artist's & Graphic Designer's Market*. He moonlights as a wise-cracking but tender-hearted detective.

How did the switch from Plume to Bleak House occur?

It wasn't actually a direct shift. I hadn't written anything but Moe Prager books for years and wanted to stretch my wings a little. And I wasn't sure if my contract for the Moe books would be renewed, so I wasn't going to write a Moe book that might never get published. I was more willing to try this new [Joe Serpe detective] series on spec as it's a bit grittier and darker than Moe or my previous Dylan Klein series. Jon Jordan, the publisher of *Crime Spree Magazine*, suggested I look into Bleak House. My former agent contacted them and we hit it off. They were willing to take bigger risks than other houses.

Your next work is under the pseudonym Tony Spinosa. What is the reasoning behind this?

It was a way to get the expectations off my back. I feel victimized by the numbers game in the publishing industry, so using Tony Spinosa as a front was a way for me to get the numbers and expectations monkey off my back. I also wanted this series to stand on its own and be judged for its own merits.

And like I said, I wasn't sure if Moe would get picked up again, but I had to wait a few months for the verdict to come in. Meanwhile, I'd already written this other book and people were willing to publish it. I had a dilemma: if Moe was picked up again, I couldn't compete with myself. If the Moe series wasn't picked up, I would have wasted months just sitting on the sidelines. That's not my style. So I figured I'd publish under a pseudonym. It was a way to create a little buzz and have some fun. I guess it worked, because I made the front page of the *Wall Street Journal* in a story about pen names.

What are the differences between Tony Spinosa and Reed Farrel Coleman? Did you find yourself writing in a different style?

There are countless differences between Reed and Tony and between the Moe books and the Joe Serpe books. There are also some unavoidable similarities. Let's start with style. Moe books are written in first person with single perspective. The Joe Serpe books are written in third person with various perspectives. The Moe books are set in the '70s and '80s mostly in Brooklyn and Manhattan. *Hose Monkey* and *Gun Bunnies*, the first two Joe Serpe books, are set in current day Long Island. Moe is Jewish. Joe is a Roman Catholic. Moe is happily married and a good father. Joe is divorced and estranged from his son and his ex wife. Moe had an unremarkable 10-year career in uniform as a member of the NYPD. Joe Serpe is a lonely, bitter, disgraced former legendary NYPD detective. Tony Spinosa writes the Joe Serpe books with way more violence and moral ambiguity than I write the Moe books. Tony also strays into the sexual arena, a place where I don't usually let a happily married man like Moe Prager venture.

You were a poet before you were a fiction writer. What caused the transition? Do you still write poetry?

I often say that if you want to be poor, be a writer. If you want to be destitute, be a poet. Even when I was studying poetry in college, I knew I wasn't good enough to make a career of it. Even people who *are* good enough can't. When I was at Brooklyn College in the mid- and late '70s, John Ashbery, Allen Ginsberg and David Lehman taught there. If Ashbery, Ginsberg and Lehman had to teach, then I wasn't going to go very far. I still love poetry and write it some. These days, I use my poetry in my prose writing more than anything else.

What made you start writing detective fiction?

Out of boredom with my "real" job, I took a night class in detective fiction at Brooklyn College. This was years after I'd left school. The first few books we read were *The Continental*

Op; *Farewell, My Lovely*; *Red Harvest*; *The Long Goodbye*; and *The Dain Curse*. It completely opened, or should I say, reopened my eyes. For me, this genre had been all about the cheesy paperbacks on my dad's nightstand. After reading Hammett and Chandler, I was transformed. I could see the genius in their work, the poetry in their work, and was inspired to try my hand at it.

Where do you get inspiration for your stories?

You know it's funny; one of the most frequently asked questions at book signings and panels is, "Where do you get your ideas from?" No matter how many times I'm asked, I'm always taken aback by the question. I get my stories from the paper, from magazines, from TV, from movies, from cop friends, from the guys I worked with in the cargo area at Kennedy airport, from my friends, from the grief in my life, from my relatives, from an innocent incident on the street, from books I've read, from. . . I often say that I could not live long enough to write the books I get ideas for in a single day.

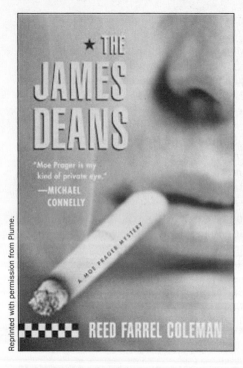

Reprinted with permission from Plume.

When you start writing a novel, how do you begin and what goals do you set for yourself? Do you make an outline or do you just start writing? How much research goes into writing a mystery?

I never outline. The whole pleasure for me in writing is being surprised. Outlines ruin the surprise for me and hence ruin my pleasure. Sometimes, like with *Walking the Perfect Square*, the entire plot just appears in my head. Bang! The whole thing, characters, twists, everything. *The James Deans* was like that too. Some books, like *Hose Monkey*, start out as short stories: I remember reading my short story called *Invisibility* one night at the Forest Hills Branch of the Queens Public Library. And S.J. Rozan said that she wanted to know more, that it would make for a good book.

I'm not big on research. I do some, but it's limited. However, I'm working on a book proposal for a broader, larger book and have enlisted the aid of a paid researcher.

How long does it usually take you to finish a story?

It took me two years to finish my first novel *Life Goes Sleeping*. My next two books took about a year each. *Walking The Perfect Square* took six months. *The James Deans* took four months, *Hose Monkey* and *Gun Bunnies* as well.

What do you do when you have writer's block?

I'm too poor to have writer's block. Ask me this question again when I make my first 10 million. Truthfully, I think writer's block is a bit of a media myth in the same way that writing is portrayed as somehow romantic. I've found neither to be true. Some writers do battle fear, especially a fear of matching past success.

The Moe Prager series has been successful. Is there extra pressure in writing a series?

Well, it hasn't been as successful as I hoped it would be from a financial and sales perspective, but as far as winning loyal fans and producing fine books, I guess you're right. I don't think there's much pressure in a series, but I can only speak for myself and don't want to generalize. There are two big dangers in writing a series, I think: boredom for the writer and repetition in the books themselves. One of the reasons I wanted to try on the new Tony Spinosa persona with the Joe Serpe character was to keep Moe fresh.

If Moe was all I kept writing, I would have gotten bored and the series would have suffered because I would have begun repeating myself. I've never been one of those writers interested in rewriting the same book over and over and over again. Now that I'm back doing a Moe book, man, it's exciting, fresh and new to me again.

Moe Prager is a great character. How did you come up with him? Did you have an idea for a story or did you have and idea for a detective?

Thank you. I think Moe's pretty cool myself. Moe Prager is the outgrowth of a character I began experimenting with in the late '80s named Moe Einstein. The original Moe was a little too cutesy for his own good and wasn't fully formed. Unfortunately, I didn't have the writing chops to pull the character off then, but there was something about him, an essential goodness and an innate and nuanced sense of morality, that kept drawing me back to him. When the idea for *Walking the Perfect Square* popped fully formed into my head, I just knew my earlier protagonist, Dylan Klein, wouldn't work as the detective. Moe Einstein forced himself into my consciousness as Moe Prager and that was that.

Reprinted with permission from Plume.

Is there any chance you'll write something outside of detective fiction?

Actually, I've written a few science fiction short stories, one of which I someday hope to turn into a novel. The story is called "Gobble." It's all very existential and would probably bore Sartre and piss off King.

I have also written a series of short essays about my life growing up in Brooklyn. I call it an automythology. My old agent told me it was great fun but until I was famous no one would publish it. I have published an essay or two, and I have a true crime essay scheduled to appear in *Brooklyn Noir 3*. There's always my poetry and maybe someday a literary novel. Hell, if I couldn't write anything else, I'd write business letters. It's a compulsion.

You are working on a graphic novel. What is different in your approach to writing a graphic novel as opposed to novel?

It's incredibly different and, much to my dismay, involves detailed outlining. I was approached by Jeff Fisher, a very talented artist and illustrator with whom I've played basketball for 15 years. He asked if I'd like to take a crack at a graphic novel. If my answer to the previous question didn't make it clear enough, I'll try anything when it comes to writing. I said yes.

So first I had to conceive an idea which leant itself to visual expression—only the visual expression would have to be someone else's. Hence, the challenge is to take the idea and describe it to Jeff in such a way as to have him produce a physical likeness of the visions in my head. What's cool is that we get to play off each other. His illustrations inspire new ideas and directions. The hard thing to cope with is the absolute economy of words needed. The bulk of the writing I'm doing for *Blood Alley* will never be seen by the reader. It's mostly for Jeff's benefit and mine. The dialogue that does appear is more akin to underlining and emphasizing. The story must basically be told by the illustrations. It's helped me with my discipline and focus. It has also given me insight into my colleagues who outline.

What was the first piece of work you had published?

The first thing I ever got published was a poem called ''Monopoly'' in my sophomore year in high school. Nothing has ever felt like seeing that poem in the high school literary magazine. I still read that poem aloud sometimes at signings. The first long piece of fiction I ever attempted was published as my first novel, *Life Goes Sleeping,* in 1991.

What is the most useful piece of writing advice you ever received?

David Lehman, my poetry-writing instructor at Brooklyn College, once gave us permission to think of ourselves as writers. He actually had us raise our right hands and repeat after him that from that moment forward we were to think of ourselves as writers. It was incredibly liberating. I recently went to a poetry reading of his in Manhattan and we sat around and talked. We hadn't seen each other in 20 years. I recounted that moment to him and told him he'd changed my life.

Can't Get Enough Whodunit?

Check out these books by Reed Farrel Coleman:
- *Hardboiled Brooklyn*, edited by Reed Farrel Coleman (Bleak House, 2006)
- *The James Deans* (Plume, 2005)
- *Redemption Steet* (Viking, 2004)
- *Walking the Perfect Square* (Permanent Press, 2001)
- *They Don't Play Stickball in Milwaukee* (Permanent Press, 1997)
- *Little Easter* (Permanent Press, 1993)
- *Life Goes Sleeping* (Permanent Press, 1991)

Resources

Where to Look for More Information

Below is a list of invaluable resources specifically for mystery writers. To order any of the Writer's Digest Books titles or to get a consumer book catalog, call (800)448-0915. You may also order Writer's Digest Books selections through www.writersdiges t.com, Amazon.com or www.barnesandnoble.com.

MAGAZINES

- *Mystery Readers Journal*, Mystery Readers International, P.O. Box 8116, Berkeley CA 94707. Web site: www.mysteryreaders.org.
- *Mystery News*, Black Raven Press, PMB 152, 105 E. Townline Rd., Vernon Hills IL 60061-1424. Web site: www.blackravenpress.com.
- *Mystery Scene*, 331 W. 57th St., Suite 148, New York NY 10019. Web site: www.mysterys cenemag.com.

BOOKS

Howdunit series (Writer's Digest Books)

- *Private Eyes: A Writer's Guide to Private Investigators*, by Hal Blythe, Charlie Sweet and John Landreth
- *Missing Persons: A Writer's Guide to Finding the Lost, the Abducted and the Escaped*, by Fay Faron
- *Deadly Doses: A Writer's Guide to Poisons*, by Serita Deborah Stevens and Anne Klarner
- *Cause of Death: A Writer's Guide to Death, Murder & Forensic Medicine*, by Keith D. Wilson, M.D.
- *Scene of the Crime: A Writer's Guide to Crime Scene Investigation*, by Anne Wingate, Ph.D.
- *Just the Facts, Ma'am: A Writer's Guide to Investigators and Investigation Techniques*, by Greg Fallis
- *Rip-off: A Writer's Guide to Crimes of Deception*, by Fay Faron

Other Writer's Digest Books for mystery writers

- *The Criminal Mind, A Writer's Guide to Forensic Psychology*, by Katherine Ramsland
- *Howdunit: How Crimes are Committed and Solved*, by John Boertlein
- *Urge to Kill: How Police Take Homicide from Case to Court*, by Martin Edwards
- *Writing Mysteries: A Handbook by the Mystery Writers of America*, edited by Sue Grafton
- *Writing and Selling Your Mystery Novel: How to Knock 'em Dead With Style*, by Hallie Ephron
- *You Can Write a Mystery*, by Gillian Roberts

ORGANIZATIONS & ONLINE

- Crime Writers of Canada. Web site: www.crimewriterscanada.com.
- Crime Writers' Association. Web site: www.thecwa.co.uk.
- Mystery Writers of America, 17 E. 47th St., 6th Floor, New York NY 10017. Web site: www.mysterywriters.org.
- The Private Eye Writers of America, 4342 Forest DeVille Dr., Apt. H, St. Louis MO 63129. Web site: http://hometown.aol.com/rrandisi/myhomepage/writing.html.
- Sisters in Crime, P.O. Box 442124, Lawrence KS 66044-8933. Web site: www.sistersincrime.org.
- Writer's Market Online. Web site: www.writersmarket.com.
- Writer's Digest Online. Web site: www.writersdigest.com.

Carly Phillips

The Writer Behind the Best-selling Brand

© Lynne McTague

by Lauren Mosko

I'm Karen, wife and mother of two, the same Karen who couldn't handle moot court in law school and hated speaking in public. I dealt with Regis on television and met my soap opera idol, Kelly Ripa. And now, I'm a New York Times Best-selling author with her first hardcover novels coming out. I'm not just Karen Drogin aka Carly Phillips, I am Carly Phillips. And proud of it.

Carly Phillips recorded these thoughts in a Web posting titled "Diary of a Cinderella Story" (www.carlyphillips.com/article7.html), which recounts her experiences before, during and after Kelly Ripa chose her first single-title novel, *The Bachelor,* as a Reading with Ripa book club pick in July of 2002.

Not only are these sentiments heartwarming—after all, self-doubt is something to which any writer can relate—they're also inspiring. They affirm that, with hard work, courage and a little luck, some of those old feelings can be replaced with a sense of pride and empowerment. And with over 20 series and single-title romances to her credit, Phillips has every right to be proud of the writer she's become.

Such a strong declaration of self also invites curiosity. Just who *is* Carly Phillips? To fans, she's at once Cinderella, who worked unrecognized for years before having her greatest wish granted. She's also their Fairy Godmother, creating worlds and heroes that are the stuff of dreams.

For Phillips, the description is a little less romantic and a lot more practical.

"Being Carly Phillips means living up to the writer whose book was chosen by Kelly Ripa," she says. "Being Carly means striving to continue to be a *New York Times* best seller. But most of all, being Carly means I owe my readers something for the hard-earned money they lay out for one of my novels. I never lose sight of that when I am writing. I can't promise everyone will love what I write, but I can promise I put everything I have into each story."

In this interview, the author gives us a window into her writing life, where she's been, and where she's headed. But no matter which pair of glass slippers she's wearing today, she'll always be Carly Phillips.

LAUREN MOSKO is the editor of *Novel & Short Story Writer's Market.*

It's clear what Kelly Ripa's endorsement of *The Bachelor* did for your public career, but did it influence you in personal ways?

Kelly Ripa's endorsement validated my writing in a way nothing else could have. I was a writer before she picked my book for her book club and I would have still been a writer had she not chosen *The Bachelor*. But when she did, she exposed my book to the public beyond the romance-reading community. Those readers could have said, "I don't like this book or this style of book" but instead they kept coming back for more. *The Bachelor*'s success was wholly because of Kelly Ripa. The continuing success is because I work hard to sustain the entrée she gave me. I will be grateful to her forever for opening my work up to a broader, national audience.

On a purely personal level, I have been a Kelly Ripa fan since she walked onto "All My Children" in a black wig playing the role of Hayley Vaughn. In many ways she has influenced my life over the years, and meeting her was truly a highlight for me, unrelated to her choosing my book. The fact that *she* chose *The Bachelor* was a thrill for me in such a personal way.

You were an attorney before your writing career took off. When did you decide to give up law and write full time? Do you find any of your former legal/rhetorical skills useful in your new career?

I gave up law after one year of practicing. I think my argumentative/aggressive skills were lacking, but the writing and the methodical parts of going through case law came easier to me. These days my law career comes in handy when I write about working women. The legal education comes in handy when dealing with contracts and other parts of my profession. I still have an agent and an attorney to look over my contracts, but I am educated in the legalese and I don't have to ask as many questions as I might otherwise have to. My dad always said I'd have my law degree forever, and I see now what he meant.

In your interview with Kelley St. John for her Web site feature "The Call" (www.kelleystjohn.com/TheCall.cfm), you described the combination of persistence and belief in your own work that it took to get your first book, *Brazen*, into the hands of the right editor. After seven years of writing and hunting for a publisher, how did you stay focused and positive?

Staying focused and positive is necessary when inundated with rejections. The best way is to find a kernel of hope within the body of the rejection letter.

At first the letters are usually form rejections, but over time, hopefully you end up with one positive line. Ultimately you look for a line that says the editor would be interested in seeing something else. Then you can submit a new book without querying first. To me, that became the goal—sometimes more than selling, because it was more realistic. So as soon as I'd mail off one completed manuscript, I'd begin working on a brand new one so if the other one came back rejected, I would immediately have something new to go out with. It became a process, and I learned how to work within it and even enjoy it sometimes.

You also need to reward yourself just for finishing because that is something to celebrate. Of course there will be many pints of ice cream for pity parties in between!

How was the process of working on *Brazen* with Brenda Chin at Temptation? What did you learn from the experience?

I learned that when published authors tell unpublished authors to be flexible and to do what an editor asks in the way of revisions, they mean it. For every new author who sells, there are hundreds of unsold authors who would love to be in that position. Translation: Editors don't have to work with difficult authors. They have a large talent pool to choose from.

I learned to have even *more* patience at the point when a first sale was so close I could taste it, but I just wasn't there yet.

And I learned things happen for a reason. The book prior to *Brazen* had been through many revisions with Brenda and had gone all the way up to the senior editor before being rejected. If I had ultimately sold that book, I believe in my heart I never would have sold again because Temptation was changing, getting hotter. The book before *Brazen* was more family oriented. I never would have understood what Temptation was becoming had I sold then. So I learned to accept what happens as necessary if things are to work out in the end.

You had 10 completed manuscripts when you finally sold *Brazen*. What happened to those other early books?

The early books were learning experiences for the most part. I did sell three of those to Kensington's Bouquet line, but I learned something from those experiences as well. Those weren't my Carly Phillips-style books.

Can you talk a little bit about the development of the Carly Phillips brand? How has it evolved?

The Carly Phillips brand began as "hot books" for Harlequin Temptation and Blaze. From the beginning, I worked to associate my name with a sizzling story. Carly Phillips preexisted "Karen Drogin" as a writer since I sold as Carly Phillips first and only wrote three books under the KD name.

Over time, sizzling evolved into "sexy fun." Besides sexy fun, the trademark of a CP book is emotional depth and character. I pride myself on giving a reader well-developed, well-motivated characters they can relate to on some level. Their conflicts, hopes and dreams are rooted in a reality someone has experienced at some time. Maybe it's loss, maybe it's insecurity, maybe it's even a learning disability such as dyslexia (*Hot Stuff*). But if you read my books, I want you to be able to relate to and fall in love with my characters.

Reprinted with permission from Harlequin.

Are you pleased with the way you've been branded and marketed? Was any of it hard to get used to?

I have had a hand in my branding and marketing every step of the way, both with my publishers and with my publicist. I take responsibility for the growth and for the steps forward (and occasionally backward!). I'm a very anal, hands-on person (just ask my agent, editor and publicist). I can't always control how things go, but I have a vision I am always working towards.

The hardest part to get used to was the pseudonym. I needed to accept that I *am* Carly Phillips. That I'm not a phony or a fraud when I sign the name Carly. It's been eight years since I sold and took the name, so by now Carly is a part of me. The next thing that was hard to get used to was the *New York Times* label. With hitting the big lists comes new pressures and concerns. Those I am still dealing with now.

At what point did you get an agent? A publicist? How do they help make your life easier?

I got an agent when I sold to Bouquet and didn't want to end up obligated to two companies and have conflict. I think authors believe they are competent enough to represent themselves, but the truth is even with a legal background, a third party can step in and do the dirty side of the business while keeping the author's relationship with their publisher nice and happy. A good agent takes stress off of an author, and that is what any writer needs.

That said, having no agent is better than having a bad agent. A writer should never pay an agent to read their work. This is where Romance Writers of America is key. Everything I learned about dos and don'ts, I learned from RWA.

I didn't get a publicist until about six months before my first single-title book, *The Bachelor*, was due to be published. Publicity and promotion is important, but a publicist is expensive, so that should only happen when an author can afford to use one. There are many things authors can do for themselves (and I did for myself) effectively, such as managing their own Web site (with an easy-to-remember URL like www.carlyphillips.com). But a writer needs to be careful because the publicity side can end up eating into writing time.

On your Web site, you said your professional dream of happiness would include a Top Five NYT book "without the angst and drama that goes into each book promotion." Which parts of book promotion cause you the most stress?

I actually love the process of promotion. I can spend hours and way too much money on PR and promotion and enjoy every minute. It's not the promotion that causes stress. It's the "how a book will do." I put a lot of pressure on myself not only in the writing process, but afterwards to ensure the book does as well as possible. So from the point where I turn in the book and begin looking towards PR and promotion for the novel, performance angst sets in.

Ultimately I would like it if each book outperforms the last, so at the very least there is a slow and steady climb, an increase in my readership. My goal is to write a book my readers will love and then to do everything possible to get the book into as many people's hands as possible. There's the angst!

Please talk about your writing process.

Every day is different for me. Sometimes I write best at 6 a.m. and sometimes at 10 p.m. If the muse strikes, I want to be able to write, and that's why I love my new Apple iBook laptop, because I can write anywhere! I can't plan in advance to write because I'm a mother and there will always be crises that come up that must come first. But the writing does get done. It's part of who I am.

The writing process, however, is a pretty consistent one for me, and it isn't pretty. I'm not a strong outliner. I write and fly by the seat of my pants. I have the basic concept of the story, a synopsis that usually includes a lot of backstory/history of the characters, and a general hook. I dive in and start writing. By the time I hit page 100, I've usually revised a gazillion times because I'll hit page 50, come up with something huge, and have to go back and weave it in from the beginning. It's a constant revising process as I write. The benefit is by the time I'm finished, I usually have a pretty solid story that only needs cleanup, not revision.

My editor shares this process with me, reading after I've completed about 100 or more pages and suggesting revisions so we catch problems early. The drawback to this process is I drive my critique partner, Janelle Denison, absolutely crazy asking her to read, reread once I've revised, and reread again. However, you can't change what works and this is my system, for better or worse!

At what point do you start showing your manuscript to your critique partner? Do you have any other constant manuscript readers besides Janelle?

Janelle looks at my manuscript as early as chapter one. We compliment one another writing-wise and it's a win-win partnership. I value her advice as a reader and as a writer. I'm more needy at the beginning of a story, needing advice and input and wanting to have a pat on the head, so to speak. She needs more help at the end of a story. But we count on each other all the way through. I have two other plot partners who don't read my work but who I go away with once a year to plot out one another's stories. Leslie Kelly, Julie Leto, Janelle and I do this together and we have an e-mail loop we use to help one another as we write. We're also a support/friendship group, and I'm lucky to have them.

You have two young daughters. Have they asked to read your books?

The nine-year-old has never asked to read my books. The 13-year-old has asked and I have given her permission, because frankly the books out there for her age go very far. She's read detail. I'd rather her read what I write because the lesson is monogamy is important. Fidelity is important. Trust in a relationship is important. I am proud of what I write and the views I convey, so once I feel my girls are emotionally ready to handle the content, I would love for them to read a whole story and discuss those things with me.

The romance market is changing, with the blending of genres and the creation of new subgenres. Do you have any desire to try something other than contemporary romance?

The things that intrigue me within romance are paranormal and time travel. Although not time travel backwards because I'm not a researcher, so I'd rather go forward and create worlds. I'm not sure what the future holds, but I'm always trying to develop my writing and stay fresh.

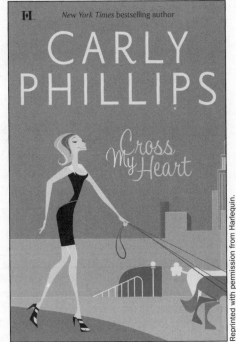

New York Times bestselling author

CARLY PHILLIPS

Cross My Heart

Reprinted with permission from Harlequin.

You've accomplished so much in the last seven years. What are your goals going forward?

What an apropos question at this particular time. I feel I am at a crossroads of sorts. It may be more of a personal feeling than one that truly exists in my career. I'm at a place where I want to make some smart and innovative choices. For now, I would like to consistently move up on the best-seller lists, because to me that would mean I am reaching more readers. I'd love to be an automatic buy for readers. That's a true goal for me.

What's the best piece of publishing advice you can give new writers?

In the end, the only thing you can control is the work itself. Everything else is truly in someone else's hands—readers, reviewers, editors, publishers, etc. You can guide your career and you should, but write the best book you can first. It's the most important thing and a direct reflection of you.

(Sexy) Voices in Your Head

Dialogue, from Imagination to Page

© Stanley Studios, Melbourne, FL

by Leslie Kelly

Some people say I talk too much. After I give my husband—er, *some* people—an indignant look, I am able to concede that, at times, I am slightly verbose. Personally, I think every writer likes really good conversation, which is not a bad thing since most of us have chats, arguments, witty repartee or sexy whispers running through our heads 24/7. (Or maybe I'm the only one with the sexy whispers. . . .) Our occupation gives us the right to hear the voices of imaginary people without being considered nuts.

So with all that conversing going on, writing dialogue ought to be a simple part of our job, right? Just tune that mental dial to the conversation going on in the old brain, eavesdrop, and type it into your work in progress.

If only it were that easy. Because despite the fact that most writers do hear their characters' voices, a lot of effort goes into writing effective dialogue that keeps our stories moving. And even if you *do* simply let those voices in your head come out into your computer, you will eventually have to edit them into something cohesive.

It *shouldn't* be this tough. There are, after all, so many other elements of fiction writing which, on the surface, appear to be much more difficult. Take plot. How many of us have ruled a country, thwarted an assassination, dabbled in serial-killing, or been on the run with a former Marine turned bodyguard who looks like Brad Pitt and wants to make-out while bullets are flying overhead? Or characterization. How many serial killers have you met? Bodyguards? Presidents? How about setting? Ever actually been to Alaska, Siberia, the jungles of South America?

Thought not.

That stuff is hard, requiring time, effort and research.

But dialogue—talking—that should be simple, right? We've all experienced the humor, pathos, anger, emotion and, at times, mortification that can come with the spoken word. (Like the time my oldest, at age three, screeched—loudly—about the amount of hair growing out of an elderly stranger's ears. Sometimes teaching them to talk isn't all it's cracked up to be.)

Still, with years of experience in talking, we shouldn't have to think so hard about what our characters say. But we do, because it's important. Just by putting a few people together

---

LESLIE KELLY, since selling her first book to Harlequin in 1999, has become known for writing sassy, sexy and sometimes irreverent stories filled with strong heroines and playful heroes. A National Reader's Choice Award winning author, Kelly has twice been nominated for the highest award in romance, the RWA Rita Award, and is a four-time nominee for the Romantic Times Bookclub Award. Kelly resides in Florida with her husband, three daughters, and a fuzzy little dog who hasn't yet been informed she's not a human.

and letting them shoot off their mouths, you can reveal character, advance plot, enhance description, heighten conflict, build tension and affect pacing.

Now you're panicking: It has to do all that? Can't I just lay down some fun words that make me grin?

Unfortunately, no. Dialogue is too important a tool to waste it. (Well, okay, I occasionally leave stuff in just because it's super clever and I like it...but not often.)

Fortunately, there are some things you can do to make the most of every spoken word in your novel.

CONSIDER THE CONTEXT

First, know what kind of book you're writing and make sure your dialogue fits. Jaunty, clever banter works well in romantic comedy. In historical, epic sagas? Not so much.

I enjoy witty, fast-paced books, so I like dialogue that bounces. Think of it as a kid's game of hot potato: Somebody lobs a comment into the air and the next person bounces it right back. Keep it going until that spud cools off, and your reader will keep turning those pages. Here's an example from my recent book, *Here Comes Trouble* (HQN, 2006):

> "Funny, I can't picture you as a saintly kid. I somehow see you as the cautionary cartoon bad boy in the young man's puberty handbook. The one with the cigarette in his hand."
> "Don't smoke."
> "The beer can, then."
> "Don't drink, either."
> Her eyes widened. "You really have no vices?"
> He smiled. Slowly. Deliberately. "I didn't say that."

The characters in my own books quite often have fast-paced, bouncy conversations, made sharper by the quick, internal dialogue going on inside the point-of-view character's head. In *Here Comes Trouble*, for instance, the hero and heroine have a snappy discussion about horror movies. The back-and-forth pacing sets up the perfect line when they finally introduce themselves: she with her real name, and he as well-known movie psycho Michael Myers. The moment wouldn't have been as effective—for the reader or for the heroine—if the preceding conversation hadn't been paced just right.

INCORPORATE MOTION

One romance and women's fiction author known for her sparkling, bouncy dialogue is *New York Times* best-selling author Jennifer Crusie. Crusie recently teamed up with Bob Mayer, a *USA Today* best-selling author of science fiction and thrillers, to collaborate on a comic romantic adventure titled *Don't Look Down* (St. Martin's Press, 2006.) When asked if they have any particular techniques for developing dialogue, Crusie says, "Honestly, I just write down what I hear in my head. Dialogue is the one thing in writing I don't have a technique for." (Remember . . . we like her anyway!) Mayer, however, says, "I think action in concert with dialogue. For example, in *Don't Look Down*, when J.T. Wilder introduced himself to the young girl Pepper, he gets down on one knee so he's at her level. He's the only one who does that and I think it was important."

Mayer's comment is a reminder that people don't exist and converse in vacuums. Most conversations take place while dinner is being prepared, wine is being poured, or guns are being pointed. Keep your characters doing something during their dialogue so you don't have "talking heads."

Physical action and reaction is a good way to convey to your reader how a line is spoken and what it *really* means. In teaching workshops about writing dialogue, I've often indulged my ham tendencies to illustrate this very point. Picture me, the serious author, standing in front of a crowd saying, "Come and get me," a half-dozen different ways: like a child playing hide-and-seek, James Cagney yelling at the coppers, a girl screaming out the window of a burning building, a serial killer taunting an FBI agent, or a redhead in a black negligee. (No, I don't typically wear the negligee. I write romance . . . not horror.)

The point of the exercise is to show that the same words can be spoken in many different ways. There have to be clues to tell the reader how they should take them, without relying on those dreadful "ly" words we've all been warned against. Inner thoughts are great, but you can also use physical actions—the tensing of an arm, the frustrated pounding of a hand—to help convey the delivery of the dialogue to the reader. A smirk from the heroine and a shrug from the hero in this scene from *Don't Open Till Chistmas* (Blaze, 2005) make the characters' feelings apparent:

> "I guess that means you just love the holiday season, hmm?"
> She smirked. "Oh, it's the most wonderful time of the year, don't you know."
> "I think I've heard that. Though, I personally prefer St. Patrick's Day."
> Grinning, she admitted. "Me, too. Irish coffee."
> "Green beer."
> "Red-nosed Irishmen instead of rosy-cheeked North Polers."
> He shrugged. "But I think the leprechaun/elf thing is pretty evenly annoying."

Studying screenplays and comparing them to movies or television shows with effective dialogue can also be helpful in illustrating this point. Seeing the way an actor delivers a line makes it patently clear what he means, especially when compared to the same line as written in the script. The actor takes the words and makes them come alive. As writers, though, we don't have that luxury and must get the message across in another way. Adding physical action is one way to do it.

SET THE PACE, FEEL THE RHYTHM

USA Today best-selling author Julie Elizabeth Leto also studies TV shows to learn more about pacing and rhythm, both of which are affected by dialogue. "I love certain television shows that have quick dialogue—shows like 'Gilmore Girls' and 'Gray's Anatomy.' I use my TiVO to rewind particularly good exchanges. It's all about timing, and while it's hard to make that work on the page instead of in the skilled hands of a trained actor, it's not impossible."

The rhythm and pace of the language you choose can also build character through dialogue. Some authors like to reveal their characters' backgrounds, ethnicity or even mood with the use of dialects, but most agree they should be used sparingly. Crusie says, "I think you do them through word choice and rhythm. No cute spellings. No apostrophes for missing letters." Mayer concurs. "I'm not a fan either. Dialect really jars the reader out of your prose." *New York Times* best-selling author Mary Jo Putney, who began her career writing

richly detailed Regency-era historical romances, feels the same way. "I think it's really easy to overdo dialect, and most readers—myself included—usually find it irritating and distracting."

New York Times best-selling author Vicki Lewis Thompson puts it very well: "Dialects are like chili pepper. A little goes a long way."

MAKE VOICES DISTINCT

Thompson, whose popular Nerd series for St. Martin's Press is full of witty, sexy banter, also comments on another challenging aspect of writing dialogue: keeping your characters "sounding" distinct from one another. "It's a challenge, but again, it's about developing your ear. Gender, age, education, personality, economic level—all those impact how a person speaks. As you crawl into your character's skin, you have to adopt the societal position of that person and speak as they would, given their circumstances."

As I mentioned, I enjoy snappy, fast-paced dialogue. But I also enjoy reading lyrical, more formal prose, which often appears in historical romance fiction. The challenges remain the same, despite the style of the dialogue. When asked how she keeps her characters' voices distinct, Putney says, "If I know the characters really well, it's automatically reflected in the dialogue. Guys talk like guys, kids talk like kids.... However, since I mostly write British set historicals, a lot of my characters tend to sound like educated Brits, because they are."

Keeping dialogue true to character becomes especially important when writing about the opposite sex. The collaboration between Jennifer Crusie and Bob Mayer helped each of them in this regard. Crusie says, "I try really hard to think like a guy. It's why my guys always sound like English teachers. Writing with Bob has been great for this. His guys are GUYS." She also adds, "Dialogue Rule #1: Guys do not chat."

Mayer also enjoyed coming at the dialogue from another angle. "I've always liked snappy, funny dialogue. It popped up in places in my other books but often got edited out because the over-all tone of those books was usually kind of grim with high body counts. Writing with Jenny has really freed that creative part of me."

You don't have to be co-writing to make sure your dialogue sounds realistic and in character. Running your work by a critique partner, or a significant other can help ensure your characters sound real. Or even running them by *yourself*. *USA Today* best-selling author Jill Shalvis does just that. "I always read my dialogue to myself out loud. It's the only way to make sure it sounds natural!"

BRILLIANT, SPARKLING, CRACKLING, SNAPPY . . . *USEFUL*

So, whether listening to those voices in your head, writing with a partner, imagining your words being spoken on the big screen, or reading them aloud, always pay special attention to what your characters are saying and how they're saying it. Keep it snappy, necessary and realistic. Make it useful.

Vicki Lewis Thompson offers a final word of caution, "One of my pet peeves is dialogue written solely to illustrate that the author is clever. Dialogue can be snappy and work fine for me, but when I start to *notice* the dialogue because it's so clever, then I'm jerked out of the story. Dialogue should serve the story, not outshine it."

Which reminds me, I have some more revising to do. Rats . . . that ear-hair story was so cute, too. . . .

Sabrina Jeffries

Writing Royal Romance but
Grounded in Reality

© Christopher J. Happel, Studio 16

by Deborah Bouziden

As Sabrina Jeffries celebrates the publication of her 26th book, *Never Seduce a Scoundrel* (Pocket, 2006), she can look back on her career and enthusiastically say she does what she wants and does it her way. Her books have landed on *The New York Times* Extended List, followed closely by the *USA Today* top 50 best-seller list. Her dream is coming true—and in romantic royal style.

"I started making up stories at 12, though I don't think I wrote them down. I do remember telling myself that one day I *would* write them down and sell them. I've been a romantic since early childhood."

These romantic fantasies were built from the many books Jeffries read as a little girl. Her parents were missionaries who traveled the world. For a time, the family lived in Bangkok, and used books were easy to come by because the international school had a library.

"My parents were big readers, so we had books everywhere, including a multivolume set of *The Junior Classics* with wonderful stories that I devoured. Still, I never had enough books to satisfy me," Jeffries says. "I started on Barbara Cartland's books in high school, but even before those, I loved romantic fairy tales."

After Jeffries finished high school, she attended college at Tulane University and earned her doctorate in English. After receiving her degree and making the college interview rounds, she realized she didn't want to spend the rest of her life teaching and she loathed academic writing.

"I wrote my first real novel after grad school. I sat down to develop a publishable academic work based on my dissertation and found it so boring I started writing a romance instead— a category romance. It didn't sell, but I enjoyed the experience so much, I kept writing. I sold the first historical I wrote," she remembers.

For new writers who are looking to be published, this may seem like a fairy tale in itself, but Jeffries understands and lives in the real world. She has faced and lived through hard times and continued publishing despite them. In her professional life, she has been rejected, received harsh reviews, and was dropped by two publishers in one year.

"I handled it all by pressing on—looking for a new publisher and looking at my writing to determine what I could improve to make myself more marketable," she says.

In her personal life, Jeffries and her husband care for an autistic son, Nick. To inform

DEBORAH BOUZIDEN, since 1985, has had hundreds of articles published and has authored or co-authored nine books including *In Their Name*, *The Journal Wheel and Guidebook* and *Oklahoma: Off The Beaten Path*, her latest project. To learn more about Bouziden, visit her Web site at www.deborahbouziden.com.

others, she speaks candidly about autism on her Web site www.sabrinajeffries.com. While she has faced challenges raising her son and balancing her career, Jeffries keeps her life in perspective.

"My son keeps me grounded," Jeffries says. "I can't quantify how my greater tolerance has shown up in my work. I'm sure it's there, but it's a subtle influence. It's more pronounced in my daily living because I put up with people's eccentricities to a greater degree than I used to.

"My son has certainly affected my writing schedule, however. I have to stay on top of the writing. I can't let it build up, then do a blitzkrieg to finish the book. Despite being a teenager, my son is always needy. When I lock myself into writing mode for days on end, he gets cranky and hard to handle. So I have to stick to a fairly rigorous daily writing schedule. I'm sure that has contributed to my success."

From her desk, which sits on a raised dais affectionately referred to as "the throne," Jeffries rules like a queen over family and career. In this interview, she offers wisdom gleaned from years of hard work and publishing success.

What fascinates you about early 19th century England?

I love the glamour of the Regency period—the costumes, the rules and the really great hairstyles for men (especially when compared to Georgian periwigs and Victorian muttonchops). I like the clash of the rising merchant class with the aristocracy. I like that the English royals then were so colorful. (Oh, wait, I guess that's still true.) And I love Romantic poetry—Byron, Shelley, Keats—the bad boys of the Regency.

I've already written a couple of Restoration-era historicals as Deborah Martin, and while I'm not quite as keen on the fashions then, I loved the clash of the Puritans with the aristocracy. The bawdy Cavaliers were rebelling against the repressed Roundheads. What's not to like?

I'm intrigued by the tidbits you put in your books—wicked whist, peep show boxes, dragon paintings, etc. Do you find these details before writing your books and set them aside to use later, or do you discover them while researching?

I don't usually do much research in the beginning—just enough to confirm that my plot will work in the period. Once I start writing, I have to research individual elements, so that takes me lots of different places. Whatever I stumble across is usually what I end up using, although once in a while I see something in a museum or article or book that piques my interest outside of the book. In the case of the peep show boxes, for example, I happened to see two of them at an exhibit at the New York Public Library while I was on vacation. I couldn't resist incorporating them into a book.

How did you come up with the Royal Brotherhood of Bastards, your third series?

It happened while I was toying with having three noble half-brothers share the same mother. I was always intrigued by the idea of three lords joined in a connection they despise. My critique partner Rexanne Becnel once wrote a secondary character whom I loved, a bastard son of a king, but she'd never centered a book around him. One night, my noble half-brothers idea melded with research I'd been doing on Prinny (King George IV, Prince of Wales) and my wish that she'd develop *her* character, and voila, a series was born.

When you write a series, do you decide on plot, setting or character first?

Of necessity (since most series are linked by character connection) I usually start with the series' characters (three bastard half-brothers or three spinster sisters), but at that point they are pretty generic. It's only when I plot the book and actually start writing it that the characters gel. I tend to be a plot-driven writer, but I work hard to develop my characters fully once I plot their books.

In your books, your characters have secrets. Do you believe everyone has secrets and those secrets are what drive them?

Absolutely. I love secrets. I think all of our relationships stem from what happens as we slowly peel away the layers of our past for other people. If they can tolerate our darkest selves, then they become our friends (or spouses) for life. If they can't, then they drift off to other people. It's the slow unpeeling that makes romance so much fun for me to write.

You have written as Deborah Nicholas, Deborah Martin and now Sabrina Jeffries. Do you feel it's important to establish a different identity for different genres? What advice would you give to a new writer regarding pseudonyms?

Reprinted with permission from Pocket.

I wrote as Deborah Martin and Deborah Nicholas almost simultaneously. My respective publishers didn't want my growing career at one publishing house to be affected adversely by my numbers at the other house, and since I was an unknown author at the time, they weren't taking any chances, so they insisted on my having two different pseudonyms. When I decided to write a completely different kind of historical, my new publisher wanted me to take a new name to reflect the new style and voice. By that point, I was an experienced writer, and I realized I'd be better off choosing something catchy rather than something close to my real name.

Incidentally, that would be my advice to any new genre author—if you have a catchy real name, use it. If you don't, choose something interesting and unique as a pseudonym because your name is part of the marketing package. Unfortunately, marketing is everything in today's publishing world. Taking a pseudonym the third time around was the best thing that ever happened to me—but I did lose most of my old readers because they couldn't find me. Sometimes, however, booksellers are more eager to take a chance on a debut author than an established one with lackluster sales, so you have to weigh whether to take a pseudonym in terms of marketing.

How has the Internet changed the way you do promotion for your books?

The Internet has made a huge difference, although I still do postal mailings. I've found ARC mailings to bookstores and fan mailing lists can be very effective.

I love interacting with readers, but I have to be careful about what I take away from that interaction. If I listen to every reader's opinion equally (and they sometimes contradict each other), I'll make myself crazy. For example, if a hundred readers complain that my characters are unlikable, maybe they are. But if two say it, I have to consider it in the same vein as all the other varying opinions I get—i.e., it doesn't mean much. There's plenty of truth to that old adage, "Too many cooks spoil the broth." As writers, we have to protect our own voice and vision or risk having it eroded by well-meaning (and not so well-meaning) critics.

Where do you think the romance genre is headed? Do you think the current changes are permanent or just trendy?

I tend to agree with those who see the changes as just one more swing of the pendulum. I remember when historicals were all the rage. Before that, contemporaries were all the rage. Now paranormals are all the rage. That may change, but I've given up predicting how. I think there will always be a market for most subgenres; they'll just be popular at different times.

Please talk about your latest book series.

Never Seduce a Scoundrel and *Only a Duke Will Do* came out in 2006 as book one and two of the series. An anthology containing novellas centered on the series comes out in December.

The series (and the anthology) is entitled The School for Heiresses, and is about a widow, Mrs. Charlotte Harris, who runs a respectable establishment called Mrs. Harris's School for Young Ladies. Since it caters to only the wealthy, society dubs it the School for Heiresses. Ever since Charlotte's exciting elopement to a scoundrel ended up depriving her of everything but her very genteel upbringing, she has been determined to keep other heiresses from making the same mistake, so she teaches such things as how to recognize a fortune-hunter, how to balance one's family's needs with one's own, how to resist seduction by a bounder, and how not to let love blind one to a man's disadvantages.

The stories will be set in and around London during a period from 1818 to 1823. *Only a Duke Will Do* is linked to the Royal Brotherhood Series. My readers clamored for it so much that I decided to work it into the new series.

What is the one thing you wish interviewers would ask you, but they never do?

Why I like to write about hot sex. I'll answer it, too—why *wouldn't* I want to write about hot sex? It's one of the best parts of life, along with chocolate, Dougie Maclean albums and Shakespeare. And if somehow you can combine all four—ooh, baby!

Resources

Where to Look for More Information

Below is a list of invaluable resources specifically for romance writers. To order any of the Writer's Digest Books titles or to get a consumer book catalog, call (800)448-0915. You may also order Writer's Digest Books selections through www.writers digest.com, Amazon.com or www.barnesandnoble.com.

MAGAZINES
- *Romance Writers Report*, Romance Writers of America, 16000 Stuebner Airline Rd., Suite 140, Spring TX 77379. (832)717-5200. Fax: (832)717-5201. E-mail: info@rwanational.org.
- *Romantic Times Bookclub Magazine*, 55 Bergen St., Brooklyn NY 11201. (718)237-1097. Web site: www.romantictimes.com.

BOOKS
- *How To Write Romances (Revised and Updated)**, by Phyllis Taylor Pianka
- *Keys to Success: The Professional Writer's Career Handbook*, Romance Writers of America
- *Writing Romances: A Handbook by the Romance Writers of America*, edited by Rita Clay Estrada and Rita Gallagher
- *You Can Write a Romance*, by Rita Clay Estrada and Rita Gallagher (Writer's Digest Books)

ORGANIZATIONS & ONLINE
- Canadian Romance Authors' Network. Web site: www.canadianromanceauthors.com.
- Romance Writers of America, Inc. (RWA), 16000 Stuebner Airline Rd., Suite 140, Spring TX 77379. (832)717-5200. Fax: (832)717-5201. E-mail: info@rwanational.org. Web site: www.rwanational.org.
- Romance Writers of America regional chapters. Contact National Office (address above) for information on the chapter nearest you.
- The Romance Club. Web site: http://theromanceclub.com.
- Romance Central. Web site: www.romance-central.com. Offers workshops and forum where romance writers share ideas and exchange advice about romance writing.
- Writer's Market Online. Web site: www.writersmarket.com.
- Writer's Digest Online. Web site: www.writersdigest.com.

* *Out of print. Check your local library.*

Laugh Until You Scream

Writing Humor and Horror

by Carol Pinchefsky

Why was the skeleton afraid to cross the road?

Because it had no guts.

Like other branches of fiction, horror has its subgenres. And while humorous horror is not a new entry—Frederic Brown employed it in the 1940s—in the last few years it's gained momentum in both sales and readership. Humorous horror involves either telling morbid tales with a witty flair or writing about wacky escapades that go horribly, grotesquely wrong. A good example of humorous horror is the role reversal of Buffy the Vampire Slayer, where the vampires are afraid of the blonde.

Writing in this style is not for the faint-hearted: It is difficult enough to make humor funny and horror scary. Compound those problems when trying to do both at the same time—it's the literary equivalent of patting one's head while rubbing one's stomach.

Writers employ humor in their horror for various reasons. Some do it to ease tension in an otherwise disturbing scene. Others, because they believe their characters would respond to a shocking occurrence with a joke.

Writer and editor Jay Lake says, "There are not a lot of people writing humor and horror. You can get career traction fairly quickly over something that most people don't even know exists. If one thinks humor combined with horror is funny and has that rather perverse sense of humor, one should just go ahead and write it. Because if you do it well, it means you have a distinctive voice."

And if done well, writers can elevate their prose to the heights of the deliciously absurd. Where horror goes to the edge, and humor goes over the top, humorous horror finds its own place—where the funny bone meets the gut.

Five authors with experience in the subgenre share their thoughts. **Charlaine Harris** is the author of over 20 books, including the Sookie Stackhouse series. **Jay Lake** is author of over 100 short stories, three collections, and a chapbook and is co-editor of the *Polyphony* anthology series from Wheatland Press. **Joe R. Lansdale** has written over 20 books and dozens of humorous horror stories, including the novella *Bubba Ho-Tep*, which was adapted for film. **Dean Wesley Smith** is the author of *All Eve's Hallows* and countless movie and TV novelizations. **Wm. Mark Simmons** is the author of eight books, including the Chris Cséjthe series.

CAROL PINCHEFSKY is a freelance writer in New York City. She has written articles on science fiction for SciFi.com, *Battlestar Galactica* magazine, *SFX* and *Orson Scott Card's Intergalactic Medicine Show*.

Why did you start combining humor and horror in your writing?

Harris: I had reached a point in my career where I could either take a leap of faith or be satisfied with my mid-list status. I decided to take the leap of faith. It seemed to me that I wanted to cross some genre boundaries; I wanted to keep my mystery audience small and select and hopefully add some new readers. So I decided to write a book I always wanted to write without regard to keeping it within any one genre.

Lansdale: It was a natural outgrowth of who I am. I don't remember making the decision. It just happened. I think it's more about how I see life.

Charlaine Harris

© Caroline Grayshock

What makes this such a good combination?

Lake: To me humor and horror are both rather idiosyncratic. Think about the difference between horror and fantasy: Fantasy is something that has happened to the world, and horror is something that happens to the individual—a definition I got from editor Ellen Datlow, by the way. Except for The Dark Tower series, characters don't typically have horror quests, but they have fantasy quests.

And humor, of course, is an incredibly individual experience, which is why humor is so terribly hard to write. So what you have is a cross section between the two pretty individualized fields.

Jay Lake

© Briant Nierstedt

Harris: I think it mirrors real life to a certain extent. My own life is a mixture of horrible moments and very funny moments. My father died in January and, at the funeral, my mother sat down in a chair under the mourner's tent. The back two legs gave way [laughs] and she just fell over backwards. The natural instinct was both to rush to her aid and to laugh.

Simmons: A close examination of comedy reveals a concept generally based on pain, loss or humiliation. Take almost any joke, any comedy sketch, and break it down to its basic components. What are we laughing at? Someone else's difficulty, problem, comeuppance. We laugh, recognizing similar events in our own lives. Or thinking, "There but for the grace of God . . ."

Horror works in the same way, though usually as a cathartic means of dealing with our deepest fears, our darkest nightmares, by proxy.

What are its challenges?

Lansdale: It's easy to fail; that's for sure. You really have to let the writing develop naturally. Too much preparation and it looks planned—*feels* planned—and isn't funny.

Smith: It takes a certain skill level to do it right, it's so easy to come down on one side or another too much. It's funny instead of horrific. Or if you're trying to be funny and it's not, it becomes too horrific for the reader to handle, and they put it down.

Harris: It's hard to balance. It's hard to decide the proportion of humor to horror, the proportion of mystery to romance. It's establishing being true to the character rather than letting the genre overtake you.

Joe R. Lansdale

© Karen Lansdale

Simmons: Balance isn't simply a matter of adjusting the left and right channels of your story for more jokes/less gore or fewer punch lines/higher body count. It's a question of audience expectations and the kind of story you're trying to tell.

Courtesy of author

Mark Simmons

Some people approach the humor/horror equation as something that should be very intense and they take their humor dark and in very small doses. Others prefer the other end of the spectrum with a thematic spoof or farce: Abbott & Costello Meet Casper the Friendly Ghost.

My approach is to straddle the line as best I can, delivering real chills at some points of the narrative while giving the reader enough wit, irony and near-absurdity that some horror tropes are heir to.

Which do you prefer, the short form or the long form?

Lansdale: The short form. I think it can wear thin in the long form. But, that doesn't mean you can't include some humor in a longer piece; it means that strong humor can become strained in longer pieces. It's not impossible, but it's hard.

Harris: It can work either way. I write books and few short stories, but I enjoyed many short stories that have the balance right. Short stories tend to be one thing or the other and not both, but that's my limitation. It depends on the writer, of getting the proportion right, no matter what the length of the work is.

What advice do you have for writers who are interested in combining humor and horror?

Lake: At least for me personally, what makes the kind of stuff work is when you push an edge. If you're going to write both humor and horror, don't hold back, say the stuff you'd

Recommended Reading

Charlaine Harris: MaryJanice Davidson's books are absolutely farcical. Her heroine is a vampire who refuses to act as a vampire in an everyday context. She insists that her parents invite her over to Thanksgiving.

Jay Lake: Howard Waldrop. Humorous horror is a particularly fertile playground for weird, and he is out there. In a book I did called *TEL:Stories*, a writer named Ken Scholes wrote "The Santaman Cycle." It's a story that has Santa Claus as a mythic figure, ravaging the world with his bloody sword.

Joe Lansdale: Fred Brown was a master of this kind of thing, as was Robert Bloch and Ambrose Bierce. Flannery O'Connor could be very funny and very dark at the same time.

Dean Wesley Smith: Dean Koontz' *Life Expectancy* was startlingly funny and startlingly horrific. He's a master of crossing the line and using both in a way of complete control. I'm a big fan of Joe Lansdale. I think anything by him has some elements of humor as well as horror.

Wm. Mark Simmons: My favorite work mixing humor with "elements" of horror is *Good Omens* by Neil Gaiman and Terry Pratchett. I also enjoy Charlaine Harris for her subtlety and Christopher Moore for his lack thereof.

be ashamed for your grandmother to read, and be outrageous. It's a sub-sub-sub-genre that works only because it goes to extremes. So you know what? Pile it on and let 'er rip.

Smith: Read a lot of the people who are crossing the line and using both in a way of complete control. Read a book four or five times and get down to the words to see how the writer managed to do a certain scene where you as the reader thought, "Wow, that's funny. No, that's horror." Write and practice a lot. It's the only way to get good at this.

Lansdale: Character is what makes it work. You have to find the character interesting, and if not, it doesn't seem real. You have to make the character someone people care about.

To me, the work itself becomes the character. That's done through style, by the way it's written, the words you can chew on. The gothic South becomes a character itself.

Dean Wesley Smith

Simmons: Never sacrifice plot or character or style for the sake of a punch line or a cheap laugh. If your characters are cardboard props with no higher purpose than to serve the joke, then your reader won't emotionally invest in them. Humor, horror or a gestalt of the two, the result is deeper, richer, if the reader actually cares about your characters—what they are thinking, feeling, what will happen to them.

Boot Camps for Writers

Whip Your Speculative Fiction into Shape

Courtesy of author

by John Joseph Adams

Writers who specialize in creating science fiction, fantasy and horror have a number of opportunities to study with luminaries in the field by participating in one of the following writers' workshops. These workshops encourage students to conduct in-depth examinations of their strengths and weaknesses, by writing and critiquing the work of others. This provides for a rather intense experience, earning this sort of workshop the affectionate title of "writer's boot camp."

In my role as assistant editor of *The Magazine of Fantasy & Science Fiction*, I've seen the results of these workshops firsthand. Some writers don't show an appreciable increase in skill or craft right away (for some it takes a while for the lessons to sink in, and for some it never sinks in at all), but for others it's as if their writing experienced a quantum leap forward—as if going to the workshop turned some key and unlocked their inner writer.

While examples of the former are fairly common, examples of the latter are harder to come by. But one such writer is David Marusek. He's what you might call a poster child for workshopping success. "I attended Clarion West in Seattle in 1992 and sold two short stories that I wrote there. I sold one on the spot to *Asimov's Science Fiction* magazine. I sold the other a month later to *Playboy*. These were my first fiction sales, and I have been publishing regularly, if not prolifically, ever since," he says. Marusek's stories have gone on to be lauded by both fans and critics alike, and in 1999, his story "The Wedding Album" was nominated for a Nebula Award and won the Theodore Sturgeon Memorial Award.

Before attending Clarion West, Marusek says that he had been writing for about seven years on his own, with no writing classes under his belt and only a few weeklong workshops. He was collecting personalized rejections from editors, but he couldn't seem to break into print. "In retrospect," he said, "I believe I had taught myself the basic elements of the craft— characterization, plotting, dialogue, etc.—but I still lacked that certain ineffable something that makes them all gel into a story. And that's what I picked up at Clarion West."

But you don't have to take Marusek's word for it; ask just about any writer who has attended one of the workshops. SF/fantasy author David Barr Kirtley, who has published fiction in *Realms of Fantasy*, *Weird Tales* and several anthologies, got so much out of his first workshop experience that he went on to attend several more. "The first workshop I

JOHN JOSEPH ADAMS is the assistant editor of *The Magazine of Fantasy & Science Fiction*. His nonfiction has appeared in *Amazing Stories*, *The Internet Review of Science Fiction*, *Kirkus*, *Locus Magazine*, *Locus Online*, *Publishers Weekly* and *Science Fiction Weekly*. He is an affiliate member of SFWA and served as a judge for the 2005 Audie Awards. You can visit his blog, The Slush God Speaketh, at www.tuginternet.com/jja/journal.

attended—Clarion—was a revelation, a truly life-changing experience," he says. "I found the workshop so fascinating that I started signing up for more. Obviously a one-week workshop isn't going to be as involving as a six-week one, and there is a point of diminishing returns after a while, but every workshop I've done has taught me new things and introduced me to great new people, and I'd endorse any of them."

Clarion graduate Daryl Gregory, whose stories have appeared in *Asimov's Science Fiction Magazine, The Magazine of Fantasy & Science Fiction* and *Amazing Stories,* says that though some people think the worst thing you can do is go to a workshop looking for validation, that's the most important thing it did for him. "I didn't know how this writing thing worked. I didn't have any friends who were published writers. The idea of becoming a writer seemed far-fetched and vaguely delusional, like deciding to become an alligator wrestler," he says. "Once I was accepted, I killed time waiting for the workshop to start by going through the archives in the Michigan State library. Every story written for or during Clarion was down there. Early work by dozens of the field's famous names, but stripped of the glamour of typesetting and binding. And the best thing? Some of the stories by these famous names sucked. Big time. I decided that if they could be this bad and get so much better, then so could I."

Attending one of the following workshops is a huge investment of time and money, so choosing the right one is of the utmost importance. The information provided will help you determine which workshop would be best for you. (*Note:* Cost information and dates are subject to change, so check the workshop Web sites for up-to-date information.)

Clarion: The Science Fiction and Fantasy Writer's Workshop

Clarion is the granddaddy of science fiction writing workshops, founded in 1968 by Robin Scott Wilson at Clarion State College (now Clarion University) in Pennsylvania. The structure of Clarion was based upon the Milford Science Fiction Writers' Conference, a professional writer's workshop.

Clarion Foundation Chairperson Kate Wilhelm says the reason to go to Clarion is because of its long-standing tradition of success. "About one third of the alumni go on to become published writers, some with spectacular success," she says. Vonda McIntyre, Octavia Butler, Kim Stanley Robinson, Lucius Shepherd, Ted Chiang and Bruce Sterling are just a few Clarion graduates who have gone on to wildly successful careers in the field.

Wilhelm also emphasizes the talented variety of instructors Clarion provides. "The first Clarion had Judy Merrill, Fritz Leiber, Harlan Ellison, Damon Knight and me. That kind of diversity and excellence has prevailed ever since."

All the tools and techniques a writer needs to know can be acquired at Clarion, says Wilhelm. "Students will develop a solid awareness of what it takes to become a professional writer: a honed critical approach to the written work, others' and one's own; a way to find an individual voice that is uniquely that writer's own voice, not derivative, not overly filtered through fleeting outside influences that change without warning."

Tuition: $1,500
Housing: $1,000
College Credit: four college credits (included with tuition)
Application Fee: $100 (nonrefundable)
Application Deadline: April 1
Workshop Schedule: six weeks, starts mid- to late-June
Location: East Lansing, MI
Max. # of Participants: 16-18
Founded: 1968
Web site: www.theclarionfoundation.org

Clarion West Writers Workshop

Clarion West is an offshoot of the original Clarion workshop, founded by SF writer Vonda McIntyre in 1971.

Clarion West Workshop Administrator Neile Graham says, "people decide to apply to Clarion West because of our reputation for excellence, our top-notch instructor lineup, and the allure of Seattle itself, not to mention the beauty of the surrounding mountains and water." Clarion West offers the same top quality instructors as the original Clarion, but Graham says that West goes the extra mile for its guests. "Clarion West staff are experienced, thoughtful and professional, and the overall workshop environment creates a positive writing retreat atmosphere. Students compliment CW on the attention paid to details that facilitate the flow of the workshop and keep everything running smoothly so students can concentrate on writing. The sorority house we live in is homey, comfortable and most meals are provided for," she says. "The supportive Seattle SF community provides us with volunteers, welcoming hosts for our Friday night parties and local authors who visit the students as 'mystery muse' guest lecturers. Readings are held at the Science Fiction Museum and Hall of Fame, where students are inspired by the great writers who have gone before them."

Here's how Graham describes the workshop experience: "It's six wild, wonderful, intense, insane weeks where the most important thing is writing. Suddenly you have 17 new friends who are as passionate about writing science fiction/fantasy as you are. You get to know six professionals who are equally passionate and who reveal hard truths about writing—your writing. It's amazing and liberating, and you'll work harder than you've ever worked in your life. There's not enough time in the day. You need your sleep; you don't dare sleep. You speak in code. Six weeks fly by, and the real world seems far away. You come out of it knowing more about yourself as a writer, as a person, and how to begin a writing career." Clarion West alumni include: Kathleen Ann Goonan, Andy Duncan, Susan Palwick, Benjamin Rosenbaum, Mary Rosenblum, David Marusek, Syne Mitchell, Eric S. Nylund, Justina Robson and many, many more.

Tuition: $1,700
Housing: $1,200
College Credit: n/a
Application Fee: $25 (nonrefundable)
Application Deadline: April 1
Workshop Schedule: six weeks, starts mid-June
Location: Seattle, WA
Max # of Participants: 18
Founded: 1971
Web site: clarionwest.org

Clarion South

In addition to the two Clarion workshops mentioned above, there is now a third Clarion, located in Australia. The Clarion South Web site announced its 2007 tutors to be Gardner Dozois, Kelly Link, Simon Brown, Robert Hood, Janeen Webb and Lee Battersby. Unlike the other annual Clarions, the Clarion South workshop, after holding concurrent 2004 and 2005 workshops, has decided to move to a biennial schedule.

Tuition: $2,600
Housing: included with tuition fee
College Credit: n/a
Application Fee: $17 (nonrefundable)
Application Deadline: June 30

Sci Fi/Fantasy/Horror

Workshop Schedule: six weeks starting in January
Location: Brisbane, Australia
Number of Participants: 17
Founded: 2004
Web site: www.clarionsouth.org

Odyssey, the Fantasy Writing Workshop

Odyssey is another well-respected six-week writing workshop, but one of the ways it differs from Clarion and Clarion West is that the entire learning process is overseen by one instructor, editor and workshop director Jeanne Cavelos. "A single instructor guides you through the six weeks, gaining in-depth knowledge of your work, providing detailed assessments of your strengths and weaknesses, helping you target your weaknesses one by one, and charting your progress," Cavelos says. "Some other workshops provide a series of instructors, which leaves you without any continuity of feedback to help you understand whether you are improving or not." Also, where the Clarion workshops focus on short fiction, Odyssey allows students to work on both short fiction and novels. And despite the name, students are allowed to work on *both* science fiction and fantasy.

Cavelos is a former senior editor at Bantam Doubleday Dell, and Odyssey is the only six-week workshop that has an editor's guidance throughout. Cavelos says that her experienced editorial perspective is key to the learning process and enables her to help writers find the writing process that will best work for them.

But going to Odyssey doesn't mean you'll miss out on being tutored by genre luminaries. Each week of the program, a different guest writer or editor spends a period of 24 hours with the students, providing additional instruction. Odyssey also features a writer-in-residence who is available the whole six weeks. Past instructors include Harlan Ellison, Dan Simmons, Ben Bova, George R. R. Martin and Terry Brooks.

Forty-six percent of Odyssey graduates have gone on to be published professionally, according to Cavelos. This is the highest percentage of post-workshop success reported by any of these programs. "I believe the journey to become the best writer you can be is a lifelong one," Cavelos said. "At the end of Odyssey, your journey will not be done. Yet I'm constantly told by graduates that they learned more at Odyssey than they learned in years of workshopping and creative writing classes. The workshop helps you advance in your journey at a much accelerated rate."

Published novelists who are Odyssey alumni include Barbara Campbell (two-book deal with DAW), Carrie Vaughn (four books sold to Warner), and Elaine Isaak (two books sold to Harper); in addition to this, Odyssey alumni have published over 200 stories in a variety of anthologies and magazines, such as *Asimov's* and *Realms of Fantasy*.

Tuition: $1,600
Housing: $625 double room-$1,250 single room
College Credit: available ($120 processing fee)
Application Fee: $25 (nonrefundable)
Application Deadline: April 14
Workshop Schedule: six weeks, starts mid- to late-June
Location: Manchester, NH
Max # of Participants: 16
Founded: 1996
Web site: www.sff.net/odyssey

Uncle Orson's Writing Workshop & Literary Boot Camp

Uncle Orson is none other than best-selling, multi-Hugo and Nebula Award-winning writer Orson Scott Card. He offers two options for prospective students: (1) attend the two-day writing workshop; or (2) attend the two-day writing workshop, then stay for the extended training provided by the boot camp.

"Uncle Orson's Writing Workshop is a two-day combination of lectures and exercises for 50-100 writers, offering a total immersion in story structure, idea generation and viewpoint—the most important yet least-taught aspects of fiction writing," Card says. "The Literary Boot Camp, for 10-15 writers, starts as part of the Writing Workshop; when the others go home, the boot campers write a story in a day, then read each other's stories and workshop them with me."

Though Card is known for his science fiction writing, writers of any genre are welcome to attend. Boot Camp participants must provide a brief writing sample to be admitted to the course. For the Writing Workshop, no sample is necessary; anyone 18 or older is welcome to attend.

Boot Camp success stories include author Mette Ivie Harrison, who sold two novels to Viking (a division of Penguin Putnam). Other graduates have sold fiction to *Analog* and *Strange Horizons* and have been finalists in the Writers of the Future contest.

The workshop's primary advantages are short length and affordable pricing. "You don't have to quit your job to attend," Card says, "or get a second job to pay for it."

Tuition (Writing Workshop): $175
Tuition (Boot Camp): $725 (includes cost of Writing Workshop)
Housing: on campus, $30 per day
College Credit: n/a
Application Fee: n/a
Application Deadline: April 1
Workshop Schedule: one week in summer
Location: various college campuses across the United States (past locations have included Southern Virginia University, UNC-Greensboro and Utah Valley State College)
Max # of Participants: 15
Founded: 2001
Web site: www.hatrack.com

Viable Paradise

Viable Paradise is a weeklong residential SF/F workshop, set against the backdrop of Martha's Vineyard. The workshop uses a rotating cycle of established professional writers and editors, including Debra Doyle, Laura J. Mixon, James D. Macdonald, Teresa Nielsen Hayden, Patrick Nielsen Hayden, Steven Gould, Lawrence Watt-Evans, Elizabeth Moon, Maureen McHugh and James Patrick Kelly.

Instructor James D. Macdonald says that Viable Paradise fills the void between the one-day or one-weekend workshops and the six-week workshops. "The former can't go into depth; the latter require more time than many people can take away from their jobs or home lives," Macdonald says. "We are also one of the few workshops that deals with novels as well as short stories."

Viable Paradise has a 4:1 student to instructor ratio, and the instructors and students both live in the same location. "Students get a great deal of individualized interaction with professional writers and acquiring editors, during and after formal class hours," Macdonald says.

Viable Paradise graduates have been nominated for the Nebula Award and the John W. Campbell Award for Best New Writer and have sold short fiction to *The Magazine of Fantasy & Science Fiction, Asimov's, Strange Horizons* and *Intergalactic Medicine Show* and have been reprinted in *The Year's Best Science Fiction* (ed. Gardner Dozois). VP graduate Sandra McDonald recently received a two-book deal from Tor Books.

Tuition $850
Housing: $125-$150 per night
College Credit: n/a
Application Fee: $25 (nonrefundable)
Application Deadline: June 15
Workshop Schedule: one week in October
Location: Martha's Vineyard, MA
Number of Participants: 24-26
Founded: 1995
Web site: www.viableparadise.com

The Center for the Study of Science Fiction Workshops

The CSSF Writers Workshop is a two-week workshop held annually at the University of Kansas. Students can expect to have three stories workshopped and will revise one story for week two based on workshop feedback. Workshop directors James Gunn and Chris McKitterick critique student stories, along with contributions from a variety of authors and editors, which often includes the winners of the Campbell and Sturgeon Awards (presented at The Campbell Conference, an academic forum that takes place the weekend after the workshop) and luminaries such as Frederik Pohl.

McKitterick says those who are just starting to publish or those who need that little bit extra to begin will get the most out of the workshop, though all others are welcome to apply.

The Center also offers an SF Novel Writers Workshop, which runs concurrently with the short fiction workshop and is led by SF author Kij Johnson. Students can expect to have three hours of manuscript critiquing each afternoon and the rest of the day for writing and/ or recreation. All students are expected to revise at least one chapter and their novel's outline during the course of the workshop.

A number of writers who have attended the CSSF workshop have gone on not only to publish numerous stories and novels but also to win the field's most prestigious awards. Among these are World Fantasy Award-winners Pat Cadigan and Bradley Denton and Nebula and Sturgeon Award-winner John Kessel.

Tuition: $400
Housing: $210-$420
College Credit: available (to earn credit, add KU per-credit costs)
Application Fee: n/a
Application Deadline: June 1
Workshop Schedule: two weeks, late June/early July
Location: University of Kansas, Lawrence, KS
Number of Participants: 10-12
Founded: 1988 (with earlier incarnations going back to the mid '70s)
Web site: www.ku.edu/~sfcenter/courses.htm

Alpha SF/F/H Workshop for Young Writers

Alpha is a 10-day residency workshop restricted to young writers (ages 14-19). Workshop administrator Diane Turnshek says it's designed to be a gentle introduction to workshopping. "It's the only workshop of its kind in the world. Alpha is shorter than Clarion or Odyssey, just long enough to write a single new story," she says.

Ideal for young beginners, Alpha takes the age of its participants into consideration, while still creating an intense learning experience. "We take a whole day for arrivals and getting to know each other and the campus. The obligatory manuscript format talk kicks off the 10-day workshop. Critiques of the submission story are done by e-mail prior to the workshop," Turnshek says. "Each student writes a new story and has it critiqued before they revise it, with step-by-step processes explained in small studio groups."

Four professional authors also participate in the workshop; they each attend for two days and provide lectures and assist in the learning process. Authors Tamora Pierce and Wen Spencer have been at each workshop to date.

Though all the participants are young, the extent of their experience—in both life and in writing—is quite varied. "We've had students who have never slept away from home before and ones who are summer camp junkies," Turnshek says. "Some students have never been told their work is anything less than perfect; some have pro writer mentors and have been critiqued for years."

After the workshop is concluded, the students attend Confluence, a small literary science fiction convention of around 300 people. Alpha graduate Thomas Seay has sold to *Realms of Fantasy* and *Boy's Life*. Fellow graduate Michail Velichansky won first place in the first quarter of the 2005 Writers of the Future contest and was twice a finalist for the Isaac Asimov Award for Undergraduate Excellence in Fantasy and Science Fiction Writing.

Tuition: $900
Housing: housing, food, local transportation included with tuition
College Credit: n/a
Application Fee: $10
Application Deadline: March 31
Workshop Schedule: 10 days in July
Location: University of Pittsburgh, Greensburg, PA (branch campus)
Founded: 2001
Web site: alpha.spellcaster.org

The Clarion/Kiddie Lit Club Young Authors Conference

The Clarion/Kiddie Lit Club Young Authors Conference is a one-day workshop that aims to cover all genres (not just science fiction/fantasy) and restricts the participants to young writers (middle school through college age). The first Conference was held at Michigan State University in East Lansing, Michigan in 2006. It's too early to tell if this workshop will be an annual event, so check the Web sites below for up-to-date information.

Unlike some of the other workshops, which look for writers with an intermediate rather than beginning level of craft, any young person who wishes to learn more about writing is welcome to attend the YA Conference, according to director Elizabeth Zernechel.

"Clarion, in conjunction with the Kiddie Lit Club, hopes to provide a number of benefits for the students of the Young Authors Conference. Among these are advice from professional writers, exposure to the Milford critiquing style, introduction to other local writers of the same age group, information about publishing opportunities, exposure for high school students to Michigan State University, and most importantly, encouragement of each student's growth as a writer," Zernechel says.

Tuition: $75 in 2006
Housing: not provided
College Credit: n/a
Application Fee: n/a
Application Deadline: early January
Workshop Schedule: one day in late January
Location: East Lansing, MI
Founded: 2005
Web sites: www.msu.edu/~clarion or www.msu.edu/~kidlit

The Best of Both Worlds

Balancing Science and Imagination

by Carol Pinchefsky

If science fiction has any rule of thumb, it is this: Good science strengthens your writing while bad science derails it.

According to research, the human body carries "junk" DNA—genetic code that has no identifiable function—which your protagonist decides to take advantage of. He breaks into a laboratory, where he stabs himself with a fully loaded syringe. In a matter of moments, he mutates into . . . a dinosaur!

It's accurate that the human body carries junk DNA, but the ability to automatically transform oneself into a dinosaur is certainly a stretch, as your readers will tell you in their sarcastically worded hate mail. While some science fiction requires the reader to suspend disbelief in order to accept a world of faster-than-light travel, many science fiction readers cannot easily suspend disbelief to include shoddy science.

So how does a writer with only hazy memories of high school chem lab take this tale of dinosaur woe and turn it into a believable science fiction story? The same way the professionals do: with a great deal of research.

FIRST, THE SCIENCE
Hit the books.

If you feel you lack a good grasp of a certain area of science and you're unsure where to begin, start with the children's department of your bookstore. Children's books are written to explain, in the most basic language possible, every branch of the sciences. Topics include astronomy, technology, the physical sciences and, of course, dinosaurs. After you understand the basics, graduate to more advanced reading.

Syne Mitchell, author of *End in Fire* (Roc, 2005), says, "I like to start with a college-sophomore-level textbook on the subject because it gives you a good science foundation and grounding."

Once you have one or two books you find helpful, Catherine Asaro, physicist and author of *Schism* (Tor, 2004), suggests, "Go to any online booksellers who have 'people who liked this book also bought this.' You can find a list of other books along those lines that people have been buying."

Magazines like *Popular Science*, *Nature*, *Science News* and the weekly British publication *New Scientist* are tremendous sources of current information on the sciences. The articles

CAROL PINCHEFSKY is a freelance writer in New York City. She has written articles on science fiction for SciFi.com, *Battlestar Galactica* magazine, *SFX* and *Orson Scott Card's Intergalactic Medicine Show*.

are written for a mass audience, so even nonscientists can understand them. Academic and professional journals offer the most technically dense information, but abstracts—short summaries at the beginning of each paper—are easier to read.

National Public Radio also offers a show called "Science Friday" (now available as podcasts at www.apple.com/itunes) that speaks to a nontechnical audience.

Search the Web and the stacks.

The Internet has proven a boon for researchers because it can provide up-to-the-minute information—at your fingertips and in your pajamas. Need to know the etymology of the word "skull"? Try Merriam-Webster online (www.m-w.com). Looking for the latest on American stem cell research? Check out the National Institutes of Health (www.nih.gov). Few facts are so arcane that the Internet does not have some mention of them.

But despite the ease of access and the relative cheapness of computers, the Internet is not the research panacea. According to Asaro, the biggest problem with the Internet is reliability. "Unless it's NASA (www.nasa.gov) or a site that you know is going to have reputable information, you always need to check the facts you take off the Internet." Make sure to restrict your browsing to the Web sites of authoritative sources. Government and university Web sites are more likely to have factual knowledge (as currently understood) than the sites of hobbyists.

Unlike the 24-hour instant gratification of the Internet, the library has limited hours and may not be easily accessible. However, Asaro feels the information is more likely to be dependable. Keep in mind, too, that many magazines and journals that have Web sites do not archive their articles online, so a trip to the library is required to find the information you may need. And whereas there are no tour guides on the World Wide Web, research librarians are often on hand to help you navigate the stacks and answer questions. If you have a little time to wander, libraries are fabulous places to browse, discovering related books or periodicals you didn't even know you were searching for.

Recommended Web sites

Web sites Science Fiction authors frequent:

- Internet Review of Science Fiction (irosf.com)
- Locus Online (www.locusmag.com)
- Hatrack River, the official site of Orson Scott Card (www.hatrack.com)
- Speculations.com
- Ralan.com
- SpeculativeLiterature.org
- Science Fiction Writer's Association (sfwa.org)

Message boards authors frequent:

- SF Site (www.sfsite.com/forum/)
- NightshadeBooks.com
- CodexWriters.com
- Science Fiction Poetry Association (sfpoetry.com)

Sci Fi/Fantasy/Horror

Interview scientists.

Once you understand the basics, it's useful to interview people working in the field whose knowledge and research projects are more cutting edge than what's in print. These conversations can be a creative springboard for you and fill in the experiential gaps left by books. Although they're often extremely busy, scientists can be accessible. If you're close to a university or science center, a wealth of information can be yours for the price of a dinner. If a meeting is out of the question, you can call a university and ask a professor for help, but be sure you've done a good bit of research before you pick up the phone.

"You don't want to go to a geneticist and say 'Hey, this microbiology, what's that about?' You want to go with specific questions that show you're not wasting their time, that you've done the work already," Mitchell says. "Then you can say, 'Hey, can I look at a DNA synthesizer and study some of the reagents?' Don't be afraid to ask for personal interviews. The worst thing that can happen is they say no."

If a personal interview isn't possible, Dr. Mike Brotherton, professor of astronomy and author of *Star Dragon* (Tor, 2003), and Asaro use first-hand accounts as the next-best thing. While reading the journals and reports of astronauts, Brotherton learned, "when you first get weightless after thrust, dust will float up off of the surfaces they've settled on, and a lot of people sneeze." He suggests: "Get those realistic details."

Asaro says, "I found these wonderful books of first-person accounts of pilot dog fights, and the different things the pilots have to worry about. Not only was it useful for doing the research but also very interesting to read."

Take a science class.

Local community colleges and online universities offer introductory science classes that won't break your budget. For those writers who aren't scientists, a beginner's class won't be too difficult or cause frustration. Of course, it won't give you the skills to write a peer-reviewed paper, but it'll give you a certain familiarity with the language of science. While a cursory glance at a textbook reveals the term "valence shells," Chemistry 101 can teach you what it actually means. All the scientific research in the world is worthless to your writing if you use the language incorrectly.

NOW, THE FICTION

In the Golden Age of Science Fiction (early 1940s to late 1950s), characters were stereotypes, and dialogue was wooden at best. Modern science fiction no longer suffers from these flaws because its writers are more sophisticated. Science fiction writers have to balance research and imagination in ways that other writers do not, as we not only are required to construct fully functional and believable universes but also create likable, sympathetic characters. In contemporary science fiction, a discussion has emerged regarding the use of research and if there's such a thing as "too much" science in speculative fiction.

According to Robert Sawyer, Hugo and Nebula Award-winning author of *Hominids* (Tor, 2002), "It's indicative of our culture's sad attitude towards science that this question gets asked so often. No one says to a romance writer, 'How do you keep the romance from getting out of hand in your novel?' No one says to a horror writer, 'Hey, this is getting really horrific—shouldn't you pull back?' No one says to a western writer, 'Gee, do you think you could maybe have fewer cowboys?' But somehow people tend to think science should be ladled out in small doses. No, it shouldn't; it's what the genre is about. It's in our very name."

Offering another point of view, Mitchell and other authors make the case that science fiction writers are storytellers, not textbooks. Sawyer's point that *science* is in the name of the genre is a valid one, but *fiction* is the other half of the label. On top of being well researched, science fiction has to engage the reader on an emotional level.

"If you're not entertaining people, they're not going to read your work," says Mitchell. "You know you're going too heavy with the science when you're readers are bored, when you're telling them things that do not immediately impact the story, when you're telling them things that can be easily cut from the book and not effect the story at all."

This rule of thumb applies to all categories of fiction. Mitchell says even the most beautiful prose should be pruned if it slows down the story.

So when should imagination trump fact? According to Sawyer, the answer is rarely. "A science fiction writer's core audience is scientifically savvy," he asserts. "If your characters are standing around telling each other things they already know, that's boring in real life, and it's boring in fiction. But if a woman is explaining to a man, even at great technical length, how she decoded the first alien transmission ever received from space, that's riveting."

> While some science fiction requires the reader to suspend disbelief in order to accept a world of faster-than-light travel, many science fiction readers cannot easily suspend disbelief to include shoddy science.

Still, writers of the story-first mindset insist that even too much good science can be off-putting to a reader. Mitchell explains, "While I encourage everybody to get the facts as right as possible, there's something I learned from my father. He would tell these stories that were wonderfully engaging, and a little bit different [each time]. I realized that he was changing the story from what had really happened to make it more interesting and more applicable to his given audience. I think we have a responsibility as writers to entertain. And while I still feel strongly that you should try to get good science information in there if you possibly can, the time to abandon good science is when you need to make the story better."

So is there a science-to-character ratio? The issue of balance is tied to what market you're targeting and your readers' expectations. If you're targeting a "hard" science fiction audience, then there's almost no limit to the amount of science you should introduce in your story.

A good way to maintain a level of scientific thought while moving the plot along is to allow the research guide your story. Let's revisit our dinosaur-man. As a matter of fact (or fiction), your protagonist can turn himself into a dinosaur without suffering the consequences of lazy writing if the transformation is explained in a logical manner: Your protagonist splices a heretofore unexplored genetic sequence into his chromosomes, which signals the non-coding DNA to express dormant functions. Voila! A dinosaur is born.

You've got the genetics down, so maybe now you think your story calls for a little more *chemistry*. While reading up on the dinosaur, you're fascinated that some dinosaurs have crests—possibly used to catch the eye of a mate. So introduce a character with a spiny crest, perhaps a female researcher in the same lab who follows up on our dino-man's experiment and transforms herself as well. What does this mean for our large, scaly and loveless protagonist?

Whether or not they live happily ever after until the next Ice Age and how they survive in the meantime is the job of a science fiction writer.

Sci Fi/Fantasy/Horror

Resources

Where to Look for More Information

B elow is a list of invaluable resources specifically for science fiction, fantasy and horror writers. To order any of the Writer's Digest Books titles or to get a consumer book catalog, call (800)448-0915. You may also order Writer's Digest Books selections through www.writersdigest.com, Amazon.com or www.barnesandnoble.com.

MAGAZINES

- *Locus*, P.O. Box 13305, Oakland CA 94661. E-mail: locus@locusmag.com. Web site: www.locusmag.com.
- *Science Fiction Chronicle*, P.O. Box 022730, Brooklyn NY 11202-0056. (718)643-9011. Fax: (718)522-3308. E-mail: sfchronicle@dnapublications.com. Web site: www.dnapublications.com.
- SPECFICME! (bi-monthly PDF newsletter). Web site: www.specficworld.com.

BOOKS (by Writer's Digest Books)

- *Aliens and Alien Societies: A Writer's Guide to Creating Extraterrestrial Life-forms*, by Stanley Schmidt
- *Worlds of Wonder, How to Write Science Fiction and Fantasy**, by David Gerrold
- *How to Write Science Fiction & Fantasy*, by Orson Scott Card
- *The Writer's Complete Fantasy Reference*, from the editors of Writer's Digest Books
- *Writing Horror**, edited by Mort Castle

ORGANIZATIONS & ONLINE

- Fantasy-Writers.org. Web site: www.fantasy-writers.org.
- Horror Writers Association, P.O. Box 50577, Palo Alto CA 94303. Web site: www.horror.org.
- Science Fiction & Fantasy Writers of America, Inc., P.O. Box 877, Chestertown MD 21620. E-mail: execdir@sfwa.org. Web site: www.sfwa.org/.
- SF Canada, 303-2333 Scarth St., Regina SK S4P 2J8. Web site: www.sfcanada.ca.
- SpecFicWorld. Web site: www.specficworld.com. Covers all 3 speculative genres (science fiction, fantasy and horror).
- Books and Writing Online. Web site: www.interzone.com/Books/books.html.
- Writer's Market Online. Web site: www.writersmarket.com.
- Locus Magazine Online. Web site: www.locusmag.com.

* Out of print. Check your local library.

New Golden Age

David, Wolfman, Salicrup and Schmidt
on Comics Writing Today

© Christine Norrie

by Greg Hatfield

From writer-creators Jerry Siegel (Superman) and Bill Finger (Batman) in the Golden Age of comics to Stan Lee (the Hulk, X-Men, the Fantastic Four, Spider-Man) and Roy Thomas (Conan the Barbarian) in the Silver Age, writers have always captured the imaginations of comics fans. In the Modern Age, writers have taken on a celebrity that has made them the new "next big thing."

With Will Eisner's *A Contract with God*, published in 1978 and considered by many to be the first graphic novel, comics took a new direction and a giant leap forward. Spearheaded by such editors as Dick Giordano and Jim Salicrup, characters in comics began experiencing a wider range of human emotions and conflicts. A new realism in comics was taking shape, thanks to a new generation of writers.

Writer Chris Claremont shaped the paths of the *Uncanny X-Men* for 16 years, adding personal drama and persecution to the group of mutants. John Byrne, Claremont's co-writer and artist, began a long run on *Fantastic Four* in 1979, returning the team to their cosmic glory and family disputes, not seen since the days of Lee and Jack Kirby. Writer/artist Frank Miller began his work on *Daredevil* in 1980, showing the grit of New York's Hell's Kitchen and the iron will of a tormented hero. In 1983, Alan Moore started writing for one of DC's lesser-known comics, *Swamp Thing*, turning a lower-tier horror creature into an elemental character with wide emotional range, while Neil Gaiman's ground-breaking run on *The Sandman* continued to enhance the maturity of comics.

Today, writers of comics are celebrated as much as film or television stars, apropos since there's so much crossover between the industries these days. *Buffy the Vampire Slayer* creator Joss Whedon now writes the *Astonishing X-Men*; *Babylon 5* creator J. Michael Straczynski writes the *Amazing Spider-Man* (among others); and film director Kevin Smith has taken turns on *Green Arrow*, *Daredevil* and *Black Cat*.

The opportunities and rewards for comics writers are greater than ever. Comics publishers, many of whom are listed in this book, are more receptive to publishing quality work from unknown writers than ever before. The Internet has opened avenues for self-publication, giving writers a forum for their art and enabling them to create a fan base before their first work is even published in print.

GREG HATFIELD has coordinated the "Impact University: How to Write and Draw Comics and Graphic Novels" panel for Comic-Con International in San Diego for the past three years and is co-coordinator of the BookExpo America/ Writer's Digest Books Writers Conference, a national writing conference held each year prior to the annual publishing trade show.

To find out about the state of the market today, we asked two renowned writers and two acclaimed editors to give us their take on writing for comics.

Peter David's current workload includes the monthly books *Friendly Neighborhood Spi-der-Man* and *X-Factor* (Marvel) and his own creator-driven book *Fallen Angel* (IDW Publishing). David is also known for his amazing 12-year run on the *Incredible Hulk* and an ongoing column for over a decade called "But I Digress . . . ," published in *Comics Buyer's Guide*. He has published over 50 novels, with numerous appearances on the *New York Times* best-seller list. His newest book, *Writing for Comics with Peter David*, has just been released by Impact Books. His Web site (www.peterdavid.net) continues to be an outstanding forum for fans.

Marv Wolfman has written for every single major comic book character. His work with George Perez on *The New Teen Titans* transformed a second-unit-team book into a major work, creating new characters and retooling older ones. Wolfman's 1985 comics series, *Crisis on Infinite Earths*, has been described with such superlatives as "ground breaking" and "earth shattering." In that work, Wolfman was responsible for cleaning up the continuity of the DC Universe (killing off Supergirl and the Silver Age Flash in the process). The events from that series still reverberate in the DC Universe today. In addition, Wolfman created the character of Blade the Vampire Hunter and revamped the characters of Robin the Boy Wonder and Lex Luthor. His current project, the novelization of the film *Superman Returns*, is out this summer. Fans can contact Marv through his Web site (www.marvwolfman.com).

Jim Salicrup began his comics career at Marvel Comics, where he worked for 20 years and spearheaded the rise of the Modern Age as editor-in-chief. He edited *Uncanny X-Men* during Claremont and Byrne's run, *Fantastic Four*, *The Avengers*, and the best-selling *Spider-Man* series by Todd McFarlane. Salicrup was also editor-in-chief of Topps Comics, where he edited *Bram Stoker's Dracula*, *The X-Files*, *The Lone Ranger and Tonto*, a line of Jack Kirby superhero titles, *Ray Bradbury Comics* and more. He is now editor-in-chief at Papercutz, publishers of the all-new *Nancy Drew, Girl Detective*; *The Hardy Boys* and *Zorro* graphic novels. He writes the weekly "Addicted to Comics" column at popcultureshock.com and a blog (http://blog.myspace.com/jimsalicrup).

Andy Schmidt has been editing comics for Marvel Entertainment for the last four years. He's put together projects such as *Secret War*, *Ms. Marvel*, *X-Factor* and *Annihilation*. He assists on the Marvel Heroes line, which includes *New Avengers*, *Fantastic Four* and *Young Avengers*. Prior to beginning his comics editing career, Schmidt was a college professor in St. Louis, where he earned his master's degree in media communications and taught classes on aesthetics, film and comics & sequential art.

This seems to be the age of the writer. So many comics writers like Alan Moore, Brad Meltzer and Neil Gaiman have become as celebrated as the artists. Writers are now signing exclusive contracts with publishers. Is this a good thing?

Salicrup: I think comics fans enjoy comics that are both well written and well drawn. Perhaps there's just more well-written and well-drawn comics now than 10 years ago. And that's certainly a good thing.

Wolfman: Writers have always signed exclusive contracts. I had one at Marvel in the '70s and DC in the '80s. Anything that promotes talent is good.

Salicrup: Most top Marvel and DC writers had exclusive contracts in the '80s.

David: I can't speak for other writers; all I can do is speak for myself. For myself, it's a great thing. Basically Marvel approached me and made an offer that boiled down to, "Hey, do you want to keep doing the exact same thing you're doing except you get medical insurance?" I don't know what Alan, Brad and Neil are doing in regards to such concerns, but I'm pushing 50 and have four kids, so the security it offers is just marvelous.

Schmidt: I'd love to say yes, but honestly, I think it's gotten a bit out of hand. I'm worried when we have to bump good writers off projects because someone else (who's also a good writer) has a contract that we have to fulfill. However, it's the climate we're in right now. It's tough.

I like all the writers Marvel has under contract, but I also like a lot of writers DC has under contract. It's a shame I can't work with all of them at the same time. And it's a shame that it limits who can work on what.

All of you have worked on and developed many of comics' most iconic characters. How important is continuous characterization? Some writers change the characteristics of long-running characters until they're no longer recognizable. One current example is Batman's character in *All-Star Batman and Robin, the Boy Wonder*. Frank Miller writes Batman like he's never been portrayed before, shocking many readers. Is this fair to the readers?

David: Sure it's fair. Many fans wring their hands and decry changes in characters and characterization as if this is something remotely new. People think what makes a character iconic is that he never changes, and that's just not right. What makes a character iconic is that he is extremely malleable. No matter what you do to them, no matter how much you may change their look, background or environment, they are still recognizably that same character. Tarzan remains Tarzan whether he's an English lord with Jane by his side or a confused New York resident with Jane now a police detective (although the TV version kinda sucked for entirely different reasons).

Wolfman: I think the answer actually depends on in what form the final product is appearing. If it's in the next issue of *Superman*, *Action*, etc. then Superman should read like Superman. You can push him right to the edge of the envelope—and you should, it's the only way to keep things fresh—but you owe it not to the readers but to the characters to portray them honestly and within their character. But if something is under a special banner, which indicates it's not canon, then you can play with the idea as much as you want because that's the nature of the beast. Now, that doesn't mean it'll be good nor does it mean anyone will want to read it, but those off-continuity titles at least let you try something different.

Salicrup: Many people I know consider the current Batman to not be "the real" Batman. As for Miller's take, it seems to me he's examining a part of Batman's history—his first encounters with Dick Grayson/Robin—that hasn't really been explored before. Or at least not in this way or in this amount of detail. I suspect critics may not be seeing the big picture here. For example, if you saw a policeman trying to scare a kid off drugs as part of those "Scared Straight" programs, wouldn't you assume the policeman's extreme behavior was not his normal behavior? Let's see where Miller's story winds up before we judge it.

Schmidt: I think Frank is within his rights, as that's supposed to be a new version of Batman. If that had been *Batman* #645, yeah, that would have been too drastic a change, in my opinion. However, for me, I want the characters I work on to grow and change. I don't want them to stay constant at all times. But, one must be careful not to break what works about each character. It happens, and characters can be fixed, but that's the danger with doing drastic changes to say, Spider-Man or Captain America.

David: It's ludicrous to say that what Frank is doing with Batman is inherently not "fair" when Batman has undergone any number of character changes from the dark horror-themed feel of the Golden Age to the science fiction goofiness of the Silver Age to the New Look Batman and so on. Changes that we take for granted now were once novel. Can you imagine if a red-and-green-clad boy sidekick were introduced to Batman for the first time *now*? The Internet would light up with the sheer idiocy of such a move. The Silver Age saw the setting aside of such high-profile heroes as Flash, Green Lantern, the Atom, etc., to be replaced with newcomers with new costumes, names and powers. As loudly as fans howled for Hal Jordan to be reinstated as Green Lantern, certainly there must have been that same grumbling from fans in the '50s demanding the return of the one, true Green Lantern, Alan Scott, not this Hal Jordan/Lensman ripoff.

Do writers have a responsibility to their readers to keep their characters constant?

Salicrup: Writers have a responsibility to tell good stories, and that includes writing consistent, believable characters. But like real people, characters can and should evolve. Sometimes they can do things that may appear totally out of character, but as long as it's believable, then it's okay.

David: Change is constant in comics. Change is good. If iconic characters couldn't survive change, they wouldn't be iconic.

Wolfman: It's a good idea to shock readers. Complacency is the death of creativity.

What's an editor's primary function? How important is it to a writer to have a good editor?

Salicrup: The editor is responsible for putting together the best comic or graphic novel possible and getting it in on time. A good editor works hard to bring the best out of his writers, artists, letterers and colorists. A bad editor can destroy a good script in an infinite amount of ways.

Schmidt: My job is to put out quality comics in a timely fashion. Primarily, this means workshopping stories with writers and reviewing layouts from artists to make sure they're telling the story in the clearest and most impacting manner. A lot of writers don't want to be edited or have input from an editor. Others really enjoy and thrive off an editor's input. And as much as I hate to say it, yeah, there are some writers who are better if I get out of their way. So, it's different with everyone. In the case of Peter David, he and I discuss stories on the phone and then he writes them. It's pretty casual and that's how it works best for the two of us. Keith Giffen and I set up meetings and hash storylines out between the two of us and that seems to work well. Brian Bendis pretty much tells me what he wants to do and we discuss and then he turns in scripts. It's different with everyone.

Salicrup: The truth is that every writer/editor relationship is different, each usually with some combination of pluses and minuses. Great work has been created under horrible conditions, and forgettable work has been produced under idyllic circumstances. Just like life, huh?

Schmidt: As for how important a good editor is: I'd say invaluable. Don't get me wrong, I'm not saying that because I'm an editor. I'm saying that because a good editor knows when to get out of the way. There are cases when a good editor does very little on a project. And there are many cases where an editor makes a poor decision to overwork a story. It's tough to know what situation you're in when you're in it. In general, I'm a pretty hands-on editor, but there are those cases, like *Secret War*, where I just let two great talents tell a great story. I reviewed scripts and layouts and then sat back and watched beautiful painting after beautiful painting come rolling in.

As an editor, what do you do differently with an established writer that you don't do with a newer one?

Salicrup: Not much. No matter whom I'm working with, I try my best to create an environment that's conducive to creating good work. Obviously, a more experienced writer may require far less guidance, but that's not always the case. With comics constantly evolving, it's a never-ending learning experience for everyone involved in the process. I often learn far more from the creators than they could ever hope to learn from me.

Schmidt: Not much. Every person is different, so I don't work with any two writers the same way. With younger writers, I'll sometimes spend more time in the outline stages.

When you're writing, how detailed are you in your plotting? I'm sure you have a plan to get from Point A to Point B and beyond, but how succinct are you writing for your artist? Does the ''Marvel style'' model of creating comics— writers providing illustrators with a rough story outline and then writing each panel later to fit illustrations—still work? How much leeway does an artist have when drawing the panels for your script?

David: I write full script. Marvel-style tends to allow for the artist to emphasize the wrong things or leave out story aspects that I had been putting in to set up for subsequent issues. Plus when I was writing Marvel-style I would sometimes pack the story in with way too much stuff and just figure the artist would sort it out, placing an unfair burden on him and expecting him to clean up after me. Full script means I control the pacing and provide a firmer guide for the artist so he'll know what to present visually. I break pages down on a panel-by-panel basis, but I offer no suggestion in terms of what the actual layout should be. I figure that's something the artist should have full license to design.

Wolfman: I write very tight plots when I work plot style, except when I'm working with an artist like George Perez who wants shorter plots. But usually every major detail is in. With nearly everyone else, my plots are as tight as any full script.

David: I think Marvel-style can still work, but it depends on the writer and artist. I could write Marvel-style with George Perez, for instance, because I fully trust his skill, experience and professionalism.

What's better, creating a new character or working on an established one?

Wolfman: Both. I've done both. I love writing, say, *Superman* and I love writing *The Man Called A-X* or *Night Force*, etc. I just love writing things that challenge me.

David: They both have advantages. The nice thing about a new character—presuming it's creator-owned like *Fallen Angel*—is that you're in total control of everything that's going on. It's a blank slate that you have total license to write on. An established character naturally has tighter rules . . . but it also presents a greater challenge to a writer in terms of finding new and different ways to keep the character interesting for changing audiences.

Obviously, there aren't many jobs on books such as Superman, Batman, Spider-Man, etc. Writers aren't going to break in and begin writing those books. We always tell new writers that the way to get ahead is to write and get published anywhere they can. Is this correct? Does the Internet offer opportunities that you didn't have when you were starting out?

Wolfman: That's absolutely right. You're not a writer unless you're writing and you're not a professional unless you're being paid. It doesn't matter where you write, just write. The Internet is like the fanzines of old, but they potentially reach a much larger audience.

Salicrup: The answer is a great big ''yes.'' If you printed your own comics back when I was first starting out, you'd be limited to selling it mainly through an ad in a couple of fanzines, at conventions, and to friends and family. Now, you can post your work online for the whole world to see. I have a page at www1.myspace.com/jimsalicrup, and I've seen all sorts of work from talented new writers and artists there. And that's without even trying.

David: It doesn't hurt. Having a résumé is always better than not having a résumé. And of course the Internet offers opportunities not available before. You can get your work out to tens of thousands of people in one shot, as opposed to sitting at a table at a convention and hoping you can convince passersby to give your material a look.

Schmidt: I don't read a lot of fan fiction on the Internet, but I certainly know people who do. Definitely try to get published somewhere. That always helps.

What is the first thing you look for when reviewing a submission from a writer?

Salicrup: In an increasingly litigious world, it becomes harder and harder for editors to actually look at writing submissions without risking future lawsuits. Someone can say, "Hey, I sent in a story where Batman battles the Joker and Catwoman at Arkham Asylum, and now they're stealing my idea!" That's why it's a good idea to submit published material. Furthermore, there are already dozens of writers I want to work with, so I'm not especially looking to find more. But, when I do read a submission, the first thing I look for is something new and exciting. If I find the story compelling, I'm sure others will as well. If a submission reads like I've read it a million times before, I'll pass.

Schmidt: Honestly, that they have a signed legal form with us so I *can* look at the submission. After that, I look for a story. There often isn't one. All stories can be boiled down to one sentence: "Protagonist is trying to accomplish goal and Antagonist is getting in his/her way." Boom. You got that and it's compelling, I'll read the next sentence or two at least.

What is the biggest mistake an aspiring writer can make?

Schmidt: When a writer is trying to get in the door with me, I understand people get nervous and ramble and what have you. The only two things that tend to terminate my conversations are if someone is rude or dismissive—if you're not willing to listen to me, then we're done—and if, after a writer's pitch for something doesn't pan out (it happens), I'm asked if there is a character available for him/her to pitch on. That's a pretty good indication that the writer doesn't have a story that he or she is passionate about. And passion is extremely important—especially when you're starting out. I may not like a story, but I can often tell if the writer is passionate, and I respect that.

Salicrup: Leaving the name and/or contact information off of the submission. If it's a submission for an established character, the writer should be sufficiently aware of the character's history to prevent proposing either a previous storyline or something totally wrong for the character. You don't want the editor to think you never read the comic he edits.

What's the one thing every writer should know?

David: Don't take rejection personally. It's not a commentary on you as a person. Keep your own self-esteem separate from your work. It helps to have a huge ego.

And that they should buy my book, *Writing Comics with Peter David*, published by Impact Books, so they can stop asking me for advice all the time.

Wolfman: Listen to criticism, understand the criticism, take what works and discard the rest. Do what you know in your gut is right.

Do you still get a kick out of seeing a finished comic?

David: Yes.

Wolfman: Always.

Craig Thompson

Chunky Rice *and* Blankets:
Cure for Ailing Comics Image

© Greg Preston

by Lauren Mosko

When Craig Thompson was in high school, he refused to set foot in a comic book store. "I loved comics as a kid, but then I fell out of love with the medium. I wanted to stop being as much of a nerd and grow up a bit and have girls like me," he laughs. "I had friends who were always trying to sell me on comics or take me to a comics store, but it always made me uncomfortable."

It wasn't that he didn't appreciate sequential art; it was the *image* of comic books that turned him off. "For one thing, I didn't think it should be a primarily masculine adolescent form," Thompson explains. "The stories you can tell [with the medium] could be much more quiet and sensitive and intimate than these terrible superhero and science fiction/fantasy stories."

He also felt the traditional saddle-stitched binding of comics and the way they were treated contributed to the notion that the material was insubstantial. "I like having books; I like having something with a spine that you can put on a bookshelf," Thompson says. "That whole collector market of people putting little comic books in plastic bags and keeping them in boxes in their dens, I found really repulsive. I just wanted to break out of that [mentality] and get back to the medium itself."

Thompson was convinced comics had the potential to reach a much broader audience. He issued a challenge to himself and re-entered the world of comics, with the intent to bend and/ or break all preconceptions about the form. He answered his own call to arms with the critically acclaimed and commercially successful graphic novels *Goodbye, Chunky Rice* (Top Shelf, 2000) and *Blankets* (2003) and the travelogue *Carnet de Voyage* (2004), which have earned not only Harvey, Eisner and Ignatz awards but also quite a devoted following among avid comics consumers. In interview after interview, however, Thompson reiterates that it's really new readers— those more reluctant or skeptical about the medium—he's trying to appeal to with his work because he remembers that time when he counted himself among them.

Here, Thompson shares his own thoughts on his work, on the comics medium and where it's headed, and on the sacrifices necessary to create art.

Please talk about your creative process. Has it changed significantly from book to book?

Well, *Chunky Rice*, being my first book, was just made up as I went along. It was page by page, and I probably got 20 or 30 pages in when it was pointed out to me that the story didn't have a beginning or an end. It was just floating in the middle of nowhere. So that's when I

LAUREN MOSKO is the editor of *Novel & Short Story Writer's Market* and a newly anointed comics geek.

went back and I thumbnailed—did like a sketchy version—of a beginning and an end. And that was kind of like a revelation.

I didn't write out a script or screenplay but drew the first draft in comics form, albeit rough thumbnails. I remember the process being really quick with *Chunky*. Maybe there was a week when I sat down and was able to thumbnail the rest of the book out. And then things made sense and flowed better for me while drawing, and I was confident about what was coming next.

I spent almost a year thumbnailing *Blankets*, and when I reached the end, it felt like an end of the book, but it didn't feel like "the" end of the book. But because things were tied up enough I went ahead and started drawing the book, and when I reached the last chapter I totally reconfigured and rewrote it. I was kind of experiencing it in real time; my life was more directly influencing what I drew and wrote.

With the new book, I'm using that same method of thumbnailing everything ahead of time, but it's kind of driving me crazy. I'm still not drawing the final artwork and I've been working a year and a half or so on the thumbnails. Just editing and redrawing and reworking everything, taking out characters and adding new ones. I haven't even gotten to the true image-making of the book. Unlike *Blankets*, which I tried to make more sparse and breathable, the new book is just a lot more dense. It's taking a long time for some legitimate reasons and some stupid reasons. I think initially I had a good flow when I was writing it, but then I hit a big creative block. I had an epiphany about restructuring the whole narrative in a nonlinear way that kind of salvaged me from that block but it also complicated the whole process. I'd written like 400 pages and then kind of made a mess out of it.

I think *Carnet* was very refreshing because there was zero editing. It is my diary, straight to paper. In fact, I sent it to press while I was still on the trip. It was back from the press before I got back to the States. And there's something really fulfilling about the instantaneous aspect of that.

In your Fear of Speed interview, you were talking about *Blankets* and you said, "When I was writing it, that was me. Now that it's written, it's a character." That's some fascinating psychology. Can you talk a little bit more about that idea?

When I was writing *Blankets*, I was working so hard to relive those experiences and pin them down on paper, and ultimately I think I failed because the book isn't those moments. It's like a paper-and-ink reenactment from watered-down memories. It's not a reproduction. But at the same time, something new is born, something that has its own life. Some readers who meet me think they can identify with me because they know this character on the pages of my book, which is not really me. It's the part of myself I choose to depict; sometimes I flatter myself, sometimes I deprecate myself. In the end, anyway, it's just these clunky drawings.

Any kind of documentation is an abstraction from the reality. Everyone who keeps a diary talks about the fact that they tend to only journal during negative moments, when they're trying to work things out. When they look back they're like, that doesn't really represent my life at all. As soon as you try to pin something down in words or drawings, you're changing it—you *have to*. That's sort of the perpetual frustration of artists. In a way, it's better to do fantasy work like I'm doing now, because it doesn't have the pretense of being reality, and in some ways it's more honest.

Talk a little more about your upcoming graphic novel, *Habibi*. You're obviously pushing yourself again narratively—moving out of your own experience and into the realm of Arabian folk tale. What's your vision for the final artwork?

One of the things about making comics—and it must apply to lots of mediums, but for me personally—after I've spent 100 . . . 200 . . . 600 pages drawing something, I'm pretty sick of it. That happened with *Chunky Rice*, where I was sick of the cute little animals with round heads and the slick brush line. I knew with my next book I wanted to do something a little more visually organic, like a looser brush line, and with human beings and with an environment that was more real to me.

But then I went crazy doing that with *Blankets*. I'd drawn 600 pages of myself as a character and of these mundane Midwestern landscapes, like pick-up trucks and these terrible ranch-style houses and cubicle-style churches. And so with the next book I wanted to do something big and fantastical and epic and outside of myself.

Actually I think I was throwing back and forth two notions of it either being this elaborate, fantastical, make-everything-up, crazy world or do something more socially and politically relevant, à la Joe Sacco. I do think *Habibi* is kind of a compromise using this Arabian Nights genre. It's fantastical but it can't escape the obvious Middle Eastern trappings. It can't avoid having certain social and political implications. And I think growing up with Biblical stories helps me write things allegorically.

Did you do photo research on the Middle East or will you draw from imagination?

It will be a combination. I definitely got really caught up in Islamic architecture and art, especially calligraphy. I think that was part of the core. There's something I'd read about beautiful Arabic calligraphy being the music of words and that echoed my own notion of comics being a music of drawings.

All I hear is how impossible it is to break into comics/graphic novels. Please talk about your dues-paying experience. How did you come to work with Top Shelf?

I don't know if it's incredibly hard to break into graphic novels. A lot of people will send me mail asking how to become a graphic novelist, how to get published, how to get someone to pay you to work on your graphic novel, but basically you just have to make the comics yourself and start shopping it around to publishers. And some of them pay advances and most of them don't, so even then you're dependent on if the book sells, then you'll make some money from royalties.

I became acquainted with Top Shelf when they were just starting out as a company too. I did the dues paying thing when I was kind of like their little grunt. (laughs) They had a Kinko's connection and could get free photocopies, so the publisher Brett Warnock and I would go there after midnight and stay until five in the morning making photocopies and binding comics together. It was a really lo-fi sort of outfit back then.

I worked as a designer for them for a while, designing other cartoonists' books. And they'd pay me a token $50 here and there; I was definitely laboring towards getting my own book published. With *Chunky Rice*, there was a tiny advance and the book started to do well and make royalties, but it still wasn't very significant financially. I paid for

Blankets

an illustrated novel by
CRAIG THOMPSON

Reprinted with permission from Top Shelf.

Blankets by working as an illustrator for three and a half years. And that's what paid the bills—*Nickelodeon* magazine.

How did you originally get the gig making copies for Top Shelf? Did you just send them a résumé and say, hey I want to help you guys out?

Reprinted with permission from Top Shelf.

When I was living in Wisconsin, I was working a bunch of terrible jobs but making my own photocopied mini-comics. I was fortunate to have a great distribution connection through this other cartoonist, John Porcellino, who has been doing mini-comics for a long time, 10-15 years, and had a distribution company called Spit and a Half. And so my little mini-comics were able to get all around the state.

Brett Warnock, who started Top Shelf, sent me a letter while I was still in Wisconsin asking if I would be a part of this anthology that he did. I remember the anthology was a real mixed bag; some of it was great and some of it was awful. So I didn't respond to his letter until I ended up in Portland myself and I didn't have any friends. I dug up his info and gave him a call. At first he disregarded my call, because apparently he was getting calls all the time from young hopefuls wanting to get their foot in the door. But then he remembered who I was and that he'd actually sent me a letter and we started hanging out. It was a very young time in the company. They hadn't done any graphic novels; they were mainly doing an anthology. It was really just Brett in his living room. At the beginning of the next year, he joined up with Chris Staros. That's also when I was signed on.

Did they know you had book aspirations at the time?

Right away when I met Brett, I showed him my work. Of the handful of pages I had, he actually liked Chunky Rice, the turtle character, more than my other work. He kind of pointed out, "Oh I like this guy; if you do a whole book of him, I'll publish it." So I had that incentive. It was just going to be a pamphlet-style comic book of 60 pages or so but it kept growing and growing, especially after I sat and wrote out the rest of it. It ended up being a book, and it was one of their first books with a spine.

Why did you decide to get an agent?

Much of that was motivated by trying to figure out what to do with my next book—if I really wanted to do it with Top Shelf or with someone else—and I was also really overwhelmed with all the business distractions. All the constant interviews and business travel, people needing this or that, tons of e-mails—and so I was asking around like, what do I *do*? I was getting all kinds of suggestions, and I think it was a writer friend who first said, you need an agent.

When I talked with other cartoonists, they said, no you don't need an agent, they're just going to take some of your money. When I talked to people in the writing world, writers and authors would say, you need an agent; that's a no-brainer. (laughs) So I went through this long phase of interviewing a lot of agents and trying to figure out if I really needed one.

It's kind of a new concept to the world of comics. I'm really happy with my decision. PJ [Mark] has helped me a lot. I'd talked to a number of people and some that were really nice but [I chose him because] he was familiar with my work and was a fan. It was nice; he said he'd be happy to help me verbally in any way, whether I chose him as an agent or not.

Are there even many agents who represent cartoonists? How did you find PJ Mark?

I already had some connections with book publishers and had done a little bit of the groundwork myself, feeling out if they were interested in publishing me, but I still didn't know how I would go about negotiating a contract or how I would compare one publisher to the other. The editors I was talking to were very helpful. PJ's name came from two entirely different publishers. There were maybe two or three other names that also came up when I was asking around, because they had represented a number of cartoonists.

In your ADDTF interview, you were talking with Sean Collins about fighting pressure to serialize *Blankets*. You said, "I guess other cartoonists have a point that they have to make a living, but they're artists, godammit. They have to make some sacrifices for their art." I was struck by the passion in your comment, and so I have to ask: What sacrifices do you feel you have made for your own art?

Well (laughs), there was a lot of starvation in those last six years. When I first moved to Portland, I worked some really bad jobs while working on my comics. There was a time when I'd go to Taco Bell and wait for people to abandon unwrapped tacos on their plate. That's what I was living off of, surviving on. After *Chunky Rice* was out and had some success, I'd get my free copies from the printer and take them straight to the used bookstore and sell all of them so I could have groceries for that week.

Just last night I was with a friend and walking by this apartment I used to live in and it was terrible *terrible*, like ghetto-style. I lived there for five years. That's where I drew *Blankets*. It was just this really trashy, noisy, chaotic place. So that's what I traded to get my work done—a lot of creature comforts.

I expect to be poor again. I feel like I'm in a good upswing right now. Graphic novel is a huge buzzword in the literary industry; I don't know how long that's going to last. I expect there to be dry spells again.

There are a lot of things we don't have access to when we're artists. But that's not our world, that's not our calling. We're not in the world of material goods and that sort of success. It kind of reminds me of my parents' Christian upbringing, like you're laboring for something spiritual.

Even though you work as a full-time illustrator, do you think, with three illustrated novels and another on the way, that you've finally found your true calling—as a novelist? Do you even feel comfortable thinking of yourself as a novelist?

I usually just use the term cartoonist, which is an admittedly broad term. It could be a Disney animator, or someone who draws political cartoons for a newspaper, or someone who draws caricatures at the circus. But it has a certain old-fashioned sensibility to it that I like, sort of like a working-class draftsman.

Novelist still sounds a bit pretentious. I feel like I've labored so hard against the format that comics were known for and wanted them to be book form and novel-length comics. I was really troubled by the trappings of comic books, pamphlet form. But beyond that now, I'm comfortable again just calling them comics. At the time I thought it was important to say "illustrated novel" and separate it from all the preconceived notions of the medium.

Do you reject the term "illustrated novel" now? What will the cover of *Habibi* say: "a very long comic"?

(laughs) I think *Habibi* won't say anything. I don't regret it. I think the whole debate is a little bit boring and silly. It goes on a lot in the comics community. People are always trying to define the label. But I feel like I can justify my decision to put that on the book; I guess I could have put "a comic book" on the cover and that alone, [being] a huge book, would have challenged preconceptions. But I didn't want to use it at the time; I just felt there was too much of a negative connotation to the term "comic book."

But I think that's starting to change. And graphic novel is just like a hip catch phrase, it seems. I was at the Frankfurt book fair with my agent and we saw an advertisement for Chicken Soup for the Soul Graphic Novel. We thought that was pretty hilarious. That someone is very proud of themselves for fusing the two (laughs) into *an amazing new form*.

You said earlier that you expect to be poor again. Do you think graphic novels are around for a little while or do you think they're cooling off? I mean, don't things stop being cool when you get Chicken Soup for the Graphic Soul or whatever? Do you think the market is a little saturated already?

There's definitely room to grow. That won't be a problem. And it will be good because out of this explosion, there will come a handful of books that will stick around for a while. For a long time, all we've had is Art Spiegelman's *Maus* as something like a literary graphic novel, and that list has already grown pretty dramatically over the last 10 years. It will continue to grow at some kind of slow rate but there will be probably a saturation point. A lot of book publishers just want to publish graphic novels now and they're not really discerning what's good and what's not.

Comic books are ultimately books, and the book market—it's kind of unfathomable that it's still alive. People say every year, this is it, publishing is over, but it's still going on. And sometimes things come along and revitalize the literary world for a bit. But it's definitely an old-fashioned medium. We've got the Internet and video games now.

So I think it's past its heyday to some extent. But maybe it will exist in different formats. Maybe it will crossover to more digital comics. Most people I know still love handling an object in their hands, the smell of ink on paper, and again the quietness of the medium. They like that they can let their computers go to sleep and go read a book. So I think that will go on for a bit.

Again, going back to growing up Christian, my parents always had a very apocalyptic view that the world was going to end any day now, and to some extent that kind of feeling persists in me. Every time I hear jet planes going overhead, I'm like, oh here it is. And I'm kind of comfortable with that, to some extent. So I'll be surprised if the world even keeps going long enough for (laughs) books to be eliminated entirely.

What's the most important thing you've learned as your writing career evolved?

That it doesn't get any easier. Definitely when you're a young cartoonist—even before you're a cartoonist—you have to come to the realization that no matter what kind of crap job you're working or if you're going to school or paying school loans, you can't let those be excuses. You have to just start drawing. And that's the first big revelation you have and progress you make towards being a cartoonist, just not letting all those excuses get in the way.

I think I still held on to a notion that with more economic freedom, the creative parts would flow even easier. That's not really the case, or it hasn't been. There's still plenty of distractions and excuses you can make for not getting work done. I guess it goes back to that core thing I learned: You can't make excuses. (laughs) You can *always* make excuses, but you've just got to draw.

The Business of Comics

Finding a Job in Hollywood's Idea Factory

by John Jackson Miller

Creating comics, it has been said, has something in common with golf. You can't watch either being done without being inspired, at some point, to try your own hand at it—advisedly or not. Indeed, there are more aspiring comic book creators in the aisles of comic book conventions than there are behind the signing tables.

That kind of power to inspire consumers to action is certainly a strength of comics, but it can also be a problem. Few markets have such fierce creative competition. One of comics' best-known scribes once famously said he had no fans—just people who wanted his job. Indeed, there have been times when the greatest fear in comics was that we were one big craft circle, selling only to ourselves.

Fortunately, comics in the 21st century are in a much better place. Bouncing back from a historic speculation-driven collapse in the early 1990s, comics have claimed a position as a factory of creative ideas for other media. With more than 170,000 comic book issues having been published in North America alone, Hollywood has found a seemingly inexhaustible supply of reader-tested material—and mass-market booksellers have taken notice.

Now, squarebound comics are no longer relegated to the "Humor" shelves of bookstores but are racked on their own in most venues. Some farsighted retailers are even beginning to rack comics alongside related prose works in their individual genres—putting comics mysteries, comics SF, and comics romances where their customers are, regardless of the format. For creators of what used to be considered a second-class or children's medium, that's a dream come true.

But comics are deceptive. Looking at the growing presence of bound editions of comics in mass-market bookstores, a novice writer might assume they're just another kind of book, as far as publishers are concerned. But however they're eventually packaged, almost all American comics begin as *magazines*, and the production model is, at heart, a magazine production model.

Understanding the product

The term "graphic novel," coined in comics in the 1970s, has become popular in the mainstream press, allowing coverage of comics to appear in places where it might not have before. But a graphic novel—correctly defined as a complete comics work (usually of more than 64

JOHN JACKSON MILLER (www.johnjacksonmiller.com) writes comics, in titles including Star Wars, Simpsons and Iron Man, and writes about them in books and magazines, including *The Standard Catalog of Comic Books* and *Comics Buyer's Guide*. He's also editorial director of collectibles for F + W Publications.

pages) appearing for the first time in a single squarebound volume—is more of a rarity in comics publishing.

In fact, 98% or more of the comics seen on the bookshelves of Borders and Barnes & Noble are collections reprinting material that's already appeared in monthly comics in the United States or in Japanese manga. They're the DVD release of the TV series, if you will. Within the comics field, they're called "trade paperbacks" (despite that term meaning something else for the book publishing world), and they helped revitalize the industry in the early 2000s by allowing periodical publishers both a second stream of income and a vital inroad into mass-market stores, many of which had surrendered their business in the 32-page monthlies to the 2,500 or so comics shops in North America.

Without the pre-existing series, few bound editions would be published. Many of the original graphic novels green-lit by major publishers are by people who've already made their names, either in comics, the outside world, or both. Before there was a place for comics in bookstores in addition to the spinner rack, Harvey Pekar's award-winning *American Splendor* (Ballantine, 2003) was serialized in periodical form. His later *Quitter* (Vertigo, 2005) was not, there being, by then, both a wider market for his work and a place for bookstores to actually stock that work. Apart from art houses and specialty imprints of major prose publishers, most comics publishers look on the original graphic novel as a prestige—and, thus, a luxury—item.

As much as sales of bound editions of comics (reprint and otherwise) have grown, prior serialization remains a must for most comics publishers. The reasons are many. Without the revenue from the periodical, the publisher loses both revenue and exposure. It's the word-of-mouth from the periodical version that helps sell the trade-paperback collection—often to the very same people who bought the individual issues.

Furthermore, the work simply won't get done. A 132-page comics story (the equivalent of a six-issue arc of a comic-book series) might take a writer a few weeks to complete. But it requires *months* of time for one or more artists, not to mention colorists and letterers involved. Experience has shown that the monthly tempo, enforcing deadlines of a chapter a month, brings more stories to market than you'd see if a graphic novel had to be completed before its initial publication.

And comics is a cash-on-delivery business. Just as with magazine writing, creators rarely, if ever, are paid in advance. Publishers usually pay on delivery of the work, which means one thing if you're turning in 22 pages at a time—and starvation at 132 pages at a time.

Creators hope that as bookstore sales of comics in bound form grow, comics publishers will increasingly adopt such prose-market devices as advances, which will then allow for longer-form original works.

But for now, aspiring comics creators with ideas for their own graphic novels have a decision to make: If they eschew serialization in comic books, the odds against publication by an existing publisher escalate. A first-time creator can find an opportunity with a longer-form work at a smaller art house (of which there are several in comics), but, with the larger firms, serialized periodicals are often a necessary part of the equation.

Breaking in—and in and in again . . .

More than 300 new comic books are released every month in North America, which would seem to suggest a lot of opportunities for new entries. Unfortunately, the publishing market is not as broad as it is deep. The two longtime market leaders, Marvel and DC, combine for nearly two-thirds of the offerings each month and nearly four-fifths of the sales. And, while getting an assignment with one or the other is an invaluable stamp of approval, the competition for positions with either reflects that.

The news is good here for artists who make it onto the larger publishers' radar screens:

So *much* material is moving through the system that the partnership with a competent and punctual creator can be an editor's most valuable commodity. Artists also have an advantage in a more streamlined path to discovery. Major publishers hold portfolio review sessions at the hobby's major conventions—and many artists have earned assignments just by setting up in "Artists Alley" and being seen when an editor in need walks by.

Here, the importance of taking any assignment at all, for however small the publisher, becomes obvious for most artists. Published work in one's portfolio isn't just the best visual cue to one's talent; it also suggests the artist both made a deadline and has had exposure. Comics fans are obsessive when it comes to indexing creators' careers—online sites and the *Standard Catalog of Comic Books* are to comics what The Internet Movie Database (IMDb) is to film—so every credit is magnified many times. The career paths of most artists working regularly in monthly comics today can be traced through the "rookie leagues" to the larger publishers, as editors see their ability (and, what's more important, reliability).

Opportunities for artists multiplied with the arrival of next-day shipping and multiplied again with the introduction of the Internet. Where most chances for work used to go to artists in New York City, now artists can live virtually anywhere, communicating with their writers and delivering their image files electronically. That's changed how comics are produced. The "Marvel method" (in which a writer dialogues pages that an artist has drawn based on an agreed-upon plot) still exists but has largely been replaced by full scripts (in which the writer has provided panel-by-panel direction). In-person collaboration has vanished for most. (I wrote an entire year of a series without ever meeting my artist, who lived in Argentina.)

> So *much* material is moving through the system that the partnership with a competent and punctual creator can be an editor's most valuable commodity.

Finding work tends to be harder for new writers. Consider the numbers: An artist may have time to draw a little more than one 22-page comic book a month—two, if he's working full-time and has the speed of Mercury. Meanwhile, it's not unusual to see full-time comics writers hammering out several titles a month. In the early 1990s, Fabian Nicieza was both editing at Marvel and writing nine monthlies and, in the 1960s, Stan Lee wrote every Marvel series! A monthly title might provide work to as many as a dozen cover artists, interior artists, and colorists in a year, yet might be only *one* of the titles a writer is scripting. Since writers are generally paid less per page than artists, they often have to take more assignments—thus, assignments tend to coalesce around a small number of contributors.

So it is that the power of being an insider—or a familiar face—is greatly magnified when it comes to writers. In periods of business contraction, many assignments understandably go to insiders-turned-freelancers. Some majors have been known to stop accepting writing submissions for years at a time. Complicating the process for comics writers, too, is that the characters being written about are usually owned by the publisher, so idea submission agreements are usually required beforehand. Which puts many writers in a Catch-22 with the majors: A pitch about Copyrighted Character X can only go to one publisher, yet publishers are not often in the market for work from beginning writers about brand new characters.

Another challenge comics creators face is remaining in the public's eye, year after year. Even the creative superstars of comics say that "paying your dues" is a process that never really stops. While longevity can translate to royalties where it couldn't before, the market is so volatile and dynamic that assignments on the corporate-owned titles must be won, and won, and won again. Even with creator-owned characters and concepts, a continuing supply of new material in periodical form makes it far easier to help retailers sell the older collections. It's a lot easier to maintain an ongoing franchise than to revive it.

However, in recent years many comics fans have gone from being brand-loyal to author-loyal—an easier thing now that the creators' names appear on the covers and elsewhere inside. (For years, they weren't listed in comic books at all!) It's increasingly possible for a creator to bring his or her fans with him to the next project, wherever it is—though this involves a great deal of personal marketing at conventions and online. With hundreds of comics released each month, it's vital for a creator to communicate where he is and what he's doing at all times—not just for the fans' information, but for the editors as well. Editors are accustomed to creators drifting into and out of the business, and without stoking the fires it's easy for a writer or artist to be counted in the latter group.

Guerilla marketing

Even without the visual advantages artists have in marketing their services, aspiring writers do have ways of being seen. The comics blogosphere and fan press is active and has generated name recognition for many who later became comics writers (myself included). Self-publishing, a mark of vanity elsewhere, is regarded as a declaration of independence in comics and has produced many writers who went on to long careers. Many, many comics series started at small presses have gone to the larger ones without much loss in the way of the creators' rights. Webcomics also can serve as a method of guerilla-marketing exposure; although comics remain—make no mistake—exclusively a print medium for most financial and artistic purposes. Finally, as with artists, traveling to major conventions is vital. Writers and artists may no longer work face-to-face, but face time with editors is necessary for both.

The major publishers do occasionally stage talent searches, whenever they're looking for fresh faces and a publicity boost. These are worth watching for, although the challenge is that the pent-up demand for consideration can be vast, resulting in a flood of proposals. These searches can work for a creator (one did for this writer), but they're always a reminder of just how many comics readers want to work behind the scenes.

As with artists, proof of reliability is everything. The writer, at the beginning of the chain, can start a cascade of delays that can upset everything.

Got what it takes?

Most everyone who reads comics wants to create them themselves. If you're an aspiring creator who's not an avid comics consumer already, the best advice is not to bother: Comics require a visual vocabulary that is learned only by reading comics. Trying to create comics without that background knowledge is like aspiring to write a prose story in a language you don't know. But, if you know the lingo, have interesting ideas, can hit a deadline, and don't mind a little competition, there may be a place for you among the *next* 170,000 comics published.

Graphic Novels & Comics

Resources

Where to Look for More Information

Below is a list of invaluable resources specifically for writers of graphic novels and comics. To order any of the Impact Books titles or to get a consumer book catalog, call (800)448-0915 or visit amazon.com or barnesandnoble.com.

MAGAZINES

- *Comic Buyer's Guide*, published by Krause Publications (a division of F + W Publications, Inc.). Subscribe online at www.cbgxtra.com. Six issues for $19.95.
- *The Comics Journal*, published by Fantagraphics Books. Subscribe by writing The Comics Journal, 7563 Lake City Way NE, Seattle, WA 98115, by calling 1-800-657-1100, or online at http://tcj.com/1_frontdesk/subscribe.html. Five issues for $36.

BOOKS

- *Alan Moore's Writing for Comics*, by Alan Moore. Avatar Press: 2003.
- *Best American Comics* anthology. Houghton Mifflin: annual.
- *Comics and Sequential Art,* by Will Eisner. Impact Books: 2004.
- *The DC Comics Guide to Writing Comics*, by Dennis O'Neil. Watson-Guptill: 2001.
- *Graphic Storytelling and Visual Narrative*, by Will Eisner. Impact Books: 2004.
- *How to Draw and Sell Comics*, by Alan McKenzie. Impact Books: 2005.
- *The Writer's Guide to the Business of Comics*, by Lurene Haines. Watson-Guptill: 1998.
- *Writing for Comics with Peter David*, by Peter David. Impact Books: 2006.

ORGANIZATIONS

- Comic Book Legal Defense Fund. "Non-profit organization dedicated to the preservation of First Amendment rights for members of the comics community." Web site: www.cbldf.org.
- Friends of Lulu. Nonprofit organization dedicated to promoting and encouraging female readership and participation in the comic book industry. Web site: www.friends-lulu.org.
- International Comic Arts Association. Non-profit organization that strives to "support, promote, and strengthen the comic industry, its products, and professionals." Web site: www.comicarts.org.
- Organized Readers of Comics Associated. International association that promotes the reading of comic books. Web site: www.orcafresh.net.

ONLINE

- Artbomb. Reviews. Web site: www.artbomb.net.
- The Big Comic Book Database. Research guide. Web site: www.comics-db.com.
- Comic Book Resources. Daily news, columns and interviews. Web site: www.comicbookresources.com.
- Egon. Coverage of independent comics, including news, events and exhibits. Web site: www.egonlabs.com.
- ICV2. Industry business news. Web site: www.icv2.com.
- Newsarama. Breaking news, columns, previews, interviews. Web site: www.newsarama.com.
- The Pulse. News and interviews, updated daily. Web site: www.comicon.com/pulse/.
- Silver Bullet Comics. News, previews and industry gossip. Web site: www.silverbulletcomicbooks.com.
- SmallPressComics.com. Focuses on the creation, distribution and promotion of small-press comics. Web site: www.smallpresscomics.com.

Literary Agents

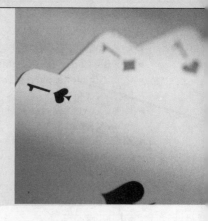

Many publishers are willing to look at unsolicited submissions, but most feel having an agent is in the writer's best interest. In this section, we include agents who specialize in or represent fiction. These agents were also selected because of their openness to submissions from writers.

The commercial fiction field is intensely competitive. Many publishers have small staffs and little time. For that reason, many book publishers rely on agents for new talent. Some publishers are even relying on agents as "first readers" who must wade through the deluge of submissions from writers to find the very best. For writers, a good agent can be a foot in the door—someone willing to do the necessary work to put your manuscript in the right editor's hands.

It would seem today that finding a good agent is as hard as finding a good publisher. Yet those writers who have agents say they are invaluable. Not only can a good agent help you make your work more marketable, an agent also acts as your business manager and adviser, protecting your interests during and after contract negotiations.

Still, finding an agent can be very difficult for a new writer. If you are already published in magazines, you have a better chance than someone with no publishing credits. (Many agents routinely read periodicals searching for new writers.) Although many agents do read queries and manuscripts from unpublished authors without introduction, referrals from their writer clients can be a big help. If you don't know any published authors with agents, attending a conference is a good way to meet agents. Some agents even set aside time at conferences to meet new writers.

Almost all the agents listed here have said they are open to working with new, previously unpublished writers as well as published writers. They do not charge a fee to cover the time and effort involved in reviewing a manuscript or a synopsis and chapters, but their time is still extremely valuable. Only send an agent your work when you feel it is as complete and polished as possible.

USING THE LISTINGS

It is especially important that you read individual listings carefully before contacting these busy agents. The first information after the company name includes the address and phone, fax, e-mail address (when available) and Web site. **Member Agents** gives the names of individual agents working at that company. (Specific types of fiction an agent handles are indicated in parenthesis after that agent's name.) The **Represents** section lists the types of fiction the agency works with. Reading the **Recent Sales** gives you the names of writers an agent is currently working with and, very importantly, publishers the agent has placed manuscripts with. **Writers' Conferences** identifies conferences an agent attends (and where you might possibly meet that agent). **Tips** presents advice directly from the agent to authors.

Also, look closely at the openness to submissions icons that precede most listings. They will indicate how willing an agency is to take on new writers.

▣ DOMINICK ABEL LITERARY AGENCY, INC.

146 W. 82nd St., #1B, New York NY 10024. Fax: (212)595-3133. E-mail: agency@dalainc.com. Estab. 1975. Member of AAR. Represents 100 clients. Currently handles: adult nonfiction books; adult novels.
How to Contact Query with SASE.
Terms Agent receives 15% commission on domestic sales; 20% commission on foreign sales.

▣ ▣ ACACIA HOUSE PUBLISHING SERVICES, LTD.

51 Acacia Rd., Toronto ON M4S 2K6 Canada. Phone/Fax: (416)484-8356. **Contact:** (Ms.) Frances Hanna. Estab. 1985. Represents 100 clients. Currently handles: 30% nonfiction books; 70% novels.
- Ms. Hanna has been in the publishing business for 30 years, first in London as a fiction editor with Barrie & Jenkins and Pan Books, and as a senior editor with a packager of mainly illustrated books. She was condensed books editor for 6 years for *Reader's Digest* in Montreal and senior editor and foreign rights manager for William Collins & Sons (now HarperCollins) in Toronto. Mr. Hanna has over 40 years of experience in the publishing business.

Member Agents Bill Hanna, vice president (business, self-help, modern history).
Represents Nonfiction books, novels. **Considers these nonfiction areas:** Animals; biography/autobiography; language/literature/criticism; memoirs; military/war; music/dance; nature/environment; theater/film; travel. **Considers these fiction areas:** Action/adventure; detective/police/crime; literary; mainstream/contemporary; mystery/suspense; thriller.
- ➤ This agency specializes in contemporary fiction—literary or commercial. Actively seeking outstanding first novels with literary merit. Does not want to receive horror, occult, or science fiction.

How to Contact Query with outline, SASE. *No unsolicited mss.* No e-mail or fax queries. Responds in 6 weeks to queries. Returns materials only with SASE.
Recent Sales Sold over 75 titles in the last year. Also made numerous international rights sales. This agency prefers not to share information on specific sales or clients.
Terms Agent receives 15% commission on English language sales; 20% commission on dramatic sales; 25% commission on foreign sales. Charges clients for photocopying, postage, courier.
Tips "We prefer that writers be previously published, with at least a few short stories or articles to their credit. Strongest consideration will be given to those with 3 or more published books. However, we would take on an unpublished writer of outstanding talent."

▣ AGENTS INK!

P.O. Box 4956, Fresno CA 93744. (559)438-8289. **Contact:** Sydney H. Harriet, director. Estab. 1987. Member of APA. Represents 20 clients. 70% of clients are new/unpublished writers. Currently handles: 80% nonfiction books; 20% novels; multimedia.
- Prior to opening his agency, Dr. Harriet was a psychologist, radio and television reporter, and professor of English. Ms. McNichols has a BA in classical Greek and an MA in classics. She has more than 20 years of experience as an editor for daily and alternative newspapers, major syndicates, and independent authors.

Member Agents Sydney Harriet; Dinah McNichols.
Represents Nonfiction books, novels. **Considers these nonfiction areas:** Animals; cooking/foods/nutrition; government/politics/law; health/medicine (mind/body healing); history; language/literature/criticism; psychology; science/technology; self-help/personal improvement; sociology; sports (medicine, psychology); Foreign affairs; international topics.
- ➤ This agency specializes in writers who have education experience in the business, legal, and health professions. It is helpful if the writer is licensed, but not necessary. Prior nonfiction book publication is not necessary. For fiction, previously published fiction is a prerequisite for representation. Does not want memoirs, autobiographies, stories about overcoming an illness, science fiction, fantasy, religious materials, or children's books.

How to Contact Query with SASE. Considers simultaneous submissions. Responds in 1 month.
Recent Sales Sold 5 titles in the last year. *Infantry Soldier*, by George Neil (University of Oklahoma Press); *SAMe, The European Arthritis and Depression Breakthrough*, by Sol Grazi and Maria Costa (Prima); *What to Eat if You Have Diabetes*, by Danielle Chase (Contemporary); *How to Turn Your Fat Husband Into a Lean Lover*, by Maureen Keane (Random House).

Terms Agent receives 15% commission on domestic sales; 20% commission on foreign sales. Offers written contract, binding for 6-12 months (negotiable).

Writers' Conferences Scheduled as a speaker at a number of conferences across the country. Contact agency to book authors and agents for conferences.

Tips "Remember, query first. Do not call to pitch an idea. The only way we can judge the quality of your idea is to see how you write. Unsolicited manuscripts will not be read if they arrive without a SASE. Currently, we are receiving more than 200 query letters and proposals each month. Send a complete proposal/manuscript only if requested. Ask yourself why someone would be compelled to buy your book. If you think the idea is unique, spend the time to create a query and then a proposal where every word counts. Fiction writers need to understand that the craft is just as important as the idea—99% of the fiction is rejected because of sloppy, overwritten dialogue, wooden characters, predictable plotting, and lifeless narrative. Once you finish your novel, put it away and let it percolate, then take it out and work on fine-tuning it some more. A novel is never finished until you stop working on it. We would love to represent more fiction writers and probably will when we read a manuscript that has gone through a dozen or more drafts. Because of rising costs, we no longer can respond to queries, proposals, and/or complete manuscripts without receiving a return envelope and sufficient postage."

🖉 THE AHEARN AGENCY, INC.

2021 Pine St., New Orleans LA 70118. E-mail: pahearn@aol.com. **Contact:** Pamela G. Ahearn. Estab. 1992. Member of MWA, RWA, ITW. Represents 25 clients. 20% of clients are new/unpublished writers. Currently handles: 10% nonfiction books; 90% novels.

- Prior to opening her agency, Ms. Ahearn was an agent for 8 years and an editor with Bantam Books.

Represents Nonfiction books, novels, short story collections (if stories have been previously published). **Considers these nonfiction areas:** Animals; child guidance/parenting; current affairs; ethnic/cultural interests; gay/lesbian issues; health/medicine; history; music/dance; popular culture; self-help/personal improvement; theater/film; true crime/investigative; women's issues/studies. **Considers these fiction areas:** Action/adventure; contemporary issues; detective/police/crime; ethnic; family saga; feminist; gay/lesbian; glitz; historical; humor/satire; literary; mainstream/contemporary; mystery/suspense; psychic/supernatural; regional; romance; thriller.

    O━ This agency specializes in historical romance and is also very interested in mysteries and suspense fiction. Does not want to receive category romance, science fiction, or fantasy.

How to Contact Query with SASE. Accepts e-mail queries (no attachments). Considers simultaneous queries. Responds in 8 weeks to queries; 10 weeks to mss. Obtains most new clients through recommendations from others, solicitations, conferences.

Recent Sales *Assassin's Touch*, by Laura Joh Rowland (St. Martin's); *To Pleasure a Prince*, by Sabrina Jeffries (Pocket); *The Templar Legacy*, by Steve Berry.

Terms Agent receives 15% commission on domestic sales; 20% commission on foreign sales. Offers written contract, binding for 1 year; renewable by mutual consent.

Writers' Conferences Moonlight & Magnolias; RWA National Conference; Virginia Romance Writers; Florida Romance Writers; Bouchercon; Malice Domestic.

Tips "Be professional! Always send in exactly what an agent/editor asks for—no more, no less. Keep query letters brief and to the point, giving your writing credentials and a very brief summary of your book. If one agent rejects you, keep trying—there are a lot of us out there!"

🖉 ALIVE COMMUNICATIONS, INC.

7680 Goddard St., Suite 200, Colorado Springs CO 80920. (719)260-7080. Fax: (719)260-8223. Web site: www.alivecom.com. Estab. 1989. Member of CBA, Authors Guild. Represents 200+ clients. 5% of clients are new/unpublished writers. Currently handles: 50% nonfiction books; 35% novels; 5% novellas; 10% juvenile books.

Member Agents Rick Christian, president (blockbusters, bestsellers); Don Pape (popular/commercial nonfiction and fiction, new authors with breakout potential); Beth Jusino (thoughtful/inspirational nonfiction, women's fiction/nonfiction, Christian living); Lee Hough (popular/commercial nonfiction and fiction, thoughtful spirituality, children's).

Represents Nonfiction books, novels, short story collections, novellas. **Considers these nonfiction areas:** Biography/autobiography; business/economics; child guidance/parenting; how-to; memoirs; religious/inspirational; self-help/personal improvement; women's issues/studies. **Considers these fiction areas:** Action/adventure; contemporary issues; detective/police/crime; family saga; historical; humor/satire; literary; mainstream/contemporary; mystery/suspense; religious/inspirational; thriller.

    O━ This agency specializes in fiction, Christian living, how-to, and commercial nonfiction. Actively seeking inspirational, literary and mainstream fiction, and work from authors with established track records and platforms. Does not want poetry, young adult paperbacks, scripts, or dark themes.

How to Contact Works primarily with well-established, bestselling, and career authors. Returns materials only with SASE. Obtains most new clients through recommendations from others.

Recent Sales Sold 300+ titles in the last year. Left Behind series, by Tim LaHaye and Jerry B. Jenkins (Tyndale); *Let's Roll*, by Lisa Beamer (Tyndale); *The Message*, by Eugene Peterson (NavPress); Every Man series, by Stephen Arterburn (Waterbrook); *One Tuesday Morning*, by Karen Kingsbury (Zondervan).

Terms Agent receives 15% commission on domestic sales; 15% commission on foreign sales. Offers written contract; 2-month written notice must be given to terminate contract.

Tips "Rewrite and polish until the words on the page shine. Endorsements and great connections may help, provided you can write with power and passion. Network with publishing professionals by making contacts, joining critique groups, and attending writers' conferences in order to make personal connections and to get feedback. Alive Communications, Inc., has established itself as a premiere literary agency. We serve an elite group of authors who are critically acclaimed and commercially successful in both Christian and general markets."

◢ MIRIAM ALTSHULER LITERARY AGENCY

53 Old Post Rd. N., Red Hook NY 12571. (845)758-9408. **Contact:** Miriam Altshuler. Estab. 1994. Member of AAR. Represents 40 clients. Currently handles: 45% nonfiction books; 45% novels; 5% story collections; 5% juvenile books.

• Ms. Altshuler has been an agent since 1982.

Represents Nonfiction books, novels, short story collections, juvenile books. **Considers these nonfiction areas:** Biography/autobiography; ethnic/cultural interests; history; language/literature/criticism; memoirs; multicultural; music/dance; nature/environment; popular culture; psychology; sociology; theater/film; women's issues/studies. **Considers these fiction areas:** Literary; mainstream/contemporary; multicultural.

○┑ Does not want self-help, mystery, how-to, romance, horror, spiritual, fantasy, poetry, screenplays, science fiction, or techno-thriller.

How to Contact Query with SASE. Prefers to read materials exclusively. If no SASE is included, no response will be sent. No unsolicited mss. No e-mail or fax queries. Considers simultaneous queries. Responds in 3 weeks to mss. Returns materials only with SASE. Obtains most new clients through recommendations from others.

Terms Agent receives 15% commission on domestic sales; 20% commission on foreign sales. Charges clients for overseas mailing, photocopies, overnight mail when requested by author.

Writers' Conferences Bread Loaf Writers' Conference; Washington Independent Writers Conference; North Carolina Writers' Network Conference.

Ⓝ ⊕ ◢ THE AMPERSAND AGENCY

Ryman's Cottages, Little Tew, Oxfordshire OX7 4JJ United Kingdom. (44)(16)868-3677. Fax: (44)(16)868-3449. E-mail: peter@theampersandagency.co.uk. Web site: www.theampersandagency.co.uk. **Contact:** Peter Buckman. Estab. 2003. Represents 30 clients. 75% of clients are new/unpublished writers.

• Prior to opening his agency, Mr. Buckman was a writer and publisher in England and America.

Member Agents Peter Buckman (literary fiction and nonfiction); Peter Janson-Smith (crime, thrillers, biography); Anne-Marie Doulton (historical and women's fiction).

Represents Nonfiction books, novels, juvenile books, scholarly books. **Considers these nonfiction areas:** Animals; biography/autobiography; cooking/foods/nutrition; current affairs; education; ethnic/cultural interests; government/politics/law; health/medicine; history; humor/satire; language/literature/criticism; memoirs; military/war; music/dance; popular culture; psychology; theater/film; translation; true crime/investigative. **Considers these fiction areas:** Action/adventure; comic books/cartoon; confession; detective/police/crime; ethnic; family saga; fantasy; historical; juvenile; literary; mainstream/contemporary; mystery/suspense; romance; thriller; young adult; Glitz.

○┑ "Being a new agency, we specialize in new writers, although we also represent well-established names. We are small, experienced, and professional. We know what we like, respond quickly, and enjoy working with the writers we take on to present their work in the best possible way. We also offer a foreign rights service and have well-established contacts on both sides of the Atlantic in film, TV, broadcasting, and publishing." Actively seeking commercial and literary fiction and nonfiction. Does not want science fiction or works with only regional appeal.

How to Contact Submit outline, 1-2 sample chapters. Accepts queries via e-mail. Considers simultaneous queries. Responds in 1 week to queries; 1 month to mss. Returns materials only with SASE. Obtains most new clients through recommendations, writers' handbooks, word of mouth.

Recent Sales Sold 14 titles in the last year. *Q&A*, by Vikas Swarup (Scribner/Doubleday); *My Side of the Story*, by Will Davis (Bloomsbury); *Digging Up the Dead*, by Dr. Druin Burch (Chatoo & Windus); *Neptune's Daughter*, by Beryl Kingston (Transita). Other clients include Geoff Baker, Max Barron, Rob Buckman, Anna Crosbie,

Andrew Cullen, Tom Darke, Francis Ellen, Justin Elliott, Cora Harrison, Georgette Heyer, Michael Hutchinson, Jim McKenna, Euan Macpherson, Bolaji Odofin, Rosie Orr, Philip Purser, Penny Rumble, Nick van Bloss, Mike Walters, Norman Welch, Kirby Wright.

Terms Agent receives 10-15% commission on domestic sales; 20% commission on foreign sales. Offers written contract. "By agreement with the author, we charge for extra photocopying in the case of multiple submissions and for any lawyers or other profesional fees required by a negotiation."

◪ BETSY AMSTER LITERARY ENTERPRISES

P.O. Box 27788, Los Angeles CA 90027-0788. **Contact:** Betsy Amster. Estab. 1992. Member of AAR. Represents over 65 clients. 35% of clients are new/unpublished writers. Currently handles: 65% nonfiction books; 35% novels.

- Prior to opening her agency, Ms. Amster was an editor at Pantheon and Vintage for 10 years, and served as editorial director for the Globe Pequot Press for 2 years. "This experience gives me a wider perspective on the business and the ability to give focused editorial feedback to my clients."

Represents Nonfiction books, novels. **Considers these nonfiction areas:** Biography/autobiography; child guidance/parenting; ethnic/cultural interests; gardening; health/medicine; history; money/finance; psychology; sociology; women's issues/studies; Career. **Considers these fiction areas:** Ethnic; literary; mystery/suspense (quirky); thriller (quirky); women's (high quality).

- ⊶ Actively seeking strong narrative nonfiction, particularly by journalists; outstanding literary fiction (the next Michael Chabon or Jhumpa Lahiri); witty, intelligent, commercial women's fiction (the next Elinor Lipman or Jennifer Weiner); and high-profile self-help and psychology, preferably research based. Does not want to receive poetry, children's books, romances, westerns, science fiction, or action/adventure.

How to Contact For fiction, send query, first 3 pages, SASE. For nonfiction, send query or proposal with SASE. No e-mail or fax queries. Considers simultaneous queries. Responds in 1 month to queries; 2 months to mss. Obtains most new clients through recommendations from others, solicitations, conferences.

Recent Sales *Wild Indigo* and *Wild Inferno*, by Sandi Ault (Berkley Prime Crime); *Famous Writers School*, by Steven Carter (Counterpoint); *The Great Black Way: L.A.'s Central Avenue in the 1940s and the Rise of African American Pop Culture*, by RJ Smith (PublicAffairs); *Rejuvenile: The Reinvention of the American Grown-Up*, by Christopher Noxon (Crown); *The Renaissance Soul: Life Design for People with Too Many Passions to Pick Just One*, by Margaret Lobenstine (Broadway). Other clients include Dr. Linda Acredolo, Dr. Susan Goodwyn, Dwight Allen, Lynette Brasfield, Dr. Elaine N. Aron, Barbara DeMarco-Barrett, Robin Chotzinoff, Rob Cohen, David Wollock, Phil Doran, Mara Amparo Escandón, Paul Mandelbaum, Wendy Mogel, Sharon Montrose, Joy Nicholson, Lynette Padwa, Diana Wells, Dr. Edward Schneider, Leigh Ann Hirschman.

Terms Agent receives 15% commission on domestic sales; 20% commission on foreign sales. Offers written contract, binding for 1 year; 3-month notice must be given to terminate contract. Charges for photocopying, postage, long distance phone calls, messengers, galleys/books used in submissions to foreign and film agents and to magazines for first serial rights.

Writers' Conferences Squaw Valley Writers Workshop; San Diego State University Writers' Conference; UCLA Extension Writers' Program; The Loft Literary Center.

Ⓝ ⊕ ◪ ANUBIS LITERARY AGENCY

7 Birdhaven Close Lighthorne Heath, Banbury Rd., Warwick Warwickshire CV35 0BE Great Britain. Phone/Fax: (44)(192)664-2588. E-mail: anubis.agency2@btopenworld.com. **Contact:** Steve Calcutt. Estab. 1994. Represents 15 clients. 50% of clients are new/unpublished writers. Currently handles: 100% novels.

- In addition to being an agent, Mr. Calcutt teaches creative writing and American history (US Civil War) at Warwick University.

Represents Novels. **Considers these fiction areas:** Horror; science fiction; Dark fantasy.

- ⊶ Actively seeking horror fiction. Does not want to receive children's books, nonfiction, journalism, or TV/film scripts.

How to Contact Query with proposal package, outline, SASE/IRCs. Returns materials only with SASE/IRCs. No e-mail or fax queries. Responds in 6 weeks to queries; 3 months to mss. Obtains most new clients through personal recommendation.

Recent Sales *Berserk* and *Dusk*, by Tim Lebbon (Dorchester); *The Beloved*, by J.F. Gonzalez; *Breeding Ground*, by Sarah Pinborough (Dorchester); *Gradisil*, by Adam Roberts (Orion). Other clients include Steve Savile, Lesley Asquith, Anthea Ingham, Brett A. Savory.

Terms Agent receives 15% commission on domestic sales; 20% commission on foreign sales.

◪ APPLESEEDS MANAGEMENT

200 E. 30th St., Suite 302, San Bernardino CA 92404. (909)882-1667. **Contact:** S. James Foiles. Estab. 1988. 40% of clients are new/unpublished writers. Currently handles: 15% nonfiction books; 85% novels.

Represents Nonfiction books, novels. **Considers these nonfiction areas:** True crime/investigative. **Considers these fiction areas:** Detective/police/crime; mystery/suspense.

How to Contact Query with SASE. Responds in 2 weeks to queries; 2 months to mss.

Recent Sales This agency prefers not to share information on specific sales.

Terms Agent receives 10-15% commission on domestic sales; 20% commission on foreign sales. Offers written contract, binding for 1-7 years.

Tips "Because readership of mysteries is expanding, Appleseeds specializes in mysteries with a detective who could be in a continuing series."

◻ ARCADIA

31 Lake Place N., Danbury CT 06810. E-mail: arcadialit@att.net. **Contact:** Victoria Gould Pryor. Member of AAR.

Represents Nonfiction books, literary and commercial fiction. **Considers these nonfiction areas:** Biography/autobiography; business/economics; current affairs; history; memoirs; psychology; science/technology; true crime/investigative; women's issues/studies; Medicine; investigative journalism; culture; classical music; life transforming self-help.

    O─ "I'm a very hands-on agent, which is necessary in this competitive marketplace. I work with authors on revisions until whatever we present to publishers is as perfect as it can be. I represent talented, dedicated, intelligent, and ambitious writers who are looking for a long-term relationship based on professional success and mutual respect." No science fiction/fantasy, horror, humor, or children's/YA. "We are only able to read fiction submissions from previously published authors."

How to Contact Query with SASE. Accepts e-mail queries (no attachments).

Recent Sales This agency prefers not to share information on specific sales.

⊠ ◻ ARTISTS AND ARTISANS INC.

104 W. 29th St., 11th Floor, New York NY 10001. Fax: (212)931-8377. E-mail: adam@artistsandartisans.com. Web site: www.artistsandartisans.com. **Contact:** Adam Chromy. Estab. 2002. Represents 40 clients. 80% of clients are new/unpublished writers. Currently handles: 63% nonfiction books; 35% novels; 2% scholarly books.

    ● Prior to becoming an agent, Mr. Chromy was an entrepreneur in the technology field for nearly a decade.

Represents Nonfiction books, novels. **Considers these nonfiction areas:** Biography/autobiography; business/economics; child guidance/parenting; cooking/foods/nutrition; current affairs; ethnic/cultural interests; health/medicine; how-to; humor/satire; language/literature/criticism; memoirs; money/finance; music/dance; popular culture; religious/inspirational; science/technology; self-help/personal improvement; sports; theater/film; true crime/investigative; women's issues/studies; Fashion/style. **Considers these fiction areas:** Confession; family saga; humor/satire; literary; mainstream/contemporary.

    O─ "My education and experience in the business world ensure that my clients' enterprise as authors gets as much attention and care as their writing." Actively seeking working journalists for nonfiction books. Does not want to receive scripts.

How to Contact Query with SASE. Considers simultaneous queries. Responds in 2 weeks to queries; 2 weeks to mss. Returns materials only with SASE. Obtains most new clients through queries, referrals, conferences.

Recent Sales Sold 12 titles in the last year.

Terms Agent receives 15% commission on domestic sales; 25% commission on foreign sales. Offers written contract; 1-month notice must be given to terminate contract. "We only charge for extraordinary expenses (e.g., client requests check via FedEx instead of regular mail)."

Writers' Conferences ASJA Writers Conference.

Tips "Please make sure you are ready before approaching us or any other agent. If you write fiction, make sure it is the best work you can do and get objective criticism from a writing group. If you write nonfiction, make sure the proposal exhibits your best work and a comprehensive understanding of the market."

⊠ ◻ THE AUGUST AGENCY LLC

E-mail: submissions@augustagency.com. Web site: www.augustagency.com. **Contact:** Cricket Pechstein, Jefferey McGraw. Estab. 2004. Represents 25-40 clients. 50% of clients are new/unpublished writers. Currently handles: 75% nonfiction books; 20% novels; 5% other.

    ● Before opening The August Agency, Ms. Pechstein was a freelance writer, magazine editor, and independant literary agent; Mr. McGraw worked for magazines and book publishers doing editorial, public relations, publicity, advertising, and promotional work.

Member Agents Jeffery McGraw (narrative/commercial nonfiction, chick lit, women's fiction, self-help, literary fiction); Cricket Pechstein (mystery/crime fiction, chick lit, thrillers).

Represents Nonfiction books, novels. **Considers these nonfiction areas:** Biography/autobiography; business/

economics; child guidance/parenting; cooking/foods/nutrition; current affairs; ethnic/cultural interests; gay/lesbian issues; government/politics/law; health/medicine; history; how-to; humor/satire; interior design/decorating; memoirs; military/war; money/finance; music/dance; popular culture; psychology; self-help/personal improvement; sociology; sports; theater/film; true crime/investigative; women's issues/studies; Inspirational. **Considers these fiction areas:** Action/adventure; detective/police/crime; ethnic; family saga; gay/lesbian; historical; humor/satire; literary; mainstream/contemporary; mystery/suspense; psychic/supernatural; thriller; Smart chick lit (non-genre romance).

O— "We actively pursue an array of fiction and nonfiction writers to represent, with an emphasis in media (seasoned journalists receive special favor here), popular culture/entertainment, political science, diet/fitness, health, cookbooks, psychology, business, memoir, highly creative nonfiction, accessible literary fiction, women's fiction, and high-concept mysteries and thrillers. When it comes to nonfiction, we favor persuasive and prescriptive works with a full-bodied narrative command and an undeniable contemporary relevance. Our favorite novelists are as eclectic as our minds are broad, yet they all share one common denominator that might explain a peculiar predisposition for what we prefer to call "emotion fiction"—a brand of storytelling defined not so much by a novel's category as by its extraordinary power to resonate universally on a deeply emotional level." Does not want to receive academic textbooks, children's books, cozy mysteries, horror, poetry, science fiction/fantasy, short story collections, westerns, or genre romance.

How to Contact Submit book summary (1-2 paragraphs), chapter outline (nonfiction only), first 1,000 words or first chapter, total page/word count, brief paragraph on why you have chosen to write the book. Send via e-mail only (no attachments). Considers simultaneous queries. Responds in 2-3 weeks to queries; 3 months to mss. Obtains most new clients through recommendations from others, solicitations, conferences.

Terms Agent receives 15% commission on domestic sales; 20% commission on foreign sales. Offers written contract; 1-month notice must be given to terminate contract.

Writers' Conferences Surrey International Writers' Conference.

AUTHENTIC CREATIONS LITERARY AGENCY

911 Duluth Hwy., Suite D3-144, Lawrenceville GA 30043. (770)339-3774. Fax: (770)339-7126. E-mail: ron@authenticcreations.com. Web site: www.authenticcreations.com. **Contact:** Mary Lee Laitsch. Estab. 1993. Member of AAR, Authors Guild. Represents 70 clients. 30% of clients are new/unpublished writers. Currently handles: 60% nonfiction books; 40% novels.

• Prior to becoming an agent, Ms. Laitsch was a librarian and an elementary school teacher; Mr. Laitsch was an attorney and a writer.

Member Agents Mary Lee Laitsch; Ronald Laitsch; Jason Laitsch.

Represents Nonfiction books, novels, scholarly books. **Considers these nonfiction areas:** Anthropology/archaeology; biography/autobiography; child guidance/parenting; crafts/hobbies; current affairs; history; how-to; science/technology; self-help/personal improvement; sports; true crime/investigative; women's issues/studies. **Considers these fiction areas:** Action/adventure; detective/police/crime; family saga; literary; mainstream/contemporary; mystery/suspense; romance; sports; thriller.

How to Contact Query with SASE. No e-mail or fax queries. Considers simultaneous queries. Responds in 2 weeks to queries; 2 months to mss.

Recent Sales Sold 20 titles in the last year. *Secret Agent*, by Robyn Spizman and Mark Johnston (Simon & Schuster); *Beauchamp Beseiged*, by Elaine Knighton (Harlequin); *Visible Differences*, by Dominic Pulera (Continuum).

Terms Agent receives 15% commission on domestic sales; 15% commission on foreign sales. Charges clients for photocopying.

Tips "We thoroughly enjoy what we do. What makes being an agent so satisfying for us is having the opportunity to work with authors who are as excited about the works they write as we are about representing them."

THE AXELROD AGENCY

55 Main St., P.O. Box 357, Chatham NY 12037. (518)392-2100. Fax: (518)392-2944. E-mail: steve@axelrodagency.com. **Contact:** Steven Axelrod. Estab. 1983. Member of AAR. Represents 20-30 clients. 1% of clients are new/unpublished writers. Currently handles: 5% nonfiction books; 95% novels.

• Prior to becoming an agent, Mr. Axelrod was a book club editor.

Represents Nonfiction books, novels. **Considers these fiction areas:** Mystery/suspense; romance; women's.

How to Contact Query with SASE. Considers simultaneous queries. Responds in 3 weeks to queries; 6 weeks to mss. Returns materials only with SASE. Obtains most new clients through recommendations from others.

Recent Sales This agency prefers not to share information on specific sales.

Terms Agent receives 15% commission on domestic sales; 20% commission on foreign sales. No written contract.

Writers' Conferences RWA National Conference

◢ BARER LITERARY, LLC

156 Fifth Ave., Suite 1134, New York NY 10010. Web site: www.barerliterary.com. **Contact:** Julie Barer. Member of AAR.

Represents Nonfiction books, novels, short story collections. **Considers these nonfiction areas:** Biography/autobiography; ethnic/cultural interests; history; memoirs; popular culture; women's issues/studies. **Considers these fiction areas:** Ethnic; family saga; historical; literary; mainstream/contemporary; young adult.

How to Contact Query with SASE.

Recent Sales *Jupiter's Palace*, by Lauren Fox (Knopf); *Then We Came to the End*, by Joshua Ferris (Little, Brown); *Why Can't We Be Friends*, by Megan Crane (Warner Books); *The Time It Takes to Fall*, by Margaret Lazarus Dean (Simon & Schuster).

Terms Agent receives 15% commission on domestic sales; 20% commission on foreign sales. Offers written contract. Charges for photocopying and books ordered.

◢ LORETTA BARRETT BOOKS, INC.

101 Fifth Ave., New York NY 10003. (212)242-3420. Fax: (212)807-9579. E-mail: mail@lorettabarrettbooks.com. **Contact:** Loretta A. Barrett, Nick Mullendore. Estab. 1990. Member of AAR. Currently handles: 60% nonfiction books; 40% novels.

• Prior to opening her agency, Ms. Barrett was vice president and executive editor at Doubleday and editor-in-chief of Anchor Books.

Represents Nonfiction books, novels. **Considers these nonfiction areas:** Biography/autobiography; business/economics; child guidance/parenting; current affairs; ethnic/cultural interests; gay/lesbian issues; government/politics/law; health/medicine; history; language/literature/criticism; memoirs; money/finance; multicultural; nature/environment; philosophy; popular culture; psychology; religious/inspirational; science/technology; self-help/personal improvement; sociology; spirituality; sports; women's issues/studies; Nutrition; creative nonfiction. **Considers these fiction areas:** Action/adventure; contemporary issues; detective/police/crime; ethnic; family saga; historical; literary; mainstream/contemporary; mystery/suspense; psychic/supernatural; thriller.

○━ This agency specializes in general interest books. No children's, juvenile, science fiction, or fantasy.

How to Contact Query with SASE. No e-mail or fax queries. Considers simultaneous queries. Responds in 2-3 weeks to queries. Returns materials only with SASE.

Recent Sales *Dark Circles*, by Lila Shaara (Ballantine); *The Secret Power of Yoga*, by Nischala Joy Devi (Harmony); *Riverside Park*, by Laura Van Wormer (Mira); *Healing the Schism*, by Mark Judge (Doubleday); The Truth series, by Mariah Stewart (Ballantine); The Reincarnationist series, by M.J. Rose (Mira).

Terms Agent receives 15% commission on domestic sales; 20% commission on foreign sales. Offers written contract. Charges clients for shipping and photocopying.

Writers' Conferences San Diego State University Writers' Conference; Pacific Northwest Writers Conference; SEAK Medical & Legal Fiction Writing Conference.

Ⓝ ◢ FAYE BENDER LITERARY AGENCY

337 W. 76th St., #E1, New York NY 10023. E-mail: info@fbliterary.com. Web site: www.fbliterary.com. **Contact:** Faye Bender. Estab. 2004. Member of AAR. Currently handles: 50% nonfiction books; 50% novels.

Represents Nonfiction books, novels. **Considers these nonfiction areas:** Memoirs; popular culture; women's issues/studies; Narrative; health; biography; popular science. **Considers these fiction areas:** Literary; young adult (middle-grade); Women's; commercial.

○━ "I choose books based on the narrative voice and strength of writing. I work with previously published and first-time authors." Does not want genre fiction (westerns, romance, horror, fantasy, science fiction).

How to Contact Query with SASE, 10 sample pages via mail or e-mail.

◢ MEREDITH BERNSTEIN LITERARY AGENCY

2095 Broadway, Suite 505, New York NY 10023. (212)799-1007. Fax: (212)799-1145. Estab. 1981. Member of AAR. Represents 85 clients. 20% of clients are new/unpublished writers. Currently handles: 50% nonfiction books; 50% fiction.

• Prior to opening her agency, Ms. Bernstein served at another agency for 5 years.

Represents Nonfiction books, novels. **Considers these nonfiction areas:** Any area of nonfiction in which the author has an established platform. **Considers these fiction areas:** Literary; mystery/suspense; romance; thriller; women's.

○━ This agency does not specialize. It is very eclectic.

How to Contact Query with SASE. No e-mail or fax queries. Considers simultaneous queries. Obtains most new clients through recommendations from others, conferences, developing/packaging ideas.

Recent Sales *No Cry Discipline Solution*, by Elizabeth Pantley (McGraw-Hill); *Asking For It*, by Tory Johnson and Robyn Spizman (St. Martin's Press); *The House of Night*, by P.C. Cast (St. Martin's press).

Terms Agent receives 15% commission on domestic sales; 20% commission on foreign sales. Charges clients $75 disbursement fee/year.

Writers' Conferences Southwest Writers Conference; Rocky Mountain Fiction Writers Colorado Gold; Pacific Northwest Writers' Conference; Willamette Writers Conference; Surrey International Writers Conference; San Diego State University Writers' Conference.

◙ BIGSCORE PRODUCTIONS, INC.

P.O. Box 4575, Lancaster PA 17604. (717)293-0247. E-mail: bigscore@bigscoreproductions.com. Web site: www.bigscoreproductions.com. **Contact:** David A. Robie. Estab. 1995. Represents 50-75 clients. 25% of clients are new/unpublished writers.

Represents Nonfiction and fiction (see Web site for categories of interest).

> O–┐ Mr. Robie specializes in inspirational and self-help nonfiction and fiction, and has been in the publishing and agenting business for over 20 years.

How to Contact See Web site for submission guidelines. Query by e-mail only. Do not fax or mail queries. Considers simultaneous queries. Only responds if interested.

Terms Agent receives 15% commission on domestic sales. Offers written contract, binding for 6 months. Charges clients for expedited shipping, ms photocopying and preparation, books for subsidiary rights submissions.

Tips "We are very open to taking on new nonfiction clients. We only consider established fiction writers. Submit a well-prepared proposal that will take minimal fine-tuning for presentation to publishers. Nonfiction writers must be highly marketable and media savvy—the more established in speaking or in your profession, the better. Bigscore Productions works with all major general and Christian publishers."

◙ BLEECKER STREET ASSOCIATES, INC.

532 LaGuardia Place, #617, New York NY 10012. (212)677-4492. Fax: (212)388-0001. **Contact:** Agnes Birnbaum. Estab. 1984. Member of AAR, RWA, MWA. Represents 60 clients. 20% of clients are new/unpublished writers. Currently handles: 75% nonfiction books; 25% novels.

- Prior to becoming an agent, Ms. Birnbaum was a senior editor at Simon & Schuster, Dutton/Signet, and other publishing houses.

Represents Nonfiction books, novels. **Considers these nonfiction areas:** Animals; biography/autobiography; business/economics; child guidance/parenting; computers/electronic; cooking/foods/nutrition; current affairs; ethnic/cultural interests; government/politics/law; health/medicine; history; how-to; memoirs; military/war; money/finance; nature/environment; New Age/metaphysics; popular culture; psychology; religious/inspirational; science/technology; self-help/personal improvement; sociology; sports; true crime/investigative; women's issues/studies. **Considers these fiction areas:** Ethnic; historical; literary; mystery/suspense; romance; thriller; women's.

> O–┐ "We're very hands-on and accessible. We try to be truly creative in our submission approaches. We've had especially good luck with first-time authors." Does not want to receive science fiction, westerns, poetry, children's books, academic/scholarly/professional books, plays, scripts, or short stories.

How to Contact Query with SASE. No email, phone, or fax queries. Considers simultaneous queries. Responds in 2 weeks to queries; 1 month to mss. Returns materials only with SASE. Obtains most new clients through recommendations from others, solicitations, conferences, "plus, I will approach someone with a letter if his/her work impresses me."

Recent Sales Sold 20 titles in the last year. *How America Got It Right*, by Bevin Alexander (Crown); *Buddha Baby*, by Kim Wong Keltner (Morrow/Avon); *American Bee*, by James Maguire (Rodale); *Guide to the Galaxy*, by Pat Barnes-Svarney (Sterling); *Phantom Warrior*, by Bryant Johnson (Berkley).

Terms Agent receives 15% commission on domestic sales; 25% commission on foreign sales. Offers written contract; 1-month notice must be given to terminate contract. Charges for postage, long distance, fax, messengers, photocopies (not to exceed $200).

Tips "Keep query letters short and to the point; include only information pertaining to the book or background as a writer. Try to avoid superlatives in description. Work needs to stand on its own, so how much editing it may have received has no place in a query letter."

◙ THE BLUMER LITERARY AGENCY, INC.

350 Seventh Ave., Suite 2003, New York NY 10001-5013. (212)947-3040. **Contact:** Olivia B. Blumer. Estab. 2002; Board member of AAR. Represents 34 clients. 60% of clients are new/unpublished writers. Currently handles: 67% nonfiction books; 33% novels.

- Prior to becoming an agent, Ms. Blumer spent 25 years in publishing (subsidiary rights, publicity, editorial).

Represents Nonfiction books, novels. **Considers these nonfiction areas:** Agriculture/horticulture; animals;

anthropology/archaeology; art/architecture/design; biography/autobiography; business/economics; cooking/foods/nutrition; ethnic/cultural interests; health/medicine; how-to; humor/satire; language/literature/criticism; memoirs; money/finance; nature/environment; photography; popular culture; psychology; religious/inspirational; self-help/personal improvement; true crime/investigative; women's issues/studies; New Age/metaphysics; crafts/hobbies; interior design/decorating. **Considers these fiction areas:** Detective/police/crime; ethnic; family saga; feminist; historical; humor/satire; literary; mainstream/contemporary; mystery/suspense; regional; thriller.

O⊸ Actively seeking quality fiction, practical nonfiction, and memoir with a larger purpose.

How to Contact Query with SASE. No e-mail or fax queries. Responds in 2 weeks to queries; 4-6 weeks to mss. Returns materials only with SASE. Obtains most new clients through recommendations from others, but significant exceptions have come from the slush pile.

Recent Sales *The Color of Law*, by Mark Gimenez; *Still Life with Chickens*, by Catherine Goldhammer. Other clients include Joan Anderson, Marialisa Calta, Ellen Rolfes, Mark Forstater, Laura Karr, Liz McGregor, Constance Snow, Lauri Ward, Michelle Curry Wright, Susann Cokal, Dennis L. Smith, Sharon Pywell, Sarah Turnbull, Naomi Duguid, Jeffrey Alford.

Terms Agent receives 15% commission on domestic sales; 20% commission on foreign sales. Charges for photocopying, overseas shipping, FedEx/UPS.

☑ BOOKENDS, LLC

136 Long Hill Rd., Gillette NJ 07933. E-mail: editor@bookends-inc.com. Web site: www.bookends-inc.com. **Contact:** Jessica Faust, Jacky Sach, Kim Lionetti. Estab. 1999. Represents 50+ clients. 20% of clients are new/unpublished writers. Currently handles: 50% nonfiction books; 50% novels.

Represents Nonfiction books, novels. **Considers these nonfiction areas:** Business/economics; child guidance/parenting; ethnic/cultural interests; gay/lesbian issues; health/medicine; how-to; money/finance; New Age/metaphysics; psychology; religious/inspirational; self-help/personal improvement; spirituality; true crime/investigative; women's issues/studies. **Considers these fiction areas:** Detective/police/crime (cozies); mainstream/contemporary; mystery/suspense; romance; thriller; Chick lit.

O⊸ BookEnds does not want to receive children's books, screenplays, science fiction, poetry, or technical/military thrillers.

How to Contact Review Web site for guidelines.

☑ BOOKS & SUCH

52 Mission Circle, Suite 122, PMB 170, Santa Rosa CA 95409. E-mail: representative@booksandsuch.biz. Web site: www.booksandsuch.biz. **Contact:** Janet Kobobel Grant, Wendy Lawton. Estab. 1996. Member of CBA (associate), American Christian Fiction Writers. Represents 80 clients. 5% of clients are new/unpublished writers. Currently handles: 49% nonfiction books; 50% novels; 1% children's picture books.

● Prior to becoming an agent, Ms. Grant was an editor for Zondervan and managing editor for *Focus on the Family*; Ms. Lawton was an author, sculptor, and designer of porcelein dolls.

Represents Nonfiction books, novels, children's picture books. **Considers these nonfiction areas:** Child guidance/parenting; humor/satire; juvenile nonfiction; religious/inspirational; self-help/personal improvement; women's issues/studies. **Considers these fiction areas:** Contemporary issues; family saga; historical; juvenile; mainstream/contemporary; picture books; religious/inspirational; romance; African American adult.

O⊸ This agency specializes in general and inspirational fiction, romance, and in the Christian booksellers market. Actively seeking well-crafted material that presents Judeo-Christian values, if only subtly.

How to Contact Query with SASE. Considers simultaneous queries. Responds in 1 month to queries; 2 months to mss. Returns materials only with SASE. Obtains most new clients through recommendations from others, conferences.

Recent Sales Sold 112 titles in the last year. *My Life As a Doormat (In Three Acts)*, by Rene Gutterridge; *Having a Mary Spirit*, by Joanna Weaver; *Finding Father Christmas*, by Robin Jones Gunn; *No More Mr. Christian Nice Guy*, by Paul Coughlin. Other clients include Janet McHenry, Jane Orcutt, Gayle Roper, Stephanie Grace Whitson, Dale Cramer, Patti Hill, Gayle Roper, Sara Horn.

Terms Agent receives 15% commission on domestic sales; 15% commission on foreign sales. Offers written contract; 2-month notice must be given to terminate contract. Charges clients for postage, photocopying, telephone calls, fax, express mail.

Writers' Conferences Mount Hermon Christian Writers Conference; Wrangling With Writing; Glorieta Christian Writers' Conference; Writing for the Soul; Blue Ridge Mountains Christian Writers Conference; Write! Canada; American Christian Fiction Writers Conference; Sandy Cove Christian Writers Conference.

Tips ''The heart of our agency's motivation is to develop relationships with the authors we serve, to do what we can to shine the light of success on them, and to help be a caretaker of their gifts and time.''

⚫ BRANDT & HOCHMAN LITERARY AGENTS, INC.

1501 Broadway, Suite 2310, New York NY 10036. (212)840-5760. Fax: (212)840-5776. Estab. 1913. Member of AAR. Represents 200 clients.

Member Agents Carl Brandt; Gail Hochman; Marianne Merola; Charles Schlessiger.

Represents Nonfiction books, novels, short story collections, juvenile books, journalism. **Considers these nonfiction areas:** Biography/autobiography; current affairs; ethnic/cultural interests; government/politics/law; history; women's issues/studies. **Considers these fiction areas:** Contemporary issues; ethnic; historical; literary; mainstream/contemporary; mystery/suspense; romance; thriller; young adult.

How to Contact Query with SASE. No e-mail or fax queries. Considers simultaneous queries. Responds in 1 month to queries. Returns materials only with SASE. Obtains most new clients through recommendations from others.

Recent Sales This agency prefers not to share information on specific sales.

Terms Agent receives 15% commission on domestic sales; 20% commission on foreign sales. Charges clients for ms duplication or other special expenses agreed to in advance.

Tips "Write a letter which will give the agent a sense of you as a professional writer—your long-term interests as well as a short description of the work at hand."

⚫ BARBARA BRAUN ASSOCIATES, INC.

104 Fifth Ave., 7th Floor, New York NY 10011. Fax: (212)604-9041. E-mail: bba230@earthlink.net. Web site: www.barbarabraunagency.com. **Contact:** Barbara Braun. Member of AAR.

Member Agents Barbara Braun; John F. Baker.

Represents Nonfiction books, novels.

    ○┰ "Our fiction is strong on women's stories, historical and multicultural stories, as well as mysteries and thrillers. We're interested in narrative nonfiction and books by journalists. We do not represent poetry, science fiction, fantasy, horror, or screenplays." Look online for more details.

How to Contact Query with SASE. Accepts e-mail queries (no full mss).

Recent Sales *Life Studies*, by Susan Vreeland (Viking/Penguin); *The Lost Van Gogh*, by A.J. Zerries (Tor/Forge); *Sakharov: Science and Freedom*, by Gennady Gorelik and Antonina Bouis (Oxford University Press); *A Strand of Corpses* and *A Friend of Need*, by J.R. Benn (Soho Press).

Terms Agent receives 15% commission on domestic sales; 20% commission on foreign sales.

Ⓝ ⚫ BROWN LITERARY AGENCY

410 7th St. NW, Naples FL 34120. (239)455-7190. E-mail: broagent@aol.com. Web site: www.brownliteraryagency.com. **Contact:** Roberta Brown. Estab. 1996. Member of AAR, RWA, Author's Guild. Represents 35 clients. 5% of clients are new/unpublished writers.

    ● Prior to becoming an agent, Ms. Brown worked in a literacy program at a local high school.

Represents Novels. **Considers these fiction areas:** Erotica; romance (single title and category); Women's.

How to Contact Submit synopsis, 3 sample chapters. No e-mail or fax queries. Considers simultaneous queries. Responds in 4-6 weeks to queries; 2 months to mss. Obtains most new clients through recommendations from others, conferences, visitors to Web site.

Recent Sales Sold 35 titles in the last year. Clients include Emma Holly, Angela Knight, Karen Kay, Jenna Mills, Dianne Castell, Lora Leigh, Shiloh Walker, Kate Angell, Sue-Ellen Welfonder.

Terms Agent receives 15% commission on domestic sales; 15% commission on foreign sales. Offers written contract; 30-day notice must be given to terminate contract.

Writers' Conferences RWA National Conference; Romantic Times Convention.

Tips "Polish your manuscript. Be professional."

⚫ CURTIS BROWN, LTD.

10 Astor Place, New York NY 10003-6935. (212)473-5400. Alternate address: Peter Ginsberg, president at CBF, 1750 Montgomery St., San Francisco CA 94111. (415)954-8566. Member of AAR; signatory of WGA.

Member Agents Laura Blake Peterson; Emilie Jacobson, senior vice president; Maureen Walters, senior vice president; Ginger Knowlton, vice president (children's); Timothy Knowlton, CEO (film, screenplays); Ed Wintle; Mitchell Waters; Elizabeth Harding.

Represents Nonfiction books, novels, short story collections, juvenile books. **Considers these nonfiction areas:** Agriculture/horticulture; americana; animals; anthropology/archaeology; art/architecture/design; biography/autobiography; business/economics; child guidance/parenting; computers/electronic; cooking/foods/nutrition; crafts/hobbies; current affairs; education; ethnic/cultural interests; gardening; gay/lesbian issues; government/politics/law; health/medicine; history; how-to; humor/satire; interior design/decorating; juvenile nonfiction; language/literature/criticism; memoirs; military/war; money/finance; multicultural; music/dance; nature/environment; New Age/metaphysics; philosophy; photography; popular culture; psychology; recreation;

regional; religious/inspirational; science/technology; self-help/personal improvement; sex; sociology; software; spirituality; sports; theater/film; translation; travel; true crime/investigative; women's issues/studies; young adult; Creative nonfiction. **Considers these fiction areas:** Action/adventure; comic books/cartoon; confession; contemporary issues; detective/police/crime; erotica; ethnic; experimental; family saga; fantasy; feminist; gay/lesbian; glitz; gothic; hi-lo; historical; horror; humor/satire; juvenile; literary; mainstream/contemporary; military/war; multicultural; multimedia; mystery/suspense; New Age; occult; picture books; plays; poetry; psychic/supernatural; regional; religious/inspirational; romance; science fiction; short story collections; spiritual; sports; thriller; translation; westerns/frontier; young adult; women's.

How to Contact Query individual agent with SASE. Prefers to read materials exclusively. *No unsolicited mss.* No e-mail or fax queries. Responds in 3 weeks to queries; 5 weeks to mss. Obtains most new clients through recommendations from others, solicitations, conferences.

Recent Sales This agency prefers not to share information on specific sales.

Terms Offers written contract. Charges for photocopying and some postage.

BROWNE & MILLER LITERARY ASSOCIATES

410 S. Michigan Ave., Suite 460, Chicago IL 60605-1465. (312)922-3063. E-mail: mail@browneandmiller.com. **Contact:** Danielle Egan-Miller. Estab. 1971. Member of AAR, RWA, MWA, Author's Guild. Represents 150 clients. 2% of clients are new/unpublished writers. Currently handles: 40% nonfiction books; 60% novels.

Represents Nonfiction books, novels. **Considers these nonfiction areas:** Agriculture/horticulture; animals; anthropology/archaeology; biography/autobiography; business/economics; child guidance/parenting; cooking/foods/nutrition; crafts/hobbies; creative nonfiction (1); current affairs; ethnic/cultural interests; health/medicine; how-to; humor/satire; memoirs; money/finance; nature/environment; popular culture; psychology; religious/inspirational; science/technology; self-help/personal improvement; sociology; sports; true crime/investigative; women's issues/studies. **Considers these fiction areas:** Detective/police/crime; ethnic; family saga; glitz; historical; literary; mainstream/contemporary; mystery/suspense; religious/inspirational; romance (contemporary, gothic, historical, regency); sports; thriller.

⊶ "We are generalists looking for professional writers with finely honed skills in writing. We are partial to authors with promotion savvy. We work closely with our authors through the whole publishing process, from proposal to after publication." Actively seeking highly commercial mainstream fiction and nonfiction. Does not represent poetry, short stories, plays, screenplays, articles, or children's books.

How to Contact Query with SASE. *No unsolicited mss.* Prefers to read material exclusively. Responds in 6 weeks to queries. Returns materials only with SASE. Obtains most new clients through referrals, queries by professional/marketable authors.

Terms Agent receives 15% commission on domestic sales; 20% commission on foreign sales. Offers written contract, binding for 2 years. Charges clients for photocopying, overseas postage, faxes, phone calls.

Writers' Conferences BookExpo America; Frankfurt Book Fair; RWA National Conference; CBA National Conference; London Book Fair; Bouchercon.

Tips "If interested in agency representation, be well informed."

PEMA BROWNE, LTD.

11 Tena Place, Valley Cottage NY 10989. Web site: www.pemabrowneltd.com. **Contact:** Pema Browne. Estab. 1966. Member of SCBWI, RWA; signatory of WGA. Represents 30 clients. Currently handles: 25% nonfiction books; 50% novels/romance novels; 25% juvenile books.

• Prior to opening her agency, Ms. Browne was an artist and art buyer.

Represents Nonfiction books, novels, juvenile books, reference books. **Considers these nonfiction areas:** Business/economics; child guidance/parenting; cooking/foods/nutrition; ethnic/cultural interests; gay/lesbian issues; health/medicine; how-to; juvenile nonfiction; military/war; money/finance; New Age/metaphysics; popular culture; psychology; religious/inspirational; self-help/personal improvement; spirituality; true crime/investigative; women's issues/studies; Reference. **Considers these fiction areas:** Action/adventure; contemporary issues; detective/police/crime; feminist; gay/lesbian; glitz; historical; humor/satire; juvenile; literary; mainstream/contemporary (commercial); mystery/suspense; picture books; psychic/supernatural; religious/inspirational; romance (contemporary, gothic, historical, regency); young adult.

⊶ "We are not accepting any new projects or authors until further notice."

How to Contact Query with SASE. No e-mail or fax queries. Responds in 6 weeks to queries; 6-8 weeks to mss. Returns materials only with SASE. Obtains most new clients through editors, authors, *LMP, Guide to Literary Agents.*

Recent Sales *The Daring Harriet Quimby*, by Suzane Whitaker (Holiday House); *One Night to Be Sinful*, by Samantha Garver (Kensington); *Point Eyes of the Dragon*, by Linda Cargill (Cora Verlag).

Terms Agent receives 20% commission on domestic sales; 20% commission on foreign sales.

Tips "We do not review manuscripts that have been sent out to publishers. If writing romance, be sure to receive guidelines from various romance publishers. In nonfiction, one must have credentials to lend credence to a proposal. Make sure of margins, double-space, and use clean, dark type."

☕ SHEREE BYKOFSKY ASSOCIATES, INC.

16 W. 36th St., 13th Floor, New York NY 10018. E-mail: shereebee@aol.com. Web site: www.shereebee.com. **Contact:** Sheree Bykofsky. Estab. 1984, incorporated 1991. Member of AAR, ASJA, WNBA. Currently handles: 80% nonfiction books; 20% novels.

- Prior to opening her agency, Ms. Bykofsky served as executive editor of The Stonesong Press and managing editor of Chiron Press. She is also the author or co-author of more than 20 books, including *The Complete Idiot's Guide to Getting Published*. Ms. Bykofsky teaches publishing at NYU and SEAK, Inc.

Member Agents Janet Rosen, associate; Caroline Woods, associate.

Represents Nonfiction books, novels. **Considers these nonfiction areas:** Americana; animals; art/architecture/ design; biography/autobiography; business/economics; child guidance/parenting; cooking/foods/nutrition; crafts/hobbies; current affairs; education; ethnic/cultural interests; gardening; gay/lesbian issues; government/ politics/law; health/medicine; history; how-to; humor/satire; interior design/decorating; language/literature/ criticism; memoirs; military/war; money/finance (personal finance); multicultural; music/dance; nature/environment; New Age/metaphysics; philosophy; photography; popular culture; psychology; recreation; regional; religious/inspirational; science/technology; self-help/personal improvement; sex; sociology; spirituality; sports; theater/film; translation; travel; true crime/investigative; women's issues/studies; Anthropolgy; creative nonfiction. **Considers these fiction areas:** Literary; mainstream/contemporary; mystery/suspense.

- ⚷ This agency specializes in popular reference nonfiction, commercial fiction with a literary quality, and mysteries. "I have wide-ranging interests, but it really depends on quality of writing, originality, and how a particular project appeals to me (or not). I take on fiction when I completely love it—it doesn't matter what area or genre." Does not want to receive poetry, material for children, screenplays, westerns, horror, science fiction, or fantasy.

How to Contact Query with SASE. No unsolicited mss, e-mail queries, or phone calls. Considers simultaneous queries. Responds in 3 weeks to queries with SASE. Responds in 1 month to requested mss. Returns materials only with SASE. Obtains most new clients through recommendations from others.

Recent Sales Sold 100 titles in the last year. *Self-Esteem Sickness*, by Albert Ellis (Prometheus); *When the Ghost Screams*, by Leslie Rule (Andrews McMeel); *225 Squares*, by Matt Gaffney (Avalon).

Terms Agent receives 15% commission on domestic sales; 20% commission on foreign sales. Offers written contract, binding for 1 year. Charges for postage, photocopying, fax.

Writers' Conferences ASJA Writers Conference; Asilomar; Florida Suncoast Writers' Conference; Whidbey Island Writers' Conference; Florida First Coast Writers' Festibal; Agents and Editors Conference; Columbus Writers Conference; Southwest Writers Conference; Willamette Writers Conferece; Dorothy Canfield Fisher Conference; Maui Writers Conference; Pacific Northwest Writers Conference; IWWG.

Tips "Read the agent listing carefully and comply with guidelines."

ⓒ CANTON SMITH AGENCY

194 Broadway, Amityville NY 11701. (631)842-9476 or (210)379-5961. E-mail: bookhold2@yahoo.com; esmith1 67@hotmail.com. Alternate address: 11955 Parliament Rd., #1008, San Antonio TX 78216. **Contact:** Eric Smith, senior partner; Chamein Canton, partner. Estab. 2001. Represents 28 clients. 100% of clients are new/unpublished writers.

- Prior to becoming agents, Mr. Smith was in advertising and bookstore retail; Ms. Canton was a writer and a paralegal.

Member Agents Eric Smith (science fiction, sports, literature); Chamein Canton (how-to, reference, literary, women's, multicultural, ethnic, crafts, cooking, health); Melissa Falcone (childrens, juvenile, young adult, teen, fantasy).

Represents Nonfiction books, novels, juvenile books, scholarly books, textbooks, movie scripts. **Considers these nonfiction areas:** Art/architecture/design; business/economics; child guidance/parenting; cooking/ foods/nutrition; education; ethnic/cultural interests; health/medicine; history; how-to; humor/satire; language/ literature/criticism; memoirs; military/war; music/dance; photography; psychology; sports; translation; women's issues/studies. **Considers these fiction areas:** Fantasy; humor/satire; juvenile; multicultural; romance; young adult; Latina fiction; chick lit; African-American fiction; entertainment. **Considers these script subject areas:** Action/adventure; comedy; romantic comedy; romantic drama; science fiction.

- ⚷ "We specialize in helping new and established writers expand their marketing potential for prospective publishers. We are currently focusing on women's fiction (chick lit), Latina fiction, African American fiction, multicultural, romance, memoirs, humor, and entertainment, in addition to more nonfiction titles (cooking, how to, fashion, home improvement, etc)."

How to Contact Query with SASE or e-mail query with synopsis (preferred); include the title and genre in the subject line. Send nonfiction snail mail to Chamein Canton at New York address. Send all other snail mail queries to Eric Smith at Texas address. Considers simultaneous queries. Responds in 3 weeks to queries; 6 weeks to mss. Obtains most new clients through recommendations from others.

Recent Sales Sold 7 titles in the last year. Clients include Robert Koger, Olivia, Jennifer DeWit, Sheila Smestad, James Weil, Jaime Nava, JC Miller, Diana Smith, Robert Beers, Marcy Gannon, Keith Maxwell, Dawn Jackson, Jeannine Carney, Mark Barlow, Robert Marsocci, Anita Ballard Jones, Deb Mohr, Seth Ahonen, Melissa Graf, Robert Zavala, Cliff Webb, John and Carolyn Osborne.

Terms Agent receives 15% commission on domestic sales; 20% commission on foreign sales. Offers written contract; 2-month notice must be given to terminate contract.

Tips "Know your market. Agents, as well as publishers, are keenly interested in writers with their finger on the pulse of their market."

◙ CASTIGLIA LITERARY AGENCY

1155 Camino Del Mar, Suite 510, Del Mar CA 92014. (858)755-8761. Fax: (858)755-7063. Estab. 1993. Member of AAR, PEN. Represents 50 clients. Currently handles: 55% nonfiction books; 45% novels.

Member Agents Julie Castiglia; Winifred Golden; Sally Van Haitsma.

Represents Nonfiction books, novels. **Considers these nonfiction areas:** Animals; anthropology/archaeology; biography/autobiography; business/economics; child guidance/parenting; cooking/foods/nutrition; current affairs; ethnic/cultural interests; health/medicine; history; language/literature/criticism; money/finance; nature/environment; psychology; religious/inspirational; science/technology; self-help/personal improvement; women's issues/studies. **Considers these fiction areas:** Ethnic; literary; mainstream/contemporary; mystery/suspense; women's.

 O➔ Does not want to receive horror, screenplays, poetry, or academic nonfiction.

How to Contact Query with SASE. No fax queries. Returns materials only with SASE. Obtains most new clients through recommendations from others, solicitations, conferences.

Recent Sales Sold 26 titles in the last year. *Never Bet the Farm*, by Anthony Iaquinto and Stephen Spinelli Jr. (Wiley); *Invisible Lives*, by Anjali Banerjee (Pocket Books); *Orphan's Destiny*, by Robert Buettner (Warner); *What Should I Eat*, by Tershia d'Elgin (Random House); *Urban Gardens*, by Brian Coleman (Gibbs Smith).

Terms Agent receives 15% commission on domestic sales; 25% commission on foreign sales. Offers written contract; 6-week notice must be given to terminate contract.

Writers' Conferences Santa Barbara Writers Conference; Southern California Writers' Conference; Surrey International Writers' Conference; San Diego State University Writers' Conference; Willamette Writers Conference.

Tips "Be professional with submissions. Attend workshops and conferences before you approach an agent."

◙ JANE CHELIUS LITERARY AGENCY

548 Second St., Brooklyn NY 11215. (718)499-0236. Fax: (718)832-7335. E-mail: queries@janechelius.com. Web site: www.janechelius.com. Member of AAR.

Represents Nonfiction books, novels. **Considers these nonfiction areas:** Humor/satire; women's issues/studies; Science; parenting; medicine; biography; military history; narrative. **Considers these fiction areas:** Fantasy; literary; mystery/suspense; science fiction; women's; Men's adventure.

 O➔ Does not want to receive children's books, stage plays, screenplays, or poetry.

How to Contact Query with synopsis, cover letter, SASE. Accepts e-mail queries. *No unsolicited chapters or mss.* Responds in 3-4 weeks to queries.

◙ WM CLARK ASSOCIATES

154 Christopher St., Suite 3C, New York NY 10014. (212)675-2784. Fax: (646)349-1658. E-mail: query@wmclark .com. Web site: www.wmclark.com. Estab. 1997. Member of AAR. 50% of clients are new/unpublished writers. Currently handles: 50% nonfiction books; 50% novels.

 ● Prior to opening WCA, Mr. Clark was an agent at the William Morris Agency.

Represents Nonfiction books, novels. **Considers these nonfiction areas:** Art/architecture/design; biography/autobiography; current affairs; ethnic/cultural interests; history; memoirs; music/dance; popular culture; religious/inspirational (Eastern philosophy only); science/technology; sociology; theater/film; translation. **Considers these fiction areas:** Contemporary issues; ethnic; historical; literary; mainstream/contemporary; Southern fiction.

 O➔ "Building on a reputation for moving quickly and strategically on behalf of his clients, and offering individual focus and a global presence, William Clark practices an aggressive, innovative, and broad-ranged approach to the representation of content and the talent that creates it. His clients range from authors of first fiction and award-winning bestselling narrative nonfiction, to international authors in translation, musicians, and artists."

How to Contact E-mail queries only. Prefers to read requested materials exclusively. Responds in 1-2 months to queries.

Recent Sales Sold 25 titles in the last year. *Fallingwater Rising: E.J. Kaufman and Frank Lloyd Wright Create the Most Exciting House in the World*, by Franklin Toker (Alfred A. Knopf); *The Balthazar Cookbook*, by Riad Nasr, Lee Hanson, and Keith McNally (Clarkson Potter); *The Book of 'Exodus': The Making and Meaning of Bob Marley's Album of the Century*, by Vivien Goldman (Crown/Three Rivers Press); *Hungry Ghost*, by Keith Kachtick (HarperCollins). Other clients include Russell Martin, Daye Haddon, Bjork, Mian Mian, Jonathan Stone, Jocko Weyland, Peter Hessler, Rev. Billy (aka Billy Talen).

Terms Agent receives 15% commission on domestic sales; 20% commission on foreign sales. Offers written contract.

Tips "WCA works on a reciprocal basis with Ed Victor Ltd. (UK) in representing select properties to the US market and vice versa. Translation rights are sold directly in the German, Italian, Spanish, Portuguese, Latin American, French, Dutch, and Scandinavian territories in association with Andrew Nurnberg Associates Ltd. (UK); through offices in China, Bulgaria, Czech Republic, Latvia, Poland, Hungary, and Russia; and through corresponding agents in Japan, Greece, Israel, Turkey, Korea, Taiwan, and Thailand."

FRANCES COLLIN, LITERARY AGENT

P.O. Box 33, Wayne PA 19087-0033. Web site: www.francescollin.com. **Contact:** Frances Collin. Estab. 1948. Member of AAR. Represents 90 clients. 1% of clients are new/unpublished writers. Currently handles: 50% nonfiction books; 48% novels; 1% textbooks; 1% poetry.

Represents Nonfiction books, fiction.

O→ "We are accepting almost no new clients unless recommended by publishing professionals or current clients." Does not want cookbooks, crafts, children's books, software, or original screenplays.

How to Contact Query with SASE, brief proposal. No phone, fax, or e-mail inquiries. Enclose sufficient IRCs if outside the US. Considers simultaneous queries.

Terms Agent receives 15% commission on domestic sales; 20% commission on foreign sales. Offers written contract. Charges clients for overseas postage for books mailed to foreign agents; photocopying of mss, books, proposals; copyright registration fees; registered mail fees; passes along cost of any books purchased.

COLLINS LITERARY AGENCY

30 Bond St., New York NY 10012. (212)529-4909. Fax: (212)358-1055. E-mail: nina@collinsliterary.com. Web site: www.collinsliterary.com. **Contact:** Nina Collins. Estab. 2005. Represents 30 clients. 40% of clients are new/unpublished writers. Currently handles: 70% nonfiction books; 20% novels; 5% story collections; 5% juvenile books.

• Prior to opening her agency, Ms. Collins was a literary scout for foreign publishers and American film companies.

Represents Nonfiction books, novels. **Considers these nonfiction areas:** Biography/autobiography; child guidance/parenting; cooking/foods/nutrition; crafts/hobbies; current affairs; health/medicine; history; humor/satire; language/literature/criticism; memoirs; popular culture; psychology; self-help/personal improvement; women's issues/studies. **Considers these fiction areas:** Literary; mainstream/contemporary; young adult.

O→ Actively seeking nonfiction in the areas of history, psychology, health, women's studies, and lifestyle. Does not want any genre fiction.

How to Contact Query with SASE. Accepts e-mail queries. Considers simultaneous queries. Responds in 1 week to queries; 1 month to mss. Returns materials only with SASE. Obtains most new clients through referrals.

Recent Sales Sold 10 titles in the last year. *The Mother Daughter Project*, by Hamkins & Schulz (Hudson St. Press); *Over the Hill and Between the Sheets*, by Gail Belsky (Warner); *Evo-lution*, by Stephanie Staal (Bloomsbury); *Gonzo Gardening*, by Katherine Whiteside (Clarkson Potter).

Terms Agent receives 15% commission on domestic sales; 20% commission on foreign sales. Offers written contract; 1-month notice must be given to terminate contract.

DON CONGDON ASSOCIATES INC.

156 Fifth Ave., Suite 625, New York NY 10010-7002. (212)645-1229. Fax: (212)727-2688. E-mail: dca@doncongdon.com. **Contact:** Don Congdon, Michael Congdon, Susan Ramer, Cristina Concepcion. Estab. 1983. Member of AAR. Represents 100 clients. Currently handles: 60% nonfiction books; 40% fiction.

Represents Nonfiction books, fiction. **Considers these nonfiction areas:** Anthropology/archaeology; biography/autobiography; child guidance/parenting; cooking/foods/nutrition; current affairs; government/politics/law; health/medicine; history; humor/satire; language/literature/criticism; memoirs; military/war; music/dance; nature/environment; popular culture; psychology; science/technology; theater/film; travel; true crime/investigative; women's issues/studies; Creative nonfiction. **Considers these fiction areas:** Action/adventure; detective/police/crime; literary; mainstream/contemporary; mystery/suspense; short story collections; thriller; women's.

○⇥ Especially interested in narrative nonfiction and literary fiction.

How to Contact Query with SASE or via e-mail (no attachments). Responds in 3 weeks to queries; 1 month to mss. Obtains most new clients through recommendations from other authors.

Terms Agent receives 15% commission on domestic sales; 19% commission on foreign sales. Charges client for extra shipping costs, photocopying, copyright fees, book purchases.

Tips "Writing a query letter with a self-addressed stamped envelope is a must. We cannot guarantee replies to foreign queries via e-mail. No phone calls. We never download attachments to e-mail queries for security reasons, so please copy and paste material into your e-mail."

◑ CONNOR LITERARY AGENCY

2911 W. 71st St., Minneapolis MN 55423. Phone/Fax: (612)866-1486. E-mail: coolmkc@aol.com. **Contact:** Marlene Connor Lynch. Estab. 1985. Represents 50 clients. 30% of clients are new/unpublished writers. Currently handles: 50% nonfiction books; 50% novels.

• Prior to opening her agency, Ms. Connor served at the Literary Guild of America, Simon & Schuster and Random House. She is author of *Welcome to the Family: Memories of the Past for a Bright Future* (Broadway Books) and *What is Cool: Understanding Black Manhood in America* (Crown).

Member Agents Deborah Coker; Nichole Shields; Ralph Crowder.

Represents Nonfiction books, novels (especially with a minority slant). **Considers these nonfiction areas:** Child guidance/parenting; cooking/foods/nutrition; crafts/hobbies; current affairs; ethnic/cultural interests; government/politics/law; health/medicine; how-to; humor/satire; interior design/decorating; language/literature/criticism; money/finance; photography; popular culture; self-help/personal improvement; sports; true crime/investigative; women's issues/studies; Relationships. **Considers these fiction areas:** Historical; horror; literary; mainstream/contemporary; multicultural; thriller; women's; Suspense.

How to Contact All unsolicited mss returned unopened. Obtains most new clients through recommendations from others, conferences, grapevine.

Recent Sales *Outrageous Commitments*, by Dr. Ronn Elmore (HarperCollins); *Seductions*, by Snow Starborn (Sourcebooks); *Simplicity's Simply the Best Sewing Book, Revised Edition; Beautiful Hair at Any Age*, by Lisa Akbari.

Terms Agent receives 15% commission on domestic sales; 25% commission on foreign sales. Offers written contract, binding for 1 year.

Writers' Conferences National Writers Union, Midwest Chapter; Agents, Agents, Agents; Texas Writer's Conference; Detroit Writer's Conference.

Tips "We are seeking previously published writers with good sales records and new writers with real talent."

⬛ ◐ THE COOKE AGENCY

278 Bloor St. E., Suite 305, Toronto ON M4W 3M4 Canada. E-mail: agents@cookeagency.ca. Web site: www.coo keagency.ca. **Contact:** Elizabeth Griffin. Estab. 1992. Represents 60 clients. 30% of clients are new/unpublished writers. Currently handles: 50% nonfiction books; 50% novels.

Represents Nonfiction books, literary novels. **Considers these nonfiction areas:** Biography/autobiography; business/economics; child guidance/parenting; current affairs; gay/lesbian issues; health/medicine; popular culture; science/technology; young adult. **Considers these fiction areas:** Literary; women's.

○⇥ "The Cooke Agency represents some of the best Canadian writers in the world. Through our contacts and sub-agents, we have built an international reputation for quality. Curtis Brown Canada is jointly owned by Dean Cooke and Curtis Brown New York. It represents Curtis Brown New York authors in Canada." Does not want to receive how-to, self-help, spirituality, or genre fiction (science fiction, fantasy, mystery, thriller, horror).

How to Contact Query with SASE. Accepts e-mail and fax queries. Considers simultaneous queries. Responds in 6-8 weeks to queries. Returns materials only with SASE. Obtains most new clients through recommendations from others.

Recent Sales Sold 20 titles in the last year. *Last Crossing*, by Guy Vanderhaeghe (Grove/Atlantic); *The Juggler's Children*, by Carolyn Abraham (Random House); *I Was a Child of Holocaust Survivors*, by Bernice Eisenstein (McClelland & Stewart); Belgian rights to *The Englishmen's Boy*, by Guy Vanderhaeghe; Indian rights to *Brahma's Dream*, by Shree Ghatage (Rol Books); Belgian rights to *Clara Callan*, by Richard B. Wright (Perseus Books). Other clients include Lauren B. Davis, Doug Hunter, Andrew Podnieks, Steven Hayward, Robertson Davies, Neil Smith.

Terms Agent receives 15% commission on domestic sales; 20% commission on foreign sales. Offers written contract. Charges clients for postage, photocopying, courier.

Tips "Check our Web site for complete guidelines rather than calling for them."

⬙ THE DOE COOVER AGENCY

P.O. Box 668, Winchester MA 01890. (781)721-6000. Fax: (781)721-6727. Estab. 1985. Represents more than 100 clients. Currently handles: 80% nonfiction books; 20% novels.

Member Agents Doe Coover (general nonfiction, cooking); Colleen Mohyde (literary and commercial fiction, general and narrative nonfiction); Amanda Lewis (children's books); Frances Kennedy, associate.

> ○→ This agency specializes in nonfiction, particularly books on history, popular science, biography, social issues, and narrative nonfiction, as well as cooking, gardening, and literary and commercial fiction. Does not want romance, fantasy, science fiction, poetry, or screenplays.

How to Contact Query with SASE, outline. No e-mail or fax queries. Considers simultaneous queries. Returns materials only with SASE. Obtains most new clients through recommendations from others, solicitations.

Recent Sales Sold 25-30 titles in the last year. *The Gourmet Cookbook, Vol. II* (Houghton Mifflin); *The Power of Play*, by David Elkind (Houghton Mifflin); *Teaching Your Dog to Read*, by Bonnie Bergin (Broadway Books); *The Assassin's Accomplice*, by Kate Clifford Larson (Basic Books); *Liberal Arts*, by Michael Berube (W.W. Norton); *Cooking from the Hip*, by Cat Cora with Anne Krueger Spivack (Houghton Mifflin). ***Movie/TV MOW script(s) optioned/sold:*** *A Crime in the Neighborhood*, by Suzanne Berne; *Mr. White's Confession*, by Robert Clark. Other clients include WGBH, New England Aquarium, Blue Balliett, Deborah Madison, Rick Bayless, Molly Stevens, David Allen, Adria Bernardi, Paula Poundstone.

Terms Agent receives 15% commission on domestic sales; 10% of original advance commission on foreign sales.

Ⓝ ⬙ SHA-SHANA CRICHTON

6940 Carroll Ave., Takoma Park MD 20912. (301)495-9663. Fax: (202)318-0050. E-mail: cricht1@aol.com; queries@crichton-associates.com. Web site: www.crichton-associates.com. **Contact:** Sha-Shana Crichton. Estab. 2002. 90% of clients are new/unpublished writers. Currently handles: 20% nonfiction books; 80% novels.

> ● Prior to becoming an agent, Ms. Crichton did commercial litigation for a major law firm.

Represents Nonfiction books, novels. **Considers these nonfiction areas:** Child guidance/parenting; ethnic/cultural interests; gay/lesbian issues; government/politics/law; true crime/investigative; women's issues/studies. **Considers these fiction areas:** Ethnic; feminist; literary; mainstream/contemporary; mystery/suspense; religious/inspirational; romance.

> ○→ Seeking women's fiction, romance, and chick lit. No poetry.

How to Contact Accepts e-mail queries (no attachments). Responds in 3-5 weeks to queries. Returns materials only with SASE.

Recent Sales *Charmed and Dangerous*, by Candace Havens (Berkley); *After the Storm*, by Cassandra Darden-Bell (BET); *Dark Desire*, by Eve Silver (Kensington); *Weapons of Seduction*, by Maureen Smith (Kensington). Other clients include Dirk Gibson, Kimberley White, Beverly Long, Jessica Trap, Altonya Washington, Ann Christopher.

Terms Agent receives 15% commission on domestic sales; 20% commission on foreign sales. Offers written contract, binding for 45 days. Only charges fees for postage and photocopying.

Writers' Conferences Silicon Valley RWA; BookExpo America.

⬙ RICHARD CURTIS ASSOCIATES, INC.

171 E. 74th St., New York NY 10021. (212)772-7363. Fax: (212)772-7393. Web site: www.curtisagency.com. Estab. 1979. Member of RWA, MWA, SFWA; signatory of WGA. Represents 100 clients. 1% of clients are new/unpublished writers. Currently handles: 70% nonfiction books; 20% genre fiction, 10% fiction.

> ● Prior to opening his agency, Mr. Curtis was an agent with the Scott Meredith Literary Agency for 7 years. He has also authored over 50 published books.

Represents Commercial nonfiction and fiction. **Considers these nonfiction areas:** Health/medicine; history; science/technology.

How to Contact Send 1-page query letter and no more than a 5-page synopsis. Don't send ms unless specifically requested. If requested, submission must be accompanied by a SASE. No e-mail or fax queries. Returns materials only with SASE.

Recent Sales Sold 150 titles in the last year. *Olympos,* by Dan Simmons; *The Side-Effects Solution*, by Dr. Frederic Vagnini and Barry Fox; *Quantico,* by Greg Bear. Other clients include Janet Dailey, Jennifer Blake, Leonard Maltin, D.J. MacHale, John Altman, Beverly Barton, Earl Mindell, Barbara Parker.

Terms Agent receives 15% commission on domestic sales; 25% commission on foreign sales. Offers written contract. Charges for photocopying, express mail, international freight, book orders.

Writers' Conferences SFWA Conference; HWA Conference; RWA National Conference; World Fantasy Convention; Backspace Writers Conference.

[N] [●] D4EO LITERARY AGENCY

7 Indian Valley Rd., Weston CT 06883. (203)544-7180. Fax: (203)544-7160. E-mail: d4eo@optonline.net. Web site: www.publishersmarketplace.com/members/d4eo. **Contact:** Bob Diforio. Estab. 1991. Represents 150 clients. 90% of clients are new/unpublished writers. Currently handles: 70% nonfiction books; 25% novels; 5% juvenile books.

● Prior to opening his agency, Mr. Diforio was a publisher.

Represents Nonfiction books, novels. **Considers these nonfiction areas:** Art/architecture/design; biography/autobiography; business/economics; child guidance/parenting; current affairs; gay/lesbian issues; health/medicine; history; how-to; humor/satire; juvenile nonfiction; memoirs; military/war; money/finance; psychology; religious/inspirational; science/technology; self-help/personal improvement; sports; true crime/investigative; women's issues/studies. **Considers these fiction areas:** Action/adventure; detective/police/crime; erotica; historical; horror; humor/satire; juvenile; literary; mainstream/contemporary; mystery/suspense; picture books; romance; science fiction; sports; thriller; westerns/frontier; young adult.

How to Contact Query with SASE. Accepts e-mail queries. Prefers to read material exclusively. Responds in 1 week to queries; several to mss. Returns materials only with SASE. Obtains most new clients through recommendations from others.

Recent Sales Sold 75 titles in the last year. *The Worry Cure*, by Robert L. Leahy (Harmony); *Havoc*, by Jack DuBrul (NAL); *Application Suicide*, by Don Dunbar (Gotham); *Thunderhorse Six*, by Wess Roberts and Doc Bahnsen (Citadel). Other clients include Robert K. Tanenbaum, Andrea DaRif, Tawny Stokes, Cathy Verge, Lynn Kerston, Bob Bly, Michael Levine, Mark Wiskup, George Parker, Michael Stodther, Evie Rhoder, Charlie Stella, Kathy Tracy.

Terms Agent receives 15% commission on domestic sales; 25% commission on foreign sales. Offers written contract, binding for 2 years; 60-day notice must be given to terminate contract. Charges for photocopying and submission postage.

[●] LAURA DAIL LITERARY AGENCY, INC.

350 7th Ave., Suite 2003, New York NY 10010. (212)239-7477. Fax: (212)947-0460. E-mail: tellman@ldlainc.com. Web site: www.ldlainc.com. Member of AAR.

Member Agents Talia Cohen; Laura Dail; Tamar Ellman.

Represents Nonfiction books, novels.

O→ "Due to the volume of queries and manuscripts received, we apologize for not answering every e-mail and letter." Specializes in historical, literary, and some young adult fiction, as well as both practical and idea-driven nonfiction.

How to Contact Query with SASE.

Recent Sales *Bras & Broomsticks*, by Sarah Mlynowski (Delacorte); *Hide Yourself Away*, by Mary Jane Clark (St. Martin's Press); *Eating in the Raw*, by Carol Alt (Clarkson Potter).

[●] DARHANSOFF, VERRILL, FELDMAN LITERARY AGENTS

236 W. 26th St., Suite 802, New York NY 10001. (917)305-1300. Fax: (917)305-1400. Estab. 1975. Member of AAR. Represents 120 clients. 10% of clients are new/unpublished writers. Currently handles: 25% nonfiction books; 60% novels; 15% story collections.

Member Agents Liz Darhansoff; Charles Verrill; Leigh Feldman.

Represents Nonfiction books, novels, short story collections.

How to Contact Obtains most new clients through recommendations from others.

[●] LIZA DAWSON ASSOCIATES

240 W. 35th St., Suite 500, New York NY 10001. (212)465-9071. **Contact:** Liza Dawson, Caitlin Blasdell. Member of AAR, MWA, Women's Media Group. Represents 50 clients. 15% of clients are new/unpublished writers. Currently handles: 60% nonfiction books; 40% novels.

● Prior to becoming an agent, Ms. Dawson was an editor for 20 years, spending 11 years at William Morrow as vice president and 2 years at Putnam as executive editor; Ms. Blasdell was a senior editor at HarperCollins and Avon.

Represents Nonfiction books, novels. **Considers these nonfiction areas:** Biography/autobiography; health/medicine; history; memoirs; psychology; sociology; women's issues/studies; Politics; business; parenting. **Considers these fiction areas:** Fantasy (Blasdell only); historical; literary; mystery/suspense; regional; science fiction (Blasdell only); thriller.

O→ This agency specializes in readable literary fiction, thrillers, mainstream historicals, women's fiction, academics, historians, business, journalists, and psychology. Does not want to receive westerns, sports, computers, or juvenile.

How to Contact Query with SASE. Responds in 3 weeks to queries; 6 weeks to mss. Obtains most new clients through recommendations from others, conferences.

Recent Sales Sold 40 titles in the last year. *Going for It*, by Karen E. Quinones Miller (Warner); *Mayada: Daughter of Iraq*, by Jean Sasson (Dutton); *It's So Much Work to Be Your Friend: Social Skill Problems at Home and at School*, by Richard Lavoie (Touchstone); *WORDCRAFT: How to Write Like a Professional*, by Jack Hart (Pantheon); *...And a Time to Die: How Hospitals Shape the End of Life Experience*, by Dr. Sharon Kaufman (Scribner); *Zeus: A Biography*, by Tom Stone (Bloomsbury).

Terms Agent receives 15% commission on domestic sales; 20% commission on foreign sales. Offers written contract. Charges clients for photocopying and overseas postage.

THE JENNIFER DECHIARA LITERARY AGENCY

254 Park Ave. S., Suite 2L, New York NY 10010. Phone/Fax: (212)777-2702. E-mail: jenndec@aol.com. Web site: www.jdlit.com. **Contact:** Jennifer DeChiara. Estab. 2001. Represents 100 clients. 50% of clients are new/unpublished writers. Currently handles: 50% nonfiction books; 25% novels; 25% juvenile books.

• Prior to becoming an agent, Ms. DeChiara was a writing consultant, freelance editor at Simon & Schuster and Random House, and a ballerina and an actress.

Represents Nonfiction books, novels, juvenile books. **Considers these nonfiction areas:** Biography/autobiography; child guidance/parenting; cooking/foods/nutrition; crafts/hobbies; current affairs; education; ethnic/cultural interests; gay/lesbian issues; government/politics/law; health/medicine; history; how-to; humor/satire; interior design/decorating; juvenile nonfiction; language/literature/criticism; memoirs; military/war; money/finance; music/dance; nature/environment; photography; popular culture; psychology; science/technology; self-help/personal improvement; sociology; sports; theater/film; true crime/investigative; women's issues/studies. **Considers these fiction areas:** Confession; detective/police/crime; ethnic; family saga; fantasy; feminist; gay/lesbian; historical; horror; humor/satire; juvenile; literary; mainstream/contemporary; mystery/suspense; picture books; regional; sports; thriller; young adult; Chick lit; psychic/supernatural; glitz.

• "We represent both children's and adult books in a wide range of ages and genres. We are a full-service agency and fulfill the potential of every book in every possible medium—stage, film, television, etc. We help writers every step of the way, from creating book ideas to editing and promotion. We are passionate about helping writers further their careers, but are just as eager to discover new talent, regardless of age or lack of prior publishing experience. This agency is committed to managing a writer's entire career. For us, it's not just about selling books, but about making dreams come true. We are especially attracted to the downtrodden, the discouraged, and the downright disgusted." Actively seeking literary fiction, chick lit, young adult fiction, self-help, pop culture, and celebrity biographies. Does not want westerns, poetry, or short stories.

How to Contact Query with SASE. Considers simultaneous queries. Responds in 3-6 months to queries; 3-6 months to mss. Returns materials only with SASE. Obtains most new clients through recommendations from others, conferences, query letters.

Recent Sales Sold 30 titles in the last year. *I Was a Teenage Popsicle*, by Bev Katz Rosenbaum (Berkley/JAM); *Hazing Meri Sugarman*, by M. Apostolina (Simon Pulse); *The 10-Minute Sexual Solution* and *Virgin Sex: A Guy's Guide to Sex*, by Dr. Darcy Luadzers (Hatherleigh Press). ***Movie/TV MOW script(s) optioned/sold:*** *Geography Club*, by Brent Hartinger (East of Doheny). Other clients include Adam Meyer, Herbie J. Pilato, Chris Demarest, Jeff Lenburg, Joe Cadora, Tiffani Amber Thiessen, Bonnie Neubauer.

Terms Agent receives 15% commission on domestic sales; 20% commission on foreign sales. Offers written contract.

JOËLLE DELBOURGO ASSOCIATES, INC.

516 Bloomfield Ave., Suite 5, Montclair NJ 07042. (973)783-6800. Fax: (973)783-6802. E-mail: info@delbourgo.com. Web site: www.delbourgo.com. **Contact:** Joëlle Delbourgo, Molly Lyons. Estab. 2000. Represents 80 clients. 40% of clients are new/unpublished writers. Currently handles: 75% nonfiction books; 25% novels.

• Prior to becoming an agent, Ms. Delbourgo was an editor and senior publishing executive at HarperCollins and Random House.

Member Agents Joëlle Delbourgo (parenting, self-help, psychology, business, serious nonfiction, narrative nonfiction, quality fiction); Molly Lyons (practical and narrative nonfiction, memoir, quality fiction).

Represents Nonfiction books, novels, short story collections. **Considers these nonfiction areas:** Biography/autobiography; business/economics; child guidance/parenting; cooking/foods/nutrition; current affairs; education; ethnic/cultural interests; gay/lesbian issues; government/politics/law; health/medicine; history; how-to; money/finance; music/dance; nature/environment; popular culture; psychology; religious/inspirational; science/technology; self-help/personal improvement; sociology; theater/film; true crime/investigative; women's issues/studies; New Age/metaphysics, interior design/decorating. **Considers these fiction areas:** Historical; literary; mainstream/contemporary; mystery/suspense; regional (southern).

○━ "We are former publishers and editors, with deep knowledge and an insider perspective. We have a reputation for individualized attention to clients, strategic management of authors' careers, and creating strong partnerships with publishers for our clients." Actively seeking history, narrative nonfiction, science/medicine, memoir, literary fiction, psychology, parenting, and biographies. Does not want to receive genre fiction or screenplays.

How to Contact Query with SASE. No e-mail or fax queries. Considers simultaneous queries. Responds in 3 weeks to queries; 2 months to mss. Returns materials only with SASE.

Recent Sales Sold 18 titles and sold 2 scripts in the last year. *Journey of a Lifetime: The Remarkable Story of Human Development from Prebirth to Death*, by Thomas Armstrong, PhD (Sterling); *Reporting the War: Freedom of the Press in Wartime From the American Revolution to the War on Terror*, by John Byrne Cooke (Palgrave/Macmillan); *Julius Caesar, A Biography*, by Philip Freeman, PhD (Simon & Schuster); *Sex Lives of Wives: The Quest for Missing Passion*, by Helarie Hollenbeck (Springboard); *He's Just Not in the Stars: Wicked Astrology and Uncensored Advice for Getting the (Almost) Perfect Guy*, by Jenni Kosarin (HarperEntertainment). Other clients include Phyllis Chesler, Pamela Duncan, Geeta Anand, Philip Mitchell Freeman, Roy Hoffman, Chris Farrell, David Cole, Marc Siegel, Joan Wester Anderson, Julie Fenster.

Terms Agent receives 15% commission on domestic sales; 20% commission on foreign sales. Offers written contract. Charges clients for postage and photocopying. "We match writers with specific editors or co-writers as needed."

Tips "Do your homework. Do not cold call. Read and follow submission guidelines before contacting us. Do not call to find out if we received your material. No e-mail queries. Treat agents with respect, as you would any other professional, such as a doctor, lawyer, or financial advisor."

◙ DHS LITERARY, INC.
10711 Preston Rd., Suite 100, Dallas TX 75230. (214)363-4422. Fax: (214)363-4423. E-mail: submissions@dhsliterary.com. Web site: www.dhsliterary.com. **Contact:** David Hale Smith, president. Estab. 1994. Represents 35 clients. 15% of clients are new/unpublished writers. Currently handles: 60% nonfiction books; 40% novels.

● Prior to opening his agency, Mr. Smith was an agent at Dupree/Miller & Associates.

Represents Nonfiction books, novels. **Considers these nonfiction areas:** Biography/autobiography; business/economics; child guidance/parenting; cooking/foods/nutrition; current affairs; ethnic/cultural interests; popular culture; sports; true crime/investigative. **Considers these fiction areas:** Detective/police/crime; ethnic; literary; mainstream/contemporary; mystery/suspense; thriller; westerns/frontier.

○━ This agency specializes in commercial fiction and nonfiction for the adult trade market. Actively seeking thrillers, mysteries, suspense, etc., and narrative nonfiction. Does not want to receive poetry, short fiction, or children's books.

How to Contact Accepts new material by referral only. *No unsolicited mss.*

Recent Sales Sold 40+ titles in the last year. *Officer Down*, by Theresa Schwegel; *Private Wars*, by Greg Rucka; *The Lean Body Promise*, by Lee Labrada.

Terms Agent receives 15% commission on domestic sales; 25% commission on foreign sales. Offers written contract; 10-day notice must be given to terminate contract. Charges for postage and photocopying. 100% of business is derived from commissions on sales.

Tips "Remember to be courteous and professional, and to treat marketing your work and approaching an agent as you would any formal business matter. If you have a referral, always query first via e-mail. Sorry, but we cannot respond to queries sent via mail, even with a SASE. Visit our Web site for more information."

◙ DUNHAM LITERARY, INC.
156 Fifth Ave., Suite 625, New York NY 10010-7002. (212)929-0994. Web site: www.dunhamlit.com. **Contact:** Jennie Dunham. Estab. 2000. Member of AAR. Represents 50 clients. 15% of clients are new/unpublished writers. Currently handles: 25% nonfiction books; 25% novels; 50% juvenile books.

● Prior to opening her agency, Ms. Dunham worked as a literary agent for Russell & Volkening. The Rhoda Weyr Agency is now a division of Dunham Literary, Inc.

Represents Nonfiction books, novels, short story collections, juvenile books. **Considers these nonfiction areas:** Anthropology/archaeology; biography/autobiography; ethnic/cultural interests; government/politics/law; health/medicine; history; language/literature/criticism; nature/environment; popular culture; psychology; science/technology; women's issues/studies. **Considers these fiction areas:** Ethnic; juvenile; literary; mainstream/contemporary; picture books; young adult.

How to Contact Query with SASE. No e-mail or fax queries. Responds in 1 week to queries; 2 months to mss. Obtains most new clients through recommendations from others, solicitations.

Recent Sales *America the Beautiful*, by Robert Sabuda; *Dahlia*, by Barbara McClintock; *Living Dead Girl*, by

Tod Goldberg; *In My Mother's House*, by Margaret McMulla; *Black Hawk Down*, by Mark Bowden; *Look Back All the Green Valley*, by Fred Chappell; *Under a Wing*, by Reeve Lindbergh; *I Am Madame X*, by Gioia Diliberto.
Terms Agent receives 15% commission on domestic sales; 20% commission on foreign sales.

DYSTEL & GODERICH LITERARY MANAGEMENT

1 Union Square W., Suite 904, New York NY 10003. (212)627-9100. Fax: (212)627-9313. E-mail: miriam@dystel. com. Web site: www.dystel.com. **Contact:** Miriam Goderich. Estab. 1994. Member of AAR. Represents 300 clients. 50% of clients are new/unpublished writers. Currently handles: 65% nonfiction books; 25% novels; 10% cookbooks.

 • Dystel & Goderich Literary Management recently acquired the client list of Bedford Book Works.

Member Agents Stacey Glick; Jane Dystel; Miriam Goderich; Michael Bourret; Jim McCarthy; Kate McKean; Lauren Abramo.

Represents Nonfiction books, novels, cookbooks. **Considers these nonfiction areas:** Animals; anthropology/ archaeology; biography/autobiography; business/economics; child guidance/parenting; cooking/foods/nutrition; current affairs; education; ethnic/cultural interests; gay/lesbian issues; government/politics/law; health/ medicine; history; humor/satire; military/war; money/finance; New Age/metaphysics; popular culture; psychology; religious/inspirational; science/technology; true crime/investigative; women's issues/studies. **Considers these fiction areas:** Action/adventure; detective/police/crime; ethnic; family saga; gay/lesbian; literary; mainstream/contemporary; mystery/suspense; thriller.

 ⚬➤ This agency specializes in cookbooks and commercial and literary fiction and nonfiction.

How to Contact Query with SASE. Considers simultaneous queries. Responds in 1 month to queries; 6 weeks to mss. Obtains most new clients through recommendations from others, solicitations, conferences.

Terms Agent receives 15% commission on domestic sales; 19% commission on foreign sales. Offers written contract. Charges for photocopying. Galley charges and book charges from the publisher are passed on to the author.

Writers' Conferences Whidbey Island Writers' Conference; Iowa Summer Writing Festival; Pacific Northwest Writer's Association; Pike's Peak Writers Conference; Santa Barbara Writers' Conference; Harriette Austin Writers Conference; Sandhills Writers Conference; Denver Publishing Institute; Love Is Murder.

Tips "Work on sending professional, well-written queries that are concise and addressed to the specific agent the author is contacting. No dear Sirs/Madam."

ETHAN ELLENBERG LITERARY AGENCY

548 Broadway, #5-E, New York NY 10012. (212)431-4554. Fax: (212)941-4652. E-mail: agent@ethanellenberg.c om. Web site: www.ethanellenberg.com. **Contact:** Ethan Ellenberg. Estab. 1983. Represents 80 clients. 10% of clients are new/unpublished writers. Currently handles: 25% nonfiction books; 75% novels.

 • Prior to opening his agency, Mr. Ellenberg was contracts manager of Berkley/Jove and associate contracts manager for Bantam.

Represents Nonfiction books, novels, children's books. **Considers these nonfiction areas:** Biography/autobiography; health/medicine; history; military/war; New Age/metaphysics; religious/inspirational; science/technology. **Considers these fiction areas:** Fantasy; mystery/suspense; picture books; romance (all genres); science fiction; thriller; young adult; women's; Middle grade.

 ⚬➤ This agency specializes in commercial fiction—especially thrillers, romance/women's, and specialized nonfiction. "We also do a lot of children's books." Actively seeking commercial and literary fiction, children's books, and breakthrough nonfiction. Does not want to receive poetry, short stories, westerns, autobiographies, or screenplays.

How to Contact For fiction, send introductory letter, outline, first 3 chapters, SASE. For nonfiction, send query letter, proposal, 1 sample chapter, SASE. For children's books, send introductory letter, up to 3 picture book mss, outline, first 3 chapters, SASE. No fax queries. Accepts e-mail queries (no attachments). Will only respond to e-mail queries if interested. Considers simultaneous queries. Responds in 4-6 weeks to mss. Returns materials only with SASE.

Recent Sales Has sold over 100 titles in the last 3 years. *Ghost Brigades*, by John Scalzi (Tor); *Dark Moon Descender*, by Sharon Shinn (Ace); *Deep, Dark and Dangerous*, by Jaid Black (Pocket Books); *The Alien in the Supermarket*, by Susan Grant (HQN); *Beyond the Limit*, by Lindsay McKenna (HQN); *Master of Darkness*, by Susan Sizemore (Pocket Books); *Peach Hill*, by Marthe Jocelyn (Random House/Wendy Lamb Books). Other clients include Mel Odom, MaryJanice Davidson, Amanda Ashley, Rebecca York, Bertrice Small, Eric Rohmann.

Terms Agent receives 15% commission on domestic sales; 10% commission on foreign sales. Offers written contract. Charges clients (with their consent) for direct expenses limited to photocopying and postage.

Writers' Conferences RWA National Conference; Novelists, Inc; and other regional conferences.

Tips "We do consider new material from unsolicited authors. Write a good, clear letter with a succinct description of your book. We prefer the first 3 chapters when we consider fiction. For all submissions, you must include a SASE or the material will be discarded. It's always hard to break in, but talent will find a home. Check our Web site for complete submission guidelines. We continue to see natural storytellers and nonfiction writers with important books."

⦿ NICHOLAS ELLISON, INC.

Affiliated with Sanford J. Greenburger Associates, 55 Fifth Ave., 15th Floor, New York NY 10003. (212)206-6050. Fax: (212)463-8718. Web site: www.greenburger.com. **Contact:** Nicholas Ellison. Estab. 1983. Represents 70 clients. Currently handles: 50% nonfiction books; 50% novels.

- Prior to becoming an agent, Mr. Ellison was an editor at Minerva Editions and Harper & Row, and editor-in-chief at Delacorte.

Member Agents Nicholas Ellison; Jennifer Cayea.

Represents Nonfiction books, novels. **Considers these nonfiction areas:** Considers most nonfiction areas. **Considers these fiction areas:** Literary; mainstream/contemporary.

How to Contact Query with SASE. Responds in 6 weeks to queries.

Recent Sales *A Dirty Job*, by Christopher Moore (HarperCollins); *I'm Not Myself*, by Sarah Dunn (Little, Brown); *The Girl from Charnelle*, by K.L. Cook (HarperCollins); next 3 Nelson DeMille Books (Warner). Other clients include Olivia Goldsmith, P.T. Deutermann, Nancy Geary, Jeff Lindsay, Lee Gruenfeld, Thomas Christopher Greene, Bill Mason; Mario Boxquez, Father Albert Cutié, Geoff Emerick, Howard Massey, Sofia Quintero.

Terms Agent receives 15% commission on domestic sales; 20% commission on foreign sales.

⦿ ANN ELMO AGENCY, INC.

60 E. 42nd St., New York NY 10165. (212)661-2880. Fax: (212)661-2883. **Contact:** Lettie Lee. Estab. 1959. Member of AAR, Authors Guild.

Member Agents Lettie Lee; Mari Cronin (plays); A.L. Abecassis (nonfiction).

Represents Nonfiction books, novels. **Considers these nonfiction areas:** Biography/autobiography; current affairs; health/medicine; history; how-to; popular culture; science/technology. **Considers these fiction areas:** Ethnic; family saga; mainstream/contemporary; romance (contemporary, gothic, historical, regency); thriller; women's.

How to Contact Only accepts mailed queries with SASE. Do not send full ms unless requested. No fax queries. Responds in 3 months to queries. Obtains most new clients through recommendations from others.

Recent Sales This agency prefers not to share information on specific sales.

Terms Agent receives 15% commission on domestic sales; 20% commission on foreign sales. Offers written contract. Charges clients for special mailings, shipping, multiple international calls. There is no charge for usual cost of doing business.

Tips "Query first, and only when asked send properly prepared manuscript. A double-spaced, readable manuscript is the best recommendation. Include a SASE, of course."

⦿ THE ELAINE P. ENGLISH LITERARY AGENCY

4701 41st St. NW, Suite D, Washington DC 20016. (202)362-5190. Fax: (202)362-5192. E-mail: elaineengl@aol.com. Web site: www.elaineenglish.com. **Contact:** Elaine English. Member of AAR. Represents 16 clients. 50% of clients are new/unpublished writers. Currently handles: 100% novels.

- Ms. English has been working in publishing for over 15 years. She is also an attorney specializing in media and publishing law.

Represents Novels. **Considers these fiction areas:** Historical; multicultural; mystery/suspense; romance (single title, historical, contemporary, romantic, suspense, chick lit, erotic); thriller; women's.

- ➜ Actively seeking women's fiction, including single-title romances. Does not want to receive any science fiction, time travel, children's, or young adult.

How to Contact Prefers e-mail queries. If requested, submit synopsis, first 3 chapters, SASE. Responds in 6-12 weeks to queries; 6 months to requested ms. Returns materials only with SASE. Obtains most new clients through recommendations from others, conferences, submissions.

Terms Agent receives 15% commission on domestic sales; 20% commission on foreign sales. Offers written contract; 30-day notice must be given to terminate contract. Charges only for expenses directly related to sales of manuscript (long distance phone calls, postage, copying).

Writers' Conferences RWA National Conference; SEAK Medical & Legal Fiction Writing Conference; Novelists, Inc; Washington Romance Writers Retreat.

⦿ FARBER LITERARY AGENCY, INC.

14 E. 75th St., #2E, New York NY 10021. (212)861-7075. Fax: (212)861-7076. E-mail: farberlit@aol.com. Web site: www.donaldfarber.com. **Contact:** Ann Farber, Dr. Seth Farber. Estab. 1989. Represents 40 clients. 50%

of clients are new/unpublished writers. Currently handles: 25% nonfiction books; 35% novels; 15% scholarly books; 25% stage plays.

Member Agents Ann Farber (novels); Seth Farber (plays, scholarly books, novels); Donald C. Farber (attorney, all entertainment media).

Represents Nonfiction books, novels, juvenile books, textbooks, stage plays. **Considers these nonfiction areas:** Child guidance/parenting; cooking/foods/nutrition; music/dance; psychology; theater/film. **Considers these fiction areas:** Action/adventure; humor/satire; juvenile; literary; mainstream/contemporary; mystery/suspense; thriller; young adult.

How to Contact Submit outline, 3 sample chapters, SASE. Prefers to read materials exclusively. Responds in 1 month to queries; 2 months to mss. Obtains most new clients through recommendations from others.

Terms Agent receives 15% commission on domestic sales; 20% commission on foreign sales. Offers written contract, binding for 1 year. Client must furnish copies of ms, treatments, and any other items for submission.

Tips "Our attorney, Donald C. Farber, is the author of many books. His services are available to the agency's clients as part of the agency service at no additional charge."

🖉 FARRIS LITERARY AGENCY, INC.

P.O. Box 570069, Dallas TX 75357. (972)203-8804. E-mail: farris1@airmail.net. Web site: www.farrisliterary.com. **Contact:** Mike Farris, Susan Morgan Farris. Estab. 2002. Represents 30 clients. 60% of clients are new/unpublished writers.

• Both Mr. Farris and Ms. Farris are attorneys.

Represents Nonfiction books, novels. **Considers these nonfiction areas:** Biography/autobiography; business/economics; child guidance/parenting; cooking/foods/nutrition; current affairs; government/politics/law; health/medicine; history; how-to; humor/satire; memoirs; military/war; music/dance; popular culture; religious/inspirational; self-help/personal improvement; sports; women's issues/studies. **Considers these fiction areas:** Action/adventure; detective/police/crime; historical; humor/satire; literary; mainstream/contemporary; mystery/suspense; religious/inspirational; romance; sports; thriller; westerns/frontier.

     ⦿ "We specialize in both fiction and nonfiction books. We are particularly interested in discovering unpublished authors. We adhere to AAR guidelines" Does not consider science fiction, fantasy, gay and lesbian, erotica, young adult, or children's.

How to Contact Query with SASE. Considers simultaneous queries. Responds in 2-3 weeks to queries; 4-8 weeks to mss. Returns materials only with SASE. Obtains most new clients through recommendations from others, solicitations, conferences.

Recent Sales Sold 4 titles in the last year. *Detachment Fault* and *Untitled*, by Susan Cummins Miller (Berkley); *Creed*, by Sheldon Russell (Oklahoma University Press); *How to Understand Autism: The Easy Way*, by Dr. Alexander Durig (Jessica Kingsley Publishers Ltd.).

Terms Agent receives 15% commission on domestic sales; 20% commission on foreign sales. Offers written contract; 30-day notice must be given to terminate contract. Charges clients for postage and photocopying.

Writers' Conferences Oklahoma Writers Federation Conference; The Screenwriting Conference in Santa Fe; Pikes Peak Writers Conference; Women Writing the West Annual Conference.

🖉 DIANA FINCH LITERARY AGENCY

116 W. 23rd St., Suite 500, New York NY 10011. (646)375-2081. E-mail: diana.finch@verizon.net. **Contact:** Diana Finch. Estab. 2003. Member of AAR. Represents 45 clients. 20% of clients are new/unpublished writers. Currently handles: 65% nonfiction books; 25% novels; 5% juvenile books; 5% multimedia.

• Prior to opening her agency, Ms. Finch worked at Ellen Levine Literary Agency for 18 years.

Represents Nonfiction books, novels, scholarly books. **Considers these nonfiction areas:** Biography/autobiography; business/economics; child guidance/parenting; computers/electronic; current affairs; ethnic/cultural interests; government/politics/law; health/medicine; history; how-to; humor/satire; juvenile nonfiction; memoirs; military/war; money/finance; music/dance; nature/environment; photography; popular culture; psychology; science/technology; self-help/personal improvement; sports; theater/film; translation; true crime/investigative; women's issues/studies. **Considers these fiction areas:** Action/adventure; detective/police/crime; ethnic; historical; literary; mainstream/contemporary; thriller; young adult.

     ⦿ Actively seeking narrative nonfiction, popular science, and health topics. Does not want romance, mysteries, or children's picture books.

How to Contact Query with SASE or via e-mail (no attachments). No phone or fax queries. Considers simultaneous queries. Returns materials only with SASE. Obtains most new clients through recommendations from others.

Recent Sales *Armed Madhouse*, by Greg Palast (Penguin US/UK); *Journey of the Magi*, by Tudor Parfitt (Farrar, Straus & Giroux); *The Queen's Soprano*, by Carol Dines (Harcourt Young Adult); *Was the 2004 Election Stolen?*, by Steven Freeman and Joel Bleifuss (Seven Stories); *Lipstick Jihad*, by Azadeh Moaveni (Public Affairs); *Great*

Customer Connections, by Rich Gallagher (Amacom). Other clients include Keith Devlin, Daniel Duane, Thomas Goltz, Hugh Pope, Owen Matthews, Joan Lambert, Dr. Robert Marion.

Terms Agent receives 15% commission on domestic sales; 20% commission on foreign sales. Offers written contract. "I charge for photocopying, overseas postage, galleys, and books purchased, and try to recap these costs from earnings received for a client, rather than charging outright."

Tips "Do as much research as you can on agents before you query. Have someone critique your query letter before you send it. It should be only 1 page and describe your book clearly—and why you are writing it—but also demonstrate creativity and a sense of your writing style."

N ◐ FLETCHER & PARRY

78 Fifth Ave., 3rd Floor, New York NY 10011. (212)614-0778. Fax: (212)614-0728. **Contact:** Christy Fletcher, Emma Parry. Estab. 2003. Member of AAR.

Represents Nonfiction books, novels. **Considers these nonfiction areas:** Current affairs; history; memoirs; sports; travel; African American; narrative; science; biography; business; health; lifestyle. **Considers these fiction areas:** Literary; young adult; Commercial.

   O⌐ Does not want genre fiction.

How to Contact Query with SASE. Responds in 4-6 weeks to queries.

◐ THE FOLEY LITERARY AGENCY

34 E. 38th St., New York NY 10016-2508. (212)686-6930. **Contact:** Joan Foley, Joseph Foley. Estab. 1961. Represents 10 clients. Currently handles: 75% nonfiction books; 25% novels.

Represents Nonfiction books, novels.

How to Contact Query with letter, brief outline, SASE. Responds promptly to queries. Obtains most new clients through recommendations from others (rarely taking on new clients).

Recent Sales This agency prefers not to share information on specific sales.

Terms Agent receives 10% commission on domestic sales; 15% commission on foreign sales. 100% of business is derived from commissions on ms sales.

N ◐ SARAH JANE FREYMANN LITERARY AGENCY

59 W. 71st St., Suite 9B, New York NY 10023. (212)362-9277. Fax: (212)501-8240. E-mail: sjfs@aol.com. **Contact:** Sarah Jane Freymann. Represents 100 clients. 20% of clients are new/unpublished writers. Currently handles: 75% nonfiction books; 23% novels; 2% juvenile books.

Represents Nonfiction books, novels, illustrated books. **Considers these nonfiction areas:** Animals; anthropology/archaeology; art/architecture/design; biography/autobiography; business/economics; child guidance/parenting; cooking/foods/nutrition; current affairs; ethnic/cultural interests; health/medicine; history; interior design/decorating; memoirs (narrative); nature/environment; psychology; religious/inspirational; self-help/personal improvement; women's issues/studies; Lifestyle. **Considers these fiction areas:** Ethnic; literary; mainstream/contemporary.

How to Contact Query with SASE. Responds in 2 weeks to queries; 6 weeks to mss. Obtains most new clients through recommendations from others.

Recent Sales *Girl Stories*, by Lauren Weinstein (Henry Holt); *The Good, Good Pig*, by Sy Montgomery (Ballantine/Random House); *The Man Who Killed the Whale*, by Linda Hogan (W.W. Norton); *Writing the Fire! Yoga and the Art of Making Your Words Come Alive*, by Gail Sher (Harmoney/Bell Tower); *Mexicocina*, by Melba Levick and Betsy McNair (Chronicle); *Holy Play*, by Kirk Byron Jones (Jossey Bass).

Terms Agent receives 15% commission on domestic sales; 20% commission on foreign sales. Offers written contract. Charges clients for long distance, overseas postage, photocopying. 100% of business is derived from commissions on ms sales.

Tips "I love fresh, new, passionate works by authors who love what they are doing and have both natural talent and carefully honed skill."

◐ GELFMAN, SCHNEIDER, LITERARY AGENTS, INC.

250 W. 57th St., Suite 2515, New York NY 10107. (212)245-1993. Fax: (212)245-8678. E-mail: mail@gelfmanschneider.com. **Contact:** Jane Gelfman, Deborah Schneider. Estab. 1981. Member of AAR. Represents 300+ clients. 10% of clients are new/unpublished writers.

Represents Nonfiction books, novels. **Considers these nonfiction areas:** Biography; health; lifestyle; politics; science. **Considers these fiction areas:** Literary; mainstream/contemporary; mystery/suspense.

   O⌐ Does not want to receive romance, science fiction, westerns, or children's books.

How to Contact Query with SASE. No e-mail queries accepted. Responds in 1 month to queries; 2 months to mss. Obtains most new clients through recommendations from others.

Literary Agents

Terms Agent receives 15% commission on domestic sales; 20% commission on foreign sales; 15% commission on dramatic rights sales. Offers written contract. Charges clients for photocopying and messengers/couriers.

◪ THE GISLASON AGENCY

219 Main St. SE, Suite 506, Minneapolis MN 55414-2160. (612)331-8033. Fax: (612)331-8115. E-mail: gislasonbj @aol.com. Web site: www.thegislasonagency.com. **Contact:** Barbara J. Gislason. Estab. 1992. Member of Minnesota State Bar Association, American Bar Association, Art & Entertainment Law Section, Animal Law, Internet Committee, Minnesota Intellectual Property Law Association Copyright Committee; SFWA, MWA, Sisters in Crime, Icelandic Association of Minnesota, American Academy of Acupuncture and Oriental Medicine. 80% of clients are new/unpublished writers. Currently handles: 10% nonfiction books; 90% novels.

- Ms. Gislason became an attorney in 1980, and continues to practice art and entertainment law. She has been nationally recognized as a Leading American Attorney and a Super Lawyer. She is also the owner of Blue Raven Press, which publishes fiction and nonfiction about animals.

Member Agents Deborah Sweeney (fantasy, science fiction); Kellie Hultgren (fantasy, science fiction); Lisa Higgs (mystery, literary fiction); Kris Olson (mystery); Kevin Hedman (fantasy, science fiction, mystery, literary fiction).

Represents Nonfiction books, novels. **Considers these nonfiction areas:** Animals (behavior/communications). **Considers these fiction areas:** Fantasy; literary; mystery/suspense; science fiction; thriller (legal).

- ⚬┮ Do not send personal memoirs, poetry, short stories, screenplays, or children's books.

How to Contact For fiction, query with synopsis, first 3 chapters, SASE. For nonfiction, query with proposal, sample chapters. Published authors may submit complete ms. No e-mail or fax queries. Responds in 2 months to queries; 3 months to mss. Obtains most new clients through recommendations from others, conferences, *Guide to Literary Agents, Literary Market Place*, other reference books.

Recent Sales *Historical Romance #4*, by Linda Cook (Kensington); *Dancing Dead*, by Deborah Woodworth (HarperCollins); *Owen Keane's Lonely Journey*, by Terence Faherty (Harlequin).

Terms Agent receives 15% commission on domestic sales; 20% commission on foreign sales. Offers written contract, binding for 1 year with option to renew. Charges clients for photocopying and postage.

Writers' Conferences Southwest Writers Conference; Willamette Writers Conference; Wrangling with Writing; other state and regional conferences.

Tips "Your cover letter should be well written and include a detailed synopsis (fiction) or proposal (nonfiction), the first 3 chapters, and author bio. Appropriate SASE required. We are looking for a great writer with a poetic, lyrical, or quirky writing style who can create intriguing ambiguities. We expect a well-researched, imaginative, and fresh plot that reflects a familiarity with the applicable genre. If submitting nonfiction work, explain how the submission differs from and adds to previously published works in the field. Scenes with sex and violence must be intrinsic to the plot. Remember to proofread. If the work was written with a specific publisher in mind, this should be communicated."

Ⓝ ⊕ ◪ GOLVAN ARTS MANAGEMENT

P.O. Box 766, Kew VIC 3101 Australia. E-mail: golvan@ozemail.com.au. Web site: www.golvanarts.com.au. **Contact:** Colin Golvan.

Represents Nonfiction books, novels, juvenile books, poetry books, movie scripts, TV scripts, stage plays.

How to Contact Query with author bio, SASE.

Recent Sales *The Runaway Circus*, by Gordon Reece (Lothian Books); *Two for the Road*, by Shirly Hardy-Rix and Brian Rix (Macmillan); *The Catch*, by Marg Vandeleur (Penguin).

Terms Agent receives 11% commission on domestic sales.

◉ GOODMAN ASSOCIATES

500 West End Ave., New York NY 10024-4317. (212)873-4806. **Contact:** Elise Simon Goodman. Estab. 1976. Member of AAR. Represents 50 clients.

- Mr. Goodman is the former chair of the AAR Ethics Committee.

Member Agents Elise Simon Goodman; Arnold P. Goodman.

Represents Nonfiction books, novels.

- ⚬┮ Accepting new clients by recommendation only. Does not want to receive poetry, articles, individual stories, children's, or young adult material.

How to Contact Query with SASE. Responds in 10 days to queries; 1 month to mss.

Terms Agent receives 15% commission on domestic sales; 20% commission on foreign sales. Charges clients for certain expenses: faxes, toll calls, overseas postage, photocopying, book purchases.

☑ JILL GROSJEAN LITERARY AGENCY

1390 Millstone Rd., Sag Harbor NY 11963-2214. (631)725-7419. Fax: (631)725-8632. E-mail: jill6981@aol.com. Web site: www.hometown.aol.com/jill6981/myhomepage/index.html. **Contact:** Jill Grosjean. Estab. 1999. Represents 33 clients. 100% of clients are new/unpublished writers.

- Prior to becoming an agent, Ms. Grosjean was manager of an independent bookstore. She has also worked in publishing and advertising.

Represents Novels. **Considers these fiction areas:** Historical; literary; mainstream/contemporary; mystery/suspense; regional; romance.

- ☞ This agency offers some editorial assistance (i.e., line-by-line edits). Actively seeking literary novels and mysteries.

How to Contact Query with SASE. No cold calls, please. Considers simultaneous queries. Responds in 1 week to queries; 1 month to mss. Returns materials only with SASE. Obtains most new clients through recommendations from others, solicitations.

Recent Sales *Stealing the Dragon*, by Tim Maleeny (Midnight Ink); *I Love You Like a Tomato*, by Marie Giordano (Forge Books); *Nectar*, by David C. Fickett (Forge Books); *Cycling* and *Sanctuary*, by Greg Garrett (Kensington); *The Smoke*, by Tony Broadbent (St. Martin's Press/Minotaur); *Fields of Gold*, by Marie Bostwick (Kensington); Spectres in the Smoke, by Tony Broadbent (St. Martin's Press/Minotaur).

Terms Agent receives 15% commission on domestic sales; 20% commission on foreign sales. No written contract. Charges clients for photocopying and mailing expenses.

Writers' Conferences Book Passage's Mystery Writers Conference; Agents and Editors Conference.

☑ REECE HALSEY NORTH

98 Main St., #704, Tiburon CA 94920. Fax: (415)789-9177. E-mail: info@reecehalseynorth.com. Web site: www.reecehalseynorth.com. **Contact:** Kimberley Cameron. Estab. 1957 (Reece Halsey Agency); 1993 (Reece Halsey North). Member of AAR. Represents 40 clients. 30% of clients are new/unpublished writers. Currently handles: 25% nonfiction books; 75% fiction.

- The Reece Halsey Agency has an illustrious client list of established writers, including the estate of Aldous Huxley, and has represented Upton Sinclair, William Faulkner, and Henry Miller.

Member Agents Dorris Halsey (Reece Halsey Agency, Los Angeles); Kimberley Cameron, Adam Marsh (Reece Halsey North).

Represents Nonfiction books, novels. **Considers these nonfiction areas:** Biography/autobiography; current affairs; history; language/literature/criticism; popular culture; science/technology; true crime/investigative; women's issues/studies. **Considers these fiction areas:** Action/adventure; contemporary issues; detective/police/crime; ethnic; family saga; historical; literary; mainstream/contemporary; mystery/suspense; science fiction; thriller; women's.

- ☞ "We are looking for a unique and heartfelt voice."

How to Contact Query with SASE, first 10 pages of novel. Please do not fax queries. Responds in 3-6 weeks to queries; 3 months to mss. Obtains most new clients through recommendations from others, solicitations.

Terms Agent receives 15% commission on domestic sales; 10% commission on dramatic rights sales. Offers written contract, binding for 1 year. Requests 6 copies of ms if representing an author.

Writers' Conferences Maui Writers Conference; Aspen Summer Words Literary Festival; Willamette Writers Conference.

Tips "Always send a well-written query and include a SASE with it."

☑ THE MITCHELL J. HAMILBURG AGENCY

149 S. Barrington Ave., #732, Los Angeles CA 90049-2930. (310)471-4024. Fax: (310)471-9588. **Contact:** Michael Hamilburg. Estab. 1937. Signatory of WGA. Represents 70 clients. Currently handles: 70% nonfiction books; 30% novels.

Represents Nonfiction books, novels. **Considers these nonfiction areas:** Anthropology/archaeology; biography/autobiography; business/economics; child guidance/parenting; cooking/foods/nutrition; current affairs; education; government/politics/law; health/medicine; history; memoirs; military/war; money/finance; psychology; recreation; regional; self-help/personal improvement; sex; sociology; spirituality; sports; travel; women's issues/studies; Creative nonfiction; romance; architecture; inspirational; true crime. **Considers these fiction areas:** Action/adventure; experimental; feminist; glitz; humor/satire; military/war; mystery/suspense; New Age; occult; regional; religious/inspirational; romance; sports; thriller; Crime; mainstream; psychic.

How to Contact Query with outline, 2 sample chapters, SASE. Responds in 1 month to mss. Obtains most new clients through recommendations from others, conferences, personal search.

Terms Agent receives 10-15% commission on domestic sales.

✪ THE JOY HARRIS LITERARY AGENCY, INC.

156 Fifth Ave., Suite 617, New York NY 10010. (212)924-6269. Fax: (212)924-6609. E-mail: agentname@jhlitagent.com. **Contact:** Joy Harris. Member of AAR. Represents over 100 clients. Currently handles: 50% nonfiction books; 50% novels.

Member Agents Joy Harris; Cheryl Pientica; Robin London.

Represents Nonfiction books, novels. **Considers these fiction areas:** Ethnic; experimental; family saga; feminist; gay/lesbian; glitz; hi-lo; historical; humor/satire; literary; mainstream/contemporary; multicultural; multimedia; mystery/suspense; regional; short story collections; spiritual; translation; young adult; women's.

    O➡ Does not want to receive screenplays.

How to Contact Query with sample chapter, outline/proposal, SASE. Considers simultaneous queries. Responds in 2 months to queries. Obtains most new clients through recommendations from clients and editors.

Recent Sales This agency prefers not to share information on specific sales.

Terms Agent receives 15% commission on domestic sales; 20% commission on foreign sales. Charges clients for some office expenses.

◗ HARTLINE LITERARY AGENCY

123 Queenston Dr., Pittsburgh PA 15235-5429. (412)829-2495. Fax: (412)829-2450. E-mail: joyce@hartlineliterary.com. Web site: www.hartlineliterary.com. **Contact:** Joyce A. Hart. Estab. 1990. Represents 40 clients. 20% of clients are new/unpublished writers. Currently handles: 40% nonfiction books; 60% novels.

Member Agents Joyce A. Hart, principal agent; Janet Benrey; Tamela Hancock Murray; Andrea Boeshaar.

Represents Nonfiction books, novels. **Considers these nonfiction areas:** Business/economics; child guidance/parenting; cooking/foods/nutrition; money/finance; religious/inspirational; self-help/personal improvement; women's issues/studies. **Considers these fiction areas:** Action/adventure; contemporary issues; family saga; historical; literary; mystery/suspense (amateur sleuth, cozy); regional; religious/inspirational; romance (contemporary, gothic, historical, regency); thriller.

    O➡ This agency specializes in the Christian bookseller market. Actively seeking adult fiction, self-help, nutritional books, devotional, and business. Does not want to receive erotica, gay/lesbian, fantasy, horror, etc.

How to Contact Submit summary/outline, author bio, 3 sample chapters. Accepts e-mail and fax queries. Considers simultaneous queries. Responds in 2 months to queries; 3 months to mss. Returns materials only with SASE. Obtains most new clients through recommendations from others.

Recent Sales *I'm Not OK and Neither Are You*, by David E. Clarke, PhD (Barbour Publishers); *Along Came Love*, by Carrie Turansky (Steeple Hill); *Glory Be*, by Ron and Janet Benrey (Steeple Hill); *Overcoing the Top Ten Reasons Singles Stay Single*, by Tom and Beverly Rodgers (NavPress); *A Clearing in the Wild*, by Jane Kirkpatrick (Waterbrook); *The Mothers-in-Law*, by Andrea Boeshaar and Jeri Odel (Focus on the Family); *Ties to Home*, by Kim Sawyer (Bethany House); The Reluctant 3-book series, by Jill Nelson (Harvest House).

Terms Agent receives 15% commission on domestic sales. Offers written contract.

N ⊕ ✪ ANTONY HARWOOD LIMITED

103 Walton St., Oxford OX2 6EB England. (44)(186)555-9615. Fax: (44)(186)531-0660. E-mail: mail@antonyharwood.com. Web site: www.antonyharwood.com. **Contact:** Antony Harwood, James Macdonald Lockhart. Estab. 2000. Represents 52 clients.

    • Prior to starting this agency, Mr. Harwood and Mr. Lockhart worked at publishing houses and other literary agencies.

Represents Nonfiction books, novels. **Considers these nonfiction areas:** Agriculture/horticulture; americana; animals; anthropology/archaeology; art/architecture/design; biography/autobiography; business/economics; child guidance/parenting; computers/electronic; cooking/foods/nutrition; creative nonfiction (1); current affairs; education; ethnic/cultural interests; gardening; gay/lesbian issues; government/politics/law; health/medicine; history; how-to; humor/satire; language/literature/criticism; memoirs; military/war; money/finance; multicultural; music/dance; nature/environment; philosophy; photography; popular culture; psychology; recreation; regional; religious/inspirational; science/technology; self-help/personal improvement; sex; sociology; software; spirituality; sports; theater/film; translation; travel; true crime/investigative; women's issues/studies. **Considers these fiction areas:** Action/adventure; comic books/cartoon; confession; detective/police/crime; erotica; ethnic; experimental; family saga; fantasy; feminist; gay/lesbian; gothic; hi-lo; historical; horror; humor/satire; literary; mainstream/contemporary; military/war; multicultural; multimedia; mystery/suspense; occult; picture books; plays; regional; religious/inspirational; romance; science fiction; spiritual; sports; thriller; translation; westerns/frontier; young adult.

    O➡ "We accept every genre of fiction and nonfiction except for children's fiction for readers ages 10 and younger. We also do not accept poetry or screenplays."

How to Contact Submit outline, 2-3 sample chapters via e-mail or postal mail (include SAE). Responds in 2 months to queries.

Recent Sales *Learning to Swim*, by Clare Chambers; *The Dark Fields*, by Alan Glynn; *Jimmy Corrigan*, by Chris Ware; *The Proposal*, by Owen Slot.

Terms Agent receives 15% commission on domestic sales; 20% commission on foreign sales.

JOHN HAWKINS & ASSOCIATES, INC.

71 W. 23rd St., Suite 1600, New York NY 10010. (212)807-7040. Fax: (212)807-9555. E-mail: jha@jhalit.com. Web site: www.jhalit.com. **Contact:** Moses Cardona (moses@jhalit.com). Estab. 1893. Member of AAR. Represents over 100 clients. 5-10% of clients are new/unpublished writers. Currently handles: 40% nonfiction books; 40% novels; 20% juvenile books.

Member Agents Moses Cardona; Warren Frazier; Anne Hawkins; John Hawkins; William Reiss.

Represents Nonfiction books, novels, juvenile books. **Considers these nonfiction areas:** Agriculture/horticulture; americana; anthropology/archaeology; art/architecture/design; biography/autobiography; business/economics; current affairs; education; ethnic/cultural interests; gardening; gay/lesbian issues; government/politics/law; health/medicine; history; how-to; interior design/decorating; language/literature/criticism; memoirs; money/finance; multicultural; nature/environment; philosophy; popular culture; psychology; recreation; science/technology; self-help/personal improvement; sex; sociology; software; theater/film; travel; true crime/investigative; young adult; Music, creative nonfiction. **Considers these fiction areas:** Action/adventure; detective/police/crime; ethnic; experimental; family saga; feminist; gay/lesbian; glitz; gothic; hi-lo; historical; literary; mainstream/contemporary; military/war; multicultural; multimedia; mystery/suspense; psychic/supernatural; religious/inspirational; short story collections; sports; thriller; translation; westerns/frontier; young adult; women's.

How to Contact Submit query, proposal package, outline, SASE. Considers simultaneous queries. Responds in 1 month to queries. Returns materials only with SASE. Obtains most new clients through recommendations from others.

Recent Sales *And Only to Deceive*, by Tasha Alexander; *The Dream Life of Sukhanov*, by Olga Grushin; *The Method Actors*, by Carl Shuker.

Terms Agent receives 15% commission on domestic sales; 20% commission on foreign sales. Charges clients for photocopying.

RICHARD HENSHAW GROUP

127 W. 24th St., 4th Floor, New York NY 10011. (212)414-1172. Fax: (212)414-1182. E-mail: submissions@henshaw.com. Web site: www.rich.henshaw.com. **Contact:** Rich Henshaw. Estab. 1995. Member of AAR, SinC, MWA, HWA, SFWA, RWA. Represents 35 clients. 20% of clients are new/unpublished writers. Currently handles: 35% nonfiction books; 65% novels.

● Prior to opening his agency, Mr. Henshaw served as an agent with Richard Curtis Associates, Inc.

Represents Nonfiction books, novels. **Considers these nonfiction areas:** Animals; biography/autobiography; business/economics; child guidance/parenting; computers/electronic; cooking/foods/nutrition; current affairs; gay/lesbian issues; government/politics/law; health/medicine; how-to; humor/satire; military/war; money/finance; music/dance; nature/environment; New Age/metaphysics; popular culture; psychology; science/technology; self-help/personal improvement; sociology; sports; true crime/investigative; women's issues/studies. **Considers these fiction areas:** Action/adventure; detective/police/crime; ethnic; family saga; fantasy; glitz; historical; horror; humor/satire; literary; mainstream/contemporary; mystery/suspense; psychic/supernatural; romance; science fiction; sports; thriller.

○— This agency specializes in thrillers, mysteries, science fiction, fantasy, and horror.

How to Contact Query with SASE. Responds in 3 weeks to queries; 6 weeks to mss. Obtains most new clients through recommendations from others, solicitations, conferences.

Recent Sales *Blindfold Game*, by Dana Stabenow (St. Martin's Press); *Eye of the Wolf*, by Margaret Coel (Berkely); *The Well-Educated Mind*, by Susan Wise Bauer (Norton); *Shadow Man*, by James D. Doss (St. Martin's Press); *Box Like the Pros*, by Joe Frazier and William Dettloff (HarperCollins). Other clients include Jessie Wise, Peter van Dijk, Jay Caselberg, Judith Laik.

Terms Agent receives 15% commission on domestic sales; 20% commission on foreign sales. No written contract. 100% of business is derived from commissions on ms sales. Charges clients for photocopying mss and book orders.

Tips "While we do not have any reason to believe that our submission guidelines will change in the near future, writers can find up-to-date submission policy information on our Web site. Always include a SASE with correct return postage."

◙ FREDERICK HILL BONNIE NADELL, INC.

1842 Union St., San Francisco CA 94123. (415)921-2910. Fax: (415)921-2802. **Contact:** Elise Proulx. Estab. 1979. Represents 100 clients.

Member Agents Fred Hill, president; Bonnie Nadell, vice president; Elise Proulx, associate.

Represents Nonfiction books, novels. **Considers these nonfiction areas:** Current affairs; language/literature/criticism; nature/environment; Biography; government/politics. **Considers these fiction areas:** Literary; mainstream/contemporary.

How to Contact Query with SASE. No e-mail or fax queries. Considers simultaneous queries. Returns materials only with SASE.

Recent Sales *It Might Have Been What He Said*, by Eden Collinsworth; *Consider the Lobster and Other Essays*, by David Foster Wallace; *The Underdog*, by Joshua Davis.

Terms Agent receives 15% commission on domestic sales; 20% commission on foreign sales; 15% commission on dramatic rights sales. Charges clients for photocopying.

◙ HOPKINS LITERARY ASSOCIATES

2117 Buffalo Rd., Suite 327, Rochester NY 14624-1507. (585)352-6268. **Contact:** Pam Hopkins. Estab. 1996. Member of AAR, RWA. Represents 30 clients. 5% of clients are new/unpublished writers. Currently handles: 100% novels.

Represents Novels. **Considers these fiction areas:** Romance (historical, contemporary, category); women's.

> O→ This agency specializes in women's fiction, particularly historical, contemporary, and category romance, as well as mainstream work.

How to Contact Submit outline, 3 sample chapters. No e-mail or fax queries. Considers simultaneous queries. Responds in 2 weeks to queries; 1 month to mss. Returns materials only with SASE. Obtains most new clients through recommendations from others, solicitations, conferences.

Recent Sales Sold 50 titles in the last year. *Lady of Sin*, by Madeline Hunter (Bantam); *Silent in the Grave*, by Deanna Raybourn (Mira); *Passion*, by Lisa Valdez (Berkley).

Terms Agent receives 15% commission on domestic sales; 20% commission on foreign sales. No written contract.

Writers' Conferences RWA National Conference.

◙ IMPRINT AGENCY, INC.

5 W. 101 St., Suite 8B, New York NY 10025. E-mail: imprintagency@earthlink.net. Web site: www.imprintagency.com. **Contact:** Stephany Evans. Member of AAR. Represents 100+ clients.

Member Agents Stephany Evans; Gary Heidt (garyheidt@yahoo.com); Meredith Phelan (mphelan@mindspring.com).

Represents Nonfiction books, novels. **Considers these nonfiction areas:** Animals; art/architecture/design; biography/autobiography; child guidance/parenting; cooking/foods/nutrition; crafts/hobbies; current affairs; ethnic/cultural interests; health/medicine; history; how-to; interior design/decorating; memoirs; music/dance; nature/environment; popular culture; psychology; self-help/personal improvement; sports; theater/film; true crime/investigative; women's issues/studies. **Considers these fiction areas:** Detective/police/crime; glitz; literary; mystery/suspense; romance; thriller; women's.

How to Contact Query with SASE. Responds in 1 week to queries; 2 months to mss.

Terms Agent receives 15% commission on domestic sales; 20% commission on foreign sales. Offers written contract. Charges clients for copying and postage if necessary.

◙ J DE S ASSOCIATES, INC.

9 Shagbark Rd., Wilson Point, South Norwalk CT 06854. (203)838-7571. **Contact:** Jacques de Spoelberch. Estab. 1975. Represents 50 clients. Currently handles: 50% nonfiction books; 50% novels.

> • Prior to opening his agency, Mr. de Spoelberch was an editor with Houghton Mifflin.

Represents Nonfiction books, novels. **Considers these nonfiction areas:** Biography/autobiography; business/economics; current affairs; ethnic/cultural interests; government/politics/law; health/medicine; history; military/war; New Age/metaphysics; self-help/personal improvement; sociology; sports; translation. **Considers these fiction areas:** Detective/police/crime; historical; juvenile; literary; mainstream/contemporary; mystery/suspense; New Age; westerns/frontier; young adult.

How to Contact Query with SASE. Responds in 2 months to queries. Obtains most new clients through recommendations from authors and other clients.

Terms Agent receives 15% commission on domestic sales; 20% commission on foreign sales. Charges clients for foreign postage and photocopying.

🙂 JABBERWOCKY LITERARY AGENCY

P.O. Box 4558, Sunnyside NY 11104-0558. (718)392-5985. Web site: www.awfulagent.com. **Contact:** Joshua Bilmes. Estab. 1994. Member of SFWA. Represents 40 clients. 15% of clients are new/unpublished writers. Currently handles: 15% nonfiction books; 75% novels; 5% scholarly books; 5% other.

Represents Nonfiction books, novels, scholarly books. **Considers these nonfiction areas:** Biography/autobiography; business/economics; cooking/foods/nutrition; current affairs; gay/lesbian issues; government/politics/law; health/medicine; history; humor/satire; language/literature/criticism; military/war; money/finance; nature/environment; popular culture; science/technology; sociology; sports; theater/film; true crime/investigative; women's issues/studies. **Considers these fiction areas:** Action/adventure; contemporary issues; detective/police/crime; ethnic; family saga; fantasy; gay/lesbian; glitz; historical; horror; humor/satire; literary; mainstream/contemporary; psychic/supernatural; regional; science fiction; sports; thriller.

> 🔾 This agency represents quite a lot of genre fiction and is actively seeking to increase the amount of nonfiction projects. It does not handle juvenile or young adult. Book-length material only—no poetry, articles, or short fiction.

How to Contact Query with SASE. Do not send mss unless requested. No e-mail or fax queries. Considers simultaneous queries. Responds in 2 weeks to queries. Returns materials only with SASE. Obtains most new clients through solicitations, recommendation by current clients.

Recent Sales Sold 25 US and 100 foreign titles in the last year. *Definitely Dead*, by Charlaine Harris (ACE); *Engaging the Enemy*, by Elizabeth Moon (Del Rey); *Mistborn*, by Brandon Sanderson (Tor); *Greywalker*, by Kathleen Richardson. Other clients include Simon Green, Tanya Huff, Tobias Buckell.

Terms Agent receives 15% commission on domestic sales; 20% commission on foreign sales. Offers written contract, binding for 1 year. Charges clients for book purchases, photocopying, international book/ms mailing.

Writers' Conferences Malice Domestic; World Fantasy Convention.

Tips ''In approaching with a query, the most important things to me are your credits and your biographical background to the extent it's relevant to your work. I (and most agents) will ignore the adjectives you may choose to describe your own work.''

🙂 JCA LITERARY AGENCY

174 Sullivan St., New York NY 10012. (212)807-0888. E-mail: tom@jcalit.com. Web site: www.jcalit.com. **Contact:** Tom Cushman. Estab. 1978. Member of AAR. Represents 100 clients. 10% of clients are new/unpublished writers. Currently handles: 20% nonfiction books; 75% novels; 5% scholarly books.

Member Agents Tom Cushman; Melanie Meyers Cushman; Tony Outhwaite.

Represents Nonfiction books, novels. **Considers these nonfiction areas:** Biography/autobiography; current affairs; government/politics/law; history; language/literature/criticism; memoirs; popular culture; sociology; sports; theater/film; translation; true crime/investigative. **Considers these fiction areas:** Action/adventure; contemporary issues; detective/police/crime; family saga; historical; literary; mainstream/contemporary; mystery/suspense; sports; thriller.

> 🔾 Does not want to receive screenplays, poetry, children's books, science fiction/fantasy, or genre romance.

How to Contact Query with SASE. No e-mail or fax queries. Considers simultaneous queries. Responds in 1 month to queries; 10 weeks to mss. Returns materials only with SASE. Obtains most new clients through recommendations from others, solicitations, conferences.

Recent Sales *Jury of One*, by David Ellis (Putnam); *The Heaven of Mercury*, by Brad Watson (Norton); *The Rope Eater*, by Ben Jones; *The Circus in Winter*, by Cathy Dial. Other clients include Ernest J. Gaines, Gwen Hunter.

Terms Agent receives 15% commission on domestic sales; 20% commission on foreign sales. No written contract. ''We work with our clients on a handshake basis.'' Charges for postage on overseas submissions, photocopying, mss for submission, books purchased for subrights submission, bank charges. ''We deduct the cost from payments received from publishers.''

Tips ''We do not provide legal, accounting, or public relations services for our clients, although some of the advice we give falls into these realms. In cases where it seems necessary, we will recommend obtaining outside advice or assistance in these areas from professionals who are not in any way connected to the agency.''

🙂 JELLINEK & MURRAY LITERARY AGENCY

2024 Muana Place, Honolulu HI 96822. (808)521-4057. Fax: (808)521-4058. E-mail: jellinek@lava.net. **Contact:** Roger Jellinek. Estab. 1995. Represents 75 clients. 90% of clients are new/unpublished writers. Currently handles: 70% nonfiction books; 30% novels.

> ● Prior to becoming an agent, Mr. Jellinek was deputy editor, *New York Times Book Review* (1966-1974); editor-in-chief, New York Times Book Co. (1975-1981); editor/packager of book/TV projects (1981-1995); editorial director, Inner Ocean Publishing (2000-2003).

Member Agents Roger Jellinek; Eden Lee Murray. Literary Associates: Grant Ching; Lavonne Leong; Jeremy Colvin. **Represents** Nonfiction books, novels, textbooks, movie scripts (from book clients), TV scripts (from book clients). **Considers these nonfiction areas:** Animals; anthropology/archaeology; art/architecture/design; biography/autobiography; business/economics; child guidance/parenting; computers/electronic; cooking/foods/nutrition; current affairs; ethnic/cultural interests; gay/lesbian issues; government/politics/law; health/medicine; history; how-to; memoirs; military/war; money/finance; nature/environment; New Age/metaphysics; popular culture; psychology; religious/inspirational; science/technology; self-help/personal improvement; travel; true crime/investigative; women's issues/studies. **Considers these fiction areas:** Action/adventure; confession; contemporary issues; detective/police/crime; erotica; ethnic; family saga; feminist; gay/lesbian; glitz; historical; horror; humor/satire; literary; mainstream/contemporary; multicultural; mystery/suspense; New Age; picture books; psychic/supernatural; regional (specific to Hawaii); thriller.

> ⚬┭ This is the only literary agency in Hawaii. "Half our clients are based in Hawaii and half are from all over the world. We prefer submissions (after query) via e-mail attachment. We only send out fully-edited proposals and manuscripts." Actively seeking first-rate writing.

How to Contact Outline. Query with SASE, outline, author bio, 2 sample chapters, credentials/platform. Accepts e-mail and fax queries. Considers simultaneous queries. Responds in 2-3 weeks to queries; 2 months to mss. Returns materials only with SASE. Obtains most new clients through recommendations from others, solicitations, conferences.

Recent Sales Sold 10 titles and 1 script in the last year.

Terms Agent receives 15% commission on domestic sales; 25% commission on foreign sales. Offers written contract, binding for indefinite period; 30-day notice must be given to terminate contract. Charges clients for photocopies and postage. May refer to editing services if author asks for recommendation. "We derive no income from our referrals. Referrals to editors do not imply representation."

Writers' Conferences Mr. Jellinek manages the publishing program at the Maui Writers Conference.

Tips "Would-be authors should be well read and knowledgeable about their field and genre."

◪ JETREID LITERARY AGENCY

Am Co Center #106, 201 E. 10th St., New York NY 10003. (718)821-4996. E-mail: jetreidliterary@earthlink.net. Web site: www.jetreidliterary.com. **Contact:** Janet Reid. Estab. 2003. Represents 22 clients. Currently handles: 50% nonfiction books; 50% novels.

• Prior to becoming an agent, Ms. Reid spent 15 years in book publicity with national and regional clients.

Represents Nonfiction books, novels. **Considers these nonfiction areas:** Animals; art/architecture/design; biography/autobiography; business/economics; current affairs; ethnic/cultural interests; history; language/literature/criticism; memoirs; music/dance; nature/environment; popular culture; science/technology; true crime/investigative. **Considers these fiction areas:** Action/adventure; detective/police/crime; ethnic; experimental; literary; mainstream/contemporary; mystery/suspense; regional; thriller; young adult.

> ⚬┭ "JetReid Literary has an eclectic list of interesting, original, and imaginative voices. We look for authors of compelling work in both fiction and nonfiction. Our mysteries range from smart girls with guns to rat pack noir best read with a martini and a sardonic sneer at danger. Our nonfiction runs from the narrative of living on an Oregon commune to the prescriptive help of what to do if you work with an abuser." Actively seeking narrative fiction and nonfiction, along with an original voice and subject matter. Does not want to receive poems, screenplays, romance, westerns, self-help, or previously published work.

How to Contact Query with SASE. Considers simultaneous queries. Responds in 10 days to queries; 2-3 months to mss. Obtains most new clients through recommendations from others, query letters.

Recent Sales Sold 7 titles in the last year. *The Greening of Ben Brown*, by Michael Strelow (Hawthorne Press); *The Electric Church*, by Jeff Somers (Warner Aspect); *Lost Dog*, by Bill Cameron (Midnight Ink); *Becoming a Great Musician*, by Stan Munslow (Schirmer Trade Books); *Master Detective: The Life and Crimes of Ellis Parker*, by John Reisinger (Kensington); *Million Dollar Baby*, by Amy Meade (Midnight Ink). Other clients include Tim Anderson, Adam Eisenberg, Kari Dell, Jeanne Erickson, Kennedy Foster, Katy King, Evan Mandery, Dan Tomasulo, Garry Wang.

Terms Agent receives 15% commission on domestic sales; 15% commission on foreign sales. Offers written contract; 30-day written notice must be given to terminate contract. Charges up to $300 for office expenses when the project is sold. Most projects don't come close to reaching the $300 maximum.

Tips "Check the Web site for guidelines that will help you send the right material. We do not accept e-mail queries."

◪ NATASHA KERN LITERARY AGENCY

P.O. Box 1069, White Salmon WA 98672. (509)493-3803. Web site: www.natashakern.com. **Contact:** Natasha Kern. Estab. 1986. Member of RWA, MWA, SinC.

- Prior to opening her agency, Ms. Kern worked as an editor and publicist for Simon & Schuster, Bantam, and Ballantine. "This agency has sold over 700 books."

Represents Adult commercial nonfiction and fiction. **Considers these nonfiction areas:** Animals; child guidance/parenting; current affairs; ethnic/cultural interests; gardening; health/medicine; nature/environment; New Age/metaphysics; popular culture; psychology; religious/inspirational; self-help/personal improvement; spirituality; women's issues/studies; Investigative journalism. **Considers these fiction areas:** Women's; chick lit; lady lit; romance (contemporary, historical); historical; mainstream/contemporary; multicultural; mystery/suspense; religious/inspirational; thriller.

- This agency specializes in commercial fiction and nonfiction for adults. "We are a full-service agency." Does not represent sports, true crime, scholarly works, coffee table books, war memoirs, software, scripts, literary fiction, photography, poetry, short stories, children's, horror, fantasy, genre science fiction, stage plays, or traditional westerns.

How to Contact See submission instructions online. Query with SASE, submission history, writing credits, length of ms. Considers simultaneous queries. Responds in 3 weeks to queries.

Recent Sales Sold 56 titles in the last year. *Wicked Pleasure*, by Nina Bangs (Berkley); *Inviting God In*, by David Aaron (Shambhala); *Perfect Killer*, by Lewis Perdue (Tor); *The Secret Lives of the Sushi Club*, by Christy Yorke (Penguin); *Extreme Exposure*, by Pamela Clare (Berkley); *Dead End Dating*, by Kimberly Raye (Ballantine); *Under the Jacaranda Tree*, by Nikki Arana (Baker Book House); *My True Love's Name*, by Diana Holquist (Warner Books).

Terms Agent receives 15% commission on domestic sales; 20% commission on foreign sales; 15% commission on dramatic rights sales.

Writers' Conferences RWA National Conference; MWA National Conference; and many regional conferences.

Tips "Your chances of being accepted for representation will be greatly enhanced by going to our Web site first. Our idea of a dream client is someone who participates in a mutually respectful business relationship, is clear about needs and goals, and communicates about career planning. If we know what you need and want, we can help you achieve it. A dream client has a storytelling gift, a commitment to a writing career, a desire to learn and grow, and a passion for excellence. We want clients who are expressing their own unique voice and truly have something of their own to communicate. This client understands that many people have to work together for a book to succeed and that everything in publishing takes far longer than one imagines. Trust and communication are truly essential."

[N] ♥ VIRGINIA KIDD AGENCY, INC.

538 E. Harford St., P.O. Box 278, Milford PA 18337. (570)296-6205. Fax: (570)296-7266. Web site: www.vk-agency.com. Estab. 1965. Member of SFWA, SFRA. Represents 80 clients.

Member Agents Christine Cohen; Vaughne Hansen; Brian Townsell.

Represents Novels. **Considers these fiction areas:** Fantasy; historical; mystery/suspense; science fiction; women's; Speculative; mainstream.

- This agency specializes in science fiction and fantasy.

How to Contact Submit synopsis (1-3 pages), cover letter, first chapter, SASE. Responds in 4-6 weeks to queries.

Recent Sales *The Wizard* and *Starwater Strains*, by Gene Wolfe (Tor); *Gifts* and *Voices*, by Ursula K. Le Guin (Harcourt); *The Galileo's Children*, by Gardner Dozois (Pry); *The Light Years Beneath My Feet* and *Running From the Deity*, by Alan Dean Foster (Del Ray); *From the Files of the Time Rangers*, by Rick Bowes (Golden Gryphon); *Chasing Fire*, by Michelle Welch. Other clients include Eleanor Arnason, Ted Chiang, Jack Skillinsgread, Kage Baker, Patricia Briggs, and the estates for James Tiptree Jr., Murray Leinster, E.E. "Doc" Smith, R.A. Lafferty.

Terms Agent receives 15% commission on domestic sales; 20-25% commission on foreign sales; 20% commission on dramatic rights sales. Offers written contract; 2-month notice must be given to terminate contract. Charges clients occasionally for extraordinary expenses.

Tips "If you have a completed novel that is of extraordinary quality, please send us a query."

◎ KIRCHOFF/WOHLBERG, INC., AUTHORS' REPRESENTATION DIVISION

866 United Nations Plaza, #525, New York NY 10017. (212)644-2020. Fax: (212)223-4387. **Contact:** Liza Pulitzer Voges. Director of Operations: John R. Whitman. Estab. 1930s. Member of AAR, AAP, Society of Illustrators, SPAR, Bookbuilders of Boston, New York Bookbinders' Guild, AIGA. Represents 50 clients. 10% of clients are new/unpublished writers. Currently handles: 5% nonfiction books; 25% novels; 5% young adult; 65% picture books.

- Kirchoff/Wohlberg has been in business for over 60 years.

- This agency specializes in only juvenile through young adult trade books.

How to Contact For novels, query with SASE, outline, a few sample chapters. For picture books, send entire ms, SASE. No e-mail or fax queries. Considers simultaneous queries. Responds in 1 month to queries; 2 months to mss. Returns materials only with SASE. Obtains most new clients through recommendations from authors, illustrators, and editors.

Recent Sales Sold over 50 titles in the last year. *Three Nasty Gnarlies*, by Keith Graves (Scholastic); *Listening for Lions*, by Gloria Whelan (HarperCollins); My Weird School series, by Dan Gutman (HarperCollins); *Biscuit*, by Alyssa Capucilli (HarperCollins).

Terms Offers written contract, binding for at least 1 year. Agent receives standard commission, depending upon whether it is an author only, illustrator only, or an author/illustrator book.

☑ HARVEY KLINGER, INC.

300 W. 55th St., New York NY 10019. (212)581-7068. E-mail: queries@harveyklinger.com. Web site: www.harveyklinger.com. **Contact:** Harvey Klinger. Estab. 1977. Member of AAR. Represents 100 clients. 25% of clients are new/unpublished writers. Currently handles: 50% nonfiction books; 50% novels.

Member Agents David Dunton (popular culture, music-related books, literary fiction, crime novels, thrillers); Sara Crowe (children's and young adult authors, some adult authors, foreign rights sales); Andrea Somberg (literary fiction, commercial fiction, quality narrative nonfiction, popular culture, how-to, self-help, humor, interior design, cookbooks, health/fitness); Nikki Van De Car (science fiction/fantasy, horror, romance, literary fiction, popular culture, how-to, memoir).

Represents Nonfiction books, novels. **Considers these nonfiction areas:** Biography/autobiography; cooking/foods/nutrition; health/medicine; psychology; science/technology; self-help/personal improvement; spirituality; sports; true crime/investigative; women's issues/studies. **Considers these fiction areas:** Action/adventure; detective/police/crime; family saga; glitz; literary; mainstream/contemporary; mystery/suspense; thriller.

   ○━ This agency specializes in big, mainstream, contemporary fiction and nonfiction.

How to Contact Query with SASE. No phone or fax queries. Responds in 2 months to queries and mss. Obtains most new clients through recommendations from others.

Recent Sales *The Red Hat Society: Fun & Friendship After Fifty*, by Sue Ellen Cooper; *Wilco: Learning How to Die*, by Greg Kot; *A Window Across the River*, by Brian Morton; *The Sweet Potato Queen's Field Guide to Men: Every Man I Love Is Either Gay, Married, or Dead*, by Jill Conner Browne; *Get Your Share: A Guide to Striking it Rich in the Stock Market*, by Julie Stav; *Wink: The Incredible Life & Epic Journey of Jimmy Winkfield*, by Ed Hotaling. Other clients include Barbara Wood, Terry Kay, Barbara De Angelis, Jeremy Jackson.

Terms Agent receives 15% commission on domestic sales; 25% commission on foreign sales. Offers written contract. Charges for photocopying mss and overseas postage for mss.

ⓃⓈ KNEERIM & WILLIAMS

225 Franklin St., Boston MA 02110. (617)542-5070. Fax: (617)542-8906. Web site: www.fr.com/kwfr. **Contact:** Melissa Grella. Estab. 1990. Represents 200 clients. 5% of clients are new/unpublished writers. Currently handles: 80% nonfiction books; 15% novels; 5% movie scripts.

   • Prior to becoming an agent, Mr. Williams was a lawyer; Ms. Kneerim was a publisher and editor; Mr. Wasserman was an editor and journalist.

Member Agents Elaine Rogers (film/TV agent and entertainment lawyer).

Represents Nonfiction books, novels. **Considers these nonfiction areas:** Anthropology/archaeology; biography/autobiography; business/economics; child guidance/parenting; current affairs; government/politics/law; health/medicine; history; language/literature/criticism; memoirs; nature/environment; popular culture; psychology; religious/inspirational; science/technology; sociology; sports; women's issues/studies. **Considers these fiction areas:** Historical; literary; mainstream/contemporary.

   ○━ This agency specializes in narrative nonfiction, history, science, business, women's issues, commercial and literary fiction, film, and television. "We have 7 agents and 2 scouts in Boston, New York, and Santa Fe." Actively seeking distinguished authors, experts, professionals, intellectuals, and serious writers. Does not want to receive blanket multiple submissions, genre fiction, children's literature, or original screenplays.

How to Contact Query with SASE. Responds in 2 weeks to queries; 2 months to mss. Returns materials only with SASE. Obtains most new clients through recommendations from others.

Recent Sales See Web site for a list of clients and recent sales.

☑ ELAINE KOSTER LITERARY AGENCY, LLC

55 Central Park W., Suite 6, New York NY 10023. (212)362-9488. Fax: (212)712-0164. **Contact:** Elaine Koster, Stephanie Lehmann. Member of AAR, MWA. Represents 40 clients. 10% of clients are new/unpublished writers. Currently handles: 30% nonfiction books; 70% novels.

   • Prior to opening her agency in 1998, Ms. Koster was president and publisher of Dutton NAL, part of the Penguin Group.

Represents Nonfiction books, novels. **Considers these nonfiction areas:** Biography/autobiography; business/

economics; child guidance/parenting; cooking/foods/nutrition; current affairs; ethnic/cultural interests; health/ medicine; history; how-to; money/finance; nature/environment; popular culture; psychology; self-help/personal improvement; spirituality; women's issues/studies. **Considers these fiction areas:** Contemporary issues; detective/police/crime; ethnic; family saga; feminist; historical; literary; mainstream/contemporary; mystery/ suspense (amateur sleuth, cozy, culinary, malice domestic); regional; thriller; Chick lit.

> O→ This agency specializes in quality fiction and nonfiction. Does not want to receive juvenile, screenplays, or science fiction.

How to Contact Query with SASE, outline, 3 sample chapters. Prefers to read materials exclusively. No e-mail or fax queries. Responds in 3 weeks to queries; 1 month to mss. Returns materials only with SASE. Obtains most new clients through recommendations from others.

Recent Sales Sold 29 titles in the last year. *A Rock and a Hard Place*, by Kimberla Lawson Roby (Morrow); *Mine to Keep*, by Sheridan Hay (Doubleday); *Body Count*, by P.D. Martin (Mira).

Terms Agent receives 15% commission on domestic sales. Bills back specific expenses incurred doing business for a client.

Tips "We prefer exclusive submissions. Don't e-mail or fax submissions. Please include biographical information and publishing history."

⬛ KRAAS LITERARY AGENCY

13514 Winter Creek Ct., Houston TX 77077. (281)870-9770. Fax: (281)679-1655. **Contact:** Irene Kraas. Alternate address: 3447 NE 23rd Ave., Portland OR 97212. (503)319-0900. **Contact:** Ashley Kraas. Estab. 1990. Represents 40 clients. 75% of clients are new/unpublished writers. Currently handles: 5% nonfiction books; 95% novels.

Member Agents Irene Kraas, principal (psychological thrillers, medical thrillers, literary fiction, young adult); Ashley Kraas, associate (romance, women's fiction, historical fiction, memoirs, biographies, self-help, spiritual). Please send appropriate submissions to the correct address (Ashley in Portland; Irene in Houston).

> O→ This agency specializes in adult fiction. Actively seeking books that are well written with commercial potential. Does not want to receive short stories, plays, or poetry.

How to Contact Submit cover letter, first 50 pages of a completed ms, SASE. No e-mail or fax queries. Considers simultaneous queries. Returns materials only with SASE.

Recent Sales *Words to Die By*, by Kyra Davis (Harlequin); St. Germain series, by Chelsea Quinn Yarbro (Tor); *Shriker*, by Janet Lee Carey (Atheneum); *Crazy Quilt*, by Paula Paul (University of New Mexico Press); *The Sword*, *The Shield* and *The Crown*, a trilogy by Hilari Bell (Simon & Schuster).

Terms Agent receives 15% commission on domestic sales. Offers written contract. Charges clients for photocopying and postage.

Writers' Conferences Irene: Southwest Writers Conference; Wrangling with Writing. Ashley: Surrey International Writers Conference; Wrangling with Writing; Willamette Writers Conference.

Tips "Material by unpublished authors will be accepted in the above areas only. Published authors seeking representation may contact us regarding any material in any area except children's picture books and chapter books."

⬛ ◻ KT PUBLIC RELATIONS & LITERARY SERVICES

1905 Cricklewood Cove, Fogelsville PA 18051. (610)395-6298. Fax: (610)395-6299. E-mail: kae@ktpublicrelatio ns.com. Web site: www.ktpublicrelations.com. **Contact:** Kae Tienstra, Jon Tienstra. Estab. 2005. Represents 5 clients. 75% of clients are new/unpublished writers. Currently handles: 50% nonfiction books; 50% novels.

> • Prior to becoming an agent, Ms. Tienstra was publicity director for Rodale, Inc. for 13 years and then founded her own publicity agency; Mr. Tienstra joined the firm in 1995 with varied corporate experience and a master's degree in library science.

Member Agents Kae Tienstra (health, parenting, psychology, how-to, crafts, foods/nutrition, beauty, women's fiction, general fiction); Jon Tienstra (nature/environment, history, cooking/foods/nutrition, war/military, automotive, health/medicine, gardening, general fiction, science fiction/fantasy, popular fiction).

Represents Nonfiction books, novels, novellas. **Considers these nonfiction areas:** Agriculture/horticulture; animals; child guidance/parenting; cooking/foods/nutrition; crafts/hobbies; health/medicine; history; how-to; military/war; nature/environment; popular culture; psychology; science/technology; self-help/personal improvement; Interior design/decorating. **Considers these fiction areas:** Action/adventure; detective/police/ crime; family saga; fantasy; historical; literary; mainstream/contemporary; mystery/suspense; romance; science fiction; thriller.

> O→ "We have worked with a variety of authors and publishers over the years and have learned what individual publishers are looking for in terms of new acquisitions. We are both mad about books and authors and we look forward to finding publishing success for all our clients." Specializes in parenting, history, cooking/foods/nutrition, crafts, beauty, war, health/medicine, psychology, how-to, gardening, science fiction, fantasy, women's fiction, and popular fiction. Does not want to see unprofessional material.

How to Contact Query with SASE. Accepts e-mail and fax queries. Considers simultaneous queries. Responds in 2 weeks to queries; 3 months to mss. Returns materials only with SASE. Obtains most new clients through recommendations from others.

Terms Agent receives 15% commission on domestic sales; 20% commission on foreign sales. No written contract. Charges clients for long-distance phone calls, fax, postage, photocopying (only when incurred). No advance payment for these out-of-pocket expenses.

◙ THE LA LITERARY AGENCY

P.O. Box 46370, Los Angeles CA 90046. (323)654-5288. E-mail: laliteraryag@aol.com. **Contact:** Ann Cashman, Eric Lasher. Estab. 1980.

• Prior to becoming an agent, Mr. Lasher worked in publishing in New York and Los Angeles.

Represents Nonfiction books, novels. **Considers these nonfiction areas:** Animals; anthropology/archaeology; art/architecture/design; biography/autobiography; business/economics; child guidance/parenting; cooking/foods/nutrition; current affairs; ethnic/cultural interests; government/politics/law; health/medicine; history; how-to; nature/environment; popular culture; psychology; science/technology; self-help/personal improvement; sociology; sports; true crime/investigative; women's issues/studies; Narrative nonfiction. **Considers these fiction areas:** Action/adventure; detective/police/crime; family saga; feminist; historical; literary; mainstream/contemporary; sports; thriller.

How to Contact Query with SASE, outline, 1 sample chapter. No e-mail or fax queries.

Recent Sales *Full Bloom: The Art and Life of Georgia O'Keeffe*, by Hunter Drohojowska-Philp (Norton); *And the Walls Came Tumbling Down*, by H. Caldwell (Scribner); *Italian Slow & Savory*, by Joyce Goldstein (Chronicle); *A Field Guide to Chocolate Chip Cookies*, by Dede Wilson (Harvard Common Press); *Teen Knitting Club* (Artisan); *The Framingham Heart Study*, by Dr. Daniel Levy (Knopf).

◙ PETER LAMPACK AGENCY, INC.

551 Fifth Ave., Suite 1613, New York NY 10176-0187. (212)687-9106. Fax: (212)687-9109. E-mail: alampack@verizon.net. **Contact:** Andrew Lampack. Estab. 1977. Represents 50 clients. 10% of clients are new/unpublished writers. Currently handles: 20% nonfiction books; 80% novels.

Member Agents Peter Lampack (psychological suspense, action/adventure, literary fiction, nonfiction, contemporary relationships); Rema Delanyan (foreign rights); Andrew Lampack (new writers).

Represents Nonfiction books, novels. **Considers these fiction areas:** Action/adventure; detective/police/crime; family saga; historical; literary; mainstream/contemporary; mystery/suspense; thriller; Contemporary relationships.

    O→ This agency specializes in commercial fiction and nonfiction by recognized experts. Actively seeking literary and commercial fiction, thrillers, mysteries, suspense, and psychological thrillers. Does not want to receive horror, romance, science fiction, westerns, or academic material.

How to Contact Query with SASE. *No unsolicited mss.* Accepts e-mail queries. No fax queries. Considers simultaneous queries. Responds in 2 months to queries and mss. Obtains most new clients through referrals made by clients.

Recent Sales *Slow Man*, by J.M. Coetzee; *Black Wind*, by Clive Cussler and Dirk Cussler; *Sacred Stone*, by Clive Cussler and Craig Dirgo; *Lost City*, by Clive Cussler with Paul Kemprecos.

Terms Agent receives 15% commission on domestic sales; 20% commission on foreign sales.

Writers' Conferences BookExpo America.

Tips "Submit only your best work for consideration. Have a very specific agenda of goals you wish your prospective agent to accomplish for you. Provide the agent with a comprehensive statement of your credentials—educational and professional."

Ⓝ ◙ LAURA LANGLIE, LITERARY AGENT

275 President St., Suite 3, Brooklyn NY 11231. (718)858-0659. Fax: (718)858-6161. E-mail: laura@lauralanglie.com. **Contact:** Laura Langlie. Estab. 2001. Represents 25 clients. 50% of clients are new/unpublished writers. Currently handles: 25% nonfiction books; 48% novels; 2% story collections; 25% juvenile books.

• Prior to opening her agency, Ms. Langlie worked in publishing for 7 years and as an agent at Kidde, Hoyt & Picard for 6 years.

Represents Nonfiction books, novels, short story collections, novellas, juvenile books. **Considers these nonfiction areas:** Animals (not how-to); anthropology/archaeology; biography/autobiography; current affairs; ethnic/cultural interests; gay/lesbian issues; government/politics/law; history; humor/satire; memoirs; nature/environment; popular culture; psychology; theater/film; women's issues/studies; History of medicine and science; language/literature. **Considers these fiction areas:** Detective/police/crime; ethnic; feminist; gay/lesbian; historical; humor/satire; juvenile; literary; mystery/suspense; romance; thriller; young adult; Mainstream.

○━ "I love working with first-time authors. I'm very involved with and committed to my clients. I also employ a publicist to work with all my clients to make the most of each book's publication. Most of my clients come to me via recommendations from other agents, clients, and editors. I've met very few at conferences. I've often sought out writers for projects, and I still find new clients via the traditional query letter." Does not want science fiction, poetry, men's adventure, or erotica.

How to Contact Query with SASE. Accepts queries via fax. Considers simultaneous queries. Responds in 1 week to queries; 1 month to mss. Returns materials only with SASE. Obtains most new clients through recommendations, submissions.

Recent Sales Sold 40 titles in the last year. *How to Be Popular*, by Meg Cabot (HarperCollins Children's); *It's About Your Husband*, by Lauren Lipton (Warner Books); *Fix*, by Leslie Margolis (Simon Pulse); Untitled work about Muslims in America since September 11, by Geneive Abdo (Oxford University Press). Other clients include Renée Ashley, Mignon F. Ballard, Jessica Benson, Joan Druett, Jack El-Hai, Sarah Elliott, Fiona Gibson, Robin Hathaway, Melanie Lynne Hauser, Mary Hogan, Jonathan Neale, Eric Pinder, Delia Ray, Cheryl L. Reed, Jennifer Sturman.

Terms Agent receives 15% commission on domestic sales; 20% commission on foreign sales. No written contract.

Tips "Be complete, forthright, and clear in your communications. Do your research as to what a particular agent represents."

◪ MICHAEL LARSEN/ELIZABETH POMADA, LITERARY AGENTS

1029 Jones St., San Francisco CA 94109-5023. (415)673-0939. E-mail: larsenpoma@aol.com. Web site: www.lar sen-pomada.com. **Contact:** Mike Larsen, Elizabeth Pomada. Estab. 1972. Member of AAR, Authors Guild, ASJA, PEN, WNBA, California Writers Club, National Speakers Association. Represents 100 clients. 40-45% of clients are new/unpublished writers. Currently handles: 70% nonfiction books; 30% novels.

• Prior to opening their agency, Mr. Larsen and Ms. Pomada were promotion executives for major publishing houses. Mr. Larsen worked for Morrow, Bantam, and Pyramid (now part of Berkley); Ms. Pomada worked at Holt, David McKay, and The Dial Press.

Member Agents Michael Larsen (nonfiction); Elizabeth Pomada (fiction, narrative nonfiction, nonfiction for women).

Represents Adult book-length fiction and nonfiction that will interest New York publishers or are irresistibly written or conceived. **Considers these nonfiction areas:** Anthropology/archaeology; art/architecture/design; biography/autobiography; business/economics; cooking/foods/nutrition; current affairs; ethnic/cultural interests; gay/lesbian issues; government/politics/law; health/medicine; history; how-to; humor/satire; memoirs; money/finance; music/dance; nature/environment; New Age/metaphysics; popular culture; psychology; religious/inspirational; science/technology; self-help/personal improvement; sociology; sports; theater/film; travel; true crime/investigative; women's issues/studies; Futurism. **Considers these fiction areas:** Action/ adventure; contemporary issues; detective/police/crime; ethnic; experimental; family saga; fantasy; feminist; gay/lesbian; glitz; historical; humor/satire; literary; mainstream/contemporary; mystery/suspense; religious/ inspirational; romance (contemporary, gothic, historical); Chick lit.

○━ "We have diverse tastes. We look for fresh voices and new ideas. We handle literary, commercial, and genre fiction, and the full range of nonfiction books." Actively seeking commercial and literary fiction. Does not want to receive children's books, plays, short stories, screenplays, pornography, poetry, or stories of abuse.

How to Contact Query with SASE, first 10 pages of completed novel, 2-page synopsis, SASE. "For nonfiction, send title, promotion plan and proposal done according to our plan (see Web site)." No e-mail or fax queries. Responds in 2 days to queries; 2 months to mss.

Recent Sales Sold at least 15 titles in the last year. *The Blonde Theory*, by Kristin Harmel (Warner 5 Spot); *The Shadowed Isle*, by Katharine Kerr (Daw); *Making Documentary Movies*, by Barry Hampe (Holt); *Hit By a Farm*, by Catherine Friend (Marlowe).

Terms Agent receives 15% commission on domestic sales; 20% (30% for Asia) commission on foreign sales. May charge for printing, postage for multiple submissions, foreign mail, foreign phone calls, galleys, books, legal fees.

Writers' Conferences BookExpo America; Santa Barbara Writers' Conference; San Francisco Writers Conference.

Tips "If you can write books that meet the needs of the marketplace and you can promote your books, now is the best time ever to be a writer. We must find new writers to make a living, so we are very eager to hear from new writers whose work will interest large houses, and nonfiction writers who can promote their books. For a list of recent sales, helpful info, and three ways to make yourself irresistible to any publisher, please visit our Web site."

◎ THE STEVE LAUBE AGENCY

5501 N. 7th Ave., #502, Phoenix AZ 85013. (602)336-8910. Fax: (602)532-7123. E-mail: krichards@stevelaube.c om. Web site: www.stevelaube.com. **Contact:** Steve Laube. Estab. 2004. Member of CBA. Represents 50 clients. 20% of clients are new/unpublished writers. Currently handles: 48% nonfiction books; 48% novels; 2% novellas; 2% scholarly books.

- Prior to becoming an agent, Mr. Laube worked 11 years as a bookseller and 11 years as editorial director of nonfiction with Bethany House Publishers.

Represents Nonfiction books, novels. **Considers these nonfiction areas:** Religious/inspirational. **Considers these fiction areas:** Religious/inspirational.

- ○━ "We primarily serve the Christian market (CBA). However, we have had success representing books in a variety of fields." Actively seeking fiction and religious nonfiction. Does not want children's picture books, poetry, or cookbooks.

How to Contact Submit proposal package, outline, 3 sample chapters, SASE. No e-mail submissions. Consult Web site for guidelines. Considers simultaneous queries. Responds in 6-8 weeks. Returns materials only with SASE. Obtains most new clients through recommendations from others, solicitations, conferences.

Recent Sales Sold 80 titles in the last year. Clients include Deborah Raney, Bright Media, Allison Bottke, H. Norman Wright, Ellie Kay, Jack Cavanaugh, Karen Ball, Tracey Bateman, Clint Kelly, Susan May Warren, Lori Copeland, Martha Bolton, Lisa Bergren.

Terms Agent receives 15% commission on domestic sales; 20% commission on foreign sales. Offers written contract; 30-day notice must be given to terminate contract.

Writers' Conferences Mount Hermon Christian Writers Conference; American Christian Fiction Writers Conference; Glorieta Christian Writers Conference.

◙ LAZEAR AGENCY, INC.

431 2nd St., Suite 300, Hudson WI 54016. (715)531-0012. Fax: (715)531-0016. E-mail: info@lazear.com. Web site: www.lazear.com. **Contact:** Editorial Board. Estab. 1984. Represents 250 clients. Currently handles: 60% nonfiction books; 30% novels; 10% juvenile books.

- The Lazear Agency opened a New York office in September 1997.

Member Agents Jonathon Lazear; Christi Cardenas; Julie Mayo; Anne Blackstone.

Represents Nonfiction books, novels, juvenile books, licensing, new media with connection to book projects. **Considers these nonfiction areas:** Agriculture/horticulture; americana; animals; anthropology/archaeology; art/architecture/design; biography/autobiography; business/economics; child guidance/parenting; computers/ electronic; cooking/foods/nutrition; crafts/hobbies; current affairs; education; ethnic/cultural interests; gardening; gay/lesbian issues; government/politics/law; health/medicine; history; how-to; humor/satire; interior design/decorating; juvenile nonfiction; language/literature/criticism; memoirs; military/war; money/finance; multicultural; music/dance; nature/environment; New Age/metaphysics; philosophy; photography; popular culture; psychology; recreation; regional; religious/inspirational; science/technology; self-help/personal improvement; sex; sociology; software; spirituality; sports; theater/film; translation; travel; true crime/investigative; women's issues/studies; young adult; Creative nonfiction. **Considers these fiction areas:** Action/adventure; comic books/cartoon; confession; detective/police/crime; erotica; ethnic; experimental; family saga; fantasy; feminist; gay/lesbian; glitz; gothic; hi-lo; historical; horror; humor/satire; juvenile; literary; mainstream/contemporary; military/war; multicultural; multimedia; mystery/suspense; New Age; occult; picture books; plays; poetry; poetry in translation; psychic/supernatural; regional; religious/inspirational; romance; science fiction; short story collections; spiritual; sports; thriller; translation; westerns/frontier; young adult; women's.

How to Contact Query with SASE, outline/proposal. No phone calls or faxes. Responds in 3 weeks to queries; 1 month to mss. Returns materials only with SASE. Obtains most new clients through recommendations from others, bestseller lists, word of mouth.

Recent Sales Sold over 50 titles in the last year. *The Truth (with Jokes)*, by Al Franken (Dutton); *Harvest for Hope*, by Jane Goodall with Gary McAvoy and Gail Hudson (Warner); *Mommy Knows Worst*, by James Lileks (Crown); *The Prop*, by Pete Hautman (Simon & Schuster); *One Phone Call Away: Secrets of a Master Networker*, by Jeffrey Meshel (Portfolio); *Full Service*, by Will Weaver (Farrar, Straus & Giroux); *101 Ways to Help Birds*, by Laura Erickson (Stackpole).

Terms Agent receives 15% commission on domestic sales; 20% commission on foreign sales. Offers written contract. Charges clients for photocopying, international express mail, bound galleys, books used for subsidiary rights sales. No fees charged if book is not sold.

Tips "The writer should first view himself as a salesperson in order to obtain an agent. Sell yourself, your idea, your concept. Do your homework. Notice what is in the marketplace. Be sophisticated about the arena in which you are writing."

◙ THE NED LEAVITT AGENCY

70 Wooster St., Suite 4F, New York NY 10012. (212)334-0999. Web site: www.nedleavittagency.com/agency.ht ml. **Contact:** Ned Leavitt. Member of AAR.
Represents Nonfiction books, novels.
How to Contact For fiction, submit cover letter, 1-2 chapters, brief synopsis, author bio. For nonfiction, submit cover letter, TOC, brief chapter synopsis or outline, 1-2 sample chapters, author bio. No materials will be returned.
Tips ''See Web site for more information on what we need.''

◙ LESCHER & LESCHER, LTD.

47 E. 19th St., New York NY 10003. (212)529-1790. Fax: (212)529-2716. **Contact:** Robert Lescher, Susan Lescher. Estab. 1966. Member of AAR. Represents 150 clients. Currently handles: 80% nonfiction books; 20% novels.
Represents Nonfiction books, novels. **Considers these nonfiction areas:** Current affairs; history; memoirs; popular culture; Biography; cookbooks/wines; law; contemporary issues; narrative nonfiction. **Considers these fiction areas:** Literary; mystery/suspense; Commercial.
  O— Does not want to receive screenplays, science fiction, or romance.
How to Contact Query with SASE. Obtains most new clients through recommendations from others.
Recent Sales Sold 35 titles in the last year. This agency prefers not to share information on specific sales. Clients include Neil Sheehan, Madeleine L'Engle, Calvin Trillin, Judith Viorst, Thomas Perry, Anne Fadiman, Frances FitzGerald, Paula Fox, Robert M. Parker Jr.
Terms Agent receives 15% commission on domestic sales; 20-25% commission on foreign sales.

◙ LEVINE GREENBERG LITERARY AGENCY, INC.

307 7th Ave., Suite 2407, New York NY 10001. (212)337-0934. Fax: (212)337-0948. Web site: www.levinegreenb erg.com. Estab. 1989. Member of AAR. Represents 250 clients. 33% of clients are new/unpublished writers. Currently handles: 70% nonfiction books; 30% novels.
  • Prior to opening his agency, Mr. Levine served as vice president of the Bank Street College of Education.
Member Agents James Levine; Arielle Eckstut; Daniel Greenberg; Stephanie Kip Roston; Jenoyne Adams.
Represents Nonfiction books, novels. **Considers these nonfiction areas:** Animals; art/architecture/design; biography/autobiography; business/economics; child guidance/parenting; computers/electronic; cooking/ foods/nutrition; gardening; gay/lesbian issues; health/medicine; money/finance; nature/environment; New Age/metaphysics; religious/inspirational; science/technology; self-help/personal improvement; sociology; spirituality; sports; women's issues/studies. **Considers these fiction areas:** Literary; mainstream/contemporary; mystery/suspense; thriller (psychological); women's.
  O— This agency specializes in business, psychology, parenting, health/medicine, narrative nonfiction, spirituality, religion, women's issues, and commercial fiction.
How to Contact See Web site for full submission procedure. Prefers e-mail queries. Obtains most new clients through recommendations from others.
Recent Sales *The Onion: Our Dumb Century*; *Alternadad*, by Neal Pollack; *The Opposite of Death Is Love*, by Nando Parrado.
Terms Agent receives 15% commission on domestic sales; 20% commission on foreign sales. Offers written contract. Charges clients for out-of-pocket expenses—telephone, fax, postage, photocopying—directly connected to the project.
Writers' Conferences ASJA Writers Conference.
Tips ''We focus on editorial development, business representation, and publicity and marketing strategy.''

◙ PAUL S. LEVINE LITERARY AGENCY

1054 Superba Ave., Venice CA 90291-3940. (310)450-6711. Fax: (310)450-0181. E-mail: pslevine@ix.netcom.c om. Web site: www.paulslevine.com. **Contact:** Paul S. Levine. Estab. 1996. Member of the State Bar of California. Represents over 100 clients. 75% of clients are new/unpublished writers. Currently handles: 30% nonfiction books; 30% novels; 10% movie scripts; 30% TV scripts.
Represents Nonfiction books, novels, movie scripts, feature film, TV scripts, TV movie of the week, episodic drama, sitcom, animation, documentary, miniseries, syndicated material. **Considers these nonfiction areas:** Art/architecture/design; biography/autobiography; business/economics; child guidance/parenting; computers/electronic; cooking/foods/nutrition; crafts/hobbies; current affairs; education; ethnic/cultural interests; gay/lesbian issues; government/politics/law; health/medicine; history; how-to; humor/satire; interior design/ decorating; language/literature/criticism; memoirs; military/war; money/finance; music/dance; nature/environment; New Age/metaphysics; photography; popular culture; psychology; religious/inspirational; science/ technology; self-help/personal improvement; sociology; sports; theater/film; true crime/investigative; women's issues/studies; Creative nonfiction. **Considers these fiction areas:** Action/adventure; comic books/cartoon;

confession; detective/police/crime; erotica; ethnic; experimental; family saga; feminist; gay/lesbian; glitz; historical; humor/satire; literary; mainstream/contemporary; mystery/suspense; regional; religious/inspirational; romance; sports; thriller; westerns/frontier. **Considers these script subject areas:** Action/adventure; biography/autobiography; cartoon/animation; comedy; contemporary issues; detective/police/crime; erotica; ethnic; experimental; family saga; feminist; gay/lesbian; glitz; historical; horror; juvenile; mainstream; multimedia; mystery/suspense; religious/inspirational; romantic comedy; romantic drama; sports; teen; thriller; western/frontier.

O→ Actively seeking commercial fiction and nonfiction. Also handles children's and young adult fiction and nonfiction. Does not want to receive science fiction, fantasy, or horror.

How to Contact Query with SASE. Accepts e-mail and fax queries. Considers simultaneous queries. Responds in 1 day to queries; 2 months to mss. Returns materials only with SASE. Obtains most new clients through conferences, referrals, listings on various Web sites and in directories.

Recent Sales Sold 25 titles in the last year. This agency prefers not to share information on specific sales.

Terms Agent receives 15% commission on domestic sales; 20% commission on foreign sales. Offers written contract. Charges clients for messengers, long distance calls, postage (only when incurred). No advance payment necessary.

Writers' Conferences California Lawyers for the Arts Workshops; Selling to Hollywood Conference; Willamette Writers Conference; and many others.

N ☑ LIPPINCOTT MASSIE MCQUILKIN

80 Fifth Ave., Suite 1101, New York NY 10011. (212)337-2044. Fax: (212)352-2059. E-mail: rob@lmqlit.com; will@lmqlit.com; maria@lmqlit.com. Web site: www.lmqlit.com. **Contact:** Makila Sands, assistant. Estab. 2003. Represents 90 clients. 30% of clients are new/unpublished writers. Currently handles: 40% nonfiction books; 40% novels; 10% story collections; 5% scholarly books; 5% poetry.

Member Agents Maria Massie (fiction, memoir, cultural criticism); Will Lippincott (politics, current affairs, history); Rob McQuilkin (fiction, history, psychology, sociology, graphic material).

Represents Nonfiction books, novels, short story collections, scholarly books, graphic novels. **Considers these nonfiction areas:** Animals; anthropology/archaeology; art/architecture/design; biography/autobiography; business/economics; child guidance/parenting; current affairs; ethnic/cultural interests; gay/lesbian issues; government/politics/law; health/medicine; history; language/literature/criticism; memoirs; military/war; money/finance; music/dance; nature/environment; popular culture; psychology; religious/inspirational; science/technology; self-help/personal improvement; sociology; theater/film; true crime/investigative; women's issues/studies. **Considers these fiction areas:** Action/adventure; comic books/cartoon; confession; family saga; feminist; gay/lesbian; historical; humor/satire; literary; mainstream/contemporary; regional.

O→ LMQ focuses on bringing new voices in literary and commercial fiction to the market, as well as popularizing the ideas and arguments of scholars in the fields of history, psychology, sociology, political science, and current affairs. Seeks fiction writers who already have credits in magazines and quarterlies, as well as nonfiction writers who already have a media platform or some kind of a university affiliation. No romance, genre fiction, or children's material.

How to Contact Send query via e-mail. Only send additional materials if requested. Considers simultaneous queries. Responds in 1 week to queries; 1 month to mss. Obtains most new clients through recommendations from others, solicitations, conferences.

Recent Sales Sold 27 titles in the last year. *The Abstinence Teacher*, by Tom Perrotta (St. Martins); *Queen of Fashion*, by Caroline Weber (Henry Holt); *Whistling Past Dixie*, by Tom Schaller (Simon & Schuster); *Pretty Little Dirty*, by Amanda Boyden (Vintage). Other clients include Peter Ho Davies, Kim Addonizio, Don Lee, Natasha Trethewey, Anotol Lieven, Sir Michael Marmot, Anne Carson, Liza Ward, David Sirota, Anne Marie Slaughter, Marina Belozerskaya, Kate Walbert.

Terms Agent receives 15% commission on domestic sales; 30% commission on foreign sales. Offers written contract; 30-day notice must be given to terminate contract. Only charges for reasonable business expenses upon successful sale.

☑ THE LITERARY GROUP

270 Lafayette St., Suite 1505, New York NY 10012. (212)274-1616. Fax: (212)274-9876. E-mail: fweimann@theliterarygroup.com. Web site: www.theliterarygroup.com. **Contact:** Frank Weimann. Estab. 1985. 65% of clients are new/unpublished writers. Currently handles: 50% nonfiction books; 50% fiction.

Member Agents Frank Weimann; Ian Kleinert.

Represents Nonfiction books, novels. **Considers these nonfiction areas:** Animals; anthropology/archaeology; biography/autobiography; business/economics; child guidance/parenting; crafts/hobbies; current affairs; education; ethnic/cultural interests; government/politics/law; health/medicine; history; how-to; humor/satire; juvenile nonfiction; language/literature/criticism; memoirs; military/war; money/finance; multicultural; music/

dance; nature/environment; popular culture; psychology; religious/inspirational; science/technology; self-help/personal improvement; sociology; sports; theater/film; true crime/investigative; women's issues/studies; Creative nonfiction. **Considers these fiction areas:** Action/adventure; contemporary issues; detective/police/crime; ethnic; family saga; fantasy; feminist; horror; humor/satire; mystery/suspense; psychic/supernatural; romance (contemporary, gothic, historical, regency); sports; thriller; westerns/frontier.

⌾ This agency specializes in nonfiction (memoir, military, history, biography, sports, how-to).

How to Contact Query with SASE, outline, 3 sample chapters. Prefers to read materials exclusively. Only responds if interested. Returns materials only with SASE. Obtains most new clients through referrals, writers' conferences, query letters.

Recent Sales Sold 150 titles in the last year. *There and Back Again: An Actor's Tale*, by Sean Astin; *The Ambassador's Son*, by Homer Hickam; *Idiot*, by Johnny Damon; *Lemons Are Not Red*, by Laura Vaccaro Seeger; *The Good Guys*, by Bill Bonanno and Joe Pistone; *Flags of Our Fathers*, by James Bradley; *One Minute Wellness*, by Dr. Ben Lerner. Other clients include Robert Anderson, Michael Reagan, J.L. King.

Terms Agent receives 15% commission on domestic sales; 20% commission on foreign sales. Offers written contract; 30-day notice must be given to terminate contract.

Writers' Conferences San Diego State University Writers' Conference; Maui Writers Conference; Agents and Editors Conference.

◍ JULIA LORD LITERARY MANAGEMENT

38 W. Ninth St., #4, New York NY 10011. (212)995-2333. Fax: (212)995-2332. E-mail: julialordliterary@nyc.rr.com. Estab. 1999. Member of AAR.

Member Agents Julia Lord, owner; Riley Kellogg, subagent.

Represents Nonfiction books, novels. **Considers these nonfiction areas:** Biography/autobiography; history; sports; travel; African-American; lifestyle; narrative nonfiction. **Considers these fiction areas:** Action/adventure; historical; literary; mainstream/contemporary; mystery/suspense.

How to Contact Query with SASE or via e-mail. Obtains most new clients through recommendations from others, solicitations.

◍ STERLING LORD LITERISTIC, INC.

65 Bleecker St., 12th Floor, New York NY 10012. (212)780-6050. Fax: (212)780-6095. E-mail: info@sll.com. Web site: www.sll.com. Estab. 1952. Member of AAR; signatory of WGA. Represents 600 clients. Currently handles: 50% nonfiction books; 50% novels.

Member Agents Marcy Posner; Philippa Brophy; Laurie Liss; Chris Calhoun; Peter Matson; Sterling Lord; Claudia Cross; Neeti Madan; George Nicholson; Jim Rutman; Charlotte Sheedy (affiliate); Douglas Stewart; Paul Rodeen; Robert Guinsler.

Represents Nonfiction books, novels.

How to Contact Query with SASE. Responds in 1 month to mss. Obtains most new clients through recommendations from others.

Recent Sales This agency prefers not to share information on specific sales. Clients include Kent Haruf, Dick Francis, Mary Gordon, Sen. John McCain, Simon Winchester, James McBride, Billy Collins, Richard Paul Evans, Dave Pelzer.

Terms Agent receives 15% commission on domestic sales; 20% commission on foreign sales. Offers written contract. Charges clients for photocopying.

◍ LOWENSTEIN-YOST ASSOCIATES

121 W. 27th St., Suite 601, New York NY 10001. (212)206-1630. Fax: (212)727-0280. Web site: www.lowensteinyost.com. **Contact:** Barbara Lowenstein. Estab. 1976. Member of AAR. Represents 150 clients. 20% of clients are new/unpublished writers. Currently handles: 60% nonfiction books; 40% novels.

Member Agents Barbara Lowenstein, president; Nancy Yost, vice president; Norman Kurz, business affairs; Rachel Vater.

Represents Nonfiction books, novels. **Considers these nonfiction areas:** Animals; anthropology/archaeology; biography/autobiography; business/economics; child guidance/parenting; creative nonfiction (1); current affairs; education; ethnic/cultural interests; government/politics/law; health/medicine; history; how-to; language/literature/criticism; memoirs; money/finance; multicultural; nature/environment; popular culture; psychology; self-help/personal improvement; sociology; travel; women's issues/studies; Music; narrative nonfiction; science; film. **Considers these fiction areas:** Detective/police/crime; erotica; ethnic; feminist; historical; literary; mainstream/contemporary; mystery/suspense; romance (contemporary, historical, regency); thriller; women's.

⌾ This agency specializes in health, business, creative nonfiction, literary fiction, and commercial fiction—especially suspense, crime, and women's issues. "We are a full-service agency, handling domestic and foreign rights, film rights, and audio rights to all of our books."

How to Contact Query with SASE. Prefers to read materials exclusively. For fiction, send outline and first chapter. *No unsolicited mss.* Responds in 6 weeks to queries. Returns materials only with SASE. Obtains most new clients through recommendations from others, solicitations, conferences.

Recent Sales Sold 75 titles in the last year. *6 Day Body Makeover*, by Michael Thurmond (Warner); *House of Dark Delights*, by Louisa Burton. Other clients include Ishmael Reed, Deborah Crombie, Stephanie Laurens, Perri O'Shaughnessy, Tim Cahill, Liz Carlyle, Valerie Frankel, Suzanne Enoch, Cordelia Fine, Rovenia Brock, Barbara Keerling.

Terms Agent receives 15% commission on domestic sales; 20% commission on foreign sales. Offers written contract. Charges for large photocopy batches, messenger service, international postage.

Writers' Conferences Malice Domestic; Bouchercon; RWA National Conference.

Tips "Know the genre you are working in and read!"

◖ DONALD MAASS LITERARY AGENCY

121 W. 27th St., Suite 801, New York NY 10001. (212)727-8383. Web site: www.maassagency.com. Estab. 1980. Member of AAR, SFWA, MWA, RWA. Represents over 100 clients. 5% of clients are new/unpublished writers. Currently handles: 100% novels.

- Prior to opening his agency, Mr. Maass served as an editor at Dell Publishing (New York) and as a reader at Gollancz (London). He also served as the president of AAR.

Member Agents Donald Maass (mainstream, literary, mystery/suspense, science fiction); Jennifer Jackson (commercial fiction, romance, science fiction, fantasy, mystery/suspense); Cameron McClure (literary, historical, mystery/suspense, fantasy, women's fiction, narrative nonfiction and projects with multicultural, international, and environmental themes); Stephen Barbara (literary fiction, young adult novels, narrative nonfiction, historical nonfiction, commercial fiction, topical nonfiction).

Represents Novels. **Considers these fiction areas:** Detective/police/crime; fantasy; historical; horror; literary; mainstream/contemporary; mystery/suspense; psychic/supernatural; romance (historical, paranormal, time travel); science fiction; thriller; women's.

- ⚲ This agency specializes in commercial fiction, especially science fiction, fantasy, romance, and suspense. Actively seeking to expand in literary fiction and women's fiction. Does not want to receive nonfiction, children's material, or poetry.

How to Contact Query with SASE, synopsis, first 5 pages. Returns material only with SASE. Considers simultaneous queries. Responds in 2 weeks to queries; 3 months to mss.

Recent Sales Sold over 100 titles in the last year. *The Shifting Tide*, by Anne Perry (Ballantine); *Midnight Plague*, by Gregg Keizer (G.P. Putnam's Sons).

Terms Agent receives 15% commission on domestic sales; 20% commission on foreign sales.

Writers' Conferences Donald Maass: World Science Fiction Convention; Frankfurt Book Fair; Pacific Northwest Writers Conference; Bouchercon. Jennifer Jackson: World Science Fiction Convention; RWA National Conference.

Tips "We are fiction specialists, also noted for our innovative approach to career planning. Few new clients are accepted, but interested authors should query with a SASE. Works with subagents in all principle foreign countries and Hollywood. No nonfiction or juvenile works will be considered."

◖ GINA MACCOBY LITERARY AGENCY

P.O. Box 60, Chappaqua NY 10514. (914)238-5630. **Contact:** Gina Maccoby. Estab. 1986. Represents 25 clients. Currently handles: 33% nonfiction books; 33% novels; 33% juvenile books; illustrators of children's books.

Represents Nonfiction books, novels, juvenile books. **Considers these nonfiction areas:** Biography/autobiography; current affairs; ethnic/cultural interests; history; juvenile nonfiction; popular culture; women's issues/studies. **Considers these fiction areas:** Juvenile; literary; mainstream/contemporary; mystery/suspense; thriller; young adult.

How to Contact Query with SASE. Considers simultaneous queries. Responds in 3 months to queries. Returns materials only with SASE. Obtains most new clients through recommendations from clients and publishers.

Recent Sales Sold 21 titles in the last year.

Terms Agent receives 15% commission on domestic sales; 25% commission on foreign sales. Charges clients for photocopying. May recover certain costs, such as legal fees or the cost of shipping books by air to Europe or Japan.

◖ CAROL MANN AGENCY

55 Fifth Ave., New York NY 10003. (212)206-5635. Fax: (212)675-4809. E-mail: will@carolmannagency.com. **Contact:** Will Sherlin. Estab. 1977. Member of AAR. Represents 200 clients. 15% of clients are new/unpublished writers. Currently handles: 70% nonfiction books; 30% novels.

Member Agents Carol Mann; Will Sherlin; Laura Yorke.

Represents Nonfiction books, novels. **Considers these nonfiction areas:** Anthropology/archaeology; art/architecture/design; biography/autobiography; business/economics; child guidance/parenting; current affairs; ethnic/cultural interests; government/politics/law; health/medicine; history; money/finance; psychology; self-help/personal improvement; sociology; sports; women's issues/studies; Music. **Considers these fiction areas:** Literary; Commercial.

> 0→ This agency specializes in current affairs, self-help, popular culture, psychology, parenting, and history. Does not want to receive genre fiction (romance, mystery, etc.).

How to Contact Query with outline/proposal, SASE. Responds in 3 weeks to queries.

Recent Sales Clients include novelists Paul Auster and Marita Golden; journalists Tim Egan, Hannah Storm, and Willow Bay; Pulitzer Prize-winner Fox Butterfield; bestselling essayist Shelby Steele; sociologist Dr. William Julius Wilson; economist Thomas Sowell; bestselling diet doctors Mary Dan and Michael Eades; ACLU president Nadine Strossen; pundit Mona Charen; memoirist Lauren Winner; photography project editors Rick Smolan and David Cohen (*America 24/7*); and Kevin Liles, executive vice president of Warner Music Group and former president of Def Jam Records.

Terms Agent receives 15% commission on domestic sales; 20% commission on foreign sales. Offers written contract.

☑ MANUS & ASSOCIATES LITERARY AGENCY, INC.

425 Sherman Ave., Suite 200, Palo Alto CA 94306. (650)470-5151. Fax: (650)470-5159. E-mail: manuslit@manus lit.com. Web site: www.manuslit.com. **Contact:** Jillian Manus, Jandy Nelson, Stephanie Lee, Donna Levin, Penny Nelson. Alternate address: 445 Park Ave., New York NY 10022. (212)644-8020. Fax (212)644-3374. **Contact:** Janet Manus. Estab. 1985. Member of AAR. Represents 75 clients. 30% of clients are new/unpublished writers. Currently handles: 70% nonfiction books; 30% novels.

> • Prior to becoming an agent, Jillian Manus was associate publisher of two national magazines and director of development at Warner Bros. and Universal Studios; Janet Manus has been a literary agent for 20 years.

Member Agents Jandy Nelson (self-help, health, memoirs, narrative nonfiction, women's fiction, literary fiction, multicultural fiction, thrillers); Stephanie Lee (self-help, narrative nonfiction, commercial literary fiction, quirky/edgy fiction, pop culture, pop science); Jillian Manus (political, memoirs, self-help, history, sports, women's issues, Latin fiction and nonfiction, thrillers); Penny Nelson (memoirs, self-help, sports, nonfiction); Dena Fischer (literary fiction, mainstream/commercial fiction, chick lit, women's fiction, historical fiction, ethnic/cultural fiction, narrative nonfiction, parenting, relationships, pop culture, health, sociology, psychology).

Represents Nonfiction books, novels. **Considers these nonfiction areas:** Biography/autobiography; business/economics; child guidance/parenting; current affairs; ethnic/cultural interests; health/medicine; how-to; memoirs; money/finance; nature/environment; popular culture; psychology; science/technology; self-help/personal improvement; women's issues/studies; Gen X and Gen Y issues; creative nonfiction. **Considers these fiction areas:** Literary; mainstream/contemporary; multicultural; mystery/suspense; thriller; women's; Quirky/edgy fiction.

> 0→ This agency specializes in commercial literary fiction, narrative nonfiction, thrillers, health, pop psychology, and women's empowerment. "Our agency is unique in the way that we not only sell the material, but we edit, develop concepts, and participate in the marketing effort. We specialize in large, conceptual fiction and nonfiction, and always value a project that can be sold in the TV/feature film market." Actively seeking high-concept thrillers, commercial literary fiction, women's fiction, celebrity biographies, memoirs, multicultural fiction, popular health, women's empowerment, and mysteries. Does not want to receive horror, romance, science fiction/fantasy, westerns, young adult, children's, poetry, cookbooks, or magazine articles.

How to Contact Query with SASE. If requested, submit outline, 2-3 sample chapters. All queries should be sent to the California office. Accepts e-mail queries. No fax queries. Considers simultaneous queries. Responds in 3 months to queries; 3 months to mss. Returns materials only with SASE. Obtains most new clients through recommendations from others, solicitations, conferences.

Recent Sales *Nothing Down for the 2000s* and *Multiple Streams of Income for the 2000s*, by Robert Allen; *Missed Fortune* and *Missed Fortune 101*, by Doug Andrew; *Cracking the Millionaire Code*, by Mark Victor Hansen and Robert Allen; *Stress Free for Good*, by Dr. Fred Luskin and Dr. Ken Pelletier; *The Mercy of Thin Air*, by Ronlyn Domangue; *The Fine Art of Small Talk*, by Debra Fine; *Bone Man of Bonares*, by Terry Tarnoff. Other clients include Dr. Lorraine Zappart, Marcus Allen, Carlton Stowers, Alan Jacobson, Ann Brandt, Dr. Richard Marrs, Mary LoVerde, Lisa Huang Fleishman, Judy Carter, Daryl Ott Underhill, Glen Kleier, Andrew X. Pham, Alexander Sanger, Lalita Tademy, Frank Baldwin, Katy Robinson, K.M. Soehnlein, Joelle Fraser, James Rogan, Jim Schutze, Deborah Santana, Karen Neuburger, Mira Tweti, Newt Gingrich, William Forstchen, Ken Walsh, Doug Wead, Nadine Schiff, Deborah Santana, Tom Dolby, Laurie Lynn Drummond, Christine Wicker, Wendy Dale, Mineko Iwasaki, Dorothy Ferebee, Reverand Run.

Terms Agent receives 15% commission on domestic sales; 20-25% commission on foreign sales. Offers written contract, binding for 2 years; 60-day notice must be given to terminate contract. Charges for photocopying and postage/UPS.

Writers' Conferences Maui Writers Conference; San Diego State University Writers' Conference; Willamette Writers Conference; BookExpo America; MEGA Book Marketing University.

Tips ''Research agents using a variety of sources, including *LMP*, guides, *Publishers Weekly*, conferences, and even acknowledgements in books similar in tone to yours.''

◙ MARCH TENTH, INC.

4 Myrtle St., Haworth NJ 07641-1740. (201)387-6551. Fax: (201)387-6552. E-mail: hchoron@aol.com. Web site: www.marchtenthinc.com. **Contact:** Harry Choron, vice president. Estab. 1982. Represents 40 clients. 30% of clients are new/unpublished writers. Currently handles: 75% nonfiction books; 25% novels.

Represents Nonfiction books, novels. **Considers these nonfiction areas:** Biography/autobiography; current affairs; health/medicine; history; humor/satire; language/literature/criticism; music/dance; popular culture; theater/film. **Considers these fiction areas:** Confession; ethnic; family saga; historical; humor/satire; literary; mainstream/contemporary.

    ○┅ Writers must have professional expertise in their field. ''We prefer to work with published/established writers.''

How to Contact Query with SASE. Considers simultaneous queries. Responds in 1 month to queries. Returns materials only with SASE.

Recent Sales Sold 24 titles in the last year. *Art of the Chopper*, by Tom Zimberoff; *Bruce Springstein Live*, by Dave Marsh; *Complete Annotated Grateful Dead Lyrics*, by David Dodd.

Terms Agent receives 15% commission on domestic sales; 20% commission on foreign sales; 20% commission on dramatic rights sales. Charges clients for postage, photocopying, overseas phone expenses. Does not require expense money upfront.

◙ THE DENISE MARCIL LITERARY AGENCY, INC.

156 Fifth Ave., Suite 625, New York NY 10010. (212)337-3402. Fax: (212)727-2688. **Contact:** Denise Marcil, Maura Kye-Casella. Estab. 1977. Member of AAR. Represents 50 clients. 10% of clients are new/unpublished writers.

    ● Prior to opening her agency, Ms. Marcil served as an editorial assistant with Avon Books and as an assistant editor with Simon & Schuster.

Represents Commercial fiction and nonfiction books.

    ○┅ Denise Marcil specializes in women's commercial fiction, thrillers, suspense, popular reference, how-to, self-help, health, business, and parenting. ''I am looking for fresh, new voices in commercial women's fiction: chick lit, mom lit—stories that capture women's experiences today. I'd love to find a well-written historical novel about a real-life woman from another century.'' Maura Kye-Casella is seeking narrative nonfiction (adventure, pop culture, parenting, cookbooks, humor, memoir) and fiction (multi-cultural, paranormal, suspense, chick lit, well-written novels with an edgy voice, quirky characters, and/or unique plots and settings).

How to Contact Query with SASE.

Recent Sales Sold 43 titles in the last year. *My Grandmother's Bones*, by Jill Althouse Wood (Algonquin); *Silent Wager*, by Anita Bunkley (Kensington/Dafina); *Duke of Scandal*, by Adele Ashworth (Avon); *Big City, Bad Blood*, by Sean Chercover (Avon/Morrow); *Consigned to Death*, by Jane Cleland (St. Martin's Press); *The Liars Club*, by Peter Spiegelman (Knopf); *Tales from the Top: Ten Crucial Questions from the World's #1 Executive Coach*, by Graham Alexander (Nelson Business Books).

Terms Agent receives 15% commission on domestic sales; 20% commission on foreign sales. Offers written contract, binding for 2 years; 100% of business is derived from commissions on ms sales. Charges $100/year for postage, photocopying, long-distance calls, etc.

Writers' Conferences Pacific Northwest Writers Conference; RWA National Conference; Oregon Writers Colony.

◙ THE EVAN MARSHALL AGENCY

Six Tristam Place, Pine Brook NJ 07058-9445. (973)882-1122. Fax: (973)882-3099. E-mail: evanmarshall@theno velist.com. Web site: www.publishersmarketplace.com/members/evanmarshall. **Contact:** Evan Marshall. Estab. 1987. Member of AAR, MWA, RWA, Sisters in Crime. Currently handles: 100% novels.

    ● Prior to opening his agency, Mr. Marshall served as an editor with Houghton Mifflin, New American Library, Everest House, and Dodd, Mead & Co., and then worked as a literary agent at The Sterling Lord Agency.

Represents Novels. **Considers these fiction areas:** Action/adventure; erotica; ethnic; historical; horror; humor/

satire; literary; mainstream/contemporary; mystery/suspense; religious/inspirational; romance (contemporary, gothic, historical, regency); science fiction; westerns/frontier.

How to Contact Query first with SASE; do not enclose material. No e-mail queries. Responds in 1 week to queries; 3 months to mss. Obtains most new clients through recommendations from others.

Recent Sales *Copycat*, by Erica Spindler (Mira); *The Closing*, by Rebecca Drake (Kensington); *Desperately Seeking Sushi*, by Jerrilyn Farmer (Morrow).

Terms Agent receives 15% commission on domestic sales; 20% commission on foreign sales. Offers written contract.

⬤ HELEN MCGRATH

1406 Idaho Ct., Concord CA 94521. (925)672-6211. Fax: (925)672-6383. E-mail: hmcgrath_lit@yahoo.com. **Contact:** Helen McGrath. Estab. 1977. Currently handles: 50% nonfiction books; 50% novels.

Represents Nonfiction books, novels. **Considers these nonfiction areas:** Biography/autobiography; business/economics; current affairs; health/medicine; history; how-to; military/war; psychology; self-help/personal improvement; sports; women's issues/studies. **Considers these fiction areas:** Detective/police/crime; literary; mainstream/contemporary; mystery/suspense; psychic/supernatural; romance; science fiction; thriller.

How to Contact Submit proposal with SASE. *No unsolicited mss.* Responds in 2 months to queries. Obtains most new clients through recommendations from others.

Terms Agent receives 15% commission on domestic sales. Offers written contract. Charges clients for photocopying.

⬤ MENDEL MEDIA GROUP LLC

254 Canal St., Suite 4018, New York NY 10013. (646)239-9896. Fax: (212)697-7777. E-mail: scott@mendelmedia.com. Web site: www.mendelmedia.com. Estab. 2002. Member of AAR. Represents 40-60 clients.

• Prior to becoming an agent, Mr. Mendel was an academic. ''I taught American literature, Yiddish, Jewish studies, and literary theory at the University of Chicago and the University of Illinois at Chicago while working on my PhD in English. I also worked as a freelance technical writer and as the managing editor of a healthcare magazine. In 1998, I began working for the late Jane Jordan Browne, a long-time agent in the book publishing world.''

Represents Nonfiction books, novels, scholarly books (with potential for broad/popular appeal). **Considers these nonfiction areas:** Americana; animals; anthropology/archaeology; art/architecture/design; biography/autobiography; business/economics; child guidance/parenting; cooking/foods/nutrition; current affairs; education; ethnic/cultural interests; gardening; gay/lesbian issues; government/politics/law; health/medicine; history; how-to; humor/satire; language/literature/criticism; memoirs; military/war; money/finance; multicultural; music/dance; nature/environment; philosophy; popular culture; psychology; recreation; regional; religious/inspirational; science/technology; self-help/personal improvement; sex; sociology; software; spirituality; sports; true crime/investigative; women's issues/studies; Jewish topics; creative nonfiction. **Considers these fiction areas:** Action/adventure; contemporary issues; detective/police/crime; erotica; ethnic; feminist; gay/lesbian; glitz; historical; humor/satire; juvenile; literary; mainstream/contemporary; mystery/suspense; picture books; religious/inspirational; romance; sports; thriller; young adult; Jewish fiction.

O➝ ''I am interested in major works of history, current affairs, biography, business, politics, economics, science, major memoirs, narrative nonfiction, and other sorts of general nonfiction. Actively seeking new, major or definitive work on a subject of broad interest, or a controversial, but authoritative, new book on a subject that affects many people's lives. I also represent more light-hearted nonfiction projects, such as gift or novelty books, when they suit the market particularly well.'' Does not want queries about projects written years ago that were unsuccessfully shopped to a long list of trade publishers by either the author or another agent. ''I am specifically not interested in reading short, category romances (regency, time travel, paranormal, etc.), horror novels, supernatural stories, poetry, original plays, or film scripts.''

How to Contact Query with SASE. Do not e-mail or fax queries. For nonfiction, include a complete, fully-edited book proposal with sample chapters. For fiction, include a complete synopsis and no more than 20 pages of sample text. Responds in 2 weeks to queries; 4-6 weeks to mss. Returns materials only with SASE. Obtains most new clients through recommendations from others.

Terms Agent receives 15% commission on domestic sales; 20% commission on foreign sales. Offers written contract, binding for 2 years; 1-month notice must be given to terminate contract. Charges clients for ms duplication, expedited delivery services (when necessary), any overseas shipping, telephone calls/faxes necessary for marketing the author's foreign rights.

Writers' Conferences BookExpo America; Frankfurt Book Fair; London Book Fair; RWA National Conference; Modern Language Association Convention; Jerusalem Book Fair.

Tips ''While I am not interested in being flattered by a prospective client, it does matter to me that she knows why she is writing to me in the first place. Is one of my clients a colleague of hers? Has she read a book by one of my clients that led her to believe I might be interested in her work? Authors of descriptive nonfiction should have real credentials and expertise in their subject areas, either as academics, journalists, or policy experts, and authors of prescriptive nonfiction should have legitimate expertise and considerable experience communicating their ideas in seminars and workshops, in a successful business, through the media, etc.''

DORIS S. MICHAELS LITERARY AGENCY, INC.

1841 Broadway, Suite 903, New York NY 10023. (212)265-9474. Fax: (212)265-9480. E-mail: query@dsmagenecy.com. Web site: www.dsmagency.com. **Contact:** Doris S. Michaels, president. Estab. 1994. Member of AAR, WNBA.

Represents Novels. **Considers these fiction areas:** Literary (with commercial appeal and strong screen potential).

How to Contact Query by e-mail; see submission guidelines on Web site. Obtains most new clients through recommendations from others, conferences.

Terms Agent receives 15% commission on domestic sales; 20% commission on foreign sales. Offers written contract, binding for 1 year; 1-month notice must be given to terminate contract. 100% of business is derived from commissions on ms sales. Charges clients for office expenses, not to exceed $150 without written permission.

Writers' Conferences BookExpo America; Frankfurt Book Fair; London Book Fair; Maui Writers Conference.

HENRY MORRISON, INC.

105 S. Bedford Rd., Suite 306A, Mt. Kisco NY 10549. (914)666-3500. Fax: (914)241-7846. **Contact:** Henry Morrison. Estab. 1965. Signatory of WGA. Represents 53 clients. 5% of clients are new/unpublished writers. Currently handles: 5% nonfiction books; 95% novels.

Represents Nonfiction books, novels. **Considers these nonfiction areas:** Anthropology/archaeology; biography/autobiography; government/politics/law; history. **Considers these fiction areas:** Action/adventure; detective/police/crime; family saga; historical.

How to Contact Query with SASE. Responds in 2 weeks to queries; 3 months to mss. Obtains most new clients through recommendations from others.

Recent Sales Sold 16 titles in the last year. *The Ambler Warning*, by Robert Ludlum (St. Martin's Press); *The Bravo Testament*, by Eric Van Lustbader (Forge); *White Flag Down*, by Joel N. Ross (Doubleday); *Encyclopedia of World War II*, by Alan Axelrod (Facts on File); *The Lucifer Gospel*, by Paul Christopher (Signet); *The Midas Touch*, by Jon J. Land (Tor); *Your Cat Is Into You*, by Molly Katz (Morrow); *Son of a Gun*, by Randye Lordon (St. Martin's Press); *Rage Therapy*, by Dan Kalla (Forge). Other clients include Samuel R. Delany, Daniel Cohen, Brian Garfield, Gayle Lynds, Christopher Hyde.

Terms Agent receives 15% commission on domestic sales; 25% commission on foreign sales. Charges clients for ms copies, bound galleys, finished books for submissions to publishers, movie producers and foreign publishers.

MUSE LITERARY MANAGEMENT

189 Waverly Place, #4, New York NY 10014. (212)925-3721. E-mail: museliterarymgmt@aol.com. **Contact:** Deborah Carter. Estab. 1998. Member of Author's Guild, SCBWI, International Thriller Writers. Represents 10 clients. 80% of clients are new/unpublished writers. Currently handles: 9% nonfiction books; 55% novels; 9% story collections; 27% juvenile books.

- Prior to starting her agency, Ms. Carter trained with an AAR literary agent and worked in the music business in artist management and as a talent scout for record companies. She has a BA in English and music from Washington Square University College at NYU.

Represents Novels, short story collections, novellas, juvenile books. **Considers these nonfiction areas:** Narrative-only nonfiction (memoir, sports, outdoors, music, writing). Please query other narrative nonfiction subjects. **Considers these fiction areas:** Action/adventure; detective/police/crime; experimental; juvenile; literary; mainstream/contemporary; mystery/suspense; picture books; thriller; young adult; Espionage; middle-grade novels; literary short story collections.

- Specializes in ms development, the sale and administration of print, performance, and foreign rights to literary works, and post-publication publicity and appearances. Actively seeking progressive, African-American, and multicultural fiction for adults and children in the US market. Does not want category fiction (romance, chick lit, fantasy, science fiction), or books with any religious or spiritual matter.

How to Contact Query via e-mail (no attachments). Discards unwanted queries. Responds in 2 weeks to queries; 2-3 weeks to mss. Obtains most new clients through recommendations from others, conferences.

Recent Sales Sold 3 titles in the last year. *Heat Sync* and *The Fund*, by Wes DeMott (Leisure Books); foreign rights sales. Other clients include Anne Shelby, Samantha Talbot.

Terms Agent receives 15% commission on domestic sales; 20% commission on foreign sales. Offers written contract, binding for 1 year; 1-day notice must be given to terminate contract. Sometimes charges for postage and photocopying. All expenses are subject to client approval.

Writers' Conferences BookExpo America; Bouchercon; SCBWI Winter Conference.

⬤ JEAN V. NAGGAR LITERARY AGENCY, INC.

216 E. 75th St., Suite 1E, New York NY 10021. (212)794-1082. **Contact:** Jean Naggar. Estab. 1978. Member of AAR, PEN, Women's Media Group, Women's Forum. Represents 80 clients. 20% of clients are new/unpublished writers. Currently handles: 35% nonfiction books; 45% novels; 15% juvenile books; 5% scholarly books.

   • Ms. Naggar has served as president of AAR.

Member Agents Jennifer Weltz, director (subsidiary rights, children's books); Alice Tasman, senior agent (commercial and literary fiction, thrillers, narrative nonfiction); Mollie Glick, agent (literary and commercial fiction with a unique premise/voice, literary and practical nonfiction); Jessica Regel, agent (young adult fiction and nonfiction).

Represents Nonfiction books, novels. **Considers these nonfiction areas:** Biography/autobiography; child guidance/parenting; current affairs; government/politics/law; health/medicine; history; juvenile nonfiction; memoirs; New Age/metaphysics; psychology; religious/inspirational; self-help/personal improvement; sociology; travel; women's issues/studies. **Considers these fiction areas:** Action/adventure; detective/police/crime; ethnic; family saga; feminist; historical; literary; mainstream/contemporary; mystery/suspense; psychic/supernatural; thriller.

   ⦿ This agency specializes in mainstream fiction and nonfiction and literary fiction with commercial potential.

How to Contact Query with SASE. Prefers to read materials exclusively. No e-mail or fax queries. Responds in 1 day to queries; 2 months to mss. Returns materials only with SASE. Obtains most new clients through recommendations from others.

Recent Sales *Dark Angels*, by Karleen Koen; *Poison*, by Susan Fromberg Schaeffer; *Unauthorized*, by Kristin McCloy; *Voyage of the Sea Turtle: The Search for the Last Dinosaurs*, by Carl Safina; *Enola Holmes*, by Nancy Springer; *The Liar's Diary*, by Patry Francis; *Closing Costs*, by Seth Margolis; *Blind Faith*, by Richard Sloan.

Terms Agent receives 15% commission on domestic sales; 20% commission on foreign sales. Offers written contract. Charges for overseas mailing, messenger services, book purchases, long-distance telephone, photocopying—all deductible from royalties received.

Writers' Conferences Willamette Writers Conference; Pacific Northwest Writers Conference; Bread Loaf Writers Conference; Marymount Manhattan Writers Conference; SEAK Medical & Legal Fiction Writing Conference.

Tips "Use a professional presentation. Because of the avalanche of unsolicited queries that flood the agency every week, we have had to modify our policy. We will now only guarantee to read and respond to queries from writers who come recommended by someone we know. Our areas are general fiction and nonfiction—no children's books by unpublished writers, no multimedia, no screenplays, no formula fiction, and no mysteries by unpublished writers. We recommend patience and fortitude: the courage to be true to your own vision, the fortitude to finish a novel and polish it again and again before sending it out, and the patience to accept rejection gracefully and wait for the stars to align themselves appropriately for success."

⬤ NELSON LITERARY AGENCY

1020 15th St., Suite 26L, Denver CO 80202. (303)463-5301. E-mail: query@nelsonagency.com. Web site: www.nelsonagency.com. **Contact:** Kristin Nelson. Estab. 2002. Member of AAR.

   • Prior to opening her own agency, Ms. Nelson worked as a literary scout and subrights agent for agent Jody Rein.

Represents Novels, select nonfiction. **Considers these nonfiction areas:** Memoirs; Narrative nonfiction. **Considers these fiction areas:** Literary; romance (includes fantasy with romantic elements, science fiction, young adult); women's; Chick lit (includes mysteries); commercial/mainstream.

   ⦿ NLA specializes in representing commercial fiction and high caliber literary fiction. Actively seeking Latina writers who tackle contemporary issues in a modern voice (think *Dirty Girls Social Club*). Does not want short story collections, mysteries (except chick lit), thrillers, Christian, horror, or children's picture books.

How to Contact Query by e-mail only.

Recent Sales *Plan B*, by Jennifer O'Connell (MTV/Pocket Books); *Code of Love*, by Cheryl Sawyer (NAL/Penguin Group); *Once Upon Stilettos*, by Shanna Swendson (Ballantine); *I'd Tell You I Love You But Then I'd Have to Kill You*, by Ally Carter (Hyperion Children's); *An Accidental Goddess*, by Linnea Sinclair (Bantam Spectra). Other clients include Paula Reed, Becky Motew, Jack McCallum, Jana Deleon.

◉ HAROLD OBER ASSOCIATES

425 Madison Ave., New York NY 10017. (212)759-8600. Fax: (212)759-9428. Estab. 1929. Member of AAR. Represents 250 clients. 10% of clients are new/unpublished writers. Currently handles: 35% nonfiction books; 50% novels; 15% juvenile books.

Member Agents Phyllis Westberg; Pamela Malpas; Knox Burger; Craig Tenney (not accepting new clients).

Represents Nonfiction books, novels, juvenile books.

   O→ "We consider all subjects/genres of fiction and nonfiction."

How to Contact Submit query letter only with SASE. No e-mail or fax queries. Responds as promptly as possible. Obtains most new clients through recommendations from others.

Terms Agent receives 15% commission on domestic sales; 20% commission on foreign sales. Charges clients for photocopying and express mail/package services.

◉ THE RICHARD PARKS AGENCY

Box 693, Salem NY 12865. Web site: www.richardparksagency.com. **Contact:** Richard Parks. Estab. 1988. Member of AAR. Currently handles: 55% nonfiction books; 40% novels; 5% story collections.

Represents Nonfiction books, novels. **Considers these nonfiction areas:** Animals; anthropology/archaeology; art/architecture/design; biography/autobiography; business/economics; child guidance/parenting; cooking/foods/nutrition; crafts/hobbies; current affairs; ethnic/cultural interests; gardening; gay/lesbian issues; government/politics/law; health/medicine; history; how-to; humor/satire; language/literature/criticism; memoirs; military/war; money/finance; music/dance; nature/environment; popular culture; psychology; science/technology; self-help/personal improvement; sociology; theater/film; travel; women's issues/studies.

   O→ Actively seeking nonfiction. Considers fiction by referral only. Does not want to receive unsolicited material.

How to Contact Query with SASE. No e-mail or fax queries. Considers simultaneous queries Responds in 2 weeks to queries. Returns materials only with SASE. Obtains most new clients through recommendations/referrals.

Terms Agent receives 15% commission on domestic sales; 20% commission on foreign sales. Charges clients for photocopying or any unusual expense incurred at the writer's request.

◉ L. PERKINS ASSOCIATES

5800 Arlington Ave., Riverdale NY 10471. (718)543-5344. Fax: (718)543-5354. E-mail: lperkinsagency@yahoo.com. **Contact:** Lori Perkins, Amy Stout (astoutlperkinsagency@yahoo.com). Estab. 1990. Member of AAR. Represents 50 clients. 10% of clients are new/unpublished writers.

   ● Ms. Perkins has been an agent for 18 years. She is also the author of *The Insider's Guide to Getting an Agent* (Writer's Digest Books).

Represents Nonfiction books, novels. **Considers these nonfiction areas:** Popular culture. **Considers these fiction areas:** Fantasy; horror; literary (dark); science fiction.

   O→ Most of Ms. Perkins' clients write both fiction and nonfiction. "This combination keeps my clients publishing for years. I am also a published author, so I know what it takes to write a good book." Actively seeking a Latino *Gone With the Wind* and *Waiting to Exhale,* and urban ethnic horror. Does not want to receive anything outside of the above categories (westerns, romance, etc.).

How to Contact Query with SASE. Considers simultaneous queries. Responds in 6 weeks to queries; 3 months to mss. Returns materials only with SASE. Obtains most new clients through recommendations from others, solicitations, conferences.

Recent Sales Sold 100 titles in the last year. *How to Make Love Like a Porn Star: A Cautionary Tale,* by Jenna Jameson (Reagan Books); *Dear Mom, I Always Wanted You to Know,* by Lisa Delman (Perigee Books); *The Illustrated Ray Bradbury,* by Jerry Weist (Avon); *The Poet in Exile,* by Ray Manzarek (Avalon); *Behind Sad Eyes: The Life of George Harrison,* by Marc Shapiro (St. Martin's Press).

Terms Agent receives 15% commission on domestic sales; 20% commission on foreign sales. No written contract. Charges clients for photocopying.

Writers' Conferences San Diego State University Writers' Conference; NECON; BookExpo America; World Fantasy Convention.

Tips "Research your field and contact professional writers' organizations to see who is looking for what. Finish your novel before querying agents. Read my book, *An Insider's Guide to Getting an Agent,* to get a sense of how agents operate."

◉ STEPHEN PEVNER, INC.

382 Lafayette St., 8th Floor, New York NY 10003. (212)674-8403. Fax: (212)529-3692. E-mail: spevner@aol.com. **Contact:** Stephen Pevner.

Represents Nonfiction books, novels, feature film, TV scripts, TV movie of the week, episodic drama, animation, documentary, miniseries. **Considers these nonfiction areas:** Biography/autobiography; ethnic/cultural interests; gay/lesbian issues; history; humor/satire; language/literature/criticism; memoirs; music/dance; New Age/metaphysics; photography; popular culture; religious/inspirational; sociology; travel. **Considers these fiction areas:** Comic books/cartoon; erotica; ethnic; experimental; gay/lesbian; glitz; horror; humor/satire; literary; mainstream/contemporary; psychic/supernatural; thriller; Urban. **Considers these script subject areas:** Comedy; contemporary issues; detective/police/crime; gay/lesbian; glitz; horror; romantic comedy; romantic drama; thriller.

- ⚡ This agency specializes in motion pictures, novels, humor, pop culture, urban fiction, and independent filmmakers.

How to Contact Query with SASE, outline/proposal. Prefers to read materials exclusively. No e-mail or fax queries. Responds in 2 weeks to queries; 1 month to mss. Obtains most new clients through recommendations from others.

Recent Sales *Matt and Ben*, by Mindy Kaling and Brenda Withers; *In the Company of Men* and *Bash: Latterday Plays*, by Neil Labote; *The Vagina Monologues*, by Eve Ensler; *Guide to Life*, by The Five Lesbian Brothers; *Noise From Underground*, by Michael Levine. Other clients include Richard Linklater, Gregg Araki, Tom DiCillo, Genvieve Turner/Rose Troche, Todd Solondz, Neil LaBute.

Terms Agent receives 15% commission on domestic sales; 20% commission on foreign sales. Offers written contract, binding for 1 year; 6-week notice must be given to terminate contract. 100% of business is derived from commissions on ms sales.

Tips "Be persistent, but civilized."

⊘ ALISON J. PICARD, LITERARY AGENT

P.O. Box 2000, Cotuit MA 02635. Phone/Fax: (508)477-7192. E-mail: ajpicard@aol.com. **Contact:** Alison Picard. Estab. 1985. Represents 48 clients. 30% of clients are new/unpublished writers. Currently handles: 40% nonfiction books; 40% novels; 20% juvenile books.

- • Prior to becoming an agent, Ms. Picard was an assistant at a literary agency in New York.

Represents Nonfiction books, novels, juvenile books. **Considers these nonfiction areas:** Animals; biography/autobiography; business/economics; child guidance/parenting; cooking/foods/nutrition; current affairs; education; ethnic/cultural interests; gay/lesbian issues; government/politics/law; health/medicine; history; how-to; humor/satire; juvenile nonfiction; memoirs; military/war; money/finance; multicultural; nature/environment; New Age/metaphysics; popular culture; psychology; religious/inspirational; science/technology; self-help/personal improvement; travel; true crime/investigative; women's issues/studies; young adult. **Considers these fiction areas:** Action/adventure; contemporary issues; detective/police/crime; erotica; ethnic; family saga; feminist; gay/lesbian; glitz; historical; horror; humor/satire; juvenile; literary; mainstream/contemporary; multicultural; mystery/suspense; New Age; picture books; psychic/supernatural; romance; sports; thriller; young adult.

- ⚡ "Many of my clients have come to me from big agencies, where they felt overlooked or ignored. I communicate freely with my clients and offer a lot of career advice, suggestions for revising manuscripts, etc. If I believe in a project, I will submit it to a dozen or more publishers, unlike some agents who give up after four or five rejections." *Closed to submissions until June.* Does not want to receive science fiction/fantasy, westerns, poetry, plays, or articles.

How to Contact Query with SASE. Considers simultaneous queries. Responds in 2 weeks to queries; 4 months to mss. Returns materials only with SASE. Obtains most new clients through recommendations from others, solicitations.

Recent Sales Sold 32 titles in the last year. *A Hard Ticket Home*, by David Housewright (St. Martin's Press); *Indigo Rose*, by Susan Miller (Bantam Books/Random House); *Fly Fishing & Funerals*, by Mary Bartek (Henry Holt & Co.); *Stage Fright*, by Dina Friedman (Farrar, Straus & Giroux); *Fashion Slaves*, by Louise de Teliga (Kensington). Other clients include Osha Gray Davidson, Amy Dean, David Housewright, Nancy Means Wright.

Terms Agent receives 15% commission on domestic sales; 20% commission on foreign sales. Offers written contract, binding for 1 year; 1-week notice must be given to terminate contract.

Tips "Please don't send material without sending a query first via mail or e-mail. I don't accept phone or fax queries. Always enclose a SASE with a query."

⊘ ALICKA PISTEK LITERARY AGENCY, LLC

302A W. 12th St., #124, New York NY 10014. E-mail: info@apliterary.com. Web site: www.apliterary.com. **Contact:** Alicka Pistek. Estab. 2003. Represents 15 clients. 50% of clients are new/unpublished writers. Currently handles: 60% nonfiction books; 40% novels.

- • Prior to opening her agency, Ms. Pistek worked at ICM and as an agent at Nicholas Ellison, Inc.

Represents Nonfiction books, novels. **Considers these nonfiction areas:** Animals; anthropology/archaeology; biography/autobiography; business/economics; child guidance/parenting; cooking/foods/nutrition; current affairs; government/politics/law; health/medicine; history; how-to; language/literature/criticism; memoirs; military/war; money/finance; nature/environment; psychology; religious/inspirational; science/technology; self-help/personal improvement; translation; travel; Creative nonfiction. **Considers these fiction areas:** Detective/police/crime; ethnic; family saga; historical; literary; mainstream/contemporary; mystery/suspense; romance; thriller.

⊶ Does not want to receive fantasy, science fiction, or westerns.

How to Contact Query with SASE, outline, 2 sample chapters. Considers simultaneous queries. Responds in 2 months to queries; 8 weeks to mss. Returns materials only with SASE.

Recent Sales *Mommy Yoga*, by Julie Tilsner; *The Pajamaist*, by Matthew Zapruder; *900 Miles From Nowhere*, by Steve Kinsella. Other clients include Michael Christopher Carroll, Alex Boese, Quinton Skinner, Erin Grady, Marcelle DiFalco, Jocelyn Herz, John Fulton.

Terms Agent receives 15% commission on domestic sales; 20% commission on foreign sales. Offers written contract. Charges for photocopying over 40 pages and international postage.

Writers' Conferences Frankfurt Book Fair.

Tips "Be sure you are familiar with the genre you are writing in and learn standard procedures for submitting your work. A good query will go a long way."

◩ JULIE POPKIN

725 Richmond Ave., Silver Spring MD 20910. (301)585-3676. **Contact:** Julie Popkin, Joel Mandelbaum. Estab. 1989. Represents 35 clients. 30% of clients are new/unpublished writers. Currently handles: 70% nonfiction books; 30% novels.

• Prior to opening her agency, Ms. Popkin taught at the university level and did freelance editing and writing.

Member Agents Julie Popkin (fiction, memoirs, biography); Alyson Sena (nonfiction).

Represents Nonfiction books, novels, translations. **Considers these nonfiction areas:** Art/architecture/design; ethnic/cultural interests; government/politics/law; history; memoirs; philosophy; women's issues/studies (feminist); Criticism. **Considers these fiction areas:** Literary; mainstream/contemporary; mystery/suspense.

⊶ This agency specializes in selling book-length fiction and nonfiction mss. Especially interested in social issues, ethnic and minority subjects, and Latin American authors. Does not want to receive New Age, spiritual, romance, or science fiction.

How to Contact Query with SASE. No e-mail or fax queries. Responds in 1 month to queries; 2 months to mss. Obtains most new clients through personal contacts and guidebooks.

Recent Sales *Out of the Shadows: Contributions of 20th Century Women to Physics*, edited by Nina Byers (Cambridge University Press); *The End of Romance: Love, Sex and Violins*, by Norma Barzman (Nation Books); *In the Dark Cave*, by Richard Watson, illustrated by Dean Norman (Star Bright); *The Docks*, by Bill Sharpsteen (Gibbs Smith); *That Inferno*, translated from Spanish by Gretta Siebentritt (Vanderbilt University Press).

Terms Agent receives 15% commission on domestic sales; 20% commission on foreign sales; 10% commission on dramatic rights sales. Sometimes asks for fee if ms requires extensive copying and mailing.

Writers' Conferences BookExpo America; Santa Barbara Writers' Conference.

Tips "Keep your eyes on the current market. Publishing responds to changes very quickly and often works toward perceived and fresh subject matter. Historical fiction seems to be rising in interest after a long, quiet period."

◩ AARON M. PRIEST LITERARY AGENCY

708 Third Ave., 23rd Floor, New York NY 10017-4103. (212)818-0344. Fax: (212)573-9417. Estab. 1974. Member of AAR. Currently handles: 25% nonfiction books; 75% novels.

Member Agents Lisa Erbach Vance (levance@aaronpriest.com); Paul Cirone (pcirone@aaronpriest.com); Aaron Priest (apriest@aaronpriest.com); Molly Friedrich (mfriedrich@aaronpriest.com); Lucy Childs (lchilds@aaronpriest.com).

Represents Commercial fiction, literary fiction, some nonfiction.

How to Contact No e-mail or fax queries. Considers simultaneous queries. Responds in 1 month if interested.

Terms Agent receives 15% commission on domestic sales. Charges for photocopying and postage expenses.

Ⓝ ◩ PROSPECT AGENCY LLC

285 Fifth Ave., PMB 445, Brooklyn NY 11215. Phone/Fax: (718)788-3217. E-mail: esk@prospectagency.com. Web site: www.prospectagency.com. **Contact:** Emily Sylvan Kim. Estab. 2005. Represents 15 clients. 50% of clients are new/unpublished writers. Currently handles: 66% novels; 33% juvenile books.

• Prior to starting her agency, Ms. Kim briefly attended law school and worked for another literary agency.

Represents Nonfiction books, novels, juvenile books. **Considers these nonfiction areas:** Memoirs; science/technology; Juvenile. **Considers these fiction areas:** Action/adventure; detective/police/crime; erotica; ethnic;

family saga; fantasy; juvenile; literary; mainstream/contemporary; mystery/suspense; picture books; romance; science fiction; thriller; westerns/frontier; young adult.

- **O—** "We are currently looking for the next generation of writers to shape the literary landscape. Our clients receive professional and knowledgeable representation. We are committed to offering skilled editorial advice and advocating our clients in the marketplace." Actively seeking romance, literary fiction, and young adult submissions. Does not want to receive poetry, short stories, textbooks, or most nonfiction.

How to Contact Upload outline and 3 sample chapters to the Web site. Considers simultaneous queries. Responds in 3 weeks to queries; 1 month to mss. Returns materials only with SASE. Obtains most new clients through recommendations from others, conferences, unsolicited mss.

Recent Sales Clients include Diane Perkins, Kate Rothwell, Regina Scott.

Terms Agent receives 15% commission on domestic sales; 20% commission on foreign sales. Offers written contract.

Writers' Conferences SCBWI Annual Winter Conference; Pikes Peak Writers Conference; RWA National Conference.

☑ MICHAEL PSALTIS

200 Bennett Ave., New York NY 10040. E-mail: michael@mpsaltis.com. **Contact:** Michael Psaltis. Member of AAR. Represents 30 clients.

Represents Nonfiction books, novels. **Considers these nonfiction areas:** Biography/autobiography; business/economics; cooking/foods/nutrition; health/medicine; history; psychology. **Considers these fiction areas:** Mainstream/contemporary.

How to Contact Submit outline/proposal. Responds in 2 weeks to queries; 6 weeks to mss.

Recent Sales *Turning the Tables*, by Steven Shaw (HarperCollins); *Why We Hate*, by David Smith (St. Martin's Press); *A Life in Twilight*, by Mark Wolverton (Joseph Henry Press); *Under a Passionate Moon*, by Donna Simpson (Berkley).

Terms Agent receives 15% commission on domestic sales; 20% commission on foreign sales. Offers written contract.

☑ QUICKSILVER BOOKS—LITERARY AGENTS

508 Central Park Ave., #5101, Scarsdale NY 10583. Phone/Fax: (914)722-4664. Web site: www.quicksilverbooks.com. **Contact:** Bob Silverstein. Estab. 1973 as packager; 1987 as literary agency. Represents 50 clients. 50% of clients are new/unpublished writers. Currently handles: 75% nonfiction books; 25% novels.

- Prior to opening his agency, Mr. Silverstein served as senior editor at Bantam Books and Dell Books/Delacorte Press.

Represents Nonfiction books, novels. **Considers these nonfiction areas:** Anthropology/archaeology; biography/autobiography; business/economics; child guidance/parenting; cooking/foods/nutrition; current affairs; ethnic/cultural interests; health/medicine; history; how-to; language/literature/criticism; memoirs; nature/environment; New Age/metaphysics; popular culture; psychology; religious/inspirational; science/technology; self-help/personal improvement; sociology; sports; true crime/investigative; women's issues/studies. **Considers these fiction areas:** Action/adventure; glitz; mystery/suspense; thriller.

- **O—** This agency specializes in literary and commercial mainstream fiction and nonfiction, especially psychology, New Age, holistic healing, consciousness, ecology, environment, spirituality, reference, cookbooks, and narrative nonfiction. Does not want to receive science fiction, pornography, poetry, or single-spaced mss.

How to Contact Query with SASE. Authors are expected to supply SASE for return of ms and for query letter responses. No e-mail or fax queries. Considers simultaneous queries. Responds in 2 weeks to queries; 1 month to mss. Returns materials only with SASE. Obtains most new clients through recommendations, listings in sourcebooks, solicitations, workshop participation.

Recent Sales Sold over 20 titles in the last year. *Nice Girls Don't Get Rich*, by Lois P. Frankel, PhD (Warner Books); *The Young Patriots*, by Charles Cerami (Sourcebooks); *The Coming of the Beatles*, by Martin Goldsmith (Wiley); *The Real Food Daily Cookbook*, by Ann Gentry (Ten Speed Press); *The Complete Book of Vinyasa Yoga*, by Srivatsa Ramaswami (Marlowe & Co.).

Terms Agent receives 15% commission on domestic sales; 20% commission on foreign sales. Offers written contract.

Writers' Conferences National Writers Union.

Tips "Write what you know. Write from the heart. Publishers print, authors sell."

☑ RAINES & RAINES

103 Kenyon Rd., Medusa NY 12120. (518)239-8311. Fax: (518)239-6029. **Contact:** Theron Raines (member of AAR); Joan Raines; Keith Korman. Represents 100 clients.

Represents Nonfiction books, novels. **Considers these nonfiction areas:** Any. **Considers these fiction areas:** Action/adventure; detective/police/crime; fantasy; historical; mystery/suspense; picture books; science fiction; thriller; westerns/frontier.

How to Contact Query with SASE. Responds in 2 weeks to queries.

Terms Agent receives 15% commission on domestic sales; 20% commission on foreign sales. Charges for photocopying.

HELEN REES LITERARY AGENCY

376 North St., Boston MA 02113-2013. (617)227-9014. Fax: (617)227-8762. E-mail: reesagency@reesagency.com. **Contact:** Joan Mazmanian, Ann Collette, Helen Rees, Lorin Rees. Estab. 1983. Member of AAR, PEN. Represents 98 clients. 50% of clients are new/unpublished writers. Currently handles: 60% nonfiction books; 40% novels.

Member Agents Ann Collette (literary fiction, women's studies, health, biography, history); Helen Rees (business, money/finance/economics, government/politics/law, contemporary issues, literary fiction); Lorin Rees (business, money/finance, management, history, narrative nonfiction, science, literary fiction, memoir).

Represents Nonfiction books, novels. **Considers these nonfiction areas:** Biography/autobiography; business/economics; current affairs; government/politics/law; health/medicine; history; money/finance; women's issues/studies. **Considers these fiction areas:** Historical; literary; mainstream/contemporary; mystery/suspense; thriller.

How to Contact Query with SASE, outline, 2 sample chapters. No unsolicited e-mail submissions. No multiple submissions. No e-mail or fax queries. Responds in 3-4 weeks to queries. Obtains most new clients through recommendations from others, conferences, submissions.

Recent Sales Sold over 35 titles in the last year. *Get Your Shipt Together*, by Capt. D. Michael Abrashoff; *Overpromise and Overdeliver*, by Rick Berrara; *Opacity*, by Joel Kurtzman; *America the Broke*, by Gerald Swanson; *Murder at the B-School*, by Jeffrey Cruikshank; *Bone Factory*, by Steven Sidor; *Father Said*, by Hal Sirowitz; *Winning*, by Jack Welch; *The Case for Israel*, by Alan Dershowitz; *As the Future Catches You*, by Juan Enriquez; *Killing Haji: A Travelogue*, by Johnny Rico; *DVD Video Movie Guide*, by Mick Martin and Marsha Porter; *Killer Words*, by Frank Luntz.

Terms Agent receives 15% commission on domestic sales; 20% commission on foreign sales.

REGAL LITERARY AGENCY

1140 Broadway, Penthouse, New York NY 10001. (212)684-7900. Fax: (212)684-7906. E-mail: office@regal-literary.com. Web site: www.regal-literary.com. **Contact:** Bess Reed, Lauren Schott Pearson. Estab. 2002. Member of AAR. Represents 90 clients. 20% of clients are new/unpublished writers. Currently handles: 48% nonfiction books; 46% novels; 2% story collections; 2% novellas; 2% poetry.

- Prior to becoming agents, Mr. Regal was a musician; Mr. Steinberg was a filmmaker and screenwriter; Ms. Reid and Ms. Schott Pearson were magazine editors.

Member Agents Joseph Regal (literary fiction, science, history, memoir); Peter Steinberg (literary and commercial fiction, history, humor, memoir, narrative nonfiction, young adult); Bess Reed (literary fiction, narrative nonfiction, self-help); Lauren Schott Pearson (literary fiction, commercial fiction, memoir, narrative nonfiction, thrillers, mysteries). Michael Psaltis of Psaltis Literary also works with Regal Literary agents to form the Culinary Cooperative—a joint-venture agency dedicated to food writing, cookbooks, and all things related to cooking. Recent sales include *The Fat Guy's Manifatso* (Bloomsbury USA); *Fish On a First-Name Basis* (St. Martin's Press); *The Reverse Diet* (John Wiley & Sons); and *The Seasoning of a Chef* (Doubleday/Broadway).

Represents Nonfiction books, novels, short story collections, novellas. **Considers these nonfiction areas:** Anthropology/archaeology; art/architecture/design; biography/autobiography; business/economics; cooking/foods/nutrition; current affairs; ethnic/cultural interests; gay/lesbian issues; history; humor/satire; language/literature/criticism; memoirs; military/war; music/dance; nature/environment; photography; popular culture; psychology; religious/inspirational; science/technology; sports; translation; women's issues/studies. **Considers these fiction areas:** Comic books/cartoon; detective/police/crime; ethnic; historical; literary; mystery/suspense; thriller; Contemporary.

- "We have discovered more than a dozen successful literary novelists in the last 5 years. We are small, but are extraordinarily responsive to our writers. We are more like managers than agents, with an eye toward every aspect of our writers' careers, including publicity and other media." Actively seeking literary fiction and narrative nonfiction. Does not want romance, science fiction, horror, or screenplays.

How to Contact Query with SASE, 5-15 sample pages. No phone calls. No e-mail or fax queries. Considers simultaneous queries. Responds in 2-3 weeks to queries; 4-12 to mss. Returns materials only with SASE. Obtains most new clients through recommendations from others, unsolicited submissions.

Recent Sales Sold 20 titles in the last year. *The Stolen Child*, by Keith Donohue (Nan Talese/Doubleday); *What Elmo Taught Me*, by Kevin Clash (HarperCollins); *The Affected Provincial's Companion*, by Lord Breaulove

Swells Whimsy (Bloomsbury); *The Three Incestuous Sisters*, by Audrey Niffenegger (Abrams); *The Traveler*, by John Twelve Hawks (Doubleday). Other clients include James Reston Jr., Tony Earley, Dennie Hughes, Mark Lee, Jake Page, Cheryl Bernard, Daniel Wallace, John Marks, Keith Scribner, Cathy Day, Alicia Erian, Gregory David Roberts, Dallas Hudgens, Tim Winton, Ian Spiegelman, Brad Barkley, Heather Hepler, Gavin Edwards, Sara Voorhees, Alex Abella.

Terms Agent receives 15% commission on domestic sales; 20% commission on foreign sales. No written contract. Charges clients for typical/major office expenses, such as photocopying and foreign postage.

JODY REIN BOOKS, INC.

7741 S. Ash Ct., Centennial CO 80122. (303)694-4430. Fax: (303)694-0687. Web site: www.jodyreinbooks.com. **Contact:** Winnefred Dollar. Estab. 1994. Member of AAR, Authors' Guild. Currently handles: 70% nonfiction books; 30% novels.

- Prior to opening her agency, Ms. Rein worked for 13 years as an acquisitions editor for Contemporary Books and as executive editor for Bantam/Doubleday/Dell and Morrow/Avon.

Represents Nonfiction books, novels. **Considers these nonfiction areas:** Business/economics; child guidance/parenting; current affairs; ethnic/cultural interests; government/politics/law; history; humor/satire; music/dance; nature/environment; popular culture; psychology; science/technology; sociology; theater/film; women's issues/studies. **Considers these fiction areas:** Literary; mainstream/contemporary.

O─ This agency specializes in commercial and narrative nonfiction and literary/commercial fiction.

How to Contact Query with SASE. No e-mail or fax queries. Considers simultaneous queries. Responds in 6 weeks to queries; 2 months to mss. Obtains most new clients through recommendations from others, solicitations.

Recent Sales *How to Remodel a Man*, by Bruce Cameron (St. Martin's Press); *8 Simple Rules for Dating My Teenage Daughter*, by Bruce Cameron (ABC/Disney); *Skeletons on the Zahara*, by Dean King (Little, Brown); *The Big Year*, by Mark Obmascik (The Free Press).

Terms Agent receives 15% commission on domestic sales; 25% commission on foreign sales; 20% commission on dramatic rights sales. Offers written contract. Charges clients for express mail, overseas expenses, photocopying mss.

Tips "Do your homework before submitting. Make sure you have a marketable topic and the credentials to write about it. We want well-written books on fresh and original nonfiction topics that have broad appeal, as well as novels written by authors who have spent years developing their craft. Authors must be well established in their fields and have strong media experience."

JODIE RHODES LITERARY AGENCY

8840 Villa La Jolla Dr., Suite 315, La Jolla CA 92037-1957. **Contact:** Jodie Rhodes, president. Estab. 1998. Member of AAR. Represents 50 clients. 60% of clients are new/unpublished writers. Currently handles: 60% nonfiction books; 35% novels; 5% middle grade/young adult books.

- Prior to opening her agency, Ms. Rhodes was a university-level creative writing teacher, workshop director, published novelist, and vice president/media director at the N.W. Ayer Advertising Agency.

Member Agents Jodie Rhodes; Clark McCutcheon (fiction); Bob McCarter (nonfiction).

Represents Nonfiction books, novels. **Considers these nonfiction areas:** Biography/autobiography; child guidance/parenting; ethnic/cultural interests; government/politics/law; health/medicine; history; memoirs; military/war; science/technology; women's issues/studies. **Considers these fiction areas:** Ethnic; family saga; historical; literary; mainstream/contemporary; mystery/suspense; thriller; young adult; women's.

O─ Actively seeking writers passionate about their books with a talent for richly textured narrative, an eye for details, and a nose for research. Nonfiction writers must have recognized credentials and expert knowledge of their subject matter. Does not want to receive erotica, horror, fantasy, romance, science fiction, religious/inspirational, or children's books (does accept young adult/teen).

How to Contact Query with brief synopsis, first 30-50 pages, SASE. No e-mail or fax queries. Considers simultaneous queries. Responds in 10 days to queries. Returns materials only with SASE. Obtains most new clients through recommendations from others, agent sourcebooks.

Recent Sales Sold 40 titles in the last year. *Chloe Doe*, by Suzanne Phillips (Little, Brown US/MacMillan UK); *Memory Matters*, by Scott Hagwood (Simon & Schuster); *Diagnosis of Love*, by Maggie Martin (Bantam); *Salaam, Paris*, by Kavita Daswani (Putnam); *Preventing Alzheimer's*, by Marwan Sabbagh (John Wiley & Sons); *Japanland*, by Karin Muller (Rodale); *Raising Drug Free Kids*, by Aletha Solter (Da Capo Press).

Terms Agent receives 15% commission on domestic sales; 20% commission on foreign sales. Offers written contract; 1-month notice must be given to terminate contract. Charges clients for fax, photocopying, phone calls, postage. Charges are itemized and approved by writers upfront.

Tips "Think your book out before you write it. Do your research, know your subject matter intimately, and write vivid specifics, not bland generalities. Care deeply about your book. Don't imitate other writers. Find your own voice. We never take on a book we don't believe in, and we go the extra mile for our writers. We welcome talented, new writers."

☻ ANN RITTENBERG LITERARY AGENCY, INC.

30 Bond St., New York NY 10012. (212)684-6936. **Contact:** Ann Rittenberg, president. Estab. 1992. Member of AAR. Represents 35 clients. 40% of clients are new/unpublished writers. Currently handles: 50% nonfiction books; 50% novels.

Represents Nonfiction books, novels. **Considers these nonfiction areas:** Biography/autobiography; history (social/cultural); memoirs; women's issues/studies. **Considers these fiction areas:** Literary.

○┑ This agent specializes in literary fiction and literary nonfiction.

How to Contact Submit outline, 3 sample chapters, SASE. Considers simultaneous queries. Responds in 6 weeks to queries; 2 months to mss. Obtains most new clients through referrals from established writers and editors.

Recent Sales Sold 20 titles in the last year. *Bad Cat*, by Jim Edgar (Workman); *A Certain Slant of Light*, by Laura Whitcomb (Houghton Mifflin); *New York Night*, by Mark Caldwell (Scribner); *In Plain Sight*, by C.J. Box (Putnam); *Improbable*, by Adam Fawer; *Colleges That Change Lives*, by Loren Pope.

Terms Agent receives 15% commission on domestic sales; 20% commission on foreign sales. Offers written contract. Charges clients for photocopying only.

☻ RIVERSIDE LITERARY AGENCY

41 Simon Keets Rd., Leyden MA 01337. (413)772-0067. Fax: (413)772-0969. E-mail: rivlit@sover.net. **Contact:** Susan Lee Cohen. Estab. 1990. Represents 40 clients. 20% of clients are new/unpublished writers.

Represents Adult nonfiction, adult novels.

How to Contact Query with SASE, outline. Accepts e-mail queries. No fax queries. Considers simultaneous queries. Responds in 2 weeks to queries. Obtains most new clients through referrals.

Recent Sales *Writing to Change the World*, by Mary Pipher, PhD (Riverhead/Penguin Putnam); *The Sociopath Next Door: The Ruthless Versus the Rest of Us*, by Dr. Martha Stout (Broadway); *Letting Go of the Person You Used to Be*, by Lama Surya Das (Broadway); *The Secret Magdalene*, by Ki Longfellow (Crown); *Right, Wrong, and Risky: A Dictionary of Today's American English Usage*, by Mark Davidson (Norton).

Terms Agent receives 15% commission on domestic sales. Offers written contract. Charges clients for foreign postage, photocopying large mss, express mail deliveries, etc.

Tips "We are very selective."

☻ B.J. ROBBINS LITERARY AGENCY

5130 Bellaire Ave., North Hollywood CA 91607-2908. (818)760-6602. Fax: (818)760-6616. E-mail: robbinsliterary@aol.com. **Contact:** (Ms.) B.J. Robbins. Estab. 1992. Member of AAR. Represents 40 clients. 50% of clients are new/unpublished writers. Currently handles: 50% nonfiction books; 50% novels.

Represents Nonfiction books, novels. **Considers these nonfiction areas:** Biography/autobiography; child guidance/parenting; current affairs; ethnic/cultural interests; health/medicine; how-to; humor/satire; memoirs; music/dance; popular culture; psychology; self-help/personal improvement; sociology; sports; theater/film; travel; true crime/investigative; women's issues/studies. **Considers these fiction areas:** Detective/police/crime; ethnic; literary; mainstream/contemporary; mystery/suspense; sports; thriller; young adult.

How to Contact Submit outline/proposal, 3 sample chapters, SASE. Accepts e-mail queries (no attachments). No fax queries. Considers simultaneous queries. Responds in 2-6 weeks to queries; 6-8 weeks to mss. Returns materials only with SASE. Obtains most new clients through conferences, referrals.

Recent Sales Sold 15 titles in the last year. *Getting Stoned with Savages*, by J. Maarten Troost (Broadway); *Hot Water*, by Kathryn Jordan (Berkley); *Between the Bridge and the River*, by Craig Ferguson (Chronicle); *I'm Proud of You*, by Tim Madigan (Gotham); *Man of the House*, by Chris Erskine (Rodale); *Bird of Another Heaven*, by James D. Houston (Knopf); *Tomorrow They Will Kiss*, by Eduardo Santiago (Little, Brown).

Terms Agent receives 15% commission on domestic sales; 20% commission on foreign sales. Offers written contract; 3-month notice must be given to terminate contract. 100% of business is derived from commissions on ms sales. Charges clients for postage and photocopying (charged only after sale of ms).

Writers' Conferences Squaw Valley Writers Workshop; San Diego State University Writers' Conference; Santa Barbara Writers' Conference.

☻ THE ROSENBERG GROUP

23 Lincoln Ave., Marblehead MA 01945. (781)990-1341. Fax: (781)990-1344. Web site: www.rosenberggroup.com. **Contact:** Barbara Collins Rosenberg. Estab. 1998. Member of AAR, recognized agent of the RWA. Represents 32 clients. 25% of clients are new/unpublished writers. Currently handles: 30% nonfiction books; 30% novels; 10% scholarly books; 30% textbooks.

• Prior to becoming an agent, Ms. Rosenberg was a senior editor for Harcourt.

Represents Nonfiction books, novels, textbooks. **Considers these nonfiction areas:** Current affairs; popular culture; psychology; sports; women's issues/studies; Women's health; food/wine/beverages. **Considers these fiction areas:** Romance; women's.

O→ Ms. Rosenberg is well-versed in the romance market (both category and single title). She is a frequent speaker at romance conferences. Actively seeking romance category or single title in contemporary chick lit, romantic suspense, and the historical subgenres. Does not want to receive time travel, paranormal, or inspirational/spiritual romances.

How to Contact Query with SASE. No e-mail or fax queries. Responds in 2 weeks to queries; 4-6 weeks to mss. Returns materials only with SASE. Obtains most new clients through recommendations from others, solicitations, conferences.

Recent Sales Sold 24 titles in the last year.

Terms Agent receives 15% commission on domestic sales; 15% commission on foreign sales. Offers written contract; 1-month notice must be given to terminate contract. Charges maximum of $350/year for postage and photocopying.

Writers' Conferences RWA National Conference; BookExpo America.

ROSENSTONE/WENDER

38 E. 29th St., 10th Floor, New York NY 10016. (212)725-9445. Fax: (212)725-9447. Member of AAR.

Member Agents Howard Rosenstone; Phyllis Wender; Sonia Pabley; Ronald Gwiazda, associate member.

O→ Interested in literary, adult, and dramatic material.

How to Contact Query with SASE.

JANE ROTROSEN AGENCY LLC

318 E. 51st St., New York NY 10022. (212)593-4330. Fax: (212)935-6985. E-mail: firstinitiallastname@janerotros en.com. Estab. 1974. Member of AAR, Authors Guild. Represents over 100 clients. Currently handles: 30% nonfiction books; 70% novels.

Member Agents Jane R. Berkey; Andrea Cirillo; Annelise Robey; Margaret Ruley; Kelly Harms; Christina Hogrebe; Peggy Gordijn, director of translation rights.

Represents Nonfiction books, novels. **Considers these nonfiction areas:** Biography/autobiography; business/economics; child guidance/parenting; cooking/foods/nutrition; current affairs; health/medicine; how-to; humor/satire; money/finance; nature/environment; popular culture; psychology; self-help/personal improvement; sports; true crime/investigative; women's issues/studies. **Considers these fiction areas:** Action/adventure; detective/police/crime; family saga; historical; horror; mainstream/contemporary; mystery/suspense; romance; thriller; women's.

How to Contact Query with SASE. No e-mail or fax queries. Responds in 2 months to mss. Responds in 2 weeks to writers who have been referred by a client or colleague. Returns materials only with SASE. Obtains most new clients through referrals.

Recent Sales This agency prefers not to share information on specific sales.

Terms Agent receives 15% commission on domestic sales; 20% commission on foreign sales. Offers written contract, binding for 3-5 years; 2-month notice must be given to terminate contract. Charges clients for photocopying, express mail, overseas postage, book purchase.

THE PETER RUBIE LITERARY AGENCY

240 W. 35th St., Suite 500, New York NY 10001. (212)279-1776. Fax: (212)279-0927. E-mail: peterrubie@prlit.c om. Web site: www.prlit.com. **Contact:** Peter Rubie, June Clark (pralit@aol.com). Estab. 2000. Member of AAR. Represents 130 clients. 20% of clients are new/unpublished writers.

● Prior to opening his agency, Mr. Rubie was a founding partner of another literary agency (Perkins, Rubie & Associates), and the fiction editor at Walker and Co; Ms. Clark is the author of several books and plays, and previously worked in cable TV marketing and promotion.

Member Agents Peter Rubie (crime, science fiction, fantasy, literary fiction, thrillers, narrative/serious nonfiction, business, self-help, how-to, popular, food/wine, history, commercial science, music, education, parenting); June Clark (celebrity biographies, parenting, pets, women's issues, teen nonfiction, how-to, self-help, offbeat business, food/wine, commercial New Age, pop culture, entertainment, gay/lesbian).

Represents Nonfiction books, novels. **Considers these nonfiction areas:** Business/economics; current affairs; ethnic/cultural interests; gay/lesbian issues; how-to; popular culture; science/technology; self-help/personal improvement; TV; creative nonfiction (narrative); health/nutrition; cooking/food/wine; music; theater/film; prescriptive New Age; parenting/education; pets; commercial academic material. **Considers these fiction areas:** Fantasy; historical; literary; science fiction; thriller.

How to Contact For fiction, submit short synopsis, first 30-40 pages. For nonfiction, submit 1-page overview of the book, TOC, outline, 1-2 sample chapters. Responds in 2 months to queries; 3 months to mss. Returns materials only with SASE. Obtains most new clients through recommendations from others.

Recent Sales Sold 50 titles in the last year. *Walking Money*, by James Born (Putnam); *Dark Hills Divide*, by Patrick Carman; *One Nation Under God*, by James P. Moore; *28 Days*, by Gabrielle Lichterman (Adams);

Shattered Dreams, by Harlan Ullman (Carroll & Graf); *Chef on Fire*, by Joseph Carey (Taylor); *Laughing with Lucy*, by Madelyn Pugh Davis (Emis); *Read My Hips*, by Eve Marx (Adams); *King Kong: The History of a Movie Icon*, by Ray Morton (Applause).

Terms Agent receives 15% commission on domestic sales; 20% commission on foreign sales. Offers written contract. Charges clients for photocopying and some foreign mailings.

Tips "We look for writers who are experts, have a strong platform and reputation in their field, and have an outstanding prose style. Be professional and open-minded. Know your market and learn your craft. Go to our Web site for up-to-date information on clients and sales."

☑ RUSSELL & VOLKENING

50 W. 29th St., #7E, New York NY 10001. (212)684-6050. Fax: (212)889-3026. **Contact:** Timothy Seldes, Jesseca Salky. Estab. 1940. Member of AAR. Represents 140 clients. 20% of clients are new/unpublished writers. Currently handles: 45% nonfiction books; 50% novels; 3% story collections; 2% novellas.

Represents Nonfiction books, novels, short story collections. **Considers these nonfiction areas:** Anthropology/ archaeology; art/architecture/design; biography/autobiography; business/economics; cooking/foods/nutrition; current affairs; education; ethnic/cultural interests; gay/lesbian issues; government/politics/law; health/ medicine; history; language/literature/criticism; military/war; money/finance; music/dance; nature/environment; photography; popular culture; psychology; science/technology; sociology; sports; theater/film; true crime/investigative; women's issues/studies; Creative nonfiction. **Considers these fiction areas:** Action/adventure; detective/police/crime; ethnic; literary; mainstream/contemporary; mystery/suspense; picture books; sports; thriller.

    ○➔ This agency specializes in literary fiction and narrative nonfiction.

Recent Sales *Digging to America*, by Anne Tyler (Knopf); *Get a Life*, by Nadine Gardiner; *The Franklin Affair*, by Jim Lehrer (Random House).

Terms Agent receives 15% commission on domestic sales; 20% commission on foreign sales. Charges clients for standard office expenses relating to the submission of materials.

Tips "If the query is cogent, well written, well presented, and is the type of book we'd represent, we'll ask to see the manuscript. From there, it depends purely on the quality of the work."

☑ VICTORIA SANDERS & ASSOCIATES

241 Avenue of the Americas, Suite 11 H, New York NY 10014. (212)633-8811. Fax: (212)633-0525. E-mail: queriesvsa@hotmail.com. Web site: www.victoriasanders.com. **Contact:** Victoria Sanders, Diane Dickensheid. Estab. 1993. Member of AAR; signatory of WGA. Represents 135 clients. 25% of clients are new/unpublished writers. Currently handles: 50% nonfiction books; 50% novels.

Represents Nonfiction books, novels. **Considers these nonfiction areas:** Biography/autobiography; current affairs; ethnic/cultural interests; gay/lesbian issues; government/politics/law; history; humor/satire; language/ literature/criticism; music/dance; popular culture; psychology; theater/film; translation; women's issues/studies. **Considers these fiction areas:** Action/adventure; contemporary issues; ethnic; family saga; feminist; gay/ lesbian; literary; thriller.

How to Contact Query by e-mail only.

Recent Sales Sold 20+ titles in the last year. *Faithless, Triptych & Skin Privilege*, by Karin Slaughter (Delacorte); *Jewels: 50 Phenomenal Black Women Over 50*, by Connie Briscoe and Michael Cunningham (Bulfinch); *B Mother*, by Maureen O'Brien (Harcourt); *Vagablonde*, by Kim Green (Warner); *Next Elements*, by Jeff Chang (Basic Civitas); *The Ties That Bind*, by Dr. Bertice Berry.

Terms Agent receives 15% commission on domestic sales; 20% commission on foreign sales. Offers written contract. Charges for photocopying, messenger, express mail. If in excess of $100, client approval is required.

Tips "Limit query to letter (no calls) and give it your best shot. A good query is going to get a good response."

☑ SCHIAVONE LITERARY AGENCY, INC.

236 Trails End, West Palm Beach FL 33413-2135. (561)966-9294. Fax: (561)966-9294. E-mail: profschia@aol.c om. Web site: www.publishersmarketplace.com/members/profschia. **Contact:** James Schiavone. Estab. 1996. Member of National Education Association. Represents 60 clients. 2% of clients are new/unpublished writers. Currently handles: 50% nonfiction books; 49% novels; 1% textbooks.

    ● Prior to opening his agency, Dr. Schiavone was a full professor of developmental skills at the City University of New York and author of 5 trade books and 3 textbooks.

Represents Nonfiction books, novels, juvenile books, scholarly books, textbooks. **Considers these nonfiction areas:** Animals; anthropology/archaeology; biography/autobiography; child guidance/parenting; current affairs; education; ethnic/cultural interests; gay/lesbian issues; government/politics/law; health/medicine; history; how-to; humor/satire; juvenile nonfiction; language/literature/criticism; military/war; nature/environment; popular culture; psychology; science/technology; self-help/personal improvement; sociology; true crime/

Literary Agents

investigative. **Considers these fiction areas:** Ethnic; family saga; historical; horror; humor/satire; juvenile; literary; mainstream/contemporary; science fiction; young adult.

> ⚬⇥ This agency specializes in celebrity biography and autobiography. Actively seeking serious nonfiction, literary fiction, and celebrity biography. Does not want to receive poetry.

How to Contact Query with SASE. One-page e-mail queries with no attachments are accepted and encouraged for a fast response. Does not accept phone or fax queries. Considers simultaneous queries. Responds in 2 weeks to queries; 6 weeks to mss. Returns materials only with SASE. Obtains most new clients through recommendations from others, solicitations, conferences.

Terms Agent receives 15% commission on domestic sales; 20% commission on foreign sales. Offers written contract. Charges clients for postage only.

Writers' Conferences Key West Literary Seminar; South Florida Writer's Conference.

Tips "I prefer to work with established authors published by major houses in New York. I will consider marketable proposals from new/previously unpublished writers."

☐ SCRIBE AGENCY, LLC

5508 Joylynne Dr., Madison WI 53716. E-mail: queries@scribeagency.com. Web site: www.scribeagency.com. **Contact:** Kristopher O'Higgins. Estab. 2004. Represents 5 clients. 60% of clients are new/unpublished writers. Currently handles: 100% novels.

> • "We have 14 years of experience in publishing and have worked on both agency and editorial sides in the past, with marketing expertise to boot. We love books as much or more than anyone you know. Check our Web site to see what we're about."

Member Agents Kristopher O'Higgins; Jesse Vogel.

Represents Nonfiction books, novels, short story collections, novellas, juvenile books, poetry books. **Considers these nonfiction areas:** Cooking/foods/nutrition; ethnic/cultural interests; gay/lesbian issues; humor/satire; memoirs; music/dance; popular culture; true crime/investigative; women's issues/studies. **Considers these fiction areas:** Action/adventure; comic books/cartoon; detective/police/crime; erotica; ethnic; experimental; fantasy; feminist; gay/lesbian; horror; humor/satire; juvenile; literary; mainstream/contemporary; mystery/suspense; psychic/supernatural; science fiction; thriller; young adult.

> ⚬⇥ Actively seeking excellent writers with ideas and stories to tell. Does not want cat mysteries or anything not listed above.

How to Contact Query with SASE. Responds in 3-4 weeks to queries; 3-4 months to mss. Returns materials only with SASE.

Recent Sales Sold 2 titles in the last year.

Terms Agent receives 17% commission on domestic sales; 25% commission on foreign sales. Offers written contract. Charges for postage and photocopying.

Writers' Conferences BookExpo America; The Writer's Institute; Spring Writer's Festival; WisCon; Wisconsin Book Festival; World Fantasy Convention.

☑ LYNN SELIGMAN, LITERARY AGENT

400 Highland Ave., Upper Montclair NJ 07043. (973)783-3631. **Contact:** Lynn Seligman. Estab. 1985. Member of Women's Media Group. Represents 32 clients. 15% of clients are new/unpublished writers. Currently handles: 70% nonfiction books; 30% novels.

> • Prior to opening her agency, Ms. Seligman worked in the subsidiary rights department of Doubleday and Simon & Schuster, and served as an agent with Julian Bach Literary Agency (which became IMG Literary Agency). Foreign rights are represented by Books Crossing Borders, Inc.

Represents Nonfiction books, novels. **Considers these nonfiction areas:** Anthropology/archaeology; art/architecture/design; biography/autobiography; business/economics; child guidance/parenting; cooking/foods/nutrition; current affairs; education; ethnic/cultural interests; government/politics/law; health/medicine; history; how-to; humor/satire; interior design/decorating; language/literature/criticism; money/finance; music/dance; nature/environment; photography; popular culture; psychology; science/technology; self-help/personal improvement; sociology; theater/film; true crime/investigative; women's issues/studies. **Considers these fiction areas:** Detective/police/crime; ethnic; fantasy; feminist; gay/lesbian; historical; horror; humor/satire; literary; mainstream/contemporary; mystery/suspense; romance (contemporary, gothic, historical, regency); science fiction.

> ⚬⇥ This agency specializes in general nonfiction and fiction. "I also do illustrated and photography books and have represented several photographers for books." This agency does not handle children's or young adult books.

How to Contact Query with SASE, sample chapters, outline/proposal. Prefers to read materials exclusively. No e-mail or fax queries. Considers simultaneous queries. Responds in 2 weeks to queries; 2 months to mss. Returns materials only with SASE. Obtains most new clients through referrals from other writers and editors.

Recent Sales Sold 15 titles in the last year. *20,001 Names for Baby, GEM edition*, by Carol McD. Wallace; *A House Divided*, by Deborah Leblanc.

Terms Agent receives 15% commission on domestic sales; 25% commission on foreign sales. Charges clients for photocopying, unusual postage, express mail, telephone expenses (checks with author first).

◙ SERENDIPITY LITERARY AGENCY, LLC

305 Gates Ave., Brooklyn NY 11216. (718)230-7689. Fax: (718)230-7829. E-mail: rbrooks@serendipitylit.com. Web site: www.serendipitylit.com. **Contact:** Regina Brooks. Estab. 2000. Represents 50 clients. 50% of clients are new/unpublished writers. Currently handles: 50% nonfiction books; 50% fiction.

● Prior to becoming an agent, Ms. Brooks was an acquisitions editor for John Wiley & Sons, Inc. and McGraw-Hill Companies.

Represents Nonfiction books, novels, juvenile books, scholarly books, children's books. **Considers these nonfiction areas:** Business/economics; current affairs; education; ethnic/cultural interests; history; juvenile nonfiction; memoirs; money/finance; multicultural; New Age/metaphysics; popular culture; psychology; religious/inspirational; science/technology; self-help/personal improvement; sports; women's issues/studies; Health/medical; narrative; popular science, biography; politics; crafts/design; food/cooking; contemporary culture. **Considers these fiction areas:** Action/adventure; confession; ethnic; historical; juvenile; literary; multicultural; picture books; thriller; Chick lit; lady lit; suspense; mystery; romance.

O➥ Actively seeking African-American nonfiction, commercial fiction, young adult novels with an urban flair, and juvenile books. "We do not represent original stage plays, screenplays, or poetry."

How to Contact Prefers to read materials exclusively. For nonfiction, submit outline, 1 sample chapter, SASE. Responds in 2 months to queries; 3 months to mss. Obtains most new clients through conferences, referrals.

Recent Sales This agency prefers not to share information on specific sales. Recent sales available upon request.

Terms Agent receives 15% commission on domestic sales; 20% commission on foreign sales. Offers written contract; 2-month notice must be given to terminate contract. Charges clients for office fees, which are taken from any advance. Does not make referrals to editing services.

Tips "We are eagerly looking for young adult books and fiction and nonfiction targeted to 20 and 30 year olds. We also represent illustrators."

◙ THE SEYMOUR AGENCY

475 Miner St., Canton NY 13617. (315)386-1831. Fax: (315)386-1037. E-mail: marysue@slic.com. Web site: www.theseymouragency.com. **Contact:** Mary Sue Seymour. Estab. 1992. Member of AAR, RWA, Authors Guild; signatory of WGA. Represents 50 clients. 5% of clients are new/unpublished writers. Currently handles: 50% nonfiction books; 50% fiction.

● Ms. Seymour is a retired New York State certified teacher.

Represents Nonfiction books, novels. **Considers these nonfiction areas:** Business/economics; health/medicine; how-to; self-help/personal improvement; Christian books; cookbooks; any well-written nonfiction that includes a proposal in standard format and 1 sample chapter. **Considers these fiction areas:** Literary; religious/inspirational (Christian books); romance (any type).

How to Contact Query with SASE, synopsis, first 50 pages for romance. Accepts e-mail queries. No fax queries. Considers simultaneous queries. Responds in 1 month to queries; 3 months to mss. Returns materials only with SASE.

Recent Sales *Interference*, by Shelley Wernlein; *The Doctor's Daughter*, by Donna MacQuigg; 2-book historical romance deal for Tracy Willouer.

Terms Agent receives 12-15% commission on domestic sales.

Writers' Conferences BookExpo America; Start Your Engines; Romantic Times Convention; ICE Escape Writers Conference; Spring Into Romance; Silicon Valley RWA Conference; Put Your Heart in a Book.

Ⓝ ◙ DENISE SHANNON LITERARY AGENCY, INC.

20 W. 22nd St., Suite 1603, New York NY 10010. (212)414-2911. Fax: (212)414-2930. E-mail: info@deniseshannonagency.com. Web site: www.deniseshannonagency.com. **Contact:** Denise Shannon. Estab. 2002. Member of AAR.

● Prior to opening her agency, Ms. Shannon worked for 16 years with Georges Borchardt and International Creative Management.

Represents Nonfiction books, novels. **Considers these nonfiction areas:** Biography/autobiography; business/economics; health/medicine; Narrative nonfiction; politics; journalism; social history. **Considers these fiction areas:** Literary.

O➥ "We are a boutique agency with a distinguished list of fiction and nonfiction authors."

How to Contact Submit query with description of project, bio, SASE. Accepts e-mail queries (submissions@deniseshannonagency.com).

Literary Agents

Recent Sales *Tête ø Tête: Simone de Beauvoir and Jean-Paul Sartre*, by Hazel Rowley (HarperCollins); *Organic, Inc.: The Marketing of Innocence*, by Samuel Fromartz (Harcourt); *Absurdistan*, by Gary Shteyngart (Random House); *Giving It Up*, by Stephen McCauley (Simon & Schuster).

✪ WENDY SHERMAN ASSOCIATES, INC.

450 Seventh Ave., Suite 2307, New York NY 10123. (212)279-9027. Fax: (212)279-8863. Web site: www.wsherman.com. **Contact:** Wendy Sherman. Estab. 1999. Member of AAR. Represents 50 clients. 30% of clients are new/unpublished writers. Currently handles: 50% nonfiction books; 50% novels.

- Prior to opening the agency, Ms. Sherman worked for The Aaron Priest agency and served as vice president, executive director, associate publisher, subsidary rights director, and sales and marketing director in the publishing industry.

Member Agents Tracy Brown; Wendy Sherman; Michelle Brower.

Represents Nonfiction books, novels. **Considers these nonfiction areas:** Psychology; Narrative; practical. **Considers these fiction areas:** Literary; women's (suspense).

- ○┅ "We specialize in developing new writers, as well as working with more established writers. My experience as a publisher has proven to be a great asset to my clients."

How to Contact Query with SASE or send outline/proposal, 1 sample chapter. No e-mail queries. Considers simultaneous queries. Responds in 1 month to queries. Returns materials only with SASE. Obtains most new clients through recommendations from others.

Recent Sales Fiction clients include: William Lashner, Nani Power, DW Buffa, Howard Bahr, Suzanne Chazin, Sarah Stonich, Ad Hudler, Mary Sharratt, Libby Street, Heather Estay, Darri Stephens, Megan Desales. Nonfiction clients include: Rabbi Mark Borovitz, Alan Eisenstock, Esther Perel, Clifton Leaf, Maggie Estep, Greg Baer, Martin Friedman, Lundy Bancroft, Alvin Ailey Dance, Lise Friedman, Liz Landers, Vicky Mainzer.

Terms Agent receives 15% commission on domestic sales; 20% commission on foreign sales. Offers written contract.

◒ ROSALIE SIEGEL, INTERNATIONAL LITERARY AGENCY, INC.

1 Abey Dr., Pennington NJ 08543. (609)737-1007. Fax: (609)737-3708. **Contact:** Rosalie Siegel. Estab. 1977. Member of AAR. Represents 35 clients. 10% of clients are new/unpublished writers. Currently handles: 45% nonfiction books; 45% novels; 10% young adult books; short story collections for current clients.

How to Contact Obtains most new clients through referrals from writers and friends.

Terms Agent receives 15% commission on domestic sales; 20% commission on foreign sales. Offers written contract; 2-month notice must be given to terminate contract. Charges clients for photocopying.

Tips "I'm not looking for new authors in an active way."

🌐 ✪ JEFFREY SIMMONS LITERARY AGENCY

15 Penn House, Mallory St., London NW8 8SX England. (44)(207)224-8917. E-mail: jasimmons@btconnect.com. **Contact:** Jeffrey Simmons. Estab. 1978. Represents 43 clients. 40% of clients are new/unpublished writers. Currently handles: 65% nonfiction books; 35% novels.

- Prior to becoming an agent, Mr. Simmons was a publisher. He is also an author.

Represents Nonfiction books, novels. **Considers these nonfiction areas:** Biography/autobiography; current affairs; government/politics/law; history; language/literature/criticism; memoirs; music/dance; popular culture; sociology; sports; theater/film; translation; true crime/investigative. **Considers these fiction areas:** Action/adventure; confession; detective/police/crime; family saga; literary; mainstream/contemporary; mystery/suspense; thriller.

- ○┅ This agency seeks to handle good books and promising young writers. "My long experience in publishing and as an author and ghostwriter means I can offer an excellent service all around, especially in terms of editorial experience where appropriate." Actively seeking quality fiction, biography, autobiography, showbiz, personality books, law, crime, politics, and world affairs. Does not want to receive science fiction, horror, fantasy, juvenile, academic books, or specialist subjects (e.g., cooking, gardening, religious).

How to Contact Submit sample chapter, outline/proposal, SASE (IRCs if necessary). Prefers to read materials exclusively. Responds in 1 week to queries; 1 month to mss. Obtains most new clients through recommendations from others, solicitations.

Recent Sales Sold 16 titles in the last year. *The Masks of Christ*, by Picknett & Prince (Time Warner UK/Simon & Schuster US); *The Complete One Foot in the Grave*, by Webber (Orion).

Terms Agent receives 10-15% commission on domestic sales; 15% commission on foreign sales. Offers written contract, binding for lifetime of book in question or until it becomes out of print.

Tips "When contacting us with an outline/proposal, include a brief biographical note (listing any previous publications, with publishers and dates). Preferably tell us if the book has already been offered elsewhere."

⚏ ◍ BEVERLEY SLOPEN LITERARY AGENCY

131 Bloor St. W., Suite 711, Toronto ON M5S 1S3 Canada. (416)964-9598. Fax: (416)921-7726. E-mail: beverly@slopenagency.ca. Web site: www.slopenagency.ca. **Contact:** Beverley Slopen. Estab. 1974. Represents 70 clients. 20% of clients are new/unpublished writers. Currently handles: 60% nonfiction books; 40% novels.

- Prior to opening her agency, Ms. Slopen worked in publishing and as a journalist.

Represents Nonfiction books, novels, scholarly books, textbooks (college). **Considers these nonfiction areas:** Anthropology/archaeology; biography/autobiography; business/economics; current affairs; psychology; sociology; true crime/investigative; women's issues/studies. **Considers these fiction areas:** Literary; mystery/suspense.

- O➥ This agency has a strong bent toward Canadian writers. Actively seeking serious nonfiction that is accessible and appealing to the general reader. Does not want to receive fantasy, science fiction, or children's books.

How to Contact Query with SAE and IRCs. Returns materials only with SASE (Canadian postage only). Accepts short e-mail queries. Considers simultaneous queries. Responds in 2 months to queries.

Recent Sales Sold over 40 titles in the last year. *Court Lady* and *Country Wife*, by Lita-Rose Betcherman (HarperCollins Canada/Morrow/Wiley UK); *Vermeer's Hat*, by Timothy Brook (HarperCollins Canada); *Midnight Cab*, by James W. Nichol (Canongate US/Droemer); *Lady Franklin's Revenge*, by Ken McGoogan (HarperCollins Canada/Bantam UK); *Understanding Uncertainty*, by Jeffrey Rosenthal (HarperCollins Canada); *Damaged Angels*, by Bonnie Buxton (Carroll & Graf US); *Sea of Dreams*, by Adam Mayers (McClelland & Stewart Canada); *Memory Book*, by Howard Engel (Carroll & Graf); *Written in the Flesh*, by Edward Shorter (University of Toronto Press); *Punch Line*, by Joey Slinger. Other clients include Modris Eksteins, Michael Marrus, Robert Fulford, Morley Torgov, Elliott Leyton, Don Gutteridge, Joanna Goodman, Roberta Rich, Jennifer Welsh, Margaret Wente, Frank Wydra.

Terms Agent receives 15% commission on domestic sales; 10% commission on foreign sales. Offers written contract, binding for 2 years; 3-month notice must be given to terminate contract.

Tips "Please, no unsolicited manuscripts."

◍ SPECTRUM LITERARY AGENCY

320 Central Park W., Suite 1-D, New York NY 10025. Web site: www.spectrumliteraryagency.com. **Contact:** Eleanor Wood, president. Represents 90 clients. Currently handles: 10% nonfiction books; 90% novels.

Member Agents Lucienne Diver.

Represents Nonfiction books, novels. **Considers these fiction areas:** Fantasy; historical; mainstream/contemporary; mystery/suspense; romance; science fiction.

How to Contact Query with SASE, include publishing credits and background information. No phone, e-mail, or fax queries. Responds in 1-3 months to queries. Obtains most new clients through recommendations from authors.

Recent Sales Sold over 100 titles in the last year. This agency prefers not to share information on specific sales.

Terms Agent receives 15% commission on domestic sales. Deducts for photocopying and book orders.

◍ SPENCERHILL ASSOCIATES

P.O. Box 374, Chatham NY 12037. (518)392-9293. Fax: (518)392-9554. E-mail: ksolem@klsbooks.com. **Contact:** Karen Solem. Estab. 2001. Member of AAR. Represents 40 clients. 5% of clients are new/unpublished writers. Currently handles: 5% nonfiction books; 90% novels; 5% novellas.

- Prior to becoming an agent, Ms. Solem was editor-in-chief at HarperCollins and an associate publisher.

Represents Nonfiction books, novels. **Considers these nonfiction areas:** Animals; religious/inspirational. **Considers these fiction areas:** Detective/police/crime; historical; mainstream/contemporary; religious/inspirational; romance; thriller.

- O➥ "I handle mostly commercial women's fiction, romance, thrillers, and mysteries. I also represent Christian fiction and nonfiction." No poetry, science fiction, juvenile, or scripts.

How to Contact Query with SASE, proposal package, outline. Responds in 1 month to queries. Returns materials only with SASE.

Recent Sales Sold 115 titles in the last year.

Terms Agent receives 15% commission on domestic sales; 20% commission on foreign sales. Offers written contract; 3-month notice must be given to terminate contract.

◖ THE SPIELER AGENCY

154 W. 57th St., 13th Floor, Room 135, New York NY 10019. **Contact:** Katya Balter. Estab. 1981. Represents 160 clients. 2% of clients are new/unpublished writers.

- Prior to opening his agency, Mr. Spieler was a magazine editor.

Member Agents Joe Spieler; John Thornton (nonfiction); Lisa M. Ross (fiction, nonfiction); Deirdre Mullane (nonfiction); Eric Myers (nonfiction, fiction); Victoria Shoemaker (fiction, nonfiction).

Represents Nonfiction books, novels, children's books. **Considers these nonfiction areas:** Biography/autobiography; business/economics; child guidance/parenting; current affairs; gay/lesbian issues; government/politics/law; history; memoirs; money/finance; music/dance; nature/environment; religious/inspirational; sociology; spirituality; theater/film; travel; women's issues/studies. **Considers these fiction areas:** Feminist; gay/lesbian; literary.

How to Contact Query with SASE. Prefers to read materials exclusively. Returns materials only with SASE; otherwise materials are discarded when rejected. No fax queries. Considers simultaneous queries. Responds in 2 weeks to queries; 2 months to mss. Obtains most new clients through recommendations, listing in *Guide to Literary Agents*.

Recent Sales *What's the Matter with Kansas*, by Thomas Frank (Metropolitan/Holt); *Natural History of the Rich*, by Richard Conniff (W.W. Norton); *Juicing the Game*, by Howard Bryant (Viking).

Terms Agent receives 15% commission on domestic sales. Charges clients for messenger bills, photocopying, postage.

Writers' Conferences London Book Fair.

PHILIP G. SPITZER LITERARY AGENCY, INC

50 Talmage Farm Ln., East Hampton NY 11937. (631)329-3650. Fax: (631)329-3651. E-mail: spitzer516@aol.com. **Contact:** Philip Spitzer. Estab. 1969. Member of AAR. Represents 60 clients. 10% of clients are new/unpublished writers. Currently handles: 50% nonfiction books; 50% novels.

- Prior to opening his agency, Mr. Spitzer served at New York University Press, McGraw-Hill, and the John Cushman Associates literary agency.

Represents Nonfiction books, novels. **Considers these nonfiction areas:** Biography/autobiography; business/economics; current affairs; ethnic/cultural interests; government/politics/law; health/medicine; history; language/literature/criticism; military/war; music/dance; nature/environment; popular culture; psychology; sociology; sports; theater/film; true crime/investigative. **Considers these fiction areas:** Detective/police/crime; literary; mainstream/contemporary; mystery/suspense; sports; thriller.

- This agency specializes in mystery/suspense, literary fiction, sports, and general nonfiction (no how-to).

How to Contact Query with SASE, outline, 1 sample chapter. Responds in 1 week to queries; 6 weeks to mss. Obtains most new clients through recommendations from others.

Recent Sales *The Narrows* and *Lost Light*, by Michael Connelly; *Shadow Man*, by Jonathon King; *Something's Down There*, by Mickey Spillane; *Missing Justice*, by Alafair Burke; *Last Car to Elysian Fields*, by James Lee Burke; *Shattered*, by Deborah Puglisi Sharp with Marjorie Perston.

Terms Agent receives 15% commission on domestic sales; 20% commission on foreign sales. Charges clients for photocopying.

Writers' Conferences BookExpo America.

NANCY STAUFFER ASSOCIATES

P.O. Box 1203, Darien CT 06820. (203)655-3717. Fax: (203)655-3704. E-mail: nanstauf@optonline.net. **Contact:** Nancy Stauffer Cahoon. Estab. 1989. Member of Authors Guild. 5% of clients are new/unpublished writers. Currently handles: 15% nonfiction books; 85% novels.

Represents Nonfiction books, novels. **Considers these nonfiction areas:** Current affairs; ethnic/cultural interests; Creative nonfiction (narrative). **Considers these fiction areas:** Contemporary issues; literary; regional.

How to Contact Obtains most new clients through referrals from existing clients.

Recent Sales New novels by Sherman Alexie, Mark Spragg, and William C. Harris.

Terms Agent receives 15% commission on domestic sales; 20% commission on foreign sales; 15% commission on dramatic rights sales.

Tips "We work with foreign agents in all major markets."

STEELE-PERKINS LITERARY AGENCY

26 Island Ln., Canandaigua NY 14424. (585)396-9290. Fax: (585)396-3579. E-mail: pattiesp@aol.com. **Contact:** Pattie Steele-Perkins. Member of AAR, RWA. Currently handles: 100% novels.

Represents Novels. **Considers these fiction areas:** Mainstream/contemporary; multicultural; romance (inspirational); women's.

How to Contact Submit outline, 3 sample chapters, SASE. Considers simultaneous queries. Responds in 6 weeks to queries. Returns materials only with SASE. Obtains most new clients through recommendations from others, queries/solicitations.

Recent Sales This agency prefers not to share information on specific sales.

Terms Agent receives 15% commission on domestic sales. Offers written contract, binding for 1 year; 1-month notice must be given to terminate contract.

Writers' Conferences RWA National Conference; BookExpo America; CBA Convention; Romance Slam Jam.

Tips "Be patient. E-mail rather than call. Make sure what you are sending is the best it can be."

STERNIG & BYRNE LITERARY AGENCY

2370 S. 107th St., Apt. #4, Milwaukee WI 53227-2036. (414)328-8034. Fax: (414)328-8034. E-mail: jackbyrne@hotmail.com. Web site: www.sff.net/people/jackbyrne. **Contact:** Jack Byrne. Estab. 1950s. Member of SFWA, MWA. Represents 30 clients. 10% of clients are new/unpublished writers. Currently handles: 5% nonfiction books; 85% novels; 10% juvenile books.

Represents Nonfiction books, novels, juvenile books. **Considers these fiction areas:** Fantasy; horror; mystery/suspense; science fiction.

- "Our client list is comfortably full and our current needs are therefore quite limited." Actively seeking science fiction/fantasy by established writers. Does not want to receive romance, poetry, textbooks, or highly specialized nonfiction.

How to Contact Query with SASE. Accepts e-mail queries (no attachments). Responds in 3 weeks to queries; 3 months to mss. Returns materials only with SASE.

Recent Sales Sold 13 new titles and 40+ reprints/foreign rights in the last year. *Magic Bites*, by Ilona Andrews; *Webmage*, by Kelly McCullough. Other clients include Lyn McConche, Betty Ren Wright, Jo Walton, Moira Moore, Sarah Monette, John C. Wright, Naomi Kritzer.

Terms Agent receives 15% commission on domestic sales; 20% commission on foreign sales. Offers written contract; 2-month notice must be given to terminate contract.

Tips "Don't send first drafts, have a professional presentation (including cover letter), and know your field. Read what's been done—good and bad."

PAM STRICKLER AUTHOR MANAGEMENT

1 Water St., New Paltz NY 12561. (845)255-0061. Web site: www.pamstrickler.com. **Contact:** Pamela Dean Strickler. Member of AAR.

- Prior to opening her agency, Ms. Strickler was senior editor at Ballantine Books.
- Specializes in romance and women's fiction. No nonfiction or children's books.

How to Contact Query via e-mail with 1-page letter of plot description and first 10 pages of ms (no attachments). *No unsolicited mss.*

Recent Sales *Lady Dearing's Masquerade*, by Elena Greene (New American Library); *Her Body of Work*, by Marie Donovan (Harlequin/Blaze); *Deceived*, by Nicola Cornick (Harlequin/HQN).

REBECCA STRONG INTERNATIONAL LITERARY AGENCY

235 W. 108th St., #35, New York NY 10025. (212)865-1569. **Contact:** Rebecca Strong. Estab. 2003. 95% of clients are new/unpublished writers. Currently handles: 50% nonfiction books; 40% novels; 10% story collections.

- Prior to opening her agency, Ms. Strong was an industry executive with experience editing and licensing in the US and UK. She has worked at Crown/Random House, Harmony/Random House, Bloomsbury, and Harvill.

Represents Nonfiction books, novels, short story collections. **Considers these nonfiction areas:** Biography/autobiography; cooking/foods/nutrition; current affairs; how-to; interior design/decorating; memoirs; self-help/personal improvement. **Considers these fiction areas:** Detective/police/crime; experimental; historical; humor/satire; literary; mainstream/contemporary; mystery/suspense; thriller.

- "We are a consciously small agency dedicated to established and buidling writers' book publishing careers rather than representing one-time projects." Does not want poetry, screenplays, or any unsolicited mss.

How to Contact Query with SASE. No e-mail or fax queries. Considers simultaneous queries. Responds in 2 months to queries. Returns materials only with SASE. Obtains most new clients through recommendations from others, conferences.

Terms Agent receives 15% commission on domestic sales; 20% commission on foreign sales. Offers written contract, binding for 10 years; 30-day notice must be given to terminate contract.

Tips "I represent writers with prior publishing experience only: journalists, magazine writers, or writers of fiction who have been published in anthologies or literary magazines. There are exceptions to this guideline, but not many."

THE STROTHMAN AGENCY, LLC

One Faneuil Hall Marketplace, 3rd Floor, Boston MA 02109. (617)742-2011. Fax: (617)742-2014. **Contact:** Wendy Strothman, Dan O'Connell. Estab. 2003. Represents 50 clients. Currently handles: 60% nonfiction books; 15% novels; 5% juvenile books; 20% scholarly books.

- Prior to becoming an agent, Ms. Strothman was head of Beacon Press (1983-1995) and executive vice president of Houghton Mifflin's Trade & Reference Division (1996-2002).

Member Agents John Ryden; Wendy Strothman; Dan O'Connell.

Represents Nonfiction books, novels, scholarly books. **Considers these nonfiction areas:** Current affairs; government/politics/law; history; language/literature/criticism; nature/environment. **Considers these fiction areas:** Literary.

> O⇥ "Because we are highly selective in the clients we represent, we increase the value publishers place on our properties. We seek out public figures, scholars, journalists, and other acknowledged and emerging experts in their fields. We specialize in narrative nonfiction, memoir, history, science and nature, arts and culture, literary travel, current affairs, and some business. We have a highly selective practice in literary fiction and children's literature." Actively seeking scholarly nonfiction written to appeal to several audiences. Does not want commercial fiction, romance, science fiction, or self-help.

How to Contact Query with SASE. Considers simultaneous queries. Responds in 3 weeks to queries; 1 month to mss. Returns materials only with SASE. Obtains most new clients through recommendations from others.

Recent Sales Sold 16 titles in the last year. *Iran Awakening: A Memoir of Revolution and Hope*, by Shirin Ebadi (Random House); *The Race Card*, by Richard T. Ford (Farrar, Straus & Giroux); *High Crimes: How a Mountain of Money Draws Thievery, Extortion, Fraud and Death to the Top of the World*, by Michael Kodas (Hyperion); *Errors and Omissions*, by Paul Goldstein (Doubleday); *IP Rules: How Law and Legal Change Drive the Risk and Reward of Intellectual Assets*, by Paul Goldstein (Viking/Portfolio); *The Collapse of the Conservative Case*, by James Galbraith (Holt); *Righteous Warrior: Jesse Helms and the Rise of Modern Conservatism*, by William A. Link (St. Martin's Press); *Addled*, by JoeAnn Hart (Little, Brown).

Terms Agent receives 15% commission on domestic sales; 20% commission on foreign sales. Offers written contract; 30-day notice must be given to terminate contract.

Ⓝ Ⓛ THE SWETKY AGENCY

2150 Balboa Way, No. 29, St. George UT 84770. E-mail: fayeswetky@amsaw.org. Web site: www.amsaw.org/swetkyagency/index-agency.html. **Contact:** Faye M. Swetky. Estab. 2000. Member of American Society of Authors and Writers. Represents 40+ clients. 80% of clients are new/unpublished writers. Currently handles: 10% nonfiction books; 30% novels; 10% juvenile books; 40% movie scripts; 10% TV scripts.

- Prior to becoming an agent, Ms. Swetky was an editor and corporate manager. She has also raised and raced thoroughbred horses.

Represents Nonfiction books, novels, short story collections, juvenile books, movie scripts, feature film, TV scripts, TV movie of the week, sitcom, documentary. **Considers these nonfiction areas:** Agriculture/horticulture; americana; animals; anthropology/archaeology; art/architecture/design; biography/autobiography; business/economics; child guidance/parenting; computers/electronic; cooking/foods/nutrition; creative nonfiction (1); current affairs; education; ethnic/cultural interests; gardening; gay/lesbian issues; government/politics/law; health/medicine; history; how-to; humor/satire; language/literature/criticism; memoirs; military/war; money/finance; multicultural; music/dance; nature/environment; philosophy; photography; popular culture; psychology; recreation; regional; religious/inspirational; science/technology; self-help/personal improvement; sex; sociology; software; spirituality; sports; theater/film; translation; travel; true crime/investigative; women's issues/studies. **Considers these fiction areas:** Action/adventure; comic books/cartoon; confession; detective/police/crime; erotica; ethnic; experimental; family saga; fantasy; feminist; gay/lesbian; gothic; hi-lo; historical; horror; humor/satire; juvenile; literary; mainstream/contemporary; military/war; multicultural; multimedia; mystery/suspense; occult; picture books; plays; poetry; poetry in translation; regional; religious/inspirational; romance; science fiction; short story collections; spiritual; sports; thriller; translation; westerns/frontier; young adult. **Considers these script subject areas:** Action/adventure; biography/autobiography; cartoon/animation; comedy; contemporary issues; detective/police/crime; erotica; ethnic; experimental; family saga; fantasy; feminist; gay/lesbian; glitz; historical; horror; juvenile; mainstream; multicultural; multimedia; mystery/suspense; psychic/supernatural; regional; religious/inspirational; romantic comedy; romantic drama; science fiction; sports; teen; thriller; western/frontier.

> O⇥ "I handle only book-length fiction and nonfiction and feature-length movie and television scripts. Please visit our Web site before submitting. All agency-related information is there, including a sample contract, e-mail submission forms, policies, clients, etc." Actively seeking young adult material. Do not send unprofessionally prepared mss and/or scripts.

How to Contact See Web site for submission instructions. Accepts e-mail queries only. Considers simultaneous queries. Response time varies. Obtains most new clients through queries from the Web site.

Recent Sales Sold 6 titles and sold 8 scripts in the last year. *Solid Stiehl*, by D.J. Herda (Archebooks); *24/7*, by Susan Diplacido (Zumaya Publications); *House on the Road to Salisbury*, by Lisa Adams (Archebooks). *Movie/TV MOW script(s) optioned/sold:* Demons 5, by Jim O'Rear (Katzir Productions); *Detention* and *Instinct Vs. Reason*, by Garrett Hargrove (Filmjack Productions).

Terms Agent receives 15% commission on domestic sales; 20% commission on foreign sales; 20% commission on dramatic rights sales. Offers written contract, binding for 1 year; 30-day notice must be given to terminate contract.

Tips "Be professional. Have a professionally prepared product. See the Web site for instructions beofre making any queries or submissions."

TALCOTT NOTCH LITERARY

276 Forest Rd., Milford CT 06460. (203)877-1146. Fax: (203)876-9517. E-mail: gpanettieri@talcottnotch.net; editorial@talcottnotch.net. Web site: www.talcottnotch.net. **Contact:** Gina Panettieri. Estab. 2003. Represents 25 clients. 30% of clients are new/unpublished writers.

• Prior to becoming an agent, Ms. Panettieri was a freelance writer and editor.

Represents Nonfiction books, novels, juvenile books, scholarly books, textbooks. **Considers these nonfiction areas:** Agriculture/horticulture; animals; anthropology/archaeology; art/architecture/design; biography/autobiography; business/economics; child guidance/parenting; computers/electronic; cooking/foods/nutrition; current affairs; education; ethnic/cultural interests; gay/lesbian issues; government/politics/law; health/medicine; history; how-to; memoirs; military/war; money/finance; music/dance; nature/environment; popular culture; psychology; science/technology; self-help/personal improvement; sociology; sports; true crime/investigative; women's issues/studies; New Age/metaphysics, interior design/decorating, juvenile nonfiction. **Considers these fiction areas:** Action/adventure; detective/police/crime; juvenile; mystery/suspense; thriller; young adult.

O— Actively seeking prescriptive nonfiction and mysteries. Does not want poetry or picture books.

How to Contact Query via e-mail (preferred) or with SASE. Considers simultaneous queries. Responds in 1 week to queries; 2 weeks to mss. Returns materials only with SASE. Obtains most new clients through "our listings with publishing-related Web sites or from writers seeing our sales listed in Publishers Marketplace."

Recent Sales Sold 24 titles in the last year. *Your Plus-Size Pregnancy*, by Dr. Bruce Rodgers and Brette Sember (Barricade Books); *The Healing Parent*, by Dr. Karyn Purvis, Dr. David Cross, and Wendy Sunshine (McGraw-Hill); *Multiple Job Offers in Ten Days*, by Jonathan Price (Career Books). Other clients include Mark Ellis (writing as James Axler), Wayne Wilson, Ron Franscell, Dr. Dawn-Michelle Baude, Gloria Petersen, Ira Berkowitz.

Terms Agent receives 15% commission on domestic sales; 20% commission on foreign sales. Offers written contract, binding for 1 year.

Tips "Present your book or project effectively in your query. Don't include links to a Web page rather than a traditional query, and take the time to prepare a thorough but brief synopsis of the material. Make the effort to prepare a thoughtful analysis of comparison titles. How is your work different, yet would appeal to those same readers?"

PATRICIA TEAL LITERARY AGENCY

2036 Vista Del Rosa, Fullerton CA 92831-1336. Phone/Fax: (714)738-8333. **Contact:** Patricia Teal. Estab. 1978. Member of AAR. Represents 20 clients. Currently handles: 10% nonfiction books; 90% fiction.

Represents Nonfiction books, novels. **Considers these nonfiction areas:** Animals; biography/autobiography; child guidance/parenting; health/medicine; how-to; psychology; self-help/personal improvement; true crime/investigative; women's issues/studies. **Considers these fiction areas:** Glitz; mainstream/contemporary; mystery/suspense; romance (contemporary, historical).

O— This agency specializes in women's fiction, commercial how-to, and self-help nonfiction. Does not want to receive poetry, short stories, articles, science fiction, fantasy, or regency romance.

How to Contact Published authors only may query with SASE. No e-mail or fax queries. Considers simultaneous queries. Responds in 10 days to queries; 6 weeks to mss. Returns materials only with SASE. Obtains most new clients through conferences, recommendations from authors and editors.

Recent Sales Sold 20 titles in the last year. *Texas Rose*, by Marie Ferrarella (Silhouette); *Watch Your Language*, by Sterling Johnson (St. Martin's Press); *The Black Sheep's Baby*, by Kathleen Creighton (Silhouette); *Man With a Message*, by Muriel Jensen (Harlequin).

Terms Agent receives 10-15% commission on domestic sales; 20% commission on foreign sales. Offers written contract, binding for 1 year. Charges clients for postage.

Writers' Conferences RWA Conferences; Asilomar; BookExpo America; Bouchercon; Maui Writers Conference.

Tips "Include SASE with all correspondence. I am taking on published authors only."

TESSLER LITERARY AGENCY, LLC

27 W. 20th St., Suite 1003, New York NY 10011. (212)242-0466. Fax: (212)242-2366. Web site: www.tessleragency.com. **Contact:** Michelle Tessler. Member of AAR.

- Prior to forming her own agency, Ms. Tessler worked at Carlisle & Co. (now a part of Inkwell Management). She has also worked at the William Morris Agency and the Elaine Markson Literary Agency.
- ○🕳 The Tessler Agency is a full-service boutique agency that represents writers of high-quality nonfiction and literary and commercial fiction.

How to Contact Submit query through Web site only.

🔲 3 SEAS LITERARY AGENCY

P.O. Box 7038, Madison WI 53708. (608)221-4306. E-mail: threeseaslit@aol.com. Web site: www.threeseaslit.com. **Contact:** Michelle Grajkowski. Estab. 2000. Member of RWA, Chicago Women in Publishing. Represents 40 clients. 15% of clients are new/unpublished writers. Currently handles: 5% nonfiction books; 80% novels; 15% juvenile books.

- Prior to becoming an agent, Ms. Grajkowski worked in both sales and purchasing for a medical facility. She has a degree in journalism from the University of Wisconsin-Madison.

Represents Nonfiction books, novels, juvenile books, scholarly books.

- ○🕳 3 Seas focuses on romance (including category, historical, regency, western, romantic suspense, paranormal), women's fiction, mysteries, nonfiction, young adult, and children's stories. Does not want to receive poetry, screenplays, or short stories.

How to Contact For fiction, query with first 3 chapters, synopsis, bio, SASE. For nonfiction, query with complete proposal, first 3 chapters, word count, bio, SASE. Considers simultaneous queries. Responds in 1 month to queries. Responds in 3 months to partials. Returns materials only with SASE. Obtains most new clients through recommendations from others, conferences.

Recent Sales Sold 75 titles in the last year. *Fire Me Up, Sex, Lies & Vampires* and *Hard Day's Knight*, by Katie MacAlister; *Calendar Girl*, by Naomi Neale; *To Die For*, by Stephanie Rowe; *The Phantom in the Bathtub*, by Eugenia Riley; *The Unknown Daughter*, by Anna DeStefano. Other clients include Winnie Griggs, Diane Amos, Pat Pritchard, Barbara Jean Hicks, Carrie Weaver, Robin Popp, Kerrelyn Sparks, Sandra Madden.

Terms Agent receives 15% commission on domestic sales; 20% commission on foreign sales. Offers written contract, binding for 1 month.

Writers' Conferences RWA National Conference.

🔲 TRIADA U.S. LITERARY AGENCY, INC.

P.O. Box 561, Sewickley PA 15143. (412)401-3376. E-mail: uwe@triadaus.com. Web site: www.triadaus.com. **Contact:** Dr. Uwe Stender. Estab. 2004. Represents 44 clients. 62% of clients are new/unpublished writers. Currently handles: 35% nonfiction books; 57% novels; 6% juvenile books; 2% scholarly books.

Member Agents Paul Hudson (science fiction, fantasy).

Represents Nonfiction books, novels, short story collections, juvenile books, scholarly books. **Considers these nonfiction areas:** Biography/autobiography; business/economics; child guidance/parenting; education; how-to; humor/satire; memoirs; popular culture; self-help/personal improvement; sports. **Considers these fiction areas:** Action/adventure; detective/police/crime; ethnic; fantasy; historical; horror; juvenile; literary; mainstream/contemporary; mystery/suspense; romance; science fiction; sports; thriller; young adult.

- ○🕳 "We are now focusing on self-help and how-to. Additionally, we specialize in literary novels and suspense. Education, business, popular culture, and narrative nonfiction are other strong suits. Our response time is fairly unique. We recognize that neither we nor the authors have time to waste, so we guarantee a 5-day response time. We usually respond within 24 hours." Actively looking for nonfiction, especially self-help, how-to, and prescriptive nonfiction. De-emphasizing fiction, although great writing will always be considered.

How to Contact E-mail queries preferred; otherwise query with SASE. Considers simultaneous queries. Responds in 1-5 weeks to queries; 2-4 weeks to mss. Returns materials only with SASE. Obtains most new clients through recommendations from others, conferences.

Recent Sales *Out of the Pocket*, by Tony Moss (University of Nebraska Press); *Lost World*, by Lynnette Porter and David Lavery (Sourcebooks).

Terms Agent receives 15% commission on domestic sales; 20% commission on foreign sales. Offers written contract; 30-day notice must be given to terminate contract.

Tips "I comment on all requested manuscripts which I reject."

🔲 TRIDENT MEDIA GROUP

41 Madison Ave., 36th Floor, New York NY 10010. E-mail: levine.assistant@tridentmediagroup.com. Web site: www.tridentmediagroup.com. **Contact:** Ellen Levine. Member of AAR.

Member Agents Jenny Bent; Scott Miller; Paul Fedarko; Alex Glass; Melissa Flashman; Eileen Cope.

- ○🕳 Actively seeking new or established authors in a variety of fiction and nonfiction genres.

How to Contact Query with SASE or via e-mail. Check Web site for more details.

Literary Agents

ⓝ ❹ BETH VESEL LITERARY AGENCY

80 Fifth Ave., Suite 1101, New York NY 10011. (212)924-4252. Fax: (212)675-1381. E-mail: bvesel@bvlit.com. **Contact:** Makila Sands, assistant. Estab. 2003. Represents 65 clients. 10% of clients are new/unpublished writers. Currently handles: 75% nonfiction books; 10% novels; 5% story collections; 10% scholarly books.

• Prior to becoming an agent, Ms. Vesel was a poet and a journalist.

Represents Nonfiction books, novels. **Considers these nonfiction areas:** Biography/autobiography; business/ economics; ethnic/cultural interests; health/medicine; how-to; memoirs; photography; psychology; self-help/ personal improvement; true crime/investigative; women's issues/studies; Cultural criticism. **Considers these fiction areas:** Detective/police/crime; literary.

  ○➤ "My specialties include serious nonfiction, psychology, cultural criticism, memoir, and women's issues." Actively seeking cultural criticism, literary psychological thrillers, and sophisticated memoirs. No uninspired psychology or run-of-the-mill first novels.

How to Contact Query with SASE. Considers simultaneous queries. Responds in 2 weeks to queries; 1 month to mss. Returns materials only with SASE. Obtains most new clients through referrals, reading good magazines, contacting professionals with ideas.

Recent Sales Sold 10 titles in the last year. *The Female Complaint*, by Laura Kipnis (Pantheon); *Uses of Literature*, by Marge Garber (Pantheon); *Inside the Mind of Scott Peterson*, by Keith Ablow (St. Martin's Press); *The Other Mother*, by Gina Hyans and Susan Davis (The Hudson Press). Other clients include Martha Beck, Linda Carroll, Tracy Thompson, Vicki Robin, Paul Raeburn, John Head, Joe Graves.

Terms Agent receives 15% commission on domestic sales; 20% commission on foreign sales. Offers written contract.

Writers' Conferences Squaw Valley Writers Workshop, Iowa Summer Writing Festival.

Tips "Try to find out if you fit on a particular agent's list by looking at his/her books and comparing yours. You can almost always find who represents a book by looking at the acknowledgements."

ⓝ ❹ VRATTOS LITERARY AGENCY

708 Gravenstein Hwy., Suite 185, Sebastopol CA 95472. Phone/Fax: (707)570-2720. E-mail: vrattoslitagency@a ol.com. Web site: www.vrattosliteraryagency.com. **Contact:** John Vrattos, Francesca Vrattos. Estab. 2003. Represents 16 clients. 80% of clients are new/unpublished writers. Currently handles: 60% nonfiction books; 40% novels.

• Prior to becoming an agent, Ms. Vrattos worked at Penguin Putnam and co-founded Writer's Showplace, Inc.

Represents Nonfiction books, novels. **Considers these nonfiction areas:** Agriculture/horticulture; animals; art/architecture/design; biography/autobiography; business/economics; child guidance/parenting; cooking/ foods/nutrition; crafts/hobbies; current affairs; education; ethnic/cultural interests; gay/lesbian issues; government/politics/law; health/medicine; history; how-to; humor/satire; interior design/decorating; language/literature/criticism; memoirs; military/war; money/finance; nature/environment; New Age/metaphysics; photography; popular culture; psychology; religious/inspirational; self-help/personal improvement; sociology; sports; true crime/investigative; women's issues/studies. **Considers these fiction areas:** Comic books/cartoon; confession; detective/police/crime; ethnic; family saga; feminist; gay/lesbian; glitz; historical; humor/satire; literary; mainstream/contemporary; mystery/suspense; psychic/supernatural; regional; religious/inspirational; romance; sports; thriller; westerns/frontier.

  ○➤ Actively seeking sports, humor, mystery, thriller, and mainstream. No horror, young adult, children's, or erotica.

How to Contact Query with SASE. Accepts e-mail queries. Considers simultaneous queries. Responds in 2 weeks to queries; 6 weeks to mss. Obtains most new clients through recommendations from others, conferences.

Recent Sales Sold 3 titles in the last year. *You Don't Say!*, by Hartley Miller (Andrews McMeel); *Spoiled Sports*, by Garret Kolb (Andrews McMeel); *Ultimate Betrayal*, by Danine Manette (Square One). Other clients include Sherry Rowlands, Bob Mann, Bob Stewart, Dawn Patitucci, Marcel Pincince, Brad Stanhope, Liz Holzemer, Nick Anderson, Sharon Anderson, Mitch Haudelsman, Guy Mirabello.

Terms Agent receives 15% commission on domestic sales; 20% commission on foreign sales. Offers written contract; 30-day notice must be given to terminate contract. Charges for postage and phone calls.

Writers' Conferences San Francisco Writers Conference; Willamette Writers Conference.

Tips "Be professional and patient."

ⓝ 🌐 ❹ WADE & DOHERTY LITERARY AGENCY

33 Cormorant Lodge, Thomas Moore St., London E1W 1AU England. (44)(20)7488-4171. Fax: (44)(20)7488-4172. E-mail: rw@rwla.com. Web site: www.rwla.com. **Contact:** Robin Wade. Estab. 2001.

• Prior to opening his agency, Mr. Wade was an author; Ms. Doherty worked as a production assistant, editor, and editorial director.

Member Agents Mark Barty-King, chairman; Robin Wade, agent; Broo Doherty, agent.

Represents Nonfiction books, novels, juvenile books.

    ⊶ "We are young and dynamic and actively seek new writers across the literary spectrum." No poetry, plays, or short stories.

How to Contact Submit synopsis (2-6 pages), bio, first 10,000 words via e-mail (Word or PDF documents only). If sending by post, include SASE or IRC. Responds in 1 week to queries; 1 month to mss.

Recent Sales *A Spin Doctor's Diary*, by Lance Price; *The Icarus Girl*, by Helen Oyeyemi; *Benedict XVI*, by Rupert Shortt; *The Truth Will Out: Unmasking the Real Shakespeare*, by Brenda James.

Terms Agent receives 10% commission on domestic sales; 20% commission on foreign sales. Offers written contract; 1-month notice must be given to terminate contract.

Tips "We seek manuscripts that are well written, with strong characters and an original narrative voice. Our absolute priority is giving the best possible service to the authors we choose to represent, as well as maintaining routine friendly contact with them as we help develop their careers."

◙ WALES LITERARY AGENCY, INC.

P.O. Box 9428, Seattle WA 98109-0428. (206)284-7114. E-mail: waleslit@waleslit.com. Web site: www.waleslit.com. **Contact:** Elizabeth Wales, Josie di Bernardo. Estab. 1988. Member of AAR, Book Publishers' Northwest, Pacific Northwest Booksellers Association, PEN. Represents 65 clients. 10% of clients are new/unpublished writers. Currently handles: 60% nonfiction books; 40% novels.

    • Prior to becoming an agent, Ms. Wales worked at Oxford University Press and Viking Penguin.

Member Agents Elizabeth Wales; Adrienne Reed.

    ⊶ This agency specializes in narrative nonfiction and quality mainstream and literary fiction. Does not handle screenplays, children's literature, genre fiction, or most category nonfiction.

How to Contact Query with cover letter, writing sample (about 30 pages), SASE. No phone or fax queries. Prefers regular mail queries, but accepts 1-page e-mail queries with no attachments. Considers simultaneous queries. Responds in 3 weeks to queries; 6 weeks to mss. Returns materials only with SASE.

Recent Sales *Breaking Ranks*, by Norman H. Stamper (Nation Books); *Birds of Central Park*, photographs by Cal Vornberger (Abrams); *Against Gravity*, by Farnoosh Moshiri (Penguin).

Terms Agent receives 15% commission on domestic sales; 20% commission on foreign sales.

Writers' Conferences Pacific Northwest Writers Conference; Willamette Writers Conference.

Tips "We are especially interested in work that espouses a progressive cultural or political view, projects a new voice, or simply shares an important, compelling story. We also encourage writers living in the Pacific Northwest, West Coast, Alaska, and Pacific Rim countries, and writers from historically underrepresented groups, such as gay and lesbian writers and writers of color, to submit work (but does not discourage writers outside these areas). Most importantly, whether in fiction or nonfiction, the agency is looking for talented storytellers."

◙ JOHN A. WARE LITERARY AGENCY

392 Central Park W., New York NY 10025-5801. (212)866-4733. Fax: (212)866-4734. **Contact:** John Ware. Estab. 1978. Represents 60 clients. 40% of clients are new/unpublished writers. Currently handles: 75% nonfiction books; 25% novels.

    • Prior to opening his agency, Mr. Ware served as a literary agent with James Brown Associates/Curtis Brown, Ltd., and as an editor for Doubleday & Co.

Represents Nonfiction books, novels. **Considers these nonfiction areas:** Anthropology/archaeology; biography/autobiography; current affairs; health/medicine (academic credentials required); history (oral history, Americana, folklore); language/literature/criticism; music/dance; nature/environment; popular culture; psychology (academic credentials required); science/technology; sports; true crime/investigative; women's issues/studies; Social commentary; investigative journalism; bird's eye views of phenomena. **Considers these fiction areas:** Detective/police/crime; mystery/suspense; thriller; Accessible literary noncategory fiction.

    ⊶ Does not want personal memoirs.

How to Contact Query with SASE. No e-mail or fax queries. Considers simultaneous queries. Responds in 2 weeks to queries.

Recent Sales *The Butterfly Hunter*, by Chris Ballard (Broadway); *Velva Jean Learns to Drive*, by Jennifer Niven (Plume); *Sunday*, by Craig Harline (Doubleday); *Man O'War*, by Dorothy Ours (St. Martin's Press); *The Family Business: A History of Tobacco*, by Jeffrey Rothfeder (HarperCollins); *Ledyard*, by William Gifford (Harcourt).

Terms Agent receives 15% commission on domestic sales; 20% commission on foreign sales; 15% commission on dramatic rights sales. Charges clients for messenger service and photocopying.

Tips "Writers must have appropriate credentials for authorship of proposal (nonfiction) or manuscript (fiction); no publishing track record required. Open to good writing and interesting ideas by new or veteran writers."

◙ WATKINS LOOMIS AGENCY, INC.

133 E. 35th St., Suite 1, New York NY 10016. (212)532-0080. Fax: (212)889-0506. **Contact:** Katherine Fausset. Estab. 1908. Represents 150 clients.

Member Agents Gloria Loomis, president; Katherine Fausset, agent.

Represents Nonfiction books, novels, short story collections. **Considers these nonfiction areas:** Art/architecture/design; biography/autobiography; current affairs; ethnic/cultural interests; history; nature/environment; popular culture; science/technology; true crime/investigative; Journalism. **Considers these fiction areas:** Literary.

O⊸ This agency specializes in literary fiction and nonfiction.

How to Contact *No unsolicited mss.*

Recent Sales This agency prefers not to share information on specific sales. Clients include Walter Mosley and Cornel West.

Terms Agent receives 15% commission on domestic sales; 20% commission on foreign sales.

⚫ WAXMAN LITERARY AGENCY, INC.

80 Fifth Ave., Suite 1101, New York NY 10011. Web site: www.waxmanagency.com. Estab. 1997. Represents 60 clients. 50% of clients are new/unpublished writers. Currently handles: 80% nonfiction books; 20% novels.

• Prior to opening his agency, Mr. Waxman was an editor at HarperCollins for 5 years.

Member Agents Scott Waxman (all categories of nonfiction, commercial fiction).

Represents Nonfiction books, novels. **Considers these nonfiction areas:** Narrative nonfiction. **Considers these fiction areas:** Literary.

O⊸ "Looking for serious journalists and novelists with published works."

How to Contact Query through Web site. All unsolicited mss returned unopened. Considers simultaneous queries. Responds in 2 weeks to queries; 6 weeks to mss. Returns materials only with SASE. Obtains most new clients through recommendations from others, solicitations, conferences.

Terms Agent receives 15% commission on domestic sales; 25% commission on foreign sales. Offers written contract; 2-month notice must be given to terminate contract.

⚫ CHERRY WEINER LITERARY AGENCY

28 Kipling Way, Manalapan NJ 07726-3711. (732)446-2096. Fax: (732)792-0506. E-mail: cherry8486@aol.com. **Contact:** Cherry Weiner. Estab. 1977. Represents 40 clients. 10% of clients are new/unpublished writers. Currently handles: 10-20% nonfiction books; 80-90% novels.

Represents Nonfiction books, novels. **Considers these nonfiction areas:** Self-help/personal improvement. **Considers these fiction areas:** Action/adventure; contemporary issues; detective/police/crime; family saga; fantasy; historical; mainstream/contemporary; mystery/suspense; psychic/supernatural; romance; science fiction; thriller; westerns/frontier.

O⊸ This agency is currently not looking for new clients except by referral or by personal contact at writers' conferences. Specializes in fantasy, science fiction, westerns, mysteries (both contemporary and historical), historical novels, Native American works, mainstream, and all genre romances.

How to Contact Query with SASE. Prefers to read materials exclusively. No fax queries. Responds in 1 week to queries; 2 months to mss. Returns materials only with SASE.

Recent Sales Sold 75 titles in the last year.

Terms Agent receives 15% commission on domestic sales; 15% commission on foreign sales. Offers written contract. Charges clients for extra copies of mss, first-class postage for author's copies of books, express mail for important documents/mss.

Writers' Conferences Western writers conventions; science fiction conventions; fantasy conventions; romance conventions.

Tips "Meet agents and publishers at conferences. Establish a relationship, then get in touch with them and remind them of the meeting and conference."

⚫ THE WEINGEL-FIDEL AGENCY

310 E. 46th St., 21E, New York NY 10017. (212)599-2959. **Contact:** Loretta Weingel-Fidel. Estab. 1989. Currently handles: 75% nonfiction books; 25% novels.

• Prior to opening her agency, Ms. Weingel-Fidel was a psychoeducational diagnostician.

Represents Nonfiction books, novels. **Considers these nonfiction areas:** Art/architecture/design; biography/autobiography; memoirs; music/dance; psychology; science/technology; sociology; women's issues/studies; Investigative journalism. **Considers these fiction areas:** Literary; mainstream/contemporary.

O⊸ This agency specializes in commercial and literary fiction and nonfiction. Actively seeking investigative journalism. Does not want to receive genre fiction, self-help, science fiction, or fantasy.

How to Contact Accepts writers by referral only. *No unsolicited mss.*

Terms Agent receives 15% commission on domestic sales; 20% commission on foreign sales. Offers written contract, binding for 1 year with automatic renewal. Bills sent back to clients are all reasonable expenses, such as UPS, express mail, photocopying, etc.

Tips "A very small, selective list enables me to work very closely with my clients to develop and nurture talent. I only take on projects and writers about which I am extremely enthusiastic."

☑ WINSUN LITERARY AGENCY

3706 NE Shady Lane Dr., Gladstone MO 64119. Phone/Fax: (816)459-8016. E-mail: mlittleton@earthlink.net. Estab. 2004. Represents 20 clients. 50% of clients are new/unpublished writers. Currently handles: 75% nonfiction books; 20% novels; 5% juvenile books.

• Prior to becoming an agent, Mr. Littleton was a writer and a speaker.

Represents Nonfiction books, novels, juvenile books. **Considers these nonfiction areas:** Biography/autobiography; child guidance/parenting; current affairs; how-to; humor/satire; memoirs; religious/inspirational; self-help/personal improvement. **Considers these fiction areas:** Action/adventure; detective/police/crime; family saga; humor/satire; juvenile; literary; mainstream/contemporary; mystery/suspense; picture books; psychic/supernatural; religious/inspirational; romance; thriller.

O➡ "We mainly serve Christian clients in the CBA."

How to Contact Query with SASE. Considers simultaneous queries. Responds in 6 weeks to queries; 3 months to mss. Returns materials only with SASE. Obtains most new clients through recommendations from others, conferences.

Recent Sales Sold 8 titles in the last year. *Footsteps* and *When the Lion Roars*, by Diann Mills; *Rockets, Rebels, and Rescue*, by Mark and Jeanette Littleton.

Terms Agent receives 15% commission on domestic sales; 20% commission on foreign sales. Offers written contract, binding for 1 year; 30-day notice must be given to terminate contract.

◎ WORDSERVE LITERARY GROUP

10152 S. Knoll Circle, Highlands Ranch CO 80130. (303)471-6675. Fax: (303)471-1297. Web site: www.wordserveliterary.com. **Contact:** Greg Johnson. Estab. 2003. Represents 30 clients. 25% of clients are new/unpublished writers. Currently handles: 30% nonfiction books; 40% novels; 10% story collections; 5% novellas; 10% juvenile books; 5% multimedia.

• Prior to becoming an agent in 1994, Mr. Johnson was a magazine editor and freelance writer of more than 20 books and 200 articles.

Represents Primarily religious books in these categories: nonfiction, fiction, short story collections, novellas. **Considers these nonfiction areas:** Biography/autobiography; business/economics; child guidance/parenting; current affairs; how-to; humor/satire; memoirs; religious/inspirational; self-help/personal improvement; sports. **Considers these fiction areas:** Action/adventure; detective/police/crime; family saga; historical; humor/satire; religious/inspirational; romance; sports; thriller.

How to Contact Query with SASE, proposal package, outline, 2-3 sample chapters. Considers simultaneous queries. Responds in 1 week to queries; 2 months to mss. Returns materials only with SASE. Obtains most new clients through recommendations from others, solicitations.

Recent Sales Sold 1,300 titles in the last 10 years. Redemption series, by Karen Kingsbury (Tyndale); *Loving God Up Close*, by Calvin Miller (Warner Faith); *Christmas in My Heart*, by Joe Wheeler (Tyndale). Other clients include Gilbert Morris, Calvin Miller, Robert Wise, Jim Burns, Ed Young Sr., Wayne Cordeiro, Denise George, Susie Shellenberger, Tim Smith, Joe Wheeler, Athol Dickson, Bob DeMoss, Patty Kirk, John Shore.

Terms Agent receives 15% commission on domestic sales; 10-15% commission on foreign sales. Offers written contract; up to 60-day notice must be given to terminate contract.

Tips "We are looking for good proposals, great writing, and authors willing to market their books, as appropriate."

☑ WRITERS HOUSE

21 W. 26th St., New York NY 10010. (212)685-2400. Fax: (212)685-1781. Web site: www.writershouse.com. Estab. 1974. Member of AAR. Represents 440 clients. 50% of clients are new/unpublished writers. Currently handles: 25% nonfiction books; 40% novels; 35% juvenile books.

Member Agents Albert Zuckerman (major novels, thrillers, women's fiction, important nonfiction); Amy Berkower (major juvenile authors, women's fiction, art/decorating, psychology); Merrilee Heifetz (quality children's fiction, science fiction/fantasy, popular culture, literary fiction); Susan Cohen (juvenile/young adult fiction and nonfiction, Judaism, women's issues); Susan Ginsburg (serious and popular fiction, true crime, narrative nonfiction, personality books, cookbooks); Michele Rubin (serious nonfiction); Robin Rue (commercial fiction and nonfiction, young adult fiction); Jodi Reamer (juvenile/young adult fiction and nonfiction, adult commercial fiction, popular culture); Simon Lipskar (literary and commercial fiction, narrative nonfiction); Steven Malk (juvenile/young adult fiction and nonfiction); Dan Lazar (pop culture, hip/edgy fiction and nonfiction).

Represents Nonfiction books, novels, juvenile books. **Considers these nonfiction areas:** Animals; art/architecture/design; biography/autobiography; business/economics; child guidance/parenting; cooking/foods/nutrition; health/medicine; history; humor/satire; interior design/decorating; juvenile nonfiction; military/war; money/finance; music/dance; nature/environment; psychology; science/technology; self-help/personal improvement; theater/film; true crime/investigative; women's issues/studies. **Considers these fiction areas:** Action/adventure; contemporary issues; detective/police/crime; erotica; ethnic; family saga; fantasy; feminist; gay/lesbian; gothic; hi-lo; historical; horror; humor/satire; juvenile; literary; mainstream/contemporary; military/war; multicultural; mystery/suspense; New Age; occult; picture books; psychic/supernatural; regional; romance; science fiction; short story collections; spiritual; sports; thriller; translation; westerns/frontier; young adult; women's; Cartoon.

> O— This agency specializes in all types of popular fiction and nonfiction. Does not want to receive scholarly, professional, poetry, plays, or screenplays.

How to Contact Query with SASE. No e-mail or fax queries. Responds in 1 month to queries. Obtains most new clients through recommendations from authors and editors.

Recent Sales Sold 200-300 titles in the last year. *Moneyball*, by Michael Lewis (Norton); *Cut and Run*, by Ridley Pearson (Hyperion); *Report from Ground Zero*, by Dennis Smith (Viking); *Northern Lights*, by Nora Roberts (Penguin/Putnam); Captain Underpants series, by Dav Pilkey (Scholastic); Junie B. Jones series, by Barbara Park (Random House). Other clients include Francine Pascal, Ken Follett, Stephen Hawking, Linda Howard, F. Paul Wilson, Neil Gaiman, Laurel Hamilton, V.C. Andrews, Lisa Jackson, Michael Gruber, Chris Paolini, Barbara Delinsky, Ann Martin, Bradley Trevor Greive, Erica Jong, Kyle Mills.

Terms Agent receives 15% commission on domestic sales; 20% commission on foreign sales. Offers written contract, binding for 1 year. Agency charges fees for copying mss/proposals and overseas airmail of books.

Tips "Do not send manuscripts. Write a compelling letter. If you do, we'll ask to see your work."

☑ ZACHARY SHUSTER HARMSWORTH

1776 Broadway, Suite 1405, New York NY 10019. (212)765-6900. Fax: (212)765-6490. E-mail: kfleury@zshliterary.com. Web site: www.zshliterary.com. Alternate address: 535 Boylston St., 11th Floor. (617)262-2400. Fax: (617)262-2468. **Contact:** Kathleen Fleury. Estab. 1996. Represents 125 clients. 20% of clients are new/unpublished writers. Currently handles: 45% nonfiction books; 45% novels; 5% story collections; 5% scholarly books.

> ● "Our principals include 2 former publishing and entertainment lawyers, a journalist, and an editor/agent." Lane Zachary was an editor at Random House before becoming an agent.

Member Agents Esmond Harmsworth (commercial mysteries, literary fiction, history, science, adventure, business); Todd Shuster (narrative and prescriptive nonfiction, biography, memoirs); Lane Zachary (biography, memoirs, literary fiction); Jennifer Gates (literary fiction, nonfiction).

Represents Nonfiction books, novels. **Considers these nonfiction areas:** Animals; biography/autobiography; business/economics; current affairs; gay/lesbian issues; government/politics/law; health/medicine; history; how-to; language/literature/criticism; memoirs; money/finance; music/dance; psychology; science/technology; self-help/personal improvement; sports; true crime/investigative; women's issues/studies. **Considers these fiction areas:** Detective/police/crime; ethnic; feminist; gay/lesbian; historical; literary; mainstream/contemporary; mystery/suspense; thriller.

> O— This agency specializes in journalist-driven narrative nonfiction and literary and commercial fiction. Interested in narrative nonfiction, mystery, commercial and literary fiction, memoirs, history, and biographies. Does not want to receive poetry.

How to Contact *No unsolicited submissions.* No e-mail or fax queries. Obtains most new clients through recommendations from others, solicitations, conferences.

Recent Sales *Christmas Hope*, by Donna Van Liere; *Female Chauvinist Pigs*, by Ariel Levy; *War Trash*, by Ha Jin; *Women Who Think Too Much*, by Susan Nolen-Hoeksema, PhD; *The Red Carpet*, by Lavanya Sankaran; *Grapevine*, by David Balter and John Butman.

Terms Agent receives 15% commission on domestic sales; 20% commission on foreign sales. Offers written contract, binding for 1 work only; 30-day notice must be given to terminate contract. Charges clients for postage, copying, courier, telephone. "We only charge expenses if the manuscript is sold."

Tips "We work closely with all our clients on all editorial and promotional aspects of their works."

☑ SUSAN ZECKENDORF ASSOC., INC.

171 W. 57th St., New York NY 10019. (212)245-2928. **Contact:** Susan Zeckendorf. Estab. 1979. Member of AAR. Represents 15 clients. 25% of clients are new/unpublished writers. Currently handles: 50% nonfiction books; 50% novels.

> ● Prior to opening her agency, Ms. Zeckendorf was a counseling psychologist.

Represents Nonfiction books, novels. **Considers these nonfiction areas:** Biography/autobiography; child guidance/parenting; health/medicine; history; music/dance; psychology; science/technology; sociology; women's issues/studies. **Considers these fiction areas:** Detective/police/crime; ethnic; historical; literary; mainstream/contemporary; mystery/suspense; thriller.

O⟶ Actively seeking mysteries, literary fiction, mainstream fiction, thrillers, social history, parenting, classical music, and biography. Does not want to receive science fiction, romance, or children's books.

How to Contact Query with SASE. No e-mail or fax queries. Considers simultaneous queries. Responds in 10 days to queries; 3 weeks to mss. Returns materials only with SASE.

Recent Sales *How to Write a Damn Good Mystery*, by James N. Frey (St. Martin's Press); *The Handscrabble Chronicles* (Berkley); *Something to Live For* (University of Michigan Press).

Terms Agent receives 15% commission on domestic sales; 20% commission on foreign sales. Charges for photocopying and messenger services.

Writers' Conferences Frontiers in Writing Conference; Oklahoma Festival of Books.

Tips "We are a small agency giving lots of individual attention. We respond quickly to submissions."

Literary Magazines

This section contains markets for your literary short fiction. Although definitions of what constitutes "literary" writing vary, editors of literary journals agree they want to publish the best fiction they can acquire. Qualities they look for in fiction include fully developed characters, strong and unique narrative voice, flawless mechanics, and careful attention to detail in content and manuscript preparation. Most of the authors writing such fiction are well read and well educated, and many are students and graduates of university creative writing programs.

Please also review our Online Markets section, page 342, for electronic literary magazines. At a time when paper and publishing costs rise while funding to small and university presses continues to be cut or eliminated, electronic literary magazines are helping generate a publishing renaissance for experimental as well as more traditional literary fiction. These electronic outlets for literary fiction also benefit writers by eliminating copying and postage costs and providing the opportunity for much quicker responses to submissions. Also notice that some magazines with Web sites give specific information about what they offer online, including updated writer's guidelines and sample fiction from their publications.

STEPPING STONES TO RECOGNITION

Some well-established literary journals pay several hundred or even several thousand dollars for a short story. Most, though, can only pay with contributor's copies or a subscription to their publication. However, being published in literary journals offers the important benefits of experience, exposure and prestige. Agents and major book publishers regularly read literary magazines in search of new writers. Work from these journals is also selected for inclusion in annual prize anthologies. (See next page for a list of anthologies.)

You'll find most of the well-known prestigious literary journals listed here. Many, including *The Southern Review* and *Ploughshares*, are associated with universities, while others like *The Paris Review* are independently published.

SELECTING THE RIGHT LITERARY JOURNAL

Once you have browsed through this section and have a list of journals you might like to submit to, read those listings again carefully. Remember this is information editors present to help you in submitting work that fits their needs. You've Got a Story, starting on page 2, will guide you through the process of finding markets for your fiction.

Note that you will find some magazines that do not read submissions all year long. Whether limited reading periods are tied to a university schedule or meant to accommodate the capabilities of a very small staff, those periods are noted within listings (when the editors notify us). The staffs of university journals are usually made up of student editors and a managing editor who is also a faculty member. These staffs often change every year. Whenever possible, we indicate this in listings and give the name of the current editor and the length of that editor's term. Also be aware that the schedule of a university journal usually coincides with that university's academic year, meaning that the editors of most university publications are difficult or impossible to reach during the summer.

FURTHERING YOUR SEARCH

It cannot be stressed enough that reading the listings for literary journals is only the first part of developing your marketing plan. The second part, equally important, is to obtain fiction guidelines and to read with great care the actual journal you'd like to submit to. Reading copies of these journals helps you determine the fine points of each magazine's publishing style and sensibility. There is no substitute for this type of hands-on research.

Unlike commercial periodicals available at most newsstands and bookstores, it requires a little more effort to obtain some of the magazines listed here. The super chain bookstores are doing a better job these days of stocking literaries, and you can find some in independent and college bookstores, especially those published in your area. The Internet is an invaluable resource for submission guidelines, as more and more journals establish an online presence. You may, however, need to send for a sample copy. We include sample copy prices in the listings whenever possible. In addition to reading your sample copies, pay close attention to the **Advice** section of each listing. There you'll often find a very specific description of the style of fiction editors at that publication prefer.

Another way to find out more about literary magazines is to check out the various prize anthologies and take note of journals whose fiction is being selected for publication in them. Studying prize anthologies not only lets you know which magazines are publishing award-winning work but it also provides a valuable overview of what is considered to be the best fiction published today. Those anthologies include:

- *Best American Short Stories*, published by Houghton Mifflin.
- *New Stories from The South: The Year's Best*, published by Algonquin Books of Chapel Hill.
- *Prize Stories: The O. Henry Awards*, published by Doubleday/Anchor.
- *Pushcart Prize: Best of the Small Presses*, published by Pushcart Press.

At the beginnings of listings, we include symbols to help you narrow your search. Keys to those symbols can be found on the inside covers of this book.

Literary Magazines

▲ ACM (ANOTHER CHICAGO MAGAZINE)

Left Field Press, 3709 N. Kenmore, Chicago IL 60613. E-mail: editors@anotherchicagomag.com. Web site: www.anotherchicagomag.com. **Contact:** Sharon Solwitz, fiction editor. Magazine: $5\frac{1}{2} \times 8\frac{1}{2}$; 200-220 pages; "art folio each issue." Biannual. Estab. 1977. Circ. 2,000.

Needs Ethnic/multicultural, experimental, feminist, gay, lesbian, literary, translations, contemporary, prose poem. No religious, strictly genre or editorial. Receives 300 unsolicited mss/month. Reads mss from February 1-August 31. Publishes ms 6-12 months after acceptance. **Publishes 10 new writers/year.** Recently published work by Stuart Dybek and Steve Almond.

How to Contact Responds in 3 months to queries; 6 months to mss. Accepts simultaneous, multiple submissions. Sample copy for $8 ppd. Writer's guidelines online.

Payment/Terms Pays small honorarium when possible, contributor's copies and 1-year subscription. Acquires first North American serial rights.

Advice "Support literary publishing by subscribing to at least one literary journal—if not ours, another. Get used to rejection slips, and don't get discouraged. Keep introductory letters short. Make sure manuscript has name and address on every page, and it is clean, neat and proofread. We are looking for stories with freshness and originality in subject angle and style, and work that encounters the world and is not stuck in its own navel."

▲ ADVOCATE, PKA'S PUBLICATION

PKA Publications, 1881 Little Westkill Rd. CO2, Prattsville NY 12468. (518)299-3103. Tabloid: $9\frac{3}{8} \times 12\frac{1}{4}$; 32 pages; newsprint paper; line drawings; color and b&w photographs. "Eclectic for a general audience." Bimonthly. Estab. 1987. Circ. 12,000.

Needs Adventure, children's/juvenile (5-9 years), ethnic/multicultural, experimental, fantasy, feminist, historical, humor/satire, literary, mainstream, mystery/suspense, regional, romance, science fiction, western, young adult/teen (10-18 years), contemporary, prose poem, senior citizen/retirement, sports. "Nothing religious, pornographic, violent, erotic, pro-drug or anti-enviroment. Currently looking for equine (horses) stories, poetry, art, photos and cartoons. The *Gaited Horse Newsletter* is currently published within the pages of PKA's *Advocate.*" Receives 60 unsolicited mss/month. Accepts 6-8 mss/issue; 34-48 mss/year. Publishes ms 4 months to 1 year after acceptance. Also publishes poetry. Sometimes comments on rejected mss.

How to Contact Send a complete ms with cover letter. Responds in 2 months to mss. No simultaneous submissions. "No work that has appeared on the Internet." Sample copy for $4 (US currency for inside US; $5.25 US currency for Canada). Writer's guidelines with purchase of sample copy.

Payment/Terms Pays contributor copies. Acquires first rights.

Advice "The highest criterion in selecting a work is its entertainment value. It must first be enjoyable reading. It must, of course, be orginal. To stand out, it must be thought provoking or strongly emotive, or very cleverly plotted. Will consider only previously unpublished works by writers who do not earn their living principally through writing. We are currently very backed up on short stories. We are mostly looking for art, photos and poetry."

$▲ AFRICAN AMERICAN REVIEW

Saint Louis University, Humanities 317, 3800 Lindell Boulevard, St. Louis MO 63108-3414. (314)977-3688. Fax: (314)977-1514. E-mail: keenanam@slu.edu. Web site: aar.slu.edu. **Contact:** Joycelyn Moody, editor; Aileen Keenan, managing editor. Magazine: 7×10; 176 pages; 60 lb., acid-free paper; 100 lb. skid stock cover; illustrations; photos. "Essays on African-American literature, theater, film, art and culture generally; interviews; poetry and fiction by African-American authors; book reviews." Quarterly. Estab. 1967. Circ. 2,067.

    ● *African American Review* is the official publication of the Division of Black American Literature and Culture of the Modern Language Association. The magazine received American Literary Magazine Awards in 1994 and 1995.

Needs Ethnic/multicultural, experimental, feminist, literary, mainstream. "No children's/juvenile/young adult/teen." Receives 50 unsolicited mss/month. Accepts 40 mss/year. Publishes ms 1-2 years after acceptance. Agented fiction 10%. Recently published work by Solon Timothy Woodward, Eugenia Collier, Jeffery Renard Allen, Patrick Lohier, Raki Jones, Olympia Vernon. Length: 2,500-5,000 words; average length: 3,000 words. Also publishes literary essays, literary criticism, poetry. Sometimes comments on rejected mss.

How to Contact Responds in 1 week to queries; 4 months to mss. Sample copy for $12. Writer's guidelines online. Reviews fiction.

Payment/Terms Pays $25-100, 1 contributor's copy and 5 offprints. Pays on publication for first North American serial rights. Sends galleys to author.

$ 🖰 🖿 AGNI

Boston University, 236 Bay State Rd., Boston MA 02215. (617)353-7135. Fax: (617)353-7134. E-mail: agni@bu.e du. Web site: www.agnimagazine.org. **Contact:** Sven Birkerts, editor. Magazine: $5^3/8 \times 8^1/2$; 240 pages; 55 lb. booktext paper; art portfolios. "Eclectic literary magazine publishing first-rate poems, essays, translations and stories." Biannual. Estab. 1972. Circ. 4,000.

- Founding editor Askold Melnyczuk won the 2001 Nora Magid Award for Magazine Editing. Work from *AGNI* has been included and cited regularly in the *Pushcart Prize* and *Best American* anthologies.

Needs Translations, stories, prose poems. "No science fiction or romance." Receives 500 unsolicited mss/ month. Accepts 3-5 mss/issue; 6-10 mss/year. Reading period September 1 through May 31 only. Publishes ms 6 months after acceptance. **Publishes 30 new writers/year.** Recently published work by Rikki Ducornet, Phong Nguyen, Jack Pulaski, David Foster Wallace, Lise Haines, Gania Barlow and Nicholas Montemarano.

How to Contact Responds in 2 weeks to queries; 4 months to mss. Accepts simultaneous submissions. Sample copy for $10 or online. Writer's guidelines for #10 SASE or online.

Payment/Terms Pays $10/page up to $150, 2 contributor's copies, 1-year subscription, and 4 gift copies. Pays on publication for first North American serial rights, rights to reprint in *AGNI* anthology (with author's consent). Sends galleys to author.

Advice "Read *AGNI* and other literary magazines carefully to understand the kinds of stories we do and do not publish. It's also important for artists to support the arts."

Ⓝ ◪ THE AGUILAR EXPRESSION

1329 Gilmore Ave., Donora PA 15033-2228. (724)379-8019. E-mail: xyz0@access995.com. Web site: www.word runner.com/xfaguilar. **Contact:** Xavier F. Aguilar, editor. Magazine: $8^1/2 \times 11$; 4-20 pages; 20 lb. bond paper; illustrations. "We are open to all writers of a general theme—something that may appeal to everyone." Publishes in October. Estab. 1986. Circ. 300.

Needs Adventure, ethnic/multicultural, experimental, horror, mainstream, mystery/suspense (romantic suspense), romance (contemporary). "No religious or erotic stories. Want more current social issues." Receives 15 unsolicited mss/month. Accepts 1-2 mss/year. Reading period: January, February, March. Publishes ms 1 month to 1 year after acceptance. **Publishes 2-4 new writers/year.** Recently published work by Ken Bennet. Length: 250-1,000 words; average length: 1,000 words. Also publishes poetry.

How to Contact Send a disposable copy of ms with SASE for reply. "We do not return any manuscripts and discard rejected works. If we decide to publish, we contact within 30 days." Responds in 1 month to mss. No simultaneous submissions. Sample copy for $8. Guidelines for first class stamp.

Payment/Terms Pays 2 contributor's copies for lead story; additional copies at a reduced rate of $3. Acquires one-time rights. Not copyrighted.

Advice "We would like to see more social issues worked into fiction."

$ ◪ ALASKA QUARTERLY REVIEW

ESB 208, University of Alaska-Anchorage, 3211 Providence Dr., Anchorage AK 99508. (907)786-6916. E-mail: ayaqr@uaa.alaska.edu. Web site: www.uaa.alaska.edu/aqr. **Contact:** Ronald Spatz, fiction editor. Magazine: 6×9; 232-300 pages; 60 lb. Glatfelter paper; 12 pt. C15 black ink or 4-color; varnish cover stock; photos on cover and photo essays. *AQR* "publishes fiction, poetry, literary nonfiction and short plays in traditional and experimental styles." Semiannual. Estab. 1982. Circ. 3,500.

- Two stories selected for inclusion in the 2004 *Prize Stories: The O'Henry Awards.*

Needs Experimental, literary, translations, contemporary, prose poem. "If the works in *Alaska Quarterly Review* have certain characteristics, they are these: freshness, honesty and a compelling subject. What makes a piece stand out from the multitude of other submissions? The voice of the piece must be strong—idiosyncratic enough to create a unique persona. We look for the demonstration of craft, making the situation palpable and putting it in a form where it becomes emotionally and intellectually complex. One could look through our pages over time and see that many of the pieces published in the *Alaska Quarterly Review* concern everyday life. We're not asking our writers to go outside themselves and their experiences to the absolute exotic to catch our interest. We look for the experiential and revelatory qualities of the work. We will, without hesitation, champion a piece that may be less polished or stylistically sophisticated, if it engages me, surprises me, and resonates for me. The joy in reading such a work is in discovering something true. Moreover, in keeping with our mission to publish new writers, we are looking for voices our readers do not know, voices that may not always be reflected in the dominant culture and that, in all instances, have something important to convey." Receives 200 unsolicited mss/month. Accepts 7-18 mss/issue; 15-30 mss/year. Does not read mss May 10-August 25. Publishes ms 6 months after acceptance. **Publishes 6 new writers/year.** Recently published work by Howard Norman, Douglas Light, Courtney Angela Brkic, Alison Baker, Lindsay Fitz-Gerald, John Fulton, Ann Stapleton, Edith Pearlman. Publishes short shorts.

How to Contact Responds in 4 months to queries; 4 months to mss. Simultaneous submissions "undesirable, but will accept if indicated." Sample copy for $6. Writer's guidelines online.

Payment/Terms Pays $50-200 subject to funding; pays in contributor's copies and subscriptions when funding is limited. Honorariums on publication when funding permits. Acquires first North American serial rights. Upon request, rights will be transferred back to author after publication.

Advice "Professionalism, patience and persistence are essential. One needs to do one's homework and know the market. The competition is very intense, and funding for the front-line journals is generally inadequate, so staffing is low. It takes time to get a response, and rejections are a fact of life. It is important not to take the rejections personally, and also to know that editors make decisions for better or worse, and they make mistakes too. Fortunately there are many gatekeepers. *Alaska Quarterly Review* has published many pieces that had been turned down by other journals—including pieces that then went on to win national awards. We also know of instances in which pieces *Alaska Quarterly Review* rejected later appeared in other magazines. We haven't regretted that we didn't take those pieces. Rather, we're happy that the authors have made a good match. Disappointment should *never* stop anyone. Will counts as much as talent, and new writers need to have confidence in themselves and stick to it."

🅽 ◪ ◎ ALIMENTUM, The Literature of Food

P.O. Box 776, New York NY 10163. E-mail: submissions@alimentumjournal.com. Web site: www.alimentumjournal.com. **Contact:** Submissions editor. Peter Selgin, editor. Literary magazine/journal: 6×7½, 128 pages, glossy cover. Contains illustrations. "All of our stories, poems and essays have food as a theme." Semiannual. Estab. 2005.

Needs Literary. Special interests: food related. Receives 60 mss/month. Accepts 20 mss/issue. Manuscript published 6-12 months after acceptance. **Publishes average of 2 new writers/year.** Published Mark Kurlansky, Oliver Sacks, Janna McMahan, Leslie McGrath, Carly Sachs. Length: 4,500 words (max). Average length: 2,000-3,000 words. Publishes short shorts. Also publishes literary essays, poetry, spot illustrations. Rarely comments on/critiques rejected manuscripts.

How to Contact Send complete ms with cover letter. Accepts submissions by e-mail "when pasted into body of message (1,200 word e-mail limit), no attachments." Responds to queries in 3 months. Responds to mss in 3 months. Send either SASE (or IRC) for return of ms or disposable copy of ms and #10 SASE for reply only. Sample copy available for $10. Guidelines available on Web site.

Payment and Terms Writers receive 1 contributor's copy. Additional copies $10. Pays on publication. Acquires first North American serial rights. Publication is copyrighted.

Advice "Write a good story, no clichés, attention to style, strong voice, memorable characters and scenes."

◪ ◎ THE ALLEGHENY REVIEW, A National Journal of Undergraduate Literature

Box 32 Allegheny College, Meadville PA 16335. E-mail: review@allegheny.edu. Web site: http://review.allegheny.edu. **Contact:** Senior editor. Magazine: 6×9; 100 pages; illustrations; photos. "*The Allegheny Review* is one of America's only nationwide literary magazines exclusively for undergraduate works fo poetry, fiction and nonfiction. Our intended audience is persons interested in quality literature." Annual. Estab. 1983.

Needs Adventure, ethnic/multicultural, experimental, family saga, fantasy, feminist, gay, historical, horror, humor/satire, lesbian, literary, mainstream, military/war, mystery/suspense, New Age, psychic/supernatural/occult, religious/inspirational (general), romance, science fiction, western. No "fiction not written by undergraduates; we accept nothing but fiction by currently enrolled undergraduate students." "We consider anything catering to an intellectual audience." Receives 50 unsolicited mss/month. Accepts 3 mss/issue. Publishes ms 2 months after deadline. **Publishes roughly 90% new writers/year.** Recently published work by Dianne Page, Monica Stahl and DJ Kinney. Publishes short shorts. Also publishes literary essays, literary criticism, poetry. Sometimes comments on rejected mss.

How to Contact Send complete mss with a cover letter. Accepts submissions on disk. Responds in 2 weeks to queries; 4 months to mss. Send disposable copy of ms and #10 SASE for reply only. Sample copy for $4. Guidelines for SASE, by e-mail or on Web site.

Payment/Terms Pays 1 contributor's copy; additional copies $3. Sponsors awards/contests.

Advice "We look for quality work that has been thoroughly revised. What stands out includes unique voice, interesting topic and playfulness with the English language. Revise, revise, revise! And be careful how you send it—the cover letter says a lot. We definitely look for diversity in the pieces we publish."

◪ THE AMERICAN DRIVEL REVIEW, A Unified Field Theory of Wit

1425, Stuart Street #1, Longmont CO 80501. (720)494-8719. E-mail: info@americandrivelreview.com. Web site: www.americandrivelreview.com. **Contact:** Tara Blaine and David Wester, editors. Magazine: 6×9; 60-80 pages; illustrations; photos. *The American Drivel Review* is a journal of literary humor dedicated to formulating a Unified Field Theory of Wit. Estab. 2004. Circ. 200.

Needs "We are delighted to consider any categories, styles, forms or genres—real or imagined. We are interested in quality humorous writing in every conceivable form." Receives 75-100 unsolicited mss/month. Accepts 10-12 mss/issue; 40-48 mss/year. Publishes ms 2 months after acceptance. **Publishes 10-15 new writers/year.** Recently published work by Willie Smith, Laird Hunt, Junior Burke, Jack Collom, Richard Froude, Takashi Kendrick and Howard Muggins. Publishes short shorts. Also publishes literary essays, literary criticism, poetry.

How to Contact Send complete ms. Accepts submissions by e-mail, disk. Send SASE for return of ms. Responds in 2-3 months to queries. Accepts multiple submissions. No simultaneous submissions. Sample copy for $4.50. Writer's guidelines for #10 SASE, online or by e-mail.

Payment/Terms Pays 2 contributor's copies. Pays on publication for one-time rights.

Advice "We look primarily for sublime funny, brilliant writing and a unique or experimental voice."

◢ AMERICAN LITERARY REVIEW

University of North Texas, P.O. Box 311307, Denton TX 76203-1307. (940)565-2755. Fax: (940)565-4355. E-mail: americanliteraryreview@gmail.com. Web site: www.engl.unt.edu/alr/. **Contact:** Ann McCutchan, prose editor. Magazine: 6×9; 128 pages; 70 lb. Mohawk paper; 67 lb. Wausau Vellum cover. "Publishes quality, contemporary poems and stories." Semiannual. Estab. 1990. Circ. 1,200.

Needs Literary, mainstream. "No genre works." Receives 150-200 unsolicited mss/month. Accepts 4-6 mss/issue; 8-16 mss/year. Reading period: September 1-May 1. Publishes ms within 2 years after acceptance. Recently published work by Dana Johnson, Bill Roorbach, Cynthia Shearer, Mark Jacobs and Sylvia Wantanabe. Also publishes literary essays, poetry. Critiques or comments on rejected mss.

How to Contact Send complete ms with cover letter. Responds in 2-4 months to mss. Accepts simultaneous submissions. Sample copy for $6. Writer's guidelines for #10 SASE.

Payment/Terms Pays in contributor's copies. Acquires one-time rights.

Advice "We would like to see more short shorts and stylistically innovative and risk-taking fiction. We like to see stories that illuminate the various layers of characters and their situations with great artistry. Give us distinctive character-driven stories that explore the complexities of human existence." Looks for "the small moments that contain more than at first possible, that surprise us with more truth than we thought we had a right to expect."

$◢ ◎ ANCIENT PATHS, A Journal of Christian Art and Literature

P.O. Box 7505, Fairfax Station VA 22039. Web site: www.literatureclassics.com/ancientpaths/magazine/table.html. **Contact:** Skylar H. Burris, editor. Magazine: digest size; 80+ pages; 20 lb. plain white paper; cardstock cover; perfect bound; illustrations. "*Ancient Paths* publishes quality fiction and creative nonfiction for a literate Christian audience. Religious themes are usually subtle, and the magazine has non-Christian readers as well as some content by non-Christian authors. However, writers should be comfortable appearing in a Christian magazine." Annual. Estab. 1998. Circ. 175-200.

Needs Historical, humor/satire, literary, mainstream, novel excerpts, religious/inspirational (general religious/literary), science fiction (Christian), slice-of-life vignettes. No retelling of Bible stories. Literary fiction favored over genre fiction. Receives 10+ unsolicited mss/month. Accepts 7-10 mss/issue. Publishes ms 2-4 months after acceptance. Recently published work by Larry Marshall Sams, Erin Tocknell, Maureen Stirsman and Chris Williams. Length: 250-2,500 words; average length: 1,500 words. Publishes short shorts. Often comments on rejected mss.

How to Contact Send complete ms. Accepts submissions by e-mail (ssburris@msn.com [only international submissions]). Include estimated word count. Send SASE for return of ms or send a disposable copy of ms and #10 SASE for reply only. Responds in 1 week to queries; 4-5 weeks to mss. Accepts simultaneous, multiple submissions and reprints. Sample copy for $5; make checks payable to Skylar Burris *not* to *Ancient Paths*. Writer's guidelines online. Reviews fiction.

Payment/Terms Pays $6, 1 copy, and discount on additional copies. Pays on publication for one-time rights. Not copyrighted.

Advice "We look for fluid prose, intriguing characters and substantial themes in fiction manuscripts."

$◢ ⛎ ANTIETAM REVIEW

Washington County Arts Council, 14 West Washington Street, Hagerstown MD 21740-5512. (301)791-3132. Fax: (240)420-1754. E-mail: antietamreview@washingtoncountyarts.com. Web site: www.washingtoncountyarts.com. **Contact:** Mary Jo Vincent, managing editor. Magazine: 8½×11; 75-90 pages; glossy paper; light card cover. A literary magazine of short fiction, poetry and black-and-white photography. Annual. Estab. 1982. Circ. 1,000.

Needs Condensed novels, ethnic/multicultural, experimental, literary ("short stories of a literary quality"), novel excerpts ("if works as an independent piece"), creative nonfiction, interviews, memoirs and book reviews. No religious, romance, erotic, confession or horror. Accepts 8-10 mss/year. Publishes ms 3-4 months after acceptance. **Publishes 2-3 new writers/year.** Recently published work by Stephen Dixon, Pinckney Benedict, Brad Barkley, Ellyn Bache, Joyce Kornblatt.

How to Contact Send complete ms. "Reading period September 1-December 1, annually. Queries accepted by mail, e-mail and phone. No electronic submissions. Manuscripts are not returned unless requested and sufficient postage and SASE is enclosed. Send #10 SASE for response only." Sample copy for $8.40 (current issue), $6.30 (back issue).

Payment/Terms Pays $50 and 2 contributor's copies. Pays on publication for first North American serial rights.

Advice "We seek high-quality, well-crafted work with significant character development and shift. No specific theme. We look for work that is interesting, involves the reader, and teaches us a new way to view the world. A manuscript stands out because of its energy and flow. Most of our submissions reflect the times more than industry trends. We also seek a compelling voice, originality, magic." Contributors are encouraged to review past issues before submitting.

$ ☑ ☑ THE ANTIGONISH REVIEW

St. Francis Xavier University, P.O. Box 5000, Antigonish NS B2G 2W5 Canada. (902)867-3962. Fax: (902)867-5563. Web site: www.antigonishreview.com. **Contact:** Bonnie McIsaac, office manager. Literary magazine for educated and creative readers. Quarterly. Estab. 1970. Circ. 1,000.

Needs Literary, translations, contemporary, prose poem. No erotica. Receives 50 unsolicited mss/month. Accepts 6 mss/issue. Publishes ms 4 months after acceptance. **Publishes some new writers/year.** Recently published work by Arnold Bloch, Richard Butts and Helen Barolini. Sometimes comments on rejected mss.

How to Contact Send complete ms. Accepts submissions by fax. Accepts electronic (disk compatible with WordPerfect/IBM and Windows) submissions. Prefers hard copy with disk submission. Responds in 1 month to queries; 6 months to mss. No simultaneous submissions. Sample copy for $7 or online. Writer's guidelines for #10 SASE or online.

Payment/Terms Pays $50 for stories. Pays on publication. Rights retained by author.

Advice "Learn the fundamentals and do not deluge an editor."

$ ☑ ANTIOCH REVIEW

P.O. Box 148, Yellow Springs OH 45387-0148. E-mail: review@antioch.edu. Web site: www.review.antioch.edu. **Contact:** Fiction editor. Magazine: 6×9; 200 pages; 50 lb. book offset paper; coated cover stock; illustrations "seldom." "Literary and cultural review of contemporary issues, and literature for general readership." Quarterly. Estab. 1941. Circ. 5,100.

Needs Experimental, literary, translations, contemporary. No science fiction, fantasy or confessions. Receives 275 unsolicited mss/month. Accepts 5-6 mss/issue; 20-24 mss/year. No mss accepted June 1-September 1. Publishes ms 10 months after acceptance. Agented fiction 1-2%. **Publishes 1-2 new writers/year.** Recently published work by William Cobb, Andrew Porter, Edith Pearlman, Peter LaSalle, Nicholas Montemarano.

How to Contact Send complete ms with SASE, preferably mailed flat. Responds in 4-6 months to mss. Sample copy for $7. Writer's guidelines online.

Payment/Terms Pays $15/printed page. Pays on publication.

Advice "Our best advice always is to *read* the *Antioch Review* to see what type of material we publish. Quality fiction requires an engagement of the reader's intellectual interest supported by mature emotional relevance, written in a style that is rich and rewarding without being freaky. The great number of stories submitted to us indicates that fiction still has great appeal. We assume that if so many are writing fiction, many must be reading it."

☑ ARABLE, A Literary Journal

514 Washburn Avenue, Louisville KY 40222. (502)802-2786. E-mail: arable@insightbb.com. **Contact:** Edmund August. Magazine: 6×9; 100 pages; 60 lb. paper; 10 pt. cover stock. "*Arable* is dedicated to the fundamental belief that creativity in literature (as well as in all arts and sciences) needs room in which to grow. Our hope is that this journal will serve as one plot of nurturing land for that growth." Triannual. Estab. 2004. Circ. 300.

Needs Ethnic/multicultural, experimental, feminist, gay, historical, literary, mainstream. Receives 50-60 unsolicited mss/month. Accepts 4-12 mss/issue; 12-36 mss/year. Publishes ms 3 months after acceptance. **Publishes 8 new writers/year.** Recently published work by Annette Allen, Reid Bush, Erin Keanem, W. Loran Smith, Amelia Blossom, Pamela Steele. Length: 500-6,000 words; average length: 2,500 words. Publishes short shorts. Also publishes literary essays, poetry. Sometimes comments on rejected mss.

How to Contact Send complete ms. Accepts submissions by e-mail. Responds in 1-4 months to mss. Accepts simultaneous, multiple submissions. Sample copy for $10. Writer's guidelines by e-mail.

Payment/Terms Pays one contributor's copy. Acquires one-time rights.

Advice "*Arable* looks for stories with consistent narrative voice, one I can hear inside my head, one that makes me stop thinking as an editor and allows me to sit back and enjoy being taken on a journey."

ARKANSAS REVIEW, A Journal of Delta Studies

Department of English and Philosophy, P.O. Box 1890, Arkansas State University, State University AR 72467-1890. (501)972-3043. Fax: (501)972-3045. E-mail: tswillia@astate.edu. Web site: www.clt.astate.edu/arkreview. **Contact:** Ted Williams, fiction editor. Magazine: 8¼×11; 64-100 pages; coated, matte paper; matte, 4-color cover stock; illustrations; photos. Publishes articles, fiction, poetry, essays, interviews, reviews, visual art evocative of or responsive to the Mississippi River Delta. Triannual. Estab. 1996. Circ. 700.

Needs Literary (essays and criticism), regional (short stories). "No genre fiction. Must have a Delta focus." Receives 30-50 unsolicited mss/month. Accepts 2-3 mss/issue; 5-7 mss/year. Publishes ms 6-12 months after acceptance. Agented fiction 1%. **Publishes 3-4 new writers/year.** Recently published work by Susan Henderson, George Singleton, Scott Ely and Pia Erhart. Also publishes literary essays, poetry. Sometimes comments on rejected mss.

How to Contact Accepts submissions by e-mail, fax. Send SASE for reply, return of ms or send a disposable copy of ms. Responds in 1 week to queries; 4 months to mss. Sample copy for $7.50. Writer's guidelines for #10 SASE.

Payment/Terms Pays 3 contributor's copies; additional copies for $5. Acquires first North American serial rights.

Advice "We see a lot of stories set in New Orleans but prefer fiction that takes place in other parts of the Delta. We'd love more innovative and experimental fiction too but primarily seek stories that involve and engage the reader and evoke or respond to the Delta natural and/or cultural experience."

THE ARMCHAIR AESTHETE

Pickle Gas Press, 31 Rolling Meadows Way, Penfield NY 14526. (585)388-6968. E-mail: bypaul@netacc.net. **Contact:** Paul Agosto, editor. Magazine: 5½×8½; 60-75 pages; 20 lb. paper; 110 lb. card stock color cover. "*The Armchair Aesthete* seeks quality writing that enlightens and entertains a thoughtful audience (ages 9-90) with a 'good read.'" Tri-annual. Estab. 1996. Circ. 100.

Needs Adventure, fantasy (science fantasy, sword and sorcery), historical (general), horror, humor/satire (satire), mainstream (contemporary), mystery/suspense (amateur sleuth, cozy, police procedural, private eye/hard-boiled, romantic suspense), science fiction (soft/sociological), western (frontier, traditional). "No racist, pornographic, overt gore; no religious or material intended for or written by children. Receives 90 unsolicited mss/month. Accepts 13-18 mss/issue; 60-80 mss/year. Publishes ms 3-9 months after acceptance. Agented fiction 5%. **Publishes 15-25 new writers/year.** Recently published work by Alan Reynolds, Frank Andreotti, Joyce G. Bradshaw, Rachel Lapidow, D'Arcy Ann Pryciak. Average length: 3,500 words. Publishes short shorts. Also publishes poetry. Sometimes comments on rejected mss.

How to Contact Accepts submissions by e-mail. Send SASE for reply, return of ms or send a disposable copy of ms. Responds in 2-3 weeks to queries; 3-6 months to mss. Accepts simultaneous, multiple submissions and reprints. Sample copy for $4 (paid to P. Agosto, Ed.) and 3 first-class stamps. Writer's guidelines for #10 SASE. Reviews fiction.

Payment/Terms Pays 1 contributor's copy; additional copies for $3 (pay to P. Agosto, editor). Pays on publication for one-time rights.

Advice "Clever, compelling storytelling has a good chance here. We look for a clever plot, thought-out characters, something that surprises or catches us off guard. Write on innovative subjects and situations. Submissions should be professionally presented and technically sound."

$ ARTFUL DODGE

Dept. of English, College of Wooster, Wooster OH 44691. (330)263-2577. Web site: www.wooster.edu/artfuldodge/home.htm. **Contact:** Editor. Magazine: 180 pages; illustrations; photos. "There is no theme in this magazine, except literary power. We also have an ongoing interest in translations from Central/Eastern Europe and elsewhere." Annual. Estab. 1979. Circ. 1,000.

Needs Experimental, literary, translations, prose poem. "We judge by literary quality, not by genre. We are especially interested in fine English translations of significant prose writers. Translations should be submitted with original texts." Receives 50 unsolicited mss/month. Accepts 5 mss/year. **Publishes 1 new writer/year.** Recently published work by Dan Chaon, Lynne Sharon Schwartz, Robert Mooney, Joan Connor, Sarah Willis; and interviews with Tim O'Brien, Lee Smith, Michael Dorris, Stuart Dybek. Average length: 2,500 words. Also publishes literary essays, literary criticism, poetry. Occasionally comments on rejected mss.

How to Contact Send complete ms with SASE. Do not send more than 30 pages at a time. Responds in 1 year to mss. Accepts simultaneous submissions if contacted immediately after being accepted elsewhere. Sample copy for $7. Writer's guidelines for #10 SASE.

Payment/Terms Pays 2 contributor's copies and honorarium of $5/page, "thanks to funding from the Ohio Arts Council." Acquires first North American serial rights.

Advice "If we take time to offer criticism, do not subsequently flood us with other stories no better than the first. If starting out, get as many *good* readers as possible. Above all, read contemporary fiction and the magazine you are trying to publish in."

AXE FACTORY REVIEW

Cynic Press, P.O. Box 40691, Philadelphia PA 19107. **Contact:** Joseph Farley, editor. Magazine: 11×17 folded to 8½×11; 30-60 pages; 20 lb. stock paper; 70 lb. stock cover; illustrations; photos on occasion. "We firmly believe that literature is a form of (and/or expression/manifestations of) madness. We seek to spread the disease called literature. We will look at any genre, but we search for the quirky, the off-center, the offensive, the annoying, but always the well-written story, poem, essay." Biannual. Estab. 1986. Circ. 200.

Needs Adventure, comics/graphic novels, erotica, ethnic/multicultural (Asian), experimental, fantasy (space fantasy, sword and sorcery), feminist, gay, historical, horror (dark fantasy, futuristic, psychological, supernatural), humor/satire, lesbian, literary, mainstream, military/war, mystery/suspense, New Age, psychic/supernatural/occult, regional (Philadelphia area), religious/inspirational (general religious, inspirational, religious mystery/suspense), romance, science fiction (hard science/technological, soft/sociological, cross genre), thriller/espionage, translations, western (frontier saga, traditional). "We would like to see more hybrid genres, literary/science fiction, Beat writing. No genteel professional gibberish." Receives 20 unsolicited mss/month. Accepts 1-2 mss/issue; 3 mss/year. Publishes ms 6-12 months after acceptance. Recently published work by Tim Gavin and Michael Hafer. Length: 500-5,000 words; average length: 3,000 words. Publishes short shorts. Also publishes literary essays, literary criticism, poetry. Often comments on rejected mss.

How to Contact Send SASE (or IRC) for return of ms. Responds in 6 weeks to mss. Accepts simultaneous, multiple submissions and reprints. Sample copy for $8. Current issue $9. Reviews fiction.

Payment/Terms Pays 1-2 contributor's copies; additional copies $8. Pays on publication for one-time rights, anthology rights.

Advice "In fiction we look for a strong beginning, strong middle, strong end; memorable characters; and most importantly language, language, language."

BACKWARDS CITY REVIEW

Backwards City Publications, P.O. Box 41317, Greensboro NC 27404-1317. (336)275-9777. E-mail: editors@backwardscity.net. Web site: www.backwardscity.net. **Contact:** Gerry Canavan, editor. Literary magazine/journal: 6×9, 128 pages, white, 50 lb. paper, 10 pt CIS cover. Contains illustrations. Includes photographs. "At Backwards City Review, we seek to gather strong voices from different genres to create a journal that caters to the world above, beyond, below, around, near, within sight of, and slightly out of tune with conventional literary outlets." Semiannual. Estab. 2004. Circ. 400. Member CLMP.

Needs Comics/graphic novels, experimental, literary, mainstream, science fiction (soft/sociological), translations. Does not want religious, historical. List of upcoming themes available on Web site. Receives 100+ mss/month. Accepts 5-6 mss/issue; 10-12 mss/year. Manuscript published 6 months after acceptance. Agented fiction 0%. **Publishes 3-5 new writers/year.** Published Chris Bachelder, Cory Doctorow, Alix Ohlin, Michael Parker, Alika Tanaka, Kurt Vonnegut. Length: 10,000 words max. Average length: 3,000-5,000 words. Publishes short shorts. Average length of short shorts: 1,000 words. Also publishes literary essays, poetry. Sometimes comments on/critiques rejected manuscripts.

How to Contact Send complete ms with cover letter. Include estimated word count, brief bio, list of publications, SASE. Responds to queries in 4 weeks. Responds to mss in 4 months. Send disposable copy of ms and #10 SASE for reply only. Considers simultaneous submissions. Sample copy available for $5. Guidelines available on Web site.

Payment and Terms Writers receive 3 contributors copies. Additional copies $3 each. Acquires first North American serial rights. Sends galleys to author. "Sponsors an Annual Fiction Contest. Deadline is April 15th. See Web site for additional contests." Cash prize for contest winners.

Advice "We're looking for something both well written and unconventional. We showcase the different. We love stories we've never seen before. Be original. Read a sample issue. Visit our blog. Send us only your best work."

BALLYHOO STORIES

Ballyhoo Stories, LLC, 18 Willoughby Ave. #3, Brooklyn NY 11205. (347)886-6033. E-mail: editors@ballyhoostories.com. Web site: www.ballyhoostories.com. **Contact:** Joshua Mandelbaum or Suzanne Pettypiece, editors. Literary magazine/journal: 88 pages, matte cover. "*Ballyhoo Stories* publishes the best in creative nonfiction and fiction. Each issue has a theme. We look for imaginative interpretation of each theme. We also have an online-only '50 States project.' The goal of this project is to collect one story with each state as either the subject or the setting." Bimonthly. Estab. 2005. Circ. 500. Member CLMP.

Needs Literary. List of upcoming themes available on Web site. Receives 100 mss/month. Accepts 10 mss/issue; 20 mss/year. Manuscript published 2 months after acceptance. **Publishes 4 new writers/year.** Length: 7,000 words (max). Average length: 5,000. Also publishes literary essays. Sometimes comments on/critiques rejected manuscripts.

How to Contact Send complete ms with cover letter. Accepts e-mail submissions for 50 States project ONLY.

Include brief bio. Responds to queries in 1 week. Responds to mss in 2 months. Send disposable copy of ms and #10 SASE for reply only. Considers simultaneous submissions. Sample copy available for $8. Guidelines available via e-mail, on Web site.

Payment and Terms Writers receive 2 contributors copies. Additional copies $8. Acquires first North American serial rights. Publication is copyrighted.

▣ THE BALTIMORE REVIEW

P.O. Box 36418, Towson MD 21286. Web site: www.baltimorereview.org. **Contact:** Susan Muaddi Darraj, managing editor. Magazine: 6×9; 150 pages; 60 lb. paper; 10 pt. CS1 gloss film cover. Showcase for the best short stories, creative nonfiction and poetry by writers in the Baltimore area and beyond. Semiannual. Estab. 1996.

Needs Ethnic/multicultural, literary, mainstream. "No science fiction, westerns, children's, romance, etc." Accepts 20 mss/issue; approx. 40 mss/year. Publishes ms 1-9 months after acceptance. **Publishes "at least a few" new writers/year.** Average length: 3,000 words. Publishes short shorts. Also publishes poetry.

How to Contact Send SASE for reply, return of ms or send a disposable copy of ms. Responds in 4-6 months to mss. Accepts simultaneous submissions. No e-mail or fax submissions. Sample copy online.

Payment/Terms Pays 2 contributor's copies. Acquires first North American serial rights.

Advice "We look for compelling stories and a masterful use of the English language. We want to feel that we have never heard this story, or this voice, before. Read the kinds of publications you want your work to appear in. Make your reader believe and care."

▣ BARBARIC YAWP

Bone World Publishing, 3700 County Rt. 24, Russell NY 13684-3198. (315)347-2609. **Contact:** Nancy Berbrich, fiction editor. Magazine: digest-size; 60 pages; 24 lb. paper; matte cover stock. "We publish what we like. Fiction should include some bounce and surprise. Our publication is intended for the intelligent, open-minded reader." Quarterly. Estab. 1997. Circ. 120.

Needs Adventure, experimental, fantasy (science, sword and sorcery), historical, horror, literary, mainstream, psychic/supernatural/occult, regional, religious/inspirational, science fiction (hard, soft/sociological). "We don't want any pornography, gratuitous violence or whining." Wants more suspense and philosophical work. Receives 30-40 unsolicited mss/month. Accepts 10-12 mss/issue; 40-48 mss/year. Publishes ms up to 6 months after acceptance. **Publishes 4-6 new writers/year.** Recently published work by Michael Fowler, Jeff Grimshaw, Robert Layden and Holly Interlandi. Length: 1,500 words; average length: 600 words. Publishes short shorts. Also publishes literary essays, literary criticism, poetry. Often comments on rejected mss.

How to Contact Send SASE for reply, return of ms or send a disposable copy of ms. Responds in 2 weeks to queries; 4 months to mss. Accepts simultaneous, multiple submissions and reprints. Sample copy for $4. Writer's guidelines for #10 SASE.

Payment/Terms Pays 1 contributor's copy; additional copies $3. Acquires one-time rights.

Advice "Don't give up. Read much, write much, submit much. Observe closely the world around you. Don't borrow ideas from TV or films. Revision is often necessary—grit your teeth and do it. Never fear rejection."

▢ BATHTUB GIN

Pathwise Press, P.O. Box 178, Erie PA 16512. (814)455-5498. E-mail: pathwisepress@hotmail.com. Web site: www.bluemarble.net/~charter/btgin.htm. **Contact:** Fiction Editor. Magazine: 8½×5½; 60 pages; reycled 20-lb. paper; 80-lb. card cover; illustrations; photos. "*Bathtub Gin* is looking for work that has some kick to it. We are very eclectic and publish a wide range of styles. Audience is anyone interested in new writing and art that is not being presented in larger magazines." Semiannual. Estab. 1997. Circ. 250.

Needs Condensed novels, experimental, humor/satire, literary. "No horror, science fiction, historical unless they go beyond the usual formula." "We want more experimental fiction." Receives 20 unsolicited mss/month. Accepts 2-3 mss/issue. Reads mss for two issues June 1st-September 15th. "We publish in mid-October and mid-April." **Publishes 10 new writers/year.** Recently published work by J.T. Whitehead and G.D. McFetridge. Publishes short shorts. Also publishes literary essays, literary criticism, poetry. Often comments on rejected mss.

How to Contact Accepts submissions by e-mail. Send cover letter with a 3-5 line bio. Send SASE for reply, return of ms or send a disposable copy of ms. Responds in 1-2 months to queries. Accepts simultaneous, multiple submissions and reprints. Sample copy for $5. Writer's guidelines for #10 SASE. Reviews fiction.

Payment/Terms Pays 2 contributor's copies; discount on additional copies. Rights revert to author upon publication.

Advice "We are looking for writing that contains strong imagery, is complex, and is willing to take a chance with form and structure."

○ BEGINNINGS PUBLISHING INC., A Magazine for the Novice Writer

Beginnings Publishing, P.O. Box 214 -W, Bayport NY 11705. (631)645-3846. E-mail: jenineb@optonline.net. Web site: www.scbeginnings.com. **Contact:** Jenine Killoran, fiction editor. Magazine: $8^{1}/_{2} \times 11$; 54 pages; matte; glossy cover; illustrations; photographs. "*Beginnings* publishes only beginner/novice writers. We do accept articles by professionals pertaining to the craft of writing. We have had many new writers go on to be published elsewhere after being featured in our magazine." Triannual. Estab. 1999. Circ. 2,500.

Needs Adventure, family saga, literary, mainstream, mystery/suspense (amateur slueth), romance (contemporary), science fiction (soft/sociological), western. "No erotica, horror." Receives 425 unsolicited mss/month. Accepts 10 mss/issue; 20 mss/year. Does not read mss during January and April. Publishes ms 3-4 months after acceptance. **Publishes 100 percent new writers/year.** Recently published work by Harvey Stanbrough, Sue Guiney, Tom Cooper and Stephen Wallace. Average length: 2,500 words. Publishes short shorts. Also publishes poetry. Usually comments on rejected mss.

How to Contact Send complete ms. Send disposable copy of ms and #10 SASE for reply only; however, will accept SASE for return of ms. Responds in 3 weeks to queries; 10-13 weeks to mss. Accepts simultaneous submissions and reprints. Sample copy for $4. Writer's guidelines for SASE, e-mail or on Web site.

Payment/Terms Pays one contributor's copy; additional copies $4. Pays on publication for first North American serial, first rights.

Advice "Originality, presentation, proper grammar and spelling a must. Non-predictable endings. Many new writers confuse showing vs. telling. Writers who have that mastered stand out. Study the magazine. Check and double check your work. Original storylines, well thought out, keep up a good pace. Presentation is important, too! Rewrite, rewrite!"

○ BELLEVUE LITERARY REVIEW, A Journal of Humanity and Human Experience

Dept. of Medicine, NYU School of Medicine, 550 First Avenue, OBV-A612, New York NY 10016. (212)263-3973. Fax: (212)263-3206. E-mail: info@blreview.org. Web site: http://blreview.org. **Contact:** Ronna Wineberg, fiction editor. Magazine: 6×9; 160 pages. "The *BLR* is a literary journal that examines human existence through the prism of health and healing, illness and disease. We encourage creative interpretations of these themes." Semiannual. Estab. 2001. Member CLMP.

Needs Literary. No genre fiction. Receives 100 unsolicited mss/month. Accepts 9 mss/issue; 18 mss/year. Publishes ms 3-6 months after acceptance. Agented fiction 1%. **Publishes 3-6 new writers/year.** Recently published work by Amy Hempel, Sheila Kohler, Abraham Verghese, Stephen Dixon. Length: 5,000 words; average length: 2,500 words. Publishes short shorts. Also publishes literary essays, poetry. Sometimes comments on rejected mss.

How to Contact Submit online at www.blreview.org (preferred). Also accepts mss via regular mail. Send complete ms. Send SASE (or IRC) for return of ms or disposable copy of the ms and #10 SASE for reply only. Online submissions now accepted, www.blreview.org. Responds in 3-6 months to mss. Accepts simultaneous submissions. Sample copy for $7. Writer's guidelines for SASE, e-mail or on Web site.

Payment/Terms Pays 2 contributor's copies, 1-year subscription and 1-year gift subscription; additional copies $5. Pays on publication for first North American serial rights. Sends galleys to author.

○ BELLINGHAM REVIEW

Mail Stop 9053, Western Washington University, Bellingham WA 98225. (360)650-4863. E-mail: bhreview@cc.wwu.edu. Web site: www.wwu.edu/~bhreview. **Contact:** Fiction Editor. Magazine: $6 \times 8^{1}/_{4}$; 150 pages; 60 lb. white paper; four-color cover." *Bellingham Review* seeks literature of palpable quality; stories, essays and poems that nudge the limits of form or execute traditional forms exquisitely. Semiannual. Estab. 1977. Circ. 1,600.

- The editors are actively seeking submissions of creative nonfiction, as well as stories that push the boundaries of the form. The Tobias Wolff Award in Fiction Contest runs December 1-March 15; see Web site for guidelines or send SASE.

Needs Experimental, humor/satire, literary, regional (Northwest). Does not want anything nonliterary. Accepts 3-4 mss/issue. Does not read ms February 2-September 30. Publishes ms 6 months after acceptance. Agented fiction 10%. **Publishes 10 new writers/year.** Recently published work by Christie Hodgen, Robert Van Wagoner and Joan Leegeant. Publishes short shorts. Also publishes poetry.

How to Contact Send complete ms. Responds in 3 months to mss. Accepts simultaneous submissions. Sample copy for $7. Writer's guidelines online.

Payment/Terms Pays on publication when funding allows. Acquires first North American serial rights.

Advice "We look for work that is ambitious, vital and challenging both to the spirit and the intellect."

○ ▨ BELLOWING ARK, A Literary Tabloid

P.O. Box 55564, Shoreline WA 98155. E-mail: bellowingark@bellowingark.org. **Contact:** Fiction Editor. Tabloid: $11^{1}/_{2} \times 17^{1}/_{2}$; 32 pages; electro-brite paper and cover stock; illustrations; photos. "We publish material we feel addresses the human situation in an affirmative way. We do not publish academic fiction." Bimonthly. Estab. 1984. Circ. 650.

● Work from *Bellowing Ark* appeared in the *Pushcart Prize* anthology.

Needs Literary, mainstream, serialized novels. "No science fiction or fantasy." Receives 10-20 unsolicited mss/month. Accepts 2-5 mss/issue; 700-1,000 mss/year. Publishes ms 6 months after acceptance. **Publishes 10-50 new writers/year.** Recently published work by Tom Cook, Diane Tryczinski, Shelley Uva, Tanyo Ravicz, Susan Montag and E.R. Romaine. Publishes short shorts. Also publishes literary essays, literary criticism, poetry. Sometimes comments on rejected mss.

How to Contact Send complete ms and SASE. Responds in 6 weeks to mss. No simultaneous submissions. Sample copy for $4, 9½×12½ SAE and $1.43 postage.

Payment/Terms Pays in contributor's copies. Acquires one-time rights.

Advice "*Bellowing Ark* began as (and remains) an alternative to the despair and negativity of the workshop/academic literary scene; we believe that life has meaning and is worth living—the work we publish reflects that belief. Learn how to tell a story before submitting. Avoid 'trick' endings; they have all been done before and better. *Bellowing Ark* is interested in publishing writers who will develop with the magazine, as in an extended community. We find *good* writers and stick with them. This is why the magazine has grown from 12 to 32 pages."

◙ BERKELEY FICTION REVIEW

10B Eshleman Hall, University of California, Berkeley CA 94720. (510)642-2892. E-mail: smh@uclink.berkeley.edu. Web site: www.OCF.Berkeley.EDU/~bfr/. **Contact:** Sarah Haufrect and Julia Simon, editors. Magazine: 5½×8½; 180 pages; perfect-bound; glossy cover; some b&w art; photographs. "The mission of *Berkeley Fiction Review* is to provide a forum for new and emerging writers as well as writers already established. We publish a wide variety of contemporary short fiction for a literary audience." Annual. Estab. 1981. Circ. 1,000.

Needs Experimental, literary, mainstream. "Quality, inventive short fiction. No poetry or formula fiction." Receives 60 unsolicited mss/month. Accepts 10-20 mss/issue. **Publishes 15-20 new writers/year.** Publishes short shorts. Occasionally comments on rejected mss.

How to Contact Responds in 6-7 months to mss. Accepts simultaneous, multiple submissions. Sample copy for $9.50. Writer's guidelines for SASE.

Payment/Terms Pays one contributor's copy. Acquires first rights. Sponsors awards/contests.

Advice "Our criteria is fiction that resonates. Voices that are strong and move a reader. Clear, powerful prose (either voice or rendering of subject) with a point. Unique ways of telling stories. These capture the editors. Work hard, don't give up. Don't let your friends or family critique your work. Get someone honest to point out your writing weaknesses, and then work on them. Don't submit thinly veiled autobiographical stories; it's been done before—and better. With the proliferation of computers, everyone thinks they're a writer. Not true, unfortunately. The plus side though is ease of transmission and layout, and diversity and range of new work."

$ BIBLIOPHILOS, A Journal of History, Literature, and the Liberal Arts

The Bibliophile Publishing Co., Inc., 200 Security Building, Fairmont WV 26554. (304)366-8107. **Contact:** Gerald J. Bobango, editor. Literary magazine: 5½×8; 68-72 pages; white glossy paper; illustrations; photos. "We see ourself as a forum for new and unpublished writers, historians, philosophers, literary critics and reviewers, and those who love animals. Audience is academic-oriented, college graduate, who believes in traditional Aristotelian-Thomistic thought and education and has a fair streak of the Luddite in him/her. Our ideal reader owns no television, has never sent or received e-mail, and avoids shopping malls at any cost. He loves books." Quarterly. Estab. 1981. Circ. 400.

Needs Adventure, ethnic/multicultural, family saga, historical (general, US, Eastern Europe), horror (psychological, supernatural), humor/satire, literary, mainstream, military/war, mystery/suspense (police procedural, private eye/hard-boiled, courtroom), novel excerpts, regional (New England, Middle Atlantic), romance (gothic, historical, regency period), slice-of-life vignettes, suspense, thriller/espionage, translations, western (frontier saga, traditional), utopian, Orwellian. "No 'I found Jesus and it turned my life around'; no 'I remember Mama, who was a saint and I miss her terribly'; no gay or lesbian topics; no drug culture material; nothing harping on political correctness; nothing to do with healthy living, HMOs, medical programs, or the welfare state, unless it is against statism in these areas." *No unsolicited submissions.* Accepts 5-6 mss/issue; 25-30 mss/year. Publishes ms 12-18 months after acceptance. **Publishes 2-6 new writers/year.** Recently published work by Mardelle Fortier, Clevenger Kehmeier, Gwen Williams, Manuel Sanchez-Lopez, Janet Tyson, Andrea C. Poe, Norman Nathan. Also publishes literary essays, literary criticism, poetry. Often comments on rejected mss.

How to Contact Query with clips of published work. Include bio, SASE and $5.25 for sample issue. Responds in 2 weeks to queries; 1 month to mss. Sample copy for $5.25. Writer's guidelines for 9½×4 SAE and 2 first-class stamps.

Payment/Terms Pays $15-40. Pays on publication for first North American serial rights.

Advice "Write for specifications, send for a sample issue, then *read* the thing, study the formatting, and follow the instructions, which say query first before sending anything. We shall not respond to unsolicited material.

We don't want touchy-feely maudlin stuff where hugging kids solves all of life's problems, and we want no references anywhere in the story to e-mail, the Internet, or computers, unless it's to berate them.''

BIG MUDDY: A JOURNAL OF THE MISSISSIPPI RIVER VALLEY

Southeast Missouri State University Press, MS2650 English Dept., Southeast MO State University, Cape Girardeau MO 63701. E-mail: sswartwout@semo.edu. Web site: www6.semo.edu/universitypress/. **Contact:** Susan Swartwout, editor. Magazine: $8\frac{1}{2} \times 5\frac{1}{2}$ perfect-bound; 150 pages; acid-free paper; color cover stock; layflat lamination; illustrations; photos. *"Big Muddy* explores multidisciplinary, multicultural issues, people, and events mainly concerning the 10-state area that borders the Mississippi River, by people who have lived here, who have an interest in the area, or who know the River Basin. We publish fiction, poetry, historical essays, creative nonfiction, environmental essays, biography, regional events, photography, art, etc.'' Semiannual. Estab. 2001. Circ. 500.

Needs Adventure, ethnic/multicultural, experimental, family saga, feminist, historical, humor/satire, literary, mainstream, military/war, mystery/suspense, regional (Mississippi River Valley; Midwest), translations. ''No romance, fantasy or children's.'' Receives 50 unsolicited mss/month. Accepts 2-4 mss/issue. Publishes ms 6 months after acceptance. Recently published work by Philip Kolin, Virgil Suarez, Stephen Graham Jones, Phil Harvey.

How to Contact Send SASE for return of ms or send a disposable copy of ms and #10 SASE for reply only. Responds in 10 weeks to mss. Accepts multiple submissions. Sample copy for $6. Writer's guidelines for SASE, e-mail, fax or on Web site. Reviews fiction.

Payment/Terms Pays 2 contributor's copies; additional copies $5. Acquires first North American serial rights.

Advice ''In fiction manuscripts we look for clear language, avoidance of clichés except in necessary dialogue, a *fresh* vision of the theme or issue. Find some excellent and honest readers to comment on your work-in-progress and final draft. Consider their viewpoints carefully. Revise.''

BIGNEWS, The Art and Literary Monthly

Grand Central Neighborhood, E-mail: BIGnewsmag@aol.com. Web site: www.mainchance.org. **Contact:** Ron Grunberg, editor. Magazine: $8\frac{1}{4} \times 17$; 10 pages; tabloid paper; 26 lb. cover stock; illustrations; photos. Quarterly. Estab. 2000. Circ. 30,000.

● Received North American Street Newspaper Association (NASNA) Awards for Best Editorial or Essay, Best Art, Best Poetry.

Needs Literary, mainstream. ''Generally, no genre fiction.'' Receives 25 unsolicited mss/month. Accepts 5 mss/year. Publishes ms 3-4 months after acceptance. **Publishes 4 new writers/year.** Recently published work by Robert Sheckley, John Ray, JR., J.L. Navarro, Ben Cheever. Length: 200-5,000 words; average length: 2,700 words. Publishes short shorts. Also publishes literary essays. Sometimes comments on rejected mss.

How to Contact Send complete ms. Accepts submissions by e-mail. Responds in 1 month to queries; 2 months to mss. Writer's guidelines online.

Payment/Terms No payment.

Advice ''A very busy editor has to want to read the whole thing through. Avoid clever. Take risks. Don't write knowingly. Make it an effort of discovery.''

BILINGUAL REVIEW

Hispanic Research Center, Arizona State University, Box 875303, Tempe AZ 85287-5303. (480)965-3867. E-mail: brp@asu.edu. Web site: www.asu.edu/brp/brp.html. **Contact:** Gary D. Keller, editor-in-chief. Magazine: 7×10; 96 pages; 55 lb. acid-free paper; coated cover stock. Scholarly/literary journal of US Hispanic life: poetry, short stories, other prose and short theater. 3 times/year. Estab. 1974. Circ. 2,000.

Needs US Hispanic creative literature. ''We accept material in English or Spanish. We publish orginal work only—no translations.'' US Hispanic themes only. Receives 50 unsolicited mss/month. Accepts 3 mss/issue; 9 mss/year. Publishes ms 1 year after acceptance. Recently published work by Daniel Olivas, Virgil Suárez, Ibis Gomez-Vega. Also publishes literary criticism, poetry. Often comments on rejected mss.

How to Contact Accepts submissions by e-mail. Responds in 1-2 months to queries. Accepts simultaneous submissions and high-quality photocopied submissions. Sample copy for $8. Reviews fiction.

Payment/Terms Pays 2 contributor's copies; 30% discount for extras. Acquires 50% of reprint permission fee given to author as matter of policy rights.

Advice ''We do not publish literature about tourists in Latin America and their perceptions of the 'native culture.' We do not publish fiction about Latin America unless there is a clear tie to the United States (characters, theme, etc.).''

THE BITTER OLEANDER

4983 Tall Oaks Dr., Fayettville NY 13066-9776. (315)637-3047. Fax: (315)637-5056. E-mail: info@bitteroleander. com. Web site: www.bitteroleander.com. **Contact:** Paul B. Roth. Zine specializing in poetry and fiction: 6×9;

128 pages; 55 lb. paper; 12 pt. CIS cover stock; photos. "We're interested in the surreal; deep image particulariza-tion of natural experiences." Semiannual. Estab. 1974. Circ. 2,000.

Needs Experimental, translations. "No pornography; no confessional; no romance." Receives 100 unsolicited mss/month. Accepts 1-2 mss/issue; 2-4 mss/year. Does not read in July. Publishes ms 4-6 months after accep-tance. Recently published work by Tom Stoner, John Michael Cummings, Sara Leslie. Average length: 2,500 words. Publishes short shorts. Also publishes literary essays, poetry. Always comments on rejected mss.

How to Contact Send SASE for reply, return of ms. Responds in 1 week to queries; 1 month to mss. Accepts multiple submissions. Sample copy for $8. Writer's guidelines for #10 SASE.

Payment/Terms Pays 1 contributor's copy; additional copies $8. Acquires first rights.

Advice "If within the first 100 words my mind drifts, the rest rarely makes it. Be yourself and listen to no one but yourself."

$☐ ◎ BLACK LACE

BLK Publishing CO., P.O. Box 83912, Los Angeles CA 90083-0912. (310)410-0808. Fax: (310)410-9250. E-mail: newsroom@blk.com. Web site: www.blacklace.org. **Contact:** Fiction Editor. Magazine: $8^1/_8 \times 10^5/_8$; 48 pages; book stock; color glossy cover; illustrations; photos. "*Black Lace* is a lifestyle magazine for African-American lesbians. Its content ranges from erotic imagery to political commentary." Quarterly. Estab. 1991.

Needs Ethnic/multicultural, lesbian. "Avoid interracial stories of idealized pornography." Accepts 4 mss/year. Recently published work by Nicole King, Wanda Thompson, Lynn K. Pannell, Sheree Ann Slaughter, Lyn Lifshin, JoJo and Drew Alise Timmens. Publishes short shorts. Also publishes literary essays, literary criticism, poetry.

How to Contact Query with published clips or send complete ms. Send a disposable copy of ms. No simultaneous submissions. Accepts electronic submissions. Sample copy for $7. Writer's guidelines free.

Payment/Terms Pays $50 and 2 contributor's copies. Acquires first North American serial rights. Right to anthologize.

Advice "*Black Lace* seeks erotic material of the highest quality. The most important thing is that the work be erotic and that it feature black lesbians or themes. Study the magazine to see what we do and how we do it. Some fiction is very romantic, other is highly sexual. Most articles in *Black Lace* cater to black lesbians between two extremes."

⊞ ☑ THE BLACK MOUNTAIN REVIEW

Black Mountain Press, P.O. Box 9, Ballyclare Co Antrim BT390JW N. Ireland. E-mail: editors@blackmountainrev iew.com. Web site: www.blackmountainreview.com. **Contact:** Editor. Magazine: A5; approximately 100 pages. "We publish short fiction with a contemporary flavour for an international audience." Semiannual. Estab. 1999.

Needs Ethnic/multicultural (general), experimental, historical (literary), literary, regional (Irish), religious/inspirational (general religious, inspirational), romance (literary), science fiction (literary), translations. Pub-lishes ms 5 months after acceptance. **Publishes many new writers/year.** Recently published work by Cathal O Searcaigh, Michael Longley and Brian Keenan. Average length: 1,500-3,000 words. Publishes short shorts. Also publishes literary essays, literary criticism, poetry. Sometimes comments on rejected mss.

How to Contact Send SASE (or IRC) for return of ms or send a disposable copy of ms and #10 SASE for reply. Material should be supplied on $3^1/_2$ inch floppy disk or by e-mail (word.txt format, preferably not attachments) with paper typescript by snail mail. Submissions *must* be accompanied with an e-mail or disk version. Responds in 2 months to queries; 4 months to mss. Accepts simultaneous submissions. Sample copy for $4.50. Writer's guidelines for SASE or by e-mail. Reviews fiction.

Payment/Terms Pays 1 contributor's copy; additional copies $4.50. Pays on publication for one-time rights.

Advice "We look for literary quality. Write well."

$☑ ⊻ BLACK WARRIOR REVIEW

P.O. Box 862936, Tuscaloosa AL 35486-0027. (205)348-4518. E-mail: bwr@ua.edu. Web site: www.webdelsol. com/bwr. **Contact:** Sarah Blackman, fiction editor. Magazine: 6×9; 160 pages; color artwork. "We publish contemporary fiction, poetry, reviews, essays and art for a literary audience. We publish the freshest work we can find." Semiannual. Estab. 1974. Circ. 2,000.

● Work that appeared in the *Black Warrior Review* has been included in the *Pushcart Prize* anthology, *Harper's Magazine, Best American Short Stories, Best American Poetry* and *New Stories from The South*.

Needs Literary, contemporary, short and short-short fiction. Wants "work that is conscious of form and well-crafted. We are open to good experimental writing and short-short fiction. No genre fiction, please." Receives 300 unsolicited mss/month. Accepts 5 mss/issue; 10 mss/year. Unsolicited novel excerpts are not considered unless the novel is already contracted for publication. Publishes ms 6 months after acceptance. **Publishes 5 new writers/year.** Recently published work by Gary Fincke, Anthony Varallo, Wayne Johnson, Jim Ruland,

Elizabeth Wetmore, Bret Anthony Johnston, Rick Bass, Sherri Flick. Length: 7,500 words; average length: 2,000-5,000 words. Occasionally comments on rejected mss.

How to Contact Send complete ms with SASE (1 story per submission). Responds in 4 months to mss. Accepts simultaneous submissions if noted. Sample copy for $10. Writer's guidelines online.

Payment/Terms Pays up to $100, copies, and a 1-year subscription. Pays on publication for first rights.

Advice "We look for attention to language, freshness, honesty, a convincing and sharp voice. Send us a clean, well-printed, proofread manuscript. Become familiar with the magazine prior to submission."

◻ ◎ BLUE MESA REVIEW

University of New Mexico, MSC03 2170, 1 University of New Mexico, Albuquerque NM 87131-0001. (505)277-6155. Fax: (505)277-5573. E-mail: bluemesa@unm.edu. Web site: www.unm.edu/~bluemesa. **Contact:** Julie Shigekuni. Magazine: 6×9; 300 pages; 55 lb. paper; 10 pt CS1 photos. "*Blue Mesa Review* publishes the best/most current creative writing on the market." Annual. Estab. 1989. Circ. 1,200.

Needs Adventure, ethnic/multicultural, experimental, feminist, gay, historical, humor/satire, lesbian, literary, mainstream, regional, western. Receives 25 unsolicited mss/month. Accepts 100 mss/year. Accepts mss July 1-October 1; all submissions must be post marked by October 1; reads mss November-December; responds in January. Publishes ms 5-6 months after acceptance. Recently published work by Kathleen Spivack, Roberta Swann and Tony Mares. Publishes short shorts. Also publishes literary essays, poetry.

How to Contact Send SASE for reply. Sample copy for $12. Writer's guidelines online. Reviews fiction.

Payment/Terms Pays 1 contributor's copy. Acquires first North American serial rights.

Advice "Contact us for complete guidelines. All submissions must follow our guidelines."

◻ BOGG, Journal of Contemporary Writing

Bogg Publications, 422 N. Cleveland St., Arlington VA 22201-1424. E-mail: boggmag@aol.com. **Contact:** John Elsberg, US editor. Magazine: 6×9; 56 pages; 70 lb. white paper; 70 lb. cover stock; line illustrations. "American and British poetry, prose poems, experimental short 'fictions,' reviews and essays on small press." Published 2 or 3 times a year. Estab. 1968. Circ. 750.

Needs Very short experimental fiction and prose poems. "We also look for work with British/Commonwealth themes and/or references." Receives 25 unsolicited mss/month. Accepts 1-2 mss/issue; 3-6 mss/year. Publishes ms 3-18 after acceptance. **Publishes 25-50 new writers/year.** Recently published work by Linda Bosson, Brian Johnson, Pamela Gay, Art Stein and Hugh Fox. Also publishes literary essays, literary criticism. Occasionally comments on rejected mss.

How to Contact Responds in 1 week to queries; 2 weeks to mss. Sample copy for $4 or $5 (current issue). Reviews fiction. Does not consider e-mail or simultaneous submissions.

Payment/Terms Pays 2 contributor's copies; reduced charge for extras. Acquires one-time rights.

Advice "We look for voice and originality. Read magazine first. We are most interested in prose of experimental or wry nature to supplement poetry and are always looking for innovative/imaginative uses of British references."

⊕ ◻ BOOK WORLD MAGAZINE

Christ Church Publishers Ltd., 2 Caversham Street, London England SW3 4AH United Kingdom. 0207 351 4995. Fax: 0207 3514995. E-mail: leonard.holdsworth@btopenworld.com. **Contact:** James Hughes. Magazine: 64 pages; illustrations; photos. "Subscription magazine for serious book lovers, book collectors, librarians and academics." Monthly. Estab. 1971. Circ. 6,000.

Needs Also publishes literary essays, literary criticism.

How to Contact Query. Send IRC (International Reply Coupon) for return of ms. Responds in 3 months to queries; 3 months to mss. Accepts simultaneous submissions. Sample copy for $7.50. Writer's guidelines for IRC.

Payment/Terms Pays on publication for one-time rights.

Advice "Always write to us before sending any mss."

$◻ BOULEVARD

Opojaz, Inc., 6614 Clayton Rd., PMB 325, Richmond Heights MO 63117. (314)862-2643. Fax: (314)862-2982. E-mail: ballymon@hotmail.com. Web site: www.richardburgin.com. **Contact:** Richard Burgin, editor. Magazine: 5½×8½; 150-250 pages; excellent paper; high-quality cover stock; illustrations; photos. "*Boulevard* is a diverse literary magazine presenting original creative work by well-known authors, as well as by writers of exciting promise." Triannual. Estab. 1985. Circ. 11,000.

Needs Confessions, experimental, literary, mainstream, novel excerpts. "We do not want erotica, science fiction, romance, western or children's stories." Receives over 600 unsolicited mss/month. Accepts about 10 mss/issue. Does not accept manuscripts between May 1 and October 1. Publishes ms 9 months after acceptance.

Agented fiction $^{1}/_{3}$-$^{1}/_{4}$%. **Publishes 10 new writers/year.** Recently published work by Joyce Carol Oates, Floyd Skloot, Alice Hoffman, Stephen Dixon and Frederick Busch. Length: 9,000 words maximum; average length: 5,000 words. Publishes short shorts. Also publishes literary essays, literary criticism, poetry. Sometimes comments on rejected mss.

How to Contact Send complete ms. Accepts submissions on disk. SASE for reply. Responds in 2 weeks to queries; 3 months to mss. Accepts multiple submissions. No simultaneous submissions. Sample copy for $8. Writer's guidelines online.

Payment/Terms Pays $50-700. Pays on publication for first North American serial rights.

Advice "We pick the stories that move us the most emotionally, stimulate us the most intellectually, are the best written and thought out. Don't write to get published—write to express your experience and vision of the world."

🅽 ⬙ ◎ BRANCHWOOD JOURNAL: A CHRISTIAN LITERARY MAGAZINE

Branchwood Christian Literary Project, Inc., P.O. Box 755, Versailles KY 40383. (859)879-9152. E-mail: editor@b ranchwood.org. Web site: http://branchwood.org. **Contact:** Danna Estridge, editor. Literary magazine/journal. $8^{1}/_{2}\times11$, 24 lb. white paper, 43 lb. color glossy cover. Contains illustrations. Includes photographs. "*Branchwood Journal* publishes fiction, creative nonfiction, poetry, essays and art (photos) with a Christian worldview/ philosophy. Nothing 'preachy' and nothing that espouses one denomination over another. Our publication is unique because it is Christian and nondenominational. Encourages new writers and artists." Semiannual. Estab. Jan 2005. Circ. 200.

Needs Religious (general, inspirational, fantasy, mystery/suspense, thriller, romance). Special interests: Must be Christian. Does not want horror, erotica. Receives 10-15 mss/month. Accepts 5-7 mss/issue; 10-14 mss/ year. Manuscript published 6-8 months after acceptance. Agented fiction 0%. **Publishes 5-7 new writers/year.** Published Bryan Auxier, Caleb Brooks (debut), Ballard Hitchcock (debut), Charles Semones, Susan Christerson Brown, Ronald Lands (debut), Beth Dotson Brown, Connie Coppings. Length: 500 words (min)-5,000 words (max). Average length: 1,500 words. Publishes short shorts. Average length of short shorts: 1,000 words. Also publishes literary essays, poetry. Often comments on/critiques rejected manuscripts.

How to Contact Send complete ms with cover letter or e-mail query. Include estimated word count, brief bio, list of publications. Responds to queries in 1-3 months; to mss in 1-3 months. Send disposable copy of ms and #10 SASE for reply only. Considers previously published submissions, multiple submissions. Sample copy available for $4. Guidelines available for SASE, via e-mail, on Web site.

Payment and Terms Writers receive 2 contributors copies. Additional copies $4. Pays on publication. Acquires first North American serial rights, one-time rights. Publication is copyrighted.

Advice "Wants well written, strong character development, well-defined central theme that reflects a Christian worldview or expands Christian or Biblical themes or ethics. Christian themes should be universal, not denominational." Will only accept submissions by e-mail if pasted within the body of the message; NO ATTACHMENTS. To break in here, "write, rewrite, revise, check spelling and punctuation. Make your manuscript as good as it can be before you submit it to us for consideration. The little things *do* count!"

⬙ THE BRIAR CLIFF REVIEW

Briar Cliff University, 3303 Rebecca St., Sioux City IA 51104-0100. (712)279-5477. E-mail: curranst@briarcliff.e du. Web site: www.briarcliff.edu/bcreview. **Contact:** Phil Hey or Tricia Currans-Sheehan, fiction editors. Magazine: $8^{1}/_{2}\times11$; 88 pages; 70 lb. Finch Opaque cover stock; illustrations; photos. "*The Briar Cliff Review* is an eclectic literary and cultural magazine focusing on (but not limited to) Siouxland writers and subjects. We are happy to proclaim ourselves a regional publication. It doesn't diminish us; it enhances us." Annual. Estab. 1989. Circ. 750.

Needs Ethnic/multicultural, feminist, historical, humor/satire, literary, mainstream, regional. "No romance, horror or alien stories. Accepts 5 mss/year. Reads mss only between August 1 and November 1. Publishes ms 3-4 months after acceptance. **Publishes 10-14 new writers/year.** Recently published work by Jenna Blum, Brian Bedard, Constance Squires, Andrew Schultz, Paul Crenshaw and Josip Novakovich. Length: 2,500-5,000 words; average length: 3,000 words. Also publishes literary essays, literary criticism, poetry. Sometimes comments on rejected mss.

How to Contact Send SASE for return of ms. Does not accept electronic submissions (unless from overseas). Responds in 4-5 months to mss. Accepts simultaneous submissions. Sample copy for $12 and 9×12 SAE. Writer's guidelines for #10 SASE. Reviews fiction.

Payment/Terms Pays 2 contributor's copies; additional copies available for $9. Acquires first rights.

Advice "So many stories are just telling. We want some action. It has to move. We prefer stories in which there is no gimmick, no mechanical turn of events, no moral except the one we would draw privately."

◐ ◎ BRILLANT CORNERS, A Journal of Jazz & Literature

Lycoming College, Williamsport PA 17701. (570)321-4279. Fax: (570)321-4090. E-mail: feinstein@lycoming.e du. **Contact:** Sascha Feinstein, editor. Journal: 6×9; 100 pages; 70 lb. Cougar opaque, vellum, natural paper; photographs. "We publish jazz-related literature—fiction, poetry and nonfiction." Semiannual. Estab. 1996. Circ. 1,200.

Needs Condensed novels, ethnic/multicultural, experimental, literary, mainstream, romance (contemporary). Receives 10-15 unsolicited mss/month. Accepts 1-2 mss/issue; 2-3 mss/year. Does not read mss May 15-September 1. Publishes ms 4-12 months after acceptance. Publishes short shorts. Also publishes literary essays, literary criticism, poetry. Rarely comments on rejected mss.

How to Contact SASE for return of ms or send a disposable copy of ms. Accepts unpublished work only. Responds in 2 weeks to queries; 1-2 months to mss. Sample copy for $7. Reviews fiction.

Payment/Terms Acquires first North American serial rights. Sends galleys to author when possible.

Advice "We look for clear, moving prose that demostrates a love of both writing and jazz. We primarily publish established writers, but we read all submissions carefully and welcome work by outstanding young writers."

Ⓝ ◐ BROKEN BRIDGE REVIEW, The Best New Work By Emerging Writers

Pomfret School, 398 Pomfret St., Pomfret CT 06258-0128. (860)963-5220. E-mail: eds@brokenbridge.us. Web site: www.brokenbridge.us. **Contact:** Brad Davis, editor. Literary magazine/journal: 6×9, 200 pages, matte color cover. "Neither for beginners nor A-list writers; think 'on the cusp'. A journal of interest for new writers, college and MFA writers, established writers—with an eye for the best new work by emerging writers." Annual. Estab. 2006.

Needs Experimental, literary, mainstream, regional. Does not read December-August. Manuscript published 10 months after acceptance. Length: 1,000 words (min)-4,000 words (max). Average length: 3,000 words. Publishes short shorts. Also publishes poetry. Never comments on/critiques rejected manuscripts.

How to Contact Send complete ms with cover letter. Include estimated word count, brief bio, list of publications, e-mail address and (if any) private school connection. Responds to mss in 1-3 months. Send disposable copy of ms. Replies by e-mail. Sample copy available for $10. Guidelines available via e-mail, on Web site.

Payment and Terms Writers receive 2 contributors copies. Additional copies $10. Pays on publication. Acquires one-time rights. Sends galleys to author.

◐ BRYANT LITERARY REVIEW

Bryant University, 1150 Douglas Pike, Faculty Suite F, Smithfield RI 02917. (401)232-6802. Fax: (401)232-6270. E-mail: blr@bryant.edu. Web site: http://web.bryant.edu/~blr. **Contact:** M.J. Kim. Magazine: 6×9; 125 pages; photos. Annual. Estab. 2000. Circ. 2,400. CLMP.

Needs Adventure, ethnic/multicultural, experimental, family saga, fantasy, feminist, historical, humor/satire, literary, mainstream, military/war, mystery/suspense, New Age, psychic/supernatural/occult, regional, science fiction, thriller/espionage, translations, western. "No novellas or serialized novels; only short stories." Receives 100 unsolicited mss/month. Accepts approx. 7 mss/issue. Does not read January through August. Publishes ms 4-5 months after acceptance. **Publishes 1-2 new writers/year.** Recently published work by Lyzette Wanzer, K.S. Phillips, Richard N. Bentley. Publishes short shorts. Also publishes poetry.

How to Contact Send a disposable copy of ms and #10 SASE for reply only. Responds in 2 weeks to queries; 12 weeks to mss. No simultaneous submissions. Sample copy for $8. Writer's guidelines by email or on Web site.

Payment/Terms Pays 2 contributor's copies; additional copies $8. Pays on publication.

Ⓝ ◐ BUTTON, New England's Tiniest Magazine of Poetry, Fiction and Gracious Living

P.O. Box 77, Westminster, MA 014 73. Web site: www.moonsigns.net. **Contact:** W.M. Davies, fiction editor. Magazine: 4×5; 34 pages; bond paper; color cardstock cover; illustrations; photos. "*Button* is New England's tiniest magazine of poetry, fiction and gracious living, published once a year. As 'gracious living' is on the cover, we like wit, brevity, cleverly-conceived essay/recipe, poetry that isn't sentimental or song lyrics. I started *Button* so that a century from now, when people read it in landfils or, preferably, libraries, they'll say, 'Gee, what a great time to have lived. I wish I lived back then.'" Annual. Estab. 1993. Circ. 1,500.

Needs Literary. "No genre fiction, science fiction, techno-thriller." Wants more of "anything Herman Melville, Henry James or Betty MacDonald would like to read." Receives 20-40 unsolicited mss/month. Accepts 1-2 mss/issue; 3-5 mss/year. Publishes ms 3-9 months after acceptance. Recently published work by Ralph Lombreglia, John Hanson Mitchell, They Might Be Giants and Lawrence Millman. Also publishes literary essays, poetry. Sometimes comments on rejected mss.

How to Contact Send complete ms with bio, list of publications and explain how you found magazine. Include SASE. Responds in 1 month to queries; 2 months to mss. Sample copy for $2.50 and one 39¢ stamp. Writer's guidelines for #10 SASE. Reviews fiction.

Payment/Terms Honorium, subscription and copies. Pays on publication for first North American serial rights.
Advice "What makes a manuscript stand out? Flannery O'Connor once said, 'Don't get subtle till the fourth page,' and I agree. We look for interesting, sympathetic, believable characters and careful setting. I'm really tired of stories that start strong then devolve into dialogue uninterrupted by further exposition. Also, no stories from a mad person's POV unless it's really tricky and skillful. Advice to prospective writers: Continue to read at least 10 times as much as you write. Read the best, and read intelligent criticism if you can find it. *No beginners please.* Please don't submit more than once a year; it's more important that you work on your craft rather than machine-gunning publications with samples, and don't submit more than 3 poems in a batch (this advice goes for other places, you'll find)."

$⬛ BYLINE

P.O. Box 5240, Edmond OK 73083-5240. (405)348-5591. E-mail: mpreston@bylinemag.com. Web site: www.bylinemag.com. **Contact:** Marcia Preston, fiction editor. Magazine "aimed at encouraging and motivating all writers toward success, with special information to help new writers. Articles center on how to write better, market smarter, sell your work." Monthly. Estab. 1981.
Needs Literary, genre, general fiction. "Does not want to see erotica or explicit graphic content. No science fiction or fantasy." Receives 100-200 unsolicited mss/month. Accepts 1 mss/issue; 11 mss/year. Publishes ms 3 months after acceptance. **Publishes many new writers/year.** Recently published work by Ami Elizabeth Reeves, David Dumitru, William Eisner. Also publishes poetry.
How to Contact No cover letter needed. Responds in 6-12 weeks to mss. Accepts simultaneous submissions "if notified." Writer's guidelines for #10 SASE or online.
Payment/Terms Pays $100 and 3 contributor's copies. Pays on acceptance for first North American serial rights.
Advice "We look for good writing that draws the reader in; conflict and character movement by story's end. We're very open to new writers. Submit a well-written, professionally prepared ms with SASE. No erotica or senseless violence; otherwise, we'll consider most any theme. We also sponsor short story and poetry contests. Read what's being published. Find a good story, not just a narrative reflection. Keep submitting."

⬛ ⬛ CAIRN

St. Andrews College Press, 1700 Dogwood Mile, Laurinburg NC 28352. (910)277-5310. Fax: (910)277-5020. E-mail: pressemail@sapc.edu. Web site: www.sapc.edu/sapress.html. **Contact:** Fiction Editor. Magazine: 50-60 lb. paper. "*Cairn* is a nonprofit, student-run literary magazine which seeks to publish established writers and talented students together." Estab. 1969. Member CLMP and AWP.
Needs Literary, short stories and short-short fiction. "We're looking for original, imaginative short fiction with style and insight." **Publishes 10-15 new writers/year.**
How to Contact Accepts submissions by e-mail. Send disposable copy of ms with SASE for reply only. Responds in 3-4 months to mss. Accepts simultaneous submissions with notice.
Payment/Terms Pays 3 contributor's copies.

⬛ ⬛ ⬛ CALLALOO, A Journal of African-American and African Diaspora Arts and Letters

Dept. of English, TAMU 4227, Texas A&M University, College Station TX 77843-4227. (979)458-3108. Fax: (979)458-3275. E-mail: callaloo@tamu.edu. Web site: http://callaloo.tamu.edu/callaloohome.htm. **Contact:** Charles H. Rowell, editor. Magazine: 7×10; 250 pages. "Devoted to publishing fiction, poetry, drama of the African diaspora, including North, Central and South America, the Caribbean, Europe and Africa. Visually beautiful and well edited, the journal publishes 3-5 short stories in all forms and styles in each issue." Quarterly. Estab. 1976. Circ. 2,000.

- One of the leading voices in African-American literature, *Callaloo* has recieved NEA literature grants. Several pieces every year are chosen for collections of the year's best stories, such as *Beacon's Best*. John Wideman's "Weight" from *Callaloo* won the 2000 O. Henry Award.

Needs Ethnic/multicultural (black culture), feminist, historical, humor/satire, literary, regional, science fiction, serialized novels, translations, contemporary, prose poem. "No romance, confessional. Would like to see more experimental fiction, science fiction and well-crafted literary fiction particularly dealing with the black middle class, immigrant communities and/or the black South." Accepts 3-5 mss/issue; 10-20 mss/year. **Publishes 5-10 new writers/year.** Recently published work by Charles Johnson, Edwidge Danticat, Thomas Glave, Nallo Hopkinson, John Edgar Wideman, Jamaica Kincaid, Percival Everett and Patricia Powell. Also publishes poetry.
How to Contact Generally accepts unpublished work, rarely accepts reprints. Responds in 2 weeks to queries; 6 months to mss. Accepts multiple submissions. Sample copy for $12. Writer's guidelines online.
Payment/Terms Pays in contributor's copies. Aquires some rights. Sends galleys to author.
Advice "We look for freshness of both writing and plot, strength of characterization, plausibilty of plot. Read what's being written and published, especially in journals such as *Callaloo*."

☑ ◎ CALYX, A Journal of Art & Literature by Women

Calyx, Inc., P.O. Box B, Corvallis OR 97339. (541)753-9384. Fax: (541)753-0515. E-mail: calyx@proaxis.com. Web site: www.proaxis.com/~calyx. **Contact:** Editor. Magazine: 6×8; 128 pages per single issue; 60 lb. coated matte stock paper; 10 pt. chrome coat cover; original art. Publishes prose, poetry, art, essays, interviews and critical and review articles. "*Calyx* exists to publish fine literature and art by women and is committed to publishing the work of all women, including women of color, older women, working class women and other voices that need to be heard. We are committed to discovering and nurturing beginning writers." Biannual. Estab. 1976. Circ. 6,000.

Needs Receives approximately 1,000 unsolicited prose and poetry mss when open. Accepts 4-8 prose mss/issue; 9-15 mss/year. Reads mss October 1-December 31; submit only during this period. Mss received when not reading will be returned. Publishes ms 4-12 months after acceptance. **Publishes 10-20 new writers/year.** Recently published work by M. Evelina Galang, Chitrita Banerji, Diana Ma, Catherine Brady. Also publishes literary essays, literary criticism, poetry.

How to Contact Responds in 4-12 months to mss. Accepts simultaneous submissions. Sample copy for $9.50 plus $3 postage. Include SASE. Reviews fiction.

Payment/Terms "Combination of free issues and 1 volume subscription.

Advice Most mss are rejected because "The writers are not familiar with *Calyx*. Writers should read *Calyx* and be familar with the publication. We look for good writing, imagination and important/interesting subject matter."

$ ☷ ☑ THE CAPILANO REVIEW

2055 Purcell Way, North Vancouver BC V7J 3H5 Canada. Web site: www.capcollege.bc.ca/thecapilanoreview. Magazine: 6×9; 90-120 pages; book paper; glossy cover; perfect-bound; visual art. "Triannual visual and literary arts magazine that publishes only what the editors consider to be the very best fiction, poetry, drama, or visual art being produced. *TCR* editors are interested in fresh, original work that stimulates and challenges readers. Over the years, the magazine has developed a reputation for pushing beyond the boundaries of traditional art and writing. We are interested in work that is new in concept and in execution." Estab. 1972. Circ. 900.

Needs "No traditional, conventional fiction. Want to see more innovative, genre-blurring work." Receives 80 unsolicited mss/month. Accepts 1 mss/issue; 3-5 mss/year. Publishes ms 2-4 months after acceptance. **Publishes some new writers/year.** Recently published work by Michael Turner, Lewis Buzbee, George Bowering. Also publishes literary essays, poetry.

How to Contact Include 2- to 3-sentence bio and brief list of publications. Send Canadian SASE or IRCs for reply. Responds in 1 month to queries; 4 months to mss. No simultaneous submissions. Sample copy for $9. Writer's guidelines for #10 SASE with IRC or Canadian stamps or online.

Payment/Terms Pays $50-200. Pays on publication for first North American serial rights.

Advice "Do not send conventional realist fiction. Read the magazine before submitting and ensure your work is technically perfect."

⊞ ◎ ☘ THE CARIBBEAN WRITER

The University of the Virgin Islands, RR 02, Box 10,000-Kinghill, St. Croix 00850 Virgin Islands. (340)692-4152. Fax: (340)692-4026. E-mail: qmars@uvi.edu. Web site: www.TheCaribbeanWriter.com. **Contact:** Quilin B. Mars, managing editor. Magazine: 6×9; 304 pages; 60 lb. paper; glossy cover stock; illustrations; photos. "*The Caribbean Writer* is an international magazine with a Caribbean focus. The Caribbean should be central to the work, or the work should reflect a Caribbean heritage, experience or perspective." Annual. Estab. 1987. Circ. 1,500.

● Work published in *The Caribbean Writer* has received two Pushcart Prizes and Quenepon Award.

Needs Historical (general), humor/satire, literary, mainstream, translations, contemporary and prose poem. Receives 65 unsolicited mss/month. Accepts 60 mss/issue. **Publishes approximately 20% new writers/year.** Recently published work by Cecil Gray, Virgil Suarez and Opal Palmer Adisa. Also publishes literary essays, poetry.

How to Contact Accepts submissions by e-mail. "Blind submissions only. Send name, address and title of manuscript on separate sheet. Title only on manuscript. Manuscripts will not be returned unless this procedure is followed." Include SASE (or IRC). Accepts simultaneous, multiple submissions. Sample copy for $7 and $4 postage.

Payment/Terms Pays 2 contributor's copies. Annual prizes for best story ($400); for best poem ($300); $200 for first time publication; best work by Caribbean Author ($500); best work by Virgin Islands author ($200). Acquires one-time rights.

Advice Looks for "work which reflects a Caribbean heritage, experience or perspective."

CAROLINA QUARTERLY

Greenlaw Hall CB #3520, University of North Carolina, Chapel Hill NC 27599-3520. (919)962-0244. Fax: (919)962-3520. E-mail: cquarter@unc.edu. Web site: www.unc.edu/depts/cqonline. **Contact:** Tessa Joseph, editor-in-chief. Literary journal: 80-100 pages; illustrations. Publishes fiction for a "general literary audience." Triannual. Estab. 1948. Circ. 900-1,000.

  • Work published in *Carolina Quarterly* has been selected for inclusion in *Best American Short Stories* and *New Stories from The South: The Year's Best.*

Needs Literary. "We would like to see more short/micro-fiction and more stories by minority/ethnic writers." Receives 150-200 unsolicited mss/month. Accepts 4-5 mss/issue; 14-16 mss/year. Does not read mss May-August. Publishes ms 4 months after acceptance. **Publishes 5-6 new writers/year.** Recently published work by Pam Durban, Elizabeth Spencer, Brad Vice, Wendy Brenner, Nanci Kincaid. Publishes short shorts. Also publishes literary essays, poetry. Occasionally comments on rejected mss.

How to Contact Responds in 3 months to queries; 6 months to mss. Does not accept e-mail submissions. No simultaneous submissions. Sample copy for $6. Writer's guidelines for SASE.

Payment/Terms Pays in contributor's copies. Acquires first rights.

CENTER, A Journal of the Literary Arts

University of Missouri, 202 Tate Hall, Columbia MO 65211. (573)882-4971. E-mail: cla@missouri.edu. Web site: www.missouri.edu/~center. **Contact:** Fiction editor. Magazine: 6×9; 125-200 pages; perfect bound, with 4-color card cover. *Center*'s goal is to publish the best in literary fiction, poetry and creative nonfiction by previously unpublished and emerging writers, as well as more established writers. Annual. Estab. 2000. Circ. 500.

Needs Ethnic/multicultural, experimental, humor/satire, literary. Receives 30-50 unsolicited mss/month. Accepts 3-5 mss/year. Reads mss from July 1-December 1 only. Publishes ms 6 months after acceptance. **Publishes 25% new writers/year.** Recently published work by Lisa Glatt and Robert Root. Publishes short shorts. Also publishes literary essays, poetry. Sometimes comments on rejected mss.

How to Contact Send SASE (or IRC) for return of ms or send a disposable copy of ms and #10 SASE for reply only. Responds in 1 month to queries; 3-4 months to mss. Accepts simultaneous, multiple submissions. Sample copy for $3, current copy $6. Writer's guidelines for SASE.

Payment/Terms Pays 2 contributor's copy; additional copies $3. Pays on publication for one-time rights.

CHAFFIN JOURNAL

English Department, Eastern Kentucky University, Case Annex 467, Richmond KY 40475-3102. (859)622-3080. E-mail: robert.witt@eku.edu. Web site: www.english.eku.edu/chaffin_journal. **Contact:** Robert Witt, editor. Magazine: 8×5½; 120-130 pages; 70 lb. paper; 80 lb. cover. "We publish fiction on any subject; our only consideration is the quality." Annual. Estab. 1998. Circ. 150.

Needs Ethnic/multicultural, historical, humor/satire, literary, mainstream, regional (Appalachia). "No erotica, fantasy." Receives 20 unsolicited mss/month. Accepts 6-8 mss/year. Does not read mss October 1 through May 31. Publishes ms 6 months after acceptance. **Publishes 2-3 new writers/year.** Recently published work by Meridith Sue Willis, Marie Manilla, Raymond Abbott, Marjorie Bixler, Chris Helvey. Length: 10,000 words; average length: 5,000 words.

How to Contact Send SASE for return of ms. Responds in 1 week to queries; 3 months to mss. Accepts simultaneous, multiple submissions. Sample copy for $6. Writer's guidelines for SASE, by e-mail or online.

Payment/Terms Pays 1 contributor's copy; additional copies $6. Pays on publication for one-time rights.

Advice "All manuscripts submitted are considered."

CHAPMAN

Chapman Publishing, 4 Broughton Place, Edinburgh Scotland EH1 3RX United Kingdom. (+44)131 557 2207. E-mail: chapman-pub@blueyonder.co.uk. Web site: www.chapman-pub.co.uk. **Contact:** Joy Hendry, fiction editor. "*Chapman*, Scotland's quality literary magazine, is a dynamic force in Scotland—publishing poetry; fiction; criticism; reviews; articles on theatre, politics, language and the arts. Our philosophy is to publish new work, from known and unknown writers, mainly Scottish, but also worldwide." Quarterly. Estab. 1970. Circ. 2,000.

Needs Experimental, historical, humor/satire, literary, Scottish/international. "No horror, science fiction." Accepts 4-6 mss/issue. Publishes ms 3 months after acceptance. **Publishes 50 new writers/year.**

How to Contact No simultaneous submissions. Writer's guidelines by e-mail.

Payment/Terms Pays by negotiation. Pays on publication for first rights.

Advice "Keep your stories for six months and edit carefully. We seek challenging work which attempts to explore difficult/new territory in content and form, but lighter work, if original enough, is welcome."

$⊘ THE CHARITON REVIEW

English Dept., Brigham Young University, Provo UT 84602. (660)785-4499. Fax: (660)785-7486. **Contact:** Jim Barnes. Magazine: 6×9; approximately 100 pages; 60 lb. paper; 65 lb. cover stock; photographs on cover. "We demand only excellence in fiction and fiction translation for a general and college readership." Estab. 1975. Circ. 600.

Needs Ethnic/multicultural, experimental, literary, mainstream, novel excerpts (if they can stand alone), translations, traditional. "We are not interested in slick or sick material." Accepts 3-5 mss/issue; 6-10 mss/year. Publishes ms 6 months after acceptance. **Publishes some new writers/year.** Recently published work by Ann Townsend, Glenn DelGrosso, Paul Ruffin, Kenneth Lincoln. Also publishes literary essays, poetry. Sometimes comments on rejected mss.

How to Contact Send complete ms. No book-length mss. Responds in 1 week to queries; 1 month to mss. No simultaneous submissions. Sample copy for $5 and 7x10 SAE with 4 first-class stamps. Reviews fiction.

Payment/Terms Pays $5/page (up to $50). Pays on publication for first North American serial rights.

Advice "Do not ask us for guidelines; the only guidelines are excellence in all matters. Write well and study the publication you are submitting to. We are interested only in the very best fiction and fiction translation. We are not interested in slick material. We do not read photocopies, dot-matrix or carbon copies. Know the simple mechanics of submission—SASE, no paper clips, no odd-sized SASE, etc. Know the genre (short story, novella, etc.). Know the unwritten laws. There is too much manufactured fiction—assembly-lined, ego-centered personal essays offered as fiction."

$⊘ ◪ THE CHATTAHOOCHEE REVIEW

Georgia Perimeter College, 2101 Womack Rd., Dunwoody GA 30338-4497. (770)274-5145. Web site: www.chattahoochee-review.org. **Contact:** Marc Fitten, editor. Magazine: 6×9; 150 pages; 70 lb. paper; 80 lb. cover stock; illustrations; photos. "We publish a number of Southern writers, but *Chattahoochee Review* is not by design a regional magazine. All themes, forms and styles are considered as long as they impact the whole person: heart, mind, intuition and imagination." Quarterly. Estab. 1980. Circ. 1,350.

- Fiction from *The Chattahoochee Review* has been included in *New Stories from The South* and was a 2003 winner of a Governor's Award in Humanities.

Needs "No juvenile, romance, science fiction." Accepts 5 mss/issue. Does not read ms June 1-August 31. Publishes ms 3 months after acceptance. **Publishes 5 new writers/year.** Recently published work by George Singleton, William Gay, Martha Witt, Ignacio Padilla. Length: 6,000 words maximum; average length: 2,500 words. Sometimes comments on rejected mss.

How to Contact Send complete ms with SASE. Responds in 2 weeks to queries; 4 months to mss. Accepts simultaneous submissions. Sample copy for $6. Writer's guidelines online. Reviews fiction.

Payment/Terms Pays $20/page ($250 max) and 2 contributor's copies. Pays on publication for first rights.

Advice "Arrange to read magazine before you submit to it."

CHELSEA

Chelsea Associates, P.O. Box 773 Cooper Station, New York NY 10276-0773. "We stress style, variety, originality. No special biases or requirements. Flexible attitudes, eclectic material. We take an active interest, as always, in cross-cultural exchanges, superior translations, and are leaning toward cosmopolitan, interdisciplinary techniques, but maintain no strictures against traditional modes." Semiannual. Estab. 1958. Circ. 2,200.

Needs Short stories. Publishes ms 6 months after acceptance.

How to Contact Send complete ms. Responds in 3-5 months to mss. Sample copy for $6. Writer's guidelines and contest guidelines available for #10 SASE.

⊘ CHICAGO QUARTERLY REVIEW

Monadnock Group Publishers, 517 Sherman Ave., Evanston IL 60202-2815. (719)633-9794. **Contact:** Syed Afzal Haider, Jane Lawrence and Lisa McKenzie, editors. Magazine: 6×9; 125 pages; illustrations; photos. Annual. Estab. 1994. Circ. 300.

Needs Literary. Receives 20-30 unsolicited mss/month. Accepts 6-8 mss/issue; 8-16 mss/year. Publishes ms 1 year after acceptance. Agented fiction 10%. **Publishes 3 new writers/year.** Length: 5,000 words; average length: 2,500 words. Publishes short shorts. Also publishes literary essays, poetry. Sometimes comments on rejected mss.

How to Contact Send a disposable copy of ms and #10 SASE for reply only. Responds in 2 months to queries; 6 months to mss. Accepts simultaneous submissions. Sample copy for $9.

Payment/Terms Pays 1 contributor's copy; additional copies $9. Pays on publication for one-time rights.

Advice "The writer's voice ought to be clear and unique and should explain something of what it means to be human. We want well-written stories that reflect an appreciation for the rhythm and music of language, work that shows passion and commitment to the art of writing."

⬛ CHICAGO REVIEW

5801 S. Kenwood Ave., Chicago IL 60637. (773)702-0887. E-mail: chicago-review@uchicago.edu. Web site: humanities.uchicago.edu/orgs/review. **Contact:** Joshua Kotin, editor. Magazine for a highly literate general audience: 6×9; 128 pages; offset white 60 lb. paper; illustrations; photos. Quarterly. Estab. 1946. Circ. 3,500.
Needs Experimental, literary, contemporary. Receives 200 unsolicited mss/month. Accepts 2 mss/issue; 8 mss/ year. Recently published work by Harry Mathews, Tom House, Viet Dinh and Doris Dörrie. Also publishes literary essays, literary criticism, poetry.
How to Contact Send complete ms with SASE. Responds in 3-6 months to mss. No simultaneous submissions. Sample copy for $10. Guidelines via Web site or SASE.
Payment/Terms Pays 3 contributor's copies and subscription.
Advice "We look for innovative fiction that avoids cliché."

$ Ⓝ ⬛ ◎ CHRYSALIS READER

1745 Gravel Hill Road, Dillwyn VA 23936. (434)983-3021. E-mail: chrysalis@hovac.com. Web site: www.swede nborg.com. **Contact:** Robert Tucker, fiction editor. Book series: 7½×10; 192 pages; archival paper; coated cover stock; illustrations; photos. "It is very important to send for writer's guidelines and sample copies before submitting. Content of fiction, articles, reviews, poetry, etc., should be directly focused on that issue's theme and directed to the educated, intellectually curious reader." Estab. 1985. Circ. 3,000.
● This journal explores contemporary questions of spirituality from the perspective of Swedenborg theology.
Needs Adventure, experimental, historical, literary, mainstream, mystery/suspense, science fiction, fiction (leading to insight), contemporary, spiritual, sports. No religious works. Upcoming theme: "Other Worlds" (Fall 2007). Receives 50 unsolicited mss/month. Accepts 15-20 mss/issue; 20-40 mss/year. Publishes ms 9 months after acceptance. **Publishes 10 new writers/year.** Recently published work by Robert Bly, Larry Dossey, Dr. Bernie Siegel, Virgil Saurez, Carol Lem, Alan Magee, John Hitchcock. Also publishes literary essays, literary criticism, poetry. Sometimes comments on rejected mss.
How to Contact Query with SASE. Accepts submissions by e-mail. Responds in 1 month to queries; 4 months to mss. No simultaneous submissions. Sample copy for $10 and 8½×11 SAE. Writer's guidelines online.
Payment/Terms Pays $50-150. Pays at page-proof stage. Acquires first rights, makes work-for-hire assignments. Sends galleys to author.
Advice Looking for "1: *Quality*; 2. appeal for our audience; 3. relevance to/illumination of an issue's theme."

⬛ CIMARRON REVIEW

Oklahoma State University, 205 Morrill Hall, Stillwater OK 74078-0135. (405)744-9476. Web site: cimarronrevie w.okstate.edu. **Contact:** Toni Graham, Andrea Koenig, fiction editors. Magazine: 6×9; 110 pages. "Poetry and fiction on contemporary themes; personal essays on contemporary issues that cope with life in the 20th century. We are eager to receive manuscripts from both established and less experienced writers who intrigue us with their unusual perspective, language, imagery and character." Quarterly. Estab. 1967. Circ. 600.
Needs Literary-quality short stories and novel excerpts. No juvenile or genre fiction. Accepts 3-5 mss/issue; 12-15 mss/year. Publishes ms 2-6 months after acceptance. **Publishes 2-4 new writers/year.** Recently published work by Adam Braver, Gary Fincke, Catherine Brady, Nona Caspers, David Ryan. Also publishes literary essays, literary criticism, poetry.
How to Contact Send complete ms with SASE. Responds in 2-6 months to mss. Accepts simultaneous submissions. Sample copy for $7. Reviews fiction.
Payment/Terms Pays 2 contributor's copies plus a year's subscription. Acquires first North American serial rights.
Advice "In order to get a feel for the kind of work we publish, please read an issue or two before submitting."

$ ⬛ THE CINCINNATI REVIEW

P.O. Box 210069, Cincinnati OH 45221-0069. (513)556-3954. E-mail: editors@cincinnatireview.com. Web site: www.cincinnatireview.com. **Contact:** Brock Clarke, fiction editor. Magazine: 6×9; 180-200 pages; 60 lb. white offset paper. "A journal devoted to publishing the best new literary fiction and poetry as well as book reviews, essays and interviews." Semiannual. Estab. 2003.
Needs Literary. Does not want genre fiction. Accepts 13 mss/year. Reads submissions September 1-May 31. Manuscripts arriving during June, July and August will be returned unread.
How to Contact Send complete ms with SASE. Does not consider e-mail submissions. Responds in 2 weeks to queries; 6 weeks to mss. Accepts simultaneous submissions with notice. Sample copy for $9, subscription $15. Writer's guidelines online or send SASE.
Payment/Terms Pays $25/page. Pays on publication for first North American serial, electronic rights. All rights revert to author upon publication.

◪ ◻ ◎ THE CLAREMONT REVIEW, The Contemporary Magazine of Young Adult Writers

The Claremont Review Publishers, 4980 Wesley Rd., Victoria BC V8Y 1Y9 Canada. (250)658-5221. Fax: (250)658-5387. E-mail: editor@theClaremontReview.ca. Web site: www.theClaremontReview.ca. **Contact:** Susan Field (business manager), Susan Stenson, editors. Magazine: 6×9; 110-120 pages; book paper; soft gloss cover; b&w illustrations. "We are dedicated to publishing emerging young writers aged 13-19 from anywhere in the English-speaking world, but primarily Canada and the U.S." Biannual. Estab. 1992. Circ. 700.

Needs Young adult/teen ("their writing, not writing for them"). No science fiction, fanatasy. Receives 20-30 unsolicited mss/month. Accepts 10-12 mss/issue; 20-24 mss/year. Publishes ms 3 months after acceptance. **Publishes 100 new writers/year.** Recently published work by Danielle Hubbard, Kristina Lucas, Taylor McKinnon. Length: 5,000 words; average length: 1,500-3,000 words. Publishes short shorts. Also publishes poetry. Always comments on rejected mss.

How to Contact Responds in 3 months to mss. Accepts multiple submissions. Sample copy for $10.

Payment/Terms Pays 1 contributor's copy. Additional copies for $6. Acquires first North American serial, one-time rights. Sponsors awards/contests.

Advice Looking for "good concrete narratives with credible dialogue and solid use of original detail. It must be unique, honest and a glimpse of some truth. Send an error-free final draft with a short cover letter and bio. Read us first to see what we publish."

Ⓝ ◻ COAL CITY REVIEW

Coal City Press, University of Kansas, Lawrence KS 66045. E-mail: coalcity@sunflower.com. **Contact:** Mary Wharff, fiction editor. Literary magazine/journal: $8\frac{1}{2} \times 5\frac{1}{2}$, 124 pages, heavy cover. Includes photographs. Annual. Estab. 1990. Circ. 200.

Needs Experimental, literary. Does not want erotica, horror, romance, mystery. Receives 10-20 mss/month. Accepts 8-10 mss/issue. Does not read November-March. Manuscript published up to 1 year after acceptance. Agented fiction 0%. **Publishes 5-10 new writers/year.** Published Daniel A. Hoyt, Bill Church, Laurie Martin-Frydman (debut), Tasha Haas, Marc Dickinson (debut), Elspeth Wood. Length: 50 words (min)—4,000 words (max). Average length: 2,000 words. Publishes short shorts. Average length of short shorts: 250 words. Also publishes literary criticism, poetry. Sometimes comments on/critiques rejected manuscripts.

How to Contact Submit via e-mail to coalcity@sunflower.com. Attach Word file. Include estimated word count, brief bio, list of publications. Responds to mss in 4 months. Send disposable copy of ms and #10 SASE for reply only. Considers simultaneous submissions. Sample copy available for $7. Guidelines available via e-mail.

Payment and Terms Writers receive 2 contributors copies. Additional copies $5. Pays on publication. Acquires one-time rights. Publication is copyrighted.

Advice "We are looking for artful stories—with great language and great heart. Please do not send work that has not been thoughtfully and carefully revised or edited."

$◪ COLORADO REVIEW

Center for Literary Publishing, Department of English, Colorado State University, Fort Collins CO 80523. (970)491-5449. E-mail: creview@colostate.edu. Web site: http://coloradoreview.colostate.edu. **Contact:** Stephanie G'Schwind, editor. Literary journal: 224 pages; 60 lb. book weight paper. Estab. 1956. Circ. 1,300.

Needs Ethnic/multicultural, experimental, literary, mainstream, contemporary. "No genre fiction." Receives 600 unsolicited mss/month. Accepts 4-5 mss/issue. Does not read mss May-August. Publishes ms within 1 year after acceptance. Recently published work by Paul Mandelbaum, Ann Hood, Kent Haruf, Kelly Magee, Bret Lott. Also publishes poetry.

How to Contact Send complete ms. Responds in 2 months to mss. Sample copy for $10. Writer's guidelines online. Reviews fiction.

Payment/Terms Pays $5/page plus two contributor's copies. Pays on publication for first North American serial rights. Rights revert to author upon publication. Sends galleys to author.

Advice "We are interested in manuscripts that show craft, imagination and a convincing voice. If a story has reached a level of technical competence, we are receptive to the fiction working on its own terms. The oldest advice is still the best: persistence. Approach every aspect of the writing process with pride, conscientiousness—from word choice to manuscript appearance. Be familiar with the *Colorado Review*; read a couple of issues before submitting your manuscript."

CONCHO RIVER REVIEW

Angelo State University, English Dept., Box 10894 ASU Station, San Angelo TX 76904. (325)942-2269, ext. 230. Fax: (325)942-2208. E-mail: me.hartje@angelo.edu. **Contact:** Charlie McMurtry, fiction editor. Magazine: $6\frac{1}{2} \times 9$; 100-125 pages; 60 lb. Ardor offset paper; Classic Laid Color cover stock; b&w drawings. "We publish any fiction of high quality—no thematic specialties." Semiannual. Estab. 1987. Circ. 300.

Needs Ethnic/multicultural, historical, humor/satire, literary, regional, western. Also publishes poetry, nonfiction, book reviews. "No erotica; no science fiction." Receives 10-15 unsolicited mss/month. Accepts 3-6 mss/ issue; 8-10 mss/year. Publishes ms 4-6 months after acceptance. **Publishes 4 new writers/year.** Recently published work by Gordon Alexander, Riley Froh, Gretchen Geralds, Kimberly Willis Holt. Length: 1,500-5,000 words; average length: 3,500 words.

How to Contact Send disk copy upon acceptance. Responds in 3 weeks to queries. Accepts simultaneous submissions (if noted). Sample copy for $4. Writer's guidelines for #10 SASE. Reviews fiction.

Payment/Terms Pays in contributor's copies; $5 charge for extras. Acquires first rights.

Advice "We prefer a clear sense of conflict, strong characterization and effective dialogue."

$□ ☑ CONFRONTATION, A Literary Journal

Long Island University, Brookville NY 11548. (516)299-2720. Fax: (516)299-2735. **Contact:** Jonna Semeiks. Magazine: 6×9; 250-350 pages; 70 lb. paper; 80 lb. cover; illustrations; photos. "We are eclectic in our taste. Excellence of style is our dominant concern." Semiannual. Estab. 1968. Circ. 2,000.

- *Confrontation* has garnered a long list of awards and honors, including the Editor's Award for Distinguished Achievement from CCLP and NEA grants. Work from the magazine has appeared in numerous anthologies including the *Pushcart Prize*, *Best Short Stories* and *O. Henry Prize Stories*.

Needs Experimental, literary, mainstream, novel excerpts (if they are self-contained stories), regional, slice-of-life vignettes, contemporary, prose poem. "No 'proselytizing' literature or genre fiction." Receives 400 unsolicited mss/month. Accepts 30 mss/issue; 60 mss/year. Does not read June-September. Publishes ms 6 months to 1 year after acceptance. Agented fiction approximately 10-15%. **Publishes 20-30 new writers/year.** Recently published work by Susan Vreeland, Lanford Wilson, Tom Stacey, Elizabeth Swados and Sallie Bingham. Publishes short shorts. Also publishes literary essays, poetry.

How to Contact Send complete ms. Accepts submissions by disk. "Cover letters acceptable, not necessary. We accept simultaneous submissions but do not prefer them." Responds in 3 weeks to queries; 2 months to mss. Sample copy for $3. Writer's guidelines not available. Reviews fiction.

Payment/Terms Pays $25-250. Pays on publication for first North American serial, first, one-time rights.

Advice "We look for literary merit. Keep trying."

☑ ☑ CONNECTICUT REVIEW

Connecticut State University System, 39 Woodland St., Hartford CT 06105-2337. (203)837-9043 for senior editor. Web site: www.connecticutreview.com. **Contact:** John Briggs, senior editor. Magazine: 6×9; 208 pages; white/ heavy paper; glossy/heavy cover; color and b&w illustrations and photos; artwork. "*Connecticut Review* presents a wide range of cultural interests that cross disciplinary lines. We' re looking for the best in literary writing in a variety of genres. Sections of our spring issues are devoted to announced themes. The editors invite the submission of academic articles of general interest, creative essays, translations, short stories, short-shorts, plays, poems and interviews." Semiannual. Estab. 1968. Circ. 2,500. Member CLMP.

* Work published in *Connecticut Review* has won the Pushcart Prize and inclusion in *Best American Poetry*, *Best American Short Stories* (2000). *CR* has also received the Phoenix Award for Significant Editorial Achievement and National Public Radio's Award for Literary Excellence (2001).

Needs Literary. "Content must be under 4,000 words and suitable for circulation to libraries and high schools." Receives 250 unsolicited mss/month. Accepts 40 mss/issue; 80 mss/year. Does not read mss May 15-September 1. Publishes ms 1-2 years after acceptance. **Publishes 15-20 new writers/year.** Has published work by John Searles, Michael Schiavone, Norman German, Tom Williams, Paul Ruffin, Dick Allen.

How to Contact Send two disposable copies of ms and #10 SASE for reply only. Responds in 6 months to queries. Accepts simultaneous submissions. Sample copy for $12. Writer's guidelines for SASE, but forms for submissions and guidelines available on Web site.

Payment/Terms Pays 2 contributor's copies; additional copies $10. Pays on publication for first rights. Rights revert to author on publication. Sends galleys to author.

☒ ☑ CONTROLLED BURN

Kirtland Community College, 10775 N. St. Helen Rd. Roscommon MI 48653. (989)275-5000, ext. 220. E-mail: crockerd@kirtland.edu. **Contact:** Dan Crocker. Literary magazine/journal: 150 pages. Includes photographs. "Our job is to take the best writing we get without regard to style, subject matter or form. We often take things that other college journals might shy away from. Send us the stories that make you laugh, cringe or send a shiver down your spine. We seldom get enough good humor." Annual. Estab. 1995. Circ. 600.

Needs Ethnic/multicultural, experimental, gay, humor/satire, literary, mainstream. Does not want badly written work. Receives 100 mss/month. Accepts 3-5 mss/issue; 3-5 mss/year. Does not read mss December-April. Manuscript published 8 months after acceptance. **Publishes 4-5 new writers/year.** Published Jim Daniels, Dennis Hinrichsen, Stephen Graham Jones, Anneliesa Frank. Length: 100-8,000. Average length: 5,000. Publishes short shorts. Average length of short shorts: 500. Also publishes poetry. Sometimes comments on/critiques rejected manuscripts.

How to Contact Send complete ms with cover letter. Include brief bio, list of publications. Responds to queries in 4-6 weeks. Responds to mss in 4-6 weeks. Send disposable copy of ms and #10 SASE for reply only. Considers previously published submissions, multiple submissions. Sample copy available for $3. Guidelines available for SASE.

Payment and Terms Writers receive 2 contributors copies. Pays on publication. Acquires one-time rights.

Advice "Don't be afraid of anything. We take a wide variety of fiction and we like it to be bold. We have no bias against touchy subject matter, humor or anything. Excellence is our only criteria."

◙ COTTONWOOD

Box J, 400 Kansas Union, University of Kansas, Lawrence KS 66045-2115. (785)864-2516. Fax: (785)864-4298. E-mail: tlorenz@ku.edu. **Contact:** Tom Lorenz, fiction editor. Magazine: 6×9; 100 pages; illustrations; photos. "*Cottonwood* publishes high quality prose, poetry and artwork and is aimed at an audience that appreciates the same. We have a national scope and reputation while maintaining a strong regional flavor." Semiannual. Estab. 1965. Circ. 500.

Needs "We publish literary prose and poetry." Receives 25-50 unsolicited mss/month. Accepts 5-6 mss/issue; 10-12 mss/year. Publishes ms 6-18 months after acceptance. Agented fiction 10%. **Publishes 1-3 new writers/year.** Recently published work by Connie May Fowler, Oakley Hall, Cris Mazza. Length: 1,000-8,000 words; average length: 2,000-5,000 words. Publishes short shorts. Also publishes literary essays, literary criticism, poetry.

How to Contact SASE for return of ms. Responds in 6 months to mss. Accepts simultaneous submissions. Sample copy for $8.50, 9×12 SAE and $1.90. Reviews fiction.

Payment/Terms Acquires one-time rights.

Advice "We're looking for depth and/or originality of subject matter, engaging voice and style, emotional honesty, command of the material and the structure. *Cottonwood* publishes high quality literary fiction, but we are very open to the work of talented new writers. Write something honest and that you care about and write it as well as you can. Don't hesitate to keep trying us. We sometimes take a piece from a writer we've rejected a number of times. We generally don't like clever, gimmicky writing. The style should be engaging but not claim all the the attention itself."

$◙ ⊠ CRAB ORCHARD REVIEW, A Journal of Creative Works

Dept. of English, Faner Hall 2380-Mail Code 4503, Southern Illinois University Carbondale, 1000 Faner Dr., Carbondale IL 62901-4503. (618)453-6833. Fax: (618)453-8224. Web site: www.siu.edu/~crborchd. **Contact:** Jon Tribble, managing editor. Magazine: 5½×8½; 275 pages; 55 lb. recycled paper, card cover; photo on cover. "We are a general interest literary journal published twice/year. We strive to be a journal that writers admire and readers enjoy. We publish fiction, poetry, creative nonfiction, fiction translations, interviews and reviews." Estab. 1995. Circ. 2,500.

• *Crab Orchard Review* has won Illinois Arts Council Literary Awards and a 2005 Program Grant from the Illinois Arts Council.

Needs Ethnic/multicultural, literary, translations, excerpted novel. No science fiction, romance, western, horror, gothic or children's. Wants more novel excerpts that also stand alone as pieces. List of upcoming themes available on Web site. Receives 800 unsolicited mss/month. Accepts 15-20 mss/issue; 20-40 mss/year. Reads during summer only for special issues. Publishes ms 9-12 months after acceptance. Agented fiction 1%. **Publishes 2 new writers/year.** Recently published work by Sefi Atta, Danit Brown, Paula Nangle, Linda Manheim. Length: 1,000-6,500 words; average length: 2,500 words. Also publishes literary essays, poetry. Rarely comments on rejected mss.

How to Contact Send SASE for reply, return of ms. Responds in 3 weeks to queries; 9 months to mss. Accepts simultaneous submissions. Sample copy for $8. Writer's guidelines for #10 SASE.

Payment/Terms Pays $100 minimum; $20/page maximum, 2 contributor's copies and a year subscription. Acquires first North American serial rights.

Advice "We look for well-written, provocative, fully realized fiction that seeks to engage both the reader's senses and intellect. Don't submit too often to the same market, and don't send manuscripts that you haven't read over carefully. Writers can't rely on spell checkers to catch all errors. Always include a SASE. Read and support the journals you admire so they can continue to survive."

$ CRAZYHORSE

College of Charleston, Dept. of English, 66 George St., Charleston SC 29424. (843)953-7740. E-mail: crazyhorse@cofc.edu. Web site: http://crazyhorse.cofc.edu. **Contact:** Anthony Varallo, fiction editor. Literary magazine: 8¾×8¼; 150 pages; illustrations; photos. "*Crazyhorse* publishes writing of fine quality regardless of style, predilection, subject. Editors are especially interested in original writing that engages in the work of honest communication.'' Raymond Carver called *Crazyhorse* ''an indispensable literary magazine of the first order.'' Semiannual. Estab. 1961. Circ. 2,000.

- Richard Jackson's ''This'' won a 2004 Pushcart Award for *Crazyhorse*.

Needs All fiction of fine quality. Receives 200 unsolicited mss/month. Accepts 8-10 mss/issue; 16-20 mss/year. Publishes ms 6-12 months after acceptance. Recently published work by W.D. Wetherell, T.M. McNally, Lia Purpura, Elizabeth Weld, Steven Schwarz. Length: 25 pages; average length: 15 pages. Publishes short shorts. Also publishes literary essays, poetry.

How to Contact Send SASE for return of ms or disposable copy of ms and #10 SASE for reply only. Responds in 1 week to queries; 3 months to mss. Accepts simultaneous submissions. Sample copy for $5. Writer's guidelines for SASE or by e-mail.

Payment/Terms Pays $20 per page and 2 contributor's copies; additional copies $5. Acquires first North American serial rights. Sends galleys to author.

Advice ''Write to explore subjects you care about. Clarity of language; subject is one in which something is at stake.''

ᴺ ◑ THE CREAM CITY REVIEW

University of Wisconsin-Milwaukee, Box 413, Milwaukee WI 53201. (414)229-4708. E-mail: tccr@uwm.edu. Web site: www.uwm.edu/dept/english/ccr. **Contact:** Bayard Godsave and Suzanne Heagy, fiction editors. Magazine: 5½×8½; 150-300 pages; 70 lb. offset/perfect bound paper; 80 lb. cover stock; illustrations; photos. ''General literary publication—an eclectic and electric selection of the best fiction we can find.'' Semiannual. Estab. 1975. Circ. 2,000.

Needs Ethnic/multicultural, experimental, literary, regional, translations, flash fiction, literary humor, magical realism, prose poem. ''Would like to see more quality fiction. No horror, formulaic, racist, sexist, pornographic, homophobic, science fiction, romance.'' Receives 300 unsolicited mss/month. Accepts 6-10 mss/issue. Does not read fiction or poetry April-September. **Publishes 10 new writers/year.** Recently published work by Stuart Dybek, Laurence Goldstein, Harold Jaffe, Bradford Morrow, Gordon Weaver, Gordon Henry, Louis Owens, Arthur Boozhoo, George Makana Clark, Kyoko Mori. Publishes short shorts. Also publishes literary essays, literary criticism, poetry, memoir.

How to Contact Responds in 6 months to mss. Accepts simultaneous, multiple submissions. Sample copy for $7 (back issue), $12 (current issue). Reviews fiction.

Payment/Terms Pays 1-year subscription. Acquires first rights. Rights revert to author after publication. Sponsors awards/contests.

Advice ''The best stories are those in which the reader doesn't know what is going to happen or what the writer is trying to do. Avoid formulas. Surprise us with language and stunning characters.''

◑ CRUCIBLE

English Dept., Barton College, College Station, Wilson NC 27893. (252)399-6343. Editor: Terrence L. Grimes. **Contact:** Fiction Editor. Magazine of fiction and poetry for a general, literary audience. Annual. Estab. 1964. Circ. 500.

Needs Ethnic/multicultural, experimental, feminist, literary, regional. Would like to see more short shorts. Receives 20 unsolicited mss/month. Accepts 5-6 mss/year. Does not normally read mss from April 30 to December 1. Publishes ms 4-5 months after acceptance. **Publishes 5 new writers/year.** Recently published work by Sally Buckner.

How to Contact Send 3 complete copies of ms unsigned with cover letter which should include a brief biography, ''in case we publish.'' Responds in 6 weeks to queries; 4 months to mss. Sample copy for $7. Writer's guidelines free.

Payment/Terms Pays in contributor's copies. Acquires first rights.

Advice ''Write about what you know. Experimentation is fine as long as the experiences portrayed come across as authentic, that is to say, plausible.''

◑ Ⓥ DESCANT, Ft. Worth's Journal of Fiction and Poetry

Texas Christian University, TCU Box 297270, Ft. Worth TX 76129. (817)257-6537. Fax: (817)257-6239. E-mail: descant@tcu.edu. Web site: www.descant.tcu.edu. **Contact:** Dave Kuhne, editor. Magazine: 6×9; 120-150 pages; acid free paper; paper cover. ''*descant* seeks high quality poems and stories in both traditional and innovative form.'' Annual. Estab. 1956. Circ. 500-750. Member CLMP.

- Offers four cash awards: The $500 Frank O'Connor Award for the best story in an issue; the $250 Gary Wilson Award for an outstanding story in an issue; the $500 Betsy Colquitt Award for the best poem in an issue; the $250 Baskerville Publishers Award for outstanding poem in an issue. Several stories first published by *descant* have appeared in *Best American Short Stories*.

Literary Magazines

Needs Literary. "No horror, romance, fantasy, erotica." Receives 20-30 unsolicited mss/month. Accepts 25-35 mss/year. Publishes ms 1 year after acceptance. **Publishes 50% new writers/year.** Recently published work by William Harrison, Annette Sanford, Miller Williams, Patricia Chao, Vonesca Stroud, Walt McDonald. Length: 1,000-5,000 words; average length: 2,500 words. Publishes short shorts. Also publishes poetry.

How to Contact Send complete ms with cover letter. Include estimated word count and brief bio. Responds in 6-8 weeks to mss. Accepts simultaneous submissions. Sample copy for $10. Guidelines for SASE, e-mail or fax.

Payment/Terms Pays 2 contributor's copies, additional copies $6. Pays on publication for one-time rights. Sponsors awards/contests.

Advice "We look for character and quality of prose. Send your best short work."

▢ ◎ DESERT VOICES

Palo Verde College, One College Drive, Blythe CA 92225. (760)921-5449. E-mail: aminyard@paloverde.edu. **Contact:** Applewhite Minyard, editor. Magazine: 6×9; 48-60 pages; illustrations; photos. "Our magazine is intended to be a showcase for our college and local/regional writers to express themselves in a creative manner, or for other writers with experiences with our area." Semiannual. Estab. 2003. Circ. 1,500.

Needs Adventure, ethnic/multicultural, feminist, humor/satire, literary, mainstream, regional (desert Southwest), science fiction, western. "No erotica, though sexual/sensual content is acceptable if essential to the story/poem." Receives 10-15 unsolicited mss/month. Accepts 4-5 mss/issue. Does not read during Summer. Publishes ms 6 months after acceptance. **Publishes 5-10 new writers/year.** Average length: 2,000 words. Publishes short shorts. Also publishes literary essays, poetry.

How to Contact Send complete ms. Accepts submissions by e-mail. Include estimated word count. Send SASE (or IRC) for return of ms or disposable copy of ms and #10 SASE for reply only. Responds in 4 weeks to queries; 3 months to mss. Accepts reprints, multiple submissions. Writer's guidelines by e-mail. Reviews fiction.

Payment/Terms Pays 2 contributor's copies on publication for one-time rights. Not copyrighted.

Advice "Write what you feel, write what you know, write what you know you feel, write clearly, write with emotion. Write and you will be heard. We are looking for good quality fiction with a regional theme. Writers should be familiar with life in the desert Southwest, though we are not interested in romanticized westerns. Poetry or artwork should meet generally accepted stylistic considerations, as well as having heart."

▢ DICEY BROWN MAGAZINE, poetry, fiction, photography

Dicey Books, 1226 Old US 421, Lillington NC 27546. E-mail: diceybrown@yahoo.com. Web site: www.diceybrown.com. **Contact:** Karen Ashburner, general editor; Lydia Copeland, fiction editor. Magazine: 8½×5; 50 pages; illustrations; photos. *Dicey Brown* is urban, gritty, raw, funny and heartbreaking. Quarterly. Estab. 2001.

Needs Comics/graphic novels, ethnic/multicultural, feminist, humor/satire, literary. Does not want western, fantasy, sci-fi, children's or religious material. Accepts 10 mss/issue; 40 mss/year. Publishes ms 3 months after acceptance. Agented fiction 1%. **Publishes 30 new writers/year.** Length: 100-2,000 words; average length: 1,500 words. Publishes short shorts. Also publishes poetry. Sometimes comments on rejected mss.

How to Contact Accepts submissions by e-mail. Does not accept submissions by regular mail. Responds in 2 months to mss. Accepts simultaneous, multiple submissions. Sample copy for $3. Writer's guidelines by e-mail.

Payment/Terms Pays on publication for first, electronic rights.

$ ▢ ◎ ▣ DOWNSTATE STORY

1825 Maple Ridge, Peoria IL 61614. (309)688-1409. Web site: www.wiu.edu/users/mfgeh/dss. **Contact:** Elaine Hopkins, editor. Magazine: includes illustrations. "Short fiction—some connection with Illinois or the Midwest." Annual. Estab. 1992. Circ. 250.

● Fiction received the Best of Illinois Stories Award.

Needs Adventure, ethnic/multicultural, experimental, historical, horror, humor/satire, literary, mainstream, mystery/suspense, psychic/supernatural/occult, regional, romance, science fiction, suspense, western. No porn. Accepts 10 mss/issue. Publishes ms 1 year after acceptance. Publishes short shorts. Also publishes literary essays.

How to Contact Send complete ms with a cover letter. SASE for return of ms. Responds "ASAP" to mss. Accepts simultaneous submissions. Sample copy for $8. Writer's guidelines online.

Payment/Terms Pays $50. Pays on acceptance for first rights.

▢ ECLIPSE, A Literary Journal

Glendale College, 1500 N. Verdugo Rd., Glendale CA 91208. (818)240-1000. Fax: (818)549-9436. E-mail: eclipse@glendale.edu. **Contact:** Michael Ritterbrown, fiction editor. Magazine: 8½×5½; 150-200 pages; 60 lb. paper. "*Eclipse* is committed to publishing outstanding fiction and poetry. We look for compelling characters and stories executed in ways that provoke our readers and allow them to understand the world in new ways." Annual. Circ. 1,800. CLMP.

Needs Ethnic/multicultural, experimental, literary. "Does not want horror, religious, science fiction or thriller mss." Receives 50-100 unsolicited mss/month. Accepts 10 mss/year. Publishes ms 6-12 months after acceptance. **Publishes 5 new writers/year.** Recently published work by Amy Sage Webb, Ira Sukrungruang, Richard Schmitt, George Rabasa. Length: 6,000 words; average length: 4,000 words. Publishes short shorts. Also publishes poetry. Sometimes comments on rejected mss.

How to Contact Send complete ms. Responds in 2 weeks to queries; 4-6 weeks to mss. Accepts simultaneous submissions. Sample copy for $6. Writer's guidelines for #10 SASE or by e-mail.

Payment/Terms Pays 2 contributor's copies; additional copies $4. Pays on publication for first North American serial rights.

Advice "We look for well-crafted fiction, experimental or traditional, with a clear unity of elements. A good story is important, but the writing must transcend the simple act of conveying the story."

ECOTONE, REIMAGINING PLACE

UNCW Dept. of Creative Writing, 601 South College Road, Wilmington NC 28403-3297. E-mail: ecotone@uncw.edu. Web site: www.uncw.edu/ecotone. **Contact:** David Gessner, editor in chief. Literary magazine/journal: 6×9. "Our magazine is focused on the writing of place and borders, be them geographical, international, sexual, spiritual, etc." Semiannual. Estab. 2005. Circ. 1,500.

Needs Ethnic/multicultural, experimental, historical, literary, mainstream. Does not want genre (fantasy, horror, sci-fi, etc.) or young adult fiction. Upcoming theme: humor- 2007-2008. Receives 30-40 mss/month. Accepts 3-4 mss/issue; 6-8 mss/year. Does not read mss May 1-August 14. Manuscript published 3-4 months after acceptance. **Publishes 5-10 new writers/year.** Published Alicia Erian, Luis Alberto Urrea, Brad Land, Paul Lisicky. Length: 2,000 words (min)-6,000 words (max). Average length: 4,500 words. Also publishes literary essays, poetry.

How to Contact Send complete ms with cover letter. Include brief bio, list of publications. Send either SASE (or IRC) for return of ms or disposable copy of ms and #10 SASE for reply only. Considers multiple submissions. Sample copy available for $10. Guidelines available for SASE, via e-mail, on Web site.

Payment and Terms Writers receive 2 contributors copies. Additional copies $5. Pays on publication. Acquires first North American serial rights. Sends galleys to author. Publication is copyrighted.

THE EDGE CITY REVIEW

Reston Review, Inc., 10912 Harpers Square Court, Reston VA 20191. E-mail: ecreds@earthlink.net. Web site: www.edge-city.com. **Contact:** T.L. Ponick, editor. Magazine: 8½×11; 44-52 pages; 60 lb. paper; 65 lb. color cover. "We publish Formalist poetry, well-plotted artistic or literary fiction, literary essays and book reviews. No left-wing screeds, please." Triannual. Estab. 1994. Circ. 500.

Needs Humor/satire, literary, serialized novels. "We see too much fiction that's riddled with four-letter words and needless vulgarity." Receives 20 unsolicited mss/month. Accepts 1-2 mss/issue; 3-6 mss/year. Publishes ms 6-8 months after acceptance. Length: 1,500-3,000 words; average length: 2,000 words. Also publishes literary essays, literary criticism, poetry. Sometimes comments on rejected mss.

How to Contact Send SASE for reply, return of ms or send a disposable copy of ms. Responds in 1 month to queries; 4-6 months to mss. Sample copy for $6. Reviews fiction.

Payment/Terms Pays 2 contributor's copies; additional copies $5. Acquires first North American serial rights. Sponsors awards/contests.

Advice "We are looking for character-based fiction. Most fiction we receive does not grow out of its characters, but finely wrought characters, fully realized, are what we want to see."

ELLIPSIS MAGAZINE

Westminster College of Salt Lake City, 1840 S. 1300 E., Salt Lake City UT 84105. (801)832-2321. Web site: www.westminstercollege.edu/ellipsis. **Contact:** Stephanie Peterson (revolving editor; changes every year). Magazine: 6×9; 110-120 pages; 60 lb. paper; 15 pt. cover stock; illustrations; photos. *Ellipsis Magazine* needs good literary poetry, fiction, essays, plays and visual art. Annual. Estab. 1967. Circ. 2,000.

Needs Receives 110 unsolicited mss/month. Accepts 4 mss/issue. Does not read mss November 1-July 31. Publishes ms 3 months after acceptance. **Publishes 2 new writers/year.** Length: 6,000 words; average length: 4,000 words. Also publishes poetry. Rarely comments on rejected mss.

How to Contact Send complete ms. Send SASE (or IRC) for return of ms or send disposable copy of the ms and #10 SASE for reply only. Responds in 6 months to mss. Accepts simultaneous submissions. Sample copy for $7.50. Writer's guidelines online.

Payment/Terms Pays $50 per story and one contributor's copy; additional copies $3.50. Pays on publication for first North American serial rights. Not copyrighted.

Advice "Have friends or mentors read your story first and make suggestions to improve it."

⬤ EMRYS JOURNAL

The Emrys Foundation, P.O. Box 8813, Greenville SC 29604. E-mail: ldishman@charter.net. Web site: www.emrys.org. **Contact:** L.B. Dishman. Catalog: $9 \times 9^{3}/_{4}$; 120 pages; 80 lb. paper. "We publish short fiction, poetry and creative nonfiction. We are particularly interested in hearing from women and other minorities." Annual. Estab. 1984. Circ. 400.

Needs Literary, contemporary. No religious, sexually explicit or science fiction mss. Accepts approx 18 mss/issue. Reading period: August 1-November 1. Publishes mss in April. **Publishes several new writers/year.** Recently published work by Jessica Goodfellow and Ron Rash. Length: 5,000 words; average length: 3,500 words. Publishes short shorts.

How to Contact Send complete ms with SASE. Responds after end of reading period. Accepts multiple submissions. Sample copy for $15 and 7×10 SAE with 4 first-class stamps. Writer's guidelines for #10 SASE.

Payment/Terms Pays in contributor's copies. Acquires first rights.

Advice Looks for previously unpublished literary fiction.

$⬤ ▨ EPOCH

251 Goldwin Smith Hall, Cornell University, Ithaca NY 14853. (607)255-3385. Fax: (607)255-6661. **Contact:** Joseph Martin, senior editor. Magazine: 6×9; 128 pages; good quality paper; good cover stock. "Well-written literary fiction, poetry, personal essays. Newcomers always welcome. Open to mainstream and avant-garde writing." Estab. 1947. Circ. 1,000.

- Work originally appearing in this quality literary journal has appeared in numerous anthologies including *Best American Short Stories*, *Best American Poetry*, *Pushcart Prize*, *The O. Henry Prize Stories*, *Best of the West* and *New Stories from the South*.

Needs Ethnic/multicultural, experimental, literary, mainstream, novel excerpts, literary short stories. "No genre fiction. Would like to see more Southern fiction (Southern US)." Receives 500 unsolicited mss/month. Accepts 15-20 mss/issue. Does not read in summer (April 15-September 15). Publishes ms an average of 6 months after acceptance. **Publishes 3-4 new writers/year.** Recently published work by Antonya Nelson, Doris Betts, Heidi Jon Schmidt. Also publishes poetry. Sometimes comments on rejected mss.

How to Contact Send complete ms. Responds in 2 weeks to queries; 6 weeks to mss. No simultaneous submissions. Sample copy for $5. Writer's guidelines for #10 SASE.

Payment/Terms Pays $5 and up/printed page. Pays on publication for first North American serial rights.

Advice "Read the journals you're sending work to."

⬤ EUREKA LITERARY MAGAZINE

300 E. College Ave., Eureka College, Eureka IL 61530-1500. (309)467-6591. E-mail: elm@eureka.edu. **Contact:** Val Perry, editor. Magazine: 6×9; 120 pages; 70 lb. white offset paper; 80 lb. gloss cover; photographs (occasionally). "We seek to be open to the best stories that are submitted to us. Our audience is a combination of professors/writers, students of writing and literature, and general readers." Semiannual. Estab. 1992. Circ. 500.

Needs Adventure, ethnic/multicultural, experimental, fantasy (science), feminist, historical, humor/satire, literary, mainstream, mystery/suspense (private eye/hard-boiled, romantic), psychic/supernatural/occult, regional, romance (historical), science fiction (soft/sociological), translations. Would like to see more "good literary fiction stories, good magic realism, historical fiction. We try to achieve a balance between the traditional and the experimental. We look for the well-crafted story, but essentially any type of story that has depth and substance to it is welcome." Receives 100 unsolicited mss/month. Accepts 10-12 mss/issue; 20-30 mss/year. Does not read mss in summer (May-August). **Publishes 5-6 new writers/year.** Recently published work by Jane Guill, Sally Asher, Ray Bradbury, Earl Coleman, Virgil Suarez, Cynthia Gallaher, Wendell Mayo. Length: 4,000-6,000 words; average length: 5,000 words. Also publishes short shorts, flash fiction and poetry.

How to Contact Accepts submissions by e-mail. Send SASE for reply, return of ms or send disposable copy of ms. Responds in 2 weeks to electronic queries; 4 months to mss. Accepts simultaneous, multiple submissions. Sample copy for $7.50.

Advice "Do something that hasn't been done a thousand times already. Give us unusual characters in unusual conflicts—clear resolution isn't always necessary, but it's nice. We don't hold to hard and fast rules about length, but most stories could do with some cutting. Make sure your title is relevant and eye-catching. Please do not send personal gifts or hate mail. Please try to limit your assumptions about our gender. We're a college-operated magazine, so we do not actually exist in summer. If we don't take a submission, that doesn't automatically mean we don't like it—we try to encourage authors who show promise to revise and resubmit. Order a copy if you can."

🆕 ⬤ EVANSVILLE REVIEW

University of Evansville, 1800 Lincoln Ave., Evansville IN 47722. (812)488-1042. **Contact:** Denis Illige-Saucier, editor. Magazine: 6×9; 180 pages; 70 lb. white paper; glossy full-color cover; perfect bound. Annual. Estab. 1989. Circ. 1,000.

Needs Does not want erotica, fantasy, experimental or children's fiction. "We're open to all creativity. No discrimination. All fiction, screenplays, nonfiction, poetry, interviews and anything in between." List of upcoming themes available for SASE. Receives 70 unsolicited mss/month. Does not read mss January-August. Agented fiction 2%. **Publishes 20 new writers/year.** Recently published work by John Updike, Arthur Miller, X.J. Kennedy, Jim Barnes, Rita Dove. Also publishes literary essays, poetry.

How to Contact Send SASE for reply, or send a disposable copy of ms. Responds in 1 month to queries; 3 months to mss. Accepts simultaneous, multiple submissions and reprints. Sample copy for $5. Writer's guidelines free.

Payment/Terms Pays 2 contributor's copies. Pays on publication for one-time rights. Not copyrighted.

Advice "Because editorial staff rolls over every 1-2 years, the journal always has a new flavor."

◪ FAULTLINE, Journal of Art and Literature

Dept. of English and Comparative Literature, University of California, Irvine, Irvine CA 92697-2650. (949)824-1573. E-mail: faultline@uci.edu. Web site: www.humanities.uci.edu/faultline. **Contact:** Editors change in September each year. Literary magazine: 6×9; 200 pages; illustrations; photos. "We publish the very best of what we recieve. Our interest is quality and literary merit." Annual. Estab. 1992.

Needs Translations, literary fiction, nonfiction up to 20 pages. Receives 150 unsolicited mss/month. Accepts 6-9 mss/year. Does not read mss April-September. Publishes ms 9 months after acceptance. Agented fiction 10-20%. **Publishes 30-40% new writers/year.** Recently published work by Maile Meloy, Aimee Bender, David Benioff, Steve Almond, Helen Maria Viramontes, Thomas Keneally. Publishes short shorts. Also publishes literary essays, poetry.

How to Contact Send SASE for reply, return of ms or send a disposable copy of ms. Responds in 2 weeks to queries; 4 months to mss. Accepts simultaneous submissions. Sample copy for $5. Writer's guidelines for business-size envelope.

Payment/Terms Pays 2 contributor's copies. Pays on publication for one-time rights.

Advice "Our commitment is to publish the best work possible from well-known and emerging authors with vivid and varied voices."

◪ ◎ FEMINIST STUDIES

0103 Taliaferro, University of Maryland, College Park MD 20742-7726. (301)405-7415. Fax: (301)405-8395. E-mail: creative@feministstudies.org. Web site: www.feministstudies.org. **Contact:** Minnie Bruce Pratt, creative writing editor. Magazine: journal-sized; about 200 pages; photographs. "Scholarly manuscripts, fiction, poetry, book review essays for professors, graduate/doctoral students; scholarly interdisciplinary feminist journal." Triannual. Estab. 1974. Circ. 7,500.

Needs Ethnic/multicultural, feminist, LGBT, contemporary. Receives 20 unsolicited mss/month. Accepts 2-3 mss/issue. "We review fiction and poetry twice a year. Deadline dates are May 1 and December 1. Authors will recieve notice of the board's decision by July 15 and February 15, respectively." Recently published work by Paola Corso, Carolyn Pajor, Minnie Bruce Pratt, Stephanie Dickinson, Eloise Klein Healy, Shouhua Qi. Sometimes comments on rejected mss.

How to Contact No simultaneous submissions. Sample copy for $17. Writer's guidelines at Web site.

Payment/Terms Pays 2 contributor's copies and 10 tearsheets.

$ ◪ ▼ FICTION

Department of English, The City College of New York, 138th St. & Convent Ave., New York NY 10031. (212)650-6319. E-mail: fictionmagazine@yahoo.com. Web site: www.fictioninc.com. **Contact:** Mark J. Mirsky, editor. Magazine: 6×9; 150-250 pages; illustrations; occasionally photos. "As the name implies, we publish only fiction; we are looking for the best new writing available, leaning toward the unconventional. *Fiction* has traditionally attempted to make accessible the unaccessible, to bring the experimental to a broader audience." Semiannual. Estab. 1972. Circ. 4,000.

- Stories first published in *Fiction* have been selected for inclusion in the *Pushcart Prize* and *Best of the Small Presses* anthologies.

Needs Experimental, humor/satire (satire), literary, translations, contemporary. No romance, science fiction, etc. Receives 200 unsolicited mss/month. Accepts 12-20 mss/issue; 24-40 mss/year. Reads mss September 15-April 15. Publishes ms 1 year after acceptance. Agented fiction 10-20%. Recently published work by Joyce Carol Oates, Robert Musil, Romulus Linney. Publishes short shorts. Sometimes comments on rejected mss.

How to Contact Send complete ms with cover letter and SASE. No e-mail submissions. Responds in 3 months to mss. Accepts simultaneous submissions. Sample copy for $5. Writer's guidelines online.

Payment/Terms Pays $114. Acquires first rights.

Advice "The guiding principle of *Fiction* has always been to go to *terra incognita* in the writing of the imagination and to ask that modern fiction set itself serious questions, if often in absurd and comical voices, interrogating the nature of the real and the fantastic. It represents no particular school of fiction, except the innovative. Its pages have often been a harbor for writers at odds with each other. As a result of its willingness to publish the difficult, experimental, unusual, while not excluding the well known, *Fiction* has a unique reputation in the U.S. and abroad as a journal of future directions.''

$\boxed{N}$ $\boxed{\$}$ $\boxed{\bowtie}$ $\boxed{\oslash}$ THE FIDDLEHEAD

University of New Brunswick, Campus House, Box 4400, Fredericton NB E3B 5A3 Canada. (506)453-3501. Web site: www.lib.und.ca/texts/fiddlehead. **Contact:** Mark A. Jarman, fiction editor. Magazine: 6×9; 128-160 pages; ink illustrations; photos. ''No criteria for publication except quality. For a general audience, including many poets and writers.'' Quarterly. Estab. 1945. Circ. 1,000.

Needs Literary. Receives 100-150 unsolicited mss/month. Accepts 4-5 mss/issue; 20-40 mss/year. Publishes ms 1 year after acceptance. Agented fiction: small percentage. **Publishes high percentage of new writers/ year.** Recently published work by Eric Miller, Tony Steele, Gina Ochsner, Liam Duncan, A.F. Moritz. Average length: 3,000 words. Publishes short shorts. Occasionally comments on rejected mss.

How to Contact Send SASE and *Canadian* stamps or IRCs for return of mss. Responds in 6 months to mss. No simultaneous submissions. Sample copy for $10 (US).

Payment/Terms Pays $20 (Canadian)/published page and 1 contributor's copy. Pays on publication for first or one-time rights.

Advice ''Less than 5% of the material received is published.''

$\boxed{\oslash}$ FIRST CLASS

Four-Sep Publications, P.O. Box 86, Friendship IN 47021. E-mail: christopherm@four-sep.com. Web site: www.f our-sep.com. **Contact:** Christopher M, editor. Magazine: 4¼×11; 60+ pages; 24 lb./60 lb. offset paper; craft cover; illustrations; photos. ''*First Class* features short fiction and poetics form the cream of the small press and killer unknowns—mingling before your very hungry eyes. I publish plays, too.'' Biannual. Estab. 1995. Circ. 200-400.

Needs Erotica, literary, science fiction (soft/sociaological), satire, drama. ''No religious or traditional poetry, or 'boomer angst'—therapy-driven self loathing.'' Receives 50-70 unsolicited mss/month. Accepts 4-6 mss/issue; 10-12 mss/year. Publishes ms 1 month after acceptance. **Publishes 10-15 new writers/year.** Recently published work by Gerald Locklin, John Bennnet, B.Z. Niditch. Length: 5,000-8,000; average length: 2,000-3,000 words. Publishes short shorts. Also publishes poetry. Sometimes comments on rejected mss.

How to Contact Send SASE for return of ms or send a disposable copy of ms and #10 SASE for reply only. Responds in 1 week to queries. Accepts simultaneous submissions and reprints. Sample copy for $6. Writer's guidelines for #10 SASE. Reviews fiction.

Payment/Terms Pays 1 contributor's copy; additional copies $5. Acquires one-time rights.

Advice ''Don't bore me with puppy dogs and the morose/sappy feeling you have about death. Belt out a good, short, thought-provoking, graphic, uncommon piece.''

$\boxed{\$}$ $\boxed{\oslash}$ $\boxed{\Psi}$ FIVE POINTS, A Journal of Literature and Art

MSC 8R0318 Georgia State University, 33 Gilmer St. SE, Unit 8, Atlanta GA 30303-3083. (404)463-9484. Fax: (404)651-3167. E-mail: msexton@gsu.edu. Web site: www.webdelsol.com/Five_Points. **Contact:** Megan Sexton, associate editor. Magazine: 6×9; 200 pages; cotton paper; glossy cover; photos. *Five Points* is ''committed to publishing work that compels the imagination through the use of fresh and convincing language.'' Triannual. Estab. 1996. Circ. 2,000.

• Fiction first appearing in *Five Points* has been anthologized in *Best American Fiction*, Pushcart anthologies, and *New Stories from The South*.

Needs List of upcoming themes available for SASE. Receives 250 unsolicited mss/month. Accepts 4 mss/issue; 15-20 mss/year. Does not read mss April 30-September 1. Publishes ms 6 months after acceptance. **Publishes 1 new writer/year.** Recently published work by Frederick Busch, Ursula Hegi, Melanie Rae Thon. Average length: 7,500 words. Publishes short shorts. Also publishes literary essays, poetry. Sometimes comments on rejected mss.

How to Contact Send SASE for reply to query. No simultaneous submissions. Sample copy for $7.

Payment/Terms Pays $15/page minimum ($250 maximum), free subscription to magazine and 2 contributor's copies; additional copies $4. Acquires first North American serial rights. Sends galleys to author. Sponsors awards/contests.

Advice ''We place no limitations on style or content. Our only criteria is excellence. If your writing has an original voice, substance and significance, send it to us. We will publish distinctive, intelligent writing that has something to say and says it in a way that captures and maintains our attention.''

$\boxed{N}$ $\boxed{\oslash}$ 580 SPLIT, A JOURNAL OF ARTS AND LETTERS

Mills College, P.O. Box 9982, Oakland CA 94613-0982. Web site: www.580split.com. **Contact:** Nina LaCour, prose editor. Literary magazine/journal: 6×10, 170 pages, matte cover. Contains illustrations. Includes photographs. "We publish innovative, risk-taking fiction, poetry, creative nonfiction and art." Annual. Estab. 1999. Circ. 600. Member of SPD.

Needs Experimental, humor/satire, literary, translations. Receives 50-70 mss/month. Accepts 7-10 mss/issue. Does not read mss November 1-July 1. Manuscript published 3 months after acceptance. **Publishes 5 new writers/year.** Published Michelle Lee, Victor LaValle, Karina Fuentes, Lisa Jarnot. Length: 4,500 words (max). Average length: 3,000 words. Publishes short shorts. Average length of short shorts: 500 words. Also publishes poetry. Never comments on/critiques rejected manuscripts.

How to Contact Send complete ms with cover letter. Include brief bio. Responds to queries in 3 weeks. Send disposable copy of ms and #10 SASE for reply only. Considers simultaneous submissions. Sample copy available for $7.50. Guidelines available for SASE.

Payment and Terms Writers receive 2 contributors copies. Additional copies $5. Pays on publication. Acquires first rights. Sends galleys to author. Publication is copyrighted.

Advice "Get a hold of a past issue, read through it, find out what we are about. Check the Web site for most recent information."

FLINT HILLS REVIEW

Dept. of English, Box 4019, Emporia State University, Emporia KS 66801-5087. (620)341-6916. Fax: (620)341-5547. E-mail: webbamy@emporia.edu. Web site: www.emporia.edu/fhr/. **Contact:** Amy Sage Webb, co-editor. Magazine: 9×6; 115 pages; 60 lb. paper; glossy cover; illustrations; photos. "*FHR* seeks work informed by a strong sense of place or region, especially Kansas and the Great Plains region. We seek to provide a publishing venue for writers of the Great Plains and Kansas while also publishing authors whose work evidences a strong sense of place, writing of literary quality, and accomplished use of language and depth of character development." Annual. Estab. 1996. Circ. 500. Member CLMP.

Needs Ethnic/multicultural, gay, historical, regional (Plains), translations. "No religious, inspirational, children's." Want to see more "writing of literary quality with a strong sense of place." List of upcoming themes online. Receives 5-15 unsolicited mss/month. Accepts 2-5 mss/issue; 2-5 mss/year. Does not read mss April-December. Publishes ms 4 months after acceptance. **Publishes 4 new writers/year.** Recently published work by Kim Stafford, Elizabeth Dodd, Bart Edelman, Jennifer Henderson. Length: 1 page-5,000; average length: 3,000 words. Publishes short shorts. Also publishes literary essays, literary criticism, poetry.

How to Contact Send a disposable copy of ms and #10 SASE for reply only. Responds in 5 weeks to queries; 6 months to mss. Accepts simultaneous, multiple submissions. Sample copy for $5.50. Writer's guidelines for SASE, by e-mail, fax or on Web site. Reviews fiction.

Payment/Terms Pays 2 contributor's copies; additional copies $5.50. Acquires one-time rights.

Advice "Strong imagery and voice, writing that is informed by place or region, writing of literary quality with depth of character development. Hone the language down to the most literary depiction that is possible in the shortest space that still provides depth of development without excess length."

FLORIDA REVIEW

Dept. of English, University of Central Florida, P.O. Box 161346, Orlando FL 32816-1346. (407)823-2038. E-mail: flreview@mail.ucf.edu. Web site: www.english.ucf.edu/~flreview. **Contact:** Jeanne Leiby, editor. Magazine: 6×9; 144 pages; semi-gloss full color cover, perfect bound. "We publish fiction of high 'literary' quality—stories that delight, instruct and take risks. Our audience consists of avid readers of fiction, poetry and creative nonfiction." Semiannual. Estab. 1972. Circ. 1,500.

Needs Experimental, literary. "We aren't particularly interested in genre fiction (sci-fi, romance, adventure, etc.) but a good story can transcend any genre." Receives 400 unsolicited mss/month. Accepts 5-7 mss/issue; 10-14 mss/year. Publishes ms 3 months after acceptance. **Publishes 2-4 new writers/year.** Recently published work by Billy Collins, David Huddle, Wendell Mayo, Virgil Suarez. Length: 2,000-7,000 words; average length: 5,000 words. Publishes short shorts. Also publishes creative nonfiction, poetry. Rarely comments on rejected mss.

How to Contact Send complete ms. Send SASE (or IRC) for return of the ms or send disposable copy of the ms and #10 SASE for reply only. Responds in 2 weeks to queries; 2 months to mss. Accepts simultaneous submissions. Sample copy for $6. Writer's guidelines for #10 SASE or online.

Payment/Terms Rights held by UCF, revert to author after publication.

Advice "We're looking for writers with fresh voices and original stories. We like risk."

FLYWAY, A Literary Review

Iowa State University, 206 Ross Hall, Ames IA 50011. (515)294-8273. Fax: (515)294-6814. E-mail: flyway@iastate.edu. Web site: www.flyway.org. **Contact:** Stephen Pett, editor. Literary magazine: 6×9; 64 pages; quality paper; cover stock; some illustrations; photos. "We publish quality fiction. Our stories are accompanied by brief commentaries by their authors, the sort of thing a writer might say introducing a piece at a reading." Biannual. Estab. 1995. Circ. 500.

Needs Literary. Receives 50 unsolicited mss/month. Accepts 2-5 mss/issue; 10-12 mss/year. Reads mss September 1-May. Publishes ms 5 months after acceptance. **Publishes 7-10 new writers/year.** Recently published work by Naomi Shihab Nye, Gina Ochsner, Ted Kooser. Length: 5,000; average length: 3,500 words. Publishes short shorts. Often comments on rejected mss.

How to Contact Send SASE. Sample copy for $8. Writer's guidelines for SASE.

Payment/Terms Pays 2 contributor's copies; additional copies $6. Acquires one-time rights.

Advice "Quality, originality, voice, drama, tension. Make it as strong as you can."

☐ FOLIATE OAK LITERARY MAGAZINE, Foliate Oak Online

University of Arkansas-Monticello, MCB 113, Monticello AR 71656. (870)460-1247. E-mail: foliate@uamont.edu. Web site: www.uamont.edu/foliateoak. **Contact**: Diane Payne, faculty advisor. Magazine: 6×9; 80 pages. Monthly. Estab. 1980. Circ. 500.

Needs Adventure, comics/graphic novels, ethnic/multicultural, experimental, family saga, feminist, gay, historical, humor/satire, lesbian, literary, mainstream, science fiction (soft/sociological). No religious, sexist or homophobic work. Receives 30 unsolicited mss/month. Accepts 7 mss/issue; 50 mss/year. Does not read mss May-August. Publishes ms 1 month after acceptance. **Publishes 20 new writers/year.** Recently published work by David Barringer, Thom Didato, Joe Taylor, Molly Giles, Patricia Shevlin, Tony Hoagland. Length: 50-3,500 words; average length: 1,500 words. Publishes short shorts. Also publishes literary essays, literary criticism, poetry. Rarely comments on rejected mss.

How to Contact Send complete ms as an e-mail attachment (Word or RTF). Postal submissions will not be read. Please include author's name and title of story/poem/essay in e-mail header. In the e-mail, please send contact information and a short bio. Responds in 8 weeks. Only accepts submissions August through April. Accepts simultaneous submissions and multiple submissions. Please contact ASAP if work is accepted elsewhere. Sample copy for SASE and 6×8 envelope. Writer's guidelines online. Reviews fiction.

Payment/Terms Pays contributor's copy. Acquires electronic rights. Sends galleys to author. Not copyrighted.

Advice "We're open to honest, experimental, offbeat, realistic and surprising writing, if it has been edited. Limit poems to five per submission, and one short story or creative nonfiction (less than 3,500 words). You may send up to three flash fictions. Please don't send more writing until you hear from us regarding your first submission. We are also looking for artwork sent as .jpg or .gif files."

☐ FOLIO, A Literary Journal at American University

Doyle, Department of Literature, American University, Washington DC 20016. (202)885-2971. E-mail: folio_editors@yahoo.com. Web site: www.foliojournal.org. **Contact:** Amina Hafiz. Magazine: about 70 pages; illustrations; photos. "*Folio* is a journal of poetry, fiction and creative nonfiction. We look for work that ignites and endures, is artful and natural, daring and elegant." Semiannual. Estab. 1984. Circ. 300.

Needs Literary. Does not want anything that is sexually offensive. Receives 50-60 unsolicited mss/month. Accepts 2-3 mss/issue; 5-8 mss/year. Does not read mss May-August. **Publishes 2-3 new writers/year.** Length: 3,500 words; average length: 2,500 words. Publishes short shorts. Also publishes poetry. Sometimes comments on rejected mss.

How to Contact Send complete ms. Send a SASE (or IRC) for return of the ms or send a disposable copy of the ms and #10 SASE for reply only. Responds in 3-4 months to mss. Accepts simultaneous, multiple submissions. Sample copy for $6. Writer's guidelines for #10 SASE or online.

Payment/Terms Pays 2 contributor's copies. Pays on publication for first North American serial rights.

Advice "Visit our Web site and/or read the journal to get a sense of *Folio* style."

$ ⊕ FRANK, An International Journal of Contemporary Writing & Art

Association Frank, 32 rue Edouard Vaillant, Montreuil France. (33)(1)48596658. Fax: (33)(1)48596668. E-mail: submissions@readfrank.com. Web site: www.readfrank.com or www.frank.ly. **Contact:** David Applefield. "Writing that takes risks and isn't ethnocentric is looked upon favorably." Published twice/year. Estab. 1983. Circ. 4,000.

Needs Experimental, novel excerpts, international. "At *Frank*, we publish fiction, poetry, literary and art interviews, and translations. We like work that falls between existing genres and has social or political consciousness." Accepts 20 mss/issue. Publishes ms 1 year after acceptance.

How to Contact Send complete ms. Send IRC or $5 cash. Must be previously unpublished in English (world). E-mail submissions as Word attachments are welcome and should be saved in RTF. Responds in 1 month to queries; 2 months to mss. Sample copy for $10. Writer's guidelines online.

Payment/Terms Pays $10/printed page. Pays on publication for one-time rights.

Advice "Send your most daring and original work. At *Frank*, we like work that is not too parochial or insular, however, don't try to write for a 'French' market."

$⚑ ☑ FREEFALL MAGAZINE

The Alexandra Writers' Centre Society, 922 Ninth Ave. SE, Calgary AB T2G 0S4 Canada. (403)264-4730. E-mail: awcs@telusplanet.net. Web site: www.alexandrawriters.org. **Contact:** Vivian Hansen, editor. Magazine: 8½×11; 40 pages; bond paper; bond stock; illustrations; photos. "*FreeFall* features the best of new, emerging writers and gives them the chance to get into print along with established writers. Now in its 14th year, *FreeFall* seeks to attract readers looking for well-crafted stories, poetry and artwork." Semiannual. Estab. 1990. Circ. Under 500. Member Alberta Magazine Publishers Association (AMPA).

Needs "No science fiction, horror." Wants to see more well-crafted literary fiction. Accepts 3-5 mss/issue; 6-10 mss/year. Does not read mss January-February, June-August. Publishes ms 6 months after acceptance. **Publishes 40% new writers/year.** Recently published work by Thomas Robert Barnes, J.L. Bond, Shirley Black, Judy Gayford, Elizabeth Lindgre-Kubitz, Renee Norman, Cheryl Sikomas, Rebecca Marshall-Courtois, Diane Stuart. Length: 500-3,000 words; average length: 2,500 words. Publishes short shorts. Also publishes poetry. Sometimes comments on rejected mss.

How to Contact Send SASE (or IRC) for return of ms, or send a disposable copy of ms with e-mail address or #10 SASE for reply only. Responds in 3 months to mss. Accepts reprint submissions. Sample copy for $10 (US). Writer's guidelines for SASE, e-mail or on Web site.

Payment/Terms Pays $5 (Canadian)/printed page and 1 contributor's copy; additional copies $10 (US). Acquires first North American serial, one-time rights.

Advice "We look for thoughtful word usage that conveys clear images and encourages further exploration of the story's idea and neat, clean presentation of work. Carefully read *FreeFall* guidelines before submitting. Do not fold manuscript, and submit 9×11 envelope. Include SASE/IRC for reply and/or return of manuscript. You may contact us by e-mail after initial hardcopy submission. For accepted pieces a request is made for disk or e-mail copy. Web presence attracts submissions from writers all over the world."

☐ FRESH BOILED PEANUTS

P.O. Box 43194, Cincinnati OH 45243-0194. E-mail: contact@freshboiledpeanuts.com. Web site: www.freshboiledpeanuts.com. "We embrace the fact that literary magazines are a dime a dozen. We have no grand illusions of money or fame. We publish for the sake of the work itself. So it better be good." Semiannual. Estab. 2004.

Needs "Open to all fiction categories." Also publishes literary essays, literary criticism, poetry. Sometimes comments on rejected mss.

How to Contact Send complete ms. Accepts submissions by e-mail (must be a .doc file or .txt file). Send SASE (or IRC) for return of ms. Responds in 2-3 months to mss. Accepts simultaneous, multiple submissions. Sample copy online. Writer's guidelines online.

Payment/Terms Pays 1 contributor's copy. Acquires one-time rights.

Advice "Please be sure to visit our Web site for up-to-date submission guidelines."

⚑ ☑ FRONT & CENTRE

Black Bile Press, 573 Gainsborough Ave., Ottawa ON K2A 2Y6 Canada. (613)729-8973. E-mail: firth@istar.ca. Web site: www.ardentdreams.com/blackbilepress. **Contact:** Matthew Firth, editor. Magazine: half letter-size; 40-50 pages; illustrations; photos. "We look for new fiction from Canadian and international writers—bold, aggressive work that does not compromise quality." Three issues per year. Estab. 1998. Circ. 500.

Needs Literary ("contemporary realism/gritty urban"). "No science fiction, horror, mainstream, romance or religious." Receives 30-40 unsolicited mss/month. Accepts 6-7 mss/issue; 10-20 mss/year. Publishes ms 6 months after acceptance. Agented fiction 10%. **Publishes 4-5 new writers/year.** Recently published work by Kenneth J. Harvey, David Rose, Laura Hird, Jon Boillard, Nichole McGill, John Swan. Length: 50-4,000 words; average length: 2,500 words. Publishes short shorts. Always comments on rejected mss.

How to Contact Send SASE (from Canada) (or IRCs from USA) for return of ms or send a disposable copy of ms with #10 SASE for reply only. Responds in 2 weeks to queries; 4 months to mss. Accepts multiple submissions. Sample copy for $6. Writer's guidelines for SASE or by e-mail. Reviews fiction.

Payment/Terms Acquires first rights. Not copyrighted.

Advice "We look for attention to detail, unique voice, not overtly derivative, bold writing, not pretentious. We should like to see more realism. Read the magazine first—simple as that!"

$☑ FUGUE

200 Brink Hall, University of Idaho, P.O. Box 441102, Moscow ID 83844-1102. (208)885-6156. Fax: (208)885-5944. E-mail: fugue@uidaho.edu. Web site: www.uidaho.edu/fugue. **Contact:** Fiction editor. Magazine: 6×9; 175 pages; 70 lb. stock paper. By allowing the voices of established writers to lend their authority to new and

emerging writers, *Fugue* strives to provide its readers with the most compelling stories, poems, essays, interviews and literary criticism possible. Semiannual. Estab. 1990. Circ. 1,400.

• Work published in *Fugue* has won the Pushcart Prize and has been cited in *Best American Essays*.

Needs Ethnic/multicultural, experimental, humor/satire, literary. Receives 80 unsolicited mss/month. Accepts 6-8 mss/issue; 12-15 mss/year. Does not read mss May 1-August 31. Publishes ms 6 months after acceptance. **Publishes 4-6 new writers/year.** Recently published work by Kent Nelson, Marilyn Krysl, Cary Holladay, Padgett Powell, Dean Young, W.S. Merwin, Matthew Vollmer. Publishes short shorts. Also publishes literary essays, literary criticism, poetry. Sometimes comments on rejected mss.

How to Contact Send complete ms. Send SASE (or IRC) for return of the ms or disposable copy of the ms and #10 SASE for reply only. Responds in 3-4 months to mss. Accepts simultaneous submissions. Sample copy for $8. Writer's guidelines for SASE or on Web site.

Payment/Terms Pays $10 minimum and 1 contributor copy as well as a one-year subscription to the magazine; additional copies $5. Pays on publication for first North American serial, electronic rights.

Advice "The best way, of course, to determine what we're looking for is to read the journal. As the name *Fugue* indicates, our goal is to present a wide range of literary perspectives. We like stories that satisfy us both intellectually and emotionally, with fresh language and characters so captivating that they stick with us and invite a second reading. We are also seeking creative literary criticism which illuminates a piece of literature or a specific writer by examining that writer's personal experience."

Ⓝ Ⓛ GAMBARA

Gambara Books, P.O. Box 3887, Santa Cruz CA 95063-3887. E-mail: editor@gambara.org. Web site: http://gambara.org. **Contact:** Scott Johnson, general editor. Literary magazine/journal: 4×6, perfect bound, 150+ pages, uncoated stock paper, CS1 cover. Contains illustrations. Includes photographs. "We publish new and interesting work from all kinds of writers. We are unique in that everything published in the book is first published—and permanently archived—on our Web site. Our audience is the general literary audience, perhaps a bit younger on average." Published continually online with an annual print edition. Estab. January 2005 (online), January 2006 (print). Circ. 2,000 for first edition.

Needs Comics/graphic novels, erotica, ethnic/multicultural (general), experimental, feminist, gay, historical (general), lesbian, literary, mainstream, regional, translations. Does not want formulaic writing. Fiction that uses elements of genre is fine so long as those elements support the "dream," as opposed to constituting the dream in its entirety. Not interested in fiction that points to a moral. Deadline for the print version is November 30 each year. Receives 1 mss/month. Accepts 15-20 (minimum) mss/year. Manuscript published 2-3 weeks after acceptance. Agented fiction 0%. **Publishes "as many as possible" new writers/year.** Length: 15,000 words (max). Average length: 5,000 words. Publishes short shorts. Also publishes literary essays, book reviews, poetry. Send review copies to Scott Johnson. Often comments on/critiques rejected manuscripts.

How to Contact Send complete ms with cover letter. Prefers submissions by e-mail. Include estimated word count, brief bio, list of publications. Responds to queries in 4-6 weeks. Responds to mss in 4-6 weeks. Send either SASE (or IRC) for return of ms or disposable copy of ms and #10 SASE for reply only. Considers simultaneous submissions, multiple submissions. Guidelines available on Web site.

Payment and Terms Writers receive 3 contributors copies. Additional copies $5. Pays on publication. Acquires first rights, electronic rights. Sends galleys to author. Publication is copyrighted.

Advice "If I can read it from beginning to end without stopping or feeling that the 'dream' has been broken, that is a special manuscript and I will consider it for publication. I will probably ask for a few changes that I believe will improve the story. Please don't be defensive. I do this work in good faith, for no compensation. I will explain my thinking, and if you disagree, I'm open to your thinking. We both want the same thing: a great piece in a great magazine. Let's cooperate."

Ⓛ GARGOYLE

3819 N. 13th St., Arlington VA 22201. (703)525-9296. E-mail: gargoyle@gargoylemagazine.com. Web site: www.gargoylemagazine.com. **Contact:** Richard Peabody and Lucinda Ebersole, editors. Literary magazine: 5½×8½; 200 pages; illustrations; photos. "*Gargoyle* began in 1976 with twin goals: to discover new voices and to rediscover overlooked talent. These days we publish a lot of fictional efforts written by poets. We have always been more interested in how a writer tells a story than in plot or story per se." Annual. Estab. 1976. Circ. 2,000.

Needs Erotica, ethnic/multicultural, experimental, gay, lesbian, literary, mainstream, translations. "No romance, horror, science fiction." Wants "good short stories with sports or music backgrounds." Wants to see more Canadian, British, Australian and Third World fiction. Receives 50-200 unsolicited mss/month. Accepts 10-15 mss/issue. Accepts submissions during June, July, Aug. Publishes ms 6-12 months after acceptance. Agented fiction 5%. **Publishes 2-3 new writers/year.** Recently published work by Randt Sue Coburn, John Dufresne, Rick Moody, Thaisa Frank, Abby Frucht, Elizabeth Hand, Kit Reed and Eileen Myles. Length: 30

pages maximum; average length: 5-10 pages. Publishes short shorts. Also publishes literary essays, literary criticism, poetry. Sometimes comments on rejected mss.

How to Contact We prefer electronic submissions. Please send in the body of a letter. For snail mail, send SASE for reply, return of ms or send a disposable copy of ms. Responds in 2 weeks to queries; 3 months to mss. Accepts simultaneous submissions. Sample copy for $12.95.

Payment/Terms Pays 1 contributor's copy; additional copies for $\frac{1}{2}$ price. Acquires first North American serial, first, first British rights. Sends galleys to author.

Advice "We have to fall in love with a particular fiction."

N ◯ GEORGETOWN REVIEW

G and R Publishing, Box 227, 400 East College St., Georgetown KY 40324. (502)863-8308. Fax: (502)868-8888. E-mail: gtownreview@georgetowncollege.edu. Web site: http://georgetownreview.georgetowncollege.edu. **Contact:** Steven Carter, editor. Literary magazine/journal: 6×9, 192 pages, 20 lb. paper, four-color 60 lb. glossy cover. "We publish the best fiction we receive, regardless of theme or genre." Annual. Estab. 1993. Circ. 1,000. Member CLMP.

Needs Ethnic/multicultural (general), experimental, literary. Does not want adventure, children's, fantasy, romance. Receives 100-125 mss/month. Accepts 8-10 mss/issue; 15-20 mss/year. Does not read March 16-August 31. Manuscript published 1 month-2 years after acceptance. Agented fiction 0%. **Publishes 3-4 new writers/year.** Published Liz Funk (debut), Laura Selby, Sallie Bingham, David Romtvedt, Carla Panciera. Average length: 4,000 words. Publishes short shorts. Average length of short shorts: 500-1,500 words. Also publishes literary essays, poetry. Sometimes comments on/critiques rejected manuscripts.

How to Contact Send complete ms with cover letter. Include brief bio, list of publications. Responds to queries in 1 month. Responds to mss in 1-3 months. Send either SASE (or IRC) for return of ms or disposable copy of ms and #10 SASE for reply only. Considers simultaneous submissions. Sample copy available for $6.50. Guidelines available on Web site.

Payment and Terms Writers receive 2 contributors copies, free subscription to the magazine. Additional copies $5. Pays on publication. Acquires first North American serial rights. Publication is copyrighted. "Sponsors annual contest with $1,000 prize. Check Web site for guidelines."

Advice "We look for fiction that is well written and that has a story line that keeps our interest. Don't send a first draft, and even if we don't take your first, second, or third submission, keep trying."

$ ◻ ☑ THE GEORGIA REVIEW

The University of Georgia, 012 Gilbert Hall, Athens GA 30602-9009. (706)542-3481. Fax: (706)542-0047. Web site: www.uga.edu/garev. **Contact:** T.R. Hummer, editor. Journal: 7×10; 208 pages (average); 50 lb. woven old-style paper; 80 lb. cover stock; illustrations; photos. "Our readers are educated, inquisitive people who read a lot of work in the areas we feature, so they expect only the best in our pages. All work submitted should show evidence that the writer is at least as well educated and well read as our readers. Essays should be authoritative but accessible to a range of readers." Quarterly. Estab. 1947. Circ. 4,000.

● Stories first published in *The Georgia Review* have been anthologized in *Best American Short Stories*, *Best American Mystery Stories*, *New Stories from The South* and the *Pushcart Prize Collection*. *The Georgia Review* was a finalist for the National Magazine Award in Fiction in 2003.

Needs "Ordinarily we do not publish novel excerpts or works translated into English, and we strongly discourage authors from submitting these." Receives 300 unsolicited mss/month. Accepts 3-4 mss/issue; 12-15 mss/year. Does not read unsolicited mss May 1-August 15. Publishes ms 6 months after acceptance. **Publishes some new writers/year.** Recently published work by Brock Clarke, Christie Hodgen, Liza Ward, Robert Olen Butler, Joyce Carol Oates, Guy Davenport, Carrie Brown. Also publishes literary essays, literary criticism, poetry. Occasionally comments on rejected mss.

How to Contact Send complete ms. Responds in 2 weeks to queries; 3-6 months to mss. No simultaneous submissions. Sample copy for $7. Writer's guidelines online.

Payment/Terms Pays $40/published page. Pays on publication for first North American serial rights. Sends galleys to author.

$ ◻ ☑ THE GETTYSBURG REVIEW

Gettysburg College, Gettysburg PA 17325. (717)337-6770. Fax: (717)337-6775. Web site: www.gettysburgreview .com. **Contact:** Peter Stitt, editor. Magazine: 6¼×10; 170 pages; acid free paper; full color illustrations. "Our concern is quality. Manuscripts submitted here should be extremely well written." Reading period September-May. Quarterly. Estab. 1988. Circ. 4,000.

● Work appearing in *The Gettysburg Review* has also been included in *Prize Stories: The O. Henry Awards*, *Pushcart Prize* anthology, *Best American Fiction*, *New Stories from The South*, *Harper's* and elsewhere. It is also the recipient of a Lila Wallace-Reader's Digest grant and NEA grants.

Needs Experimental, historical, humor/satire, literary, mainstream, novel excerpts, regional, serialized novels, contemporary. "We require that fiction be intelligent and esthetically written." Receives 350 unsolicited mss/month. Accepts 15-20 mss/issue; 60-80 mss/year. Publishes ms within 1 year after acceptance. **Publishes 1-5 new writers/year.** Recently published work by Robert Olen Butler, Joyce Carol Oates, Naeem Murr, Tom Perrotta, Alison Baker, Alice Fulton. Length: 2,000-7,000 words; average length: 3,000 words. Publishes short shorts. Also publishes literary essays, literary criticism, poetry. Sometimes comments on rejected mss.

How to Contact Send complete ms with SASE. Responds in 1 month to queries; 3-6 months to mss. Accepts simultaneous submissions. Sample copy for $7. Writer's guidelines online.

Payment/Terms Pays $30/page. Pays on publication for first North American serial rights.

Advice "Reporting time can take more than three months. It is helpful to look at a sample copy of *The Gettysburg Review* to see what kinds of fiction we publish before submitting."

⚫ GINOSKO

P.O. Box 246, Fairfax CA 94978. (415)785-2802. E-mail: ginoskoeditor@aol.com. **Contact:** Robert Cesaretti, editor. Magazine: $5^1/_2 \times 8^1/_2$; 50-60 pages; standard paper; photo glossy cover. Ghin-*oce*-koe: to perceive, understand, come to know; knowledge that has an inception, an attainment; the recognition of truth by personal experience. "Writing that lifts up the grace and beauty of human frailty yet carries with it the strength and veracity of humility, compassion, belief." Published semiannually. Estab. 2003. Circ. 1,000.

Needs Experimental, literary, stylized; "consider 'Pagan Night' by Kate Braverman, 'Driving the Heart' by Jason Brown, 'Customs of the Country' by Madison Smartt Bell." Strong on theme, imagistic writing. Receives 30-50 unsolicited mss/month. **Publishes 4 new writers/year.** Recently published work by Stephanie Dickinson, Michael Hettich.

How to Contact Send complete ms. Accepts submissions by e-mail (ginoskoeditor@aol.com) and snail mail. Responds in 1-3 months to mss. Accepts simultaneous and reprints submissions.

Payment/Terms Pays one contributor's copy. Pays on publication for one-time rights. Not copyrighted.

Advice "I am looking for a style that conveys spiritual hunger and yearning, yet avoids religiosity and convention—*between literary vision and spiritual realities*."

$⚫ ⚫ GLIMMER TRAIN STORIES

Glimmer Train Press, Inc., 1211 NW Glisan St. #207, Portland OR 97209. (503)221-0836. Fax: (503)221-0837. Web site: www.glimmertrain.org. **Contact:** Susan Burmeister-Brown and Linda Swanson-Davies. Magazine: $7^1/_4 \times 9^1/_4$; 260 pages; recycled; acid-free paper; 12 photographs. "We are interested in well-written, emotionally-moving short stories published by unknown, as well as known, writers." Quarterly. Estab. 1991. Circ. 16,000.

● The magazine also sponsors an annual short story contest for new writers and a very short fiction contest.

Needs Literary. Receives 4,000 unsolicited mss/month. Accepts 10 mss/issue; 40 mss/year. Reads in January, April, July, October. Publishes ms up to 2 years after acceptance. Agented fiction 10%. **Publishes 12 new writers/year.** Recently published work by Judy Budnitz, Nancy Reisman, Herman Carrillo, Andre Dubus III, William Trevor, Alberto Rios, Alice Mattison. Sometimes comments on rejected mss.

How to Contact Submit work online at www.glimmertrain.org. Accepted work published in *Glimmer Train Stories*. Responds in 3 months to mss. No simultaneous submissions. Sample copy for $9.95 on Web site. Writer's guidelines online.

Payment/Terms Pays $700. Pays on acceptance for first rights.

Advice "When a story stays with us after the first reading, it gets another reading. Those stories that simply don't let us set them aside get published. Read good fiction. It will often improve the quality of your own writing."

$⚫ ⚫ GRAIN LITERARY MAGAZINE

Saskatchewan Writers Guild, P.O. Box 67, Saskatoon SK S7K 3K1 Canada. (306)244-2828. Fax: (306)244-0255. Web site: www.grainmagazine.ca. **Contact:** Kent Bruyneel, editor. Literary magazine: 6×9; 128 pages; Chinook offset printing; chrome-coated stock; some photos. "*Grain* publishes writing of the highest quality, both traditional and innovative in nature. *Grain* aim: To publish work that challenges readers; to encourage promising new writers; and to produce a well-designed, visually interesting magazine." Quarterly. Estab. 1973. Circ. 1,500.

Needs Experimental, literary, mainstream, contemporary, prose poem, poetry. "No romance, confession, science fiction, vignettes, mystery." Receives 80 unsolicited mss/month. Accepts 8-12 mss/issue; 32-48 mss/year. Publishes ms 11 months after acceptance. Recently published work by Yann Martel, Tom Wayman, Lorna Crozier. Also publishes poetry. Occasionally comments on rejected mss.

How to Contact Send complete ms with SASE (or IRC) and brief letter. Accepts queries by e-mail, mail, fax, phone. Responds in 1 month to queries; 4 months to mss. No simultaneous submissions. Sample copy for $13 or online. Writer's guidelines for #10 SASE or online.

Payment/Terms Pays $50-225. Pays on publication for first Canadian serial rights.

Advice "Submit a story to us that will deepen the imaginative experience of our readers. *Grain* has established itself as a first-class magazine of serious fiction. We receive submissions from around the world. Do not use U.S. postage stamps on your return envelope. Without sufficient Canadian postage or an International Reply Coupon, we *will not* read or reply to your submission. We look for attention to detail, credibility, lucid use of language and metaphor and a confident, convincing voice. Make sure you have researched your piece, that the literal and metaphorical support one another."

GRANTA, The Magazine of New Writing

Granta Publications, 2-3 Hanover Yard, Noel Rd., London England NI 8BE United Kingdom. (44)(0)20 7704 9776. E-mail: editorial@granta.com. Web site: www.granta.com. **Contact:** Ian Jack, editor. Magazine: paperback, 256 pages approx; photos. "*Granta* magazine publishes fiction, reportage, biography and autobiography, history, travel and documentary photography. It does not publish 'writing about writing.' The realistic narrative—the story—is its primary form." Quarterly. Estab. 1979. Circ. 80,000.

Needs Literary, novel excerpts. No genre fiction. Themes decided as deadline approaches. Receives 100 unsolicited mss/month. Accepts 0-1 mss/issue; 1-2 mss/year. **Publishes 1-2 new writers/year.**

How to Contact Send SAE and IRCs for reply, return of ms or send a disposable copy of ms. Responds in 3 months to mss. Accepts simultaneous submissions. Sample copy for $14.95. Writer's guidelines online.

Payment/Terms Payment varies. Pays on publication. Buys world English language rights, first serial rights (minimum). "We hold more rights in pieces we commission." Sends galleys to author.

Advice "We are looking for the best in realistic stories; originality of voice, without jargon, connivance or self-conscious 'performance'—writing that endures."

$ GRASSLIMB

Grasslimb, P.O. Box 420816, San Diego CA 92142. E-mail: valerie@grasslimb.com. Web site: www.grasslimb. com/journal/. **Contact:** Valerie Polichar, editor. Magazine: 14×20; 8 pages; 60 lb. white paper; illustrations. "*Grasslimb* is sold in cafés as well as in bookstores. Our readers like some insight into both the pain and the strange joys of life along with their cups of coffee. Loss, alienation and grief are subjects which draw us. Conversely, we find the beauty of the natural world compelling. Fiction is best when it is short and avant-garde or otherwise experimental." Semiannual. Estab. 2002. Circ. 300.

Needs Comics/graphic novels, ethnic/multicultural, experimental, gay, literary, mystery/suspense (crime), regional, thriller/espionage, translations. Does not want romance or religious writings. Accepts 2-4 mss/issue; 4-8 mss/year. Does not read mss in December, January, June or July. Publishes ms 3 months after acceptance. **Publishes 2 new writers/year.** Recently published work by Leonard Crino, Josey Foo, Madeline Malan, James Sallis. Length: 500-2,000 words; average length: 1,500 words. Publishes short shorts. Also publishes poetry. Rarely comments on rejected mss.

How to Contact Send complete ms. Send SASE for return of ms or disposable copy of ms and #10 SASE for reply only. Responds in 2 months to mss. Accepts simultaneous, multiple submissions and reprints. Sample copy for $2. Writer's guidelines for SASE, e-mail or on Web site. Reviews fiction.

Payment/Terms Writers receive $5 minimum; $50 maximum, and 2 contributor's copies; additional copies $2. Pays on acceptance for first North American serial rights. Sends galleys to author.

Advice "We publish brief fiction work that can be read in a single sitting over a cup of coffee. Work can be serious or light, but is generally 'literary' in nature, rather than mainstream. Experimental work welcome. Remember to have you work proofread and to send short work."

THE GREEN HILLS LITERARY LANTERN

Published by Truman State University, Division of Language & Literature, Kirksville MO 63501. (660)785-4487. E-mail: adavis@truman.edu. Web site: http://ll.truman.edu/ghllweb. **Contact:** Fiction editor. "The mission of *GHLL* is to provide a literary market for quality fiction writers, both established and beginners, and to provide quality literature for readers from diverse backgrounds. We also see ourselves as a cultural resource for North Missouri. Our publication works to publish the highest quality fiction—dense, layered, subtle—and, at the same time, fiction which grabs the ordinary reader. We tend to publish traditional short stories, but we are open to experimental forms." Annual. Estab. 1990. Circ.

Needs Ethnic/multicultural, experimental, feminist, humor/satire, literary, mainstream, regional. "Our main requirement is literary merit. Wants more quality fiction about rural culture. No adventure, crime, erotica, horror, inspirational, mystery/suspense, romance." Receives 40 unsolicited mss/month. Accepts 15-17 mss/issue. Publishes ms 6-12 months after acceptance. **Publishes 0-3 new writers/year.** Recently published work by Karl Harshbarger, Mark Jacobs, J. Morris, Gary Fincke, Dennis Vannatta. Length: 7,000 words; average length: 3,000 words. Publishes short shorts. Also publishes poetry. Sometimes comments on rejected mss.

How to Contact SASE for return of ms. Responds in 4 months to mss. Accepts simultaneous, multiple submissions. Electronic submissions in .doc or .txt format also acceptable, but our manuscript readers still prefer hardcopy. E-mail attachment to adavis@truman.edu.

Payment/Terms No payment. Acquires one-time rights.

Advice "We look for strong character development, substantive plot and theme, visual and forceful language within a multilayered story. Make sure your work has the flavor of life, a sense of reality. A good story, well crafted, will eventually get published. Find the right market for it, and above all, don't give up."

GREEN MOUNTAINS REVIEW

Johnson State College, Johnson VT 05656. (802)635-1350. E-mail: greenmountainsreview@jsc.vsc.edu. **Contact:** Leslie Daniels, fiction editor. Magazine: digest-sized; 160-200 pages. Semiannual. Estab. 1975. Circ. 1,700.

 • *Green Mountains Review* has received a Pushcart Prize and Editors Choice Award.

Needs Adventure, experimental, humor/satire, literary, mainstream, serialized novels, translations. Receives 100 unsolicited mss/month. Accepts 6 mss/issue; 12 mss/year. "Manuscripts will not be read and will be returned between March 1 and September 1." Publishes ms 6-12 months after acceptance. **Publishes 0-4 new writers/year.** Recently published work by Howard Norman, Debra Spark, Valerie Miner, Peter LaSalle. Publishes short shorts. Also publishes literary criticism, poetry. Sometimes comments on rejected mss.

How to Contact Send complete ms and SASE. Responds in 1 month to queries; 6 months to mss. Accepts simultaneous submissions if advised. Sample copy for $7.

Payment/Terms Pays contributor's copies, 1-year subscription and small honorarium, depending on grants. Acquires first North American serial rights. Rights revert to author upon request.

Advice "We're looking for more rich, textured, original fiction with cross-cultural themes. The editors are open to a wide spectrum of styles and subject matter as is apparent from a look at the list of fiction writers who have published in its pages. One issue was devoted to Vermont fiction, another issue filled with new writing from the People's Republic of China, and a recent issue devoted to literary ethnography."

THE GREENSBORO REVIEW

English Dept., 134 McIver Bldg., UNC Greensboro, P.O. Box 26170, Greensboro NC 27402-6170. (336)334-5459. E-mail: jlclark@uncg.edu. Web site: www.greensbororeview.com. **Contact:** Jim Clark, editor. Magazine: 6×9; approximately 128 pages; 60 lb. paper; 80 lb. cover. Literary magazine featuring fiction and poetry for readers interested in contemporary literature. Semiannual. Circ. 800.

 • Stories for *The Greensboro Review* have been included in *Best American Short Stories, Prize Stories: The O. Henry Awards, New Stories from The South*, and *Pushcart Prize.*

Needs Accepts 6-8 mss/issue; 12-16 mss/year. Unsolicited manuscripts must arrive by September 15 to be considered for the spring issue and by February 15 to be considered for the fall issue. Manuscripts arriving after those dates may be held for the next consideration. **Publishes 10% new writers/year.** Recently published work by Robert Morgan, George Singleton, Robert Olmstead, Brock Clarke, Dale Ray Phillips, Kelly Cherry.

How to Contact Responds in 4 months to mss. Accepts multiple submissions. No simultaneous submissions. Sample copy for $5.

Payment/Terms Pays in contributor's copies. Acquires first North American serial rights.

Advice "We want to see the best being written regardless of theme, subject or style."

THE GRIFFIN

Gwynedd-Mercy College, P.O. Box 901, 1325 Sumneytown Pike, Gwynedd Valley PA 19437-0901. (215)641-5518. Fax: (215)641-5552. E-mail: fazzini.j@gmc.edu or allego.d@gmc.edu. **Contact:** Donna Allego and Jill Fazzini, editors. Literary magazine: 8½×5½; 112 pages. "*The Griffin* is a literary journal sponsored by Gwynedd-Mercy College. Its mission is to enrich society by nurturing and promoting creative writing that demonstrates a unique and intelligent voice. We seek writing which accurately reflects the human condition with all its intellectual, emotional and ethical challenges." Annual. Estab. 1999. Circ. 500.

Needs Short stories, essays and poetry. Open to genre work. "No slasher, graphic violence or sex." Accepts mss depending on the quality of work submitted. Receives 10-12 unsolicited mss/month. Publishes ms 6 months after acceptance. **Publishes 10-15 new writers/year.** Length: 2,500 words; average length: 2,000 words. Publishes short shorts. Also publishes literary essays, poetry.

How to Contact Send complete ms. Send SASE for return of ms or send disposable copy of ms and #10 SASE for reply only. Responds in 2-3 months to queries; 6 months to mss. Accepts simultaneous submissions "if notified." Sample copy for $6.

Payment/Terms Pays 2 contributor's copies; additional copies for $6.

Advice "Looking for well-constructed works that explore universal qualities, respect for the individual and community, justice and integrity. Check our description and criteria. Rewrite until you're sure every word counts. We publish the best work we find regardless of industry needs."

◪ THE GSU REVIEW

Georgia State University, Campus P.O. Box 1894, MSC 8R0322 Unit 8, Atlanta GA 30303-3083. (404)651-4804. Fax: (404)651-1710. Web site: www.gsu.edu/~wwwrev/. **Contact:** Jody Brooks, fiction editor. Literary journal. "*The GSU Review* is a biannual literary magazine publishing poetry, fiction, creative nonfiction and artwork. We're looking for original voices and well-written manuscripts. No subject or form biases." Semiannual.

Needs Literary. "No pornography." Receives 200 unsolicited mss/month. Publishes short shorts.

How to Contact Include SASE for notification. Responds in 1-2 months. Sample copy for $5. Writer's guidelines for SASE or on Web site.

Payment/Terms Pays in contributor's copy. Acquires one-time rights.

$◪ ◪ GULF COAST, A Journal of Literature & Fine Arts

Dept. of English, University of Houston, Houston TX 77204-3013. (713)743-3223. Fax: (713)743-3229. Web site: www.gulfcoastmag.org. **Contact:** Tiphanie Yanique Galiber, fiction editor. Magazine: 7×9; approx. 300 pages; stock paper, gloss cover; illustrations; photos. "Innovative fiction for the literary-minded." Estab. 1987. Circ. 2,300.

• Work published in *Gulf Coast* has been selected for inclusion in the *Pushcart Prize* anthology, *O'Henry Prize* anthology and *Best American Short Stories*.

Needs Ethnic/multicultural, experimental, literary, regional, translations, contemporary. "No children's, genre, religious/inspirational." Wants more "cutting-edge, experimental" fiction. Receives 300 unsolicited mss/month. Accepts 4-8 mss/issue; 12-16 mss/year. Publishes ms 6 months-1 year after acceptance. Agented fiction 5%. **Publishes 2-8 new writers/year.** Recently published work by Justin Cronin, Cary Holladay, Holiday Reinhorn, Michael Martone, Joe Meno, Karen An-hwei Lee. Publishes short shorts. Sometimes comments on rejected mss.

How to Contact Responds in 6 months to mss. Accepts simultaneous submissions. Back issue for $7, 7×10 SASE with 4 first-class stamps. Writer's guidelines for #10 SASE or on Web site.

Payment/Terms Pays $50-100. Acquires one-time rights.

Advice "Rotating editorship, so please be patient with replies. As always, please send one story at a time."

◪ GULF STREAM MAGAZINE

Florida International University, English Dept., Biscayne Bay Campus, 3000 N.E. 151st St., N. Miami FL 33181-3000. (305)919-5599. E-mail: gulfstreamfiu@yahoo.com. Editor: John Dufresne. **Contact:** Fiction Editor. Magazine: 5½×8½; 96 pages; recycled paper; 80 lb. glossy cover; cover illustrations. "We publish *good quality—* fiction, nonfiction and poetry for a predominately literary market." Semiannual. Estab. 1989. Circ. 1,000.

Needs Literary, mainstream, contemporary. Does not want romance, historical, juvenile or religious work. Receives 250 unsolicited mss/month. Accepts 5 mss/issue; 10 mss/year. Does not read mss during the summer. Publishes ms 3-6 months after acceptance. **Publishes 2-5 new writers/year.** Recently published work by Maureen Seaton, Charles Harper Webb, Lise Saffran, Janice Eidus, Susan Neville. Length: 7,500 words; average length: 5,000 words. Publishes short shorts. Also publishes poetry.

How to Contact Send complete ms with SASE. Responds in 3 months to mss. Accepts simultaneous submissions "if noted." Sample copy for $5. Writer's guidelines for #10 SASE.

Payment/Terms Pays in gift subscriptions and contributor's copies. Acquires first North American serial rights.

Advice "Looks for good concise writing—well plotted with interesting characters. Usually longer stories do not get accepted. There are exceptions, however."

$◪ HAPPY

46 St. Paul's Avenue, Jersey City, NJ 07306. E-mail: bayardx@gmail.com. **Contact:** Bayard, fiction editor. Magazine: 5½×8; 150-200 pages; 60 lb. text paper; 150 lb. cover; perfect-bound; illustrations; photos. Quarterly. Estab. 1995. Circ. 500.

Needs Erotica, ethnic/multicultural, experimental, fantasy, feminist, gay, horror, humor/satire, lesbian, literary, novel excerpts, psychic/supernatural/occult, science fiction, short stories. No "television rehash or religious nonsense." Wants more work that is "strong, angry, empowering, intelligent, God-like, expressive." Receives 300-500 unsolicited mss/month. Accepts 30-40 mss/issue; 100-150 mss/year. Publishes ms 6-12 months after acceptance. **Publishes 25-30 new writers/year.** Length: 6,000 words maximum; average length: 1,000-3,500 words. Publishes short shorts. Often comments on rejected mss.

How to Contact Send complete ms. Include estimated word count. Send SASE for reply, return of ms or send a disposable copy of ms. Responds in 1 month to queries. Accepts simultaneous submissions. Sample copy for $20. Writer's guidelines for #10 SASE.

Payment/Terms Pays 1-5¢/word. Pays on publication for one-time rights.

Advice "Excite me!"

☑ ◎ HARD ROW TO HOE

Potato Eyes Foundation, P.O. Box 541-I, Healdsburg CA 95448. (707)433-9786. **Contact:** Joe E. Armstrong, editor. Magazine: 8½×12; 12 pages; 60 lb. white paper; illustrations; photos. "We look for literature of rural life, including environmental, Native American and foreign (English only) subjects. Book reviews, short story, poetry and a regular column. So far as we know, we are the only literary newsletter that features rural subjects." Triannual. Estab. 1982. Circ. 200.

Needs Rural, enviromental, Native American, foreign (English only). "No urban subjects. We would like to see more fiction on current rural lifestyles." Receives 5-10 unsolicited mss/month. Accepts 2-3 mss/issue; 6-8 mss/year. Publishes ms 10 months after acceptance. **Publishes 2 new writers/year.** Recently published work by Gary Every, Victoria Gorton, Jane Bradbury. Average length: 1,200 words. Publishes short shorts. Also publishes literary essays, poetry. Often comments on rejected mss.

How to Contact Send complete ms. Send SASE for return of ms or send a disposable copy of ms and #10 SASE for reply only. Responds in 2 weeks to queries; 6 weeks to mss. Accepts multiple submissions. Sample copy for $3. Writer's guidelines for SASE. Reviews fiction.

Payment/Terms Pays 2 contributor's copies; additional copies $3. Pays on publication for one-time rights.

Advice "Work must exhibit authentic setting and dialogue."

☑ HARPUR PALATE, A Literary Journal at Binghamton University

English Department, P.O. Box 6000, Binghamton University, Binghamton NY 13902-6000. E-mail: hpfiction@ho tmail.com. Web site: harpurpalate.binghamton.edu. **Contact:** J.D. Schraffenberger, editor. Magazine: 6×9; 180-200 pages; coated or uncoated paper; 100 lb. coated cover; 4-color photography insert. "We have no restrictions on subject matter or form. Quite simply, send us your highest-quality fiction and poetry." Semiannual. Estab. 2000. Circ. 500.

• Stories published in *Harpur Palate* have been chosen for *Best American Mystery Stories 2003* and *Best of the Rest 3*.

Needs Adventure, ethnic/multicultural, experimental, historical, humor/satire, mainstream, mystery/suspense, novel excerpts, science fiction, suspense, literary, fabulism, magical realism, metafiction, slipstream. Receives 150 unsolicited mss/month. Accepts 5-10 mss/issue; 12-20 mss/year. Publishes ms 1-2 months after acceptance. **Publishes 5 new writers/year.** Recently published work by Lee K. Abbott, Jaimee Wriston Colbert, Joan Connor, Viet Dinh, Andrew Farkas, Mary Ann Mohanraj, Michael Steinberg, Martha Witt. Length: 250-8,000 words; average length: 2,000-4,000 words. Publishes short shorts. Also publishes poetry. Sometimes comments on rejected mss.

How to Contact Send complete ms with a cover letter. Include e-mail address on cover. Include estimated word count, brief bio, list of publications. Send a disposable copy of ms and #10 SASE for reply only. Responds in 1-3 week to queries; 4-6 months to mss. Accepts simultaneous submissions if stated in the cover letter. Sample copy for $8. Writer's guidelines online.

Payment/Terms Pays 2 copies. Pays on publication for first North American serial, electronic rights. Sponsors awards/contests.

Advice "*Harpur Palate* now accepts submissions all year; deadline for the Winter issue is October 15, for the Summer issue March 15. *Harpur Palate* also sponsors a fiction contest for the Summer issue. Due to concerns about computer viruses, we no longer accept submissions via e-mail. Also, due to the large number of submissions we receive, we cannot answer queries about the status of a particular story. Almost every literary magazine already says this, but it bears repeating: look at a recent copy of our publication to get an idea of the kind of writing published."

☑ HARVARD REVIEW

Harvard University, Lamont Library, Level 5, Cambridge MA 02138. (617)495-9775. E-mail: harvrev@fas.harvar d.edu. Web site: http://hcl.harvard.edu/harvardreview. **Contact:** Christina Thompson, editor. Magazine: 6×9; 192-240 pages; illustrations; photographs. Semiannual. Estab. 1992. Circ. 2,000.

Needs Literary. Receives 100-120 unsolicited mss/month. Accepts 4 mss/issue; 8 mss/year. Publishes ms 3-6 months after acceptance. **Publishes 3-4 new writers/year.** Recently published work by Joyce Carol Oates, Peter Orner, Jim Crace, Gore Vidal, Mary Swan, Karen Bender, Rishi Reddi. Length: 1,000-7,000 words; average length: 3,000-5,000 words. Publishes short shorts. Also publishes literary essays, literary criticism, poetry. Sometimes comments on rejected mss.

How to Contact Send SASE for return of ms or disposable copy of ms and SASE for reply only. Responds in 2 months to queries; 3-6 months to mss. Accepts simultaneous submissions. Writer's guidelines online.

Payment/Terms Pays 2 contributor's copies; additional copies $7. Pays on publication for first North American serial rights. Sends galleys to author.

⦿ HAWAI'I PACIFIC REVIEW

Hawai'i Pacific University, 1060 Bishop St., Honolulu HI 96813. (808)544-1108. Fax: (808)544-0862. E-mail: pwilson@hpu.edu. Web site: www.hpu.edu. **Contact:** Patrice M. Wilson, editor. Magazine: 6×9; 100 pages; glossy coated cover. *"Hawai'i Pacific Review* is looking for poetry, short fiction and personal essays that speak with a powerful and unique voice. We encourage experimental narrative techniques and poetic styles, and we welcome works in translation." Annual.

Needs Ethnic/multicultural (general), experimental, fantasy, feminist, historical (general), humor/satire, literary, mainstream, regional (Pacific), translations. "Open to all types as long as they're well done. Our audience is adults, so nothing for children/teens." Receives 25-40 unsolicited mss/month. Accepts 5-10 mss/year. Does not read mss January-August each year. Publishes ms 10 months after acceptance. **Publishes 1-2 new writers/ year.** Recently published work by Wendell Mayo, Elizabeth Crowell, Janet Flora. Publishes short shorts. Also publishes literary essays, poetry. Sometimes comments on rejected mss.

How to Contact Send SASE for return of ms or send a disposable copy of ms and SASE for reply only. Responds in 2 weeks to queries; 15 weeks to mss. Accepts simultaneous submissions but must be cited in the cover letter. Sample copy for $5.

Payment/Terms Pays 2 contributor's copies; additional copies $5. Pays on publication for first North American serial rights.

Advice "We look for the unusual or original plot; prose with the texture and nuance of poetry. Character development or portrayal must be unusual/original; humanity shown in an original insightful way (or characters); sense of humor where applicable. Be sure it's a draft that has gone through substantial changes, with supervision from a more experienced writer, if you're a beginner. Write about intense emotion and feeling, not just about someone's divorce or shaky relationship. No soap-opera-like fiction."

$⦿ ▨ HAYDEN'S FERRY REVIEW

The Virginia G. Piper Center for Creative Writing at Arizona State University, Box 875002, Arizona State University, Tempe AZ 85287-1502. (480)965-1243. E-mail: hfr@asu.edu. Web site: www.haydensferryreview.org. **Contact:** Fiction editor. Editors change every 1-2 years. Magazine: 7×9¾; 128 pages; fine paper; illustrations; photos. *"Hayden's Ferry Review* publishes best quality fiction, poetry, and creative nonfiction from new, emerging and established writers." Semiannual. Estab. 1986. Circ. 1,300.

● Work from *Hayden's Ferry Review* has been selected for inclusion in *Pushcart Prize* anthologies.

Needs Ethnic/multicultural, experimental, humor/satire, literary, regional, slice-of-life vignettes, contemporary, prose poem. Possible special fiction issue. Receives 250 unsolicited mss/month. Accepts 5 mss/issue; 10 mss/ year. Publishes ms 6 months after acceptance. Recently published work by T.C. Boyle, Raymond Carver, Ken Kesey, Rita Dove, Chuck Rosenthal and Rick Bass. Publishes short shorts. Also publishes literary criticism.

How to Contact Send complete ms with SASE. Responds in 2 weeks to queries; 3 months to mss. Accepts simultaneous submissions. Sample copy for $7.50. Writer's guidelines online.

Payment/Terms Pays $25-100. Pays on publication for first North American serial rights. Sends galleys to author.

⦿ ◎ HEARTLANDS, A Magazine of Midwest Life and Art

(formerly *The Heartlands Today*), The Firelands Writing Center, Firelands College of BGSU, Huron OH 44839. (419)433-5560. E-mail: lsmithdog@aol.com. Web site: www.theheartlandstoday.org. **Contact:** Fiction editor. Magazine: 8½×11; perfect bound; 96 pages; b&w illustrations; 15 photos. *Material must be set in the Midwest.* "We prefer material that reveals life in the Midwest today for a general, literate audience." Biannual. Estab. 1991.

Needs Ethnic/multicultural, humor/satire, literary, mainstream, regional (Midwest). Receives 15 unsolicited mss/month. Accepts 6 mss/issue. Does not read August-December. "We edit between January 1 and May 15. Submit then." Publishes ms 6 months after acceptance. Recently published work by Wendell Mayo, Tony Tomassi, Gloria Bowman. Also publishes literary essays, poetry. Sometimes comments on rejected mss.

How to Contact Send SASE for ms, not needed for query. Responds in 2 months to mss. Accepts simultaneous submissions If noted. Sample copy for $5.

Payment/Terms Pays $10-20 and 2 contributor's copies. Pays on publication for first rights.

Advice "We look for writing that connects on a human level, that moves us with its truth and opens our vision of the world. If writing is a great escape for you, don't bother with us. We're in it for the joy, beauty or truth of the art. We look for a straight, honest voice dealing with human experiences. We do not define the Midwest, we hope to be a document of the Midwest. If you feel you are writing from the Midwest, send your work to us. We look first at the quality of the writing."

⦿ ▨ HOME PLANET NEWS

Home Planet Publications, P.O. Box 455, High Falls NY 12440. (845)687-4084. **Contact:** Donald Lev, editor. Tabloid: 11½×16; 24 pages; newsprint; illustrations; photos. *"Home Planet News* publishes mainly poetry

Literary Magazines

along with some fiction, as well as reviews (books, theater and art) and articles of literary interest. We see *HPN* as a quality literary journal in an eminently readable format and with content that is urban, urbane and politically aware.'' Triannual. Estab. 1979. Circ. 1,000.

• *HPN* has received a small grant from the Puffin Foundation for its focus on AIDS issues.

Needs Ethnic/multicultural, experimental, feminist, gay, historical, lesbian, literary, mainstream, science fiction (soft/sociological). No ''children's or genre stories (except rarely some science fiction).'' Upcoming themes: ''Midrash.'' Publishes special fiction issue or anthology. Receives 12 unsolicited mss/month. Accepts 1 mss/issue; 3 mss/year. Publishes ms 1 year after acceptance. Recently published work by Maureen McNeil, Eugene Stein, Hugh Fox, Walter Jackman, Layle Silbert. Length: 500-2,500 words; average length: 2,000 words. Publishes short shorts. Also publishes literary criticism.

How to Contact Send complete ms. Send SASE for reply, return of ms or send a disposable copy of the ms. Responds in 6 months to mss. Sample copy for $4. Writer's guidelines for SASE.

Payment/Terms Pays 3 contributor's copies; additional copies $1. Acquires one-time rights.

Advice ''We use very little fiction, and a story we accept just has to grab us. We need short pieces of some complexity, stories about complex people facing situations which resist simple resolutions.''

☒ HOTEL AMERIKA

English Department, 360 Ellis Hall, Ohio University, Athens OH 45701. (740)597-1360. E-mail: editors@hotelam erika.net. Web site: www.hotelamerika.net. **Contact:** David Lazar, editor. Magazine: 130 pages; cardstock cover stock; photos. *Hotel Amerika* is a literary journal open to all genres and schools of writing, from the most formalistic to the most avant garde. Biannual. Estab. 2002. Circ. 2,000.

• Work published in *Hotel Amerika* was selected for the 2003 Pushcart Prize anthology.

Needs Literary. Receives 30-40 unsolicited mss/month. Accepts 3-5 mss/issue; 6-10 mss/year. Does not read mss May 1-August 31. Publishes ms 4-12 months after acceptance. Recently published work by Louise Wareham, Edith Pearlman, William Black. Publishes short shorts. Also publishes literary essays, poetry. Sometimes comments on rejected mss.

How to Contact Send complete ms. Send SASE (or IRC) for return of ms or send disposable copy of ms and #10 SASE for reply only. Responds in 3 months to mss. Accepts multiple submissions. Writer's guidelines for #10 SASE or online.

Payment/Terms Pays contributor's copies. Pays on publication for first North American serial rights. Sends galleys to author.

$ THE HUDSON REVIEW, A magazine of literature and the arts

The Hudson Review, Inc., 684 Park Ave., New York NY 10021. (212)650-0020. Fax: (212)774-1911. E-mail: info@hudsonreview.com. Web site: www.hudsonreview.com. **Contact:** Ronald Koury. Quarterly. Estab. 1948. Circ. 5,000.

Needs Reads between September 1 and November 30 only. Publishes ms 6 months after acceptance.

How to Contact Responds in 2 months to queries; 3 months to mss. No simultaneous submissions. Sample copy for $9. Writer's guidelines for #10 SASE.

Payment/Terms Pays 2½¢/word. Pays on publication. Only assigned reviews are copyrighted.

$ ☒ THE ICONOCLAST

1675 Amazon Rd., Mohegan Lake NY 10547-1804. **Contact:** Phil Wagner, editor. Journal: 8½×5½; 44-96 pages; 20 lb. white paper; 50 lb. cover stock; illustrations. ''Aimed for a literate general audience with interests in fine (but accessible) fiction and poetry.'' Bimonthly. Estab. 1992. Circ. 700.

Needs Adventure, ethnic/multicultural, experimental, humor/satire, literary, mainstream, novel excerpts, science fiction, literary. No character studies, slice-of-life, pieces strong on attitude/weak on plot. Receives 150 unsolicited mss/month. Accepts 3-6 mss/issue; 25-30 mss/year. Publishes ms 9-12 months after acceptance. **Publishes 8-10 new writers/year.** Publishes short shorts. Also publishes literary essays, poetry. Sometimes comments on rejected mss.

How to Contact Send complete ms. Send SASE for reply, return of ms or send a disposable copy of the ms labeled as such. Responds in 2 weeks to queries; 5 weeks to mss. No simultaneous submissions. Sample copy for $5. Writer's guidelines for #10 SASE. Reviews fiction.

Payment/Terms Pays 1¢/word. Pays on publication for first North American serial rights.

Advice ''We like fiction that has something to say (and not about its author). We hope for work that is observant, intense and multi-leveled. Follow Pound's advice—'make it new.' Write what you want in whatever style you want without being gross, sensational or needlessly explicit—then pray there's someone who can appreciate your sensibility. Read good fiction. It's as fundamental as learning how to hit, throw and catch is to baseball. With the increasing American disinclination towards literature, stories must insist on being heard. Read what is being published—then write something better—and different. Do all rewrites before sending a story out. Few editors have time to work with writers on promising stories; only polished ones.''

🔲 🔲 THE IDAHO REVIEW

Boise State University, English Dept., 1910 University Dr., Boise ID 83725. (208)426-1002. Fax: (208)426-4373. E-mail: mwieland@boisestate.edu. **Contact:** Mitch Wieland, editor. Magazine: 6×9; 180-200 pages; acid-free accent opaque paper; coated cover stock; photos. ''A literary journal for anyone who enjoys good fiction.'' Annual. Estab. 1998. Circ. 1,000. Member CLMP.

- Recent stories reprinted in *The Best American Short Stories*, The O. Henry Awards, The Pushcart Prize, and *New Stories from The South.*

Needs Experimental, literary. ''No genre fiction of any type.'' Receives 150 unsolicited mss/month. Accepts 5-7 mss/issue; 5-7 mss/year. ''We do not read from May 1-August 31.'' Publishes ms 1 year after acceptance. Agented fiction 5%. **Publishes 1 new writer/year.** Recently published work by Rick Bass, Melanie Rae Thon, Ron Carlson, Joy Williams, Madison Smart Bell, Carolyn Cooke. Length: open; average length: 7,000 words. Publishes short shorts. Also publishes literary essays, poetry. Sometimes comments on rejected mss.

How to Contact Send SASE for return of ms or send a disposable copy of ms and #10 SASE for reply only. Responds in 3-5 months to mss. Accepts simultaneous, multiple submissions. Sample copy for $8.95. Writer's guidelines for SASE. Reviews fiction.

Payment/Terms Pays $100 when funds are available, plus 2 contributor's copies; additional copies $5. Pays on publication for first North American serial rights. Sends galleys to author.

Advice ''We look for strongly crafted work that tells a story that needs to be told. We demand vision and intelligence and mystery in the fiction we publish.''

🔲 THE IDIOT

E-mail: idiotsubmission@yahoo.com. Web site: www.theidiotmagazine.com. **Contact:** Brian Campbell and Toni Plummer, lackeys. Magazine: 5½×8½; 48 pages; 20 lb. white paper; cardboard glossy cover; illustrations. ''For people who enjoy Triumph The Insult Comic Dog, *The Daily Show*, *South Park*, *Ali G*, Louis Black, old Woody Allen, S.J. Perelman, James Thurber and Albert Camus. We're looking for black comedy. Death, disease, God, religion and micronauts are all potential subjects of comedy. Nothing is sacred, but it needs to be funny. I don't want whimsical, I don't want amusing, I don't want some fanciful anecdote about a trip you took with your uncle when you were eight. I want laugh-out-loud-fall-on-the-floor-funny. If it's cute, give it to your mom, your sweetheart, or your puppy dog. Length doesn't matter, but most comedy is like soup. It's an appetizer, not a meal. Short is often better. Bizarre, obscure, referential and literary are all appreciated. My audience is mostly comprised of bitter misanthropes who play Russian Roulette between airings of *The Simpsons* each day. I want dark.'' Annual. Estab. 1993. Circ. 1,000.

Needs Humor/satire. Wants more short, dark humor. Publishes ms 6-12 after acceptance. **Publishes 1-3 new writers/year.** Recently published work by Judd Trichter, Freud Pachenko, Brad Hufford and Johnny ''John-John'' Kearns. Length: 2,000 words; average length: 500 words. Publishes short shorts. Also publishes poetry. Sometimes comments on rejected mss.

How to Contact Accepts submissions by e-mail only. Responds in 1-12 months to mss. Accepts simultaneous and reprints submissions. Sample copy for $5, subscription $10.

Payment/Terms Pays 1 contributor's copy when applicable. Acquires one-time rights. Sends galleys to author.

Advice ''We almost never use anything over 1,500 words, but if it's really funny I'll take a look at it.''

🔲 ILLUMINATIONS, An International Magazine of Contemporary Writing

Dept. of English, College of Charleston, 66 George St., Charleston SC 29424-0001. (843)953-1920. Fax: (843)953-1924. E-mail: lewiss@cofc.edu. Web site: www.cofc.edu/illuminations. **Contact:** Simon Lewis, editor. Magazine: 5×8; 80 pages; illustrations. ''*Illuminations* is one of the most challengingly eclectic little literary magazines around, having featured writers from the United States, Britain and Romania, as well as Southern Africa.'' Annual. Estab. 1982. Circ. 500.

Needs Literary. Receives 5 unsolicited mss/month. Accepts 1 mss/year. **Publishes 1 new writer/year.** Recently published work by John Michael Cummings. Also publishes poetry. Sometimes comments on rejected mss.

How to Contact Send SASE for reply, return of ms or send a disposable copy of ms. Responds in 2 weeks to queries; 2 months to mss. No simultaneous submissions. Sample copy for $10 and 6×9 envelope. Writer's guidelines free.

Payment/Terms Pays 2 contributor's copies of current issue; 1 of subsequent issue. Acquires one-time rights.

🔲 ILLYA'S HONEY

The Dallas Poets Community, a nonprofit corporation, P.O. Box 700865, Dallas TX 75370. E-mail: info@dallaspo ets.org. Web site: www.dallaspoets.org. **Contact:** Ann Howells, editor. Magazine: 5½×8½; 34 pages; 24 lb.

paper; glossy cover; photos. "We publish poetry and flash fiction under 200 words. We try to present quality work by writers who take time to learn technique—aimed at anyone who appreciates good literature." Quarterly. Estab. 1994. Circ. 125.

Needs Ethnic/multicultural, experimental, feminist, gay, historical, humor/satire, lesbian, literary, mainstream, regional, flash fiction. "We accept only flash (also known as micro) fiction." Receives 10 unsolicited mss/month. Accepts 2-8 mss/issue. Publishes ms 3-5 months after acceptance. **Publishes 2-3 new writers/year.** Recently published work by Paul Sampson, Susanne Bowers, Denworthy. Also publishes poetry. Sometimes comments on rejected mss.

How to Contact Send complete ms. Send SASE for return of ms or send a disposable copy of ms and #10 SASE for reply only. Responds in 6 months to mss. Sample copy for $4. Writer's guidelines for SASE.

Payment/Terms Pays 1 contributor's copy; additional copies $6. Pays on publication for first North American serial rights.

Advice "We would like to see more character studies, humor."

$ ▢ ◎ IMAGE, Art, Faith, Mystery

3307 Third Ave. W, Seattle WA 98119. (206)281-2988. E-mail: image@imagejournal.org. Web site: www.imagej ournal.org. **Contact:** Gregory Wolfe. Magazine: 7×10; 136 pages; glossy cover stock; illustrations; photos. "*Image* is a showcase for the encounter between religious faith and world-class contemporary art. Each issue features fiction, poetry, essays, memoirs, an in-depth interview and articles about visual artists, film, music, etc. and glossy 4-color plates of contemporary visual art." Quarterly. Estab. 1989. Circ. 4, 500. Member CLMP.

Needs Literary, translations. Receives 100 unsolicited mss/month. Accepts 2 mss/issue; 8 mss/year. Publishes ms 1 year after acceptance. Agented fiction 5%. Recently published work by Annie Dillard, David James Duncan, Robert Olen Butler, Bret Lott, Melanie Rae Thon. Length: 4,000-6,000 words; average length: 5,000 words. Also publishes literary essays, poetry.

How to Contact Send SASE for reply, return of ms or send disposable copy of ms. Responds in 1 month to queries; 3 months to mss. Sample copy for $16. Reviews fiction.

Payment/Terms Pays $10/page and 4 contributor's copies; additional copies for $6. Pays on acceptance. Sends galleys to author.

Advice "Fiction must grapple with religious faith, though the settings and subjects need not be overtly religious."

$ ▢ ▨ INDIANA REVIEW

Indiana University, Ballantine Hall 465, 1020 E. Kirkwood, Bloomington IN 47405-7103. (812)855-3439. Web site: www.indiana.edu/~inreview. **Contact:** Fiction editor. Magazine: 6×9; 160 pages; 50 lb. paper; Glatfelter cover stock. "*Indiana Review*, a nonprofit organization run by IU graduate students, is a journal of previously unpublished poetry and fiction. Literary interviews and essays also considered. We publish innovative fiction and poetry. We're interested in energy, originality and careful attention to craft. While we publish many well-known writers, we also welcome new and emerging poets and fiction writers." Semiannual. Estab. 1976. Circ. 2,000.

• Work published in *Indiana Review* received a Pushcart Prize (2001) and was included in *Best New American Voices* (2001). *IR* also received an Indiana Arts Council Grant and a NEA grant.

Needs Ethnic/multicultural, experimental, literary, mainstream, novel excerpts, regional, translations. No genre fiction. Receives 300 unsolicited mss/month. Accepts 7-9 mss/issue. Does not read mss mid-December-mid-January. Publishes ms an average of 3-6 months after acceptance. **Publishes 6-8 new writers/year.** Recently published work by Stuart Dybek, Marilyn Chin, Ray Gonzalez, Abby Frucht. Also publishes literary essays, poetry.

How to Contact Send complete ms. Accepts submissions by e-mail. Cover letters should be *brief* and demonstrate specific familiarity with the content of a recent issue of *Indiana Review*. Include SASE. Responds in 4 months to mss. Accepts simultaneous submissions if notified *immediately* of other publication. Sample copy for $9. Writer's guidelines online.

Payment/Terms Pays $5/page, plus 2 contributor's copies. Pays on publication for first North American serial rights. Sponsors awards/contests.

Advice "Because our editors change each year, so do our literary preferences. It's important that potential contributors are familiar with our most recent issue of *Indiana Review* via library, sample copy or subscription. Beyond that, we look for prose that is well crafted and socially relevant. Dig deep. Don't accept your first choice descriptions when you are revising. Cliché and easy images sink 90% of the stories we reject. Understand the magazines you send to—investigate!"

▢ INKWELL MAGAZINE

Manhattanville College, 2900 Purchase St., Purchase NY 10577. (914)323-7239. E-mail: inkwell@mville.edu. Web site: www.inkwelljournal.org. **Contact:** Fiction editor. Literary Journal: 5½×7½; 120-170 pages; 60 lb.

paper; 10 pt C1S, 4/c cover; illustrations; photos. *"Inkwell Magazine* is committed to presenting top quality poetry, prose and artwork in a high quality publication. *Inkwell* is dedicated to discovering new talent and to encouraging and bringing talents of working writers and artists to a wider audience. We encourage diverse voices and have an open submission policy for both art and literature." Annual. Estab. 1995. Circ. 1,000. Member CLMP.

Needs Experimental, humor/satire, literary. "No erotica, children's literature, romance, religious." Receives 120 unsolicited mss/month. Accepts 45 mss/issue. Does not read mss December-July. Publishes ms 2 months after acceptance. **Publishes 3-5 new writers/year.** Recently published work by Alice Quinn, Margaret Gibson, Benjamin Cheever. Length: 5,000 words; average length: 3,000 words. Publishes short shorts. Also publishes poetry.

How to Contact Send a disposable copy of ms and #10 SASE for reply only. Responds in 1 month to queries; 4-6 months to mss. Sample copy for $6. Writer's guidelines for SASE.

Payment/Terms Pays 2 contributor's copies; additional copies $8. Acquires first North American serial, first rights. Sponsors awards/contests.

Advice "We look for well-crafted original stories with a strong voice."

$⬛ THE IOWA REVIEW

308 EPB, The University of Iowa, Iowa City IA 52242. (319)335-0462. Fax: (319)335-2535. Web site: www.iowareview.org. **Contact:** Fiction Editor. Magazine: $5^1/_2 \times 8^1/_2$; 200 pages; first-grade offset paper; Carolina CS1 10-pt. cover stock. "Stories, essays, poems for a general readership interested in contemporary literature." Triannual magazine. Estab. 1970. Circ. 2,500.

Needs "We are open to a range of styles and voices and always hope to be surprised by work we then feel we need." Receives 600 unsolicited mss/month. Accepts 4-6 mss/issue; 12-18 mss/year. Does not read mss January-August. Publishes ms an average of 12-18 months after acceptance. Agented fiction less than 2%. **Publishes some new writers/year.** Recently published work by Ann Joslin Williams, Robert Coover, Lucia Nevai. Also publishes literary essays, literary criticism, poetry.

How to Contact Send complete ms with cover letter. "Don't bother with queries." SASE for return of ms. Responds in 3 months to queries; 3 months to mss. "We discourage simultaneous submissions." Sample copy for $8 and online. Writer's guidelines online. Reviews fiction.

Payment/Terms Pays $25 for the first page and $15 for each additional page, plus 2 contributor's copies; additional copies 30% off cover price. Pays on publication for first North American serial, nonexclusive anthology, classroom, online serial rights.

Advice "We have no set guidelines as to content or length; we look for what we consider to be the best writing available to us and are pleased when writers we believe we have discovered catch on with a wider range of readers. It is never a bad idea to look through an issue or two of the magazine prior to a submission."

⬛ ◎ IRIS, A Journal About Women

P.O. Box 800588, University of Virginia, Charlottesville VA 22908. (434)924-4500. E-mail: iris@virginia.edu. **Contact:** Fiction Editor. Magazine: $8^1/_2 \times 11$; 80 pages; glossy paper; heavy cover; illustrations; artwork; photos. "Material of particular interest to women. For a feminist audience, college educated and above." Semiannual. Estab. 1980. Circ. 3,500.

Needs Experimental, feminist, lesbian, literary, mainstream. "We're just looking for well-written stories of interest to women (particularly feminist women)." Receives 25 unsolicited mss/month. Accepts 5 mss/year. Publishes ms 1 year after acceptance. **Publishes 1-2 new writers/year.** Recently published work by Sheila Thorne, Lizette Wanzer, Marsha Recknagel and Denise Laughlin. Average length: 2,500-4,000 words. Sometimes comments on rejected mss.

How to Contact Accepts submissions by e-mail or send complete ms with SASE. Responds in 3 months to mss. Accepts simultaneous submissions. Sample copy for $5. Writer's guidelines for SASE. Label: Fiction Editor.

Payment/Terms Pays in contributor's copies and 1-year subscription. Acquires one-time rights.

Advice "My major complaint is with stories that don't elevate the language above the bland sameness we hear on the television everyday. Read the work on the outstanding women writers, such as Alice Munro and Louise Erdrich."

Ⓝ ⬛ ◎ ISOTOPE

A Journal of Literary Nature and Science Writing, 3200 Old Main Hill, Logan UT 84322-3200. (435)797-3697. Fax: (435)797-3797. E-mail: lbrown@cc.usu.edu. Web site: isotope.usu.edu. **Contact:** Charles Waugh, fiction editor. Literary magazine/journal: $8^1/_2 \times 11$, 44 pages. Contains illustrations. Includes photographs. "Focus on nature and science writing that meditates on and engages in the varied and complex relations among the human and non-human worlds." Semiannual. Estab. 2003. Circ. 670. Member CLMP and CELJ.

Needs Experimental, humor/satire, literary, translations. Special interests: nature and science. Receives 10 mss/month. Accepts 1-2 mss/issue; 2-4 mss/year. Does not read November 16-August 1. Manuscript published 6-18 months after acceptance. **Publishes 2 new writers/year.** Published Jill Stegman, Emily Doak, Janette Fecteau. Length: 250-7,500. Average length: 5,000. Publishes short shorts. Average length of short shorts: 500. Also publishes literary essays, poetry. Rarely comments on/critiques rejected mss.

How to Contact Send complete ms with cover letter. Include brief bio, list of publications. Send either SASE (or IRC) for return of ms or disposable copy of ms and #10 SASE for reply only. Considers simultaneous submissions, multiple submissions. Sample copy available for $5. Guidelines available on Web site.

Payment and Terms Writers receive 4 contributors copies, free subscription to the magazine. Additional copies $4. Pays on publication. Acquires first North American serial rights. Sends galleys to author. Publication is copyrighted.

Ⓝ ☑ THE JABBERWOCK REVIEW

Mississippi State University, Drawer E, Dept. of English, Mississippi State MS 39762. (662)325-3644. E-mail: jabberwock@org.msstate.edu. Web site: www.msstate.edu/org/jabberwock. **Contact:** Fiction Editor (revolving editorship). Magazine: $8^{1}/_{2} \times 5^{1}/_{2}$; 120 pages; glossy cover; illustrations; photos. "We are located in the South—love the South—but we publish good writing from anywhere and everywhere. And from anyone. We respect writers of reputation—and print their work—but we take great delight in publishing new and emerging writers as well." Semiannual. Estab. 1979. Circ. 500.

Needs Ethnic/multicultural, experimental, feminist, gay, literary, mainstream, regional, translations. "No science fiction, romance." Receives 150 unsolicited mss/month. Accepts 7-8 mss/issue; 15 mss/year. "We do not read during the summer (May 1 to September 1). Publishes ms 4-6 months after acceptance. Agented fiction 5%. **Publishes 1-5 new writers/year.** Recently published work by James Wilcox, Clarinda Harriss, Alan Elysheritz, Margo Rabb, Chris Mazza, Richard Lyons. Length: 250-5,000 words; average length: 4,000 words. Publishes short shorts. Also publishes literary essays, poetry. Sometimes comments on rejected mss.

How to Contact Send SASE (or IRC) for return of ms. Responds in 5 months to mss. Accepts simultaneous submissions "with notification of such." Sample copy for $6. Writer's guidelines for SASE.

Payment/Terms Pays 2 contributor's copies. Sponsors awards/contests.

Advice "It might take a few months to get a response from us, but your manuscript will be read with care. Our editors enjoy reading submissions (really!) and will remember writers who are persistent and commited to getting a story 'right' through revision."

$ ☑ THE JOURNAL

The Ohio State University, 164 W. 17th Ave., Columbus OH 43210. (614)292-4076. Fax: (614)292-7816. E-mail: thejournal@osu.edu. Web site: english.osu.edu/journals/the_journal/. **Contact:** Kathy Fagan (poetry); Michelle Herman (fiction). Magazine: 6×9; 150 pages. "We're open to all forms; we tend to favor work that gives evidence of a mature and sophisticated sense of the language." Semiannual. Estab. 1972. Circ. 1,500.

Needs Novel excerpts, literary short stories. No romance, science fiction or religious/devotional. Receives 100 unsolicited mss/month. Accepts 2 mss/issue. Publishes ms 1 year after acceptance. Agented fiction 10%. **Publishes some new writers/year.** Recently published work by Michael Martone, Gregory Spatz and Stephen Graham Jones. Sometimes comments on rejected mss.

How to Contact Send complete ms with cover letter and SASE. Responds in 2 weeks to queries; 2 months to mss. Accepts simultaneous submissions. No electronic submissions. Sample copy for $7 or online. Writer's guidelines online.

Payment/Terms Pays $25. Pays on publication for first North American serial rights. Sends galleys to author.

Advice Manuscripts are rejected because of "lack of understanding of the short story form, shallow plots, undeveloped characters. Cure: Read as much well-written fiction as possible. Our readers prefer 'psychological' fiction rather than stories with intricate plots. Take care to present a clean, well-typed submission."

☑ KALLIOPE, a journal of women's literature & art

Florida Community College at Jacksonville, 11901 Beach Blvd., Jacksonville FL 32246. (904)646-2081. E-mail: maclark@fccj.edu. Web site: www.fccj.org/kalliope. **Contact:** Fiction Editor. Magazine: $7^{1}/_{4} \times 8^{1}/_{4}$; 120 pages; 70 lb. coated matte paper; Bristol cover; 16-18 halftones per issue. "*Kalliope* publishes poetry, short fiction, reviews and b&w art, usually by women artists. We look for artistic excellence." Estab. 1978. Circ. 1,600.

Needs Ethnic/multicultural, experimental, novel excerpts, literary. "Quality short fiction by women writers. No science fiction or fantasy. Would like to see more experimental fiction." Receives approximately 100 unsolicited mss/month. Accepts up to 10 mss/issue. Does not read mss May-August. Publishes ms 3 months after acceptance. **Publishes 3 new writers/year.** Recently published work by Edith Pearlman, Bette Howland, Ruth Knafo Setton and Leslea Newman. Publishes short shorts. Also publishes poetry. Sometimes comments on rejected mss.

How to Contact Send complete ms. Responds in 1 week to queries; 3 months to mss. No simultaneous submissions. Sample copy for $9 (recent issue) or $4 (back copy), or see sample issues on Web site. Writer's guidelines online. Reviews fiction.

Payment/Terms Pays $10 honorarium if funds are available, otherwise 2 copies or subscription. Pays on publication for first rights. "We accept only unpublished work. Copyright returned to author upon request."

Advice "Read our magazine. The work we consider for publication will be well written and the characters and dialogue will be convincing. We like a fresh approach and are interested in new or unusual forms. Make us believe your characters; give readers an insight which they might not have had if they had not read you. We would like to publish more work by minority writers." Manuscripts are rejected because "1) nothing *happens!*, 2) it is thinly disguised autobiography (richly disguised autobiography is OK), 3) ending is either too pat or else just trails off, 4) characterization is not developed, and 5) point of view falters."

⏹ 🔲 KARAMU

English Dept., Eastern Illinois University, 600 Lincoln Ave., Charleston IL 61920. (217)581-6297. E-mail: cfoxa@ eiu.edu. **Contact**: Fiction Editor. Literary magazine: 5×8; 132-136 pages; illustrations; photos. "*Karamu* is a literary magazine of ideas and artistic expression independently produced by the faculty members and associates of Eastern Illinois University. We publish writing that captures something essential about life, which goes beyond superficial, and which develops voice genuinely. Contributions of creative nonfiction, fiction, poetry and artwork of interest to a broadly educated audience are welcome." Annual. Estab. 1966. Circ. 500.

• *Karamu* has received three Illinois Arts Council Awards.

Needs Adventure, ethnic/multicultural, experimental, feminist, gay, historical, humor/satire, lesbian, literary, mainstream, regional. "No pornographic, science fiction, religious, political or didactic stories—no dogma or proselytizing." List of upcoming editorial themes available for SASE. Receives 80-90 unsolicited mss/month. Accepts 10-15 mss/issue. Does not read February 16-September 1. Publishes ms 1 year after acceptance. **Publishes 3-6 new writers/year.** Recently published work by Jan Shoemaker, Beth Epstein, David Snyder, Rob Magnuson Smith, Craig Loomis and Debra Anne Davis. Publishes short shorts. Also publishes poetry. Sometimes comments on rejected mss.

How to Contact Send SASE for reply. Responds in 1 week to queries. Does not accept simultaneous submissions. Sample copy for $8 or $6 for back issues. Writer's guidelines for SASE.

Payment/Terms Pays 1 contributor's copy; additional copies at discount. Acquires one-time rights.

Advice Looks for "convincing, well-developed characters and plots expressing aspects of human nature or relationships in a perceptive, believable and carefully considered and written way."

$⏹ 🔲 THE KENYON REVIEW

Walton House, 104 College Dr., Gambier OH 43022. (740)427-5208. Fax: (740)427-5417. E-mail: kenyonreview @kenyon.edu. Web site: www.kenyonreview.org. **Contact:** Fiction Editor. An international journal of literature, culture and the arts dedicated to an inclusive representation of the best in new writing (fiction, poetry, essays, interviews, criticism) from established and emerging writers. Estab. 1939. Circ. 6,000.

• Work published in the *Kenyon Review* has been selected for inclusion in *Pushcart Prize* anthologies, *Best American Short Stories* and *Best American Poetry*.

Needs Condensed novels, ethnic/multicultural, experimental, feminist, gay, historical, humor/satire, lesbian, literary, mainstream, translations, contemporary. Receives 400 unsolicited mss/month. Unsolicited mss typically read only from September 1-March 31. Publishes ms 1 year after acceptance. Recently published work by Alice Hoffman, Beth Ann Fennelly, Romulus Linney, John Koethe, Albert Goldbarth, Erin McGraw.

How to Contact Now accepting mss via online submissions program. Please visit Web site for instructions. No simultaneous submissions. Sample copy $12 single issue, includes postage and handling. Please call or e-mail to order. Writer's guidelines online.

Payment/Terms Pays $15-40/page. Pays on publication for first rights.

Advice "We look for strong voice, unusual perspective, and power in the writing."

🔲 ⊚ KEREM, Creative Explorations in Judaism

Jewish Study Center Press, Inc., 3035 Porter St. NW, Washington DC 20008. (202)364-3006. E-mail: langner@er ols.com. Web site: www.kerem.org. **Contact:** Sara R. Horowitz and Gilah Langner, editors. Magazine: 6×9; 128 pages; 60 lb. offset paper; glossy cover; illustrations; photos. "*Kerem* publishes Jewish religious, creative, literary material—short stories, poetry, personal reflections, text study, prayers, rituals, etc." Estab. 1992. Circ. 2,000.

Needs Jewish: feminist, humor/satire, literary, religious/inspirational. Receives 10-12 unsolicited mss/month. Accepts 1-2 mss/issue. Publishes ms 2-10 months after acceptance. **Publishes 2 new writers/year.** Also publishes literary essays, poetry.

How to Contact Accepts submissions by e-mail. Send SASE for reply, return of ms or send disposable copy of ms. Responds in 2 months to queries; 5 months to mss. Accepts simultaneous, multiple submissions. Sample copy for $8.50. Writer's guidelines online.

Payment/Terms Pays free subscription and 2-10 contributor's copies. Acquires one-time rights.

Advice "Should have a strong Jewish content. We want to be moved by reading the manuscript!"

$☐ THE KIT-CAT REVIEW

244 Halstead Ave., Harrison NY 10528. (914)835-4833. **Contact:** Claudia Fletcher, editor. Magazine: 8½×5½; 75 pages; laser paper; colored card cover stock; illustrations. "*The Kit-Cat Review* is named after the 18th Century Kit-Cat Club, whose members included Addison, Steele, Congreve, Vanbrugh and Garth. Its purpose is to promote/discover excellence and originality." *The Kit-Cat Review* is part of the collections of the University of Wisconsin (Madison) and State University of New York (Buffalo). Quarterly. Estab. 1998. Circ. 500.

Needs Ethnic/multicultural, experimental, literary, novel excerpts, slice-of-life vignettes. No stories with "O. Henry-type formula endings. Shorter pieces stand a better chance of publication." No science fiction, fantasy, romance, horror or new age. Receives 40 unsolicited mss/month. Accepts 6 mss/issue; 24 mss/year. Publishes ms 6-12 months after acceptance. **Publishes 14 new writers/year.** Recently published work by Chayym Zeldis, Michael Fedo, Louis Phillips, Elisha Porat. Length: 5,000 words maximum; average length: 2,000 words. Publishes short shorts. Also publishes literary essays, literary criticism, poetry.

How to Contact Send complete ms. Accepts submissions by disk. Send SASE (or IRC) for return of ms, or send disposable copy of ms and #10 SASE for reply only. Responds in 1 week to queries; 2 months to mss. Accepts simultaneous, multiple submissions. Sample copy for $7 (payable to Claudia Fletcher). Writer's guidelines not available.

Payment/Terms Pays $25-200 and 2 contributor's copies; additional copies $5. Pays on publication for first rights.

☑ LAKE EFFECT, A Journal of the Literary Arts

Penn State Erie, Humanities and Social Sciences, 5091 Station Rd., Erie PA 16563-1501. (814)898-6281. Fax: (814)898-6032. E-mail: goL1@psu.edu. **Contact:** George Looney, editor-in-chief. Magazine: 5½×8½; 136-150 pages; 55 lb. natural paper; 12 pt. C1S cover. "In addition to seeking strong, traditional stories, *Lake Effect* is open to more experimental, language-centered fiction as well." Annual. Estab. as *Lake Effect*, 2001; as *Tempest*, 1978. Circ. 500. Member CLMP.

Needs Experimental, literary, mainstream. "No children's/juvenile, fantasy, science fiction, romance or young adult/teen." Receives 120 unsolicited mss/month. Accepts 5-9 mss/issue. Publishes ms 1 year after acceptance. **Publishes 6 new writers/year.** Recently published work by Edith Pearlman, Abby Frucht, Cris Mazza, Joan Connor, Rick Henry, Joanna Howard. Length: 4,500 words; average length: 2,600 words. Publishes short shorts. Also publishes literary essays, poetry.

How to Contact Send SASE for return of ms or send a disposable copy of ms and #10 SASE for reply only. Responds in 3 weeks to queries; 4-6 months to mss. Accepts simultaneous submissions. Sample copy for $6. Writer's guidelines for SASE.

Payment/Terms Pays 2 contributor's copies; additional copies $2. Acquires first, one-time rights. Not copyrighted.

Advice "We're looking for strong, well-crafted stories that emerge from character and language more than plot. The language is what makes a story stand out (and a strong sense of voice). Be sure to let us know immediately should a submitted story be accepted elsewhere."

☑ ◎ THE LAMP-POST, of the Southern California C.S. Lewis Society

1106 W. 16th St., Santa Ana CA 92706. (714)836-5257. E-mail: dgclark@adelphia. net. **Contact:** David G. Clark, editor. Magazine: 5½×8½; 34 pages; 7 lb. paper; 8 lb. cover; illustrations. "We are a literary review focused on C.S. Lewis and like writers." Quarterly. Estab. 1977. Circ. 200.

Needs "Literary fantasy and science fiction for children to adults." Publishes ms 3-12 months after acceptance. **Publishes 3-5 new writers/year.** Length: 1,000-5,000 words; average length: 2,500 words. Also publishes literary essays, literary criticism, poetry. Sometimes comments on rejected mss.

How to Contact Send via e-mail as Word file or rich text format. Send SASE for reply, return of ms or send a disposable copy of ms. Responds in 2 weeks to mss. Accepts reprint submissions. No simultaneous submissions. Sample copy for $3. Writer's guidelines for #10 SASE. Reviews fiction.

Payment/Terms Pays 2 contributor's copies; additional copies $3. Acquires first North American serial, one-time rights.

Advice "We look for fiction with the supernatural, mythic feel of the fiction of C.S. Lewis and Charles Williams. Our slant is Christian but we want work of literary quality. No inspirational. Is it the sort of thing Lewis, Tolkien and Williams would like—subtle, crafted fiction? If so, send it. Don't be too obvious or facile. Our readers aren't stupid."

◫ LAND-GRANT COLLEGE REVIEW

P.O. Box 1164, New York NY 10159-1164. E-mail: editors@land-grantcollegereview.com. Web site: www.lgcr.o rg. **Contact:** Fiction Submission. Magazine: 6×9; 196 pages; 70 lb. natural stock paper; 12 point cover stock. "The *Land-Grant College Review* is a nationally distributed literary journal. Recent contributors include Aimee Bender, Josip Novakovich, Robert Olmstead, Ron Carlson and Stephen Dixon." Semiannual. Estab. 2002. Circ. 4,000.

Needs Literary. No genre fiction, humor for its own sake, or anything "cutesy-pooh." Accepts 16 mss/issue; 32 mss/year. Publishes ms 3-4 months after acceptance. Agented fiction 10%. **Publishes 2 new writers/year.** Recently published work by Aimee Bender, Josip Novakovich, Robert Olmstead, Ron Carlson, Arthur Bradford, Alan Chuese. Average length: 2,750 words. Publishes short shorts.

How to Contact Send complete ms. Responds in 1 week to queries; 3 months to mss. Accepts simultaneous submissions and reprints. Sample copy for $8. Writer's guidelines online.

Payment/Terms Pays in copies. Acquires first North American serial rights.

Advice "Read the magazine first and familiarize yourself with stories we've selected in the past. Lots of additional information (and additional stories) are available on our Web sites."

⊕ LANDFALL/UNIVERSITY OF OTAGO PRESS

University of Otago Press, P.O. Box 56, Dunedin New Zealand. Fax: (643)479-8385. E-mail: landfall@otago.ac. nz. **Contact:** Fiction Editor.

Needs Publishes fiction, poetry, commentary and reviews of New Zealand books.

How to Contact Send copy of ms with SASE. Sample copy not available.

Advice "We concentrate on publishing work by New Zealand writers, but occasionally accept work from elsewhere."

◉ THE LAUREL REVIEW

Northwest Missouri State University, Dept. of English, Maryville MO 64468. (660)562-1739. E-mail: tlr@nwmiss ouri.edu. Web site: http://info.nwmissouri.edu/~m500025/laurel/lr_submit.html. **Contact:** Nancy Mayer, Rebeca Aronson, John Gallaher. Magazine: 6×9; 124-128 pages; good quality paper. "We publish poetry and fiction of high quality, from the traditional to the avant-garde. We are eclectic, open and flexible. Good writing is all we seek." Biannual. Estab. 1960. Circ. 900.

Needs Literary, contemporary. "No genre or politically polemical fiction." Receives 120 unsolicited mss/month. Accepts 3-5 mss/issue; 6-10 mss/year. Reading period: September 1-May 1. Publishes ms 1-12 months after acceptance. **Publishes 1-2 new writers/year.** Recently published work by Bruce Tallerman, Judith Kitchen, John Vanderslice. Also publishes literary essays, poetry.

How to Contact Responds in 4 months to mss. No simultaneous submissions. Sample copy for $5.

Payment/Terms Pays 2 contributor's copies and 1-year subscription. Acquires first rights. Copyright reverts to author upon request.

Advice "Nothing really matters to us except our perception that the story presents something powerfully felt by the writer and communicated intensely to a serious reader. (We believe, incidentally, that comedy is just as serious a matter as tragedy, and we don't mind a bit if something makes us laugh out loud; we get too little that makes us laugh, in fact.) We try to reply promptly, though we don't always manage that. In short, we want good poems and good stories. We hope to be able to recognize them, and we print what we believe to be the best work submitted."

◪ ◎ LE FORUM, Supplement Littéraire

Franco-American Research Opportunity Group, University of Maine, Franco American Center, Orono ME 04469-5719. (207)581-3764. Fax: (207)581-1455. E-mail: lisa_michaud@umit.maine.edu. Web site: www.francomaine .org. **Contact:** Lisa Michaud, managing editor. Magazine format: 56 pages; illustrations; photos. Publication was founded to stimulate and recognize creative expression among Franco-Americans, all types of readers, including literary and working class. This publication is used in classrooms. Circulated internationally. Quarterly. Estab. 1986. Circ. 5,000.

Needs "We will consider any type of short fiction, poetry and critical essays having to with Franco-American experience. They must be of good quality in French or English. We are also looking for Canadian writers with French-North American experiences." Receives 10 unsolicited mss/month. Accepts 2-4 mss/issue. **Publishes some new writers/year.** Length: 750-2,500 words; average length: 1,000 words. Occasionally comments on rejected mss.

How to Contact Include SASE. Responds in 3 weeks to queries; 1 month to mss. Accepts simultaneous submissions and reprints. Sample copy not available.

Payment/Terms Pays 3 copies. Acquires one-time rights.

Advice "Write honestly. Start with a strongly felt personal Franco-American experience. If you make us feel what you have felt, we will publish it. We stress that this publication deals specifically with the Franco-American experience.''

N ◙ THE LEDGE MAGAZINE

40 Maple Ave., Bellport NY 11713-2011.(631)286-5252. E-mail: tkmonaghan@aol.com. Web site: www.theledge magazine.com. **Contact:** Tim Monaghan, publisher. Literary magazine/journal: 6×9, 192 pages, offset paper, glossy stock cover. *"The Ledge Magazine* publishes cutting-edge contemporary fiction by emerging and established wirters.'' Annual. Estab. 1988. Circ. 1,500.

Needs Erotica, ethnic/multicultural (general), literary. Receives 30 mss/month. Accepts 3-4 mss/issue. Manuscript published 6 months after acceptance. Published Jim Thomson, Louis Gallo, Elissa Minor Rust. Length: 2,500 words (min)-7,500 words (max). Average length: 6,000 words. Also publishes poetry. Rarely comments on/critiques rejected mss.

How to Contact Send complete ms with cover letter. Include estimated word count, brief bio. Responds to queries in 4 weeks. Responds to mss in 3 months. Send SASE (or IRC) for return of ms. Considers simultaneous submissions. Sample copy available for $10. Guidelines available for SASE.

Payment and Terms Writers receive 1 contributor's copy. Additional copies $6. Pays on publication. Acquires first North American serial rights. Sends galleys to author. Publication is copyrighted.

Advice ''We seek stories that utilize language in a fresh, original way. We dislike sloppy or hackneyed writing.''

◙ THE LISTENING EYE

Kent State University Geauga Campus, 14111 Claridon-Troy Rd., Burton OH 44021. (440)286-3840. E-mail: grace_butcher@msn.com. **Contact:** Grace Butcher, editor. Magazine: $5^{1}/_{2} \times 8^{1}/_{2}$; 60 pages; photographs. ''We publish the occasional very short stories (750 words/3 pages double spaced) in any subject and any style, but the language must be strong, unusual, free from cliché and vagueness. We are a shoestring operation from a small campus but we publish high-quality work.'' Annual. Estab. 1970. Circ. 250.

Needs Literary. ''Pretty much anything will be considered except porn.'' Does not read mss April 15-January 1. Publishes ms 3-4 months after acceptance. Recently published work by Elizabeth Scott, Sam Ruddick, H.E. Wright. Publishes short shorts. Also publishes poetry. Sometimes comments on rejected mss.

How to Contact Send SASE for return of ms or disposable copy of ms with SASE for reply only. Responds in 4 weeks to queries; 4 months to mss. Accepts reprint submissions. Sample copy for $3 and $1 postage. Writer's guidelines for SASE.

Payment/Terms Pays 2 contributor's copies; additional copies $3 with $1 postage. Pays on publication for one-time rights.

Advice ''We look for powerful, unusual imagery, content and plot. Short, short.''

◙ ☷ THE LITERARY REVIEW, An International Journal of Contemporary Writing

Fairleigh Dickinson University, 285 Madison Ave., Madison NJ 07940. (973)443-8564. Fax: (973)443-8364. E-mail: tlr@fdu.edu. Web site: www.theliteraryreview.org. **Contact:** René Steinke, editor-in-chief. Magazine: 6×9; 160 pages; professionally printed on textpaper; semigloss card cover; perfect-bound. ''Literary magazine specializing in fiction, poetry and essays with an international focus. Our audience is general with a leaning toward scholars, libraries and schools.'' Quarterly. Estab. 1957. Circ. 2,000.

● Work published in *The Literary Review* has been included in *Editor's Choice, Best American Short Stories* and *Pushcart Prize* anthologies.

Needs Works of high literary quality only. Does not want to see ''overused subject matter or pat resolutions to conflicts.'' Receives 90-100 unsolicited mss/month. Accepts 20-25 mss/year. Does not read submissions during June, July and August. Publishes ms $1^{1}/_{2}$-2 years after acceptance. Agented fiction 1-2%. **Publishes 80% new writers/year.** Recently published work by Irvin Faust, Todd James Pierce, Joshua Shapiro, Susan Schwartz Senstadt. Also publishes literary essays, literary criticism, poetry. Occasionally comments on rejected mss.

How to Contact Responds in 3-4 months to mss. Accepts multiple submissions. Sample copy for $7. Writer's guidelines for SASE. Reviews fiction.

Payment/Terms Pays 2 contributor's copies; $3 discount for extras. Acquires first rights.

Advice ''We want original dramatic situations with complex moral and intellectual resonance and vivid prose. We don't want versions of familiar plots and relationships. Too much of what we are seeing today is openly derivative in subject, plot and prose style. We pride ourselves on spotting new writers with fresh insight and approach.''

◙ THE LONG STORY

18 Eaton St., Lawrence MA 01843. (978)686-7638. E-mail: rpburnham@mac.com. Web site: http://homepage.m ac.com/rpburnham/longstory.html. **Contact:** R.P. Burnham. Magazine: $5^{1}/_{2} \times 8^{1}/_{2}$; 150-200 pages; 60 lb. cover stock; illustrations (b&w graphics). For serious, educated, literary people. Annual. Estab. 1983. Circ. 1,200.

Needs Ethnic/multicultural, feminist, literary, contemporary. "No science fiction, adventure, romance, etc. We publish high literary quality of any kind but especially look for stories that have difficulty getting published elsewhere—committed fiction, working class settings, left-wing themes, etc." Receives 30-40 unsolicited mss/month. Accepts 6-7 mss/issue. Publishes ms 3 months to 1 year after acceptance. **Publishes 90% new writers/year.** Length: 8,000-20,000 words; average length: 8,000-12,000 words.

How to Contact Include SASE. Responds in 2 months to mss. Accepts simultaneous submissions "but not wild about it." Sample copy for $7.

Payment/Terms Pays 2 contributor's copies; $5 charge for extras. Acquires first rights.

Advice "Read us first and make sure submitted material is the kind we're interested in. Send clear, legible manuscripts. We're not interested in commercial success; rather we want to provide a place for long stories, the most difficult literary form to publish in our country."

N $ ◨ LORRAINE AND JAMES, Global Urban Literature

3727 W. Magnolia Blvd. Box 406, Burbank CA 91505. E-mail: editor@lorraineandjames.com. Web site: www.lorraineandjames.com. **Contact:** Jasai Madden, editor. Literary magazine/journal: 6×9, 190 pages. "Our main mission is to till the urban landscape in search of new writers and give attention to the noncommercial work of established writers from the U.S. and around the globe." Triannual. Estab. 2005. Circ. 1,000. Member Publishers Marketing Association and CLMP.

Needs Experimental, feminist, humor/satire, literary, mainstream. Does not want fantasy, children's, adventure, horror and romance. Receives 350 mss/month. Accepts 10-12 mss/issue; 35 mss/year. Manuscript published 6-10 months after acceptance. Agented fiction 1%. **Publishes 5 new writers/year.** Length: 500 words (min)-5,000 words (max). Average length: 3,500 words. Publishes short shorts. Also publishes literary essays, poetry.

How to Contact Send complete ms with cover letter. Accepts submissions by e-mail. Include estimated word count, brief bio, list of publications. Responds to queries in 2 weeks. Responds to mss in 12 weeks. Send either SASE (or IRC) for return of ms or disposable copy of ms and #10 SASE for reply only. Considers simultaneous submissions, multiple submissions. Sample copy available for $12. Guidelines available on Web site.

Payment and Terms Writers receive $50-$200 flate-rate payment. Pays on publication. Acquires first North American serial rights. Publication is copyrighted.

Advice "Be honest and be brave. Tell the story without compromise and let that be enough. If you feel like you need to explain it, you should probably re-work it."

◨ ◎ LOUISIANA LITERATURE, A Review of Literature and Humanities

Southeastern Louisiana University, SLU 792, Hammond LA 70402. (504)549-5783. Fax: (504)549-5021. E-mail: ngerman@selu.edu. Web site: www.selu.edu. **Contact:** Norman German, fiction editor. Magazine: 6¾×9¾; 150 pages; 70 lb. paper; card cover; illustrations. "Essays should be about Louisiana material; preference is given to fiction and poetry with Louisiana and Southern themes, but creative work can be set anywhere." Semiannual. Estab. 1984. Circ. 400 paid; 500-700 printed.

Needs Literary, mainstream, regional. "No sloppy, ungrammatical manuscripts." Receives 100 unsolicited mss/month. May not read mss June-July. Publishes ms 6-12 after acceptance. **Publishes 4 new writers/year.** Recently published work by Anthony Bukowski, Tim Parrish, Robert Phillips, Andrew Otis Haschemeyer. Length: 1,000-6,000 words; average length: 3,500 words. Also publishes literary essays, literary criticism, poetry. Sometimes comments on rejected mss.

How to Contact Include SASE. Responds in 3 months to mss. Sample copy for $8. Reviews fiction.

Payment/Terms Pays usually in contributor's copies. Acquires one-time rights.

Advice "Cut out everything that is not a functioning part of the story. Make sure your manuscript is professionally presented. Use relevant specific detail in every scene. We love detail, local color, voice and craft. Any professional manuscript stands out."

◎ THE LOUISIANA REVIEW

Division of Liberal Arts, Louisiana State University at Eunice, P.O. Box 1129, Eunice LA 70535. (337)550-1315. E-mail: bfonteno@lsue.edu. **Contact:** Dr. Jason Ambrosiano and Dr. Billy Fontenot, editors. Magazine: 5½×8½; 100-200 pages; illustrations. "While we will accept some of the better works submitted by our own students, we prefer excellent work by Louisiana writers as well as those outside the state who tell us their connection to it." Annual. Estab. 1999. Circ. 300-600.

Needs Ethnic/multicultural (Cajun or Louisiana culture), historical (Louisiana-related or setting), regional (Louisiana), romance (gothic). Receives 25 unsolicited mss/month. Accepts 5-7 mss/issue. Reads year-round. Publishes ms 11 months after acceptance. Recently published work by Tom Bonner, Laura Cario, Sheryl St. Germaine. Length: 1,000-5,000 words; average length: 2,000 words. Publishes short shorts. Also publishes poetry. Sometimes comments on rejected mss.

How to Contact Send SASE (or IRC) for return of ms. Responds in 5 weeks to queries; 10 weeks to mss. Accepts multiple submissions. Sample copy for $5.

Payment/Terms Pays 1-2 contributor's copies; additional copies $3. Pays on publication for one-time rights. Not copyrighted but has an ISSN number.

Advice "We do like to have fiction play out visually as a film would rather than static and undramatized."

☑ THE LOUISVILLE REVIEW

Spalding University, 851 S. Fourth St., Louisville KY 40203. (502)585-9911, ext. 2777. E-mail: louisvillereview@spalding.edu. Web site: www.louisvillereview.org. **Contact:** Sena Jeter Naslund, editor. Literary magazine. "We are a literary journal seeking original stories with fresh imagery and vivid language." Semiannual. Estab. 1976.

Needs Literary. Receives 200+ unsolicited mss/month. Accepts 4-6 fiction mss/issue; 8-12 fiction mss/year. Publishes ms 6 months after acceptance. **Publishes 8-10 new writers/year.** Recently published work by Peter Macuck, Aleda Shirley. Publishes essays, fiction, nonfiction and poetry.

How to Contact Send a disposable copy of ms and #10 SASE for reply only. Responds in 6 months to queries; 6 months to mss. Accepts multiple submissions.

Payment/Terms Pays 2 contributor's copies.

ℕ $☐ LUNCH HOUR STORIES

Lunch Hour Publications, 22833 Bothell-Everett Hwy, STE 102-PMB 1117, Bothell WA 98021-9366. (425)246-3726. Fax: (425)486-0631. E-mail: editor@lunchhourbooks.com. Web site: www.lunchhourstories.com. **Contact:** Nina Bayer, editor. Literary magazine/journal: $5\frac{1}{2} \times 8\frac{1}{2}$, 20 pages, natural linen paper, natural linen cover. "*Lunch Hour Stories*, dedicated to promoting excellent works of literary fiction, publishes only short stories and distributes them only to paid subscribers. *Lunch Hour Stories* are thin, easy-to-carry booklets that contain one short story each. They are designed to fit easily into a purse or briefcase and be read in less than 60 minutes. They are distributed by mail approximately 16 times a year (minimum of one issue per month). First consideration for publication is given to previously unpublished and authors that reside in the Northwestern U.S. Our goal is to publish a minimum of 6 stories each year from previously unpublished authors." 16 issues/year (min. 1 per month). Estab. Jan 2007.

Needs Literary, mainstream. Special interests: "Literary only." Does not want genre (romance, sci-fi, horror, etc.); experimental; religious; children's/young adult; feminist/gay. Accepts 1 mss/issue; 16 mss/year. Manuscript published 6-12 months after acceptance. **Publishes 6+ new writers/year.** Length: 4,000 words (min)-8,000 words (max). Average length: 6,000 words. Often comments on/critiques rejected mss.

How to Contact Send 2 print copies with a cover letter. Include estimated word count, brief bio, list of publications, contact information, SASE, synopsis of 100 words. Responds to mss in 3-6 months. Send disposable copies of ms and #10 SASE for reply only. Considers multiple submissions. Sample copy free with SASE (6×9). Guidelines available on Web site.

Payment and Terms Writers receive $50 flat-rate payment, 10 contributor's copies, free subscription to the magazine, and an interview on Web site. Additional copies $2. Pays on publication. Acquires first worldwide English language serial rights. All stories must be previously unpublished. Rights revert back to author following publication, with some limitations for the first year. Sends galleys to author. Publication is copyrighted.

Advice "Stories should be well written and carefully edited. They should be engrossing, humorous, warm or moving. They should make us want to read it more than once and then share it with a friend. We advise new writers to step out and take a chance! Do your best work, share it with a workshop or critique group, and then share it with us."

☑ THE MACGUFFIN

Schoolcraft College, Department of English, 18600 Haggerty Rd., Livonia MI 48152-2696. (734)462-4400, ext. 5327. Fax: (734)462-4679. E-mail: macguffin@schoolcraft.edu. Web site: www.macguffin.org. **Contact:** Steven A. Dolgin, editor; Nausheen S. Khan, managing editor; Elizabeth Kircos, fiction editor; Carol Was, poetry editor. Magazine: 6×9; 164+ pages; 60 lb. paper; 110 lb. cover; b&w illustrations; photos. "The *MacGuffin* is a literary magazine which publishes a range of material including poetry, creative nonfiction and fiction. Material ranges from traditional to experimental. We hope our periodical attracts a variety of people with many different interests." Triannual. Estab. 1984. Circ. 600.

Needs Adventure, ethnic/multicultural, experimental, historical (general), humor/satire, literary, mainstream, translations, contemporary, prose poem. "No religious, inspirational, juvenile, romance, horror, pornography." Receives 35-55 unsolicited mss/month. Accepts 10-15 mss/issue; 30-50 mss/year. Does not read mss between July 1-August 15. Publishes ms 6 months to 2 years after acceptance. Agented fiction 10-15%. **Publishes 30 new writers/year.** Recently published work by Gerry LaFemina, Gail Waldstein, Margaret Karmazin, Linda Nemec Foster, Laurence Lieberman, Conrad Hilberry. Length: 100-5,000 words; average length: 2,000-2,500 words. Publishes short shorts. Also publishes literary essays. Occasionally comments on rejected mss.

How to Contact Send SASE or e-mail. Responds in 6 months to mss. Sample copy for $6; current issue for $9. Writer's guidelines free.

Payment/Terms Pays 2 contributor's copies. Acquires one-time rights.

Advice "We want to give promising new fiction writers the opportunity to publish alongside recognized writers. Be persistent. If a story is rejected, try to send it somewhere else. When we reject a story, we may accept the next one you send us. When we make suggestions for a rewrite, we may accept the revision. There seems to be a great number of good authors of fiction, but there are far too few places for publication. However, this is changing. Make your characters come to life. Even the most ordinary people become fascinating if they live for your readers."

THE MADISON REVIEW

Department of English, Helen C. White Hall, 600 N. Park St., University of Wisconsin, Madison WI 53706. (608)263-0566. E-mail: madisonreview@yahoo.com. **Contact:** Laura Weingarten and Abram Foley, fiction editors. Magazine: 6×9; 180 pages. "Magazine for fiction and poetry with special emphasis on literary stories and some emphasis on Midwestern writers." Semiannual. Estab. 1978. Circ. 1,000.

Needs Experimental, literary, novel excerpts, translations, prose poems. "We would like to see more contemporary fiction; however, we accept fiction of any creative form and content. No historical fiction." Receives 10-50 unsolicited mss/month. Accepts 6 mss/issue. Does not read May-September. Publishes ms 4 months after acceptance. **Publishes 4 new writers/year.** Recently published work by Maurice Glenn Taylor and John McNally. Average length: 4,000 words. Also publishes poetry.

How to Contact Responds in 4 months to mss. Accepts multiple submissions. Sample copy for $3 via postal service or e-mail.

Payment/Terms Pays 2 contributor's copies; $2.50 charge for extras. Acquires first North American serial rights.

$ THE MALAHAT REVIEW

The University of Victoria P.O. Box 1700, STN CSC, Victoria BC V8W 2Y2 Canada. (250)721-8524. E-mail: malahat@uvic.ca. Web site: www.malahatreview.ca. **Contact:** John Barton, editor. "We try to achieve a balance of views and styles in each issue. We strive for a mix of the best writing by both established and new writers." Quarterly. Estab. 1967. Circ. 1,000.

• *The Malahat Review* has received the National Magazine Award for poetry and fiction.

Needs "General ficton and poetry." Accepts 3-4 mss/issue. Publishes ms 6 months after acceptance. **Publishes 4-5 new writers/year.** Recently published work by Michael Kenyon, Elise Levine, Bill Gaston, Marilyn Bowering.

How to Contact Send complete ms. "Enclose proper postage on the SASE (or send IRC)." Responds in 2 weeks to queries; 3 months to mss. No simultaneous submissions. Sample copy for $15 (US). Writer's guidelines online.

Payment/Terms Pays $30/magazine page. Pays on acceptance for second serial (reprint), first world rights.

Advice "We do encourage new writers to submit. Read the magazines you want to be published in, ask for their guidelines and follow them. Write for information on *Malahat*'s novella competition."

$ MANOA, A Pacific Journal of International Writing

English Dept., University of Hawaii, Honolulu HI 96822. (808)956-3070. Fax: (808)956-3083. E-mail: mjournal-l@hawaii.edu. Web site: http://www2.hawaii.edu/mjournal/. **Contact:** Frank Stewart, editor. Magazine: 7×10; 240 pages. "High quality literary fiction, poetry, essays, personal narrative, reviews. Most of each issue devoted to new work from Pacific and Asian nations. Our audience is primarily in the U.S., although expanding in Pacific countries. U.S. writing need not be confined to Pacific settings or subjects. " Semiannual. Estab. 1989. Circ. 2,500.

• *Manoa* has received numerous awards, and work published in the magazine has been selected for prize anthologies.

Needs Literary, mainstream, translations (from U.S. and nations in or bordering on the Pacific), contemporary, excerpted novel. No Pacific exotica. Accepts 1-2 mss/issue. Agented fiction 10%. **Publishes 1-2 new writers/year.** Recently published work by Ha Jin, Catherine Ryan Hyde, Samrat Upadhyay, Josip Novakovich. Also publishes poetry.

How to Contact Please query first before sending in mss. Include SASE. Does not accept submissions by e-mail. Responds in 3 weeks to queries; 1 month to poetry mss; 6 months to fiction to mss. Accepts simultaneous submissions. Sample copy for $10 (U.S.). Writer's guidelines online. Reviews fiction.

Payment/Terms Pays $100-500 normally ($25/printed page). Pays on publication for first North American serial, non-exclusive, one-time print rights. Sends galleys to author.

◨ ◩ THE MARLBORO REVIEW

The Marlboro Review Inc., P.O. Box 243, Marlboro VT 05344-0243. (802)254-4938. E-mail: marlboro@marlboro review.com. Web site: www.marlbororeview.com. **Contact:** Ellen Dudley, fiction editor. Magazine: 6×9; 80-120 pages; 60 lb. paper; photos. "We are interested in cultural, philosophical, scientific and literary issues approached from a writer's sensibility. Our only criterion for publication is strength of work." Semiannual. Estab. 1996. Circ. 1,000. Member CLMP, AWP.

- Works published in *The Marlboro Review* have received Pushcart Prizes.

Needs Literary, translations. Receives 400-500 unsolicited mss/month. Accepts 2-3 mss/issue; 4-6 mss/year. "Accepts manuscripts September through May." Publishes ms 1 year after acceptance. Recently published work by Stephen Dobyns, Jean Valentine, Joseph Shuster, Chana Bloch, William Matthews and Alberto Rios. Length: 500-12,000 words; average length: 7,000 words. Publishes short shorts. Also publishes literary essays, literary criticism, poetry.

How to Contact Send SASE for return of ms or send a disposable copy of ms and #10 SASE for reply only. No summer or e-mail submissions. Responds in 3 months to queries; 4 months to mss. Accepts simultaneous, multiple submissions. Sample copy for $20. Writer's guidelines for SASE or on Web site. Reviews fiction.

Payment/Terms Pays 2 contributor's copies; additional copies $8. All rights revert to author on publication.

Advice "We're looking for work with a strong voice and sense of control. Do your apprenticeship first. The minimalist impulse seems to be passing and for that we are grateful. We love to see great, sprawling, musical, chance-taking fiction."

$ ◨ ◩ THE MASSACHUSETTS REVIEW

South College, University of Massachusetts, Amherst MA 01003-9934. (413)545-2689. Fax: (413)577-0740. E-mail: massrev@external.umass.edu. Web site: www.massreview.org. **Contact:** Fiction Editor. Magazine: 6×9; 172 pages; 52 lb. paper; 65 lb. vellum cover; illustrations; photos. Quarterly. Estab. 1959. Circ. 1,200.

- Stories from *The Massachusetts Review* have been anthologized in the *100 Best American Short Stories of the Century* and the *Pushcart Prize* anthology.

Needs Short stories. Wants more prose less than 30 pages. Does not read fiction mss June 1-October 1. Publishes ms 18 months after acceptance. Agented fiction Approximately 5%. **Publishes 3-5 new writers/year.** Recently published work by Ahdaf Soueif, Elizabeth Denton, Nicholas Montemarano. Also publishes poetry. Sometimes comments on rejected mss.

How to Contact Send complete ms. No returned ms without SASE. Responds in 3 months to mss. Accepts simultaneous, multiple submissions. Sample copy for $7. Writer's guidelines online.

Payment/Terms Pays $50. Pays on publication for first North American serial rights.

Advice "Shorter rather than longer stories preferred (up to 28-30 pages)." Looks for works that "stop us in our tracks." Manuscripts that stand out use "unexpected language, idiosyncrasy of outlook and are the opposite of ordinary."

◯ METAL SCRATCHES

P.O. Box 685, Forest Lake MN 55025. E-mail: metalscratches@aol.com. **Contact:** Kim Mark, editor. Magazine: 5½×8½; 35 pages; heavy cover-stock. "*Metal Scratches* focuses on literary fiction that examines the dark side of humanity. We are not looking for anything that is 'cute' or 'sweet'." Semiannual. Estab. 2000.

Needs Erotica, experimental, horror (psychological), literary. "No poetry, science fiction, rape, murder or horror as in gore." Receives 20 unsolicited mss/month. Accepts 5-6 mss/issue; 20 mss/year. Publishes ms 6 months after acceptance. **Publishes 3 new writers/year.** Length: 3,500 words; average length: 3,000 words. Publishes short shorts. Sometimes comments on rejected mss.

How to Contact Send complete ms. Accepts submissions by e-mail. (No attachments.) Send disposable copy of ms and #10 SASE for reply only. Responds in 1 month to mss. Accepts simultaneous, multiple submissions. Sample copy for $3. Writer's guidelines for SASE or by e-mail.

Payment/Terms Pays 2 contributor's copies; additional copies for $2.50. Pays on publication for one-time rights. Not copyrighted.

Advice "Clean manuscripts prepared according to guidelines are a must. Send us something new and inventive. Don't let rejections from any editor scare you. Keep writing and keep submitting."

$ ◩ MICHIGAN QUARTERLY REVIEW

3574 Rackham Bldg., 915 E. Washington, University of Michigan, Ann Arbor MI 48109-1070. (734)764-9265. E-mail: mqr@umich.edu. Web site: www.umich.edu/~mqr. **Contact:** Fiction Editor. "An interdisciplinary journal which publishes mainly essays and reviews, with some high-quality fiction and poetry, for an intellectual, widely read audience." Quarterly. Estab. 1962. Circ. 1,500.

- Stories from *Michigan Quarterly Review* have been selected for inclusion in *The Best American Short Stories*, *O. Henry* and *Pushcart Prize* volumes.

Needs Literary. "No genre fiction written for a market. Would like to see more fiction about social, political, cultural matters, not just centered on a love relationship or dysfunctional family." Receives 200 unsolicited mss/month. Accepts 2 mss/issue; 8 mss/year. Publishes ms 1 year after acceptance. **Publishes 1-2 new writers/ year.** Recently published work by Robert Boyers, Herbert Gold, Alice Mattison, Joyce Carol Oates, Vu Tran. Length: 1,500-7,000 words; average length: 5,000 words. Also publishes literary essays, poetry.

How to Contact Send complete ms. "I like to know if a writer is at the beginning, or further along, in his or her career. Don't offer plot summaries of the story, though a background comment is welcome." Include SASE. Responds in 2 months to queries; 2 months to mss. No simultaneous submissions. Sample copy for $4. Writer's guidelines online.

Payment/Terms Pays $10/published page. Pays on publication. Buys first serial rights. Sponsors awards/ contests.

Advice "There's no beating a good plot, interesting characters and a fresh use of the English language. (Most stories fail because they're written in such a bland manner, or in TV-speak.) Be ambitious, try to involve the social world in the personal one, be aware of what the best writing of today is doing, don't be satisfied with a small slice-of-life narrative but think how to go beyond the ordinary."

MID-AMERICAN REVIEW

Department of English Box W, Bowling Green State University, Bowling Green OH 43403. (419)372-2725. Fax: (419)372-6805. Web site: www.bgsu.edu/midamericanreview. **Contact:** Michael Czyzniejewski, fiction editor. Magazine: 6×9; 192 pages; 60 lb. bond paper; coated cover stock. "We try to put the best possible work in front of the biggest possible audience. We publish serious fiction and poetry, as well as critical studies in contemporary literature, translations and book reviews." Semiannual. Estab. 1981.

● Work published in *Mid-American Review* has received the Pushcart Prize.

Needs Experimental, literary, translations, memoir, prose poem, traditional. "No genre fiction. Would like to see more short shorts." Receives 500 unsolicited mss/month. Accepts 6-8 mss/issue. Publishes ms 6 months after acceptance. Agented fiction 5%. **Publishes 4-8 new writers/year.** Recently published work by Dan Chaon, Steve Almond, Robert Olmstead. Also publishes literary essays, poetry. Occasionally comments on rejected mss.

How to Contact Accepts submissions by disk. Send complete ms with SASE. Responds in 4 months to mss. Sample copy for $7 (current issue), $5 (back issue); rare back issues $10. Writer's guidelines online. Reviews fiction.

Payment/Terms Pays $10/page up to $50, pending funding. Pays on publication when funding is available. Acquires first North American serial, one-time rights. Sponsors awards/contests.

Advice "We look for well-written stories that make the reader want to read on past the first line and page. Cliché themes and sloppy writing turn us off immediately. Read literary journals to see what's being published in today's market. We tend to publish work that is more nontraditional in style and subject, but are open to all literary nongenre submissions."

MINDPRINTS, A Literary Journal

Learning Assistance Program, Allan Hancock College, 800 S. College Dr., Santa Maria CA 93454-6399. (805)922-6966, ext. 3274. Fax: (805)922-3556. E-mail: pafahey@hancockcollege.edu. Web site: www.imindprints.com. **Contact:** Paul Fahey, editor. Magazine: 6×9; 125-150 pages; 70 lb. matte coated paper; glossy cover; illustrations; photos. "*Mindprints, A Literary Journal* is one of a very few college publications created as a forum for writers and artists with disabilities or for those with an interest in the field. The emphasis on flash fiction, as well as the fact that we are a national journal, puts us on the cutting edge of today's market." Annual. Estab. 2000. Circ. 600.

Needs Flash fiction: literary, mainstream. Receives 20-30 unsolicited mss/month. Accepts 75 mss/year. Does not read mss June-August. Publishes ms 6 months after acceptance. **Publishes 25-30 new writers/year.** Recently published work by Lori Maupas, Margaret A. Fry, Yolanda Falron, Carolyn-Howard Johnson, Barbara Jacksha. Length: 250-750 words; average length: 500 words. Publishes short shorts. Also publishes poetry. Often comments on rejected mss.

How to Contact Accepts submissions by e-mail (only from outside of the United States). Send a disposable copy of ms and cover letter and #10 SASE for reply only. Responds in 1 week to queries; 4 months to mss. Accepts simultaneous, multiple submissions and reprints. Sample copy for $6 and $2 postage or IRCs. Writer's guidelines for SASE, by e-mail or fax.

Payment/Terms Pays 1 contributor's copy; additional copies $5. Pays on publication for one-time rights. Not copyrighted.

Advice "We look for a great hook; a story that grabs us from the beginning; fiction and memoir with a strong voice and unusual themes; stories with a narrowness of focus yet broad in their appeal. Read and study the flash fiction genre. Revise, revise, revise. Do not send manuscripts that have not been proofed. Our mission is to showcase as many voices and worldviews as possible. We want our readers to sample creative talent from a national and international group of published and unpublished writers and artists.''

☑ THE MINNESOTA REVIEW, A Journal of Committed Writing

Dept. of English, Carnegie Mellon University, Pittsburgh PA 15213. (412)268-1977. E-mail: editors@ theminnesotareview.org. Web site: http://theminnesotareview.org. **Contact:** Jeffrey Williams, editor. Magazine: 5¼×7½; approximately 200 pages; some illustrations; occasional photos. ''We emphasize socially and politically engaged work.'' Semiannual. Estab. 1960. Circ. 1,500.

Needs Experimental, feminist, gay, historical, lesbian, literary. Receives 50-75 unsolicited mss/month. Accepts 3-4 mss/issue; 6-8 mss/year. Publishes ms 6-12 months after acceptance. **Publishes 3-5 new writers/year.** Recently published work by E. Shaskan Bumas, Carlos Fuentes, Maggie Jaffe, James Hughes. Publishes short shorts. Also publishes literary essays, literary criticism, poetry. Occasionally comments on rejected mss.

How to Contact Include SASE. Responds in 3 weeks to queries; 3 months to mss. Accepts simultaneous, multiple submissions. Sample copy for $12. Reviews fiction.

Payment/Terms Pays in contributor's copies. Charge for additional copies. Acquires first rights.

Advice ''We look for socially and politically engaged work, particularly short, striking work that stretches boundaries.''

☑ MISSISSIPPI REVIEW

University of Southern Mississippi, 118 College Dr. #5144, Hattiesburg MS 39406-0001. (601)266-4321. Fax: (601)266-5757. E-mail: rief@mississippireview.com. Web site: www.mississippireview.com. **Contact:** Rie Fortenberry, managing editor. Semiannual. Estab. 1972. Circ. 1,500.

Needs Annual fiction and poetry competition. $1,000 awarded in each category plus publication of all winners and finalists. Fiction entries 5,000 words or less. Poetry entry equals 1-3 poems, page limit is 10. $15 entry fee includes copy of prize issue. No limit on number of entries. Deadline October 1. No manuscripts returned. Does not read mss in summer. **Publishes 10-20 new writers/year.**

How to Contact Sample copy for $8. Writer's guidelines online.

Payment/Terms Acquires first North American serial rights.

$☑ ☑ THE MISSOURI REVIEW

1507 Hillcrest Hall, University of Missouri, Columbia MO 65211. (573)882-4474. Fax: (573)884-4671. E-mail: question@missourireview.com. Web site: www.missourireview.com. **Contact:** Speer Morgan, editor. Magazine: 6¾×10; 200 pages. ''We publish contemporary fiction, poetry, interviews, personal essays, cartoons, special features—such as 'History as Literature' series and 'Found Text' series—for the literary and the general reader interested in a wide range of subjects.'' Estab. 1978. Circ. 5,500.

● This magazine had stories anthologized in the *Pushcart Prize, Best American Short Stories, O. Henry Awards, Best American Essays, Best American Mystery Stories, Best American Nature and Science Writing,- Best American Erotica*, and *New Stories from The South.*

Needs Literary fiction on all subjects, novel excerpts. No genre fiction. Receives 500 unsolicited mss/month. Accepts 5-7 mss/issue; 16-20 mss/year. **Publishes 6-10 new writers/year.** Recently published work by Paul Eggers, Penelope Lively, Susan Perabo, Steve Almond. Also publishes literary essays, poetry. Often comments on rejected mss.

How to Contact Send complete ms. May include brief bio and list of publications. Send SASE for reply, return of ms or send disposable copy of ms. International submissions via Web site. Responds in 2 weeks to queries; 10 weeks to mss. Sample copy for $8 or online. Writer's guidelines online.

Payment/Terms Pays $30/printed page up to $750. Offers signed contract. Sponsors awards/contests.

☑ MOBIUS, The Journal of Social Change

505 Christianson, Madison WI 53714. (608)242-1009. E-mail: fmschep@charter.net. Web site: www.mobiusma gazine.com. **Contact:** Fred Schepartz, editor. Magazine: 8½×11; 16-24 pages; 60 lb. paper; 60 lb. cover. ''Looking for fiction which uses social change as either a primary or secondary theme. This is broader than most people think. Need social relevance in one way or another. For an artistically and politically aware and curious audience.'' Quarterly. Estab. 1989. Circ. 1,500.

Needs Ethnic/multicultural, experimental, fantasy, feminist, gay, historical, horror, humor/satire, lesbian, literary, mainstream, science fiction, contemporary, prose poem. ''No porn, no racist, sexist or any other kind of - ist. No Christian or spirituality proselytizing fiction.'' Wants to see more science fiction, erotica ''assuming it relates to social change.'' Receives 15 unsolicited mss/month. Accepts 3-5 mss/issue. Publishes ms 3-9 months after acceptance. **Publishes 10 new writers/year.** Recently published work by Margaret Karmazin, Benjamin Reed, John Tuschen, Ken Byrnes. Length: 500-5,000 words; average length: 3,500 words. Publishes short shorts. Always comments on rejected mss.

How to Contact Include SASE. Responds in 4 months to mss. Accepts simultaneous, multiple submissions and reprints. Sample copy for $2, 9×12 SAE and 3 first class stamps. Writer's guidelines for SASE.

Payment/Terms Pays contributor's copies. Acquires one-time rights, electronic rights for www version.

Advice "Note that fiction and poetry may be simultaneously published in e-version of *Mobius*. Due to space constraints of print version, some works may be accepted in e-version, but not print version. We like high impact, we like plot and character-driven stories that function like theater of the mind. Looks for first and foremost, good writing. Prose must be crisp and polished; the story must pique my interest and make me care due to a certain intellectual, emotional aspect. Second, *Mobius* is about social change. We want stories that make some statement about the society we live in, either on a macro or micro level. Not that your story neeeds to preach from a soapbox (actually, we prefer that it doesn't), but your story needs to have *something* to say."

Ⓔ NASSAU REVIEW

Nassau Community College, State University of New York, 1 Education Dr., Garden City NY 11530-6793. (516)572-7792. **Contact:** Editorial Board. Magazine: 6½×9½; 200 pages; heavy stock paper and cover; illustrations; photos. "Looking for high-level, professionally talented fiction on any subject matter except science fiction. Intended for a college and university faculty-level audience. Not geared to college students or others of that age who have not yet reached professional competency." Annual. Estab. 1964. Circ. 1,200. Member Council of Literary Magazines & Presses.

Needs Historical (general), humor/satire, literary, mainstream, mystery/suspense (amateur sleuth, cozy). "No science fiction." Receives 200-400 unsolicited mss/month. Accepts 5-6 mss/year. Does not read mss April-October. Publishes ms 6 months after acceptance. **Publishes 3-4 new writers/year.** Recently published work by Louis Phillips, Dick Wimmer, Norbert Petsch, Mike Lipstock. Length: 2,000-6,000 words; average length: 3,000-4,000 words. Publishes short shorts. Also publishes literary essays, literary criticism, poetry.

How to Contact Send 3 disposable copies of ms and #10 SASE for reply only. Responds in 2 weeks to queries; 6 months to mss. No simultaneous submissions. Sample copy free.

Payment/Terms Pays contributor's copies. Acquires one-time rights. Sponsors awards/contests.

Advice "We look for narrative drive, perceptive characterization and professional competence. Write concretely. Does not want over-elaborate details, and avoid digressions."

Ⓜ NERVE COWBOY

Liquid Paper Press, P.O. Box 4973, Austin TX 78765. Web site: www.onr.com/user/jwhagins/nervecowboy.html. **Contact:** Joseph Shields or Jerry Hagins, editors. Magazine: 7×8½; 64 pages; 20 lb. paper; card stock cover; illustrations. "*Nerve Cowboy* publishes adventurous, comical, disturbing, thought-provoking, accessible poetry and fiction. We like to see work sensitive enough to make the hardest hard-ass cry, funny enough to make the most helpless brooder laugh and disturbing enough to make us all glad we're not the author of the piece." Semiannual. Estab. 1996. Circ. 350.

Needs Literary. No "racist, sexist or overly offensive work. Wants more unusual stories with rich description and enough twists and turns that leave the reader thinking." Receives 40 unsolicited mss/month. Accepts 2-3 mss/issue; 4-6 mss/year. Publishes ms 6-12 months after acceptance. **Publishes 5-10 new writers/year.** Recently published work by Lori Jakiela, Tina Vincenti, Dave Newman, Brad Kohler, d.n. simmers, Paul Rogalus. Length: 1,500 words; average length: 750-1,000 words. Publishes short shorts. Also publishes poetry.

How to Contact Send SASE for reply, return of ms or send a disposable copy of ms. Responds in 2 weeks to queries; 3 months to mss. Accepts reprint submissions. No simultaneous submissions. Sample copy for $5. Writer's guidelines for #10 SASE or online.

Payment/Terms Pays 1 contributor's copy. Acquires one-time rights.

Advice "We look for writing which is very direct and elicits a visceral reaction in the reader. Read magazines you submit to in order to get a feel for what the editors are looking for. Write simply and from the gut."

Ⓔ Ⓜ NEW DELTA REVIEW

Louisiana State University, Dept. of English, 214 Allen Hall, Baton Rouge LA 70803-5001. (225)578-4079. E-mail: new-delta@lsu.edu. Web site: www.english.lsu.edu/journals/ndr. **Contact:** Editors change every year. Check Web site. Magazine: 6×9; 75-125 pages; high quality paper; glossy card cover; color artwork. "We seek vivid and exciting work from new and established writers. We have published fiction from writers such as Stacy Richter, Mark Poirier and George Singleton." Semiannual. Estab. 1984. Circ. 500.

- *New Delta Review* also sponsors the Matt Clark Prizes for fiction and poetry. Work from the magazine has been included in the *Pushcart Prize* anthology.

Needs Humor/satire, literary, mainstream, translations, contemporary, prose poem. "No Elvis stories, overwrought 'Southern' fiction, or cancer stories." Receives 150 unsolicited mss/month. Accepts 3-4 mss/issue; 6-8 mss/year. Reads from August 15-April 15. **Publishes 1-3 new writers/year.** Length: 250 words; average length: 15 ms pages words. Publishes short shorts. Also publishes poetry. Rarely comments on rejected mss.

Lachard. Length: 500-5,000 words; average length: 2,000 words. Also publishes literary essays, literary criticism, poetry.

How to Contact Accepts submissions by e-mail, fax or send complete ms with SASE. Responds in 2 months to mss. Accepts simultaneous submissions and reprints. Sample copy for $3. Writer's guidelines for SASE. Reviews fiction.

Payment/Terms Acquires one-time rights.

Advice "Tell your story with no padding, as if telling it to a person standing with one hand on the door ready to run out to a meeting. Have a good lead. This is the 'alpha & omega' of all good story writing. Don't start with 'This is a story about a boy and a girl.' Avoid writing how life 'ought to be,' rather write how life is."

◨ POINTED CIRCLE

Portland Community College-Cascade, 705 N. Killingsworth St., Portland OR 97217. (503)978-5251. E-mail: kimball@pcc.edu. **Contact:** Cynthia Kimball, English instructor, faculty advisor. Magazine: 80 pages; b&w illustrations; photos. "Anything of interest to educationally/culturally mixed audience." Annual. Estab. 1980.

Needs Ethnic/multicultural, literary, regional, contemporary, prose poem. "We will read whatever is sent, but encourage writers to remember we are a quality literary/arts magazine intended to promote the arts in the community. No pornography. Be mindful of deadlines and length limits." Accepts submissions only October 1-March 1, for July 1 issue.

How to Contact Accepts submissions by e-mail, fax. Submitted materials will not be returned; SASE for notification only. Accepts multiple submissions. Writer's guidelines for #10 SASE.

Payment/Terms Pays 2 copies. Acquires one-time rights.

Advice "Looks for quality—topicality—nothing trite. The author cares about language and acts responsibly toward the reader, honors the reader's investment of time and piques the reader's interest."

N ◻ ◎ POLYPHONY H.S., A Student-run National Literary Magazine for High School Writers

The Latin School of Chicago, 59 W. North Blvd., Chicago IL 60610.(312)582-6405. Fax: (312)582-6401. E-mail: blombardo@latinschool.org. Web site: www.polyphonyhs.com. **Contact:** Billy Lombardo, editor-in-chief. Literary magazine/journal: 9×6, 70-120 pages; silk finish 80 lb. white paper, silk finish 100 lb. cover. "Our goal is to seek out the finest high school writers in the country, to work with them to grow as writers, and to exhibit their fiction before a national audience. Their work is edited by an actual staff of high school editors." Annual. Estab. 2005. Circ. 1,050.

Needs Literary works. Does not want erotica. Receives 20 mss/month. Accepts 20-40 mss/issue. **Publishes 20-40 new writers/year.** Published Matt Ruggirello, Emily Cook, Taylor Rice. Length: 250 words (min)-4,000 words (max). Average length: 2,000 words. Publishes short shorts. Also publishes poetry. Always comments on/critiques rejected mss.

How to Contact Send complete ms as Word attachment and also paste within the e-mail text. Accepts submissions by e-mail. Include brief bio, name of school. Responds to mss in 6 weeks. Send disposable copy of ms and #10 SASE for reply only. Considers simultaneous submissions. Sample copy available for $5. Guidelines available via e-mail.

Payment and Terms Writers receive 2 contributors copies. Additional copies $3.50. Pays on publication. Acquires first rights. Publication is not copyrighted.

Advice "Revise, revise, revise. All first drafts are crappy, but absolutely essential to the final product. Care about the story."

◨ PORCUPINE LITERARY ARTS MAGAZINE

P.O. Box 259, Cedarburg WI 53012-0259. (262)375-3128. E-mail: ppine259@aol.com. Web site: www.porcupine literaryarts.com. **Contact:** Chris Skoczynski, fiction editor. Magazine: 5×8½; 150 pages; glossy color cover stock; art work and photos. Publishes "primarily poetry and short fiction. Novel excerpts are acceptable if self-contained. No restrictions as to theme or style." Semiannual. Estab. 1996. Circ. 1,500.

Needs Condensed novels, ethnic/multicultural, literary, mainstream. "No pornographic or religious." Receives 40 unsolicited mss/month. Accepts 3 mss/issue; 6 mss/year. Publishes ms 6-12 months after acceptance. **Publishes 4-6 new writers/year.** Recently published work by Richard Thieme, Halina Duraj, Lauro Palomba, Jane Summer, Carol Lee Lorenzo. Length: 2,000-7,500 words; average length: 3,500 words. Also publishes literary essays, poetry. Sometimes comments on rejected mss.

How to Contact Accepts submissions by e-mail. Send SASE for reply, return of ms or send a disposable copy of ms. Responds in 2 weeks to queries; 2 months to mss. Sample copy for $5. Writer's guidelines for #10 SASE.

Payment/Terms Pays 1 contributor's copy; additional copies for $8.95. Pays on publication for one-time rights.

Advice Looks for "believable dialogue and a narrator I can see and hear and smell. Form or join a writers' group. Read aloud. Rewrite extensively."

⬛ PORTLAND REVIEW

Portland State University, Box 347, Portland OR 97207-0347. (503)7254533. E-mail: ncj@pdx.edu. Web site: www.portlandreview.org. **Contact:** Nina Jett. Magazine: 9×6; 100 pages; b&w art and photos. Triannual. Estab. 1956. Circ. 500.

Needs Experimental, historical, humor/satire, novel excerpts, regional, slice-of-life vignettes. Wants more humor. No fantasy, detective, western or science fiction. Receives 100 unsolicited mss/month. Accepts 10-12 mss/issue; 30-40 mss/year. Publishes ms 3-6 months after acceptance. Recently published work by Katy Williams, Tina Boscha, Kathryn Ma, Brian Turner.

How to Contact Send complete ms. Send SASE for return of ms. Responds in 6 weeks to queries; 2-4 months to mss. Accepts simultaneous submissions. Sample copy for $8. Writer's guidelines online.

Payment/Terms Pays contributor's copies. Acquires first North American serial rights.

⬛ POTOMAC REVIEW, The Journal for Arts & Humanities

Montgomery College, Paul Peck Humanities Institute, 51 Mannakee St., Rockville MD 20850. (301)251-7417. Fax: (301)738-1745. Web site: www.montgomerycollege.edu/potomacreview. **Contact:** Julie Wakeman-Linn, editor. Magazine: 5½×8½; 248 pages; 50 lb. paper; 65 lb. color cover; art; illustrations; photos. *Potomac Review* "explores the inner and outer terrain of the Mid-Atlantic and beyond via a challenging diversity of prose, poetry and b&w artwork." Annual. Estab. 1994. Circ. 500.

Needs "Seeks stories with a vivid, individual quality that get at 'the concealed side' of life." Humor (plus essays, cogent nonfiction of all sorts) welcome. Accepts 50-60 mss/issue. Publishes ms within 1 year after acceptance. Agented fiction 2%. **Publishes new writers.** Recently published work by Kate Blackwell, Francine Witte, Clarissa Sligh, Herman Asarnow, Ivan Amato, Lyn Lifshin, Judith McCombs, J.D. Smith, Fay Picardi, E. Ethelbert Miller, Ann Knox, Hilary Tham. Length: 5,000 words; average length: 2,000 words. Publishes short shorts. Also publishes poetry.

How to Contact Send SASE for reply, return of ms or send a disposable copy of ms. Responds in 3 weeks to queries; 6 months to mss. Accepts simultaneous submissions. Sample copy for $10. Writer's guidelines for #10 SASE or on Web site.

Payment/Terms Pays 2 or more contributor's copies; additional copies for a 40% discount.

Advice "Have something to say in a original voice; check the magazine first; rewriting often trumps the original."

$ ⬛ ⬛ THE PRAIRIE JOURNAL, Journal of Canadian Literature

Prairie Journal Trust, P.O. Box 61203, Brentwood P.O., Calgary AB T2L 2K6 Canada. Web site: www.geocities.com/prairiejournal. **Contact:** A.E. Burke, editor. Journal: 7×8½; 50-60 pages; white bond paper; Cadillac cover stock; cover illustrations. "The audience is literary, university, library, scholarly and creative readers/writers." Semiannual. Estab. 1983. Circ. 600.

Needs Literary, regional. No genre (romance, horror, western—sagebrush or cowboys—erotic, science fiction, or mystery). Receives 100 unsolicited mss/month. Accepts 10-15 mss/issue; 20-30 mss/year. Suggested deadlines: April 1 for spring/summer issue; October 1 for fall/winter. Publishes ms 4-6 months after acceptance. **Publishes 60 new writers/year.** Recently published work by Robert Clark, Sandy Campbell, Darcie Hasack, Christopher Blais. Length: 100-3,000 words; average length: 2,500 words. Also publishes literary essays, literary criticism, poetry. Sometimes comments on rejected mss.

How to Contact Send complete ms with SASE (IRC). Include cover letter of past credits, if any. Reply to queries for SAE with 55¢ for postage or IRC. No American stamps. Responds in 2 weeks to queries; 6 months to mss. No simultaneous submissions. No e-mail submissions. Sample copy for $6. Writer's guidelines online. Reviews fiction.

Payment/Terms Pays $10-75. Pays on publication for first North American serial rights. In Canada, author retains copyright with acknowledgement appreciated.

Advice "We like character-driven rather than plot-centered fiction." Interested in "innovational work of quality. Beginning writers welcome! There is no point in simply republishing known authors or conventional, predictable plots. Of the genres we receive, fiction is most often of the highest calibre. It is a very competitive field. Be proud of what you send. You're worth it."

⬛ ⬛ PRAIRIE SCHOONER

University of Nebraska, English Department, 201 Andrews Hall, P.O. Box 880334, Lincoln NE 68588-0334. (402)472-0911. Fax: (402)472-9771. Web site: http://prairieschooner.unl.edu. **Contact:** Hilda Raz, editor. Magazine: 6×9; 200 pages; good stock paper; heavy cover stock. "A fine literary quarterly of stories, poems, essays and reviews for a general audience that reads for pleasure." Estab. 1926. Circ. 3,000.

• *Prairie Schooner*, one of the oldest publications in this book, has garnered several awards and honors over the years. Work appearing in the magazine has been selected for anthologies including the *Pushcart Prize* anthology and *Best American Short Stories*.

Needs Good fiction (literary). Receives 500 unsolicited mss/month. Accepts 4-5 mss/issue. Mss are read September through May only. **Publishes 5-10 new writers/year.** Recently published work by Robert Olen Butler, Janet Burroway, Aimee Phan, Valerie Sayers, Daniel Stern. Also publishes poetry.

How to Contact Send complete ms with SASE and cover letter listing previous publications—where, when. Responds in 4 months to mss. Sample copy for $6. Writer's guidelines and excerpts online. Reviews fiction.

Payment/Terms Pays in contributor's copies and prize money awarded. Will reassign rights upon request after publication. Sponsors awards/contests.

Advice *"Prairie Schooner* is eager to see fiction from beginning and established writers. Be tenacious. Accept rejection as a temporary setback and send out rejected stories to other magazines. *Prairie Schooner* is not a magazine with a program. We look for good fiction in traditional narrative modes as well as experimental, meta-fiction or any other form or fashion a writer might try. Create striking detail, well-developed characters, fresh dialogue; let the images and the situations evoke the stories' themes. Too much explication kills a lot of otherwise good stories. Be persistent. Keep writing and sending out new work. Be familiar with the tastes of the magazines where you're sending. We are receiving record numbers of submissions. Prospective contributors must sometimes wait longer to receive our reply."

$ 🌐 ⬭ PRETEXT

Pen & Inc. Press, School of Literature & Creative Writing, University of East Anglia, Norwich, Norfolk NR1 4HE United Kingdom. (+44)(0)1603592783. Fax: (+44)(0)1603507728. E-mail: info@penandinc.co.uk. Web site: www.inpressbooks.co.uk/penandinc. **Contact:** Katri Skala, managing editor. Magazine: 210×148 mm; 170 pages; Albury 80gsm paper; 4-color 240gsm art board cover stock; illustrations; photos. Semiannual. Estab. 1999. Member of Inpress Ltd.

Needs Literary, translations. No mass-market or non-literary work. Receives 70-80 unsolicited mss/month. Accepts 3 mss/issue; 6 mss/year. Publishes ms 6 months after acceptance. Agented fiction 10%. **Publishes 4 new writers/year.** Recently published work by Seamus Heaney, J.G. Ballard, Michael Holroyd, Tim Guest, Luisa Valenzuela, Dubravka Ugresic. Length: 6,000 words; average length: 3,000-4,000 words. Publishes short stories. Also publishes literary essays, literary criticism, poetry. Often comments on rejected mss.

How to Contact Send complete ms. Send SASE (or IRC) for return of the ms. Responds in 2 days to queries; 6 months to mss. Accepts simultaneous, multiple submissions. Sample copy for £7.99(UK), £8.99(Europe), £9.99 (rest of world). Writer's guidelines for SASE, fax, e-mail or online.

Payment/Terms Pays £50 and 1 contributor's copy. Pays on publication. Sends galleys to author.

Advice "Looking for good writing with a sense of purpose and an awareness of literary context. Never send until you are sure it's the best it can be."

📝 📷 PRIMAVERA

P.O. Box 37-7547, Chicago IL 60637-7547. (312)324-5920. **Contact:** Editorial Board. Magazine: 5½×8½; 128 pages; 60 lb. paper; glossy cover; illustrations; photos. Literature and graphics reflecting the experiences of women: poetry, short stories, photos, drawings. "We publish original fiction that reflects the experience of women. We select works that encompass the lives of women of different ages, races, sexual orientations and social class." Annual. Estab. 1975. Circ. 1,000.

• *Primavera* has won grants from the Illinois Arts Council, the Puffin Foundation and from Chicago Women in Publishing.

Needs Fantasy, feminist, gay, humor/satire, lesbian, literary, science fiction. "We dislike slick stories packaged for more traditional women's magazines. We publish only work reflecting the experiences of women, but also publish manuscripts by men." Receives 40 unsolicited mss/month. Accepts 6-10 mss/issue. Publishes ms 1 year after acceptance. **Publishes some new writers/year.** Recently published work by Elizabeth Keller Whitehurst, Gayle Whittier, Christine Stark, Robert Wallace, Alice Stern. Also publishes poetry. Sometimes comments on rejected mss.

How to Contact Send complete ms. Responds in 6 months to mss. No simultaneous submissions. Sample copy for $5; $10 for recent issues. Writer's guidelines for SASE.

Payment/Terms Pays 2 contributor's copies. Acquires first rights.

Advice "We're looking for artistry and deftness of untrendy, unhackneyed themes; an original slant on a well-known theme, an original use of language, and the highest quality we can find."

$ 📨 📝 📑 PRISM INTERNATIONAL

Department of Creative Writing, Buch E462-1866 Main Mall, University of British Columbia, Vancouver BC V6T 1Z1 Canada. (604)822-2514. Fax: (604)822-3616. E-mail: prism@interchange.ubc.ca. Web site: prism.arts. ubc.ca. **Contact:** Editor. Magazine: 6×9; 80 pages; Zephyr book paper; Cornwall, coated one-side cover; artwork on cover. "An international journal of contemporary writing—fiction, poetry, drama, creative nonfiction and translation.'' Readership: ''public and university libraries, individual subscriptions, bookstores—a worldwide audience concerned with the contemporary in literature.'' Quarterly. Estab. 1959. Circ. 1,200.

- *Prism International* has won numerous magazine awards, and stories first published in *Prism International* have been included in the *Journey Prize Anthology* every year since 1991.

Needs Experimental, traditional. New writing that is contemporary and literary. Short stories and self-contained novel excerpts (up to 25 double-spaced pages). Works of translation are eagerly sought and should be accompanied by a copy of the original. Would like to see more translations. ''No gothic, confession, religious, romance, pornography, or sci-fi.'' Also looking for creative nonfiction that is literary, not journalistic, in scope and tone. Receives over 100 unsolicited mss/month. Accepts 70 mss/year. ''*PRISM* publishes both new and established writers; our contributors have included Franz Kafka, Gabriel Garcia Marquez, Michael Ondaatje, Margaret Laurence, Mark Anthony Jarman, Gail Anderson-Dargatz and Eden Robinson.'' Publishes ms 4 months after acceptance. **Publishes 7 new writers/year.** Recently published work by S.A. Afolabi, Tammy Armstrong, Tim Bowling, Wayde Compton, David Zieroth. Publishes short shorts. Also publishes poetry.

How to Contact Send complete ms. Accepts submissions by fax, disk. ''Keep it simple. U.S. contributors take note: Do not send U.S. stamps, they are not valid in Canada. Send International Reply Coupons instead.'' Responds in 4 months to queries; 3-6 months to mss. Sample copy for $10 or on Web site. Writer's guidelines online.

Payment/Terms Pays $20/printed page and 1-year subscription. Pays on publication for first North American serial rights. Selected authors are paid an additional $10/page for digital rights. Sponsors awards/contests.

Advice ''Read several issues of our magazine before submitting. We are committed to publishing outstanding literary work. We look for strong, believeable characters; real voices; attention to language; interesting ideas and plots. Send us fresh, innovative work which also shows a mastery of the basics of good prose writing.''

⬛ PUCKERBRUSH REVIEW

Puckerbrush Press, 76 Main St., Orono ME 04473. (207)866-4868/581-3832. **Contact:** Constance Hunting, editor/publisher. Magazine: 9×12; 80-100 pages; illustrations. ''We publish interviews, fiction, reviews, poetry for a literary audience.'' Semiannual. Estab. 1979. Circ. 500.

Needs Experimental, gay (occasionally), literary, Belles-lettres. ''Wants to see more original, quirky and well-written fiction. No genre fiction. Nothing cliché, nothing overly sensational except in its human interest.'' Receives 30 unsolicited mss/month. Accepts 6 mss/issue; 12 mss/year. Publishes ms 1 year after acceptance. Recently published work by John Sullivan, Beth Thorpe, Chenoweth Hall, Merle Hillman, Wayne Burke. Publishes short shorts. Also publishes literary essays, literary criticism, poetry. Sometimes comments on rejected mss.

How to Contact Include SASE. Responds in 2 months to mss. Accepts simultaneous, multiple submissions. Sample copy for $3. Writer's guidelines for SASE. Reviews fiction and poetry.

Payment/Terms Pays in contributor's copies.

Advice ''I don't want to see tired plots or treatments. I want to see respect for language—the right words, true views of human nature. Don't follow clichés, but don't be too outré either.''

⬜ PUERTO DEL SOL

New Mexico State University, Box 3E, Las Cruces NM 88003-0001. (505)646-2345. Fax: (505)646-7755. E-mail: PUERTO@nmsu.edu. Web site: www.nmsu.edu/~puerto/welcome.html. **Contact:** Kevin McIlvoy, editor-in-chief and fiction editor; Kathleene West, poetry editor. Magazine: 6×9; 200 pages; 60 lb. paper; 70 lb. cover stock. ''We publish quality material from anyone. Poetry, fiction, interviews, reviews, parts-of-novels, long poems.'' Semiannual. Estab. 1964. Circ. 2,000.

Needs Ethnic/multicultural, experimental, literary, mainstream, novel excerpts, translations, contemporary, prose poem. Accepts 8-10 mss/issue; 12-15 mss/year. Does not accept mss January-September. **Publishes 8-10 new writers/year.** Recently published work by Dagoberto Gilb, Wendell Mayo, William H. Cobb. Also publishes literary essays, poetry. Always comments on rejected mss.

How to Contact Responds in 3-6 months to mss. Accepts simultaneous submissions. Sample copy for $8.

Payment/Terms Pays 2 contributor's copies. Acquires one-time rights. Rights revert to author after publication.

Advice ''We are open to all forms of fiction, from the conventional to the wildly experimental and we are pleased to work with emerging writers.''

🌐 ⬛ QUALITY WOMEN'S FICTION, Extending the Boundaries of Women's Fiction

QWF, P.O. Box 1768, Rugby CV21 4ZA United Kingdom. E-mail: sallyzigmond@gmail.com. Web site: www.qwf magazine.co.uk. **Contact:** Sally Zigmond, assistant editor. Magazine: A5; 80 pages; glossy paper. ''*QWF* gets under the skin of the female experience and exposes emotional truth.'' Bimonthly. Estab. 1994. Circ. 1,800.

Needs Experimental, feminist, literary. Receives 30 unsolicited mss/month. Accepts 12 mss/issue; 78 mss/year. Does not read mss June-August. Publishes ms 6-12 months after acceptance. **Publishes 15 new writers/**

year. Recently published work by Kathryn Kulpa, Ruth Latta, Kirsten Marek. Length: 1,500-5,000 words; average length: 2,500 words. Publishes short shorts. Also publishes literary essays, literary criticism. Always comments on rejected mss.

How to Contact Send complete ms. Accepts submissions by e-mail. Send SASE (or IRC) for return of ms or send disposable copy of the ms and #10 SASE for reply only. Responds in 2 months to queries; 2 months to mss. Accepts reprint submissions. Sample copy for SASE. Writer's guidelines by e-mail. Reviews fiction.

Payment/Terms Pays a free 3-issue subscription, including copy of magazine featuring writer's story. Pays on publication for first British serial rights.

Advice "Study the stories published on the *QWF* Web site."

☑ ◎ QUARTER AFTER EIGHT, A Journal of Prose and Community

QAE, Ellis Hall, Ohio University, Atens OH 45701. (740)593-2827. E-mail: editor@quarteraftereight.org. Web site: www.quarteraftereight.org. **Contact:** Hayley Haugen, co-editor-in-chief. Magazine: 6×9; 310 pages; 20 lb. glossy cover stock; photos. "We look to publish work which challenges boundaries of genre, style, idea and voice." Annual.

Needs Condensed novels, erotica, ethnic/multicultural, experimental, gay, humor/satire, lesbian, literary, mainstream, translations. "No traditional, conventional fiction." Send SASE for list of upcoming themes. Receives 150-200 unsolicited mss/month. Accepts 40-50 mss/issue. Does not read mss mid-March-mid-September. Publishes ms 6-12 months after acceptance. **Publishes 20-30 new writers/year.** Recently published work by Virgil Suárez, Maureen Sexton, John Gallagher and Amy England. Length: 10,000 words; average length: 3,000 words. Publishes short shorts. Also publishes literary essays, literary criticism, poetry. Sometimes comments on rejected mss.

How to Contact Send SASE for return of ms or send a disposable copy of ms. Responds in 3 months to mss. Accepts simultaneous, multiple submissions. Sample copy for $10, 8×11 SAE and $1.60 postage. Writer's guidelines for #10 SASE. Reviews fiction.

Payment/Terms Pays 2 contributor's copies; additional copies $7. Acquires first North American serial rights. Rights revert to author upon publication. Sponsors awards/contests.

Advice "We look for fiction that is experimental, exploratory, devoted to and driven by language—that which succeeds in achieving the *QAE* aesthetic. Please subscribe to our journal and read what is published. We do not publish traditional lined poetry or straightforward conventional stories. We encourage writers to submit after they have gotten acquainted with the *QAE* aesthetic."

Ⓝ ☑ QUICK FICTION

P.O. Box 4445, Salem MA 01970. E-mail: editors@jppress.org. Web site: http://quickfiction.org. **Contact:** Jennifer Pieroni, editor in chief. Literary magazine/journal: 6×6, 50 pages. Contains illustrations. "Publishes stories and narrative prose poems under 500 words." Semiannual. Estab. 2001. Circ. 1,000. Member CLMP.

Needs Literary. Does not want religious, children's, romance. Receives 50+ mss/month. Accepts 20-30 mss/issue; 40-60 mss/year. Manuscript published 4-6 months after acceptance. Agented fiction 0%. **Publishes 3 new writers/year.** Published Kevin Sampsell, Pamela Painter, David Barringer. Length: 500 words (max). Average length: 400 words. Rarely comments on/critiques rejected mss.

How to Contact Send complete ms with cover letter. Send disposable copy of ms and #10 SASE for reply only. Considers previously published submissions, multiple submissions. Sample copy available for $6.50. Guidelines available for SASE, via e-mail, on Web site.

Payment and Terms Writers receive 2 contributors copies and discount on additional copies. Acquires first North American serial rights. Sends galleys to author. Publication is copyrighted.

Advice Looks for "authenticity." "Read previous issues to understand our editorial sensibility."

☑ RAINBOW CURVE

P.O. Box 93206, Las Vegas NV 89193-3206. E-mail: rainbowcurve@sbcglobal.net. Web site: www.rainbowcurve.com. **Contact:** Daphne Young and Julianne Bonnet, editors. Magazine: 5½×8½; 100 pages; 60 lb. paper; coated cover. "*Rainbow Curve* publishes fiction and poetry that dabble at the edge; contemporary work that evokes emotion. Our audience is interested in exploring new worlds of experience and emotion; raw, visceral work is what we look for." Semiannual. Estab. 2002. Circ. 500.

Needs Ethnic/multicultural, experimental, feminist, gay, lesbian, literary. "No genre fiction (romance, western, fantasy, sci-fi)." Receives 60 unsolicited mss/month. Accepts 10-15 mss/issue; 20-30 mss/year. Publishes ms 6 months after acceptance. Agented fiction 1%. **Publishes 80% new writers/year.** Recently published work by Jonathan Barrett, Trent Busch, Rob Carney, Peter Fontaine, Bridget Hoida, Karen Toloui. Length: 500-10,000 words; average length: 7,500 words. Publishes short shorts. Sometimes comments on rejected mss.

How to Contact Send SASE for return of ms or send a disposable copy of ms and #10 SASE for reply only.

Responds in 3 months to mss. Accepts simultaneous submissions. Sample copy for $6. Writer's guidelines for SASE or on Web site.

Payment/Terms Pays 1 contributor's copy; additional copies $5. Acquires one-time rights. Sends galleys to author.

Advice "Unusual rendering of usual subjects and strong narrative voice make a story stand out. Unique glimpses into the lives of others—make it new."

ℕ $⬚ THE RAMBLER: GREAT STORIES, GREAT CONVERSATION

Rambler Publications, LLC, P.O. Box 5070, Chapel Hill NC 27514-5001. (919)545-9789. Fax: (919)545-0921. E-mail: editor@ramblermagazine.com. Web site: www.ramblermagazine.com. **Contact:** Elizabeth Oliver, editor. Magazine: 8⅛×10⅞, 64 pages, full color. Contains illustrations. Includes photographs. "Each isssue of *The Rambler* features in-depth, personal interviews with artists, writers and performers as well as selections of fiction, poetry and essays." Bimonthly. Estab. Jan/Feb 2004. Circ. 4,000. Member IPA.

Needs Literary. Does not want any kind of genre fiction. Receives 50-100 mss/month. Accepts 1-2 mss/issue; 6-12 mss/year. We accept 3-4 fiction manuscripts for our annual fiction issue (Jan/Feb). Manuscript published 6-12 months after acceptance. Agented fiction 5%. **Publishes 15 new writers/year.** Published Marjorie Kemper, Lawrence Naumoff, Amanda Ver Meulen (debut), Steve Cushman, Stephanie Johnson (debut), Judith Cox, Jen Provenzano (debut), Marianne Gingher. Length: 10,000 words max. Average length: 8,000 words. Publishes short shorts. Average length of short shorts: 800-1,000 words. Also publishes literary essays, poetry. Sometimes comments on/critiques rejected mss.

How to Contact Send complete ms with cover letter. Include estimated word count, brief bio, list of publications. Responds to queries in 2 months. Responds to mss in 4-6 months. Send either SASE (or IRC) for return of ms or disposable copy of ms and #10 SASE for reply only. Considers multiple submissions. Sample copy available for $7. Guidelines available for SASE, on Web site.

Payment and Terms Writers receive $25-$50 flat-rate payment, 1 contributors copy, free subscription to the magazine. Additional copies $6. Pays on publication. Acquires first North American serial rights. Sends galleys to author. Publication is copyrighted.

Advice "We're looking for stories that are well written with well-developed characters, believable dialogue and satisfying plots. A story that moves us in some way, connects us to something larger. Something that stays with us long after the story is finished."

⬚ RATTAPALLAX

Rattapallax Press, 532 La Guardia Place, Suite 353, New York NJ 10012. E-mail: info@rattapallax.com. Web site: www.rattapallax.com. **Contact:** Alan Cheuse, fiction editor. Literary magazine: 9×12; 128 pages; bound; some illustrations; photos. "General readership. Our stories must be character driven with strong conflict. All accepted stories are edited by our staff and the writer before publication to ensure a well-crafted and written work." Semiannual. Estab. 1999. Circ. 2,000.

Needs Literary. Receives 15 unsolicited mss/month. Accepts 3 mss/issue; 6 mss/year. Publishes ms 3-6 months after acceptance. Agented fiction 15%. **Publishes 3 new writers/year.** Recently published work by Stuart Dybek, Howard Norman, Molly Giles, Rick Moody. Length: 1,000-10,000 words; average length: 5,000 words. Publishes short shorts. Also publishes poetry. Often comments on rejected mss.

How to Contact Send SASE for return of ms. Responds in 3 months to queries; 3 months to mss. Sample copy for $7.95. Writer's guidelines for SASE or on Web site.

Payment/Terms Pays 2 contributor's copies; additional copies for $7.95. Pays on publication for first North American serial rights. Sends galleys to author.

Advice "Character driven, well crafted, strong conflict."

ℕ $⬚ THE RAVEN CHRONICLES, A Magazine of Transcultural Art, Literature and the Spoken Word

The Raven Chronicles, 1634 11th Ave., Seattle WA 98122-2419. (206)364-2045. E-mail: editors@ravenchronicles .org. Web site: www.ravenchronicles.org. **Contact:** Fiction editor. Jeannine Hall Gailey, poetry. Magazine: 8½×11; 96 pages; 50 lb. book; glossy cover; b&w illustrations; photos. "*The Raven Chronicles* is designed to promote transcultural art, literature and the spoken word." Triannual. Estab. 1991. Circ. 2,500-5,000.

Needs Ethnic/multicultural, literary, regional, political, cultural essays. "No romance, fantasy, mystery or detective." Receives 300-400 unsolicited mss/month. Accepts 35-60 mss/issue; 105-150 mss/year. Publishes ms 3-6 after acceptance. **Publishes 50-100 new writers/year.** Recently published work by David Romtvedt, Sherman Alexie, D.L. Birchfield, Nancy Redwine, Diane Glancy, Greg Hischak, Sharon Hashimoto. Length: 2,500 words (but negotiable); average length: 2,000 words. Publishes short shorts. Also publishes literary essays, literary criticism, poetry. Sometimes comments on rejected mss.

How to Contact Send SASE for return of ms. Does not accept unsolicited submissions by e-mail (except foreign submissions). Responds in 3 months to mss. Does not accept simultaneous submissions. Sample copy for $6.50. Writer's guidelines for #10 SASE.

Payment/Terms Pays $10-40 and 2 contributor's copies; additional copies at half cover cost. Pays on publication for first North American serial rights. Sends galleys to author.

Advice Looks for "clean, direct language, written from the heart, and experimental writing. Read sample copy, or look at *Before Columbus* anthologies and *Greywolf Annual* anthologies."

RE:AL, The Journal of Liberal Arts

Stephen F. Austin State University, P.O. Box 13007-SFA Station, Nacogdoches TX 75962-3007. (936)468-2059. Web site: http://libweb.sfasu.edu/real/default.htm. **Contact:** Dr. Christine Butterworth-McDermott, editor. Literary journal: 8×10; perfect-bound; 120-170 pages; "top" stock. Editorial content: 40% fiction, 40% poetry, 20% creative nonfiction. "Work is based on the intrinsic merit and its appeal to a sophisticated readership." Spring & Fall issues. Semiannual. Estab. 1968. Circ. 500.

Needs Realistic poetry and fiction. Open to well-crafted magical realism and exceptional genre work. No longer publishes scholarly articles. Receives 300 unsolicited mss/month. Accepts 10-20 mss/issue. Publishes ms 6-12 months after acceptance.

How to Contact Include SASE. Responds in 3-4 month to mss. Accepts simultaneous submissions. Sample copy for $12. Writer's guidelines for #10 SASE or online.

Payment/Terms Pays contributor copy; additional copies at reduced rate. Rights revert to author upon publication.

Advice "We are looking for the best work, whether you are established or not. Please submit a clean, neatly typed (or well-photocopied) manuscript. Please include all contact information in a cover letter. Please correspond with the editors in writing until your submission has been accepted."

RED ROCK REVIEW

Community College of Southern Nevada, 3200 E. Cheyenne Ave. N., Las Vegas NV 89030. (702)651-4094. Fax: (702)651-4639. E-mail: richard_logsdon@ccsn.nevada.edu. Web site: www.ccsn.edu/english/redrockreview/index/html. **Contact:** Dr. Richard Logsdon, senior editor. Magazine: 5×8; 125 pages. "We're looking for the very best literature. Stories need to be tightly crafted, strong in character development, built around conflict. Poems need to be tightly crafted, characterised by expert use of language." Semiannual. Estab. 1995. Circ. 250.

Needs Experimental, literary, mainstream. Receives 350 unsolicited mss/month. Accepts 40-60 mss/issue; 80-120 mss/year. Does not read mss during summer. Publishes ms 3-5 after acceptance. **Publishes 5-10 new writers/year.** Recently published work by Charles Harper Webb, Mary Sojourner, Mark Irwin. Length: 1,500-5,000 words; average length: 3,500 words. Publishes short shorts. Also publishes literary essays, literary criticism, poetry. Sometimes comments on rejected mss.

How to Contact Send SASE (or IRC) for return of ms. Responds in 2 weeks to queries; 3 months to mss. Accepts simultaneous, multiple submissions. Sample copy for $5.50. Writer's guidelines for SASE, by e-mail or on Web site.

Payment/Terms Pays 2 contributor's copies. Pays on acceptance for first rights.

RED WHEELBARROW

De Anza College, 21250 Stevens Creek Blvd., Cupertino CA 95014-5702. (408)864-8600. E-mail: splitterrandolph @fhda.edu. Web site: www.deanza.edu/redwheelbarrow. **Contact:** Randolph Splitter, editor-in-chief. Magazine: 6×9; 140-216 pages; photos. "Contemporary poetry, fiction, creative nonfiction, b&w graphics, comics and photos." Annual. Estab. 1976 as *Bottomfish*; 2000 as *Red Wheelbarrow*. Circ. 250-500.

Needs "Thoughtful, personal writing. We welcome submissions of all kinds, and we seek to publish a diverse range of styles and voices from around the country and the world." Receives 75 unsolicited mss/month. Accepts 30-50 mss/issue. Reads mss September through February. Submission deadline: January 31; publication date: Spring or Summer. Publishes ms 2-4 months after acceptance. Agented fiction 1%. **Publishes 0-2 new writers/year.** Recently published work by Mark Brazaitis, Christopher Buckley, Liesl Jobson, Virgil Suárez. Length: 4,000 words; average length: 2,500 words. Publishes short shorts. Also publishes poetry.

How to Contact Accepts submissions by e-mail. Responds in 2-4 months to mss. Accepts simultaneous submissions. Sample copy for $10; back issues $2.50. Writer's guidelines online.

Payment/Terms Pays 2 contributor's copies. Acquires first North American serial rights.

Advice "Write freely, rewrite carefully. Resist clichés and stereotypes. We are not affiliated with Red Wheelbarrow Press or any similarly named publication."

REDIVIDER

120 Boylston St., Emerson College, Boston MA 02116. E-mail: beaconstreetreview@hotmail.com. Web site: http://pages.emerson.edu/publications/redivider. **Contact:** Prose Editor. Editors change each year. Magazine:

$5^{1}/_{2} \times 8^{1}/_{2}$; 100 pages; 60 lb. paper. *Redivider*, a journal of new prose and poetry, is published twice a year by students in the graduate writing, literature and publishing department of Emerson College. Biannual. Estab. 1986. Circ. 100.

Needs Literary. Receives 20-30 unsolicited mss/month. Accepts 6-8 mss/issue; 10-12 mss/year. Publishes ms 3-6 months after acceptance. Publishes short shorts. Also publishes poetry. Sometimes comments on rejected mss.

How to Contact Send disposable copy of ms. Accepts simultaneous submissions with notification. Sample copy for $6 with a #10 SASE. Writer's guidelines for SASE.

Payment/Terms Pays 3 contributor's copies; additional copies $2. Pays on publication for one-time rights. Sponsors awards/contests.

REFLECTIONS LITERARY JOURNAL

Piedmont Community College, P.O. Box 1197, Roxboro NC 27573. (336)599-1181. E-mail: reflect@piedmont.cc. nc.us. **Contact:** Ernest Avery, editor. Magazine: 100-150 pages. Annual. Estab. 1999. Circ. 250.

• Publication suspended until 2008. Will accept submissions beginning January 1, 2007.

Needs Literary. Receives 30 unsolicited mss/month. Accepts 10-20 mss/issue. Publishes ms 4-6 months after acceptance. **Publishes 3-5 new writers/year.** Recently published work by Tim McLaurin, Peter Rennebohm, J. Dixon Hearne, Christopher Stanton. Length: 4,000 words; average length: 2,500 words. Publishes short shorts. Also publishes poetry.

How to Contact Send SASE for return of ms or #10 SASE for reply only. Sample copy for $6. Writer's guidelines for SASE or by e-mail.

Payment/Terms Pays 1 contributor's copy; additional copies $6 pre-publication; $7 post-publication. Acquires first North American serial rights. Sponsors awards/contests.

Advice "We look for good writing with a flair, which captivates an educated lay audience. Don't take rejection letters personally. We turn away many submissions simply because we don't have room for everything we like. For that reason, we're more likely to accept shorter well-written stories than longer stories of the same quality. Also, stories containing profanity that doesn't contribute to the plot, structure or intended tone are rejected immediately."

$ THE REJECTED QUARTERLY, A Journal of Quality Literature Rejected at Least Five Times

Black Plankton Press, P.O. Box 1351, Cobb CA 95426. E-mail: bplankton@juno.com. **Contact:** Daniel Weiss, Jeff Ludecke, fiction editors. Magazine: $8^{1}/_{2} \times 11$; 40 pages; 60 lb. paper; 10 pt. coated cover stock; illustrations. "We want the best literature possible, regardless of genre. We do, however, have a bias toward the unusual and toward speculative fiction. We aim for a literate, educated audience. *The Rejected Quarterly* believes in publishing the highest quality rejected fiction and other writing that doesn't fit anywhere else. We strive to be different, but will go for quality every time, whether conventional or not." Semiannual. Estab. 1998.

Needs Experimental, fantasy, historical, humor/satire, literary, mainstream, mystery/suspense, romance (futuristic/time travel only), science fiction (soft/sociological), sports. Accepts poetry about being rejected. Receives 30 unsolicited mss/month. Accepts 4-6 mss/issue; 8-12 mss/year. Publishes ms 1-12 months after acceptance. **Publishes 1-2 new writers/year.** Recently published work by Matthew Babcock, RC Cooper, Stephen Jones. Length: 8,000 words; average length: 5,000 words. Publishes short shorts. Also publishes literary essays, literary criticism, poetry. Often comments on rejected mss.

How to Contact Accepts submissions by e-mail. Send SASE for reply, return of ms or send a disposable copy of ms. Responds in 2 weeks to queries; 9 months to mss. Accepts reprint submissions. Sample copy for $6 (IRCs for foreign requests). Reviews fiction.

Payment/Terms Pays $7.50 and 1 contributor's copy; additional copies $5. Pays on acceptance for first rights. Sends galleys to author.

Advice "We are looking for high-quality writing that tells a story or expresses a coherent idea. We want unique stories, original viewpoints and unusual slants. We are getting far too many inappropriate submissions. Please be familiar with the magazine. Be sure to include your rejection slips! Send out quality rather than quantity. Work on one piece until it is as close to a masterpiece in your own eyes as you can get it. Find the right place for it. Be selective in ordering samples, but do be familiar with where you're sending your work."

RIVERWIND

Hocking College, 3301 Hocking Park Way, Nelsonville OH 45764. (740)753-3591. E-mail: williams_k@hocking.e du. **Contact:** Kristine Williams, co-editor. Magazine: 7×7; 125-150 pages; 60 lb. offset paper; illustrations; photos. *Riverwind* is an established magazine that prints fiction, poetry, black and white photos and prints, drawings, creative nonfiction, book reviews and plays. Special consideration is given to writers from the Appalachian region. Annual. Estab. 1976. Circ. 200-400.

Needs Adventure, ethnic/multicultural (Appalachian), humor/satire, literary, mainstream, regional. Does not want erotica, fantasy, horror, experimental, religious, children's/juvenile. Receives 25 unsolicited mss/month. Does not read mss June-September. Publishes ms 6-9 months after acceptance. **Publishes many new writers/ year.** Recently published work by Gerald Wheeler, Wendy McVicker, Roy Bentley, Perry A. White, Tom Montag, Beau Beadreaux. Length: 500-2,500 words; average length: 1,750 words. Publishes short shorts. Also publishes literary essays, literary criticism, poetry. Rarely comments on rejected mss.

How to Contact Send complete ms. Accepts submissions by e-mail, disk. Send disposable copy of ms and #10 SASE for reply only. Responds in 4 weeks to queries; 8-16 weeks to mss. Accepts simultaneous, multiple submissions. Sample copy for $5. Writer's guidelines for #10 SASE or by e-mail.

Payment/Terms Pays 2 contributor's copies. Pays on publication for first North American serial rights.

Advice "Avoid stereotypical plots and characters. We tend to favor realism but not sentimentality."

$⊘ ROANOKE REVIEW

Roanoke College, 221 College Lane, Salem VA 24153-3794. (540)375-2380. E-mail: review@roanoke.edu. **Contact:** Paul Hanstedt, editor. Magazine: 6×9; 200 pages; 60 lb. paper; 70 lb. cover. "We're looking for fresh, thoughtful material that will appeal to a broader as well as literary audience. Humor encouraged." Annual. Estab. 1967. Circ. 500.

Needs Feminist, gay, humor/satire, lesbian, literary, mainstream, regional. No pornography, science fiction or horror. Receives 150 unsolicited mss/month. Accepts 5-10 mss/year. Does not read mss February 1-September 1. Publishes ms 6 months after acceptance. **Publishes 1-5 new writers/year.** Recently published work by Robert Morgan, Lucy Ferriss, Francine Witte. Length: 1,000-6,000 words; average length: 1,500 words. Publishes short shorts. Also publishes poetry. Sometimes comments on rejected mss.

How to Contact Send SASE for return of ms or send a disposable copy of ms and #10 SASE for reply only. Responds in 1 month to queries; 6 months to mss. Sample copy for 8×11 SAE with $2 postage. Writer's guidelines for SASE.

Payment/Terms Pays $10-50/story (when budget allows) and 2 contributor's copies; additional copies $5. Pays on publication for one-time rights.

Advice "Pay attention to sentence-level writing—verbs, metaphors, concrete images. Don't forget, though, that plot and character keep us reading. We're looking for stuff that breaks the MFA story style."

⊘ THE ROCKFORD REVIEW

The Rockford Writers Guild, P.O. Box 858, Rockford IL 61105. E-mail: davecconnieross@aol.com. Web site: http://writersguild1.tripod.com. **Contact:** David Ross, editor. Magazine: 100 pages; perfect bound; color illustrations; b&w photos. "We look for prose and poetry with a fresh approach to old themes or new insights into the human condition." Semiannual. Estab. 1971. Circ. 600.

Needs Ethnic/multicultural, experimental, fantasy, humor/satire, literary, regional, science fiction (hard science, soft/sociological). "No graphic sex, translations or overly academic work." Recently published work by James Bellarosa, Sean Michael Rice, John P. Kristofco, L.S. Sedishiro. Also publishes literary essays.

How to Contact Include SASE. Responds in 2 months to mss. Accepts simultaneous, multiple submissions. Sample copy for $9. Writer's guidelines for SASE or online.

Payment/Terms Pays contributor's copies. "Two $25 editor's choice cash prizes per issue." Acquires first North American serial rights.

Advice "We're wide open to new and established writers alike—particularly short satire."

ℕ $⊠ ⊘ ◎ ROOM OF ONE'S OWN, A Canadian Quarterly of Women's Literature and Criticism

West Coast Feminist Literary Magazine Society, P.O. Box 46160, Station D, Vancouver BC V6J 5G5 Canada. Web site: www.roommagazine.com. **Contact:** Growing Room Collective. Magazine: 112 pages; illustrations; photos. "*Room of One's Own* is Canada's oldest feminist literary journal. Since 1975, *Room* has been a forum in which women can share their unique perspectives on the world, each other and themselves." Quarterly. Estab. 1975. Circ. 1,000.

Needs Feminist literature—short stories, creative nonfiction, essays—by, for and about women. "No humor, science fiction, romance." Receives 60-100 unsolicited mss/month. Accepts 18-20 mss/issue; 75-80 mss/year. Publishes ms 1 year after acceptance. **Publishes 15-20 new writers/year.** Also publishes poetry.

How to Contact Send complete ms with a cover letter. Include estimated word count and brief bio. Send a disposable copy of ms and #10 SASE or IRC for reply only. Responds in 6 months to mss. Sample copy for $13 or online. Writer's guidelines online. Reviews fiction.

Payment/Terms Pays $50 (Canadian) and a 1-year subscription. Pays on publication for first North American serial rights.

⊘ ⚑ SALMAGUNDI

Skidmore College, 815 North Broadway, Saratoga Springs NY 12866. Fax: (518)580-5188. E-mail: pboyes@skidmore.edu. **Contact:** Peg Boyers. Magazine: 8×5; 200-300 pages; illustrations; photos. "*Salmagundi* publishes an eclectic variety of materials, ranging from short-short fiction to novellas from the surreal to the realistic. Authors include Nadine Gordimer, Russell Banks, Steven Millhauser, Gordon Lish, Clark Blaise, Mary Gordon, Joyce Carol Oates and Cynthia Ozick. Our audience is a generally literate population of people who read for pleasure.'' Quarterly. Estab. 1965. Circ. 4,800. Member CLMP.

- *Salmagundi* authors are regularly represented in *Pushcart* collections and *Best American Short Story* collections.

Needs Ethnic/multicultural (multicultural), experimental, family saga, gay, historical (general), literary, poetry. Receives 300-500 unsolicited mss/month. Accepts 2 mss/year. Read mss October 1-May 1. Publishes ms up to 2 years after acceptance. Agented fiction 10%. Also publishes literary essays, literary criticism, poetry.

How to Contact Send complete ms. Accepts submissions by e-mail (pboyes@skidmore.edu). Responds in 6 months to mss. Sample copy for $5. Writer's guidelines for #10 SASE.

Payment/Terms Pays 6-10 contributor's copies and subscription to magazine. Acquires first, electronic rights.

Advice ''I look for excellence and a very unpredictable ability to appeal to the interests and tastes of the editors. Be brave. Don't be discouraged by rejection. Keep stories in circulation. Of course, it goes without saying: Work hard on the writing. Revise tirelessly. Study magazines and send only to those whose sensibility matches yours.''

SANSKRIT, Literary Arts Magazine of UNC Charlotte

University of North Carolina at Charlotte, 168 Conf. University Center, 9201 University City Blvd., Charlotte NC 28223-0001. (704)687-2326. Fax: (704)687-3394. E-mail: sanskrit@email.uncc.edu. Web site: www.uncc.edu/sanskrit. **Contact:** Sanskrit editor. ''*Sanskrit* is an award-winning magazine produced with two goals in mind: service to the student staff and student body, and promotion of unpublished and beginning artists. Our intended audience is the literary/arts community of UNCC, Charlotte, other schools and contributors, and specifically individuals who might never have read a literary magazine before.'' Annual. Estab. 1968.

- *Sanskrit* has received the Pacemaker Award, Associated College Press, Gold Crown Award and Columbia Scholastic Press Award.

Needs ''Not looking for any specific category—just good writing.'' Receives 50 unsolicited mss/month. Accepts 2-3 mss/issue. Recently published work by Bayard. Publishes short shorts. Also publishes poetry. Rarely comments on rejected mss.

How to Contact Send complete ms. Accepts submissions by e-mail (sanskrit@email.uncc.edu), fax. Include complete manuscript with cover letter. Accepts simultaneous, multiple submissions. Sample copy for $10. Writer's guidelines for #10 SASE.

Payment/Terms Pays contributor's copy. Acquires one-time rights.

Advice ''Remember that you are entering a market often saturated with mediocrity—an abundance of cute words and phrases held together by clichés simply will not do.''

SANTA MONICA REVIEW

Santa Monica College, 1900 Pico Blvd., Santa Monica CA 90405. (310)434-4242. **Contact:** Andrew Tonkovich, editor. Magazine: 250 pages. ''The editors are committed to fostering new talent as well as presenting new work by established writers. There is also a special emphasis on presenting and promoting writers who make their home in Southern California.'' Estab. 1989. Circ. 4,000.

Needs Experimental, literary, memoirs. ''No crime and detective, misogyny, footnotes, TV, dog stories. We want more self-conscious, smart, political, humorous, digressive, meta-fiction.'' Receives 250 unsolicited mss/month. Accepts 10 mss/issue; 20 mss/year. Agented fiction 10%. **Publishes 5 new writers/year.** Recently published work by Ed Skoog, Trini Dalton, Judith Grossman, John Peterson. Also publishes literary essays.

How to Contact Send complete disposable copy of ms. Responds in 3 months to mss. Accepts simultaneous, multiple submissions. Sample copy for $7.

Payment/Terms Pays 5 contributor's copies. Acquires first North American serial rights. Sends galleys to author.

THE SARANAC REVIEW

Suny Plattsburgh, Dept. of English, Champlain Valley Hall, Plattsburgh NY 12901. (518)564-5151. Fax: (518)564-2140. E-mail: saranacreview@plattsburgh.edu. Web site: http://research.plattsburgh.edu/saranacreview/. **Contact:** Fiction editor. Magazine: $5\frac{1}{2} \times 8\frac{1}{2}$; 180-200 pages; 80 lb. cover/70 lb. paper; glossy cover stock; illustrations; photos. ''*The Saranac Review* is committed to dissolving boundaries of all kinds, seeking to publish a diverse array of emerging and established writers from Canada and the U.S. *The Saranac Review* aims to be a textual clearing in which a space is opened for cross-pollination between American and Canadian writers. In this way the magazine reflects the expansive bright spirit of the etymology of it's name, Saranac, meaning 'cluster of stars.''' Annual. Estab. 2004.

Needs Ethnic/multicultural, historical, literary. Publishes ms 8 months after acceptance. Publishes short shorts. Also publishes poetry and literary/creative nonfiction. Sometimes comments on rejected mss.

How to Contact Send complete ms. Send SASE (or IRC) for return of ms or send disposable copy of the ms and #10 SASE for reply only. Responds in 4 months to mss. Accepts simultaneous submissions. Sample copy for $6. Writer's guidelines online, or by e-mail. "Please send one story at a time." Maximum length: 7,000 words.
Payment/Terms Pays 2 contributor's copies. Pays on publication for first North American serial, first rights.
Advice "We publish serious, generous fiction."

▣ THE SEATTLE REVIEW

Box 354330, University of Washington, Seattle WA 98195. (206)543-2302. E-mail: seaview@u.washington.edu. Web site: www.seattlereview.org. **Contact:** Caroline Simpson, editor-in-chief. Magazine: 6×9; 150 pages; illustrations; photos. "Includes fiction, nonfiction, poetry and one interview per issue with an established writer." Semiannual. Estab. 1978. Circ. 1,000.
Needs Literary. Nothing in "bad taste (porn, racist, etc.)." Receives 200 unsolicited mss/month. Accepts 2-4 mss/issue; 4-8 mss/year. Does not read mss May 31-October 1. Publishes ms 1-2½ years after acceptance. **Publishes 1-2 new writers/year.** Recently published work by Rick Bass, Lauren Whitehurst, Martha Hurwitz. Length: 5,500 words; average length: 3,000 words.
How to Contact Send complete ms. Send SASE (or IRC) for return of ms or send disposable copy of ms and #10 SASE for reply only. Responds in 4-6 months to mss. Accepts simultaneous, multiple submissions. Sample copy for $8. Writer's guidelines for #10 SASE, online or by e-mail.
Payment/Terms Pays 2 contributor's copies. Acquires first North American serial rights.
Advice "Know what we publish: no genre fiction; look at our magazine and decide if your work might be appreciated."

ℕ $THE SEWANEE REVIEW

University of the South, 735 University Ave., Sewanee TN 37383-1000. (931)598-1246. Web site: www.sewanee.edu/sreview/home.html. **Contact:** Fiction Editor. "A literary quarterly, publishing original fiction, poetry, essays on literary and related subjects, and book reviews for well-educated readers who appreciate good American and English literature." Quarterly. Estab. 1892. Circ. 2,000.
Needs Literary, contemporary. No erotica, science fiction, fantasy or excessively violent or profane material.
How to Contact Responds in 6 weeks to mss. Sample copy for $8.50. Writer's guidelines online.
Payment/Terms Pays $10-12/printed page; 2 contributor copies. Pays on publication for first North American serial, second serial (reprint) rights.

$SHENANDOAH, The Washington and Lee University Review

Washington and Lee University, Mattingly House, 2 Lee Avenue, Washington and Lee University, Lexington VA 24450-2116. (540)458-8765. E-mail: shenandoah@wlu.edu. Web site: http://shenandoah.wlu.edu. Triannual. Estab. 1950. Circ. 2,000.
Needs Mainstream, novel excerpts. No sloppy, hasty, slight fiction. Publishes ms 10 months after acceptance.
How to Contact Send complete ms. Responds in 2 months to mss. Sample copy for $10. Writer's guidelines online.
Payment/Terms Pays $25/page. Pays on publication for first North American serial, one-time rights.

SHORT STUFF, For Grown-ups

Bowman Publications, 712 W. 10th St., Loveland CO 80537. (970)669-9139. "We are perhaps an enigma in that we publish only clean stories in any genre. We'll tackle any subject, but don't allow obscene language or pornographic description. Our magazine is for grown-ups, *not* X-rated 'adult' fare." Bimonthly. Estab. 1989. Circ. 10,400.
Needs Adventure, historical, humor/satire, mainstream, mystery/suspense, romance, science fiction (seldom), suspense, western. "We want to see more humor—not essay format—real stories with humor; 1,000-word mysteries, modern lifestyles. The 1,000-word pieces have the best chance of publication. We are no longer accepting essays for publication in the magazine. In particular, we are absolutely, positively not accepting any Erma Bombeck-like essays, e.g. essays proclaiming how wonderful hubby is or bemoaning how your children are sticking pencils up their noses." No erotica; nothing morbid or pornographic. Issues are Valentine (February/March); Easter (April/May); Mom's and Dad's (June/July); Americana (August/September); Halloween (October/November); and Holiday (December/January). Receives 500 unsolicited mss/month. Accepts 9-12 mss/issue; 76 mss/year. **Publishes 90% new writers/year.** Recently published work by Bill Hallstead, Dede Hammond, Skye Gibbons.
How to Contact Send complete ms. Responds in 6 months to mss. Sample copy for $1.50 and 9×12 SAE with 5 first-class stamps. Writer's guidelines for #10 SASE.
Payment/Terms Payment varies. Payment and contract upon publication. Acquires first North American serial rights.

Advice "We seek a potpourri of subjects each issue. A new slant, a different approach, fresh viewpoints—all of these excite us. We don't like gore, salacious humor or perverted tales. Prefer third person, past tense. Be sure it is a story with a beginning, middle and end. It must have dialogue. Many beginners do not know an essay from a short story. Essays frequently used if *humorous*. We'd like to see more young (25 and over) humor; 'clean' humor is hard to come by. Length is a big factor. Writers who can tell a good story in a thousand words are true artists and their work is highly prized by our readers. Stick to the guidelines. We get manuscripts of up to 10,000 words because the story is 'unique and deserving.' We don't even read these. Too many writers fail to include SASE. These submissions are not considered."

☐ ◎ SINISTER WISDOM, A Journal for the Lesbian Imagination in the Arts and Politics

Sinister Wisdom, Inc., Box 3252, Berkeley CA 94703. Web site: www.sinisterwisdom.org. Magazine: 5½×8½; 128-144 pages; 55 lb. stock; 10 pt. C1S cover; illustrations; photos. Lesbian-feminist journal, providing fiction, poetry, drama, essays, journals and artwork. Past issues included "Lesbians of Color," "Old Lesbians/Dykes" and "Lesbians and Religion." Triannual. Estab. 1976. Circ. 2,000.

Needs Lesbian (erotica, ethnic, experimental). No heterosexual or male-oriented fiction; no '70s amazon adventures; nothing that stereotypes or degrades women. List of upcoming themes available for SASE or on Web site. Receives 30 unsolicited mss/month. Accepts 6 mss/issue; 24 mss/year. Publishes ms 3-12 months after acceptance. **Publishes some new writers/year.** Recently published work by Jacqueline Miranda, Amanada Esteva, Sharon Bridgeforth. Length: 500-4,000 words; average length: 2,000 words. Publishes short shorts. Also publishes literary essays, literary criticism, poetry. Sometimes comments on rejected mss.

How to Contact Send complete ms and SASE. Accepts submissions by e-mail. Responds in 6 months to mss. Accepts simultaneous, multiple submissions. Sample copy for $7.50. Writer's guidelines for #10 SASE. Reviews fiction.

Payment/Terms Pays 2 contributor's copies. Acquires one-time rights.

Advice *Sinister Wisdom* is "a multicultural lesbian journal reflecting the art, writing and politics of our communities."

Ⓝ ◙ SLEEPINGFISH

Calamari Press, 35 Essex St. #7B, New York NY 10002. (212)533-4024. E-mail: white@sleppingfish.net. Web site: www.sleepingfish.net. **Contact:** Derek White, editor. Literary magazine/journal: 6×8, 128 pages, 60 lb. vellum paper, card stock cover. Contains illustrations. Includes photographs. "*Sleepingfish* publishes an eclectic mix of flash fiction, prose and visual poetry, experimental texts, text/image and art." Published every 9 months. Estab. 2003. Circ. 300.

Needs Adventure, comics/graphic novels, ethnic/multicultural, experimental, literary. Does not want to see any fiction or writing that fits into a genre or that is written for any other reason except for the sake of art. Receives 250 mss/month. Accepts 25 mss/issue; 25 mss/year. Manuscript published less than 3 months after acceptance. **Publishes 2-3 new writers/year.** Published Norman Lock, Michael Kimball, Peter Markus, Kevin Sampsell, George Sich, Christian Peet, Peter Conners, Daryl Scroggins. Length: 1 word (min)-2,500 words (max). Average length: 500 words. Publishes short shorts. Average length of short shorts: 500 words. Also publishes poetry. Rarely comments on/critiques rejected mss.

How to Contact Send complete ms with cover letter. Accepts submissions by e-mail. Include brief bio. Responds to queries in 2 weeks. Responds to mss in 2 months. Send SASE (or IRC) for return of ms. Considers simultaneous submissions, multiple submissions. Guidelines available on Web site.

Payment and Terms Writers receive 1 contributor copy. Additional copies $6. Pays on publication. Acquires first rights. Sends galleys to author. Publication is copyrighted.

Advice "Write or create what's true to yourself and find a publication where you think your work honestly fits in."

$◙ SNOWY EGRET

The Fair Press, P.O. Box 29, Terre Haute IN 47808. **Contact:** Editors. Magazine: 8½×11; 60 pages; text paper; heavier cover; illustrations. "We publish works which celebrate the abundance and beauty of nature and examine the variety of ways in which human beings interact with landscapes and living things. Nature writing from literary, artistic, psychological, philosophical and historical perspectives." Semiannual. Estab. 1922. Circ. 400.

Needs "No genre fiction, e.g., horror, western, romance, etc." Receives 25 unsolicited mss/month. Accepts up to 6 mss/issue; up to 12 mss/year. Publishes ms 6 months after acceptance. **Publishes 20 new writers/year.** Recently published work by James Hinton, Ron Gielgun, Tom Noyes, Alice Cross, Maeve Mullin Ellis. Length: 500-10,000 words; average length: 1,000-3,000 words. Publishes short shorts. Sometimes comments on rejected mss.

How to Contact Send complete ms with SASE. Cover letter optional: do not query. Responds in 2 months to mss. Accepts simultaneous submissions if noted. Sample copy for 9×12 SASE and $8. Writer's guidelines for #10 SASE.

Payment/Terms Pays $2/page plus 2 contributor's copies. Pays on publication for first North American serial, one-time anthology rights, or reprint rights. Sends galleys to author.

Advice Looks for "honest, freshly detailed pieces with plenty of description and/or dialogue which will allow the reader to identify with the characters and step into the setting; fiction in which nature affects character development and the outcome of the story."

⬤ ◎ SO TO SPEAK, A Feminist Journal of Language and Art

George Mason University, 4400 University Dr., MS 2D6, Fairfax VA 22030. (703)993-3625. E-mail: sts@gmu.edu. Web site: www.gmu.edu/org/sts. **Contact:** Courtney Campbell; Amy Amoroso, fiction editor. Magazine: 5½×8½; approximately 100 pages. "We are a feminist journal of language and art." Semiannual. Estab. 1993. Circ. 1,000.

Needs Ethnic/multicultural, experimental, feminist, lesbian, literary, mainstream, regional, translations. "No science fiction, mystery, genre romance." Receives 100 unsolicited mss/month. Accepts 3-5 mss/issue; 6-10 mss/year. Publishes ms 6 months after acceptance. **Publishes 5 new writers/year.** Length: For fiction, up to 5,000 words; for poetry, 3-5 pages per submission; average length: 4,000 words. Publishes short shorts. Also publishes literary essays, literary criticism, poetry.

How to Contact Send complete ms. Include bio (50 words maximum) and SASE for return of ms or send a disposable copy of ms. Responds in 6 months to mss. Accepts simultaneous submissions. Sample copy for $7. Reviews fiction.

Payment/Terms Pays contributor copies. Acquires first North American serial rights. Sponsors awards/contests.

Advice "We do not read between March 15 and August 15. Every writer has something they do exceptionally well; do that and it will shine through in the work. We look for quality prose with a definite appeal to a feminist audience. We are trying to move away from strict genre lines. We want high quality fiction, nonfiction, poetry, art, innovative and risk-taking work."

⬤ SOUTH CAROLINA REVIEW

611 Strode Tower Box 340522, Clemson University, Clemson SC 29634-0522. (864)656-5399. Fax: (864)656-1345. E-mail: cwayne@clemson.edu. Web site: www.clemson.edu/caah/cedp. **Contact:** Wayne Chapman, editor. Magazine: 6×9; 200 pages; 60 lb. cream white vellum paper; 65 lb. cream white vellum cover stock. Semiannual. Estab. 1967. Circ. 500.

Needs Literary, mainstream, poetry, essays, reviews. Does not read mss June-August or December. Receives 50-60 unsolicited mss/month. Recently published work by Joyce Carol Oates, Rosanne Coggeshal, Fred Chappell, Stephen Dixon. Rarely comments on rejected mss.

How to Contact Send complete ms. Requires text on disk upon acceptance in WordPerfect or Microsoft Word in PC format. Responds in 2 months to mss. Sample copy for $12 plus $1.50 postage. Reviews fiction.

Payment/Terms Pays in contributor's copies.

⬤ SOUTHERN CALIFORNIA ANTHOLOGY

University of Southern California, Waite Phillips Hall, Room 404, Los Angeles CA 90089-4034. (213)740-3252. Fax: (213)740-5775. E-mail: mpw@usc.edu. Web site: www.usc.edu/dept/LAS/mpw. **Contact:** Editor. Magazine: 5½×8½; 142 pages; semiglosss cover stock. "The *Southern California Anthology* is a literary review that contains an eclectic collection of previously unpublished, quality contemporary fiction, poetry and interviews with established literary people, published for adults of all professions, particularly those interested in serious contemporary literature." Annual. Estab. 1983. Circ. 1,500.

Needs Ethnic/multicultural, experimental, feminist, historical, humor/satire, literary, mainstream, regional, serialized novels. "No juvenile, religious, confession, romance, science fiction or pornography." Receives 40 unsolicited mss/month. Accepts 1-2 mss/issue. Publishes ms 4 months after acceptance. **Publishes 1-2 new writers/year.** Recently published work by James Ragan, James Tate, Alice Fulton, John Updike, Joyce Carol Oates, Hubert Selby Jr., Marge Piercy, Stephen Dunn, Ruth Stone, Gay Talese. Publishes short shorts.

How to Contact Send complete ms. Cover letter should include list of previous publications. Responds in 4 months to mss. Sample copy for $4. Writer's guidelines for #10 SASE.

Payment/Terms Pays in contributor copies. Acquires first rights.

Advice "The *Anthology* pays particular attention to craft and style in its selection of narrative writing."

⬤ ◎ SOUTHERN HUMANITIES REVIEW

Auburn University, 9088 Haley Center, Auburn University AL 36849. Web site: www.auburn.edu/english/shr/home.htm. **Contact:** Fiction Editor. Magazine: 6×9; 100 pages; 60 lb neutral pH, natural paper; 65 lb. neutral pH medium coated cover stock; occasional illustration; photos. "We publish essays, poetry, fiction and reviews.

Our fiction has ranged from very traditional in form and content to very experimental. Literate, college-educated audience. We hope they read our journal for both enlightenment and pleasure." Quarterly. Estab. 1967. Circ. 800.

Needs Feminist, humor/satire, regional. Slower reading time in summer. Receives 25 unsolicited mss/month. Accepts 1-2 mss/issue; 4-6 mss/year. Recently published work by William Cobb, R.T. Smith, Heimito von Doderer, Greg Johnson, Elke Heidenreich, Dieter Kuhn. Also publishes literary essays, literary criticism, poetry. Sometimes comments on rejected mss.

How to Contact Send complete ms, cover letter with an explanation of the topic chosen—"special, certain book, etc., a little about the author if he/she has never submitted." No e-mail submissions. No simultaneous submissions. Responds in 3 months to mss.

Payment/Terms Pays in contributor copies. Rights revert to author on publication.

Advice "Send us the ms with SASE. If we like it, we'll take it or we'll recommend changes. If we don't like it, we'll send it back as promptly as possible. Read the journal. Send typewritten, clean copy, carefully proofread. We also award the annual Hoepfner Prize of $100 for the best published essay or short story of the year. Let someone whose opinion you respect read your story and give you an honest appraisal. Rewrite, if necessary, to get the most from your story."

$ 🖊 🖊 THE SOUTHERN REVIEW

Old President's House, Louisiana State University, Baton Rouge LA 70803. (225)578-5108. Fax: (225)578-5098. E-mail: southernreview@lsu.edu. Web site: www.lsu.edu/thesouthernreview. **Contact:** Bret Lott, editor. Magazine: 6¼×10; 240 pages; 50 lb. Glatfelter paper; 65 lb. #1 grade cover stock. Quarterly. Estab. 1935. Circ. 3,100.

● Several stories published in *The Southern Review* were *Pushcart Prize* selections.

Needs Literary. "We desire fiction that crystalizes immediately the author's voice and vision." Receives approximately 300 unsolicited mss/month. Accepts 6-7 mss/issue. Reading period: September-May. Publishes ms 6 months after acceptance. Agented fiction 1%. **Publishes 10-12 new writers/year.** Recently published work by Diane Abu-Jabar, James Lee Burke, Shelby Hearon, Keith Lee Morris. Also publishes literary essays, literary criticism, poetry.

How to Contact Send complete ms with cover letter and SASE. No queries. "Prefer brief letters giving information on author concerning where he/she has been published before, biographical info and what he/she is doing now." Responds in 2 months to mss. Sample copy for $8. Writer's guidelines online. Reviews fiction.

Payment/Terms Pays $30/page. Pays on publication for first North American serial rights. Sends galleys to author. Sponsors awards/contests.

Advice "Careful attention to craftsmanship and technique combined with a compelling sense of the importance of story will always make us pay attention."

🖊 SOUTHWEST REVIEW

P.O. Box 750374, Dallas TX 75275-0374. (214)768-1037. Fax: (214)768-1408. E-mail: swr@mail.smu.edu. Web site: www.southwestreview.org. **Contact:** Jennifer Cranfill, managing editor. Magazine: 6×9; 144 pages. "The majority of our readers are college-educated adults who wish to stay abreast of the latest and best in contemporary fiction, poetry, literary criticism and books in all but the most specialized disciplines." Quarterly. Estab. 1915. Circ. 1,600.

Needs "High literary quality; no specific requirements as to subject matter, but cannot use sentimental, religious, western, poor science fiction, pornographic, true confession, mystery, juvenile or serialized or condensed novels." Receives 200 unsolicited mss/month. Publishes ms 6-12 months after acceptance. Recently published work by Tracy Daugherty, Millicent Dillon, Mark Jacobs. Also publishes literary essays, poetry. Occasionally comments on rejected mss.

How to Contact Send complete ms. Responds in 6 months to mss. Accepts multiple submissions. Sample copy for $6. Writer's guidelines for #10 SASE or on Web site.

Payment/Terms Pays negotiable rate and 3 contributor copies. Acquires first North American serial rights. Sends galleys to author.

Advice "We have become less regional. A lot of time would be saved for us and for the writer if he or she looked at a copy of review before submitting. We like to receive a cover letter because it is some reassurance that the author has taken the time to check a current directory for the editor's name. When there isn't a cover letter, we wonder whether the same story is on 20 other desks around the country."

🖊 🖊 SOUTHWESTERN AMERICAN LITERATURE

Center for the Study of the Southwest, Texas State University-San Marcos, 601 University Drive, San Marcos TX 78666. (512)245-2224. Fax: (512)245-7462. E-mail: mb13@txstate.edu. Web site: www.english.txstate.edu/css.sal.html. **Contact:** Twister Marquiss, assistant editor; Mark Busby, co-editor; Dick Maurice Heaberlin, co-editor. Magazine: 6×9; 125 pages; 80 lb. cover stock. "We publish fiction, nonfiction, poetry, literary criticism and book reviews. Generally speaking, we want material covering the Greater Southwest, or material written by Southwest writers.'' Biannual. Estab. 1971. Circ. 300.

Needs Ethnic/multicultural, literary, mainstream, regional. "No science fiction or romance." Receives 10-15 unsolicited mss/month. Accepts 1-2 mss/issue; 4-5 mss/year. Publishes ms 6 months after acceptance. **Publishes 1-2 new writers/year.** Recently published work by Greg Garrett, Andrew Geyer, Robert Flynn, Walt McDonald, Carol Hamilton, Larry D. Thomas. Length: 6,250 words; average length: 4,000 words. Also publishes literary essays, literary criticism, poetry. Sometimes comments on rejected mss.

How to Contact Send complete ms. Include cover letter, estimated word count, 2-5 line bio and list of publications. Does not accept e-mail submissions. Responds in 3-6 months to mss. Sample copy for $8. Writer's guidelines free.

Payment/Terms Pays 2 contributor copies. Acquires first rights.

Advice "We look for crisp language, an interesting approach to material; a regional approach is desired but not required. Read widely, write often, revise carefully. We are looking for stories that probe the relationship between the tradition of Southwestern American literature and the writer's own imagination in creative ways. We seek stories that move beyond stereotype and approach the larger defining elements and also ones that, as William Faulkner noted in his Nobel Prize acceptance speech, treat subjects central to good literature—the old verities of the human heart, such as honor and courage and pity and suffering, fear and humor, love and sorrow."

SPEAK UP

Speak Up Press, P.O. Box 100506, Denver CO 80250. (303)715-0837. Fax: (303)715-0793. Web site: www.speakuppresss.org. **Contact:** Senior editor. Magazine: $5^{1}/_{2} \times 8^{1}/_{2}$; 128 pages; 55 lb. Glat. Supple Opaque Recycled Natural paper; 12 CIS cover; illustrations; photos. "*Speak Up* features the original fiction, nonfiction, poetry, plays, photography and artwork of young people 13-19 years old. *Speak Up* provides a place for teens to be creative, honest and expressive in an uncensored environment." Annual. Estab. 1999. Circ. 2,900.

Needs Teen writers. Receives 30 unsolicited mss/month. Accepts 30 mss/issue; 30 mss/year. Publishes ms 3-12 months after acceptance. **Publishes 20 new writers/year.** Length: 5,000 words; average length: 500 words. Publishes short shorts. Also publishes literary essays, poetry.

How to Contact Send complete ms. Accepts submissions by e-mail, fax. Responds in 3 months to queries; 3 months to mss. Accepts simultaneous, multiple submissions and reprints. Sample copy free. Please include required submission forms. See Web site for details.

Payment/Terms Pays 2 contributor copies. Acquires first North American serial, one-time rights.

SPIRE, The Future of Arts & Literature

532 La Guardia Pl. Ste. 298, New York NY 10012. E-mail: editor@spirepress.org. Web site: www.spirepress.org. **Contact:** Shelly Reed. Magazine: $8^{1}/_{2} \times 11$; 70 pages; color, laminated cover stock; illustrations; photos. "We are a nonprofit and encourage low-income and minority writers. We publish at least two poets and writers under 18 per issue." Semiannual. Estab. 2002. Circ. 800. Member PMA, CLMP.

Needs Literary. No horror, romance, or religious work. Accepts 4-6 mss/issue; 12 mss/year. Publishes ms 3 months after acceptance. **Publishes 20 new writers/year.** Recently published work by Sandra Kelly-Green, Yoon Choi, Richard Weems. Length: 500-3,000 words; average length: 1,600 words. Publishes short shorts. Also publishes literary essays, poetry. Rarely comments on rejected mss.

How to Contact Send complete ms. Accepts submissions by e-mail. Send disposable copy of ms and #10 SASE for reply only. Responds in 3 months to mss. Accepts simultaneous submissions. Sample copy for $9. Writer's guidelines for #10 SASE or online.

Payment/Terms Pays 1 contributor's copy. Pays on publication for one-time, electronic rights.

Advice "Have a plot please."

STAND MAGAZINE

Department of English, VCU, Richmond VA 23284-2005. (804)828-1331. E-mail: dlatane@vcu.edu. Web site: www.standmagazine.org. "*Stand Magazine* is concerned with what happens when cultures and literatures meet, with translation in its many guises, with the mechanics of language, with the processes by which the policy receives or disables its cultural makers. *Stand* promotes debate of issues that are of radical concern to the intellectual community worldwide." Quarterly. Estab. 1952. Circ. 3,000 worldwide.

Needs "No genre fiction." Publishes ms 10 months after acceptance.

How to Contact Send complete ms. Responds in 6 weeks to queries; 3 months to mss. Sample copy for $12. Writer's guidelines for #10 SASE with sufficient number of IRCs or online.

Payment/Terms Payment varies. Pays on publication. Aquires first world rights.

STAPLE MAGAZINE

74 Rangeley Road, Walkley, Sheffield S6 5DW United Kingdom. E-mail: e.barrett@shu.ac.uk. **Contact:** Elizabeth Barrett, editor. Magazine: A5; 100 pages; illustrations; photos. Quarterly. Estab. 1982. Circ. 500.

Needs Receives 1,000 unsolicited mss/month. Recently published work by David Swann, Penny Feeny. Length: 5,000 words; average length: 3,000 words. Publishes short shorts. Also publishes literary essays, literary criticism, poetry. Sometimes comments on rejected mss.

How to Contact Send complete ms. Send SASE (or IRC) for return of ms. Responds in 8 weeks to queries; 12 weeks to mss. Sample copy for $12. Writer's guidelines for SASE.

Payment/Terms Pays 2 contributor's copies; additional copies $12. Pays on publication for one-time rights.

$ ☐ ◎ ☒ STONE SOUP, The Magazine by Young Writers and Artists

Children's Art Foundation, P.O. Box 83, Santa Cruz CA 95063-0083. (831)426-5557. Fax: (831)426-1161. Web site: www.stonesoup.com. **Contact:** Ms. Gerry Mandel, editor. Magazine: 7×10; 48 pages; high quality paper; photos. Audience is children, teachers, parents, writers, artists. "We have a preference for writing and art based on real-life experiences; no formula stories or poems. We only publish writing by children ages 8 to 13. We do not publish writing by adults." Bimonthly. Estab. 1973. Circ. 20,000.

• This is known as "the literary journal for children." *Stone Soup* has previously won the Ed Press Golden Lamp Honor Award and the Parent's Choice Award.

Needs Adventure, ethnic/multicultural, experimental, fantasy, historical, humor/satire, mystery/suspense, science fiction, slice-of-life vignettes, suspense. "We do not like assignments or formula stories of any kind." Receives 1,000 unsolicited mss/month. Accepts 10 mss/issue. Publishes ms 4 months after acceptance. **Publishes some new writers/year.** Also publishes literary essays, poetry.

How to Contact Send complete ms. "We like to learn a little about our young writers, why they like to write, and how they came to write the story they are submitting." Please do not include SASE. Do not send originals. Responds only to those submissions being considered for possible publication. "If you do not hear from us in 4 to 6 weeks it means we were not able to use your work. Don't be discouraged! Try again!" No simultaneous submissions. Sample copy for $5 or online. Writer's guidelines online.

Payment/Terms Pays $40 for stories. Authors also receive 2 copies, a certificate, and discounts on additional copies and on subscriptions. Pays on publication.

Advice Mss are rejected because they are "derivatives of movies, TV, comic books, or classroom assignments or other formulas. Go to our Web site, where you can see many examples of the kind of work we publish."

$ ⊕ ◑ STORIE, All Write

Leconte Press, Via Suor Celestina Donati 13/E, Rome 00167 Italy. (+39)06 614 8777. Fax: (+39)06 614 8777. E-mail: storie@tiscali.it. Web site: www.storie.it. **Contact:** Gianluca Bassi, editor; Barbara Pezzopane, assistant editor; George Lerner, foreign editor. Magazine: 186 pages; illustrations; photographs. "*Storie* is one of Italy's leading literary magazines. Committed to a truly crossover vision of writing, the bilingual (Italian/English) review publishes high quality fiction and poetry, interspersed with the work of alternative wordsmiths such as filmmakers and musicians. Through writings bordering on narratives and interviews with important contemporary writers, it explores the culture and craft of writing." Bimonthly. Estab. 1989. Circ. 20,000.

Needs Literary. Receives 150 unsolicited mss/month. Accepts 6-10 mss/issue; 30-50 mss/year. Does not read mss in August. Publishes ms 2 months after acceptance. **Publishes 20 new writers/year.** Recently published work by Joyce Carol Oates, Haruki Murakami, Paul Aster, Robert Coover, Raymond Carver, T.C. Boyle, Ariel Dorfman, Tess Gallagher. Length: 2,000-6,000 words; average length: 3,000 words. Publishes short shorts. Also publishes literary essays, literary criticism, poetry. Sometimes comments on rejected mss.

How to Contact Accepts submissions by e-mail or on disk. Include brief bio. Send complete ms with cover letter. "Manuscripts may be submitted directly by regular post without querying first; however, we do not accept unsolicited manuscripts via e-mail. Please query via e-mail first. We only contact writers if their work has been accepted. We also arrange for and oversee a high-quality, professional translation of the piece." Responds in 1 month to queries; 6 months to mss. Accepts multiple submissions. Sample copy for $8. Writer's guidelines online.

Payment/Terms Pays $30-600 and 2 contributor's copies. Pays on publication for first (in English and Italian) rights.

Advice "More than erudite references or a virtuoso performance, we're interested in the recording of human experience in a genuine, original voice. *Storie* reserves the right to include a brief review of interesting submissions not selected for publication in a special column of the magazine."

◑ ☒ STORYQUARTERLY

431 Sheridan Rd., Kenilworth IL 60043. (847)256-6998. Web site: www.storyquarterly.com. **Contact:** Fiction Editors. Magazine: 5½×8¼; 550 pages; good quality paper. An all-story annual anthology, committed to a full range of styles and forms. "*StoryQuarterly*, an annual anthology of short stories, publishes contemporary American and international literature of high quality in a full range of styles and forms—outstanding writing and unusual insights." Estab. 1975. Circ. 6,000.

- *StoryQuarterly* received recognitions in *New Stories from The South*, *Best American Mystery Stories*, *O. Henry Prize Stories*, *Best American Short Stories*, *Best American Essays* and *Pushcart Prize Collection* in the last 3 years. The publication also won Illinois Arts Council Awards, two apiece each of the last 5 years.

Needs "Well-written stories, serious or humorous, that get up and go from the first page." Receives 1,500 unsolicited mss/month. Accepts 40-50 mss/yr. **New authors in every issue.** Recently published work by Chris Abni, J.M. Coetzee, Robert Olen Butler, T.C. Boyle, Stuart Dybek, Stephen Dixon, Reginald Gibbons, Alice Hoffman, Alice McDermott, Charles Johnson, Romulus Linney and other notables.

How to Contact Submissions accepted online through Web site www.storyquarterly.com. "Online submissions site notifies receipt of submission, and online file tracks status. We decide in about two months; the online process is that much faster." Back issue sample copy, $7. Year subscription, $9.

Payment/Terms Pays 10 copies, plus lifetime subscription (a $350 value). Acquires one-time rights. Copyright reverts to author after publication. Electronic publishing agreement available.

Advice Subscribe to and study magazine and market. *SQ* fiction is selected for author control, subject matter, absence of cliché, originality of voice and insight. Fiction Prize awarded to one story among those accepted, judged independently. Judge in 2006 was Scott Turow. Our third winner, Sylvia Sellers-Garcia, won with a first-fiction. Winners have also included Edward Schwarzschild, Emily Rapp, Emily Raboteau and Sharon May.

N ◯ STRAYLIGHT

UW-Parkside, English Dept., 900 Wood Rd., P.O. Box 2000, Kenosha WI 53141. (262)595-2139. Fax: (262)595-2271. E-mail: admin@straylightontheweb.net. Web site: www.straylightontheweb.net. **Contact:** Leo Carbajal, fiction editor. Magazine has revolving editor. Editorial term: 2 years. Literary magazine/journal: $6^{1}/_{4} \times 9^{1}/_{2}$, 75 pages, quality paper, uncoated index stock cover. Contains illustrations. Includes photographs. "Straylight is a new literary journal. We are interested in publishing high quality, character-based fiction of any style. We tend not to publish strict genre pieces, though we may query them for future special issues. We do not publish erotica." Biannual with special issues. Estab. 2005.

Needs Ethnic/multicultural (general), experimental, gay, lesbian, literary, mainstream, regional. Special interests: genre fiction in special theme issues. Accepts 5-7 mss/issue; 10-14 mss/year. Does not read June-August. Manuscript published 6 months after acceptance. Agented fiction 0%. Length: 1,000 words (min)-5,000 words (max). Average length: 2,500 words. Publishes short shorts. Also publishes poetry. Rarely comments on/critiques rejected mss.

How to Contact Send complete ms with cover letter. Accepts submissions by e-mail. Include brief bio, list of publications. Responds to queries in 2 weeks. Responds to mss in 2 months. Send either SASE (or IRC) for return of ms or disposable copy of ms and #10 SASE for reply only. Sample copy available for $4. Guidelines available for SASE, on Web site.

Payment and Terms Writers receive 3 contributors copies. Additional copies $2. Pays on publication. Acquires first North American serial rights. Publication is copyrighted.

Advice "We tend to publish character-based and inventive fiction with cutting-edge prose. We are unimpressed with works based on strict plot twists or novelties. Read a sample copy to get a feel for what we publish."

◪ STRUGGLE, A Magazine of Proletarian Revolutionary Literature

Detroit MI 48213-0261. (213)273-9039. E-mail: timhall11@yahoo.com. **Contact:** Tim Hall, editor. Magazine: $5^{1}/_{2} \times 8^{1}/_{2}$; 36-72 pages; 20 lb. white bond paper; colored cover; illustrations; occasional photos. Publishes material related to "the struggle of the working class and all progressive people against the rule of the rich—including their war policies, repression, racism, exploitation of the workers, oppression of women and general culture, etc." Quarterly. Estab. 1985.

Needs Ethnic/multicultural, experimental, feminist, historical, humor/satire, literary, regional, science fiction, translations, young adult/teen (10-18), prose poem, senior citizen/retirement. "The theme can be approached in many ways, including plenty of categories not listed here. Readers would like fiction about anti-globalization, the fight against racism, prison conditions, neo-conservatism and the Iraq War. Would also like to see more fiction that depicts life, work and struggle of the working class of every background; also the struggles of the 1930s and '60s illustrated and brought to life. No romance, psychic, mystery, western, erotica, religious." Receives 10-12 unsolicited mss/month. Recently published work by Gregory Alan Norton, Paris Smith, Keith Laufenberg. Length: 4,000 words; average length: 1,000-3,000 words. Publishes short shorts. Normally comments on rejected mss.

How to Contact Send complete ms. Accepts submissions by e-mail. "Tries to" report in 3-4 months to queries. Accepts simultaneous, multiple submissions and reprints. Sample copies for $3; $5 for double-size issues; subscriptions $10 for 4 issues; make checks payable to Tim Hall, Special Account, not to *Struggle*.

Payment/Terms Pays 1 contributor's copy. No rights acquired. Not copyrighted.

Advice "Write about the oppression of the working people, the poor, the minorities, women and, if possible, their rebellion against it—we are not interested in anything which accepts the status quo. We are not too

Literary Magazines

worried about plot and advanced technique (fine if we get them!)—we would probably accept things others would call sketches, provided they have life and struggle. For new writers: just describe for us a situation in which some real people confront some problem of oppression, however seemingly minor. Observe and put down the real facts. Experienced writers: try your 'committed'/experimental fiction on us. We get poetry all the time. We have increased our fiction portion of our content in the last few years. The quality of fiction that we have published has continued to improve. If your work raises an interesting issue of literature and politics, it may get discussed in letters and in my editorial. I suggest ordering a sample.''

$ ☒ ◯ SUBTERRAIN, Strong words for a polite nation

P.O. Box 3008, MPO, Vancouver BC V6B 3×5 Canada. (604)876-8710. Fax: (604)879-2667. E-mail: subter@port al.ca. Web site: www.subterrain.ca. **Contact:** Fiction editor. Magazine: 8¼×10⅞; 46-52 pages; gloss stock paper; color gloss cover stock; illustrations; photos. ''Looking for unique work and perspectives from Canada and beyond.'' Triannual. Estab. 1987. Circ. 3,000.

Needs Literary. Does not want genre fiction or children's fiction. Receives 100 unsolicited mss/month. Accepts 4 mss/issue; 10-15 mss/year. Publishes ms 4 months after acceptance. Recently published work by John Moore. Also publishes literary essays, literary criticism. Rarely comments on rejected mss.

How to Contact Send complete ms. Include disposable copy of the ms and #10 SASE for reply only. Responds in 3-4 weeks to queries; 2-4 months to mss. Accepts multiple submissions. Sample copy for $5. Writer's guidelines for #10 SASE or online.

Payment/Terms Pays $25 per page for prose. Pays on publication for first North American serial rights.

Advice ''Read the magazine first. Get to know what kind of work we publish.''

◯ SULPHUR RIVER LITERARY REVIEW

P.O. Box 19228, Austin TX 78760-9228. (512)292-9456. **Contact:** James Michael Robbins, editor. Magazine: 5½×8½; 145 pages; illustrations; photos. ''*SRLR* publishes literature of quality—poetry and short fiction with appeal that transcends time. Audience includes a broad spectrum of readers, mostly educated, many of whom are writers, artists and educators.'' Semiannual. Estab. 1978. Circ. 350.

Needs Ethnic/multicultural, experimental, feminist, humor/satire, literary, mainstream, translations. ''No religious, juvenile, teen, sports, romance or mystery. Wants to see more experimental, surreal and imaginative fiction.'' Receives 20 unsolicited mss/month. Accepts 4-5 mss/issue; 8-10 mss/year. Publishes ms 1-2 years after acceptance. Recently published work by William Jablonsky, Richard Vaughn, Frederic Boutet. Publishes short shorts. Also publishes literary essays, literary criticism, poetry.

How to Contact Send complete ms. Include short bio and list of publications. Send SASE for reply, return of ms, or send disposable copy of ms. Responds in 1 week to queries; 1 month to mss. Sample copy for $7.

Payment/Terms Pays 2 contributor copies. Additional copies $7. Acquires first North American serial rights.

Advice Looks for ''quality. Imagination served perfectly by masterful control of language.''

$ ◯ THE SUN

The Sun Publishing Co., 107 N. Roberson St., Chapel Hill NC 27516. (919)942-5282. Fax: (919)932-3101. Web site: www.thesunmagazine.org. **Contact:** Sy Safransky, editor. Magazine: 8½×11; 48 pages; offset paper; glossy cover stock; photos. ''We are open to all kinds of writing, though we favor work of a personal nature.'' Monthly. Estab. 1974. Circ. 70,000.

Needs Literary. Open to all fiction. Receives 500 unsolicited mss/month. Accepts 2 mss/issue. Publishes ms 6-12 months after acceptance. Recently published work by Ronald F. Currie Jr., Davy Rothbart, Lindsay Fitzgerald, Jenny Bitner. Also publishes poetry.

How to Contact Send complete ms. Accepts reprint submissions. Sample copy for $5. Writer's guidelines online.

Payment/Terms Pays $300-750. Pays on publication for first, one-time rights.

Advice ''We favor honest, personal writing with an intimate point of view.''

◯ SYCAMORE REVIEW

Purdue University, Department of English, 500 Oval Drive, West Lafayette IN 47907. (765)494-3783. Fax: (765)494-3780. E-mail: sycamore@purdue.edu. Web site: www.sla.purdue.edu/sycamore. **Contact:** Fiction Editor. Magazine: 5½×8½; 150-200 pages; heavy, textured, uncoated paper; heavy laminated cover. ''Journal devoted to contemporary literature. We publish both traditional and experimental fiction, personal essay, poetry, interviews, drama and graphic art. Novel excerpts welcome if they stand alone as a story.'' Semiannual. Estab. 1989. Circ. 1,000.

Needs Experimental, humor/satire, literary, mainstream, regional, translations. ''We generally avoid genre literature but maintain no formal restrictions on style or subject matter. No romance, children's.'' Would like to see more experimental fiction. Publishes ms 11 months after acceptance. Recently published work by Lucia Perillo, June Armstrong, W.P. Osborn, William Giraldi. Also publishes poetry. Sometimes comments on rejected mss.

How to Contact Send complete ms with SASE, cover letter with previous publications and address. Responds in 4 months to mss. Accepts simultaneous submissions. Sample copy for $7. Writer's guidelines for #10 SASE or online.

Payment/Terms Acquires one-time rights.

Advice "We publish both new and experienced authors but we're always looking for stories with strong emotional appeal, vivid characterization and a distinctive narrative voice; fiction that breaks new ground while still telling an interesting and significant story. Avoid gimmicks and trite, predictable outcomes. Write stories that have a ring of truth, the impact of felt emotion. Don't be afraid to submit, send your best."

$ ⬛ TAKAHE

P.O. Box 13-335, Christchurch 8001 New Zealand. (03)359-8133. **Contact:** Isa Moynihan, editor. "A literary magazine which appears three or four times a year and publishes short stories and poetry by both established and emerging writers. The publisher is Takahe Collective Trust, a charitable trust formed by established writers to help new writers and get them into print." The magazine is published in hard copy.

Needs "We are particularly losing interest in stories by 'victims' of various kinds . . . morbid stories. We would like to see more humorous and light-hearted stories." **Publishes 20 new writers/year.** Recently published work by Jenny Argante, Lyn McConchie, David Hill, Virgil Suarez, David Clarkson, Chrissie Ward.

How to Contact Send complete ms. Include e-mail address, brief bio and SASE (IRC for overseas submissions). Single spacing, indented paragraphs and double quotation marks for direct speech. Any use of foreign languages must be accompanied by English translation. Accepts multiple submissions.

Payment/Terms Pays $15 ($30 NZ). Copyright reverts to author on publication.

Advice "We pay a flat rate to each writer/poet appearing in a particular issue regardless of the number/length of items. Amount is subject to change according to circumstances. Editorials and literary commentaries are by invitation only and, not being covered by our grant, are not paid for. All contributors receive two hard copies of the issue in which their work appears."

⬛ TALKING RIVER REVIEW

Lewis-Clark State College, Division of Literature and Languages, 500 8th Ave., Lewiston ID 83501. (208)792-2307. Fax: (208)792-2324. **Contact:** Mark Sanders, editor. Magazine: 6×9; 150 pages; 60 lb. paper; coated, color cover; illustrations; photos. "We look for new voices with something to say to a discerning general audience." Semiannual. Estab. 1994. Circ. 500.

Needs Condensed novels, ethnic/multicultural, feminist, historical, humor/satire, literary, mainstream, regional. "Wants more well-written, character-driven stories that surprise and delight the reader with fresh, arresting yet unself-conscious language, imagery, metaphor, revelation." No stories that are sexist, racist, homophobic, erotic for shock value, romance. Receives 200 unsolicited mss/month. Accepts 5-8 mss/issue; 10-15 mss/year. Reads mss September 1-May 1 only. Publishes ms up to 1 year after acceptance. Agented fiction 10%. **Publishes 10-15 new writers/year.** Recently published work by X.J. Kennedy and Clair Davis. Length: 7,500 words; average length: 3,000 words. Also publishes literary essays, poetry. Sometimes comments on rejected mss.

How to Contact Send complete manuscript with cover letter. Include estimated word count, 2-sentence bio and list of publications. Send SASE for reply, return of ms or send disposable copy of ms. Responds in 3 months to mss. Accepts simultaneous submissions if indicated. Sample copy for $6. Writer's guidelines for #10 SASE.

Payment/Terms Pays contributor's copies; additional copies $4. Acquires one-time rights.

Advice "We look for the strong, the unique; we reject clichéd images and predictable climaxes."

$ ⬛ TAMPA REVIEW

University of Tampa Press, 401 W. Kennedy Blvd., Tampa FL 33606. (813)253-6266. Fax: (813)258-7593. Web site: tampareview.ut.edu. **Contact:** Lisa Birnbaum and Kathleen Ochshorn, fiction editors. Magazine: 7½×10½; hardback; approximately 100 pages; acid-free paper; visual art; photos. An international literary journal publishing art and literature from Florida and Tampa Bay as well as new work and translations from throughout the world. Semiannual. Estab. 1988. Circ. 500.

Needs Ethnic/multicultural, experimental, fantasy, historical, literary, mainstream, translations. "We are far more interested in quality than in genre. Nothing sentimental as opposed to genuinely moving, nor self-conscious style at the expense of human truth." Accepts 4-5 mss/issue. Reads September-December; reports January-May. Publishes ms 10 months after acceptance. Agented fiction 20%. Recently published work by Elizabeth Spencer, Lee K. Abbott, Lorrie Moore, Gordon Weaver, Tim O'Brien. Publishes short shorts. Also publishes literary essays, poetry.

How to Contact Send complete ms. Include brief bio. Responds in 5 months to mss. Accepts multiple submissions. Sample copy for $7. Writer's guidelines online.

Payment/Terms Pays $10/printed page. Pays on publication for first North American serial rights. Sends galleys to author.

Advice "There are more good writers publishing in magazines today than there have been in many decades. Unfortunately, there are even more bad ones. In T. Gertler's *Elbowing the Seducer*, an editor advises a young writer that he wants to hear her voice completely, to tell (he means 'show') him in a story the truest thing she knows. We concur. Rather than a trendy workshop story or a minimalism that actually stems from not having much to say, we would like to see stories that make us believe they mattered to the writer and, more importantly, will matter to a reader. Trim until only the essential is left, and don't give up belief in yourself. And it might help to attend a good writers' conference, e.g. Wesleyan or Bennington."

⬤ TAPROOT LITERARY REVIEW

Taproot Writer's Workshop, Inc., Box 204, Ambridge PA 15003. (724)266-8476. E-mail: taproot10@aol.com. **Contact:** Tikvah Feinstein, editor. Magazine: $5^{1}/_{2} \times 8^{1}/_{2}$; 93 pages; 20 lb. paper; hardcover; attractively printed; saddle-stitched. "We select on quality, not topic. Variety and quality are our appealing features." Annual. Estab. 1987. Circ. 500.

Needs Literary. "No pornography, religious, popular, romance fiction. Wants more multicultural-displaced people living among others in new places." The majority of ms published are received through annual contest. Receives 20 unsolicited mss/month. Accepts 6 mss/issue. **Publishes 2-4 new writers/year.** Recently published work by Anita Swanson, Tony Concannon, Lonnie Goldman, E. Peregrine Til, Susan Williams. Publishes short shorts. Also publishes poetry. Sometimes comments on rejected mss.

How to Contact Accepts submissions by e-mail. Send for guidelines first. Send complete ms with a cover letter. Include estimated word count and bio. Responds in 6 months to mss. No simultaneous submissions. Sample copy for $5, 6×12 SAE with 5 first-class stamps. Writer's guidelines for #10 SASE.

Payment/Terms Awards $25 in prize money for first place fiction and poetry winners each issue; certificate for 2nd and 3rd place; 1 contributor's copy. Additionally, *Taproot* offers a coveted literary prize, promotion, and $15 for the winner. Acquires first rights. Sponsors awards/contests.

Advice "Taproot is getting more fiction submissions, and every one is read entirely. This takes time, so response can be delayed at busy times of year. Our contest is a good way to start publishing. Send for a sample copy and read it through. Ask for a critique and follow suggestions. Don't be offended by any suggestions—just take them or leave them and keep writing. Looks for a story that speaks in its unique voice, told in a well-crafted and complete, memorable style, a style of signature to the author. Follow writer's guidelines. Research markets. Send cover letter. Don't give up."

⬤ THE TEXAS REVIEW

Texas Review Press at Sam Houston State University, P.O. Box 2146, Huntsville TX 77341-2146. (936)294-1992. Fax: (936)294-3070 (inquiries only). E-mail: eng_pdr@shsu.edu. Web site: www.shsu.edu. **Contact:** Paul Ruffin, editor. Magazine: 6×9; 148-190 pages; best quality paper; 70 lb. cover stock; illustrations; photos. "We publish top quality poetry, fiction, articles, interviews and reviews for a general audience." Semiannual. Estab. 1976. Circ. 1,200. A member of the Texas A&M University Press consortium.

Needs Humor/satire, literary, mainstream, contemporary fiction. "We are eager enough to consider fiction of quality, no matter what its theme or subject matter. No juvenile fiction." Receives 40-60 unsolicited mss/ month. Accepts 4 mss/issue; 6 mss/year. Does not read mss May-September. Publishes ms 6-12 months after acceptance. **Publishes some new writers/year.** Recently published work by George Garrett, Ellen Gilchrist, Fred Chappell. Also publishes literary essays, literary criticism, poetry. Sometimes comments on rejected mss.

How to Contact Send complete ms. No mss accepted via fax. Send disposable copy of ms and #10 SASE for reply only. Responds in 2 weeks to queries; 3-6 months to mss. Accepts multiple submissions. Sample copy for $5. Writer's guidelines for SASE and on Web site.

Payment/Terms Pays contributor's copies and one year subscription. Pays on publication for first North American serial, one-time rights. Sends galleys to author.

Advice "Submit often; be aware that we reject 90% of submissions due to overwhelming number of mss sent."

Ⓝ $⬤ THEMA

Box 8747, Metairie LA 70011-8747. (504)887-1263. **Contact:** Virginia Howard, editor. Magazine: $5^{1}/_{2} \times 8^{1}/_{2}$; 150 pages; Grandee Strathmore cover stock; b&w illustrations. "*Thema* is designed to stimulate creative thinking by challenging writers with unusual themes, such as 'safety in numbers' and 'the power of whim.' Appeals to writers, teachers of creative writing, and general reading audience." Estab. 1988. Circ. 350.

Needs Adventure, ethnic/multicultural, experimental, fantasy, historical, humor/satire, literary, mainstream, mystery/suspense, novel excerpts, psychic/supernatural/occult, regional, religious/inspirational, science fiction, slice-of-life vignettes, western, contemporary, sports, prose poem. "No erotica." 2006 themes were "*Rage Over a Lost Penny*" (March 1); "*The Perfect Cup of Coffee*" (July 1); "*Written in Stone*" (November 1). Write for 2007 themes. Publishes ms within 6 months after acceptance. **Publishes 9 new writers/year.** Recently published work by Kristine Guile, Jennifer Hubbard, Serena Alibhai, Carol V. Paul. Publishes short shorts. Also publishes poetry. Sometimes comments on rejected mss.

How to Contact Send complete ms with SASE, cover letter, include "name and address, brief introduction, specifying the intended target issue for the mss." Responds in 1 week to queries; 5 months to mss. Accepts simultaneous, multiple submissions and reprints. Sample copy for $8. Writer's guidelines for #10 SASE.

Payment/Terms Pays $10-25. Pays on acceptance for one-time rights.

Advice "Do not submit a manuscript unless you have written it for a specified theme. If you don't know the upcoming themes, send for guidelines first, before sending a story. We need more stories told in the Mark Twain/O. Henry tradition in magazine fiction."

TICKLED BY THUNDER, Helping Writers Get Published Since 1990

Tickled By Thunder Publishing Co., 14076 86A Ave., Surrey BC V3W 0V9 Canada. (604)591-6095. E-mail: info@tickledbythunder.com. Web site: www.tickledbythunder.com. **Contact:** Larry Lindner, publisher. Magazine: digest-sized; 24 pages; bond paper; bond cover stock; illustrations; photos. "*Tickled By Thunder* is designed to encourage beginning writers of fiction, poetry and nonfiction." Quarterly. Estab. 1990. Circ. 1,000.

Needs Fantasy, humor/satire, literary, mainstream, mystery/suspense, science fiction, western. "No overly indulgent horror, sex, profanity or religious material." Receives 25 unsolicited mss/month. Accepts 3 mss/issue; 12 mss/year. Publishes ms 3-9 months after acceptance. **Publishes 10 new writers/year.** Recently published work by Rick Cook and Jerry Shane. Length: 2,000 words; average length: 1,500 words. Also publishes literary essays, literary criticism, poetry.

How to Contact Send complete ms. Include estimated word count and brief bio. Send SASE or IRC for return of ms; or send disposable copy of ms and #10 SASE for reply only. No e-mail submissions. Responds in 3 months to queries; 6 months to mss. Accepts simultaneous, multiple submissions and reprints. Writer's guidelines online.

Payment/Terms Pays on publication for first, second serial (reprint) rights.

Advice "Make your characters breathe on their own. Use description with action."

TOUCHSTONE LITERARY JOURNAL

P.O. Box 130233, Spring TX 77393-0233. E-mail: panthercreek3@hotmail.com. **Contact:** Julia Gomez-Rivas, fiction editor. Magazine: 5½×8½; 56 pages; linen paper; coated stock cover; perfect bound; b&w illustrations; occasional photos. "We publish literary and mainstream fiction but enjoy experimental and multicultural work as well. Our audience is middle-class, heavily academic. We are eclectic and given to whims—i.e., two years ago we devoted a 104-page issue to West African women writers." Annual. Estab. 1976. Circ. 1,000.

Needs Humor/satire, literary, translations. "No erotica, religious, juvenile, stories written in creative writing programs that all sound alike." List of upcoming themes available for SASE. Receives 20-30 unsolicited mss/month. Accepts 3-4 mss/issue. Publishes ms "within the year" after acceptance. Recently published work by Ann Alejandro, Lynn Bradley, Roy Fish, Julia Mercedes Castilla. Length: 250-5,000 words; average length: 2,500 words. Publishes short shorts. Also publishes literary essays, literary criticism, poetry.

How to Contact Send complete ms. Include estimated word count and three-sentence bio. Send SASE for return of ms. Responds in 6 weeks to mss. Accepts multiple submissions. Sample copy not available. Writer's guidelines for #10 SASE.

Payment/Terms Pays 2 contributor's copies. Acquires one-time rights. Sends galleys to author.

Advice "We like to see fiction that doesn't read as if it had been composed in a creative writing class. If you can entertain, edify or touch the reader, polish your story and send it in. Don't worry if it doesn't read like our other fiction."

UNBOUND

Suny Potsdam Dept. of English and Communications, Morey Hall, SUNY Potsdam, Potsdam NY 13676. (315)267-2043. E-mail: unbound@potsdam.edu. Web site: www2.potsdam.edu/henryrm/unbound.html. **Contact:** Rick Henry, editor. Magazine. "*Unbound* seeks fiction that exceeds the page. We are interested in collage, avant-garde, experimental, new media, multi-media fiction that maintains a strong narrative thread." Annual. Estab. 2002.

Needs Experimental. "No genre fiction." Publishes short shorts.

How to Contact Send complete ms. Include brief bio. Send SASE for return of ms or send a disposable copy of ms and #10 SASE for reply only. Responds in 2 months to queries; 10 weeks to mss. Accepts simultaneous submissions. Sample copy not available. Writer's guidelines by e-mail.

Payment/Terms Pays 1 contributor copy. Pays on publication for first North American serial rights.

Advice "We look for an intelligent relationship between a fiction's form and content. Fiction need not be limited by the borders of 8½×11 sheets of paper."

[N] [⊕] [✓] UNDERSTANDING

Dionysia Press, 127 Milton Rd. West, 7 Duddingston House Courtyard, Edinburgh Scotland EH15 1JG United Kingdom. Fax: (0131)6611156. Magazine: A5; 200 pages. Annual. Estab. 1989. Circ. 500. Member: Scottish Publishing Association.

Needs Translations. Publishes ms 10 months after acceptance. **Publishes 100 new writers/year.** Publishes short shorts. Also publishes literary essays, poetry. Sometimes comments on rejected mss.

How to Contact Responds in 1 year to queries. Sample copy for $4.50 + postage. Writer's guidelines for SASE.

Payment/Terms Pays in contributor's copies.

[✓] UNMUZZLED OX

Unmuzzled Ox Foundation Ltd., 105 Hudson St., New York NY 10013. (212)226-7170. E-mail: mandreox@aol.com. **Contact:** Michael Andre, editor. Magazine: 5½ × 8½. "Magazine about life for an intelligent audience." Irregular frequency. Estab. 1971. Circ. 7,000.

- Recent issues of this magazine have included art, poetry and essays only. Check before sending submissions.

Needs Literary, mainstream, translations, prose poetry. "No commercial fiction." Receives 20-25 unsolicited mss/month. Also publishes poetry. Sometimes comments on rejected mss.

How to Contact "Please no phone calls and no e-mail submissions. Correspondence by *mail* only. Cover letter is significant." Responds in 1 month to queries; 1 month to mss. Sample copy not available.

Payment/Terms Pays in contributor's copies.

Advice "You may want to check out a copy of the magazine before you submit."

[N] [⊕] [✓] VERSAL

wordsinhere, Amsterdam, The Netherlands. E-mail: versal@wordsinhere.com. Web site: http://versal.wordsinhere.com. **Contact:** Robert Glick, fiction editor. Literary magazine/journal: 20 cm × 20 cm, 100 pages, offset, perfect bound paper, acid free color cover. Contains illustrations. Includes photographs. "Versal is the only English-language literary magazine in the Netherlands and publishes new poetry, prose and art from around the world. We publish writers with an instinct for language and line break, content and form that is urgent, involved and unexpected." Annual. Estab. 2002. Circ. 500.

Needs Experimental, literary. Receives 15 mss/month. Accepts 8 mss/year. Does not read mss January 16-September 14. Manuscript published 3 months after acceptance. **Publishes 2 new writers/year.** Published Russell Edson, Kathe Gray, Sandy Florian, Marius Benta, Rhonda Waterfall. Length: 2,500 words (max). Publishes short shorts. Average length of short shorts: 500 words. Also publishes poetry. Sometimes comments on/critiques rejected mss.

How to Contact Send complete ms with cover letter. Accepts submissions by e-mail. Include brief bio. Responds to queries in 1 week. Responds to mss in 4 months. Considers simultaneous submissions, multiple submissions. Guidelines available on Web site.

Payment and Terms Writers receive 1 contributor copy. Additional copies $8. Pays on publication. Acquires one-time rights. Sends galleys to author. Publication is copyrighted.

Advice "We are drawn to good pacing, varied tone and something out of the ordinary. Above all, we look for surprise and richness of detail in representing this surprise. We especially love something written in an unusual voice that also contains depth in content. For more traditional voices, we look for surprise within the story—either by giving us an unusual situation or by having characters surprise us with their actions. Nasty sex and drug adventures don't really shock us, so unless there's a fantastic twist to the tale, they don't provide a jump out of the slush pile. In flash fiction, we are less inclined to the purely anecdotal than to work that somehow manages to convey depth and/or tension."

[$] [✓] VIRGINIA QUARTERLY REVIEW

University of Virginia, One West Range, P.O. Box 400223, Charlottesville VA 22904-4223. (434)924-3124. Fax: (434)924-1397. Web site: www.vqronline.org. **Contact:** Ted Genoways, editor. "A national journal of literature and discussion, featuring nonfiction, fiction, and poetry for both educated general readers and the academic audience." Quarterly. Estab. 1925. Circ. 6,000.

- Offers Emily Clark Balch Award for best short story and poetry, and the Staige D. Blackford prize for the best essay, published in its pages in the past year.

Needs Adventure, ethnic/multicultural, feminist, historical, humor/satire, literary, mainstream, mystery/suspense, novel excerpts, romance, serialized novels, translations. "No pornography." Accepts 3 mss/issue; 20 mss/year. Publishes ms 1 year after acceptance.

How to Contact Send complete ms. SASE. No queries. Responds in 3-4 months to mss. Sample copy for $6. Writer's guidelines online.

Payment/Terms Pays $100/page maximum. $5 per line for poetry. Pays on publication for first North American rights and nonexclusive online rights.

⟨N⟩ $WESTERN HUMANITIES REVIEW

University of Utah, English Department, 255 S. Central Campus Dr., Room 3500, Salt Lake City UT 84112-0494. (801)581-6070. Fax: (801)585-5167. Web site: www.hum.utah.edu/whr. **Contact:** Karen Brennan and Robin Hemley, fiction editors. Biannual. Estab. 1947. Circ. 1,000.

Needs Experimental (any type), literary. Does not want genre (romance, sci-fi, etc.). Receives 100 unsolicited mss/month. Accepts 3-4 mss/issue; 6-8 mss/year. Does not read mss May-August. Publishes ms 1 year after acceptance. Agented fiction 10%. **Publishes 5 new writers/year.** Recently published work by Philip Graham, Judith Grossman, Kevin McIlvoy, Michael Martone. Publishes short shorts. Also publishes literary essays, literary criticism, poetry. Rarely comments on rejected mss.

How to Contact Send complete ms. Accepts simultaneous submissions. Sample copy for $10. Writer's guidelines online.

Payment/Terms Pays $5/published page (when funds available). Pays on publication.

⟨⟩ WHISKEY ISLAND MAGAZINE

Dept. of English, Cleveland State University, Cleveland OH 44115-2440. (216)687-2056. Fax: (216)687-6943. E-mail: whiskeyisland@csuohio.edu. Web site: www.csuohio.edu/whiskey_island. Editors change each year. Magazine of fiction and poetry. "We provide a forum for new writers and new work, for themes and points of view that are both meaningful and experimental, accessible and extreme." Semiannual. Estab. 1978. Circ. 2,500.

Needs "Would like to see more short shorts, flash fiction." Receives 100 unsolicited mss/month. Accepts 46 mss/issue. **Publishes 5-10 new writers/year.** Recently published work by Nin Andrews, Reginald Gibbons, Jim Daniels, Allison Luterman. Also publishes poetry.

How to Contact Send complete ms. Accepts submissions by e-mail. Responds in 4 months to queries; 4 months to mss. Sample copy for $6.

Payment/Terms Pays 2 contributor copies and 1-year subscription. Acquires one-time rights. Sponsors awards/contests.

Advice "We read manuscripts year round. We seek engaging writing of any style."

⟨⟩ THE WILLIAM AND MARY REVIEW

The College of William and Mary, P.O. Box 8795, Williamsburg VA 23187. (757)221-3290. E-mail: review@wm.edu. Web site: www.wm.edu/so/wmreview. **Contact:** Justin Fowler, editor-in-chief. Magazine: 6×9; 96 pages; coated paper; 4-color card cover; photos. "We encourage good fiction and nonfiction that can be literary, though we are not bound by tradition. Genre stories are acceptable only if the work transcends the genre. Our journal is read by a sophisticated audience of subscribers, professors and university students. Annual. Estab. 1962. Circ. 2,000.

Needs Experimental, family saga, historical, horror (psychological), humor/satire, literary, mainstream, science fiction, thriller/espionage, translations. "We do not want to see typical genre pieces. Do not bother sending fantasy or erotica." Receives 35 unsolicited mss/month. Accepts 6-8 mss/year. Does not read mss from February to August. Publishes ms 1-2 months after acceptance. **Publishes 1-2 new writers/year.** Length: 250-7,000 words; average length: 3,500 words. Publishes short shorts. Also publishes literary essays, poetry. Rarely comments on rejected mss.

How to Contact Send complete ms. Send SASE (or IRC) for return of the mss or send disposable copy of the ms and #10 SASE for reply only. Responds in 5-6 months to queries. Accepts simultaneous, multiple submissions. Sample copy for $5.50.

Payment/Terms Pays 5 contributor's copies; additional copies $5. Pays on publication for first North American serial rights.

Advice "We do not give much weight to prior publications; each piece is judged on its own merit. New writers should be bold and unafraid to submit unorthodox works that depart from textbook literary tradition. We would like to see more quality short shorts and nonfiction works. We receive far too many mediocre genre stories."

⟨⟩ WILLARD & MAPLE, The Literary Magazine of Champlain College

163 South Willard Street, Freeman 302, Box 34, Burlington VT 05401. (802)860-2700 ext.2462. E-mail: willardandmaple@champlain.edu. **Contact:** Fiction editor. Magazine: perfect bound; 125 pages; illustrations; photos. "*Willard & Maple* is a student-run literary magazine from Champlain College that publishes a wide array of poems, short stories, creative essays, short plays, pen and ink drawings, black and white photos, and computer graphics. We now accept color." Annual. Estab. 1996.

Needs We accept all types of mss. Receives 20 unsolicited mss/month. Accepts 5 mss/year. Does not read mss

September 1-March 31. Publishes ms within 1 year after acceptance. **Publishes 10 new writers/year.** Recently published work by Shannon Sevakian, Bill Mosler, Sandy Johnson, Bill Trippe, David Jacobs. Length: 5,000 words; average length: 2,500 words. Publishes short shorts. Also publishes literary essays, poetry. Sometimes comments on rejected mss.

How to Contact Send complete ms. Send SASE for return of ms or send disposable copy of mss and #10 SASE for reply only. Responds in 2 months to queries; 2 months to mss. Accepts simultaneous, multiple submissions. Sample copy for $8.50. Writer's guidelines for SASE or send e-mail. Reviews fiction.

Payment/Terms Pays 2 contributor's copies; additional copies $10. Pays on publication for one-time rights.

Advice ''Work hard; be good; never surrender!''

N WILLOW REVIEW

College of Lake County, 19351 W. Washington, Grayslake IL 60030.(847)543-2956. E-mail: com426@clcillinois. edu. **Contact:** Michael Latza, editor. Literary magazine/journal: 6×9, 110 pages. Annual. Estab. 1969. Circ. 125.

Needs Literary. Receives 10 mss/month. Accepts 3-5 mss/issue. Does not read mss May 1-September 1. **Publishes 2-3 new writers/year.** Published Patricia Smith, Tim Joycek. Length: 7,500 words (max). Publishes short shorts. Average length of short shorts: 500 words. Also publishes literary criticism. Rarely comments on/ critiques rejected manuscripts.

How to Contact Send complete ms with cover letter. Include estimated word count, brief bio, list of publications. Responds to mss in 3-4 months. Send either SASE (or IRC) for return of ms or disposable copy of ms and #10 SASE for reply only. Considers simultaneous submissions, multiple submissions. Sample copy available for $5. Guidelines available for SASE, via e-mail.

Payment and Terms Writers receive 2 contributors copies. Additional copies $7. Pays on publication. Acquires one-time rights.

N ⃠ ✓ WILLOW SPRINGS

705 W. First Ave., Spokane WA 99201. (509)623-4349. Web site: http://willowsprings.ewu.edu. **Contact:** Fiction Editor. Magazine: 9×6; 144 pages; 80 lb. glossy cover. ''We publish quality contemporary fiction, poetry, nonfiction, interviews with notable authors, and works in translation.'' Semiannual. Estab. 1977. Circ. 1,500. Member CLMP, AWP.

- *Willow Springs* has received grants from the NEA and a CLMP excellence award.

Needs Literary short shorts, nonfiction, translations, short stories, prose poems, poems. ''No genre fiction, please.'' Receives 200 unsolicited mss/month. Accepts 2-4 mss/issue; 4-8 mss/year. Reads mss year round, but expect slower response between July and October. Publishes ms 4 months after acceptance. **Publishes some new writers/year.** Recently published work by Imad Rahman, Deb Olin Unferth, Jim Daniels, Kirsten Sundberg Lunstrum, Robert Lopez, Stacey Richter. Also publishes literary essays, literary criticism, poetry. Rarely comments on rejected mss.

How to Contact Send complete ms. Prose submissions now accepted online. Responds in 2 months to queries; 2 months to mss. Simultaneous submissions encouraged. Sample copy for $6. Writer's guidelines for #10 SASE.

Payment/Terms Pays 2 contributor's copies. Acquires first North American serial, first rights.

Advice ''We hope to attract good fiction writers to our magazine, and we've made a commitment to publish 3-4 stories per issue. We like fiction that exhibits a fresh approach to language. Our most recent issues, we feel, indicate the quality and level of our conmmitment.''

⃝ WINDHOVER, A Journal of Christian Literature

University of Mary Hardin-Baylor, P.O. Box 8008, 900 College St., Belton TX 76513. (254)295-4561. E-mail: windhover@umhb.edu. **Contact:** D. Audell Shelburne, editor. Magazine: 6×9; white bond paper. ''We accept poetry, short fiction, nonfiction, creative nonfiction. *Windhover* is devoted to promoting writers and literature with a Christian perspective and with a broad definition of that perspective.'' Annual. Estab. 1997. Circ. 500.

Needs Ethnic/multicultural, experimental, fantasy, historical, humor/satire, literary. No erotica. Receives 30 unsolicited mss/month. Accepts 5 mss/issue; 5 mss/year. Publishes ms 1 year after acceptance. **Publishes 5 new writers/year.** Recently published work by Walt McDonald, Cleatus Rattan, Greg Garrett, Barbara Crooker. Length: 1,500-4,000 words; average length: 3,000 words. Publishes short shorts. Also publishes literary essays, poetry. Sometimes comments on rejected mss.

How to Contact Send complete ms. Estimated word count, brief bio and list of publications. Include SASE postcard for acknowledgement. No submissions by e-mail. Responds in 4-6 weeks to queries; 4-6 months to mss. Accepts simultaneous submissions. Sample copy for $10. Writer's guidelines by e-mail.

Payment/Terms Pays 2 contributor copies. Pays on publication for first rights.

Advice ''Be patient. We have an editorial board and it sometimes takes longer than I like. We particularly look for convincing plot and character development.''

☑ ☒ WISCONSIN REVIEW

University of Wisconsin-Oshkosh, 800 Algoma Blvd., Oshkosh WI 54902. (920)424-2267. E-mail: wisconsin.revi ew@gmail.com. Web site: http://www.english.uwosh.edu/review.html. **Contact:** Jason Book, senior fiction editor. Magazine: 6×9; 60-100 pages; illustrations. ''We seek literary prose and poetry. The publication is for an adult contemporary audience. Fiction including fantastic imagery and fresh voices is published. We seek to publish quality, not quantity.'' Biannual. Estab. 1966. Circ. 2,000.

• *Wisconsin Review* won the Pippistrelle Best of the Small Press Award #13.

Needs Experimental, literary. Receives 30 unsolicited mss/month. Publishes ms 1-3 months after acceptance. **Publishes 3-6 new writers/year.** Publishes short shorts.

How to Contact Send complete ms. Sample copy for $5.

Payment/Terms Pays 2 contributor copies. Acquires first rights.

Advice ''We accept fiction that displays strong characterization, dialogue that provides pertinent information and transports the story, vivid imagery, and unique plots and themes.''

☑ THE WORCESTER REVIEW

Worcester County Poetry Association, Inc., 1 Ekman St., Worcester MA 01607. (508)797-4770. Web site: www.g eocities.com/Paris/LeftBank/6433. **Contact:** Fiction Editor. Magazine: 6×9; 100 pages; 60 lb. white offset paper; 10 pt. CS1 cover stock; illustrations; photos. ''We like high quality, creative poetry, artwork and fiction. Critical articles should be connected to New England.'' Annual. Estab. 1972. Circ. 1,000.

Needs Literary, prose poem. ''We encourage New England writers in the hopes we will publish at least 30% New England but want the other 70% to show the best of writing from across the U.S.'' Receives 20-30 unsolic-ited mss/month. Accepts 2-4 mss/issue. Publishes ms 11 months after acceptance. Agented fiction less than 10%. Recently published work by Robert Pinsky, Marge Piercy, Wes McNair, Ed Hirsch. Length: 1,000-4,000 words; average length: 2,000 words. Publishes short shorts. Also publishes literary essays, literary criticism, poetry. Sometimes comments on rejected mss.

How to Contact Send complete ms. Responds in 1 year to mss. Accepts simultaneous submissions only if other markets are clearly identified. Sample copy for $6. Writer's guidelines free.

Payment/Terms Pays 2 contributor copies and honorarium if possible. Acquires one-time rights.

Advice ''Send only one short story—reading editors do not like to read two by the same author at the same time. We will use only one. We generally look for creative work with a blend of craftsmanship, insight and empathy. This does not exclude humor. We won't print work that is shoddy in any of these areas.''

☑ XAVIER REVIEW

Xavier University, 1 Drexel Dr., New Orleans LA 70125-1098. (504)520-7549. Fax: (504)485-7197. E-mail: rcollin s@xula.edu (correspondence only—no mss). **Contact:** Richard Collins, editor. Mark Whitaker, associate editor. Magazine: 6×9; 75 pages; 50 lb. paper; 12 pt. CS1 cover; photographs. Magazine of ''poetry/fiction/nonfiction/ reviews (contemporary literature) for professional writers, libraries, colleges and universities.'' Semiannual. Estab. 1980. Circ. 500.

Needs Ethnic/multicultural, experimental, historical, literary, mainstream, regional (Southern, Latin Ameri-can), religious/inspirational, serialized novels, translations. Receives 40 unsolicited mss/month. Accepts 2 mss/ issue; 4 mss/year. **Publishes 2-3 new writers/year.** Recently published work by Andrei Codrescu, Terrance Hayes, Naton Leslie, Alvin Aubert. Also publishes literary essays, literary criticism. Occasionally comments on rejected mss.

How to Contact Send complete ms. Include 2-3 sentence bio. Sample copy for $5.

Payment/Terms Pays 2 contributor copies.

$☑ XCONNECT

P.O. Box 2317, Philadelphia PA 19103. (215)898-5324. Fax: (215)898-9348. E-mail: editors@xconnect.org. Web site: www.xconnect.org. **Contact:** David Deifer. Journal: 5½×8½; trade paper; 200 pages. ''*Xconnect* publishes on the World Wide Web and annually in print, with the best of our Web issues. *Xconnect: writers of the information age* is a nationally distributed, full color, journal sized book.''

Needs Experimental, literary. ''Our mission—like our name—is one of connection. *Xconnect* seeks to promote and document the emergent creative artists as well as established artists who have made the transition to the new technologies of the Information Age.'' **Publishes 25 new writers/year.** Recently published work by Russell Banks, John Edgar Wideman, David Jauss. Rarely comments on rejected mss.

How to Contact Accepts simultaneous and reprint submissions. Sample copy not available.

Payment/Terms Pays 1 contributor's copy and $150-250 for stories used in print. Author retains all rights. Regularly sends prepublication galleys.

Advice ''Persistence.''

Ⓝ $THE YALE REVIEW

Yale University, P.O. Box 208243, New Haven CT 06520-8243. (203)432-0499. Web site: www.yale.edu/yalerevi ew. Quarterly. Estab. 1911. Circ. 7,000.
Needs Publishes ms 6 months after acceptance.
How to Contact Responds in 2 months to queries; 2 months to mss. Sample copy for $9, plus postage. Writer's guidelines online.
Payment/Terms Pays $400-500. Pays prior to publication. Acquires one-time rights.

Ⓐ THE YALOBUSHA REVIEW, The Literary Journal of the University of Mississippi

Dept. of English, P.O. Box 1848, University MS 38677. (662)915-3175. Fax: (662)915-7419. E-mail: yalobusha@o lemiss.edu. Magazine: 5×10; 125 pages; illustrations; photos. Annual. Estab. 1995. Circ. 1,000.
Needs Experimental, family saga, historical, humor/satire, literary, mainstream, genre. Receives 100 unsolicited mss/month. Accepts 8-10 mss/issue. Reading period: July 15-November 15. Publishes ms 4 months after acceptance. **Publishes 3-4 new writers/year.** Recently published work by Steve Almond, Shay Youngblood, Dan Chaon. Length: 1,000-5,000 words; average length: 4,000 words. Publishes short shorts. Also publishes poetry.
How to Contact Send complete ms. Include a brief bio. Send disposable copy of ms and #10 SASE for reply only. Responds in 3 months to mss. Sample copy for $5. Writer's guidelines for #10 SASE.
Payment/Terms Pays 2 contributor's copies. Acquires first North American serial rights.
Advice "We look for writers with a strong, distinct voice and good stories to tell. Thrill us."

Ⓐ Ⓦ YEMASSEE, The literary journal of the University of South Carolina

Department of English, University of South Carolina, Columbia SC 29208. (803)777-2085. Fax: (803)777-9064. E-mail: yemassee@gwm.sc.edu. Web site: www.cla.sc.edu/ENGL/yemassee/index.htm. **Contact:** Editors. Magazine: 5¹/₂×8¹/₂; 70-90 pages; 60 lb. natural paper; 65 lb. cover; cover illustration. "We are open to a variety of subjects and writing styles. We publish primarily fiction and poetry, but we are also interested in one-act plays, brief excerpts of novels, and interviews with literary figures. Our essential consideration for acceptance is the quality of the work." Semiannual. Estab. 1993. Circ. 500.
● Stories from *Yemassee* have been selected for publication in *New Stories from The South.*
Needs Condensed novels, ethnic/multicultural, experimental, feminist, gay, historical, humor/satire, lesbian, literary, regional. "No romance, religious/inspirational, young adult/teen, children's/juvenile, erotica. Wants more experimental work." Receives 30 unsolicited mss/month. Accepts 1-3 mss/issue; 2-6 mss/year. "We read from August-May and hold ms over to the next year if they arrive in the summer." **Publishes 6 new writers/ year.** Recently published work by Robert Coover, Chris Railey, Virgil Suárez, Susan Ludvigson, Kwame Dawes. Publishes short shorts. Also publishes literary essays, poetry.
How to Contact Send complete ms. Include estimated word count, brief bio, list of publications. Send SASE for reply, return of ms, or send disposable copy of ms. Responds in 2 weeks to queries; 4 months to mss. Accepts simultaneous submissions. Sample copy for $5. Writer's guidelines for #10 SASE.
Payment/Terms Acquires first rights.
Advice "Our criteria are based on what we perceive as quality. Generally that is work that is literary. We are interested in subtlety and originality, interesting or beautiful language, craft and precision. Read our journal and any other journal before you submit to see if your work seems appropriate. Send for guidelines and make sure you follow them."

Ⓝ $Ⓞ ZEEK, A JEWISH JOURNAL OF THOUGHT AND CULTURE

Metatronics Inc., 104 West 14th St., 4th Floor, New York NY 10011. E-mail: zeek@zeek.net. Web site: www.zee k.net. **Contact:** Joshua Furst, fiction editor. Literary magazine/journal, online magazine: 6×9, 96 pages, card cover. Contains illustrations. Includes photographs. "*Zeek* is a new Jewish journal of thought and culture. Our mission is to present alternative Jewish voices of criticism, literature and religious thought, in an intelligent, but non-academic, context. *Zeek* exists both online and in print, in semi-annual journal form. *Zeek* believes in expansive definitions of what constitutes Jewish writing and culture, and is dedicated toward enriching those definitions within its pages. While it would be reductive to label any writing produced by Jews as 'Jewish writing,' *Zeek* believes that vibrant Jewish writing embraces a wide variety of media, opinions and perspectives that often express their Jewishness in subtle and unexpected ways, and often presents Jewish readings of non-Jewish culture. This may mean, for example, expressing an ethical/humanist sensibility in art criticism, or engaging the alterity of Jewishness with that of queer sexuality, or immersing oneself in the many diasporic cultures of Jewish character, from New York's Broadway to Marxism. Sometimes it may mean content that grapples with explicitly Jewish cultural themes, and sometimes it may mean Jews interacting with other cultures in a way in which Jewishness is relevant and informative." Semiannual. Estab. 2003. Circ. 500. Member IPA.
Needs Comics/graphic novels, ethnic/multicultural (general, Jewish), feminist, gay, historical (general, Jewish), humor/satire, lesbian, literary, religious (Jewish), translations. Does not want "cynical, inspirational. No

ethnocentric writing or simplistic ranting. If someone else can say it, let them; define new boundaries." Receives 20 mss/month. Accepts 2-4 (with more online) mss/issue; 4-8 (with more online) mss/year. Manuscript published 4 months after acceptance. Agented fiction 0%. **Publishes 5-7 new writers/year.** Published David Ehrlich, Jill Hammer, Rebecca Mostov (debut), Leah Koenig (debut), Hayyim Obadiah. Length: 750 words (min)-3,000 words (max). Average length: 1,500 words. Publishes short shorts. Average length of short shorts: 500 words. Also publishes literary essays, literary criticism, book reviews, poetry. Send review copies to Review Editor. Often comments on/critiques rejected mss.

How to Contact Accepts submissions by e-mail. Send ms attachment to cover letter to zeek@zeek.net. Include estimated word count, brief bio, list of publications. Responds to queries in 4 weeks. Responds to mss in 4 weeks. Send disposable copy of ms and #10 SASE for reply only, "but prefers e-mail submissions." Considers simultaneous submissions, multiple submissions. Guidelines available on Web site.

Payment and Terms Writers receive $25-$50 flate-rate payment, contibutor's copies, free subscription to the magazine. Additional copies $7/each. Pays on publication. Acquires first rights. Publication is copyrighted.

Advice "Seeks quality, freshness of perspective. Something intangibly Jewish and questioning of Jewish mores. Read the online archives. Ask yourself what questions your fiction poses."

ZOETROPE: ALL STORY

916 Kearny St., San Francisco CA 94133. (415)788-7500. Web site: www.all-story.com. **Contact:** Michael Ray, editor. Magazine specializing in the best of contemporary short fiction. *"Zoetrope: All Story* presents a new generation of classic stories." Quarterly. Estab. 1997. Circ. 20,000.

Needs Literary short stories, one-act plays. Accepts 25-35 mss/year. Publishes ms 5 months after acceptance. Length: 7,000 words (max).

How to Contact Send complete ms. Does not accept mss between June 1-August 1, or via e-mail. Responds in 5 months (if SASE included) to mss. Accepts simultaneous submissions. Sample copy for $6.95. Writer's guidelines online.

Payment/Terms Acquires first serial rights.

$ ☺ ZYZZYVA, The Last Word: West Coast Writers & Artists

P.O. Box 590069, San Francisco CA 94159-0069. (415)752-4393. Fax: (415)752-4391. E-mail: editor@zyzzyva.o rg. Web site: www.zyzzyva.org. **Contact:** Howard Junker, editor. "We feature work by writers currently living on the West Coast or in Alaska and Hawaii only. We are essentially a literary magazine, but of wide-ranging interests and a strong commitment to nonfiction." Estab. 1985. Circ. 3,500.

Needs Ethnic/multicultural, experimental, humor/satire, mainstream. Receives 300 unsolicited mss/month. Accepts 10 mss/issue; 30 mss/year. Publishes ms 3 months after acceptance. Agented fiction 1%. **Publishes 15 new writers/year.** Recently published work by Amanda Field, Katherine Karlin, Margaret Weatherford. Publishes short shorts. Also publishes literary essays, poetry.

How to Contact Send complete ms. Responds in 1 week to queries; 1 month to mss. Sample copy for $7 or online. Writer's guidelines online.

Payment/Terms Pays $50. Pays on acceptance for first North American serial and one-time anthology rights.

Small Circulation Magazines

his section of *Novel & Short Story Writer's Market* contains general interest, special interest, regional and genre magazines with circulations under 10,000. Although these magazines vary greatly in size, theme, format and management, the editors are all looking for short stories. Their specific fiction needs present writers of all degrees of expertise and interests with an abundance of publishing opportunities. Among the diverse publications in this section are magazines devoted to almost every topic, every level of writing, and every type of writer. Some of the markets listed here publish fiction about a particular geographic area or by authors who live in that locale.

Although not as high-paying as the large-circulation consumer magazines, you'll find some of the publications listed here do pay writers 1-5¢/word or more. Also, unlike the big consumer magazines, these markets are very open to new writers and relatively easy to break into. Their only criteria are that your story be well written, well presented and suitable for their particular readership.

In this section you will also find listings for zines. Zines vary greatly in appearance as well as content. Some paper zines are photocopies published whenever the editor has material and money, while others feature offset printing and regular distribution schedules. A few have evolved into very slick four-color, commercial-looking publications.

SELECTING THE RIGHT MARKET

First, zero in on those markets most likely to be interested in your work. Begin by looking at the Category Index starting on page 588. If your work is more general—or conversely, very specialized—you may wish to browse through the listings, perhaps looking up those magazines published in your state or region. Also check the Online Markets section for other specialized and genre publications.

In addition to browsing through the listings and using the Category Index, check the openness icons at the beginning of listings to find those most likely to be receptive to your work. This is especially true for beginning writers, who should look for magazines that say they are especially open to new writers ($\square$) and for those giving equal weight to both new and established writers ($\blacksquare$). For more explanation about these icons, see the inside covers of this book.

Once you have a list of magazines you might like to try, read their listings carefully. Much of the material within each listing carries clues that tell you more about the magazine. You've Got a Story, starting on page 2, describes in detail the listing information common to all the markets in our book.

The physical description appearing near the beginning of the listings can give you clues about the size and financial commitment to the publication. This is not always an indication of quality, but chances are a publication with expensive paper and four-color artwork on the cover has more prestige than a photocopied publication featuring a clip-art cover. For more information on some of the paper, binding and printing terms used in these descriptions, see Printing and Production Terms Defined on page 550.

FURTHERING YOUR SEARCH

It cannot be stressed enough that reading the listing is only the first part of developing your marketing plan. The second part, equally important, is to obtain fiction guidelines and read the actual magazine. Reading copies of a magazine helps you determine the fine points of the magazine's publishing style and philosophy. There is no substitute for this type of hands-on research.

Unlike commercial magazines available at most newsstands and bookstores, it requires a little more effort to obtain some of the magazines listed here. You may need to send for a sample copy. We include sample copy prices in the listings whenever possible. See The Business of Fiction Writing on page 79 for the specific mechanics of manuscript submission. Above all, editors appreciate a professional presentation. Include a brief cover letter and send a self-addressed, stamped envelope for a reply. Be sure the envelope is large enough to accommodate your manuscript, if you would like it returned, and include enough stamps or International Reply Coupons (for replies from countries other than your own) to cover your manuscript's return. Many publishers today appreciate receiving a disposable manuscript, eliminating the cost to writers of return postage and saving editors the effort of repackaging manuscripts for return.

Most of the magazines listed here are published in the U.S. You will also find some English-speaking markets from around the world. These foreign publications are denoted with a ⊕ symbol at the beginning of listings. To make it easier to find Canadian markets, we include a 🔛 symbol at the start of those listings.

N ⊕ ◯ ◎ THE ABIKO ANNUAL WITH JAMES JOYCE, Finnegans Wake Studies
ALP Ltd., 8-1-7 Namiki, Abiko, Chiba 270-1165 Japan. (011)81-471-69-8036. E-mail: hamada-tatsuo@jcom.home.ne.jp. Web site: http://members.jcom.home.ne.jp/hamada-tatsuo/. **Contact:** Tatsuo Hamada. Magazine: A5; 350 pages; illustrations; photos. "We primarily publish James Joyce *Finnegans Wake* essays from writers here in Japan and abroad." Annual. Estab. 1989. Circ. 300.
Needs Experimental (in the vein of James Joyce), literary, inspirational. Also essays on James Joyce's *Finnegans Wake* from around the world. Receives very few unsolicited mss/month. Also publishes literary essays, literary criticism, poetry. Always comments on rejected mss.
How to Contact Send a disposable copy of ms or e-mail attachment. Responds in 1 week to queries; 3 months to mss. Accepts multiple submissions. Sample copy for $20. Guidelines for SASE. Reviews fiction.
Payment/Terms Pays 1 contributor's copy; additional copies $25. Copyright reverts to author upon publication.
Advice "We require camera-ready copy. The writer is welcome to accompany it with appropriate artwork."

⊕ ▣ ◎ ALBEDO ONE, The Irish Magazine of Science Fiction, Fantasy and Horror
Albedo One, 2 Post Rd., Lusk, Co Dublin Ireland. (+353)1-8730177. E-mail: bobn@yellowbrickroad.ie. Web site: www.albedo.com. **Contact:** Editor, *Albedo One*. Magazine: A4; 44 pages. "We hope to publish interesting and unusual fiction by new and established writers. We will consider anything, as long as it is well written and entertaining, though our definitions of both may not be exactly mainstream. We like stories with plot and characters that live on the page. Most of our audience are probably committed genre fans, but we try to appeal to a broad spectrum of readers—the narrow focus of our readership is due to the public-at-large's unwillingness to experiment with their reading/magazine purchasing rather than any desire on our part to be exclusive." Triannual. Estab. 1993. Circ. 900.
Needs Comics/graphic novels, experimental, fantasy, horror, literary, science fiction. Receives more than 80 unsolicited mss/month. Accepts 15-18 mss/year. Publishes ms 1 year after acceptance. **Publishes 6-8 new writers/year.** Length: 2,000- 6,000 words; average length: 4,000 words. Also publishes literary criticism. Sometimes comments on rejected mss.
How to Contact Responds in 4 months to mss. Sample copy not available. Guidelines available by e-mail or on Web site. Reviews fiction.

Payment/Terms Pays 100 Euro for best-in-issue story and 1 contributor's copy; additional copies $5 plus p&p. Pays on publication for first rights.

Advice "We look for good writing, good plot, good characters. Read the magazine, and don't give up."

$AMAZING JOURNEYS

Journey Books Publishing, 3205 Hwy. 431, Spring Hill TN 37174. (615)791-8006. Web site: www.journeybooksp ublishing.com. "We are seeking the best in up-and-coming authors who produce great stories that appeal to a wide audience. Each issue will be packed with exciting, fresh material. *Amazing Journeys* will be a fun read, designed to stimulate the senses without offending them. With the introduction of *Amazing Journeys*, we intend to reintroduce the style of writing that made the Golden Age of science fiction "golden." If you are tired of 'shock culture' stories or stories written strictly to appeal to a commercial audience, then *Amazing Journeys* is the right magazine for you." Quarterly. Estab. 2003.

Needs Fantasy, science fiction. "Absolutely no sexual content will be accepted. Profanity is greatly restricted (none is preferred). Publishes ms 6-12 months after acceptance.

How to Contact Send complete ms. Accepts submissions by e-mail. Responds in 1 week to queries; 2 months to mss. Sample copy for $6.99, plus 1 SAE with 3 first-class stamps. Writer's guidelines for #10 SASE.

Payment/Terms Pays $1/4$¢-1¢/word. Pays on acceptance for first North American serial rights.

✪ ANY DREAM WILL DO REVIEW, Short Stories and Humor from the Secret Recesses of our Minds

Any Dream Will Do, Inc., 1830 Kirman Ave., C1, Reno NV 89502-3381. (775)786-0345. E-mail: cassjmb@iqemail .com. Web site: www.willigocrazy.org/Ch08.htm. **Contact:** Dr . Jean M. Bradt, editor and publisher. Magazine: $5^{1}/_{2} \times 8^{1}/_{2}$; 52 pages; 20 lb. bond paper; 12pt. Carolina cover stock. "The 52-page *Any Dream Will Do Review* showcases a new literary genre, Fiction In The Raw, which attempts to fight the prejudice against consumers of mental-health services by touching hearts, that is, by exposing the consumers' deepest thoughts and emotions. In the *Review*'s stories, accomplished authors honestly reveal their most intimate secrets. See www.willi gocrazy.org/Ch09a.htm for detailed instructions on how to write Fiction In The Raw." Annual. Estab. 2001. Circ. 200.

Needs Ethnic/multicultural, mainstream, psychic/supernatural/occult, romance (contemporary), science fiction (soft/sociological). No pornography, true life stories, black humor, political material, testimonials, experimental fiction, or depressing accounts of hopeless or perverted people. Accepts 10 mss/issue; 20 mss/year. Publishes ms 12 months after acceptance. **Publishes 10 new writers/year.** Publishes short shorts. Often comments on rejected mss.

How to Contact Send complete ms. Accepts submissions by e-mail (cassjmb@iqemail.com). Please submit by e-mail, if possible. If you must submit by hardcopy, please send disposable copies. No queries, please. Responds in 8 weeks to mss. Sample copy for $4 plus postage. Writer's guidelines online.

Payment/Terms Pays in contributor's copies; additional copies $4 plus postage. Acquires first North American serial rights.

Advice "Read several stories on www.willigocrazy.org before starting to write. Proof your story many times before submitting. Make the readers think. Above all, present people (preferably diagnosed with mental illness) realistically rather than with prejudice."

Ⓝ $✪ APEX SCIENCE FICTION AND HORROR DIGEST

Apex Publications, P.O. Box 2223, Lexington KY 40588. (859)312-3974. E-mail: jason@apexdigest.com. Web site: www.apexdigest.com. **Contact:** Jason Sizemore, editor-in-chief. Magazine: $5^{1}/_{2} \times 8^{1}/_{2}$, 128 pages, 70 lb. white offset paper, glossy #120 cover. Contains illustrations. "We publish dark sci-fi with horror elements. Our readers are those who enjoy speculative fiction with dark themes." Quarterly. Estab. 2005. Circ. 3,000.

Needs Dark science fiction. "We're not fans of 'monster' fiction." Receives 75-150 mss/month. Accepts 8 mss/ issue; 32 mss/year. Manuscript published 3 months after acceptance. **Publishes 10 new writers/year.** Published Ben Bova, William F. Nolan, Tom Piccirilli, M.M. Buckner, JA Rourath, James P. Hogan. Length: 200 words (min)-10,000 words (max). Average length: 4,000 words. Publishes short shorts. Average length of short shorts: 500 words. Also publishes literary essays. Often comments on/critiques rejected manuscripts.

How to Contact Send complete ms with cover letter. Include estimated word count, brief bio. Responds to queries in 3-4 weeks. Responds to mss in 3-4 weeks. Prefers submissions by e-mail, or send disposable copy of ms and #10 SASE for reply only. Considers previously published submissions; "must query, however." Sample copy available for $5. Guidelines available via e-mail, on Web site.

Payment and Terms Writers receive 1¢/word and two comp copies of magazine. Additional copies $4. Pays on publication. Acquires first North American serial rights. Publication is copyrighted.

Advice "Be professional. Be confident. Remember that any criticisms offered are given for your benefit."

THE BINNACLE

University of Maine at Machias, 9 O'Brien Ave., Machias ME 04654. E-mail: ummbinnacle@maine.edu. Web site: www.umm.maine.edu/binnacle. "We publish an alternative format journal of literary and visual art. We are restless about the ossification of literature and what to do about it." Semiannual. Estab. 1957. Circ. 300.

Needs Ethnic/multicultural, experimental, humor/satire, mainstream, slice-of-life vignettes. No extreme erotica, fantasy, horror, or religious, but any genre attuned to a general audience can work. Publishes ms 3 months after acceptance.

How to Contact Send complete ms. Accepts submissions by e-mail (ummbinnacle@maine.edu). Responds in 1 month to queries; 3 months to mss. Accepts simultaneous submissions. Sample copy for $5. Writer's guidelines online at Web site or by e-mail.

Payment/Terms Acquires one-time rights.

$ BRUTARIAN, The Magazine of Brutiful Art

9405 Ulysses Ct., Burke VA 22015. E-mail: brutarian@msn.com. Web site: www.brutarian.com. "A healthy knowledge of the great works of antiquity and an equally healthy contempt for most of what passes today as culture." Quarterly. Estab. 1991. Circ. 5,000.

Needs Adventure, confessions, erotica, experimental, fantasy, horror, humor/satire, mystery/suspense, novel excerpts. Publishes ms 3 months after acceptance.

How to Contact Send complete ms. Responds in 1 week to queries; 2 months to mss. Accepts simultaneous submissions. Sample copy for $6. Writer's guidelines online.

Payment/Terms Pays up to 10¢/word. Pays on publication for first, electronic rights.

$ ◎ CHARACTERS, Kids Short Story & Poetry Outlet

Davis Publications, P.O. Box 708, Newport NH 03773. (603)864-5896. Fax: (603)863-8198. E-mail: hotdog@nhvt .net. **Contact:** Cindy Davis, editor. Magazine: 5½×8½; 45 pages; saddle bound cover stock; illustrations. "We want to give kids a place to showcase their talents." Quarterly. Estab. 2003.

Needs "We accept all subjects of interest to kids. Particularly would like to see humor , mystery and adventure." Receives 60 unsolicited mss/month. Accepts 8-12 mss/issue; 36-48 mss/year. Publishes ms 1-6 months after acceptance. Publishes short shorts. Sometimes comments on rejected mss.

How to Contact Send complete ms. Accepts submissions by e-mail, fax. Send disposable copy of the ms and #10 SASE or e-mail address for reply. Responds in 2-4 weeks to mss. Accepts simultaneous submissions and reprints. Sample copy for $5. Writer's guidelines for #10 SASE or by e-mail.

Payment/Terms Pays $5 and contributor's copy; additional copies $4. Pays on publication for one-time rights. Not copyrighted.

Advice "We love to see a well-thought-out plot and interesting, varied characters."

N $ CHURCH EDUCATOR

Educational Ministries, Inc., 165 Plaza Dr., Prescott AZ 86303. (928)771-8601. Fax: (928)771-8621. E-mail: edmin2@aol.com. "*Church Educator* has programming ideas for the Christian educator in the mainline Protestant church. We are *not* on the conservative, fundamental side theologically, so slant articles to the liberal side. Programs should offer lots of questions and not give pat answers." Monthly. Estab. 1978. Circ. 2,500.

Needs Religious/inspirational; seasonal programs. Publishes ms 2 months after acceptance.

How to Contact Send complete ms. Accepts submissions by e-mail, fax, disk. Responds in 2 weeks to queries; 4 months to mss. Accepts simultaneous submissions. Sample copy for 9×12 SAE and 4 first-class stamps. Writer's guidelines free.

Payment/Terms Pays 3¢/word. Pays 60 days after publication. Acquires first rights.

◻ THE CIRCLE MAGAZINE

Circle Publications, 173 Grandview Road, Wernersville PA 19565. (610)678-6550. E-mail: circlemag@aol.com. Web site: www.circlemagazine.com. **Contact:** Penny Talbert, editor. Magazine: 5½×8½; 48-52 pages; white offset paper; illustrations; photos. "*The Circle* is an eclectic mix of culture and subculture. Our goal is to provide the reader with thought-provoking reading that they will remember." Quarterly.

Needs Adventure, experimental, humor/satire, literary, mainstream, mystery/suspense, New Age, psychic/supernatural/occult, romance, science fiction, thriller/espionage. No religious fiction. Receives 400 unsolicited mss/month. Accepts 3-5 mss/issue; 12-20 mss/year. Publishes ms 1-4 months after acceptance. Recently published work by David McDaniel, Bart Stewart, Ace Boggess, Stephen Forney. Length: 2,000-6,000 words; average length: 2,500 words. Publishes short shorts. Also publishes literary essays, literary criticism, poetry. Sometimes comments on rejected mss.

How to Contact Send complete ms with cover letter. Accepts submissions by e-mail (circlemag@aol.com). Include estimated word count, brief bio and list of publications. Responds in 1 month to queries; 4 months to mss. Accepts simultaneous, multiple submissions and reprints. Sample copy for $4. Writer's guidelines online.

Payment/Terms Pays 1 contributor's copy; additional copies $4. Pays on publication for one-time, electronic rights.

Advice "The most important thing is that submitted fiction keeps our attention and interest. The most typical reason for rejection: bad endings! Proofread your work, and send it in compliance with our guidelines."

$⬚ ◎ CITY SLAB, Urban Tales of the Grotesque

City Slab Publications, 1705 Summit Ave. #314, Seattle WA 98122. (206)568-4343. E-mail: dave@cityslab.com. Web site: www.cityslab.com. **Contact**: Dave Lindschmidt, editor. Magazine: 8½×11; 60 pages; color covers; illustrations; photos. "*City Slab* presents the best in urban horror today. *City Slab* offers an intriguing mix of familiar voices with new discoveries. Each page is a cold, wet kiss to the genre."—Evan Wright, *Rolling Stone Magazine*. Quarterly. Estab. 2002.

Needs "We're looking for taut, multi-leveled urban horror. Start the story with action. Capture the feel of your city whether it's real or imagined and have a story to tell! We love crime fiction but there has to be a horror slant to it. Steer away from first person point of view." Publishes ms 3-6 months after acceptance. **Publishes 6 new writers/year.** Recently published work by Gerard Houarner, Christa Faust, Yvonne Navarro, Patricia Russo, Robert Dunbar.

How to Contact Accepts submissions by e-mail (submission@cityslab.com with a copy to Scott@cityslab.com). Include estimated word count, brief bio and list of publications. Send disposable copy of ms and #10 SASE for reply only. Responds in 6 weeks to queries; 2 months to mss. Sample copy for $6. Writer's guidelines online.

Payment/Terms Pays 1-5¢ per word within 60 days of publication for first serial rights.

$⬚ THE COUNTRY CONNECTION

Pinecone Publishing, P.O. Box 100, Boulter ON K0L 1G0 Canada. (613)332-3651. E-mail: editor@pinecone.on. ca. Web site: www.pinecone.on.ca. "*The Country Connection* is a magazine for true nature lovers and the rural adventurer. Building on our commitment to heritage, cultural, artistic and environmental themes, we continually add new topics to illuminate the country experience of people living within nature. Our goal is to chronicle rural life in its many aspects, giving 'voice' to the countryside." Estab. 1989. Circ. 10,000.

Needs Ontario history and heritage, humor/satire, nature, environment, the arts, country living. Publishes ms 4 months after acceptance.

How to Contact Send complete ms. Accepts submissions by e-mail, disk. Sample copy for $5.70. Writer's guidelines online.

Payment/Terms Pays 10¢/word. Pays on publication for first rights.

⬚ CREATIVE WITH WORDS PUBLICATIONS

Creative With Words Publications, P.O. Box 223226, Carmel CA 93922. Fax: (831)655-8627. E-mail: cwwpub@u sa.net. Web site: members.tripod.com/CreativeWithWords. **Contact:** Brigitta Geltrich, general editor. Booklet: 5½×8½; up to 50 pages; bond paper; illustrations/computer art work. "We want writers to look at the world from a different perspective, research topics thoroughly, be creative, apply brevity, tell the story from a character's point of view, tighten dialogue, be less descriptive, proofread before submitting and be patient." 12 times/year. Estab. 1975. Circ. varies.

Needs Ethnic/multicultural, humor/satire, mystery/suspense (amateur sleuth, private eye), regional (folklore), young adult/teen (adventure, historical). "Do not submit essays." No violence or erotica, overly religious fiction or sensationalism. "Once a year we publish an anthology of the writings of young writers, titled, *We are Writers, Too!*" List of upcoming themes available for SASE. Limit poetry to 20 lines or less, 46 characters per line or less. Receives 250-500 unsolicited mss/month. Accepts 50-80 mss/year. Publishes ms 1-2 months after acceptance. Recently published work by Najwa Salam Brax, June K. Silconas, William Bridge and David Napolin. Average length: 800 words. Publishes short shorts. Also publishes poetry. Sometimes comments on rejected mss.

How to Contact Send complete ms, cover letter, SASE. Include estimated word count. Responds in 2 weeks to queries; 2 months to mss. Sample copy for $6. Writer's guidelines for #10 SASE.

Payment/Terms Offers 20% reduction cost on 1-9 copies ordered, 30% reduction on order of 10 or more. Acquires one-time rights.

Advice "We offer a great variety of themes. We look for clean family-type fiction. Also, we ask the writer to look at the world from a different perspective, research topic thoroughly, be creative, apply brevity, tell the story from a character's viewpoint, tighten dialogue, be less descriptive, proofread before submitting and be patient. We will not publish every manuscript we receive. It has to be in standard English, well written, proofread. We do not appreciate receiving manuscripts where we have to do the proofreading and the correcting of grammar."

$☐ ⊚ CTHULHU SEX MAGAZINE, Blood, Sex and Tentacles

Cthulhu Sex, P.O. Box 3678, Grand Central Station, New York NY 10163. E-mail: stcthulhu@cthulhusex.com. Web site: www.cthulhusex.com. **Contact:** Michael Amorel, editor-in-chief. Magazine: $8^1/_4 \times 10^5/_8$; 80 pages; 24 lb. white paper; 80 lb. glossy color cover stock; illustrations; photos. "We intend to corrupt the mainstream ideals of the apparent mutual exclusivity of beauty and horror. We generally publish poetry, short stories and artwork that evoke a dark and sensual atmosphere in the genre of erotic horror. We particularly look for edgy and experimental works that explore the dark side of sensuality and have a subtle yet powerful impact. We cater to mature readers and connoisseurs of sensual horror." Quarterly. Estab. 1998. Circ. 2,500.

Needs Fantasy (dark), horror (dark fantasy, futuristic, psychological, supernatural, erotic), psychic/supernatural/occult, science fiction (dark). "We do not want to see explicit pornography, rape, rehashed vampire stories, erotica without a darker edge, serials." Receives 40-50 unsolicited mss/month. Accepts 5-7 mss/issue; 25-30 mss/year. Publishes ms 4 months after acceptance. **Publishes 5 new writers/year.** Recently published work by C.J. Henderson, Robert Masterson, Wrath James White, J.F. Gonzalez and Mark McLaughlin. Length: 800-5,000 words; average length: 2,500 words. Publishes short shorts. Also publishes poetry. Sometimes comments on rejected mss.

How to Contact Send complete ms. Prefers submissions by e-mail. Send disposable copy of ms and #10 SASE for reply only. Responds in 1 month to queries; 3 months to mss. No simultaneous submissions or multiple submissions. Sample copy for $4.95. Writer's guidelines for SASE, e-mail or Web site.

Payment/Terms Pays 2¢/word for original fiction or $5 for an original poem and 1 contributor's copy; additional copies $4. Pays on publication for one-time printing and promotional rights.

Advice "We look for work that explores at least one of the elements of the theme blood, sex and tentacles. Well-edited pieces are always appreciated. We want authors to use good writing to evoke a response instead of cheap TADA tactics. Have a unique plotline. We recommend prospective contributors read at least one copy of the magazine to get an idea of our content style. Do not try to sell your story; let it speak for itself."

$☐ DAN RIVER ANTHOLOGY

Conservatory of American Letters, P.O. Box 298, Thomaston ME 04861. (207)354-0998. Web site: www.america nletters.org. **Contact:** R.S. Danbury III, editor. Book: 6×9; 192 pages; 60 lb. paper; gloss 10 pt. full-color cover. Deadline every year is March 31, with acceptance/rejection by May 15, proofs out by June 15, and book released December 7. Annual. Estab. 1984. Circ. 750.

Needs Adventure, ethnic/multicultural, experimental, fantasy, historical, horror, humor/satire, literary, mainstream, psychic/supernatural/occult, regional, romance (contemporary and historical), science fiction, suspense, western, contemporary, prose poem, senior citizen/retirement. "Virtually anything but porn, evangelical, juvenile. Would like to see more first-person adventure." Reads "mostly in April." Length: 800-3,500 words; average length: 2,000-2,400 words. Also publishes poetry.

How to Contact Send complete ms. No simultaneous submissions. Nothing previously published. Sample copy for $16.95 paperback, $39.95 cloth, plus $3.25 shipping. Writer's guidelines available for #10 SASE or online.

Payment/Terms Payment "depends on your experience with us, as it is a nonrefundable advance against royalties on all sales that we can attribute to your influence. For first-timers, the advance is about 1¢/word." Pays on acceptance for first rights.

Advice "Read an issue or two, know the market. Don't submit without reading guidelines on the Web or send #10 SASE."

☐ DOWN IN THE DIRT, The Publication Revealing all your Dirty Little Secrets

Scars Publications and Design, 829 Brian Court, Gurnee IL 60031-3155. (847)281-9070. E-mail: alexrand@scars. tv. Web site: scars.tv. **Contact:** Alexandria Rand, editor. Magazine: $5^1/_2 \times 8^1/_2$; 60 lb. paper; illustrations; photos. As material gathers. Estab. 2000.

Needs Adventure, ethnic/multicultural, experimental, fantasy, feminist, gay, historical, horror, lesbian, literary, mystery/suspense, New Age, psychic/supernatural/occult, science fiction. No religious or rhyming or family-oriented material. Publishes ms within 1 year after acceptance. Recently published work by Simon Perchik, Jim Dewitt, Jennifer Connelly, L.B. Sedlacek, Aeon Logan, Helena Wolfe. Average length: 1,000 words. Publishes short shorts. Also publishes poetry. Always, if asked, comments on rejected mss.

How to Contact Query with published clips or send complete ms. Accepts submissions by e-mail. Send SASE (or IRC) for return of ms or disposable copy of ms and #10 SASE for reply only. Responds in 1 month to queries; 1 month to mss. Accepts simultaneous, multiple submissions and reprints. Sample copy for $6. Writer's guidelines for SASE, e-mail or on Web site. Reviews fiction.

$⊞ ⊚ DREAMS & VISIONS, Spiritual Fiction

Skysong Press, 35 Peter St. S., Orillia ON L3V 5A8 Canada. (705)329-1770. Fax: (705)329-1770. E-mail: skysong @bconnex.net. Web site: www.bconnex.net/~skysong. **Contact:** Steve Stanton, editor. Magazine: $5^1/_2 \times 8^1/_2$;

56 pages; 20 lb. bond paper; glossy cover. "Innovative literary fiction for adult Christian readers." Semiannual. Estab. 1988. Circ. 200.

Needs Experimental, fantasy, humor/satire, literary, mainstream, mystery/suspense, novel excerpts, religious/inspirational, science fiction, slice-of-life vignettes. "We do not publish stories that glorify violence or perversity. All stories should portray a Christian world view or expand upon Biblical themes or ethics in an entertaining or enlightening manner." Receives 20 unsolicited mss/month. Accepts 7 mss/issue; 14 mss/year. Publishes ms 4-8 months after acceptance. **Publishes 3 new writers/year.** Recently published work by Fred McGavran, Steven Mills, Donna Farley, Michael Vance. Length: 2,000-6,000 words; average length: 2,500 words.

How to Contact Send complete ms. Responds in 3 weeks to queries; 3 months to mss. Accepts simultaneous submissions. Sample copy for $4.95. Writer's guidelines online.

Payment/Terms Pays 1¢/word. Pays on publication for first North American serial, one-time, second serial (reprint) rights.

Advice "In general we look for work that has some literary value, that is in some way unique and relevant to Christian readers today. Our first priority is technical adequacy, though we will occasionally work with a beginning writer to polish a manuscript. Ultimately, we look for stories that glorify the Lord Jesus Christ, stories that build up rather than tear down, that exalt the sanctity of life, the holiness of God, and the value of the family."

$ 🎯 ☑ THE FIRST LINE

Blue Cubicle Press, LLC, P.O. Box 250382, Plano TX 75025-0382. (972)824-0646. E-mail: submissions@thefirstline.com. Web site: www.thefirstline.com. **Contact:** Robin LaBounty, manuscript coordinator. Magzine: 8×5; 64-72 pages; 20 lb. bond paper; 80 lb. cover stock. "We only publish stories that start with the first line provided. We are a collection of tales—of different directions writers can take when they start from the same place. Quarterly. Estab. 1999. Circ. 800.

Needs Adventure, ethnic/multicultural, fantasy, gay, humor/satire, lesbian, literary, mainstream, mystery/suspense, regional, romance, science fiction, western. Receives 100 unsolicited mss/month. Accepts 12 mss/issue; 48 mss/year. Publishes ms 1 month after acceptance. **Publishes 6 new writers/year.** Length: 300-3,000 words; average length: 1,500 words. Publishes short shorts. Also publishes literary essays, literary criticism. Often comments on rejected mss.

How to Contact Send complete ms. Accepts submissions by e-mail. Send SASE for return of ms or disposable copy of the ms and #10 SASE for reply only. Responds in 1 week to queries; 3 months to mss. Accepts multiple submissions. No simultaneous submissions. Sample copy for $3.50. Writer's guidelines for SASE, e-mail or on Web site. Reviews fiction.

Payment/Terms Pays $20 maximum and contributor's copy; additional copy $2. Pays on publication.

Advice "Don't just write the first story that comes to mind after you read the sentence. If it is obvious, chances are other people are writing about the same thing. Don't try so hard. Be willing to accept criticism."

$ ☑ 🎯 🔱 FLESH AND BLOOD, Tales of Horror & Dark Fantasy

Flesh & Blood Press, 121 Joseph St., Bayville NJ 08721. E-mail: harrorjackf@aol.com. Web site: www.fleshandbloodmagazine.com. **Contact:** Jack Fisher, editor-in-chief/publisher; Teri A. Jacobs, assistant editor. Magazine: full-sized; 80 + pages; thick/glossy, full-color cover; "fully and lavishly illustrated." "We publish fiction with heavy emphasis on the fantastic and bizarre." Quarterly. Estab. 1997. Circ. 1,000.

● The magazine recently won the 2001 Zine Publishing Competition Award in *Writer's Digest Magazine*, 2002 Bram Stoker Award nominee, and won The Best Magazine of the Year Award in the *Jobs In Hell* newsletter contest.

Needs Horror (dark fantasy, supernatural), slice-of-life vignettes, dark fantasy. "Nothing that isn't dark, strange, odd and/or offbeat." Receives 250 unsolicited mss/month. Accepts 7-10 mss/issue; 21-36 mss/year. Publishes ms 10 months after acceptance. Agented fiction 1%. **Publishes 4-6 new writers/year.** Recently published work by Wendy Rathbone, Teri Jacobs, Tim Piccirrilli, China Melville, Doug Clegg, Jay Bonansigna and Jack Ketchum. Length: 100-5,000 words; average length: 2,000 words. Publishes short shorts. Also publishes poetry.

How to Contact Accepts submissions by e-mail. Send complete ms with cover letter. Include brief bio and list of publications. Send SASE (or IRC) for return of ms. Responds in 2 weeks to queries; 1 month to mss. No simultaneous submissions. Sample copy for $6 (check payable to Jack Fisher). Writer's guidelines online.

Payment/Terms Pays 2-5¢/word. Pays on publication.

Advice "Stories that mix one or more of the following elements with a horrific/weird idea/plot have a good chance: the fantastical, whimsical, supernatural, bizarre; stories should have unique ideas and be strongly written; the weirder and more offbeat, the better."

$ 🎯 FUN FOR KIDZ

Bluffton News Publishing and Printing Company, P.O. Box 227, 103 N. Main Street, Bluffton OH 45817-0227. (419)358-4610. Fax: (419)358-5027. Web site: www.funforkidz.com. **Contact:** Virginia Edwards, associate editor. Magazine: 7×8; 49 pages; illustrations; photographs. *"Fun for Kidz* focuses on activity. The children are encouraged to solve problems, explore and develop character. Target age: 6-13 years." Bimonthly. Estab. 2002. Circ. 8,000.

Needs Children's/juvenile (adventure, animal, easy-to-read, historical, mystery, preschool, series, sports). Previous themes: Bugs; Oceans; Animals; Camping; Fun with Stars; Healthy Fun; Summer Splash; In the Mountains; Fun with Words. List of upcoming themes for SASE. Accepts 10 mss/issue; 60 mss/year. Publishes short shorts. Also publishes poetry. Sometimes comments on rejected mss.

How to Contact Send complete ms with cover letter. Include estimated word count and brief bio. Responds in 6 weeks to queries; 6 months to mss. Accepts simultaneous, multiple submissions. Sample copy for $5. Writer's guidelines for #10 SASE.

Payment/Terms Pays 5¢/word and 1 contributor's copy. Pays on publication for first rights.

Advice "Work needs to be appropriate for a children's publication ages 6-13 years. Request a theme list so story submitted will work into an upcoming issue."

☐ THE FUNNY PAPER

F/J Writers Service, 615 NW Jacob Dr. #206, Lee's Summit, MO 64081. E-mail: felixkcmo@aol.com. Web site: www.funnypaper.info. **Contact:** F.H. Fellhauer, editor. Zine specializing in humor, contest and poetry: 8½×11; 8 pages. Published 4 times/year. No summer or Christmas. Estab. 1984.

Needs Children's/juvenile, humor/satire, literary. "No controversial fiction." Receives 10-20 unsolicited mss/month. Accepts 1 mss/issue; 4-5 mss/year. Length: 1,000 words; average length: 295 words. Publishes short shorts. Also publishes poetry. Sometimes comments on rejected mss.

How to Contact Accepts submissions by e-mail. Send for guidelines. Include estimated word count with submission. Send disposable copy of ms and #10 SASE for reply only. Responds in 2 weeks to queries; 1-3 months to mss. Accepts simultaneous submissions and reprints. Sample copy for $3.

Payment/Terms Prizes for stories, jokes and poems for $5-100 (humor, inspirational, fillers). Additional copies $3. Pays on publication for first, one-time rights.

Advice "Do your best work, no trash. We try to keep abreast of online publishing and provide information."

Ⓝ $☐ HA!

Writers' Haven Press, P.O. Box 368, Seabeck WA 98380-0368. (360)830-5772. Fax: (360)830-5772. E-mail: svend@sinclair.net. Web site: www.writershavenpress.com. **Contact:** Janie Danesh, fiction editor. Magazine: 8½×11, 56 pages, white 60 lb. paper paper, colored cover stock cover. "HA! is a humor magazine, as if you couldn't tell!" Quarterly. Estab. 2004. Circ. 230. Member SPAN.

Needs Comics/graphic novels, humor/satire. Receives 30-50 mss/month. Accepts 7 mss/issue; 28 mss/year. **Publishes 7 new writers/year.** Length: 500-1,500. Average length: 1,000. Publishes short shorts. Average length of short shorts: 500. Also publishes poetry. Rarely comments on/critiques rejected mss.

How to Contact Send complete ms with cover letter. Include estimated word count, brief bio. Responds to mss in 4 months. Send either SASE (or IRC) for return of ms or disposable copy of ms and #10 SASE for reply only. Considers simultaneous submissions, previously published submissions, multiple submissions. Sample copy available for $5 plus $1.50 postage. Guidelines available for SASE, via e-mail.

Payment and Terms Writers receive $5 flate-rate payment, 1 contributor copy. Additional copies $5. Pays on publication. Acquires first North American serial rights, one-time rights, reprint rights. Publication is copyrighted.

Advice "Read your work to others; see if they laugh."

$☐ ◎ HARDBOILED

Gryphon Publications, P.O. Box 209, Brooklyn NY 11228. Web site: www.gryphonbooks.com. **Contact:** Gary Lovisi, editor. Magazine: Digest-sized; 100 pages; offset paper; color cover; illustrations. "Hard-hitting crime fiction and private-eye stories—the newest and most cutting-edge work and classic reprints." Semiannual. Estab. 1988. Circ. 1,000.

Needs Mystery/suspense (private eye, police procedural, noir), hard-boiled crime and private-eye stories, all on the cutting edge. No "pastches, violence for the sake of violence." Wants to see more non-private-eye hard-boiled. Receives 40-60 unsolicited mss/month. Accepts 10-20 mss/issue. Publishes ms 18 months after acceptance. **Publishes 5-10 new writers/year.** Recently published work by Andrew Vachss, Stephen Solomita, Joe Hensley, Mike Black. Sometimes comments on rejected mss.

How to Contact Query with or without published clips or send complete ms. Accepts submissions by fax. Query with SASE only on anything over 3,000 words. All stories must be submitted in hard copy. If accepted, e-mail as an attachment in a Word document. Responds in 2 weeks to queries; 1 month to mss. Accepts simultaneous submissions and reprints. Sample copy for $10 or double issue for $20 (add $1.50 book postage). Writer's guidelines for #10 SASE.

Payment/Terms Pays $5-50. Pays on publication for first North American serial, one-time rights.

Advice By "hardboiled" the editor does not mean rehashing of pulp detective fiction from the 1940s and 1950s but, rather, realistic, gritty material. We look for good writing, memorable characters, intense situations. Lovisi could be called a pulp fiction "afficionado," however he also publishes *Paperback Parade* and holds an annual vintage paperback fiction convention each year. "It is advisable new writers try a subscription to the magazine to better see the type of stories and writing I am looking for. $35 gets you the next 4 hard-hitting issues."

HYBOLICS, Da Literature and Culture of Hawaii

Hybolics, Inc., P.O. Box 3016, Aiea HI 96701. (808)366-1272. E-mail: hybolics@lava.net. **Contact:** Lee Tonouchi, co-editor. Magazine: 8½×11; 80 pages; 80 lb. coated paper; cardstock cover; illustrations; photos. "We publish da kine creative and critical work dat get some kine connection to Hawaii." Annual. Estab. 1999. Circ. 1,000.
Needs Comics/graphic novels, ethnic/multicultural, experimental, humor/satire, literary. "No genre fiction. Wants to see more sudden fiction." Receives 50 unsolicited mss/month. Accepts 10 mss/year. Publishes ms 1 year after acceptance. **Publishes 3 new writers/year.** Recently published work by Darrell Lum, Rodney Morales, Lee Cataluna and Lisa Kanae. Length: 1,000-8,000 words; average length: 4,000 words. Publishes short shorts. Also publishes literary essays, literary criticism, poetry.
How to Contact Send complete ms with a cover letter. Include estimated word count, brief bio and list of publications. Responds in 5 weeks to queries; 5 months to mss. Sample copy for $13.35. Writer's guidelines for #10 SASE.
Payment/Terms Pays 2 contributor's copies; additional copies $7.25. Pays on publication for first rights.

ITALIAN AMERICANA

URI/CCE, 80 Washington Street, Providence RI 02903-1803. (401)277-5306. Fax: (401)277-5100. E-mail: bonom oal@etal.uri.edu. Web site: www.uri.edu/prov/italian/italian.html. **Contact:** C.B. Albright, editor. Magazine: 6×9; 240 pages; varnished cover; perfect bound; photos. "*Italian Americana* contains historical articles, fiction, poetry and memoirs, all concerning the Italian experience in the Americas." Semiannual. Estab. 1974. Circ. 1,200.
Needs Literary, Italian American. No nostalgia. Wants to see more fiction featuring "individualized characters." Receives 10 unsolicited mss/month. Accepts 3 mss/issue; 6-7 mss/year. Publishes ms up to 1 year after acceptance. Agented fiction 5%. **Publishes 2-4 new writers/year.** Recently published work by Mary Caponegro and Sal LaPuma. Publishes short shorts. Also publishes literary essays, literary criticism, poetry. Sometimes comments on rejected mss.
How to Contact Send complete ms (in duplicate) with a cover letter. Include 3-5 line bio, list of publications. Responds in 1 month to queries; 2 months to mss. No simultaneous submissions. Sample copy for $7. Writer's guidelines for #10 SASE. Reviews fiction.
Payment/Terms Pays 1 contributor's copy; additional copies $7. Acquires first North American serial rights.
Advice "Please individualize characters, instead of presenting types (i.e., lovable uncle, etc.). No nostalgia."

KELSEY REVIEW

Mercer County College, P.O. Box B, Trenton NJ 08690. (609)586-4800. Fax: (609)586-2318. E-mail: kelsey.revie w@mccc.edu. Web site: www.mccc.edu. **Contact:** Ed Carmien, Holly-Katherine Johnson, editors. Magazine: 7×14; 98 pages; glossy paper; soft cover. "Must live or work in Mercer County, NJ." Annual. Estab. 1988. Circ. 1,900.
Needs Regional (Mercer County only), open. Receives 10 unsolicited mss/month. Accepts 24 mss/issue. Reads mss only in May. **Publishes 10 new writers/year.** Recently published work by Thom Beachamps, Janet Kirk, Bruce Petronio. Publishes short shorts. Also publishes literary essays, poetry. Always comments on rejected mss.
How to Contact SASE for return of ms. Responds in June to mss. Accepts multiple submissions. Sample copy free.
Payment/Terms Pays 5 contributor's copies. Rights revert to author on publication.
Advice Look for "quality, intellect, grace and guts. Avoid sentimentality, overwriting and self-indulgence. Work on clarity, depth and originality."

KRAX MAGAZINE

63 Dixon Lane, Leeds Yorkshire Britain LS12 4RR United Kingdom. **Contact:** A. Robson, co-editor. "*Krax* publishes lighthearted, humorous and whimsical writing. It is for anyone seeking light relief at a gentle pace. Our audience has grown middle-aged along with us, especially now that we're annual and not able to provide the instant fix demanded by teens and twenties."
Needs "No war stories, horror, space bandits, boy-girl soap opera. We publish mostly poetry of a lighthearted nature but use comic or spoof fiction, witty and humorous essays. Would like to see more whimsical items,

trivia ramblings or anything daft.'' Accepts 1 mss/issue. **Publishes 1 new writer/year.** Recently published work by Charles Stevens, Neil Lombard.

How to Contact No specific guidelines but cover letter appreciated. Sample copy for $2.

Advice ''Don't spend too long on scene-setting or character construction, as this inevitably produces an anti-climax in a short piece. We look for original settings, distinctive pacing, description related to plot, i.e. only dress character in bow tie and gumboots if you're having a candlelight dinner in The Everglades. Look at what you enjoy in all forms of fiction—from strip cartoons to novels, movies to music lyrics—then try to put some of this into your own writing.''

$⊘ LADY CHURCHILL'S ROSEBUD WRISTLET

Small Beer Press, 176 Prospect Ave., Northampton MA 01060. E-mail: info@lcrw.net. Web site: www.lcrw.net/lcrw. **Contact:** Gavin Grant, editor. Zine: half legal size; 40 pages; 60 lb. paper; glossy cover; illustrations; photos. Semiannual. Estab. 1996. Circ. 700.

Needs Comics/graphic novels, experimental, fantasy, feminist, literary, science fiction, translations, short story collections. Receives 25 unsolicited mss/month. Accepts 4-6 mss/issue; 8-12 mss/year. Publishes ms 6-12 months after acceptance. **Publishes 2-4 new writers/year.** Recently published work by Amy Beth Forbes, Jeffrey Ford, Carol Emshwiller and Theodora Goss. Length: 200-7,000 words; average length: 3,500 words. Also publishes literary essays, poetry. Sometimes comments on rejected mss.

How to Contact Send complete ms with a cover letter. Include estimated word count. Send SASE (or IRC) for return of ms, or send a disposable copy of ms and #10 SASE for reply only. Responds in 2 weeks to queries; 1-3 months to mss. Sample copy for $5. Writer's guidelines online. Reviews fiction.

Payment/Terms Pays $.01/word, $20 minimum and 2 contributor's copies; additional copies contributor's discount 40%. Pays on publication for first, one-time rights.

Advice ''I like fiction that tends toward the speculative.''

$◻ LEADING EDGE, Magazine of Science Fiction and Fantasy

4 198 JFFSB Provo UT 84602. (801)378-4455. E-mail: fiction@leadingedgemagazine.com. Web site: www.leadingedgemagazine.com. **Contact:** Fiction director. Zine specializing in science fiction: $5^1/_2 \times 8^1/_2$; 170 pages; card stock; some illustrations. ''*Leading Edge* is dedicated to helping new writers make their way into publishing. We send back critiques with every story. We don't print anything with heavy swearing, violence that is too graphic, or explicit sex.'' Semiannual. Estab. 1981. Circ. 500.

Needs Fantasy (space fantasy, sword/sorcery), science fiction (hard science/technological, soft/sociological). Receives 100 unsolicited mss/month. Accepts 8 mss/issue; 16 mss/year. Publishes ms 1-6 months after acceptance. **Publishes 9-10 new writers/year.** Recently published work by Orson Scott Card and Dave Wolverton. Length: 17,000; average length: 10,000 words. Publishes short shorts. Also publishes poetry. Always comments on rejected mss.

How to Contact Send complete ms with cover letter. Include estimated word count, brief bio and list of publications. Send disposable copy of ms and #10 SASE for reply only. Responds in 2 months to mss. Sample copy for $4.95. Writer's guidelines for SASE. Reviews fiction.

Payment/Terms Pays 1¢/word; $100 maximum and 2 contributor's copies; additional copies $4.95. Pays on publication for first North American serial rights. Sends galleys to author.

Advice ''Don't base your story on your favorite TV show, book or game. Be original, creative and current. Base science fiction on recent science, not '50s horror flicks.''

LEFT CURVE

P.O. Box 472, Oakland CA 94604-0472. (510)763-7193. E-mail: editor@leftcurve.org. Web site: www.leftcurve.org. **Contact:** Csaba Polony, editor. Magazine: $8^1/_2 \times 11$; 144 pages; 60 lb. paper; 100 pt. C1S gloss layflat lamination cover; illustrations; photos. ''*Left Curve* is an artist-produced journal addressing the problem(s) of cultural forms emerging from the crises of modernity that strive to be independent from the control of dominant institutions, based on the recognition of the destructiveness of commodity (capitalist) systems to all life.'' Published irregularly. Estab. 1974. Circ. 2,000.

Needs Ethnic/multicultural, experimental, historical, literary, regional, science fiction, translations, contemporary, prose poem, political. ''No topical satire, religion-based pieces, melodrama. We publish critical, open, social/political-conscious writing.'' Receives 50 unsolicited mss/month. Accepts 3-4 mss/issue. Publishes ms 6-12 months after acceptance. Recently published work by Mike Standaert, Susan Emerling, Paul E. Wolf. Length: 500-5,000 words; average length: 1,200 words. Publishes short shorts. Sometimes comments on rejected mss.

How to Contact Accepts submissions by e-mail (editor@leftcurve.org). Send complete ms with cover letter. Include ''statement of writer's intent, brief bio and reason for submitting to *Left Curve*.'' Accepts electronic submissions; ''prefer $3^1/_2$ disk and hard copy, though we do accept e-mail submissions.'' Responds in 6 months to mss. Sample copy for $10, 9×12 SAE and $1.42 postage. Writer's guidelines for 1 first-class stamp.

Payment/Terms Contributor's copies. Rights revert to author.

Advice "We look for continuity, adequate descriptive passages, endings that are not simply abandoned (in both meanings). Dig deep; no superficial personalisms, no corny satire. Be honest, realistic and gouge out the truth you wish to say. Understand yourself and the world. Have writing be a means to achieve or realize what is real."

$ ⊕ THE LONDON MAGAZINE, Review of Literature and the Arts

32 Addison Grove, London England W4 1ER United Kingdom. (00)44 0208 400 5882. Fax: (00)44 0208 994 1713. E-mail: admin@thelondonmagazine.net. Web site: www.thelondonmagazine.ukf.net. Bimonthly. Estab. 1732. Circ. 1,000.

Needs Adventure, confessions, erotica, ethnic/multicultural, experimental, fantasy, historical, humor/satire, mainstream, mystery/suspense, novel excerpts, religious/inspirational, romance, slice-of-life vignettes, suspense. Publishes ms 4 months after acceptance.

How to Contact Send complete ms. Include SASE. Responds in 1 month to queries; 4 months to mss. Accepts simultaneous submissions. Sample copy for £8.75. Writer's guidelines free.

Payment/Terms Pays minimum £20; maximum rate is negotiable. Pays on publication for first rights.

◪ LOW BUDGET ADVENTURE STORIES

Cynic Press, P.O. Box 40691, Philadelphia PA 19107. **Contact:** Joseph Farley. Magazine: 8½×11; 28 pages; 20 lb. stock paper; 70 lb. cover stock; illustrations. Annual. Estab. 2004. Circ. 70.

Needs Adventure, military/war, mystery/suspense (amateur sleuth, cozy, police procedural, private eye/hard-boiled). Receives 5 unsolicited mss/month. Accepts 4-6 mss/issue. Publishes ms 6 months to 2 years after acceptance. **Publishes some new writers/year.** Length: 1,000-15,000 words; average length: 4,000 words. Publishes short shorts. Sometimes comments on rejected mss.

How to Contact Send complete ms. Send SASE (or IRC) for return of the ms. Responds in 1 month to queries. Accepts simultaneous, multiple submissions and reprints. Sample copy for $7.

Payment/Terms Pays in 2 contributor's copies and free subscription to the magazine. Pays on publication for one-time rights.

LOW BUDGET SCIENCE FICTION

Cynic Press, P.O. Box 40691, Philadelphia PA 19107. **Contact:** Joseph Farley, editor. Magazine specializing in science fiction: 8½×11; 24-40 pages; 20 lb. paper; 70 lb. cover; illustrations; photographs. "Quirky science fiction, horror and fantasy have a home here." Biannual. Estab. 2002. Circ. 100.

Needs Fantasy (space fantasy, sword and sorcery, cross-over), science fiction (erotica, experimental, hard science/technological, cross-genre). Receives 5 unsolicited mss/month. Accepts 4-10 mss/issue. Recently published work by Ernest Swallow, Joseph Farley, Brad Wells. Publishes short shorts. Sometimes comments on rejected mss.

How to Contact Send complete ms with cover letter. Include brief bio and list of publications. Send SASE for return of ms, or send disposable copy of ms with SASE for reply only. Responds in 4 months to mss. Accepts simultaneous, multiple submissions and reprints. Sample copy for $7. Reviews fiction.

Payment/Terms Pays 1 contributor's copy; additional copies $7. Pays on publication for one-time rights.

Advice "Finding a good manuscript is like falling in love: you may know it when you first see it, or you may need to get familiar with it for a while."

◻ ◉ MOUNTAIN LUMINARY

P.O. Box 1187, Mountain View AR 72560-1187. (870)585-2260. E-mail: ecomtn@mvtel.net. **Contact:** Julia Thiel, editor. Magazine: photos. "*Mountain Luminary* is dedicated to bringing information to people about the Aquarian Age, how to grow with its new and evolutionary energies, and how to work with the resultant changes in spirituality, relationships, environment and the planet. *Mountain Luminary* provides a vehicle for people to share ideas, philosophies and experiences that deepen understanding of this evolutionary process and humankind's journey on Earth." Quarterly. Estab. 1985.

Needs Humor/satire, metaphor/inspirational/Aquarian-Age topics. Accepts 8-10 mss/year. Publishes ms 6 months after acceptance. **Publishes 2 new writers/year.**

How to Contact Accepts submissions by mail or e-mail (ecomtn@mvtel.net). Query with clips of published work. SASE for return of ms. Accepts simultaneous submissions. Sample copy free. Writer's guidelines free.

Payment/Terms Pays 1 contributor's copy. "We may offer advertising space as payment." Acquires one-time rights.

Advice "We look for stories with a moral—those with insight into problems on the path, which raise the reader's awareness. Topical interests include: New Age/Aquarian Age, astrology, crystals, cultural and ethnic concerns, dreams, ecosystems, the environment, extraterrestrials, feminism, folklore, healing and health, holistic and natural health, inspiration, juvenile and teen issues, lifestyle, meditation, men's issues, metaphysics, mysticism, nutrition, parallel dimensions, prayer, psychic phenomenon, self-help, spirituality and women's issues."

☑ MUDROCK: STORIES & TALES

MudRock Press, P.O. Box 31688, Dayton OH 45437. E-mail: mudrockpress@hotmail.com. Web site: www.mudr ockpress.com. **Contact:** Brady Allen and Scott Geisel, editors. Magazine: $7 \times 8^{1}/_{2}$; 80-120 pages; bond paper; color cover; illustrations. "*MudRock* is an eclectic collection of stories, odd or not so, that people can follow, stories based in North America. We both like road stories, but we accept a wide range of genres from mainstream and realism to humor, horror and sci-fi." Triannual. Estab. 2003. Circ. 250-500.

Needs Ethnic/multicultural (North America), feminist, horror (dark fantasy, futuristic, psychological, supernatural), humor/satire, literary, mainstream, mystery/suspense (amateur sleuth, cozy, police procedural, private eye/hard-boiled), psychic/supernatural/occult, regional (North America), science fiction (hard science/technological, soft/sociological), thriller/espionage, western, road stories. Accepts 8-10 mss/issue; 25-30 mss/year. Publishes ms up to 12 months after acceptance. **Publishes 20-25 new writers/year.** Length: max 7,000 words; preferred length: 2,500-5,000 words. Publishes short shorts. Often comments on rejected mss.

How to Contact Send disposable copy of ms and #10 SASE for reply only. We do not return mss. Responds in 4 months to mss. Accepts simultaneous submissions. No multible submissions. Sample copy for $5 (past issue), $6 current issue. Writer's guidelines for SASE or on Web site.

Payment/Terms Pays 2 contributor's copies; additional copies $4 (up to 4). Pays on publication for one-time rights. Sends proofs if requested.

Advice "Stories first, style second. We want vivid characters and setting and compelling action and storylines. If you have a story and aren't sure where it fits, try us. *MudRock* is an eclectic mix, so long as the stories relate somehow to the North American experience. Simply put: Something's gotta happen in your tale that readers will give a squat about. Check our editors' preferences and other info on our Web site, and send us something you think is as good as what we publish."

☐ ◎ THE NOCTURNAL LYRIC, Journal of the Bizarre

The Nocturnal Lyric, P.O. Box 542, Astoria OR 97103. E-mail: nocturnallyric@melodymail.com. Web site: www.angelfire.com/ca/nocturnallyric. **Contact:** Susan Moon, editor. Magazine: $8^{1}/_{2} \times 11$; 40 pages; illustrations. "Fiction and poetry submitted should have a bizarre horror theme. Our audience encompasses people who stand proudly outside of the mainstream society." Annual. Estab. 1987. Circ. 400.

Needs Horror (dark fantasy, futuristic, psychological, supernatural, satirical). "No sexually graphic material—it's too overdone in the horror genre lately." Receives 25-30 unsolicited mss/month. Accepts 10-11 mss/year. Publishes ms 1 year after acceptance. **Publishes 20 new writers/year.** Recently published work by Mary Blais, Brian Biswas, John Sunseri, J.A. Davidson. Length: 2,000 words maximum; average length: 1,500 words. Publishes short shorts. Also publishes literary essays, poetry. Rarely comments on rejected mss.

How to Contact Send complete ms with cover letter. Include estimated word count. Responds in 3 month to queries; 8 months to mss. Accepts simultaneous, multiple submissions and reprints. Sample copy for $2 (back issue); $3 (current issue). Writer's guidelines online.

Payment/Terms Pays with discounts on subscriptions and discounts on copies of issue. Pays on acceptance. Not copyrighted.

Advice "A manuscript stands out when the story has a very original theme and the ending is not predictable to Don't be afraid to be adventurous with your story. Mainstream horror can be boring. Surreal, satirical horror is what true nightmares are all about."

Ⓝ $◎ NOVA SCIENCE FICTION MAGAZINE

Nova Publishing Company, 17983 Paseo Del Sol, Chino Hills CA 91709-3947. (909)393-0806. **Contact:** Wesley Kawato, editor. Zine specializing in evangelical Christian science fiction: $8^{1}/_{2} \times 5^{1}/_{2}$; 64 pages; cardstock cover. "We publish religious science fiction short stories, no fantasy or horror. One story slot per issue will be reserved for a story written from an evangelical Christian viewpoint. We also plan to carry one article per issue dealing with science fiction wargaming." Quarterly. Estab. 1999. Circ. 25.

Needs Science fiction (hard science/technological, soft/sociological, religious). "No stories where the villain is a religious fanatic and stories that assume the truth of evolution." Accepts 3 mss/issue; 12 mss/year. Publishes ms 3 months after acceptance. **Publishes 7 new writers/year.** Recently published work by Lawrence Dagstine, Martha Jean Gable, Megan James, Michael Cooper, Don Kerr, Robert Anderson, Robert Santa, Francis Alexander. Length: 250-7,000 words; average length: 4,000 words. Publishes short shorts. Sometimes comments on rejected mss.

How to Contact Query first. Include estimated word count and list of publications. Responds in 3 months to queries and mss. Send SASE (or IRC) for return of ms. Accepts reprints, multiple submissions. Sample copy for $6. Guidelines free for SASE.

Payment/Terms Pays $1.25-35. Pays on publication for first North American serial rights. Not copyrighted.

Advice "Make sure your plot is believable and describe your characters well enough so I can visualize them. If I like it, I buy it. I like happy endings and heroes with a strong sense of faith."

NTH DEGREE, The Fiction and Fandom 'Zine

Big Blind Productions, 9623 Hollyburgh Terrace, Charlotte NC 28215. (704)597-5597. E-mail: editor@nthzine.com. Web site: www.nthzine.com. **Contact**: Michael Pederson, editor. Magazine: 8½×11; 48 pages; 50 lb. white off-set paper; 80 lb. glossy cover stock; illustrations; photos. "We print the best SF/Fantasy from the genre's newest writers and run artwork by the hottest new artists. Our goal is to help make it easier for new artists and writers to break into the field." Quarterly. Estab. 2002. Circ. 3,500.

Needs Fantasy (space fantasy, sword and sorcery), historical (alternate history), horror (dark fantasy, futuristic, psychological, supernatural), humor/satire, science fiction (hard science/technological), young adult/teen (fantasy/science fiction), comic strips. Receives 3 unsolicited mss/month. Accepts 4 mss/issue; 6 mss/year. Publishes ms 6 months after acceptance. **Publishes 6 new writers/year.** Recently published work by Michail Velichensky, James R. Stratton, C.J. Henderson, Robert Balder, Matt McIrvin. Length: 2,000-7,000 words; average length: 3,500 words. Publishes short shorts. Also publishes poetry. Always comments on rejected mss.

How to Contact Send complete ms. Accepts submissions by e-mail, disk. Send SASE (or IRC) for return of ms, or send disposable copy of the ms and #10 SASE for reply only. Responds in 2 weeks to queries; 2 months to mss. Accepts simultaneous, multiple submissions. Sample copy for $3. Writer's guidelines online or by e-mail.

Payment/Terms Pays 5 contributor's copies and free subscription to the magazine. Pays on publication for one-time rights.

Advice "Don't submit anything that you may be ashamed of 10 years later."

NUTHOUSE, Your Place for Humor Therapy

Twin Rivers Press, P.O. Box 119, Ellenton FL 34222. E-mail: nuthous449@aol.com. Web site: hometown.aol.com/nuthous499/index2.html. **Contact:** Dr. Ludwig "Needles" Von Quirk, chief of staff. Zine: digest-sized; 12-16 pages; bond paper; illustrations; photos. "Humor of all genres for an adult readership that is not easily offended." Published every 2-3 months. Estab. 1993. Circ. 100.

Needs Humor/satire (erotica, experimental, fantasy, feminist, historical [general], horror, literary, mainstream/contemporary, mystery/suspense, psychic/supernatural/occult, romance, science fiction and westerns). Receives 30-50 unsolicited mss/month. Accepts 5-10 mss/issue; 50-60 mss/year. Publishes ms 6-12 months after acceptance. **Publishes 10-15 new writers/year.** Recently published work by Michael Fowler, Dale Andrew White, Jim Sullivan. Length: 100-1,000 words; average length: 500 words. Publishes short shorts. Also publishes literary essays, literary criticism, poetry. Often comments on rejected mss.

How to Contact Send complete ms with a cover letter. Include estimated word count, bio (paragraph) and list of publications. SASE for return of ms or send disposable copy of ms. Sample copy for $1.25 (payable to Twin Rivers Press). Writer's guidelines for #10 SASE.

Payment/Terms Pays 1 contributor's copy. Acquires one-time rights. Not copyrighted.

Advice Looks for "laugh-out-loud prose. Strive for original ideas; read the great humorists—Saki, Woody Allen, Robert Benchley, Garrison Keillor, John Irving—and learn from them. We are turned off by sophomoric attempts at humor built on a single, tired, overworked gag or pun; give us a story with a beginning, middle and end."

THE OAK

1530 Seventh Street, Rock Island IL 61201. (309)788-3980. **Contact:** Betty Mowery, editor. Magazine: 8½×11; 8-10 pages. "To provide a showcase for new authors while showing the work of established authors as well; to publish wholesome work, something with a message." Bimonthly. Estab. 1991. Circ. 300.

Needs Adventure, experimental, fantasy, humor/satire, mainstream, contemporary, poems. No erotica or love poetry. "Gray Squirrel" appears as a section in *Oak*, accepts poetry and fiction from seniors age 50 and up. Length: 500 words. Receives 25 unsolicited mss/month. Accepts 12 mss/issue. Publishes ms 3 months after acceptance. **Publishes 25 new writers/year.**

How to Contact Send complete ms. Responds in 1 week to mss. Accepts simultaneous, multiple submissions and reprints. Sample copy for $3; subscription $10. Writer's guidelines for #10 SASE.

Payment/Terms None, but not necessary to buy a copy in order to be published. Acquires first rights.

Advice "I do not want erotica, extreme violence or killing of humans or animals for the sake of killing. Just be yourself when you write. Also, write *tight*. Please include SASE or manuscripts will be destroyed. Be sure name and address are on the manuscript. Study the markets for length of manuscript and what type of material is wanted. *The Shepherd* needs inspirational fiction up to 500 words, poetry, and Biblical character profiles. Same address as *The Oak*. Sample $3."

$ ⬛ ✅ ON SPEC

P.O. Box 4727, Station South, Edmonton AB T6E 5G6 Canada. (780)413-0215. Fax: (780)413-1538. E-mail: onspec@onspec.ca. Web site: www.onspec.ca. **Contact:** Diane L. Walton, editor. Magazine: 5¼×8; 112 pages; illustrations. "We publish speculative fiction by new and established writers, with a strong preference for Canadian authored works." Quarterly. Estab. 1989. Circ. 2,000.

Needs Fantasy, horror, science fiction, magic realism. No media tie-in or shaggy-alien stories. No condensed or excerpted novels, religious/inspirational stories, fairy tales. "We would like to see more horror, fantasy, science fiction—well developed stories with complex characters and strong plots." Receives 100 unsolicited mss/month. Accepts 10 mss/issue; 40 mss/year. "We read manuscripts during the month after each deadline: February 28/May 31/August 31/November 30." Publishes ms 6-18 months after acceptance. **Publishes 10-15 new writers/year.** Recently published work by Tony Pi, Robert Burke Richardson, Cliff Burns. Length: 1,000-6,000 words; average length: 4,000 words. Also publishes poetry. Often comments on rejected mss.

How to Contact Send complete ms. Accepts submissions by disk. SASE for return of ms or send a disposable copy of ms plus #10 SASE for response. Include Canadian postage or IRCs. No e-mail or fax submissions. Responds in 2 weeks to queries 4 months after deadline to mss. Accepts simultaneous submissions. Sample copy for $7. Writer's guidelines for #10 SASE or on Web site.

Payment/Terms Pays $50-180 for fiction. Short stories (under 1,000 words): $50 plus 1 contributor's copy. Pays on acceptance for first North American serial rights.

Advice "We're looking for original ideas with a strong SF element, excellent dialogue, and characters who are so believable, our readers will really care about them."

⬛ ✅ ◎ OPEN MINDS QUARTERLY, A Psychosocial Literary Journal

NISA/Northern Initiative for Social Action, 680 Kirkwood Dr., Bldg 1, Sudbury ON P3E 1X3 Canada. (705)675-9193, ext. 8286. Fax: (705)675-3501. E-mail: openminds@nisa.on.ca. Web site: www.nisa.on.ca. **Contact**: Dinah Lapraine, editor. Magazine: 8½×11; 28 pages; illustrations; photos. "*Open Minds Quarterly* publishes quality, insightful writing from consumer/survivors of mental illness who have experiences to share and voices to be heard. We inform mental health professionals, family and friends, fellow consumer/survivors, and society at large of the strength, intelligence and creativity of our writers. The purpose is to eliminate the stigma associated with mental illness." Quarterly. Estab. 1998. Circ. 750.

Needs Mental illness, mental health. Receives 5-10 unsolicited mss/month. Accepts 1-2 mss/issue; 4-8 mss/year. **Publishes many new writers/year.** Occasionally publishes short shorts. Also publishes literary essays, poetry. Sometimes comments on rejected mss.

How to Contact Send complete ms with cover letter. Accepts submissions by e-mail, mail, disk. Send disposable copy of the ms and #10 SASE for reply only. Responds in 1 week to queries; 16 weeks to mss. Accepts simultaneous, multiple submissions and reprints. Sample copy for $5. Writer's guidelines for #10 SASE, online, or by e-mail.

Payment/Terms Pays 2-3 contributor's copies. Acquires first, one-time rights.

✅ ORACLE STORY & LETTERS

Rising Star Publishers, 7510 Lake Glen Drive, Glen Dale MD 20769. (301)352-233. Fax: (301)352-2529. E-mail: hekwonna@aol.com. **Contact:** Obi H. Ekwonna, publisher. Magazine: 5½×8½; 60 lb. white bound paper. Quarterly. Estab. 1989. Circ. 1,000.

Needs Adventure, children's/juvenile (adventure, fantasy, historical, mystery, series), comics/graphic novels, ethnic/multicultural, family saga, fantasy (sword and sorcery), historical, literary, mainstream, military/war, romance (contemporary, historical, suspense), thriller/espionage, western (frontier saga), young adult/teen (adventure, historical). Does not want gay/lesbian or erotica works. Receives 10 unsolicited mss/month. Accepts 7 mss/issue. Publishes ms 4 months after acceptance. **Publishes 5 new writers/year.** Recently published work by Joseph Manco, I.B.S. Sesay. Publishes short shorts. Also publishes literary essays, literary criticism, poetry. Rarely comments on rejected mss.

How to Contact Send complete ms. Accepts submissions by disk. Send SASE (or IRC) for return of the ms, or send a disposable copy of the ms and #10 SASE for reply only. Responds in 1 month to mss. Accepts multiple submissions. Sample copy for $10. Writer's guidelines for #10 SASE or by e-mail.

Payment/Terms Pays 1 contributor's copy. Pays on publication for first North American serial rights.

Advice "Read anything you can lay your hands on."

⬛ ✅ THE ORPHAN LEAF REVIEW

Orphan Leaf Press, J. Wallis, ℅ A Hirshmann, 7 Brean Down Avenue, Bristol BS4 7AE United Kingdom. E-mail: orphanleaf@jpwallis.co.uk. Web site: www.orphanleaf.co.uk. **Contact:** James Paul Wallis, editor. Zine specializing in creative writing: A5, 40 pages, mixed paper, card cover. Contains illustrations. "Each issue is a collection of orphan leaves. An orphan leaf is a page, seemingly torn from some parent book. Each page is a different size and texture. Read to the end of the leaf, let your imagination do the rest." Triannual. Estab. 2004. Circ. 100.

Needs All categories considered, but submission must be an orphan leaf. Receives 15 mss/month. Accepts 15 mss/issue. Manuscript published 2 months after acceptance. Length: 500 words (min)-800 words (max). Average length: 700 words. Also publishes literary essays, literary criticism, poetry. Never comments on/critiques rejected manuscripts.

How to Contact Accepts submissions by e-mail. Responds to queries in 1 week. Responds to mss in 6 months. Considers simultaneous submissions, previously published submissions, multiple submissions. Sample copy available for $10.

Payment and Terms Writers receive 1 contributor copy. Additional copies $10. Pays on publication. Publication is copyrighted.

Advice "Buy a copy to view the general standard. I have a surplus of fiction and poetry. So nonfiction and pieces from other types of books stand a greater chance of selection."

☑ ☒ OUTER DARKNESS, Where Nightmares Roam Unleashed

Outer Darkness Press, 1312 N. Delaware Place, Tulsa OK 74110. **Contact:** Dennis Kirk, editor. Zine: $8^1/_2 \times 5^1/_2$; 60-80 pages; 20 lb. paper; 90 lb. glossy cover; illustrations. Specializes in imaginative literature. "Variety is something I strive for in *Outer Darkness*. In each issue we present readers with great tales of science fiction and horror along with poetry, cartoons and interviews/essays. I seek to provide readers with a magazine which, overall, is fun to read. My readers range in age from 16 to 70." Quarterly. Estab. 1994. Circ. 500.

● Fiction published in *Outer Darkness* has received honorable mention in *The Year's Best Fantasy and Horror*.

Needs Fantasy (science), horror, mystery/suspense (with horror slant), psychic/supernatural/occult, romance (gothic), science fiction (hard science, soft/sociological). No straight mystery, pure fantasy—works which do not incorporate elements of science fiction and/or horror. Also, no slasher horror with violence, gore, sex instead of plot. Wants more "character driven tales—especially in the genre of science fiction and well-developed psychological horror. I do not publish works with children in sexual situations, and graphic language should be kept to a minimum." Receives 75-100 unsolicited mss/month. Accepts 7-9 mss/issue; 25-40 mss/year. **Publishes 2-5 new writers/year.** Recently published work by Tim Curran, Jim Lee, Erin McCole-Cupp and Steve Vertlieb. Length: 1,500-5,000 words; average length: 3,000 words. Also publishes poetry. Always comments on rejected mss.

How to Contact Send complete ms with a cover letter. Include estimated word count, 50- to 75-word bio, list of publications and "any awards, honors you have received." Send SASE for reply, return of ms, or send a disposable copy of ms. Responds in 2 weeks to queries; 4 months to mss. Accepts simultaneous, multiple submissions. Sample copy for $4.95. Writer's guidelines for #10 SASE.

Payment/Terms Pays 3 contributor's copies for fiction; 2 for poetry and 3 for art. Pays on publication for one-time rights.

Advice "I look for strong characters and well developed plot. And I definitely look for suspense. I want stories which move—and carry the reader along with them. Be patient and persistent. Often it's simply a matter of linking the right story with the right editor. I've received many stories which were good, but not what I wanted at the time. However, these stories worked well in another horror-sci-fi zine."

$ ☑ ◎ PANGAIA, A Pagan Journal for Thinking People

B.B.I. Media, P.O. Box 641, Point Arena CA 95468. (707)882-2052. Fax: (707)882-2793. Web site: www.pangaia. com. **Contact:** Anne Niven, chief editor. Magazine: $8^1/_2 \times 11$; 80 pages; 50 lb. recycled book paper; 80 lb. book cover stock. "We are the only publication of this type. *PanGaia* explores Pagan and Gaian earth-based spirituality at home and around the world. We envision a world in which living in spirit and living on earth support and enrich each other; a spirituality that honors what is sacred in all life; a future in which ancient ritual and modern science both have a place. Intended audience: thinking adult Pagans of every sort. Women and men of all earth-affirming spiritual paths." Quarterly. Estab. 1997. Circ. 10,000. Member IPA.

● Nominated for the *Utne* Reader's Alternative Press Award for best spirituality coverage.

Needs Humor/satire, New Age, psychic/supernatural/occult, religious/inspirational (fantasy, mystery/suspense, thriller), science fiction (Pagan themes), Pagan/Gaian. No romance or juvenile stories. Receives 2-4 unsolicited mss/month. Accepts 1-4 mss/year. Publishes ms 6 months after acceptance. **Publishes some new writers/year.** Length: 500-5,000 words; average length: 3,500 words. Publishes short shorts. Also publishes poetry. Sometimes comments on rejected mss.

How to Contact Send complete ms. Accepts submissions by e-mail, fax, disk. Include SASE (or IRC) for return of ms, or send disposable copy of the ms and #10 SASE for reply only. Responds in 3-6 weeks to mss. Accepts reprint submissions. Sample copy free. Writer's guidelines for #10 SASE, online or by e-mail.

Payment/Terms Pays .025¢-4¢/word. Pays on publication for first North American serial, electronic rights.
Advice "Read the magazine! Must know who we are and what we like."

◎ PARADOXISM

University of New Mexico, 200 College Rd., Gallup NM 87301. Fax: (503)863-7532. E-mail: smarand@unm.edu.
Web site: www.gallup.unm.edu/~smarandache/a/paradoxism.htm. **Contact:** Dr. Florentin Smarandache.
Magazine: 8½×11; 100 pages; illustrations. "*Paradoxism* is an avant-garde movement based on excessive use
of antinomies, antitheses, contradictions, paradoxes in the literary creations set up by the editor in the 1980s as
an anti-totalitarian protest." Annual. Estab. 1993. Circ. 500.
Needs Experimental, literary. "Contradictory, uncommon, experimental, avant garde." Plans specific themes
in the next year. Publishes annual special fiction issue or anthology. Receives 5 unsolicited mss/month. Accepts
10 mss/issue. Recently published work by Mirecea Monu, Doru Motoc and Patrick Pinard. Publishes short
shorts. Also publishes literary essays, literary criticism, poetry. Sometimes comments on rejected mss.
How to Contact Send a disposable copy of ms. Responds in 2 months to mss. Accepts simultaneous submissions.
Sample copy for $19.95 and 8½×11 SASE. Writer's guidelines online.
Payment/Terms Pays subscription. Pays on publication. Not copyrighted.
Advice "We look for work that refers to the paradoxism or is written in the paradoxist style. The Basic Thesis
of the paradoxism: everything has a meaning and a non-meaning in a harmony with each other. The Essence
of the paradoxism: a) the sense has a non-sense, and reciprocally B) the non-sense has a sense. The Motto of
the paradoxism: 'All is possible, the impossible too!' The Symbol of the paradoxism: a spiral—optic illusion,
or vicious circle."

☐ ◎ THE PEGASUS REVIEW

P.O. Box 88, Henderson MD 21640-0088. (410)482-6736. **Contact:** Art Bounds, editor. Magazine: 5½×8½; 6-
8 pages; illustrations. "*The Pegasus Review* is a bimonthly, done in a calligraphic format and occasionally
illustrated. Each issue is based on a specific theme." Estab. 1980. Circ. 120.
 • Because *The Pegasus Review* is done is a calligraphic format, fiction submissions must be very short. Two
   pages, says the editor, are the ideal length.
Needs Humor/satire, literary, religious/inspirational, prose poem. Wants more short-shorts (2½ pages ideal
length) and essays. For 2007 themes please send SASE.
How to Contact Send complete ms. Send brief cover letter with author's background, name and prior credits,
if any. Responds in 2 months to mss. Accepts simultaneous submissions. Sample copy for $2.50. Writer's
guidelines for #10 SASE.
Payment/Terms Pays 2 contributor's copies. Acquires one-time rights. Sponsors awards/contests.
Advice "Write and continue to read as well, especially what is being published today. Don't overlook the
classics. They have achieved that status for a reason—quality. Seek every opportunity to have your work read
at various organizations. The reading of a work can give you a new slant on it. Avove all, believe in your craft
and stick to it!"

☐ ◎ PRAYERWORKS, Encouraging God's people to do real work of ministry—intercessory prayer

The Master's Work, P.O. Box 301363, Portland OR 97294-9363. (503)761-2072. E-mail: vannm1@aol.com. Web
site: www.prayerworksnw.org. **Contact:** V. Ann Mandeville, editor. Newsletter: 5½×8; 4 pages; bond paper.
"Our intended audience is 70% retired Christians and 30% families. We publish 350-500 word devotional
material—fiction, nonfiction, biographical, poetry, clean quips and quotes. Our philosophy is evangelical Christian serving the body of Chirst in the area of prayer." Estab. 1988. Circ. 1,100.
Needs Religious/inspirational. "No nonevangelical Christian. Subject matter may include anything which will
build relationship with the Lord—prayer, ways to pray, stories of answered prayer, teaching on a Scripture
portion, articles that will build faith, or poems will all work." We even use a series occasionally. Publishes ms
2-6 months after acceptance. **Publishes 30 new writers/year.** Recently published work by Allen Audrey and
Petey Prater. Length: 350-500 words; average length: 350-500 words. Publishes short shorts. Also publishes
poetry. Often comments on rejected mss.
How to Contact Send complete ms with cover letter. Include estimated word count and a very short bio.
Responds in 1 month to mss. Accepts simultaneous, multiple submissions and reprints. Writer's guidelines for
#10 SASE.
Payment/Terms Pays free subscription to the magazine and contributor's copies. Pays on publication. Not
copyrighted.
Advice Stories "must have a great take-away—no preaching; teach through action. Be thrifty with words—
make them count."

$ ☑ PSI

P.O. Box 6218, Charlottesville VA 22906-6218. E-mail: asam@publisherssyndication.com. Web site: www.publisherssyndication.com. **Contact:** A.P. Samuels, editor. Magazine: $8^1/_2 \times 11$; 32 pages; bond paper; self cover. "Mystery and romance." Bimonthly. Estab. 1987.

Needs Adventure, mystery/suspense (private eye), romance (contemporary, historical, young adult), western (traditional). No ghoulish, sex, violence. Wants to see more believable stories. Accepts 1-2 mss/issue. **Publishes 1-3 new writers/year.** Average length: 30,000 (novelettes) words. Publishes short shorts. Rarely comments on rejected mss.

How to Contact Send complete ms with cover letter. Responds in 2 weeks to queries; 6 weeks to mss.

Payment/Terms Pays 1-4¢/word, plus royalty. Pays on acceptance.

Advice "Manuscripts must be for a general audience. Just good plain story telling (make it compelling). No explicit sex or ghoulish violence."

$ ☐ PURPOSE

616 Walnut Ave., Scottdale PA 15683-1999. (724)887-8500. Fax: (724)887-3111. E-mail: horsch@mph.org. Web site: www.mph.org. **Contact:** James E. Horsch, editor. Magazine: $5^3/_8 \times 8^3/_8$; 8 pages; illustrations; photos. Weekly. Estab. 1968. Circ. 9,000.

Needs Historical (related to discipleship theme), humor/satire, religious/inspirational. No militaristic, narrow patriotism, or racist themes. Receives 150 unsolicited mss/month. Accepts 3 mss/issue; 140 mss/year. Publishes ms 1 year after acceptance. **Publishes 15-25 new writers/year.** Length: 700 words; average length: 400 words. Occasionally comments on rejected mss.

How to Contact Send complete ms. Send all submissions by word attachment via e-mail. Responds in 3 months to queries. Accepts simultaneous submissions, reprints, multiple submissions. Sample copy and writer's guidelines for $2, 6×9 SAE and 2 first-class stamps. Writer's guidelines online.

Payment/Terms Pays up to 6¢/word for stories, 2 contributor's copies. Pays on acceptance for one-time rights.

Advice "Many stories are situational, how to respond to dilemmas. Looking for first-person storylines. Write crisp action, moving, personal style, focused upon an individual, a group of people, or an organization. The story form is an excellent literary device to help readers explore discipleship issues. The first two paragraphs are crucial in establishing the mood/issue to be resolved in the story. Work hard on the development of these."

$ ☑ ◎ QUEEN OF ALL HEARTS

Montfort Missionaries, 26 S. Saxon Ave., Bay Shore NY 11706-8993. (631)665-0726. Fax: (631)665-4349. E-mail: montfort@optonline.net. Web site: www.montfortmissionaries.com. **Contact:** Roger M. Charest, S.M.M., managing editor. Magazine: $7^3/_4 \times 10^3/_4$; 48 pages; self cover stock; illustrations; photos. Magazine of "stories, articles and features on the Mother of God by explaining the Scriptural basis and traditional teaching of the Catholic Church concerning the Mother of Jesus, her influence in fields of history, literature, art, music, poetry, etc." Bimonthly. Estab. 1950. Circ. 2,000.

Needs Religious/inspirational. "Wants mss only about Our Lady, the Mother of God, the Mother of Jesus." Publishes ms 6-12 months after acceptance. **Publishes 6 new writers/year.** Recently published work by Richard O'Donnell and Jackie Clements-Marenda. Sometimes comments on rejected mss.

How to Contact Send complete ms. Accepts submissions by e-mail, fax, disk. Accepts queries/mss by e-mail and fax (mss by permission only). Responds in 2 months to queries. Sample copy for $2.50 with 9×12 SAE.

Payment/Terms Pays $40-60. Pays on publication. Not copyrighted.

Advice "We are publishing stories with a Marian theme."

$ ▧ ☐ ◎ QUEEN'S QUARTERLY, A Canadian Review

Queen's University, Kingston ON K7L 3N6 Canada. (613)533-2667. Fax: (613)533-6822. E-mail: qquarter@post. queensu.ca. Web site: info.queensu.ca/quarterly. **Contact:** Boris Castel, editor. Magazine: 6×9; 800 pages/year; illustrations. "A general interest intellectual review, featuring articles on science, politics, humanities, arts and letters. Book reviews, poetry and fiction." Quarterly. Estab. 1893. Circ. 3,000.

Needs Historical, literary, mainstream, novel excerpts, short stories, women's. "Special emphasis on work by Canadian writers." Accepts 2 mss/issue; 8 mss/year. Publishes ms 6-12 months after acceptance. **Publishes 5 new writers/year.** Recently published work by Gail Anderson-Dargatz, Tim Bowling, Emma Donohue, Viktor Carr, Mark Jarman, Rick Bowers and Dennis Bock. Also publishes literary essays, literary criticism, poetry.

How to Contact "Send complete ms with SASE and/or IRC. No reply with insufficient postage." Responds in 2-3 months to queries. Sample copy online. Writer's guidelines online. Reviews fiction.

Payment/Terms Pays $100-300 for fiction, 2 contributor's copies and 1-year subscription; additional copies $5. Pays on publication for first North American serial rights. Sends galleys to author.

◪ RHAPSOIDIA

E-mail: catrhap@hotmail.com. Web site: http://rhapsoidia.com. **Contact:** Catlyn Marcuri, Jennifer Redelle Carey, fiction editors. Magazine: Digest size; 40-56 pages; illustrations; photos. "Our fiction tastes lean toward experimental fiction, magical realism, metafiction or works of any genre told in innovative or different ways." Quarterly. Estab. 2002. Circ. 350.

Needs Experimental. No young adult/teen, children/juvenile. Receives 30 unsolicited mss/month. Accepts 10 mss/issue; 40 mss/year. Publishes ms 3 months after acceptance. **Publishes some new writers/year.** Recently published work by Debra Di Blasi, Stephanie Hammer, Lance Olsen, Steve Redwood. Length: 2,500-5,000 words; average length: 3,000 words. Also publishes poetry. Rarely comments on rejected mss.

How to Contact Send complete ms. Accepts submissions by e-mail. Responds in 1 month to queries; 4 months to mss. Sample copy for $2.95 plus $1 s&h. Writer's guidelines online.

Payment/Terms Pays one contributor's copy. Pays on publication for first North American serial rights.

Advice "Visit our Web site for more detailed submission guidelines. We only accept online submissions. Please work long and hard on fine tuning your pieces before sending them out."

◻ ◉ SLATE & STYLE, Magazine of the National Federation of the Blind Writers Division

NFB Writer's Division, 2704 Beach Drive, Merrick NY 11566. (516)868-8718. E-mail: loristay@aol.com. **Contact:** Lori Stayer, fiction editor. Newsletter: 8×10; 28 print/40 Braille pages; e-mail, cassette and large print. "Articles of interest to writers and resources for blind writers." Quarterly. Estab. 1982. Circ. 200.

Needs Adventure, fantasy, humor/satire, contemporary, blindness. No erotica. "Avoid theme of death." Does not read mss in June or July. **Publishes 2 new writers/year.** Recently published work by Bonnie Lannom, Jane Lansaw, Christina Oakes, Patricia Hubschman. Publishes short shorts. Also publishes literary criticism, poetry. Sometimes comments on rejected mss.

How to Contact Accepts submissions by e-mail. Responds in 3-6 weeks to queries; 3-6 weeks to mss. Sample copy for $3.

Payment/Terms Pays in contributor's copies. Acquires one-time rights. Not copyrighted. Sponsors awards/contests.

Advice "The best advice I can give is to send your work out; manuscripts left in a drawer have no chance at all."

◻ THE STORYTELLER, A Writer's Magazine

2441 Washington Road, Maynard AR 72444. (870)647-2137. Fax: (870)647-2454. E-mail: storyteller1@cox-internet.com. Web site: http://freewebz.com/fossilcreek. **Contact:** Regina Cook Williams, editor. Tabloid: 8½×11; 72 pages; typing paper; glossy cover; illustrations. "This magazine is open to all new writers regardless of age. I will accept short stories in any genre and poetry in any type. Please keep in mind, this is a family publication." Quarterly. Estab. 1996.

● Offers *People's Choice Awards* and nominates for a *Pushcart Prize.*

Needs Adventure, historical, humor/satire, literary, mainstream, mystery/suspense, religious/inspirational, romance, western, young adult/teen, senior citizen/retirement, sports. "I will not accept pornography, erotica, science fiction, new age, foul language, graphic horror or graphic violence." Wants more well-plotted mysteries. Publishes ms 3-9 months after acceptance. **Publishes 30-50 new writers/year.** Recently published work by Jodi Thomas, Jory Sherman, David Marion Wilkinson, Dusty Richards and Tony Hillerman. Publishes short shorts. Also publishes literary essays, poetry. Sometimes comments on rejected mss.

How to Contact Send complete ms with cover letter. Include estimated word count and 5-line bio. Submission by mail only. Responds in 1-2 weeks to mss. No queries. Accepts simultaneous submissions and reprints. Sample copy for $6. Writer's guidelines for #10 SASE.

Payment/Terms Sponsors awards/contests.

Advice "Follow the guidelines. No matter how many times this has been said, writers still ignore this basic and most important rule." Looks for "professionalism, good plots and unique characters. Purchase a sample copy so you know the kind of material we look for." Would like more "well-plotted mysteries and suspense and a few traditional westerns. Avoid sending anything that children or young adults would not (or could not) read, such as really bad language."

◷ ◪ STUDIO, A Journal of Christians Writing

727 Peel Street, Albury 2640. Australia. (+61)26021-1135. E-mail: studio00@bigpond.net.au. **Contact:** Paul Grover, managing editor. Quarterly. Circ. 300.

Needs "*Studio* publishes prose and poetry of literary merit, offers a venue for new and aspiring writers, and seeks to create a sense of community among Christians writing." Accepts 30-40 mss/year. **Publishes 40 new writers/year.** Recently published work by Andrew Lansdown and Benjamin Gilmour.

How to Contact Accepts submissions by e-mail. Send SASE. "Overseas contributors must use International

postal coupons in place of stamped envelope." Responds in 1 month to mss. Sample copy for $10 (Aus).
Payment/Terms Pays in copies; additional copies are discounted. Subscription $60 (Australian) for 4 issues (1 year). International draft in Australian dollars and IRC required, or Visa and Mastercard facilities available. "Copyright of individual published pieces remains with the author, while each collection is copyright to *Studio*."

ⓝ $ⓩ TABARD INN, Tales of Questionable Taste

468 E. Vallette St., Elmhurst IL 60126. E-mail: tabardinnedgewoodent@yahoo.com. Web site: www.talesofquestionabletaste.com. **Contact:** John Bruni, editor. Magazine: 8½×11, 60 pages, 60 lb. opaque smooth cover. Includes photographs. "*Tabard Inn* is a place for edgy stories that don't usually find a home in other magazines due to 'questionable' content." Estab. 2005. Circ. 560.
Needs Adventure, erotica, ethnic/multicultural, experimental, feminist, gay, historical, horror (dark fantasy, futuristic, psychological, supernatural), humor/satire, lesbian, literary, mainstream, military/war, mystery (amateur sleuth, cozy, police procedural, private eye/hard-boiled) religious (general), science fiction (soft/sociological), western. Does not want children's or fantasy works. Accepts 12 mss/issue. Manuscript published 6 months after acceptance. **Publishes 3 new writers/year.** Published John Bruni, Anthony Haversham, Jesse Russell, Edgar Wells and David Fuller. Length: 1 word (min)-5,000 words (max). Average length: 2,000 words. Publishes short shorts. Average length of short shorts: 1,000 words. Also publishes poetry. Always comments on/critiques rejected mss.
How to Contact Send complete ms with cover letter. Accepts submissions by e-mail, on disk. Include estimated word count, brief bio, list of publications. Responds to queries in 2 weeks. Responds to mss in 1 month. Send either SASE (or IRC) for return of ms or disposable copy of ms and #10 SASE for reply only. Considers simultaneous submissions, multiple submissions. Sample copy available for $6. Guidelines available for SASE, via e-mail.
Payment and Terms Writers receive $1 flat-rate payment, 2 contributors copies. Additional copies $3.50. Pays on publication. Acquires first North American serial rights. Publication is copyrighted.
Advice "Follow your heart. Write what you want to, not what you think has a good shot at getting published."

ⓩ TALEBONES, Fiction on the Dark Edge

Fairwood Press, 5203 Quincy Avenue SE, Auburn WA 98092-8723. (253)735-6552. E-mail: info@talebones.com. **Contact:** Patrick and Honna Swenson, editors. Magazine: digest size; 100 pages; standard paper; glossy cover stock; illustrations; photos. "We like stories that have punch but still entertain. We like science fiction and dark fantasy, humor, psychological and experimental works." Published 2-3 times a year. Estab. 1995. Circ. 700.
Needs Fantasy (dark), humor/satire, science fiction (hard science, soft/sociological, dark). "No straight slash and hack horror. No cat stories or stories told by young adults. Would like to see more science fiction." Receives 200 unsolicited mss/month. Accepts 8-10 mss/issue; 16-30 mss/year. Publishes ms 3-4 months after acceptance. **Publishes 2-3 new writers/year.** Recently published work by Jack Cady, Louise Marley, Tom Piccirilli, Kay Kenyon, Nina Kiriki Hoffman. Length: 1,000-6,000 words; average length: 3,000-4,000 words. Publishes short shorts. Also publishes poetry.
How to Contact Send complete ms with cover letter. Include estimated word count and 1-paragraph bio. Responds in 1 week to queries; 1-2 months to mss. Sample copy for $7. Writer's guidelines for #10 SASE. Reviews fiction.

$ⓩ Ⓥ TALES OF THE TALISMAN

(formerly Hadrosaur Tales), Hadrosaur Productions, P.O. Box 2194, Mesilla Park NM 88047-2194. E-mail: hadrosaur@zianet.com. Web site: www.hadrosaur.com. **Contact:** David L. Summers, editor. Zine specializing in science fiction: 8½×11; 84 pages; 50 lb. white stock; 80 lb. cover. "*Tales of the Talisman* is a literary science fiction and fantasy magazine published 4 times a year. We publish short stories, poetry and articles with themes related to science fiction and fantasy. Above all, we are looking for thought-provoking ideas and good writing. Speculative fiction set in the past, present and future is welcome. Likewise, contemporary or historical fiction is welcome as long as it has a mythic or science fictional element. Our target audience includes adult fans of the science fiction and fantasy genres along with anyone else who enjoys thought-provoking and entertaining writing." Quarterly. Estab. 1995. Circ. 150.
 • Received an honorable mention in *The Year's Best Science Fiction* 2004 edited by Gardner Dozois.
Needs Fantasy (space fantasy, sword and sorcery), horror, science fiction (hard science/technological, soft/sociological). "We do not want to see stories with graphic violence. Do not send 'mainstream' fiction with no science fictional or fantastic elements. Do not send stories with copyrighted characters, unless you're the copyright holder." Receives 15 unsolicited mss/month. Accepts 7-10 mss/issue; 21-30 mss/year. Does not read May 1-June 15 and November 1-December 15. Publishes ms 9 months after acceptance. **Publishes 8 new writers/year.** Recently published work by Tim Myers, Neal Asher, Ken Goldman, Sonya Taaffe, Mark Fewell,

Christina Sng, and Julie Shiel. Length: 1,000-6,000 words; average length: 4,000 words. Also publishes poetry. Often comments on rejected mss.

How to Contact Send complete ms. Accepts submissions by e-mail (hadrosaur@zianet.com). Include estimated word count, brief bio and list of publications. Send SASE (or IRC) for return of ms or send a disposable copy of ms and #10 SASE for reply only. Responds in 1 week to queries; 1 month to mss. Accepts reprint submissions No simultaneous submissions. Sample copy for $8. Writer's guidelines online.

Payment/Terms Pays $6-10. Pays on acceptance for one-time rights.

Advice "First and foremost, I look for engaging drama and believable characters. With those characters and situations, I want you to take me someplace I've never been before. The story I'll buy is the one set in a new world or where the unexpected happens, but yet I cannot help but believe in the situation because it feels real. Read absolutely everything you can get your hands on, especially stories and articles outside your genre of choice. This is a great source for original ideas."

$ 🖂 TIMBER CREEK REVIEW

P.O. Box 16542, Greensboro NC 27416. E-mail: timber_creek_review@hoopsmail.com. **Contact:** John M. Freiermuth, editor; Rosyln Willette, associate editor. Newsletter: $5^{1}/_{2} \times 8^{1}/_{2}$; 80-88 pages; computer generated on copy paper; saddle-stapled with colored paper cover; some illustrations. "Fiction, humor/satire, poetry and travel for a general audience." Quarterly. Estab. 1992. Circ. 140-160.

Needs Adventure, ethnic/multicultural, feminist, historical, humor/satire, literary, mainstream, mystery/suspense, regional, western, literary nonfiction, and one-act plays. "No religious, children's, gay, modern romance, and no reprints please!" Receives 50 unsolicited mss/month. Accepts 30-40 stories and 80-90 poems a year. Publishes ms 2-6 months after acceptance. **Publishes 0-3 new writers/year.** Recently published work by Christopher Dungey, Chris Brown, Richard Thieme, Hunter Huckabay, Kathleen Wheaton, Joan Fox, Carol Firth, Sid Miller, Susan V. Carlos.

How to Contact Cover letter required. Accepts simultaneous submissions. Sample copy for $4.75, subscription $17.

Payment/Terms Pays $10-35, plus subscription. Acquires first North American serial rights. Not copyrighted.

Advice "Stop watching TV and read that literary magazine where your last manuscript appeared. There are no automatons here, so don't treat us like machines. We may not recognize your name at the top of the manuscript. Include a statement that the mss have previously not been published on paper or on the internet, nor have they been accepted by others. A few lines about yourself breaks the ice, the names of three or four magazines that have published you in the last year or two would show your reality, and a bio blurb of 27 words including the names of 2 or 3 of the magazines you send the occasional subscription check (where you aspire to be?) could help. If you are not sending a check to some little magazine that is supported by subscriptions and the blood, sweat and tears of the editors, why would you send your manuscript to any of them and expect to receive a warm welcome? No requirement to subscribe or buy a sample, but they're available and are encouraged. There are no phony contests and never a reading fee. We read all year long, but may take 1 to 6 months to respond."

🅽 ◯ ◎ TRAIL OF INDISCRETION

Fortress Publishing, Inc., 3704 Hartzdale Dr., Camp Hill PA 17011. (717)350-8760. E-mail: fortresspublishinginc @yahoo.com. Web site: www.fortresspublishinginc.com. **Contact:** Brian Koscienski, editor in chief. Zine specializing in genre fiction: digest ($5^{1}/_{2} \times 8^{1}/_{2}$), 48 pages, 24 lb. paper, glossy cover. "We publish genre fiction—sci-fi, fantasy, horror, etc. We'd rather have a solid story containing great characters than a weak story with a surprise 'trick' ending." Quarterly. Estab. 2006. Circ. <100.

Needs Adventure, fantasy (space fantasy, sword and sorcery), horror (dark fantasy, futuristic, psychological, supernatural), humor/satire, psychic/supernatural/occult, science fiction (hard science/technological, soft/ sociological). Does not want "touchy-feely 'coming of age' stories or stories where the protagonist mopes about contemplating his/her own mortality." Accepts 5-7 mss/issue. Manuscript published 3-9 months after acceptance. **Publishes 2-10 new writers/year.** Published Nellie Batz (debut), Jeff Young, Den Wilson, Eric Hardenbrook (debut), Danielle Ackley-McPhail. Length: 5,000 words (max). Average length: 3,000 words. Publishes short shorts. Sometimes comments on/critiques rejected mss.

How to Contact Send complete ms with cover letter. Accepts submissions by e-mail. Include estimated word count, brief bio, list of publications. Responds to queries in 1-2 weeks. Responds to mss in 1-10 weeks. Send either SASE (or IRC) for return of ms or disposable copy of ms and #10 SASE for reply only. Considers simultaneous submissions, previously published submissions. Sample copy available for $4 or on Web site. Guidelines available for SASE, via e-mail, on Web site.

Payment and Terms Writers receive 2 contributors copies. Additional copies $2. Pays on publication. Acquires one-time rights. Publication is copyrighted.

Advice "If your story is about a 13-year-old girl coping with the change to womanhood while poignantly reflecting the recent passing of her favorite aunt, then we *don't* want it. However, if your story is about the 13-year-old daughter of a vampire cowboy who stumbles upon a government conspiracy involving unicorns and aliens while investigating the grizzly murder of her favorite aunt, then we'll look at it. Please read the magazine to see what we want. Love your story, but listen to advice."

N: ◪ ◎ TRANSCENDENT VISIONS
Toxic Evolution Press, 251 S. Olds Blvd., 84-E, Fairless Hills PA 19030-3426. (215)547-7159. **Contact:** David Kime, editor. Zine: letter size; 24 pages; xerox paper; illustrations. "*Transcendent Visions* is a literary zine by and for people who have been labeled mentally ill. Our purpose is to illustrate how creative and articulate mental patients are." Annual. Estab. 1992. Circ. 200.

• *Transcendent Visions* has received excellent reviews in many underground publications.

Needs Experimental, feminist, gay, humor/satire, lesbian. Especially interested in material dealing with mental illness. "I do not like stuff one would find in a mainstream publication. No porn." Would like to see more "quirky, non-mainstream fiction." Receives 5 unsolicited mss/month. Accepts 7 mss/year. Publishes ms 3-4 months after acceptance. Recently published work by Brian McCarvill, Michael Fowler, Thomas A. Long, Lisa Donnelly, Roger D. Coleman and Emil Vachas. Publishes short shorts. Also publishes poetry.

How to Contact Send complete ms with cover letter. Include half-page bio. Send disposable copy of ms. Responds in 3 month to mss. Accepts simultaneous and reprint submissions. Sample copy for $3.

Payment/Terms Pays 1 contributor's copy. Pays on publication for one-time rights.

Advice "We like unusual stories that are quirky. We like shorter pieces. Please do not go on and on about what zines you have been published in or awards you have won, etc. We just want to read your material, not know your life story. Please don't swamp me with tons of submissions. Send up to five stories. Please print or type your name and address."

$ ◪ ◎ WEBER STUDIES, Voices and Viewpoints of the Contemporary West
1214 University Circle, Ogden UT 84408-1214. (801)626-6473. E-mail: blroghaar@weber.edu. Web site: weberst udies.weber.edu. **Contact:** Brad L. Roghaar, editor. Magazine: 7½×10; 120-140 pages; coated paper; 4-color cover; illustrations; photos. "We seek the following themes: preservation of and access to wilderness, environmental cooperation, insight derived from living in the West, cultural diversity, changing federal involvement in the region, women and the West, implications of population growth, a sense of place, etc. We love good writing that reveals human nature as well as natural environment." Triannual. Estab. 1984. Circ. 1,000.

Needs Adventure, comics/graphic novels, ethnic/multicultural, experimental, feminist, historical, humor/satire, literary, mainstream, military/war, mystery/suspense, New Age, psychic/supernatural/occult, regional (contemporary western US), translations, western (frontier sage, tradtional, contemporary), short story collections. No children's/juvenile, erotica, religious or young adult/teen. Receives 50 unsolicited mss/month. Accepts 3-6 mss/issue; 9-18 mss/year. Publishes ms up to 18 months after acceptance. **Publishes "few" new writers/year.** Recently published work by Gary Gildner, Ron McFarland and David Duncan. Publishes short shorts. Also publishes literary essays, poetry, art. Sometimes comments on rejected mss.

How to Contact Send complete ms with a cover letter. Include estimated word count, bio (if necessary), and list of publications (not necessary). Responds in 3 months to mss. Accepts multiple submissions. Sample copy for $10.

Payment/Terms Pays $150-$300. Pays on publication for first, electronic rights. Requests electronic archive permission. Sends galleys to author.

Advice "Is it true? Is it new? Is it interesting? Will the story appeal to educated readers who are concerned with the contemporary western United States? Declining public interest in reading generally is of concern. We publish both print media and electronic media because we believe the future will expect both options. The Dr. Neila C. Seshachari Fiction Award, a $500 prize, is awarded annually to the best fiction appearing in *Weber Studies* each year."

$ ◪ WEIRD TALES
121 Crooked Lane, King of Prussia PA 19406. (610)275-4463. E-mail: weirdtales@comcast.net. **Contact:** George H. Seithers and Darrell Schweitzer, editors. Magazine: 8½×11; 68 pages; white, non-glossy paper; glossy 4-color cover; illustrations. "We publish fantastic fiction, supernatural horror for an adult audience." Published 6 times a year. Estab. 1923. Circ. 5,000.

Needs Fantasy (sword and sorcery), horror, psychic/supernatural/occult, translations. No hard science fiction or non-fantasy. "We want to see a wide range of fantasy, from sword and sorcery to supernatural horror. We can use some unclassifiables." Receives 400 unsolicited mss/month. Accepts 8 mss/issue; 48 mss/year. Publishes ms 6-18 months after acceptance. Agented fiction 10%. **Publishes 8 new writers/year.** Recently published work by Tanith Lee, Thomas Ligotti, Ian Watson, Lord Dunsany. Length: 10,000 words; average length: 4,000 words. Publishes short shorts. Also publishes poetry. Always comments on rejected mss.

How to Contact Send complete ms. Send SASE for reply, return of ms or send a disposable copy of ms with

SASE. Responds in 2-3 weeks to mss. Accepts multiple submissions No simultaneous submissions. Sample copy for $5.95. Writer's guidelines for #10 SASE or by e-mail. Reviews fiction.

Payment/Terms Pays 3¢/word and 2 contributor's copies on publication. Acquires first North American serial, plus anthology option rights. Sends galleys to author.

Advice "We look for imagination and vivid writing. Read the magazine. Get a good grounding in the contemporary horror and fantasy field through the various 'best of the year' anthologies. Avoid the obvious cliches of technicalities of the hereafter, the mechanics of vampirism, generic Tolkien-clone fantasy. In general, it is to be honest and emotionally moving rather than clever. Avoid stories which have nothing of interest for the allegedly 'surprise' ending."

WORDS OF WISDOM

P.O. Box 16542, Greensboro NC 27416. E-mail: wowmail@hoopsmail.com. **Contact:** Mikhammad Abdel-Ishara, editor. Newsletter: $5^{1}/_{2} \times 8^{1}/_{2}$; 76-88 pages; computer-generated on copy paper; saddle-stapled with colored paper cover; some illustrations. "Fiction, satire/humor, poetry and travel for a general audience." Estab. 1981. Circ. 150-160.

Needs Adventure, ethnic/multicultural, feminist, historical, humor/satire, literary, mainstream, mystery/suspense (private eye, cozy), regional, western, one-act plays. "No religious, children, gay or romance." Receives 50 unsolicited mss/month. Accepts 65-75 mss/year. Publishes ms 2-6 months after acceptance. **Publishes 0-5 new writers/year.** Recently published work by Debra Leigh Scott, Margaret Karmazin, Frank Marvin, James O'Gorman, Lorraine Tolliver, Kent Kameron, Margene Whittler Hucek. Length: 1,500-5,000 words; average length: 3,000 words. No previously published work.

How to Contact Send complete ms. Accepts submissions by U.S. mail only. Responds in 1-6 months to mss. Accepts simultaneous submissions. Sample copy free, or for $4.75.

Payment/Terms Offers subscription to magazine for first story published. Acquires first North American serial rights. Not copyrighted.

Advice "A few lines about yourself in the cover letter breaks the ice, the names of three or four magazines that have published your work in the last year would show your reality, and a bio blurb of about 27 words including the names of two or three magazines you send your subscription money to would show your dreams. No requirements to subscribe or buy a sample, but they are available at $17 and $4.75 and would be appreciated. There are no phony contests and never a reading fee. We read all year long, but it may take one to six months to respond."

ZAHIR, Unforgettable Tales

Zahir Publishing, 315 South Coast Hwy. 101, Suite U8, Encinitas CA 92024. E-mail: stempchin@zahirtales.com. Web site: www.zahirtales.com. **Contact:** Sheryl Tempchin, editor. Magazine: Digest-size; 80 pages; heavy stock paper; glossy, full color cover stock. "We publish quality speculative fiction for intelligent adult readers. Our goal is to bridge the gap between literary and genre fiction." Triannual. Estab. 2003.

Needs Fantasy, literary, psychic/supernatural/occult, science fiction, surrealism, magical realism. No children's stories, excessive violence or pornography. Accepts 6-8 mss/issue; 18-24 mss/year. Publishes ms 2-12 months after acceptance. **Publishes 6 new writers/year.** Sometimes comments on rejected mss.

How to Contact Send complete ms. Send SASE (or IRC) for return of ms, or send disposable copy of the ms and #10 SASE for reply only. E-mail queries okay. No e-mail mss except from writers living outside the U.S. Responds in 1-2 weeks to queries; 1-3 months to mss. Accepts reprint submissions. No simultaneous submissions. Sample copy for $6.50 (US). Writer's guidelines for #10 SASE, by e-mail, or online.

Payment/Terms Pays $10 and 2 contributor's copies. Pays on publication for first, second serial (reprint) rights.

Advice "The stories we are most likely to buy are well written, have interesting, well-developed characters and/or ideas that fascinate, chill, thrill, or amuse us. They must have some element of the fantastic or surreal."

Online Markets

As production and distribution costs go up and the number of subscribers falls, more and more magazines are giving up print publication and moving online. Relatively inexpensive to maintain and quicker to accept and post submissions, online fiction sites are growing fast in numbers and legitimacy. Jason Sanford, editor of *storySouth*, explains, "Online journals reach for greater audiences than print journals with far less cost. I have a friend who edits a print literary journal and he is constantly struggling to cover the cost of printing 500 copies twice a year. At *storySouth*, we reach 1,000 individual readers every single day without having to worry that we're going to break the bank with our printing budget. The benefit for writers is that your stories tend to gain more attention online than in small literary journals. Because small journals have print runs of 500-1,000 copies, there is a limit on how many people will read your work. Online, there is no limit. I've been published in both print and online literary journals, and the stories I've published online have received the most attention and feedback."

Writers exploring online opportunities for publication will find a rich and diverse community of voices. Genre sites are strong, in particular those for science fiction/fantasy and horror. (See *Far Sector SFFH* and *Dargonzine*.) Mainstream short fiction markets are also growing exponentially. (See *Toasted Cheese* and *Paperplates*, among many others.) Online literary journals range from the traditional (*The Barcelona Review*, *Carve Magazine*) to those with a decidedly more quirky bent (*Timothy McSweeney's Internet Tendency*, *The Glut*). Writers will also find here more highly experimental and multimedia work. (See *Words on Walls: Literary Fresco* and *Diagram*.)

Online journals are gaining respect for the writers who appear on their sites. As Jill Adams, publisher and editor of *The Barcelona Review*, says: "We see our Internet review, like the small independent publishing houses, as a means of counterbalancing the big-business mentality of the multi-national publishing houses. At the same time, we want to see our writers 'make it big.' Last year we heard from more and more big houses asking about some of our new writers, wanting contact information, etc. So I see a healthy trend in that big houses are finally—after being skeptical and confused—looking at it seriously and scouting online."

While the medium of online publication is different, the traditional rules of publishing apply to submissions. Writers should research the sites and archives carefully, looking for a match in sensibility for their work. They should then follow submission guidelines exactly and submit courteously. True, these sites aren't bound by traditional print schedules, so your work theoretically may be published more quickly. But that doesn't mean online journals have a larger staff, so exercise patience with editors considering your manuscript.

Also, while reviewing the listings in this market section, notice they are grouped differently from other market listings. In our literary magazines section, for example, you'll find primarily only publications searching for literary short fiction. But Online Markets are grouped by medium, so you'll find publishers of mystery short stories listed next to those looking for horror next to those specializing in flash fiction, so review with care. In addition, online markets with print counterparts, such as *North American Review*, can be found listed in the print markets sections.

A final note about online publication: Like literary journals, the majority of these markets are either nonpaying or very low paying. In addition, writers will not receive print copies of the publications because of the medium. So in most cases, do not expect to be paid for your exposure.

$☑ THE ABSINTHE LITERARY REVIEW

P.O. Box 328, Spring Green WI 53588. E-mail: staff@absinthe-literary-review.com. Web site: www.absinthe-literary-review.com. **Contact:** Charles Allen Wyman, editor. Electronic literary magazine; print issue coming 2007. "*ALR* publishes short stories, novel excerpts, poems, book reviews and literary essays. Our target audience is the literate individual who enjoys creative language use, character-driven fiction and the clashing of worlds— real and surreal, poetic and prosaic, sacred and transgressive."

Needs "Transgressive works dealing with sex, death, disease, madness and the like; the clash of archaic with modern-day; archetype, symbolism; surrealism, philosophy, physics; existential and post-modern flavoring; experimental or flagrantly textured (but not sloppy or casual) fiction; intense crafting of language from the writer's writer. See Web site for information on our annual Eros and Thanatos. Anathemas: mainstream storytellers, 'Oprah' fiction, high school or beginner fiction, poetry or fiction that contains no capital letters or punctuation, 'hot' trends, genre, utterly normal prose or poetry, first, second or third drafts, pieces that exceed our stated word count (5,000 max.) by thousands of words." **Publishes 3-6 new writers/year.** Recently published work by Bruce Holland Rogers, David Schneiderman, Virgil Suarez, John Tisdale, James Reidel and Dan Pope.

How to Contact Prefers submissions by e-mail. Read online guidelines, then send a single fiction submission per reading period to fiction@absinthe-literary-review.com; 3-7 poems to poetry@absinthe-literary-review.com or a single essay on a literary topic to essays@absinthe-literary-review.com. Sample copy online.

Payment/Terms Pays $2-10 for fiction and essays; $1-10 for poetry.

Advice "Be erudite and daring in your writing. Draw from the past to drag meaning from the present. Kill ego and cliché. Invest your work with layers of meaning that subtly reveal multiple realities. Do not submit pieces that are riddled with spelling errors and grammatical snafus. Above all, be professional. For those of you who don't understand exactly what this means, please send your manuscripts elsewhere until you have experienced the necessary epiphany."

☑ ALIENSKIN MAGAZINE, An Online Science Fiction, Fantasy & Horror Magazine

Froggy Bottom Press, P.O. Box 495, Beaver PA 15009. E-mail: alienskin@alienskinmag.com. Web site: www.alienskinmag.com. **Contact:** Feature fiction: K. A. Patterson; Flash fiction: Phil Adams. Online magazine. "Our magazine was created for, and strives to help, aspiring writers of SFFH. We endeavor to promote and educate genre writers, helping them learn and develop the skills they need to produce marketable short stories." Bimonthly. Estab. 2002. Circ. 1,000+ Internet.

Needs Fantasy (dark fantasy, sword and sorcery), horror (dark fantasy, futuristic, psychological, psychic/supernatural/occult), science fiction (hard science/technological, soft/sociological). "No excessive blood, gore, erotica or vulgarity. No experimental or speculative fiction that does not use basic story elements of character, conflict, action and resolution. No esoteric ruminations." Receives 100-200 unsolicited mss/month. Accepts 24-30 mss/issue; 144-180 mss/year. Publishes ms 30-60 days after acceptance. **Publishes 10-15 new writers/year.** Recently published work by Michael Kechula, Manfred Gabriel, Francis Alexander, Daniel Smith. Length: 1,000-3,500 words; average length: 2,200 words. Publishes short shorts. Also publishes poetry. Always comments on rejected mss.

How to Contact Send complete ms. Accepts submissions by e-mail. Include estimated word count, brief bio, name, address, e-mail address. Responds in 1-2 weeks to queries; 2 months to mss. Accepts multiple submissions. Sample copy online. Writer's guidelines online.

Payment/Terms Pays ½¢/word for 1,001-3,500 words; $5 flat pay for 500-1,000 words. Pays on publication for first, electronic rights. Sponsors awards/contests.

Advice "We look for interesting stories that offer something unique; stories that use basic story elements of character, conflict, action and resolution. We like the dark, twisted side of SFFH genres. Read our guidelines and follow the rules, treating the submission process as a serious business transaction. Only send stories that have been spell-checked, and proofread at least twice. Try to remember that editors who offer a critique on manuscripts do so to help you as a writer, not to hamper or dissuade you as a writer."

◑ THE ALSOP REVIEW

1880 Lincoln Ave., Calistoga, CA 94515. E-mail: alsop@alsopreview.com. Web site: www.alsopreview.com. **Contact:** Jaimes Alsop, editor. Web zine. *"The Alsop Review* is primarily a literary resource and as such does not solicit manuscripts. However, the review operates an e-zine which accepts manuscripts. *Octavo* is a quarterly magazine that accepts short stories and poetry. Send submissions to Andrew Boobier at andrew@netstep.co.uk.

Needs Experimental, literary. "No genre work or humor for its own sake. No pornography. We would like to see more experimental and unconventional works. Surprise me." Recently published work by Kyle Jarrard, Dennis Must, Kristy Nielsen, Bob Riche and Linda Sue Park.

How to Contact Accepts submissions by e-mail (alsop@alsopreview.com). Accepts reprint submissions. Sample copy not available.

Payment/Terms "None. We offer a permanent 'home' on the Web for writers and will pull and add material to their pages upon request."

Advice "Read, read, read. Treat submissions to Web zines as carefully as you would a print magazine. Research the market first. For every great Web zine, there are a hundred mediocre ones. Remember that once your work is on the Web, chances are it will be there for a very long time. Put your best stuff out there and take advantage of the opportunities to re-publish work from print magazines."

$◻ ANTI MUSE

502 S. Main St., Saint Joseph TN 38481. (931)845-4838. E-mail: antimuse@antimuse.org. Web site: http://antimuse.org. **Contact:** Michael Haislip, editor. *Anti Muse* appeals to readers with a somewhat jaded and cynical outlook on life. Monthly. Estab. 2004. Circ. 10,000.

Needs Adventure, comics/graphic novels, erotica, ethnic/multicultural, experimental, fantasy, feminist, gay, historical, horror, humor/satire, lesbian, literary, mainstream, military/war, New Age, psychic/supernatural/occult, regional, science fiction, thriller/espionage, western. Receives 300 unsolicited mss/month. Accepts 5-10 mss/issue; 50 mss/year. Publishes ms 1 month after acceptance. **Publishes 50 new writers/year.** Recently published work by Robert Levin, Corey Mesler, Trevor Davis. Length: 200-10,000 words; average length: 1,000 words. Publishes short shorts. Also publishes literary essays, literary criticism, poetry. Sometimes comments on rejected mss.

How to Contact Send complete ms. Accepts submissions by e-mail. Send SASE (or IRC) for return of the ms, or send disposable copy of the ms and #10 SASE for reply only. Responds in 1 month to mss. Accepts simultaneous, multiple submissions and reprints. Sample copy free. Writer's guidelines online.

Payment/Terms Pays $5-20. Pays on publication for one-time rights.

Advice "I want to be entertained by your submission. I want to feel as if I'd be foolish to put down your manuscript."

Ⓝ ◑ APPLE VALLEY REVIEW, A Journal of Contemporary Literature

P.O. Box 5766, Collegeville MN 56321. E-mail: editor@leahbrowning.net. Web site: www.applevalleyreview.com. **Contact:** Leah Browning, editor. Online literary magazine. Includes photographs/artwork on cover. "Each issue features a selection of beautifully crafted poetry, short fiction and essays. We prefer work that has both mainstream and literary appeal. As such, we avoid erotica, work containing explicit language and anything violent or extremely depressing. Our audience includes teens and adults of all ages." Semiannual. Estab. 2005. Member CLMP.

Needs Ethnic/multicultural (general), experimental, humor/satire, literary, mainstream, regional (American South, Southwest), translations, literary women's fiction (e.g. Barbara Kingsolver, Anne Tyler, Lee Smith, Elinor Lipman, Perri Klass). Does not want genre fiction, erotica, work containing explicit language, or anything violent or extremely depressing. Receives 20+ mss/month. Accepts 1-4 mss/issue; 2-8 mss/year. Manuscript published 3-6 months after acceptance. Published Hal Sirowitz, Anna Evans, David Thornbrugh, Steve Klepetar, Louie Crew, Arlene L. Mandell, Jéanpaul Ferro, Janet Zupan. Length: 100 words (min)-3,000 words (max). Average length: 2,000 words. Publishes short shorts. Average length of short shorts: 1,200 words. Also publishes literary essays, poetry. Sometimes comments on/critiques rejected manuscripts.

How to Contact Send complete ms with cover letter. Accepts submissions only via e-mail. Include estimated word count, brief bio. Responds to mss in 1 week-3 months. Considers multiple submissions. Guidelines available via e-mail, on Web site. Sample copy on Web site.

Payment and Terms Acquires first rights, right to archive online. Publication is copyrighted.

Advice "Excellent writing always makes a manuscript stand out. Beyond that, I look for stories and poems that I want to read again and that I want to give to someone else to read—work so interesting for one reason or another that I feel compelled to share it. Please read at least some of the previously published work to get a feel for our style, and follow the submission guidelines as closely as possible. We accept submissions only via e-mail."

⚅ ⬭ ASCENT ASPIRATIONS

Ascent, 1560 Arbutus Dr., Nanoose Bay BC C9P 9C8 Canada. E-mail: ascent aspirations@shaw.com. Web site: www.ascentaspirations.ca. **Contact:** David Fraser, editor. E-zine specializing in short fiction (all genres) and poetry, essays, visual art: 40 electronic pages; illustrations; photos. "*Ascent Aspirations* magazine publishes quarterly online and semi-annually in print. The print issues are operated as contests. Please refer to current guidelines before submitting. *Ascent* is a quality electronic publication dedicated to the promotion and encouragement of aspiring writers of any genre. The focus however is toward interesting experimental writing in dark mainstream, literary, science fiction, fantasy and horror. Poetry can be on any theme. Essays need to be unique, current and have social, philosophical commentary." Quarterly online. Estab. 1997.

Needs Erotica, experimental, fantasy (space fantasy), feminist, horror (dark fantasy, futuristic, psychological, supernatural), literary, mainstream, mystery/suspense, New Age, psychic/supernatural/occult, science fiction (hard science/technological, soft/sociological). Receives 70- 100 unsolicited mss/month. Accepts 10-15 mss/issue; 70 mss/year. Publishes ms 3 months after acceptance. **Publishes 5-10 new writers/year.** Recently published work by Taylor Graham, Janet Buck, Jim Manton, Steve Cartwright, Don Stockard, Penn Kemp, Sam Vargo, Vernon Waring, Margaret Karmazin, Bill Hughes. Length: 2,000 words or less; average length: 1, 500 words. Publishes short shorts. Also publishes literary essays, literary criticism, poetry. Sometimes comments on rejected mss.

How to Contact "Query by e-mail with word attachment." Include estimated word count, brief bio and list of publications. If you have to submit by mail because it is your only avenue, provide a SASE with either International Coupons or Canadian stamps only. Responds in 1 week to queries; 3 months to mss. Accepts simultaneous, multiple submissions and reprints. Guidelines by e-mail or on Web site. Reviews fiction.

Payment/Terms "No payment at this time. Rights remain with author."

Advice "Short fiction should first of all tell a good story, take the reader to new and interesting imaginary or real places. Short fiction should use language lyrically and effectively, be experimental in either form or content and take the reader into realms where they can analyze and think about the human condition. Write with passion for your material, be concise and economical and let the reader work to unravel your story. In terms of editing, always proofread to the point where what you submit is the best it possibly can be. Never be discouraged if your work is not accepted; it may just not be the right fit for a current publication."

BABEL, the Multilingual, Multicultural Online Journal and Community of Arts and Ideas

E-mail: malcolm@towerofbabel.com. Web site: www.towerofbabel.com. **Contact**: Malcolm Lawrence, editor-in-chief. Electronic zine. "We publish regional reports from international stringers all over the planet, as well as feature round table discussions, fiction, columns, poetry, erotica, travelogues, reviews of all the arts and editorials. We are an online community involving an extensive group of over 100 artists, writers and programmers, and over 300 translators representing (so far) 75 of the world's languages."

Needs "There are no specific categories of fiction that we are not interested in. Possible exceptions: laywers/vampires, different genders hailing from different planets, cold war military scenarios and things that go bump in the suburban night." Recently published work by Neal Robbins, Jennifer Prado, Nicholas P. Snoek, Yves Jacques, Doug Williamson, A.L. Fern, Laura Feister, Denzel J. Hankinson, Pete Hanson and Malcolm Lawrence.

How to Contact Query. Accepts submissions by e-mail. Reviews fiction.

Advice "We would like to see more fiction with first-person male characters written by female authors as well as more fiction with first-person female characters written by male authors. The best advice we could give to writers wanting to be published is simply to know what you're writing about and to write passionately about it. We should also mention that the phrase 'dead white men' will only hurt your chances. The Internet is the most important invention since the printing press and will change the world in the same way. One look at *Babel* and you'll see our predictions for the future of electronic publishing."

⊕ ⬭ ⬭ THE BARCELONA REVIEW

Correu Vell 12-2, Barcelona 08002 Spain. (00) 34 93 319 15 96. E-mail: editor@barcelonareview.com. Web site: www.barcelonareview.com. **Contact:** Jill Adams, editor. "*TBR* is an international review of contemporary, cutting-edge fiction published in English, Spanish and Catalan. Our aim is to bring both new and established writers to the attention of a larger audience. Well-known writers such as Alicia Erian in the U.S., Michel Faber in the U.K., Carlos Gardini in Argentina, and Nuria Amat in Spain, for example, were not known outside their countries until appearing in *TBR*. Our multilingual format increases the audience all the more. Internationally-known writers, such as Irvine Welsh and Douglas Coupland, have contributed stories that ran in small press anthologies available only in one country. We try to keep abreast of what's happening internationally and to present the best finds every two months. Our intended audience is anyone interested in high-quality contemporary fiction that often (but not always) veers from the mainstream; we assume that our readers are well read and familiar with contemporary fiction in general."

Needs Short fiction. "Our bias is towards potent and powerful cutting-edge material; given that general criteria, we are open to all styles and techniques and all genres. No slice-of-life stories, vignettes or reworked fables, and nothing that does not measure up, in your opinion, to the quality of work in our review, which we expect submitters to be familiar with.'' **Publishes 20 new writers/year.** Recently published work by Niall Griffiths, Adam Haslett, G.K. Wuori, Adam Johnson, Mary Wornov, Emily Carter, Jesse Shepard, Julie Orringer.

How to Contact Send submissions by e-mail as an attached file. Hard copies accepted but cannot be returned. No simultaneous submissions.

Payment/Terms ''In lieu of pay, we offer a highly professional Spanish translation to English language writers and vice versa to Spanish writers.''

Advice ''Send top drawer material that has been drafted two, three, four times—whatever it takes. Then sit on it for a while and look at it afresh. Keep the text tight. Grab the reader in the first paragraph and don't let go. Keep in mind that a perfectly crafted story that lacks a punch of some sort won't cut it. Make it new, make it different. Surprise the reader in some way. Read the best of the short fiction available in your area of writing to see how yours measures up. Don't send anything off until you feel it's ready and then familiarize yourself with the content of the review/magazine to which you are submitting.''

☐ ☑ BIG COUNTRY PEACOCK CHRONICLE, Online Magazine

RR1, Box 89K-112, Aspermont TX 79502. (806)254-2322. E-mail: publisher@peacockchronicle.com. Web site: www.peacockchronicle.com. **Contact:** Audrey Yoeckel, owner/publisher. Online magazine. ''We publish articles, commentaries, reviews, interviews, short stories, serialized novels and novellas, poetry, essays, humor and anecdotes. Due to the nature of Internet publication, guidelines for length of written works are flexible and acceptance is based more on content. Content must be family friendly. Writings that promote hatred or violence will not be accepted. *The Big Country Peacock Chronicle* is dedicated to the preservation of community values and traditional folk cultures. In today's society, we are too often deprived of a solid feeling of community which is so vital to our security and well-being. It is our attempt to keep the best parts of our culture intact. Our goal is to build a place for individuals, no matter the skill level, to test their talents and get feedback from others in a non-threatening, friendly environment. The original concept for the magazine was to open the door to talented writers by providing not only a publishing medium for their work but support and feedback as well. It was created along the lines of a smalltown publication in order to remove some of the anxiety about submitting works for first-time publication.'' Quarterly. Estab. 2000.

Needs Adventure, children's/juvenile (adventure, easy-to-read, fantasy, historical, mystery, preschool, series, sports), ethnic/multicultural (general), family saga, fantasy (space fantasy, sword and sorcery), gay, historical (general), horror (futuristic, supernatural, psychological), humor/satire, literary, military/war, mystery/suspense (amateur sleuth, police procedural, private eye/hard-boiled), psychic/supernatural/occult, regional, religious/inspirational (children's religious), romance (gothic, historical, romantic suspense), science fiction (soft/sociological), thriller/espionage, translations (frontier saga, traditional), western. 'While the genre of the writing or the style does not matter, excessive or gratuitous violence, foul language and sexually explicit material is not acceptable.'' Accepts 2-3 (depending on length) mss/issue. Publishes ms 3 months after acceptance. Average length: 2,500 words. Publishes short shorts. Also publishes literary essays, literary criticism, poetry. Always comments on rejected mss.

How to Contact Include estimated word count, brief bio, list of publications and Internet contact information (i.e. e-mail, Web site address). Responds in 3 weeks to queries; 6 weeks to mss. Accepts simultaneous, multiple submissions and reprints. Writer's guidelines online. Reviews fiction.

Payment/Terms Acquires electronic rights. Sends galleys to author.

Advice ''We look for continuity and coherence. The work must be clean with a minimum of typographical errors. The advantage to submitting works to us is the feedback and support. We work closely with our writers, offering promotion, resource information, moral support and general help to achieve success as writers. While we recommend doing businesss with us via the Internet, we have also published writers who do not have access. For those new to the Internet, we also provide assistance with the best ways to use it as a medium for achieving success in the field.''

$ ☑ BLACKBIRD, an online journal of literature and the arts

Virginia Commonwealth University Department of Fiction, P.O. Box 843082, Richmond VA 23284. (804)225-4729. E-mail: blackbird@vcu.edu. Web site: www.blackbird.vcu.edu. **Contact:** Mary Flinn, Gregory Donovan, editors. Online journal: 80+ pages if printed; illustrations; photos. ''We strive to maintain the highest quality of writing and design, bringing the best things about a print magazine to the outside world. We publish fiction that is carefully crafted, thoughtful and suprising.'' Semiannual. Estab. 2001. Circ. 30,000 readers per month.

Needs Adventure, comics/graphic novels, confessions, ethnic/multicultural, experimental, family saga, fantasy, feminist, gay, glitz, historical, humor/satire, lesbian, literary, mainstream, military/war, mystery/suspense, New Age, novel excerpts, psychic/supernatural/occult, regional, serialized novels, slice-of-life vignettes, suspense, thriller/espionage, translations, western, young adult/teen. Does not want science fiction, religious/inspirational, condensed novels, horror, romance, children's. Receives 200- 300 unsolicited mss/month. Accepts

4-5 mss/issue; 8-10 mss/year. Does not read from April 15-September 15. Publishes ms 3-6 months after acceptance. **Publishes 1-2 new writers/year.** Length: 5,000-10,000 words; average length: 5,000-6,500 words. Also publishes literary essays, literary criticism, poetry. Sometimes comments on rejected mss.

How to Contact Send complete ms. Include cover letter, name, address, telephone number, brief biographical comment. Responds in 6 months to mss. Accepts simultaneous submissions. Sample copy online. Writer's guidelines online.

Payment/Terms Pays $200 for fiction, $40 for poetry. Pays on publication for first North American serial rights.

Advice "We like a story that invites us into its world, that engages our senses, soul and mind."

$⬚⬚⬚ THE CAFE IRREAL, International Imagination

E-mail: editors@cafeirreal.com. Web site: www.cafeirreal.com. **Contact:** Alice Whittenburg, G.S. Evans, editors. E-zine: illustrations. *"The Cafe Irreal* is a Web zine focusing on short stories and short shorts of an irreal nature." Quarterly. Estab. 1998. Member Council of Literary Magazine and Presses.

Needs Experimental, fantasy (literary), science fiction (literary), translations. "No horror or 'slice-of-life' stories; no genre or mainstream fiction or fantasy." Accepts 8-10 mss/issue; 30-40 mss/year. Recently published work by Emilio Martinez, Charles Simic, Alexandra Berkova, M.E. McMullen. Publishes short shorts. Also publishes literary essays, literary criticism. Sometimes comments on rejected mss.

How to Contact Accepts submissions by e-mail. "No attachments, include submission in body of e-mail. Include estimated word count." Responds in 2-4 months to mss. No simultaneous submissions. Sample copy online. Writer's guidelines online.

Payment/Terms Pays 1¢/word, $2 minimum. Pays on publication for first-time electronic rights. Sends galleys to author.

Advice "Forget formulas. Write about what you don't know, take me places I couldn't possibly go, don't try to make me care about the characters. Read short fiction by writers such as Franz Kafka, Kobo Abe, Donald Barthelme, Leonora Carrington, Ana Maria Shua and Stanislaw Lem. Also read our Web site and guidelines."

⬚⬚ CARVE MAGAZINE

P.O. Box 1573, Tallahassee FL 32302. E-mail: editor@carvezine.com. Web site: www.carvezine.com. **Contact:** Melvin Sterne, editor. Bimonthly online journal, annual printed anthology. Bimonthly. Estab. 2000. "One of the most widely read fiction magazines in the world. 3,250 regular subscribers. Web site visited by more than 12,000 readers per month.

● Fiction appearing in *Carve Magazine* has been nominated for the Pushcart, O. Henry, Best American and other anthologies.

Needs Literary (fiction). No poetry, reviews, criticism or etc. Accepts 70-80 mss/year. **Publishes 10-20 new writers/year.** Recently published work by Stephen Kallos, Bill Ransom, Lynn Stegner, Dominic Smith, Clarinda Harris, Mike Lubow.

How to Contact Send complete ms by mail or e-mail. Responds in 1-6 months to mss. Accepts simultaneous submissions. Writer's guidelines online.

Payment/Terms Sponsors awards/contests.

Advice "We look for stories with strong characterization, conflict and tightly written prose. We are not a market for amateurs. We publish work by new and established authors from the United States and around the world."

Ⓝ ⬚ CEZANNE'S CARROT, A Literary Journal of Fresh Observations

Spiritual, Transformational & Visionary Art, Inc., P.O. Box 6037, Santa Fe NM 87502-6037. E-mail: editors@cezannescarrot.org. Web site: www.cezannescarrot.org. **Contact:** Barbara Jackson, editor. Online magazine. *"Cezanne's Carrot* publishes fiction, creative nonfiction and poetry that explores spiritual, transformational, visionary or contemplative themes. We publish work that explores the higher, more expansive aspects of human nature, the integration of inner and outer worlds, and the exciting thresholds where the familiar meets the unknown." Quarterly. Estab. 2005.

Needs Ethnic/multicultural (general), experimental, fantasy (speculative), gay, humor/satire, lesbian, literary, mainstream, new age, psychic/supernatural/occult, religious, science fiction (soft/sociological), magical realism, irrealism, visionary, surrealism, spiritual. "Does not want horror, gore, murder, serial-killers, abuse stories, drug stories, vampires or other monsters, political stories, stories written for children, stories that primarily promote an agenda or a particular religion. We're not interested in dogma in any form." Receives 40 mss/month. Accepts 10-15 mss/issue; 40-60 mss/year. Manuscript published 4-12 weeks after acceptance. **Publishes 1-5 new writers/year.** Published Mary Estrada, Antonios Maltezos, Paul Allen Fahey. Length: 100 words (min)-3,000 words (max). Average length: 1,800 words. Publishes short shorts. Also publishes poetry. Always comments on/critiques rejected manuscripts.

How to Contact Send complete ms with cover letter. Accepts submissions by e-mail (fiction@cezannescarrot-.org). Include estimated word count, brief bio, list of publications. Responds to mss in 1-4 months. Considers simultaneous submissions, previously published submissions. Guidelines available on Web site.

Payment and Terms Acquires one-time rights, reprint rights.

Advice "Read our guidelines and mission statement carefully. Read previous issues to understand the kind of work we're looking for. Please send submissions to the e-mail address given in our guidelines."

$ ☒ ◯ CHALLENGING DESTINY, New Fantasy & Science Fiction

Crystalline Sphere Publishing, RR #6, St. Marys ON N4X 1C8 Canada. (519)885-6012. E-mail: csp@golden.net. Web site: challengingdestiny.com. **Contact:** David M. Switzer, editor. "We publish all kinds of science fiction and fantasy short stories." Quarterly. Estab. 1997. Circ. 200.

Needs Fantasy, science fiction. No horror, short short stories. Receives 40 unsolicited mss/month. Accepts 6 mss/issue; 24 mss/year. Publishes ms 5 months after acceptance. **Publishes 6 new writers/year.** Recently published work by Uncle River, A.R. Morlan, Jay Lake and Ken Rand. Length: 2,000-10,000 words; average length: 6,000 words. Often comments on rejected mss.

How to Contact Send complete ms. Send SAE and IRC for reply, return of ms or send disposable copy of ms. Responds in 1 week to queries; 1 month to mss. Accepts simultaneous submissions. Writer's guidelines for #10 SASE, 1 IRC, or online. Reviews fiction.

Payment/Terms Pays 1¢/word (Canadian), plus 1 contributor's copy (PDF format). Pays on publication for first North American serial, electronic rights. Sends galleys to author.

Advice "Manuscripts with a good story and interesting characters stand out. We look for fiction that entertains and makes you think. If you're going to write short fiction, you need to read lots of it. Don't reinvent the wheel. Use your own voice."

Ⓝ $ ☒ CLUB ROMANCE

Romantic Short Love Stories, P.O. Box 397, Brice OH 43109. (740)739-3327. E-mail: editor@romantic-short-love-stories.com. Web site: www.romantic-short-love-stories.com. **Contact:** Tameka Norris, senior editor. Online magazine. Contains illustrations. Includes photographs. "Publishes romantic fiction and nonfiction, including true love stories, romantic short stories, love poetry and articles. Audience is avid romance fans. The publication's uniqueness lies in the fact that fantasy and reality reside in one place. Romance fans get the best of both worlds." Monthly. Estab. 2006. Circ. 100.

Needs Fantasy (space fantasy, sword and sorcery), religious (fantasy), romance (contemporary, futuristic/time travel, gothic, historical, regency, suspense, paranormal, fantasy). Does not want erotica. Receives 200 mss/month. Accepts 8 mss/issue; 96 mss/year. Manuscript published 3-4 months after acceptance. Agented fiction 0%. **Publishes 36 new writers/year.** Published Amy Blizzard, Stephan Dukofsky, Kelly Adolph, Aaron Jackson. Length: 2,000 words (min)-10,000 words (max). Average length: 5,000 words. Also publishes poetry. Sometimes comments on/critiques rejected mss.

How to Contact Send complete ms with cover letter. Accepts submissions by e-mail. Include estimated word count, brief bio. Responds to mss in 1-4 weeks. Send either SASE (or IRC) for return of ms or disposable copy of ms and #10 SASE for reply only. Considers simultaneous submissions, previously published submissions. Sample copy and guidelines available on Web site.

Payment and Terms Writers receive $25-50 flat-rate payment. Pays on publication. Acquires electronic rights. Sends galleys to author. Publication is copyrighted.

Advice "Selects fiction by length. We want stories that generally read like a novel, with the ability to make the reader feel as though they read a novel although it's a short story. Stories that take the reader on a ride are a plus and don't just seem like they exist for the writer's sake." Check out Web site before submitting to get a thorough idea of what we accept.

☒ COLLECTEDSTORIES.COM, The Story on Short Stories

collectedstories.com, Columbia U. Station, P.O. Box 250626, New York NY 10025. (718)755-1966. E-mail: info@collectedstories.com. Web site: www.collectedstories.com. **Contact:** Dara Albanese or Wendy Ball, co-publishers. Online magazine: photos. "An online magazine devoted exclusively to literary short fiction, *collectedstories.com* publishes original short stories but also reports on various aspects related to the short form, featuring upcoming releases, author interviews, news on short story book deals, etc." Quarterly. Estab. 2000.

Needs Literary. "No young adult or children's fiction." Receives 50-75 unsolicited mss/month. Accepts 4 mss/issue; 12 mss/year. Publishes ms 1 month after acceptance. **Publishes 7 new writers/year.** Recently published work by David Levinson, Hannah Holborn, Sean Conway. Average length: 1,800 words.

How to Contact Query without published clips. Accepts submission via online form only or by e-mail. Responds in 1 week to queries; 6 months to mss. Accepts multiple submissions. Sample copy online. Writer's guidelines online. Reviews fiction.

Payment/Terms Writers retain copyright.

Advice "Since stories are accepted on a revolving basis, criteria may vary in that a story is up against the best of only that particular batch under consideration for the next issue. We select the most readable stories, that is, stories that are original, compelling, or with a sense of character, and evidence of talent with prose. Writers should become familiar with a publication before submission, develop a strong hold on grammar, and thereby submit only clean, finished works for consideration."

☑ CONVERGENCE

P.O. Box 1127, Magalia CA 95954. E-mail: editor@convergence-journal.com. Web site: www.convergence-journal.com. **Contact:** Lara Gularte, editor. *Convergence* seeks to unify the literary and visual arts and draw new interpretations of the written word by pairing poems and flash fiction with complementary art. Quarterly. Estab. 2003. Circ. 400.

Needs Ethnic/multicultural, experimental, feminist, gay, lesbian, literary, regional, translations. Accepts 10 mss/issue. Publishes ms 3 weeks after acceptance. Recently published work by Andrena Zawinski, Grace Cavalieri, Lola Haskins, Molly Fisk, Renato Rosaldo. Publishes short shorts. Also publishes poetry. Sometimes comments on rejected mss.

How to Contact Send complete ms. E-mail submissions only. No simultaneous submissions. Responds in 2 weeks to queries; 4 months to mss. Writer's guidelines online.

Payment/Terms Acquires electronic rights.

Advice "We look for freshness and originality and a mastery of the craft of flash fiction."

☑ ◎ THE COPPERFIELD REVIEW, A Journal for Readers and Writers of Historical Fiction

E-mail: info@copperfieldreview.com. Web site: www.copperfieldreview.com. **Contact:** Meredith Allard, executive editor. "We are an online literary journal that publishes historical fiction and articles, reviews and interviews related to historical fiction. We believe that by understanding the lessons of the past through historical fiction we can gain better insight into the nature of our society today, as well as a better understanding of ourselves." Quarterly. Estab. 2000.

Needs Historical (general), romance (historical), western (frontier saga, traditional). "We will consider submissions in most fiction categories, but the setting must be historical in nature. We don't want to see anything not related to historical fiction." Receives 30 unsolicited mss/month. Accepts 7-10 mss/issue; 28-40 mss/year. Responds to mss during the months of January, April, July and October. **Publishes "between 30 and 40 percent" new writers/year.** Publishes short shorts. Also publishes literary essays, literary criticism, poetry. Seldom comments on rejected mss.

How to Contact Send complete ms. Accepts submissions by e-mail. Responds in 6 weeks to queries. Accepts simultaneous, multiple submissions and reprints. Sample copy online. Writer's guidelines online. Reviews fiction.

Payment/Terms Acquires one-time rights.

Advice "We wish to showcase the very best in literary historical fiction. Stories that use historical periods and details to illuminate universal truths will immediately stand out. We are thrilled to receive thoughtful work that is polished, poised and written from the heart. Be professional, and only submit your very best work. Be certain to adhere to a publication's submission guidelines, and always treat your e-mail submissions with the same care you would use with a traditional publisher. Above all, be strong and true to your calling as a writer. It is a difficult, frustrating but wonderful journey. It is important for writers to review our online submission guidelines prior to submitting."

$☑ DANA LITERARY SOCIETY ONLINE JOURNAL

Dana Literary Society, P.O. Box 3362, Dana Point CA 92629-8362. E-mail: ward@danaliterary.org. Web site: www.danaliterary.org. **Contact:** Robert L. Ward, director. Online journal. "Fiction we publish must be thought-provoking and well crafted. We prefer works that have a message or moral." Monthly. Estab. 2000. Circ. 8,000.

Needs Humor/satire. "Most categories are acceptable if work is mindful of a thinking audience. No romance, children's/juvenile, religious/inspirational, pornographic, excessively violent or profane work. Would like to see more humor/satire." Receives 120 unsolicited mss/month. Accepts 6 mss/issue; 72 mss/year. Publishes ms 3 months after acceptance. **Publishes 8 new writers/year.** Recently published work by A.B. Jacobs, Barbara Anton, Gerald Eisman. Length: 800-2,500 words; average length: 2,000 words. Also publishes literary essays, poetry. Often comments on rejected mss.

How to Contact Send complete ms. Responds in 2 weeks to mss. Accepts simultaneous submissions and reprints. Sample copy online. Writer's guidelines online.

Payment/Terms Pays $50. Pays on publication for one-time rights. Not copyrighted.

Advice "Success requires two qualities: ability and tenacity. Perfect your technique through educational resources, expansion of your scope of interests and regular re-evaluation and, as required, revision of your works. Profit by a wide exposure to the writings of others. Submit works systematically and persistently, keeping accurate records so you know what went where and when. Take to heart responses and suggestions and plan your follow-up accordingly."

◎ DARGONZINE

E-mail: dargon@dargonzine.org. Web site: dargonzine.org. **Contact:** Ornoth D.A. Liscomb, editor. Electronic zine specializing in fantasy. *"DargonZine* is an electronic magazine that prints original fantasy fiction by aspiring Internet writers. The Dargon Project is a collaborative anthology whose goal is to provide a way for aspiring fantasy writers on the Internet to meet and become better writers through mutual contact and collaboration as well as contact with a live readership via the Internet."

Needs Fantasy. "Our goal is to write fantasy fiction that is mature, emotionally compelling and professional. Membership in the Dargon Project is a requirement for publication." **Publishes 4-12 new writers/year.**

How to Contact Guidelines available on Web site. Sample copy online. Writer's guidelines online.

Payment/Terms "As a strictly noncommercial magazine, our writers' only compensation is their growth and membership in a lively writing community. Authors retain all rights to their stories."

Advice "The Readers and Writers FAQs on our Web site provide much more detailed information about our mission, writing philosophy and the value of writing for *DargonZine.*"

$☑ DEATHLINGS.COM, Dark Fiction for the Discerning Reader

130 E. Willamette Ave., Colorado Springs CO 80903-1112. E-mail: cvgelvin@aol.com. Web site: www.deathlings .com. **Contact:** CV Gelvin, editor. E-zine specializing in dark fiction. "Our wonderfully quirky themes for the short story contests have included "Frozen Smiles" (dolls), "Burbian Horrors," "Technology Run Amuck" and "Love Gone Bad." Quarterly. Estab. 2000.

Needs Horror (futuristic, psychological, supernatural). "No children's, fantasy, poetry or romance." List of upcoming themes available on Web site. Receives 20-30 unsolicited mss/month. Accepts 3-4 mss/issue. Publishes ms 1-2 months after acceptance. **Publishes 3-6 new writers/year.** Recently published work by David Ballard, Fiona Curnow, Denise Dumars, Jason Franks, dgk Golberg, Darren O. Godfrey and CV Gelvin. Length: 4,000 words; average length: 3,000 words. Publishes short shorts. Sometimes comments on rejected mss.

How to Contact E-mail story attached in RTF. Include estimated word count, brief bio and list of publications with submission. Responds in 1-3 months to mss. Accepts simultaneous, multiple submissions and reprints. Guidelines free by e-mail or on Web site.

Payment/Terms Pays 3¢/word. Pays on publication for electronic rights. Sponsors awards/contests.

◪ DIAGRAM, A Magazine of Art, Text, and Schematic

New Michigan Press, 648 Crescent NE, Grand Rapids MI 49503. E-mail: prose@thediagram.com. Web site: http:// thediagram.com. **Contact:** Ander Monson, editor. "We specialize in work that pushes the boundaries of traditional genre or work that is in some way schematic. We do publish traditional fiction and poetry, too, but hybrid forms (short stories, prose poems, indexes, tables of contents, etc.) are welcome! We also publish diagrams and schematics (original and found). Bimonthly. Estab. 2001. Circ. 150,000 hits/month. Member CLMP.

Needs Experimental, literary. "We don't publish genre fiction, unless it's exceptional and transcends the genre boundaries." Receives 100 unsolicited mss/month. Accepts 2-3 mss/issue; 15 mss/year. **Publishes 15 new writers/year.** Average length: 250-1,000 words. Publishes short shorts. Also publishes literary essays, poetry. Often comments on rejected mss.

How to Contact Send complete ms. Accepts submissions by e-mail. Send SASE (or IRC) for return of the ms, or send disposable copy of the ms and #10 SASE for reply only. Responds in 2 weeks to queries; 1 month to mss. Accepts simultaneous submissions. Sample copy for $12 for print version. Writer's guidelines online.

Payment/Terms Acquires first, electronic rights.

Advice "We value invention, energy, experimentation and voice. When done very well, we like traditional fiction, too. Nearly all the work we select is propulsive and exciting."

⊕ ◪ DOTLIT, The Online Journal of Creative Writing

Creating Writing & Cultural Studies, Queensland University of Technology, Victoria Park Rd., Kelvin Grove Q 4059 Australia. E-mail: dotlitsubmissions@qut.edu.au. Web site: www.dotlit.qut.edu.au. Semiannual. Estab. 2000. "*dotlit* publishes a selection of the best new and innovative fiction, creative nonfiction and hypertexts, including commissioned pieces by established authors and new works by emerging writers. The journal's emphasis is on quality stories well told. Although it is by no means a prescriptive requirement, stories that innovate in terms of voice, structure or other literary convention will be highly regarded."

Needs Children's/juvenile (10 and above), experimental, literary, young adult/teen. Receives 400 unsolicited mss/month. Accepts 12-20 mss/issue; 24-40 mss/year. Publishes ms 6-12 months after acceptance. Recently published work by Ian McNeil, Olga Pavlinova and Lee Gutkind. Publishes short shorts. Also publishes literary essays, literary criticism, poetry.

How to Contact Send complete ms (double-spaced in MS Word), 50-100 word biography of the author, including a relevant e-mail address. Length: 4,000 words (max). Accepts submissions only by e-mail. Responds in 10 weeks to mss. Submissions must be unpublished. Writer's guidelines online.

Payment/Terms Acquires electronic rights.

N $ ◨ DRAGONS, KNIGHTS & ANGELS, The Magazine of Christian Fantasy and Science Fiction
Double-Edged Publishing, 9618 Misty Brook Cove, Cordova TN 38016. (901)213-3768. Fax: (901)213-3878. E-mail: editor@dkamagazine.com. Web site: www.dkamagazine.com. **Contact:** Johne Cook, managing editor. Online magazine. Contains illustrations and photographs. "Stories submitted to *DKA* for publication will be examined first on their merit as works of sci-fi/fantasy/poetry. A good short story needs a beginning, middle and end. A good story is all about conflict. All the classic tools are in evidence—foreshadowing, resonance, economy of words, and a poetic bent. Stories submitted to *DKA* are also viewed as to how well they entertain, uplift and enlighten. *DKA* is looking for smart, daring stories that keep the balance between Providence and Sci-fi/fantasy. Ask God what it is that He wants to get across to the public through fiction, and use your feelings and your intellect to deliver that in your writing." Estab. 1999. Circ. 2,000.
Needs Fantasy (space fantasy, sword and sorcery), religious, science fiction (hard science/technological, soft/sociological), young adult/teen (adventure, fantasy/science fiction, horror, mystery/suspense, romance). Does not want lesbian, gay, erotica. Promotion of values and principles not compatible with Christianity will not be published. Receives 20-30 mss/month. Accepts 4-6 mss/issue; 48-60 mss/year. Manuscript published 2-6 weeks after acceptance. **Publishes 6 new writers/year.** Published Catherine Knutsson, Robert Barlow, David Cassel, Melissa Pinol, Kevin Beuckert, Amy M. Smith and Lori Z. Scott. Average length: 3,500 words. Publishes short shorts. Average length of short shorts: 1,100 words. Also publishes poetry. Always comments on/critiques rejected mss.
How to Contact Submit via Web site through online submission system. Responds to queries in 1 week. Responds to mss in 6 weeks. Considers previously published submissions, multiple submissions. Guidelines available on Web site.
Payment and Terms Writers receive $5 flate-rate payment. Pays on acceptance.
Advice "The first step is to understand the submission guidelines. Read them, and then read published stories. After getting a sense of the publication, you will have a sense of 'goodness of fit' between it and your story. Writing stories with a moral core is a tricky line. We are not at all interested in stories that preach. Stories submitted to *DKA* for publication will be examined first on their merit as works of sci-fi/fantasy/poetry. Writing is a privilege and an honor, and it is as much art as craft. As God is the Great Creator, we expect great stories as He fills your cup to overflowing. To that end, we will be challenging you as writers."

◨ DUCTS
P.O. Box 3203, Grand Central Station, New York NY 10163. (718)383-6728. E-mail: editor@ducts.org. Web site: http://ducts.org. **Contact:** Jonathan Kravetz. *DUCTS* is a Web zine of personal stories, fiction, essays, memoirs, poetry, humor, profiles, reviews and art. "*DUCTS* was founded in 1999 with the intent of giving emerging writers a venue to regularly publish their compelling, personal stories. The site has been expanded to include art and creative works of all genres. We believe that these genres must and do overlap. *DUCTS* publishes the best, most compelling stories and we hope to attract readers who are drawn to work that rises above." Semiannual. Estab. 1999. Circ. 12,000. Member CLMP.
Needs Ethnic/multicultural, humor/satire, literary, mainstream. "Please do not send us genre work, unless it is extraordinarily unique." Receives 50 unsolicited mss/month. Accepts 40 mss/issue; 80 mss/year. Publishes ms 1-6 months after acceptance. **Publishes 10-12 new writers/year.** Recently published work by Charles Salzberg, Mark Goldblatt, Richard Kostelanz, Helen Zelon. Publishes short shorts. Also publishes literary essays, literary criticism, poetry. Sometimes comments on rejected mss.
How to Contact Send complete ms. Accepts submissions by e-mail to appropriate departments. Responds in 1-4 weeks to queries; 1-6 months to mss. Accepts simultaneous submissions and reprints. Writer's guidelines on ducts.org.
Payment/Terms Acquires one-time rights.
Advice "We prefer writing that tells a compelling story with a strong narrative drive."

◨ ▩ FAILBETTER.COM
Failbetter, 3222 Hanover Avenue, Richmond, VA 23221. E-mail: submissions@failbetter.com. Web site: www.failbetter.com. **Contact:** Thom Didato, editor. "We are a quarterly online magazine published in the spirit of a traditional literary journal—dedicated to publishing quality fiction, poetry and artwork. While the Web plays host to hundreds, if not thousands, of genre-related sites (many of which have merit), we are not one of them." Quarterly. Estab. 2000. Circ. 35,000. Member Council of Literary Magazines and Presses.
Needs Literary, novel excerpts. "No genre fiction—romance, fantasy or science fiction." Always would like to see more "character-driven literary fiction where something happens!" Receives 50-75 unsolicited mss/month. Accepts 3-5 mss/issue; 12-20 mss/year. Publishes ms 4-8 months after acceptance. **Publishes 4-6 new writers/year.** Recently published work by Susan Daitch, Geoffrey Becker, Frances Sherwook, Don Lee. Publishes short shorts. Often comments on rejected mss.
How to Contact Accepts submissions by e-mail. Include the word "submission" in the subject line. Responds

in 8-12 weeks to queries; 4-6 month to mss. Accepts simultaneous submissions. Sample copy online. Writer's guidelines online.

Payment/Terms Acquires one-time rights.

Advice "Read an issue. Read our guidelines! We place a high degree of importance on originality, believing that even in this age of trends, it is still possible. We are not looking for what is current or momentary. We are not concerned with length: One good sentence may find a home here, as the bulk of mediocrity will not. Most importantly, know that what you are saying could only come from you. When you are sure of this, please feel free to submit."

THE FAIRFIELD REVIEW

544 Silver Spring Rd., Fairfield CT 06824. (203)256-1960. Fax: (203)256-1970. E-mail: fairfieldreview@hpmd.com. Web site: www.fairfieldreview.org. **Contact:** Edward and Janet Granger-Happ, Pamela Pollak, editors. Electronic magazine. "Our mission is to provide an outlet for poetry, short stories and essays, from both new and established writers and students. We are accessible to the general public."

Needs Literary. "Would like to see more stories rich in lyrical imagery and those that are more humorous." **Publishes 20 new writers/year.** Recently published work by Nan Leslie (Pushcart nominee) and Richard Boughton.

How to Contact Strongly prefers submissions by e-mail. Replies by e-mail only. Sample copy online.

Payment/Terms Acquires first rights. Right to retain publication in online archive issues, and the right to use in "Best of The Fairfield Review" anthologies.

Advice "We encourage students and first-time writers to submit their work. In addition to the submission guidelines found in each issue on our Web site, we recommend reading the essay 'Writing Qualities to Keep in Mind' from our Editors and Authors page on the Web site. Keep to small, directly experienced themes; write crisply using creative, poetic images, avoid the trite expression."

$ FAR SECTOR SFFH

(formerly Deep Outside SFFH), PMB 600973, Grantville Station, Mission Gorge, San Diego CA 92120. Web site: www.farsector.com. **Contact:** John Cullen, editor. Web-only magazine. "We are a paying, professional magazine for science fiction and dark imaginative fiction, aimed at people who love to read well-plotted and character-driven fiction." Monthly. Estab. 1998. Circ. 5,000+.

Needs Science fiction (hard science/technological, soft/sociological) and horror (dark fantasy, futuristic, psychological). "No porn, excessive gore or vulgarity unless it directly furthers the story (sparingly, at that)." No sword and sorcery, elves, high fantasy, cookie-cutter space opera. Receives 100-150 unsolicited mss/month. Accepts 1 mss/issue; 12 mss/year. Publishes ms 3 months after acceptance. **Publishes 1-6 new writers/year.** Recently published work by Pat York, Melanie Tem, Paul Martens and Dennis Latham.

How to Contact Send complete ms. Accepts submissions by e-mail only. (No snail mail.) Responds in 3 months to mss. Writer's guidelines online.

Payment/Terms Pay rate online. Pays within 90 days of acceptance. Acquires first, electronic rights.

Advice "We look for the best quality story. Genre comes second. We look for publishable, first-rate, professional fiction. It is most important to grab us from the first three paragraphs—not only as a common standard but because that's how we lead with the main page of the magazine. Please read the tips and guidelines at the magazine's Web site for up-to-the-moment details. Do not send envelopes asking for guidelines, please. All the info is online at our Web site."

5-TROPE

E-mail: editor.5trope@gmail.com. Web site: www.webdelsol.com/5_trope. **Contact:** Gunnar Benediktsson, editor. Online literary journal. "We aim to publish the new and original in fiction, poetry and new media. We are seeking writers with a playful seriousness about language and form." Quarterly. Estab. 1999. Circ. 5,000.

Needs Comics/graphic novels, experimental, literary. "No religious, horror, fantasy, espionage." Receives 50 unsolicited mss/month. Accepts 6 mss/issue; 30 mss/year. Publishes ms 1-6 months after acceptance. **Publishes 5 new writers/year.** Recently published work by Cole Swensen, Christopher Kennedy, Mike Topp, Norman Lock, Jeff Johnson, Peter Markus, Mandee Wright, Jane Unrue. Length: 25-5,000 words; average length: 1,000 words. Publishes short shorts. Also publishes poetry. Sometimes comments on rejected mss.

How to Contact Accepts submissions by e-mail. Send complete mss electronically. Sample copy online.

Payment/Terms Acquires first rights. Sends galleys to author.

Advice "Before submitting, please visit our site, read an issue, and consult our guidelines for submission. Include your story within the body of an e-mail, not as an attachment."

$ FLASHQUAKE, An Online Journal of Flash Literature

River Road Studios, P.O. Box 2154, Albany NY 12220-0154. E-mail: dorton@flashquake.org. Web site: www.flashquake.org. **Contact:** Debi Orton, publisher. E-zine specializing in flash literature. "*flashquake* is a quarterly online literary journal featuring flash literature—flash fiction, flash nonfiction and short poetry. Send us works that will leave readers thinking. We define flash as works less than 1,000 words, shorter pieces will impress us. Poetry can be up to 35 lines. We want the best story you can tell us in the fewest words you need to do it! Move us, engage us, give us a complete story with characters, plot and a beginning, middle and end."

Needs Ethnic/multicultural (general), experimental, literary, flash literature of all types: fiction, memoir, creative nonfiction, poetry and artwork. "Not interested in romance, graphic sex, graphic violence, gore, vampires or work of a religious nature." Receives 100-150 unsolicited mss/month. Accepts 30 mss/issue. Publishes ms 1-3 months after acceptance. Publishes only short shorts. Comments on rejected mss.

How to Contact Accepts submissions by e-mail (submit@flashquake.org) only. No land mail. Include brief bio, mailing address and e-mail address. Guidelines and submission instructions on Web site.

Payment/Terms Pays $5-25 plus CD copy of site. Pays within two weeks of publication for electronic rights. Sponsors occasional awards/contests.

Advice "Read our submission guidelines before submitting. Proofread your work thoroughly! We will instantly reject your work for spelling and grammar errors. Save your document as plain text and paste it into an e-mail message. We do not open attachments. We like experimental work, but that is not a license to forget narrative clarity, plot, character development or reader satisfaction."

✓ FLUENT ASCENSION

Fierce Concepts, P.O. Box 6407, Glendale AZ 85312. E-mail: submissions@fluentascension.com. Web site: www.fluentascension.com. **Contact:** Warren Norgaard, editor. Online magazine. Quarterly. Estab. 2003.

Needs Comics/graphic novels, erotica, ethnic/multicultural, experimental, gay, humor/satire, lesbian, literary, translations. Receives 6-10 unsolicited mss/month. Accepts 1-3 mss/issue. Publishes short shorts. Also publishes literary essays, literary criticism, poetry. Sometimes comments on rejected mss.

How to Contact Send complete ms. Accepts submissions by e-mail. Include estimated word count, brief bio and list of publications. Send SASE (or IRC) for return of ms or send disposable copy of ms and #10 SASE for reply only. Responds in 4-8 weeks to queries; 4-8 weeks to mss. Accepts simultaneous, multiple submissions. Sample copy online. Writer's guidelines online.

Payment/Terms Acquires electronic rights. Sponsors awards/contests.

◻ THE FURNACE REVIEW

E-mail: editor@thefurnacereview.com. Web site: www.furnacereview.com. **Contact:** Ciara LaVelle, editor. "We reach out to a young, well-educated audience, bringing them new, unique, fresh work they won't find elsewhere." Quarterly. Estab. 2004.

Needs Erotica, experimental, feminist, gay, historical, humor/satire, lesbian, literary, mainstream, military/war. Does not want children's, science fiction or religious submissions. Receives 50-60 unsolicited mss/month. Accepts 3-4 mss/issue; 9-12 mss/year. **Publishes 5 new writers/year.** Recently published work by Amy Greene, Dominic Preziosi, Sandra Soson. Length: 7,000 words; average length: 4,000 words. Publishes short shorts. Also publishes poetry.

How to Contact Send complete ms. Accepts submissions by e-mail. Responds in 1 month to queries; 4 months to mss. Accepts simultaneous submissions.

Payment/Terms Acquires first North American serial rights.

✓ ◎ GATEWAY S-F MAGAZINE, Stories of Science and Faith

GateWay Publishing House, B. Joseph Fekete, Jr, 12141 Medocino Place, Chino CA 90006. (909)591-1481. E-mail: gateway59@hotmail.com. Web site: www.geocities.com/scifieditor/index.html. **Contact:** John A.M. Darnell, editor; johnamdarnell@gmail.com. Christian SF E-Zine. "We are a e-zine, specializing in hard science fiction plots with Christian themes." Released every 3 months. Estab. 2000. Web hits: 1,000 per month.

Needs Science fiction (futuristic, time travel, hard science, technological, soft/sociological, Christian), young adult/teen (science fiction). No fantasy, horror or romance. No experimental forms such as local dialects. Receives 20-30 unsolicited mss/month. Accepts 10-20 mss/issue; 80 mss/year. Publishes ms 6 months after acceptance. **Publishes 40 new writers/year.** Length: 500-7,500 words; average length: 2,500 words. Publishes short shorts. Sometimes comments on rejected mss.

How to Contact Send complete ms. Accepts submissions by e-mail only (johnamdarnell@gmail.com or kawilkes @gmail.com). "We prefer electronic submissions via e-mail or accompanied by disk if snail mail." Include estimated word count, brief bio, postal address, e-mail address and phone number. No longer accepts reprint submissions.

Payment/Terms Supplies author a CD contributor copy for all stories.

Advice "We look for good, solid writing with hard SF plots and Christian themes having no typos or weak grammar, a good hook, rapid advance of plot, no experimental forms. The story must establish within the first few pages that it is both Science Fiction and Christian. Visit us online for a sense of what we publish."

✍ ◎ THE GLUT, Online journal of prose and praise of gluttony

P.O. Box 362, Walnut Creek CA 94597. E-mail: calvin@theglut.com. Web site: www.theglut.com. **Contact:** Calvin Liu, editor. *"The Glut* seeks all forms of prose, with a slight bias toward things related to food or gluttony—eating, overeating, cooking, overcooking, digesting, indigesting and so on. Irreverence is key. Also, please do not be fooled by our apparent meat-centrism; we like vegetables, too. Except peas. We hate peas." Bimonthly. Estab. 2003.

Needs Experimental, humor/satire, literary. Receives 30-40 unsolicited mss/month. Accepts 4-5 mss/issue. Publishes ms 1-2 months after acceptance. Recently published work by Blake Butler, Magdalen Powers, Avital Gad-Cykman, Jensen Whelan, Liz Tascio, Elizabeth Glixman. Length: 1,500 words; average length: 750 words. Publishes short shorts. Often comments on rejected mss.

How to Contact Send complete ms. Responds in 2 weeks to queries; 1 month to mss. Accepts simultaneous submissions. Writer's guidelines online.

Payment/Terms Acquires one-time rights.

Advice "Make us laugh, even if it's nervous laughter from our inability to comprehend."

✍ ◎ KENNESAW REVIEW

Kennesaw State University, Dept. of English, Building 27, 1000 Chastain Rd., Kennesaw GA 30144-5591. (770)423-6346. Web site: www.kennesawreview.org. **Contact:** Robert W. Hill, editor. Online literary journal. "Just good literary fiction, all themes, for a eclectic audience." Biannual. Estab. 1987.

Needs Short stories and flash fiction. "No formulaic genre fiction." Receives 25 unsolicited mss/month. Accepts 2-4 mss/issue. Publishes ms 12-18 months after acceptance. Recently published work by Jon Hansen, Donna Vitucci, Joan Frank, Luke Whisnant.

How to Contact Send complete ms. Include previous publications. Responds in 2 months to mss. Accepts simultaneous, multiple submissions. Writer's guidelines online.

Payment/Terms Acquires first rights.

Advice "Use the language well and tell an interesting story."

$ ⊕ ✍ LONE STAR STORIES, Speculative Fiction and Poetry

E-mail: submissions@erictmarin.com. Web site: www.lonestarstories.com. **Contact:** Eric T. Marin, editor. On-line magazine. Contains illustrations and photographs. "Lone Star Stories publishes quality speculative fiction and poetry that has not found a home elsewhere." Bimonthly. Estab. 2004.

Needs Speculative fiction (fantasy, dark fantasy, science fiction, interstitial). Receives 100+ mss/month. Accepts 3 mss/issue; 18 mss/year. Manuscript published 2 months after acceptance. Average length: 5,000 words. Publishes short shorts. Average length of short shorts: 500 words. Also publishes poetry.

How to Contact Send complete ms with cover letter. Accepts submissions by e-mail. Include estimated word count. Responds to queries in 1 week. Responds to mss in 1 week. Considers simultaneous submissions, previously published submissions. Guidelines available on Web site.

Payment and Terms Writers receive $20 per story; $5 per poem. Pays on acceptance. Publication is copyrighted.

Advice "The standard advice applies: read the current issue of Lone Star Stories to get a feel for what is likely to be published."

◎ 🏵 MARGIN, Exploring Modern Magical Realism

321 High School Road, N.E., PMB #204, Bainbridge Island WA 98110. E-mail: magicalrealismmaven@yahoo.com. Web site: www.magical-realism.com. **Contact:** Tamara Kaye Sellman, editor. Electronic anthology special-izing in literary magical realism. *"Margin* seeks, in a variety of ways, to answer the question 'what is magical realism?'" Estab. 2000. Circ. 30,000.

- *Margin* has received the Arete "Wave of a Site" award and the Point of Life Gold Award of Excellence. Member CLMP since 2001. Nominates for *Pushcart*.

Needs Translations, magic realism. "No magical realist knockoffs, no stock fantasy with elves or angels. Nothing gratuitous. If you are unsure what magical realism is, visit the Web site and look at our discussion of criteria before sending. Interested in academic writing; query first." Receives 100 unsolicited mss/month. Publishes ms 6 months after acceptance. Recently published work by Gayle Brandeis, Virgil Suárez, Brian Evenson. Also publishes literary essays, literary criticism. Sometimes comments on rejected mss.

How to Contact Send complete ms. Accepts submissions by e-mail. No attachments or surface mail. Please enclose SASE for return of mss or e-mail address for reply. Sample copy online. Writer's guidelines for SASE or online. Reviews fiction.

Payment/Terms Pay negotiable.

Advice "Technical strength, unique, engaging style, well-developed and inventive story. Surprise us by avoiding what has already been done. Manuscript must be magical realism. Do not send more than one submission at a time. You will not get a fair reading if you do. Always enclose SASE. Do not inquire before 3 months. Send us your A-list, no works in progress.''

TIMOTHY MCSWEENEY'S INTERNET TENDENCY

826 Valencia Street, San Francisco CA 94110. E-mail: websubmissions@mcsweeneys.net. Web site: www.mcsw eeneys.net. **Contact:** Dave Eggers, John Warner, editors. Online literary journal. *"Timothy McSweeney's Internet Tendency* is an offshoot of *Timothy McSweeney's Quarterly Concern*, a journal created by nervous people in relative obscurity, and published four times a year.'' Daily.

Needs Literate humor, sestinas. Sometimes comments on rejected mss.

How to Contact Accepts submissions by e-mail. ''For submissions to the Web site, paste the entire piece into the body of an e-mail. Absolute length limit of 1,500 words, with a preference for pieces significantly shorter (700-1,000 words).'' Sample copy online. Writer's guidelines online.

Advice ''Do not submit your work to both the print submissions address and the Web submissions address, as seemingly hundreds of writers have been doing lately. If you submit a piece of writing intended for the magazine to the Web submissions address, you will confuse us, and if you confuse us, we will accidentally delete your work without reading it, and then we will laugh and never give it another moment's thought, and sleep the carefree sleep of young children. This is very, very serious.''

☐ MIDNIGHT TIMES

1731 Shadwell Dr., Barnhart MO 63012. E-mail: editor@midnighttimes.com. Web site: www.midnighttimes.c om. **Contact:** Jay Manning, editor. The intention of this online publication is to provide a forum for new writers to get exposure. The primary theme is darkness, but this doesn't necessarily mean evil. There can be a light at the end of the tunnel. Quarterly. Estab. 2003.

Needs Fantasy (sword and sorcery), horror (dark fantasy, futuristic, psychological, supernatural), literary, mainstream, psychic/supernatural/occult, science fiction, vampires. No pornography. Accepts 3-6 mss/issue; 12-24 mss/year. Publishes ms 3-9 months after acceptance. **Publishes many new writers/year.** Length: 500-10,000 words; average length: 4,000 words. Publishes short shorts. Also publishes poetry. Sometimes comments on rejected mss.

How to Contact Send complete ms. Accepts submissions by e-mail. Send SASE (or IRC) for return of the ms, or send disposable copy of the ms and #10 SASE for reply only. Responds in 2 weeks to queries; 1 month to mss. Accepts simultaneous submissions and reprints. Writer's guidelines for SASE or by e-mail or on Web site.

Payment/Terms No payment. Acquires one-time, electronic rights.

Advice ''A good vampire story does not have to be a 'horror' story. Eternal darkness is a universal theme that transcends all genres.''

Ⓝ ☑ NEW WORKS REVIEW

P.O. Box 54, Friendswood TX 77549-0054. (281)482-7300. Fax: (281)482-7300. E-mail: timhealy@hal-pc.org. Web site: www.new-works.org. **Contact:** Tim Healy, editor-in-chief. Online magazine. Contains illustrations and photographs. ''Our philosphy is to publish outstanding work suitable for all readers. All genres are published.'' Quarterly. Estab. 1998.

Needs Adventure, family saga, humor/satire, literary, mainstream, military/war, mystery/suspense (amateur sleuth, cozy, police procedural, private eye/hard-boiled), thriller/espionage, translations, western. Does not want porn, anit-religious, erotica or use of obscenities. Receives 30 mss/month. Accepts 10 mss/issue; 40 mss/year. Manuscript published 3 months after acceptance. **Publishes 5-10 new writers/year.** Published Irving Greenfield, Lynn Strongin, Tom Sheehan, Michael Corrigan, Brett Alan Sanders and Diane Sawyer. Average length: 3,000 words. Also publishes literary essays, literary criticism, poetry, book reviews. Often comments on/critiques rejected mss.

How to Contact Send complete ms with cover letter. Accepts submissions by e-mail, on disk. Include estimated word count. Responds to queries in 1 week. Considers simultaneous submissions, previously published submissions, multiple submissions. Guidelines available on Web site.

Payment and Terms Rights retained by author. Sends galleys to author. Publication is copyrighted.

Advice ''Read established writers, edit and re-edit your stories, follow the guidelines.''

$ ☑ ◎ NOCTURNAL OOZE, an Online Horror Magazine

Froggy Bottom Press, P.O. Box 495, Beaver PA 15009-0495. E-mail: submit@nocturnalooze.com. Web site: www.nocturnalooze.com. **Contact:** Katherine Patterson, Marty Hiller; senior editors. ''*Nocturnal Ooze* blends sight and sound in a themed enviroment, to create an atmosphere of the macabre which enhances the reading experience of visitors to our site. We seek to promote dark fiction, tales that make our spines tingle.'' Monthly. Estab. 2003. Circ. 650+. Member HWA.

Needs Horror (dark fantasy, psychological, supernatural), psychic/supernatural/occult. ''No silly or humorous horror. No excessive blood and gore just for mere shock value. No child abuse or baby mutilation stories." Receives 40-80 unsolicited mss/month. Accepts 10-12 mss/issue; 72 mss/year. Publishes ms 1-2 months after acceptance. **Publishes 10% new writers/year.** Recently published work by Mark Allan Gunnells, David Debeer, David McGillvera, Yolanda Sfetsos, Lawrence Barker. Length: 750-3,500 words; average length: 1,250 words. Also publishes poetry. Always comments on rejected mss.

How to Contact Send complete ms. Accepts submissions by e-mail. Responds in 2 months to mss. Accepts multiple submissions. Writer's guidelines online.

Payment/Terms Pays $5-17.50. Pays on publication for first, electronic rights.

Advice "We look for a story that grabs us at the start and draws us into the darkness of the unknown. Stories that put us on the brink of peril then either save us in the end or shove us into the abyss."

NUVEIN ONLINE

(626)401-3466. Fax: (626)401-3460. E-mail: editor@nuvein.com. Web site: www.nuvein.com. **Contact:** Ahn Lottman, editor; Enrique Diaz, publisher. Electronic Zine. "We are open to short works that explore topics divergent from the mainstream. Our vision is to provide a forum for new and experienced voices rarely heard in our global community."

• Nuvein Online has received the Visionary Media Award.

Needs Fiction, poetry, plays and art. Wants more "experimental fiction, ethnic works and pieces dealing with the exploration of sexuality." **Publishes 20 new writers/year.** Recently published work by J. Knight, Paul A. Toth, Rick Austin, Robert Levin and Scott Essman.

How to Contact Query. Accepts submissions by e-mail. Send work as attachment. Sample copy online.

Advice "Read over each submission before sending it, and if you, as the writer, find the piece irresistable, e-mail it to us immediately!"

OPIUM MAGAZINE

Literary Humor for the Deliriously Captivated, 40 E. 3rd St., Suite 8, New York NY 10003-9213. (347)229-2443. E-mail: todd@opiummagazine.com. Web site: www.opiummagazine.com. **Contact:** Todd Zuniga, editor-in-chief. Online magazine. Contains illustrations and photographs. "OpiumMagazine.com displays an eclectic mix of stories, poetry, reviews, cartoons, interviews and much more. It features 'estimated reading times' that precede each piece. It is updated daily. While the focus is often humorous literature, we love to publish heart-breaking, serious work. Our rule is that all work must be well written and engaging. While we publish traditional pieces, we're primarily engaged by writers who take risks." Updated daily. Estab. 2001. Circ. 25,000 hits/month. Member CLMP.

Needs Comics/graphic novels, experimental, humor/satire, literary, mainstream. "Vignettes and first-person 'look at what a whacky time I had going to Spain' stories aren't going to get past first base with us." Receives 400 mss/month. Accepts 275 mss/year. Manuscript published 4 months after acceptance. Agented fiction 10%. **Publishes 50-75 new writers/year.** Published Darby Larson, John Leary, Grant Bailie, Angela Lovell, Tao Lin. Length: 50-1,200 words. Average length: 700 words. Publishes short shorts. Average length of short shorts: 400 words. Also publishes literary essays, literary criticism, poetry. Sometimes comments on/critiques rejected mss.

How to Contact Send complete ms with cover letter. Accepts submissions by e-mail. Include estimated word count, brief bio, list of publications, and your favorite book. Responds to queries in 1 week. Responds to mss in 2 weeks. Considers simultaneous submissions. Guidelines available via e-mail or on Web site.

Payment and Terms Acquires first North American serial rights. Publication is copyrighted.

Advice "We love sparkling, surprising, well-penned, brilliant stories. If you don't strike out in that first paragraph to expose something definitive or new, then you better by the second. We get scores of stories, and like the readers we want to attract, we demand to be engaged immediately. Every publication will say the same thing: read the magazine, read the site. And we, too, encourage that (obviously). But if you're short on time, send us your absolute best story. Tell us it's your first time, we'll be gentle, and our editors usually give thoughts and encouragement if a piece has promise, even if we reject it."

THE ORACULAR TREE, A Transformational E-Zine

The Oracular Tree, 208-167 Morgan Ave., Kitchener ON N2A 2M4 Canada. E-mail: editor@oraculartree.com. Web site: www.oraculartree.com. **Contact:** Teresa Hawkes, publisher. E-zine specializing in practical ideas for transforming our lives. "The stories we tell ourselves and each other predict the outcome of our lives. We can affect gradual social change by transforming our deeply rooted cultural stories. The genre is not as important as the message and the high quality of the writing. We accept stories, poems, articles and essays which will reach well-educated, open-minded readers around the world. We offer a forum for those who see a need for change, who want to add their voices to a growing search for positive alternatives." Weekly. Estab. 1977. Circ. 75,000 hits/month.

Needs Serial fiction, poetry, essays, novels and novel excerpts, visual art, short fiction, news. "We'll look at any genre that is well written and can examine a new cultural paradigm. No tired dogma, no greeting card poetry, please.'' Receives 20-30 unsolicited mss/month. Accepts 80-100 mss/year. Publishes ms 3 months after acceptance. **Publishes 20-30 new writers/year.** Recently published work by Elisha Porat, Lyn Lyfshin, Rattan Mann, Dr. Elaine Hatfield. Publishes short shorts. Also publishes literary essays, poetry. Often comments on rejected mss.

How to Contact Send complete ms. Accepts submissions by e-mail. Responds in 2 weeks to queries; 2 months to mss. Accepts simultaneous, multiple submissions and reprints. Sample copy online. Writer's guidelines online.

Payment/Terms Author retains copyright; one-time archive posting.

Advice ''The underlying idea must be clearly expressed. The language should be appropriate to the tale, using creative license and an awareness of rhythm. We look for a juxtaposition of ideas that creates resonance in the mind and heart of the reader. Write from your honest voice. Trust your writing to unfold.''

OUTER ART, the worst possible art in world
The University of New Mexico, 200 College Road, Gallup NM 87301. (505)863-7647. Fax: (505)863-7532. E-mail: smarand@unm.edu. Web site: www.gallup.unm.edu/~smarandache/a/outer-art.htm. **Contact:** Florentin Smarandache, editor. E-zine. Annual. Estab. 2000.

Needs Experimental, literary, outer-art. Publishes ms 1 month after acceptance. Publishes short shorts. Also publishes literary essays, literary criticism.

How to Contact Accepts submissions by e-mail. Send SASE (or IRC) for return of the ms. Responds in 1 month to mss. Accepts simultaneous submissions and reprints. Writer's guidelines online.

OUTSIDER INK
Outsider Media, 201 W. 11th St., New York NY 10014. (646)373-3117. E-mail: editor@outsiderink.com. Web site: www.outsiderink.com. **Contact:** Sean Meriwether, editor. E-zine specializing in alternative fiction, poetry and artwork. ''We are an online quarterly only. Each issue contains an average of six short stories, one poet and one visual artist. A monthly feature spotlights an individual, normally an underpublished writer or poet. *Outsider Ink* has established an international readership by publishing new material with a diverse range of adult themes. We are all outsiders, artist and non-artist alike, but there are those brave enough to share their experiences with the world. Rattle my cage and demand my attention, tell me your story the way you want it to be told. I am looking for the harsh and sometimes ugly truths. Dark humor is especially appealing. We want to see more work by women.'' Quarterly. Estab. 1999. Circ. 50,000.

Needs Literary. ''No mainstream, genre fiction, children's or religious.'' Receives 200 unsolicited mss/month. Accepts 7 mss/issue; 28 mss/year. Publishes ms 3 months after acceptance. **Publishes 15 new writers/year.** Recently published work by Linda Boroff, Greg Wharton, Maryanne Stahl. Average length: 2,000 words. Publishes short shorts. Also publishes poetry. Often comments on rejected mss.

How to Contact Send complete ms. Accepts submissions by e-mail. Responds in 1 week to queries; 3 months to mss. Accepts simultaneous, multiple submissions and reprints. Sample copy online. Writer's guidelines online.

Payment/Terms Acquires electronic rights. Sends galleys to author. Not copyrighted.

Advice ''*Outsider Ink* publishes work that isn't afraid to cover unexplored territory, both emotionally and physically. Though we want work that pushes the envelope, it should maintain a literary foundation. We aren't looking for fiction or poetry that is weird for the sake of being weird, we want prose with a purpose. Please familiarize yourself with the e-zine before submitting. The bulk of submissions are not accepted because they are inappropriate for the venue. We encourage new writers and act as a launching pad to other venues. Trust your own voice when editing your own material. If you think it isn't ready yet, don't submit it—finish it first.''

OXFORD MAGAZINE
Bachelor Hall, Miami University, Oxford OH 45056. (513)529-1279. E-mail: oxmag@muohio.edu. Web site: www.oxfordmagazine.org. **Contact:** Fiction editor. Annual. Estab. 1985. Circ. 1,000.
• *Oxford* has been awarded two Pushcart Prizes.

Needs Wants quality fiction and prose, genre is not an issue but nothing sentimental. Receives 150 unsolicited mss/month. **Publishes some new writers/year.** Recently published work by Stephen Dixon, Andre Dubus and Stuart Dybek. Publishes short shorts. Also publishes poetry.

How to Contact Send complete ms with SASE. Also accepts e-mail submissions (attached as Word.doc files). Include name, address, e-mail address. Responds in 2 months, depending upon time of submissions; mss received after December 31 will be returned. Accepts simultaneous submissions if notified. Sample copy for $7.

Payment/Terms Acquires one-time rights.

Advice ''*Oxford Magazine* accepts fiction, poetry, and essays (this last genre is a catch-all, much like the space under your couch cushions, and includes creative nonfiction, critical work exploring writing, and the like). Appearing once a year, OxMag is a Web-based journal that acquires first North American serial rights, one-time anthology rights and online serial rights. Simultaneous submissions are okay if you would kindly let us know if and when someone beats us to the punch."

⚡ ◻ PAPERPLATES, a magazine for fifty readers

Perkolator Kommunikation, 19 Kenwood Ave., Toronto ON M6C 2R8 Canada. (416)651-2551. E-mail: magazine @paperplates.org. Web site: www.paperplates.org. **Contact:** Bethany Gibson, fiction editor. Electronic magazine. Quarterly. Estab. 1990.

Needs Condensed novels, ethnic/multicultural, feminist, gay, lesbian, literary, mainstream, translations. "No science fiction, fantasy or horror." Receives 12 unsolicited mss/month. Accepts 2-3 mss/issue; 6-9 mss/year. Publishes ms 6-8 months after acceptance. Recently published work by Lyn Fox, David Bezmozgis, Fraser Sutherland and Tim Conley. Length: 1,500-3,500 words; average length: 3,000 words. Publishes short shorts. Also publishes literary essays, literary criticism, poetry.

How to Contact Accepts submissions by e-mail and land mail. Responds in 6 weeks to queries; 6 months to mss. Accepts simultaneous submissions. Sample copy online. Writer's guidelines online.

Payment/Terms Pays 1 contributor's copy. Acquires first North American serial rights.

◻ PBW

513 N. Central Ave., Fairborn OH 45324. (937)878-5184. E-mail: rianca@aol.com. Electronic disk zine; 700 pages, specializing in avant-garde fiction and poetry. "*PBW* is an experimental floppy disk that prints strange and 'unpublishable' in an above-ground-sense writing." Twice per year. Estab. 1988.

How to Contact "Manuscripts are only taken if they are submitted on disk or by e-mail." Send SASE for reply, return of ms. Sample copy not available.

Payment/Terms All rights revert back to author. Not copyrighted.

$◻ 🌀 PERIDOT BOOKS, Tri-Annual Online Magazine of SF, Fantasy & Horror

1225 Liberty Bell Dr., Cherry Hill NJ 08003. (856)354-0786. E-mail: submissions@peridotbooks.com. Web site: www.peridotbooks.com. **Contact:** Ty Drago, editor. Online magazine specializing in science fiction, fantasy and horror. "We are an e-zine by writers for writers. Our articles focus on the art, craft and business of writing. Our links and editorial policy all focus on the needs of fiction authors." Triannual. Estab. 1998.

• Peridot Books won the Page One Award for Literary Contribution.

Needs Fantasy (space fantasy, sword and sorcery, sociological), horror (dark fantasy, futuristic, supernatural), science fiction (hard science/technological, soft/sociological). "No media tie-ins (Star Trek, Star Wars, etc., or space opera, vampires)." Receives 150 unsolicited mss/month. Accepts 8 mss/issue; 24 mss/year. Publishes ms 1-2 months after acceptance. Agented fiction 5%. **Publishes 10 new writers/year.** Length: 1,500-7,500 words; average length: 4,500 words. Also publishes literary essays, literary criticism. Often comments on rejected mss.

How to Contact Send complete ms with a cover letter, electronic only. Include estimated word count, brief bio, list of publications and name and e-mail address in the body of the message. Responds in 8 weeks to mss. Accepts simultaneous, multiple submissions and reprints. Writer's guidelines online.

Payment/Terms Pays $1/2$¢/word. Pays on publication for one-time, electronic rights.

Advice "Give us something original, preferably with a twist. Avoid gratuitous sex or violence. Funny always scores points. Be clever, imaginative, but be able to tell a story with proper mood and characterization. Read the site and get a feel for it before submitting."

THE PINK CHAMELEON

E-mail: dpfreda@juno.com. Web site: http://www.geocities.com/thepinkchameleon/index.html. **Contact:** Mrs. Dorothy Paula Freda, editor/publisher. Family-oriented electronic magazine. Annual. Estab. 2000. Reading period from January to April and September to October.

Needs Adventure, family saga, fantasy, humor/satire, literary, mainstream, mystery/suspense, religious/inspirational, romance, science fiction, thriller/espionage, western, young adult/teen, psychic/supernatural. "No violence for the sake of violence." Receives 50 unsolicited mss/month. Publishes ms within 1 year after acceptance. **Publishes 50% new writers/year.** Recently published work by Deanne F. Purcell, Martin Green, Albert J. Manachino, James W. Collins, Ken Sieben, Glenn D. Hayes, C.T. VanHoose. Length: 500-2,500 words; average length: 2,000 words. Publishes short shorts. Also publishes literary essays, poetry. Sometimes comments on rejected mss.

How to Contact Send complete ms in the body of the e-mail. No attachments. Responds in 1 month to mss. Accepts reprints, multiple submissions. No simultaneous submissions. Sample copy online. Writer's guidelines online.

Payment/Terms "Non-profit. Acquires one-time rights for one year but will return rights earlier on request."
Advice "Simple, honest, evocative emotion, upbeat submissions that give hope for the future; well-paced plots; stories, poetry, articles, essays that speak from the heart. Read guidelines carefully. Use a good, but not ostentatious, opening hook. Stories should have a beginning, middle and end that make the reader feel the story was worth his or her time. This also applies to articles and essays. In the latter two, wrap your comments and conclusions in a neatly packaged final paragraph. Turnoffs include violence, bad language. Simple, genuine and sensitive work does not need to shock with vulgarity to be interesting and enjoyable."

🌐 ◖ PREMONITIONS

Pigasus Press, 13 Hazely Combe, Arreton Isle of Wight PO30 3AJ United Kingdom. Web site: www.pigasuspress. co.uk. **Contact:** Tony Lee, editor. "A magazine of science fiction, horror stories, genre poetry and fantastic artwork." Biannual.
Needs Science fiction (hard, contemporary science fiction/fantasy). "No sword and sorcery, supernatural horror." Accepts 12 mss/issue.
How to Contact "Unsolicited submissions are always welcome, but writers must enclose SAE/IRC for reply, plus adequate postage to return ms if unsuitable. No fiction or poetry submissions accepted via e-mail." Sample copy online.
Advice "Potential contributors are advised to study recent issues of the magazine."

Ⓝ ◖ R-KV-R-Y, A Quarterly Literary Journal

90 Meetings in 90 Days Press, 499 North Canon Dr., Suite 400, Beverly Hills CA 90210. (323)217-5162. Fax: (323)852-1535. E-mail: recovery@ninetymeetingsinninetydays.com. Web site: www.ninetymeetingsinninetyda ys.com. **Contact:** Victoria Pynchon, editor-in-chief. Online magazine. 25 Web pages. Contains illustrations. Includes photographs. "R-KV-R-Y publishes half a dozen short stories of high literary quality every quarter. We publish fiction that varies widely in style. We prefer stories of character development, psychological penetration, and lyricism, without sentimentality or purple prose. We ask that all submissions address issues related to recovery from any type of physical, psychological or cultural loss, dislocation or oppression. We include but do not limit ourselves to issues of substance abuse. We do not publish the standard 'what it was like, what happened and what it is like now' recovery narrative. Works published by R-KV-R-Y embrace almost every area of adult interest related to recovery: literary affairs, history, folklore, fiction, poetry, literary criticism, art, music and the theatre. Material should be presented in a fashion suited to a quarterly that is neither journalistic nor academic. We welcome academic articles from varying fields. We encourage our academic contributors to free themselves from the contraints imposed by academic journals, letting their knowledge, wisdom and experience rock and roll on these pages. Our intended audience is people of discriminating taste, original ideas, heart, and love of narrative and language." Quarterly. Estab. 2004. Circ. 14,000 readers.
Needs Literary. List of upcoming themes available on Web site. Receives 5 mss/month. Accepts 5 mss/issue; 20 mss/year. Manuscript published 2-3 months after acceptance. Agented fiction 0%. **Publishes 5-6 new writers/year.** Published Rita Coleman (debut fiction), Anne LaBorde (debut literary nonfiction), Richard Wirick, Joseph Mockus, Birute Serota, Zoe Kiethley, Lee Patton, Nathan Leslie, Kathleen Wakefield, Sherry Lynne Maze (debut). Length: 5,000 words (max). Average length: 2,000 words. Publishes short shorts. Average length of short shorts: 1,000 words. Also publishes literary essays, book reviews, poetry. Sometimes comments on/ critiques rejected mss.
How to Contact Send complete ms with cover letter. Accepts submissions by e-mail. Include brief bio, list of publications. Responds to queries in 2 weeks. Responds to mss in 1-3 months. Considers simultaneous submissions, previously published submissions. Guidelines available on Web site.
Payment and Terms Acquires electronic rights. Sends galleys to author. Publication is copyrighted.
Advice "Wants strong focus on character development and lively writing style with strong voice. Read our present and former issues (archived online) as well as fiction found in such journals and magazines as *Granta*, *The New Yorker*, *Tri-Quarterly*, *The Atlantic*, *Harper's*, *Story* and similar sources of the highest quality fiction."

◖ REALPOETIK, A Little Magazine of the Internet

840 W. Nickerson #11, Seattle WA 98119. (206)282-3776. E-mail: salasin@scn.org. Web site: www.scn.org/ realpoetik. **Contact:** Fiction Editor. "We publish the new, lively, exciting and unexpected in vernacular English. Any vernacular will do." Weekly. Estab. 1993.
Needs "We do not want to see anything that fits neatly into categories. We subvert categories." Publishes ms 2-4 months after acceptance. **Publishes 20-30 new writers/year.** Average length: 250-500 words. Publishes short shorts. Also publishes literary essays, literary criticism, poetry. Sometimes comments on rejected mss.
How to Contact Query with or without published clips or send complete ms. Accepts submissions by e-mail. Responds in 1 month to queries. Sample copy online.
Payment/Terms Acquires one-time rights. Sponsors awards/contests.

Advice "Be different but interesting. Humor and consciousness are always helpful. Write short. We're a post-modern e-zine."

◘ REFLECTIONS EDGE

E-mail: editor@reflectionsedge.com. Web site: www.reflectionsedge.com. **Contact:** Sharon Dodge, editor-in-chief. "We're an ezine with a small staff; editor, staff writer/assistant, several tech members. Our focus is genre fiction." Estab. 2004.

Needs Adventure, erotica, fantasy, horror, mystery/suspense, psychic/supernatural/occult, science fiction (hard and soft), western, magical realism. Accepts 110 mss/year. Publishes ms 2 months after acceptance.

How to Contact Submit fiction with name, title, genre, length to fictionsubmissions@reflectionsedge.com. Accepts queries by e-mail only. No attachments. Responds in 1 week to queries; 2 months to mss. Accepts simultaneous submissions. Writer's guidelines online.

Payment/Terms Acquires electronic rights.

Advice "We're drawn to great writing first, but great ideas are close behind. We're a 'zine for marginalized fiction—don't send us anything mainstream!"

◘ ▼ THE ROSE & THORN LITERARY E-ZINE, Showcasing Emerging and Established Writers and A Writer's Resource

E-mail: BAQuinn@aol.com. Web site: www.theroseandthornezine.com. **Contact:** Barbara Quinn, fiction editor, publisher, managing editor. E-zine specializing in literary works of fiction, nonfiction, poetry and essays. "We created this publication for readers and writers alike. We provide a forum for emerging and established voices. We blend contemporary writing with traditional prose and poetry in an effort to promote the literary arts." Quarterly. Circ. 12,000.

Needs Adventure, ethnic/multicultural, experimental, fantasy, historical, horror (dark fantasy, futuristic, psychological, supernatural), humor/satire, literary, mainstream, mystery/suspense, New Age, regional, religious/inspirational, romance (contemporary, futuristic/time travel, gothic, historical, regency, romantic suspense), science fiction, thriller/espionage, western. Receives "several hundred" unsolicited mss/month. Accepts 8-10 mss/issue; 40-50 mss/year. **Publishes many new writers/year.** Publishes short shorts. Also publishes literary essays, poetry. Sometimes comments on rejected mss.

How to Contact Query with or without published clips or send complete ms. Accepts submissions by e-mail. Include estimated word count, 150-word bio, list of publications and author's byline. Responds in 1 week to queries; 1 month to mss. Accepts simultaneous submissions and reprints. Sample copy free. Writer's guidelines online. 200 word limit.

Payment/Terms Writer retains all rights. Sends galleys to author.

Advice "Clarity, control of the language, evocative stories that tug at the heart and make their mark on the reader long after it's been read. We look for uniqueness in voice, style and characterization. New twists on old themes are always welcome. Use all aspects of good writing in your stories, including dynamic characters, strong narrative voice and a riveting original plot. We have eclectic tastes, so go ahead and give us a shot. Read the publication and other quality literary journals so you'll see what we look for. Always check your spelling and grammar before submitting. Reread your submission with a critical eye and ask yourself, 'Does it evoke an emotional response? Have I completely captured my reader?' Check your submission for 'it' and 'was' and see if you can come up with a better way to express yourself. Be unique."

◘ RPPS/FULLOSIA PRESS

Rockaway Park Philosophical Society, P.O. Box 280, Ronkonkoma NY 11779. E-mail: deanofrpps@aol.com. Web site: rpps_fullosia_press.tripod.com. **Contact:** J.D. Collins, editor. E-zine. "One-person, part-time. Publishes fiction and nonfiction. Our publication is right wing and conservative, leaning to views of Patrick Buchanan but amenable to the opposition's point of view. We promote an independent America. We are anti-global, anti-UN. Collects unusual news from former British or American provinces. Fiction interests include military, police, private detective, courthouse stories." Monthly. Estab. 1999. Circ. 150.

Needs Historical (American), military/war, mystery/suspense, thriller/espionage. Special issues: Christmas, St. Patrick's Day, Fourth of July. Publishes ms 1 week after acceptance. **Publishes 10 new writers/year.** Recently published work by Laura Stamps, John Grey, Dr. Kelly White, James Davies, Andy Martin, Michael Levy, Peter Vetrano's class. Length: 500-2,000 words; average length: 750 words. Publishes short shorts. Also publishes literary essays. Always comments on rejected mss.

How to Contact Query with or without published clips. Accepts submissions by e-mail. Include brief bio and list of publications. Mail submissions must be on 3¼ floppy disk. Responds in 1 month to mss. Accepts simultaneous submissions, reprints, multiple submissions. Sample copy online. Reviews fiction.

Payment/Terms Acquires electronic rights.

Advice "Make your point quickly. If you haven't done so after five pages, everybody hates you and your characters."

◻ SNREVIEW, Starry Night Review—A Literary E-Zine

197 Fairchild Ave., Fairfield CT 06825-4856. (203)366-5991. E-mail: editor@snreview.org. Web site: www.snrev iew.org. **Contact:** Joseph Conlin, editor. E-zine specializing in literary short stories, essays and poetry. ''We search for material that not only has strong characters and plot but also a devotion to imagery.'' Quarterly. Estab. 1999.

Needs Literary, mainstream. Receives 50 unsolicited mss/month. Accepts 8 mss/issue; 32 mss/year. Publishes ms 6 months after acceptance. **Publishes 25 new writers/year.** Recently published work by Frank X. Walker, Adrian Louis, Barbara Burkhardt, E. Lindsey Balkan, Marie Griffin and Jonathan Lerner. Length: 1,000-7,000 words; average length: 4,000 words. Also publishes literary essays, literary criticism, poetry.

How to Contact Accepts submissions by e-mail only. Include 100 word bio and list of publications. Responds in 3 months to mss. Accepts simultaneous submissions and reprints. Sample copy online. Writer's guidelines online.

Payment/Terms Acquires first rights.

◙ STORY BYTES, Very Short Stories

E-mail: editor@storybytes.com. Web site: www.storybytes.com. **Contact:** M. Stanley Bubien, editor. Electronic zine. ''We are strictly an electronic publication, appearing on the Internet in three forms. First, the stories are sent to an electronic mailing list of readers. They also get placed on our Web site, both in PDF and HTML format.''

Needs ''Stories must be very short—having a length that is the power of 2, specifically: 2, 4, 8, 16, 32, etc.'' No sexually explicit material. ''Would like to see more material dealing with religion—not necessarily 'inspirational' stories, but those that show the struggles of living a life of faith in a realistic manner.'' **Publishes 33 percent new writers/year.** Recently published work by Richard K. Weems, Joseph Lerner, Lisa Cote and Thomas Sennet.

How to Contact Not accepting submissions for most of 2006/2007. Please query first. Query with or without published clips or send complete ms. Accepts submissions by e-mail. ''I prefer plain text with story title, authorship and word count. Only accepts electronic submissions. See Web site for complete guidelines.'' Sample copy online. Writer's guidelines online.

Advice ''In *Story Bytes*, the very short stories themselves range in topic. Many explore a brief event—a vignette of something unusual, unique and at times something even commonplace. Some stories can be bizarre, while others quite lucid. Some are based on actual events, while others are entirely fictional. Try to develop conflict early on (in the first sentence if possible!), and illustrate or resolve this conflict through action rather than description. I believe we'll find an audience for electronic published works primarily in the short story realm.''

◙ STORYSOUTH, The best from New South writers

898 Chelsea Ave., Columbus OH 43209. (614)545-0754. E-mail: storysouth@yahoo.com. Web site: www.storyso uth.com. **Contact:** Jason Sanford, editor. ''*storySouth* is interested in fiction, creative nonfiction and poetry by writers from the New South. The exact definition of *New South* varies from person to person and we leave it up to the writer to define their own connection to the southern United States.'' Quarterly. Estab. 2001.

Needs Experimental, literary, regional (South), translations. Receives 70 unsolicited mss/month. Accepts 5 mss/issue; 20 mss/year. Publishes ms 1 month after acceptance. **Publishes 5-10 new writers/year.** Average length: 4,000 words. Publishes short shorts. Also publishes literary essays, literary criticism, poetry. Often comments on rejected mss.

How to Contact Send complete ms. Accepts submissions by e-mail. Responds in 2 months to mss. Accepts simultaneous, multiple submissions. Writer's guidelines online.

Payment/Terms Acquires one-time rights.

Advice ''What really makes a story stand out is a strong voice and a sense of urgency—a need for the reader to keep reading the story and not put it down until it is finished.''

$◙ THE SUMMERSET REVIEW

25 Summerset Dr., Smithtown NY 11787. E-mail: editor@summersetreview.org. Web site: www.summersetrevi ew.org. **Contact:** Joseph Levens, editor. Online magazine: illustrations and photographs. ''Our goal is simply to publish the highest quality literary fiction and essays intended for a general audience. We love lighter pieces. We love romance and fantasy, as long as it isn't pure genre writing but rather something that might indeed teach us a thing or two. This a simple online literary journal of high quality material, so simple you can call it unique.'' Quarterly. Estab. 2002.

    ● Several editors-in-chief of very prominent literary publications have done interviews for *The Summerset Review*: M.M.M. Hayes of *StoryQuarterly*, Gina Frangello of *Other Voices*, Jennifer Spiegel of *Hayden's Ferry Review*.

Needs Fantasy, humor/satire, literary, romance. No sci-fi, horror or graphic erotica. Receives 50 unsolicited mss/month. Accepts 4 mss/issue; 18 mss/year. Publishes ms 2-3 months after acceptance. **Publishes 5-10 new writers/year.** Length: 8,000 words; average length: 3,000 words. Publishes short shorts. Also publishes literary essays. Usually critiques mss that were almost accepted.

How to Contact Send complete ms. Accepts submissions by e-mail. Responds in 1-2 weeks to queries; 4-12 weeks to mss. Accepts simultaneous submissions and reprints. Writer's guidelines online.

Payment/Terms Pays $25 per story/essay. Acquires no rights other than one-time publishing, although we request credit if first published in *The Summerset Review*. Sends galleys to author.

Advice "Style counts. We prefer innovative or at least very smooth, convincing voices. Even the dullest of premises or the complete lack of conflict make for an interesting story if it is told in the right voice and style. We like to find little, interesting facts and/or connections subtly sprinkled throughout the piece. Harsh language should be used only if/when necessary. If we are choosing between light and dark subjects, the light will usually win."

N $ THE SWORD REVIEW

Double-Edged Publishing, 9618 Misty Brook Cove, Cordova TN 38016. (901)213-3768. Fax: (901)213-3878. E-mail: editor@theswordreview.com. Web site: www.theswordreview.com. **Contact:** Bill Snodgrass, editor. Online magazine. Contains illustrations and photographs. "The purpose of *The Sword Review* is to entertain, uplift and enlighten. It is a publication targeted to adult readers, with consideration to readers aged 14 and up. Although not a teen publication, we acknowledge that the fantasy and science fiction genres attract many readers in that demographic. While not all stories and articles will appeal to all readers, it is our intention to provide content that appeals across a wide range of ages." Estab. 2005. Circ. 3,000 plus.

Needs Adventure, ethnic/multicultural, fantasy (space fantasy, sword and sorcery), historical, horror, literary, mainstream, mystery/suspense, religious (inspirational, fantasy, mystery/suspense, thriller, romance), science fiction (hard science/technological, soft/sociological), thriller/espionage, young adult/teen (fantasy/science fiction, horror, mystery/suspense, romance). Does not want lesbian, gay, erotica. Promotion of values and principles not compatible with Christianity will not be published. Receives 20-30 mss/month. Accepts 4-6 mss/issue; 48-60 mss/year. Manuscript published 2-6 weeks after acceptance. **Publishes 6 new writers/year.** Published Terry Weide, Michale Ouellette, Marsheila Rockwell, Sean T. M. Stiennon, and Marcie Lynn Tentchoff. Average length: 5,500 words. Publishes short shorts. Average length of short shorts: 1,100 words. Also publishes literary essays, literary criticism, poetry. Always comments on/critiques rejected mss.

How to Contact Submit via Web site through online submissions system. Responds to queries in 1 week. Responds to mss in 6 weeks. Considers previously published submissions, multiple submissions. Guidelines available on Web site.

Payment and Terms Writers receive $5-25 flate-rate payment. Pays on acceptance. Acquires one-time rights, electronic rights and/or nonexclusive print rights (English language). Publication is copyrighted.

Advice "Meticulous editing is a must. Many begininning writers leave out details that are important to conveying the plot, themes and character development. Other beginning writers include details that are unneeded. Be sure you know what your story is trying to do, then edit away what is not needed, and add what is lacking."

THE 13TH WARRIOR REVIEW

Asterius Press, P.O. Box 5122, Seabrook NJ 08302-3511. E-mail: theeditor@asteriuspress.com. Web site: www.asteriuspress.com. **Contact:** John C. Erianne, publisher/editor. Online magazine. Estab. 2000.

Needs Erotica, experimental, humor/satire, literary, mainstream. Receives 200 unsolicited mss/month. Accepts 4-5 mss/issue; 10-15 mss/year. Publishes ms 6 months after acceptance. **Publishes 1-2 new writers/year.** Recently published work by Marjolyn Deurloo, Suzanne Nelson, Stoyan Valev, Paul A. Toth and D. Olsen. Length: 300-3,000 words; average length: 1,500 words. Publishes short shorts. Also publishes literary essays, literary criticism, poetry. Sometimes comments on rejected mss.

How to Contact Send complete ms. Include estimated word count, brief bio and address/e-mail. Send SASE or IRC for return of ms or send a disposable copy of ms and #10 SASE for reply only. Accepts submissions by e-mail (text in in message body only, no file attachements). Responds in 1 week to queries; 1-2 months to mss. Accepts simultaneous submissions. Sample copy online. Reviews fiction.

Payment/Terms Acquires first, electronic rights.

TOASTED CHEESE

E-mail: editors@toasted-cheese.com. Web site: www.toasted-cheese.com. **Contact:** submit@toasted-cheese.com. E-zine specializing in fiction, creative nonfiction, poetry and flash fiction. "*Toasted Cheese* accepts submissions of previously unpublished fiction, flash fiction, creative nonfiction and poetry. Our focus is on quality of work, not quantity. Some issues will therefore contain fewer/more pieces than previous issues. We don't restrict publication based on subject matter. We encourage submissions from innovative writers in all genres." Quarterly. Estab. 2001.

Needs Adventure, children's/juvenile, ethnic/multicultural, fantasy, feminist, gay, historical, horror, humor/satire, lesbian, literary, mainstream, mystery/suspense, New Age, psychic/supernatural/occult, romance, science fiction, thriller/espionage, western. "No fan fiction. No chapters or excerpts unless they read as a stand-alone story. No first drafts." Receives 70 unsolicited mss/month. Accepts 1-10 mss/issue; 5-30 mss/year. **Publishes 15 new writers/year.** Publishes short shorts. Also publishes poetry.

How to Contact Send complete ms. Accepts submissions by e-mail. Responds in 4 months to mss. No simultaneous submissions. Sample copy online. Writer's guidelines online.

Payment/Terms Acquires electronic rights. Sponsors awards/contests.

Advice "We are looking for clean, professional writing from writers of any level. Accepted stories will be concise and compelling. We are looking for writers who are serious about the craft: tomorrow's literary stars before they're famous. Take your submission seriously, yet remember that levity is appreciated. You are submitting not to traditional 'editors' but to fellow writers who appreciate the efforts of those in the trenches."

WEB DEL SOL

E-mail: submissions@webdelsol.com. Web site: www.webdelsol.com. **Contact:** Michael Neff, editor-in-chief. Electronic magazine. "The goal of *Web Del Sol* is to use the medium of the Internet to bring the finest in contemporary literary arts to a larger audience. To that end, *WDS* not only Web-publishes collections of work by accomplished writers and poets, but hosts over 25 literary arts publications on the WWW such as *Del Sol Review*, *North American Review*, *Global City Review*, *The Literary Review* and *The Prose Poem*." Estab. 1994.

Needs Literary. "*WDS* publishes work considered to be literary in nature, i.e. nongenre fiction. *WDS* also publishes poetry, prose poetry, essays and experimental types of writing." **Publishes 100-200 new writers/year.**

How to Contact "Submissions by e-mail from September through November and from January through March only. Submissions must contain some brief bio, list of prior publications (if any), and a short work or portion of that work, neither to exceed 1,000 words. Editors will contact if the balance of work is required." Sample copy online.

Advice "*WDS* wants fiction that is absolutely cutting edge, unique and/or at a minimum, accomplished with a crisp style and concerning subjects not usually considered the objects of literary scrutiny. Read works in such publications as *Conjunctions* (www.conjunctions.com) and *North American Review* (webdelsol.com/NorthAmReview/NAR) to get an idea of what we are looking for."

$ WEE SMALL HOURS

Wolf Moon Publications, 4212 Derby Lane, Evansville IN 47715-1568. E-mail: wolfmoonpub@aol.com. Web site: www.hellnotes.com/fiction.html. **Contact:** Judi Rohrig, editor. Online magazine. "The chosen Prompts from which writers are to pen their stories come from INSTIGATION, a weekly column written by Professor Michael Arnzen (Seton Hill) for *HELLNOTES* (a newsletter that serves the horror/sci-fi/mystery communities of writers)." Bimonthly. Estab. 2005. Circ. 300 hits/month. *HELLNOTES*, the parent publication has been honored with a Bram Stoker Award and a International Horror Guild Award.

Needs Fantasy, horror, mystery/suspense, supernatural, science fiction, thriller, western. Does not want fanfic. Receives 60 mss/month. Publishes 1 mss/issue; 6 mss/year. Published Daniel Robichaud, R.W. Day, James Stuart and Michael Fountain. Length: 500 words (min)-1,000 words (max). Average length: 800 words. Publishes short shorts. No reprints.

How to Contact Follow online guidelines. (E-mail submissions only.) Include estimated word count, brief bio. Considers multiple submissions. Guidelines available on Web site.

Payment and Terms Writers receive $50 max flate-rate payment, free 1-year subscription *HELLNOTES* newsletter. Pays on publication. Acquires electronic rights. Publication is copyrighted.

Advice "Write the best story using one of the Prompts listed for the period submitting. There are three editors who read all submissions."

WILD VIOLET

Wild Violet, P.O. Box 39706, Philadelphia PA 19106-9706. E-mail: wildvioletmagazine@yahoo.com. Web site: www.wildviolet.net. **Contact:** Alyce Wilson, editor. Online magazine: illustrations, photos. "Our goal is to make a place for the arts: to make the arts more accessible and to serve as a creative forum for writers and artists. Our audience includes English-speaking readers from all over the world, who are interested in both 'high art' and pop culture." Quarterly. Estab. 2001.

Needs Comics/graphic novels, ethnic/multicultural, experimental, fantasy (space fantasy, sword and sorcery), feminist, gay, horror (dark fantasy, futuristic, psychological, supernatural), humor/satire, lesbian, literary, New Age, psychic/supernatural/occult, science fiction. "No stories where sexual or violent content is just used to shock the reader. No racist writings." Receives 30 unsolicited mss/month. Accepts 5 mss/issue; 20 mss/year. **Publishes 30 new writers/year.** Recently published work by Deen Borok, Wayne Scheer, Jane McDonald and

Eric Brown. Length: 500-6,000 words; average length: 3,000 words. Also publishes literary essays, literary criticism, poetry. Sometimes comments on rejected mss.

How to Contact Send complete ms. Accepts submissions by e-mail. Include estimated word count and brief bio. Send SASE for return of ms or send a disposable copy of ms and #10 SASE for reply only. Responds in 1 week to queries; 3-6 months to mss. Accepts simultaneous, multiple submissions. Sample copy online. Writer's guidelines by e-mail.

Payment/Terms Writers receive bio and links on contributor's page. Request limited electronic rights, for online publication and archival only. Sponsors awards/contests.

Advice "We look for stories that are well paced and show character and plot development. Even short shorts should do more than simply paint a picture. Manuscripts stand out when the author's voice is fresh and engaging. Avoid muddying your story with too many characters and don't attempt to shock the reader with an ending you have not earned. Experiment with styles and structures, but don't resort to experimentation for its own sake."

☑ WORD RIOT, A Communication-Breakdown Production

Word Riot Press, P.O. Box 414, Middletown NJ 07748-3143. (732)706-1272. Fax: (732)706-5856. E-mail: submissions@wordriot.org. Web site: www.wordriot.org. **Contact:** Brian Ames and David Barringer, fiction editors. Online magazine. Monthly. Estab. 2002. Member CLMP.

Needs Humor/satire, literary, mainstream. "No fantasy, science fiction, romance." Accepts 10-12 mss/issue; 120-144 mss/year. Publishes ms 3 weeks after acceptance. Agented fiction 5%. **Publishes 8-10 new writers/year.** Length: 300-6,000 words; average length: 2,700 words. Publishes short shorts. Also publishes literary essays, poetry. Often comments on rejected mss.

How to Contact Accepts submissions by e-mail. Include estimated word count and brief bio. Responds in 4-6 weeks to mss. Accepts multiple submissions. Sample copy online. Writer's guidelines online.

Payment/Terms Acquires electronic rights. Not copyrighted. Sponsors awards/contests.

Advice "We're always looking for something edgy or quirky. We like writers who take risks."

☑ WORDS ON WALLS

3408 Whitfield Ave. Apt 4, Cincinnati OH 45220. (513)961-1475. E-mail: editor@wordsonwalls.net. Web site: http://wordsonwalls.net. **Contact:** Kathrine Wright; Ariana-Sophia Kartsonis. Quarterly. Estab. 2003.

Needs Experimental, feminist, gay, literary. Receives 25-35 unsolicited mss/month. Accepts 2-3 mss/issue; 6-12 mss/year. Publishes ms 3-4 months after acceptance. Publishes short shorts. Also publishes literary essays, poetry. Often comments on rejected mss.

How to Contact Accepts submissions by e-mail. Accepts simultaneous, multiple submissions and reprints. Writer's guidelines online.

Payment/Terms Writer retains all rights.

Advice "We like work that is edgy, beautifully written with a strong sense of voice and music."

Consumer Magazines

I n this section of *Novel & Short Story Writer's Market* are consumer magazines with circulations of more than 10,000. Many have circulations in the hundreds of thousands or millions. Among the oldest magazines listed here are ones not only familiar to us but also to our parents, grandparents and even great-grandparents: *The Atlantic Monthly* (1857); *The New Yorker* (1925); *Esquire* (1933); and *Ellery Queen's Mystery Magazine* (1941).

Consumer periodicals make excellent markets for fiction in terms of exposure, prestige and payment. Because these magazines are well known, however, competition is great. Even the largest consumer publications buy only one or two stories an issue, yet thousands of writers submit to these popular magazines.

Despite the odds, it is possible for talented new writers to break into print in the magazines listed here. Your keys to breaking into these markets are careful research, professional presentation and, of course, top-quality fiction.

TYPES OF CONSUMER MAGAZINES

In this section you will find a number of popular publications, some for a broad-based, general-interest readership and others for large but select groups of readers—children, teenagers, women, men and seniors. There are also religious and church-affiliated magazines, publications devoted to the interests of particular cultures and outlooks, and top markets for genre fiction.

SELECTING THE RIGHT MARKET

Unlike smaller journals and publications, most of the magazines listed here are available at newsstands and bookstores. Many can also be found in the library, and guidelines and sample copies are almost always available by mail or online. Start your search by reviewing the listings, then familiarize yourself with the fiction included in the magazines that interest you.

Don't make the mistake of thinking that just because you are familiar with a magazine, their fiction is the same today as when you first read it. Nothing could be further from the truth. Consumer magazines, no matter how well established, are constantly revising their fiction needs as they strive to expand their audience base.

In a magazine that uses only one or two stories an issue, take a look at the nonfiction articles and features as well. These can give you a better idea of the audience for the publication and clues to the type of fiction that might appeal to them.

If you write genre fiction, look in the Category Index beginning on page 588. There you will find a list of markets that say they are looking for a particular subject.

FURTHERING YOUR SEARCH

See You've Got a Story (page 2) for information about the material common to all listings in this book. In this section in particular, pay close attention to the number of submissions a magazine receives in a given period and how many they publish in the same period. This will give you a clear picture of how stiff your competition can be.

While many of the magazines listed here publish one or two pieces of fiction in each issue, some also publish special fiction issues once or twice a year. When possible, we have indicated this in the listing information. We also note if the magazine is open to novel excerpts as well as short fiction, and we advise novelists to query first before submitting long work.

The Business of Fiction Writing, beginning on page 79, covers the basics of submitting your work. Professional presentation is a must for all markets listed. Editors at consumer magazines are especially busy, and anything you can do to make your manuscript easy to read and accessible will help your chances of being published. Most magazines want to see complete manuscripts, but watch for publications in this section that require a query first.

As in the previous section, we've included our own comments in many of the listings, set off by a bullet (●). Whenever possible, we list the publication's recent awards and honors. We've also included any special information we feel will help you in determining whether a particular publication interests you.

The maple leaf symbol (![maple leaf]) identifies our Canadian listings. You will also find some English-speaking markets from around the world. These foreign magazines are denoted with ![globe] at the beginning of the listings. Remember to use International Reply Coupons rather than stamps when you want a reply from a country other than your own.

Periodicals of Interest

For More Info

For more on consumer magazines, see issues of *Writer's Digest* (F + W Publications) and other industry trade publications available in larger libraries.

For news about some of the genre publications listed here and information about a particular field, there are a number of magazines devoted to genre topics, including *The Drood Review of Mystery*; *Locus* (for science fiction); *Science Fiction Chronicle*; and *Romance Writers' Report* (available to members of Romance Writers of America).

ADVENTURES

WordAction Publications, 6401 The Paseo, Kansas City MO 64131-1213. (816)333-7000. **Contact:** Julie Smith, editor. Magazine: 8¼×11; 4 pages; self cover; color illustrations. "This weekly take-home paper connects Sunday school learning to life for first and second graders (ages 6-8)." Weekly. Circ. 45,000.

How to Contact *Adventures* will begin accepting new submissions in September 2006.

$✉ AFRICAN VOICES

African Voices Communications, Inc., 270 W. 96th St., New York NY 10025. (212)865-2982. Fax: (212)316-3335. Web site: www.africanvoices.com. **Contact:** Kim Horne, fiction editor. Magazine: 52 pages; illustrations; photos. "*African Voices* is dedicated to highlighting the art, literature and history of people of color." Quarterly. Estab. 1992. Circ. 20,000.

Needs Adventure, children's/juvenile, condensed novels, erotica, ethnic/multicultural, experimental, fantasy, gay, historical (general), horror, humor/satire, literary, mainstream, mystery/suspense, novel excerpts, psychic/supernatural/occult, religious/inspirational, romance, science fiction, serialized novels, slice-of-life vignettes, suspense, young adult/teen (adventure, romance), African-American. List of upcoming themes available for SASE. Publishes special fiction issue. Receives 20-50 unsolicited mss/month. Accepts 20 mss/issue. Publishes ms 3-6 months after acceptance. Agented fiction 5%. **Publishes 30 new writers/year.** Recently published work by Anton Nimblett, Latoya Wolfe and novelist Ngugiwa Thiong'o. Length: 500-2,500 words; average length: 2,000 words. Publishes short shorts. Also publishes literary essays, poetry.

How to Contact Send complete ms. Include short bio. Send SASE for return of ms. Responds in 3 months to queries. Accepts simultaneous submissions and reprints. Sample copy for $5 or online. Writer's guidelines online. Reviews fiction.

Payment/Terms Pays $25-50. Pays on publication for first North American serial rights.

Advice "A manuscript stands out if it is neatly typed with a well-written and interesting story line or plot. Originality encouraged. We are interested in more horror, erotic and drama pieces. *AV* wants to highlight the diversity in our culture. Stories must touch the humanity in us all."

$✉ AIM MAGAZINE

Aim Publishing Co., P.O. Box 1174, Maywood IL 60153. (708)344-4414. Fax: (206)543-2746. Web site: aimmagazine.org. **Contact:** Ruth Apilado, associate editor. Magazine: 8½×11; 48 pages; slick paper; photos and illustrations. Publishes material "to purge racism from the human bloodstream through the written word—that is the purpose of *Aim Magazine*." Quarterly. Estab. 1975. Circ. 10,000.

Needs Ethnic/multicultural, historical, mainstream, suspense. Open. No "religious" mss. Published special fiction issue last year; plans another. Receives 25 unsolicited mss/month. Accepts 15 mss/issue; 60 mss/year. Publishes ms 3 months after acceptance. **Publishes 40 new writers/year.** Recently published work by Christina Touregny, Thomas Lee Harris, Michael Williams and Jake Halpern. Publishes short shorts. Sometimes comments on rejected mss.

How to Contact Send complete ms. Accepts submissions by e-mail. Include SASE with cover letter and author's photograph. Responds in 2 months to queries; 1 month to mss. Accepts simultaneous submissions. Sample copy and writer's guidelines for $4 and 9×12 SAE with $1.70 postage or online.

Payment/Terms Pays $25-35. Pays on publication for first, one-time rights.

Advice "Search for those who are making unselfish contributions to their community and write about them. Write about your own experiences. Be familar with the background of your characters. Known for stories with social significance, proving that people from different ethnic, racial backgrounds are more alike than they are different."

$✉ ▣ ANALOG SCIENCE FICTION & FACT

Dell Magazine Fiction Group, 475 Park Ave. S., 11th Floor, New York NY 10016. (212)686-7188. Fax: (212)686-7414. E-mail: analog@dellmagazines.com. Web site: www.analogsf.com. **Contact:** Stanley Schmidt, editor. Magazine: 144 pages; illustrations; photos. Monthly. Estab. 1930. Circ. 50,000.

● Fiction published in *Analog* has won numerous Nebula and Hugo Awards.

Needs Science fiction (hard science/technological, soft/sociological). "No fantasy or stories in which the scientific background is implausible or plays no essential role." Receives 500 unsolicited mss/month. Accepts 6 mss/issue; 70 mss/year. Publishes ms 10 months after acceptance. Agented fiction 5%. **Publishes 3-4 new writers/year.** Recently published work by Ben Bova, Stephen Baxter, Larry Niven, Michael F. Flynn, Timothy Zahn, Robert J. Sawyer, Joe Haldeman. Length: 2,000-80,000 words; average length: 10,000 words. Publishes short shorts. Sometimes comments on rejected mss.

How to Contact Send complete ms with a cover letter. Accepts queries for serials and fact articles only; query by mail. Include estimated word count. Send SASE for return of ms or send a disposable copy of ms and #10

SASE for reply only. Responds in 1 month to queries. Accepts multiple submissions. No simultaneous submissions. Sample copy for $5. Writer's guidelines online. Reviews fiction.

Payment/Terms Pays 4¢/word for novels; 5-6¢/word for novelettes; 6-8¢/word for shorts under 7,500 words; $450-600 for intermediate lengths. Pays on acceptance for first North American serial, nonexclusive foreign serial rights. Sends galleys to author. Not copyrighted.

Advice "I'm looking for irresistibly entertaining stories that make me think about things in ways I've never done before. Read several issues to get a broad feel for our tastes, but don't try to imitate what you read."

$ ⬚ ◲ ◎ THE ANNALS OF SAINT ANNE DE BEAUPRÉ

Redemptorist Fathers, 9795 St. Anne Blvd., St. Anne de Beaupré QC G0A 3C0 Canada. (418)827-4538. Fax: (418)827-4530. **Contact:** Father R. Théberge, C.Ss.R., editor. Magazine: 8×11; 32 pages; glossy paper; photos. "Our mission statement includes dedication to Christian family values and devotion to St. Anne." Releases 10 issues/year; July/August and November/December are each one issue. Estab. 1885. Circ. 32,000.

Needs Religious/inspirational. "No senseless mockery." Receives 50-60 unsolicited mss/month. Recently published work by Beverly Sheresh. Always comments on rejected mss.

How to Contact Send complete ms. Include estimated word count. Send SASE for reply or return of ms. Responds in 4-6 weeks to queries. No simultaneous submissions.

Payment/Terms Pays 3-4¢/word. Pays on acceptance for first North American serial rights. Please state "rights" for sale.

$ ◲ ART TIMES, Commentary and Resources for the Fine and Performing Arts

P.O. Box 730, Mount Marion NY 12456-0730. (914)246-6944. Fax: (914)246-6944. Web site: www.arttimesjournal.com. **Contact:** Raymond J. Steiner, fiction editor. Magazine: 12×15; 24 pages; Jet paper and cover; illustrations; photos. "*Art Times* covers the art fields and is distributed in locations most frequented by those enjoying the arts. Our copies are distributed throughout the Northeast region as well as in most of the galleries of Soho, 57th Street and Madison Avenue in the metropolitan area; locations include theaters, galleries, museums, cultural centers and the like. Our readers are mostly over 40, affluent, art-conscious and sophisticated. Subscribers are located across U.S. and abroad (Italy, France, Germany, Greece, Russia, etc.)." Monthly. Estab. 1984. Circ. 27,000.

Needs Adventure, ethnic/multicultural, fantasy, feminist, gay, historical, humor/satire, lesbian, literary, mainstream, science fiction, contemporary. "We seek quality literary pieces. Nothing violent, sexist, erotic, juvenile, racist, romantic, political, etc." Receives 30-50 unsolicited mss/month. Accepts 1 mss/issue; 10 mss/year. Publishes ms 3 years after acceptance. **Publishes 6 new writers/year.** Publishes short shorts.

How to Contact Send complete ms with SASE. Responds in 6 months to mss. Accepts simultaneous, multiple submissions. Sample copy for 9×12 SAE and 6 first-class stamps. Writer's guidelines for #10 SASE or on Web site.

Payment/Terms Pays $25 maximum (honorarium) and 1-year's free subscription. Pays on publication for first North American serial, first rights.

Advice "Competition is greater (more submissions received), but keep trying. We print new as well as published writers."

$ ◲ ⬚ ASIMOV'S SCIENCE FICTION

Dell Magazine Fiction Group, 475 Park Ave. S., 11th Floor, New York NY 10016. (212)686-7188. Fax: (212)686-7414. E-mail: asimovs@dellmagazines.com. Web site: www.asimovs.com. **Contact:** Sheila Williams, editor. Magazine: 5¼×8¼ (trim size); 144 pages; 30 lb. newspaper; 70 lb. to 8 pt. C1S cover stock; illustrations; rarely photos. Magazine consists of science fiction and fantasy stories for adults and young adults. Publishes "the best short science fiction available." Estab. 1977. Circ. 50,000.

• Named for a science fiction "legend," *Asimov's* regularly receives Hugo and Nebula Awards. Editor Gardner Dozois has received several awards for editing including Hugos and those from *Locus* magazine.

Needs Fantasy, science fiction (hard science, soft sociological). No horror or psychic/supernatural. Would like to see more hard science fiction. Receives approximately 800 unsolicited mss/month. Accepts 10 mss/issue. Publishes ms 6-12 months after acceptance. Agented fiction 10%. **Publishes 6 new writers/year.** Recently published work by Ursula LeGuin and Larry Niven. Publishes short shorts. Sometimes comments on rejected mss.

How to Contact Send complete ms with SASE. Responds in 2 months to queries; 3 months to mss. Accepts reprint submissions. No simultaneous submissions. Sample copy for $5. Writer's guidelines for #10 SASE or online. Reviews fiction.

Payment/Terms Pays 5-8¢/word. Pays on acceptance. Buys first North American serial, nonexclusive foreign serial rights; reprint rights occasionally. Sends galleys to author.

Advice "We are looking for character stories rather than those emphasizing technology or science. New writers will do best with a story under 10,000 words. Every new science fiction or fantasy film seems to 'inspire' writers—and this is not a desirable trend. Be sure to be familiar with our magazine and the type of story we like; workshops and lots of practice help. Try to stay away from trite, clichéd themes. Start in the middle of the action, starting as close to the end of the story as you possibly can. We like stories that extrapolate from up-to-date scientific research, but don't forget that we've been publishing clone stories for decades. Ideas must be fresh.''

$ THE ATLANTIC MONTHLY

The Watergate, 600 New Hampshire Ave. NW, Washington DC 20037. (617)854-7749. Fax: (617)854-7877. Web site: www.theatlantic.com. **Contact:** C. Michael Curtis, senior editor. General magazine for an educated readership with broad cultural interests. Monthly. Estab. 1857. Circ. 500,000.

Needs Literary and contemporary fiction. ''Seeks fiction that is clear, tightly written with strong sense of 'story' and well-defined characters.'' Receives 1,000 unsolicited mss/month. Accepts 10 mss/year. **Publishes 3-4 new writers/year.** Recently published work by Mary Gordon, Donald Hall, Roxana Robinson.

How to Contact Send complete ms. Responds in 2 months to mss. Accepts multiple submissions. No simultaneous submissions. Writer's guidelines online.

Payment/Terms Pays $3,000. Pays on acceptance for first North American serial rights.

Advice When making first contract, ''cover letters are sometimes helpful, particularly if they cite prior publications or involvement in writing programs. Common mistakes: melodrama, inconclusiveness, lack of development, unpersuasive characters and/or dialogue.''

$ BACKROADS, Motorcycles, Travel & Adventure

Backroads, Inc., P.O. Box 317, Branchville NJ 07826. (973)948-4176. Fax: (973)948-0823. E-mail: editor@backroadsusa.com. Web site: www.backroadsusa.com. ''*Backroads* is a motorcycle tour magazine geared toward getting motorcyclists on the road and traveling. We provide interesting destinations, unique roadside attractions and eateries, plus Rip & Ride Route Sheets. We cater to all brands. If you really ride, you need *Backroads*.'' Monthly. Estab. 1995. Circ. 40,000.

Needs Travel, motorcycle-related stories. Publishes ms 3 months after acceptance.

How to Contact Query. Accepts submissions by e-mail. Responds in 3 weeks to queries. Accepts reprint submissions. Sample copy for $2. Writer's guidelines free.

Payment/Terms Pays 5¢/word. Pays on publication for one-time rights.

$ 🔲 THE BEAR DELUXE MAGAZINE

Orlo, P.O. Box 10342, Portland OR 97296. (503)242-1047. E-mail: bear@orlo.org. Web site: www.orlo.org. **Contact:** Tom Webb, editor. Magazine: 9×12; 48 pages; newsprint paper; Kraft paper cover illustrations; photos. ''*The Bear Deluxe Magazine* provides a fresh voice amid often strident and polarized environmental discourse. Street level, solution-oriented and nondogmatic, *The Bear Deluxe* presents lively creative discussion to a diverse readership.'' Semiannual. Estab. 1993. Circ. 20,000.

• *The Bear Deluxe* has received publishing grants from the Oregon Council for the Humanities, Literary Arts, Regional Arts and Culture Council, Tides Foundation.

Needs Adventure, condensed novels, historical, horror, humor/satire, mystery/suspense, novel excerpts, western. ''No detective, children's or horror.'' Environmentally focused: humor/satire, literary, science fiction. ''We would like to see more nontraditional forms.'' List of upcoming themes available for SASE. Receives 20-30 unsolicited mss/month. Accepts 2-3 mss/issue; 8-12 mss/year. Publishes ms 3 months after acceptance. **Publishes 5-6 new writers/year.** Recently published work by Peter Houlahan, John Reed and Karen Hueler. Length: 750-4,500 words; average length: 2,500 words. Publishes short shorts. Also publishes literary essays, literary criticism, poetry. Sometimes comments on rejected mss.

How to Contact Query with or without published clips or send complete ms. Send disposable copy of mss. Responds in 3 months to queries; 6 months to mss. Accepts simultaneous submissions and reprints. Sample copy for $3. Writer's guidelines for #10 SASE or on Web site. Reviews fiction.

Payment/Terms Pays free subscription to the magazine, contributor's copies and 5¢/word; additional copies for postage. Pays on publication for first, one-time rights.

Advice ''Keep sending work. Write actively and focus on the connections of man, nature, etc., not just flowery descriptions. Urban and suburban environments are grist for the mill as well. Have not seen enough quality humorous and ironic writing. Interview and artist profile ideas needed. Juxtaposition of place welcome. Action and hands-on great. Not all that interested in environmental ranting and simple 'walks through the park.' Make it powerful, yet accessible to a wide audience.''

$ 🔲 BOMB MAGAZINE

80 Hanson Place, Suite 703, Brooklyn NY 11217. (718)636-9100. Fax: (718)636-9200. E-mail: info@bombsite.com. Web site: www.bombsite.com. Magazine: 11×14; 104 pages; 70 lb. glossy cover; illustrations; photos. Written, edited and produced by industry professionals and funded by those interested in the arts. Publishes

writing which is unconventional and contains an edge, whether it be in style or subject matter. Quarterly. Estab. 1981. Circ. 36,000.

Needs Experimental, novel excerpts, contemporary. No genre: romance, science fiction, horror, western. Receives 200 unsolicited mss/month. Accepts 6 mss/issue; 24 mss/year. Publishes ms 3-6 months after acceptance. Agented fiction 70%. **Publishes 2-3 new writers/year.** Recently published work by Lynne Tillman, Brenda Shaughnessy, Susan Wheeler and Steve Almond.

How to Contact Send complete ms with SASE. Responds in 3-5 months to mss. Accepts multiple submissions. Sample copy for $7, plus $1.42 postage and handling. Writer's guidelines by e-mail.

Payment/Terms Pays $100, and contributor's copies. Pays on publication for first, one-time rights. Sends galleys to author.

Advice "We are committed to publishing new work that commercial publishers often deem too dangerous or difficult. The problem is, a lot of young writers confuse difficult with dreadful. Read the magazine before you even think of submitting something."

$🖉 🔽 BOSTON REVIEW

E53-407, M.I.T., Cambridge MA 02139. (617)258-0805. Fax: (617)252-1549. E-mail: review@mit.edu. Web site: www.bostonreview.net. **Contact:** Junot Diaz, fiction editor. Magazine: 10³/₄×14³/₄; 60 pages; newsprint. "The editors are committed to a society and culture that foster human diversity and a democracy in which we seek common grounds of principle amidst our many differences. In the hope of advancing these ideals, the *Review* acts as a forum that seeks to enrich the language of public debate." Bimonthly. Estab. 1975. Circ. 20,000.

• *Boston Review* is the recipient of a Pushcart Prize in poetry.

Needs Ethnic/multicultural, experimental, literary, regional, translations, contemporary, prose poem. Receives 150 unsolicited mss/month. Accepts 4-6 mss/year. Publishes ms 4 months after acceptance. Recently published work by David Mamet, Rhonda Stamell, Jacob Appel, Elisha Porat and Diane Williams. Length: 1,200-5,000 words; average length: 2,000 words. Occasionally comments on rejected mss.

How to Contact Send complete ms. Responds in 4 months to queries. Accepts simultaneous submissions if noted. Sample copy for $5 or online. Writer's guidelines online. Reviews fiction.

Payment/Terms Pays $50-100, and 5 contributor's copies. Acquires first North American serial, first rights.

$◎ BOWHUNTER, The Number One Bowhunting Magazine

Primedia Consumer Media & Magazine Group, 6405 Flank Dr., Harrisburg PA 17112. (717)657-9555. Fax: (717)657-9552. E-mail: bowhunter_magazine@primediamags.com. Web site: www.bowhunter.com. **Contact:** Dwight Schuh, editor. Magazine: 7³/₄×10¹/₂: 150 pages; 75 lb. glossy paper; 150 lb. glossy cover stock; illustrations; photos. "We are a special-interest publication, produced by bowhunters for bowhunters, covering all aspects of the sport. Material included in each issue is designed to entertain and inform readers, making them better bowhunters." Bimonthly. Estab. 1971. Circ. 154,446.

Needs Bowhunting, outdoor adventure. "Writers must expect a very limited market. We buy only one or two fiction pieces a year. Writers must know the market—bowhunting—and let that be the theme of their work. No 'me and my dog' types of stories; no stories by people who have obviously never held a bow in their hands." Receives 25 unsolicited mss/month. Accepts 30 mss/year. Publishes ms 3 months to 2 years after acceptance. **Publishes 3-4 new writers/year.** Length: 500-2,000 words; average length: 1,500 words. Publishes short shorts. Sometimes comments on rejected mss.

How to Contact Send complete ms. Accepts submissions by e-mail, fax. Responds in 2 weeks to queries; 1 month to mss. Sample copy for $2 and 8¹/₂×11 SAE with appropriate postage. Writer's guidelines for #10 SASE or on Web site.

Payment/Terms Pays $100-350. Pays on acceptance. Buys exclusive first, worldwide publication rights.

Advice "We have a resident humorist who supplies us with most of the 'fiction' we need. But if a story comes through the door which captures the essence of bowhunting and we feel it will reach out to our readers, we will buy it. Despite our macho outdoor magazine status, we are a bunch of English majors who love to read. You can't bull your way around real outdoor people—they can spot a phony at 20 paces. If you've never camped out under the stars and listened to an elk bugle and try to relate that experience without really experiencing it, someone's going to know. We are very specialized; we don't want stories about shooting apples off people's heads or of Cupid's arrow finding its mark. James Dickey's *Deliverance* used bowhunting metaphorically, very effectively . . . while we don't expect that type of writing from everyone, that's the kind of feeling that characterizes a good piece of outdoor fiction."

$🖉 BUGLE

Rocky Mountain Elk Foundation, P.O. Box 8249, 5705 Grant Creek Rd., Missoula MT 59808. (406)523-4538. Fax: (406)543-7710. E-mail: bugle@rmef.org. Web site: www.elkfoundation.org. **Contact:** Don Burgess, hunting/human interest editor, dburgess@rmef.org; Lee Lamb, conservation editor, lcromrich@rmef.org. Magazine:

114-172 pages; 55 lb. Escanaba paper; 80 lb. Sterling cover, b&w, 4-color illustrations; photos. *Bugle* is the membership publication of the Rocky Mountain Elk Foundation, a nonprofit wildlife conservation group. "Our readers are predominantly hunters, many of them conservationists who care deeply about protecting wildlife habitat." Bimonthly. Estab. 1984. Circ. 132,000.

Needs Adventure, children's/juvenile, historical, humor/satire, novel excerpts, slice-of-life vignettes, western, human interest, natural history, conservation. "We accept fiction and nonfiction stories pertaining in some way to elk, other wildlife, hunting, habitat conservation, and related issues. We would like to see more humor." Upcoming themes: "Bowhunting for Elk"; "Lost: Stories of Disorientation"; "Bears". Receives 20-30 unsolicited mss/month. Accepts 3-4 mss/issue; 18-24 mss/year. Publishes ms 1-36 months after acceptance. **Publishes 12 new writers/year.** Recently published work by Rick Bass and Susan Ewing. Length: 1,500-4,500 words; average length: 2,500 words. Publishes short shorts. Also publishes literary essays, poetry.

How to Contact Query with or without published clips or send complete ms. Prefers submissions by e-mail. Send SASE for reply, return of ms or send a disposable copy of ms. Responds in 1 month to queries; 3 months to mss. Accepts reprints, multiple submissions. Sample copy for $5. Writer's guidelines online.

Payment/Terms Pays 20¢/word. Pays on acceptance for one-time rights.

Advice "Hunting stories and essays should celebrate the hunting experience, demonstrating respect for wildlife, the land, and the hunt. Articles on elk behavior or elk habitat should include personal observations and entertain as well as educate. No freelance product reviews or formulaic how-to articles accepted. Straight action-adventure hunting stories are in short supply, as are "Situation Ethics" manuscripts."

$⊘ ◎ CADET QUEST MAGAZINE

P.O. Box 7259, Grand Rapids MI 49510-7259. (616)241-5616. Fax: (616)241-5558. E-mail: submissions@calvinistcadets.org. Web site: www.calvinistcadets.org. **Contact:** G. Richard Broene, editor. Magazine: $8^{1}/_{2} \times 11$; 24 pages; illustrations; photos. "*Cadet Quest Magazine* shows boys 9-14 how God is at work in their lives and in the world around them." Estab. 1958. Circ. 10,000.

Needs Adventure, children's/juvenile, religious/inspirational (Christian), spiritual, sports, comics. "Needs material based on Christian perspective and articles on Christian role models. Avoid long dialogue and little action." No fantasy, science fiction, fashion, horror or erotica. List of upcoming themes available for SASE or on Web site. Receives 60 unsolicited mss/month. Accepts 3 mss/issue; 18 mss/year. Publishes ms 4-11 months after acceptance. **Publishes 0-3 new writers/year.** Length: 900-1,500 words; average length: 1,200 words. Publishes short shorts.

How to Contact Send complete ms by mail, or send submissions in the body of the e-mail, not as an attachment. Responds in 2 months to queries. Accepts simultaneous, multiple submissions and reprints. Sample copy for 9×12 SASE. Writer's guidelines for #10 SASE.

Payment/Terms Pays 4-6¢/word, and 1 contributor's copy. Pays on acceptance for first North American serial, one-time, second serial (reprint), simultaneous rights. Rights purchased vary with author and material.

Advice "On a cover sheet, list the point your story is trying to make. Our magazine has a theme for each issue, and we try to fit the fiction to the theme. All fiction should be about a young boy's interests—sports, outdoor activities, problems—with an emphasis on a Christian perspective. No simple moralisms."

$⊠ CALLIOPE, Exploring World History

Cobblestone Publishing Co., 30 Grove St., Suite C, Peterborough NH 03458-1454. (603)924-7209. Fax: (603)924-7380. Web site: www.cobblestonepub.com. **Contact:** Rosalie Baker, editor. Magazine. "*Calliope* covers world history (east/west), and lively, original approaches to the subject are the primary concerns of the editors in choosing material. For 8-14 year olds." Estab. 1990. Circ. 13,000.

● Cobblestone Publishing also publishes the children's magazines *Appleseeds, Dig, Footsteps, Odyssey, Cobblestone* and *Faces*, some listed in this section. *Calliope* has received the Ed Press Golden Lamp and One-Theme Issue awards.

Needs Material must fit upcoming theme; write for themes and deadlines. Childrens/juvenile (8-14 years). "Authentic historical and biographical fiction, adventure, retold legends, folktales, etc. relating to the theme." Send SASE for guidelines and theme list. Published after theme deadline. **Publishes 5-10 new writers/year.** Recently published work by Diane Childress and Jackson Kuhl. Publishes short shorts.

How to Contact Query with or without published clips. Send SASE (or IRC) for reply. Responds in several months (if interested, responds 5 months before publication date) to mss. No simultaneous submissions. Sample copy for $5.95 and $7^{1}/_{2} \times 10^{1}/_{2}$ SASE with 4 first-class stamps or online. Writer's guidelines for #10 SAE and 1 first-class stamp or on Web site.

Payment/Terms Pays 20-25¢/word. Pays on publication.

Advice "We primarily publish historical nonfiction. Fiction should be retold legends or folktales related to appropriate themes."

⬛ CANADIAN WRITER'S JOURNAL

P.O. Box 1178, New Liskeard ON P0J 1P0 Canada. (705)647-5424. Fax: (705)647-8366. Web site: www.cwj.ca. Accepts well-written articles by all writers. Bimonthly. Estab. 1984. Circ. 350.

Needs Requirements being met by annual contest. Send SASE for rules, or see guidelines on Web site. "Does not want gratuitous violence, sex subject matter." Publishes ms 9 months after acceptance. **Publishes 40 new writers/year.** Also publishes poetry. Rarely comments on rejected mss.

How to Contact Accepts submissions by e-mail, fax, disk. Responds in 2 months to queries. Sample copy for $8, including postage. Writer's guidelines online.

Payment/Terms Pays on publication for one-time rights.

$ CLUB CONNECTION, A Missionettes Magazine for Girls

The General Council of the Assemblies of God, 1445 N. Boonville Ave., Springfield MO 65802. (417)862-2781. Fax: (417)862-0503. E-mail: clubconnection@ag.org. Web site: www.clubconnection.ag.org. "*Club Connection* is a Christian-based magazine for girls ages 6-12." Quarterly. Estab. 1997. Circ. 12,000.

Needs Adventure, confessions, ethnic/multicultural, historical, humor/satire, mainstream, mystery/suspense, religious/inspirational. No songs or poetry. Publishes ms 6-12 months after acceptance.

How to Contact Send complete ms. Accepts submissions by e-mail (clubconnection@ag.org), fax and snail mail. Responds in 1 month to queries; 1-2 months to mss. Sample copy $1 back issues, $1.95 current issues. Writer's guidelines online and model release forms found at www.missionettes.org/clubconnection/.

Payment/Terms Pays $25-50. Pays on publication for first, one-time rights.

$ ⬛ ◎ CLUBHOUSE JR.

Focus on the Family, 8605 Explorer Drive, Colorado Springs CO 80920. (719)531-3400. Web site: www.clubhous ejr.com. **Contact:** Mary Busha, editorial assistant. Magazine: $8^1/2 \times 11$; 16-24 pages; illustrations; photos. *Clubhouse Jr.* is designed to inspire, entertain, and teach Christian values to children 4-8. Estab. 1988. Circ. 100,000.

Needs Children's/juvenile (adventure, animal, preschool, sports), ethnic/multicultural, religious/inspirational. Receives 160 unsolicited mss/month. Accepts 1 mss/issue; 12 mss/year. Publishes ms 1 year after acceptance. Agented fiction 50%. **Publishes 2-3 new writers/year.** Recently published work by Laura Sassi, Nancy Sanders, Manfred Koehler, Mary Manz Simon. Length: 250-1,000 words; average length: 250-700 words. Publishes short shorts. Also publishes poetry. Sometimes comments on rejected mss.

How to Contact Send complete ms. Send SASE (or IRC) for return of the ms or send disposable copy of the ms and #10 SASE for reply only. Responds in 4-6 weeks to mss. Accepts simultaneous submissions. Sample copy for $1.25. Writer's guidelines for #10 SASE.

Payment/Terms Pays $125-200. Pays on acceptance for first, one-time, electronic rights.

Advice "Fresh, inviting, creative; stories that explore a worthy theme without an obvious *moral*. Characters are well developed, story line fast-moving and interesting; built on Christian beliefs and values."

$ ⬛ ◎ CLUBHOUSE MAGAZINE

Focus on the Family, 8605 Explorer Dr., Colorado Springs CO 80920. (719)531-3400. Web site: www.clubhouse magazine.com. **Contact**: Mary Busha, editorial assistant. Magazine: 8×11; 24 pages; illustrations; photos. "*Clubhouse* readers are 8-12 year old boys and girls who desire to know more about God and the Bible. Their parents (who typically pay for the membership) want wholesome, educational material with Scriptural or moral insight. The kids want excitement, adventure, action, humor or mystery. Your job as a writer is to please both the parent and child with each article." Monthly. Estab. 1987. Circ. 114,000.

Needs Adventure, children's/juvenile (8-12 years), humor/satire, mystery/suspense, religious/inspirational, holiday. Avoid contemporary, middle-class family settings (existing authors meet this need), stories dealing with boy-girl relationships. "No science fiction." Receives 150 unsolicited mss/month. Accepts 1 mss/issue. Publishes ms 6-12 months after acceptance. Agented fiction 15%. **Publishes 8 new writers/year.** Recently published work by Sigmund Brower and Nancy Rue.

How to Contact Send complete ms. Send SASE for reply, return of ms or send a disposable copy of ms. Responds in 2 months to mss. Sample copy for $1.50 with 9×12 SASE. Writer's guidelines for #10 SASE.

Payment/Terms Pays $200 and up for first-time contributor and 5 contributor's copies; additional copies available. Pays on acceptance for first North American serial, first, one-time, electronic rights.

Advice Looks for "humor with a point, historical fiction featuring great Christians or Christians who lived during great times; contemporary, exotic settings; holiday material (Christmas, Thanksgiving, Easter, President's Day); parables; fantasy (avoid graphic descriptions of evil creatures and sorcery); mystery stories; choose-your-own adventure stories. No contemporary, middle-class family settings (we already have authors who can meet these needs) or stories dealing with boy-girl relationships."

N $⊞ COSMOS, A MAGAZINE OF IDEAS, SCIENCE, SOCIETY AND THE FUTURE

Luna Media Pty Ltd, P.O. Box 302, Strawberry Hills, NSW 2012, Sydney Australia. (61)(2)9219 2500. Fax: (61)(2)9281 2360. E-mail: fiction@cosmosmagazine.com. Web site: www.cosmosmagazine.com. **Contact:** Damien Broderick, fiction editor. Magazine: 230 mm × 275 mm, 112 pages, 80 gsm paper, 150 gsm cover. Contains illustrations and photographs. "We look for stories that are well written, stylistically and imaginatively executed, and polished. They should involve some element of science: a new technology, a new idea, a different society or alternative reality, but based on scientific premises, principles and possibilities. It doesn't have to be set in the future, but it's kind of fun if it is." Monthly. Estab. 2005. Circ. 25,000.

Needs Science fiction (hard science/technological, soft/sociological). Does not want thinly-disguised lectures, poetic effusions with no science or quasi-science content, media spinoffs or fantasy. Accepts 1 mss/issue. Manuscript published 6 months after acceptance. Published Gregory Benford, Charles Stross, Paul Di Filippo, Joe Haldeman and others. Required length: "as close as possible to 2,000 words." Rarely comments on/critiques rejected mss.

How to Contact E-mail complete ms with cover letter. Include brief bio, list of publications. Responds to queries in 2 weeks. Responds to mss in 2 weeks. No simultaneous submissions, multiple submissions. Guidelines available on Web site.

Payment and Terms Writers receive $500 flat-rate payment, 2 contributors copies. Additional copies $4. **Pays on acceptance.** Acquires first worldwide rights for 3 months following date of first publication. Publication is copyrighted.

Advice "Because both our standards and our pay rates are so high, we are only interested in seeing the best writing. Unless you are convinced that your work is of top-shelf, global standard—the sort of excellent fiction published by, for example, *Asimov's*—please don't bother."

$⊚ DISCIPLESWORLD, A Journal of News, Opinion, and Mission for the Christian Church

DisciplesWorld, Inc., 6325 N. Guilford Ave., Dyr. 213, Indianapolis IN 46202. E-mail: editor@disciplesworld.com. Web site: www.disciplesworld.com. "We are the journal of the Christian Church (Disciples of Christ) in North America. Our denomination numbers roughly 800,000. Disciples are a mainline Protestant group. Our readers are mostly laity, active in their churches, and interested in issues of faithful living, political and church news, ethics, and contemporary social issues." Monthly. Estab. 2002. Circ. 14,000.

Needs Ethnic/multicultural, mainstream, novel excerpts, religious/inspirational, serialized novels, slice-of-life vignettes. "We're a religious publication, so use common sense! Stories do not have to be overtly 'religious,' but they should be uplifting and positive." Publishes ms 6 months after acceptance.

How to Contact Send complete ms. Accepts submissions by e-mail (editor@disciplesworld.com). Responds in 2 weeks to queries; 2 months to mss. Accepts simultaneous submissions. Sample copy for #10 SASE. Writer's guidelines online.

Payment/Terms Pays 16¢/word. Pays on publication for first North American serial rights.

$⊠ ⊞ ESQUIRE

Hearst, 1790 Broadway, 13th Floor, New York NY 10019. (212)649-4050. Web site: www.esquire.com. **Contact:** Adrienne Miller, literary editor. Magazine. Monthly magazine for smart, well-off men. General readership is college educated and sophisticated, between ages 30 and 45. Written mostly by contributing editors on contract. Rarely accepts unsolicited manuscripts. Monthly. Estab. 1933. Circ. 750,000.

• *Esquire* is well respected for its fiction and has received several National Magazine Awards. Work published in *Esquire* has been selected for inclusion in the *Best American Short Stories* and *O. Henry* anthologies.

Needs Novel excerpts, short stories, some poetry, memoirs, plays. No "pornography, science fiction or 'true romance' stories." Publishes special fiction issue in July. Receives 800 unsolicited mss/month. Rarely accepts unsolicited fiction. Publishes ms 2-6 months after acceptance. Recently published work by Russell Banks, Tim O'Brien, Richard Russo and David Means.

How to Contact Send complete ms. Accepts simultaneous submissions. Writer's guidelines for SASE.

Payment/Terms Pays in cash on acceptance, amount undisclosed. Retains first worldwide periodical publication rights for 90 days from cover date.

Advice "Submit one story at a time. We receive over 10,000 stories a year, so worry a little less about publication, a little more about the work itself."

$⊠ ⊚ EVANGEL

Free Methodist Publishing House, P.O. Box 535002, Indianapolis IN 46253-5002. (317)244-3660. Magazine: 5½×8½; 8 pages; 2 and 4-color illustrations; color and b&w photos. Sunday school take-home paper for distribution to adults who attend church. Fiction involves people coping with everday crises, making decisions that show spiritual growth. Weekly distribution. Printed quarterly. Estab. 1897. Circ. 10,000.

Needs Religious/inspirational. "No fiction without any semblance of Christian message or where the message clobbers the reader. Looking for more short pieces of devotional nature of 500 words or less." Receives 300 unsolicited mss/month. Accepts 3-4 mss/issue; 156-200 mss/year. Publishes ms 18-36 months after acceptance. **Publishes 7 new writers/year.** Recently published work by Karen Leet and Dennis Hensley.

How to Contact Send complete ms. Responds in 4-6 weeks to queries. Accepts multiple submissions. Sample copy and writer's guidelines for #10 SASE.

Payment/Terms Pays 4¢/word and 2 contributor's copies. Pays on publication. Buys second serial (reprint) or one-time rights.

Advice "Choose a contemporary situation or conflict and create a good mix for the characters (not all-good or all-bad heroes and villians). Don't spell out everything in detail; let the reader fill in some blanks in the story. Keep him guessing." Rejects mss because of "unbelievable characters and predictable events in the story."

$ ⊚ FIFTY SOMETHING MAGAZINE

Linde Graphics Co., 1168 S. Beachview Rd., Willoughby OH 44094. (440)951-2468. Fax: (440)951-1015. "We are focusing on the 50-and-better reader." Quarterly. Estab. 1990. Circ. 10,000.

Needs Adventure, confessions, ethnic/multicultural, experimental, fantasy, historical, humor/satire, mainstream, mystery/suspense, novel excerpts, romance, slice-of-life vignettes, suspense, western. No erotica or horror. Receives 150 unsolicited mss/month. Accepts 5 mss/issue. Publishes ms 6 months after acceptance. **Publishes 20 new writers/year.** Recently published work by Gail Morrisey, Sally Morrisey, Jenny Miller, J. Alan Witt, Sharon McGreagor. Length: 500-1,000 words; average length: 1,000 words. Publishes short shorts.

How to Contact Send complete ms. Responds in 3 months to queries; 3 months to mss. Accepts simultaneous submissions and reprints. Sample copy for 9×12 SAE and 4 first-class stamps. Writer's guidelines for #10 SASE.

Payment/Terms Pays $10-100. Pays on publication for one-time, second serial (reprint), simultaneous rights.

$ ⊚ FIRST HAND, Experiences For Loving Men

Firsthand, Ltd., 310 Cedar Lane, Teaneck NJ 07666. (201)836-9177. Fax: (201)836-5055. **Contact:** Don Dooley, editor. Magazine: digest-size; 130 pages; illustrations. "Half of the magazine is made up of our readers' own gay sexual experience. Rest is fiction and video reviews." Monthly. Estab. 1980. Circ. 70,000.

Needs Erotica, gay. "Should be written in first person." No science fiction or fantasy. Erotica should detail experiences based in reality. Receives 75-100 unsolicited mss/month. Accepts 6 mss/issue; 72 mss/year. Publishes ms 9-18 months after acceptance. Length: 2,500-3,750 words; average length: 3,000 words. Sometimes comments on rejected mss.

How to Contact Send complete ms. Include name, address, telephone and Social Security number and "advise on use of a pseudonym if any. Also whether selling all rights or first North American rights." Responds in 2 months to queries; 4 months to mss. No simultaneous submissions. Sample copy for $5.99. Writer's guidelines for #10 SASE.

Payment/Terms Pays $75. Pays on publication. Aquires all rights (exceptions made) and second serial (reprint) rights.

Advice "Avoid the hackneyed situations. Be original. We like strong plots."

$ FRICTION ZONE, Motorcycle Travel and Information

60166 Hop Patch Spring Road, Mountain Center CA 92561. (951)659-9500. Fax: (951)659-8182. E-mail: editor@friction-zone.com. Web site: www.friction-zone.com. **Contact:** Amy Holland. Monthly. Estab. 1999. Circ. 33,000.

Needs "Want stories concerning motorcycling or motorcyclists. No 'first-person' fiction." Accepts 1 mss/issue; 12 mss/year. Publishes ms 1 month after acceptance. **Publishes 20 new writers/year.** Length: 1,000-2,000 words; average length: 1,500 words. Publishes short shorts. Often comments on rejected mss.

How to Contact Query. Sample copy for $4.50 or on Web site. Writer's guidelines online.

Payment/Terms Pays 20¢/word. Pays on publication for first North American serial rights.

Advice "If you are not familar with the lifestyle of a motorcyclist, i.e. if you're not a motorcycle rider, your work will likely not be accepted."

◪ GRIT, American Life and Traditions

Ogden Publications, 1503 SW 42nd St., Topeka KS 66609-1265. (785)274-4300. Fax: (785)274-4305. E-mail: grit@grit.com. Web site: www.grit.com. **Contact:** Fiction Department. Magazine: 48-64 pages; 30 lb. newsprint; illustrations; photos. "*Grit* is good news. As a wholesome, family-oriented magazine published for more than a century and distributed nationally, *Grit* features articles about family lifestyles, traditions, values and pastimes. *Grit* accents the best of American life and traditions—past and present. Our readers are ordinary people doing extraordinary things, with courage, heart, determination and imagination. Many of them live in small towns and rural areas across the country; others live in cities but share many of the values typical of small-town America." Monthly. Estab. 1882. Circ. 100,000.

• *Grit* is considered one of the leading family-oriented publications.

Needs Adventure, mainstream, mystery/suspense, inspiring, romance (contemporary, historical), western (frontier, traditional), nostalgia. "No sex, violence, drugs, obscene words, abuse, alcohol or negative diatribes." "Special Storytellers issue in December; 5-6 manuscripts needed; submit in June." Accepts 1-2 mss/issue; 12-24 mss/year. **Publishes 12-15 new writers/year.** Length: 1,200-4,000 words; average length: 1,500-3,000 words. Also publishes poetry; send in batches of no more than 5.

How to Contact Send complete ms. Send SASE for return of ms. No e-mail submissions. No simultaneous submissions. Sample copy and writer's guidelines for $4 and 11×14 SASE with 4 first-class stamps. Sample nonfiction articles and writer's guidelines on Web site.

Payment/Terms Pays on acceptance for shared rights.

Advice "Keep trying and be patient."

$⬛ FUNNY TIMES, A Monthly Humor Review

Funny Times, Inc., P.O. Box 18530, Cleveland Heights OH 44118. (216)371-8600. Fax: (216)371-8696. Web site: www.funnytimes.com. **Contact:** Ray Lesser and Susan Wolpert, editors. Zine specializing in humor: tabloid; 24 pages; newsprint; illustrations. "*Funny Times* is a monthly review of America's funniest cartoonists and writers. We are the *Reader's Digest* of modern American humor with a progressive/peace-oriented/environmental/politically activist slant." Monthly. Estab. 1985. Circ. 74,000.

Needs Humor/satire. "Anything funny." Receives hundreds unsolicited mss/month. Accepts 5 mss/issue; 60 mss/year. Publishes ms 3 months after acceptance. Agented fiction 10%. **Publishes 10 new writers/year.** Publishes short shorts.

How to Contact Query with published clips. Include list of publications. Send SASE for return of ms or disposable copy of ms. Responds in 3 months to mss. Accepts simultaneous submissions and reprints. Sample copy for $3 or 9×12 SAE with 4 first-class stamps (83¢ postage). Writer's guidelines online.

Payment/Terms Pays $50-150. Pays on publication for one-time, second serial (reprint) rights.

Advice "It must be funny."

$◎ 🅥 HADASSAH MAGAZINE

50 W. 58th St., New York NY 10019. (212)451-6289. Fax: (212)451-6257. Web site: www.hadassah.org/magazine. **Contact:** Zelda Shluker, managing editor. Jewish general interest magazine: 7⅞×10½; 64-80 pages; coated and uncoated paper; slick, medium weight coated cover; drawings and cartoons; photos. "*Hadassah* is a general interest Jewish feature and literary magazine. We speak to our readers on a vast array of subjects ranging from politics to parenting, midlife crisis to Mideast crisis. Our readers want coverage on social and economic issues, Jewish women's (feminist) issues, the arts, travel and health." Monthly. Circ. 243,000.

• *Hadassah* has been nominated for a National Magazine Award and has received numerous Rockower Awards for Excellence in Jewish Journalism.

Needs Ethnic/multicultural (Jewish). No personal memoirs, "schmaltzy" or shelter magazine fiction. Receives 20-25 unsolicited mss/month. **Publishes some new writers/year.** Recently published work by Joanne Greenberg and Jennifer Traig.

How to Contact Must submit appropriate sized SASE. Responds in 4 months to mss. Sample copy and writer's guidelines for 9×12 SASE.

Payment/Terms Pays $700 minimum. Pays on acceptance for first North American serial, first rights.

Advice "Stories on a Jewish theme should be neither self-hating nor schmaltzy."

$⬛ HARPER'S MAGAZINE

666 Broadway, 11th Floor, New York NY 10012. (212)420-5720. Fax: (212)228-5889. Web site: www.harpers.org. **Contact:** Ben Metcalf. Magazine: 8×10¾; 80 pages; illustrations. "*Harper's Magazine* encourages national discussion on current and significant issues in a format that offers arresting facts and intelligent opinions. By means of its several shorter journalistic forms—Harper's Index, Readings, Forum, and Annotation—as well as with its acclaimed essays, fiction and reporting, *Harper's* continues the tradition begun with its first issue in 1850: to inform readers across the whole spectrum of political, literary, cultural and scientific affairs." Monthly. Estab. 1850. Circ. 230,000.

Needs Humor/satire. Stories on contemporary life and its problems. Receives 50 unsolicited mss/month. Accepts 12 mss/year. Publishes ms 3 months after acceptance. **Publishes some new writers/year.** Recently published work by Rebecca Curtis, George Saunders, Haruki Murakami, Margaret Atwood, Allan Gurganus, Evan Connell and Dave Bezmosgis.

How to Contact Query. Responds in 3 months to queries. Accepts reprint submissions. SASE required for all unsolicited material. Sample copy for $6.95.

Payment/Terms Generally pays 50¢-$1/word. Pays on acceptance. Vary with author and material. Sends galleys to author.

$☑ ⊻ HIGHLIGHTS FOR CHILDREN

803 Church St., Honesdale PA 18431-1824. (570)253-1080. Fax: (570)251-7847. Web site: www.highlights.com. **Contact:** Marileta Robinson, senior editor. Magazine: $8^{1}/_{2} \times 11$; 42 pages; uncoated paper; coated cover stock; illustrations; photos. "This book of wholesome fun is dedicated to helping children grow in basic skills and knowledge, in creativeness, in ability to think and reason, in sensitivity to others, in high ideals and worthy ways of living—for children are the world's most important people. We publish stories for beginning and advanced readers. Up to 500 words for beginners (ages 3-7), up to 800 words for advanced (ages 8-12)." Monthly. Estab. 1946. Circ. more than 2,000,000.

- *Highlights* has won the Parent's Guide to Children's Media Award, Parent's Choice Award, and Editorial Excellence Awards from the Association of Educational Publishers.

Needs Adventure, children's/juvenile (ages 2-12), fantasy, historical, humor/satire, animal, contemporary, folktales, multicultural, problem-solving, sports. "No war, crime or violence." Unusual stories appealing to both girls and boys; stories with good characterization, strong emotional appeal, vivid, full of action. "Needs stories that begin with action rather than description, have strong plot, believable setting, suspense from start to finish." Receives 600-800 unsolicited mss/month. **Publishes 30 new writers/year.** Recently published work by Eileen Spinelli, James M. Janik, Teresa Bateman, Maryilyn Kratz, Ruskin Bond. Occasionally comments on rejected mss.

How to Contact Send complete ms. Responds in 2 months to queries. Accepts multiple submissions. Sample copy free. Writer's guidelines for SASE or on Web site.

Payment/Terms Pays $150 minimum, plus 2 contributor's copies. **Pays on acceptance.** Sends galleys to author.

Advice "We accept a story on its merit whether written by an unpublished or an experienced writer. Mss are rejected because of poor writing, lack of plot, trite or worn-out plot, or poor characterization. Children *like* stories and learn about life from stories. Children learn to become lifelong fiction readers by enjoying stories. Feel passion for your subject. Create vivid images. Write a child-centered story; leave adults in the background."

☑ ⊻ ALFRED HITCHCOCK'S MYSTERY MAGAZINE

Dell Magazines, 475 Park Ave. S., 11th Floor, New York NY 10016. Web site: www.themysteryplace.com. **Contact:** Linda Landrigan, editor. Mystery fiction magazine: $5^{1}/_{2} \times 8^{3}/_{8}$; 144 pages; 28 lb. newsprint paper; 70 lb. machine-coated cover stock; illustrations; photos. Monthly. Estab. 1956. Circ. 125,000.

- Stories published in *Alfred Hitchcock's Mystery Magazine* have won Edgar Awards for "Best Mystery Story of the Year," Shamus Awards for "Best Private Eye Story of the Year" and Robert L. Fish Awards for "Best First Mystery Short Story of the Year."

Needs Mystery/suspense (amateur slueth, private eye, police procedural, suspense, etc.). No sensationalism. Number of mss/issue varies with length of mss. Recently published work by Rhys Bowen, Doug Allyn, I.J. Parker, Martin Limón.

How to Contact Send complete ms. Responds in 3 months to mss. Sample copy for $5. Writer's guidelines for SASE or on Web site.

Payment/Terms Payment varies. Pays on publication for first serial, foreign rights.

$ INDY MEN'S MAGAZINE, The Guy's Guide to the Good Life

Table Moose Media, 8500 Keystone Crossing, Indianapolis IN 46240. (317)255-3850. E-mail: lou@indymensmag azine.com. Web site: www.indymensmagazine.com. "We are very, very selective when it comes to fiction and have even put our fiction department on hold for a couple of months because we haven't found the pieces. Stories must be outstanding and must stand alone. From square one they must hold our attention and convince us that we are in the hands of a professional. Character and plot are important, but so are rhythm and style. Send complete manuscript for fiction. Query first for nonfiction." Monthly. Estab. 2002. Circ. 50,000.

Needs Adventure, fantasy, historical, horror, humor/satire, mainstream, mystery/suspense, science fiction, suspense.

How to Contact Send complete ms. Accepts submissions by e-mail (lou@indynewsmagazine.com). Responds in 2 months to mss. Accepts simultaneous submissions. Sample copy for $5. Writer's guidelines by e-mail.

Payment/Terms Pays $50-150. Pays on publication for first North American serial rights.

◎ JEWISH CURRENTS MAGAZINE

45 E. 33rd Street, New York NY 10016-1919. (845)626-2427. E-mail: lawrencebush@earthlink.net. **Contact:** Lawrence Bush. Magazine: $8^{1}/_{2} \times 11$; 48 pages. "We are a secular, progressive, independent Jewish bimonthly, printing fiction, poetry, articles and reviews on Jewish politics and history. Holocaust/Resistance, Mideast peace process, Black-Jewish relations, labor struggles, women's issues. Audience is secular, left/progressive, Jewish, mostly urban." Bimonthly. Estab. 1946. Circ. 16,000.

Needs Ethnic/multicultural, feminist, historical, humor/satire, translations, contemporary; senior citizen/retirement. "No religious, sectarian; no porn or hard sex, no escapist stuff. Go easy on experimentation, but we're interested." Must be well written! We are interested in *authentic* experience and readable prose; humanistic orientation. Must have Jewish theme. Could use more humor; short, smart, emotional and intellectual impact." Upcoming Themes: (submit at least 6 months in advance): "Black-Jewish Relations" (January/February); "International Women's Day, Holocaust/Resistance, Passover" (March/April); "Israel" (May/June); "Jews in the USSR and Ex-USSR" (July/August); "Jewish Book Month, Hanuka" (November/December). Receives 6-10 unsolicited mss/month. Accepts 0-1 mss/issue; 8-10 mss/year. Publishes ms 2-24 months after acceptance. Recently published work by Lanny Lefkowitz, Esther Cohen, Paul Beckman, Shirley Adelman, Galena Vromen, Alex B. Stone. Length: 1,000-3,000 words; average length: 1,800 words. Publishes short shorts. Also publishes literary essays, literary criticism, poetry.

How to Contact Send complete ms with cover letter, SASE. "Writers should include brief biographical information, especially their publishing histories." Responds in 2 months to mss. Sample copy for $3 with SAE and 3 first class stamps. Reviews fiction.

Payment/Terms Pays complimentary one-year subscription and 6 contributor's copies. "We readily give reprint permission at no charge." Sends galleys to author.

Advice Noted for "stories with Jewish content and personal Jewish experience—e.g., immigrant or Holocaust memories, assimilation dilemmas, dealing with Jewish conflicts OK. Space is increasingly a problem. Be intelligent, imaginative, intuitive and absolutely honest. Have a musical ear, and an ear for people: how they sound when they talk and also hear what they don't say."

$⬚⬚⬚⬚ KALEIDOSCOPE, Exploring the Experience of Disability Through Literature and the Fine Arts

Kaleidoscope Press, 701 S. Main St., Akron OH 44311-1019. (330)762-9755. Fax: (330)762-0912. Web site: www.udsakron.org. **Contact:** Gail Willmott, editor-in-chief. Magazine: $8^{1/2} \times 11$; 64 pages; non-coated paper; coated cover stock; illustrations (all media); photos. Subscribers include individuals, agencies and organizations that assist people with disabilities and many university and public libraries. Open to new writers but appreciates work by established writers as well. Especially interested in work by writers with a disability, but features writers both with and without disabilities. "Writers without a disability must limit themselves to our focus, while those with a disability may explore any topic (although we prefer original perspectives about experiences with disability)." Semiannual. Estab. 1979. Circ. 1,000.

• *Kaleidoscope* has received awards from the American Heart Association, the Great Lakes Awards Competition and Ohio Public Images.

Needs "We look for well-developed plots, engaging characters and realistic dialogue. We lean toward fiction that emphasizes character and emotions rather than action-oriented narratives. No fiction that is stereotypical, patronizing, sentimental, erotic or maudlin. No romance, religious or dogmatic fiction; no children's literature." Receives 20-25 unsolicited mss/month. Accepts 10 mss/year. Agented fiction 1%. **Publishes 1 new writer/ year.** Recently published work by Mark Wellman, Tamara B. Titus and Elizabeth Cohen. Also publishes poetry.

How to Contact Accepts submissions by fax. Query first or send complete ms and cover letter with SASE. Include author's education and writing background and, if author has a disability, how it influenced the writing. Responds in 3 weeks to queries; 6 months to mss. Accepts simultaneous, multiple submissions and reprints. Sample copy for $6 prepaid. Writer's guidelines online.

Payment/Terms Pays $10-125, 2 contributor's copies; additional copies $6. Pays on publication for first rights, reprints permitted with credit given to original publication. Rights revert to author upon publication.

Advice "Read the magazine and get submission guidelines. We prefer that writers with a disability offer original perspectives about their experiences; writers without disabilities should limit themselves to our focus in order to solidify a connection to our magazine's purpose. Do not use stereotypical, patronizing and sentimental attitudes about disability."

$⬚ KENTUCKY MONTHLY

Vested Interest Publications, 213 St. Clair St., Frankfort KY 40601. (502)227-0053. Fax: (502)227-5009. E-mail: membry@kentuckymonthly.com. Web site: www.kentuckymonthly.com. **Contact:** Michael Embry, editor. "We publish stories about Kentucky and by Kentuckians, including those who live elsewhere." Monthly. Estab. 1998. Circ. 40,000.

Needs Adventure, historical, mainstream, novel excerpts. Publishes ms 3 months after acceptance.

How to Contact Query with published clips. Accepts submissions by e-mail, fax. Responds in 3 weeks to queries; 1 month to mss. Accepts simultaneous submissions. Sample copy online. Writer's guidelines online.

Payment/Terms Pays $50-100. Pays within 3 months of publication. Acquires first North American serial rights.

$⬚⬚ LIGUORIAN

One Liguori Dr., Liguori MO 63057-9999. (636)464-2500. Fax: (636)464-8449. E-mail: liguorianeditor@liguori.org. Web site: www.liguorian.org. **Contact:** Fr. William Parker, C.Ss.R, editor-in-chief. Magazine: $10^{5/8} \times 8$; 40 pages; 4-

color illustrations; photos. "Our purpose is to lead our readers to a fuller Christian life by helping them better understand the teachings of the gospel and the church and by illustrating how these teachings apply to life and the problems confronting them as members of families, the church, and society." Estab. 1913. Circ. 200,000.

● *Liguorian* received Catholic Press Association awards for 2004 including second and third place for Best Short Story.

Needs Religious/inspirational, young adult/teen, senior citizen/retirement. "Stories submitted to *Liguorian* must have as their goal the lifting up of the reader to a higher Christian view of values and goals. We are not interested in contemporary works that lack purpose or are of questionable moral value." Receives 25 unsolicited mss/month. Accepts 12 mss/year. **Publishes 8-10 new writers/year.**

How to Contact Send complete ms. Accepts submissions by e-mail, fax, disk. Responds in 3 months to mss. Sample copy for 9×12 SAE with 3 first-class stamps or online. Writer's guidelines for #10 SASE and on Web site.

Payment/Terms Pays 10-15¢/word and 5 contributor's copies. Pays on acceptance. Buys first rights.

Advice "First read several issues containing short stories. We look for originality and creative input in each story we read. Since most editors must wade through mounds of manuscripts each month, consideration for the editor requires that the market be studied, the manuscript be carefully presented and polished before submitting. Our publication uses only one story a month. Compare this with the 25 or more we receive over the transom each month. Also, many fiction mss are written without a specific goal or thrust, i.e., an interesting incident that goes nowhere is *not a story*. We believe fiction is a highly effective mode for transmitting the Christian message and also provides a good balance in an unusually heavy issue."

$☐ LISTEN MAGAZINE, Celebrating Positive Choices

The Health Connection, 55 W. Oak Ridge Dr., Hagerstown MD 21740. (301)393-4010. Fax: (301)393-2294. E-mail : editor@ listenmagazine.org. Web site: www.listenmagazine.org. **Contact:** Celeste Perrino-Walker, editor. Magazine: 32 pages; glossy paper; illustrations; photos. "*Listen* is used in many high school classes and by professionals: medical personnel, counselors, law enforcement officers, educators, youth workers, etc. *Listen* publishes true lifestories about giving teens choices about real-life situations and moral issues in a secular way." Monthly. Circ. 40,000.

Needs Young adult/teen (easy-to-read, sports), anti-drug, alcohol, tobacco, positive role models. Publishes ms 6 months after acceptance. Length: 800-1,000; average length: 800 words.

How to Contact Query with published clips or send complete ms. Prefers submissions by e-mail. Responds in 2 months to queries. Accepts simultaneous, multiple submissions and reprints. Sample copy for $2 and 9×12 SASE. Writer's guidelines for SASE, by e-mail, fax or on Web site.

Payment/Terms Pays $50-150, 3 contributor's copies; additional copies $2. Pays on acceptance for first rights.

$☐ ⊚ LIVE, A Weekly Journal of Practical Christian Living

Gospel Publishing House, 1445 N. Boonville Ave., Springfield MO 65802-1894. (417)862-2781. Fax: (417)862-6059. E-mail: rl-live@gph.org. Web site: www.radiantlife.org. **Contact:** Richard Bennett, editor. "*LIVE* is a take-home paper distributed weekly in young adult and adult Sunday school classes. We seek to encourage Christians in living for God through fiction and true stories which apply Biblical principles to everyday problems." Weekly. Estab. 1928. Circ. 60,000.

Needs Religious/inspirational, prose poem. No preachy fiction, fiction about Bible characters, or stories that refer to religious myths (e.g., Santa Claus, Easter Bunny, etc.). No science fiction or Bible fiction. No controversial stories about such subjects as feminism, war or capital punishment. "Inner city, ethnic, racial settings." Accepts 2 mss/issue. Publishes ms 18 months after acceptance. **Publishes 75-100 new writers/year.** Recently published work by Tiffany Stuart, David Faust, Joanne Schulte, Michael W. Reed.

How to Contact Send complete ms. Accepts submissions by e-mail, fax. Responds in 2 weeks to queries; 6 weeks to mss. Accepts simultaneous submissions. Sample copy for #10 SASE. Writer's guidelines for #10 SASE.

Payment/Terms Pays 7-10¢/word. Pays on acceptance for first, second serial (reprint) rights.

Advice "Study our publication and write good, inspirational stories that will encourage people to become all they can be as Christians. Stories should go somewhere! Action, not just thought; interaction, not just insights. Heroes and heroines, suspense and conflict. Avoid simplistic, pietistic conclusions, preachy, critical or moralizing. We don't accept science fiction or Bible fiction. Stories should be encouraging, challenging, humorous. Even problem-centered stories should be upbeat." Reserves the right to change the titles, abbreviate length and clarify flashbacks for publication.

$☒ ⊚ LIVING LIGHT NEWS

Living Light Ministries, 5306 89th St., #200, Edmonton AB T6E 5P9 Canada. (780)468-6872. Fax: (780)468-6872. Web site: www.livinglightnews.org. **Contact**: Jeff Caporale. Newspaper: 11×17; 40 pages; newsprint; electrobrite cover; illustrations; photos. "Our publication is a seeker-sensitive evangelical outreach-oriented newspaper focusing on glorifying God and promoting a personal relationship with Him." Bimonthly. Estab. 1995. Circ. 30,000.

Needs Religious/inspirational. No Victorian-era or strongly American fiction. "We are a Northern Canadian publication interested in Christmas-related fiction focusing on the true meaning of Christmas, humorous Christmas pieces." Christmas deadline is November 1st. Receives 3-4 unsolicited mss/month. Accepts 5 mss/year. Publishes ms 2-6 months after acceptance. **Publishes 2-6 new writers/year.** Length: 300-1,250 words; average length: 700 words. Publishes short shorts. Always comments on rejected mss.

How to Contact Query with or without published clips or send complete ms. Accepts submissions by e-mail. Responds in 5 days to queries; 2 weeks to mss. Accepts simultaneous, multiple submissions and reprints. Sample copy for 9×13 SAE with $2.50 in IRCs or Canadian postage. Writer's guidelines for SASE, e-mail or on Web site.

Payment/Terms Pays $10-100. Pays on publication.

Advice "We are looking for lively, humorous, inviting, heart-warming Christmas-related fiction that focuses on the non-materialistic side of Christmas or shares God's love and grace with others. Try to write with pizzazz. We get many bland submissions. Do not be afraid to use humor and have fun."

$◎ THE LUTHERAN JOURNAL

Apostolic Publishing Co., Inc., P.O. Box 28158, Oakdale MN 55128. (651)702-0086. Fax: (651)702-0074. E-mail: lutheran2@msn.com. **Contact:** Vance E. Lichty. "A family magazine providing wholesome and inspirational reading material for the enjoyment and enrichment of Lutherans." Semiannual. Estab. 1938. Circ. 200,000.

Needs Literary, religious/inspirational, romance (historical), young adult/teen, senior citizen/retirement. Must be appropriate for distribution in the churches. Accepts 3-6 mss/issue.

How to Contact Send complete ms. Responds in 4 months to queries. Accepts simultaneous submissions. Sample copy for 9×12 SAE with 60¢ postage.

Payment/Terms Pays $50-300 and one contributor's copy. Pays on publication for first rights.

$⬛ ⬛ THE MAGAZINE OF FANTASY & SCIENCE FICTION

Spilogale, Inc., P.O. Box 3447, Hoboken NJ 07030. E-mail: fsfmagf@fsmag.com. Web site: www.fsfmag.com. **Contact:** Gordon Van Gelder, editor. Magazine: 5×8; 160 pages; groundwood paper; card stock cover; illustrations on cover only. "*The Magazine of Fantasy & Science Fiction* publishes various types of science fiction and fantasy short stories and novellas, making up about 80% of each issue. The balance of each issue is devoted to articles about science fiction, a science column, book and film reviews, cartoons, and competitions." Monthly. Estab. 1949. Circ. 50,00.

● The *Magazine of Fantasy & Science Fiction* won a Nebula Award for Best Novella for "Bronte's Egg" by Richard Chwedyk and a Nebula Award for Best Short Story for "Creature" by Carol Emshwiller. Also won the 2002 World Fantasy Award for Best Short Story for "Queen for a Day" by Albert E. Cowdrey.

Needs Adventure, fantasy (space fantasy, sword and sorcery), horror (dark fantasy, futuristic, psychological, supernatural), psychic/supernatural/occult, science fiction (hard science/technological, soft/sociological), young adult/teen (fantasy/science fiction, horror). No electronic submissions. "We're always looking for more science fiction." Receives 500-700 unsolicited mss/month. Accepts 5-8 mss/issue; 75-100 mss/year. Publishes ms 9-12 months after acceptance. **Publishes 1-5 new writers/year.** Recently published work by Ray Bradbury, Ursula K. Le Guin, Alex Irvine, Pat Murphy, Joyce Carol Oates and Robert Sheckley. Length: Up to 25,000 words; average length: 7,000 words. Publishes short shorts. Sometimes comments on rejected mss.

How to Contact Send complete ms with SASE (or IRC). Responds in 2 months to queries. Accepts reprint submissions. Sample copy for $5. Writer's guidelines for SASE, by e-mail or on Web site.

Payment/Terms Pays 6-9¢/word; additional copies $2.10. Pays on acceptance for first North American serial, foreign serial rights.

Advice "A well-prepared manuscript stands out better that one with fancy doo-dads. Fiction that stands out tends to have well-developed characters and thinks through the implications of its fantasy elements. It has been said 100 times before, but read an issue of the magazine before submitting. In the wake of the recent films, we are seeing more fantasy stories about sorcerers than we can possibly publish. Humorous stories about the future are in short supply nowadays."

⬛ $◻ ◎ MATURE LIVING: A Magazine for Christian Senior Adults

Lifeway Christian Resources, One Lifeway Plaza, Nashville TN 37234-0175. (615)251-2485. **Contact:** David Seay, editor-in-chief. Magazine: 8½×11; 52 pages; slick cover stock; full-color illustrations; photos. "Our magazine is Christian in content, and the material required is what would appeal to 55 and over age group: inspirational, informational, nostalgic, humorous. Our magazine is distributed mainly through churches (especially Southern Baptist churches) that buy the magazine in bulk and distribute it to members in this age group." Monthly. Estab. 1977. Circ. 315,000.

Needs Humor/satire, religious/inspirational, senior citizen/retirement. No reference to liquor, dancing, drugs, gambling; no pornography, profanity or occult. Accepts 8-10 mss/issue. Publishes ms 7-8 months after acceptance. Length: 600-1,200 words preferred; average length: 1,000 words.

How to Contact Send complete ms. "No queries please." Responds in 2 months to mss. Sample copy for 9×12 SAE with 4 first-class stamps. Writer's guidelines for #10 SASE.

Payment/Terms Pays $75-105 for feature articles; 3 contributor's copies. Pays on publication.

Advice Mss are rejected because they are too long or subject matter unsuitable. "Our readers seem to enjoy an occasional short piece of fiction. It must be believable, however, and present senior adults in a favorable light."

$ ✍ ◎ MATURE YEARS

The United Methodist Publishing House, 201 Eighth Ave. S., Nashville TN 37202-0801. (615)749-6292. Fax: (615)749-6512. E-mail: matureyears@umpublishing.org. **Contact:** Marvin Cropsey, editor. Magazine: 8½×11; 112 pages; illustrations; photos. Magazine "helps persons in and nearing retirement to appropriate the resources of the Christian faith as they seek to face the problems and opportunities related to aging." Quarterly. Estab. 1954. Circ. 55,000.

Needs Humor/satire, religious/inspirational, slice-of-life vignettes, retirement years issues, intergenerational relationships. "We don't want anything poking fun at old age, saccharine stories or anything not for older adults. Must show older adults (age 55 plus) in a positive manner." Accepts 1 mss/issue; 4 mss/year. Publishes ms 1 year after acceptance. **Publishes some new writers/year.** Recently published work by Terril Lee Shorb, Donita K. Paul and Suzanne Waring.

How to Contact Send complete ms. Responds in 2 weeks to queries; 2 months to mss. No simultaneous submissions. Sample copy for $5.25 and 9×12 SAE. Writer's guidelines for #10 SASE or by e-mail.

Payment/Terms Pays $60-125. Pays on acceptance for first North American serial rights.

Advice "Practice writing dialogue! Listen to people talk; take notes; master dialogue writing! Not easy, but well worth it! Most inquiry letters are far too long. If you can't sell me an idea in a brief paragraph, you're not going to sell the reader on reading your finished article or story."

$ 🌐 ◎ MSLEXIA, For Women Who Write

Mslexia Publications Ltd., P.O. Box 656, Newcastle Upon Tyne NE99 1PZ United Kingdom. (00)44-191-2616656. Fax: (00)44-191-2616636. E-mail: postbag@mslexia.demon.co.uk. Web site: www.mslexia.co.uk. **Contact:** Debbie Taylor, editor. Magazine: A4; 60 pages; some illustrations; photos. "*Mslexia* is for women who write, who want to write, who have a specialist interest in women's writing or who teach creative writing. *Mslexia* is a blend of features, articles, advice, listings, and original prose and poetry. Many parts of the magazine are open to submission from any women. Please request contributor's guidelines prior to sending in work." Quarterly. Estab. 1999. Circ. 20,000.

Needs No work from men accepted, except on letters' page. Prose and poetry in each issue is to a specific theme (e.g. fairy tales, flying, deadly sins). Send SASE for themes. Publishes ms 1-2 months after acceptance. **Publishes 40-50 new writers/year.** Length: 3,000 words; average length: 2,000 words. Publishes short shorts to a specific theme and autobiography (800 words). Also publishes poetry.

How to Contact Accepts submissions by e-mail (postbag@mslexia.demon.co.uk). Query first. Responds in 3 months to mss. Guidelines for SAE, e-mail, fax or on Web site.

Payment/Terms Pays £25 per poem; £15 per 1,000 words prose; features by negotiation. Plus contributors' copies.

Advice "Well structured, short pieces preferred. We look for intelligence and a strong sense of voice and place. Consider the obvious interpretations of the theme—then try to think of a new slant. Dare to be different. Make sure the piece is strong on craft as well as content. Extracts from novels are unlikely to be suitable."

$ ✍ ◎ MY FRIEND, The Catholic Magazine for Kids

Pauline Books & Media/Daughters of St. Paul, 50 Saint Pauls Ave., Jamaica Plain, Boston MA 02130-3491. (617)522-8911. Fax: (617)541-9805. E-mail: myfriend@pauline media. com. Web site: www.myfriendmagazine. com. **Contact:** Sister Maria Grace Dateno, editor. Magazine: 8½×11; 32 pages; smooth, glossy paper and cover stock; illustrations; photos. "*My Friend* is a 32-page monthly Catholic magazine for boys and girls ages 7-12. Its goal is to communicate religious truths and positive values in an enjoyable and attractive way." Theme list available. Send a SASE to the above address. Estab. 1979. Circ. 8,000.

Needs Children's/juvenile, religious/inspirational, sports, holidays. Receives 100 unsolicited mss/month. Accepts 3-4 mss/issue; 30-40 mss/year. Publishes ms 6 months after acceptance. **Publishes some new writers/year.** Recently published work by Diana Jenkins and Sandra Humphrey. Length: 600-1,200 words; average length: 850 words.

How to Contact Send complete ms. Responds in 2 months to mss. Sample copy for $2 and 9×12 SASE ($1.35). Writer's guidelines and theme list available at the Web site.

Payment/Terms Pays $75-150. Pays on acceptance. Buys worldwide publication rights.
Advice "We are particularly interested in fun and amusing stories with backbone. Good dialogue, realistic character development, current lingo are necessary. We have a need for each of these types at different times. We prefer child-centered stories in a real-world setting."

$ 🖸 THE NEW YORKER

The New Yorker, Inc., 4 Times Square, New York NY 10036. (212) 286-5900. E-mail: fiction@newyorker.com; fiction@newyorker.com. Web site: www.newyorker.com. **Contact:** Deborah Treisman, fiction editor. A quality magazine of interesting, well-written stories, articles, essays and poems for a literate audience. Weekly. Estab. 1925. Circ. 750,000.
Needs Accepts 1 mss/issue.
How to Contact Send complete ms. Accepts submissions by e-mail. No more than 1 story or 6 poems should be submitted. No attachments. Responds in 3 months to mss. No simultaneous submissions. Writer's guidelines online.
Payment/Terms Payment varies. Pays on acceptance.
Advice "Be lively, original, not overly literary. Write what you want to write, not what you think the editor would like. Send poetry to Poetry Department."

$ 🖸 OVER THE BACK FENCE, Southern Ohio's Own Magazine

Panther Publishing, LLC, P.O. Box 756, Chillicothe OH 45601. (740)772-2165. Fax: (740)773-7626. Web site: www.pantherpublishing.com. "We are a regional magazine serving 40 counties in Southern Ohio. *Over The Back Fence* has a wholesome, neighborly style. It appeals to readers from young adults to seniors, showcasing art and travel opportunities in the area." Quarterly. Estab. 1994. Circ. 15,000.
Needs Humor/satire. Receives 20 unsolicited mss/month. Accepts 2-3 mss/issue; 8-12 mss/year. Publishes ms 1 year after acceptance. **Publishes 4 new writers/year.** Recently published work by Debbie Farmer, Carol Lucas and Marcia Shonberg. Publishes short shorts. Also publishes poetry. Sometimes comments on rejected mss.
How to Contact Query with published clips. Responds in 3 months to queries. Accepts simultaneous submissions. Sample copy for $4 or on Web site. Writer's guidelines online.
Payment/Terms Pays 10¢/word minimum, negotiable depending on experience. Pays on publication for one-time North American serial rights, makes work-for-hire assignments.
Advice "Submitted pieces should have a neighborly, friendly quality. Our publication is a positive piece on the good things in Ohio."

$ 🖸 🖾 PLAYBOY MAGAZINE

730 5th Avenue, New York NY 10019. (212)261-5000. Web site: www.playboy.com. **Contact:** Fiction Department. "As the world's largest general interest lifestyle magazine for men, *Playboy* spans the spectrum of contemporary men's passions. From hard-hitting investigative journalism to light-hearted humor, the latest in fashion and personal technology to the cutting edge of the popular culture, *Playboy* is and always has been guidebook and dream book for generations of American men . . . the definitive source of information and ideas for over 10 million readers each month. In addition, *Playboy*'s 'Interview' and '20 Questions' present profiles of politicians, athletes and today's hottest personalities." Monthly. Estab. 1953. Circ. 3,283,000.
Needs Humor/satire, mainstream/literary, mystery/suspense. Does not consider poetry, plays, story outlines or novel-length mss. Writers should remember that the magazine's appeal is chiefly to a well-informed, young male audience. Fairy tales, extremely experimental fiction and outright pornography all have their place, but it is not in *Playboy*. Handwritten submissions will be returned unread. Writers who submit mss without including a SASE will receive neither the ms nor a printed rejection. "We will not consider stories submitted electronically or by fax."
How to Contact Query. Responds in 1 month to queries. No simultaneous submissions. Writer's guidelines for #10 SASE or online at Web site.
Payment/Terms Acquires first North American serial rights.
Advice "*Playboy* does not consider poetry, plays, story outlines or novel-length manuscripts."

$ 🖸 POCKETS

The Upper Room, 1908 Grand Ave., P.O. Box 340004, Nashville TN 37203-0004. (615)340-7333. Fax: (615)340-7267. E-mail: pockets@upperroom.org. Web site: www.pockets.org. **Contact**: Lynn W. Gilliam, editor. Magazine: 7×11; 48 pages; some photos. "We are a Christian, interdenominational publication for children 6-11 years of age. Each issue reflects a specific theme." Estab. 1981. Circ. 96,000.
   ● *Pockets* has received honors from the Educational Press Association of America.
Needs Adventure, ethnic/multicultural, historical (general), religious/inspirational, slice-of-life vignettes. No fantasy, science fiction, talking animals. "All submissions should address the broad theme of the magazine. Each issue is built around one theme with material which can be used by children in a variety of ways. Scripture stories, fiction, poetry, prayers, art, graphics, puzzles and activities are included. Submissions do not need to be overtly religious. They should help children experience a Christian lifestyle that is not always a neatly-

wrapped moral package, but is open to the continuing revelation of God's will. Seasonal material, both secular and liturgical, is desired. No violence, horror, sexual, racial stereotyping or fiction containing heavy moralizing." Receives 200 unsolicited mss/month. Accepts 3-4 mss/issue; 33-44 mss/year. Publishes ms 1 year to 18 months after acceptance. **Publishes 15 new writers/year.** Length: 600-1,400 words; average length: 1,200 words.

How to Contact Send complete ms with SASE. Cover letter not required. Responds in 6 weeks to mss. Accepts one-time reprints, multiple submissions. For a sample copy, themes and/or guidelines send 9×12 SASE with 4 first-class stamps. Writer's guidelines, themes and due dates available online.

Payment/Terms Pays 14¢/word, plus 2-5 contributor's copies. Pays on acceptance for first North American serial rights. Sponsors awards/contests.

Advice "Listen to children as they talk with each other. Send for a sample copy. Study guidelines and themes before submitting. Many manuscripts we receive are simply inappropriate. Each issue is theme-related. Please send for list of themes. New themes published in December of each year. We strongly advise sending for themes or checking the Web site before submitting."

☑ ◎ PORTLAND MONTHLY, Maine's City Magazine

722 Congress St., Portland ME 041012. (207)775-4339. Fax: (207)775-2334. E-mail: editor@portlandmonthly.com. Web site: www.portlandmagazine.com. **Contact:** Colin Sargent, editor. Magazine: 200 pages; 60 lb. paper; 100 lb. cover stock; illustrations; photos. "City lifestyle magazine—fiction, style, business, real estate, controversy, fashion, cuisine, interviews and art relating to the Maine area." Monthly. Estab. 1986. Circ. 100,000.

Needs Historical, literary (Maine connection). Query first. Receives 20 unsolicited mss/month. Accepts 1 mss/issue; 10 mss/year. **Publishes 50 new writers/year.** Recently published work by C.D.B Bryan, Joan Connor, Mameve Medwed, Jason Brown, Sebastian Junger.

How to Contact Send complete ms with SASE.

Payment/Terms Pays on publication for first North American serial rights.

Advice "We publish ambitious short fiction featuring everyone from Frederick Barthelme to newly discovered fiction by Edna St. Vincent Millay."

$☑ ☒ ELLERY QUEEN'S MYSTERY MAGAZINE

Dell Magazines Fiction Group, 475 Park Ave. S., 11th Floor, New York NY 10016. (212)686-7188. Fax: (212)686-7414. E-mail: elleryqueen@dellmagazines.com. Web site: www.themysteryplace.com. **Contact:** Janet Hutchings, editor. Magazine: $5^3/_8 \times 8^1/_2$; 144 pages with special 240-page combined March/April and September/October issues. "*Ellery Queen's Mystery Magazine* welcomes submissions from both new and established writers. We publish every kind of mystery short story: the psychological suspense tale, the deductive puzzle, the private eye case—the gamut of crime and detection from the realistic (including the policeman's lot and stories of police procedure) to the more imaginative (including "locked rooms" and "impossible crimes"). *EQMM* has been in continuous publication since 1941. From the beginning, three general criteria have been employed in evaluating submissions: We look for strong writing, an original and exciting plot, and professional craftsmanship. We encourage writers whose work meets these general criteria to read an issue of *EQMM* before making a submission." Magazine for lovers of mystery fiction. Estab. 1941. Circ. 180,780 readers.

• *EQMM* has won numerous awards and sponsors its own award yearly for the best *EQMM* stories nominated by its readership.

Needs Mystery/suspense. No explicit sex or violence, no gore or horror. Seldom publishes parodies or pastiches. "We accept only mystery, crime, suspense and detective fiction." 2,500-8,000 words is the preferred range. Also publishes minute mysteries of 250 words; novellas up to 20,000 words from established authors. Publishes ms 6-12 months after acceptance. Agented fiction 50%. **Publishes 10 new writers/year.** Recently published work by Jeffery Deaver, Joyce Carol Oates and Margaret Maron. Sometimes comments on rejected mss.

How to Contact Send complete ms. Responds in 3 months to mss. Accepts simultaneous, multiple submissions. Sample copy for $5. Writer's guidelines for SASE or online.

Payment/Terms Pays 5-8¢/word, occasionally higher for established authors. Pays on acceptance for first North American serial rights.

Advice "We have a Department of First Stories and usually publish at least one first story an issue, i.e., the author's first published fiction. We select stories that are fresh and of the kind our readers have expressed a liking for. In writing a detective story, you must play fair with the reader, providing clues and necessary information. Otherwise you have a better chance of publishing if you avoid writing to formula."

$☑ SEEK

Standard Publishing, 8121 Hamilton Ave., Cincinnati OH 45231. (513)931-4050, ext. 351. Fax: (513)931-0950. E-mail: seek@standardpub.com. Web site: www.standardpub.com. Magazine: $5^1/_2 \times 8^1/_2$; 8 pages; newsprint paper; art and photo in each issue. "Inspirational stories of faith-in-action for Christian adults; a Sunday School take-home paper." Quarterly. Estab. 1970. Circ. 27,000.

Needs Religious/inspirational, religious fiction and religiously slanted historical and humorous fiction. No poetry. List of upcoming themes available online. Accepts 150 mss/year. Publishes ms 1 year after acceptance. **How to Contact** Send complete ms. Prefers submissions by e-mail. Writer's guidelines online. **Payment/Terms** Pays 7¢/word. Pays on acceptance for first North American serial, pays 5¢ for second serial (reprint) rights. **Advice** "Write a credible story with a Christian slant—no preachments; avoid overworked themes such as joy in suffering, generation gaps, etc. Most manuscripts are rejected by us because of irrelevant topic or message, unrealistic story, or poor charater and/or plot development. We use fiction stories that are believable."

$⊘◎▼ SHINE BRIGHTLY

GEMS Girls' Clubs, P.O. Box 7259, Grand Rapids MI 49510. (616)241-5616. Fax: (616)241-5558. E-mail: christina @gemsgc.org. Web site: www.gemsgc.org. **Contact:** Christina Malone, managing editor. Magazine: 8½×11; 24 pages; 50 lb. paper; 50 lb. cover stock; illustrations; photos. "Our purpose is to lead girls into a living relationship with Jesus Christ and to help them see how God is at work in their lives and the world around them. Puzzles, crafts, stories and articles for girls ages 9-14." Monthly. Estab. 1971. Circ. 18,000.

● *SHINE brightly* has received awards for fiction and illustrations from the Evangelical Press Association.

Needs Adventure (that girls could experience in their hometowns or places they might realistically visit), children's/juvenile, ethnic/multicultural, historical, humor/satire, mystery/suspense (believable only), religious/inspirational (nothing too preachy), romance (stories that deal with awakening awareness of boys are appreciated), slice-of-life vignettes, suspense (can be serialized). Write for upcoming themes. Each year has an overall theme and each month has a theme to fit with yearly themes. Receives 50 unsolicited mss/month. Accepts 3 mss/issue; 30 mss/year. Publishes ms 1 year after acceptance. **Publishes some new writers/year.** Recently published work by A.J. Schut. Length: 400-1,000 words; average length: 800 words. **How to Contact** Send complete ms. Responds in 2 months to queries. Accepts simultaneous submissions and reprints. Sample copy for 9×12 SAE with 3 first class stamps and $1. Writer's guidelines online. **Payment/Terms** Pays 3¢/word. Pays on publication for first North American serial, second serial (reprint), simultaneous rights. **Advice** "Try new and refreshing approaches. No fluffy fiction with Polyanna endings. We want stories dealing with real issues facing girls today. The one-parent, new girl at school is a bit overdone in our market. We have been dealing with issues like AIDS, abuse, drugs, and family relationships in our stories—more awareness-type articles."

$⊘◎▼ ST. ANTHONY MESSENGER

28 W. Liberty St., Cincinnati OH 45202-6498. (513)241-5615. Fax: (513)241-0399. E-mail: patm@americancathol ic.org. Web site: www.americancatholic.org. **Contact:** Father Pat McCloskey, O.F.M., editor. Magazine: 8×10¾; 60 pages; illustrations; photos. "*St. Anthony Messenger* is a Catholic family magazine which aims to help its readers lead more fully human and Christian lives. We publish articles which report on a changing church and world, opinion pieces written from the perspective of Christian faith and values, personality profiles, and fiction which entertains and informs." Estab. 1893. Circ. 308,884.

● This is a leading Catholic magazine but has won awards for both religious and secular journalism and writing from the Catholic Press Association, the International Association of Business Communicators, and the Society of Professional Journalists.

Needs Mainstream, religious/inspirational, senior citizen/retirement. "We do not want mawkishly sentimental or preachy fiction. Stories are most often rejected for poor plotting and characterization; bad dialogue—listen to how people talk; inadequate motivation. Many stories say nothing, are 'happenings' rather than stories." No fetal journals, no rewritten Bible stories. Receives 60-70 unsolicited mss/month. Accepts 1 mss/issue; 12 mss/year. Publishes ms 1 year after acceptance. **Publishes 3 new writers/year.** Recently published work by Geraldine Marshall Gutfreund, John Salustri, Beth Dotson, Miriam Pollikatsikis and Joseph Pici. Sometimes requests revisions before acceptance. **How to Contact** Send complete ms. Accepts submissions by e-mail, fax. "For quickest response send self-addressed stamped postcard with choices: Yes, we're interested in publishing; Maybe, we'd like to hold for future consideration; No, we've decided to pass on the publication." Responds in 3 weeks to queries; 2 months to mss. No simultaneous submissions. Sample copy for 9×12 SAE with 4 first-class stamps. Writer's guidelines online. Reviews fiction. **Payment/Terms** Pays 16¢/word maximum and 2 contributor's copies; $1 charge for extras. Pays on acceptance for first North American serial, electronic rights. **Advice** "We publish one story a month and we get up to 1,000 a year. Too many offer simplistic 'solutions' or answers. Pay attention to endings. Easy, simplistic, *deus ex machina* endings don't work. People have to feel characters in the stories are real and have a reason to care about them and what happens to them. Fiction entertains but can also convey a point and sound values."

$ST. JOSEPH'S MESSENGER & ADVOCATE OF THE BLIND

Sisters of St. Joseph of Peace, St. Joseph's Home, P.O. Box 288, Jersey City NJ 07303-0288. **Contact:** Sister Mary Kuiken, editor. Magazine: $8^1/_4 \times 11$; 12-16 pages. Semiannual. Estab. 1898. Circ. 13,000.

Needs Mainstream, religious/inspirational, romance, suspense, contemporary. Publishes ms 6 months after acceptance. Length: 700-900 words; average length: 800 words. Publishes short shorts. Also publishes poetry. Rarely comments on rejected mss.

How to Contact Send complete ms. Send SASE (or IRC) for return of the ms or send disposable copy of the ms and #10 SASE for reply only. Responds in 2 weeks to queries; 2 months to mss. Accepts simultaneous submissions and reprints. Sample copy and writer's guidelines for 9×12 SAE and 2 first-class stamps.

Payment/Terms Pays $10-20. Pays on acceptance. Buys first serial and second serial (reprint) rights; reassigns rights back to author after publication in return for credit line in next publication.

$ 🖪 🔘 STANDARD

Nazarene International Headquarters, 6401 The Paseo, Kansas City MO 64131. (816)333-7000. Fax: (816)333-4439. E-mail: cyourdon@nazarene.org. Web site: www.nazarene.org. **Contact:** Everett Leadingham, editor; Charlie L. Yourdon, managing editor. Magazine: $8^1/_2 \times 11$; 8 pages; illustrations; photos. Inspirational reading for adults. "In *Standard* we want to show Christianity in action, and we prefer to do that through stories that hold the reader's attention." Weekly. Estab. 1936. Circ. 130,000.

Needs "Looking for stories that show Christianity in action." Accepts 200 mss/year. Publishes ms 14-18 months after acceptance. **Publishes some new writers/year.**

How to Contact Send complete ms with SASE. Accepts submissions by e-mail. Accepts simultaneous submissions but pays at reprint rates. Writer's guidelines and sample copy for SAE with 2 first-class stamps.

Payment/Terms Pays $3^1/_2$¢/word for first rights; 2¢/word for reprint rights, and contributor's copies. Pays on acceptance for one-time rights, whether first or reprint rights.

Advice "Be conscientious in your use of Scripture; don't overload your story with quoatations. When you quote the Bible, quote it exactly and cite chapter, verse, and version used. (We prefer NIV.) *Standard* will handle copyright matters for Scripture. Except for quotations from the Bible, written permission for the use of any other copyrighted material (especially song lyrics) is the responsibility of the writer. Keep in mind the international audience of *Standard* with regard to geographic references and holidays. We cannot use stories about cultural, national, or secular holidays. Do not mention specific church affiliations. *Standard* is read in a variety of denominations. Do not submit any manuscrips which have been submitted to or published in any of the following: *Vista, Wesleyan Advocate, Holiness Today, Preacher's Magazine, World Mission, Women Alive*, or various teen and children's publications produced by WordAction Publishing Company. These are overlapping markets."

$ 🖪 🔘 THE STRAND MAGAZINE

P.O. Box 1418, Birmingham MI 48012-1418. (248)788-5948. Fax: (248)874-1046. E-mail: strandmag@strandmag .com. Web site: www.strandmag.com. **Contact:** A.F. Gulli, editor. "After an absence of nearly half a century, the magazine known to millions for bringing Sir Arthur Conan Doyle's ingenious detective, Sherlock Holmes, to the world has once again appeared on the literary scene. First launched in 1891, *The Strand* included in its pages the works of some of the greatest writers of the 20th century: Agatha Christie, Dorothy Sayers, Margery Allingham, W. Somerset Maugham, Graham Greene, P.G. Wodehouse, H.G. Wells, Aldous Huxley and many others. In 1950, economic difficulties in England caused a drop in circulation which forced the magazine to cease publication." Quarterly. Estab. 1998. Circ. 50,000.

Needs Horror, humor/satire, mystery/suspense (detective stories), suspense, tales of the unexpected, tales of terror and the supernatural "written in the classic tradition fo this century's great authors. We are NOT interested in submissions with any sexual content. Stories can be set in any time or place, provided they are well written and the plots interesting and well thought out." Publishes ms 4 months after acceptance.

How to Contact Query first with SASE (IRCs if outside the US). Responds in 1 month to queries. Sample copy not available. Writer's guidelines for #10 SASE.

Payment/Terms Pays $50-175. Pays on acceptance for first North American serial rights.

$ 🖪 🔘 TRUE CONFESSIONS

333 Seventh Ave. 11th Floor, New York NY 10001. (212)780-3500. Fax: (212)979-4825. E-mail: Nbrooks-harris@ dorchestermedia.com. **Contact:** Natasha Brooks-Harris, editor. Magazine: $8 \times 10^1/_2$; 112 pages; photos. "*True Confessions* is a women's magazine featuring true-to-life stories about working class women and their families." Monthly. Circ. 100,000.

Needs "Family problems, relationship issues, realistic romances, working woman and single mom, single woman problems, abuse, etc. Stories should help women lead better lives. Also stories about multicultural experience—Latino, African-American, Caribbean, Asian, Aboriginal and Native American, Alaskan/Aleut, Native Pacific Islander stories encouraged. Must be written in first-person. No science fiction or third person stories. Wants to see more first-person inspirationals, thrillers, mysteries, romances with an edge. Don't be afraid to take a risk when writing these stories. Be daring. We need seasonal stories, so consult a book of holidays—major and minor and craft stories with that theme in mind. However please send seasonal stories six months before the holiday. Mark the outside of your envelopes SEASONAL MATERIAL." Publishes ms on average 6 months after acceptance.

How to Contact Query. Accepts submissions by e-mail. Responds in 3 months to queries; 15 months to mss. Send ms and stories saved on disk or CD, saved as an MS Word file. No WP, MS Works, or .rtf files, please." Sample copy for $4.49.

Payment/Terms Pays 3¢/word or a flat $100 rate for mini-stories, 1 contributor's copy. Pays 2 months after publication.

Advice "Emotionally charged stories with a strong emphasis on characterization and well-defined plots are preferred. Stories should be intriguing, suspenseful, humorous, romantic or tragic. The plots and characters should reflect American life. I want stories that cover the wide spectrum of America. I want to feel as though I intimately know the narrator and his/her motivation. If your story is dramatically gripping and/or humorous, features three-dimensional characters, and a realistic conflict, you have an excellent chance of making a sale at *True Confessions*. I suggest writers read three to four issues of *True Confessions* before sending submissions. Do not talk down to our readers. Contemporary problems should be handled with insight and a fresh angle. Timely, first-person stories told by a sympathetic narrator are always needed as well as good romantic stories."

$▢ WOMAN'S WORLD

Bauer Publishing Co., 270 Sylvan Ave., Englewood Cliffs NJ 07632. (201)569-6699. Fax: (201)569-3584. E-mail: dearww@aol.com. **Contact:** Johnene Granger, fiction editor. Magazine: 9½×11; 54 pages. "We publish short romances and mini-mysteries for all woman, ages 18-68." Weekly. Estab. 1980. Circ. 1,600,000.

Needs Mystery/suspense, romance (contemporary). Not interested in science fiction, fantasy, historical romance or foreign locales. No explicit sex, graphic language or steamy settings. "We buy contemporary romances of 1,400 words. Stories must revolve around a compelling, true to life relationship dilemma; may feature a male or female protagonist, and may be written in either first or third person. We are *not* interested in stories of life-or-death, or fluffy, fly-away style romances. When we say romance, what we really mean is relationship, whether it's just beginning or is about to celebrate its 50th anniversary." Receives 2,500 unsolicited mss/month. Accepts 2 mss/issue; 104 mss/year. Publishes ms 4 months after acceptance. Recently published work by Linda S. Reilly, Linda Yellin and Tim Myers. Publishes short shorts.

How to Contact Send complete ms with SASE. *No queries.* Responds in 2 months to mss. Sample copy not available. Writer's guidelines for #10 SASE.

Payment/Terms Pays $500-1,000. Pays on acceptance. Buys first North American serial rights for 6 months.

Advice "Familiarize yourself totally with our format and style. Read at least a year's worth of *Woman's World* fiction. Analyze and dissect it. Regarding romances, scrutinize them not only for content but tone, mood and sensibility."

$▦ ▢ WRITERS' FORUM, Britain's Best Magazine for Writers

Writers International Ltd., P.O. Box 3229, Bournemouth Dorset BH1 1ZS United Kingdom. (44)1202 589828. Fax: (44)1202 587758. E-mail: editorial@writers-forum.com. Web site: www.writers-forum.com. **Contact:** John Jenkins, editor. Monthly: A4; 76 pages; illustrations; photos. "In each issue *Writers' Forum* covers the *who, why, what, where, when* and *how* of writing. You will find the latest on markets, how-to articles, courses/holidays for writers and much more. There is also a short story competition in every issue—that means you have 10 chances to get published and win some cash. Prizes range from £150 to 250 and there's £1,000 for the best story of the year. Monthly. Estab. 1995. Circ. 25,000.

Needs Erotica, historical, horror (psychological), literary, mainstream, mystery/suspense (cozy, private eye/hard-boiled), romance (contemporary, futuristic/time travel, historical, romantic suspense), science fiction (soft/sociological), thriller/espionage, western (frontier saga, traditional), young adult/teen (adventure, easy-to-read, historical, problem novels, romance). Receives hundreds unsolicited mss/month. Accepts 3-4 mss/issue; 20 mss/year. Publishes ms 2-3 months after acceptance. Length: 1,000-3,000 words; average length: 1,500 words. Also publishes literary essays, literary criticism, poetry. Always comments on rejected mss.

How to Contact Query. Accepts submissions by e-mail, fax. Send SASE (or IRC) for return of ms or send disposable copy of the ms and #10 SASE for reply only. Responds in 2-3 weeks to queries; 2-3 weeks to mss. Accepts simultaneous submissions. Sample copy online. Writer's guidelines online. Reviews fiction.

Payment/Terms Pays $120 maximum and 1 contributor's copy; additional copies $5. Pays 1 month following publication. Acquires first rights. Sponsors awards/contests.

Advice "A good introduction and an original slant on a common theme. Always read the competition rules and our guidelines."

WRITERS' JOURNAL, The Complete Writer's Magazine
Val-Tech Media, P.O. Box 394, Perham MN 56573-0394. (218)346-7921. Fax: (218)346-7924. E-mail: editor@writersjournal.com. Web site: www.writersjournal.com. *"Writers' Journal* is read by thousands of aspiring writers whose love of writing has taken them to the next step: writing for money. We are an instructional manual giving writers the tools and information necessary to get their work published. We also print works by authors who have won our writing contests." Bimonthly. Estab. 1980. Circ. 26,000.

Needs "We only publish winners of our fiction contests—16 contests/year." Receives 200 contest entries unsolicited mss/month. Accepts 5-7 mss/issue; 30-40 mss/year. Publishes ms 10 months after acceptance. Agented fiction 3%. **Publishes 100 new writers/year.** Also publishes poetry.

How to Contact Accepts submissions by e-mail (not as attachment). Responds in 6 weeks to queries; 6 months to mss. Accepts simultaneous submissions. Sample copy for $5.

Payment/Terms Pays on publication for one-time rights.

Book Publishers

I n this section, you will find many of the "big name" book publishers. Many of these publishers remain tough markets for new writers or for those whose work might be considered literary or experimental. Indeed, some only accept work from established authors, and then often only through an author's agent. Although having your novel published by one of the big commercial publishers listed in this section is difficult, it is not impossible. The trade magazine *Publishers Weekly* regularly features interviews with writers whose first novels are being released by top publishers. Many editors at large publishing houses find great satisfaction in publishing a writer's first novel.

On page 544, you'll find the publishing industry's "family tree," which maps out each of the large book publishing conglomerates' divisions, subsidiaries and imprints. Remember, most manuscripts are acquired by imprints, not their parent company, so avoid submitting to the conglomerates themselves. (For example, submit to Dutton or Berkley Books, not their parent Penguin.)

Also listed here are "small presses" publishing four or more titles annually. Included among them are independent presses, university presses and other nonprofit publishers. Introducing new writers to the reading public has become an increasingly important role of these smaller presses at a time when the large conglomerates are taking fewer chances on unknown writers. Many of the successful small presses listed in this section have built their reputations and their businesses in this way and have become known for publishing prize-winning fiction.

These smaller presses also tend to keep books in print longer than larger houses. And, since small presses publish a smaller number of books, each title is equally important to the publisher, and each is promoted in much the same way and with the same commitment. Editors also stay at small presses longer because they have more of a stake in the business—often they own the business. Many smaller book publishers are writers themselves and know firsthand the importance of a close editor-author or publisher-author relationship.

TYPES OF BOOK PUBLISHERS

Large or small, the publishers in this section publish books "for the trade." That is, unlike textbook, technical or scholarly publishers, trade publishers publish books to be sold to the general consumer through bookstores, chain stores or other retail outlets. Within the trade book field, however, there are a number of different types of books.

The easiest way to categorize books is by their physical appearance and the way they are marketed. Hardcover books are the more expensive editions of a book, sold through bookstores and carrying a price tag of around $20 and up. Trade paperbacks are soft-bound books, also sold mostly in bookstores, that carry a more modest price tag of usually around $10 to $20. Today a lot of fiction is published in this form because it means a lower financial risk than hardcover.

Mass market paperbacks are another animal altogether. These are the smaller ''pocket-size'' books available at bookstores, grocery stores, drug stores, chain retail outlets, etc. Much genre or category fiction is published in this format. This area of the publishing industry is very open to the work of talented new writers who write in specific genres like science fiction, romance and mystery.

At one time publishers could be easily identified and grouped by the type of books they produce. Today, however, the lines between hardcover and paperback books are blurred. Many publishers known for publishing hardcover books also publish trade paperbacks and have paperback imprints. This enables them to offer established authors (and a very few lucky newcomers) hard-soft deals in which their book comes out in both versions. Thanks to the mergers of the past decade, too, the same company may own several hardcover and paperback subsidiaries and imprints, even though their editorial focuses may remain separate.

CHOOSING A BOOK PUBLISHER

In addition to checking the bookstores and libraries for books by publishers that interest you, you may want to refer to the Category Index at the back of this book to find publishers divided by specific subject categories. The subjects listed in the Index are general. Read individual listings to find which subcategories interest a publisher. For example, you will find several romance publishers listed, but read the listings to find which type of romance is considered—gothic, contemporary, regency or futuristic. See You've Got a Story on page 2 for more on how to refine your list of potential markets.

The icons appearing before the names of the publishers will also help you in selecting a publisher. These codes are especially important in this section, because many of the publishing houses listed here require writers to submit through an agent. The ◩ symbol indicates that a publisher accepts agented submissions only. A ◪ icon identifies those that mostly publish established and agented authors, while a ◻ points to publishers most open to new writers. See the inside front cover of this book for a complete list and explanations of symbols used in this book.

IN THE LISTINGS

As with other sections in this book, we identify new listings with a ◪ symbol. In this section, most with this symbol are not new publishers, but instead are established publishers who were unable or decided not to list last year and are therefore new to this edition.

In addition to the ◪ symbol indicating new listings, we include other symbols to help you in narrowing your search. English-speaking foreign markets are denoted by a ◉ . The maple leaf symbol ◪ identifies Canadian presses. If you are not a Canadian writer but are interested in a Canadian press, check the listing carefully. Many small presses in Canada receive grants and other funds from their provincial or national government and are, therefore, restricted to publishing Canadian authors.

We also include editorial comments set off by a bullet (●) within listings. This is where we include information about any special requirements or circumstances that will help you know even more about the publisher's needs and policies. The star ◪ signals that this market is an imprint or division of a larger publisher. The ◪ symbol identifies publishers who have recently received honors or awards for their books. The ◪ denotes publishers who produce comics and graphic novels.

Each listing includes a summary of the editorial mission of the house, an overarching principle that ties together what they publish. Under the heading **Contact** we list one or more editors, often with their specific area of expertise.

Book editors asked us again this year to emphasize the importance of paying close attention to the **Needs** and **How to Contact** subheads of listings for book publishers. Unlike magazine editors who want to see complete manuscripts of short stories, most of the book publishers listed here ask that writers send a query letter with an outline and/or synopsis and several chapters of their novel. The Business of Fiction Writing, beginning on page 79 of this book, outlines how to prepare work to submit directly to a publisher.

There are no subsidy book publishers listed in *Novel & Short Story Writer's Market*. By subsidy, we mean any arrangement in which the writer is expected to pay all or part of the cost of producing, distributing and marketing his book. We feel a writer should not be asked to share in any cost of turning his manuscript into a book. All the book publishers listed here told us that they *do not charge writers* for publishing their work. **If any of the publishers listed here ask you to pay any part of publishing or marketing your manuscript, please let us know**. See our Complaint Procedure on the copyright page of this book.

A NOTE ABOUT AGENTS

Some publishers are willing to look at unsolicited submissions, but most feel having an agent is in the writer's best interest. In this section more than any other, you'll find a number of publishers who prefer submissions from agents. That's why we've included a section of agents open to submissions from fiction writers (page 152).

If you use the Internet or another resource to find an agent not listed in this book, be wary of any agents who charge large sums of money for reading a manuscript. Reading fees do not guarantee representation. Think of an agent as a potential business partner and feel free to ask tough questions about his or her credentials, experience and business practices.

Periodicals of Interest

For More Info

Check out issues of *Publishers Weekly* for publishing industry trade news in the U.S. and around the world or *Quill & Quire* for book publishing news in the Canadian book industry.

For more small presses see the *International Directory of Little Magazines and Small Presses* published by Dustbooks. To keep up with changes in the industry throughout the year, check issues of two small press trade publications: *Small Press Review* (also published by Dustbooks) and *Independent Publisher* (Jenkins Group, Inc.).

⊕ A&C BLACK PUBLISHERS, LTD.

Bloomsbury plc, 38 Soho Square, London W1D 3QZ United Kingdom. +44 (020)7758-0200. E-mail: childrens@a cblack.com. Web site: www.acblack.com. **Contact:** Reader, children's editorial department. Publishes hardcover and trade paperback originals, trade paperback reprints. Averages 170 total titles/year.

Imprint(s) Adlard Coles Nautical (Janet Murphy, editor); Christopher Helm/Pica Press (Nigel Redman, editor); Herbert Press (Linda Lambert, editor).

Needs Juvenile.

How to Contact Submit 2 sample chapter(s), synopsis or submit complete ms. Responds in 1 month to queries; 2 months to mss. Accepts simultaneous submissions.

Terms Pays royalty on retail price or net receipts; makes outright purchase very occasionally on short children's books.

HARRY N. ABRAMS, INC.

La Martiniere Groupe, Attn: Managing Editor, 115 West 18th St., New York NY 10011. (212)206-7715. Fax: (212)645-8437. Web site: www.abramsbooks.com. **Contact:** Managing editor. Estab. 1949. Publishes hardcover and "a few" paperback originals. Averages 150 total titles/year.

Imprint(s) Abrams Books; Stewart, Tabori & Chang; Abrams Books for Young Readers (including Amulet Books for Middle Grade and Young Adult); Abrams Gifts and Stationery.

How to Contact Responds in 6 months to queries. No simultaneous submissions, electronic submissions.

Terms Pays royalty. Average advance: variable. Publishes ms 2 years after acceptance. Book catalog for $5.

⊘ ABSEY & CO.

45 West 21st Street Ste. 5, New York NY 10010. (212)277-8028. E-mail: abseyandco@aol.com. Web site: www.a bsey.com. **Contact:** Edward E. Wilson, publisher. "We are interested in book-length fiction of literary merit with a firm intended audience." Publishes hardcover, trade paperback and mass market paperback originals. **Published 3-5 debut authors within the last year.** Averages 6-10 total titles, 6-10 fiction titles/year.

Needs Juvenile, mainstream/contemporary, short story collections. Published *Where I'm From*, by George Ella Lyon; *Blast Man Standing*, by Robert V. Spelleri.

How to Contact Accepts unsolicited mss. Query with SASE. Responds in 3 months to queries; 9 months to mss. No simultaneous submissions, electronic submissions.

Terms Royalty and advance vary. Publishes ms 1 year after acceptance. Ms guidelines online.

Advice "Since we are a small, new press looking for good manuscripts with a firm intended audience, we tend to work closely and attentively with our authors. Many established authors who have been with the large New York houses have come to us to publish their work because we work closely with them."

⊘ ACADEMY CHICAGO PUBLISHERS

363 W. Erie St., Suite 7E., Chicago IL 60610-3125. (312)751-7300. Fax: (312)751-7306. E-mail: info@academychicag o.com. Web site: www.academychicago.com. **Contact:** Anita Miller, senior editor. Estab. 1975. Midsize independent publisher. Publishes hardcover originals and trade paperback reprints. Averages 15 total titles/year.

Needs Historical, mainstream/contemporary, military/war, mystery. "We look for quality work, but we do not publish experimental, avant-garde novels." Biography, history, academic and anthologies. Only the most unusual mysteries, no private-eyes or thrillers. No explicit sex or violence. Serious fiction, no romance/adventure. "We will consider historical fiction that is well researched. No science fiction/fantasy, no religious/inspirational, no how-to, no cookbooks. In general, we are very conscious of women's roles. We publish very few children's books." Published *Clean Start*, by Patricia Margaret Page (first fiction); *Cutter's Island: Caesar in Captivity*, by Vincent Panella (first fiction, historical); *Murder at the Paniomic Games*, by Michael B. Edward.

How to Contact Accepts unsolicited mss. Submit 3 sample chapter(s), synopsis. Accepts queries by mail. Include cover letter briefly describing the content of your work. Send SASE or IRC. "Manuscripts without envelopes will be discarded. *Mailers* are a *must* even from agents." Responds in 3 months to queries. No electronic submissions.

Terms Pays 7-10% royalty on wholesale price. Average advance: modest. Publishes ms 18 months after acceptance. Ms guidelines online.

Advice "At the moment we are swamped with manuscripts and anything under consideration can be under consideration for months."

★ ⊘ ◎ ACE SCIENCE FICTION AND FANTASY

The Berkley Publishing Group, Penguin Group (USA), Inc., 375 Hudson St., New York NY 10014. (212)366-2000. Web site: www.penguin.com. **Contact:** Susan Allison, editor-in-chief; Anne Sowards, editor. Estab. 1953. Publishes hardcover, paperback and trade paperback originals and reprints. Averages 75 total titles, 75 fiction titles/year.

Needs Fantasy, science fiction. No other genre accepted. No short stories. Published *Iron Sunrise*, by Charles Stross; *Neuromancer*, by William Gibson; *King Kelson's Bride*, by Katherine Kurtz.

How to Contact Does not accept unsolicited mss. Submit 1-2 sample chapter(s), synopsis. Send SASE or IRC. Responds in 2-3 months to queries. Accepts simultaneous submissions.

Terms Pays royalty. Offers advance. Publishes ms 1-2 years after acceptance. Ms guidelines for #10 SASE.

Advice "Good science fiction and fantasy are almost always written by people who have read and loved a lot of it. We are looking for knowledgeable science or magic, as well as sympathetic characters with recognizable motivation. We are looking for solid, well-plotted science fiction: good action adventure, well-researched hard science with good characterization, and books that emphasize characterization without sacrificing plot. In fantasy we are looking for all types of work, from high fantasy to sword and sorcery." Submit fantasy and science fiction to Anne Sowards.

N ◎ ACME PRESS

P.O. Box 1702, Westminster MD 21158-1702. (410)848-7577. **Contact:** (Ms.) E.G. Johnston, managing editor. Estab. 1991. "We operate on a part-time basis." Publishes hardcover and trade paperback originals. **Published some debut authors within the last year.** Averages 1-2 total titles/year.

Needs Humor. "We accept submissions on any subject as long as the material is humorous; prefer full-length novels. No cartoons or art (text only). No pornography, poetry, short stories or children's material." Published *She-Crab Soup* by Dawn Langley Simmons (fictional memoir/humor); *Biting the Wall*, by J.M. Johnston (humor/mystery); and *SuperFan*, by Lyn A. Sherwood (comic/sports).

How to Contact Accepts unsolicited mss. Agented fiction 25%. Responds in 2 weeks to queries; 2 months to mss. Accepts simultaneous submissions. Always comments on rejected mss.

Terms Pays 25 author's copies and 50% of profits. Average advance: small. Publishes ms 1 year after acceptance. Book catalog and ms guidelines for #10 SASE.

◢ ◎ AGELESS PRESS

3759 Collins St., Sarasota FL 34232. E-mail: irishope@comcast.net. Web site: http://irisforrest.com. **Contact:** Iris Forrest, editor. Estab. 1992. Independent publisher. Publishes paperback originals. Books: acid-free paper; notched perfect binding; no illustrations. Averages 1 total title/year.

Needs Experimental, fantasy, humor, literary, mainstream/contemporary, mystery, new age/mystic, science fiction, short story collections, thriller/espionage. Looking for material "based on personal computer experiences." Stories selected by editor. Published *Computer Legends, Lies & Lore*, by various (anthology); and *Computer Tales of Fact and Fantasy*, by various (anthology).

How to Contact Does not accept unsolicited mss. Query with SASE. Accepts queries by e-mail, fax, mail. Responds in 1 week to queries; 1 week to mss. Accepts simultaneous submissions, electronic submissions, submissions on disk. Sometimes comments on rejected mss.

Terms Average advance: negotiable. Publishes ms 6-12 months after acceptance.

Advice "Query! Don't send work without a query!"

⊠ ALGONQUIN BOOKS OF CHAPEL HILL

Workman Publishing, P.O. Box 2225, Chapel Hill NC 27515-2225. (919)967-0108. Web site: www.algonquin.com. **Contact:** Editorial Department. Publishes hardcover originals. Averages 24 total titles/year.

Needs Literary fiction and nonfiction, cookbooks and lifestyle books (about family, animals, food, flowers, adventure, and other topics of interest). No poetry, genre fiction (romance, science fiction, etc.) or children's books. Recently published *Saving the World*, by Julia Alvarez; *Which Brings Me to You*, by Steve Almond and Julianna Baggott; *Hope and Other Dangerous Pursuits*, by Laila Lalami.

How to Contact Query by mail before submitting work. No phone, e-mail or fax queries or submissions. Visit our Web site for full submission policy to queries.

Terms Ms guidelines online.

⊘ ▼ ALLEN-AYERS BOOKS

4621 S. Atlantic Ave. #7603, Ponce Inlet FL 32127. E-mail: allen-ayers@cfl.rr.com. Web site: http://home.att.net/~allen-ayers. Estab. 2000. Allen-Ayers Books is a two-person operation on a part-time basis. Publishes paperback originals. Distributes through Ingram Books.

- *Never by Blood*, by Noel Carroll, received Scribs World's Reviewers Choice Award.

Needs Humor, science fiction (hard science/technological), short story collections, thriller/espionage. Published *Broken Odyssey*, by Noel Carroll (thriller); *Never by Blood*, by Noel Carroll (thriller); *Hey, God; Got A Minute?*, by John Barr (humor/satire); *Starve The Devil*, by Noel Carroll (thriller).

How to Contact Does not accept unsolicited queries. Never comments on rejected mss.

Terms Pays royalty. Ms guidelines for #10 SASE.

⊘ ⓒ ALTERNATIVE COMICS

503 NW 37th Ave., Gainsville FL 32609-2204. Web site: www.indyworld.com/altcomics. **Contact:** Jeff Mason, publisher. Estab. 1993.
How to Contact "Not currently accepting submissions."

⊘ ◎ ALYSON PUBLICATIONS

245 West 17th Street Suite 1200, New York, NY 10011. (212)242-8100. Fax: (212)727-7939. E-mail: mail@alyson.com. Web site: www.alyson.com. Estab. 1980. Medium-sized publisher specializing in lesbian- and gay-related material. Publishes hardcover and trade paperback originals and reprints. Books: paper and printing varies; trade paper, perfect bound. **Published some debut authors within the last year.** Averages 50 total titles, 25 fiction titles/year.
Imprint(s) Alyson Wonderland, Advocate Books.
Needs "We are interested in all categories; *all* materials must be geared toward lesbian and/or gay readers." Publishes anthologies. Authors may submit to them directly. Recently published *Back Where He Started*, by Jay Quinn; *My One-Night Stand With Cancer*, by Tania Katan; *Cruise Control*, by Robert Weiss; *Clay's Way*, by Blair Mastbaum.
How to Contact Query with SASE. Accepts queries by mail. Responds in 4 months to queries. Accepts simultaneous submissions.
Terms Pays 8-15% royalty on net receipts. Average advance: $1,500-5,000. Book catalog and ms guidelines for 6×9 SAE with 3 first-class stamps. Ms guidelines also online.

◎ AMBASSADOR BOOKS, INC.

91 Prescott St., Worcester MA 01605. (508)756-2893. Fax: (508)757-7055. Web site: www.ambassadorbooks.com. **Contact:** Chris Driscoll, acquisitions editor. Publishes hardcover and trade paperback originals. **Published 50% debut authors within the last year.** Averages 7 total titles/year.
Needs Juvenile, literary, picture books, religious, spiritual, sports, young adult, women's. Published *A Child's Bedtime Companion*, by Sandy Henry, illustrated by Vera Pavlova (children's); *Praying for a Miracle*, by Gilda D'Agostino (nonfiction inspirational); *Behind the Green Monster*, by Bill Ballou (sports).
How to Contact Query with SASE or submit complete ms. Responds in 3-4 months to queries. Accepts simultaneous submissions.
Terms Pays 8-10% royalty on retail price. Publishes ms 1 year after acceptance. Book catalog free or online.

↙ ⊘ ◎ ANVIL PRESS

278 East First Avenue, Vancouver BC V5T 1A6 Canada. (604)876-8710. Fax: (604)879-2667. E-mail: info@anvilpress.com. Web site: www.anvilpress.com. **Contact:** Brian Kaufman, publisher. Estab. 1988. "Three-person operation with volunteer editorial board." Publishes trade paperback originals. Canadian authors *only*. Books: offset or web printing; perfect bound. **Published some debut authors within the last year.** Averages 8-10 total titles/year.
Needs Experimental, literary, short story collections. Contemporary, modern literature—no formulaic or genre. Published *The Beautiful Dead End*, by Clint Hutzulack; *Knucklehead*, by W. Mark Giles (short stories); *Bogman's Music*, by Tammy Armstrong (poetry); *Shylock*, by Mark Leiren-Young (drama); *Socket*, by David Zimmerman.
How to Contact Accepts unsolicited mss, or query with SASE. Include estimated word count, brief bio. Send SASE for return of ms or send a disposable ms and SASE for reply only. Responds in 2 months to queries; 6 months to mss. Accepts simultaneous submissions.
Terms Pays 15% royalty on net receipts. Average advance: $500. Publishes ms 8 months after acceptance. Book catalog for 9×12 SAE with 2 first-class stamps. Ms guidelines online.
Advice "We are only interested in writing that is progressive in some way—form, content. We want contemporary fiction from serious writers who intend to be around for a while and be a name people will know in years to come. Read back titles, look through our catalog before submitting."

Ⓐ ◐ ARCADE PUBLISHING

141 Fifth Ave., New York NY 10010. (212)475-2633. **Contact:** Richard Seaver, Jeannette Seaver, Cal Barksdale, and Casey Ebro. Estab. 1988. Independent publisher. Publishes hardcover originals, trade paperback reprints. Books: 50-55 lb. paper; notch, perfect bound; illustrations. **Published some debut authors within the last year.** Averages 45 total titles, 12-15 fiction titles/year. Distributes titles through Time Warner Book Group.
Needs Ethnic, literary, mainstream/contemporary, short story collections. Published *Trying to Save Piggy Sneed*, by John Irving; *Judge Savage*, by Tim Parks; *Music of a Life*, by Andrei Makine; *The Last Song of Dusk*, by Siddharth Dhanvant Shanghvi; *Bibliophilia*, by Michael Griffith.
How to Contact Does not accept unsolicited mss. *Agented submissions only*. Agented fiction 100%. Responds in 2 weeks to queries; 4 months to mss.

Terms Pays royalty on retail price, 10 author's copies. Offers advance. Publishes ms within 18 months after acceptance. Ms guidelines for #10 SASE.

ARIEL STARR PRODUCTIONS, LTD.

P.O. Box 17, Demarest NJ 07627. E-mail: darkbird@aol.com. Cynthia Sorona, president. Estab. 1991. Publishes paperback originals. **Published 2 debut authors within the last year.**

How to Contact Submit outline, 1 sample chapter(s). Accepts queries by e-mail, mail. Include brief bio. Send SASE or IRC. Responds in 6 weeks to queries; 4 months to mss. Sometimes comments on rejected mss.

Terms Publishes ms one year after acceptance.

ARTE PUBLICO PRESS

University of Houston, 452 Cullen Performance Hall, Houston TX 77204-2004. Fax: (713)743-3080. Web site: www.artepublicopress.com. **Contact:** Dr. Nicolas Kanellos, editor. Estab. 1979. "Small press devoted to the publication of contemporary U.S.-Hispanic literature." Publishes hardcover originals, trade paperback originals and reprints. Averages 36 total titles/year.

- Arte Publico Press is the oldest and largest publisher of Hispanic literature for children and adults in the United States.

Imprint(s) Pinata Books featuring children's and young adult literature by U.S.-Hispanic writers.

Needs Ethnic, literary, mainstream/contemporary, written by U.S.-Hispanic authors. Published *Project Death*, by Richard Bertematti (novel, mystery); *A Perfect Silence*, by Alba Ambert; *Song of the Hummingbird*, by Graciela Limon; *Little Havana Blues: A Cuban-American Literature Anthology*.

How to Contact Accepts unsolicited mss. Query with SASE or submit 2 sample chapter(s), synopsis or submit complete ms. Agented fiction 1%. Responds in 2-4 months to queries; 3-6 months to mss. Accepts simultaneous submissions. Sometimes comments on rejected mss.

Terms Pays 10% royalty on wholesale price. Provides 20 author's copies; 40% discount on subsequent copies. Average advance: $1,000-3,000. Publishes ms 2 years after acceptance. Ms guidelines online.

Advice "Include cover letter in which you 'sell' your book—why should we publish the book, who will want to read it, why does it matter, etc."

ARTEMIS PRESS

SRS Internet Publishing, 236 W. Portal Avenue #525, San Francisco CA 94127. (866)216-7333. E-mail: submissions@artemispress.com. Web site: www.artemispress.com. **Contact:** Susan R. Skolnick, publisher and editor-in-chief; Hedda James, editor. Estab. 2000. "Publisher of fiction and nonfiction titles of interest to the worldwide women's community. We specialize in feminist and lesbian-related titles but are interested in all women-centered titles. We are open to working with new authors and provide extremely personalized services." Publishes electronic and paperback editions of original, out-of-print and previously published titles. **Published 2 debut authors within the last year.** Plans 4 first novels this year. Titles distributed and promoted online and offline to target market.

Needs Feminist, historical, lesbian, literary, mystery, psychic/supernatural, romance, science fiction. Published *Zoo Gang Girls*, by Joan Arndt (science fiction); *Against a White Sky: A Memoir of Closets and Classrooms*, by Laurie Stapleton (lesbian studies/gender studies); *Clicking Stones*, by Nancy Tyler Glenn (new age/mystic); *Moon Madness and Other Stories*, by Liann Snow (short story collection); *Faith in Love*, by Liann Snow (humor/satire); *Luna Ascending: Stories of Love and Magic*, by Renee Brown (short story collection); *Windrow Garden*, by Janet McClellan (romance); *Never Letting Go*, by Suzanne Hollo (humor/satire); *Minding Therapy*, by Ros Johnson (humor/satire).

How to Contact Does not accept unsolicited mss. Agented fiction 10%. Responds in 3 months to queries. Accepts simultaneous submissions. Often comments on rejected mss.

Terms Pays 30% royalty. Publishes ms 6 months after acceptance. Ms guidelines online.

Advice "We like to see clean manuscripts and an indication that the author has proofed and self-edited before submitting. We work collaboratively with our authors in all phases of publication and expect the same efforts of our authors in return."

ATHENEUM BOOKS FOR YOUNG READERS

Simon & Schuster, 1230 Avenue of the Americas, New York NY 10020. (212)698-2715. Fax: (212)698-2796. Web site: www.simonsayskids.com. **Contact:** Caitlyn Dlouhy, executive editor; Richard Jackson, editorial director, Richard Jackson Books; Anne Schwartz, vice president and editorial director; Anne Schwartz Books. Estab. 1960. Atheneum Books for Young Readers is a hardcover imprint with a focus on literary fiction and fine picture books for preschoolers through young adults. Publishes special interest, first novels and new talent. Books: illustrations for picture books, some illustrated short novels. Averages 75 total titles/year.

• In the past year, three books by Atheneum have received awards: *House of the Scorpion*, by Nancy Farmer, National Book Award; *Clever Beatrice*, by Margaret Willey, Charlotte Zolotow Award; and *Silent Night*, by Sandy Turner, Ragazzi Award.

Needs Adventure, ethnic, experimental, fantasy, gothic, historical, horror, humor, mainstream/contemporary, mystery, science fiction, sports, suspense, western, animal. "We have few specific needs except for books that are fresh, interesting and well written. Fad topics are dangerous, as are works you haven't polished to the best of your ability. (The competition is fierce.) Other things we don't need at this time are safety pamphlets, ABC books, coloring books and board books. In writing picture book texts, avoid the coy and 'cutesy,' such as stories about characters with alliterative names." Published *Ben Franklin's Almanac*, by Candace Fleming (non-fiction); *If I were a Lion*, by Sarah Weeks and Heather Soloman; *Seadogs*, by Lisa Wheeler; *Friction*, by E.R. Frank (YA novel); and *Audrey and Barbara*, by Janet Lawson (picture book fiction; debut author).

How to Contact Does not accept unsolicited mss. Query with SASE or IRC. Accepts queries by mail. Agented fiction 70%. Responds in 3 months to queries. Accepts simultaneous submissions.

Terms Pays 10% royalty on retail price. Average advance: $5,000-6,500. Publishes ms 18 months after acceptance. Ms guidelines for #10 SASE.

Advice "Write about what you know best. We look for original stories, unique and flavor-filled voices, and strong, evocative characters with whom a reader will readily embark on a literary journey. *Query letter only is best.* We do not accept unsolicited mss."

AUNT LUTE BOOKS

P.O. Box 410687, San Francisco CA 94141. (415)826-1300. Fax: (415)826-8300. E-mail: books@auntlute.com. Web site: www.auntlute.com. **Contact:** Shahara Godfrey, first reader. Small feminist and women-of-color press. Publishes hardcover and paperback originals. Averages 4 total titles/year.

Needs Ethnic, feminist, lesbian.

How to Contact Accepts unsolicited mss. Query with SASE or submit outline, sample chapter(s), synopsis. Send SASE or IRC. Responds in 4 months to mss.

Terms Pays royalty.

Advice "We seek manuscripts, both fiction and nonfiction, by women from a variety of cultures, ethnic backgrounds and subcultures; women who are self-aware and who, in the face of all contradictory evidence, are still hopeful that the world can reserve a place of respect for each woman in it. We seek work that explores the specificities of the worlds from which we come, and which examines the intersections between the borders which we all inhabit."

AVALON BOOKS

Thomas Bouregy & Co., Inc., 160 Madison Ave., 5th Floor, New York NY 10016. (212)598-0222. Fax: (212)979-1862. E-mail: editorial@avalonbooks.com. Web site: www.avalonbooks.com. **Contact:** Erin Cartwright-Niumata, editorial director; Abby Holcomb, assistant editor. Estab. 1950. Publishes hardcover originals. **Published some debut authors within the last year.** Averages 60 total titles/year. Distributes titles through Baker & Taylor, libraries, Barnes&Noble.com and Amazon.com. Promotes titles through *Library Journal*, *Booklist*, *Publisher's Weekly* and local papers.

Needs Historical (romance), mystery, romance, western. "We publish wholesome contemporary romances, mysteries, historical romances and westerns. Our books are read by adults as well as teenagers, and the characters are all adults. All mysteries are contemporary. We publish contemporary romances (four every two months), historical romances (two every two months), mysteries (two every two months) and westerns (two every two months). Submit first 3 sample chapters, a 2-3 page synopsis and SASE. The manuscripts should be between 40,000 to 70,000 words. Manuscripts that are too long will not be considered. Time period and setting are the author's preference. The historical romances will maintain the high level of reading expected by our readers. The books shall be wholesome fiction, without graphic sex, violence or strong language. We are actively looking for romantic comedy, chick lit." Published *Last One Down*, by Joyce and Jim Lavene (mystery); *The Bride Wore Blood*, by Vicky Hunnings (mystery); *Cruising for Love*, by Tami D. Cowden (romantic comedy); *Pickup Lines*, by Holly Jacobs (romantic comedy).

How to Contact Does not accept unsolicited mss. Query with SASE or IRC. Responds in 1 month to queries; 6-10 months to mss.

Terms Average advance: $1,000. Publishes ms 8-12 months after acceptance. Ms guidelines online.

BAEN PUBLISHING ENTERPRISES

P.O. Box 1403, Riverdale NY 10471-0671. (718)548-3100. E-mail: slush@baen.com. Web site: www.baen.com. **Contact:** Jim Baen, publisher and editor; Toni Weisskopf, executive editor. Estab. 1983. "We publish books at the heart of science fiction and fantasy." Publishes hardcover, trade paperback and mass market paperback

originals and reprints. **Published some debut authors within the last year.** Plans 2-3 first novels this year. Averages 120 total titles, 120 fiction titles/year. Distributes titles through Simon & Schuster.
Imprint(s) Baen Science Fiction and Baen Fantasy.
Needs Fantasy, science fiction. Interested in science fiction novels (based on real science) and fantasy novels "that at least strive for originality." Length: 100,00-130,000 words. Published *A Civil Campaign*, by Lois McMaster Bujold; *Ashes of Victory*, by David Weber; *Sentry Peak*, by Harry Turtledove.
How to Contact Submit synopsis and complete ms. "Electronic submissions are strongly preferred. Attach manuscript as a Rich Text Format (.rtf) file. Any other format will not be considered." Additional submission guidelines online. Include estimated word count, brief bio. Send SASE or IRC. Responds in 9-12 months. No simultaneous submissions. Sometimes comments on rejected mss.
Terms Pays royalty on retail price. Offers advance. Ms guidelines online.
Advice "Keep an eye and a firm hand on the overall story you are telling. Style is important but less important than plot. Good style, like good breeding, never calls attention to itself. Read *Writing to the Point*, by Algis Budrys. We like to maintain long-term relationships with authors."

Ⓐ ✖ BALLANTINE BOOKS
Random House, Inc., 1745 Broadway, New York NY 10019. (212)782-9000. Web site: www.randomhouse.com/ BB. Estab. 1952. "Ballantine's list encompasses a large, diverse offering in a variety of formats." Publishes hardcover, trade paperback, mass market paperback originals
Imprint(s) Ballantine Books; Del Ray; Fawcett (mystery line); Ivy (romance); The Modern Library; One World; Strivers Row; Presidio Press; Random House Trade Paperbacks; Villard Books.
Needs Confession, ethnic, fantasy, feminist, gay/lesbian, historical, humor, literary, mainstream/contemporary (women's), military/war, multicultural, mystery, romance, short story collections, spiritual, suspense, general fiction.
How to Contact *Agented submissions only.*
Terms Pays 8-15% royalty. Average advance: variable. Ms guidelines online.

Ⓐ ◎ BANCROFT PRESS
P.O. Box 65360, Baltimore MD 21209-9945. (410)358-0658. Fax: (410)764-1967. Web site: www.bancroftpress.c om. **Contact:** Bruce Bortz, publisher (health, investments, politics, history, humor); Fiction Editor (literary novels, mystery/thrillers, young adult). "Small independent press publishing literary and commercial fiction, often by journalists." Publishes hardcover and trade paperback originals. Also packages books for other publishers (no fee to authors). **Published 2 debut authors within the last year.** Plans several first novels this year. Averages 4 total titles, 2-4 fiction titles/year.
• *The Re-Appearance of Sam Webber*, by Scott Fugua is an ALEX Award winner.
Needs Ethnic (general), family saga, feminist, gay/lesbian, glitz, historical, humor, lesbian, literary, mainstream/contemporary, military/war, mystery (amateur sleuth, cozy, police procedural, private eye/hardboiled), new age/mystic, regional, science fiction (hard science/technological, soft/sociological), thriller/espionage, young adult (historical, problem novels, series). "Our No. 1 priority is publishing books appropriate for young adults, ages 10-18. All quality books on any subject that fit that category will be considered." Published *Those Who Trespass*, by Bill O'Reilly (thriller); *The Re-Appearance of Sam Webber*, by Scott Fugua (literary); and *Malicious Intent*, by Mike Walker (Hollywood).
How to Contact Accepts unsolicited mss. Query with SASE or submit outline, 2 sample chapter(s), synopsis, by mail or e-mail or submit complete ms. Accepts queries by e-mail, fax. Include brief bio, list of publishing credits. Send SASE for return of ms or send a disposable ms and SASE for reply only. Agented fiction 100%. Responds in 6-12 months to mss. Accepts simultaneous submissions. Sometimes comments on rejected mss.
Terms Pays various royalties on retail price. Average advance: $750. Publishes ms up to 3 years after acceptance. Ms guidelines online.
Advice "Be patient, send a sample, know your book's audience."

Ⓐ ✖ BANTAM DELL PUBLISHING GROUP
Random House, Inc., 1745 Broadway, New York NY 10019. (212)782-9000. Fax: (212)782-8890. Web site: www.bantamdell.com. Estab. 1945. "In addition to being the nation's largest mass market paperback publisher, Bantam publishes a select yet diverse hardcover list." Publishes hardcover, trade paperback and mass market paperback originals; mass market paperback reprints. Averages 350 total titles/year.
Imprint(s) Bantam Hardcover; Bantam Trade Paperback; Bantam Mass Market; Crimeline; Dell; Delta; Domain; DTP; Delacorte Press; The Dial Press; Fanfare; Island; Spectra.
Needs Adventure, fantasy, horror.
How to Contact Agented submissions only.
Terms Offers advance. Publishes ms 1 year after acceptance.

Ⓐ ⊠ Ⓨ BANTAM DOUBLEDAY DELL BOOKS FOR YOUNG READERS

Random House Children's Publishing, Random House, Inc., 1745 Broadway, New York NY 10019. (212)782-9000. Fax: (212)782-8234. Web site: www.randomhouse.com/kids. **Contact:** Michelle Poplof, editorial director. Publishes hardcover, trade paperback and mass market paperback series originals, trade paperback reprints. Averages 300 total titles/year.

• *Bud, Not Buddy*, by Christopher Paul Curtis won the Newberry Medal and the Coretta Scott King Award.

Imprint(s) Delecorte Books for Young Readers; Doubleday Books for Young Readers; Laurel Leaf; Skylark; Starfire; Yearling Books.

Needs Adventure, fantasy, historical, humor, juvenile, mainstream/contemporary, mystery, picture books, suspense, chapter books, middle-grade. Published *Bud, Not Buddy*, by Christopher Paul Curtis; *The Sisterhood of the Traveling Pants*, by Ann Brashares.

How to Contact Does not accept unsolicited mss. *Agented submissions only.* Responds in 2 months to queries; 4 months to mss. No simultaneous submissions.

Terms Pays royalty. Average advance: varied. Publishes ms 2 years after acceptance. Book catalog for 9×12 SASE.

Ⓝ Ⓞ BARBOUR PUBLISHING, INC.

P.O. Box 719, Uhrichsville OH 44683. (740)922-6045. Fax: (740)922-5948. E-mail: info@barbourbooks.com. Web site: www.barbourpublishing.com. **Contact:** Rebecca Germany, senior editor (fiction). Estab. 1981. Publishes hardcover, trade paperback and mass market paperback originals and reprints. **Published 40% debut authors within the last year.** Averages 250 total titles/year.

Imprint(s) Heartsong Presents; Barbour Books and Heartsong Presents Mysteries.

Needs Historical, contemporary, religious, romance, western, mystery. All submissions must be Christian mss. "Heartsong romance is 'sweet'—no sex, no bad language. All stories must have Christian faith as an underlying basis. Common writer's mistakes are a sketchy proposal, an unbelieveable story, and a story that doesn't fit our guidelines for inspirational romances." Published *The Storekeeper's Daughter*, by Wanda E. Brunstetter (fiction).

How to Contact Submit 3 sample chapter(s), synopsis by e-mail. Responds in 3 months to mss. Accepts simultaneous submissions.

Terms Pays 8-16% royalty on net price or makes outright purchase of $1,000-5,000. Average advance: $1,000-8,000. Publishes ms 1-2 years after acceptance. Book catalog online or for 9×12 SAE with 2 first-class stamps; ms guidelines for #10 SASE or online.

Advice "Audience is evangelical/Christian conservative, non-denominational, young and old. We're looking for *great concepts*, not necessarily a big name author or agent. We want to publish books with mass appeal."

Ⓞ BAREFOOT BOOKS

2067 Massachusetts Avenue, Cambridge MA 02140. Web site: www.barefootbooks.com. **Contact:** Submissions editor. Publishes hardcover and trade paperback originals. **Published 35% debut authors within the last year.** Averages 30 total titles/year.

Needs Juvenile. Barefoot Books only publishes children's picture books and anthologies of folktales. "We do not publish novels. We do accept query letters but prefer full manuscripts." *Daddy Island*, by Philip Wells (picture book); *Fiesta Femenina: Celebrating Women in Mexican Folktale*, by Mary-Joan Gerson (illustrated anthology).

How to Contact Query with SASE or submit first page of ms. Responds in 4 months to mss. Accepts simultaneous submissions. No phone calls please.

Terms Pays 2½-5% royalty on retail price or makes outright purchase. Offers advance. Publishes ms 2 years after acceptance. Book catalog for 9×12 SAE stamped with $1.80 postage. Ms guidelines online.

Advice "Our audience is made up of children and parents, teachers and students of many different ages and cultures. Since we are a small publisher and we definitely publish for a 'niche' market, it is helpful to look at our books and our Web site before submitting, to see if your book would fit into our list."

◯ Ⓞ BARKING DOG BOOKS

758 Peralta Avenue, Berkeley CA 94708. (510)527-6274. E-mail: barkingdogbooks@yahoo.com. **Contact:** Michael Mercer, editor. Estab. 1996. "Focuses on expatriate life, especially in Mexico, and America viewed from exile." Publishes paperback originals. Books: quality paper; offset printing; perfect bound. Average print order: 1,000. Titles distributed through Sunbelt Publications.

Needs Ethnic (Mexican), experimental, historical, humor, literary, regional (Mexico/Southwest), short story collections, expatriate life. Published *Bandidos*, by Michael Mercer.

How to Contact Accepts unsolicited mss. Submit outline, 3 sample chapter(s). Accepts queries by mail. Include brief bio, list of publishing credits. Send copy of ms and SASE. Responds in 2 months to queries; 6 months to mss. Accepts simultaneous submissions. No submissions on disk. Sometimes comments on rejected mss.

Terms Publishes ms 1 year after acceptance.

Advice "Don't try to write for a market; write for yourself, be authentic, and trust readers to gravitate to an authentic voice."

[N] [◎] BARRON'S EDUCATIONAL SERIES, INC.

250 Wireless Blvd., Hauppauge NY 11788. (631)434-3311. Fax: (631)434-3394. Web site: barronseduc.com. **Contact:** Wayne Barr, managing editor/director of acquisitions. Estab. 1941. Publishes hardcover, paperback and mass market originals and software. **Published 40% debut authors within the last year.** Averages 400 total titles/year.

Needs Middle grade, YA.

How to Contact Submit sample chapter(s), synopsis. Responds in 3 months to queries; 8 months to mss. Accepts simultaneous submissions.

Terms Pays 12-14% royalty on net receipts. Average advance: $3-4,000. Publishes ms 18 months after acceptance. Ms queries online.

Advice "Audience is mostly educated self-learners and hobbyists. The writer has the best chance of selling us a book that will fit into one of our series. Children's books have less chance for acceptance because of the glut of submissions. SASE must be included for the return of all materials. Please be patient for replies."

[◎] FREDERIC C. BEIL, PUBLISHER, INC.

609 Whitaker St., Savannah GA 31401. (912)233-2446. Fax: (912)233-6456. Web site: www.beil.com. **Contact:** Frederic C. Beil III, president; Mary Ann Bowman, editor. Estab. 1982. "Our objectives are (1) to offer to the reading public carefully selected texts of lasting value; (2) to adhere to high standards in the choice of materials and bookmaking craftsmanship; (3) to produce books that exemplify good taste in format and design; and (4) to maintain the lowest cost consistent with quality." Publishes hardcover originals and reprints. Books: acid-free paper; letterpress and offset printing; Smyth-sewn, hardcover binding; illustrations. Plans 10 first novels this year. Averages 13 total titles, 4 fiction titles/year.

Imprint(s) The Sandstone Press, Hypermedia, Inc.

Needs Historical, literary, regional, short story collections, biography. Published *Dancing by The River*, by Marlin Barton; *Joseph Jefferson*, by Arthur Bloom (biography); *The Invisible Country*, by H.E. Francis (fiction).

How to Contact Does not accept unsolicited mss. Query with SASE. Responds in 2 weeks to queries. Accepts simultaneous submissions.

Terms Pays 7½% royalty on retail price. Publishes ms 20 months after acceptance.

Advice "Write about what you love."

[◎] BEN BELLA BOOKS

6440 N. Central Expy Suite 508, Dallas TX 75206. (214)750-3600. Fax: (214)750-3645. E-mail: shanna@benbella books.com. Web site: www.benbellabooks.com. **Contact:** Shanna Caughey, editor; Leah Wilson, associate editor. Estab. 2001. Small, growing independent publisher specializing in popular culture, smart nonfiction and science fiction; our fiction is largely reprints or by established authors. Publishes harcover and paperback originals and paperback reprints. **Published 1 debut author within the last year.** Averages 20 total titles, 5-10 fiction titles/year. Distributed through the Independent Publishers Group.

Needs Currently not accepting fiction submissions.

[A] [✭] THE BERKLEY PUBLISHING GROUP

Penguin Putnam, Inc., 375 Hudson St., New York NY 10014. (212)366-2000. E-mail: online@penguinputnam.c om. Web site: www.penguinputnam.com. Estab. 1954. "Berkley is proud to publish in paperback some of the country's most significant best-selling authors." Publishes paperback and mass market originals and reprints. Averages approximately 800 total titles/year.

Imprint(s) Ace Books, Berkley Books, HP Books, Perigee, Riverhead Books.

Needs Adventure, historical, literary, mystery, romance, spiritual, suspense, western, young adult.

How to Contact Does not accept unsolicited mss.

Terms Pays 4-15% royalty on retail price. Offers advance. Publishes ms 2 years after acceptance.

[◎] [◎] BETHANY HOUSE PUBLISHERS

11400 Hampshire Ave. S., Minneapolis MN 55438. (952)829-2500. Fax: (952)996-1304. Web site: www.bethany house.com. Estab. 1956. "The purpose of Bethany House Publisher's publishing program is to relate biblical truth to all areas of life—whether in the framework of a well-told story, of a challenging book for spiritual growth, or of a Bible reference work." Publishes hardcover and trade paperback originals, mass market paperback reprints. Averages 90-100 total titles/year.

Needs Adventure, children's/juvenile, historical, young adult. Published *The Still of Night*, by Kristen Heitzmann (fiction).

How to Contact Does not accept unsolicited mss. Accepts queries only by fax. Accepts simultaneous submissions. Query guidelines online.

Terms Pays negotiable royalty on net price. Average advance: negotiable. Publishes ms 1 year after acceptance.

BIRCH BROOK PRESS

P.O. Box 81, Delhi NY 13753. Fax: (607)746-7453. Web site: www.birchbrookpress.info. **Contact:** Tom Tolnay, publisher. Estab. 1982. Small publisher of popular culture and literary titles in handcrafted letterpress editions. Specializes in fiction anthologies with specific theme, and an occasional novella. "Not a good market for full-length novels." Publishes hardcover and trade paperback originals. Books: 80 lb. vellum paper; letterpress printing; wood engraving illustrations. Averages 4 total titles, 2 fiction titles/year. Member, Small Press Center, Publishers Marketing Association, Academy of American Poets. Distributes titles through Baker and Taylor, Barnes&Noble.com, Amazon.com, Gazelle Book Services in Europe. Promotes titles through Web site, catalogs, direct mail and group ads.

Imprint(s) Birch Brook Press; Persephone Press and Birch Brook Impressions.

Needs Literary, regional (Adirondacks), popular culture, special interest (flyfishing, baseball, books about books, outdoors). "Mostly we do anthologies around a particular theme generated inhouse. "We make specific calls for fiction when we are doing an anthology." Published *Magic and Madness in the Library*, edited by Eric Graeber (fiction collection); *Life & Death of a Book*, by William MacAdams; *Fateful Choices*, edited by Marshall Brooks and Stephanie Greene; *A Punk in Gallows America*, by P.W. Fox; *White Buffalo*, by Peter Skinner; *Cooperstown Chronicles*, by Peter Rutkoff; *The Suspense of Loneliness* (anthology); *Tales for the Trail* (anthology); *Sexy Sixties*, by Harry Smith.

How to Contact Query with SASE or submit sample chapter(s), synopsis. Responds in 1-2 months to queries. Accepts simultaneous submissions. Sometimes comments on rejected mss.

Terms Modest flat fee on anthologies. Publishes ms 1-2 years after acceptance. Ms guidelines for #10 SASE.

Advice "Write well on subjects of interest to BBP, such as outdoors, flyfishing, baseball, music, literary novellas, books about books."

BKMK PRESS

University of Missouri-Kansas City, 5101 Rockhill Rd., Kansas City MO 64110-2499. (816)235-2558. Fax: (816)235-2611. E-mail: bkmk@umkc.edu. Web site: www.umkc.edu/bkmk. Estab. 1971. Publishes trade paperback originals. Averages 4 total titles/year.

Needs Literary, short story collections.

How to Contact Query with SASE or submit 2-3 sample chapter(s). Responds in 8 months to mss. Accepts simultaneous submissions.

Terms Pays 10% royalty on wholesale price. Publishes ms 1 year after acceptance. Ms guidelines online.

BL PUBLISHING

Games Workshop Ltd., Willow Road, Lenton, Nottingham NG7 2WS. (44)(115) 900-4100. Fax: (44)(115) 900-4111. E-mail: publishing@games-workshop.co.uk. Web site: www.blacklibrary.com. **Contact:** Christian Dunn. Estab. 1997. Publishes paperback originals. Published 4 new writers last year. Averages 85 total titles/year; 85 fiction titles/year.

Imprint(s) Black Library, Black Flame.

Needs Fantasy (space fantasy, sword and sorcery), horror (dark fantasy, futuristic), science fiction (hard science/technological, soft/sociological), short story collection, young adult/teen (fantasy/science fiction, horror). Published *Salvation*, by CS Goto (science fiction); *The Daemon's Curse*, by Dan Abnett (fantasy); *Fifteen Hours*, by Mitchel Scanlon (science fiction).

How to Contact Submit through agent only. Accepts queries by snail mail, e-mail. Include brief bio, list of publishing credits. Send SASE or IRC for return of ms or disposable copy of ms and SASE/IRC for reply only. Agented fiction: 5%. Responds to mss in 3 months. No unsolicited mss. Considers simultaneous submissions, e-mail submissions. Rarely critiques/comments on rejected mss.

Terms Sends pre-production galleys to author. Writer's guidelines on Web site.

Advice "Please check our Web site."

BLACK LACE BOOKS

Virgin Books, Thames Wharf Studio, Rainville Road, London England W6 9HA United Kingdom. +44 (0207) 386 3300. Fax: +44 (0207) 386 3360. E-mail: anevil@virgin-books.co.uk. Web site: www.blacklace-books.co.uk. **Contact:** Adam Nevill, erotica editor. Estab. 1993. Publishes paper originals.

Imprint(s) Nexus Fetish Erotic Fiction for Men; Black Lace Erotic Fiction for Women. ''Nexus and Black Lace are the leading imprints of erotic fiction in the UK.''

Needs Erotica. ''Female writers only for the Black Lace Series.'' Especially needs erotic fiction in contemporary and paranormal erotica settings. Also considers exceptional historical and erotic memoir. Publishes 4 erotic short story anthologies by women per year, called *Wicked Words*. Also published 6 novels within the softer Erotica Cheek imprint, chick-lit with erotic content aimed at 20-30 somethings.

How to Contact Accepts unsolicited mss. Query with SASE. Include estimated word count. Agented fiction 25%. Responds in 1 month to queries; 6-8 months to mss. No simultaneous submissions. Always comments on rejected mss.

Terms Pays 7½% royalty. Average advance: £1,000. Publishes ms 7 months after acceptance. Ms guidelines online.

Advice ''Black Lace is open to female authors only. Read the guidelines first.''

⬛ ◎ JOHN F. BLAIR, PUBLISHER

1406 Plaza Dr., Winston-Salem NC 27103-1470. (336)768-1374. Fax: (336)768-9194. Web site: www.blairpub.com. **Contact:** Carolyn Sakowski, president. Estab. 1954. Small, independent publisher. Publishes hardcover originals and trade paperbacks. Books: Acid-free paper; offset printing; illustrations. Averages 20 total titles/year.

Needs Prefers regional material dealing with southeastern U.S. ''We publish one work of fiction per season relating to the Southeastern U.S. Our editorial focus concentrates mostly on nonfiction.'' Published *The Minotaur Takes a Cigarette Break*, by Steven Sherrill; *Lord Baltimore*, by Stephen Doster.

How to Contact Accepts unsolicited mss. Query with SASE or submit complete ms with SASE or IRC. Responds in 3 months to queries. Accepts simultaneous submissions.

Terms Royalty negotiable. Offers advance. Publishes ms 18 months after acceptance. Book catalog for 9×12 SAE with 5 first-class stamps. Ms guidelines online.

Advice ''We are primarily interested in nonfiction titles. Most of our titles have a tie-in with North Carolina or the southeastern United States. Please enclose a cover letter and outline with the manuscript. We prefer to review queries before we are sent complete manuscripts. Queries should include an approximate word count.''

⬛ BLEAK HOUSE BOOKS

923 Williamson St., Madison WI 53703. (608)259-8370. Web site: www.bleakhousebooks.com. Benjamin Le-Roy, publisher. Estab. 1995. Publisher hardcover and paperback originals. Averages 15-20 titles annually.

Needs ''Good psychological engagement. We aren't looking for big budget special effects and car chases. The best part of the story isn't in the distractions, it's in the heart. Characters need to be well drawn. We don't want formula fiction. We don't want rehashes of CSI. We don't want unqualified 'experts' writing books with plot holes. We don't want authors who are so married to their words that they can't see when something doesn't work.'' Published *The Blood Knot*, by John Galligan; *Chasing the Wolf*, by Nathan Singer; *Provincetown Follies: Bangkok Blues*, by Randall Peffer; *Hardboiled Brooklyn*, edited by Reed Farrel Coleman; *Hose Monkey*, by Tony Spinosa.

How to Contact Does not accept unsolicited mss. Any unsolicited mss we receive will be recycled without ever being read. Query with SASE. We accept queries during January, February, July and August. Materials received in any other month will be returned unopened and unread. Include estimated word count, brief bio, list of publishing credits. Agented fiction 75%. ''Responds as fast as we can to queries. Depending on when we receive them, it may take a while. Same holds true for submitted manuscripts, but we'll keep you abreast of what's going on when we know it.'' Responds in 2 weeks to queries; 2 months to mss. Accepts simultaneous submissions. No electronic submissions. Check Web site for up-to-date guidelines.

Terms All contracts negotiable depending on author, market viability, etc. Our average royalty rate is somewhere between 7.5-15% depending on hardcover/paperback, print run, and many other factors. Advances range from $500-$10,000. Publishes ms 12-18 months after acceptance.

Advice ''We've grown from a two book a year publishing house to doing 20-25 books a year (combined with our sister company, Intrigue Press). We're still willing to take a chance on first-time authors with extraordinary books. We're still willing to take a chance on offbeat fiction. We are very busy in our office and sometimes our response time isn't as fast as we'd like it to be. But, between working with the books in house or looking at submissions, we feel it's very important to take care of our family of authors first. Please, if you value your work and you are serious about being published, do not send out first drafts. Edit your book. Then edit it again. Please also understand that for a book to be successful, the author and the publisher (and sometimes the agent) have to work together as a team. Good publishers need good writers as much as good writers need good publishers. It's a two-way street. Best of luck and keep writing.''

❤ ◎ BOOKS FOR ALL TIMES, INC.

P.O. Box 202, Warrenton VA 20188. Web site: www.bfat.com. **Contact:** Joe David, publisher/editor. Estab. 1981. One-man operation. Publishes paperback originals.

Needs Literary, mainstream/contemporary, short story collections. "No novels at the moment; hopeful, though, of publishing a collection of quality short stories. No popular fiction or material easily published by the major or minor houses specializing in mindless entertainment. Only interested in stories of the Victor Hugo or Sinclair Lewis quality."

How to Contact Query with SASE. Responds in 1 month to queries. Sometimes comments on rejected mss.

Terms Pays negotiable advance. "Publishing/payment arrangement will depend on plans for the book."

Advice Interested in "controversial, honest stories which satisfy the reader's curiosity to know. Read Victor Hugo, Fyodor Dostoyevsky and Sinclair Lewis for example."

◻ ◎ BOYDS MILLS PRESS

Highlights for Children, 815 Church St., Honesdale PA 18431-1895. (570)253-1164. E-mail: contact@boydsmills press.com. Web site: www.boydsmillspress.com. **Contact:** Larry Rosler, editorial director. Estab. 1990. "Independent publisher of quality books for children of all ages." Publishes hardcover originals and trade paperback reprints. Books: coated paper; offset printing; case binding; 4-color illustrations. **Published 5 debut authors within the last year.** Averages 50 total titles, 4 fiction titles/year. Distributes titles through independent sales reps and via order line directly from Boyds Mills Press. Promotes titles through sales and professional conferences, sales reps, reviews.

Needs Adventure, ethnic, historical, humor, juvenile, mystery, picture books, young adult (adventure, animal, contemporary, ethnic, historical, humor, mystery, sports). "We look for imaginative stories or concepts with simple, lively language that employs a variety of literary devices, including rhythm, repetition and, when composed properly, rhyme. The stories may entertain or challenge, but the content must be age appropriate for children. For middle and young adult fiction we look for stories told in strong, considered prose driven by well-imagined characters." Published *Sharks! Strange and Wonderful*, by Laurence Pringle; *Groover's Heart*, by Carole Crowe; *Storm's Coming!*, by Audrey B. Baird.

How to Contact Accepts unsolicited mss. Query with SASE. Agented fiction 30%. Responds in 1 month to mss. Accepts simultaneous submissions.

Terms Pays royalty on retail price. Average advance: variable.

Advice "Read through our recently published titles and review our catalogue. If your book is too different from what we publish, then it may not fit our list. Feel free to query us if you're not sure."

Ⓝ ◻ GEORGE BRAZILLER, INC.

171 Madison Avenue, Suite 1105, New York NY 10016. (212)889-0909. **Contact:** Mary Taveras, production editor. Publishes hardcover and trade paperback originals and reprints.

Needs Ethnic, gay/lesbian, literary. "We rarely do fiction but when we have published novels, they have mostly been literary novels." *Blindsight*, by Herve Guibert; *Papa's Suitcase*, by Gerhard Kopf (literary fiction).

How to Contact Submit 4-6 sample chapter(s), SASE. Agented fiction 20%. Responds in 3 months to proposals.

Terms Publishes ms 10 months after acceptance.

◻ ◎ BREAKAWAY BOOKS

P.O. Box 24, Halcottsville NY 12438. (212)898-0408. E-mail: information@breakawaybooks.com. Web site: www.breakawaybooks.com. **Contact:** Garth Battista, publisher. Estab. 1994. "Small press specializing in fine literary books on sports. We have a new line of children's illustrated books (ages 3-7)—dealing with sports, especially running, cycling, triathlon, swimming, and boating (canoes, kayaks, sailboats). Publishes hardcover and trade paperback originals. **Published 3 debut authors within the last year.** Averages 8-10 total titles, 5 fiction titles/year.

Needs Short story collections (sports stories).

How to Contact Accepts unsolicited mss. Query with SASE or submit complete ms. Accepts queries by e-mail. Include brief bio, list of publishing credits. Send SASE for return of ms or send a disposable ms and SASE for reply only. Agented fiction 50%. Responds in 1 month to queries; 2 months to mss. Accepts simultaneous submissions, electronic submissions. Rarely comments on rejected mss.

Terms Pays 6-15% royalty on retail price. Average advance: $2,000-3,000. Publishes ms 9 months after acceptance. Book catalog and ms guidelines free. Ms guidelines online.

★ ◻ ◎ BROADMAN & HOLMAN

LifeWay Christian Resources, 127 Ninth Ave. N., Nashville TN 37234. (615)251-2392. Fax: (615)251-3752. Web site: www.broadmanholman.com. **Contact:** Leonard G. Goss, editorial director (historical, romance, contemporary, suspense, western, thrillers, etc.). Estab. 1934. "Large, commericial, evangelical Christian publishing firm.

We publish Christian fiction in all genres.'' Publishes hardcover and paperback originals. **Published 10 debut authors within the last year.** Averages 90 total titles, 25 fiction titles/year. Member: ECPA. Distributes and promotes titles "on a national and international scale through a large sales organization."

Needs Adventure, mystery, religious (general religious, inspirational, religious fantasy, religious mystery/suspense, religious thriller, religious romance), western. "We publish fiction in all the main genres. We want not only a very good story, but also one that sets forth Christian values. Nothing that lacks a positive Christian emphasis (but do NOT preach, however); nothing that fails to sustain reader interest." Published *Sea of Glory*, by Ken Wales and David Poling (historical, debut author); *The Third Dragon*, by Frank Simon (mystery/intrique); *Friends and Enemies*, by Steve Bly (western).

How to Contact Does not accept unsolicited mss. Query with SASE. Accepts queries by e-mail. Include estimated word count, brief bio, list of publishing credits. Send copy of ms and SASE. Agented fiction 50%. Responds in 3 months to queries. Accepts simultaneous submissions. No electronic submissions, submissions on disk. Sometimes comments on rejected mss.

Terms Pays negotiable royalty. Publishes ms 10 months after acceptance. Ms guidelines for #10 SASE.

Ⓐ ✯ BROADWAY BOOKS

Doubleday Broadway Publishing Group, Random House, Inc., 1745 Broadway, New York NY 10019. (212)782-9000. Fax: (212)782-9411. E-mail: (first initial_last name)@randomhouse.com. Web site: www.broadwaybooks .com. **Contact:** William Thomas, editor-in-chief. Estab. 1995. Broadway publishes general interest nonfiction and fiction for adults. Publishes hardcover and trade paperback originals and reprints.

Needs Publishes a limited list of commercial literary fiction. Published *Freedomland*, by Richard Price.

How to Contact *Agented submissions only.*

⊕ ◎ BROWN SKIN BOOKS

Pentimento, Ltd., P.O. Box 46504, London England N1 3NT United Kingdom. E-mail: info@brownskinbooks.co. uk. Web site: www.brownskinbooks.co.uk. Estab. 2002. Publishes trade paperback originals. Averages 7 total titles/year.

Needs Erotica. "We are looking for erotic short stories or novels written by women of color."

How to Contact Submit proposal package including 2 sample chapter(s), synopsis. Responds in 1 month to queries; 2 months to mss. Accepts simultaneous submissions.

Terms Pays 5-50% royalty or makes outright purchase. Publishes ms 12 months after acceptance. Ms guidelines online.

Ⓝ ◲ CALAMARI PRESS

35 Essex St. #7B, New York NY 10002. E-mail: derek@calamaripress.com. Web site: www.calamaripress.com. **Contact:** Derek White, editor. Estab. 2003. "Calamari Press is a tiny, one-person operation on a part-time basis that devotes special attention to creating books that stand alone as pieces of art. It has no preconceived notions of what exactly that means and tastes are admittedly whimsical." Publishes paperback originals. Format: 60 lb. natural finch opaque paper; digital printing; perfect or saddle-stitched bound. Average print order: 200. Debut novel print order: 200. Averages 4 total titles/year; 2 fiction titles/year.

Needs Adventure, comics/graphic novels, ethnic/multicultural, experimental, literary, short story collections. Published *Land of the Snow Men*, by George Belden (Norman Lock) (fictional literary canard with illustrations); *The Singing Fish*, by Peter Markus (prose poem/short fiction collection).

How to Contact Query with outline/synopsis and 3 sample chapters. Accepts queries by e-mail. Include brief bio. Send SASE or IRC for return of ms. Responds to queries in 2 weeks. Accepts unsolicited mss. Considers e-mail submissions. Sometimes critiques/comments on rejected mss. Responds to mss in 2 weeks.

Terms Sends pre-production galleys to author. Manuscript published 2-6 months after acceptance. Writer's guidelines on Web site. Pays in author's copies. Book catalogs free upon request.

Advice "Find your voice and write what's true to yourself. Find a press that fits what you're doing, and if you can't find one then publish it yourself."

◲ ◎ CALYX BOOKS

P.O. Box B, Corvallis OR 97339-0539. (541)753-9384. Fax: (541)753-0515. **Contact:** M. Donnelly, director. Estab. 1986 for Calyx Books; 1976 for Calyx, Inc. "Calyx exists to publish women's literary and artistic work and is committed to publishing the works of all women, including women of color, older women, lesbians, working-class women, and other voices that need to be heard." Publishes fine literature by women, fiction, nonfiction and poetry. Publishes hardcover and paperback originals. Books: offset printing; paper and cloth binding. **Published 1 debut author within the last year.** Averages 1-2 total titles/year. Distributes titles through Consortium Book Sale and Distribution. Promotes titles through author reading tours, print advertising (trade and individuals), galley and review copy mailings, presence at trade shows, etc.

Needs Ethnic, experimental, feminist, gay/lesbian, lesbian, literary, mainstream/contemporary, short story collections. Published *Forbidden Stitch: An Asian American Women's Anthology; Women and Aging: Present Tense; Writing and Art by Young Women*; and *A Line of Cutting Women*.
How to Contact Closed to submissions until further notice.
Terms Pays 10-15% royalty on net receipts. Average advance: depends on grant support. Publishes ms 2 years after acceptance. Ms guidelines for #10 SASE.

CANDLEWICK PRESS

2067 Massachusetts Ave., Cambridge MA 02140. (617)661-3330. Fax: (617)661-0565. E-mail: bigbear@candlewick.com. Web site: www.candlewick.com. **Contact:** Joan Powers, editor-at-large; Amy Ehrlich, editor-at-large; Deb Wayshak Noyes, senior editor; Liz Bicknell, editorial director/associate publisher (poetry, picture books, fiction); Mary Lee Donovan, executive editor (picture books, fiction); Sarah Ketchersid, editor (board, toddler). Estab. 1991. "We are a truly child-centered publisher." Publishes hardcover originals, trade paperback originals and reprints. Averages 200 total titles/year.
• *The Tale of Despereaux*, by Kate DiCamillo won the 2004 Newbery Medal.
Needs Juvenile, picture books, young adult. Published *The Tale of Despereaux*, by Kate DiCamillo; *Judy Moody*, by Megan McDonald, illustrated by Peter Reynolds; *Feed*, by M.T. Anderson; *Fairieality*, by David Ellwando.
How to Contact Does not accept unsolicited mss.

CARNIFEX PRESS

P.O. Box 1686, Ormond Beach FL 32175. E-mail: armand@carnifexpress.net. Web site: www.carnifexpress.net. **Contact:** Armand Rosamilia (fantasy and horror), Boone Dryden (science fiction). Estab. 2005. "Small press publisher of fantasy, horror and science fiction chapbooks and books from the fresh faces in the genres. We publish themed anthologies and single-author novellas. We try to be the midpoint between big publishers and the non-paying markets." Publishes paperback originals. Format: 24# paper with glossy cover; off-set printing; side-stapled (chapbooks) or perfect bound (books). Average print order: 1,000. Debut novel print order: 2,000. **Published 6 new writers last year.** Plans 4 debut novels this year. Averages 9 total titles/year; 8 fiction titles/year. Distributes/promotes titles through our Web site and small-press distributors like Shocklines and ProjectPulp.
Needs Children's/juvenile (fantasy), fantasy (space fantasy, sword and sorcery), horror (dark fantasy, futuristic, psychological, supernatural), romance (gothic), science fiction (hard science/technological, soft/sociological), young adult/teen (fantasy/science fiction). Plans three themed fantasy and three themed horror anthologies. Writers may submit work during specific reading periods. See Web site for details. Published *Shards of Faith: A Will Scarlet Tale*, by Heather Lee Fleming (fantasy); *Clash of Steel: Book Two-Assassin*, anthology of various authors (fantasy); *Revenant: A Horror Anthology*, by various authors (horror). Plans Freehold, a shared world fantasy book series.
How to Contact Accepts unsolicited mss. Query with outline/synopsis and 3 sample chapters. Reads all year for novellas in the 20,000 word range. Accepts queries by snail mail, e-mail. Include estimated word count, brief bio. Send disposable copy of ms and SASE for reply only. Responds to queries in 1-2 weeks. Responds to mss in 2-3 months. Considers e-mail submissions. Sometimes critiques/comments on rejected mss.
Terms Pays royalties of 10% and 3 author's copies. Sends pre-production galleys to author. Manuscript published 8 months after acceptance. Writer's guidelines on Web site. Book catalogs on Web site.
Advice "Small press is such a wide business but easy to get into, which is good and bad. So many new publishers are springing up but then closing only a few short months later without a business model and cash flow. Carnifex Press is new, but Armand Rosamilia has been in the small-press market for over 10 years and knows the challenges and rewards of the fantasy/horror/science fiction niche. Send us the best possible copy of your work! Despite what some think, an editor isn't going to spend hours fixing grammar mistakes and rewriting paragraphs. We're looking for finished books ready to sell with a few minor changes to either plot or characterization that you make yourself. Small press doesn't rely on big advertising campaigns, we rely on word of mouth and the author to get behind their own work and hit book fairs, conventions, and do online promotion with us."

CAROLINA WREN PRESS

120 Morris St., Durham NC 27701. (919)560-2738. E-mail: carolina@carolinawrenpress.org. Web site: www.carolinawrenpress.org. **Contact:** Andrea Selch, president. Estab. 1976. "We publish poetry, fiction, nonfiction, biography, autobiography, literary nonfiction work by and/or about people of color, women, gay/lesbian issues, health and mental health topics in children's literature." Books: 6×9 paper; typeset; various bindings; illustrations. **Published 1 debut author within the last year.** Plans 1 novel this year. Distributes titles through Amazon.com, Barnes & Noble, Borders, Ingram and Baker & Taylor.
Needs "We read unsolicited manuscripts of fiction and nonfiction September-December."

How to Contact Accepts unsolicited mss. Accepts queries by e-mail, mail. Include brief bio. Send SASE or IRC. Responds in 3 months to queries; 6 months to mss.

Terms Publishes ms 1 year after acceptance. Ms guidelines online.

Advice "Please read our mission statement online before submitting."

✦ ⬙ ◎ CAROLRHODA BOOKS, INC.

Lerner Publishing Group, 241 First Ave. N., Minneapolis MN 55401. Fax: (612)332-7615. Web site: www.lernerb ooks.com. **Contact:** Zelda Wagner, submissions editor. Estab. 1969. Carolrhoda Books seeks creative picture books, middle-grade fiction, historical fiction and K-6 children's nonfiction. Publishes hardcover originals. Averages 50-60 total titles/year.

Needs Historical, juvenile, multicultural, picture books, young reader, middle grade and young adult fiction. "We continue to add fiction for middle grades and 8-10 picture books per year. Not looking for folktales or anthropomorphic animal stories." Recently published *The Perfect Shot*, by Elaine Marie Alphin; *Noel*, by Tony Johnston.

How to Contact Submit complete ms. Responds in 8 months to queries. Accepts simultaneous submissions. Accepts submissions only in November.

Terms Pays royalty on wholesale price or makes outright purchase. Negotiates payments of advance against royalty. Average advance: varied. Book catalog for 9×12 SAE with $3.50 postage. Ms guidelines online.

Ⓐ ✦ ♥ CARROLL & GRAF PUBLISHERS, INC.

Avalon Publishing Group, 245 W. 17th St. 11th floor, New York NY 10011. (212)981-9919. Fax: (646)375-2571. Web site: www.avalonpub.com. **Contact:** Will Balliett, publisher; Phillip Turner, editor-in-chief; Don Weise, senior editor. Estab. 1982. Publishes hardcover and trade paperback originals. Averages 120 total titles, 50 fiction titles/year.

Needs Literary, mainstream/contemporary, mystery, science fiction, suspense, thriller. Published *The Woman Who Wouldn't Talk*, by Susan McDougal.

How to Contact Does not accept unsolicited mss. *Agented submissions only.*

Terms Pays 10-15% royalty on retail price for hardcover, 6-7½% for paperback. Offers advance commensurate with the work. Publishes ms 9-18 months after acceptance.

◎ CAVE BOOKS

277 Clamer Rd., Trenton NJ 08628-3204. (609)530-9743. E-mail: pddb@juno.com. Web site: www.cavebooks.c om. **Contact:** Paul Steward, managing editor. Estab. 1980. Small press devoted to books on caves, karst and speleology. Fiction: novels about cave exploration only. Publishes hardcover and trade paperback originals and reprints. Books: acid-free paper; offset printing. Averages 2 total titles, 1 fiction title/year.

Needs Adventure, historical, literary, caves, karst, speleology. Recently published *True Tales of Terror in The Caves of the World*, by Paul Jay Steward; *Prehistoric Cavers of Mammoth Cave*, by Colleen O'Connor Olson.

How to Contact Accepts unsolicited mss. Query with SASE or submit complete ms. Accepts queries by e-mail. Send SASE for return of ms or send a disposable ms and SASE for reply only. Responds in 2 weeks to queries; 3 months to mss. Accepts simultaneous submissions, electronic submissions. Sometimes comments on rejected mss.

Terms Pays 10% royalty on retail price. Publishes ms 18 months after acceptance.

Advice "In the last 3 years we have received only 3 novels about caves, and we have published one of them. We get dozens of inappropriate submissions. We only print books about caves."

CHARLESBRIDGE PUBLISHING, SCHOOL DIVISION

85 Main St., Watertown MA 02472. Web site: www.charlesbridge.com/school. Estab. 1980. Publishes educational curricula and hardcover and paperback nonfiction and fiction children's books. Averages 30 total titles/year.

Needs Multicultural, nature, science, social studies, bedtime, etc. Non-rhyming stories. Recently published *A Mother's Journey*, by Sandra Markle; *Ace Lancewing: Bug Detective*, by David Biedrzycki.

How to Contact Submit complete ms.

Terms Royalty and advance vary. Publishes ms 2 years after acceptance. Ms guidelines online.

⊕ CHRISTCHURCH PUBLISHERS LTD

2 Caversham St., London England SW3 4AH United Kingdom. Fax: 0044 171 351 4995. **Contact:** James Hughes, fiction editor.

Needs "Miscellaneous fiction, also poetry. More 'literary' style of fiction, but also thrillers, crime fiction, etc."

How to Contact Query with SASE.

Terms Pays royalty. Offers advance. "We have contacts and agents worldwide."

CHRONICLE BOOKS

Adult Trade Division, 85 Second St., 6th Floor, San Francisco CA 94105. (415)537-4200. Fax: (415)537-4440. Web site: www.chroniclebooks.com. **Contact:** Editorial Dept., Adult Trade Division. Estab. 1966. Publishes hardcover and trade paperback originals. Averages 175 total titles/year.

Needs Novels and story collections. No genre fiction.

How to Contact Submit complete ms and SASE. Responds in 3 months to mss. Accepts simultaneous submissions.

Terms Publishes ms 18 months after acceptance. Ms guidelines online.

▩ ◎ CHRONICLE BOOKS FOR CHILDREN

85 Second St., 6th Floor, San Francisco CA 94105. (415)537-4200. Fax: (415)537-4460. E-mail: frontdesk@chroniclebooks.com. Web site: www.chroniclekids.com. **Contact:** Victoria Rock, associate publisher. Publishes hardcover and trade paperback originals. **Published 5% debut authors within the last year.** Averages 50-60 total titles/year.

Needs Mainstream/contemporary, multicultural, young adult, picture books, middle grade fiction, young adult projects. Published *The Man Who Went to the Far Side of the Moon*; by Bea Uusma Shyffert; *Just a Minute: A Trickster Tale and Counting Book*; by Yuyi Morales; *Mama, Do You Love Me?*, by Barbara Joosse and Barbara Lavallee.

How to Contact Query with SASE. Responds in 2-4 weeks to queries; 3 months to mss. Accepts simultaneous submissions. No electronic submissions, submissions on disk.

Terms Royalty varies. Average advance: variable. Publishes ms 18-24 months after acceptance. Ms guidelines online.

Advice "We are interested in projects that have a unique bent to them—be it in subject matter, writing style or illustrative technique. As a small list, we are looking for books that will lend our list a distinctive flavor. Primarily, we are interested in fiction and nonfiction picture books for children ages up to 8 years, and nonfiction books for children ages up to 12 years. We publish board, pop-up and other novelty formats as well as picture books. We are also interested in early chapter books, middle grade fiction and young adult projects."

◎ ▨ CIRCLET PRESS, INC.

1770 Massachusetts Ave., #278, Cambridge MA 02140. (617)864-0492. E-mail: ctan@circlet.com. Web site: www.circlet.com. **Contact:** Cecilia Tan, publisher. Estab. 1992. Small, independent specialty book publisher. "We are the only book publisher specializing in science fiction and fantasy of an erotic nature." Publishes hardcover and trade paperback originals. Books: perfect binding; illustrations sometimes. **Published 20 debut authors within the last year.** Averages 4 titles/year. Distributes titles through SCB Distribution in the US/Canada, Turnaround UK in the UK, and Bulldog Books in Australia. Promotes titles through reviews in book trade and general media, mentions in *Publishers Weekly, Bookselling This Week* and regional radio/TV.

● "Our titles were finalists in the Independent Publisher Awards in both science fiction and fantasy."

Imprint(s) The Ultra Violet Library (non-erotic lesbian/gay fantasy and science fiction).

Needs Short stories only. "Fiction must combine both the erotic and the fantastic. The erotic content needs to be an integral part of a science fiction story, and vice versa. Writers should not assume that any sex is the same as erotica." All books are anthologies of short stories. Published *Nymph*, by Francesca Lia Block; *The Darker Passions*, by Amarantha Knight.

How to Contact Accepts unsolicited mss only between April 15 and August 15. Check Web site for anthology topics which change annually. Query with SASE. Include estimated word count, brief bio, list of publishing credits. Send SASE for return of ms or send a disposable ms and SASE for reply only. Agented fiction 5%. Responds in 1 month to queries; 6-18 months to mss. Accepts simultaneous submissions, electronic submissions only from overseas authors. Always comments on rejected mss.

Terms Pays 4-12% royalty on retail price or makes outright purchase. Also pays in books, if author prefers. Publishes ms 18 months after acceptance. Ms guidelines online.

Advice "Read what we publish, learn to use lyrical but concise language to portray sex positively. No horror. Make sex and erotic interaction integral to your plot. Stay away from genre stereotypes. Use depth of character, internal monologue and psychological introspection to draw me in."

CITY LIGHTS BOOKS

261 Columbus Ave., San Francisco CA 94133. (415)362-8193. Fax: (415)362-4921. E-mail: staff@citylights.com. Web site: www.citylights.com. **Contact:** Robert Sharrard, editor. Estab. 1955. Publishes paperback originals. Plans 1-2 first novels this year. Averages 12 total titles, 4-5 fiction titles/year.

Needs Fiction, essays, memoirs, translations, poetry and books on social and political issues.

How to Contact Submit one-page description of the book and a sample chapter or two with SASE. Does not accept unsolicited mss. Does not accept queries by e-mail. See Web site for guidelines.

✪ ◎ ⚅ CLARION BOOKS

Houghton Mifflin Co., 215 Park Ave. S., New York NY 10003. Web site: www.houghtonmifflinbooks.com. **Contact:** Dinah Stevenson, vice-president and publisher (YA, middle-grade, chapter book); Jennifer B. Greene, senior editor (YA, middle-grade, chapter book); Jennifer Wingertzahn, editor (YA, middle-grade, chapter book); Lynne Polvino, associate editor (YA, middle-grade, chapter book). Estab. 1965. "Clarion is a strong presence in the fiction market for young readers. We are highly selective in the areas of historical and contemporary fiction. We publish chapter books for children ages 7-10 and middle-grade novels for ages 9-12, as well as picture books and nonfiction." Publishes hardcover originals for children. Averages 50 total titles/year.

- Clarion author Linda Sue Park received the 2002 Newbery Award for her book, *A Single Shard*. David Wiesner received the 2002 Caldecott Award for *The Three Pigs*.

Needs Adventure, historical, humor, mystery, suspense, strong character studies. Clarion is highly selective in the areas of historical fiction, fantasy and science fiction. A novel must be superlatively written in order to find a place on the list. Mss that arrive without an SASE of adequate size will *not* be responded to or returned. Accepts fiction translations. Published *The Great Blue Yonder*, by Alex Shearer (contemporary, middle-grade); *When My Name Was Keoko*, by Linda Sue Park (historical fiction); *Dunk*, by David Lubar (contemporary YA).

How to Contact Submit complete ms. Responds in 2 months to queries. Prefers no multiple submissions to mss.

Terms Pays 5-10% royalty on retail price. Average advance: minimum of $4,000. Publishes ms 2 years after acceptance. Ms guidelines for #10 SASE.

◎ ⚅ COFFEE HOUSE PRESS

27 N. Fourth St., Suite 400, Minneapolis MN 55401. Fax: (612)338-4004. **Contact:** Chris Fischbach, senior editor. Estab. 1984. "Nonprofit publisher with a small staff. We publish literary titles: fiction and poetry." Publishes hardcover and trade paperback originals. Books: acid-free paper; cover illustrations. **Published some debut authors within the last year.** Averages 12 total titles, 6 fiction titles/year.

- This successful nonprofit small press has received numerous grants from various organizations including the NEA, the McKnight Foundation and Target.

Needs Ethnic, experimental, literary, mainstream/contemporary, short story collections, novels. Publishes anthologies, but they are closed to unsolicited submissions. Published *Miniatures*, by Norah Labiner (novel); *Circle K Cycles*, by Karen Yamashita (stories); *Little Casino*, by Gilbert Sorrentino (novel).

How to Contact Accepts unsolicited mss. Query with SASE. Agented fiction 10%. Responds in 1 month to queries; up to 4 months to mss. No electronic submissions.

Terms Pays 8% royalty on retail price. Provides 15 author's copies. Publishes ms 18 months after acceptance. Book catalog and ms guidelines for #10 SASE with 2 first-class stamps. Ms guidelines for #10 SAE with 55¢ first-class stamps.

⚙ ◎ COTEAU BOOKS

Thunder Creek Publishing Co-operative Ltd., 2517 Victoria Ave., Regina SK S4P 0T2 Canada. (306)777-0170. Fax: (306)522-5152. E-mail: coteau@coteaubooks.com. Web site: www.coteaubooks.com. **Contact:** Nik L. Burton, managing editor. Estab. 1975. "Coteau Books publishes the finest Canadian fiction, poetry, drama and children's literature, with an emphasis on western writers." Publishes trade paperback originals and reprints. Books: 2 lb. offset or 60 lb. hi-bulk paper; offset printing; perfect bound; 4-color illustrations. Averages 16 total titles, 4-6 fiction titles/year. Distributes titles through Fitzhenry & Whiteside.

- 2003 Sask Book Award, Book of the Year for *Nobody Goes to Earth Anymore*, by Donald Ward.

Needs Ethnic, fantasy, feminist, gay/lesbian, historical, humor, juvenile, literary, mainstream/contemporary, multicultural, multimedia, mystery, regional, short story collections, spiritual, sports, young adult. *Canadian authors only*. Published *Grasslands*, by Michael Hetherton (fiction); *Peacekeepers*, by Dianne Unden (young adult); *Residual Desire*, by Jill Robinson (fiction).

How to Contact Accepts unsolicited mss. Submit 3-4 sample chapter(s), author bio. Responds in 2 months to queries; 6 months to mss. No simultaneous submissions. Sometimes comments on rejected mss.

Terms Pays 10% royalty on retail price. "We're a co-operative and receive subsidies from the Canadian, provincial and local governments. We do not accept payments from authors to publish their works." Publishes ms 1 year after acceptance. Ms guidelines online.

Advice "We publish short-story collections, novels, drama, nonfiction and poetry collections. Canadian authors only! This is part of our mandate. The work speaks for itself! Be bold. Be creative. Be persistent!"

◎ COVENANT COMMUNICATIONS, INC.

920 E. State Rd., American Fork UT 84003-0416. (801)756-9966. E-mail: info@covenant-lds.com. Web site: www.covenant-lds.com. Averages 50+ total titles/year.

Needs Adventure, historical, humor, juvenile, literary, mainstream/contemporary, mystery, picture books, regional, religious, romance, spiritual, suspense, young adult.

How to Contact Responds in 4 months to mss.

Terms Pays 6½-15% royalty on retail price. Publishes ms 6-12 months after acceptance. Ms guidelines online.

Advice Our audience is exclusively LDS (Latter-Day Saints, "Mormon").

N ⊕ ◪ CRESCENT MOON PUBLISHING

P.O. Box 393, Maidstone Kent ME14 5XU United Kingdom. Web site: www.crescentmoon.org.uk. **Contact:** J. Robinson, director. Estab. 1988. Small independent publisher. Publishes hardcover and trade paperback originals. **Published some debut authors within the last year.** Plans 1-2 first novels this year. Averages 25 total titles, 1-2 fiction titles/year.

Needs Erotica, experimental, feminist, gay/lesbian, literary, new age/mystic, short story collections. "We do not publish much fiction at present, but will consider high quality new work." Plans anthology. Send short stories to editor.

How to Contact Does not accept whole unsolicited mss. Submit outline, 2 sample chapter(s), synopsis. Include estimated word count, list of publishing credits. Send SASE for return of ms or send a disposable ms and SASE for reply only. Agented fiction 10%. Responds in 2 months to queries; 4 months to mss. Accepts simultaneous submissions. Sometimes comments on rejected mss.

Terms Pays royalty. Average advance: negotiable. Publishes ms 18 months after acceptance.

Advice "We publish a small amount of fiction, and mainly in *Pagan Magazine* and *Passion Magazine*.

CROSSQUARTER PUBLISHING GROUP

P.O. Box 8756, Santa Fe NM 87504. (505)438-9846. Web site: www.crossquarter.com. **Contact:** Anthony Ravenscroft. Publishes case and trade paperback originals and reprints. **Published 90% debut authors within the last year.** Averages 5-10 total titles/year.

Needs Science fiction, visionary fiction.

How to Contact Query with SASE. Responds in 3 months to queries. Accepts simultaneous submissions.

Terms Pays 8-10% royalty on wholesale or retail price. Publishes ms 1 year after acceptance. Book catalog for $1.75. Ms guidelines online.

Advice "Audience is earth-conscious people looking to grow into balance of body, mind, heart and spirit."

✴ ◪ CROSSTIME

Crossquarter Publishing Group, P.O. Box 8756, Santa Fe NM 87504. (505)438-9846. Fax: (505)438-9846. E-mail: info@crossquarter.com. Web site: www.crossquarter.com. **Contact:** Anthony Ravenscroft. Estab. 1985. Small Publisher. Publishes paperback originals. Books: recycled paper; docutech or offset printing; perfect bound. **Published 2 debut authors within the last year.** Plans 2 first novels this year. Member SPAN, PMA.

Needs Mystery (occult), new age/mystic, psychic/supernatural, romance (occult), science fiction, young adult (fantasy/science fiction). Plans an anthology of Paul B. Duquette Memorial Short Science Fiction contest winners. Guidelines on Web site. Recently published *The Shamrock and the Feather*, by Dori Dalton (debut author); *Shyla's Initiative*, by Barbara Casey (occult romance); *Emperor of Portland*, by Anthony Ravenscroft (occult mystery); *CrossTIME SF Anthology Vol. II* (science fiction).

How to Contact Does not accept unsolicited mss. Query with SASE. No longer accepts queries by e-mail. Include estimated word count, brief bio, list of publishing credits. Send SASE for return of ms or send a disposable ms and SASE for reply only. Responds in 3 months to queries; 6 months to mss. Accepts simultaneous submissions, electronic submissions, submissions on disk.

Terms Pays 6-10% royalty. Publishes ms 6-9 months after acceptance. Ms guidelines online.

✴ ⊘ ◎ CROSSWAY BOOKS

Division of Good News Publishers, 1300 Crescent St., Wheaton IL 60187-5800. (630)682-4300. Fax: (630)682-4785. Web site: www.crossway.com. **Contact:** Jill Carter. Estab. 1938. " 'Making a difference in people's lives for Christ' as its maxim, Crossway Books lists titles written from an evangelical Christian perspective." Midsize evangelical Christian publisher. Publishes hardcover and trade paperback originals. Averages 85 total titles, 5 fiction titles/year. Member ECPA. Distributes titles through Christian bookstores and catalogs. Promotes titles through magazine ads, catalogs.

Needs *Currently not accepting fiction manuscripts.*

How to Contact Does not accept unsolicited mss. Agented fiction 5%.

Terms Pays negotiable royalty. Average advance: negotiable. Publishes ms 18 months after acceptance. Ms guidelines online.

Advice "With so much Christian fiction on the market, we are carefully looking at our program to see the direction we wish to proceed. Be sure your project fits into our guidelines and is written from an evangelical Christian worldview. 'Religious' or 'Spiritual' viewpoints will not fit."

☐ DAN RIVER PRESS
Conservatory of American Letters, P.O. Box 298, Thomaston ME 04861-0298. (207)354-0998. E-mail: cal@ameri canletters.org. Web site: www.americanletters.org. **Contact:** Richard S. Danbury, III, fiction editor. Estab. 1977. "Small press publisher of fiction and biographies owned by a non-profit foundation." Publishes hardcover and paperback originals. Books: paperback; offset printing; perfect and cloth binding; illustrations. Averages 3-4 fiction titles/year, plus the annual (since 1984) *Dan River Anthology, (Year)*. Promotes titles through the author's sphere of influence. Distributes titles by mail order to libraries and bookstores, as well as by Amazon, Barnesan-dnoble.com, Baker & Taylor, Ingrams, 10 UK distributors, and author's influence.
Needs Adventure, family saga, fantasy (space fantasy, sword and sorcery), historical (general), horror (dark fantasy, futuristic, psychological, supernatural), humor, literary, mainstream/contemporary, military/war, mystery (amateur sleuth, police procedural, private eye/hard-boiled), new age/mystic, psychic/supernatural, religious (general religious, inspirational, religious mystery/suspense, religious thriller, religious romance), romance (contemporary, futuristic/time travel, gothic, historical, romantic suspense), science fiction (hard science/technological, soft/sociological), short story collections, thriller/espionage, western (frontier saga, traditional), young adult, outdoors/fishing/hunting/camping/trapping. Accepts anything but porn, sedition, evangelical, and children's literature. Publishes poetry and fiction anthology (submission guidelines to *Dan River Anthology* on the Web).
How to Contact Accepts unsolicited mss. Accepts queries by mail. Include estimated word count, brief bio, list of publishing credits. Send SASE for return of ms or send a disposable ms and SASE for reply only. Responds in 2-3 days to queries; 1-2 weeks to mss. Accepts simultaneous submissions. No electronic submissions.
Terms Pays 10-15% royalty and 5 author's copies. Average advance: occasional. Publishes ms 3-4 months after acceptance. Book catalog for 6×9 SAE with 60¢ postage affixed. Ms guidelines online.
Advice "Spend some time developing a following."

JOHN DANIEL AND CO.
Daniel & Daniel, Publishers, Inc., P.O. Box 2790, McKinleyville CA 95519. (707)839-3495. Fax: (707)839-3242. E-mail: dand@danielpublishing.com. Web site: www.danielpublishing.com. **Contact:** John Daniel, publisher. Estab. 1980. "We publish small books, usually in small editions, but we do so with pride." Publishes hardcover originals and trade paperback originals. Publishes poetry, fiction and nonfiction. Averages 4 total titles/year. Distributes through SCB Distributors. Promotes through direct mail, reviews.
Needs Literary, short story collections. Publishes poetry, fiction and nonfiction; specializes in belles lettres, literary memoir. Published *Mary Lou's War*, by Lia Schallert (novel); *Kissing Kate*, by Bradford Dillman (novel); *Till I'm With You Again*, by Edna Jeffrey (novel).
How to Contact Accepts unsolicited mss. Query with SASE or submit synopsis, 50 pages. Responds in 1 month to queries; 2 months to mss. Accepts simultaneous submissions.
Terms Pays 10% royalty on wholesale price. Average advance: $0-500. Publishes ms 1 year after acceptance. Ms guidelines online.
Advice "Write for the joy of writing. That's as good as it gets."

☑ DARK HORSE COMICS, INC.
10956 SE Main St., Milwaukie OR 97222. (503)652-8815. Web site: www.darkhorse.com. "In addition to publishing comics from top talent like Frank Miller, Mike Mignola, Stan Sakai and internationally-renowned humorist Sergio Aragonés, Dark Horse is recognized as the world's leading publisher of licensed comics."
Needs Comic books, graphic novels. Published *Astro Boy Volume 10 TPB*, by Osamu Tezuka and Reid Fleming; *Flaming Carrot Crossover #1* by Bob Burden and David Boswell.
How to Contact Submit synopsis.
Advice "If you're looking for constructive criticism, show your work to industry professionals at conventions."

☑ ◎ MAY DAVENPORT, PUBLISHERS
26313 Purissima Rd., Los Altos Hills CA 94022. (650)947-1275. Fax: (650)947-1373. E-mail: mdbooks@earthlink .net. Web site: www.maydavenportpublishers.com. **Contact:** May Davenport, editor/publisher. Estab. 1976. "We prefer books which can be *used* in high schools as supplementary readings in English or creative writing courses. Reading skills have to be taught, and novels by humourous authors can be more pleasant to read than Hawthorne's or Melville's novels, war novels, or novels about past generations. Humor has a place in literature." Publishes hardcover and paperback originals. Averages 4 total titles/year. Distributes titles through direct mail order.
Imprint(s) md Books (nonfiction and fiction).

Needs Humor, literary. "We want to focus on novels junior and senior high school teachers can share with the reluctant readers in their classrooms." Published *Charlie and Champ*, by Allyson Wagoner; *Senioritis*, by Tate Thompson; *A Life on The Line*, by Michael Horton; *Making My Escape*, by David Lee Finkle.

How to Contact Query with SASE. Responds in 1 month to queries.

Terms Pays 15% royalty on retail price. Publishes ms 1 year after acceptance. Ms guidelines for #10 SASE.

Advice "Just write humorous novels about today's generation with youthful, admirable, believable characters to make young readers laugh. TV-oriented youth need role models in literature, and how a writer uses descriptive adjectives and similes enlightens youngsters who are so used to music, animation, special effects with stories."

★ ▢ ◎ DAW BOOKS, INC.

Penguin Putnam, Inc., 375 Hudson St., 3rd Floor, New York NY 10014-3658. (212)366-2096. Fax: (212)366-2090. E-mail: daw@penguinputnam.com. Web site: www.dawbooks.com. **Contact:** Peter Stampfel, submissions editor. Estab. 1971. Publishes hardcover and paperback originals and reprints. Averages 60-80 total titles/year.

Needs Fantasy, science fiction. "We are interested in science fiction and fantasy novels. We need science fiction more than fantasy right now, but we're still looking for both. We like character-driven books with attractive characters. We accept both agented and unagented manuscripts. Long books are absolutely not a problem. We are not seeking collections of short stories or ideas for anthologies. We do not want any nonfiction manuscripts." Published *The War of the Flowers*, by Tad Williams (fantasy).

How to Contact Query with SASE or submit complete ms. "Please type your name, address and phone number in the upper right hand corner of the first page of your manuscript. Right under this, please put the length of your manuscript in number of words." Responds in 6 weeks to queries.

Terms Pays in royalties with an advance negotiable on a book-by-book basis. Ms guidelines online.

Advice "We strongly encourage new writers. Research your publishers and submit only appropriate work."

Ⓐ ★ ◎ DEL REY BOOKS

The Random House Publishing Group, Random House, Inc., 1745 Broadway, 18th Floor, New York NY 10019. (212)782-9000. Web site: www.delreybooks.com. **Contact:** Betsy Mitchell, editor-in-chief; Shelly Shapiro, editorial director; Steve Saffel, executive editor. Estab. 1977. "We are a long-established imprint with an eclectic frontlist. We're seeking interesting new voices to add to our best-selling backlist. Publishes hardcover, trade paperback, and mass market originals and mass market paperback reprints. Averages 120 total titles, 80 fiction titles/year.

Imprint(s) Imprints: Del Rey Manga, edited by Dallas Middaugh, publishes translations of Japanese comics.

Needs Fantasy (should have the practice of magic as an essential element of the plot), science fiction (well-plotted novels with good characterizations and interesting extrapolations), alternate history. Published *The Iron Council*, by China Mieville; *The Charnel Prince*, by Greg Keyes; *Marque and Reprisal*, by Elizabeth Moon; *Dragon's Kin*, by Ann McCaffrey and Todd McCaffrey; *Star Wars: Yoda: Dark Rendezvous*, by Sean Stewart.

How to Contact Does not accept unsolicited mss. *Agented submissions only.* Responds in 6 months to queries. No simultaneous submissions. Sometimes comments on rejected mss.

Terms Pays royalty on retail price. Average advance: competitive. Publishes ms 1 year after acceptance. Ms guidelines online.

Advice Has been publishing "more fiction and hardcovers, because the market is there for them. Read a lot of science fiction and fantasy, such as works by Anne McCaffrey, David Eddings, China Mieville, Arthur C. Clarke, Terry Brooks, Richard K. Morgan, Elizabeth Moon. When writing, pay particular attention to plotting (and a satisfactory conclusion) and characters (sympathetic and well rounded) because those are what readers look for."

▢ DENLINGER'S PUBLISHERS, LTD.

P.O. Box 1030, Edgewater FL 32132-1030. (386)416-0009. Fax: (386)236-0517. E-mail: acquisitions@thebookden.com. Web site: www.thebookden.com. **Contact:** Cecelia Peters, acquisitions editor (fiction-all). Estab. 1926. Denlinger's Publishers has a small dedicated staff that is interested in new technology in the field of publishing. Publishes paperback and hardcover originals. **Published 75% debut authors within the last year.** Plans 6 first novels this year. Member PMA. Distributes titles through Baker & Taylor, BN.com, direct mail, Amazon.com and company Web site.

- Delinger's Publishers won the Grand Prize Fiction Award at the 2000 Frankfurt International E-book Awards.

Needs Adventure, ethnic, family saga, feminist, historical, horror, military/war, mystery, new age/mystic, religious, romance, science fiction, short story collections, thriller/espionage, western, young adult. Published *A Greater Pox*, by C.B. Mosher (historical/medical); *My Carl*, by Chris Bower (general fiction); *Blauser's Building*, by Alan Neff (dark comedy). Publishes the ongoing series *Cricket Mysteries* (young adult/animal).

How to Contact Accepts unsolicited mss by e-mail only. See Web site for guidelines. Responds in 3-6 weeks to queries. Accepts simultaneous submissions, electronic submissions, submissions on disk. Never comments on rejected mss.

Terms Pays 10% royalty, 6 contributor's copies. Publishes ms 6-12 months after acceptance.

Advice "Read the material on the Web site carefully. Do your research on questions regarding publishing *prior* to submission. We do not have time to explain the whole industry to each prospective submitter. Make sure you are comfortable with the publishing arrangement *prior* to submission. Our contract is online at www.thebookden.com/agree.html."

⭐ ◎ DIAL BOOKS FOR YOUNG READERS

Penguin Group USA, 345 Hudson St., 14th Floor, New York NY 10014. (212)366-2000. Web site: www.penguinputnam.com. **Contact:** Submissions Editor. Estab. 1961. Trade children's book publisher. Publishes hardcover originals. Averages 50 total titles/year.

Needs Adventure, fantasy, juvenile, picture books, young adult. Especially looking for "lively and well-written novels for middle grade and young adult children involving a convincing plot and believable characters. The subject matter or theme should not already be overworked in previously published books. The approach must not be demeaning to any minority group, nor should the roles of female characters (or others) be stereotyped, though we don't think books should be didactic, or in any way message-y. No topics inappropriate for the juvenile, young adult and middle grade audiences. No plays." Published *A Year Down Yonder*, by Richard Peck; *The Missing Mitten Mystery*, by Steven Kellog.

How to Contact Accepts unsolicited mss. "Submit entire picture book manuscript or the first three chapters of longer works. Please include a cover letter with brief bio and publication credits. Please note that, unless interested in publishing your book, Dial will not respond to unsolicited submissions. Please do NOT include a SASE. If Dial is interested, expect a reply from us within four months."

Terms Pays royalty. Average advance: varies.

Ⓐ ⭐ DIAL PRESS

Bantam Dell Publishing Group, Random House, Inc., 1745 Broadway, New York NY 10019. (212)782-9000. Fax: (212)782-9523. Web site: www.randomhouse.com/bantamdell/. **Contact:** Susan Kamil, vice president, editorial director. Estab. 1924. Averages 6-12 total titles/year.

Needs Literary (general). Published *Mary and O'Neil* (short story collection); *Niagara Falls Over Again*, by Elizabeth Mccracken(fiction).

How to Contact *Agented submissions only.* Accepts simultaneous submissions.

Terms Pays royalty on retail price. Offers advance. Publishes ms 18 months after acceptance.

◖ DISKUS PUBLISHING

P.O. Box 43, Albany IN 47320. E-mail: submissions@diskuspublishing.com. Web site: www.diskuspublishing.com. **Contact:** Marilyn Nesbitt, editor-in-chief; Joyce McLaughlin, inspirational and children's editor; Holly Janey, submissions editor. Estab. 1997. Publishes paperback originals and e-books. **Published 10 debut authors within the last year.** Averages 100 total titles, 80 fiction titles/year. Member AEP, PMA, EPIC.

  • *Elrod McBugle On The Loose*, by Jeff Strand was the 2001 Eppie Finalist; *Camper of The Year*, by Ann Herrick was a 2003 Eppie Finalist.

Needs Adventure, children's/juvenile, ethnic (general), family saga, fantasy (space fantasy), historical, horror, humor, juvenile, literary, mainstream/contemporary, military/war, multicultural (general), mystery, psychic/supernatural, religious, romance, science fiction, short story collections, suspense, thriller/espionage, western, young adult. "We are actively seeking confessions for our Diskus Confessions line. As well as short stories for our Quick Pick line. We only accept e-mailed submissions for these lines." *The Quest for the White Jewel*, by Janet Lane Walters; *Brazen*, by Lori Foster (adventure/romance); *A Change of Destiny*, by Marilynn Mansfield (science fiction/futuristic)

How to Contact Accepts unsolicited mss. Submit publishing history, author bio, estimated word count and genre and complete ms. Send SASE for return of ms or send a disposable ms and SASE for reply only. Prefers submissions by e-mail. Agented fiction 5%. Accepts simultaneous submissions. Sometimes comments on rejected mss.

Terms Pays 40% royalty. Publishes ms usually within the year after acceptance. Ms guidelines online.

Ⓐ ⭐ DOUBLEDAY

Doubleday Broadway Publishing Group, Random House, Inc., 1745 Broadway, New York NY 10019. (212)782-9000. Fax: (212)782-9700. Web site: www.randomhouse.com. Estab. 1897. Publishes hardcover originals. Averages 70 total titles/year.

Needs Adventure, confession, ethnic, experimental, feminist, gay/lesbian, historical, humor, literary, mainstream/contemporary, religious, short story collections.

How to Contact *Agented submissions only.* No simultaneous submissions.

Terms Pays royalty on retail price. Offers advance. Publishes ms 1 year after acceptance.

Ⓐ ⊠ ⊠ DOUBLEDAY CANADA

Random House of Canada, 1 Toronto Street, Suite 300, Toronto ON M5C 2V6 Canada. (416)364-4449. Web site: www.randomhouse.ca. Publishes hardcover and paperback originals. Averages 50 total titles/year.

Imprint(s) Doubleday Canada (hardcover and paperback publisher); Bond Street Books Canada (hardcover publisher of international titles); Seal Books (mass market publisher); Anchor Canada (trade paperback publisher).

How to Contact Does not accept unsolicited mss. *Agented submissions only.*

Ⓐ ⊠ ◎ DOUBLEDAY RELIGIOUS PUBLISHING

Doubleday Broadway Publishing Group, Random House, Inc., 1745 Broadway, New York NY 10019. (212)782-9000. Web site: www.randomhouse.com. **Contact:** Eric Major, vice president, religious division; Trace Murphy, executive editor; Andrew Corbin, editor. Estab. 1897. Publishes hardcover and trade paperback originals and reprints. Averages 45-50 total titles/year.

Imprint(s) Image Books, Anchor Bible Commentary, Anchor Bible Reference, Galilee, New Jerusalem Bible.

Needs Religious.

How to Contact *Agented submissions only.* Accepts simultaneous submissions.

Terms Pays 7½-15% royalty. Offers advance. Publishes ms 1 year after acceptance. Book catalog for SAE with 3 first-class stamps.

⊠ ◯ ◎ DRAGON MOON PRESS

3521 43A Ave, Red Deer AB T4N 3W9 Canada. E-mail: publisher@dragonmoonpress.com. Web site: www.dragonmoonpress.com. **Contact:** Gwen Gades, publisher. Estab. 1994. "Dragon Moon Press is dedicated to new and exciting voices in science fiction and fantasy." Publishes trade paperback and electronic originals. Books: 60 lb. offset paper; short run printing and offset printing. Average print order: 250-3,000. **Published several debut authors within the last year.** Plans 5 first novels this year. Averages 4-6 total titles, 4-5 fiction titles/year. Distributed through Baker & Taylor. Promoted locally through authors and online at leading retail bookstores like Amazon, Barnes & Noble, Chapters, etc.

Imprint(s) Dragon Moon Press, Gwen Gades and Christine Mains, editors (fantasy and science fiction).

Needs Fantasy, science fiction (soft/sociological). No horror or children's fiction. "At Dragon Moon Press, continue to seek out quality manuscripts and authors who are eager to participate in the marketing of their book. We are receiving many high quality manuscripts that we feel deserve to be published." Published *The Magister's Mask*, by Deby Fredericks; *The Complete Guide to Writing Fantasy*, by Darin Park and Tom Dullemond; *The Dragon Reborn*, by Kathleen H. Nelson (fantasy).

How to Contact Does not accept unsolicited mss. Accepts simultaneous submissions. No submissions on disk.

Terms Pays 8-15% royalty on retail price. Publishes ms 2 years after acceptance. Ms guidelines online.

Advice "First, be patient. Read our guidelines at dragonmoonpress.com. Not following our submission guidelines can be grounds for automatic rejection. Second, we view publishing as a family affair. Be ready to participate in the process and show some enthusiasm and understanding in what we do. Remember also, this is a business and not about egos, so keep yours on a leash! The reward with Dragon Moon Press is not so much in money as it is in the experience and the satisfaction in the final work. Show us a great story with well-developed characters and plot lines, show us that you are interested in participating in marketing and developing as an author, and show us your desire to create a great book and you may just find yourself published by Dragon Moon Press."

Ⓝ ◎ DRAGONON

Dragonon, Inc., 9378 Mason Montgomery Rd. #108, Mason OH 45040. E-mail: dmeyer@dragonon.com. Web site: www.dragonon.com. **Contact:** Deborah Meyer (adult trade fiction). Estab. 2004. "Small independent publisher of adult trade fiction. Interested in religious fiction, fantasy, sci-fi mostly." Publishes hardcover originals, paperback originals, paperback reprints. Format: smythsewn perfect bound. Average print order: 5,000. **Published 2 new writers last year.** Averages 3 total titles/year; 3 fiction titles/year. Member SPAN, PMA. Distributes/promotes titles through Baker & Taylor, the News Group (wholesalers).

Needs Fantasy, mainstream, religious (fantasy, mystery/suspense, thriller), science fiction (soft/sociological), thriller/espionage. Especially wants "quality religious fiction." Published *Chosen: The Final Potential is Discovered*, by Deborah Meyer (religious fiction, debut); *Russell's Revenge*, by Dennis Fishel (young adult, debut);

Bang! A Love Story, by Anthony Mora (adult trade). Also planning upcoming series Chosen: Battle for Creation (religious fiction).

How to Contact "As a result of the tremendous volume of recent submissions, Dragonon is no longer accepting manuscripts." Please continue to check Web site for updates. Query with outline/synopsis and 3 sample chapters. Accepts queries by snail mail. Include brief bio, list of publishing credits. Send disposable copy of ms and SASE for reply only. Agented fiction: 5%. Responds to queries in 6 months. No unsolicited mss. Considers simultaneous submissions. Rarely critiques/comments on rejected mss. Does not return rejected mss.

Terms Pays royalties of 10%-15%. Sends pre-production galleys to author. Manuscript published 1 year after acceptance. Writer's guidelines on Web site. Book catalogs not available.

⚡ ◯ ◎ THE DUNDURN GROUP

3 Church St., Suite 500, Toronto ON M5E 1M2 Canada. (416)214-5544. Web site: www.dundurn.com. **Contact:** Acquisitions Editor. Estab. 1972. Dundurn prefers work by Canadian authors. First-time authors are welcome. Publishes hardcover and trade paperback originals and reprints.

• *Shoulder the Sky*, by Lesley Choyce, won the 2003 Ann Connor Brimer Children's Literature Prize.

Imprint(s) Simon & Pierre (literary fiction); Castle Street Mysteries (mystery); Boardwalk Books (young adult).

Needs Literary, mystery, young adult. Published *The Unexpected and Fictional Career Change of Jim Kearns*, by David Munroe (literary fiction); *Overexposed*, by Michael Blair (mystery); *Deconstructing Dylan*, by Lesley Choyce (young adult).

How to Contact Query with SASE or submit 3 sample chapter(s), synopsis. Accepts queries by mail. Include estimated word count. Responds in 3-4 months to queries. Accepts simultaneous submissions. No electronic submissions.

Terms Pays 10% royalty on net receipts. Publishes ms an average of 1 year after acceptance. Ms guidelines online.

Ⓐ ⚡ ◉ DUTTON (ADULT TRADE)

Penguin Putnam, Inc., 375 Hudson St., New York NY 10014. (212)366-2000. Web site: www.penguinputnam.com. **Contact:** Editor-in-Chief: Brian Tart. Estab. 1852. Publishers hardcover originals. Averages 40 total titles/year.

Needs Adventure, historical, literary, mainstream/contemporary, mystery, short story collections, suspense. Published *The Darwin Awards II*, by Wendy Northcutt (humor); *Falling Angels*, by Tracy Chevalier (fiction); *The Oath*, by John Lescroart (fiction).

How to Contact *Agented submissions only.* Responds in 6 months to queries. Accepts simultaneous submissions.

Terms Pays royalty. Average advance: negotiable. Publishes ms 12-18 months after acceptance.

Advice "Write the complete manuscript and submit it to an agent or agents. They will know exactly which editor will be interested in a project."

⚡ ◯ ◎ DUTTON CHILDREN'S BOOKS

Penguin Group, Inc., 345 Hudson St., New York NY 10014. (212)414-3700. Fax: (212)414-3397. Web site: www.penguin.com. **Contact:** Stephanie Owens Lurie, president and publisher (picture books and fiction); Maureen Sullivan, executive editor (upper young adult, fiction and nonfiction); Lucia Monfried, senior editor (picture books, easy-to-read books, fiction); Mark McVeigh, senior editor (picture books and fiction); Julie Strauss-Gabel, senior editor (picture books and young adult fiction). Estab. 1852. Dutton Children's Books publishes fiction and nonfiction for readers ranging from preschoolers to young adults on a variety of subjects. Publishes hardcover originals as well as novelty formats. Averages 100 total titles/year.

Needs Dutton Children's Books has a diverse, general-interest list that includes picture books, easy-to-read books and fiction for all ages, from "first chapter" books to young adult readers. Published *My Teacher for President*, by Kay Winters, illustrated by Denise Brunkus (picture book); *The Best Pet of All*, by David LaRochelle, illustrated by Hanako Wakiyama (picture book); *The Schwa was Here*, by Neal Shusteman (novel); *Guitar Girl*, by Sarra Manning (novel).

How to Contact Does not accept unsolicited mss. Query with SASE.

Terms Pays royalty on retail price. Offers advance.

⚡ ECW PRESS

2120 Queen St. E., Suite 200, Toronto ON M4E 1E2 Canada. (416)694-3348. Fax: (416)698-9906. E-mail: info@ecwpress.com. Web site: www.ecwpress.com. **Contact:** Jack David, publisher. Estab. 1979. Publishes hardcover and trade paperback originals. Averages 40 total titles/year.

Needs Literary, mystery, poetry, short story collections, suspense.

How to Contact Accepts simultaneous submissions.

Terms Pays 8-12% royalty on net receipts. Average advance: $300-5,000. Publishes ms 18 months after acceptance. Book catalog and ms guidelines free. Ms guidelines online.

Advice "Make sure to include return postage (SASE, IRC if outside of Canada) it you wish your material to be returned."

⚡ ◎ EDGE SCIENCE FICTION AND FANTASY PUBLISHING

Box 1714, Calgary AB T2P 2L7 Canada. (403)254-0160. Fax: (403)254-0456. E-mail: publisher@hadespublications.com. Web site: www.edgewebsite.com. **Contact:** Kimberly Gammon, editorial manager (science fiction/fantasy). Estab. 1996. "We are an independent publisher of science fiction and fantasy novels in hard cover or trade paperback format. We produce high-quality books with lots of attention to detail and lots of marketing effort. We want to encourage, produce and promote thought-provoking and fun-to-read science fiction and fantasy literature by 'bringing the magic alive: one world at a time' (as our motto says) with each new book released." Publishes hardcover and trade paperback originals. Books: natural offset paper; offset/web printing; HC/perfect binding; b&w illustration only. Average print order: 2,000-3,000. Plans 8 first novels this year. Averages 6-8 total titles/year. Member of Book Publishers Association of Alberta (BPAA), Independent Publishers Association of Canada (IPAC), Publisher's Marketing Association (PMA), Small Press Center.

Imprint(s) Edge, Alien Vistas, Riverbend.

Needs Fantasy (space fantasy, sword and sorcery), science fiction (hard science/technological, soft/sociological). "We are looking for all types of fantasy and science fiction, except juvenile/young adult, horror, erotica, religious fiction, short stories, dark/gruesome fantasy, or poetry." Published *Throne Price*, by Lynda Williams and Alison Sinclair (science fantasy); *Keaen*, by Till Noever (fantasy); *Orbital Burn*, by K.A. Bedford.

How to Contact Accepts unsolicited mss. Query with SASE or submit outline, 3 sample chapter(s), synopsis, Check Web site for guidelines or send SAE & IRCs for same. Include estimated word count. Responds in 1 month to queries; 4-5 months to mss. No simultaneous submissions, electronic submissions. Rarely comments on rejected mss.

Terms Pays 10% royalty on wholesale price. Average advance: negotiable. Publishes ms 18 months after acceptance. Ms guidelines online.

Advice "Send us your best, polished, completed manuscript. Use proper manuscript format. Take the time before you submit to get a critique from people who can offer you useful advice. When in doubt, visit our Web site for helpful resources, FAQs and other tips."

⚡ EERDMANS BOOKS FOR YOUNG READERS

William B. Eerdmans Publishing Co., 255 Jefferson Ave. SE, Grand Rapids MI 49503. (616)459-4591. Fax: (616)459-6540. **Contact:** Judy Zylstra, editor. Publishes picture books and middle reader and young adult fiction and nonfiction. Averages 12-15 total titles/year.

Needs Juvenile, picture books, young adult, middle reader. Published *Going for The Record*, by Julie Swanson; *Dancing With Elvis*, by Lynda Stephenson.

How to Contact Responds in 6 weeks to 3 months to queries. Accepts exclusive submissions.

Terms Pays 5-7½% royalty on retail price. Publishes middle reader and YA books in 1-2 years; publishes picture books 2-4 years after acceptance.

◢ ◎ ⚡ WILLIAM B. EERDMANS PUBLISHING CO.

255 Jefferson Ave. SE, Grand Rapids MI 49503. (616)459-4591. Fax: (616)459-6540. E-mail: info@eerdmans.com. Web site: www.eerdmans.com. **Contact:** Jon Pott, editor-in-chief, fiction editor (adult fiction); Judy Zylstra, fiction editor (children). Estab. 1911. "Although Eerdmans publishes some regional books and other nonreligious titles, it is essentially a religious publisher whose titles range from the academic to the semi-popular. We are a midsize independent publisher. We publish the occasional adult novel, and these tend to engage deep spiritual issues from a Christian perspective." Publishes hardcover and paperback originals and reprints. **Published some debut authors within the last year.** Averages 120-130 total titles, 6-8 (mostly for children) fiction titles/year.

• Wm. B. Eerdmans Publishing Co.'s titles have won awards from the American Library Association and The American Bookseller's Association.

Imprint(s) Eerdmans Books for Young Readers.

Needs Religious (children's, general, fantasy). Published *I Wonder as I Wander*, by Gwenyth Swain, illustrated by Ronald Himler; *Gilgamesh the Herd*, by Geraldine McCaughrean, illustrated by David Parkins; *The Enemy Has a Face*, by Gloria D. Miklowitz (young adult); *Down in the Piney Woods* and *Mariah's Pond*, by Ethel Footman Smothers.

How to Contact Accepts unsolicited mss. Submit outline, 2 sample chapter(s), synopsis. Include brief bio, list of publishing credits. Send SASE for return of ms or send a disposable ms and SASE for reply only. Agented fiction 5%. Responds in 6 weeks to queries. Accepts simultaneous submissions. Sometimes comments on rejected mss.

Terms Pays royalty. Average advance: occasional. Publishes ms usually within 1 year after acceptance.
Advice "Our readers are educated and fairly sophisticated, and we are looking for novels with literary merit."

THE EIGHTH MOUNTAIN PRESS

624 SE 29th Ave., Portland OR 97214. E-mail: ruth@eighthmountain.com. Estab. 1985. Publishes original trade paperbacks. Averages 1 total title/year.
How to Contact No longer accepts unsolicted mss.
Terms Pays 7% royalty.

◎ ELLORA'S CAVE PUBLISHING, INC.

1056 Home Avenue, Akron OH 44310-3205. E-mail: submissions@ellorascave.com. Web site: www.ellorascave.com and www.cerridwenpress.com. Estab. 2000. Publishes trade paperback and electronic originals and reprints. Averages 300 total titles/year.
Needs Erotica, fantasy, gay/lesbian, gothic, historical, horror, mainstream/contemporary, multicultural, mystery, romance, science fiction, suspense, western. All must be under genre romance. All must have erotic content. For Cerridwen Press, all mainstream fiction genres.
How to Contact Submit proposal package including detailed full synopsis, first three chapters, last chapter. Responds in 3-12 months to mss. Accepts simultaneous submissions.
Terms Pays royalty of 37.5% of cover price for digital, 7.5% of cover for print. Ms guidelines online.

✓ ◎ EMPIRE PUBLISHING SERVICE

P.O. Box 1344, Studio City CA 91614-0344. Estab. 1960. Midsize publisher with related imprints. Publishes hardcover reprints and trade paperback originals and reprints. Book: paper varies; offset printing; binding varies. Average print order: 5,000-10,000. First novel print order: 2,500-5,000. **Published 4 debut authors within the last year.** Averages 60 total titles, 5 fiction titles/year. Distributes and promotes titles by "Sales & Marketing Distribution offices in five countries."
Imprint(s) Paul Mould Publishing, Paul Mould, editor (historical); Gaslight Publications (Sherlock Holmes); Collectors Publications (erotica).
Needs Historical (pre-18th century), mystery (Sherlock Holmes). Plans anthology of Sherlock Holmes short stories. Published *Gods Hammer*, by Eric Shumacher.
How to Contact Does not accept unsolicited mss. Query with SASE. Include estimated word count, brief bio, list of publishing credits, general background. Send SASE for return of ms or send a disposable ms and SASE for reply only. Agented fiction 2%. Responds in 1 month to queries; up to 1 year to mss. No simultaneous submissions, electronic submissions, submissions on disk.
Terms Pays 6-10% royalty on retail price. Average advance: variable. Publishes ms 6 months to 2 years after acceptance. Ms guidelines for $1 or #10 SASE.
Advice "Send query with SASE for only the type of material we publish, historical and Sherlock Holmes."

✂ ✓ EMPYREAL PRESS

P.O. Box 1746, Place Du Parc, Montreal QC HZX 4A7 Canada. E-mail: empyrealpress@hotmail.com. Web site: www.skarwood.com. **Contact:** Colleen B. McCool. "Our mission is the publishing of literature which doesn't fit into any standard 'mold'—writing which is experimental yet grounded in discipline, imagination." Publishes trade paperback originals. **Published 50% debut authors within the last year.** Averages 1-2 total titles/year.
Needs Experimental, feminist, gay/lesbian, literary, short story collections. Empyreal Press is not currently accepting unsolicited manuscripts "due to extremely limited resources."

🅽 ✓ ◎ EROS BOOKS

463 Barlow Ave., Staten Island NY 10308. (718)317-7484. E-mail: marynicholaou@aol.com. Web site: www.geocities.com/marynicholaou/classic_blue.html. **Contact:** Mary Nicholaou, fiction editor. Estab. 2000. "Small independent publisher of postmodern romance, short fiction and translations." Publishes paperback originals, e-books. Format: 20 lb. paper; offset printing. Average print order: 500. Debut novel print order: 500. **Published 5 new writers last year.** Plans 10 debut novels this year. Averages 5 total titles/year; 4 fiction titles/year.
Needs Postmodern, short, romance fiction, translations. Published *Cracks*, by Mary Nicholaou (postmodern romance); *Chimera*, by Clara Smith (postmodern romance).
How to Contact Query with outline/synopsis. Reads submissions June-September. Accepts queries by snail mail, e-mail. Include social security number. Send SASE or IRC for return of ms or disposable copy of ms and SASE/IRC for reply only. Agented fiction: 10%. Responds to queries in 2 weeks. Considers simultaneous submissions, submissions on CD or disk. Always critiques/comments on rejected mss. Responds to mss in 2 months.

Terms Pays in author's copies. Manuscript published 12 months after acceptance. Writer's guidelines available for SASE. Book catalogs available for SASE.

Ⓐ ☑ M. EVANS AND CO., INC.

216 E. 49th St., New York NY 10017-1502. (212)688-2810. Fax: (212)688-2810. Web site: www.mevans.com. **Contact:** Editor. Estab. 1960. Small, general trade publisher specializing in nonfiction titles on health, nutrition, diet, cookbooks, parenting, popular psychology. Publishes hardcover and trade paperback originals. Averages 30-40 total titles/year.

Needs "Our very small general fiction list represents an attempt to combine quality with commercial potential. We publish no more than one novel per season." Published *Dying Embers* and *Private Heat*, both by R. Bailey (mystery).

How to Contact Does not accept unsolicited mss. Query with SASE. Agented fiction 100%. Responds in 2 months to queries.

Terms Pays negotiable royalty. Offers advance. Publishes ms 8 months after acceptance.

Ⓝ ☑ ☒ ☒FANTAGRAPHICS BOOKS

7563 Lake City Way NE, Seattle WA 98115. Fax: (206)524-2104. E-mail: fbicomix@fantagraphics.com. Web site: www.fantagraphics.com. **Contact:** Michael Dowers (all genres). Estab. 1976. "Fantagraphics Books has been a leading proponent of comics as a legitimate form of art and literature since it began publishing the critical trade magazine *The Comics Journal* in 1976. By the early 1980s, Fantagraphics found itself at the forefront of the burgeoning movement to establish comics as a medium as eloquent and expressive as the more established popular arts of film, literature, poetry, et al. Fantagraphics quickly established a reputation as an advocacy publisher that specialized in seeking out and publishing the kind of innovative work that traditional comics corporations who dealt almost exclusively in superheroes and fantasy either didn't know existed or wouldn't touch: serious, dramatic, historical, journalistic, political and satirical work by a new generation of alternative cartoonists, as well as many artists who gained prominence as part of the seminal underground comix movement of the '60s. Fantagraphics has since gained an international reputation for its literate and audacious editorial standards and its exacting production values." Publishes hardcover originals, paperback originals, hardcover reprints, paperpack reprints. Average print run: 3,000 (debut writer). **Publishes 3-4 debut writers/year.** Publishes 60 titles/year. Titles promoted/distributed by W.W. Norton & Co. Awards: Harvey Awards, Eisner Awards, Ignatz Awards, Quills nomination.

Needs All categories. Does not want superheros. Anthologies: MOME, Hotwire, Blab. Editors select stories.

How to Contact Prefers submissions from writer-artists. Detailed submission guidelines at www.fantagraphics.com/submissions.html. Agented submissions: less than 5%. Responds to queries and ms/art packages in 4 months. Often comments on rejected manuscripts.

Terms Creators paid royalty. Sends pre-publication galleys to author. Writer's and artist's guidelines on Web site. Book catalog free upon request.

Ⓐ FARRAR, STRAUS & GIROUX

19 Union Square West, New York NY 10003. (212)741-6900. E-mail: fsg.editorial@fsgbooks.com. Web site: www.fsgbooks.com. Publishes hardcover and trade paperback books. Averages 180 total titles/year.

Needs Literary.

How to Contact Does not accept unsolicited mss.

✦ ◯ ◎ ☒ FARRAR, STRAUS & GIROUX BOOKS FOR YOUNG READERS

Farrar Straus Giroux, Inc., 19 Union Square W., New York NY 10003. (212)741-6900. Fax: (212)633-2427. **Contact:** Margaret Ferguson, editorial director (children's); Wesley Adams, executive editor (children's); Beverly Reingold, executive editor (children's); Janine O'Malley, editor (children's). Estab. 1946. "We publish original and well-written materials for all ages." Publishes hardcover originals and trade paperback reprints. **Published some debut authors within the last year.** Averages 75 total titles/year.

Imprint(s) Frances Foster Books, edited by Frances Foster (children's); Melanie Kroupa Books, edited by Melanie Kroupa (children's).

Needs Children's/juvenile, picture books, young adult, nonfiction. "Do not query picture books; just send manuscript. Do not fax queries or manuscripts." Published *The Tree of Life*, by Peter Sis; *Tadpole*, by Ruth White.

How to Contact Query with SASE. Include brief bio, list of publishing credits. Agented fiction 25%. Responds in 2 months to queries; 4 months to mss. Accepts simultaneous submissions. No electronic submissions, submissions on disk.

Terms Pays 2-6% royalty on retail price for paperbacks, 3-10% for hardcovers. Average advance: $3,000-25,000. Publishes ms 18 months after acceptance. Book catalog for 9×12 SAE with $1.87 postage. Ms guidelines for #10 SASE.

Advice "Study our list to avoid sending something inappropriate. Send query letters for long manuscripts; don't ask for editorial advice (just not possible, unfortunately); and send SASEs!"

🅰 ✖ FARRAR, STRAUS & GIROUX PAPERBACKS

19 Union Square W., New York NY 10003. (212)741-6900. FSG Paperbacks emphasizes literary nonfiction and fiction, as well as poetry. Publishes hardcover and trade paperback originals and reprints. Averages 180 total titles/year.

Needs Literary. Published *The Corrections*, by Jonathan Franzen; *The Haunting of L.*, by Howard Norman.

How to Contact Does not accept unsolicited mss. Agented submissions only.

FC2

Publications Unit, Campus Box 4241 Illinois University, Normal IL 61790. E-mail: fc2@english.fsu.edu. Web site: http://fc2.org. **Contact:** R.M. Berry, publisher (fiction); Brenda L. Mills, managing editor. Estab. 1974. Publisher of innovative fiction. Publishes hardcover and paperback originals. Books: perfect/Smyth binding; illustrations. Average print order: 2,200. **Published some debut authors within the last year.** Plans 2 first novels this year. Averages 6 total titles, 6 fiction titles/year. Titles distributed through Northwestern U.P. $10 reader's fee. With your returned submission/notification, you will receive a coupon for 50% off your next purchase on the FC2 Web site.

Needs Experimental, feminist, gay/lesbian, innovative; modernist/postmodern; avant-garde; anarchist; minority; cyberpunk. Published *Book of Lazarus*, by Richard Grossman; *Is It Sexual Harassment Yet?*, by Cris Mazza; *Liberty's Excess*, by Lidia Yuknavitch; *Aunt Rachel's Fur*, by Raymond Federman.

How to Contact Accepts unsolicited mss. Query with SASE or submit outline, publishing history, synopsis, author bio. Agented fiction 5%. Responds in 3 weeks to queries; 2-6 months to mss. Accepts simultaneous submissions.

Terms Pays 10% royalty. Publishes ms 1-3 years after acceptance. Ms guidelines online.

Advice "Be familiar with our list."

⊘ ◎ THE FEMINIST PRESS AT THE CITY UNIVERSITY OF NEW YORK

365 Fifth Ave., Suite 5406, New York NY 10016. (212)817-7917. Fax: (212)817-1593. E-mail: fhowe@gc.cuny.e du. Web site: www.feministpress.org. **Contact:** Florence Howe. Estab. 1970. Small, nonprofit literary and educational publisher. "The Feminist Press publishes only fiction reprints by classic American women authors and translations of distinguished international women writers." Publishes hardcover and trade paperback originals and reprints. Publishes original fiction rarely; exceptions are anthologies and international works. "We use an acid-free paper, perfect-bind our books, four color covers; and some cloth for library sales if the book has been out of print for some time; we shoot from the original text when possible. We always include a scholarly and literary afterword, since we are introducing a text to a new audience. Average print run: 2,500." Averages 15-20 total titles, 4-8 fiction titles/year. Member: CLMP, Small Press Association. Distributes titles through Consortium Book Sales and Distribution. Promotes titles through author tours, advertising, exhibits and conferences. Charges "permission fees (reimbursement)."

Needs Ethnic, feminist, gay/lesbian, literary, short story collections, women's. "The Feminist Press publishes only fiction reprints by classic American women authors and imports and translations of distinguished international women writers. Absolutely no original fiction is considered." Needs fiction by "U.S. women of color writers from 1920-1970 who have fallen out of print." Published *Apples From the Desert*, by Savyon Liebrecht (short stories, translation); *The Parish and the Hill*, by Mary Doyle Curran (fiction reprint); *Allegra Maud Goldman*, by Edith Konecky (fiction, reprint); and *Still Alive*, by Ruth Kluger (memoir).

How to Contact Does not accept unsolicited mss. Include estimated word count, brief bio, list of publishing credits. Responds immediately to queries. Accepts simultaneous submissions, electronic submissions.

Terms Pays 10% royalty on net receipts. Pays 5-10 author's copies. Average advance: $500. Publishes ms 18-24 months after acceptance. Ms guidelines online.

FLORIDA ACADEMIC PRESS

P.O. Box 540, Gainesville FL 32602. (352)332-5104. Fax: (352)331-6003. E-mail: fapress@worldnet.att.net. **Contact:** Max Vargas, CEO (nonfiction/self-help); Sam Decalo, managing editor (academic); Florence Dusek, assistant editor (fiction). Publishes hardcover and trade paperback originals. **Published 85% debut authors within the last year.** Averages 10 total titles/year.

Needs Serious fiction.

How to Contact Submit complete ms. Responds in 4-12 weeks to mss.

Terms Pays 5-8% royalty on retail price, depending if paperback or hardcover. Publishes ms 3-5 months after acceptance.

Advice Considers complete mss only. "Manuscripts we decide to publish must be re-submitted in camera-ready form."

✦ ⬛ ◪ FORGE AND TOR BOOKS

Tom Doherty Associates, LLC, 175 Fifth Ave. 14th Floor, New York NY 10010. (212)388-0100. Fax: (212)388-0191. Web site: www.tor.com. **Contact:** Melissa Ann Singer, senior editor (general fiction, mysteries, thriller); Patrick Nielsen Hayden, senior editor (science fiction, fantasy). Estab. 1980. ''Tor Books are science fiction, fantasy and horror, and occasionally, related nonfiction. Forge books are everything else—general fiction, historical fiction, mysteries and suspense, women's fiction and nonfiction. Orb titles are trade paperback reprint editions of science fiction, fantasy and horror books.'' Publishes hardcover, trade paperback and mass market paperback originals, trade and mass market paperback reprints. **Published some debut authors within the last year.**

● Tor was named Best Publisher at the Locus Awards for the sixteenth consecutive year.

Imprint(s) Forge, Tor, Orb.

Needs Historical, horror, mainstream/contemporary, mystery (amateur sleuth, police procedural, private eye/hard-boiled), science fiction, suspense, thriller/espionage, western (frontier saga, traditional), thriller; general fiction and fantasy.

How to Contact Accepts unsolicited mss. Do not query; ''submit only the first three chapters of your book and a synopsis of the entire book. Your cover letter should state the genre of the submission and previous sales or publications if relevant.'' Include estimated word count, brief bio, list of publishing credits. Agented fiction 95%. Sometimes comments on rejected mss. Responds in 4-6 months. No simultaneous submissions. Additional guidelines on Web site.

Terms Paperback: Pays 6-8% royalty for first-time authors, 8-10% royalty for established authors. Hardcover: Pays 10% first 5,000; $12\frac{1}{2}$% second 5,000; 15% thereafter. Offers advance. Publishes ms 12-18 months after acceptance.

Advice ''The writing must be outstanding for a new author to break into today's market.''

◎ FORT ROSS INC. RUSSIAN-AMERICAN PUBLISHING PROJECTS

26 Arthur Place, Yonkers NY 10701. (914)375-6448. Fax: (914)375-6439. E-mail: fort.ross@verizon.net. Web site: www.fortrossinc.com. **Contact:** Dr. Vladimir P. Kartsev. Estab. 1992. ''We welcome Russia-related manuscripts as well as books from well-established fantasy and romance novel writers who would like to have their novels translated in Russia and Eastern Europe by our publishing house in cooperation with the local publishers.'' Publishes paperback originals. **Published 3 debut authors within the last year.** Averages 40 total titles/year.

Needs Adventure, fantasy (space fantasy, sword and sorcery), horror, mainstream/contemporary, mystery (amateur sleuth, police procedural, private eye/hard-boiled), romance (contemporary, regency), science fiction (hard science/technological, soft/sociological), suspense, thriller/espionage.

How to Contact Does not accept unsolicited mss. Query with SASE. Include estimated word count, brief bio, list of publishing credits. Send SASE for return of ms or send a disposable ms and SASE for reply only. Responds in 1 month to queries; 3 months to mss. Accepts simultaneous submissions.

Terms Pays 5-10% royalty on wholesale price or makes outright purchase of $500-1,500. Average advance: $500-$1,000; negotiable.

⬛ ◎ ◪ FRONT STREET

862 Haywood Rd., Asheville NC 28806. (828)236-5940. Fax: (828)236-5935. E-mail: submissions@frontstreetbooks.com. Web site: www.frontstreetbooks.com. **Contact:** Joy Neaves, editor. Estab. 1994. ''Small publisher of high-quality picture books and literature for children and young adults.'' Publishes hardcover originals. Averages 10-15 total titles/year. Titles promoted on the Internet, in catalog, by sales representatives, at library and education conferences.

● *A Step from Heaven*, by An Na won the Michael L. Printz Award for 2002. *Carver: A Life in Poems*, by Marilyn Nelson won a Newberry Honor 2002 and a Coretta Scott King Honor.

Needs Adventure, historical, humor, juvenile, literary, picture books, young adult (adventure, fantasy/science fiction, historical, mystery/suspense, problem novels, sports). Published *Honeysuckle House*, by Andrea Cheng (YA); *Hunger Moon*, by Sarah Lamstein (YA); *Black Brothers*, by Liza Tetzner and Hans Binder (YA graphic novel).

How to Contact Accepts unsolicited mss. Query with SASE or submit 3 sample chapters. Accepts queries by e-mail and mail. Include contact info, brief bio, list of publishing credits. Send SASE for return of ms or send a disposable ms and SASE for reply only. Agented fiction 10%. Responds in 1 month to queries; 3 months to mss. Accepts simultaneous submissions.

Terms Pays royalty on retail price. Offers advance. Publishes ms 1 year after acceptance. Ms guidelines online.

✦ ◎ GASLIGHT PUBLICATIONS

Empire Publishing Services, P.O. Box 1344, Studio City CA 91614. (818)784-8918. **Contact:** Simon Waters, fiction editor (Sherlock Holmes only). Estab. 1960. Publishes hardcover and paperback originals and reprints. Books: paper varies; offset printing; binding varies; illustrations. Average print order: 5,000. **Published 1 debut**

author within the last year. Averages 4-12 total titles, 2-4 fiction titles/year. Promotes titles through sales reps, trade, library, etc.

Needs Sherlock Holmes only. Recently published *Sherlock Holmes, The Complete Bagel Street Saga*, by Robert L. Fish; *Subcutaneously: My Dear Watson*, by Jack Tracy (all Sherlock Holmes).

How to Contact Accepts unsolicited mss. Query with SASE. Include estimated word count, brief bio, list of publishing credits. Send SASE for return of ms or send a disposable ms and SASE for reply only. Agented fiction 10%. Responds in 2 weeks to queries; 1 year to mss.

Terms Pays 8-10% royalty. Royalty and advance dependent on the material. Publishes ms 1-6 months after acceptance.

Advice "Please send only Sherlock Holmes material. Other stuff just wastes time and money."

LAURA GERINGER BOOKS

HarperCollins Children's Books, 1350 Avenue of the Americas, New York NY 10019. (212)261-6500. Web site: www.harperchildrens.com. **Contact:** Laura Geringer, senior vice president/publisher. "We look for books that are out of the ordinary, authors who have their own definite take, and artists who add a sense of humor to the text." Publishes hardcover originals. **Published some debut authors within the last year.** Averages 15-20 total titles/year.

Needs Adventure, fantasy, historical, humor, juvenile, literary, picture books, young adult. Recently published *Regular Guy*, by Sarah Weeks; *Throwing Smoke*, by Bruce Brooks.

How to Contact Does not accept unsolicited mss. Query with SASE. Agented fiction 90%. Responds in 3 months to queries.

Terms Pays 10-12½% royalty on retail price. Average advance: variable.

Advice "A mistake writers often make is failing to research the type of books an imprint publishes, therefore sending inappropriate material."

GERTRUDE PRESS

P.O. Box 83948, Portland OR 97283. Web site: www.gertrudepress.org. **Contact:** Justus Ballard (all fiction). Estab. 2005. "Gertrude Press is a nonprofit organization developing and showcasing the creative talents of lesbian, gay, bisexual, trans, queer-identified and allied individuals. We publish limited-edition fiction and poetry chapbooks plus the biannual literary journal, *Gertrude*." Publishes paperback originals. Format: 60 lb. paper; high-quality digital printing; perfect (lit mag) or saddle-stitch (chapbook) bound. Average print order: 250. **Published 5-10 new writers last year.** Averages 4 total titles/year; 1 fiction title/year.

Needs Ethnic/multicultural, experimental, feminist, gay, humor/satire, lesbian, literary, mainstream, short story collections.

How to Contact Submit complete ms with cover letter. Submissions accepted year-round. Accepts queries by snail mail, e-mail. Include estimated word count, brief bio, list of publishing credits. Send disposable copy of ms and SASE for reply only. Responds to queries in 3-4 weeks; mss in 3-6 months. Accepts unsolicited mss. Considers simultaneous submissions, e-mail submissions. Sometimes critiques/comments on rejected mss.

Terms Manuscript published 3 months after acceptance. Writer's guidelines on Web site. Pays in author's copies (1 for lit mag, 50 for chapbook). Book catalogs not available.

Advice Sponsors poetry and fiction chapbook contest. Prize is $50 and 50 contributor copies. Submission guidelines and fee information on Web site. "Read the journal and sample published work. We are not impressed by pages of publications; your work should speak for itself."

GIVAL PRESS

P.O. Box 3812, Arlington VA 22203. (703)351-0079. E-mail: givalpress@yahoo.com. Web site: www.givalpress.com. **Contact:** Robert L. Giron, publisher. Estab. 1998. A small, award-winning independent publisher that publishes quality works by a variety of authors from an array of walks of life. Works are in English, Spanish and French and have a philosophical or social message. Publishes paperback originals and reprints and e-books. Books: perfect-bound. Average print order: 500. **Published 4 debut authors within the last year.** Plans 2 first novels this year. Member AAP, PMA, Literary Council of Small Presses and Magazines. Distributes books through Ingram and BookMasters, Inc.

- Received a DIY Book Festival award for Compilations/Anthologies; Silver Award, 2003 *Foreword Magazine* for fiction—translation.

Needs Ethnic, gay/lesbian, historical, literary. "Looking for French books with English translation." The Annual Gival Press Novel Award contest deadline is May 30th. The Annual Gival Press Short Story Award contest deadline is August 8th. Guidelines on Web site. Recently published *A Change of Heart*, by David Garrett Izzo; *The Gay Herman Melville Reader*, by Ken Schellenberg; *Secret Memories*, by Carlos Rubio (memoir).

How to Contact Does not accept unsolicited mss. Query with SASE or submit outline, 2 sample chapter(s). Reading period open from September to November. Accepts queries by e-mail, mail. Include estimated word count, brief bio, list of publishing credits. Send SASE for return of ms or send a disposable ms and SASE for reply only. Agented fiction 5%. Responds in 4 months to queries; 5 months to mss. Rarely comments on rejected mss.

Terms Pays 20 contributor's copies. Offers advance. Publishes ms 1 year after acceptance. Book catalog for SASE and on Web site. Ms guidelines for SASE or on Web site.

Advice "Study the types of books we have published—literary works with a message of high quality."

THE GLENCANNON PRESS

P.O. Box 633 1428, El Cerrito CA 94530. (510)528-4216. Fax: (510)528-3194. E-mail: merships@yahoo.com. Web site: www.glencannon.com. **Contact:** Bill Harris (maritime, maritime children's). Estab. 1993. "We publish quality books about ships and the sea." Publishes hardcover and paperback originals and hardcover reprints. Books: Smyth: perfect binding; illustrations. Average print order: 1,000. First novel print order: 750. Averages 4-5 total titles, 1 fiction titles/year. Member PMA, BAIPA. Distributes titles through Quality Books, Baker & Taylor. Promotes titles through direct mail, magazine advertising and word of mouth.

Imprint(s) Palo Alto Books (any except maritime); Glencannon Press (merchant marine and Navy).

Needs Adventure, children's/juvenile (adventure, fantasy, historical, mystery, preschool/picture book), ethnic (general), historical (maritime), humor, mainstream/contemporary, military/war, mystery, thriller/espionage, western (frontier saga, traditional maritime), young adult (adventure, historical, mystery/suspense, western). Currently emphasizing children's maritime, any age. Recently published *Good Shipmates*, by Ernest F. Imhoff (anthology, merchant marine); *Fort Ross*, by Mark West (Palo Alto Books, western).

How to Contact Accepts unsolicited mss. Submit complete ms. Include brief bio, list of publishing credits. Send SASE for return of ms or send a disposable ms and SASE for reply only. Responds in 1 month to queries; 2 months to mss. Accepts simultaneous submissions. Often comments on rejected mss.

Terms Pays 10-20% royalty. Publishes ms 6-24 months after acceptance.

Advice "Write a good story in a compelling style."

DAVID R. GODINE, PUBLISHER, INC.

9 Hamilton Place, Boston MA 02108. (617)451-9600. Fax: (617)350-0250. E-mail: info@godine.com. Web site: www.godine.com. **Contact:** David R. Godine, president. Estab. 1970. Small independent publisher (5-person staff). Publishes hardcover and trade paperback originals and reprints. Averages 35 total titles/year.

Imprint(s) Nonpareil Books (trade paperbacks), Verba Mundi (translations), Imago Mundi (photography).

Needs Children's/juvenile, historical, literary. *No unsolicited mss.*

How to Contact Does not accept unsolicited mss. Query with SASE.

Terms Pays royalty on retail price. Publishes ms 3 years after acceptance.

Advice "Have your agent contact us. Please no phone queries."

GOOSE LANE EDITIONS

469 King St., Fredericton NB E3B 1E5 Canada. (506)450-4251. Fax: (506)459-4991. Web site: www.gooselane.c om. **Contact:** Laurel Boone, editorial director. Estab. 1954. Publishes hardcover and paperback originals and occasional reprints. Books: some illustrations. Average print order: 3,000. First novel print order: 1,500. Averages 16-18 total titles, 6-8 fiction titles/year. Distributes titles through University of Toronto Press (UTP).

- *Elle*, by Douglas Glover, won the 2004 Governor General's Award for Fiction and was shortlisted for the International IMPAC Dublin Literary Award.

Needs Literary (novels), mainstream/contemporary, short story collections. "Our needs in fiction never change: substantial, character-centered literary fiction." Published *Tattycoram*, by Audrey Thomas.

How to Contact Accepts unsolicited mss. Query with SASE. Responds in 6 months to mss. No simultaneous submissions.

Terms Pays 8-10% royalty on retail price. Average advance: $200-1,000, negotiable. Ms guidelines online.

Advice "We do not consider submissions from outside Canada."

GOTHIC CHAPBOOK SERIES

Gothic Press, 1701 Lobdell Avenue, No. 32, Baton Rouge LA 70806-8242. E-mail: gothicpt12@aol.com. Web site: www.gothicpress.com. **Contact:** Gary W. Crawford, editor (horror, fiction, poetry and scholarship). Estab. 1979. "One person operation on a part-time basis." Publishes paperback originals. Books: printing or photocopying. Average print order: 150-200. Distributes titles through direct mail and book dealers.

Needs Horror (dark fantasy, psychological, supernatural). Need novellas and short stories.

How to Contact Accepts unsolicited mss. Query with SASE. Accepts queries by e-mail, phone. Include estimated word count, brief bio, list of publishing credits. Send SASE for return of ms or send a disposable ms and SASE for reply only. Responds in 2 weeks to queries; 2 months to mss. Sometimes comments on rejected mss.

Terms Pays 10% royalty. Ms guidelines for #10 SASE.

Advice "Know gothic and horror literature well."

◐ GRAYWOLF PRESS

2402 University Ave., Suite 203, St. Paul MN 55114. E-mail: wolves@graywolfpress.org. Web site: www.graywo lfpress.org. **Contact:** Anne Czarniecki, executive editor; Katie Dublinski, editor. Estab. 1974. Growing small literary press, nonprofit corporation. Publishes trade cloth and paperback originals. Books: acid-free quality paper; offset printing; hardcover and soft binding. Average print order: 3,000-10,000. First novel print order: 3,000-7,500. Averages 22 total titles, 6-8 fiction titles/year. Distributes titles nationally through Farrar, Straus & Giroux. "We have an in-house marketing staff and an advertising budget for all books we publish."

Needs Literary, short story collections. "Familiarize yourself with our list first." Published *Wounded*, by Percival Everett; *Pocketfull of Names*, by Joe Coomer; *Record Palace*, by Susan Wheeler; *Times Like These*, by Rachel Ingalis.

How to Contact Query or submit 1 sample chapter. Include SASE/IRC, estimated word count, brief bio, list of publishing credits. Agented fiction 90%. Responds in 3 months to queries.

Terms Pays royalty on retail price, author's copies. Average advance: $2,500-15,000. Publishes ms 18-24 months after acceptance. Ms guidelines online.

Advice "Please review our catalog and submission guidelines before submitting your work. We rarely publish collections or novels by authors who have not published work previously in literary journals or magazines."

⬛ ◉ GREENWILLOW BOOKS

HarperCollins Publishers, 1350 Avenue of the Americas, New York NY 10019. (212)261-6500. Web site: www.ha rperchildrens.com. **Contact:** Fiction Editor. Estab. 1974. Publishes hardcover originals and reprints. Averages 50-60 total titles/year.

Needs Fantasy, humor, literary, mystery, picture books. *The Queen of Attolia*, by Megan Whalen Turner; *Bo & Mzzz Mad*, by Sid Fleishman; *Whale Talk*, by Chris Crutcher; *Year of the Griffen*, by Diana Wynne Jones.

How to Contact Does not accept unsolicited mss.

Terms Pays 10% royalty on wholesale price for first-time authors. Average advance: variable. Publishes ms 2 years after acceptance.

Ⓐ GROVE/ATLANTIC, INC.

841 Broadway 4th Floor, New York NY 10003. (212)614-7850. Fax: (212)614-7886. Web site: www.groveatlantic .com. Estab. 1952. Publishes hardcover originals, trade paperback originals and reprints. Averages 60-70 total titles/year.

Imprint(s) Grove Press (estab. 1952), Atlantic Monthly Press (estab. 1917).

Needs Literary. Published *Halfway House*, by Katharine Noel; *A Killing in This Town*, by Olympia Vernon; *I Love You More Than You Know*, by Jonathan Ames.

How to Contact Does not accept unsolicited mss. *Agented submissions only.* Accepts simultaneous submissions.

Terms Pays 7½-15% royalty on retail price. Average advance: varies. Publishes ms 1 year after acceptance.

◖ GRYPHON BOOKS

P.O. Box 209, Brooklyn NY 11228. (718)646-6126 (after 6 p.m. EST). Web site: www.gryphonbooks.com. **Contact:** Gary Lovisi, owner/editor. Estab. 1983. Publishes paperback originals and trade paperback reprints. Books: bond paper; offset printing; perfect binding. Average print order: 500-1,000. **Published some debut authors within the last year.** Averages 10-15 total titles, 12 fiction titles/year.

Imprint(s) Gryphon Books, Gryphon Doubles, Gryphon SF Rediscovery Series.

Needs Mystery (private eye/hard-boiled, crime), science fiction (hard science/technological, soft/sociological). Published *The Dreaming Detective*, by Ralph Vaughn (mystery-fantasy-horror); *The Woman in the Dugout*, by Gary Lovisi and T. Arnone (baseball novel); *A Mate for Murder*, by Bruno Fischer (hard-boiled pulp).

How to Contact "Not looking for novels right now; *will only see a 1-2 page synopsis with SASE.*" Include estimated word count, brief bio, list of publishing credits. Agented fiction 5-10%. Often comments on rejected mss.

Terms Publishes ms 1-3 years after acceptance. Ms guidelines for #10 SASE.

Advice "I am looking for better and better writing, more cutting-edge material with *impact*! Keep it lean and focused."

⬛ ◖ ⬛ GUERNICA EDITIONS

Box 117, Station P, Toronto ON M5S 2S6 Canada. (416)658-9888. Fax: (416)657-8885. E-mail: guernicaeditions @cs.com. Web site: www.guernicaeditions.com. **Contact:** Antonio D'Alfonso, fiction editor (novel and short story). Estab. 1978. "Guernica Editions is a small press that produces works of fiction and nonfiction on the viability of pluriculturalism." Publishes trade paperback originals, reprints and software. Books: various paper; offset printing; perfect binding. Average print order: 1,000. **Published 6 debut authors within the last year.** Averages 25 total titles, 18-20 fiction titles/year. Distributes titles through professional distributors.

• Two titles by Guernica Editions have won American Book Awards.

Imprint(s) Prose Series (original); Picas Series (reprints).

Needs Erotica, feminist, gay/lesbian, literary, multicultural. ''We wish to open up into the fiction world and focus less on poetry. We specialize in European, especially Italian, translations.'' Publishes anthology of Arab women/Italian women writers. Published *Dark Man*, by Roberto Pace; *Hard Edge*, by F.G. Paci; *A Mystery in Napels*, by Ermanno Rea; *Olivo Oliva*, by Philippe Poloni.

How to Contact Accepts unsolicited mss. Query with SASE. Include estimated word count, brief bio, list of publishing credits. Responds in 1 month to queries; 1 year to mss. No simultaneous submissions.

Terms Pays 8-10% royalty on retail price. Or makes outright purchase of $200-5,000. Average advance: $200-2,000. Publishes ms 15 months after acceptance.

Advice ''Know what publishers do, and send your works only to publishers whose writers you've read and enjoyed.''

◑ HARBOR HOUSE

111 Tenth St., Augusta GA 30901. (706)738-0354. Fax: (706)738-0354. E-mail: harborhouse@harborhousebooks .com. Web site: www.harborhousebooks.com. **Contact:** Carrie McCullough, publisher. Estab. 1997. Harbor House seeks to publish the best in original fiction (southern, thrillers, horror) and current events/social issue nonfiction. Publishes hardcover originals and paperback originals. Average print order: 5,000. **Published 8 debut authors within the last year.** Member: Publishers Association of the South. Distribution with Ingram; Baker & Taylor; Anderson and American Wholesale.

• Received a Golden Eye Literary Award.

Imprint(s) Batwing Press, Southern Winds, Savannah River Press.

Needs Horror, thriller, civil war, new age/mystic, unsolved mysteries.

How to Contact Accepts queries by mail. Does not accept phone queries or proposals by e-mail. Accepts unsolicited mss or send outline, 3 sample chapter(s). Include estimated word count, brief bio, list of publishing credits, marketing plans, SASE. Agented fiction 10%. Responds in 4 weeks to queries; 2 months to mss. Accepts simultaneous submissions. Does not accept previously published works. Sometimes comments on rejected mss.

Terms Royalty rates vary, depending on hardcover or paperback. Minimum advance: $500.

Advice ''We strongly encourage authors to consult our Web site before submitting material. We are particularly interested in developing unpublished authors.''

★ ◪ ◎ HARLEQUIN AMERICAN ROMANCE

a Harlequin book line, 233 Broadway, Suite 1001, New York NY 10279. (212)553-4200. Web site: www.eharlequi n.com. **Contact:** Melissa Jeglinski, associate senior editor. ''Upbeat and lively, fast paced and well plotted, American Romance celebrates the pursuit of love in the backyards, big cities and wide-open spaces of America.'' Publishes paperback originals and reprints. Books: newspaper print paper; web printing; perfect bound.

Needs Romance (contemporary, American). Needs ''all-American stories with a range of emotional and sensual content that are supported by a sense of community within the plot's framework. In the confident and caring heroine, the tough but tender hero, and their dynamic relationship that is at the center of this series, real-life love is showcased as the best fantasy of all!''

How to Contact Query with SASE. No simultaneous submissions, electronic submissions, or submissions on disk.

Terms Pays royalty. Offers advance. Ms guidelines online.

◪ ★ ◪ ◎ HARLEQUIN BLAZE

a Harlequin book line, 225 Duncan Mill Road, Don Mills ON M3B 3K9 Canada. (416)445-5860. Web site: www.eharlequin.com. **Contact:** Brenda Chin, associate senior editor. ''Harlequin Blaze is a red-hot series. It is a vehicle to build and promote new authors who have a strong sexual edge to their stories. It is also *the* place to be for seasoned authors who want to create a sexy, sizzling, longer contemporary story.'' Publishes paperback originals. Books: newspaper print; web printing; perfect bound. **Published some debut authors within the last year.**

Needs Romance (contemporary). ''Sensuous, highly romantic, innovative plots that are sexy in premise and execution. The tone of the books can run from fun and flirtatious to dark and sensual. Submissions should have a very contemporary feel—what it's like to be young and single today. We are looking for heroes and heroines in their early 20s and up. There should be a a strong emphasis on the physical relationship between the couples. Fully described love scenes along with a high level of fantasy and playfulness.''

How to Contact No simultaneous submissions, electronic submissions, submissions on disk.

Terms Pays royalty. Offers advance. Ms guidelines online.

Advice ''Are you a *Cosmo* girl at heart? A fan of *Sex and the City*? Or maybe you have a sexually adventurous spirit. If so, then Blaze is the series for you!''

⬛ ⬛ ◪ ◎ HARLEQUIN EVERLASTING

Harlequin Enterprises, Ltd., 225 Duncan Mill Rd., Don Mills ON M3B 3K9. Web site: www.eharlequin.com. **Contact:** Paula Eykelhof, executive editor. Estab. February 2007. ''The novels in this series will follow the life and relationship/s of one couple. The books will therefore span considerably more time than the typical series romance—it could be years or even an entire lifetime. The focus of Harlequin Everlasting is on much more of the characters' lives, not just the weeks or months during which the romantic relationship develops and its initial resolution takes place.'' Publishes paperback originals. Format: newsprint paper; web printing; perfect bound. Averages 24 fiction titles/year. •

Needs Romance. ''We are looking for emotionally intense stories with a strong emphasis on well-rendered and psychologically credible characters (who influence each other's lives over time). The series will be open to a wide range of plots and situations; each story will require a significant conflict that creates urgency, excitement and momentum. Structurally, there will be many more options—interesting and nonlinear ways of structuring the story—than the traditional series romance typically allows. The narrative can start at any point, can include diaries or letters, can move freely back and forth in time, etc. Points of view can vary—and first-person narrative can be used. We're looking for writers who can create a complex and believable world for the characters and their romance. We want to see an individual and engaging style that is appropriate to the scope of the story. Above all, we want you to write a romance that matters—a sweeping narrative, a memorable story that touches the reader emotionally.''

How to Contact Query with outline/synopsis and 1-3 sample chapters. Accepts submissions by snail mail.

Terms Pays royalties, advance. Writer's guidelines on Web site. Book catalogs on Web site.

⬛ ✪ ◻ ◎ HARLEQUIN HISTORICALS

a Harlequin book line, Eton House, 18-24 Paradise Road, Richmond Surrey TW9 1SR United Kingdom. (212)553-4200. Web site: www.eharlequin.com. **Contact:** Linda Fildew, senior editor. ''The primary element of a Harlequin Historical novel is romance. The story should focus on the heroine and how her love for one man changes her life forever. For this reason, it is very important that you have an appealing hero and heroine, and that their relationship is a compelling one. The conflicts they must overcome—and the situations they face—can be as varied as the setting you have chosen, but there must be romantic tension, some spark between your hero and heroine that keeps your reader interested.'' Publishes paperback originals and reprints. Books: newsprint paper; perfect bound. **Published some debut authors within the last year.**

Needs Romance (historical). ''We will not accept books set after 1900. We're looking primarily for books set in North America, England or France between 1100 and 1900 A.D. We do not buy many novels set during the American Civil War. We are, however, flexible and will consider most periods and settings. We are not looking for gothics or family sagas, nor are we interested in the kind of comedy of manners typified by straight Regencies. Historical romances set during the Regency period, however, will definitely be considered.''

How to Contact Submit the first three chapters along with a 1-2 page synopsis of your novel.

Terms Pays royalty. Offers advance. Ms guidelines online.

✪ ◻ ◎ HARLEQUIN INTRIGUE

a Harlequin Book line, 233 Broadway, Suite 1001, New York NY 10279. (212)553-4200. Web site: www.eharlequin.com. **Contact:** Denise O'Sullivan, senior editor. ''These novels are taut, edge-of-the-seat, contemporary romantic suspense tales of intrigue and desire. Kidnappings, stalkings and women in jeopardy coupled with bestselling romantic themes are the examples of story lines we love most.'' Publishes paperback originals and reprints. Books: newspaper print; perfect bound. **Published some debut authors within the last year.**

Needs Romance (romantic suspense). ''Murder mystery, psychological suspense or thriller, the love story must be inextricably bound to the resolution where all loose ends are tied up neatly—and shared dangers lead right to shared passions. As long as they're in jeopardy and falling in love, our heroes and heroines may traverse a landscape as wide as the world itself. Their lives are on the line—and so are their hearts!''

How to Contact Accepts unsolicited mss. Query with SASE. Send SASE for return of ms or send a disposable ms and SASE for reply only. No simultaneous submissions, electronic submissions, submissions on disk.

Terms Pays royalty. Offers advance. Ms guidelines online.

⬛ ✪ HARLEQUIN MILLS & BOON, LTD.

Harlequin Enterprises, Ltd., Eton House, 18-24 Paradise Rd., Richmond Surrey TW9 1SR United Kingdom. (44)0208-288-2800. Web site: www.millsandboon.co.uk. **Contact:** K. Stoecker, editorial director; Tessa Shapcott, senior editor (Mills &Boon Modern Romance); Bryony Green, senior editor (Mills & Boon Tender Romance); Linda Fildew, senior editor (Mills & Boon Historicals); Sheila Hodgson, senior editor (Mills & Boon Medicals). Estab. 1908-1909. Publishes mass market paperback originals. **Published some debut authors within the last year.** Plans 3-4 first novels this year.

Imprint(s) Mills & Boon Modern Romance (Harlequin Presents); Mills & Boon Tender Romance (Harlequin Romance); Mills & Boon Historicals; Mills & Boon Medicals.

Needs Romance (contemporary, historical, regency period, medical).

How to Contact Send query letter. No simultaneous submissions.

Terms Pays advance against royalty. Publishes ms 2 years after acceptance. Ms guidelines online.

⚉ ⚉ ◯ HARLEQUIN SUPERROMANCE

a Harlequin book line, 225 Duncan Mill Road, Don Mills ON M3B 3K9 Canada. (416)445-5860. Web site: www.eharlequin.com. **Contact:** Laura Shin, senior editor. ''The aim of Superromance novels is to produce a contemporary, involving read with a mainstream tone in its situations and characters, using romance as the major theme. To achieve this, emphasis should be placed on individual writing styles and unique and topical ideas.'' Publishes paperback originals. Books: newspaper print; perfect bound. **Published 5 debut authors in 2006.**

Needs Romance (contemporary). ''The criteria for Superromance books are flexible. Aside from length, the determining factor for publication will always be quality. Authors should strive to break free of stereotypes, clichés and worn-out plot devices to create strong, believable stories with depth and emotional intensity. Superromance novels are intended to appeal to a wide range of romance readers.''

How to Contact Accepts unsolicited submissions. Submit 3 sample chapter(s) and synopsis. Send SASE for return of ms or send a disposable ms and SASE for reply only. No simultaneous submissions, electronic submissions, submissions on disk.

Terms Pays royalty. Offers advance. Ms guidelines online.

Advice ''A general familiarity with current Superromance books is advisable to keep abreast of ever-changing trends and overall scope, but we don't want imitations. We look for sincere, heartfelt writing based on true-to-life experiences the reader can identify with. We are interested in innovation.''

A ⚉ ◎ HARPERCOLLINS CANADA LTD.

2 Bloor St. East, 20th Floor, Toronto ON M4W 1A8 Canada. (416)975-9334. Fax: (416)975-5223. Web site: www.harpercanada.com. Harpercollins is not accepting unsolicited material at this time.

A ⚉ HARPERCOLLINS CHILDREN'S BOOKS

HarperCollins Publishers, 1350 Avenue of the Americas, New York NY 10019. (212)261-6500. Fax: (212)261-6689. Web site: www.harperchildrens.com. Publishes hardcover originals. Averages 350 total titles/year.

Imprint(s) Amistad, Avon, Joanna Cotler, EOS, Greenwillow Books, Laura Geringer Books, HarperFestival, HarperKids Entertainment, HarperTrophy, HarperTempest, Katherine Tegen Books, Rayo Books.

Needs Adventure, fantasy, historical, humor, juvenile, literary, picture books, young adult.

How to Contact *Agented submissions only.*

Terms Pays 10-12½% royalty on retail price. Average advance: variable. Publishes ms 1 year (novels) or 2 years (picture books) after acceptance.

⚉ HARPERCOLLINS GENERAL BOOKS GROUP

Division of HarperCollins Publishers, 10 East 53 Street, New York NY 10022. (212)207-7000. Fax: (212)207-7633. Web site: www.harpercollins.com. ''HarperCollins, one of the largest English language publishers in the world, is a broad-based publisher with strengths in academic, business and professional, children's, educational, general interest, and religious and spiritual books, as well as multimedia titles.'' Publishes hardcover and paperback originals and paperback reprints.

Imprint(s) Amistad Press, Avon, Caedmon, Ecco, Eos, Haper Perennial, HarperAudio, HarperCollins, HarperEntertainment, HarperLargePrint, HarperSanFranciso, HarperTorch PerfectBound, Rayo, ReganBooks, William Morrow.

How to Contact See imprint for specific guidelines.

A ◎ HARVEST HOUSE PUBLISHERS

990 Owen Loop N., Eugene OR 97402. (541)343-0123. Fax: (541)302-0731. E-mail: manuscriptcoordinator@harvesthousepublishers.com. Web site: www.harvesthousepublishers.com. **Contact:** Acquisitions. Estab. 1974. ''Our mission is to glorify God by providing high-quality books and products that affirm biblical values, help people grow spiritually strong, and proclaim Jesus Christ as the answer to every human need.'' Publishes hardcover originals and reprints, trade paperback originals and reprints, and mass market paperback originals and reprints. Books: 40 lb. ground wood paper; offset printing; perfect binding. Average print order: 10,000. First novel print order: 10,000-15,000. **Published 5-6 debut authors within the last year.** Averages 160 total titles, 15-20 fiction titles/year.

Needs Harvest House no longer accepts unsolicited manuscripts, proposals, or artwork.

How to Contact Does not accept unsolicited mss.

Advice "Attend a writer's conference where you have an opportunity to pitch your book idea to an editor face to face. We also look at fiction represented by a reputable agent."

◙ HAWK PUBLISHING GROUP

7107 S. Yale Ave., #345, Tulsa OK 74136. (918)492-3677. Fax: (918)492-2120. Web site: www.hawkpub.com. Estab. 1999. Independent publisher of general trade/commercial books, fiction and nonfiction. Publishes hardcover and trade paperback originals. **Published 4 debut authors within the last year.** Plans 2 first novels this year. Averages 6-8 total titles, 3 fiction titles/year. Member PMA. Titles are distributed by NBN/Biblio Distribution.

Needs Looking for good books of all kinds. Not interested in juvenile, poetry or short story collections. Published *The Darkest Night,* by Jodie Larsen; *All the Angels and Saints*, by r.r. bryan.

How to Contact Accepts unsolicited mss. Submit first 20 pages of your book, synopsis, author bio. Include list of publishing credits. Accepts simultaneous submissions.

Terms Pays royalty. Publishes ms 1-2 years after acceptance. Ms guidelines online.

Advice "Prepare a professional submission and follow the guidelines. The simple things really do count; use 12 pt. pitch with 1-inch margins and only send what is requested."

◖ HELICON NINE EDITIONS

Subsidiary of Midwest Center for the Literary Arts, Inc., P.O. Box 22412, Kansas City MO 64113. (816)753-1016. E-mail: helicon9@aol.com. Web site: www.heliconnine.com. **Contact:** Gloria Vando Hickok. Estab. 1990. Small not-for-profit press publishing poetry, fiction, creative nonfiction and anthologies. Publishes paperback originals. Also publishes one-story chapbooks called *feuillets*, which come with envelope, 250 print run. Books: 60 lb. paper; offset printing; perfect bound; 4-color cover. Average print order: 1,000-5,000. **Published 1 debut author within the last year.** Distributes titles through Baker & Taylor, Brodart, Ingrams, Follet (library acquisitions), Midwest Library Service, all major distributors and booksellers. Promotes titles through reviews, readings, radio and television interviews.

How to Contact Does not accept unsolicited mss.

Terms Pays royalty. Author's copies. Offers advance. Publishes ms 6-12 months after acceptance.

Advice "We accept short story collections. We welcome new writers and first books. Submit a clean, readable copy in a folder or box—paginated with title and name on each page. Also, do not pre-design book, i.e., no illustrations. We'd like to see books that will be read 50-100 years from now."

◎ HENDRICK-LONG PUBLISHING CO., INC.

10635 Toweroaks D., Houston TX 77070. (832)912-7323. Fax: (832)912-7353. E-mail: hendrick-long@worldnet. att.net. Web site: hendricklongpublishing.com. **Contact:** Vilma Long. Estab. 1969. Only considers manuscripts with Texas theme. Publishes hardcover and trade paperback originals and hardcover reprints. Averages 4 total titles/year.

Needs Juvenile, young adult.

How to Contact Submit outline, 2 sample chapter(s), synopsis. Responds in 3 months to queries. No simultaneous submissions.

Terms Pays royalty on selling price. Offers advance. Publishes ms 18 months after acceptance. Book catalog for 8½×11 or 9×12 SASE with 4 first-class stamps. Ms guidelines online.

HERITAGE BOOKS, INC.

65 E. Main St., Westminster MD 21157. E-mail: submissions@heritagebooks.com. Web site: www.heritagebook s.com. Estab. 1978. Publishes hardcover and paperback originals and reprints. Averages 200 total titles/year.

Needs Historical (relating to early American life, 1600-1900).

How to Contact Query with SASE. Responds in 1 month to queries. Accepts simultaneous submissions.

Terms Pays 10% royalty on list price.

Ⓐ ⊕ HESPERUS PRESS

4 Rickett Street, London England SW6 1RU United Kingdom. 44 20 7610 3331. Fax: 44 20 7610 3217. Web site: www.hesperus.com. Estab. 2001. Hesperus is a small independent publisher mainly of classics and literary fiction. Publishes paperback originals. Books: munken paper; traditional printing; sewn binding. Average print order: 5,000. Distributes titles through Trafalgar Square in the US, Grantham Book Services in the UK.

Needs Literary. Published *Carlyle's House*, by Virginia Woolf (rediscovered modern classic); *No Man's Land*, by Graham Greene (rediscovered modern classic); *The Princess of Mantua*, by Marie Ferranti (award-winning fiction in translation); *Talking About It,* by Tim Parks (new fiction).

How to Contact Does not accept unsolicited mss. *Agented submissions only.* Query with SASE. Accepts queries by mail. Include estimated word count, brief bio, list of publishing credits. Agented fiction 100%. Responds in

8-10 weeks to queries; 8-10 weeks to mss. Accepts simultaneous submissions. No electronic submissions, submissions on disk.

Advice Find an agent to represent you.

N ◻ ✐ HOLLOWAY HOUSE PUBLISHING CO.

8060 Melrose Ave., Los Angeles CA 90046. (323)653-8060. Fax: (323)655-9452. **Contact:** Neal Colgrass, editor (multicultural). Estab. 1960. Publishes paperback originals. Book: Groundwood paper; offset printing; perfect binding; illustrations. Average print order: 10,000. Distributes through the National Distributer.

Imprint(s) Mankind Books (multicultural).

Needs Comic books, erotica, ethnic, multicultural.

How to Contact Accepts unsolicited mss. Query with SASE. Accepts queries by mail. Include estimated word count, list of publishing credits. Send SASE or IRC. Agented fiction 10%. No simultaneous submissions. Sometimes comments on rejected mss.

Terms Publishes ms 6-12 months after acceptance.

⊡ ◎ HENRY HOLT & CO. BOOKS FOR YOUNG READERS

Henry Holt & Co., LLC, 175 Fifth Avenue, New York NY 10010. (646)307-5282. Web site: www.henryholtchildrensbooks.com. **Contact:** Submissions editor, Books for Young Readers. Henry Holt Books for Young Readers publishes excellent books of all kinds (fiction, nonfiction, illustrated) for all ages, from the very young to the young adult. Publishes hardcover originals of picture books, chapter books, middle grade and young adult novels. Averages 70-80 total titles/year.

Needs Adventure, fantasy, historical, mainstream/contemporary, multicultural, picture books, young adult. Juvenile: adventure, animal, contemporary, fantasy, history, multicultural. Picture books: animal, concept, history, mulitcultural, sports. Young adult: contemporary, fantasy, history, multicultural, nature/environment, problem novels, sports. Published *When Zachary Beaver Came to Town*, by Kimberly Willis Holt (middle grade fiction); *The Gospel According to Larry*, by Janet Tashjian (YA fiction); *Visiting Langston*, by Willie Perdomo, illustrated by Bryan Collier (picture book); *Keeper of the Night*, by Kimberly Willis Holt; *Alphabet Under Construction*, by Denise Fleming (picture book).

How to Contact Accepts unsolicited mss. Include estimated word count, brief bio, list of publishing credits. Do not send SASE; publisher will not respond unless making an offer for publication.

Terms Pays royalty on retail price. Average advance: $3,000 and up. Publishes ms 18-36 months after acceptance. Book catalog for 8½×11 SAE. Ms guidelines at www.henryholtchildrensbooks.com/submissions.htm.

Ⓐ ⊡ HENRY HOLT

Henry Holt and Company, 175 Fifth Avenue, New York NY 10011. (212)886-9200. Web site: www.henryholt.com. Publishes hardcover and paperback originals and reprints.

Imprint(s) Metropolitan Books; Times Books; Henry Holt; Owl Books; Jack Macrae Books.

How to Contact Closed to submissions. *Agented submissions only.*

◖ ◎ HOMA & SEKEY BOOKS

3rd Floor, North Tower, Mack-Cali Center III, 140 East Ridgewood Ave, Paramus NJ 07652. (201)261-8810. Fax: (201)261-8890. E-mail: info@homabooks.com. Web site: www.homabooks.com. **Contact:** Shawn Ye, editor-in-chief. Estab. 1997. "We focus on publishing Asia-related titles. Both translations and original English manuscripts are welcome. Publishes hardcover and paperback originals. Books: natural paper; web press; perfect bound; illustrations. **Published 3 debut authors within the last year.** Averages 7 total titles, 3 fiction titles/year. Member PMA. Distributes titles through Ingram, Baker & Taylor, etc.

• Received the Notable Book Award for *Father and Son: A Novel*, by Han Sung-Won (Yu Young-Man, Julie Pickering, translators).

Needs Ethnic (Asian), literary, mystery, young adult (adventure, historical, mystery/suspense, romance). Wants China-related titles. Published *Willow Leaf, Maple Leaf: A Novel of Immigration Blue*, by David Ke; *The Curse of Kim's Daughter,* by Park Kyong-Ni (translation); *A Floating City on The Water* (translation).

How to Contact Accepts unsolicited mss. Query with SASE or submit outline, 2 sample chapter(s). Accepts queries by e-mail, mail. Include estimated word count, brief bio, list of publishing credits and marketing analysis. Send SASE for return of ms or send a disposable ms and SASE for reply only. Responds in 8 weeks to queries; 20 weeks to mss. Accepts simultaneous submissions, electronic submissions. Sometimes comments on rejected mss.

Terms Pays 5-10% royalty. Publishes ms 1 year after acceptance. Book catalog for 9×12 SASE. Ms guidelines online.

Advice "Authors must be willing and able to actively participate in the publicity and promotion of their books."

☒ ◯ HOT HOUSE PRESS

760 Cushing Hwy, Cohasset MA 02025. (781)383-8360. Fax: (781)383-8346. E-mail: hothousepress@aol.com. Web site: www.hothousepress.com. **Contact:** Sally Weltman, senior editor. Estab. 2000. Small, independent publisher with over four decades of experience. Publishes hardcover and paperback originals. Average print order: 5,000. First novel print order: 3,000. **Published 2 debut authors within the last year.** Member Independent Publishers Association. Distributes through NBN.

Needs Historical, literary, mystery, memoir. Recently published *Behind the Mystery*, by Stuart Kaminsky (biography); *Accidental Encounters With History (and some lessons learned)*, by Lincoln Palmer Bloomfield (memoir); *The God Symposium*, by Edward Draugelis (mystery).

How to Contact Accepts unsolicited mss. Query with SASE. Accepts queries by e-mail, mail. Include estimated word count, brief bio, list of publishing credits. Send SASE for return of ms or send a disposable ms and SASE for reply only. Agented fiction 30%. Responds in 3 months to queries; 4-6 months to mss. Accepts simultaneous submissions.

Terms Pays 50% of revenue after outside production and marketing costs. Average advance: $100. Publishes ms within a year after acceptance. Ms guidelines for SASE.

Advice "Make sure you have your manuscript in good shape, and outline what you can/will do to promote and publicize the book."

★ ▣ ◎ HOUGHTON MIFFLIN BOOKS FOR CHILDREN

Houghton Mifflin Company, 222 Berkeley St., Boston MA 02116. (617)351-5959. Fax: (617)351-1111. E-mail: children's_books@hmco.com. Web site: www.houghtonmifflinbooks.com. **Contact:** Submissions coordinator; Kate O'Sullivan senior editor; Ann Rider, senior editor; Margaret Raymo, editorial director. "Houghton Mifflin gives shape to ideas that educate, inform and, above all, delight." Publishes hardcover originals and trade paperback originals and reprints. **Published 12 debut authors within the last year.** Averages 100 total titles/year. Promotes titles through author visits, advertising, reviews.

Imprint(s) Clarion Books, New York City, Walter Lorraine Books, King Fisher Books.

Needs Adventure, ethnic, historical, humor, juvenile (early readers), literary, mystery, picture books, suspense, young adult, board books. *Gathering Blue*, by Lois Lowry; *The Circuit*, by Francisco Jimenez; *When I Was Older*, by Garret Freymann-Weyr.

How to Contact Accepts unsolicited mss. Responds only if interested. Do not send SASE. Accepts simultaneous submissions. No electronic submissions.

Terms Pays 5-10% royalty on retail price. Average advance: variable. Publishes ms 18-24 months after acceptance. Book catalog for 9×12 SASE with 3 first-class stamps. Ms guidelines online.

▣ HOUGHTON MIFFLIN CO.

222 Berkeley St., Boston MA 02116. (617)351-5000. Web site: www.hmco.com. **Contact:** Submissions Editor. Estab. 1832. Publishes hardcover originals and trade paperback originals and reprints. **Published 5 debut authors within the last year.** Averages 250 total titles/year.

Needs Literary. "We are not a mass market publisher. Study the current list." Published *Extremely Loud and Incredibly Close*, by Jonathan Safran Foer; *The Plot Against America*, by Philip Roth; *Heir to the Glimmering World*, by Cynthia Ozick.

How to Contact Does not accept unsolicited mss. *Agented submissions only.* Accepts simultaneous submissions.

Terms Hardcover: pays 10-15% royalty on retail price, sliding scale or flat rate based on sales; paperback: 7½% flat rate, but negotiable. Average advance: variable. Publishes ms 3 years after acceptance.

▣ ★ ◎ HYPERION BOOKS FOR CHILDREN

Hyperion, 114 Fifth Ave., New York NY 10011. (212)633-440. Fax: (212)807-5880. Web site: www.hyperionbooksforchildren.com. **Contact:** Editorial director. "The aim of Hyperion Books for Children is to create a dynamic children's program informed by Disney's creative vision, direct connection to children, and unparalleled marketing and distribution." Publishes hardcover and trade paperback originals. Averages 210 total titles/year.

Needs Juvenile, picture books, young adult. Published *McDuff*, by Roesmary Wells and Susan Jeffers (picture book); *Split Just Right*, by Adele Griffin (middle grade).

How to Contact *Agented submissions only.* Accepts simultaneous submissions.

Terms Pays royalty. Average advance: varies. Publishes ms 1 year after acceptance.

Advice "Hyperion Books for Children are meant to appeal to an upscale children's audience. Study your audience. Look at and research current children's books. Who publishes what you like? Approach them."

★ ◎ IMAGES SI, INC

Imprint of Images Publishing, 109 Woods of Arden Rd., Staten Island NY 10312. (718)966-3964. Fax: (718)966-3695. Web site: www.imagesco.com/publishing/index.html. **Contact:** Acquisitions Editor. Estab. 1990. Publishes 2 audio books a year.

Needs Hard science fiction for audiocassettes and CDs. Published *Centauri III*, by George L. Griggs (science fiction print book); *Nova-Audio, Issues 1-3*, by Hoyt, Franklin, Schoen, Wild, Silverberg and Catelli (science fiction audio).

How to Contact Closed to submissions until 2007.

Terms Pays 10-20% royalty on wholesale price. Publishes stories 6 months-2 years after acceptence.

✦ INGALLS PUBLISHING GROUP, INC

197 New Market Center, #135, Boone NC 28607. (828)964-0590. Fax: (828)262-1973. E-mail: editor@highcountrypublishers.com. Web site: www.highcountrypublishers.com. **Contact:** Judith Geary, senior editor. Estab. 2001. "We are a small regional house focusing on popular fiction and memoir. At present, we are most interested in regional fiction, historical fiction and mystery fiction." Publishes hardcover orginals, paperback originals and paperback reprints. Books: 60# paper; offset printing; b&w illustrations. Average print order: 1,500-5,000. First novel print order: 1,500-3,000. **Published 1 debut author within the last year.** Plans 3 first novels this year. Member PMA, PAS, SEBA. Distributes titles through Biblio Distribution, sister company of NBN books.

Needs Ethnic, feminist, historical, mystery (amateur sleuth, cozy, police procedural, private eye/hard-boiled), regional (southern appalachian), romance (contemporary, historical, romantic suspense adventure), young adult (historical, mystery/suspense). Published *Dirty Deeds*, by Mark Terry (mystery); *Once Upon a Different Time*, by Marian Coe; *Gloria*, by Ann Chamberlin (historical fiction); *Mount Doomsday*, by Don Berman (thriller).

How to Contact Accepts unsolicited mss. Query with SASE or submit outline, 3 sample chapter(s). Reading period open from July to October. Accepts queries by e-mail, mail. Include estimated word count, brief bio, list of publishing credits. Send copy of ms and SASE. Agented fiction 10%. Responds in 6 months to queries; 6 months to mss. Accepts simultaneous submissions, electronic submissions. No submissions on disk. Often comments on rejected mss.

Terms Pays 10% royalty. Publishes ms 6 months-2 years after acceptance. Ms guidelines online.

INTERLINK PUBLISHING GROUP, INC.

46 Crosby St., Northampton MA 01060. (413)582-7054. Fax: (413)582-7057. E-mail: editor@interlinkbooks.com. Web site: www.interlinkbooks.com. **Contact:** Michel Moushabeck, publisher; Pam Thompson, editor. Estab. 1987. "Midsize independent publisher specializing in world travel, world literature, world history and politics." Publishes hardcover and trade paperback originals. Books: 55 lb. Warren Sebago Cream white paper; web offset printing; perfect binding. Average print order: 5,000. **Published new writers within the last year.** Averages 50 total titles, 2-4 fiction titles/year. Distributes titles through Baker & Taylor. Promotes titles through book mailings to extensive, specialized lists of editors and reviews; authors read at bookstores and special events across the country.

Imprint(s) Interlink Books and Olive Branch Press.

Needs Ethnic, international. "Adult—We are looking for translated works relating to the Middle East, Africa or Latin America." Recently published *Everything Good Will Come*, by Sefi Atta (first novel); *The Gardens of Light*, by Amin Maalouf (novel translated from French); *War in the Land of Egypt*, by Yusef Al-Qaid (novel translated from Arabic).

How to Contact Does not accept unsolicited mss. Query with SASE and a brief sample. Responds in 3 months to queries. Accepts simultaneous submissions. No electronic submissions.

Terms Pays 6-8% royalty on retail price. Average advance: small. Publishes ms 18 months after acceptance. Ms guidelines online.

Advice "Our Interlink International Fiction Series is designed to bring to North American writers who have achieved wide acclaim at home, but have not been recognized beyond the borders of their native lands."

✦ INVERTED-A

P.O. Box 267, Licking MO 65542. E-mail: amnfn@well.com. **Contact:** Aya Katz, chief editor (poetry, novels, political); Nets Katz, science editor (scientific, academic). Estab. 1985. Publishes paperback originals. Books: offset printing. Average print order: 1,000. Average first novel print order: 500. Distributes through Baker & Taylor, Amazon, Bowker.

Needs Utopian, political. Needs poetry submission for our newsletter, *Inverted-A Horn*.

How to Contact Does not accept unsolicited mss. Query with SASE. Reading period open from January 2 to March 15. Accepts queries by e-mail. Include estimated word count. Responds in 1 month to queries; 3 months to mss. Accepts simultaneous submissions. Sometimes comments on rejected mss.

Terms Pays in 10 author's copies. Publishes ms 1 year after acceptance. Ms guidelines for SASE.

Advice "Read our books. Read the Inverted-A Horn. We are different. We do not follow industry trends."

ION IMAGINATION PUBLISHING

Ion Imagination Entertainment, Inc., P.O. Box 210943, Nashville TN 37221-0943. Fax: (615)646-6276. E-mail: ionimagin@aol.com. Web site: www.flumpa.com. **Contact:** Keith Frickey, editor. Estab. 1994. Small independent publisher of science-related children's fiction, multimedia and audio products. Publishes hardcover and paperback originals. Average first novel print order: 10,000. Member SPAN and PMA.

• Received the Parents Choice, National Parenting Centers Seal of Approval, Dr. Toy, Parent Council.

Needs Children's/juvenile (adventure, animal, preschool/picture book, science).

How to Contact Does not accept unsolicited mss. Query with SASE. Include brief bio, list of publishing credits. Send copy of ms and SASE. Responds in 1 month to queries; 1 month to mss. Accepts simultaneous submissions. Sometimes comments on rejected mss.

Terms Pays royalty.

ITALICA PRESS

595 Main St., Suite 605, New York NY 10044-0047. (212)935-4230. Fax: (212)838-7812. E-mail: inquiries@italica press.com. Web site: www.italicapress.com. **Contact:** Ronald G. Musto and Eileen Gardiner, publishers. Estab. 1985. Small independent publisher of Italian fiction in translation. "First-time translators published. We would like to see translations of Italian writers well-known in Italy who are not yet translated for an American audience." Publishes trade paperback originals. Books: 50-60 lb. natural paper; offset printing; illustrations. Average print order: 1,500. Averages 6 total titles, 2 fiction titles/year. Distributes titles through Web site. Promotes titles through Web site.

Needs Translations of 20th century Italian fiction. Published *Eruptions*, by Monica Sarsini; *The Great Bear*, by Ginevra Bompianai; *Sparrow*, by Giovanni Verga.

How to Contact Accepts unsolicited mss. Query with SASE. Accepts queries by e-mail, fax. Responds in 1 month to queries; 2 months to mss. Accepts simultaneous submissions, electronic submissions, submissions on disk.

Terms Pays 7-15% royalty on wholesale price. Pays author's copies. Publishes ms 1 year after acceptance. Ms guidelines online.

Advice "Remember we publish *only* fiction that has been previously published in Italian. A *brief* call saves a lot of postage. 90% of proposals we receive are completely off base—but we are very interested in things that are right on target. Please send return postage if you want your manuscript back."

IVY PUBLICATIONS

72 Hyperion House, Somers Road, London England SW21HZ United Kingdom. Estab. 1989. Small book publisher. Publishes paperback originals.

Needs Adventure, children's/juvenile (adventure, historical), historical, humor, military/war, young adult (adventure, historical). "We are on the lookout for genius; a P.G. Wodehouse or Raymond Chandler would be most welcome."

How to Contact Accepts unsolicited mss. Query with SASE. Accepts queries by mail. Include list of publishing credits. Send SASE or IRC. Accepts simultaneous submissions. No electronic submissions, submissions on disk. Sometimes comments on rejected mss.

Terms "We pay all costs." Profit: 50% to author, 50% to publisher.

Advice "Write in top-class English that is used by top American, British, Indian, South African writers. Meaning of words, style and grammar are our yardsticks."

JIREH PUBLISHING COMPANY

P.O. Box 1911, Suisun City CA 94585-1911. E-mail: jireh_subms@yahoo.com. Web site: www.jirehpublishing.c om. Estab. 1995. Small independent publisher. "We have just begun our fiction line." Publishes hardcover, trade paperback and electronic originals. Books: paper varies; digital and offset printed; binding varies. Average print order: varies. First novel print order: varies. Plans 2 first novels this year. Averages 2-5 total titles, 1-2 fiction titles/year. Distributes titles through online bookstores and booksellers (retailers).

Needs Mystery/suspense, religious (Christian e-books, general religious, mystery/suspense, thriller, romance). "We are looking for Christian values in the books that we publish."

How to Contact Accepts unsolicited mss. Query by e-mail only. Include brief bio, list of publishing credits. Go to Web site for guidelines. Responds in 2 months to queries; 8 months to mss. Accepts simultaneous submissions, electronic submissions. No submissions on disk. Sometimes comments on rejected mss.

Terms Pays 10-12% royalty on wholesale price. Publishes ms 9-12 months after acceptance. Ms guidelines online.

JOURNEYFORTH

BJU Press, 1700 Wade Hampton Blvd., Greenville SC 29614-0001. (864)242-5100, ext. 4350. E-mail: jb@bjup.c om. Web site: www.bjupress.com. **Contact:** Nancy Lohr, acquisitions editor (juvenile fiction). Estab. 1974.

''Small independent publisher of excellent, trustworthy novels, information books, audio tapes and ancillary materials for readers pre-school through high school. We desire to develop in our children a love for and understanding of the written word, ultimately helping them love and understand God's word.'' Publishes paperback originals and reprints. Books: 50 lb. white paper; Webb lithography printing; perfect binding. Average print order: 5,000. **Published some debut authors within the last year.** Averages 10 total titles, 10 fiction titles/year. Distributes titles through Spring Arbor and Appalachian. Promotes titles through CBA Marketplace.
Needs Adventure (children's/juvenile, young adult), historical (children's/juvenile, young adult), juvenile (animal, easy-to-read, series), mystery (children's/juvenile, young adult), sports (children's/juvenile, young adult), suspense (young adult), western (young adult), young adult (series). ''Our fiction is all based on a moral and Christian wordview.'' Published *Susannah and the Secret Coins*, by Elaine Schulte (historical children's fiction); *Arby Jenkins Meets His Match*, by Sharon Hambrick (contemporary children's fiction); *Over the Divide*, by Catherine Farnes (young adult fiction).
How to Contact Accepts unsolicited mss. Query with SASE or submit outline, 5 sample chapters or submit complete ms. Include estimated word count, brief bio, social security number, list of publishing credits. Send SASE for return of ms or send a disposable ms and SASE for reply only. Responds in 1 month to queries; 3 months to mss. Accepts simultaneous submissions.
Terms Pays royalty. Publishes ms 12-18 months after acceptance. Ms guidelines online.
Advice ''Study the publisher's guidelines. Make sure your work is suitable or you waste time for you and the publisher.''

JOURNEY BOOKS PUBLISHING

Journey Books, 3205 Hwy. 431, Spring Hill TN 37174. (615)791-8006. E-mail: journey@journeybookspublishing.com. Web site: www.journeybookspublishing.com. **Contact:** Edward Knight (science fiction/fantasy). Estab. 1996. Publishes paperback originals and *Amazing Journeys* magazine. ''Writers must be published in our magazine, *Amazing Journeys*, before being considered for antholoties or book-length work.'' Distributes books through the Internet, Amazon, Abebooks.com, BarnesandNoble.com and other online venues.
Needs Fantasy (high fantsay, space fantasy, sword and sorcery), science fiction (hard science/technological, soft/sociological), young adult (fantasy/science fiction).
How to Contact Accepts unsolicited mss. Query with SASE. Accepts queries by mail and e-mail. Include estimated word count, brief bio, social security number, list of publishing credits. Send SASE for return of ms or send a disposable ms and SASE for reply only. Responds in 6 weeks to queries; 12 weeks to mss. No simultaneous submissions, electronic submissions, submissions on disk. Often comments on rejected mss.
Terms Pays by the word. Ms guidelines online.
Advice ''Read our guidelines before submitting. Authors must be published in our magazine, *Amazing Journeys Magazine*, before they are considered for anthologies or books.''

JUSTIN, CHARLES & CO., PUBLISHERS

236 Huntington Ave., Ste 311, Boston MA 02115. (617)536-8601. E-mail: info@justincharlesbooks.com. Web site: www.justincharles.com. **Contact:** Stephen Hull, publisher (general fiction, mystery). Carmen Mitchell, assistant editor (general fiction, mystery). Estab. 2002. Publishes hardcover originals and paperback originals. **Published 4 debut authors within the last year.** Plans 2 first novels this year. Distributes in the U.S. and Canada through the National Book Network.
Imprint(s) Kate's Mystery Books.
Needs Humor, popular culture, mystery (amateur sleuth, police procedural, private eye/hard-boiled). Published *Las Vegas Little Black Book*, by David Demontmollin and Hiram Todd Norman (nonfiction); *Boyos*, by Richard Marinick (hard-boiled); *Second Sight*, Philip Craig and William Tapply (private eye); *The White Trilogy*, by Ken Bruen (mystery/police procedural).
How to Contact Accepts unsolicited mss. Query with SASE or submit 3-4 sample chapter(s), synopsis. Accepts queries by mail. Include brief bio, list of publishing credits. Send SASE for return of ms or send a disposable ms and SASE for reply only. Agented fiction 90%. Responds in 2 months to queries; 2-3 months to mss. Accepts simultaneous submissions. No electronic submissions, submissions on disk. Rarely comments on rejected mss.
Terms Publishes ms 1-2 years after acceptance. Ms guidelines online.
Advice ''Please look at the types of books we have on our Web site and our writers guidelines.''

KEARNEY STREET BOOKS

P.O. Box 2021, Bellingham WA 98227. (360)738-1355. E-mail: garyrmc@mac.com. Web site: http://kearneystreetbooks.com. **Contact** Gary McKinney, managing editor. Estab. 2003. ''Books that rock—written by or about musicians or music.'' Publishes paperback originals. Perfect bound. Average print order: 200-2,000. Debut novel print order: 200. Plans 1 debut novel this year. Averages 1-2 total titles/year; 1-2 fiction titles/year. Member PMA, BPNW, PNBA. Distributes/promotes titles ''marginally.''

Needs Only publishes books about music or musicians. Published *Such a Killing Crime*, Robert Lopresti (mystery).

How to Contact Send query letter. Accepts queries by e-mail. Send disposable copy of ms and SASE for reply only. Responds to queries in 1 week. Accepts unsolicited mss. Responds to mss in 6-10 months. Considers simultaneous submissions, submissions on CD or disk. Never critiques/comments on rejected mss. Does not return rejected mss.

Terms Sends pre-production galleys to author. Manuscript published 18 months after acceptance. Pays "after expenses, profits split 50/50."

Advice "We publish very few titles. Nobody makes any money. This is all about the love of good fiction shunned by the corporations."

Ⓝ ⭐ ⊘ ◎ KIMANI PRESS

Harlequin Enterprises, Ltd., 233 Broadway, Suite 1001, New York NY 10279. Web site: www.eharlequin.com. Estab. 2006. "Kimani Press, a new division of Harlequin, is proud to bring you books that celebrate the beauty, spirit and love of a diverse people. At Kimani Press, you will find the new home to three of the industry's leading imprints targeting the African-American reader including: Arabesque, Sepia and New Spirit. Starting in July 2006, Kimani Press launched Kimani Romance, the industry's only African-American series romance program." Publishes paperback originals. Format: newsprint paper; web printing; perfect bound.

Imprint(s) Kimani Romance (series romance), Mavis Allen, associate senior editor; Sepia (mainstream fiction), Glenda Howard, senior editor; Arabesque Romance (single-title romance), Evette Porter, editor; Arabesque Inspirational Romance (inspirational single-title), Evette Porter, editor; New Spirit (inspirational fiction and nonfiction), Glenda Howard, senior editor.

Needs African-American romance, both mainstream and inspirational.

How to Contact Published writers query with detailed outline/synopsis and 3 sample chapters. Unpublished writers submit complete ms with detailed synopsis. Accepts submissions by snail mail. Send SASE or IRC for return of ms.

Terms Pays royalties, advance. Writer's guidelines on Web site. Book catalogs on Web site.

Ⓝ ALLEN A. KNOLL, PUBLISHERS

200 W. Victoria Street, Santa Barbara CA 93101. (805)564-3377. E-mail: bookinfo@knollpublishers.com. Web site: www.knollpublishers.com. **Contact:** Submissions. Estab. 1990. Small independent publisher, a few titles a year. Specializes in 'books for intelligent people who read for fun.' Publishes hardcover originals. Books: offset printing; sewn binding. Titles distributed through Ingram, Baker & Taylor.

Needs Published *They Fall Hard*, by Alistair Boyle (mystery); *To Die For*, by David Champion (mystery); *The Duchess to the Rescue*, by Alexandra Eden (children's fiction).

How to Contact Does not accept unsolicited mss.

Terms Varies.

Ⓐ ⭐ ALFRED A. KNOPF

Knopf Publishing Group, Random House, Inc., 1745 Broadway, 21st Floor, New York NY 10019. Web site: www.randomhouse.com/knopf. **Contact:** Senior Editor. Estab. 1915. Publishes hardcover and paperback originals. **Published some debut authors within the last year.** Averages 200 total titles/year.

Needs Publishes book-length fiction of literary merit by known or unknown writers. Length: 40,000-150,000 words. Published *Gertrude and Claudius*, by John Updike; *The Emperor of Ocean Park*, by Stephen Carter; *Balzac and the Little Chinese Seamstress*, by Dai Sijie.

How to Contact *Agented submissions only.* Query with SASE or submit sample chapter(s). Responds in 2-6 months to queries. Accepts simultaneous submissions.

Terms Pays 10-15% royalty. Royalty and advance vary. Offers advance. Must return advance if book is not completed or is unacceptable. Publishes ms 1 year after acceptance. Book catalog for 7½×10½ SAE with 5 first-class stamps.

Ⓐ ◎ KREGEL PUBLICATIONS

Kregel, Inc., P.O. Box 2607, Grand Rapids MI 49501. (616)451-4775. Fax: (616)451-9330. Web site: www.kregelpublications.com. **Contact:** Acquisitions Editor. Estab. 1949. Midsize independent Christian publisher. Publishes hardcover and trade paperback originals and reprints. Averages 90 total titles, 10-15 fiction titles/year. Member ECPA.

Imprint(s) Kregel Academic & Professional, Jim Weaver (academic/pastoral); Kregel Kid Zone, Steve Barclift (children).

Needs Adventure, children's/juvenile (adventure, historical, mystery, preschool/picture book, series, sports, Christian), historical, mystery, religious (children's, general, inspirational, fantasy/sci-fi, mystery/suspense, religious thriller, relationships), young adult (adventure). Fiction should be geared toward the evangelical

Christian market. Wants "books with fast-paced, contemporary storylines—strong Christian message presented in engaging, entertaining style as well as books for juvenile and young adults, especially young women." Published *Divided Loyalties*, by L.K. Malone (action/thriller); *A Test of Love*, by Kathleen Scott (relationships); *Jungle Hideout*, by Jeanette Windle (juvenile/adventure).

How to Contact No longer accepting unsolicited material. *Agented submissions only.*

Terms Pays 8-16% royalty on wholesale price. Average advance: $200-2,000. Publishes ms 14 months after acceptance. Book catalog for 9×12 SASE. Submissions policy online.

Advice "Visit our Web site and review the titles listed under various subject categories. Does your proposed work duplicate existing titles? Does it address areas not covered by existing titles? Does it break new ground?"

N X O WENDY LAMB BOOKS

Random House Children's Books Group, 1745 Broadway, New York NY 10019. Estab. 2001. Publishes hardcover originals. Averages 10-12 total titles/year.

Needs Juvenile (ages 8-18). "We are not currently accepting picture book submissions."

How to Contact Query with SASE. Responds in 1 month to queries. Accepts simultaneous submissions.

Terms Pays royalty on retail price. Ms guidelines for #10 SASE.

LAST KNIGHT PUBLISHING COMPANY

P.O. Box 270006, Fort Collins CO 80527. (970)391-6857. Fax: (720)596-6778. E-mail: ckaine@lastknightpublishing.com. Web site: www.LastKnightPublishing.com. **Contact:** Charles Kaine, publisher/owner. "Small independent publisher changing focus to narrow in on science fiction and fantasy. We are interested in making high quality books, both by the words written and how it is printed." Publishes paperback originals. Books: 70 lb. Vellum opaque paper; offset printed; perfect bound. Average print order: 1,500-4,000. Average first novel print order: 1,500. **Published 1 debut author within the last year.** Plans 2-3 first novels this year.

Needs Fantasy (space fantasy, sword and sorcery), magical realism, speculative fantasy, science fiction of all forms. Published *Ace on The River*, by Barry Greenstein, *The Breach*, by Brian Kaufman (historical fiction).

How to Contact Accepts unsolicited mss. Query with SASE or submit 3 sample chapter(s), synopsis. Accepts submissions by mail only. We do not respond to e-mail queries. Include estimated word count, brief bio, explanation of "why people will want to read the work." Send SASE for return of ms or send a disposable ms and SASE for reply only. Responds in 6 weeks to queries; 2-3 months to mss. Accepts simultaneous submissions. Often comments on rejected mss.

Terms Pays royalty. Average advance: negotiable. Publishes ms 9 months after acceptance. Ms guidelines online.

⊘ O LEE & LOW BOOKS

95 Madison Ave., New York NY 10016. (212)779-4400. Fax: (212)532-6035. Web site: www.leeandlow.com. **Contact:** Louise May, editor-in-chief. Estab. 1991. "Our goals are to meet a growing need for books that address children of color, and to present literature that all children can identify with. We only consider multicultural children's fiction and nonfiction works. Of special interest are stories set in contemporary America." Publishes hardcover originals—picture books and middle grade works only. Averages 12-16 total titles/year.

Imprint(s) Bebop Books.

Needs Children's/juvenile (historical, multicultural, books for children ages 5-12), ethnic/multicultural, illustrated. Published *Shanghai Messenger*, by Andrea Cheng; *Brothers in Hope*, by Mary Williams.

How to Contact Accepts unsolicited mss. Send SASE for return of ms or send a disposable ms and SASE for reply only. Agented fiction 30%. Responds in 4 months to queries; 4 months to mss. Accepts simultaneous submissions. Sometimes comments on rejected mss.

Terms Pays royalty. Offers advance. Book catalog for SASE with $2.07 postage. Ms guidelines online.

Advice "Writers should familarize themselves with the styles and formats of recently published children's books. Lee & Low Books is a multicultural children's book publisher. Animal stories and folktales are not considered at this time."

X ⊘ LEISURE BOOKS

Dorchester Publishing Co., 200 Madison Ave., Suite 2000, New York NY 10016. (212)725-8811. Fax: (212)532-1054. Web site: www.dorchesterpub.com. **Contact:** Linda Sawicki or Tricia Philip, editorial assistants. Estab. 1970. Publishes mass market paperback originals and reprints. Publishes romances, westerns, horrors, chick lit and thrillers only. Books: newsprint paper; offset printing; perfect bound. Average print order: variable. First novel print order: variable. Plans 25 first novels this year. Averages 255 total titles/year. Promotes titles through national reviews, ads, author readings, promotional items and on the Web site.

Imprint(s) Leisure Books (contact: Alicia Condon); Love Spell Books (contact: Christopher Keeslar); Making It (contact: Leah Hultenschmidt).

Needs Horror, romance, western, thrillers, chick lit. "We are strongly backing historical romance. All historical romance should be set pre-1900. Horrors and westerns are growing as well. No sweet romance, science fiction, cozy mysteries." Published *A Knight's Honor*, by Connie Mason (historical romance); *Shadow Touch*, by Marjorie M. Liu (paranormal romance); *The Lake*, by Richard Laymon (horror).

How to Contact Accepts unsolicited mss. Query with SASE or submit outline, first 3 sample chapters, synopsis. Agented fiction 70%. Responds in 6 months to queries. No simultaneous submissions, electronic submissions.

Terms Pays royalty on retail price. Average advance: negotiable. Publishes ms 18 months after acceptance. Book catalog for free (800)481-9191. Ms guidelines online.

Advice Encourage first novelists "if they are talented and willing to take direction *and* write the kind of genre fiction we publish. Please include a brief synopsis if sample chapters are requested."

⬟ ◪ ARTHUR A. LEVINE BOOKS

Scholastic Inc., 557 Broadway, New York NY 10012. (212)343-4436. Web site: www.scholastic.com. **Contact:** Arthur Levine, editorial director. "Arthur A. Levine is looking for distinctive literature, for children and young adults, for whatever's extraordinary." Averages 10-14 total titles/year.

Needs Juvenile, picture books, young adult, middle grade novels. Published *Frida*, by Jonah Winter, illustrated by Ana Juan; *Millicent Min, Girl Genius*, by Lisa Yee; *The Slightly True Story of Cedar B. Hartley*, by Martine Murray (middle-grade, debut author); *At the Crossing-Places*, by Kevin Crossley-Holland (YA fantasy).

How to Contact Query with SASE.

Terms Pays variable royalty on retail price. Average advance: variable. Book catalog for 9×12 SASE.

⬜ ◪ LIONHEARTED PUBLISHING, INC.

P.O. Box 618, Zephyr Cove NV 89448-0618. (775)588-1388. E-mail: submissions@LionHearted.com. Web site: www.lionhearted.com. **Contact:** Historical or Contemporary Acquistions Editor. Estab. 1994. "Multiple award-winning, independent publisher of single title, mass market paperback, trade and e-book romance novels." Books: mass market paperback; perfect binding. **Published 10-12 debut authors within the last year.** Averages 12-72 total titles, 12 fiction titles/year. Distributes through Ingram, Barnes & Noble, Baker & Taylor, Amazon and Internet Web site. Promotes titles through trade romance reader magazines, Web site and Internet.

Needs Romance (contemporary, futuristic/time travel, historical, regency period, romantic suspense; over 65,000 words only), romantic comedies. Published *Before an Autumn Wind*, by Katherine Smith (historical romance); *The London Claimant*, by Sharon Sobel (regency romance); *Starjumper's Bride*, by Joy Clarke (sci-fi romance); *Kiss Me Kat*, by Beverly Pironti (western romance); *Outside the Fire*, by Catherine Berlin (contemporary romance); *Beneath a Blazing Sun*, by J.A. Clarke (contemporary omance); *A Hallow Heart*, by John Strysik (contemporary paranormal romance).

How to Contact Accepts unsolicited mss. Submit outline, 3 sample chapter(s), publishing history, synopsis, estimated word count, cover letter and 1 paragraph story summary in cover letter. Accepts queries by e-mail. Agented fiction less than 10%. Responds in 1 month to queries; 3 months to mss. No simultaneous submissions. Always comments on rejected mss.

Terms Royalties of 10% maximum on paperbacks; 30% on electronic books. Average advance: $100. Publishes ms 18-24 months after acceptance. Ms guidelines online.

Advice "If you are not an avid reader and fan of romance novels, don't waste your time or an editor's by submitting to a publisher of romance. You have probably not written a romance, and likely do not understand the hidden code and language of romance. Read at least three of our novels; they are a bit different from the normal category romance. Reading our books is the smart way to discover what our editors like."

⬜ ◩ ◪ LISBETH

11 Peachtree Rd., Maplewood NJ 07040. (201)406-4452. E-mail: lisbethpublishing@hotmail.com. **Contact:** Carolanne E. Marie, publisher. Estab. March 2004. "Midsize publisher." Publishes hardcover originals, paperback originals, hardcover reprints, paperback reprints, e-books. Format: fine milled paper; lithograph metal-plate printing; case book bound; color and halftone illustrations. Average print order: 115,000. Debut novel print order: 115,000. **Published 1 new writer last year.** Plans 1-3 debut novels this year. Averages 3-5 total titles/year; 3 fiction titles/year. Distributes/promotes titles online and through direct mail and independent bookstores.

Imprint(s) International Story, Carolann E. Marie (short story, popular fiction, financial success); Unseen Split Breeze, Carolann E. Marie (short stories).

Needs Family saga, historical (general), literary, mystery/suspense (amateur sleuth, cozy, police procedural, private eye/hard-boiled), regional (North), religious (inspirational), romance (contemporary, futuristic/time travel, historical, romantic suspense), thriller/espionage, translations. Also publishes nonfiction (autobiography, biography, culinary, financial success, relationships). Published *Twelve Short Stories* and *Bliss*, both by

Carolann E. Marie (short story and literary fiction); *The June Wars*, by Beth Vogelsang. Plans ongoing series: Peter Charles Talbot Mysteries.

How to Contact Submit through agent only. No unsolicited mss. Considers simultaneous submissions. Never critiques/comments on rejected mss.

Terms Pays royalties of 5%-15%, $2,500 advance, 3 author's copies. Pay depends on grants/awards. Sends pre-production galleys to author. Manuscript published 12-18 months after acceptance. Writer's guidelines available for SASE. Book catalogs not available.

Advice "Grammar is of utmost importance. Seeking unforgettable stories. Write from your heart. No pulp, obscenities, erotica and/or explicit sex."

Ⓐ ⚝ LITTLE, BROWN AND CO. ADULT TRADE BOOKS

Hachette Book Group USA (formerly Time Warner Book Group), 1271 Avenue of the Americas, New York NY 10020. (212)522-8700. Fax: (212)522-2067. Web site: www.twbookmark.com. **Contact:** Editorial dept. Estab. 1837. "The general editorial philosophy for all divisions continues to be broad and flexible, with high quality and the promise of commercial success as always the first considerations." Publishes hardcover originals and paperback originals and reprints. Averages 100 total titles/year.

Imprint(s) Little, Brown; Arcade Books; Back Bay Books; Bulfinch Press.

Needs Literary, mainstream/contemporary. Published *When the Wind Blows*, by James Patterson; *Angels Flight*, by Michael Connelly; *Sea Glass*, by Anita Shreve; *City of Bones*, by Michael Connelly.

How to Contact *Agented submissions only.*

Terms Pays royalty. Offers advance. Ms guidelines online.

Ⓐ ⚝ ⓞ LITTLE, BROWN AND CO. BOOKS FOR YOUNG READERS

Division of Hachette Book Group USA (formerly AOL Time Warner Book Group), Time Life Building, 1271 Avenue of the Americas, 11th Floor, New York NY 10020. (212)522-8700. Web site: www.twbookmark.com/children/index.html. **Contact:** Submissions editor. Estab. 1837. "We are looking for strong writing and presentation but no predetermined topics." Publishes hardcover originals, trade paperback reprints. Averages 70-100 total titles/year.

Imprint(s) Back Bay Books; Megan Tingley Books (Megan Tingley, associate publisher).

Needs Adventure, ethnic, fantasy, historical, humor, juvenile, mystery, picture books, science fiction, suspense, young adult. "We are looking for strong fiction for children of all ages in any area, including multicultural. We always prefer full manuscripts for fiction."

How to Contact *Agented submissions only.*

Terms Pays royalty on retail price. Average advance: negotiable. Publishes ms 2 years after acceptance. Ms guidelines online.

ⓞ LLEWELLYN PUBLICATIONS

Llewellyn Worldwide, Ltd., P.O. Box 64383, St. Paul MN 55164-0383. (651)291-1970. Fax: (651)291-1908. E-mail: lwlpc@llewellyn.com. Web site: www.llewellyn.com. **Contact:** Barbara Moore, acquisitions editor (mystery: Midnight Ink imprint); Eava Palma Zuniga (Spanish); Elysia Gallo (magic); Andrew Karre (YA); Lisa Finander (astrology). Estab. 1901. Publishes trade and mass market paperback originals. **Published 30% debut authors within the last year.** Averages 100 total titles/year.

Needs Occult, spiritual (metaphysical), mystery, teen/YA. "Authentic and educational, yet entertaining."

How to Contact Responds in 3 months to queries. Accepts simultaneous submissions.

Terms Pays 10% royalty on wholesale price or retail price. Book catalog for 9×12 SAE with 4 first-class stamps. Ms guidelines online.

Ⓙ ⓞ LOST HORSE PRESS

105 Lost Horse Lane, Sandpoint ID 83864. (208)255-4410. Fax: (208)255-1560. E-mail: losthorsepress@mindspring.com. Web site: www.losthorsepress.org. **Contact:** Christine Holbert, publisher. Estab. 1998. Publishes hardcover and paperback originals. Books: 60-70 lb. natural paper; offset printing; b&w illustration. Average print order: 1,000-2,500. First novel print order: 500. **Published 2 debut authors within the last year.** Averages 4 total titles/year. Distributed by Small Press Distribution.

- *Woman on the Cross*, by Pierre Delattre, won the *ForeWord Magazine's* 2001 Book of the Year Award for literary fiction.

Needs Literary, regional (Pacific NW), short story collections, poetry. Published *Tales of a Dalai Lama*, by Pierre Delattre (literary fiction); *Love*, by Valerie Martin (short stories); *Hiding From Salesmen*, by Scott Poole; *Woman on the Cross*, by Pierre Delattre (literary).

Terms Publishes ms 1-2 years after acceptance. Please check submission guidelines on Web site before submitting ms.

✪ ☑ ◎ LOVE SPELL

Dorchester Publishing Co., Inc., 200 Madison Ave., 20th Floor, New York NY 10016. (212)725-8811. Fax: (212)532-1054. Web site: www.dorchesterpub.com. **Contact:** Leah Hulltenschmidt, editor (romance). Love Spell publishes the quirky sub-genres of romance: time-travel, paranormal, futuristic. "Despite the exotic settings, we are still interested in character-driven plots." Publishes mass market paperback originals. Books: newsprint paper; offset printing; perfect bound. Average print order: varies. First novel print order: varies. Plans 15 first novels this year. Averages 48 total titles/year.

Needs Romance (futuristic, time travel, paranormal, historical), whimsical contemporaries. "Books industry-wide are getting shorter; we're interested in 90,000 words." Published *A Knight's Honor,* by Connie Mason (historical romance); *Shadow Touch*, by Marjorie M. Liu (paranormal romance).

How to Contact Accepts unsolicited mss. Query with SASE or submit 3 sample chapter(s), synopsis. Send SASE or IRC. Agented fiction 70%. Responds in 6 months to mss. No simultaneous submissions.

Terms Pays royalty on retail price. Average advance: varies. Publishes ms 1 year after acceptance. Book catalog for free (800)481-9191. Ms guidelines online.

Advice "The best way to learn to write a Love Spell Romance is by reading several of our recent releases. The best-written stories are usually ones writers feel passionate about—so write from your heart! Also, the market is very tight these days so more than ever we are looking for refreshing, standout original fiction."

◙ ☑ LUATH PRESS LTD.

543/2 Castlehill, The Royal Mile, Edinburgh Scotland EH1 2ND United Kingdom. 0044 (0)131 225 4326. Fax: 0044 (0)131 225 4324. E-mail: gavin.macdougall@luath.co.uk. Web site: www.luath.co.uk. **Contact:** Gavin MacDougall, editor. Estab. 1981. Committed to publishing well-written books worth reading. Publishes paperback and hardcover originals. **Published 5-10 debut authors within the last year.** Plans 5-10 first novels this year. Member Scottish Publishers Association.

Needs Literary, thriller, mystery/suspense, short story collections, humor/satire, speculative fiction, translations. "The best of fiction with a distinctly Scottish twist."

How to Contact Accepts unsolicited mss. Query with SASE or submit complete ms and SASE. Accepts queries by e-mail, fax, phone, mail. Include estimated word count, brief bio, list of publishing credits. No submissions on disk. Never comments on rejected mss.

Terms Pays royalty.

Advice "Check out our Web site and our books, and then get in touch with us."

N ☑ MACADAM/CAGE PUBLISHING, INC.

155 Sansome St., Suite 550, San Francisco CA 94104. (415)986-7502. Fax: (415)986-7414. E-mail: info@macadamcage.com. Web site: www.macadamcage.com. **Contact:** Kate Nitze, editor; Jason Wood, editor; Karan Mahajan, associate editor; Khristina Wenzinger, associate editor. Estab. 1999. Mid-size independent publisher. Publishes hardcover and trade paperback originals. Books: web offset printing; case binding. Average first novel print order: 5,000-15,000. **Published 10 debut authors within the last year.** Averages 25-30 total titles/year. Member PMA, ABA, NCIBA. Distributes titles through Baker & Taylor, Ingram, Brodart, Koen and American Wholesale. Promotes titles via in-house marketing/publicity department.

Needs Historical, literary, mainstream/contemporary. Published *How To Be Lost*, by Amanda Eyre Ward (fiction); *The Time Traveler's Wife*, by Audrey Niffenegger (fiction); *Pinkerton's Sister*, by Peter Rushforth (fiction); *The God File*, by Frank Turner Hollon (fiction).

How to Contact Accepts unsolicited mss. Check Web site for ms submission guidelines. Submit proposal package including cover letter, brief synopsis, 30-page sample, SASE to ATTN: Manuscript Submissions. Agented fiction 50%. Responds in 4 months to queries; 4 months to mss. Accepts simultaneous submissions.

Terms Pays negotiable royalties. Average advance: negotiable. Publishes ms up to 1 year after acceptance. Ms guidelines on Web site.

◘ MARCH STREET PRESS

3413 Wilshire, Greensboro NC 27408. E-mail: rbixby@aol.com. Fax: (336)282-9754. Web site: www.marchstreetpress.com. Estab. 1988. Publishes 5-7 fiction titles/year.

Needs Literary.

How to Contact Accepts unsolicited mss. Submit complete ms. Accepts queries by e-mail, mail or fax. Send SASE for return of ms or send a disposable ms and SASE for reply only.

Terms Ms guidelines online.

Advice "If someone gives you advice, the appropriate response is, 'Thank you,' not 'Who do you think you are?' There's a reason why some writing is good and other writing is not and I can usually explain the reason. I've been doing this for a while. If you don't want an editor's comments, don't send your work to an editor."

◎ MARINE TECHNIQUES PUBLISHING, INC.

126 Western Ave., Suite 266, Augusta ME 04330-7249. (207)622-7984. Fax: (207)621-0821. E-mail: marinetechniques@midmaine.com. **Contact:** James L. Pelletier, president/CEO (commercial marine or maritime international); Christopher S. Pelletier, vice president operations; Jenelle M. Pelletier, editor in chief (national and international maritime related properties). **Published 15% debut authors within the last year.** Averages 3-5 total titles/year.

Needs Must be commercial maritime/marine related.

How to Contact Submit complete ms. Responds in 2 months to queries; 6 months to mss. Accepts simultaneous submissions.

Terms Pays 25-43% royalty on wholesale or retail price. Publishes ms 6-12 months after acceptance.

Advice "Audience consists of commercial marine/maritime firms, persons employed in all aspects of the marine/maritime commercial and recreational fields, persons interested in seeking employment in the commercial marine industry; firms seeking to sell their products and services to vessel owners, operators and mangers in the commercial marine industry worldwide, etc."

Ⓝ Ⓐ ◎ Ⓨ MARINER BOOKS

Houghton Mifflin, 222 Berkeley St., Boston MA 02116. (617)351-5000. Fax: (617)351-1202. Web site: www.hmco.com. **Contact:** Paperback division. Estab. 1997. Publishes trade paperback originals and reprints.

• Mariner Books' *Interpreter of Maladies*, by debut author Jhumpa Lahiri, won the 2000 Pulitzer Prize for fiction and *The Caprices*, by Sabina Murray, received the 2003 PEN/Faulkner Award.

Needs Literary, mainstream/contemporary. Recently published Bella Bathurst, Anita Desai, Perri Klass and Samrat Upadhyay.

How to Contact *Agented submissions only.* Responds in 4 months to mss.

Terms Pays royalty on retail price or makes outright purchase. Average advance: variable.

▢ Ⓖ MARVEL COMICS

417 5th Ave., New York NY 10016. (212)576-4000. Fax: (212)576-8547. Web site: www.marvel.com. Publishes hardcover originals and reprints, trade paperback reprints, mass market comic book originals, electronic reprints. Averages 650 total titles/year.

Needs Adventure, comic books, fantasy, horror, humor, science fiction, young adult. "Our shared universe needs new heroes and villains; books for younger readers and teens needed."

How to Contact "Please send us an inquiry letter, detailing your writing experience and why you would like to write for Marvel. Based on your inquiry letter, we may request to read a sample of your work. Please note: Unsolicited writing samples will not be read. Any unsolicited or solicited writing sample received without a signed Marvel Idea Submission Form will be destroyed unread." (Download Marvel Idea Submission Form from Web site). Responds only if interested in 3-5 weeks.

Terms Pays on a per page work-for-hire basis which is contracted. Ms guidelines online.

◎ ◎ MCBOOKS PRESS

10 Booth Building, 520 N. Meadow St., Ithaca NY 14850. (607)272-2114. Fax: (607)273-6068. E-mail: jackie@mcbooks.com. Web site: www.mcbooks.com. **Contact:** Editorial director. Estab. 1979. "Small independent publisher; specializes in historical fiction, American publisher of Alexander Kent's Richard Bolitho series, Dudley Pope's Ramage novels." Publishes trade paperback and hardcover originals and reprints. Averages 20 total titles, 14 fiction titles/year. Distributes titles through National Book Network.

Needs General historical, nautical (British and American naval), military historical.

How to Contact Does not accept unsolicited mss. Query with SASE. Include list of publishing credits. Responds in 2 months to queries. Accepts simultaneous submissions.

Terms Pays 5-10% royalty on retail price. Average advance: $1,000-5,000.

Advice "We are small and do not take on many unpublished writers. Historical and military accuracy is a must. Our readers know their time periods as well as their guns and their ships. Especially looking for stories with at least one strong female character."

▣ MCCLELLAND & STEWART, LTD.

75 Sherbourne St., 5th Floor, Toronto ON M5A 2P9 Canada. (416)598-1114. Fax: (416)598-7764. Web site: www.mcclelland.com. Publishes hardcover, trade paperback and mass market paperback originals and reprints. Averages 80 total titles/year.

Needs Historical, humor, literary, mainstream/contemporary, mystery, short story collections.

How to Contact Query with SASE.

Terms Offers advance.

⊠ ◎ ⛟ MARGARET K. MCELDERRY BOOKS

Simon & Schuster Children's Publishing Division, Simon & Schuster, 1230 Sixth Ave., New York NY 10020. (212)698-2761. Fax: (212)698-2797. Web site: www.simonsayskids.com. **Contact:** Emma D. Dryden, vice president/associate publisher. Estab. 1971. Publishes quality material for preschoolers to 18-year-olds. Publishes hardcover originals. Books: high quality paper; offset printing; three piece and POB bindings; illustrations. Average print order: 12,500. First novel print order: 7,500. **Published some debut authors within the last year.** Averages 35 total titles/year.

- Books published by Margaret K. McElderry Books have received numerous awards, including the Newbery and Caldecott Awards.

Needs Adventure, fantasy, historical, mainstream/contemporary, mystery, picture books, young adult (or middle grade). All categories (fiction and nonfiction) for juvenile and young adult. "We will consider any category. Results depend on the quality of the imagination, the artwork and the writing." Published *Bear Stays Up for Christmas*, by Karma Wilson and illustrated by Jane Chapman (picture books); *Permanent Rose*, by Hilary McKay (middle-grade fiction); *The Water Mirror*, by Kai Meyer (young adult fiction).

Terms Average print order is 5,000-10,000 for a first middle grade or young adult book; 7,500-20,000 for a first picture book. Pays royalty on hardcover retail price: 10% fiction; 5% author, 5% illustrator (picture book). Offers $5,000-8,000 advance for new authors. Publishes ms up to 3 years after acceptance. Ms guidelines for #10 SASE.

Advice "Imaginative writing of high quality is always in demand; also picture books that are original and unusual. Keep in mind that McElderry is a very small imprint, so we are very selective about the books we will undertake for publication. We try not to publish any 'trend' books. Be familiar with our list and with what is being published this year by all publishing houses."

⊘ MEDALLION PRESS, INC.

27825 N. Forest Garden Rd., Wauconda IL 60084. Web site: www.medallionpress.com. **Contact:** Wenda Burbank, acquisitions editor. Estab. 2003. "We are an independent publisher looking for books that are outside of the box. Please do not submit to us if you are looking for a large advance. We reserve our funds for marketing the books." Publishes paperback originals. Average print order: 5,000. **Published 20+ debut authors within the last year.**

Imprint(s) Platinum/Hardcover; Gold/Mass Market; Silver/Trade Paper; Bronze/Young Adult; Jewel/Romance; Amethyst/Fantasy, Sci-Fi, Paranormal; Emerald/Suspense; Ruby/Contemporary; Sapphire/Historical.

Needs Adventure, ethnic, fantasy (space fantasy, sword and sorcery), glitz, historical, horror (dark fantasy, futuristic, psychological, supernatural), humor, literary, mainstream/contemporary, military/war, mystery (amateur slueth, police procedural, private eye/hard-boiled), romance, science fiction (hard science/technological, soft/sociological), thriller/espionage, western (frontier saga), young adult. Published *Siren's Call*, by Mary Ann Mitchell (horror); *Grand Traverse*, by Michael Beres (mainstream fiction); *Memories of Empire*, by Django Wexler (epic fantasy).

How to Contact Does not accept unsolicited mss. "Minimum word count 80K for adult fiction, 55K for YA, no exceptions." No poetry, anthologies, erotica or inspirational. Submit first 3 consecutive chapters and a chapter-by-chapter synopsis. "Without the synopsis, the submission will be rejected." Accepts queries only by mail. No e-mail queries. Include estimated word count, brief bio, list of publishing credits. Send SASE or IRC. Agented fiction 20%. Responds in 6-12 months to mss. Accepts simultaneous submissions. Sometimes comments on rejected mss.

Terms Pays 6-8% royalty. Offers advance. Publishes ms 1-2 years after acceptance. Ms guidelines online.

Advice "We are not affected by trends. We are simply looking for well crafted, original, grammatically correct works of fiction. Please visit our Web site for the most current guidelines prior to submitting anything to us."

⊡ MEISHA MERLIN PUBLISHING, INC.

P.O. Box 7, Decatur GA 30031. E-mail: email@meishamerlin.com. Web site: www.meishamerlin.com. **Contact:** Stephen Pagel, senior editor. Estab. 1996. Midsize independent publisher devoted exclusively to science fiction, fantasy and horror. Publishes hardcover and paperback originals and reprints. Also publishes e-books. **Published 2 debut authors within the last year.**

Needs Fantasy (space fantasy, sword and sorcery), science fiction (hard science/technological, soft/sociological). Recently published *Traitor's Knot*, by Janny Wurts; *Crystal Soldier*, by Sharon Lee and Steve Miller.

How to Contact Query with SASE or submit first 75 pages. Accepts queries by mail. Include estimated word count, brief bio, list of publishing credits. Send SASE for return of ms or send a disposable ms and SASE for reply only. Often comments on rejected mss.

Advice "We look for quality and originality first, specific genre or style second."

◎ MERIWETHER PUBLISHING, LTD.

885 Elkton Dr., Colorado Springs CO 80907-3557. (719)594-4422. Fax: (719)594-9916. Web site: www.meriweth erpublishing.com; www.contemporarydrama.com. **Contact:** Rhonda Wray, associate editor (church plays); Ted Zapel, editor (school plays, comedies, books). Estab. 1969. "Mid-size, independent publisher of plays. We publish plays for teens, mostly one-act comedies, holiday plays for churches and musical comedies. Our books are on the theatrical arts." Publishes paperback originals and reprints. Books: quality paper; printing house specialist; paperback binding. Average print order: 5,000-10,000. **Published 25-35 debut authors within the last year.**

Needs Mainstream/contemporary, comedy, religious (children's plays and religious Christmas and Easter plays), suspense—all in playscript format. Published *Murder in the Manor*, by Bill Hand (comic mystery play); *Acting for Life*, by Jack Frakes (textbook).

How to Contact Accepts unsolicited mss. Query with SASE. Accepts queries by e-mail. Include list of publishing credits. Send SASE for return of ms or send a disposable ms and SASE for reply only. Responds in 3 weeks to queries; 2 months to mss. Accepts simultaneous submissions. Sometimes comments on rejected mss.

Terms Pays 10% royalty on retail price or makes outright purchase. Publishes ms 6-12 months after acceptance. Book catalog and ms guidelines for $2 postage.

Advice "If you're interested in writing comedy/farce plays, we're your best publisher."

◻ MID-LIST PRESS

4324 12th Ave S., Minneapolis MN 55407-3218. (612)432-8062. Fax: (612)823-8387. E-mail: guide@midlist.org. Web site: www.midlist.org. **Contact:** Marianne Nora, executive director. Estab. 1989. "We are a nonprofit literary press dedicated to the survival of the mid-list, those quality titles that are being neglected by the larger commercial houses. Our focus is on first-time writers, and we are probably best known for the Mid-List Press First Series Awards." Publishes hardcover and trade paperback originals. Books: acid-free paper; offset printing; perfect or Smyth-sewn binding. Average print order: 2,000. **Published 6 debut authors within the last year.** Averages 5 total titles, 2 fiction titles/year. Distributes titles through Small Press Distribution, Ingram, Baker & Taylor, Midwest Library Service, Brodart, Follett and Emery Pratt. Promotes titles through publicity, direct mail, catalogs, author's events and review and awards.

Needs General fiction. Published *The Trouble with You Is*, by Susan Jackson Rodgers (first fiction, short fiction); *Pleasant Drugs*, by Kathryn Kulpa; *The Woman Who Never Cooked*, by Mary L. Tabor.

How to Contact Accepts unsolicited mss. Agented fiction less than10%. Responds in 3 weeks to queries; 3 months to mss. Accepts simultaneous submissions.

Terms Pays 40-50% royalty on net receipts. Average advance: $1,000. Publishes ms 12-18 months after acceptance. Ms guidelines online.

Advice "Write first for guidelines or visit our Web site before submitting a query, proposal or manuscript. And take the time to read some of the titles we've published."

◻ ▼ MILKWEED EDITIONS

1011 Washington Ave. S., Suite 300, Minneapolis MN 55415. (612)332-3192. Fax: (612)215-2550. E-mail: editor @milkweed.org. Web site: www.milkweed.org. **Contact:** Daniel Slager, editor-in-chief; Elisabeth Fitz, first reader. Estab. 1984. Nonprofit publisher. Publishes hardcover originals and paperback originals and reprints. Books: book text quality—acid-free paper; offset printing; perfect or hardcover binding. Average print order: 4,000. First novel print order depends on book. **Published some debut authors within the last year.** Averages 15 total titles/year. Distributes through Publisher's Group West. Each book has its own marketing plan involving print ads, tours, conferences, etc.

• Seth Kantner's *Ordinary Wolves* received a Pacific Northwest Booksellers Award.

Needs Literary. Novels for adults and for readers 8-13. High literary quality. For adult readers: literary fiction, nonfiction, poetry, essays; for children (ages 8-13): literary novels. Translations welcome for both audiences. Published *Gardenias*, by Faith Sullivan; *Visigoth*, by Gary Amdahl (first fiction, short stories); *Sky Bridge*, by Laura Pritchett.

How to Contact Submit complete ms. Responds in 2 months to queries; 6 months to mss. Accepts simultaneous submissions.

Terms Pays 6% royalty on retail price. Average advance: varied. Publishes ms 1-2 years after acceptance. Book catalog for $1.50 postage. Ms guidelines online.

Advice "Read good contemporary literary fiction, find your own voice, and persist. Familiarize yourself with our list before submitting."

✖ ◎ ▼ MILKWEEDS FOR YOUNG READERS

Milkweed Editions, 1011 Washington Ave. S., Suite 300, Minneapolis MN 55415. (612)332-3192. Fax: (612)215-2550. Web site: www.milkweed.org. **Contact:** Daniel Slager, editor in chief; Elisabeth Fitz, children's reader.

Edgar & Ellen: Rare Beasts, by Charles Ogden (middle grade series); *Truth Is a Bright Star*, by Joan Price (middle grade adventure).

How to Contact Accepts unsolicited mss. Include brief bio, list of publishing credits, e-mail address. Send SASE for return of ms or send a disposable ms and SASE for reply only. Agented fiction 60%. Responds in 4-6 months to mss. Accepts simultaneous submissions.

Terms Pays 15-20% royalty on net receipts. Average advance: $0-9,000. Publishes ms 1-2 years after acceptance. Book catalog and ms guidelines for 9×12 SASE with 3 first-class stamps, or visit the Web site.

☑ ◎ TRIUMVIRATE PUBLICATIONS

497 West Avenue 44, Los Angeles CA 90065-3917. (818)340-6770. Fax: (818)340-6770. E-mail: triumpub@aol.com. Web site: www.triumpub.com. **Contact:** Carolyn Porter, executive editor. Estab. 1985. Publishes hardcover and paperback originals. Books: Antique/natural paper; offset printing; case and perfect bound; illustrations. Average print order 5,000-10,000. Member PMA. Distributes books through wholesalers using direct mail, fax/e-mail/telephone, trade/consumer advertising, book exhibits, reviews, listings and Internet.

Needs Adventure, fantasy, historical, horror, military/war, mystery, psychic/supernatural, science fiction, thriller/espionage. Published *A Continent Adrift*, by Vladimir Chernozemsky (science fiction); *Dark Side of Time*, by Vladimir Chernozemsky (supernatural).

How to Contact Does not accept unsolicited mss. Submit outline, 2 sample chapter(s). Accepts queries by fax, mail. Include brief bio, list of publishing credits. Send SASE for return of ms or send a disposable ms and SASE for reply only. Responds in 6 weeks to queries; 3 months to mss. Sometimes comments on rejected mss.

Terms Pays royalty. Publishes ms 6-12 months after acceptance.

Advice "Please query first. If interested, we will request the manuscript. Query should include: cover letter, short synopsis/description, 2-3 sample chapters, author bio, and writing/publishing credits. Send by mail. Do not fax except for short, 1-2 page query letters only. Please do not submit by e-mail or phone. We will respond if interested."

☑ ☒ TURTLE BOOKS

866 United Nations Plaza, Suite #525, New York NY 10017. (212)644-2020. Fax: (212)223-4387. Web site: www.turtlebooks.com. "We are an independent publishing house. Our goal is to publish a small, select list of quality children's picture books in both English and Spanish editions." Publishes hardcover and trade paperback originals. Averages 6-8 total titles/year. Member Association of American Publishers. Distrubed by Publishers Group West.

● Received the Willa Cather Award for Best Children's Book of the Year.

Needs Children's/juvenile. Subjects suitable for children's picture books. "We are looking for good stories which can be illustrated as children's picture books." Published *The Crab Man*, by Patricia Van West; *Keeper of The Swamp*, by Ann Garret; *Prairie Dog Pioneers*, by Jo Harper.

How to Contact Accepts unsolicited mss. Submit complete ms and SASE. Include list of publishing credits. Accepts simultaneous submissions.

Terms Pays royalty on retail price. Offers advance. Publishes ms 12 months after acceptance.

Advice "We only publish children's books. Every book we've published has been under 2,000 words in length. Queries are a waste of time. Please send only complete manuscripts."

◻ UNBRIDLED BOOKS

200 North 9th Street, Suite A, Columbia MO 65201. 573-256-4106. Fax: 573-256-5207. Web site: www.unbridledbooks.com. **Contact:** Greg Michalson and Fred Ramey, editors. Estab. 2004. "Unbridled Books aspires to become a premier publisher of works of rich literary quality that appeal to a broad audience." Publishes both fiction and creative nonfiction. Hardcover and trade paperback originals. **Published 1 debut author within the last year.** Averages 10-12 total titles, 8-10 fiction titles/year.

Needs Literary, nonfiction, memoir. *The Green Age of Asher Witherow*, by M. Allen Cunningham; *The Distance Between Us*, by Masha Hamilton; *Fear Itself*, by Candida Lawrence; *Lucky Strike*, by Nancy Zafris.

How to Contact Query with SASE. Accepts queries by mail. No electronic submissions.

☑ ◎ UNITY HOUSE

1901 NW Blue Parkway, Unity Village MO 64065-0001. (816)524-3559 ext. 3190. Fax: (816)251-3559. Web site: www.unityonline.org. **Contact:** Adrianne Ford, product manager. Estab. 1903. "We are a bridge between traditional Christianity and New Age spirituality. Unity is based on metaphysical Christian principles, spiritual values and the healing power of prayer as a resource for daily living." Publishes hardcover and trade paperback originals and reprints. **Published 2 debut authors within the last year.** Averages 16 total titles/year.

Needs Spiritual, visionary fiction, inspirational, metaphysical.

How to Contact Send complete mss (3 copies). Responds in 6-8 weeks. No simultaneous submissions.

Terms Pays 10-15% royalty on net receipts. Offers advance. Publishes ms 13 months after acceptance. Ms guidelines online.

Book Publishers

UNIVERSITY OF GEORGIA PRESS

330 Research Dr., Athens GA 30602-4901. (706)369-6130. E-mail: books@ugapress.uga.edu. Web site: www.ugapress.org. Estab. 1938. University of Georgia Press is a midsized press that publishes fiction *only* through the Flannery O'Connor Award for Short Fiction competition. Publishes hardcover originals, trade paperback originals and reprints. Averages 75 total titles/year.

Needs Short story collections published in Flannery O'Connor Award Competition. Most recent titles include *Copy Cats*, by David Crouse; *Sorry I Worried You*, by Gary Finke; *The Send-Away Girl*, by Barbara Sutton.

How to Contact Manuscripts for Flannery O'Connor Award for Short Fiction accepted in April and May. Please see submissions guidelines on Web site for full details. Responds in 2 months to queries. No simultaneous submissions.

Terms Pays 7-10% royalty on net receipts. Average advance: rare, varying. Publishes ms 1 year after acceptance. Book catalog and ms guidelines for #10 SASE. Ms guidelines online.

Advice "Please visit our Web site to view our book catalogs and for all manuscript submission guidelines."

UNIVERSITY OF IOWA PRESS

100 Kuhl House, Iowa City IA 52242-1000. (319)335-2000. Fax: (319)335-2055. Web site: www.uiowapress.org. **Contact:** Holly Carver, director; Joe Parsons, acquisitions editor. Estab. 1969. Publishes paperback originals. Average print run for a first book is 1,000-1,500. Averages 35 total titles/year.

Needs Currently publishes the Iowa Short Fiction Award selections.

How to Contact Responds in 6 months to queries. See Web site for details.

Terms Pays 7-10% royalty on net receipts. Publishes ms 1 year after acceptance. Ms guidelines online.

UNIVERSITY OF MICHIGAN PRESS

839 Greene St., Ann Arbor MI 48106. (734)764-4388. Fax: (734)615-1540. E-mail: ump.fiction@umich.edu. Web site: www.press.umich.edu. **Contact:** Chris Hebert, editor (fiction). Midsize university press. Publishes hardcover originals. Member AAUP.

Imprint(s) Sweetwater Fiction Originals (literary/regional).

Needs Literary, short story collections, novels.

How to Contact Accepts unsolicited mss. Query with SASE or submit outline, 3 sample chapter(s). Accepts queries by mail. Include brief bio, list of publishing credits. Responds in 4-6 weeks to queries; 6-8 weeks to mss. Accepts simultaneous submissions. No electronic submissions, submissions on disk. Sometimes comments on rejected mss.

Terms Ms guidelines online.

Advice "Aside from work published through the Michigan Literary Fiction Awards, we seek only fiction set in the Great Lakes region."

UNIVERSITY OF NEVADA PRESS

MS 166, Reno NV 89557. (775)784-6573. Fax: (775)784-6200. Web site: www.nvbooks.nevada.edu. **Contact:** Margaret Dalrymple (fiction). Estab. 1961. "Small university press. Publishes fiction that primarily focuses on the American West." Publishes hardcover and paperback originals and reprints. Averages 25 total titles, 2 fiction titles/year. Member AAUP.

• *Strange White Male*, by Gerald Haslam won the WESTAF Award for Fiction in 2000 and *Foreword Magazine's* second place winner for Book of the Year.

Needs "We publish in Basque Studies, Gambling Studies, Western literature and Western history."

How to Contact Submit outline, 2-4 sample chapter(s), synopsis. Include estimated word count, brief bio, list of publishing credits. Send SASE or IRC. Responds in 2 months to queries. No simultaneous submissions.

Terms Publishes ms 18 months after acceptance. Book catalog and ms guidelines free Ms guidelines online.

Advice Publishes fiction in Western American Literature series only.

UNIVERSITY PRESS OF NEW ENGLAND

1 Court St., Suite 250, Lebanon NH 03766. (603)448-1533. Fax: (603)448-7006. E-mail: university.press@dartmouth.edu. Web site: www.upne.com. **Contact:** Phyllis Deutsch, acquisitions editor-in-chief. Estab. 1970. Publishes hardcover originals. Averages 85 total titles, 6 fiction titles/year.

Needs Literary. Only New England novels, literary fiction and reprints. Published *Rebecca Wentworth's Distraction*, by Robert J. Begiebing; *The Private Revolution of Geoffrey Frost*, by I.E. Fender; *The Romance of Eleanor Gray*; by Raymond Kennedy; and *the Nature Notebooks*, by Don Mitchell.

How to Contact "For publication in the Hardscrabble series, it is not essential that the author live in the New England area, but the work should evoke themes and characters, and at the very least be set, in the region. Since much of what constitutes 'regional' fiction is fairly subjective, it is best to send a query letter." Query with SASE or submit sample chapter(s). Responds in 2 months to queries.

Terms Pays standard royalty. Average advance: occasional. Book catalog and ms guidelines for 9×12 SASE and 5 first-class stamps. Detailed ms and query guidelines online.

VANDAMERE PRESS

P.O. Box 149, St. Petersburg FL 33731. **Contact:** Jerry Frank, senior acquistions editor. Estab. 1984. Publishes hardcover and trade paperback originals and reprints. **Published 25% debut authors within the last year.** Averages 6-12 total titles/year.

Needs Adventure, mystery, suspense. Recently published *Classified Waste*, by Alexander M. Grace (fiction).

How to Contact Submit 5-10 sample chapter(s), synopsis. Responds in 6 months to queries. Accepts simultaneous submissions.

Terms Pays royalty on revenues generated. Offers advance. Publishes ms 1-3 years after acceptance.

Advice "Author's who can provide endorsements from significant published writers, celebrities, etc., will *always* be given serious consideration. Clean, easy-to-read, *dark* copy is essential. Patience in waiting for replies is essential. All unsolicited work is looked at, but at certain times of the year our review schedule will stop. No electronic submissions. No response without SASE."

☒ ◎ VÉHICULE PRESS

Box 125, Place du Parc Station, Montreal QC H2X 4A3 Canada. (514)844-6073. Fax: (514)844-7543. Web site: www.vehiculepress.com. **Contact:** Andrew Steinmetz, fiction editor. Estab. 1973. Small publisher of scholarly, literary and cultural books. Publishes trade paperback originals by *Canadian authors only*. Books: good quality paper; offset printing; perfect and cloth binding; illustrations. Average print order: 1,000-3,000. Averages 15 total titles/year.

Imprint(s) Signal Editions (poetry), Esplande Books (fiction).

Needs Literary, regional, short story collections. Published *Garbage Head*, by Christopher Willard; *Seventeen Tomatoes: Tales from Kashmir*, by Jaspreet Singh; *A Short Journey by Car*, by Liam Duran.

How to Contact Query with SASE. Responds in 4 months to queries.

Terms Pays 10-15% royalty on retail price. Average advance: $200-500. "Depends on press run and sales. Translators of fiction can receive Canada Council funding, which publisher applies for." Publishes ms 1 year after acceptance. Book catalog for 9×12 SAE with IRCs.

Advice "Quality in almost any style is acceptable. We believe in the editing process."

☒ ☒ VIKING

Penguin Putnam Inc., 375 Hudson St., New York NY 10014. (212)366-2000. **Contact:** Acquisitions Editor. Publishes a mix of literary and popular fiction and nonfiction. Publishes hardcover and originals.

Needs Literary, mainstream/contemporary, mystery, suspense. Published *Lake Wobegon Summer 1956*, by Garrison Keillor; *A Day Late and A Dollar Short*, by Terry McMillian; *A Common Life*, by Jan Karon; *In the Heart of the Sea*, by Nathaniel Philbrick.

How to Contact *Agented submissions only.* Responds in 6 months to queries. Accepts simultaneous submissions.

Terms Pays 10-15% royalty on retail price. Average advance: negotiable. Publishes ms 12-18 months after acceptance.

☒ ☒ ◎ VIKING CHILDREN'S BOOKS

A division of Penguin Young Readers Group, 345 Hudson St., New York NY 10014. (212)366-3600. Web site: www.penguin.com. **Contact:** Catherine Frank, Tracy Gates, Joy Peskin, Anne Gunton, Kendra Levin. "Viking Children's books publishes high quality trade hardcover books for children through young adults. These include fiction and nonfiction." Publishes hardcover originals. **Published some debut authors within the last year.** Averages 70 total titles/year. Promotes titles through press kits, institutional ads.

Needs Juvenile, picture books, young adult. Published *Just Listen*, by Sarah Dessen (novel); *Llama, Llama Red Pajama*, by Anna Dewdney (picture book).

How to Contact Only accepts solicited mss. Submit complete ms. Send SASE. Responds in 12 months to queries.

Terms Pays 5-10% royalty on retail price. Average advance: negotiable. Publishes ms 1 year after acceptance.

Advice No "cartoony" or mass-market submissions for picture books.

☒ ☒ VILLARD BOOKS

Random House Publishing Group, 1745 Broadway 18th Fl., New York NY 10019. (212)572-2600. Web site: www.atrandom.com. Estab. 1983. Publishes hardcover and trade paperback originals. Averages 40-50 total titles/year.

Needs Commercial fiction.

How to Contact *Agented submissions only.* Agented fiction 95%. Accepts simultaneous submissions.

Terms Pays negotiable royalty. Average advance: negotiable.

A ★ VINTAGE ANCHOR PUBLISHING

The Knopf Publishing Group, A Division of Random House, Inc., 1745 Broadway, New York NY 10019. Web site: www.randomhouse.com. **Contact:** Furaha Norton, editor. Publishes trade paperback originals and reprints.
Needs Literary, mainstream/contemporary, short story collections. Published *Snow Falling on Cedars*, by Guterson (contemporary); *Martin Dressler*, by Millhauser (literary).
How to Contact *Agented submissions only.* Accepts simultaneous submissions. No electronic submissions.
Terms Pays 4-8% royalty on retail price. Average advance: $2,500 and up. Publishes ms 1 year after acceptance.

A ★ ◎ WARNER ASPECT

Imprint of Warner Books, 1271 Avenue of the Americas, New York NY 10020. (212)522-7200. Web site: www.tw bookmark.com. **Contact:** Jaime Levine, editorial director. "We're looking for 'epic' stories in both fantasy and science fiction." Publishes hardcover, trade paperback, mass market paperback originals and mass market paperback reprints. **Published 2 debut authors within the last year.** Averages 30 total titles/year. Distributes titles through nationwide sales force.
Needs Fantasy, science fiction. Published *Kitty and The Midnight Hour*, by Carrie Vaughn.
How to Contact *Agented submissions only.* "Mistake writers often make is hoping against hope that being unagented won't make a difference. We simply don't have the staff to look at unagented projects." Responds in 3 months to mss.
Terms Pays royalty on retail price. Average advance: $5,000-up. Publishes ms 14 months after acceptance.
Advice "Think epic! Our favorite stories are big-screen science fiction and fantasy, with plenty of characters and subplots. Sample our existing titles—we're a fairly new list and pretty strongly focused. Also seeking writers of color to add to what we've already published by Octavia E. Butler, Nalo Hopkinson, Walter Mosley, etc."

A ★ WARNER BOOKS

Hachette Book Group USA, Time & Life Building, 1271 Avenue of the Americas, New York NY 10020. (212)522-7200. Fax: (212)522-7993. Web site: www.twbookmark.com. **Contact:** (Ms.) Jamie Raab, senior vice president/publisher (general nonfiction and fiction); Les Pockell, associate publisher (general nonfiction); Amy Einhorn, vice president, executive editor; Beth de Guzman, vice president, editor-in-chief, Warner Paperbacks; Rick Wolff, vice president/executive editor (business, humor, sports); Caryn Karmatz Rudy, senior editor (fiction, general nonfiction, popular culture); Diana Baroni, executive editor (health, fitness, general nonfiction and fiction); John Aherne, editor (popular culture, men's health, New Age, movie tie-ins, general fiction); Rolf Zettersten, vice president/Warner Faith (books for the CBA market); (Ms.) Jaime Levine, editor/Aspect (science fiction); Karen Koszto Inyik, senior editor (women's fiction); Colin Fox, senior editor. Estab. 1960. Warner publishes general interest fiction. Publishes hardcover, trade paperback and mass market paperback originals and reprints and e-books. Averages 250 total titles/year.
Imprint(s) Mysterious Press; Warner Business; Warner Forever; Warner Vision; Warner Wellness; 5 Spot; Warner Twelve; Solana.
Needs Fantasy, horror, mainstream/contemporary, mystery, romance, science fiction, suspense, thriller/espionage, thrillers. Published *Up Country*, by Nelson DeMille; *A Bend in the Road*, by Nicholas Sparks.
How to Contact *Agented submissions only.* Accepts no unsolicited mss to queries.
Terms Pays variable royalty. Average advance: variable. Publishes ms 2 years after acceptance.

A ★ WATERBROOK PRESS

Subsidiary of Random House, 12265 Oracle Blvd., Suite 200, Colorado Springs CO 80921. (719)590-4999. Fax: (719)590-8977. Web site: www.waterbrookpress.com. Estab. 1996. Publishes hardcover and trade paperback originals. Averages 70 total titles/year.
Needs Adventure, historical, literary, mainstream/contemporary, mystery, religious (inspirational, religious mystery/suspense, religious thriller, religious romance), romance (contemporary, historical), science fiction, spiritual, suspense. Published *A Name of Her Own*, by Jane Kirkpatrick (historical); *Women's Intuition*, by Lisa Samson (contemporary); *Thorn in My Heart*, by Liz Curtis Higgs (historical).
How to Contact Does not accept unsolicited mss. *Agented submissions only.* Responds in 1-2 months to queries; 1-2 months to mss. Accepts simultaneous submissions, electronic submissions.
Terms Pays royalty. Publishes ms 11 months after acceptance.

◖ ◎ WHITE MANE KIDS

White Mane Publishing, P.O. Box 708, Shippensburg PA 17257. (717)532-2237. Fax: (717)532-6110. E-mail: marketing@whitemane.com. Web site: www.whitemane.com. Publishes hardcover orginals and paperback originals.
Needs Children's/juvenile (historical), young adult (historical). Published *Anybody's Hero: Battle of Old Men & Young Boys*, by Phyllis Haslip; *Crossroads at Gettysburg*, by Alan Kay.

How to Contact Accepts unsolicited mss. Query with SASE. Accepts queries by fax, mail. Include estimated word count, brief bio, summary of work and marketing ideas. Send SASE for return of ms or send a disposable ms and SASE for reply only. Responds in 1 month to queries; 3-4 months to mss. Accepts simultaneous submissions. Rarely comments on rejected mss.

Terms Pays royalty. Publishes ms 12-18 months after acceptance. Ms guidelines for #10 SASE.

Advice "Make your work historically accurate."

N A ✪ WILLIAM MORROW

HarperCollins, 10 E. 53rd St., New York NY 10022. (212)207-7000. Fax: (212)207-7606. Web site: www.harperco llins.com. **Contact:** Acquisitions Editor. Estab. 1926. Approximately half of the books published are fiction. Averages 160 total titles/year.

Needs Publishes adult fiction. "Morrow accepts only the highest quality submissions" in adult fiction.

How to Contact *Agented submissions only.*

Terms Pays standard royalty on retail price. Average advance: varying. Publishes ms 2 years after acceptance.

Ø WILLOWGATE PRESS

P.O. Box 6529, Holliston MA 01746. (508)429-8774. E-mail: willowgatepress@yahoo.com. Web site: www.willo wgatepress.com. **Contact:** Robert Tolins, editor. Publishes trade paperback and mass market paperback originals. **Published 50% debut authors within the last year.** Averages 1-2 total titles/year.

Needs Fantasy, gothic, historical, horror, humor, literary, mainstream/contemporary, military/war, mystery, occult, regional, science fiction, short story collections, sports. "We are not interested in children's, erotica or experimental."

Advice "At the present time we are closed to new submissions, and will remain so until we can work through our backlog. Our Web site will have updates."

N Ø ◎ WILSHIRE BOOK CO.

9731 Variel Ave., Chatsworth, CA 92311-4315. (818)700-1522. Fax: (818)700-1527. E-mail: mpowers@mpowers .com. Web site: www.mpowers.com. **Contact:** Melvin Powers, publisher; editorial department (adult fables). Estab. 1947. "You are not only what you are today, but also what you choose to become tomorrow." Looking for adult fables that teach principles of psychological growth. Publishes trade paperback originals and reprints. **Published 7 debut authors within the last year.** Averages 25 total titles/year. Distributes titles through wholesalers, bookstores and mail order. Promotes titles through author interviews on radio and television.

Needs Adult allegories that teach principles of psychological growth or offer guidance in living. Minimum 25,000 words. Published *The Princess Who Believed in Fairy Tales*, by Marcia Grad; *The King in Rusty Armor*, by Robert Fisher; *The Dragon Slayer With a Heavy Heart*, by Marcia Powers.

How to Contact Accepts unsolicited mss. Query with SASE or submit 3 sample chapter(s), synopsis or submit complete ms. Accepts queries by e-mail. Responds in 2 months to queries. Accepts simultaneous submissions.

Terms Pays standard royalty. Offers advance. Publishes ms 6 months after acceptance. Ms guidelines online.

Advice "We are vitally interested in all new material we receive. Just as you hopefully submit your manuscript for publication, we hopefully read every one submitted, searching for those that we believe will be successful in the marketplace. Writing and publishing must be a team effort. We need you to write what we can sell. We suggest that you read the successful books mentioned above or others that are similar: *Greatest Salesman in the World*, *Illusions*, *Way of the Peaceful Warrior*, *Celestine Prophecy*. Analyze them to discover what elements make them winners. Duplicate those elements in your own style, using a creative new approach and fresh material, and you will have written a book we can successfully market."

Ø WIND RIVER PRESS

E-mail: submissions@windriverpress.com. Web site: www.windriverpress.com. **Contact:** Katherine Arline, editor (mainstream, travel, literary, historical, short story collections, translations). Estab. 2002. Publishes full and chapbook length paperback originals and reprints and electronic books. "Wind River Press works closely with the author to develop a cost-effective production, promotion and distribution strategy."

Needs Historical, literary, mainstream/contemporary, short story collections. Plans anthology of works selected from Wind River Press's magazines (*Critique* and *The Paumanok Review*). Recently published books by Elisha Porat, Gaither Stewart and Rochelle Mass.

How to Contact Accepts unsolicited mss. Accepts queries by e-mail. Include estimated word count, brief bio, list of publishing credits. Agented fiction 5%. Responds in 3 weeks to queries; 2 months to mss. Accepts simultaneous submissions. Always comments on rejected mss.

Terms Individual arrangement depending on book formats and target audience. Publishes ms 6 months after acceptance. Guidelines and book catalog available on Web site.

WINDRIVER PUBLISHING, INC.

72 N. Windriver Road, Silverton ID 83867-0446. (208)752-1836. Fax: (208)752-1876. E-mail: info@windriverpublishing.com. Web site: www.windriverpublishing.com. Estab. 2003. Publishes hardcover originals and reprints, trade paperback originals, mass market originals. Averages 8 total titles/year.

Needs Adventure, fantasy, historical, humor, juvenile, literary, military/war, mystery, religious, science fiction, spiritual, suspense, young adult.

How to Contact Responds in 2 months to queries; 4-6 months to mss. Accepts simultaneous submissions.

Terms Pays 8-15% royalty on wholesale price. Publishes ms 12-18 months after acceptance. Ms guidelines online.

⃝ ⃝ WIZARDS OF THE COAST

P.O. Box 707, Renton WA 98057-0707. (425)226-6500. Web site: www.wizards.com. **Contact:** Peter Archer, editorial director. "We publish shared-world fiction set in the worlds of Dungeons & Dragons, Magic: The Gathering. We also publish young reader ficiton, in such series as Knights of the Silver Dragon, and select speculative fiction." Publishes hardcover and trade paperback originals and trade paperback reprints. Wizards of the Coast publishes games as well, including Dungeons & Dragons role-playing game. Books: standard paperbacks; offset printing; perfect binding; b&w (usually) illustrations. Averages 50-60 total titles/year. Distributes titles through Holtzbrinck Publishing.

Imprint(s) Dragonlance Books; Forgotten Realms Books; Magic: The Gathering Books; Mirrorstone Books.

Needs Fantasy, short story collections. "We currently publish work-for-hire novels set in our trademarked worlds. No violent or gory fantasy or science fiction." Recently published *Empire of Blood*, by Richard A. Knaak; *Promise of the Witch-King*, by R.A. Salvatore (fantasy); *Resurrection*, by Paul S. Kemp.

How to Contact Agented fiction 65%. Responds in 4 months to queries. Accepts simultaneous submissions.

Terms Pays 4-8% royalty on retail price. Average advance: $4,000-6,000. Publishes ms 1 year after acceptance. Ms guidelines for #10 SASE.

⃝ ⃝ WOODLEY MEMORIAL PRESS

English Dept., Washburn University, Topeka KS 66621. (785)234-1032. E-mail: paul.fecteau@washburn.edu. Web site: www.washburn.edu/reference/woodley-press. **Contact:** Paul Fecteau, corresponding editor. Estab. 1980. "Woodley Memorial Press is a small, nonprofit press which publishes book-length poetry and fiction collections by Kansas writers only; by 'Kansas writers' we mean writers who reside in Kansas or have a Kansas connection." Publishes paperback originals.

Needs Literary, mainstream/contemporary, short story collections. Published *Great Blues*, by Steve Semken; *The Trouble With Campus Security*, by G.W. Clift; and *Loading The Stone*, by Harley Elliot.

How to Contact Accepts unsolicited mss. Accepts queries by e-mail. Responds in 2 weeks to queries; 3 months to mss. Often comments on rejected mss.

Terms Publishes ms 1 year after acceptance. Ms guidelines online.

Advice "We only publish one work of fiction a year, on average, and definitely want it to be by a Kansas author. We are more likely to do a collection of short stories by a single author."

⃝ ⃝ ⃝ ⃝ WORLDWIDE LIBRARY

Division of Harlequin Enterprises Limited, 225 Duncan Mill Rd., Don Mills ON M3B 3K9 Canada. (416)445-5860. Fax: (416)445-8655/8736. **Contact:** Feroze Mohammed, executive editor. Estab. 1979. Large commercial category line. Publishes paperback originals and reprints. "Mystery program is reprint; no originals please."

Imprint(s) Worldwide Mystery; Gold Eagle.

Needs "Action-adventure series and future fiction."

How to Contact Send SASE or IRC. Responds in 10 weeks to queries. Accepts simultaneous submissions.

Terms Advance and sometimes royalties; copyright buyout. Publishes ms 1-2 years after acceptance.

Advice "Publishing fiction in very selective areas."

⃝ ⃝ ⃝ WRITERS DIRECT

Imprint of Titlewaves Publishing, Book Division of H&S Publishing LLC, 1579 Kuhio Highway Suite 104, Kapaa HI 96746. (808)822-7449. Fax: (808)822-2312. E-mail: sales@hshawaii.com. Web site: www.bestplacesonearth.com. **Contact:** Rob Sanford, editor. Estab. 1985. "Small independent publishing house founded and run by published authors." Publishes hardcover and paperback orginals and reprints. Books: recycled paper; digital printing; perfect binding; illustrations.

Needs Adventure, humor, literary, mainstream/contemporary, new age/mystic, regional (Hawaii), inspirational, religious mystery/suspense, religious thriller, thriller/espionage.

How to Contact Send 1st chapter and synopsis. Include estimated word count, why author wrote book and marketing plan. Send SASE for return of ms or send a disposable ms and SASE for reply only. Responds in 1

month to queries; 3 months to mss. Accepts simultaneous submissions. Sometimes comments on rejected mss.
Terms Pays 15-35% royalty. Book catalog for legal-size SASE.
Advice "Do what you do best and enjoy most. Your writing is an outcome of the above."

☐ YELLOW SHOE FICTION SERIES

Louisiana State University Press, P.O. Box 25053, Baton Rouge LA 70894-5053. Web site: www.lsu.edu/lsupress.
Contact: Michael Griffith, editor. Estab. 2004. Literary fiction series. Averages 1 title/year.
Needs Literary. "Looking first and foremost for literary excellence, especially good manuscripts that have fallen through the cracks at the big commercial presses. I'll cast a wide net." Published *If the Sky Falls,* by Nicholas Montemarano.
How to Contact Does not accept unsolicited mss. Accepts queries by mail. No electronic submissions.
Terms Pays royalty. Offers advance. Ms guidelines online.

Contests & Awards

In addition to honors and, quite often, cash prizes, contests and awards programs offer writers the opportunity to be judged on the basis of quality alone without the outside factors that sometimes influence publishing decisions. New writers who win contests may be published for the first time, while more experienced writers may gain public recognition of an entire body of work.

Listed here are contests for almost every type of fiction writing. Some focus on form, such as short stories, novels or novellas, while others feature writing on particular themes or topics. Still others are prestigious prizes or awards for work that must be nominated, such as the Pulitzer Prize in Fiction. Chances are no matter what type of fiction you write, there is a contest or award program that may interest you.

SELECTING AND SUBMITTING TO A CONTEST

Use the same care in submitting to contests as you would sending your manuscript to a publication or book publisher. Deadlines are very important, and where possible, we've included this information. At times contest deadlines were only approximate at our press deadline, so be sure to write, call or look online for complete information.

Follow the rules to the letter. If, for instance, contest rules require your name on a cover sheet only, you will be disqualified if you ignore this and put your name on every page. Find out how many copies to send. If you don't send the correct amount, by the time you are contacted to send more, it may be past the submission deadline. An increasing number of contests invite writers to query by e-mail, and many post contest information on their Web sites. Check listings for e-mail and Web site addresses.

One note of caution: Beware of contests that charge entry fees that are disproportionate to the amount of the prize. Contests offering a $10 prize, but charging $7 in entry fees, are a waste of your time and money.

If you are interested in a contest or award that requires your publisher to nominate your work, it's acceptable to make your interest known. Be sure to leave the publisher plenty of time, however, to make the nomination deadline.

"BEST OF OHIO WRITER" CONTEST

Ohio Writer Magazine, 12200 Fairhill Rd., Townhouse #3A, Cleveland OH 44120. (216)421-0403. Fax: (216)421-8874. E-mail: pwlgc@yahoo.com. Web site: www.pwlgc.com. **Contact:** Darlene Montonaro, executive director. Award "to promote and encourage the work of writers in Ohio." Prize: $150, $50. Judged by "a selected panel of prominent Ohio writers." Entry fee: $15, which includes 1-yr. subscription to the magazine. Deadline: July 31. Entries must be unpublished. Ohio residents only. Guidelines available after January 1 for SASE or e-mail. Accepts inquiries by e-mail and phone. Length: 2,500 words, "No cliché plots; we're looking for fresh unpublished voices." Results announced November 1. Winners notified by mail. For contest results, send SASE or e-mail after November 1.

AIM MAGAZINE SHORT STORY CONTEST

P.O. Box 1174, Maywood IL 60153-8174. (708)344-4414. E-mail: apiladoone@aol.com. Web site: www.aimmagazine.org. **Contact:** Ruth Apilado, associate editor. $100 prize offered to contest winner for best unpublished short story (4,000 words maximum) "promoting brotherhood among people and cultures." Judged by staff members. No entry fee. Deadline: August 15. Competition receives 20 submissions per category. Guidelines available anytime. Accepts inquiries by e-mail and phone. Winners are announced in the autumn issue and notified by mail on September 1. List of winners available for SASE. Open to any writer.

ALABAMA STATE COUNCIL ON THE ARTS INDIVIDUAL ARTIST FELLOWSHIP

201 Monroe St., Montgomery AL 36130-1800. (334)242-4076, ext. 224. Fax: (334)240-3269. E-mail: randy.shoults@arts.alabama.gov. Web site: www.arts.state.al.us. **Contact:** Randy Shoults, literature program manager. "To recognize the achievements and potential of Alabama writers." Judged by independent peer panel. Guidelines available in January. For guidelines, fax, e-mail, visit Web site. Accepts inquiries by fax, e-mail and phone. "Two copies of the following should be submitted: a résumé and a list of published works with reviews, if available. A minimum of 10 pages of poetry or prose, but no more than 20 pages. Please label each page with title, artist's name and date. If published, indicate where and the date of publication." Winners announced in June and notified by mail. List of winners available for SASE, fax, e-mail or visit Web site. No entry fee. Deadline: March. Competition receives 25 submissions annually. Two-year residency required. Open to any writer.

NELSON ALGREN SHORT FICTION CONTEST

Chicago Tribune, Nelson Algren Awards, 435 N. Michigan Ave., LL2, Chicago IL 60611. E-mail: efigula@tribune.com. Web site: about.chicagotribune.com/community/literaryawards.htm. **Contact:** Erin Figula, senior marketing specialist. "Honors excellence in short story writing by previously unpublished authors." Prize: $5,000 grand prize, $1,500 runners-up prizes (3). Judged by a group of *Chicago Tribune* editors and contributors. No entry fee. Cover letter should include name, address, phone, e-mail, word count, title. "No info on manuscript besides title and page numbers." Results announced October. Winners notified by mail or phone in September. For contest results, visit Web site or in the *Chicago Tribune*. Deadline: February 28. Entries must be unpublished. Competition for short stories. Open to any writer. Guidelines also available by e-mail and on Web site. Accepts inquiries by e-mail.

AMERICAN ASSOCIATION OF UNIVERSITY WOMEN AWARD IN JUVENILE LITERATURE

North Carolina Literary and Historical Association, 4610 Mail Service Center, Raleigh NC 27699-4610. (919)807-7290. Fax: (919)733-8807. E-mail: michael.hill@ncmail.net. **Contact:** Michael Hill, awards coordinator. Award's purpose is to "select the year's best work of literature for young people by a North Carolina writer." Annual award for published books. Award: cup. Competition receives 10-15 submissions per category. Judged by three-judge panel. No entry fee. Deadline: July 15. Entries must be previously published. Contest open to "residents of North Carolina (three-year minimum)." Guidelines available July 15. For guidelines, send SASE, fax, e-mail or call. Accepts inquiries by fax, e-mail, phone. Winners announced October 15. Winners notified by mail. List of winners available for SASE, fax, e-mail.

AMERICAN MARKETS NEWSLETTER SHORT STORY COMPETITION

American Markets Newsletter, 1974 46th Ave., San Francisco CA 94116. E-mail: sheila.oconnor@juno.com. Award is "to give short story writers more exposure." Accepts fiction and nonfiction up to 2,000 words. Entries are eligible for cash prizes and all entries are eligible for worldwide syndication whether they win or not. Send double-spaced manuscripts with your story/article title, byline, word count and address on the first page above your article/story's first paragraph (no need for separate cover page). There is no limit to the number of entries you may send. Prize: 1st Place: $300; 2nd Place: $100; 3rd Place: $50. Judged by a panel of independent judges. Entry fee: $10 per entry; $15 for 2; $20 for 3; $23 for 4; $4 each entry thereafter. For guidelines, send SASE, fax or e-mail. Deadline:

June 30 and December 31. Contest offered biannually. Published and unpublished stories are actively encouraged. Add a note of where and when previously published. Open to any writer. "All kinds of fiction are considered. We especially want women's pieces—romance, with a twist in the tale—but all will be considered." Results announced within 3 months of deadlines. Winners notified by mail if they include SASE.

◖ THE SHERWOOD ANDERSON FOUNDATION FICTION AWARD

The Sherwood Anderson Foundation, 216 College Rd., Richmond VA 23229. (804)289-8324. Fax: (804)287-6052. E-mail: mspear@richmond.edu. Web site: www.richmond.edu/~mspear/sahome.html. **Contact:** Michael M. Spear, foundation co-president. Contest is "to honor, preserve and celebrate the memory and literary work of Sherwood Anderson, American realist for the first half of the 20th century." Annual award for short stories and chapters of novels to "encourage and support developing writers." Entrants must have published at least 1 book of fiction or have had several short stories published in major literary and/or commercial publications. Do not send your work by e-mail. Only mss in English will be accepted. Prize: $15,000 grant. Judged by a committee established by the foundation. Entry fee: $20 application fee (payable to The Sherwood Anderson Foundation). Deadline: April 1. Send a detailed résumé that provides a bibliography of your publications. Self-published stories do not qualify. Include a cover letter that provides a history of your writing experience and your future plans for writing projects. Also, submit 2 or 3 examples of what you consider to be your best work. Open to any writer. Accepts inquiries by e-mail. Mail your application to the above address. No mss or publications will be returned. "Send in your best, most vivid prose that clearly shows talent."

◨ ◪ ◉ ANNUAL ATLANTIC WRITING COMPETITION

Writer's Federation of Nova Scotia, 1113 Marginal Road, Halifax NS B3H 4P7 Canada. (902)423-8116. Fax: (902)422-0881. E-mail: talk@writers.ns.ca. Web site: www.writers.ns.ca. **Contact:** Susan Mersereau, executive assistant. Award's purpose is "to provide feedback to emerging writers and create a venue for their work to be considered against that of other beginning authors. Annual award to residents of Atlantic Canada for short stories and novels as well as children's literature, YA novels, poetry and essay." Prize: In Canadian money: $200, $150, $100 for adult novel; $150, $75, $50 for children's literature and YA novel; $100, $75, $50 for short stories and essay/magazine article. Judged by a jury of professionals from the writing/literature field—authors, librarians, publishers, teachers. Entry fee: $25 per novel entry ($20 for WFNS members); $15 per entry in other categories ($10 members). Deadline: first Friday in December of each year. Entries must be unpublished. Length: story 3,000 words maximum; novel 100,000 words maximum; children's writing 20,000 words maximum, YA novel 75,000 words maximum. Writers must use pseudonym; use $8^1/_2 \times 11$ white paper; and format entry typed and double-spaced. To be eligible, writers must be residents of Atlantic Canada, older than 16 and not extensively published in the category they are entering. Guidelines available by SASE or on website. Accepts inquiries by e-mail, phone. Winners announced in March. Winners notified by mail in late February. List of winners available on Web site.

◨ ◉ ANNUAL BOOK COMPETITION

Washington Writers' Publishing House, Elisavietta Ritchie, P.O Box 298, Broomes Island MD 20615. E-mail: megan@bcps.org. Web site: www.wwph.org. **Contact:** Moira Egan, president. "To award literary excellence in the greater Washington DC-Baltimore area." Annual. Competition/award for novels, story collections. Prize: $500, publication, and 50 copies of book. Categories: fiction (novel or collection of short stories). Receives about 50 entries per category. Judged by members of the press. Entry fee: $25. Make checks payable to WWPH. Guidelines available all year with SASE, on Web site. Accepts inquiries by e-mail. Deadline: Nov. 1. Entries should be unpublished. "Individual stories or excerpts may have been published in journals and anthologies." Open to fiction writers living within 60 miles of the Capitol (Baltimore area included). Length: no more than 350 pages, double or $1^1/_2$ spaced. Cover letter should include name, address, phone, e-mail, novel/collection title, place(s) where stories/excerpts were previously published. None of this information should appear on the actual manuscript. Writers may submit own work. Results announced January of each year. Winners notified by phone, by e-mail. Results made available to entrants on Web site.

◗ ANNUAL FICTION CONTEST

Women in the Arts, P.O. Box 2907, Decatur IL 62524. (217)872-0811. **Contact:** Vice President. Annual competition for essays, fiction, fiction for children, plays, rhymed poetry, unrhymed poetry. Prize: $50, $35, $15 in all categories. Categories: Essay (up to 1,500 words); fiction (up to 1,500 words); fiction for children (up to 1,500 words); play (one act, 10-page limit); rhymed and unrhymed poetry (up to 32 lines). Judged by published, professional writers who live outside the state of Illinois. All entries will be subject to blind judging. Entry fee: $2 per entry, unlimited entries. Deadline: November 1. Do not submit drawings for any category. Double-space prose. Entries must be typed on $8^1/_2 \times 11$ paper and must be titled. Do not put your name on any page of the ms. Do put your name, address, telephone number, e-mail and titles of your entries on a cover sheet. Submit one cover sheet and one check, with all entries mailed flat in one envelope. Do not staple. No entries published by WITA, author retains rights. Open to any writer. Results announced March 15 annually. Winners notified by mail. "Send a perfect manuscript—no typos, Liquid Paper or holes from 3-ring binders."

◎ ANNUAL JUVENILE FICTION CONTEST

Women in the Arts, P.O. Box 2907, Decatur IL 62524. (217)872-0811. **Contact:** Vice President. Annual competition for essays, fiction, fiction for children, plays, rhymed poetry, unrhymed poetry. Prize: $15-$50. Judged by anonymous judges who are published, professional writers who live outside Illinois. Entry fee: $2 per entry. Word length: 1,500 maximum for fiction, essay, fiction for children; one act for plays; up to 32 lines for poetry. Deadline: November 1. Entries must be original work of the author. Entries must be typed on $8^{1}/_{2} \times 11$ white paper and must be titled. Do not put your name on any page of the entry. Instead, put your name, address, telephone number, e-mail and titles of your entries on a cover sheet. Submit one cover sheet and one check. Mail all entries flat in a single envelope. Do not staple. Open to any writer. "Entrants must send for contest rules and follow the specific format requirements."

◨ ◻ ANNUAL POETRY & FICTION COMPETITIONS

Inkwell, Manhattanville College, 2900 Purchase St., Box 1379, Purchase NY 10577. (914)323-7239. E-mail: inkwell@mville.org. Web site: www.inkwelljournal.org. **Contact:** Editor. Annual. Competition/award for short stories. Prize: $1,500 for fiction, $1,000 for poetry. Categories: fiction and poetry. Receives about 500 (fiction) and 1,000 (poetry) entries per category. Judged by different judges every year. Entry fee: $15 per story. Make checks payable to Manhattanville—Inkwell. Guidelines available in May/June on Web site. Accepts inquiries by e-mail. Submission period: August 1-October 31. Entries should be unpublished. Length: 6,000 words (fiction). Cover letter should include name, address, phone, e-mail, word count, novel/story title. None of this information should appear on the manuscript. Writers may submit own work. Winners notified by mail, by phone, by e-mail, on Web site. Results made available to entrants with SASE, on Web site.

◻ ANTIETAM REVIEW ANNUAL LITERARY AWARD

Antietam Review, 14 West Washington Street, Hagerstown MD 21740. (301)791-3132. Fax: (240)420-1754. E-mail: antietamreview@washingtoncountyarts.com (for queries only). Web site: www.washingtoncountyarts.com. **Contact:** Philip Bufithis, executive editor. Review estab. 1982. Circ. 1,000. To encourage and give recognition to excellence in short fiction and poetry. Prize: $150 for selected prose and $100 for selected poem. Both categories receive two copies of magazine. Categories: "Fiction: Contributors may submit only 1 entry with fewer than 5,000 words. Editors seek high quality, well-crafted work with significant character development and shift. A manuscript stands out because of its energy and flow. Short stories are preferred; however, novel excerpts are considered if they work as independent pieces. Poetry: Up to three poems with no more than 30 lines. No haiku, religious or rhyme." Entry fee: $15 for fiction (three poems considered one fee); check, credit card and money orders accepted. Entries must be unpublished. Open to any writer.

◎ THE ART OF MUSIC ANNUAL WRITING CONTEST

Piano Press, P.O. Box 85, Del Mar CA 92014-0085. (619)884-1401. Fax: (858)755-1104. E-mail: pianopress@pianopress.com. Web site: www.pianopress.com. **Contact:** Elizabeth C. Axford. Offered annually. Categories are: essay, short story, poetry and song lyrics. All writings must be on music-related topics. The purpose of the contest is to promote the art of music through writing. Acquires one-time rights. All entries must be accompanied by an entry form indicating category and age; parent signature is required of all writers under age 18. Poems may be of any length and in any style; essays and short stories should not exceed five double-spaced, typewritten pages. All entries shall be previously unpublished (except poems and song lyrics) and the original work of the author. Guidelines and entry form for SASE, on Web site or by e-mail. Prize: Cash, medal, certificate, publication in the biannual anthology/chapbook titled *The Art of Music: A Collection of Writings*, and copies of the book. Judged by a panel of published poets, authors and songwriters. Entry fee: $20 fee. Inquiries accepted by fax, e-mail, phone. Deadline: June 30. Short stories should be no longer than five pages typed and double spaced. Open to any writer. "Make sure all work is fresh and original. Music-related topics only." Results announced October 31. Winners notified by mail. For contest results, send SASE or visit Web site.

◪ ◎ THE ATHENAEUM LITERARY AWARD

The Athenaeum of Philadelphia, 219 S. Sixth St., Philadelphia PA 19106-3794. (215)925-2688. Fax: (215)925-3755. E-mail: erose@PhilaAthenaeum.org. Web site: www.PhilaAthenaeum.org. **Contact:** Ellen L. Rose, circulation director. Annual award to recognize and encourage outstanding literary achievement in Philadelphia and its vicinity. Prize: a certificate bearing the name of the award, the seal of the Athenaeum, the title of the book, the name of the author and the year. Categories: The Athenaeum Literary Award is granted for a work of general literature, not exclusively for fiction. Judged by a committee appointed by the Board of Directors. No entry fee.

Deadline: December. Entries must be previously published. Nominations shall be made in writing to the Literary Award Committee by the author, the publisher, or a member of the Athenaeum, accompanied by a copy of the book. Open to work by residents of Philadelphia and its vicinity. Guidelines available for SASE, by fax, by e-mail and on Web site. Accepts inquiries by fax, e-mail and phone. Juvenile fiction is not included. Results announced in Spring. Winners notified by mail. For contest results, see Web site.

AWP AWARD SERIES IN THE NOVEL, CREATIVE NONFICTION AND SHORT FICTION

The Association of Writers & Writing Programs, Mail Stop 1E3, George Mason University, Fairfax VA 22030. (703)993-4301. Fax: (703)993-4302. E-mail: awp@awpwriter.org. Web site: www.awpwriter.org. **Contact:** Supriya Bhatnagar, director of publications. The AWP Award Series was established in cooperation with several university presses in order to publish and make fine fiction and nonfiction available to a wide audience. Offered annually to foster new literary talent. Guidelines for SASE and on Web site. Categories: novel ($2,000), Donald Hall Prize in Poetry ($4,000), Grace Paley Prize in Short Fiction ($4,000), and creative nonfiction ($2,000). Entry fee: $20 for nonmembers, $10 for members. Entries must be unpublished. Mss must be postmarked between January 1-February 28. Cover letter should include name, address, phone number, e-mail and title. ''This information should appear in cover letter only.'' Open to any writer. Guidelines available on Web site in November. No phone calls, please. Manuscripts published previously in their entirety, including self-publishing, are not eligible. No mss returned. Results announced in August. Winners notified by mail or phone. For contest results send SASE, or visit Web site. No phone calls, please.

AWP INTRO JOURNALS PROJECT

Dept. of English, Bluffton University, 1 University Drive, Bluffton OH 45817-2104. E-mail: awp@gmu.edu. Web site: www.awpwriter.org. **Contact:** Jeff Gundy. ''This is a prize for students in AWP member university creative writing programs only. Authors are nominated by the head of the creative writing department. Each school may nominate no more than one work of nonfiction, one work of short fiction and three poems.'' Prize: $100 plus publication in participating journal. 2006 journals included *Puerto del Sol*, *Quarterly West*, *Mid-American Review*, *Willow Springs*, *Tampa Review*, *Controlled Burn*, *Artful Dodge* and *Hayden's Ferry Review*. Categories: Short stories, nonfiction and poetry. Judged by AWP. No entry fee. Deadline: December 1. Entries must be unpublished. Open to students in AWP Member University Creative Writing Programs only. Accepts inquiries by e-mail, fax and phone. Guidelines available for SASE or on Web site. Results announced in Spring. Winners notified by mail in Spring. For contest results, send SASE or visit Web site.

BARD FICTION PRIZE

Bard College, P.O. Box 5000, Annandale-on-Hudson NY 12504-5000. (845)758-7087. Fax: (845)758-7043. E-mail: bfp@bard.edu. Web site: www.bard.edu/bfp. **Contact:** Irene Zedlacher. The Bard Fiction Prize is intended to encourage and support young writers of fiction to pursue their creative goals and to provide an opportunity to work in a fertile and intellectual environment. Prize: $30,000 cash award and appointment as writer-in-residence at Bard College for 1 semester. Judged by committee of 5 judges (authors associated with Bard College). No entry fee. Cover letter should include name, address, phone, e-mail and name of publisher where book was previously published. Guidelines available by SASE, fax, phone, e-mail or on Web site. Deadline: July 15. Entries must be previously published. Open to US citizens aged 39 and below. Accepts inquiries by fax, e-mail and phone. Results announced by October 15. Winners notified by phone. For contest results, e-mail or visit Web site.

GEORGE BENNETT FELLOWSHIP

Phillips Exeter Academy, 20 Main St., Exeter NH 03833-2460. Web site: www.exeter.edu. Annual award for fellow and family ''to provide time and freedom from material considerations to a person seriously contemplating or pursuing a career as a writer. Applicants should have a manuscript in progress which they intend to complete during the fellowship period.'' Duties: To be in residency for the academic year; to make oneself available informally to students interested in writing. Guidelines for SASE or on Web site. The committee favors writers who have not yet published a book with a major publisher. Residence at the Academy during the fellowship period required. Prize: $10,000 stipend, room and board. Judged by committee of the English department. No entry fee. Application form and guidelines for SASE and on Web site. Deadline: December 1. Results announced in March. Winners notified by letter or phone. List of winners available in March. All entrants will receive an announcement of the winner. ''Stay within a few pages of the limit. (We won't read more anyway.) Trust us to recognize that what you are sending is a work in progress. (You have the chance to talk about that in your statement.) Hope, but don't expect anything. If you don't win, some well-known writers have been in your shoes—at least as many as have won the fellowship.''

N ◎ BEST LESBIAN EROTICA

Cleis Press, P.O. Box 4108, Grand Central Station, New York NY 10163. E-mail: tristan@puckerup.com. **Contact:** Tristan Taormino, series editor. Categories: Novel excerpts, short stories, other prose; poetry will be considered but is not encouraged. No entry fee. Include cover page with author's name, title of submission(s), address, phone, fax, e-mail. All submissions must be typed and double-spaced. Also number the pages. Length: 5,000 words. You may submit a maximum of 3 different pieces of work. Submit 2 hard copies of each submission. No e-mail submissions will be accepted; accepts inquiries by e-mail. Accepts both previously published and unpublished material. Open to any writer. All submissions must include SASE or an e-mail address for response. No mss will be returned.

◎ BINGHAMTON UNIVERSITY JOHN GARDNER FICTION BOOK AWARD

Binghamton Center for Writers, State University of New York, P.O. Box 6000, Binghamton NY 13902. (607)777-2713. Fax: (607)777-2408. E-mail: cwpro@binghamton.edu. Web site: english.binghamton.edu/cwpro. **Contact:** Maria Mazziotti Gillan, director. Award's purpose is "to serve the literary community by calling attention to outstanding books of fiction." Prize: $1,000. Categories: novels and short story collections. Judged by "rotating outside judges." No entry fee. Entry must have been published in book form with a minimum press run of 500. Each book submitted must be accompanied by an application form, available online or send SASE to above address. Submit three copies of the book; copies will not be returned. Publishers may submit more than one book for prize consideration. Deadline: March 1. Entries must have appeared in print between January 1 and December 31 of the year preceding the award. Open to any writer. Results announced in Summer. Winners notified by e-mail or phone. For contest results, send SASE or visit Web site.

◎ ◎ IRMA S. AND JAMES H. BLACK AWARD

Bank Street College of Education, 610 W. 112th St., New York NY 10025. (212)875-4450. Fax: (212)875-4558. E-mail: lindag@bnkst.edu. Web site: streetcat.bnkst.edu/html/isb.html. **Contact:** Linda Greengrass, award director. Offered annually for a book for young children, for excellence of both text and illustrations. Entries must have been published during the previous calendar year. Prize: press function and scroll and seals by Maurice Sendak for attaching to award winner's book run. Judged by adult children's literature experts and children 6-10 years old. No entry fee. Guidelines for SASE, fax, e-mail or on Web site. Accepts inquiries by phone, fax, e-mail. Deadline: December 15. Entries must be previously published. "Write to address above. Usually publishers submit books they want considered, but individuals can too. No entries are returned." Winners notified by phone in April and announced in May. A list of winners will be available on Web site.

⊕ ◎ JAMES TAIT BLACK MEMORIAL PRIZES

Department of English Literature, University of Edinburgh, David Hume Tower, George Square, Edinburgh Scotland EH8 9JX United Kingdom. (44-13)1650-3619. Fax: (44-13)1650-6898. E-mail: s.strathdee@ed.ac.uk. Web site: www.englit.ed.ac.uk/jtbinf.htm. **Contact:** Sheila Strathdee, Department of English Literature. "Two prizes each of £10,000 are awarded: one for the best work of fiction, one for the best biography or work of that nature, published during the calendar year January 1 to December 31." Judged by the professor of English Literature. No entry fee. Guidelines available September 30. Accepts inquiries by fax, e-mail, phone. Deadline: January 31. Entries must be previously published. "Eligible works are those written in English and first published or co-published in Britain in the year of the award. Works should be submitted by publishers." Open to any writer. Winners notified by phone, via publisher. Contact department of English Literature for list of winners or check Web site.

◎ BLACK WARRIOR REVIEW FICTION CONTEST

Black Warrior Review, P.O. Box 862936, Tuscaloosa AL 35486. Web site: www.webdelsol.com/bwr. **Contact:** Fiction Contest. Prize: $1,000 and publication in Spring issue. All entrants receive 1-yr subscription to journal. Entry fee: $15 per short story. Make checks payable to the University of Alabama. Send name, phone number, e-mail, SASE and reading fee with ms. Deadline: October 1. Entries must be unpublished. Open to any writer. Winners announced in December.

◎ THE BRIAR CLIFF POETRY, FICTION & CREATIVE NONFICTION COMPETITION

The Briar Cliff Review, Briar Cliff University, 3303 Rebecca St., Sioux City IA 51104-0100. (712)279-5321. Fax: (712)279-5410. E-mail: curranst@briarcliff.edu. Web site: www.briarcliff.edu/bcreview. **Contact:** Tricia Currans-Sheehan, editor. Award "to reward good writers and showcase quality writing." Offered annually for unpublished poem, story and essay. Prize: $500, and publication in Spring issue. All entrants receive a copy of the magazine with winning entries. Judged by editors. "We guarantee a considerate reading." Entry fee: $15. Guidelines available in August for SASE. Inquiries accepted by e-mail. Deadline: Submissions between August 1 and November 1. No mss returned. Entries must be unpublished. Length: 6,000 words maximum. Open to any writer. Results announced in December or January. Winners notified by phone or letter around December 20. For contest results, send SASE with submission. "Send us your best. We want stories with a plot."

🌐 ▢ THE BRIDPORT PRIZE

Bridport Arts Centre, South Street, Bridport, Dorset DT6 3NR United Kingdom. (01308)485064. Fax: (01308)485120. E-mail: frances@poorton.demon.co.uk. Web site: www.bridportprize.org.uk. **Contact:** Frances Everitt, administrator. Award to "promote literary excellence, discover new talent." Prize: £5,000 sterling; £1,000 sterling; £500 sterling, plus various runners-up prizes and publication of approximately 10 best stories in anthology. Categories: short stories and poetry. Judged by 1 judge for fiction (in 2006, Jane Gardam) and 1 judge for poetry (in 2006, Lavinia Greenlaw). Entry fee: £6 sterling for each entry. Deadline: June 30. Entries must be unpublished. Length: 5,000 maximum for short stories; 42 lines for poetry. Open to any writer. Guidelines available in January for SASE or visit Web site. Accepts inquiries by fax, e-mail, phone. Results announced in November of year of contest. Winners notified by phone or mail in September. For contest results, send SASE.

🔁 ◎ BURNABY WRITERS' SOCIETY CONTEST

Burnaby Writers' Society, 6584 Deer Lake Ave., Burnaby BC V5G 3T7 Canada. E-mail: info@bws.bc.ca. Web site: www.bws.bc.ca. Offered annually for unpublished work. Open to all residents of British Columbia. Categories vary from year to year. Send SASE for current rules. Purpose is to encourage talented writers in all genres. Prize: 1st Place: $200; 2nd Place: $100; 3rd Place: $50; and public reading. Entry fee: $5. Guidelines available by e-mail, for SASE or on Web site. Accepts inquiries by e-mail. Deadline: May 31. Results announced in September. Winners notified by mail, phone, e-mail. Results available for SASE or on Web site.

◎ BUSH ARTIST FELLOWS PROGRAM

Bush Foundation, 332 Minnesota St., Suite E-900, St. Paul MN 55101. Fax: (651)297-6485. E-mail: kpolley@bush foundation.org. Web site: www.bushfoundation.org. **Contact:** Kathi Polley, program assistant. Award to "provide artists with significant financial support that enables them to further their work and their contributions to their communities. Fellows may decide to take time for solitary work or reflection, engage in collaborative or community projects, or embark on travel or research." Prize: $48,000 for 12-24 months. Categories: fiction, creative nonfiction, poetry. Judged by a panel of artists and arts professionals who reside outside of Minnesota, South Dakota, North Dakota or Wisconsin. No entry fee. Applications available in August. Accepts inquiries by fax and e-mail. Applicants must be at least 25 years old, U.S. citizens or Permanent Residents, and residents of Minnesota, South Dakota, North Dakota or Western Wisconsin. Students not eligible. Open to any writer. Must meet certain publication requirements. Results announced in Spring. Winners notified by letter. List of winners available in May and sent to all applicants.

▢ ◎ BYLINE MAGAZINE AWARDS

P.O. Box 5240, Edmond OK 73083-5240. (405)348-5591. E-mail: mpreston@bylinemag.com. Web site: www.byl inemag.com. **Contact:** Marcia Preston, award director. Several monthly contests, open to anyone, in various categories that include fiction, nonfiction, poetry and children's literature; a semi-annual poetry chapbook award which is open to any poet; and an annual *ByLine* Short Fiction and Poetry Award open only to our subscribers. For chapbook award and subscriber awards, publication constitutes part of the prize; winners grant first North American rights to *ByLine*. Prize: for monthly contests, cash and listing in magazine; for chapbook award, publication of chapbook, 50 copies and $200; for *ByLine* Short Fiction and Poetry Award, $250 in each category, plus publication in the magazine. Entry fee: $3-5 for monthly contests and $15 for chapbook contest. Deadline: varies. Entries must be unpublished.

🌐 ▣ ◎ THE CAINE PRIZE FOR AFRICAN WRITING

51a Southwark St., London England SE1 1RU United Kingdom. E-mail: info@caineprize.com. Web site: www.ca ineprize.com. **Contact:** Nick Elam, administrator. Annual award for a short story (3,000-15,000 words) by an African writer. "An 'African writer' is normally taken to mean someone who was born in Africa, who is a national of an African country, or whose parents are African, and whose work has reflected African sensibilities." Entries must have appeared for the first time in the 5 years prior to the closing date for submissions, which is January 31 each year. Publishers should submit 12 copies of the published original with a brief cover note (no pro forma application). Prize: $15,000 (£10,000). Judged by a panel of judges appointed each year. No entry fee. Cover letter should include name, address, phone, e-mail, title and publication where story was previously published. Deadline: January 31. Entries must be previously published. Word length: 3,000-15,000 words. "Manuscripts not accepted. Entries must be submitted in published form." Writer's work is submitted by publisher. Writing must reflect its "African-ness." Results announced in mid-July. Winners notified at event/ banquet. For contest results, send fax, e-mail or visit our Web site.

◉ **JOHN W. CAMPBELL MEMORIAL AWARD FOR BEST SCIENCE FICTION NOVEL OF THE YEAR**
Center for the Study of Science Fiction, English Department, University of Kansas, Lawrence KS 66045. (785)864-3380. Fax: (785)864-1159. E-mail: jgunn@ku.edu. Web site: www.ku.edu/~sfcenter. **Contact:** James Gunn, professor and director. Award to "honor the best science fiction novel of the year." Prize: Certificate. Winners receive tropies and an expense-paid trip to the university to receive their award. Their names are also engraved on a permanent trophy. Categories: novels. Judged by a jury. No entry fee. Deadline: see Web site. Entries must be previously published. Open to any writer. Accepts inquiries by e-mail and fax. "Ordinarily publishers should submit work, but authors have done so when publishers would not. Send for list of jurors." Results announced in July. For contest results, send SASE.

◻ **THE ALEXANDER PATTERSON CAPPON FICTION AWARD**
New Letters, 5101 Rockhill Rd., Kansas City MO 64110. (816)235-1168. Fax: (816)235-2611. Web site: www.newl etters.org. Offered annually for unpublished work to discover and to reward new and upcoming writers. Buys first North American serial rights. Prize: 1st place: $1,500 and publication in a volume of *New Letters*; 1 runner-up will receive a copy of a recent book of poetry or fiction from affiliate BkMk Press. All entries will be given consideration for publication in future issues of *New Letters*. Judged by renowned writers. Previous judges have included Philip Levine, Charles Simic, Joyce Carol Oates, Rosellen Brown, Phillip Lopate, Maxine Kumin. Entry fee: $15 (includes a 1-year subscription to *New Letters*); $10 for each entry after first. Entries in fiction are not to exceed 8,000 words. Send two cover sheets—the first with complete name, address, e-mail/phone, category and title(s); the second with category and title(s) only. Personal information should not appear anywhere else on the entry. Also enclose a stamped, self-addressed postcard if you would like notification of receipt and entry number and an SASE for list of winners. Note that manuscripts will not be returned. Deadline: third week in May. Entries must be unpublished. Simultaneous and multiple submissions welcome. Winners announced mid-September. Open to any writer.

◻ **THE CHELSEA AWARD FOR POETRY AND SHORT FICTION**
P.O. Box 773, Cooper Station, New York NY 10276-0773. E-mail: chelseaassoc@aol.com. **Contact:** Alfredo de Palchi. Prize: $1,000, winning entries published in *Chelsea*, 2 free copies and discount on additional copies. Judged by the editors. Entry fee: $10 (includes free subscription to *Chelsea*). Guidelines available for SASE. Deadline: June 15. Entries must be unpublished. Mss must not exceed 30 typed pages, or about 7,500 words. The stories must not be under consideration elsewhere or scheduled for book publication within 8 months of the competition deadline. Absolutely no simultaneous submissions. Open to any writer. Include separate cover sheet with entrant's name; no name on ms. Mss will not be returned; include SASE for notification of results. Results announced August 15. Winners notified by phone. "Read first what kind of fiction is published in *Chelsea*. No submissions, notification or guidelines will be sent or responded to by e-mail. Read and follow contest guidelines. Manuscripts on which the author's name appears will be destroyed unread."

Ⓝ ◻ ◎ **THE CHRISTOPER AWARDS**
The Christophers, 12 E. 48th St., New York NY 10017-1091. (212)759-4050. Fax: (646)843-1547. E-mail: awardsi nfo@christophers.org. Web site: www.christophers.org. **Contact:** Judith Trojan, program director. Award "to encourage authors and illustrators to continue to produce works which affirm the highest values of the human spirit in adult and children's books." Prize: bronze medallion. Categories: Adult nonfiction and young adult novels and nonfiction. Judged by a panel of juvenile reading and subject experts. Juvenile titles are "children tested." No entry fee. Submission period: June 1 through November 1 every year. Entries must be previously published. Potential winners are nominated and reviewed throughout the year by juvenile book professionals, members of the Christopher staff, and by specially supervised children's reading groups. Open to any writer. For guidelines send 6×9 SASE, e-mail or visit Web site. Inquiries accepted by letter, fax, e-mail and phone. Winners chosen in early January and notified by mail in late January. Awards are presented annually in March at a black tie gala in New York City. For contest results, send SASE, fax or visit Web site. Example of book award: *Love That Dog*, by Sharon Creech (children's book category 2001). "Publishers generally submit fiction/ nonfiction books for young people. Authors and illustrators should familiarize themselves with our awards criteria and encourage their publishers to submit applicable titles."

✠ ◎ **CITY OF TORONTO BOOK AWARDS**
City of Toronto, 100 Queem St. West, City Hall, 10th Floor, West Tower, Toronto ON M9W 3X3 Canada. (416)392-8191. Fax: (416)392-1247. Web site: www.toronto.ca/book_awards. **Contact:** Bev Kurmey, protocol officer. "The Toronto Book Awards honour authors of books of literary or artistic merit that are evocative of Toronto." Categories: short stories, novels, story collections, translations. Judged by committee. No entry fee. Guidelines available by e-mail, on Web site. Accepts inquiries by phone, fax, e-mail. Writers may submit their own fiction. Cover letter should include name, address, phone, e-mail, title. Deadline: Feb. 28. Entries must be

previously published. Books must have been published during the year prior to the award (i.e. in 2006 for the 2007 deadline). Open to any writer. Results announced in Sept., short list in June. Winners notified by mail, e-mail. Results available on Web site.

☐ CNW/FFWA ANNUAL FLORIDA STATE WRITING COMPETITION

% CNW Publishing, Florida Freelance Writers Association, P.O. Box A, North Stratford NH 03590-0167. E-mail: contest@writers-editors.com. Web site: www.writers-editors.com. **Contact:** Dana K. Cassell, executive director. Annual award "to recognize publishable talent." Divisions & Categories: Nonfiction (previously published article/essay/column/nonfiction book chapter; unpublished or self-published article/essay/column/nonfiction book chapter); Fiction (unpublished or self-published short story or novel chapter); Children's Literature (unpublished or self-published short story/nonfiction article/book chapter/poem); Poetry (unpublished or self-published free verse/traditional). Prize: 1st Place: $100, plus certificate; 2nd Place: $75, plus certificate; 3rd Place: $50, plus certificate. Honorable Mention certificates will be awarded in each category as warranted. Judged by editors, librarians and writers. Entry fee: $5 (active or new CNW/FFWA members) or $10 (nonmembers) for each fiction/nonfiction entry under 3,000 words; $10 (members) or $20 (nonmembers) for each entry of 3,000 words or longer; and $3 (members) or $5 (nonmembers) for each poem. Guidelines for SASE or on website. Accepts inquiries by e-mail, phone and mail. Deadline: March 15. Open to any writer. Results announced May 31. Winners notified by mail and posted on Web site. Results available for SASE or visit Web site.

⬛ ◎ CONSEIL DE LA VIE FRANCAISE EN AMERIQUE/PRIX CHAMPLAIN

Conseil de la Vie Francaise en Amerique, Maison de la Francophonie, 39 rue Dalhousie, Quebec City QC G1K 8R8 Canada. (418)646-9117. Fax: (418)644-7670. E-mail: cvfa@cvfa.ca. Web site: www.cvfa.ca. **Contact:** Director General. Award to encourage literary work in novel or short story in French by Francophiles living outside Quebec, in the US or Canada. Prize: $1,500 Canadian. Judged by 3 different judges each year. No entry fee. Deadline: December 31. Entries must be previously published. "There is no restriction as to the subject matter. If the author lives in Quebec, the subject matter must be related to French-speaking people living outside of Quebec." Submissions must have been published no more than 3 years before award. Open to any writer. Guidelines for SASE or IRC or on Web site. Author must furnish 4 examples of work, curriculum vitae, address and phone number.

☐ CRAZYHORSE FICTION PRIZE

College of Charleston, Dept. of English, 66 George St., Charleston SC 29424. (843)953-7740. E-mail: crazyhorse@cofc.edu. Web site: crazyhorse.cofc.edu. **Contact:** Editors. Prize: $2,000 and publication in *Crazyhorse*. Judged by anonymous writer whose identity is disclosed when the winners are announced in April. Past judges: Charles Baxter (2002), Michael Martone (2003), Diana Abu-Jaber (2004), T.M. McNally (2005). Entry fee: $15 (covers 1-yr subscription to *Crazyhorse*; make checks payable to *Crazyhorse*). To enter, please send up to 25 pages of prose. Include a detachable cover sheet with your name, address and telephone number; please do not include this information on the ms itself. Send SASE or see Web site for additional details. Deadline: December 16th of each year; see Web site. Open to any writer.

☐ ◎ CROSSTIME SHORT SCIENCE FICTION CONTEST

Crossquarter Publishing Group, P.O. Box 23749, Santa Fe NM 87502. (505)438-9846. Web site: www.crossquarter.com. **Contact:** Therese Francis, owner. Original short (up to 8,500 words) science fiction stories that demonstrate the best of the human spirit. Stories may be science fiction, fantasy or urban fantasy. No horror. No dystopia. Prize: 1st place: $250 plus publication in next volume of *CrossTIME Anthology*; 2nd place: $125 plus publication in the anthology; 3rd place: $75 plus publication in the anthology; 4th place: $50 plus publication in the anthology; 5th through 15th places: a distinctive certificate honoring their accomplishment plus publication in the anthology. Judges are not required to award all 15 positions; ties are possible. Each entrant will receive one copy of the resulting anthology highlighting the 1st through 15th place winners. Entry fee: $15 for first submission, $10 for each additional submission. The official entry form is required (available online), along with entry fee (check, money order, Visa, Mastercard, American Express). If you are entering more than one ms, you may mail all entries in the same envelope and write one check for the total entry fee. Submission should be typewritten on $8^{1}/_2 \times 11$ white paper. Your name, address, phone number and word count must appear in the upper left-hand corner of the first page. Staple or paperclip the pages together. Team writing is acceptable, but only one copy of the anthology will be sent. The "team leader" should complete the official entry form. Deadline: January 15. Entries must be unpublished. Your entry must be original, unpublished and unproduced, not accepted by any other publisher or producer at the time of submission. However, stories previously printed for copies only or for less than $25 are acceptable, provided all rights have reverted to you. (Example would be school newspapers. Include information on where and when previously published.) Open to any writer. Byline given. Publisher buys all rights for five years (early buy-out negotiable). To receive notification of the receipt of your ms, include self-addressed, stamped postcard.

☐ THE CRUCIBLE POETRY AND FICTION COMPETITION

Crucible, Barton College, College Station, Wilson NC 27893. (252)399-6456. E-mail: tgrimes@barton.edu. **Contact:** Terrence L. Grimes, editor. Offered annually for unpublished short stories. Prize: $150 (1st Prize); $100 (2nd Prize) and publication in *Crucible*. Competition receives 300 entries. Categories: Fiction should be 8,000 words or less. Judged by in-house editorial board. No entry fee. Guidelines available in January for SASE, e-mail or in publication. Deadline: April. Open to any writer. "The best time to submit is December through April." Results announced in July. Winners notified by mail. For contest rules, send e-mail.

☐ DEAD OF WINTER

E-mail: editors@toasted-cheese.com. Web site: www.toasted-cheese.com. **Contact:** Stephanie Lenz, editor. The contest is a winter-themed short fiction contest with a new topic each year. Topic and word limit announced Nov. 1. The topic is usually geared toward a supernatural theme. Prize: Amazon gift certificates in the amount of $25, $15 and $10; publication in *Toasted Cheese*. Also offers honorable mention. Categories: short stories. Judged by two *Toasted Cheese* editors who blind judge each contest. Each judge uses her own criteria to rate entries. No entry fee. Cover letter should include name, address, e-mail, word count and title. Deadline: December 21. Entries must be unpublished. Word limit varies each year. Open to any writer. Guidelines available in November on Web site. Accepts inquiries by e-mail. "Follow guidelines. Write a smart, original story. We have further guidelines on the Web site." Results announced January 31. Winners notified by e-mail. List of winners on Web site.

☐ EATON LITERARY AGENCY'S ANNUAL AWARDS PROGRAM

Eaton Literary Agency, P.O. Box 49795, Sarasota FL 34230. (941)366-6589. Fax: (941)365-4679. E-mail: eatonlit @aol.com. Web site: www.eatonliterary.com. **Contact:** Richard Lawrence, vice president. Offered biannually for unpublished mss. Prize: $2,500 (over 10,000 words); $500 (under 10,000 words). Judged by an independent agency in conjunction with some members of Eaton's staff. No entry fee. Guidelines available for SASE, by fax, e-mail, or on Web site. Accepts inquiries by fax, phone and e-mail. Deadline: March 31 (mss under 10,000 words); August 31 (mss over 10,000 words). Entries must be unpublished. Open to any writer. Results announced in April and September. Winners notified by mail. For contest results, send SASE, fax, e-mail or visit Web site.

⌦ ◘ EMERGING VOICES ROSENTHAL FELLOWSHIP

PEN USA, % Antioch University, 400 Corporate Pointe, Culver City CA 90230. (310)862-1555. Fax: (310)862-1556. E-mail: ev@penusa.org. Web site: www.penusa.org. **Contact:** Leslie Schwartz, program coordinator. "To serve up-and-coming writers from traditionally underserved communities. To help these not-yet-published authors gain the creative and professional skills needed to flourish in the literary world." Annual. Competition/award for short stories, novels, story collections. Prize: $1,000 and 1-yr mentorship wtih established author, plus classes and workshops and the opportunity to meet authors, agents, editors and publishers. Categories: fiction, poetry, creative nonfiction. Receives about 30-60 entries per category. Entries judged by EV selection committee composed of PEN USA board members, former EV fellows and prominent local authors. Entry fee: $10. Make checks payable to PEN USA. Guidelines available in May by phone, on Web site, in publication. Accepts inquiries by e-mail, phone. Deadline: September 2007. "Candidates should be minimally published, with no full-length books." Fellowship is geared towards writers from traditionally underserved communities (immigrants, ethnic minorities, women) though anyone may apply. Length: 20 pages max. Entrants must complete EV application, which is available on PEN's Web site. Writers may submit own work. "Utilize EV application. Follow all instructions. Don't wait until the last minute to assemble letters of recommendation." Results announced November. Winners notified by mail, phone, e-mail. Results made available to entrants on Web site.

⌦ EMERGING WRITERS NETWORK SHORT FICTION CONTEST

Emerging Writers Network, 1334 Woodbourne Street, Westland MI 48186.E-mail: wickettd@yahoo.com. Web site: www.emergingwriters.typepad.com. **Contact:** Dan Wickett, president. Purpose to "find an excellent short story, get it published in *Frostproof Review*, and award the author." Annual. Competition/award for short stories. Prize: $500, publication on EWN Blog, publication in spring issue of *Frostproof Review*. Judging: All stories initially read by Dan Wickett. Top 20 go without author names to guest judge who chooses winner. 2006 guest judge was Charles D' Ambrosio. Entry fee: $10. Make checks payable to Dan Wickett. Guidelines available in March on Web site. Accepts inquiries by e-mail. Submission period: January 1 through August 15, 2007. Entries should be unpublished. Open only to authors who have had, or will have had, less than 3 books published by December prior to contest. Length: 3,000-8,000 words. Cover letter should include name, address, e-mail, word count, story title. Writers may submit own work. "Have an idea of the type of fiction the Emerging Writers Network supports and is generally excited about by reading the Web site." Results announced during the month of December. Winners notified by mail, e-mail. Results made available to entrants on Web site.

THE EMILY CONTEST

West Houston Chapter Romance Writers of America, 5603 Chantilly Lane, Houston TX 77092. E-mail: ellen_watkins@juno.com. Web site: www.whrwa.com. **Contact:** Ellen Watkins, Emily Contest chair. Award "to help people writing romance novels learn to write better books and to help them make contacts in the publishing world." Prize: first place entry in each category receives the Emily brooch; all finalists receive certificates. Judged by authors and experienced critiquers in the first round; final round judges are editors at a major romance publishing house. Entry fee: $20 for WHRWA members; $30 for non-members. Deadline: October 1. Entries must be unpublished. Length: first 35 pages of a novel. Open to all unpublished romance writers. Guidelines available in July for SASE, by e-mail or on Web site. Accepts inquiries by e-mail. "We look for dynamic, interesting romance stories with a hero and heroine readers can relate to and love. Hook us from the beginning and keep the level of excitement high." Results announced in February. Winners notified by mail or phone. For contest results, send SASE or visit Web site.

FISH ONE PAGE PRIZE

Fish Publishing, Durrus, Bantry, County Cork Ireland. E-mail: vssp@fishpublishing.com. Web site: www.fishpublishing.com. **Contact:** Clem Cairns, editor. Prize: 1st prize: 1,000 Euro (approx. $1,300). Nine runners up get 100 Euro (approx. $130). The authors of the 10 best works of short short fiction will be published in the Fish Short Story Prize Anthology. Entry fee: $15 per story. Enter online. Deadline: March 4. Entries must be unpublished. Stories must fit on one A4 page. Entries can be in any style or format and can be on any subject. The competition is open to writers from all countries, but entries must be written in English. Open to any writer. Guidelines on Web site or by e-mail.

FISH SHORT STORY PRIZE

Fish Publishing, Durrus, Bantry Co. Cork Ireland. 353 (0)27 55645. E-mail: info@fishpublishing.com. Web site: www.fishpublishing.com. **Contact:** Clem Cairns, editor. Purpose is to "find and publish new and exciting short fiction from all over the world; to support the short story and those who practice it." Offered annually for unpublished fiction mss. Prize: 1st Prize: 10,000 Euros (approx. $13,000); 2nd Prize: 1 week at Anam Cara Writers' Retreat in the west of Ireland plus 250 Euros; third prize is 250 Euros. The top 15 stories will be published in Fish's anthology, which is launched at the West Cork Literary Festival in June, and will be read by literary agents, including Shirley Stewart, Merric Davidson and others. Judged by a panel of international judges which changes every year. Entry fee: $30 per story. Guidelines available in July by e-mail, on Web site or in publication. Enter online at www.fishpublishing.com. Accepts inquiries by mail, phone. Deadline: November 30. Length: 5,000 words maximum. Open to any writer except those who have won before or who have been a runner up twice. "Don't be afraid to write with your own voice. We value originality. Do make sure that your story is as good as you can get it. Don't try to please a judge or judges. Make sure it is neat and easy to read." Results announced March 17 every year. Winners notified by mail, phone or e-mail and at prize ceremony book launch in Bantry, County Cork, last Saturday in June. For contest results, send SASE, e-mail, or visit Web site. See Web site for additional contests, including "One Page Story Prize," "Short Fiction Prize" and "Unpublished Novel Award."

FLORIDA FIRST COAST WRITERS' FESTIVAL NOVEL, SHORT FICTION, PLAYWRITING & POETRY AWARDS

Writers' Festival & Florida Community College at Jacksonville, FCCJ North Campus, 4501 Capper Road, Jacksonville FL 32218-4499. (904)766-6559. Fax: (904)766-6654. E-mail: dathomas@fccj.edu or sturner@fccj.edu. Web site: www.fccj.edu/wf. **Contact:** Dana Thomas, festival contest director. Conference and contest "to create a healthy writing environment, honor writers of merit and find a novel manuscript to recommend to New York publishers for 'serious consideration.'" Judged by university faculty and freelance and professional writers. Entry fee: $45 (novels); $25 (plays); $15 (short fiction); $10 (poetry). Deadline: December 15 for novels; February 1 for plays, poetry and short fiction. Entries must be unpublished. Word length: no limit for novel; 6,000 words for short fiction; 30 lines for poetry. Open to any writer. Guidelines available on the Web site or in the fall for SASE. Accepts inquiries by fax and e-mail. "For stories and novels, make the opening pages sparkle. For plays, make them at least two acts and captivating. For poems, blow us over with imagery and insight and avoid clichés and wordiness." Results announced on the Web site and at FCCJ's Florida First Coast Writers' Festival held in the spring.

☐ FLORIDA STATE WRITING COMPETITION

Florida Freelance Writers Association, P.O. Box A, Stratford NH 03590-0167. (603)922-8338. E-mail: contest@writers-editors.com. Web site: www.writers-editors.com. **Contact:** Dana K. Cassell, executive director. Award "to offer additional opportunities for writers to earn income and recognition from their writing efforts." Prize: varies from $50-100. Categories: novels and short stories. Judged by authors, editors and teachers. Entry fee: $5-20. Deadline: March 15. Entries must be unpublished. Open to any writer. Guidelines are revised each year and are subject to change. New guidelines are available in summer of each year. Accepts inquiries by e-mail. Results announced May 31. Winners notified by mail. For contest results, send SASE marked "winners" or visit Web site.

☐ H.E. FRANCIS SHORT STORY AWARD

The Ruth Hindman Foundation, University of Alabama English Dept., Department of English, Huntsville AL 35899. E-mail: MaryH71997@aol.com. Web site: www.uah.edu/colleges/liberal/english/whatnewcontest.html. **Contact:** Patricia Sammon. Offered annually for unpublished work not to exceed 5,000 words. Acquires first time publication rights. Prize: $1,000. Judged by a panel of nationally recognized, award-winning authors, directors of creative writing programs, and editors of literary journals. Entry fee: $15 reading fee (make check payable to the Ruth Hindman Foundation). Deadline: December 31.

ℕ ☐ GIVAL PRESS NOVEL AWARD

Gival Press LLC, P.O. Box 3812, Arlington VA 22203. (703)351-0079. E-mail: givalpress@yahoo.com. Web site: www.givalpress.com. **Contact:** Robert L. Giron, publisher. "To award the best literary novel." Annual. Prize: $3,000 (USD), publication and author's copies. Categories: literary novel. Receives about 60-80 entries per category. Judge for 2005 was Richard Peabody. Entries read anonymously. Entry fee: $50 (USD). Make checks payable to Gival Press, LLC. Guidelines with SASE, by phone, by e-mail, on Web site, in journals. Accepts inquiries by e-mail. Deadline: May 30, 2007. Entries should be unpublished. Open to any author who writes original work in English. Length: 30,000-100,000 words. Cover letter should include name, address, phone, e-mail, word count, novel title. Only the title and word count should appear on the actual ms. Writers may submit own work. "Review the types of mss Gival Press has published. We stress literary works." Results announced late fall of same year. Winners notified by phone. Results made available to entrants with SASE, by e-mail, on Web site.

ℕ ☐ GIVAL PRESS SHORT STORY AWARD

Gival Press, P.O. Box 3812, Arlington VA 22203. (703)351-0079. E-mail: givalpress@yahoo.com. Web site: www.givalpress.com. **Contact:** Robert L. Giron, publisher. "To award the best literary short story." Annual. Prize: $1,000 and publication on Web site. Category: literary short story. Receives about 60-80 entries per category. Entries are judged anonymously. Entry fee: $25. Make checks payable to Gival Press, LLC. Guidelines available online, via e-mail, or by mail. Deadline: Aug. 8th of every year. Entries must be unpublished. Open to anyone who writes original short stories in English. Length: 5,000-10,000 words. Include name, address, phone, e-mail, word count, title on cover letter. Only the title and word count should be found on ms. Writers may submit their own ficiton. "We publish literary works." Results announced in the fall of the same year. Winners notified by phone. Results available with SASE, by e-mail, on Web site.

◪ THE GLASGOW PRIZE FOR EMERGING WRITERS

Washington and Lee University/*Shenandoah*, Mattingly House, 2 Lee Ave., Lexington VA 24450-2116. (540)458-8765. Fax: (540)458-8461. E-mail: lleech@wlu.edu. Web site: shenandoah.wlu.edu. **Contact:** Lynn Leech, managing editor. Award for writer with only one published book in genre being considered. (Genre rotates: 2006, short story; 2007, poetry; 2008, creative nonfiction . . . etc.) Prize: $2,500, publication of new work in *Shenandoah*, and a reading at Washington and Lee University. Judged by anonymous writer/editor, announced after prize winner is selected. Entry fee: $22 (includes 1-yr subscription to *Shenandoah*; send credit card information or make checks payable to *Shenandoah*). To apply, send first book, one unpublished piece of work (poem for 2007), SASE, and vita, along with check for $22 (from either author or publisher). Cover letter should include name, address, phone and e-mail. Guidelines available on Web site. Accepts inquiries by e-mail. Results announced on Web site and winners notified by mail or e-mail in May. Deadline: March 15-31. Open to any writer.

☐ GLIMMER TRAIN'S FALL SHORT-STORY AWARD FOR NEW WRITERS

Glimmer Train Press, Inc., 1211 NW Glisan St., Suite 207, Portland OR 97209. (503)221-0836. Fax: (503)221-0837. Web site: www.glimmertrain.org. Offered for any writer whose fiction hasn't appeared in a nationally distributed publication with a circulation over 5,000. Word limit: 1,200-10,000 words. Contest open August 1-September 30. Follow online submission procedure at www.glimmertrain.org. Notification on January 2. Prize:

Winner receives $1,200, publication in *Glimmer Train Stories*, and 20 copies of that issue. First/second runners-up receive $500/$300, respectively. Entry fee: $12/story. Entries must be unpublished.

☐ GLIMMER TRAIN'S SPRING SHORT-STORY AWARD FOR NEW WRITERS

Glimmer Train Press, Inc., 1211 NW Glisan St., Suite 207, Portland OR 97209. (503)221-0836. Fax: (503)221-0837. Web site: www.glimmertrain.org. Offered for any writer whose fiction hasn't appeared in a nationally distributed publication with a circulation over 5,000. Word limit: 1,200-10,000 words. Contest open February 1-March 31. Follow online submission procedure at www.glimmertrain.org. Notification on July 1. Prize: Winner receives $1,200, publication in *Glimmer Train Stories*, and 20 copies of that issue. First/second runners-up receive $500/$300, respectively. Entry fee: $12/story.

☐ GLIMMER TRAIN'S SUMMER FICTION OPEN

Glimmer Train Press, Inc., 1211 NW Glisan St., Suite 207, Portland OR 97209. (503)221-0836. Fax: (503)221-0837. Web site: www.glimmertrain.org. Offered annually for unpublished stories as "a platform for all themes, all lengths, all writers." Prize: 1st place: $2,000, publication in *Glimmer Train Stories*, and 20 copies of that issue; 2nd place: $1,000, and possible publication in *Glimmer Train Stories*; 3rd place: $600, and possible publication in *Glimmer Train Stories*. Entry fee: $15/story. Deadline: June 30. Open to any writer. Make your submissions online at www.glimmertrain.org. Winners will be notified and results posted by October 15.

☐ GLIMMER TRAIN'S WINTER FICTION OPEN

Glimmer Train Press, Inc., 1211 NW Glisan St., Suite 207, Portland OR 97209. (503)221-0836. Fax: (503)221-0837. Web site: www.glimmertrain.org. Offered annually for unpublished work as "a platform for all themes, all lengths, and all writers." Prize: 1st place: $2,000, publication in *Glimmer Train Stories*, and 20 copies of that issue; 2nd place: $1,000, possible publication in *Glimmer Train Stories*; 3rd place: $600, possible publication in *Glimmer Train Stories*. Entry fee: $15/story. Deadline: January 15. Open to any writer. Make your submissions online (www.glimmertrain.org). Winners will be notified and results posted April 15.

THE GOODHEART PRIZE FOR FICTION

Shenandoah: The Washington and Lee University Review, Mattingly House, 2 Lee Ave., Lexington VA 24450-2116. (540)458-8765. Fax: (540)458-8461. E-mail: shenandoah@wlu.edu. Web site: shenandoah.wlu.edu. **Contact:** Lynn Leech, managing editor. Awarded to best story published in *Shenandoah* during a volume year. Prize: $1,000. Judged by writer whose identity is revealed after the prize winner has been selected. No entry fee. All stories published in the review are automatically considered for the prize. Winners are notified by mail or e-mail each Spring. Results are available on Web site. "Read *Shenandoah* to familiarize yourself with the work we publish."

☐ THE GREAT BLUE BEACON SHORT-SHORT STORY CONTEST

The Great Blue Beacon: The Newsletter for Writers of All Genres and Skill Levels, 1425 Patriot Drive, Melbourne FL 32940-6881. (321)253-5869. E-mail: ajircc@juno.com. **Contact:** A.J. Byers, editor/publisher. Award to "recognize outstanding short-short stories." Prize: $50 (first prize), $25 (second prize), $10 (third prize) and publication of winning entry in *The Great Blue Beacon*. Judged by outside panel of judges. Entry fee: $5 ($4 for subscribers). Make checks out to A.J. Byers. Guidelines available periodically when announced. Length: 1,000 words or fewer. Cover letter and first page of ms should include name, address, phone, e-mail, word count and title. Deadline: TBA. Entries must be unpublished. Open to any writer. Two-three contests a year for short-short stories. Receives 50-75 entries per contest. For guidelines, send SASE or e-mail. Accepts inquiries by e-mail and phone. Results announced two months after contest deadline. Winners notified by SASE or e-mail. For contest results, send SASE or e-mail.

◪ ◎ GREAT CANADIAN STORY CONTEST

Storyteller, Canada's Short Story Magazine, 3687 Twin Falls Place, Ottawa ON K1 V 1 W6 Canada. (613) 822-9734. E-mail: info@storytellermagazine.com. Web site: www.storytellermagazine.com. **Contact:** Terry Tyo, publisher/managing editor. "Purpose of competition is to publish great Canadian stories. Stories must have a uniquely Canadian element (theme, setting, history, institution, politics, social phenomenon, etc.)." Prize: Varies from year to year. Short list determined by editors; judges choose from short list. Entry fee: $5 Canadian (make cheque or money order payable to TYO Communications). Deadline: sometime in mid-April every year. Entries must be unpublished. Canadian citizens or residents only. Guidelines available in February by SASE or on Web site. Length: 2,000-6,000 words. No simultaneous submissions or e-mail submissions. *Storyteller* cannot return mss unless accompanied by SASE. "Read the magazine. The short list comprises our summer issue, so all stories must be suitable for publication in *Storyteller* to qualify. Results announced on or around July 1st. Winners notified by phone or e-mail. For contest results, send SASE or visit Web site.

❷ GREAT LAKES COLLEGES ASSOCIATION NEW WRITERS AWARD

Great Lakes Colleges Association Inc., 535 W. William, Suite 301, Ann Arbor MI 48103. (734)761-4833. Fax: (734)761-3939. E-mail: shackelford@glca.org. **Contact:** Dr. Mark Andrew Clark. Award for first publication in fiction or poetry. Writer must be nominated by publisher. Prize: Winners are invited to tour the GLCA colleges. An honorarium of $300 will be guaranteed the author by each GLCA member college they visit. Judged by professors from member colleges. No entry fee. Deadline: February 28. Open to any writer. Submit 4 copies of the book to Dr. Mark Andrew Clark, Faculty of Writing, Literature & Education, Great Lakes Colleges Association, Director, New Writers Awards, The Philadelphia Center, North American Bldg., 121 S. Broad St., 7th Floor, Philadelphia PA 19107. Guidelines available after November 1. Accepts inquiries by fax and e-mail. Results announced in May. Letters go to publishers who have submitted.

❑ THE GREENSBORO REVIEW LITERARY AWARD IN FICTION AND POETRY

The Greensboro Review, English Department, 134 McIver Bldg., P.O. Box 26170, Greensboro NC 27402-6170. (336)334-5459. E-mail: anseay@uncg.edu. Web site: www.uncg.edu/eng/mfa. **Contact:** Allison Seay, assistant editor. Offered annually for fiction (7,500 word limit) and poetry; the best work is published in the Spring issue of *The Greensboro Review*. Sample issue for $5. Prize: $500 each for best short story and poem. Judged by editors of *The Greensboro Review*. No entry fee. Guidelines for SASE or on Web site. Deadline: September 15. Entries must be unpublished. No simultaneous submissions or submissions by e-mail. Open to any writer. Winners notified by mail, phone or e-mail. List of winners published in Spring issue. "All manuscripts meeting literary award guidelines will be considered for cash award as well as for publication in the Spring issue of *The Greensboro Review*."

❑ GSU REVIEW WRITING CONTEST

The GSU Review, Georgia State University, Campus Box 1894, MSC 8R0322, Unit 8, Atlanta GA 30303-3083. (404)651-4804. Web site: www2.gsu.edu/~wwwrev. **Contact:** Jody Brooks, editor. To promote quality work of emerging writers. Prize: Publication for finalists (up to 10 stories). $1,000 first prize; $250 second prize. Categories: fiction, poetry; receives more than 250 entries each. Judged by staff at *The Review* (finalists); 2005 winners picked by Tom Franklin (fiction) and Thomas Lux (poetry). Entry fee: $15, includes copy of Spring issue with contest results. Make checks payable to The GSU Review. Deadline: March 4. Entries must be unpublished. Length: should not exceed 7,500 words. Address fiction submissions to Jody Brooks, Fiction Editor. Mss must be typed or letter-quality printed. On the first page of the ms include name, address, phone, e-mail, word count. Limit each submission to one short story. Guidelines available by SASE or on Web site. Accepts inquiries by e-mail, phone. Contest open to all except faculty, staff, students of Georgia State University. Winners notified by e-mail. All entrants receive contest issue. "We look for engagement with language and characters we care about."

◎ HAMMETT PRIZE

Internatonal Association of Crime Writers/North American Branch, P.O. Box 8674, New York NY 10116-8674. Fax: (815)361-1477. E-mail: mfrisque@igc.org. Web site: www.crimewritersna.org. **Contact:** Mary A. Frisque, executive director, North American Branch. Award established "to honor a work of literary excellence in the field of crime writing by a U.S. or Canadian author." Award for novels, story collections, nonfiction by one author. Prize: trophy. Judged by committee. "Our reading committee seeks suggestions from publishers and they also ask the membership for recommendations. Eligible books are read by a committee of members of the organization. The committee chooses five nominated books, which are then sent to three outside judges for a final selection. Judges are outside the crime writing field." No entry fee. For guidelines, send SASE or e-mail. Accepts inquiries by e-mail. Deadline: December 1. Entries must be previously published. To be eligible "the book must have been published in the U.S. or Canada during the calendar year." The author must be a U.S. or Canadian citizen or permanent resident. Nominations announced in January, winners announced in fall. Winners notified by mail, phone and recognized at awards ceremony in June. For contest results, send SASE or e-mail.

◎ DRUE HEINZ LITERATURE PRIZE

University of Pittsburgh Press, 13400 Forbes Ave., 5th Floor, Eureka Building, Pittsburgh PA 15260. (412)383-2492. Fax: (412)383-2466. E-mail: susief@pitt.edu. Web site: www.pitt.edu/~press. **Contact:** Christine Pollock, assistant to the director. Award to "support the writer of short fiction at a time when the economics of commercial publishing make it more and more difficult for the serious literary artist working in the short story and novella to find publication." Prize: $15,000 and publication by the University of Pittsburgh Press. No entry fee. "It is imperative that entrants request complete rules of the competition by sending an SASE before submitting a manuscript." Deadline: Submissions received only during the months of May and June. Competition for story collections. No previously published collections. Manuscripts must be unpublished in book form. Length: 150-

Contests & Awards

300 typed pages. The award is open to writers who have published a book-length collection of fiction or three short stories or novellas in commmercial magazines or literary journals of national distribution. Cover letter should include name, address, phone, e-mail, title, name of publications where work was originally published. This information should not appear on the ms. Results announced in February. Winners notified by phone. For contest results, send SASE with manuscript.

⬜ LORIAN HEMINGWAY SHORT STORY COMPETITION

P.O. Box 993, Key West FL 33041-0993. (305)294-0320. E-mail: calico2419@aol.com. Web site: www.shortstory competition.com. **Contact:** Carol Shaughnessy, co-director. Award to "encourage literary excellence and the efforts of writers who have not yet had major-market success." Competition for short stories. Prize: $1,000 (first prize), $500 (second prize), $500 (third prize), honorable mentions. Judged by a panel of writers, editors and literary scholars selected by author Lorian Hemingway. Guidelines available in January for SASE, by e-mail or on Web site. Accepts inquiries by SASE, e-mail or visit Web site. Deadline: May 15. Entries must be unpublished. Length: 3,000 words maximum. "Open to all writers whose work has not appeared in a nationally distributed publication with a circulation of 5,000 or more." Entry fee is $10 for each story postmarked by May 1, and $15 for stories postmarked between May 1 and May 15. "We look for excellence, pure and simple—no genre restrictions, no theme restrictions. We seek a writer's voice that cannot be ignored." Results announced at the end of July during Hemingway Days festival. Winners notified by phone prior to announcement. For contest results, send e-mail or visit Web site. "All entrants will receive a letter from Lorian Hemingway and a list of winners, via mail or e-mail, by October 1."

⬜ ◎ HIGHLIGHTS FOR CHILDREN FICTION CONTEST

Highlights for Children, 803 Church St., Honesdale PA 18431-1824. (570)253-1080. Fax: (570)251-7847. E-mail: eds@highlights-corp.com. Web site: www.highlights.com. **Contact:** Marileta Robinson, senior editor. Award "to honor quality stories (previously unpublished) for young readers and to encourage children's writers." Offered for stories for children ages 2-12; category varies each year. No crime or violence, please. Specify that ms is a contest entry. Prize: $1,000 to 3 winners, plus publication in *Highlights*. Categories: Short stories. Judged by *Highlights* editors, with input given by outside readers. No entry fee. "There is a different contest theme each year. We generally receive about 1,400 entries." Cover letter should include name, address, phone, e-mail, word count and title. "We prefer that these things appear on the first page of the manuscript as well." Deadline: January 1-February 28 (postmarked). Entries must be unpublished. Length: 500 words maximum for stories for beginning readers (to age 8) and 800 words for more advanced readers (ages 9-12). No minimum word count. Open to anyone 16 years of age or older. Results announced in June. Winners notified by mail or phone. For contest results, send SASE. See www.highlights.com for current theme and guidelines.

ℕ ◎ TONY HILLERMAN MYSTERY SHORT STORY CONTEST

Tony Hillerman Writers Conference and *Cowboys & Indians* magazine, 304 Calle Oso, Sante Fe NM 87501. E-mail: wordharvest@yahoo.com. Web site: www.sfworkshops.com. **Contact:** Anne Hillerman, contest administrator. "Purpose is to encourage mystery short stories set in the West or Southwest in the tradition of Tony Hillerman." Annual. Competition/award for short stories. Prize: publication in *Cowboys & Indians* magazine, a successful glossy national publication; signed Hillerman books; and tickets to the award banquet held in conjunction with the Tony Hillerman Writers Conference: Focus on Mystery in Albuqurque the first weekend of November. Category: mystery short story set in West or Southwest with at least one Native American or cowboy character. Receives about 160 entries per year. Entries are judged by a professional writer/editor with connections to both the conference and *Cowboys & Indians* magazine. Entry fee: $10. Make checks payable to Wordharvest. Guidelines available in June on Web site, in publication. Accepts inquiries by e-mail. Deadline: Oct. 1, 2007. Entries should be unpublished. Open to all, as long as the entry is a previously unpublished mystery story that meets the guidelines. Length: 2,500 words. Cover letter should include name, address, phone, e-mail, word count, story title. Include only title on ms. Writers may submit own work. "Look at previous year's winner (published in March issue) for reference and info about the contest. Know that next year's winner must be different in terms of setting, plot and characters. Look at the magazine for info about the readers. Humor is a plus! Graphic sex, violence and four-letter words do not fit the magazine's tone." Winners notified by phone in October. Results made available to entrants on Web site.

ℕ ◎ PEARL HOGREFE FELLOWSHIP

The Pearl Hogrefe Fund and Department of English, 203 Ross Hall, Iowa State University, Ames IA 50011. (515)294-2477. Fax: (515)294-6814. E-mail: englgrad@iastate.edu. Web site: www.engl.iastate.edu. **Contact:** Helen Ewald, graduate studies coordinator. Award "to provide new Iowa State MA students with writing time." Competition for manuscript sample of 25 pages, any genre. Prize: $1,200/month for 9 months and full payment of tuition and fees. Judged by the creative writing staff at Iowa State University. No entry fee. Deadline: January

15. Open to published and unpublished manuscripts. "No restrictions, except the applicant cannot hold or expect to receive a master's degree in English or creative writing during the current year." Open to any writer. Guidelines available by e-mail. Accepts inquiries by fax, e-mail, phone. Results announced April 1. Winners notified by phone.

N ☐ TOM HOWARD/JOHN H. REID SHORT STORY CONTEST

Tom Howard Books, Mail to: Winning Writers, 351 Pleasant St., PMB 22, Northampton MA 01060-3961. (866)946-9748. Fax: (431)280-0539. E-mail: johnreid@mail.qango.com. Web site: www.winningwriters.com/contests/tomstory/ts_guidelines.php. **Contact:** John H. Reid, award director. "Established in 1993, this award honors the best short stories, essays and other works of prose being written today." Annual. Prize: $1,000 (first prize), $600 (second prize), $400 (third prize). There will also be four High Distinction Awards of $250 each. All seven winning entries will be published on Mr. Reid's Web site and announced in Tom Howard Contest News and the Winning Writers Newsletter, a combined audience of nearly 20,000 readers. The top entry will also be published in a triennial anthology. Other entries may also be published in the anthology. Categories: All entries are judged in one category. "We received 1,492 entries for the 2005 contest." Judged by a former journalist and magazine editor, John H. Reid. Mr. Reid has judged literary contests for over 15 years. He has published several novels, a collection of poetry, a guide to winning literary contests, and 15 books of film criticism and movie history. He is assisted by Dee C. Konrad, a leading educator and published author, who served as Associate Professor of English at Barat College of DePaul University and dean of Liberal Arts and Sciences for the year 2000-2001. Entry fee: $12 per entry. Make checks payable to Winning Writers. (U.S. funds only, please.) Guidelines available in Sept. on Web site. Prefers inquiries by e-mail. Deadline: March 31, 2007. "Both published and unpublished works are accepted. In the case of published work, the contestant must own the anthology and online publication rights." Open to all writers. Length: 5,000 words max per entry. Cover letter should include name, address, phone, e-mail, word count, story title, place(s) where story was previously published. Only the title should be on the actual ms. Writers may submit own work. "Read past winning entries at www.winningwriters.com/contests/tomstory/ts_pastwinners.php." Results announced May 15. Winners notified by e-mail. Winners announced in early May. Results made available to entrants on Web site.

☐ ◎ L. RON HUBBARD'S WRITERS OF THE FUTURE CONTEST

Author Services Inc., P.O. Box 1630, Los Angeles CA 90078. (323)466-3310. Fax: (323)466-6474. E-mail: contests @authorservicesinc.com. Web site: www.writersofthefuture.com. **Contact:** Judy, contest administrator. Established in 1983. Foremost competition for new and amateur writers of unpublished science fiction or fantasy short stories or novelettes. Offered "to find, reward and publicize new speculative fiction writers so they may more easily attain professional writing careers." Open to new and amateur writers who have not professionally published a novel or short novel, more than 1 novelette, or more than 3 short stories. Eligible entries are previously unpublished short stories or novelettes (under 17,000 words) of science fiction or fantasy. Guidelines for SASE or on Web site. Accepts inquiries by fax, e-mail, phone. Prize: awards quarterly: 1st place: $1,000; 2nd place: $750; and 3rd place: $500. Annual grand prize: $5,000. "Contest has four quarters. There shall be 3 cash prizes in each quarter. In addition, at the end of the year, the 4 first-place, quarterly winners will have their entries rejudged, and a grand prize winner shall be determined." Judged by K.D. Wentworth (initial judge), then by a panel of 4 professional authors. Deadline: December 31, March 31, June 30, September 30. Entries must be unpublished. Limit one entry per quarter. No entry fee; entrants retain all rights to their stories. Open to any writer. Manuscripts: white paper, black ink; double-spaced; typed; each page appropriately numbered with title, no author name. Include cover page with author's name, address, phone number, e-mail address (if available), as well as estimated word count and the title of the work. Results announced quarterly in e-newsletter. Winners notified by phone.

◎ INDIANA REVIEW ½ K (SHORT-SHORT/PROSE-POEM) CONTEST

Indiana Review, Ballantine Hall 465/Indiana University, 1020 E. Kirkwood Ave., Bloomington IN 47405-7103. (812)855-3439. Fax: (812)855-4253. E-mail: inreview@indiana.edu. Web site: www.indiana.edu/~inreview. **Contact:** Grady Jaynes, editor. Competition for fiction and prose poems no longer than 500 words. Prize: $1,000 plus publication, contributor's copies and a year's subscription. All entries considered for publication. Judged by *Indiana Review* staff and outside judges. Entry fee: $15 fee for no more than 3 pieces (includes a year's subscription, two issues). Make checks payable to *Indiana Review*. Deadline: June 10. Entries must be unpublished. Guidelines available in March for SASE, by phone, e-mail, on Web site, or in publication. Length: 500 words, 3 mss per entry. Open to any writer. Cover letter should include name, address, phone, e-mail, word count and title. No identifying information on ms. "We look for command of language and form." Results announced in August. Winners notified by mail. For contest results, send SASE or visit Web site.

☐ INDIANA REVIEW FICTION CONTEST

Indiana Review, BH 465/Indiana University, 1020 E. Kirkwood Ave., Bloomington IN 47405-7103. (812)855-3439. Fax: (812)855-4253. E-mail: inreview@indiana.edu. Web site: www.indiana.edu/~inreview. **Contact:** Tracy Truels, editor. Contest for fiction in any style and on any subject. Prize: $1,000, publication in the *Indiana Review* and contributor's copies. Judged by *Indiana Review* staff and outside judges. Entry fee: $15 fee (includes a year's subscription). Deadline: Mid-October. Entries must be unpublished. Mss will not be returned. No previously published work, or works forthcoming elsewhere, are eligible. Simultaneous submissions accepted, but in the event of entrant withdrawal, contest fee will not be refunded. Length: 15,000 words (about 40 pages) maximum, double spaced. Open to any writer. Cover letter must include name, address, phone number and title of story. Entrant's name should appear only in the cover letter, as all entries will be considered anonymously. Results announced January. Winners notified by mail. For contest results, send SASE. "We look for a command of language and structure, as well as a facility with compelling and unusual subject matter. It's a good idea to obtain copies of issues featuring past winners to get a more concrete idea of what we are looking for."

Ⓝ Ⓘ INDIVIDUAL EXCELLENCE AWARDS

Ohio Arts Council, 727 E. Main St., Columbus OH 43205-1796. (614)466-2613. Fax: (614)466-4479. E-mail: ken.emeride@oac.state.oh.us. Web site: www.oac.state.oh.us. **Contact:** Ken Emeride, Director, Individual Creativity. "An award of excellence for completed work for Ohio residents who are not students." Annual. Competition/award for short stories, novels, story collections. Prize: $5,000 or $10,000, determined by review panel. Categories: fiction/nonfiction, poetry, criticism, playwriting/screenplays. Receives about 125 poetry, 125 fiction/nonfiction, 10-15 criticism, 25-30 playwriting entries per year. Judged by three-person panel of out-of-state panelists, anonymous review. No entry fee. Guidelines available in June on Web site. Accepts inquiries by e-mail, phone. Deadline: Sept. 1. Open to Ohio residents living and working in the state for at least one year prior to the deadline who are also not students. Length: 20-30 pages fiction/nonfiction, 10-15 pages poetry, 30-50 pages criticism, 1 play or 2 short 1-act plays. Cover letter should include name, address, title of work. None of this information should appear on the actual manuscript. Writers may submit own work. "Submit concise bodies of work or sections, not a sampling of styles." Results announced Jan. Winners notified by mail. Results made available to entrants on Web site.

Ⓘ THE IOWA SHORT FICTION AWARD

Iowa Writers' Workshop, 102 Dey House, 507 N. Clinton St., Iowa City IA 52242-1000. (319)335-2000. Fax: (319)335-2055. Web site: www.uiowapress.org. **Contact:** Holly Carver, director. Award "to give exposure to promising writers who have not yet published a book of prose." Prize: publication by University of Iowa Press. Judged by Senior Iowa Writers' Workshop members who screen manuscripts; published fiction author of note makes final selections. No entry fee. Submission period: Aug. 1-Sept. 30. Entries must be unpublished, but stories previously published in periodicals are eligible for inclusion. "The manuscript must be a collection of short stories of at least 150 word-processed, double-spaced pages." Open to any writer. No application forms are necessary. Do not send original ms. Include SASE for return of ms. Announcement of winners made early in year following competition. Winners notified by phone.

☐ Ⓘ JOSEPH HENRY JACKSON AWARD

The San Francisco Foundation, Administered by Intersection for the Arts, 446 Valencia St., San Francisco CA 94103. (415)626-2787. Fax: (415)626-1636. Web site: www.theintersection.org. **Contact:** Kevin B. Chen, program director. Award "to encourage young, unpublished writers." Offered annually for unpublished, work-in-progress fiction (novel or short story), nonfiction or poetry by an author age 20-35, with 3-year consecutive residency in northern California or Nevada prior to submission. Prize: $2,000 and certificate. Categories: short stories, novels and short story collections. No entry fee. Deadline: March 31. Entries must be unpublished. Work cannot exceed 40 double-spaced, typed pages. Entry form and rules available in mid-January for SASE. "Submit a serious, ambitious portion of a book-length manuscript." Results announced August. Winners notified by mail. Winners will be announced in letter mailed to all applicants.

☐ E.M. KOEPPEL SHORT FICTION AWARD

Writecorner Press, P.O. Box 140310, Gainesville FL 32614-0310. Web site: www.writecorner.com. **Contact:** Mary Sue Koeppel, editor. Award for short stories. Prize: $1,100 first prize, and $100 for Editors' Choices. Judged by award-winning writers. Entry fee: $15 first story, $10 each additional story. Make checks payable to Writecorner Press. Send 2 title pages: One with title only and one with title, name, address, phone, e-mail, short bio. Place no other identification of the author on the ms that will be used in the judging. Guidelines available in January for SASE or on Web site. Accepts inquiries by e-mail and phone. Expects 300+ entries. Deadline: October 1-April 30. Entries must be unpublished. Open to any writer. Results announced in Summer. Winners notified by mail, phone in July (or earlier). For results, send SASE or check Web site. "Send well-crafted stories."

◎ LAWRENCE FOUNDATION PRIZE

Michigan Quarterly Review, 3574 Rackham Building, Ann Arbor MI 48109-1070. (734)764-9265. E-mail: mqr@u mich.edu. Web site: www.umich.edu/ ~ mqr. **Contact:** Vicki Lawrence, managing editor. Competition for short stories. Prize: $1,000. Judged by editorial board. No entry fee. No deadline. "An annual cash prize awarded to the author of the best short story published in *Michigan Quarterly Review* each year. Stories must be already published in *Michigan Quarterly Review*. This is not a competition in which manuscripts are read outside of the normal submission process." Guidelines available for SASE or on Web site. Accepts inquires by e-mail and phone. Results announced in December. Winners notified by phone or mail.

🅝 ◗ LC PRESS DISCOVERY AWARD/ LC PRESS EXPEDITION AWARD

Lewis-Clark Press, Humanities Division, Lewis Clark State Collge, Lewiston ID 83501.(208)792-2301. E-mail: mesanders@lcsc.edu. **Contact:** Mark Sanders, associate editor. "The Discovery Award is for a first book and the Expedition Award is for all previously published authors." Annual. Competition/award for novels, story collections. Prize: $1,000. Receives about 200-300 entries per category. Judge by editors of the press; final selections picked by writers of national reputation. Entry fee: $15. Make checks payable to LC Press. Guidelines available Dec.-May with SASE, by phone, by e-mail. Accepts inquiries by e-mail, phone. **Deadline:** July 15. Entries should be unpublished. "Individual stories may be published in journals; acknowledgments page should be part of ms." Open to all. Length: 150-275 pages. Cover letter should include name, address, phone, e-mail, word count, novel/story title, place(s) where novel/story was previously published. Please include two cover sheets—one with personal info and one with title only. Writers may submit own work. Results announced in the fall. Winners notified by mail. Winners announced by Dec. 15. Results made available to entrants with SASE, by e-mail.

✚ ◎ STEPHEN LEACOCK MEMORIAL MEDAL FOR HUMOUR

Stephen Leacock Association, Box 854, Orrillia ON L3V 6K8 Canada. (705)835-3218 or (705)835-3408. Fax: (705)835-5171 or (705)835-3689. E-mail: drapson@encode.com or moonwood@sympatico.ca. Web site: www.l eacock.com. **Contact:** Judith Rapson, award chair. Award for humorous writing by a Canadian, given in memory of Stephen B. Leacock, Canada's best-known writer of humorous fiction. Prize: silver medal and $10,000 given by TD Financial Group. Categories: novels, short story collections, drama, poetry, translations. Judged by five judges from across Canada, plus a local reading committee which has one vote. Entry fee: $100; make checks payable to Stephen Leacock Association. Entry must be a book published in the year prior to the presentation of the award and must be accompanied by a short biographical sketch and photograph of the author. Cover letter should include publisher's name, address, e-mail and name of contact person. Deadline: December 31. Authors must be Canadian citizens or landed immigrants; no more than two authors permitted for any given entry. Guidelines available in August for fax or on Web site. Book may be nominated by author or publisher. Books are judged primarily on humorous content but also on literary merit and general appeal. Results announced in April at luncheon in Orillia; winner required to attend Award Dinner in Orillia in June and deliver address. Results available for SASE, by fax, e-mail or on Web site.

⊕ ◖ LONG STORY CONTEST, INTERNATIONAL

White Eagle Coffee Store Press, P.O. Box 383, Fox River Grove IL 60021. (847)639-9200. E-mail: wecspress@aol. com. Web site: http://members.aol.com/wecspress. **Contact:** Frank E. Smith, publisher. Offered annually since 1993 for unpublished work to recognize and promote long short stories of 8,000-14,000 words (about 30-50 pages). Sample of previous winner: $5.95, including postage. Open to any writer, no restrictions on materials. Prize: (A.E. Coppard Prize) $500 and publication, plus 25 copies of chapbook; 40 additional copies sent to agents; and 10 press kits. Categories: No limits on style or subject matter. Entry fee: $15 fee, $10 for second story in same envelope. Guidelines available in April by SASE, e-mail or on Web site. Accepts inquiries by e-mail. Length: 8,000-14,000 words (30-50 pages double-spaced) single story; may have multiparts or be a self-contained novel segment. Deadline: December 15. Accepts previously unpublished submissions, but previous publication of small parts with acknowledgment is okay. Simultaneous submissions okay. Send cover with name, address, phone; second title page with title only. Submissions are not returned; they are recycled. "SASE for most current information." Results announced in late spring. Winners notified by phone. For contest results, send SASE or visit Web site in late spring. "Write with richness and depth."

⊕ ◎ MARSH AWARD FOR CHILDREN'S LITERATURE IN TRANSLATION

Marsh Christian Trust, Roehampton University, Froebel College, Roehampton Lane, London England SW15 5PJ United Kingdom. E-mail: G.Lathey@roehampton.ac.uk. **Contact:** Dr. Gillian Lathey. Award "to promote the publication of translated children's books in the UK." Biennial award for children's book translations. Judged by Patricia Crampton, Caroline Horn, Wendy Cooling, Elizabeth Hammill. No entry fee. Entries must be previously published. Entries should be translations into English first published in the UK. Entries must be nominated by publishers. Open to any writer. Guidelines available for SASE. Cover letter should include name, address, phone, e-mail and title. Accepts inquiries by e-mail. Results announced in January. Winners notified by mail and at presentation event.

WALTER RUMSEY MARVIN GRANT

Ohioana Library Association, 274 E. First Ave., Suite 300, Columbus OH 43201. (614)466-3831. Fax: (614)728-6974. E-mail: ohioana@sloma.state.oh.us. Web site: www.ohioana.org. **Contact:** Linda Hengst. Award "to encourage young, unpublished writers 30 years of age or younger." Competition for short stories. Prize: $1,000. No entry fee. Up to 6 pieces of prose may be submitted; maximum 60 pages, minimum 10 pages double-spaced, 12-point type. Deadline: January 31. Entries must be unpublished. Open to unpublished authors born in Ohio or who have lived in Ohio for a minimum of five years. Must be 30 years of age or younger. Guidelines for SASE. Winner notified in May or June. Award given in October.

MASTERS LITERARY AWARDS

Titan Press, P.O. Box 17897, Encino CA 91416-7897. Web site: www.titanpress.info. Offered annually and quarterly for work published within 2 years (preferred) and unpublished work (accepted). Fiction, 15-page maximum; poetry, 5 pages or 150-lines maximum; and nonfiction, 10 pages maximum. "A selection of winning entries may appear in our national literary publication." Winners may also appear on the Internet. Titan Press retains one-time publishing rights to selected winners. Prize: $1,000, and possible publication in the *Titan Press Internet* journal. Judged by 3 literary professionals. Entry fee: $15. Deadline: Ongoing (nominations made March 15, June 15, September 15, December 15). Any submission received prior to an award date is eligible for the subsequent award. Submissions accepted throughout the year. All entries must be in the English language. Guidelines for #10 SASE. "Be persistent, be consistent, be professional."

THE JOHN H. MCGINNIS MEMORIAL AWARD

Southwest Review, P.O. Box 750374, Dallas TX 75275-0374. (214)768-1037. Fax: (214)768-1408. E-mail: swr@mail.smu.edu. Web site: www.southwestreview.org. **Contact:** Jennifer Cranfill, managing editor. Award for short fiction and nonfiction. Prize: $500. Judged by *Southwest Review*'s editor in chief and managing editor. No entry fee. Stories or essays must have been published in the *Southwest Review* prior to the announcement of the award. Pieces are not submitted directly for the award but for publication in the magazine. Open to any writer. Guidelines available for SASE and on Web site. Results announced in first issue of the year. Winners notified in January by mail, phone and e-mail.

MEMPHIS MAGAZINE FICTION AWARDS

Memphis Magazine, P.O. Box 1738, Memphis TN 38101. (901)521-9000. E-mail: sadler@memphismagazine.com. Web site: www.memphismagazine.com. **Contact:** Marilyn Sadler, senior editor/contest coordinator. Annual. Competition/award for short stories. Prize: $1,000 grand prize and publication in *Memphis*; two $500 honorable mention awards. Judged by a panel of five, all with fiction writing experience and publications. Entry fee: $10/story. Guidelines available in April by phone, on Web site, in publication. Accepts inquiries by fax, e-mail, phone. Deadline: Aug. 1. Entries should be unpublished. "Manuscripts may be previously published as long as previous publication was not in a national magazine with over 20,000 circulation or in a regional publication within Shelby County." Open to all authors who live within 150 miles of Memphis. Length: 3,000-4,5000 words. Cover letter should include name, address, phone, story title. Do not put your name anywhere on the ms itself. Writers may submit own work. "Each story should be typed, double-spaced, with unstapled, numbered pages. Stories are not required to have a Memphis or Southern theme, but we do want a compelling story and first-rate writing." Winners announced Sept.

MICHIGAN LITERARY FICTION AWARDS

University of Michigan Press, 839 Greene St., Ann Arbor MI 48104. Fax: (734)615-1540. E-mail: ump.fiction@umich.edu. Web site: www.press.umich.edu/fiction. Award to "attract the work of writers of literary fiction looking for, and deserving, a second chance." Prize: $1,000 and publication. Categories: novels and short story collections. No entry fee. Guidelines for SASE or on Web site. Accepts inquiries by e-mail. Deadline: July 1. Entries must be unpublished. Contest open to writers who have previously published at least one book-length work of literary fiction. Cover letter should include name, address, phone, e-mail and title; title only on every page of ms. Results announced in November. Winners notified by mail. For contest results, send SASE or visit Web site.

A MIDSUMMER TALE

E-mail: editors@toasted-cheese.com. Web site: www.toasted-cheese.com. **Contact:** Theryn Fleming, editor. A Midsummer Tale is a summer-themed creative nonfiction contest. Topic changes each year. Check Web site for current focus and word limit. "We usually receive around 20 entries." Prize: First prize: $20 Amazon gift certificate, publication; Second prize: $15 Amazon gift certificate, publication; Third prize: $10 Amazon gift certificate, publication. Some feedback is often given to entrants. Categories: creative nonfiction. Judged by two Toasted Cheese editors who blind-judge each contest. Each judge has her own criteria for selecting winners. No entry fee. Guidelines, including the e-mail address to which you should send your entry and instructions for what to include and how to format, are available May 1 on Web site. Accepts inquiries by e-mail. Deadline: June 21. Entries must be unpublished. Open to any writer. Results announced July 31 on Web site. Winners notified by e-mail.

▣ ◐ MILKWEED EDITIONS NATIONAL FICTION PRIZE

Milkweed Editions, 1011 Washington Ave. S., Suite 300, Minneapolis MN 55415. (612)332-3192. Fax: (612)215-2550. E-mail: editor@milkweed.org. Web site: www.milkweed.org. **Contact:** Elisabeth Fitz, first editor. Annual award for unpublished works. "Milkweed is looking for a novel, novella, or a collection of short stories. Manuscripts should be of high literary quality and must be double-spaced and between 150-400 pages in length. Due to new postal regulations, writers who need their work returned must include a check for $5 rather than a SAS book mailer. Manuscripts not accompanied by a check for postage will be recycled." Winner will be chosen from the mss Milkweed accepts for publication each year. All mss submitted to Milkweed will automatically be considered for the prize. Submission directly to the contest is no longer necessary. "Must be written in English. Writers should have previously published a book of fiction or 3 short stories (or novellas) in magazines/journals with national distribution." Catalog available on request for $1.50. Guidelines for SASE or online. Prize: Publication by Milkweed Editions, and a cash advance of $5,000 against royalties agreed upon in the contractual arrangement negotiated at the time of acceptance. Judged by Milkweed Editions. No entry fee. Deadline: rolling, but 2007 winner chosen by October 2006. Entries must be unpublished. "Please look at previous winners: *Crossing Bully*, by Margaret Erhart; *Ordinary Wolves*, by Seth Kantner; *Roofwalker*, by Susan Power; *Hell's Bottom, Colorado* by Laura Pritchett—this is the caliber of fiction we are searching for." Winners are notified by phone and announced in November.

◎ MILLION WRITERS AWARD

StorySouth, 898 Chelsea Ave., Columbus OH 43209. (614)545-0754. E-mail: storysouth@yahoo.com. Web site: www.storysouth.com. **Contact:** Jason Sanford, editor. Contest "to honor and promote the best fiction published annually in online journals and magazines. The reason for the Million Writers Award is that most of the major literary prizes for short fiction (such as the O. Henry Awards) ignore Web-published fiction. This award aims to show that world-class fiction is being published online and to promote this fiction to the larger reading and literary community." Prize: publicity for the author and story. Categories: short stories. Judged by *StorySouth* judges. No entry fee. Cover letter should include e-mail address, word count, title and publication where story was previously published. Guidelines available in December on Web site. Deadline: January. Entries must be previously published. All stories must be 1,000 words or longer. Open to any writer. Results announced in March on Web site. Winners notified by e-mail.

◎ THE MILTON CENTER POSTGRADUATE FELLOWSHIP

The Milton Center at *Image*, 3307 Third Ave. West, Seattle WA 98119. (206)281-2988. E-mail: miltoncenter@imagejournal.org. Web site: www.imagejournal.org/milton. **Contact:** Gregory Wolfe, director. Award "to bring emerging writers of Christian commitment to the Center, where their primary goal is to complete their first book-length manuscript in fiction, poetry or creative nonfiction." No entry fee. Guidelines on Web site. Deadline: March 15. Open to any writer.

▢ THE MISSOURI REVIEW EDITORS' PRIZE CONTEST

Missouri Review, 1507 Hillcrest Hall, Columbia MO 65211. (573)882-4474. Fax: (573)884-4671. Web site: www. missourireview.org. **Contact:** Richard Sowienski, managing editor. Prize: $3,000 for fiction, poetry, essay and publication in *The Missouri Review*. Judged by *The Missouri Review* editors. Entry fee: $20; make checks payable to *Missouri Review*. Each fee entitles entrant to a one-year subscription to the journal, an extension of a current subscription, or a gift subscription. Guidelines and inquiries accepted on Web site. Expects to receive 1,800 entries. Deadline: October 1. Entries must be unpublished. Page length restrictions: 25 typed, double-spaced for fiction and essays; 10 for poetry. Open to any writer. Guidelines available in June for SASE. Outside of envelope should be marked "fiction" or "essay" or "poetry." On first page of submission include the author's name, address, e-mail address and telephone number. Results announced in January. Winners notified by phone and mail. For contest results, send SASE. "Send only fully realized work with a distinctive voice, style and subject."

⬩ ◎ MUNICIPAL CHAPTER OF TORONTO IODE BOOK AWARD

Municipal Chapter of Toronto IODE (Imperial Order of the Daughters of the Empire), 40 St. Clair Ave., Suite 205, Toronto ON M4T 1M9 Canada. (416)925-5078. Fax: (416)925-5127. **Contact:** Mary K. Anderson, education officer. To acknowledge authors and/or illustrators in the Greater Toronto Area. Prize: $1,000 to author and/or illustrator. Categories: short stories, novels, story collections. Judged by committee comprised of IODE education officer, president and other officers (approx. 5). No entry fee. Guidelines available by fax. Accepts inquiries by fax, phone. Cover letter should include name, address, phone, e-mail, title, place of original publication. Deadline: Nov. 1. Entries must be previously published. Open to books geared toward 6-12 year olds. Must be Canadian citizens. Authors/illustrators may submit their own work. "Submit books directly to the attention of Theo Heras at the Lillian Smith Library, Toronto. She compiles submissions and short-lists them." Results announced in January and available by fax. Award given at annual dinner meeting in March. Winners notified by mail in December.

NEW LETTERS LITERARY AWARDS

New Letters, 5101 Rockhill Rd., Kansas City MO 64110-2499. (816)235-1168. Fax: (816)235-2611. E-mail: newletters@umkc.edu. Web site: www.newletters.org. Award to "find and reward good writing from writers who need the recognition and support." Award has 3 categories (fiction, poetry and creative nonfiction) with 1 winner in each. Offered annually for previously unpublished work. Prize: 1st place: $1, 500, plus publication; all entries are considered for publication. Judged by 2 rounds of regional writers (preliminary judging). Winners picked by an anonymous judge of national repute. Entry fee: $15/entry (includes year's subscription). Make checks payable to *New Letters* or send credit card information. Deadline: May 18. Entries must be unpublished. Open to any writer. Guidelines available in January for SASE, e-mail, on Web site and in publication. Cover letter should include name, address, phone, e-mail and title. Results announced in September. Winners notified by phone. For contest results, send SASE, e-mail or visit Web site.

NEW MILLENNIUM WRITING AWARDS

New Millennium Writings, Room M2, P.O. Box 2463, Knoxville TN 37901. (423)428-0389. Fax: (865)428-2302. E-mail: DonWilliams7@charter.net. Web site: www.newmillenniumwritings.com/awards.html. **Contact:** Don Williams, editor. Award "to promote literary excellence in contemporary fiction." Offered twice annually for unpublished fiction, poetry, essays or nonfiction prose to encourage new fiction writers, poets and essayists and bring them to attention of publishing industry. Entrants receive an issue of *NMW* in which winners appear. Prize: $1,000 (fiction, poetry, nonfiction); winners published in *NMW* and on Web site. Judged by novelists and short story writers. Entry fee: $17 for each submission. Deadline: November 17 and June 17. Entries must be unpublished. Biannual competition. Length: 1,000-6,000 words. Guidelines available year round for SASE and on Web site. "Provide a bold, yet organic opening line, sustain the voice and mood throughout, tell an entertaining and vital story with a strong ending. *New Millennium Writings* is a forward-looking periodical for writers and lovers of good reading. It is filled with outstanding poetry, fiction, essays and other speculations on subjects both topical and timeless about life in our astonishing times. Our pages brim with prize-winning essays, humor, full-page illustration, writing advice and poetry from writers at all stages of their careers. First-timers find their work displayed alongside such well-known writers as John Updike, Sharyn McCrumb, Lee Smith, Norman Mailer, Madison Smartt Bell and Cormac McCarthy." Results announced October and April. Winners notified by mail and phone. All entrants will receive a list of winners, plus a copy of the annual anthology. Send letter-sized SASE with entry for list.

NEW YORK STORIES FICTION PRIZE

New York Stories, English Department, E-103, LaGuardia Community College/CUNY, 31-10 Thomson Ave., Long Island City NY 11101. E-mail: nystories@lagcc.cuny.edu. Web site: www.newyorkstories.org. **Contact:** Daniel Caplice Lynch, editor-in-chief. Offered annually for unpublished work to showcase new, quality short fiction. Stories must not exceed 6,000 words. Prize: 1st place: $500 and publication; 2nd place: $250 and consideration for publication. Judged by the editor. Entry fee: $15. Each submission should be accompanied by a separate, non-refundable check for $15, payable to *New York Stories*. Mss are not returned. Please write "New York Stories Fiction Prize" on the outer envelope and the title page. Deadline: September 15. Entries must be unpublished. Open to any writer. Guidelines on Web site and in publication. Accepts inquires by e-mail. Cover letter should include name, address, phone, e-mail, word count and title. "Also include this information on the manuscript." Winners notified by phone or e-mail. For contest results, send SASE or visit Web site.

JOHN NEWBERY AWARD

American Library Association (ALA), Association for Library Service to Children, 50 E. Huron St., Chicago IL 60611. (312)280-2163. Fax: (312)944-7671. E-mail: alsc@ala.org. Web site: www.ala.org/alsc. **Contact:** ALSC, Attn: Newbery Medal. Prize: Medal. Judged by Newbery Award Selection Committee. No entry fee. Deadline: December 31. Entries must be previously published. Only books for children published in the U.S. during the preceeding year are eligible. Entry restricted to U.S. citizens, residents. Guidelines available on Web site, by fax, phone or e-mail. Accepts inquiries by fax and e-mail. Results announced at the ALA Midwinter Meeting. Winners notified by phone. For contest results, visit Web site in February or contact via phone, fax, e-mail or SASE.

THE NOMA AWARD FOR PUBLISHING IN AFRICA

P.O. Box 128, Witney, Oxon 0X8 5XU. United Kingdom. E-mail: maryljay@aol.com. Web site: www.nomaaward .org. **Contact:** Mary Jay. Sponsored by Kodansha Ltd. Award "to encourage publication of works by African writers and scholars in Africa, instead of abroad as is still too often the case at present." Categories: scholarly or academic; books for children; literature and creative writing, including fiction, drama and poetry. Judged by a committee of African scholars and book experts and representatives of the international book community. Chairman: Walter Bgoya. No entry fee. Deadline: March 31. Entries must be previously published. Guidelines and entry forms available in December by fax, e-mail or on Web site. Submissions are through publishers only. "Publisher must complete entry form and supply six copies of the published work." Maximum number of entries per author is three. Results announced in October. Winners notified through publisher. List of winners available from Secretariat or on Web site. "The award is for an outstanding book. Content is the overriding criterion, but standards of publication are also taken into account."

NORTH CAROLINA ARTS COUNCIL WRITERS' RESIDENCIES

221 E. Lane St., Raleigh NC 27699-4632. (919)715-1519. Fax: (919)733-4834. E-mail: debbie.mcgill@ncmail.net. Web site: www.ncarts.org. **Contact:** Deborah McGill, literature director. Award "to encourage and recognize North Carolina's finest creative writers. Every year we offer a 2-month residency for 1 writer at Headlands Center for the Arts (California) and a 1-month residency for 1 writer at Vermont Studio Center. Judged by panels of writers and editors convened by the residency centers. No entry fee. Deadline: early June; see Web site for details. Writers must be over 18 years old, not currently enrolled in a degree-granting program on undergraduate or graduate level, must have been a resident of North Carolina for 1 full year as of application deadline and must plan to remain a resident for the following year. Please see website for other eligibility requirements. Guidelines available after March 1 by phone or online. Accepts inquiries by fax and e-mail. Results announced in the fall. Winners notified by phone. Other applicants notified by mail.

NORTHERN CALIFORNIA BOOK AWARDS

Northern California Book Reviewers Association, % Poetry Flash, 1450 Fourth St. #4, Berkeley CA 94710. (510)525-5476. Fax: (510)525-6752. E-mail: editor@poetryflash.org. Web site: www.poetryflash.org. **Contact:** Joyce Jenkins, executive director. "Award is to celebrate books published by Northern California authors in poetry, fiction, nonfiction, translation and children's literature." Annual. Competition/award for novels, story collections, translations. Prize: awards publicity from a professional publicist, $100 gift certificate, and reading at awards ceremony. Awards $1,000 for lifetime achievement award. Categories: novels and short story collections. Judged by members of the association, active book reviewers, and book editors. No entry fee. Deadline: Dec. 1 for entries published in that calendar year. Entries should be previously published. Open to authors living in Northern California. Winners announced in April. Results made available to entrants with SASE, by fax, by e-mail, on Web site.

NOVEL MANUSCRIPT CONTEST

Writers' League of Texas, 1501 W. 5th St., #E-2, Austin TX 78703. (512)499-8914. Fax: (512)499-0441. E-mail: wlt@writersleague.org. Web site: www.writersleague.org. **Contact:** Kristy Bordine. Prize: First place winners meet individually with an agent at the Writers' League of Texas Agents Conference in June. Categories: mainstream fiction, mystery, thriller/action adventure, romance, science fiction/fantasy/horror, historical/western, biography, narrative nonfiction, and children's long and short works. Judged by preliminary judges (first round), then published authors (advancing entries); agent or editor reads finalists' ms. Entry fee: $50 for score sheet with comments. Send credit card information or make check payable to Writer's League of Texas. Cover letter should include name, address, phone, e-mail, title. Entries must be unpublished. Submit first 10 pages of novel, double-spaced. Open to any writer. Guidelines available in January for SASE, by e-mail or on Web site. Accepts inquiries by e-mail. Results announced at the June conference. Winners notified after conference. Results available on Web site.

NOVELLO LITERARY AWARD

Novello Festival Press, 310 N. Tryon St., Charlotte NC 28202. (704)432-0153. Web site: www.novellopress.org. **Contact:** A. Rogers, executive editor. "To recognize a writer of a book-length work of literary fiction or nonfiction who resides in North Carolina or South Carolina." Annual. Competition/award for novels, story collections. Prize: $1,000 advance against royalties, publication, national distribution of the winning book. Categories: Literary fiction/nonfiction (including novel, short story collection, memoir, biography, history). Receives about 100 entries per year. Judged by the editor(s), staff, advisory committee of the press, and others in the literary arts community whom they may designate. No entry fee. Guidelines available in Nov. on Web site and in regional writers resources. Submission period: Nov.-June 1. Entries should be unpublished. "Portions may be previously published (e.g. a short story within a collection)." Open to writers over the age of 18 who reside in NC or SC. Length: 200-400 pages, typed and double-spaced. Cover letter should include name, address, phone, e-mail, word count, novel/collection title. Identifying information may or may not be included on the actual ms; "this is not a blind competition." Writers may submit own work. No agent submissions. "Do not send genre fiction, poetry, or work for children. Literary fiction and/or literary nonfiction only." Results announced Oct. during The Novello Festival of Reading. Winners notified by mail, by phone. Winners announced Oct. Results made available to entrants on Web site.

☐ ◎ THE FLANNERY O'CONNOR AWARD FOR SHORT FICTION

The University of Georgia Press, 330 Research Dr., Athens GA 30602-4901. Web site: www.ugapress.uga.edu. **Contact:** Andrew Berzanskis, coordinator. Does not return mss. Manuscripts must be 200-275 pages long. Authors do not have to be previously published. Prize: $1,000 and publication under standard book contract; selects two prize winners a year. Categories: Wants collections of short stories. Stories that have previously appeared in magazines or in anthologies may be included. Collections that include long stories or novellas (50-150 pages) are acceptable. However, novels or single novellas will not be considered. Stories previously published in a book-length collection of the author's own work may not be included. Entry fee: $20; checks payable to University of Georgia Press. Complete submission guidelines online. Submission Period: April 1-May 31. Open to all writers in English. "Manuscripts under consideration for this competition may be submitted elsewhere at the same time. Please notify us immediately, however, if your manuscript is accepted by another publisher while it is under review with our press. Authors may submit more than one manuscript to the competition as long as each submission is accompanied by a $20 entry fee, meets all eligibility requirements, and does not duplicate material sent to us in another manuscript." Winners are usually notified before the end of November. Entrants who have enclosed an SASE will receive a letter announcing the winners.

◎ FRANK O'CONNOR FICTION AWARD

descant, Texas Christian University, TCU Box 297270, Fort Worth TX 76129. (817)257-6537. Fax: (817)257-6239. E-mail: descant@tcu.edu. Web site: www.descant.tcu.edu. **Contact:** David Kuhne, editor. Annual award to honor the best published fiction in *descant* for its current volume. Prize: $500. No entry fee. Guidelines available for SASE or on Web site. Deadline: April 1. Entries must be previously published. Results announced in August. Winners notified by phone in July. For contest results, send SASE. Also offers the Gary Wilson Award for short fiction. Prize: $250. Send SASE for guidelines.

☐ THE OHIO STATE UNIVERSITY PRIZE IN SHORT FICTION

The Ohio State University Press and the MFA Program in Creative Writing at The Ohio State University, 1070 Carmack Rd., Columbus OH 43210-1002. (614)292-1462. Fax: (614)292-2065. Web site: ohiostatepress.org. Offered annually to published and unpublished writers. Submissions may include short stories, novellas or a combination of both. Manuscripts must be 150-300 typed pages; novellas must not exceed 125 pages. No employee or student of The Ohio State University is eligible. Prize: $1,500, publication under a standard book contract. Entry fee: $20. Deadline: Must be postmarked during the month of January.

◎ (ALICE WOOD MEMORIAL) OHIOANA AWARD FOR CHILDREN'S LITERATURE

Ohioana Library Association, 274 E. First Ave., Suite 300, Columbus OH 43201. (614)466-3831. Fax: (614)728-6974. E-mail: ohioana@sloma.state.oh.us. Web site: www.ohioana.org. **Contact:** Linda Hengst, executive director. Offered to an author whose body of work has made, and continues to make, a significant contribution to literature for children or young adults and through their work as a writer, teacher, or administrator, or through their community service, interest in children's literature has been encouraged and children have become involved with reading. Nomination forms for SASE. Recipient must have been born in Ohio or lived in Ohio at least 5 years. Prize: $1,000. No entry fee. Deadline: December 31. Guidelines for SASE. Accepts inquiries by fax and e-mail. Results announced in August or September. Winners notified by letter in May. For contest results, call or e-mail.

☑ ◎ OHIOANA BOOK AWARDS

Ohioana Library Association, 274 E. 1st Ave., Suite 300, Columbus OH 43201-3673. (614)466-3831. Fax: (614)728-6974. E-mail: ohioana@sloma.state.oh.us. Web site: www.ohioana.org. **Contact:** Linda Hengst, executive director. Offered annually to bring national attention to Ohio authors and their books, published in the last 2 years. (Books can only be considered once.) Categories: Fiction, nonfiction, juvenile, poetry, and books about Ohio or an Ohioan. Writers must have been born in Ohio or lived in Ohio for at least 5 years, but books about Ohio or an Ohioan need not be written by an Ohioan. Prize: certificate and glass sculpture. Judged by a jury selected by librarians, book reviewers, writers and other knowledgeable people. Each Spring the jury considers all books received since the previous jury. No entry fee. Deadline: December 31. Two copies of the book must be received by the Ohioana Library by December 31 prior to the year the award is given; literary quality of the book must be outstanding. No entry forms are needed, but they are available July 1 of each year. "We will be glad to answer letters or e-mails asking specific questions." Results announced in August or September. Winners notified by mail in May.

◐ ORANGE BLOSSOM FICTION CONTEST

The Oak, 1530 Seventh St., Rock Island IL 61201. (309)788-3980. **Contact:** Betty Mowery, editor. Award "to build up circulation of publication and give new authors a chance for competition and publication along with seasoned writers." Prize: subscription to *The Oak*. Categories: short fiction. Judged by published authors. Entry fee: six 39¢ stamps. Deadline: April 1. "May be on any subject, but avoid gore and killing of humans or animals." Open to any writer. Guidelines available in January for SASE. Prefers name, address, contest deadline and title on ms; no cover letter. Guidelines for other contests available for SASE. "No reply will be made without SASE." Results announced a week after deadline. Winners notified by mail. "Material is judged on content and tightness of writing as well as word lengths, since there is a 500-word limit. Always include a SASE with submissions. Entries without six 39¢ stamps will not be judged."

◎ OREGON BOOK AWARDS

Literary Arts, 224 NW 13th Ave., Ste. 306, #219, Portland OR 97209. (503)227-2583. E-mail: kristy@literary-arts.org. Web site: www.literary-arts.org. **Contact:** Kristy Athens, program coordinator. The annual Oregon Book Awards celebrate Oregon authors in the areas of poetry, fiction, nonfiction, drama and young readers' literature published between April 1, 2005 and March 31, 2006. Prize: Finalists are invited on a statewide reading tour and are promoted in bookstores and libraries across the state. Judged by writers who are selected from outside Oregon for their expertise in a genre. Past judges include Mark Doty, Colson Whitehead and Kim Barnes. Entry fee determined by initial print run; see Web site for details. Deadline: last Friday in May. Entries must be previously published. Oregon residents only. Guidelines available in February for SASE and on Web site. Accepts inquiries by phone and e-mail. Finalists announced in October. Winners announced at an awards ceremony in November. List of winners available in November.

◐ PATERSON FICTION PRIZE

The Poetry Center at Passaic County Community College, One College Blvd., Paterson NJ 07505-1179. (973)684-6555. Fax: (973)523-6085. E-mail: mgillan@pccc.edu. Web site: www.pccc.edu/poetry. **Contact:** Maria Mazziotti Gillan, executive director. Award "to encourage recognition of high-quality writing." Offered annually for a novel or collection of short fiction published the previous calendar year. Prize: $1,000. Judges rotate each year. No entry fee. Deadline: Submissions accepted after January 10. Open to any writer. Guidelines available for SASE, e-mail or on Web site. Accepts inquiries by e-mail or phone. Results announced in July. Winners notified by mail. For contest results, send SASE or visit Web site.

◐ PEARL SHORT STORY PRIZE

*Pearl*Magazine, 3030 E. Second St., Long Beach CA 90803-5163. (562)434-4523. E-mail: Pearlmag@aol.com. Web site: www.pearlmag.com. **Contact:** Marilyn Johnson, fiction editor. Award to "provide a larger forum and help widen publishing opportunities for fiction writers in the small press and to help support the continuing publication of *Pearl*." Prize: $250, publication in *Pearl* and 10 copies of the journal. Judged by the editors of *Pearl*: Marilyn Johnson, Joan Jobe Smith, Barbara Hauk. Entry fee: $10/story. Include a brief bio and SASE for reply or return of mss. Accepts simultaneous submissions, but asks to be notified if story is accepted elsewhere. Deadline: May 31. Entries must be unpublished. "Although we are open to all types of fiction, we look most favorably on coherent, well-crafted narratives containing interesting, believable characters in meaningful situations." Length: 4,000 words maximum. Open to any writer. Guidelines for SASE or on Web site. Accepts queries by e-mail or fax. Results announced in September. Winners notified by mail. For contest results, send SASE, e-mail or visit Web site.

◎ PEN CENTER USA ANNUAL LITERARY AWARDS

PEN Center USA, %Antioch University Los Angeles, 400 Corporate Pointe, Culver Citty CA 91030. (310)862-1555 ext. 361. Fax: (310)862-1556. E-mail: awards@penusa.org. Web site: www.penusa.org. Offered annually for fiction, creative nonfiction, poetry, children's/young adult literature, or translation published January 1-December 31 of 2006. Prize: $1,000 and honored at a ceremony in Los Angeles. Judged by panel of writers, editors and critics. Entry fee: $35. Guidelines available in July for SASE, fax, e-mail or on Web site. Accepts inquiries by fax, phone and e-mail. All entries must include 4 non-returnable copies of each submission and a completed entry form. Deadline: December 15. Entries must be previously published. Open to authors west of the Mississippi River, including all of Minnesota and Louisiana. Results announced in May. Winners notified by phone and mail. For contest results, send SASE or visit Web site.

☐ ◎ POCKETS FICTION-WRITING CONTEST

Upper Room Publications, 1908 Grand Ave. AV, P.O. Box 340004, Nashville TN 37203-0004. (615)340-7333. Fax: (615)340-7267. E-mail: pockets@upperroom.org. Web site: www.pockets.org. *Pockets* is a devotional magazine for children between the ages of 6 and 11. Contest offered annually for unpublished work to discover new children's writers. Prize: $1,000 and publication in *Pockets*. Categories: short stories. Judged by *Pockets* staff and staff of other Upper Room Publications. No entry fee. Guidelines available for #10 SASE or on Web site. Deadline: Must be postmarked between March 1-August 15. Entries must be unpublished. Because the purpose of the contest is to discover new writers, previous winners are not eligible. No violence, science fiction, romance, fantasy or talking animal stories. Word length 1,000-1,600 words. Open to any writer. Winner announced November 1 and notified by U.S. mail. Contest submissions accompanied by SASE will be returned Nov. 1. "Send SASE with 4 first-class stamps to request guidelines and a past issue, or go to www.pockets.org."

N ☐ KATHERINE ANNE PORTER PRIZE IN SHORT FICTION

The University of North Texas Press, Dept. of English, P.O. Box 311307, Denton TX 76203. (940)565-2142. Fax: (940)565-4590. E-mail: kdevinney@unt.edu. Web site: www.unt.edu/untpress. **Contact:** Karen DeVinney, managing editor. "Purpose is to encourage and promote short fiction." Annual. Competition/award for story collections. Prize: $1,000 and publication by UNT Press. Categories: short fiction, which may be a combination of short-shorts, short stories and novellas. Judged by anonymous judge (2005 was Sharon Oard Warner). Entry fee: $20. Make checks payable to UNT Press. Guidelines available in Jan. with SASE, by fax, by phone, by e-mail, on Web site, in publication. Accepts inquiries by fax, e-mail, phone. Submission period: July & August. Entries should be unpublished. "Unpublished and previously published stories, or a combination of both, are accepted; however, the submitted collection itself must be unpublished. If a portion is previously published, permissions are needed." Open to all. Length: 27,500-50,000 words. Cover letter should include name, address, phone, e-mail, word count, novel/story title, place(s) where story or stories were previously published. None of this information should appear on the actual manuscript. Writers may submit own work. "Simply follow the rules and do your best." Results announced in January. Winners notified by mail, by phone, by e-mail. Results made available to entrants with SASE, by fax, by e-mail, on Web site.

◎ PUSHCART PRIZE

Pushcart Press, P.O. Box 380, Wainscott NY 11975. (516)324-9300. Web site: www.pushcartprize.com. **Contact:** Bill Henderson, president. Award to "publish and recognize the best of small press literary work." Prize: Publication in *Pushcart Prize: Best of the Small Presses* anthology. Categories: short stories, poetry, essays on any subject. No entry fee. Deadline: December 1. Entries must be previously published. Must have been published during the current calendar year. Open to any writer. Nomination by small press publishers/editors only.

N ☒ ◎ QUEBEC WRITERS' FEDERATION BOOK AWARDS

Quebec Writers' Federation, 1200 Atwater, Montreal QC H3Z 1X4 Canada. (514)933-0878. E-mail: admin@qwf.org. Web site: www.Qwf.org. **Contact:** Lori Schubert, executive director. Award "to honor excellence in writing in English in Quebec." Prize: $2,000 (Canadian) in each category. Categories: fiction, poetry, nonfiction, first book and translation. Each prize judged by panel of 3 jurors, different each year. $10 entry fee. Guidelines for submissions sent to Canadian Publishers and posted on Web site in March. Accepts inquiries by e-mail. Deadline: May 31, August 15. Entries must be previously published. Length: must be more than 48 pages. "Writer must have resided in Quebec for 3 of the previous 5 years." Books may be published anywhere. Winners announced in November at Annual Awards Gala and posted on Web site.

☑ ◎ SIR WALTER RALEIGH AWARD

North Carolina Literary and Historical Association, 4610 Mail Service Center, Raleigh NC 27699-4610. (919)807-7290. **Contact:** Michael Hill, awards coordinator. "To promote among the people of North Carolina an interest in their own literature." Prize: statue of Sir Walter Raleigh. Categories: novels and short story collections. Judged by university English and history professors. No entry fee. Guidelines available in August for SASE. Accepts inquiries by fax. Deadline: July 15. Entries must be previously published. Book must be an original work published during the 12 months ending June 30 of the year for which the award is given. Writer must be a legal or physical resident of North Carolina for the 3 years preceeding the close of the contest period. Authors or publishers may submit 3 copies of their book to the above address. Results announced in October. Winners notified by mail. For contest results, send SASE.

☐ RAMBUNCTIOUS REVIEW FICTION CONTEST

Rambunctious Review, 1221 W. Pratt Blvd., Chicago IL 60626. **Contact:** N. Lennon, Editor. Annual themed contest for unpublished stories. Acquires one-time publication rights. Open to any writer. "There are no stylistic limitations, but the story should reflect the writer's philosophy on the theme of the next issue." Last year's theme: Milestones. Prize: 1st prize: $100; 2nd prize: $75; 3rd prize: $50; all winning stories will be published in future issues of *Rambunctious Review*. Judged by previous contest winners. Entry fee: $4/story. The writer's name and address must be on each page. Stories will not be returned. Entrants will be notified of contest results the following March. Guidelines available for SASE or in publication in September. Deadline: December 31. Entries must be unpublished. Looking for "originality; short, clear exposition; character-driven" stories.

☑ ◎ THE REA AWARD FOR THE SHORT STORY

Dungannon Foundation, 53 W. Church Hill Rd., Washington CT 06794. Web site: www.reaaward.org. **Contact:** Elizabeth Rea, president. "Sponsored by the Dungannon Foundation, the Rea Award was established in 1986 by Michael M. Rea to honor a living U.S. or Canadian writer who has made a significant contribution to the short story form." Prize: $30,000. Categories: short stories. Judged by 3 jurors (2005 judges were Sherman Alexie, Ron Carlson and Tess Gallagher). No entry fee. Award cannot be applied for. The recipient is selected by an annually appointed jury. Award announced in fall annually. List of winners available on Web site. 2005 winner was Ann Beattie.

Ⓝ ☐ RED HEN SHORT FICTION AWARD

Red Hen Press, P.O. Box 3537, Granada Hills CA 91394. Web site: www.redhen.org. **Contact:** Mark E. Cull, publisher. "To find new experimental fiction." Annual. Competition/award for short stories. Prize: $1,000 and publication. Categories: short fiction. Judged by a single rotating judge who is also the fiction editor of *The Los Angeles Review* for the issue the story will be included in. Entry fee: $20. Make checks payable to Red Hen Press. Guidelines available in Jan. on Web site. Deadline: June 30. Entries should be unpublished. Open to all. Length: 25 pages max. Cover letter should include name, address, phone, e-mail, word count, story title. Nothing should appear on ms except title. Writers may submit own work. Results announced by Oct. Winners notified by phone. Results made available to entrants on Web site.

🌐 ◎ THE RED HOUSE CHILDREN'S BOOK AWARD

(formerly The Children's Book Award), Federation of Children's Book Groups, The Old Malt House, Aldbourne, Marlborough, Wiltshire SN8 2DW United Kingdom. E-mail: marianneadey@aol.com. Web site: www.redhousec hildrensbookaward.co.uk. **Contact:** Marianne Adey, national coordinator. Purpose of award is "to find out what children choose among books of fiction published in the United Kingdom." Prize: silver bowl, portfolio of children's letters and pictures. Categories: Books for Younger Children, Books for Younger Readers, Books for Older Children. No entry fee. Deadline: Closing date is Dec. 31. Entries must be previously published. UK authors only. Either author or publisher may nominate title. Guidelines available on Web site. Accepts inquiries by fax, e-mail and phone. Results announced in June for books published the previous year. Winners notified at event/banquet and via the publisher. For contest results, visit Web site.

Ⓝ THE LOUISE E. REYNOLDS MEMORIAL FICTION AWARD

the new renaissance, 26 Heath Rd. #1, Arlington MA 02474. (781)646-0118. Web site: www.trnlitmag.net. **Contact:** Louise T. Reynolds, editor in chief. "To honor *tnr*'s founding manager, Louise T. Reynolds; to reward *tnr*'s writers; and to help promote quality writing." For fiction in a 3-issue volume of *tnr* judged "best" by independent judges. Competition/award for short stories, translations of stories. Prize: first place, $500; second place, $250, third place, $125; honorable mention, $50. About 400-500 eligible entries per award. Judged by independent judges; "judge is always a fiction writer with publishing credits and ideally someone already familiar to some extent with *tnr* (e.g. writers we've published, a subscriber and/or a reviewer/critic)." Entry fee: $16.50 (U.S.), $18.50 (foreign). Make checks payable to *the new renaissance*. All entrants will receive a past issue with award-winning fiction. Accepts inquiries by e-mail. Send complete ms, SASE, entry fee. Submission period: January 1-June 30, September-October '07. Award given to "any fiction already published in *tnr*, long or short, serious or satire, literary or academic (occasionally experimental)." Length: 2-36 pages. Cover letter should include name, address, e-mail, story title. Name and title should appear on actual ms. Writers may submit own work. "Read the issue sent to entrants to see samples of award-winning fiction." Results announced after the third issue of a 3-issue volume is published. Winners notified by mail or by phone before announcement is made public. Results made available to entrants with SASE, on Web site.

☑ ◎ HAROLD U. RIBALOW AWARD

Hadassah Magazine, 50 W. 58th St., New York NY 10019. (212)451-6289. Fax: (212)451-6257. E-mail: imarks@h adassah.org. **Contact:** Ian Marks, Ribalow Prize Coordinator. Offered annually for English-language books of fiction (novel or short stories) on a Jewish theme published the previous calendar year. Books should be submitted by the publisher. "Harold U. Ribalow was a noted writer and editor who devoted his time to the discovery and encouragement of young Jewish writers." Prize: $3,000 and excerpt of book in *Hadassah Magazine*. No entry fee. Deadline: March 1. Book should have been published the year preceding the award.

THE SCARS/CC&D EDITOR'S CHOICE AWARDS

Scars Publications and Design, 829 Brian Court, Gurnee IL 60031-3155. E-mail: editors@scars.tv. Web site: http://scars.tv. **Contact:** Janet Kuypers, editor/publisher. Award "to showcase good writing in an annual book." Prize: publication of story/essay and 1 copy of the book. Categories: short stories. Entry fee: $15/short story. Deadline: revolves for appearing in different upcoming books as winners. Entries may be unpublished or previously published. Open to any writer. For guidelines, visit Web site. Accepts inquiries by e-mail. Length: "We appreciate shorter works. Shorter stories, more vivid and more real storylines in writing have a good chance." Results announced at book publication, online. Winners notified by mail when book is printed. For contest results, send SASE or e-mail or look at the contest page at Web site."

SCIENCE FICTION WRITERS OF EARTH (SFWOE) SHORT STORY CONTEST

Science Fiction Writers of Earth, P.O. Box 121293, Fort Worth TX 76121-1293. E-mail: sfwoe@flash.net. Web site: www.flash.net/~sfwoe. **Contact:** Gilbert Gordon Reis, SFWoE administrator. Award to "promote the art of science fiction/fantasy short story writing." Prize: $200, $100, $50, $25; $75 paid to place the winning story on the SFWoE Web Site for 180 days. Categories: short story. Judged by author Edward Bryant. Entry fee: $5 for membership and first entry; $2 each for additional entries (make checks payable to SFWoE). Cover letter or entry form from Web Site should include name, address, phone, e-mail address, word count and title. Same information should appear on ms title page. Deadline: October 30. Entries must be unpublished. The author must not have received payment for a published piece of fiction. Stories should be science fiction or fantasy, 2,000-7,500 words. Guidelines available after November for SASE, e-mail or on Web site. Accepts inquiries by e-mail and mail. "Visit our website and read the winning story. Read our online newsletter to know what the judge looks for in a good story. Contestants enjoy international competition." Results announced January 31. Winners notified by mail, phone or e-mail. "Each contestant is mailed the contest results, judge's report, and a listing of the top 10 contestants." Send separate SASE for complete list of the contest stories and contestants (or print from Web site).

SCRIPTAPALOOZA TELEVISION WRITING COMPETITION

Supported by Writers Guild of America West, 7775 Sunset Blvd., PMB #200, Hollywood CA 90046. (323)654-5809. E-mail: info@scriptapalooza.com. Web site: www.scriptapaloozatv.com. "Seeking talented writers who have an interest in American television writing." Prize: $500 to top winner in each category (total $1,500), production company consideration. Categories: sitcoms, pilots and one-hour dramas. Entry fee: $40; accepts Paypal credit card or make checks payable to Scriptapalooza. Deadline: April 15 and November 15 of each year. Entries must be unpublished. Length: standard television format whether one hour, one-half hour or pilot. Open to any writer 18 or older. Guidelines available now for SASE or on Web Site. Accepts inquiries by e-mail, phone. "Pilots should be fresh and new and easy to visualize. Spec scripts should stay current with the shows, up-to-date story lines, characters, etc." Winners announced February 15 and August 15. For contest results, visit Web Site.

SHORT GRAIN WRITING CONTEST

Grain Magazine, Box 67, Saskatoon SK S7K 3K1 Canada. (306)244-2828. Fax: (306)244-0255. E-mail: grainmag@sasktel.net. Web site: www.grainmagazine.ca. **Contact:** Kent Bruyneel. Competition for postcard (flash) fiction, prose poems, dramatic monologues, nonfiction. Prize: 3 prizes of $500 in each category. Entry fee: $28 fee for 2 entries, plus $8 for additional entries; US and international entries $28, and $6 postage in US funds (non-Canadian). Guidelines available by fax, e-mail, on Web Site or for SASE. Deadline: January 31. Contest entries must be either an original postcard story (narrative fiction in 500 words or less); prose poem (lyric poem written as a prose paragraph or paragraphs in 500 words or less); dramatic monologue (a self-contained speech given by a single character in 500 words or less). Cover document for each entry should include name, address, phone, e-mail, word count and title; title only on ms. Results announced in May. Winners notified by phone, e-mail, fax or mail. For contest results, send SASE, e-mail, fax or visit Web Site.

JOHN SIMMONS SHORT FICTION AWARD

University of Iowa Press, 102 Dey House, 507 N. Clinton St., Iowa City IA 52242-1000. (319)335-2000. Fax: (319)335-2055. Web site: www.uiowapress.org. **Contact:** Holly Carver, director. Award "to give exposure to promising writers who have not yet published a book of prose." Offered annually for a collection of short stories. Anyone who has not published a book of prose fiction is eligible to apply. Prize: Publication by the

University of Iowa Press. Judged by Senior Iowa Writers' Workshops members who screen manuscripts; published fiction author of note makes final two selections. No entry fee. For guidelines, send SASE or visit Web site. Accepts inquiries by fax, phone. No application forms are necessary. A SASE must be included for return of ms. Submission period: August 1-September 30. "Individual stories can be previously published (as in journals), but never in *book* form." Stories must be in English. Length: "at least 150 word-processed, double-spaced pages; 8-10 stories on average for ms." Results announced early in year following competition. Winners notified by phone.

◎ SKIPPING STONES HONOR AWARDS

P.O. Box 3939, Eugene OR 97403-0939. Phone/fax: (541)342-4956. E-mail: editor@skippingstones.org. Web site: www.skippingstones.org. **Contact:** Arun N. Toké, executive editor. Award to "promote multicultural and/or nature awareness through creative writings for children and teens." Prize: honor certificates; seals; reviews; press release/publicity. Categories: short stories, novels, story collections, poetry and nonfiction. Judged by "a multicultural committee of teachers, librarians, parents, students and editors." Entry fee: $50 ($25 for small, low-income publishers/self-publishers). Deadline: January 20. Entries must be previously published. Open to previously published books and resources that appeared in print between January 2005 and January 2007. Guidelines for SASE or e-mail and on Web site. Accepts inquiries by e-mail, fax, phone. "We seek authentic, exceptional, child/youth friendly books that promote intercultural, international, intergenerational harmony and understanding through creative ways. Writings that come out of your own experiences and cultural understanding seem to have an edge." Results announced in May. Winners notified through personal notifications, press release and by publishing reviews of winning titles. For contest results, send SASE, e-mail or visit Web site.

◎ SKIPPING STONES YOUTH AWARDS

Skipping Stones Magazine, P.O. Box 3939, Eugene OR 97403-0903. Phone/fax: (541)342-4956. E-mail: editor@skippingstones.org. Web site: www.skippingstones.org. **Contact:** Arun N. Toké, executive editor. Award to "promote creativity and multicultural and nature awareness in youth." Prize: publication in Autumn issue, honor certificate, subscription to magazine, plus 5 multicultural or nature books. Categories: short stories. Entry fee: $3/entry, make checks payable to *Skipping Stones*. Cover letter should include name, address, phone and e-mail. Deadline: June 20. Entries must be unpublished. Length: 750 words maximum. Open to any writer between 7 and 17. Guidelines available by SASE, e-mail or on Web site. Accepts inquiries by e-mail or phone. "Be creative. Do not use stereotypes or excessive violent language or plots. Be sensitive to cultural diversity." Results announced in the September-October issue. Winners notified by mail. For contest results, visit Web site. Everyone who enters receives the issue which features the award winners.

Ⓝ ◎ SOCIETY OF MIDLAND AUTHORS AWARD

Society of Midland Authors, P.O. Box 10419, Chicago IL 60610-0419. E-mail: tomfrisbie@aol.com. Web site: http://midlandauthors.com. **Contact:** Thomas Frisbie, president. "Established in 1915, the Society of Midland Authors Award (SMA) is presented to one title in each of six categories 'to stimulate creative effort,' one of SMA's goals, to be honored at the group's annual awards banquet in May." Annual. Competition/award for novels, story collections. Prize: cash prize of at least $300 and a plaque that is awarded at the SMA banquet. Categories: children's nonfiction and fiction, adult nonfiction and fiction, adult biography, and poetry. Received about 125 entries last year for adult fiction category. Judging is done by a panel of three judges for each category that includes a mix of experienced authors, reviewers, book sellers, university faculty and librarians. No entry fee. Guidelines available in September-November with SASE, on Web site, in publication. Accepts inquiries by e-mail, phone. Deadline: Feb. 1, 2007. Entries should be previously published. "The contest is open to any title with a recognized publisher that has been published within the year prior to the contest year." Open to any author with a recognized publisher who lives in a Midland state, which includes Illinois, Iowa, Kansas, Michigan, Minnesota, Missouri, Nebraska, North Dakota, South Dakota, Ohio and Wisconsin. SMA only accepts published work accompanied by a completed award form. Writers may submit own work. Entries can also be submitted by the publisher's rep. "Write a great story and be sure to follow contest rules by sending a copy of the book to each of the three judges for the given category who are listed on SMA's Web site." Results announced at the SMA Awards Banquet each May. Other announcements follow in the media. Winners notified by mail, by phone. Results made available to entrants on Web site, in our monthly membership newsletter. Results will also go to local media in the form of press releases.

Ⓝ ◎ SOUTH CAROLINA ARTS COMMISSION AND THE POST AND COURIER SOUTH CAROLINA FICTION CONTEST

1800 Gervais St., Columbia SC 29201. (803)734-8696. Web site: www.southcarolinaarts.com. **Contact:** Sara June Goldstein, program director for the literary arts. "This annual writing competition calls for previously unpublished short stories of 2,500 words or less. The stories do not need to be Southern, nor do they need to be set in South Carolina, although such stories are acceptable for consideration. Up to 12 short stories will be selected for publication; each writer whose work is selected will receive $500 from *The Post and Courier*, which purchases first publication rights. Stories will also be published electronically by posting them on *The Post and Courier*'s Web site, which links to the Art Commission's Web site. No entry fee. Deadline: January 15. Applicant must be a legal resident of South Carolina and be 18 years of age or older at the time of application. Guidelines and application available on the Arts Commission's Web site.

◎ SOUTH DAKOTA ARTS COUNCIL

800 Governors Drive, Pierre SD 57501-2294. (605)773-3131. E-mail: sdac@state.sd.us. Web site: www.sdarts.org. **Contact:** Dennis Holub, executive director. "Individual Artist Grants (up to $3,000) and Artist Collaboration Grants (up to $6,000) are planned for fiscal 2007." No entry fee. Deadline: March 1. Open to South Dakota residents only. Students pursuing an undergraduate or graduate degree are ineligible. Guidelines and application available on Web site or by mail. Applicants must submit application form with an original signature; current résumé no longer than 5 pages; appropriate samples of artistic work (see guidelines); up to 5 pages additional documentation; SASE with adequate postage for return of ms (if desired).

◻ SOUTHWEST WRITERS (SWW) CONTESTS

SouthWest Writers (SWW), 3721 Morris St. NE, Suite A, Albuquerque NM 87111-3611. (505)265-9485. Fax: (505)265-9483. E-mail: SWriters@aol.com. Web site: www.southwestwriters.org. **Contact:** Joanne Bodin, chair. The SouthWest Writers (SWW) Contest encourages and honors excellence in writing. There are 19 catagories, including a Spanish category, in which writers may enter their work. (Please see Category Specific Guidelines on Web site for more details.) Prize: Finalists in all categories are notified by mail and are listed on the SWW Web site with the title of their entry. First, second and third place winners in each category also receive cash prizes of $150, $100, and $50 (respectively), as well as a certificate of achievement. First place winners also compete for the $1,000 Storyteller Award. Winners will be honored at a contest awards banquet (date and time TBA). Categories: Eleven categories—broken down by genre—are for short story and novel writers. For novels: Mainstream and Literary; Mystery, Suspense, Thriller, or Adventure; Romance; Science Fiction, Fantasy, or Horror; Historical or American Frontier/Western; Middle Grade (4th-6th grade) or Young Adult (7th grade and up); Spanish Language Nonfiction article/essay. For short stories: Science Fiction, Fantasy, or Horror; Mainstream and Literary; Mystery or Romance; Other Genres: Historical, Western, etc; Middle Grade (4th-6th grade) or Young Adult (7th grade and up). Judged by editors and agents (most from New York publishing houses) who are chosen by the contest chairs. Judges critique the top three entries in each category. All entries also receive a written critique by a qualified consultant (usually, but not always, a published author). Entry fee: $29 for members, $44 for nonmembers (make checks payable to SouthWest Writers). No cover letter is required; send signed copy of the SWW Contest Entry Form. Personal information should not appear anywhere else on ms. NOVELS: The first 20 pages or less, beginning with the prologue and/or first chapter, plus a 1-page synopsis. SHORT STORIES: 5,000 words or less. (For all children's writing, you must type *Middle Grade* or *Young Adult* in the top right corner of the first page.) Please follow detailed instructions for submission in Category Specific Guidelines on Web site. Deadline: May 1. Entries must be unpublished. Open to all writers from around the world. All entries should be submitted in English and follow standard ms format. "Entrants should read the SWW Contest Entry Form, General Contest Rules and the Category Specific Guidelines for complete information. A Tips & Resources page (as well as all contest info/entry form) is also available on the SWW Web site." Guidelines available in January by SASE, e-mail, on Web site or in SouthWest Sage SWW newsletter. Accepts inquiries by e-mail, phone.

◎ SPUR AWARDS

Western Writers of America, Inc., 1012 Fair St., Franklin TN 37064. (615)791-1444. E-mail: tncrutch@aol.com. Web site: www.westernwriters.org. **Contact:** Awards Coordinator. Purpose of award is "to reward quality in the fields of western fiction and nonfiction." Prize: Trophy. Categories: short stories, novels, poetry and nonfiction. No entry fee. Deadline: December 31. Entries must be published during the contest year. Open to any writer. Guidelines available in Sept./Oct. for SASE or by phone. Inquiries accepted by e-mail or phone. Results announced annually in Summer. Winners notified by mail. For contest results, send SASE.

N ◻ ST. LOUIS SHORT STORY CONTEST

P.O. Box 9337, St. Louis MO 63117. (314)646-8515. Fax: (314)646-8515. E-mail: Form on Web site. Web site: http://stlshortstory.com. **Contact:** Brian Jones, contest administrator. "To provide an opportunity and national platform for serious writers to showcase their talents." Annual. Competition/award for short stories. Prize: $5,000 to the 1st place winner. (This is a "winner take all" format.) The winner and the top 20 quarterfinalists will have their stories posted on the contest Web site as well as published in the 2007 St. Louis Short Story Anthology. Categories: short story (all-encompassing, not genre specific). Each entry will be judged by a panel of five judges who are professional writers from five separate fields: poetry, novel, short story, screenplay and technical writing. Entry fee: $10. Make checks payable to St. Louis Short Story Contest. Accepts inquiries by e-mail form on Web site. Deadline: May 19. Entries should be unpublished. Open to all. Length: 3,500 words. Cover letter should include name, address, phone, e-mail, word count, novel/story title. Only title should appear on actual ms. Writers may submit own work. "Be bold, be clear, and think outside the box with regards to story." Winners notified by phone, by e-mail. Winners announced Dec. 1. Results made available to entrants on Web site.

◎ STONY BROOK SHORT FICTION PRIZE

Department of English, State University of New York, Stony Brook NY 11794-5350. (631)632-7400. Web site: www.stonybrook.edu/fictionprize. **Contact:** John Westermann. Award "to recognize excellent undergraduate fiction." Prize: $1,000 and publication on Web site. Categories: Short stories. Judged by faculty of the Department of English & Creative Writing Program. No entry fee. Guidelines available on Web site. Inquiries accepted by e-mail. Expects 300 entries. Deadline: March 1. Word length: 7,500 words or less. "Only undergraduates enrolled full time in American or Canadian colleges and universities for the 2005-2006 academic year are eligible. Proof required. Students of all races and backgrounds are encouraged to enter. Guidelines for SASE or on website. Ms should include name, permanent address, phone, e-mail, word count and title. Winners notified by phone; results posted on Web site by June.

✂ ◎ THEODORE STURGEON MEMORIAL AWARD FOR BEST SHORT SF OF THE YEAR

Center for the Study of Science Fiction, English Department, University of Kansas, Lawrence KS 66045. (785)864-3380. Fax: (785)864-1159. E-mail: jgunn@ku.edu. Web site: www.ku.edu/~sfcenter. **Contact:** James Gunn, professor and director. Award to "honor the best science fiction short story of the year." Prize: certificate. Winners receive trophy and have their names engraved on permanent trophy. Categories: short stories. Judged by jury. No entry fee. Entries must be previously published. Guidelines available in December by phone, e-mail or on Web site. Accepts inquiries by e-mail and fax. Entrants for the Sturgeon Award are by nomination only. Results announced in July. For contest results, send SASE.

▣ ○ SUBTERRAIN ANNUAL LITERARY AWARDS COMPETITION: THE LUSH TRIUMPHANT

subTERRAIN Magazine, P.O. Box 3008 MPO, Vancouver BC V6B 3×5 Canada. (604)876-8710. Fax: (604)879-2667. E-mail: subter@portal.ca. Web site: www.subterrain.ca. **Contact:** Jenn Farrell, managing editor. Offered annually to foster new and upcoming writers. Prize: $500 (Canadian) cash prizes in each category, publication in summer issue, and 1-year subscription to *subTERRAIN*. Runners up also receive publication. Categories: short stories, poetry, nonfiction. Judged by an editorial collective. Entry fee: $20. Entrants may submit as many entries in as many categories as they like. Guidelines on Web site. "Contest kicks off in November." Deadline: May 15. Entries must be unpublished. Length: Fiction: 3,000 words maximum; Poetry: max 3 poems per entry, max 45 lines per poem; creative nonfiction: max 4,000 words. Results announced on Web site. Winners notified by phone call and in press release. "All entries must be previously unpublished material. Submissions will not be returned, so do not send originals. If you would like to receive information regarding the outcome of the contest prior to their publication in the magazine, please include a regular letter-size SASE with your entry. If submitting from outside Canada, please include International Reply Coupons to cover return postage."

○ TALL GRASS WRITERS GUILD LITERARY ANTHOLOGY/CONTEST

2036 North Winds Drive, Dyer IN 46311. (219)322-7085. Fax: (219)322-7085. E-mail: outriderpress@sbcglobal.net. Web site: www.outriderpress.com. **Contact:** Whitney Scott, senior editor. Competition to collect diverse writings by authors of all ages and backgrounds on the theme of "vacations" (spiritual as well as physical). Prize: publication in anthology, free copy to all published authors, $2,000 in cash prizes. Judge is Pulitzer Prize-winning author Rober Olen Butler. Categories: short stories, poetry and creative nonfiction. Entry fee: $16; $12 for members (make check payable to Tallgrass Writers Guild). Deadline: February 28. Word length: 2,500 words or less. Previously published and unpublished submissions accepted. Send SASE. Open to any writer. Guidelines and entry form available for SASE, by fax, e-mail and on Web site. Accepts inquiries by e-mail. Cover letter and ms should include name, address, phone, e-mail, word count and title. Results announced in May. "Must include e-mail address and SASE for response." For contest results, send e-mail.

◎ SYDNEY TAYLOR MANUSCRIPT COMPETITION

Association of Jewish Libraries, 315 Maitland Ave., Teaneck NJ 07666. (201)862-0312. Fax: (201)862-0362. E-mail: rkglasser@aol.com. Web site: www.jewishlibraries.org. **Contact:** Rachel Glasser, coordinator. Award "to identify and encourage writers of fiction for ages 8-11 with universal appeal of Jewish content; story should deepen the understanding of Judaism for all children, Jewish and non-Jewish, and reveal positive aspects of Jewish life. No short stories or plays. Length: 64-200 pages." Judged by 5 AJL member librarians. Prize: $1,000.

No entry fee. Guidelines available by SASE, e-mail or on Web site. Deadline: December 30. Entries must be unpublished. Cover letter should include name, address, phone, e-mail and title. Results announced April 15. Winners notified by phone or e-mail. For contest information, send e-mail or visit Web site. Check Web site for more specific details and to download release forms which must accompany entry.

☐ THE PETER TAYLOR PRIZE FOR THE NOVEL

Knoxville Writers' Guild and University of Tennessee Press, 100 S. Gay Street, Suite 101, Knoxville TN 37902. Web site: www.knoxvillewritersguild.org. Offered annually for unpublished work to discover and publish novels of high literary quality. Guidelines for SASE or on Web site. Only full-length, unpublished novels will be considered. Short story collections, translations, or nonfiction cannot be considered. Prize: $1,000, publication by University of Tennessee Press (a standard royalty contract). Judged by a widely published novelist who chooses the winner from a pool of finalists. 2005 judge: Jill McCorkle; 2006 judge: Jon Manchip White. Entry fee: $25, payable to KWG. Multiple and simultaneous submissions okay. Manuscripts should be a minimum of 40,000 words and should be of letter-quality print on standard white paper. Text should be double-spaced, paginated and printed on one side of the page only. Please do not use a binder; use two rubber bands instead. Please use a padded mailer for shipping. The mss should be accompanied by two title pages: one with the title only; the other with the title and author's name, address and phone number. The author's name or other identifying information should not appear anywhere else on the ms. Manuscripts will not be returned. Each ms must be accompanied by a self-addressed, stamped postcard for confirmation of receipt, along with an SASE for contest results. No FedEx or UPS, please. Deadline: February 1-April 30. Entries must be unpublished. The contest is open to any U.S. resident writing in English. Members of the Knoxville Writers' Guild, current or former students of the judge, and employees and students of the University of Tennessee system are not eligible. Contest results will be announced in November.

◎ TEDDY CHILDREN'S BOOK AWARD

Writers' League of Texas, 1501 W. 5th St., Suite E-2, Austin TX 78703-5155. (512)499-8914. Fax: (512)499-0441. E-mail: wlt@writersleague.org. Web site: www.writersleague.org. **Contact:** Kristy Bordine, membership administrator. Award established to "honor an outstanding book for children published by a member of the Writers' League of Texas." Prize: $1,000. Categories: long works and short works. Entry fee: $25. Deadline: May 31. Entries should be previously published children's books (during the period of June 1 to May 31) by Writers' League of Texas members. League members reside all over the U.S. and in some foreign countries. Persons may join the league when they send in their entries. Guidelines available in January for SASE, fax, e-mail, or visit Web site. Results announced in September. Winners notified at ceremony.

☐ THREE CHEERS AND A TIGER

E-mail: editors@toasted-cheese.com. Web site: www.toasted-cheese.com. **Contact:** Stephanie Lenz, editor. Purpose of contest is to write a short story (following a specific theme) within 48 hours. Prize: an Amazon gift certificate, a tiger-themed prize and publication. Also a few lines of feedback and judges' comments are often provided on entries. Categories: short stories. Judged by two *Toasted Cheese* editors. The entries are presented to the judges by a third editor who removes author info for blind judging. Each judge uses her own criteria to choose entries. No entry fee. Cover letter should include name, address, e-mail, word count and title. Information should be in the body of the e-mail. It will be removed before the judging begins. Entries must be unpublished. Contest offered biannually. Word limit announced at the start of the contest. Contest-specific information is announced 48 hours before the contest submission deadline. Open to any writer. Accepts inquiries by e-mail. "Follow the theme, word count and other contest rules. We have more suggestions at our Web site." Results announced in April and October. Winners notified by e-mail. List of winners on Web site.

☑ ◎ THE THURBER PRIZE FOR AMERICAN HUMOR

Thurber House, 77 Jefferson Ave., Columbus OH 43215. (614)464-1032. Fax: (614)280-3645. E-mail: eswartzlander@thurberhouse.org. Web site: www.thurberhouse.org. **Contact:** Emily Schwartzlander, marketing manager. Award "to give the nation's highest recognition of the art of humor writing." Prize: $5,000. Judged by well-known members of the national arts community. Entry fee: $50 per title. Deadline: April 1. Published submissions or accepted for publication in U.S. for the first time. Primarily pictorial works such as cartoon collections are not considered. Word length: no requirement. Work must be nominated by publisher. Guidelines available for SASE. Accepts inquiries by phone and e-mail. Results announced in November. Winners notified in person at the Algonquin Hotel in New York City. For contest results, visit Web site.

☒ ☐ TICKLED BY THUNDER ANNUAL FICTION CONTEST

Tickled By Thunder, 14076-86A Ave., Surrey BC V3W 0V9 Canada. E-mail: info@tickledbythunder.com. Web site: www.tickledbythunder.com. **Contact:** Larry Lindner, editor. Award to encourage new writers. Prize: $150

Canadian, 4-issue subscription (one year) plus publication. Categories: short stories. Judged by the editor and other writers. Entry fee: $10 Canadian (free for subscribers but more than one story requires $5 per entry). Deadline: February 15. Entries must be unpublished. Word length: 2,000 words or less. Open to any writer. Guidelines available for SASE, e-mail, on Web site. Accepts inquiries by e-mail. Results announced in May. Winners notified by mail. For contest results, send SASE.

TORONTO BOOK AWARDS

Toronto Protocol, City Clerk's Office, 100 Queen St. West, City Hall, 10th Floor, West Tower, Toronto ON M5H 2N2 Canada. (416)392-8191. Fax: (416)392-1247. E-mail: bkurmey@toronto.ca. Web site: www.toronto.ca/book_awards. **Contact:** Bev Kurmey, protocol officer. The Toronto Book Awards honor authors of books of literary or artistic merit that are evocative of Toronto. Annual award for short stories, novels, poetry or short story collections. Prize: $15,000. Each short-listed author (usually 4-6) receives $1,000 and the winner receives the remainder. Categories: No separate categories—novels, short story collections, books of poetry, biographies, history, books about sports, children's books—all are judged together. Judged by jury of five who have demonstrated interest and/or experience in literature, literacy, books and book publishing. No entry fee. Cover letter should include name, address, phone, e-mail and title of entry. Six copies of the entry book are also required. Deadline: February 28. Entries must be previously published. Guidelines available in September on Web site. Accepts inquires by fax, e-mail, phone. Finalists announced in June; winners notified in September at a gala reception. More information and results available on Web site.

THE TROLLOPE SOCIETY SHORT STORY PRIZE

The Trollope Society, 9A North St., London England SW4 OHN United Kingdom. E-mail: pamela@tvdox.com. Web site: www.trollopestoryprize.org. **Contact:** Pamela Neville-Sington. Competition to "encourage interest in the novels of Anthony Trollope among young people; the emphasis is on reading and writing—for fun." Prize: $1,400 to the winner; story published in the Society's quarterly journal *Trollopiana* and on Web site; occasionally a runner up prize of $140. Categories: short stories. Judged by a panel of writers and academics. No entry fee. Guidelines available on Web site. Deadline: January 15. Length: 3,500 words maximum. Open to students worldwide, 21 and under. Guidelines available in May on Web site. Accepts inquiries by fax, e-mail, phone. Cover letter should include name, address, phone, e-mail, word count and title. Results announced in March each year. Winners notified by e-mail.

VERY SHORT FICTION SUMMER AWARD

Glimmer Train Press, Inc., 1211 NW Glisan St., Suite 207, Portland OR 97209. (503)221-0836. Fax: (503)221-0837. Web site: www.glimmertrain. org. **Contact:** Linda Swanson-Davies, editor. Award to encourage the art of the very short story. "We want to read your original, unpublished, very short story (2,000 words or less)." Prize: $1,200 and publication in *Glimmer Train Stories* and 20 author's copies (1st place); $500; $300. Entry fee: $10 reading fee. Deadline: July 31. Open to any writer. Make your submissions online at www.glimmertrain.org. Winners will be notified, and top 25 places will be posted by November 1.

VERY SHORT FICTION WINTER AWARD

Glimmer Train Press, Inc., 1211 NW Glisan St., Suite 207, Portland OR 97209. (503)221-0836. Fax: (503)221-0837. Web site: www.glimmertrain.org. **Contact:** Linda Swanson-Davies. Award offered to encourage the art of the very short story. "We want to read your original, unpublished, very short story (2,000 words or less)." Prize: $1,200 and publication in *Glimmer Train Stories* and 20 author's copies (1st place); $500; $300. Entry fee: $10 reading fee. Deadline: January 31. Open to any writer. Make your submissions online at www.glimmertrain. org. Winners will be notified, and top 25 places will be posted by November 1.

VIOLET CROWN BOOK AWARD

Writers' League of Texas, 1501 W. Fifth St., Suite E-2, Austin TX 78703-5155. (512)499-8914. Fax: (512)499-0441. E-mail: wlt@writersleague.org. Web site: www.writersleague.org. **Contact:** Kristy Bordine, membership administrator. Award "to recognize the best books published by Writers' League of Texas members from June 1 to May 31 in fiction, nonfiction, literary poetry and literary prose categories." Prize: three $1,000 cash awards and 3 trophies. Judged by a panel of judges who are not affiliated with the League. Entry fee: $25. Send credit card information or make checks payable to Writers' League of Texas. "Anthologies that include the work of several authors are not eligible." Deadline: May 31. Entries must be previously published. "Entrants must be Writers' League of Texas members. League members reside all over the U.S. and in some foreign countries. Persons may join the League when they send in their entries." Publisher may also submit entry in author's name. Guidelines available after January for SASE, fax, e-mail or on Web site. Accepts inquiries by fax, e-mail or on phone. Results announced in September. Winners notified at awards ceremony. For contest results, send SASE or visit Web site. "Special citations are presented to finalists."

☐ KURT VONNEGUT FICTION PRIZE

North American Review, University of Northern Iowa, 1222 W. 27th St., Cedar Falls IA 50614-0516. (319)273-6455. Fax: (319)273-4326. E-mail: nar@uni.edu. Web site: webdelsol.com/NorthAmReview/NAR/HTMLpages/NARToday.htm. Prize: 1st: $1,000; 2nd: $100; 3rd: $50. All winners and finalists will be published. Judged by acclaimed writer. Entry fee: $18 (includes a 1-yr subscription). Send two copies of one story (7,000 words max). No names on mss. Include cover letter with name, address, phone, e-mail, title. Stories will not be returned, so do not send SASE for return. For acknowledgment of receipt, please include a SASE. Make your check or money order out to *North American Review*. If you are outside the U.S., please make sure the entry fee is in U.S. currency and routed through a U.S. bank. Deadline: Dec. 31. Entries must be unpublished. Simultaneous submission is not allowed. Stories entered must not be under consideration for publication elsewhere. Open to any writer. For list of winners, send business-sized SASE. Winners will be announced on Web site and in writers' trade magazines.

◎ EDWARD LEWIS WALLANT BOOK AWARD

Irving and Fran Waltman, 3 Brighton Rd., West Hartford CT 06117. (860)232-1421. **Contact:** Mrs. Fran Waltman, co-sponsor. To recognize an American writer whose creative work of fiction has significance for the American Jew. Prize: $500 and a scroll. Judged by panel of 3 judges. No entry fee. Accepts inquiries by phone. Writers may submit their own work. Deadline: Dec. 31. Entries must be previously published. Open to novels or story collections. Open to all American writers. Winner announced in Jan./Feb. and notified by phone.

☐ WISCONSIN INSTITUTE FOR CREATIVE WRITING FELLOWSHIP

University of Wisconsin—Madison, Creative Writing/English Dept., 6195B H.C. White Hall, 600 N. Park St., Madison WI 53706. (608)263-3374. E-mail: rfkuka@wisc.edu. Web site: www.wisc.edu/english/cw. **Contact:** Ron Kuka, program coordinator. Fellowship provides time, space and an intellectual community for writers working on first books. Receives approximately 300 applicants a year. Prize: $25,000 for a 9-month appointment. Judged by English Department faculty and current fellows. Entry fee: $20, payable to the Department of English. Applicants should submit up to 10 pages of poetry or one story of up to 30 pages and a résumé or vita directly to the program during the month of February. An applicant's name must not appear on the writing sample (which must be in ms form) but rather on a separate sheet along with address, social security number, phone number, e-mail address and title(s) of submission(s). Candidates should also supply the names and phone numbers of two recommendations. Accepts inquiries by e-mail and phone. Deadline: February. Entries must be unpublished. Open to any writer. Please enclose a SASE for notification of results. Results announced by May 1. "Send your best work. Stories seem to have a small advantage over novel excerpts."

☐ TOBIAS WOLFF AWARD IN FICTION

Bellingham Review, Mail Stop 9053, Western Washington University, Bellingham WA 98225. (360)650-4863. E-mail: bhreview@cc.wwu.edu. Web site: www.wwu.edu/~bhreview. **Contact:** Fiction Editor. Offered annually for unpublished work. Guidelines for SASE or online. Prize: $1,000, plus publication and subscription. Categories: novel excerpts and short stories. Entry fee: $15 for 1st entry; $10 each additional entry. Guidelines available in August for SASE or on Web site. Deadline: Contest runs: Dec. 1-March 15. Entries must be unpublished. Length: 8,000 words or less per story or chapter. Open to any writer. Winner announced in August and notified by mail. For contest results, send SASE.

◎ WORLD FANTASY AWARDS

World Fantasy Awards Association, P.O. Box 43, Mukilteo WA 98275-0043. E-mail: sfexecsec@aol.com. Web site: www.worldfantasy.org. **Contact:** Peter Dennis Pautz, president. Award "to recognize excellence in fantasy literature worldwide." Offered annually for previously published work in several categories, including life achievement, novel, novella, short story, anthology, collection, artist, special award-pro and special award-nonpro. Works are recommended by attendees of current and previous 2 years' conventions and a panel of judges. Prize: Bust of HP Lovecraft. Judged by panel. No entry fee. Guidelines available in December for SASE or on Web site. Deadline: June 1. Entries must be previously published. Published submissions from previous calendar year. Word length: 10,000-40,000 for novella, 10,000 for short story. "All fantasy is eligible, from supernatural horror to Tolkien-esque to sword and sorcery to the occult, and beyond." Cover letter should include name, address, phone, e-mail, word count, title and publications where submission was previously published. Results announced November 1 at annual convention. For contest results, visit Web site.

Ⓝ ◎ WRITER'S DIGEST ANNUAL SHORT SHORT STORY COMPETITION

Writer's Digest, 4700 E. Galbraith Rd., Cincinnati OH 45236. E-mail: short-short-competition@fwpubs.com. Web site: www.writersdigest.com. **Contact:** Terri Boes, contest administrator. Annual. Competition/award for short-shorts. Prize: 1st place receives $3,000 and option for free "Best Seller Publishing Package" from Trafford

Publishing; 2nd place receives $1,500; 3rd place receives $500; 4th-10th place receive $100; 11th-25th place receive $50 gift certificate for Writer's Digest Books. The names and story titles of the 1st-10th place winners will be printed in the June issue of *Writer's Digest*, and winners will receive the latest edition of *Novel & Short Story Writer's Market*. Judged by the editors of *Writer's Digest*. Entry fee: $12/story. Make checks payable to Writer's Digest. Deadline: Dec. 1. Entries should be unpublished. *"Writer's Digest* reserves the one-time publication rights to the 1st-25th place winning entries to be published in a *Writer's Digest* publication.*"* Open to all except employees of F + W Publications, Inc., and their immediate families and *Writer's Digest* contributing editors and correspondents as listed on the masthead. Length: 1,500 words or fewer. Type the word count on the first page of your entry, along with your name, address, phone number and e-mail address. All entries must be typewritten and double-spaced on one side of $8^{1}/_{2} \times 11$ A4 white paper. Mss will not be returned. Enclose a self-addressed, stamped postcard with your entry if you wish to be notified of its receipt. Write, see publication, or visit Web site for official entry form. Writers may submit own work. Results announced June. Winners notified in Feb. Results made available to entrants on Web site, in publication.

⬛ ◯ WRITER'S DIGEST ANNUAL WRITING COMPETITION

Writer's Digest, 4700 E. Galbraith Rd., Cincinnati OH 45236. (513)531-2690, ext. 1328. E-mail: writing-competiti on@fwpubs.com. Web site: www.writersdigest.com. **Contact:** Terri Boes, contest administrator. Annual. Competition/award for short stories, articles, poems, scripts. Prize: Grand prize is $3,000 cash and an all-expenses-paid trip to New York City to meet with editors and agents. *Writer's Digest* will fly you and a guest to The Big Apple, where you'll spend 3 days and 2 nights in the publishing capital of the world. While you're there, a *Writer's Digest* editor will escort you to meet and share your work with four editors or agents. You'll also receive a free Diamond Publishing Package from Outskirts Press. First place in each category receives $1,000 cash, a ms critique and marketing advice from a *Writer's Digest* editor or advisory board member, commentary from an agent, and $100 worth of Writer's Digest Books. Second place in each category receives $500 cash, plus $100 worth of Writer's Digest Books. Third place in each category receives $250 cash, plus $100 worth of Writer's Digest Books. Fourth place in each category receives $100 cash, the latest editon of *Writer's Market Deluxe*, and a 1-yr subscription to *Writer's Digest*. Fifth place in each category receives $50 cash, the latest edition of *Writer's Market Deluxe*, and a 1-yr subscription to *Writer's Digest*. Sixth-tenth place in each category receives $25 cash. First through tenth place winners also receive a copy of *Writer's Market Deluxe* and a one-year subscription to Writer's Digest mgazine. All other winners receive distinctive certificates honoring their accomplishment. Categories: Inspirational Writing (spiritual/religious); Article: Memoir/Personal Essay; Article: Magazine Feature; Short Story: Genre; Short Story: Mainstream/Literary; Poetry: Rhyming; Poetry: Non-rhyming; Script: Stage Play; Script: TV/Movie; Children's Fiction. Judged by the editors of *Writer's Digest*. Entry fee: $10 for first poem, $5 each additional poem; all other entries are $15 for first ms, $10 each additional ms. Make checks payable to Writer's Digest. Accepts inquiries by e-mail. Deadline: May 15. Entries should be unpublished. "Entries in the Magazine Feature Article category may be previously published. *Writer's Digest* retains one-time publication rights to the grand prize and first place winning entries in each category to be published in a *Writer's Digest* publication." Open to all writers except employees of F + W Publications, Inc, and their immediate families, *Writer's Digest* contributing editors and correspondents as listed on the masthead, Writer's Online Workshops instructors, and Grand Prize winners from the previous three years. Length: 2,000 words max for Memoir/Personal Essay, Feature Article, and Children's Fiction; 2,500 words max for Insipira-tional Writing; 4,000 words max for Short Story categetories; 32 lines max for Poetry categories; 15 pages in standard format plus 1-pg synopsis for Script categories. Write, visit Web site, or see publication for official entry form. Your name, address, phone number, and competition category must appear in the upper left-hand corner of the first page, otherwise your entry is disqualified. See additional guidelines in publication or on Web site. Winners notified by mail. Winners notified by Oct. Results made available to entrants on Web Site.

⬛ ◯ WRITER'S DIGEST POPULAR FICTION AWARDS

Writer's Digest Magazine, 4700 East Galbraith Rd., Cincinnati OH 45236. (513)531-2690, ext. 1328. E-mail: popularfictionawards@fwpubs.com. **Contact:** Terri Boes, contest administrator. Annual. Competition/award for short stories. Prizes: Grand Prize is $2,500 cash, $100 worth of Writer's Digest Books, plus a ms critique and marketing advice from a *Writer's Digest* editor or advisory board member; First Prize in each of the five categories receives $500 cash, $100 worth of Writer's Digest Books, plus a ms critique and marketing advice from a *Writer's Digest* editor or advisory board member; Honorable Mentions receive promotion in *Writer's Digest* and the next edition of *Novel & Short Story Writer's Market*. Categories: Romance, Mystery/Crime, Sci-Fi/Fantasy, Thriller/Suspense, Horror. Judged by *Writer's Digest* editors. Entry fee: $12.50. Make checks payable to *Writer's Digest*. Accepts inquiries by mail, e-mail, phone. Deadline: Nov. 1. Entries should be unpublished. Open to all "except employees of F + W Publications, Inc., and their immediate family members, *Writer's Digest* contributing editors and correspondents as listed on our masthead, Writer's Online Workshops instructors, and Grand Prize Winners from the previous three years in any *Writer's Digest* competitions." Length: 4,000 words or fewer. Entries must be accompanied by an Official Entry Form or facsimile. Your name, address, phone number and competition category must appear in the upper left-hand corner of the first page of your manuscript, otherwise it is disqualified. Writers may submit own work. Results announced in the July issue of *Writer's Digest*. Winners notified by mail before March 1.

◎ WRITERS' FELLOWSHIP

NC Arts Council, Department of Cultural Resources, Raleigh NC 27699-4632. (919)715-1519. Fax: (919)733-4834. E-mail: debbie.mcgill@ncmail.net. Web site: www.ncarts.org. **Contact:** Deborah McGill, literature director. Fellowships are awarded to support the creative development of NC writers and to stimulate the creation of new work. Prize: $8,000. Categories: short stories, novels, literary nonfiction, literary translation, spoken word. Work for children also invited. Judged by a panel of literary professionals appointed by the NC Arts Council, a state agency. No entry fee. Deadline: November 1, 2006. Mss must not be in published form. We receive approximately 300 applications. Word length: 20 double-spaced pages (max). The work must have been written within the past 5 years. Only writers who have been full-time residents of NC for at least 1 year as of the application deadline and who plan to remain in the state during the grant year may apply. Guidelines available in late August on Web site. Accepts inquiries by fax, e-mail, phone. Results announced in late summer. All applicants notified by mail.

▦ ◻ WRITERS' FORUM SHORT STORY COMPETITION

Writers International Ltd., P.O. Box 3229, Bournemouth BH1 1ZS United Kingdom. E-mail: editorial@writers-forum.com. Web site: www.writers-forum.com. **Contact:** Zena O'Toole, editorial assistant. "The competition aims to promote the art of short story writing." Prize: Prizes are £300 for 1st place, £150 for 2nd place and £100 for 3rd place. Categories: short stories. Judged by a panel who provides a short list to the editor. Entry fee: £10 or £7 for subscribers to *Writers' Forum*. Cover letter should include name, address, phone, e-mail, word count and title. Entries must be unpublished. "The competition is open to all nationalities, but entries must be in English." Length: 1,500-3,000 words. Open to any writer. Guidelines available for e-mail, on Web site and in publication. Accepts inquiries by fax, e-mail, phone. Make entry fee cheques payable to Writers International Ltd., or send credit card information. Winners notified by mail. List of winners available in magazine.

◻ WRITERS' JOURNAL ANNUAL FICTION CONTEST

Val-Tech Media, P.O. Box 394, Perham MN 56573. (218)346-7921. Fax: (218)346-7924. E-mail: writersjournal@writersjournal.com. Web site: www.writersjournal.com. **Contact:** Leon Ogroske, editor (editor@writersjournal.com). Offered annually for previously unpublished fiction. Open to any writer. Prize: 1st Place: $500; 2nd Place: $200; 3rd Place: $100, plus honorable mentions. Prize-winning stories and selected honorable mentions published in *Writers' Journal*. Entry fee: $15 reading fee. Guidelines and entry forms available for SASE and on Web site. Accepts inquiries by fax, e-mail and phone. Deadline: January 30. "Writer's name must not appear on submission. A separate cover sheet must include name of contest, title, word count and writer's name, address, phone and e-mail (if available)." Results announced in July. Winners notified by mail. A list of winners is published in July/August issue and posted on Web site or available for SASE.

◻ ◎ WRITERS' JOURNAL ANNUAL HORROR/GHOST CONTEST

Val-Tech Media, P.O. Box 394, Perham MN 56573. (218)346-7921. Fax: (218)346-7924. E-mail: writersjournal@writersjournal.com. Web site: www.writersjournal.com. **Contact:** Leon Ogroske, editor. Offered annually for previously unpublished works. Open to any writer. Prize: 1st place: $50; 2nd place: $25; 3rd place: $15, plus honorable mentions. Prize-winning stories and selected honorable mentions published in *Writers' Journal*. Entry fee: $5. Guidelines available for SASE, by fax, phone, e-mail, on Website and in publication. Accepts inquiries by e-mail, phone, fax. Deadline: March 30. Entries must be unpublished. Length: 2,000 words. Cover letter should include name, address, phone, e-mail, word count and title; just title on ms. Results announced in September annually. Winners notified by mail. For contest results, send SASE, fax, e-mail or visit Web site.

◻ ◎ WRITERS' JOURNAL ANNUAL ROMANCE CONTEST

Val-Tech Media, P.O. Box 394, Perham MN 56573. (218)346-7921. Fax: (218)346-7924. E-mail: writersjournal@writersjournal.com. Web site: www.writersjournal.com. **Contact:** Leon Ogroske, editor. Offered annually for previously unpublished works. Open to any writer. Prize: 1st place: $50; 2nd place: $25; 3rd place: $15, plus honorable mentions. Prize-winning stories and selected honorable mentions published in *Writers' Journal*. Entry fee: $5 fee. No limit on entries per person. Guidelines for SASE, by fax, phone, e-mail, on Web site and in publication. Accepts inquiries by fax, e-mail, phone. Deadline: July 30. Entries must be unpublished. Length: 2,000 words maximum. Open to any writer. Cover letter should include name, address, phone, e-mail, word count and title; just title on ms. Results announced in January/February issue. Winners notified by mail. Winners list published in *Writer's Journal* and on Web site. Enclose SASE for winner's list or send fax or e-mail.

WRITERS' JOURNAL ANNUAL SHORT STORY CONTEST

Val-Tech Media, P.O. Box 394, Perham MN 56573. (218)346-7921. Fax: (218)346-7924. E-mail: writersjournal@ writersjournal.com. Web site: www.writersjournal.com. **Contact:** Leon Ogroske. Offered annually for previously unpublished short stories less than 2,000 words. Open to any writer. Guidelines for SASE and online. Prize: 1st place: $300; 2nd place: $100; 3rd place: $50, plus honorable mentions. Prize-winning stories and selected honorable mentions published in *Writers' Journal*. Entry fee: $7 reading fee. Deadline: May 30.

ZOETROPE SHORT STORY CONTEST

Zoetrope: All-Story, 916 Kearny St., San Francisco CA 94133. (415)788-7500. Fax: (415)989-7910. E-mail: contest s@all-story.com. Web site: www.all-story.com. **Contact:** Francis Ford Coppola, publisher. Annual contest for unpublished short stories. Prize: 1st place: $1,000; 2nd place: $500, 3rd place: $250; plus 10 honorable mentions. Judged by Robert Olen Butler in 2005. Entry fee: $15 fee. Guidelines for SASE, by fax and e-mail, in publication, or on Web site. Deadline: October 1. Entries must be unpublished. Word length: 5,000 words maximum. Open to any writer. ''Please mark envelope clearly 'short fiction contest'.'' Winners notified by phone or e-mail in November. Results announced December 1. A list of winners will be posted on Web site and published in spring issue.

Conferences & Workshops

Why are conferences so popular? Writers and conference directors alike tell us it's because writing can be such a lonely business—at conferences writers have the opportunity to meet (and commiserate) with fellow writers, as well as meet and network with publishers, editors and agents. Conferences and workshops provide some of the best opportunities for writers to make publishing contacts and pick up valuable information on the business, as well as the craft, of writing.

The bulk of the listings in this section are for conferences. Most conferences last from one day to one week and offer a combination of workshop-type writing sessions, panel discussions and a variety of guest speakers. Topics may include all aspects of writing from fiction to poetry to scriptwriting, or they may focus on a specific type of writing, such as those conferences sponsored by the Romance Writers of America for writers of romance or by SCBWI for writers of children's books.

Workshops, however, tend to run longer—usually one to two weeks. Designed to operate like writing classes, most require writers to be prepared to work on and discuss their fiction while attending. An important benefit of workshops is the opportunity they provide writers for an intensive critique of their work, often by professional writing teachers and established writers.

Each of the listings here includes information on the specific focus of an event as well as planned panels, guest speakers and workshop topics. It is important to note, however, some conference directors were still in the planning stages for 2007 when we contacted them. If it was not possible to include 2007 dates, fees or topics, we have provided information from 2006 so you can get an idea of what to expect. For the most current information, it's best to send a self-addressed, stamped envelope to the director in question about three months before the date(s) listed or check the conference Web site.

FINDING A CONFERENCE

Many writers try to make it to at least one conference a year, but cost and location count as much as subject matter or other considerations when determining which conference to attend. There are conferences in almost every state and province and even some in Europe open to North Americans.

To make it easier for you to find a conference close to home—or to find one in an exotic locale to fit into your vacation plans—we've divided this section into geographic regions. The conferences appear in alphabetical order under the appropriate regional heading.

Note that conferences appear under the regional heading according to where they will be held, which is sometimes different from the address given as the place to register or send for information. The regions are as follows:

To find a conference based on the month in which it occurs, check out our Conference Index by Date at the back of this book.

LEARNING AND NETWORKING

Besides learning from workshop leaders and panelists in formal sessions, writers at conferences also benefit from conversations with other attendees. Writers on all levels enjoy sharing insights. Often, a conversation over lunch can reveal a new market for your work or let you know which editors are most receptive to the work of new writers. You can find out about recent editor changes and about specific agents. A casual chat could lead to a new contact or resource in your area. For more about networking, see Making the Connection, by Dena Harris, starting on page 59.

Many editors and agents make visiting conferences a part of their regular search for new writers. A cover letter or query that starts with "I met you at the Green Mountain Writers Conference," or "I found your talk on your company's new romance line at the Moonlight and Magnolias Writer's Conference most interesting . . ." may give you a small leg up on the competition.

While a few writers have been successful in selling their manuscripts at a conference, the availability of editors and agents does not usually mean these folks will have the time there to read your novel or six best short stories (unless, of course, you've scheduled an individual meeting with them ahead of time). While editors and agents are glad to meet writers and discuss work in general terms, usually they don't have the time (or energy) to give an extensive critique during a conference. In other words, use the conference as a way to make a first, brief contact.

SELECTING A CONFERENCE

Besides the obvious considerations of time, place and cost, choose your conference based on your writing goals. If, for example, your goal is to improve the quality of your writing, it will be more helpful to you to choose a hands-on craft workshop rather than a conference offering a series of panels on marketing and promotion. If, on the other hand, you are a science fiction novelist who would like to meet your fans, try one of the many science fiction conferences or "cons" held throughout the country and the world.

Look for panelists and workshop instructors whose work you admire and who seem to be writing in your general area. Check for specific panels or discussions of topics relevant to what you are writing now. Think about the size—would you feel more comfortable with a small workshop of eight people or a large group of 100 or more attendees?

If your funds are limited, start by looking for conferences close to home, but you may want to explore those that offer contests with cash prizes—and a chance to recoup your expenses. A few conferences and workshops also offer scholarships, but the competition is stiff and writers interested in these should find out the requirements early. Finally, students may want to look for conferences and workshops that offer college credit. You will find these options included in the listings here. Again, send a self-addressed, stamped envelope for the most current details.

NORTHEAST (CT, MA, ME, NH, NY, RI, VT)

N BOOKEXPO AMERICA/WRITER'S DIGEST BOOKS WRITERS CONFERENCE

4700 East Galbraith Rd., Cincinnati OH 45236. (513) 531-2690. Fax: (513) 891-7185. E-mail: publicity@fwpubs.com. Web site: www.writersdigest.com/bea or www.bookexpoamerica.com/writersconference. **Contact:** Greg Hatfield, publicity manager. Estab. 2003. Annual. Conference duration: one day, May 30, 2007. Average attendance: 600. "The purpose of the conference is to prepare writers hoping to get their work published. We offer instruction on the craft of writing, as well as advice for submitting their work to publications, publishing houses and agents. We provide breakout sessions on these topics, including expert advice from industry professionals, and offer workshops on fiction and nonfiction, in the various genres (literary, children's, mystery, romance, etc.). We also provide attendees the opportunity to actually pitch their work to agents." Site: The conference facility varies from year to year, as we are part of the BookExpo America trade show. The 2007 conference will take place in New York City. Themes and panels have included Writing Genre Fiction, Children's Writing, Brutal Truths About the Book Publishing Industry, Crafting a Strong Nonfiction Book Proposal, Crafting Your Novel Pitch, and Secrets to Irresistible Magazine Queries. Past speakers included Jerry B. Jenkins, Jonathan Karp, Steve Almond, John Warner, Heather Sellers, Donald Maass and Michael Cader.
Costs The price in 2006 was $189, which included a one-year subscription to *Writer's Digest* magazine.
Additional Information Information available in February. For brochure, visit Web site. Agents and editors participate in conference.

BREAD LOAF WRITERS' CONFERENCE

Middlebury VT 05753. (802)443-5286. Fax: (802)443-2087. E-mail: blwc@middlebury.edu. Web site: www.middlebury.edu/~blwc. **Contact:** Noreen Cargill, administrative manager. Estab. 1926. Annual. Last conference held August 16-27, 2006. Conference duration: 11 days. Average attendance: 230. For fiction, nonfiction, poetry. Site: Held at the summer campus in Ripton, Vermont (belongs to Middlebury College).
Costs In 2006, $2,164 (included room and board). Fellowships available.
Accommodations Accommodations are at Ripton. Onsite accommodations included in fee.
Additional Information 2007 conference information available December 2006 on Web site. Accepts inquiries by fax, e-mail and phone.

GOTHAM WRITERS' WORKSHOP

WritingClasses.com (online division), 1841 Broadway, Suite 809, New York NY 10023-7603. (212)974-8377. Fax: (212)307-6325. E-mail: dana@write.org. Web site: www.writingclasses.com. **Contact:** Dana Miller, director of student affairs. Estab. 1993. "Classes held throughout the year. There are four terms, beginning in January, April, June/July, September/October." Conference duration: 10-week, 1-day, and online courses offered. Average attendance: approximately 1,300 students per term, 6,000 students per year. Offers craft-oriented creative writing courses in fiction writing, screenwriting, nonfiction writing, memoir writing, novel writing, children's book writing, playwriting, poetry, songwriting, mystery writing, science fiction writing, romance writing, television writing, documentary film writing, feature article writing, travel writing and business writing. Also, Gotham Writers' Workshop offers a teen program, private instruction and classes on selling your work. Site: Classes are held at various schools in New York City as well as online at www.writingclasses.com. View a sample online class on the Web site.
Costs 10-week and online courses—$420 (includes $25 registration fee); 1-day courses—$150 (includes $25 registration fee). Meals and lodging not included.
Additional Information "Participants do not need to submit workshop material prior to their first class." Sponsors a contest for a free 10-week online creative writing course (value = $420) offered each term. Students should fill out a form online at www.writingclasses.com to participate in the contest. The winner is randomly selected. For brochure send e-mail, visit Web site, call or fax. Accepts inquiries by e-mail, phone, fax. Agents and editors participate in some workshops.

◎ HIGHLIGHTS FOUNDATION WRITING FOR CHILDREN

814 Court St., Honesdale PA 18431. (570)253-1192. Fax: (570)253-0179. E-mail: contact@highlightsfoundation. org. Web site: www.highlightsfoundation.org. **Contact:** Kent Brown, executive director. Workshops geared

toward those interested in writing for children; beginner, intermediate and advanced levels. Dozens of Classes include: Writing Poetry, Book Promotion, Characterization, Developing a Plot, Exploring Genres, The Publishing Business, What Makes a Good Book, and many more. Annual workshop. Held July 14-21, 2007, at the Chautauqua Institution, Chautauqua, NY. Registration limited to 100.
Costs $2,200, less discount for early registration; Includes tuition, meals, conference supplies. Cost does not include housing. Call for availability and pricing. Scholarships are available for first-time attendees. Phone, e-mail, or visit our Web site for more information.

IWWG MEET THE AGENTS AND EDITORS: THE BIG APPLE WORKSHOPS
% International Women's Writing Guild, P.O. Box 810, Gracie Station, New York NY 10028-0082. (212)737-7536. Fax: (212)737-9469. E-mail: iwwg@iwwg.com. Web site: www.iwwg.com. **Contact:** Hannelore Hahn, executive director. Estab. 1976. Biannual. Workshops held the second weekend in April and the second weekend in October. Average attendance: 200. Workshops to promote creative writing and professional success. Site: Private meeting space of Scandinavia House, mid-town New York City. Saturday: 1-day writing workshop. Sunday afternoon: open house/meet the agents, independent presses and editors.
Costs $125 for members; $155 for non-members for the weekend.
Accommodations Information on transportation arrangements and overnight accommodations available.
Additional Information Accepts inquiries by fax, e-mail.

IWWG SUMMER CONFERENCE
% International Women's Writing Guild, P.O. Box 810, Gracie Station, New York NY 10028-0082. (212)737-7536. Fax: (212)737-9469. E-mail: iwwg@iwwg.org. Web site: www.iwwg.org. **Contact:** Hannelore Hahn, executive director. Estab. 1977. Annual. Conference held for one week in June. Average attendance: 450, including international attendees. Conference to promote writing in all genres, personal growth and professional success. Conference is held "on the tranquil campus of Skidmore College in Saratoga Springs, NY, where the serene Hudson Valley meets the North Country of the Adirondacks." 65 different workshops are offered every day. Overall theme: "Writing Towards Personal and Professional Growth."
Costs $945 single/$860 double (members); $1,025 single/$890 double (non-members) for weeklong program, includes room and board. Weekend and also 5-day overnight accommodations are also available. Commuters are welcome, too.
Accommodations Conference attendees stay on campus. Transportation by air to Albany, NY, or Amtrak train available from New York City.
Additional Information Conference information available with SASE. Accepts inquiries by fax, e-mail.

ℕ ◎ LEGAL FICTION WRITING FOR LAWYERS
SEAK Inc., P.O. Box 729, Falmouth MA 02541. (508)548-7023. Fax: (508)540-8304. E-mail: seakinc@aol.com. Web site: www.seak.com. **Contact:** Karen Babitsky, director of marketing. Estab. 2003. Annual. October 2007. Conference duration: 2 days. Average attendance: 150. Conference focuses on writing legal fiction. Site: Sea Crest Ocean Front Resort, Falmouth MA on Cape Cod. 2006 faculty included Lisa Scottoline and Stephen Horn, both from *Esquire*.
Costs $995 conference only.
Accommodations Provides list of area hotels and lodging options.
Additional Information A writing exercise will be mailed to attendees. Send in a sample of your work to be reviewed if you register before August. Accepts inquiries by e-mail, phone and fax.

THE MACDOWELL COLONY
100 High St., Peterborough NH 03458. (603)924-3886. Fax: (603)924-9142. E-mail: admissions@macdowellcolony.org. Web site: www.macdowellcolony.org. **Contact:** Admissions Director. Estab. 1907. Open to writers and playwrights, composers, visual artists, film/video artists, interdisciplinary artists and architects. Site: includes main building, library, 3 residence halls and 32 individual studios on over 450 mostly wooded acres, 1 mile from center of small town in southern New Hampshire. Available up to 8 weeks year-round. Provisions for the writer include meals, private sleeping room, individual secluded studio. Accommodates variable number of writers, 10 to 20 at a time.
Costs "There are no residency fees. Grants for travel to and from the Colony are available based on need. The MacDowell Colony is pleased to offer grants up to $1,000 for writers in need of financial assistance during a residency at MacDowell. At the present time, only artists reviewed and accepted by the literature panel are eligible for this grant." Application forms available. Application deadline: January 15 for summer (June 1-Sept. 30), April 15 for fall (Oct. 1-Jan. 31), September 15 for winter/spring (Feb. 1-May 31). Submit 6 copies of a writing sample, no more than 25 pages. For novel, send a chapter or section. For short stories, send 2-3, work in progress strongly recommended. Brochure/guidelines available; SASE appreciated.

MARYMOUNT MANHATTAN COLLEGE WRITERS' CONFERENCE

Marymount Manhattan College, 221 E. 71st St., New York NY 10021. (212)774-4810. Fax: (212)774-4814. E-mail: lfrumkes@mmm.edu. **Contact:** Alexandra Smith and Dana Thompson. Estab. 1993. Annual. June. Conference duration: "Actual conference is one day, and there is a three-day intensive preceeding." Average attendance: 200. "We present workshops on several different writing genres and panels on publicity, editing and literary agents." Site: College/auditorium setting. 2006 conference featured 2 fiction panels, a children's book writing panel, a mystery/thriller panel and a literary agent panel. 2006 3-day intensive included fiction writer Erica Jong, magazine writer and editor Pamela Fiori, and memoir writer Malachy McCourt. The conference itself included more than 50 authors.

Costs $165, includes lunch and reception.

Accommodations Provides list of area lodging.

Additional Information 2007 conference information will be available in March by fax or phone. Also accepts inquiries by e-mail. Editors and agents sometimes attend conference.

⊚ MEDICAL FICTION WRITING FOR PHYSICIANS

SEAK, Inc., P.O. Box 729, Falmouth MA 02541. (508)548-7023. Fax: (508)540-8304. E-mail: mail@seak.com. Web site: www.seak.com. **Contact:** Karen Babitsky, director of marketing. Estab. 2003. Annual. September 3-5, 2006. Conference duration: 2 days. Average attendance: 150. Workshop focuses on writing medical fiction and is geared for physicians. Site: Sea Crest Ocean Front Resort, Falmouth MA on Cape Cod. 2006 speakers are Michael Palmer, MD; Tess Garritsen, MD; and 10 literary agents.

Accommodations Provides list of area hotels and lodging options.

Additional Information Accepts inquiries by e-mail, phone, fax. Agents and editors attend this conference.

NEW ENGLAND WRITERS CONFERENCE

P.O. Box 5, 151 Main St., Windsor VT 05089-0483. (802)674-2315. E-mail: newvtpoet@aol.com. Web site: www.newenglandwriters.org. **Contact:** Dr. Frank or Susan Anthony, co-directors. Estab. 1986. Annual. Conference held third Saturday in July. Conference duration: 1 day. Average attendance: 150. The purpose is "to bring an affordable literary conference to any writers who can get there and to expose them to emerging excellence in the craft." Site: The Old South Church on Main St. in Windsor, VT. Offers panel and seminars by prominent authors, agents, editors or publishers; open readings, contest awards and book sales/signings. Featured guest speakers have included Reeve Lindbergh, Rosanna Warren and John Kenneth Galbraith.

Costs $20 (includes refreshments). No pre-registration required.

Accommodations Provides a list of area hotels or lodging options.

Additional Information Sponsors poetry and fiction contests as part of conference (award announced at conference). Conference information available in May. For brochure send SASE or visit Web site. Accepts inquiries by SASE, e-mail, phone. "Be prepared to listen to the speakers carefully and to network among participants."

ℕ NY STATE SUMMER WRITERS INSTITUTE

Skidmore College, 815 N. Broadway, Saratoga Springs NY 12866. (518)580-5593. Fax: (518)580-5548. E-mail: cmerrill@skidmore.edu. Web site: www.skidmore.edu/summer. **Contact:** Christine Merrill, program coordinator. Estab. 1987. Annual. Conference duration: Two-week or four-week session. Average attendance: 80 per two-week session. This event features fiction, nonfiction, poetry and short story workshops. College credit is available for four-week attendees. Site: held on Skidmore campus—dorm residency and dining hall meals. "Summer in Saratoga is beautiful." Past faculty has included Amy Hempel, Nick Delbanco, Margot Livesey, Jay McInerney, Rick Moody and Lee K. Abbott. Visiting faculty has included Joyce Carol Oates, Russell Banks, Ann Beattie, Michael Cunningham and Michael Ondaatje.

Costs Tuition is $1,000 for 2 weeks and $2,000 for 4 weeks. Room and board is additional—$630 for 2 weeks and $1,260 for 4 weeks. "These are 2006 rates."

Additional Information "Writing samples are required with applications: fiction, 5-20 pages; poetry, 2-3 poems; nonfiction prose, 5-20 pages."

⊚ ODYSSEY FANTASY WRITING WORKSHOP

P.O. Box 75, Mont Vernon NH 03057-1420. Phone/fax: (603)673-6234. E-mail: jcavelos@sff.net. Web site: www.sff.net/odyssey. **Contact:** Jeanne Cavelos, director. Estab. 1996. Annual. Last workshop held June 12 to July 21, 2006. Conference duration: 6 weeks. Average attendance: limited to 16. "A workshop for fantasy, science fiction and horror writers that combines an intensive learning and writing experience with in-depth feedback on students' manuscripts. The only workshop to combine the overall guidance of a single instructor with the varied perspectives of guest lecturers. Also, the only such workshop run by a former New York City book editor." Site: conference held at Saint Anselm College in Manchester, New Hampshire. Previous guest lecturers included: George R.R. Martin, Harlan Ellison, Ben Bova, Dan Simmons, Jane Yolen, Elizabeth Hand, Terry Brooks, Craig Shaw Gardner, Patricia McKillip and John Crowley.

Costs In 2006: $1,600 tuition, $625 housing (double room), $1,250 (single room); $25 application fee, $500-600 food (approximate), $150 processing fee to receive college credit.

Accommodations "Workshop students stay at Saint Anselm College Apartments and eat at college."

Additional Information Students must apply and include a writing sample. Students' works are critiqued throughout the 6 weeks. Workshop information available in October. For brochure/guidelines send SASE, e-mail, visit Web site, call or fax. Accepts inquiries by SASE, e-mail, fax, phone.

Ⓝ THE POWER OF WORDS

Goddard College, 123 Pitkin Rd., Plainfield VT 05667. (802)454-8311. E-mail: TLAconfernce@goddard.edu. Web site: www.goddard.edu. **Contact:** Jill Washburn, events coordinator. Estab. 2003. Annual. Last conference held Oct. 6-9, 2006. Conference duration: 4 days. Average attendance: 100. "Purpose is to explore social and personal transformation through the spoken, written and sung word and to share resources for making a living using writing, storytelling, drama, etc. in local communities." Site: A small college campus nestled in the Green Mountains of Vermont; campus was once historic farm, and historic buildings still in use. Woodlands (with trails), dorms, meeting halls and offices. "Keynoters include Shaun McNiff, author and expressive arts pioneer; Gail Rosen, international storyteller and founder of The Healing Story Alliance; Cheryl Savageau, award-winning poet and writer and member of the Abenaki Tribe; and other writers and performers to be announced.

Costs $180 early bird registration/$210 afterwards/$240 at the door.

Accommodations Offers ride-sharing and taxi-sharing from airport via electronic boards. Offers overnight accommodations. $35 double/$45 single per night + $10/meal.

Additional Information Submit workshop material prior to festival; deadline for proposals is Feb 1. Information available in March. For brochure, send SASE, call, e-mail, visit Web site. "Please visit www.goddard.edu/academic/TLAConference.html for more information."

THE PUBLISHING GAME

Peanut Butter and Jelly Press, P.O. Box 590239, Newton MA 02459. E-mail: alyza@publishinggame.com. Web site: www.publishinggame.com. **Contact:** Alyza Harris, manager. Estab. 1998. Monthly. Conference held monthly, in different locales across North America: Boston, New York City, Philadelphia, Washington DC, Boca Raton, San Francisco, Los Angeles, Toronto, Seattle, Chicago. Conference duration: 9 a.m. to 4 p.m. Maximum attendance: 18 writers. "A one-day workshop on finding a literary agent, self-publishing your book, creating a publishing house and promoting your book to bestsellerdom!" Site: "Elegant hotels across the country. Boston locations alternate between the Four Seasons Hotel in downtown Boston and The Inn at Harvard in historic Harvard Square, Cambridge." Fiction panels in 2005 included Propel Your Novel from Idea to Finished Manuscript; How to Self-Publish Your Novel; Craft the Perfect Book Package; How to Promote Your Novel; Selling Your Novel to Bookstores and Libraries. Workshop led by Fern Reiss, author and publisher of The Publishing Game series.

Costs $195.

Accommodations "All locations are easily accessible by public transportation." Offers discounted conference rates for participants who choose to arrive early. Offers list of area lodging.

Additional Information Brochures available for SASE. Accepts inquiries by SASE, e-mail, phone, fax, but e-mail preferred. Agents and editors attend conference. "If you're considering finding a literary agent, self-publishing your novel or just want to sell more copies of your book, this conference will teach you everything you need to know to successfully publish and promote your work."

Ⓒ REMEMBER THE MAGIC IWWG ANNUAL SUMMER CONFERENCE

International Women's Writing Guild, P.O. Box 810, Gracie Station, New York NY 10028-0082. (212)737-7536. Fax: (212)737-9469. Web site: www.iwwg.com. **Contact:** Hannelore Hahn. Estab. 1978. Annual. Conference held in the summer. Conference duration: 1 week. Average attendance: 500. The conference features 65 workshops held every day on every aspect of writing and the arts. Site: Saratoga Springs, 30 minutes from Albany, NY, and 4 hours from New York City. Conference is held "on the tranquil campus of Skidmore College in Saratoga Springs, where the serene Hudson Valley meets the North Country of the Adirondacks."

Costs $995 single, $860 double (members); $1,025 single, $890 double (non-members). Includes meals and lodging.

Accommodations Modern, air-conditioned and non-air-conditioned dormitories—single and/or double occupancy. Equipped with spacious desks and window seats for gazing out onto nature. Meals served cafeteria-style with choice of dishes. Variety of fresh fruits, vegetables and salads have been found plentiful, even by vegetarians. Conference information is available in January. For brochure send SASE, e-mail, visit Web site or fax. Accepts inquiries by SASE, e-mail, phone or fax. "The conference is for women only."

◎ SCBWI WINTER CONFERENCE, NYC

(formerly SCBWI Midyear Conference), 8271 Beverly Blvd., Los Angeles CA 90048. (323)782-1010. Fax: (323)782-1892. E-mail: conference@scbwi.org. Web site: www.scbwi.org. **Contact:** Stephen Mooser. Estab. 2000. Annual. Conference held in February. Average attendance: 800. Conference is to promote writing and illustrating for children: picture books; fiction; nonfiction; middle grade and young adult; network with professionals; financial planning for writers; marketing your book; art exhibition; etc. Site: Manhattan.
Costs See Web site for current cost and conference information.

SEACOAST WRITERS ASSOCIATION SPRING AND FALL CONFERENCES

59 River Road, Stratham NH 03885-2358. E-mail: patparnell@comcast.net. **Contact:** Pat Parnell, conference coordinator. Annual. Conferences held in May and October. Conference duration: 1 day. Average attendance: 60. ''Our conferences offer workshops covering various aspects of fiction, nonfiction and poetry.'' Site: Chester College of New England in Chester, New Hampshire.
Costs Appr. $50.
Additional Information ''We sometimes include critiques. It is up to the speaker.'' Spring meeting includes a contest. Categories are fiction, nonfiction (essays) and poetry. Judges vary from year to year. Conference information available for SASE April 1 and September 1. Accepts inquiries by SASE, e-mail and phone.

◎ VERMONT COLLEGE POSTGRADUATE WRITERS' CONFERENCE

36 College St., Montpelier VT 05602. (802)223-2133. Fax: (802)828-8585. E-mail: roger.weingarten@tui.edu. Web site: www.tui.edu/conferences. **Contact:** Roger Weingarten, director. Estab. 1995. Annual. August. Conference duration: 6 days. Average attendance: 65. This workshop covers the following areas of writing: novels, short stories, creative nonfiction, poetry, poetry manuscript and translation. Site: Union Institute & University's historic Vermont College campus in Montpelier. Workshops are centered on craft and often include exercises. 2006 faculty included Short Story: Antonya Nelson, Michael Martone and Pamela Painter; Novel: Ellen Lesser and Laurie Alberts; Creative Nonfiction: Robin Hemley and Sue William Silverman; Poetry Manuscript: Clare Rossini, Charles Harper Webb and Bruce Weigl; Poetry: Mary Ruefle, Bruce Weigl and Roger Weingarter.
Costs Tuition is $800-875; private dorm room: $330; shared dorm room is $180; meals: $140.
Accommodations Shuttles from airport available.
Additional Information Workshop material must be submitted 6 weeks prior to conference. Submit 25 pages of prose, 6 pages of poetry, 50 pages of poetry ms. Brochures available in January for SASE, by e-mail, on Web site or in publication. ''This conference is for advanced writers with postgraduate degrees or equivalent experience. Workshops are limited to 5-7 participants. Scholarship support available. Contact director.''

WESLEYAN WRITERS CONFERENCE

Wesleyan University, 294 High St., room 207, Middletown CT 06459. (860)685-3604. Fax: (860)685-2441. E-mail: agreene@wesleyan.edu. Web site: www.wesleyan.edu/writers. **Contact:** Anne Greene, director. Estab. 1956. Annual. Conference held the third week of June. Average attendance: 100. For fiction techniques, novel, short story, poetry, screenwriting, nonfiction, literary journalism, memoir. Site: The conference is held on the campus of Wesleyan University, in the hills overlooking the Connecticut River. Meals and lodging are provided on campus. Features daily seminars, lectures and workshops; optional mss consultations and guest speakers on a range of topics including publishing. ''Both new and experienced writers are welcome.''
Costs In 2006, day students' rate $780 (included tuition and meals); boarding students' rate of $920 (included tuition, meals and room for 5 nights).
Accommodations ''Participants can fly to Hartford or take Amtrak to Meriden, CT. We are happy to help participants make travel arrangements.'' Overnight participants stay on campus or in hotels.
Additional Information ''Award-winning faculty. Participants are welcome to attend seminars in a range of genres if they are interested. Scholarships and teaching fellowships are available, including the Jakobson Scholarships for new writers of fiction, poetry and nonfiction and the Jon Davidoff Scholarships for journalists.'' Accepts inquiries by e-mail, phone, fax.

THE ''WHY IT'S GREAT'' WRITING WORKSHOP & RETREAT

21 Aviation Road, Albany NY 12205. (518)453-0890. E-mail: workshop@whyitsgreat.com. Web site: www.whyitsgreat.com. **Contact:** David Vigoda, director. Estab. 2003. Annual. Conference held in July. Conference duration: 4 days. Average attendance: 30. The fundamental activity is the appreciation and understanding of what makes great writing great. The key insight is realizing that no analysis of technique alone can be sufficient. Great writing is the melding of great technique with great heart and each must be able to get out of the way of the other even as they complete each other. Technique without heart is meaningless; heart without technique is incoherent. There are workshops about one and workshops about the other, but this is the one about cultivating and resolving the struggle between them. Writers of fiction, poetry, nonfiction are full participants. Issues

include thematic material, narration and voice. Examples are drawn from all types of writing. Site: World Fellowship Center is a secular educational camp founded in 1941 to promote peace, justice and freedom. The vacation resort is situated on 450 undeveloped acres of beautiful woods, wetlands and a large "forever wild" sanctuary pond in the New Hampshire Whithe Mountains. It is perfect for a writer's retreat and attracts singles, couples and families. There are always interesting conversations to join and lots of recreational choices, including swimming, boating and hiking. Themes are determined by particpants, according to their preferences. David Vidoda, novelist and poet, directs the workshop.

Costs The workshop fee for 2006 was $185. The cost to stay at the World Fellowship Center ranges from $42-$81 per day per adult (less for children), including all meals, facilities and programs. Weekly rates are available.

Accommodations Guests arrange their own transportation. Shuttle service is available for those arriving by bus. Carpools may be available from Massachusetts and metro New York/New Jersey.

Additional Information Brochure available by phone, e-mail or on the Web site. "No proof of ability is required. It doesn't matter if someone has written three novels or is still trying to get the first one started—or wrote 30 pages and froze. The workshop is non-competitive so all participants can feel safe in a group setting as they share their own work, insights and experience."

WRITER'S VOICE OF THE WEST SIDE YMCA

5 West 63rd Street, New York NY 10023. (212)875-4124. Fax: (212)875-4184. E-mail: graucher@ymcanyc.org. **Contact:** Glenn Raucher. Estab. 1981. Workshop held 4 times/year (Summer, Spring, Winter and Fall). Conference duration: 10 weeks (8 weeks in summer); 2 hours, one night/week. Average attendance: 12. Workshop on "fiction, poetry, writing for performance, nonfiction, multi-genre, playwriting and memoir." Special one-day intensives throughout the year. Frequent Visiting Author readings, which are free and open to the public. Site: Workshop held at the Westside YMCA.

Costs $400/workshop, $320 for summer session, free for West Side Y members.

Additional Information For workshop brochures/guidelines send e-mail or call. Accepts inquiries by SASE, e-mail, fax, phone. "The Writer's Voice of the Westside Y is the largest non-academic literary arts center in the U.S."

YADDO

Box 395, Saratoga Springs NY 12866-0395. (518)584-0746. Fax: (518)584-1312. E-mail: yaddo@yaddo.org. Web site: www.yaddo.org. **Contact:** Candace Wait, program director. Estab. 1900. Two seasons: large season is in mid-May-August; small season is late September-May (stays from 2 weeks to 2 months; average stay is 5 weeks). Average attendance: Accommodates approximately 32 artists in large season, 12-15 in the small season. "Those qualified for invitations to Yaddo are highly qualified writers, visual artists, composers, choreographers, performance artists and film and video artists who are working at the professional level in their fields. Artists who wish to work collaboratively are encouraged to apply. An abiding principle at Yaddo is that applications for residencies are judged on the quality of the artists' work and professional promise." Site: includes four small lakes, a rose garden, woodland.

Costs No fee is charged; residency includes room, board and studio space. Limited travel expenses are available to artists accepted for residencies at Yaddo.

Accommodations Provisions include room, board and studio space. No stipends are offered.

Additional Information To apply: Filing fee is $20 (checks payable to Corporation of Yaddo). Two letters of recommendation are requested. Applications are considered by the Admissions Committee and invitations are issued by March 15 (deadline: January 1) and October 1 (deadline: August 1). Information available for SASE (63¢ postage), by e-mail, fax or phone and on Web site. Accepts inquiries by e-mail, fax, SASE, phone.

MIDATLANTIC (DC, DE, MD, NJ, PA)

Ⓝ BAY TO OCEAN WRITERS' CONFERENCE

42 E. Dover St., Easton MD 21601. (410)820-8822. E-mail: clj@goeaston.net. Web site: www.talb.lib.md.us/. **Contact:** Carolyn Jaffe. Estab. 1998. Annual. Conference held in February. Conference duration: 1 day. Average attendance: 100. Conference focuses on publishing, agenting, marketing, craft, fiction, journalism, memoir-writing, nonfiction and freelance writing. Site: the historic Tidewater Inn in downtown Easton, on Maryland's Eastern Shore. Accessible to individuals with disabilities. 2006 classes were presented by Maryland's Poet Laureate Dr. Michael Glaser; publishers Gregg Wilhelm, Marci Andrews and Dan Patrell; literary agent Nina Graybill; writers Austin Camacho, Dr. Ann Hennessy, Judy Reveal and Diane Marquette.

Costs $80; includes sessions, continental breakfast and networking lunch.

Additional Information Brochures available in December at www.talb.lib.md.us/. Accepts inquiries by e-mail and phone. Agents and editors attend this conference. "Mostly for beginning and intermediate writers."

GREATER LEHIGH VALLEY WRITERS GROUP 'THE WRITE STUFF' WRITERS CONFERENCE

P.O. Box 96, Nazareth PA 18064-0096. (908)479-6581. Fax: (908)479-6744. E-mail: write@glvwg.org. Web site: www.glvwg.org. **Contact:** JoAnn Dahan, chair. Estab. 1993. Annual. Last conference was April 7-8, 2006. Conference duration: 1 day. Average attendance: 140. This conference features workshops in all genres. Site: ''The Four Points Sheraton is located in the beautiful Lehigh Valley. The spacious hotel has an indoor swimming pool where our keynote will address the conference over a wonderful, three-course meal. The hotel rooms are very inviting after a long day's drive. We try to offer a little bit of everything to satisfy all our attendees.'' 2006 keynote speaker was Stephen Fried, investigative journalist and essayist.

Costs In 2006, for members, $95, which includes all workshops, 2 meals and a chance to pitch your work to an editor or agent. Also a book fair with book signing. For non-members, cost is $115. Late registration: $130.

Additional Information For more information, see the Web site. Sponsors contest for conferees. The Writer's Flash contest is judged by conference participants. Write 100 words or less in fiction, creative nonfiction or poetry. Brochures available in March for SASE, or by phone, e-mail or on Web site. Accepts inquiries by SASE, e-mail, phone, fax. Agents and editors attend conference. ''Be sure to refer to the Web site, as often with conferences things change. Greater Lehigh Valley Writers Group has remained one of the most friendly conferences and we give the most for your money. Breakout rooms offer craft topics, editor and agent panels, a 'chick lit' panel and more.''

◎ HIGHLIGHTS FOUNDATION FOUNDERS WORKSHOPS

814 Court St., Honesdale PA 18431. (570)253-1192. Fax: (570)253-0179. E-mail: contact@highlightsfoundation. org. Web site: www.highlightsfoundation.org. **Contact:** Kent L. Brown Jr., executive director. Estab. 2000. Workshops held seasonally from March through November. Conference duration: 3-7 days. Average attendance: limited to 8-15. Conference focuses on children's writing: fiction, nonfiction, poetry, promotions, picture books, writing from nature, young adult novels, and much more. ''Our goal is to improve, over time, the quality of literature for children by educating future generations of children's authors.'' Recent faculty/speakers have included Joy Cowley, Patricia Lee Gauch, Carolyn Yoder, Sandy Asher, Rebecca Dotlich, Rich Wallace, Neil Waldman, Kent L. Brown, Jr. and Peter Jacobi.

Costs Range from $495-995, including meals, lodging, materials.

Accommodations ''Participants stay in guest cabins on the wooded grounds surrounding Highlights Founders' home adjacent to the house/conference center, near Honesdale, PA.''

Additional Information ''Some workshops require pre-workshop assignment.'' Brochure available for SASE, by e-mail, on Web site, by phone, by fax. Accepts inquiries by phone, fax, e-mail, SASE. Editors attend conference. ''Applications will be reviewed and accepted on a first-come, first-served basis, applicants must demonstrate specific experience in writing area of workshop they are applying for—writing samples are required for many of the workshops.''

◎ MONTROSE CHRISTIAN WRITER'S CONFERENCE

5 Locust Street, Montrose Bible Conference, Montrose PA 18801-1112. (570)278-1001 or (800)598-5030. Fax: (570)278-3061. E-mail: mbc@montrosebible.org. Web site: www.montrosebible.org. **Contact:** Donna Kosik, MBC Secretary/Registrar. Estab. 1990. Annual. Conference held in July 2007. Average attendance: 85. ''We try to meet a cross-section of writing needs, for beginners and advanced, covering fiction, poetry and writing for children. It is small enough to allow personal interaction between conferees and faculty. We meet in the beautiful village of Montrose, Pennsylvania, situated in the mountains. The Bible Conference provides hotel/motel-like accommodation and good food. The main sessions are held in the chapel with rooms available for other classes. Fiction writing has been taught each year.''

Costs In 2005 registration (tuition) was $140.

Accommodations Will meet planes in Binghamton, NY and Scranton, PA. On-site accomodations: room and board $245-290/conference; $55-65/day including food (2005 rates). RV court available.

Additional Information ''Writers can send work ahead of time and have it critiqued for a small fee.'' The attendees are usually church related. The writing has a Christian emphasis. Conference information available April 2007. For brochure send SASE, visit Web site, e-mail, call or fax. Accepts inquiries by SASE, e-mail, fax, phone.

PENNWRITERS CONFERENCE

RR #2, Box 241, Middlebury Center PA 16935. E-mail: conferenceco@pennwriters.org. Web site: www.pennwriters.org. **Contact:** Vicky Fisher, conference coordinator. Estab. 1987. Annual. Conference held the third or fourth weekend of May. Average attendance: 100. ''We encompass all genres and will be aiming for workshops to cover many areas, including fiction (long and short), nonfiction, etc.'' Site: Past workshops held in Harrisburg, Pittsburgh, Grantsville. Theme for 2006 was ''Rekindling the Spark.'' Speakers included Anne Sowards and Evan Fogelman.

Costs Approximately $145 for members, $170 for nonmembers (2006 rate).

Accommodations See Web site for current information.

Additional Information Sponsors contest. Published authors judge fiction in 2 categories, short stories and Great Beginnings (novels). For conference information send SASE. Accepts inquiries by fax and e-mail. "Agent/editor appointments are available on a first-come, first serve basis."

🎯 SANDY COVE CHRISTIAN WRITERS CONFERENCE AND MENTORING RETREAT

60 Sandy Cove Rd., North East MD 21901-5436. (800)234-2683. Fax: (410)287-3196. E-mail: info@sandycove. org or sandycove@jameswatkins.com. Web site: www.sandycove.org. **Contact:** Jim Watkins, director of conference. Estab. 1982. Annual. Last conference held October 1-4, 2006. Average attendance: 130. Focus is on "all areas of writing from a Christian perspective such as: periodicals, devotionals, fiction, juvenile fiction, Sunday School curriculum, screenwriting, self-publishing, Internet writing, etc." Site: "Sandy Cove is conveniently located mid-way between Baltimore and Philadelphia, just off I-95." Located on 220 acres of Maryland woodland, near headwaters of the Chesapeake Bay. Past faculty included Christy Allen Scannel, Bonnie Brechbill, Michael Davis, Sharon Ewell Foster, Lisa Halls Johnson, Curtis Lundgren, Doug Newton, Kristi Rector, John Riddle, Kathy Scott, Olivia Seaton, Brian Taylor, Claudia Tynes, Jim Watkins, Carol Wedeven.

Costs In 2006, costs were full package: $488 per person (single room occupancy) or $398 per person (double room occupancy)—includes lodging, meals, materials, seminars, sessions, private appointments and 2 ms evaluations. Add $15/night for bay-view room.

Accommodations No arrangements for transportation. "Hotel-style rooms, bay view available. Suites available for additional fee."

Additional Information "For manuscript evaluations, participants may submit their manuscripts between six and two weeks prior to the conference. One copy should be sent in a 9×12 manila envelope. Include a self-addressed, stamped postcard if you want confirmation that it arrived safely." Accepts inquiries by e-mail, phone, fax. Editors and publishers participate in conference. Also offers 1-day student training for high school and college age as well as a writer's retreat—24 hours of uninterrupted writing and mentoring.

🅽 🎯 SPX (SMALL PRESS EXPO)

E-mail: stevec@spxpo.com. Web site: www.spxpo.com. **Contact:** Steve Conley, executive director. Estab. 1996. Annual. Last festival held October 13-14, 2006. Conference duration: 2 days. Average attendance: 2,000+. "North America's premier independent comics arts and cartooning festival, SPX brings together over 300 artists and publishers to meet their readers, booksellers, distributors and each other. In its tenth year, SPX now serves as the preeminent showcase for the exhibition of independent comic books and the discovery of new creative talent." Site: In 2006, Marriott Bethesda North Hotel & Conference Center in Bethesda, MD.

Costs $8/day or $15 for weekend pass. "As with every year, all profits from SPX will go to support the Comic Book Legal Defense Fund, protecting the First Amendment rights of comic book readers and professionals."

Accommodations Detailed directions and transportation options offered on Web site. The Marriott Bethesda North Hotel & Conference Center offers reduced rates for expo attendees at $119 per night.

Additional Information Sponsors contest. "The Ignatz Award is a festival prize awarded at SPX to recognize outstanding achievement in comics and cartooning. A panel of five cartoonists develop the ballot, which is then voted on by SPX attendees. You do not need to submit your comic for the panel to consider you for nomination to the Ignatz ballot. However, if you would like to guarantee that you are considered, you can send six (6) copies of your comic to Jeff Alexander, Ignatz Awards Coordinator, ℅ Big Planet Comics, 426 Maple Avenue East, Vienna, VA 22180." Additional guidelines on Web site. For brochure, visit Web site. Editors participate in conference.

WASHINGTON INDEPENDENT WRITERS (WIW) WASHINGTON WRITERS CONFERENCE

1001 Connecticut Ave. NW, Ste. 70, Washington DC 20036. (202)775-5150. Fax: (202)775-5810. E-mail: info@w ashwriter.org. Web site: www.washwriter.org. **Contact:** Donald Graul Jr., executive director. Estab. 1975. Annual. Conference held in June. Conference duration: Saturday. Average attendance: 450. "Gives participants a chance to hear from and talk with dozens of experts on book and magazine publishing as well as meet one-on-one with literary agents." Site: George Washington University Cafritz Center. Past keynote speakers included Erica Jong, Diana Rehm, Kitty Kelley, Lawrence Block, John Barth, Stephen Hunter. 2006 Keynote Speaker, Brian Lamb, C-SPAN's award-winning founder and Book Notes host.

Additional Information Send inquiries to info@washwriter.org.

MIDSOUTH (NC, SC, TN, VA, WV)

AMERICAN CHRISTIAN WRITERS CONFERENCES

P.O. Box 110390, Nashville TN 37222. (800)21-WRITE. Fax: (615)834-7736. E-mail: ACWriters@aol.com. Web site: www.ACWriters.com. **Contact:** Reg Forder, director. Estab. 1988. Annual. Conferences held throughout

the year in over 2 dozen cities. Conference duration: 2 days. Average attendance: 30-80. Conference's purpose is to promote all forms of Christian writing. Site: Usually located at a major hotel chain like Holiday Inn.
Costs $109 for 1 day; $199 for 2 days. Plus meals and accommodations.
Accommodations Special rates available at host hotel.
Additional Information Conference information available for SASE, e-mail, phone or fax. Accepts inquiries by fax, e-mail, phone, SASE.

BLUE RIDGE MOUNTAINS CHRISTIAN WRITERS CONFERENCE

(800)588-7222. E-mail: ylehman@bellsouth.net. Web site: www.lifeway.com/christianwriters. **Contact:** Yvonne Lehman, director. Estab. 1999. Annual. Last conference held May 21-25, 2006. Average attendance: 240. All areas of Christian writing, including fiction, nonfiction, scriptwriting, devotionals, greeting cards, etc. For beginning and advanced writers. Site: LifeWay Ridgecrest Conference Center, 18 miles east of Asheville NC. "Companies represented this year include AMG Publications, Broadman and Holman, Focus on the Family, Howard Publishers, Upper Room, LifeWay Christian Resources, Lawson Falle Greeting Cards & Gift Books, Christian Film & TV, Crosswalk, Evangel, Christian Writers Guild, Light and Life, Living Ink Books, NavPress, WestBow Press, MovieGuide, Hartline Literary Agency, Les Stobbe Agency, Bethany House, God Allows U-turns, Forevermore, Publisher's Weekly, Lifeline Journal Magazine, Hensley Publishing, Veggie Tales. " Faculty includes professional authors, agents and editors.
Costs In 2006: $315, which includes all sessions, breaks, and a special Wednesday evening banquet. Additional on-campus meal package available for $98/person.
Accommodations LifeWay Ridgecrest Conference Center. See Web site for on-campus room rates.
Additional Information Sponsors contests for unpublished in categories for poetry and lyrics, articles and short stories, novels and novellas, nonfiction, greeting cards and scripts. Awards include trophy and $200 scholarship toward next year's conference. See Web site for critique service and daily schedule—offering keynote sessions, continuing classes and workshops.

HIGHLAND SUMMER CONFERENCE

Box 7014, Radford University, Radford VA 24142-7014. (540)831-5366. Fax: (540)831-5951. E-mail: jasbury@radford.edu. Web site: www.radford.edu/~arsc. **Contact:** Jo Ann Asbury, assistant to director. Estab. 1978. Annual. Conference held first 2 weeks of June. Conference duration: 2 weeks. Average attendance: 25. Three hours graduate or undergraduate credits. Site: The Highland Summer Conference is held at Radford University, a school of about 9,000 students. Radford is in the Blue Ridge Mountains of southwest Virginia, about 45 miles south of Roanoke, VA. "The HSC features one (two weeks) or two (one week each) guest leaders each year. As a rule, our leaders are well-known writers who have connections, either thematic or personal or both, to the Appalachian region. The genre emphasis depends upon the workshop leader(s). In the past we have had as guest lecturers Nikki Giovanni, Sharyn McCrumb, Gurney Norman, Denise Giardinia, George Ella Lyon, Jim Wayne Miller, Wilma Dykeman and Robert Morgan."
Costs "The cost is based on current Radford tuition for 3 credit hours plus an additional conference fee. On-campus meals and housing are available at additional cost. 2005 conference tuition was $594 for in-state undergraduates, $678 for graduate students."
Accommodations "We do not have special rate arrangements with local hotels. We do offer accommodations on the Radford University Campus in a recently refurbished residence hall. (In 2005 cost was $24.04-33.44 per night.)"
Additional Information "Conference leaders typically critique work done during the two-week conference, but do not ask to have any writing submitted prior to the conference beginning." Conference information available after February for SASE. Accepts inquiries by e-mail, fax.

HILTON HEAD ISLAND WRITERS RETREAT

52 Brams Point Road, Hilton Head Island SC 29926. E-mail: bob@bobmayer.org. Web site: www.bobmayer.org. **Contact:** Bob Mayer. Estab. 2002. Every 3 months. Last conferences: March, June, September, December 2006. Conference duration: 4 days. Site: Held at the Marriott Beach & Golf Resort, oceanside, Hilton Head Island.
Costs $550 in 2006.
Accommodations At Marriott.
Additional Information Participants will submit cover letter, one-page synopsis, and first 15 pages of ms.

NORTH CAROLINA WRITERS' NETWORK FALL CONFERENCE

P.O. Box 954, Carrboro NC 27510-0954. (919)967-9540. Fax: (919)929-0535. E-mail: mail@ncwriters.org. Web site: www.ncwriters.org. **Contact:** Cynthia Barnett, executive director. Estab. 1985. Annual. Average attendance: 450. "The conference is a weekend full of classes, panels, readings and informal gatherings. The Network serves writers at all stages of development from beginning, to emerging, to established. We also encourage readers who might be considering writing. We have several genres represented. In the past we have offered fiction, nonfiction, poetry, screenwriting, writing for children, journalism and more. We always invite New York editors and agents and offer craft classes in editing, pitching and marketing." Site: "We hold the conference at a conference center with hotel rooms available."

Costs "Conference registration fee for NCWN members is approximately $250 and includes at least two meals."

Accommodations "Special conference hotel rates are available, but the individual makes his/her own reservations."

Additional Information Conference information available September 1. For brochure, e-mail us or visit our Web site. Online secure registration available at www.ncwriters.org.

◎ OUTDOOR WRITERS ASSOCIATION OF AMERICA ANNUAL CONFERENCE

158 Lower Georges Valley Rd., Spring Mills PA 16875. (814)364-9557. Fax: (814)364-9558. E-mail: eking4owaa @cs.com. Web site: www.owaa.org. **Contact:** Eileen King, meeting planner. Estab. 1927. Annual. Conference held June 16-19, 2007, in Roanoke, Virginia. Average attendance: 700-750. Conference concentrates on outdoor communications (all forms of media). Featured speakers have included Don Ranley, University of Missouri, Columbia; Brig. General Chuck Yeager; Nina Leopold Bradley (daughter of Aldo Leopold); Secretary of the Interior, Gail Norton; Bill Irwin, the only blind man to hike the Appalachian Trail.

Costs $325 for nonmembers; "applicants must have prior approval from the Executive Director." Registration fee includes cost of most meals.

Accommodations List of accommodations available after February. Special room rates for attendees.

Additional Information Sponsors contests, "but all is done prior to the conference and you must be a member to enter them." Conference information available February 2007. For brochure visit Web site, send e-mail, call or fax. Accepts inquiries by e-mail, fax.

SEWANEE WRITERS' CONFERENCE

735 University Ave., Sewanee TN 37383-1000. (931)598-1141. E-mail: cpeters@sewanee.edu. Web site: www.se waneewriters.org. **Contact:** Cheri B. Peters, creative writing programs manager. Estab. 1990. Annual. 2006 conference held in July. Average attendance: 110. "We offer genre-based workshops in fiction, poetry and playwriting and a full schedule of readings, craft lectures, panel discussions, talks, Q&A sessions and the like." Site: "The Sewanee Writers' Conference uses the facilities of the University of the South. Physically, the University is a collection of ivy-covered Gothic-style buildings, located on the Cumberland Plateau in mid-Tennessee." Invited editors, publishers and agents structure their own presentations, but there is always opportunity for questions from the audience." 2006 faculty included John Casey, Barry Hannah, John Hollander, Arlene Hutton, Randall Kenan, Romulus Linney, Margot Livesey, Jill McCorkle, Alice McDermott, Erin McGraw, Claire Messud, Mary Jo Salter, Alan Shapiro and Dave Smith.

Costs Full conference fee (tuition, board and basic room) is $1,560; a single room costs an additional $75.

Accommodations Participants are housed in university dormitory rooms. Motel or B&B housing is available but not abundantly so. The cost of shared dormitory housing is included in the full conference fee. Complimentary chartered bus service is available—on a limited basis—on the first and last days of the conference.

Additional Information "We offer each participant (excepting auditors) the opportunity for a private manuscript conference with a member of the faculty. These manuscripts are due one month before the conference begins." Conference information available after February. For brochure send address and phone number, e-mail, visit Web site or call. "The conference has available a limited number of fellowships and scholarships; these are awarded on a competitive basis." Accepts inquiries by Web site, e-mail, phone, regular mail (send address and phone number).

SOUTH CAROLINA WRITERS WORKSHOP ANNUAL CONFERENCE

P.O. Box 7104, Columbia SC 29202. (803)794-0832. Web site: www.scwriters.com. Estab. 1990. Annual. Conference held in October. Conference duration: 3 days. Average attendance: 150. Conference theme varies each year. Hands-on and lecture-style sessions in both craft and the business of writing are featured for all major genres.

Additional Information Please check Web site for more information. Accepts inquiries by e-mail. Agents and editors attend this conference.

◎ STELLARCON

Box I-1, Elliott University Center, UNCG, Greensboro NC 27412. (336)294-8041. E-mail: stellarcon@yahoo.com. Web site: www.stellarcon.org. **Contact:** James Fulbright, convention manager. Estab. 1976. Annual. Last conference held February 17-19, 2006. Average attendance: 500. Conference focuses on "general science fiction and fantasy (horror also) with an emphasis on literature." Site: Downtown Radisson, High Point, NC. See Web site for 2007 speakers.

Costs See Web site for 2007 rates.
Accommodations "Lodging is available at the Radisson."
Additional Information Accepts inquiries by e-mail. Agents and editors participate in conference.

Ⓝ WILDACRE WRITERS WORKSHOP

233 S. Elm St., Greensboro NC 27401-2602. (336)370-9188. Fax: (336)370-9188. E-mail: judihill@aol.com. Web site: www.Wildacres.com. **Contact:** Judith Hill, director. Estab. 1985. Annual. Residential workshop held second week in July. Conference duration: 1 week. Average attendance: 110. Workshop focuses on novel, short story, poetry, creative nonfiction. Site: Beautiful retreat center on top of a mountain in the Blue Ridge Mountains of North Carolina. Faculty 2006: Ann Hood, Ron Rash, Gail Adams, Luke Whisnant, Rand Cooper, Thorpe Moeckel, Janice Fuller, Rebecca McClanahan, Philip Gerad.
Costs $550 (everything is included: workshop, ms critique, double room, all meals).
Accommodations Vans available, $50 round trip.
Additional Information "New people must submit a writing sample to be accepted. Those attending send their manuscript one month prior to arrival." Workshop information is available mid-January. For brochure send e-mail or visit Web site. Accepts inquiries by e-mail and phone. Agents and editors participate in conference.

SOUTHEAST (AL, AR, FL, GA, LA, MS, PR [PUERTO RICO])

ALABAMA WRITERS' CONCLAVE

137 Sterline Dr., Hueytown AL 35023. E-mail: harrisjc@bellsouth.net. Web site: www.alabamawritersconclave.org. **Contact:** Jimmy Carl Harris, program chair; E. Don Johnson, treasurer. Estab. 1923. Las event held July 21-23, 2006. Average attendance: 80-100. Conference to promote "all phases" of writing. Now also offers ms critiques. Site: Dixon Conference Center and Auburn Hotel at Auburn University, Auburn, Alabama.
Costs Fees for 3 days were $145 (member)/$175 (nonmember), including 3 meals, in 2006.
Accommodations Special conference rate. Was $84 (+tax)/night at Auburn Hotel.
Additional Information "We have major speakers and faculty members who conduct intensive, energetic workshops. Our annual writing contest guidelines and all other information is available at www.alabamawritersconclave.org."

AWP ANNUAL CONFERENCE AND BOOKFAIR

MS 1E3, George Mason University, Fairfax VA 22030. (703)993-4303. Fax: (703)993-4302. E-mail: awpconf@gmu.edu. Web site: www.awpwriter.org. **Contact:** Matt Scanlon, director of conferences. Estab. 1967. Annual. Conference held February 28-March 3, 2007, in Atlanta, GA. Conference duration: 4 days. Average attendance: 3,000. The annual conference is a gathering of 3,000+ students, teachers, writers, readers and publishers. All genres are represented. Site: This year the conference will be held at Hilton Atlanta. "We will offer 175 panels on everything from writing to teaching to critical analysis." In 2006, Walter Mosley, Antonya Nelson, Tim O'Brien and Naomi Shibah Nye were special speakers.
Costs Early registration fees: $35/student; $135/AWP member; $155/non-member.
Accommodations Provide airline discounts and rental-car discounts. Special rate at Hilton.
Additional Information Check Web site for more information.

FLORIDA FIRST COAST WRITERS' FESTIVAL

D315 4501 Capper Rd., Jacksonville FL 32218. (904)766-6731. Fax: (904)713-4858. E-mail: sturner@fccj.edu. Web site: opencampus.fccj.org/WF/. **Contact:** Sara Turner, conference coordinator. Estab. 1985. Annual. Last festival held in March 30-April 2, 2006. Average attendance: 300-350. All areas; mainstream plus genre. Site: Held at Radisson Riverwalk Hotel in Jacksonville.
Costs $100-$380, depending on days attended and meal packages.
Accommodations Radisson Riverwalk Hotel, (904)396-5100 or (800)333-3333, has a special festival rate.
Additional Information Sponsors contests for short fiction, poetry, novels, playwriting. Conference information available in January. For brochures/guidelines visit Web site, e-mail, fax, call. Accepts inquiries by e-mail, phone, fax. E-mail contest inquiries to hdenson@fccj.edu.

GEORGIA WRITERS ASSOCIATION'S SPRING FESTIVAL OF WORKSHOPS

1071 Steeple Run, Lawrenceville GA 30043. (678)407-0703. Fax: (678)407-9917. E-mail: festival2007@georgiawriters.org. Web site: www.georgiawriters.org; link to festival page: www.georgiawriters.org/Festival-2007.htm. **Contact:** Geri Taran, executive director. Estab. 1995. Annual. Last conference held May 22, 2006. Conference duration: 1 day. Average attendance: 200. Conference is comprehensive—all genres and business aspects of a writing career, and agents, publishers, editors. Site: Smyrna Community Center (Atlanta vicinity), large main

area, separate rooms for sessions. Presenters/speakers have included Bobbie Christmas, Michael Lucker, Peter Bowerman, Eric Haney, Barbara LeBey, David Fulmer and many others.
Costs 2006: $85 at the door; $75 in advance; $95 includes annual membership expiring on June 30, 2008 ($45 annual dues).

HOW TO BE PUBLISHED WORKSHOPS
P.O. Box 100031, Birmingham AL 35210-3006. (205)907-0140. E-mail: mike@writing2sell.com. Web site: www.writing2sell.com. **Contact:** Michael Garrett. Estab. 1986. Workshops are offered continuously year-round at various locations. Conference duration: 1 session. Average attendance: 10-15. Workshops to "move writers of category fiction closer to publication." Focus is not on how to write, but how to get published. Site: Workshops held at college campuses and universities. Themes include marketing, idea development and manuscript critique.
Costs $49-79.
Additional Information "Special critique is offered, but advance submission is not required." Workshop information available on Web site. Accepts inquiries by e-mail.

OXFORD CONFERENCE FOR THE BOOK
Center for the Study of Southern Culture, The University of Mississippi, University MS 38677-1848. (662)915-5993. Fax: (662)915-5814. E-mail: aabadie@olemiss.edu. Web site: www.olemiss.edu/depts/south. **Contact:** Ann J. Abadie, associate director. Estab. 1993. Annual. Conference held in March or April. Average attendance: 300. "The conference celebrates books, writing and reading and deals with practical concerns on which the literary arts depend, including literacy, freedom of expression and the book trade itself. Each year's program consists of readings, lectures and discussions. Areas of focus are fiction, poetry, nonfiction and—occasionally—drama. We have, on occasion, looked at science fiction and mysteries. We always pay attention to children's literature." Site: University of Mississippi campus. Annual topics include Submitting Manuscripts/Working One's Way into Print; Finding a Voice/Reaching an Audience; The Endangered Species: Readers Today and Tomorrow. In 2006, among the more than 50 were T.A. Barron, Ellen Douglas, Barry Hannah, Larry L. King, James Meek, Lewis Nordan, Jack Pendarvis, George Saunders, Annalyn Swan and Natasha Trethewey. Also on the program were publisher Sara Gorham and agent Alex Glass.
Costs "The conference is open to participants without charge."
Accommodations Provides list of area hotels.
Additional Information Brochures available in February by e-mail, on Web Site, by phone, by fax. Accepts inquiries by e-mail, phone, fax. Agents and editors participate in conference.

MARJORIE KINNAN RAWLINGS: WRITING THE REGION
P.O. Box 12246, Gainesville FL 32604. (888)917-7001. Fax: (352)373-8854. E-mail: shakes@ufl.edu. Web site: www.writingtheregion.com. **Contact:** Norma M. Homan, executive director. Estab. 1997. Annual. Last conference held July 26-30, 2006. Conference duration: 5 days. Average attendance: 100. Conference concentrates on fiction, writing for children, poetry, nonfiction, drama, screenwriting, writing with humor, setting, character, etc. Site: Conference held at historic building, formerly the Thomas Hotel.
Costs $365 for 5 days including meals; $340 "early bird" registration (breakfast and lunch); $125 single day; $75 half day.
Accommodations Special conference rates at area hotels available.
Additional Information Optional trip and dinner at Rawlings Home at Crosscreek offered. Evening activities and banquets also planned. Manuscript consultation on an individual basis by application only and $100 additional fee. Sponsors essay contest for registrants on a topic dealing with Marjorie Kinnan Rawlings. Call for brochures/guidelines. Accepts inquiries by fax, e-mail. Call toll free 888-917-7001

SCBWI SOUTHERN BREEZE FALL CONFERENCE
Writing and Illustrating for Kids, P.O. Box 26282, Birmingham AL 35260. E-mail: jskittinger@bellsouth.net. Web site: www.southern-breeze.org. **Contact:** Jo Kittinger, co-regional advisor. Estab. 1992. Annual. Conference held in October (usually the third Saturday). Conference duration: One-day Saturday conference. Average attendance: 125. "All Southern Breeze SCBWI conferences are geared to the production and support of quality children's literature." Keynote speakers TBA.
Costs About $100 for SCBWI members, $125 for non-members.
Accommodations "We have a room block with a conference rate. The conference is held at a nearby school."
Additional Information "The fall conference offers approximately 28 workshops on craft and the business of writing, including a basic workshop for those new to the children's field." Ms critiques are offered; mss must be sent by deadline. Conference information is included in the Southern Breeze newsletter, mailed in September. Brochure is available for SASE, by e-mail or visit Web site for details. Accepts inquiries by SASE or e-mail. Agents and editors attend/participate in conference. "Familiarize yourself with the works of the speakers before the event."

◎ SCBWI SOUTHERN BREEZE SPRING CONFERENCE

Springmingle '07, P.O. Box 26282, Birmingham AL 35260. E-mail: jskittinger@bellsouth.net. Web site: www.southern-breeze.org. **Contact:** Jo Kittinger, co-regional advisor. Estab. 1992. Annual. Conference held in February or March each year. Average attendance: 75. "All Southern Breeze SCBWI conferences are geared to the production and support of quality children's literature." Site: Event is held "in a hotel in one of the 3 states which compose our region: Alabama, Georgia or Mississippi. The 2006 conference was in Alabama." Speakers generally include editors, agents, authors, art directors and/or illustrators of children's books.

Costs "About $200; SCBWI non-members pay $10-15 more. Some meals are included."

Accommodations "We have a room block with a conference rate in the hotel conference site. Individuals make their own reservations."

Additional Information There will be ms critiques available this year for an additional fee. Manuscripts must be sent ahead of time. Conference information is included in the Southern Breeze newsletter, mailed in January. Brochure is available for SASE, by e-mail or visit Web site in January for details. Accepts inquiries by SASE, e-mail.

SOUTHEASTERN WRITERS ASSOCIATION

SWA, P.O. Box 82115 Athens GA 30608. E-mail: purple@southeasternwriters.com. Web site: www.southeasternwriters.com. **Contact:** Marilyn Marsh, treasurer. Estab. 1975. Annual. Conference held third week of June every year. Average attendance: 75 (limited to 100). Conference offers classes in fiction, nonfiction, juvenile, inspirational writing, poetry, etc. Site: Epworth-by-the-Sea, St. Simons Island, GA.

Costs 2006 costs: $295 early bird tuition, $345 after April 15, $100 daily tuition.

Accommodations Offers overnight accommodations. 2006 rates were approximately $650/single to $425/double and included motel-style room and 3 meals/day per person.

Additional Information Sponsors numerous contests in several genres and up to 3 free ms evaluation conferences with instructors. Agents and editors participate in conference panels and/or private appointments. Complete information is available on the Web site in March of each year, including registration forms. E-mail or send SASE for brochure.

TENNESSEE WILLIAMS/NEW ORLEANS LITERARY FESTIVAL

938 Lafayette St., Suite 328, New Orleans LA 70113. (504)581-1144. E-mail: info@tennesseewilliams.net. Web site: www.tennesseewilliams.net. **Contact:** Paul J. Willis, executive director. Estab. 1987. Annual. Conference held in late March. Average attendance: "10,000 audience seats filled." Conferences focus on "all aspects of the literary arts including editing, publishing and the artistic process. Other humanities areas are also featured, including theater and music." Site: "The festival is based at historic Le Petit Theatre du Vieux Carré and continues at other sites throughout the French Quarter."

Costs "Ticket prices range from $7 for a single event to $60 for a special event. Master classes are $35 per class. Theatre events are sold separately and range from $10-25."

Accommodations "Host hotel is the Monteleone Hotel."

Additional Information "In conjunction with the University of New Orleans, we sponsor a one-act play competition. Entries are accepted from September 1 through December 1. There is a $25 fee which must be submitted with the application form. There is a $1,000 cash prize and a staged reading at the festival, as well as a full production of the work at the following year's festival." Conference information is available in late January. For brochure send e-mail, visit Web site or call. Accepts inquiries by e-mail and phone. Agents and editors participate in conference.

WRITE IT OUT

P.O. Box 704, Sarasota FL 34230-0704. (941)359-3824. E-mail: rmillerwio@aol.com. Web site: www.writeitout.com. **Contact:** Ronni Miller, director. Estab. 1997. Workshops held 2-3 times/year in March, June, July and August. Conference duration: 5-10 days. Average attendance: 4-10. Workshops on "fiction, poetry, memoirs. We also offer intimate, motivational, in-depth free private conferences with instructors." Site: Workshops in Italy in a Tuscan villa, in Sarasota at a hotel, and in Cape Cod at an inn. Theme: "Feel It! Write It!" Past speakers included Arturo Vivante, novelist.

Costs 2006 fees: Italy, $1,795; Cape Cod, $800. Price includes tution, room and board in Italy. Cape Cod just tuition. Airfare not included.

Additional Information "Critiques on work are given at the workshops." Conference information available year round. For brochures/guidelines e-mail, call or visit Web site. Accepts inquiries by phone, e-mail. Workshops have "small groups, option to spend time writing and not attend classes, with personal appointments with instructors."

⦿ WRITING STRATEGIES FOR THE CHRISTIAN MARKET

2712 S. Peninsula Dr., Daytona Beach FL 32118-5706. (386)322-1111. Fax: (386)322-1111. E-mail: rupton@cfl.rr
.com. Web site: www.ruptonbooks.com. **Contact:** Rosemary Upton. Estab. 1991. Independent studies with
manual. Includes Basics I, Marketing II, Business III, Building the Novel. Critique by mail with SASE. Question
and answer session via e-mail or U.S. mail. Critique shop included once a month, except summer (July and
August). Instructor: Rosemary Upton, novelist.

Costs $30 for manual and ongoing support.

Additional Information "Designed for correspondence students as well as the classroom experience, the courses
are economical and include all materials, as well as the evaluation assignments." Those who have taken Writing
Strategies instruction are able to attend an on-going monthly critiqueshop where their peers critique their work.
Manual provided. For brochures/guidelines send SASE, e-mail, fax or call. Accepts inquiries by fax, e-mail.
Independent study by mail only offered at this time.

MIDWEST (IL, IN, KY, MI, OH)

ANTIOCH WRITERS' WORKSHOP

P.O. Box 494, Yellow Springs OH 45387. (937)475-7357. E-mail: info@antiochwritersworkshop.com. Web site:
www.antiochwritersworkshop.com. **Contact:** Laura Carlson, director. Estab. 1984. Annual. Conference held
July 7-13, 2007. Conference duration: 1 week. Average attendance: 80. Workshop concentration: poetry, nonfiction, fiction, personal essay, memoir, mystery. Site: Workshop located in the idyllic Glen Helen Nature Preserve
and in locations around the charming village of Yellow Springs. Past faculty have included Sue Grafton, Natalie
Goldberg, Michael Marriott, Kathy Hogen Trocheck, Larry Beinhart, Ann Hagedorn, Katrina Kittle, Silas House,
John McCluskey, Ralph Keyes, Crystal Wilson-Harris.

Costs Tuition is $610 (regular) or $550 (alumni and local participants), plus meals.

Accommodations Accomodations are available in local homes through the village host program ($150 for the
week) or at area hotels and B&Bs.

Additional Information Intensive sessions for beginning and experienced writers, small group lunches with
faculty, optional ms critiques.

COLUMBUS WRITERS CONFERENCE

P.O. Box 20548, Columbus OH 43220. (614)451-3075. Fax: (614)451-0174. E-mail: AngelaPL28@aol.com. Web
site: www.creativevista.com. **Contact:** Angela Palazzolo, director. Estab. 1993. Annual. Conference held in
August. Average attendance: 350+. "In addition to agent and editor consultations, the conference covers a
wide variety of fiction and nonfiction topics presented by writers, editors and literary agents. Writing topics
have included novel, short story, children's, young adult, poetry, historical fiction, science fiction, fantasy,
humor, mystery, playwriting, screenwriting, magazine writing, travel, humor, cookbook, technical, queries,
book proposals and freelance writing. Other topics have included finding and working with an agent/author/
editor, targeting markets, time management, obtaining grants, sparking creativity and networking." The Conference has included many writers and editors, including Lee K. Abbott, Jeff Kleinman, Jennifer DeChiara, Simon
Lipskar, Doris S. Michaels, Kim Meisner, Tracy Bernstein, Hallie Ephron, Oscar Collier, Nancy Zafris, Patrick
E. Dils, Donald Maass, Rita Rosenkrantz, Sheree Bykofsky and Patrick Lobrutto, as well as many other professionals in the writing field.

Costs To be announced.

Additional Information To receive a brochure, available mid-summer, contact the conference by e-mail, phone,
or postal mail, or check the Web site at www.creativevista.com.

⦿ FESTIVAL OF FAITH AND WRITING

Calvin College/Department of English, 1795 Knollcrest Circle SE, Grand Rapids MI 49546. (616)526-6770. Fax:
(616)526-8508. E-mail: ffw@calvin.edu. Web site: www.calvin.edu/festival. **Contact:** English Dept. Estab.
1990. Biennial. Conference usually held in April of even years. Conference duration: 3 days. Average attendance:
1,800. The Festival of Faith and Writing encourages serious, imaginative writing by all writers interested in the
intersections of literature and belief. Site: The festival is held at Calvin College in Grand Rapids, MI, 180 miles
north of Chicago. Focus is on fiction, nonfiction, memoir, poetry, drama, children's, young adult, literary
criticism, film and song lyrics. Past speakers have included Annie Dillard, John Updike, Katherine Paterson,
Elie Wiesel, Joyce Carol Oates, Leif Enger.

Costs Registration: consult Web site. Registration includes all sessions during the 3-day event but does not
include meals, lodging or evening concerts.

Accommodations Shuttles are available to and from select local hotels. Consult festival Web site for a list of
hotels with special conference rates.

Additional Information Brochures available in October of the year prior to the festival. Also accepts inquiries by e-mail, phone and fax. Agents and editors attend the festival and consult with prospective writers.

GREEN RIVER NOVELS-IN-PROGRESS WORKSHOP

2011 Lauderdale Rd., Louisville KY 40205. (502)417-5514. E-mail: nipw@greenriverwriters.org. Web site: www.nipw.org. **Contact:** Jeff Yocom, workshop director. Estab. 1991. Annual. Conference usually held in March. Conference duration: 1 week. Average attendance: 50. Conference covers fiction writing in various genres. Site: Held on the urban campus of Spalding University; small dormitories and class rooms/meeting rooms. Features faculty-led breakout sessions on subjects such as character development, plot, contacting agents, etc. Includes individual mentoring and opportunities to pitch to editors and agents. 2006 speakers included Liz Bevarly, Kit Ehrman, J. Ardian (Julianne) Lee, Keith Snyder, and Elaine Fowler Palencia.
Costs $449 with personal instruction option, $299 without.
Accommodations $18 per night for private dorm room.
Additional Information Brochures available in December for SASE, by phone, e-mail or on Web site. 2007 agents in attendance to include Castiglia Literary Agency, Sarah Jane Freymann Literary Agency, Triada US, and Grosvenor Literary Agency. Editors in attendance from Echelon Press.

INDIANA UNIVERSITY WRITERS' CONFERENCE

464 Ballantine Hall, Bloomington IN 47405-7103. (812)855-1877. Fax: (812)855-9535. E-mail: writecon@indiana.edu. Web site: www.indiana.edu/~writecon. **Contact:** Amy Locklin, director. Estab. 1940. Annual. Conference/workshops held in June (June 11-16 in 2006). Average attendance: 115. "The Indiana University Writers' Conference believes in a craft-based teaching of writing. We emphasize an exploration of creativity through a variety of approaches, offering workshop-based craft discussions, classes focusing on technique, and talks about the careers and concerns of a writing life." Site: Located on the campus of Indiana University, Bloomington. Participants in the week-long conference join faculty-led workshops in fiction, poetry and creative nonfiction; take classes on various aspects of writing; engage in one-on-one consultation with faculty members; and attend a variety of readings and social events. Previous faculty include: Raymond Carver, Gwendolyn Brooks, Andre Dubus, Kurt Vonnegut Jr., Mark Doty, Robert Olen Butler, Aimee Bender, Jean Thompson, Brenda Hillman, Li-Young Lee and Brigit Pegeen Kelly.
Costs Approximately $300 for all classes and $500 for all classes and a workshop; does not include food or housing. Scholarships and college credit options are available.
Additional Information "In order to be accepted in a workshop, the writer must submit the work they would like critiqued. Work is evaluated before accepting applicant. Scholarship awards are based on the quality of the manuscript and are determined by an outside judge." For brochures/guidelines send SASE, visit our Web site, e-mail or call. Deadline for scholarship application is April 15. Apply early, as workshops fill up quickly.

KENTUCKY WRITER'S WORKSHOP

Pine Mountain State Resort Park, 1050 State Park Rd., Pineville KY 40977. (606)337-3066. Fax: (606)337-7250. E-mail: dean.henson@ky.gov. Web site: http://parks.ky.gov/resortparks/pm/index.htm. **Contact:** Dean Henson, event coordinator. Estab. 1995. Annual. Workshop held each March. Average attendance: 50-65. "Focuses on writing in various genres, including fiction, mystery, poetry, novels, short stories, essays, etc." Site: Pine Mountain State Resort Park (a Kentucky State Park).
Costs Registration fee is $30 for non-package participants.
Accommodations Special all-inclusive event packages are available. Call for information.
Additional Information Brochures available 2 months in advance by e-mail or phone. Accepts inquiries by SASE, e-mail, phone, fax. "Our conference features successful and celebrated Kentucky authors speaking and instructing on various topics of the writing endeavor. This workshop is designed to help developing authors improve their writing craft."

KENYON REVIEW WRITERS WORKSHOP

The Kenyon Review, Kenyon College, Gambier OH 43022. (740)427-5207. Fax: (740)427-5417. E-mail: reacha@kenyon.edu. Web site: www.kenyonreview.org. **Contact:** Anna Duke Reach, director. Estab. 1990. Annual. Workshop held late June. Conference duration: 8 days. Average attendance: 40-50. Participants apply in poetry, fiction or creative nonfiction, and then participate in intensive daily workshops which focus on the generation and revision of significant new work. Site: The conference takes place on the campus of Kenyon College in the rural village of Gambier, Ohio. Students have access to college computing and recreational facilities and are housed in campus housing. Fiction faculty: Jane McCafferty, Courtney Angela Brkic, Nancy Zafris. Poetry faculty: David Baker, Maurya Simon, Janet McAdams. Nonfiction faculty: Rebecca McClanahan.
Costs $2,195 including room and board.

Accommodations The workshop operates a shuttle from Gambier to the airport in Columbus, Ohio. Offers overnight accommodations. Participants are housed in Kenyon College student housing. The cost is covered in the tuition.

Additional Information Application includes a writing sample. Admission decisions are made on a rolling basis beginning January 15. Workshop information is available November 1. For brochure send e-mail, visit Web site, call, fax. Accepts inquiries by SASE, e-mail, phone, fax.

MID-MISSISSIPPI WRITERS CONFERENCE

John Wood Community College, 1301 S. 48th St., Quincy IL 62305. (217)641-4903. Fax: (217)641-4900. E-mail: ssparks@jwcc.edu. **Contact:** Sherry Sparks. Estab. 2001. Conference in April. Conference duration: 1 weekend. Average attendance: 30-50. Workshop/conference covers all areas of writing, for beginners and more advanced. "We encourage and invite beginning-level writers." Site: John Wood Community College.

Costs $35-$50; some meals included.

Accommodations List of area hotels available.

Additional Information Sponsors contest. Brochures/registration forms available in February; send SASE, visit Web site, e-mail, fax or call. "Come ready to make new friends, see a beautiful city and be inspired to write!"

Ⓝ MIDWEST WRITERS WORKSHOP

Dept. of Journalism, Ball State University, Muncie IN 47306. (765)282-1055. Fax: (765)285-5997. E-mail: info@ midwestwriters.org. Web site: www.midwestwriters.org. **Contact:** Jama Bigger. Estab. 1974. Annual. Workshops to be in July. Average attendance: 150. Site: Conference held at New Alumni Center, Ball State University.

Costs $275 for 3-day workshop; $90 for 1-day Intensive Session including opening reception, hospitality room and closing banquet.

Accommodations Special hotel rates offered.

Additional Information Manuscript evaluation for extra fee. Conference brochures/guidelines are available for SASE.

OPEN WRITING WORKSHOPS

Creative Writing Program, Department of English, Bowling Green State University, Bowling Green OH 43403. (419)372-8370. Fax: (419)372-6805. E-mail: mmcgowa@bgsu.edu. Web site: www.bgsu.edu/departments/crea tive-writing/. "Check our Web site for next workshop dates." Conference duration: 1 day. Average attendance: 10-15. Workshop covers fiction and poetry. Site: Workshops are held in a conference room, roundtable setting, on the campus of Bowling Green State University. Provides close reading and ms critique. 2005 faculty included fiction writer Wendell Mayo and poet/editor Karen Craigo.

Costs $50 for workshop; does not include lodging or other services; $35 for alums and students.

Accommodations Parking provided on campus.

Additional Information Participants need to submit workshop material prior to conference. Fiction or non-fiction: 1 story, 15 pages double-spaced maximum; send 2 copies. Poetry: 3 poems, a total of 100 lines for all 3; send 2 copies. "Deadlines are set about 3 weeks before the workshop. This gives us time to copy all the manuscripts and mail to all participants with detailed instructions." For brochure or inquiries, e-mail, visit Web site, call or fax. "These are no-nonsense workshops whose purpose is to 'open' doors for writers who are writing in comparative isolation. We provide guidance on preparation of manuscripts for publication as well."

Ⓝ THE RAGDALE FOUNDATION

1260 North Green Bay Road, Lake Forest IL 60045. (847)234-1036 ext. 206. Fax: (847)234-1063. E-mail: admissio ns@ragdale.org. Web site: www.ragdale.org. **Contact:** Director of the Artist-In-Residence Program. Estab. 1976. Conference duration: Residencies are 2-8 weeks in length, year-round. Average attendance: 12 artists, writers and composers at one time; nearly 200 residents per year. "Emerging and established artists, writers and composers from all over the world apply for residencies, in order to be awarded time and space to focus on their work and escape day-to-day distractions." Site: Ragdale is located 30 miles north of Chicago. Arts and crafts architect Howard Van Doren Shaw designed two of the main residency buildings. Twelve people are in residence at any given time. It is an historical, home-like setting adjacent to 55 acres of preserved prairie. Dinners are prepared and communal 6 nights a week.

Costs The application fee is $30. The residency fee is just $25/day even though the actual cost to Ragdale is $240/day. The fee includes food and a private room in which to work.

Additional Information "Interested people must submit materials according to application guidelines. Applications may be attained from the Web site, by e-mail or phone request. For brochure, send SASE, call, e-mail, visit Web site. "The small group atmosphere is conducive to productivity, inspiration, interaction (if desired) and creative exploration."

READERS AND WRITERS HOLIDAY CONFERENCE

Central Ohio Fiction Writers (COFW), P.O. Box 1981, Westerville OH 43086-1981. E-mail: mollygbg@columbus. rr.com. Web site: www.cofw.org. **Contact:** Molly Greenberg, president. Estab. 1990. Annual. Conference held in October in Columbus, OH. Dates TBA. Average attendance: 120. COFW is a chapter of Romance Writers of America. The conference focuses on all romance subgenres and welcomes published writers, pre-published writers and readers. Conference theme: connecting with the romance market. Jennifer Cruise and Bob Mayer are workshop and keynote presenters. Two national agents and one editor will speak and take short appointments. Appointments to early registrants who have completed at least one manuscript.

Costs Price will include Saturday lunch. Friday and Saturday night dinner extra.

Accommodations See www.cofw.org for exact location. There will be a special conference rate for hotel rooms.

Additional Information Registration form and information available on Web site or by e-mail.

N ◎ SPACE (SMALL PRESS AND ALTERNATIVE COMICS EXPO)

Back Porch Comics, P.O. Box 20550, Columbus OH 43220. E-mail: bpc13@earthlink.net. Web site: www.backpor chcomics.com/space.htm. **Contact:** Bob Corby. Last conference held May 13, 2006. Conference duration: 1 day. "The Midwest's largest exhibition of small press, alternative and creator-owned comics." Site: 2006 held at the Aladdin Shrine Complex multipurpose room. 2006 special guests were Dave Sim and Gerhard.

Additional Information For 2007 brochure, visit Web site. Editors participate in conference.

N TOUCH OF SUCCESS WRITER'S CONFERENCE

P.O. Box 59, Glendale KY 42740. (270)769-1823. Web site: www.touchofsuccess.com. **Contact:** Bill Thomas, author/director. Estab. 1978. Annual. Conference held April 22-23, 2007. Conference duration: 2 days. Workshop focuses on journalism, nonfiction, fiction. Site: Oakbrook Farm Center for the Arts, 3 miles from historic railroad village of Glendale on family pioneer farm amidst Amish country. Workshops led by Bill Thomas, who has published hundreds of magazine articles, some poetry, and more than 25 books.

Costs $395, includes lunches (we have our own chef) and some local transportation including pickup and delivery from Louisville Regional Airport.

Additional Information Brochures available after Jan. 1, 2007, by SASE or on Web site. Accepts inquiries by SASE and phone. "Submit letter of application giving background, purpose and goals for attending this event."

WALLOON WRITERS' RETREAT

P.O. Box 304, Royal Oak MI 48068-0304. (248)589-3913. Fax: (248)589-9981. E-mail: johndlamb@ameritech.n et. Web site: www.springfed.org. **Contact:** John D. Lamb, director. Estab. 1999. Annual. Last conference held September 28-October 1, 2006. Average attendance: 75. Focus includes fiction, poetry and creative nonfiction. Site: Michigania is owned and operated by the University of Michigan Alumni Association. Located on Walloon Lake. Attendees stay in spruce-paneled cabins, and seminars are held in a large conference lodge with fieldstone fireplaces and dining area. Past faculty included Billy Collins, Jacquelyn Mitchard, Jane Hamilton, Thomas Lux, Joyce Maynard, Craig Holden, Laurel Blossom.

Costs Single occupancy is $600, $535 (3 nights, 2 nights, all meals included). $360 non-lodging.

Accommodations Shuttle rides from Traverse City Airport or Pellston Airport. Offers overnight accommodations. Provides list of area lodging options.

Additional Information Optional: Attendees may submit 3 poems or 5 pages of prose for conference with a staff member. Brochures available mid-June by e-mail, on Web site or by phone. Accepts inquiries by SASE, e-mail, phone. Editors participate in conference. "Walloon Lake in Northern Michigan is the same lake at which Ernest Hemingway spent the first 19 years of his life at his family's Windemere Cottage. The area plays a role in some of his early short stories, notably in a couple Nick Adams stories."

WESTERN RESERVE WRITERS & FREELANCE CONFERENCE

Lakeland Community College, 7700 Clocktower Dr., Kirtland OH 44094. (440) 525-7000. E-mail: deencr@aol.c om. **Contact:** Deanna Adams or Nancy Piazza, co-coordinators. Estab. 1983. Biannual. Last conference held September 17, 2005. Conference duration: One day. Average attendance: 120. "The Western Reserve Writers Conferences are designed for all writers, aspiring and professional, and offer presentations in all genres— nonfiction, fiction, poetry, essays, creative nonfiction and the business of writing, including Web sites and freelancing ." Site: Located in the main building of Lakeland Community College, the conference is easy to find and just off the I-90 freeway. The Fall 2005 conference featured "top notch writers presenting on book publishing, mystery writing, children's and women's fiction, and other fiction genres with a focus on characterization and plotting. The Fall 2005 conference featured *Plain Dealer* columnist Michael Heaton as keynote speaker. Also featured renowned mystery writer Les Roberts and prolific writer Paul Raymond Martin. Also featured presentations on book proposals, contracts and copyrights."

Costs Fall conference, including lunch: $69. Spring conference, no lunch: $45.

Additional Information Brochures for the 2007 conferences will be available in January 2006 with SASE, e-mail or by fax. Also accepts inquiries by e-mail and phone, or see Web site. Editors and agents often attend the conferences.

◎ WRITE-TO-PUBLISH CONFERENCE

9118 W Elmwood Dr., Suite 1G, Niles IL 60714-5820. (847)296-3964. Fax: (847)296-0754. E-mail: lin@writetopublish.com. Web site: www.writetopublish.com. **Contact:** Lin Johnson, director. Estab. 1971. Annual. Conference held in early June. Average attendance: 275. Conference on "writing all types of manuscripts for the Christian market." Site: Wheaton College, Wheaton, IL.

Costs $425.

Accommodations In campus residence halls or discounted hotel rates. Cost $210-290.

Additional Information Optional ms evaluation available. College credit available. Conference information available in January. For brochures/guidelines, visit Web site, e-mail, fax or call. Accepts inquiries by e-mail, fax, phone.

WRITERS ONLINE WORKSHOPS

F + W Publications, Inc., 4700 E. Galbraith Rd., Cincinnati OH 45236. (800)759-0963. Fax: (513)531-0798. E-mail: wdwowadmin@fwpubs.com. Web site: www.writersonlineworkshops.com. **Contact:** Joe Stollenwerk, educational services manager. Estab. 2000. Online workshop; ongoing. Conference duration: From 4-28 weeks. Average attendance: 10-15 per class. "We have workshops in fiction, nonfiction, memoir, poetry, proposal writing and more." Site: Internet-based, operated entirely on the Web site. Current fiction-related courses include Fundamentals of Fiction, Focus on the Novel, Focus on the Short Story, Advanced Novel Writing, Advanced Story Writing, Creating Dynamic Characters, Writing Effective Dialogue, Writing the Novel Proposal and others. New in 2005-06: Writing the Query Letter, Essentials of Mystery Writing, Essentials of Science Fiction Writing, Marketing Short Stories, and Mastering Point of View.

Costs $119-579.

Additional Information Additional information always available on Web site. Accepts inquiries by e-mail and phone.

NORTH CENTRAL (IA, MN, NE, ND, SD, WI)

🅽 GREAT LAKES WRITERS FESTIVAL

Lakeland College, P.O. Box 359, Sheboygan WI 53082-0359. (920)565-1276. Fax: (920)565-1260. E-mail: elderk @lakeland.edu. Web site: www.greatlakeswritersfestival.org. **Contact:** Karl Elder, coordinator. Estab. 1991. Annual. Last conference held Nov. 2-3, 2006. Conference duration: 2 days. "Festival celebrates the writing of poetry, fiction and creative nonfiction." Site: Lakeland College is a small, 4-yr. liberal arts college of 235 acres, a beautiful campus in a rural setting, founded in 1862. No themes or panels, just readings and workshops. 2005 faculty included Beth Ann Fennelly and Larry Watson.

Costs Free and open to the public. Participants may purchase meals and must arrange for their own lodging.

Accommodations Does not offer overnight accommodations. Provides list of area hotels or lodging options.

Additional Information All participants who would like to have their writing considered as an object for discussion during the festival workshops must submit it to Karl Elder electronically by Oct. 15. Participants may submit material for workshops in one genre only (poetry, fiction or creative nonfiction). Sponsors contest. Contest entries must contain the writer's name and address on a separate title page, be in type, and be submitted as clear, hard copy on Friday at the festival registration table. Entries may be in each of three genres per participant, yet only one poem, one story, and/or one nonfiction piece may be entered. There are two categories—high school students on one hand, all other on the other—of cash awards for first place in each of the three genres. The judges reserve the right to decline to award a prize in one or more of the genres. Judges will be the editorial staff of *Seems*, excluding the festival coordinator, Karl Elder. Information available in September. For brochure, visit Web site. Editors participate in conference. "Much information is available on the festival Web site."

🅽 GREEN LAKE WRITERS CONFERENCE

W2511 State Hwy 23, Green Lake WI 54941. (800)558-8898. Fax: (920)294-3848. E-mail: program@glcc.org. Web site: www.glcc.org. **Contact:** Program department. Estab. 1948. Annual. Conference held early August. Conference duration: one week. Average attendance: 75. The week is open to beginning as well as experienced writers. "We provide gifted instructors in areas of children's, nonfiction, poetry, fiction and inspirational writing." Site: 1,000 acres, including conference lodging and meeting rooms, dining facilities, and lake frontage for recreation, 36-hole golf course. "Barbara Smith is our fiction instructor. Barbara is a freelance writer, editor and medical ethicist from West Virginia.'' Our faculty includes Ellen Kort, Sharon Hart Addy, Mort Castle, Patricia Lorenz and more.

Costs Double occupancy—approximately $627—includes lodging, meals and program fee. Reduced rates for triple and quad occupancy. Scholarships available. Daily commuter program fee $150.

Accommodations Provides a shuttle service from airport, train station, bus station.

Additional Information Brochures available in January on Web site, and by e-mail, phone and fax.

INTERNATIONAL MUSIC CAMP CREATIVE WRITING WORKSHOP

1930 23rd Ave. SE, Minot ND 58701. Phone/fax: (701)838-8472. E-mail: joe@internationalmusiccamp.com. Web site: www.internationalmusiccamp.com. **Contact:** Joseph T. Alme, executive director. Estab. 1956. Annual. Last conference held June 25-July 1, 2006. Average attendance: 35. ''The workshop offers students the opportunity to refine their skills in thinking, composing and writing in an environment that is conducive to positive reinforcement. In addition to writing poems, essays and stories, individuals are encouraged to work on their own area of interest with conferencing and feedback from the course instructor.'' Site: International Peace Garden on the border between the US and Canada. ''Similar to a university campus, several dormitories, classrooms, lecture halls and cafeteria provide the perfect site for such a workshop. The beautiful and picturesque International Peace Garden provides additional inspiration to creative thinking.'' 2006 instructor was Colin Kapeiovitz, Dickinson State University, ND.

Costs $300, includes tuition, room and board. Early bird registration (postmarked by May 15) $275.

Accommodations Airline and depot shuttles are available upon request. Housing is included in the $275 fee.

Additional Information Conference information is available in September. For brochure visit Web site, e-mail, call or fax. Accepts inquiries by e-mail, phone and fax. Agents and editors participate in conference.

IOWA SUMMER WRITING FESTIVAL

C215 Seashore Hall, University of Iowa, Iowa City IA 52242-1802. (319)335-4160. E-mail: iswfestival@uiowa.edu. Web site: www.uiowa.edu/~iswfest. **Contact:** Amy Margolis, director. Estab. 1987. Annual. Festival held in June and July. Workshops are one week or a weekend. Average attendance: limited to 12/class—over 1,500 participants throughout the summer. ''We offer workshops across the genres, including novel, short story, poetry, essay, memoir, humor, travel, playwriting, screenwriting, writing for children and more. All writers 21 and over are welcome. You need only have the desire to write.'' Site: University of Iowa campus. Guest speakers are undetermined at this time. Readers and instructors have included Lee K. Abbott, Susan Power, Abraham Verghese, Robert Olen Butler, Ethan Canin, Clark Blaise, Gerald Stern, Donald Justice, Michael Dennis Browne, Marvin Bell, Hope Edelman, Lan Samantha Chang.

Costs $475-500 for full week; $225 for weekend workshop. Discounts available for early registration. Housing and meals are separate.

Accommodations Iowa House, $70/night; Sheraton, $88/night, Heartland Inn, $62/night (rates subject to change).

Additional Information Conference information available in February. Accepts inquiries by fax, e-mail, phone. ''Register early. Classes fill quickly.''

SOUTH CENTRAL (CO, KS, MO, NM, OK, TX)

⊚ THE AFRICAN AMERICAN BOOK CLUB SUMMIT

PMB 120, 2951 Marina Bay Dr., Suite 130, League City TX 77573. (866)875-1044. E-mail: pwsquare@pageturner.net. Web site: www.summitatsea.com. **Contact:** Pamela Walker Williams, literary events chairman. Estab. 2000. Annual. Conference held each October on board a Carnival cruise ship; the last event was October 15-26, 2006. (Check Web site for 2007 dates and prices.) Average attendance: 200. ''The purpose of the conference is to bring authors and readers together. Aspiring writers will have an opportunity to discuss and obtain information on self-publishing, marketing and writing fiction.'' Site: on board cruise ship. Includes pool, jacuzzi, restaurant, bar, spa, room service, wheelchair accessible, fitness center, children's facilities, air conditioning.

Costs 2006 fees: for inside cabin, $881; for ocean view, $991. Includes cruise, conference, on-board meals, port charges and gratuities.

Accommodations ''Participants have the option to add airfare and/or shuttle service.'' Provides a list of area accommodations for people who choose to arrive early.

Additional Information Brochures available on Web site. Accepts inquiries by e-mail, phone, fax. Agents and editors attend conference.

AGENTS & EDITORS CONFERENCE

(formerly Agents! Agents! Agents! & Editors Too!), Writers' League of Texas, 1501 W. Fifth St., Suite E-2, Austin TX 78703. (512)499-8914. Fax: (512)499-0441. E-mail: wlt@writersleague.org. Web site: www.writerslea

gue.org. **Contact:** Kristy Bordine, membership director. Estab. 1982. Conference held in Summer. Conference duration: Friday-Sunday. Average attendance: 300. "Each Summer the League holds its annual Agents & Editors Conference, which provides writers with the opportunity to meet top literary agents and editors from New York and the West Coast." Open to writers of both fiction and nonfiction. Topics include: Finding and working with agents and publishers; writing and marketing fiction and nonfiction; dialogue; characterization; voice; research; basic and advanced fiction writing/focus on the novel; business of writing; also workshops for genres. Agents/speakers have included Malaika Adero, Stacey Barney, Sha-Shana Crichton, Jessica Faust, Dena Fischer, Mickey Freiberg, Jill Grosjean, Anne Hawkins, Jim Hornfischer, Jennifer Joel, David Hale Smith and Elisabeth Weed. Agents and editors will be speaking and available for meetings with attendees.

Costs $220-275. Contests and awards programs are offered separately.

Additional Information Brochures/guidelines are available on request.

ANNUAL RETREATS, WORKSHOPS AND CLASSES

(formerly Spring and Fall Workshops and Classes), 1501 W. Fifth St., Suite E-2, Austin TX 78703-5155. (512)499-8914. Fax: (512)499-0441. E-mail: wlt@writersleague.org. Web site: www.writersleague.org. **Contact:** Kristy Bordine, membership director. All year long, except for the month of December. "Classes and workshops provide practical advice and guidance on various aspects of fiction, creative nonfiction and screenwriting." Site: Writers' League of Texas resource center or as indicated on Web site. Some classes are by e-mail. "Topics for workshops and classes have included E-publishing; Creative Nonfiction; Screenwriting Basics; Novel in Progress; Basics of Short Fiction; Technique; Writing Scenes; Journaling; Manuscript Feedback; Essays; Newspaper Columns." Instructors include Suzy Spencer, Barbara Burnett Smith, Scott Wiggerman, Diane Fanning, Marion Winik, Emily Vander Veer, Annie Reid, Bonnie Orr, Jan Epton Seale, Susan Wade, Lila Guzman, Laurie Lynn Drummond, David Wilkinson, John Pipkin, Ann McCutchan and Dao Strom.

Costs $45-$250.

Additional Information Available on our Web site.

ASPEN SUMMER WORDS WRITING RETREAT & LITERARY FESTIVAL

110 E. Hallam St., #116, Aspen CO 81611. (970)925-3122. Fax: (970)925-5700. E-mail: info@aspenwriters.org. Web site: www.aspenwriters.org. **Contact:** Jamie Abbot, director of programs. Estab. 1976. Annual. Conference held in late June. Conference duration: 5 days. Average attendance: writing retreat, 96; literary festival, 200 passholders, 1,800 visitors. For fiction, creative nonfiction, poetry, personal essay, screenwriting, literature, author readings and agent/editor meetings, industry panels and social readings and talks. 2006 faculty/speakers included Pam Houston, Ron Carlson, Amy Bloom, Ted Conover, Christopher Merrill, Laura Fraser, Gary Ferguson, Gretel Ehrlich.

Costs $375/retreat; $200/festival; $525/both; $35/private meetings with agents and editors.

Accommodations In-town housing in 2006 was $165/night 1-bedroom condo; $125/night shared single in a 2-bedroom condo. Call for other hotel rates. Free shuttle.

Additional Information Application deadline: April 1. Mss must be submitted prior to conference for review by faculty, for most workshops. A limited number of partial-tuition scholarships are available. Brochures available for SASE, by e-mail and phone request, and on Web site.

◎ EAST TEXAS CHRISTIAN WRITER'S CONFERENCE

East Texas Baptist University, School of Humanities, 1209 N. Grove, Marshall TX 75670. (903)923-2269. E-mail: jhopkins@etbu.edu or dgribble@etbu.edu. Web site: www.etbu.edu/News/CWC. **Contact:** Donna Gribble. Estab. 2002. Annual. Conference held first Saturday of June each year. Conference duration: 1 day (Saturday). Average attendance: 60. "Primarily we are interested in promoting quality Christian writing that would be accepted in mainstream publishing." Site: "We use the classrooms, cafeterias, etc. of East Texas Baptist University. Past conference themes were 10 Commandments of Powerful Writers; Editor's Perspective Do's and Don'ts; The Writer's Life; 7 Effective Habits for Christian Writers; Writing for Youth/Children; Scholarly Publications; E-Publishing and Publishing on Demand; Creative Nonfiction; Writing Grants; Inspirational Writing. Past conference speakers were David Jenkins, Chris Collins, Carolyn Pedison, Kathy Holdway, Jim Pence, Archie McDonald, Faye Field, Fredna Stuckey, Marv Knox and Marcia Preston.

Costs $50 for individual; $40 student. Price includes meal.

Additional Information "Would like to expand to an opportunity to meet with agents or an editor."

FORT BEND WRITERS GUILD WORKSHOP

12523 Folkcrest Way, Stafford TX 77477-3529. E-mail: roger@rogerpaulding.net. Web site: www.fortbendwriter sguild.com. **Contact:** Roger Paulding. Estab. 1997. Annual. Last conference held April 8, 2006. Conference duration: 1 day. Average attendance: 75. Focuses on fiction (novels) and screenwriting. Site: Held at Holiday Inn Southwest.

Costs $50 (including buffet lunch).

Additional Information Sponsors a contest. Submit for novel competition first 15 pages plus one page synopsis, entry fee $15; for short story competition 10 pages complete, $10 each. "Judges are published novelists." First prize: $300 if attending workshop, second place: $200, third place: 100. For brochure send SASE, e-mail or check Web site.

◎ THE GLEN WORKSHOP

Image, 3307 Third Avenue W, Seattle WA 98119. (206)281-2988. Fax: (206)281-2335. E-mail: glenworkshop@imagejournal.org. Web site: www.imagejournal.org. Estab. 1991. Annual. Workshop held in August. Conference duration: 1 week. Average attendance: 140-150. Workshop focuses on "fiction, poetry and spiritual writing, essay, memoir. Run by *Image*, a literary journal with a religious focus. The Glen welcomes writers who practice or grapple with religious faith." Site: 2006 conference held in Santa Fe, NM in the first week of August and features "presentations and readings by the faculty." Faculty has included Erin McGraw (fiction), Lauren F. Winner (spiritual writing), Paul Mariani and Andrew Hudgins (poetry) and Jeanne Murray Walker (playwriting).

Costs $630-855, including room and board; $365-440 for commuters (lunch only).

Accommodations Arrange transportation by shuttle. Accommodations included in conference cost.

Additional Information Prior to arrival, participants may need to submit workshop material depending on the teacher. "Usually 10-25 pages." Conference information is available in February. For brochure send SASE, e-mail, visit Web site, call or fax. "Like *Image*, the Glen is grounded in a Christian perspective, but its tone is informal and hospitable to all spiritual wayfarers."

◎ GLORIETA CHRISTIAN WRITERS CONFERENCE

Glorieta Conference Center, 3311 Candelaria NE, Ste. I, Albuquerque NM 87107-1952. (800)433-6633. Fax: (505)899-9282. E-mail: info@classervices.com. Web site: www.glorietacwc.com or www.lifeway.com. **Contact:** Marita Littauer, director. Estab. 1997. Annual. Conference held October 11-15, 2006. Conference duration: 5 days. Average attendance: 350. For "beginners, professionals, fiction, poetry, writing for children, drama, magazine writing, nonfiction books." To train Christian writers in their craft, provide them with an understanding of the industry, and give opportunities to meet with publishers. Site: "Located just north of historic Santa Fe, NM, conference center with hotels and dining hall with buffet-style meals." Plans "continuing course for fiction writers and numerous one-hour workshops."

Costs 2006 rates were $350 for early registration or $390 regular registration plus applicable tax; meals and lodging were additional and range from $200-500 depending on housing and meal plans.

Additional Information "The craft of writing is universal, but attendees should be aware this conference has a Christian emphasis."

◎ TONY HILLERMAN WRITERS CONFERENCE

304 Calle Oso, Santa FE NM 87501. (505)471-1565. E-mail: wordharvest@yahoo.com. Web site: http://sfworkshops.com. **Contact:** Jean Schaumberg, co-director. Estab. 2004. Annual. November. Conference duration: 4 days. Average attendance: 160. Site: Albuquerque Hilton hotel, mid-town Albuquerque. Previous faculty included Tony Hillerman, David Morrell, Michael McGarrity, and Jonathan and Faye Kellerman.

Costs Previous year's costs: $395.

Accommodations Previous year $69 per night at the Albuquerque Hilton.

Additional Information Sponsors on-site contest for an opening paragraph and short-story contest with *Cowboys & Indians Magazine*. Judged by a magazine editor familiar with *Cowboys & Indians*. Brochures available in July for SASE, by phone, e-mail, fax and on Web site. Accepts inquiries by SASE, phone, e-mail.

Ⓝ THE NEW LETTERS WEEKEND WRITERS CONFERENCE

University of Missouri-Kansas City, College of Arts and Sciences Continuing Ed. Division, 5300 Rockhill Rd., Kansas City MO 64110-2499. (816)235-2736. Fax: (816)235-5279. Web site: www.newletters.org. **Contact:** Robert Stewart. Estab. mid-'70s as The Longboat Key Writers Conference. Annual. Conference held in June. Conference duration: 3 days. Average attendance: 75. For "craft and the creative process in poetry, fiction, screenwriting, playwriting and journalism; but the program also deals with matters of psychology, publications and marketing. The conference is appropriate for both advanced and beginning writers." Site: "The conference meets at the beautiful Diastole conference center of The University of Missouri-Kansas City."

Costs Several options are available. Participants may choose to attend as a non-credit student or they may attend for 1-3 hours of college credit from the University of Missouri-Kansas City. Conference registration includes continental breakfasts, Saturday and Sunday lunch. For complete information, contact the university.

Accommodations Information on area accomodations is made available.

Additional Information Those registering for college credit are required to submit a ms in advance. Manuscript reading and critque are included in the credit fee. Those attending the conference for non-credit also have the option of having their ms critiqued for an additional fee. Accepts inquiries by phone, fax.

NIMROD ANNUAL WRITERS' WORKSHOP

University of Tulsa, 600 S. College Ave., Tulsa OK 74104. (918)631-3080. Fax: (918)631-3033. E-mail: nimrod@u tulsa.edu. Web site: www.utulsa.edu/nimrod. **Contact:** Eilis O'Neal, managing editor. Estab. 1978. Annual. Conference held in October. Conference duration: 1 day. Average attendance: 100-150. Workshop in fiction and poetry. "Prize winners (*Nimrod*/Hardman Prizes) conduct workshops as do contest judges." Past judges: Rosellen Brown, Stanley Kunitz, Toby Olson, Lucille Clifton, W.S. Merwin, Ron Carlson, Mark Doty, Anita Shreve and Francine Prose.

Costs Approximately $50. Lunch provided. Scholarships available for students.

Additional Information *Nimrod International Journal* sponsors *Nimrod*/Hardman Literary Awards: The Katherine Anne Porter Prize for fiction and The Pablo Neruda Prize for poetry. Poetry and fiction prizes: $2,000 each and publication (1st prize); $1,000 each and publication (2nd prize). Deadline: must be postmarked no later than April 30.

◎ ROMANCE WRITERS OF AMERICA NATIONAL CONFERENCE

3707 FM 1960 West, Suite 555, Houston TX 77068. (281)440-6885, ext. 27. Fax: (281)440-7510. E-mail: info@rw anational.com. Web site: www.rwanational.com. **Contact:** Nicole Kennedy, PR manager. Estab. 1981. Annual. Average attendance: 1,500. Over 100 workshops on writing, researching and the business side of being a working writer. Publishing professionals attend and accept appointments. Site: Conference will be held in Dallas in 2007 and San Francisco in 2008. Keynote speaker is renowned romance writer.

Costs In 2006, early registration $340 for RWA members/$415 nonmembers; late registration, $390 for RWA members/$465 nonmembers.

Additional Information Annual RITA awards are presented for romance authors. Annual Golden Heart awards are presented for unpublished writers. Conference brochures/guidelines and registration forms are available for SASE and on Web site in May. Accepts inquiries by SASE, e-mail, fax, phone.

SAN JUAN WRITERS WORKSHOP

P.O. Box 841, Ridgeway CO 81432. (806)438-2385. E-mail: inkwellliterary@mac.com. Web site: http://homepage.m ac.com/inkwellliterary. **Contact:** Jill Patterson, director. Estab. 2002. Annual. Workshop held July or August each year. Last conference was July 22-30, 2006. Conference duration: up to 10 days. Average attendance: 40 per session. Focuses on "fiction, poetry, creative nonfiction in each session. Sessions focus on generating new material, workshopping manuscripts, revising and submitting for publication. "The goal of the San Juan Workshops is to remove writers from the hectic pace of everyday life and give them the inspiration, space and quiet to attend to their writing." Site: "The Workshops are held for one week, each summer, in Ouray, CO, Switzerland of America. In this cozy mountain village, everything is within walking distance, including the Ouray Hot Springs Pool, Cascade Falls, the local movie theater in the historical Wright Opera House, several fine restaurants, lodging and the Community Center where workshop events take place." 2006 panels included Generating New Material, Craft and Critique, Revising and Submitting for Publication. Panelists in 2006 included Lee Martin, Philip Gerard, Ron Carlson, Mark Jarman, Dani Shapiro, Stanley Plumly, Gary Short, Lee Gutkind, Pam Houston.

Costs $350-475, includes workshop instruction, faculty readings, breakfast each day and admission to all receptions. "All sessions will require an additional, non-refundable application fee of $25. There are substantial discounts for attending multiple sessions. There are also $100 scholarships available."

Accommodations Offers shuttle to/from airport in Montrose, CO. Provides a list of hotels.

Additional Information Accepts inquiries by SASE, e-mail, phone. "There are social activities, including mountain cookout, concerts in the local park, the annual pub crawl, champagne brunch and readings." See Web site for more information.

SMALL PUBLISHERS MARKETING CONFERENCE AND TRADE SHOW

Small Publishers Association of North America, 1618 West Colorado Ave., Colorado Springs CO 80904. (719)475-1726. Fax: (719)471-2182. E-mail: span@spannet.org. Web site: www.spannet.org. **Contact:** Jennifer Quintana, coordinator. Estab. 1996. Annual. Last conference was October 2006. Conference duration: 3 days. Average attendance: 85. Conference/workshop and trade show for the self-publisher or independent/small press. Intensive one-on-one time with seven expert speakers and 27 industry leaders and vendors. Attendees learn how to sell more books, increase profits, create a more effective message and boost their professional standing. Site: East Coast in 2007.

Costs $345, early registration price for members. Marketing workbook and meals are included in registration fee. Hotel rooms discounted for attendees.

Additional Information Brochures available in June by fax, e-mail and on Web site. Accepts inquiries for SASE and by e-mail, phone and fax.

SOUTHWEST LITERARY CENTER OF RECURSOS DE SANTA FE

826 Camino de Monte Rey, Santa Fe NM 87505. (505)577-1125. Fax: (505)982-7125. Web site: www.santafewrit ersconference.com. **Contact:** Literary Center director. Estab. 1984. Annual. 2006 conference was held June 20-25. Conference duration: 6 days. Average attendance: 50. Last year's conference included workshops, afternoon talks, and private conferences on fiction, nonfiction and poetry. Faculty included Lisa D. Chavez, Elizabeth Benedict, Brian Kiteley and Judy Reeves.
Costs $575-700. Scholarships may be available.
Additional Information Brochure available by e-mail, fax, phone and on Web site.

SOUTHWEST WRITERS CONFERENCE

3271 Morris NE Ste A, Albuquerque NM 87111. (505)265-9485. Fax: (505)265-9483. E-mail: swwriters@aol.c om. Web site: www.southwestwriters.org. **Contact:** Conference Chair. Estab. 1983. Annual. Conferences held throughout the year. Average attendance: 50. "Conferences concentrate on all areas of writing and include appointments and networking." Workshops and speakers include writers, editors and agents of all genres for all levels from beginners to advanced.
Costs $99 and up (members); $159 and up (nonmembers); includes conference sessions and lunch.
Accommodations Usually have official airline and discount rates. Special conference rates are available at hotel. A list of other area hotels and motels is available.
Additional Information Sponsors an annual contest judged by authors, editors and agents from New York, Los Angeles, etc., and from other major publishing houses. Eighteen categories. Deadline: See Web site. Entry fee is $29 (members) or $44 (nonmembers). For brochures/guidelines send SASE, visit Web site, e-mail, fax, call. "An appointment (10 minutes, one-on-one) may be set up at the conference with the editor/agent of your choice on a first-registered/first-served basis."

STEAMBOAT SPRINGS WRITERS GROUP

Steamboat Arts Council, P.O. Box 774284, Steamboat Springs CO 80477. (970)879-8079. E-mail: sswriters@cs.c om. Web site: www.steamboatwriters.com. **Contact:** Harriet Freiberger, director. Estab. 1982. Annual. Group meets year-round on Thursdays, 12:00 to 2:00 at Arts Depot; guests welcome. Conference held in July. Conference duration: 1 day. Average attendance: 30. "Our conference emphasizes instruction within the seminar format. Novices and polished professionals benefit from the individual attention and camaraderie which can be established within small groups. A pleasurable and memorable learning experience is guaranteed by the relaxed and friendly atmosphere of the old train depot. Registration is limited." Site: Restored train depot.
Costs $35 before June 1, $45 after. Fee covers all conference activities, including lunch.
Accommodations Lodging available at Steamboat Resorts.
Additional Information Optional dinner and activities during evening preceding conference. Accepts inquiries by e-mail, phone, mail.

SUMMER WRITING PROGRAM

Naropa University, 2130 Arapahoe Ave., Boulder CO 80302. (303)245-4600. Fax: (303)546-5287. E-mail: swpr@ naropa.edu/swp. Web site: www.naropa.edu/swp. **Contact:** Corrina Lesser, registration manager. Estab. 1974. Annual. Last workshop held: June 19-July 16, 2006. Workshop duration: 4 weeks. Average attendance: 250. Offers college credit. "With 14 workshops to choose from each of the four weeks of the program, students may study poetry, prose, hybrid/cross-genre writing, small press printing, or book arts." Site: All workshops, panels, lectures and readings are hosted on the Naropa University main campus. Located in downtown Boulder, the campus is within easy walking distance of restaurants, shopping and the scenic Pearl Street Mall. Prose-related panels include Ecology, Poetics of Prose, Telling Stories, The Informant "Other." Faculty has included Samuel Delany, David Antin, Amiri Baraka, Laird Hunt, Thomas Glave, Rebecca Brown, Chris Tysh, Brian Evenson, Bobbie Louise Hawkins, Fiona Templeton, David Levi Strauss, Tonya Foster, Richard Tuttle, Anne Waldman, Miguel Algarin, Sonia Sanchez, Robin Blaser.
Costs In 2006: $375/week, $1,500 for all four weeks (non-credit students); $900/week, $3,600 for all four weeks (BA students); $1,230/week, $4,920 for all four weeks (MFA students).
Accommodations Offers overnight accommodations. Dormitory housing is available at Sangha House. Large room is $50/night or $350/week, medium room is $45/night or $315/week, small room is $40/night or $280/week.
Additional Information If students would like to take the Summer Writing Program for academic credit, they must submit a visiting student application, transcripts, a letter of intent, and 5-10 pages of their creative work. Information available in April. For brochure, call, e-mail. Accepts inquiries by e-mail, phone. Editors participate in conference.

◎ TEXAS CHRISTIAN WRITERS' CONFERENCE

First Baptist Church, 6038 Greenmont, Houston TX 77092. (713)686-7209. E-mail: marthalrogers@sbcglobal.net. **Contact:** Martha Rogers. Estab. 1990. Annual. Conference held in August. Conference duration: 1 day. Average attendance: 60-65. "Focus on all genres." Site: Held at the First Baptist Church fellowship center and classrooms. 2006 faculty: Wayne Holmes, Dennis Hensley, Mona Gansberg Hodgson, Cheri Fuller, Anita Higman, Janice Thompson, Kathleen Y'Barbo.

Costs $60 for members of IWA, $75 nonmembers, discounts for seniors (60+) and couples, meal at noon, continental breakfast and breaks.

Accommodations Offers list of area hotels or lodging options.

Additional Information Open conference for all interested writers. Sponsors a contest for short fiction; categories include articles, devotionals, poetry, short story, book proposals, drama. Fees: $8 member, $10 nonmember. Conference information available with SASE or e-mail. Agents participate in conference. Senior discounts available.

THUNDER WRITER'S RETREATS

Durango CO 81301-3408. (970)385-5884. Fax: (970)247-5327. E-mail: thunder@thunderforwriters.com. Web site: www.thunderforwriters.com. **Contact:** Michael Thunder. Estab. 2000. On demand, per client's need. Conference duration: 1-2 weeks. Average attendance: 1 individual/session. Focus is on fiction and scriptwriting. Site: Durango, Colorado, "beautiful mountain environment."

Costs $1,000/week coaching fee. Meals and lodging are dependent on the writer's taste and budget.

Accommodations Provides a list of area hotels or lodging options.

Additional Information "These writer's retreats are geared toward concepting a project or project development. Usually writers stay one week and receive 10 hours of one-on-one coaching. The rest of their time is spent writing. One and sometimes two interviews are required to design a course of action adapted to the writer's needs." Please call, e-mail, fax or send SASE for more information.

MARK TWAIN CREATIVE WRITING WORKSHOPS

University House, 5101 Rockhill Rd., Kansas City MO 64110-2499. (816)235-1168. Fax: (816)235-2611. E-mail: BeasleyM@umkc.edu. Web site: www.newletters.org. **Contact:** Betsy Beasley, adminstrative associate. Estab. 1990. Annual. Held first 3 weeks of June, from 9:30 to 12:30 each weekday morning. Conference duration: 3 weeks. Average attendance: 40. "Focus is on fiction, poetry and literary nonfiction." Site: University of Missouri-Kansas City Campus. Panels planned for next conference include the full range of craft essentials. Staff includes Robert Stewart, editor-in-chief of *New Letters* and BkMk Press.

Costs Fees for regular and noncredit courses.

Accommodations Offers list of area hotels or lodging options.

Additional Information Submit for workshop 6 poems/one short story prior to arrival. Conference information is available in March by SASE, e-mail or on Web site. Editors participate in conference.

UNIVERSITY OF NEW MEXICO'S TAOS SUMMER WRITERS' CONFERENCE

Department of English Language and Literature MSC03 2170, 1 University of New Mexico, Albuquerque NM 87131-0001. (505)277-6248. Fax: (505)277-2950. E-mail: taosconf@unm.edu. Web site: www.unm.edu/~taosconf. **Contact:** Sharon Oard Warner, director. Estab. 1999. Annual. Held each year in mid-July. Average attendance: 180. Workshops in novel writing, short story writing, screenwriting, poetry, creative nonfiction, publishing, and special topics such as yoga and writing and writing for social change. Master classes in novel, memoir and poetry. For beginning and experienced writers. "Taos itself makes our conference unique. We also offer daily visits to the D.H. Lawrence Ranch, the Harwood Museum and other local historical sites." Site: Workshops and readings are all held at the Sagebrush Inn Conference Center, part of the Sagebrush Inn, an historic hotel and Taos landmark since 1929.

Costs Weeklong workshop tuition is $550, includes a Sunday evening New Mexican buffet dinner, a Friday evening barbecue and other special events. Weekend workshop tuition is $275.

Accommodations We offer a discounted car rental rate through the Sagebrush Inn or the adjacent Comfort Suites. Conference participants receive special discounted rates $59-99/night. Room rates at both hotels include a full, hot breakfast.

Additional Information "We offer three Merit Scholarships, the Taos Resident Writer Award, the Hispanic Writer Award and one D.H. Lawrence Fellowship. Scholarship awards are based on submissions of poetry, fiction and creative nonfiction." They provide tuition remission; transportation and lodging not provided. To apply for a scholarship, submit 10 pages of poetry, nonfiction or fiction along with registration and deposit. Applicants should be registered for the conference. The Fellowship is for emerging writers with one book in print, provides tuition remission and cost of lodging. Brochures available late January-early February 2006. "The conference offers a balance of special events and free time. If participants take a morning workshop, they'll have the afternoons free and vice versa. We've also included several outings, including a tour of the Harwood Arts Center and a visit to historic D.H. Lawrence Ranch outside Taos.''

⊚ WRITERS WORKSHOP IN SCIENCE FICTION

Lawrence KS 66045-2115. (785)864-3380. Fax: (785)864-1159. E-mail: jgunn@ku.edu. Web site: www.ku.edu/ ~sfcenter. **Contact:** James Gunn, professor. Estab. 1984. Annual. Workshop held in late June to early July. Conference duration: 2 weeks. Average attendance: 10-14. The workshop is ''small, informal and aimed at writers on the edge of publication or regular publication.'' For writing and marketing science fiction. Site: ''Housing is provided and classes meet in university housing on the University of Kansas campus. Workshop sessions operate informally in a lounge.'' Past guests included Frederik Pohl, SF writer and former editor and agent; John Ordover, writer and editor; and Kij Johnson and Christopher McKittrick, writers. A novel workshop in science fiction and fantasy is also available.

Costs $400 tuition. Housing and meals are additional.

Accommodations Several airport shuttle services offer reasonable transportation from the Kansas City International Airport to Lawrence. During past conferences, students were housed in a student dormitory at $14/day double, $28/day single.

Additional Information ''Admission to the workshop is by submission of an acceptable story. Two additional stories should be submitted by the end of May. These three stories are distributed to other participants for critquing and are the basis for the first week of the workshop; one story is rewritten for the second week. The workshop offers a 3-hour session manuscript critiquing each afternoon. The rest of the day is free for writing, study, consultation and recreation.'' Information available in December. For brochures/guidelines send SASE, visit Web site, e-mail, fax, call. The workshop concludes with The Campbell Conference, a round-table discussion of a single topic, and the presentation of the Campbell and Sturgeon Awards for the Best SF Novel and Short Story of the Year. ''The Writers Workshop in Science Fiction is intended for writers who have just started to sell their work or need that extra bit of understanding or skill to become a published writer.''

WEST (AZ, CA, HI, NV, UT)

Ⓝ ⊚ ALTERNATIVE PRESS EXPO (APE)

Comic-Con International, P.O. Box 128458, San Diego CA 92112-8458 .(619)491-2475. Fax: (619)414-1022. E-mail: cci-info@comic-con.org. Web site: www.comic-con.org/ape/. **Contact:** Gary Sassaman, director of programming. Annual. Last conference held April 8-9, 2006, in San Francisco. Conference duration: 2 days. ''Hundreds of artists and publishers converge for the largest gathering of alternative and self-published comics in the country.'' Includes panels on graphic novels, Web comics, how to pitch your comic to publishers, and the traditional APE 'queer cartoonists' panel. Site: Large conference or expo center in host city. Check Web site for 2007 location. 2006 special guests included Black Olive, Justin Green, Keith Knight, Alex Robinson, Raina Telgemeier and C. Tyler.

Costs $7 single day; $10 both days.

Accommodations Does not offer overnight accommodations. Provides list of area hotels or lodging options on Web site.

Additional Information For brochure, visit Web site. Editors participate in conference.

BIG BEAR WRITER'S RETREAT

P.O. Box 1441, Big Bear Lake CA 92315-1441. (909)585-0059. Fax: (909)266-0710. E-mail: mike@writers-review. com. **Contact:** Mike Foley, director. Estab. 1995. Biannual. Last conferences held July, October 2005. Conference duration: 3 days. Average attendance: 15-25. Past themes included Finding New Creativity, Character and Setting, Avoiding Common Errors, Character Depth, Embracing Yourself as a Writer. Site: ''A small, intimate lodge in Big Bear, San Bernardino mountains of Southern California.'' Retreat is hosted annually by Mike Foley, editor of *Dream Merchant Magazine*, and Tom Foley, Ph.D., artistic psychologist.

Costs $499, includes meals and lodging.

Accommodations Offers overnight accommodations. On-site facilites included in retreat fee.

Additional Information Prior to arrival, submit a fiction or nonfiction sample, 10 double-spaced pages maximum. 2007 conference information is available March 2006. For brochure send SASE, e-mail, call or fax. Accepts inquiries by SASE, e-mail, phone and fax. Editors participate in conference. ''This is unlike the standard writer's conference. Participants will live as writers for a weekend. Retreat includes workshop sessions, open writing time and private counseling with retreat hosts. A weekend of focused writing, fun and friendship. This is a small group retreat, known for its individual attention to writers, intimate setting and strong bonding among participants.''

BLOCKBUSTER PLOT INTENSIVE WRITING WORKSHOPS

708 Blossom Hill Rd. #146, Los Gatos CA 95032. Fax: (408)356-1798. E-mail: martha@blockbusterplots.com. Web site: www.blockbusterplots.com. **Contact:** Martha Alderson, instructor. Estab. 2000. Held four times per year. Conference duration: 2 days. Average attendance: 6-8. Workshop is intended to help writers create an action, character and thematic plotline for a screenplay, memoir, short story, novel or creative nonfiction. Site: a house.
Costs $135 per day.
Accommodations Provides list of area hotels and lodging options.
Additional Information Brochures available by fax, e-mail or on Web site. Accepts inquiries by SASE, e-mail and fax.

JAMES BONNET'S STORYMAKING: THE MASTER CLASS

P.O. Box 841, Burbank CA 91503-0841. (818)567-0521. Fax: (818)567-0038. E-mail: bonnet@storymaking.com. Web site: www.storymaking.com. **Contact:** James Bonnet. Estab. 1990. Conference held February, May, June, November. Conference duration: 2 days. Average attendance: 40. Conferences focus on fiction, mystery and screenwriting. Site: In 2006, Sportsmen's Lodge, Studio City, California and Hilton Resort, Palm Springs, California. Panels for next conference include High Concept, Anatomy of A Great Idea, the Creative Process, Metaphor, The Hook, The Fundamentals of Plot, Structure, Genre, Character, Complications, Crisis, Climax, Conflict, Suspense and more. James Bonnet (author) is scheduled to participate as speaker.
Costs $350 per weekend.
Accommodations Provides a list of area hotels or lodging options.
Additional Information For brochure send SASE, e-mail, visit Web site, call or fax. Accepts inquiries by SASE, e-mail, phone and fax. "James Bonnet, author of *Stealing Fire From the Gods*, teaches a story structure and storymaking seminar that guides writers from inspiration to final draft."

◎ BYU WRITING FOR YOUNG READERS WORKSHOP

348 HCEB, Brigham Young University, Provo UT 84602. (801)422-2568. E-mail: cw348@byu.edu. Web site: http://wfyr.byu.edu. **Contact:** Bill Kelly. Estab. 2000. Annual. Workshop held June or July each year. Average attendance: 150. Conference focuses on "all genres for children and teens." Site: Brigham Young University's Conference Center. Mornings feature small group workshop sessions with a published author. Afternoon break-out sessions on a variety of topics of interest to writers. Sessions for picture book, novel, illustration, fantasy, beginners, general writing. Two editors and an agent are in attendance. Past faculty has included Eve Bunting, Tony Johnston, Tim Wynne-Jones, John H. Ritter, Alane Ferguson, Lael Little, Laura Torres, Gloria Skurzynski, Claudia Mills.
Costs $399 conference fee and closing banquet.
Accommodations Provides list of area hotels.
Additional Information Brochures available in March by phone and on Web site. Accepts inquiries by SASE, e-mail, phone. Agents and editors participate in conference. "Bring the manuscript you are currently working on."

COMMUNITY OF WRITERS AT SQUAW VALLEY

P.O. Box 1416, Nevada City CA 95959-1416. (530)470-8440. Fax: (530)470-8446. E-mail: info@squawvalleywrit ers.org. Web site: www.squawvalleywriters.org. **Contact:** Brett Hall Jones, executive director. Estab. 1969. Annual. Conference held in August. Conference duration: 7 days. Average attendance: 132. "The writers work-shops in fiction, nonfiction and memoir assist talented writers by exploring the art and craft as well as the business of writing." Offerings include daily morning workshops led by writer-teachers, editors, or agents of the staff, limited to 12-13 participants; seminars; panel discussions of editing and publishing; craft colloquies; lectures; and staff readings. Past themes and panels included Personal History in Fiction, Narrative Structure, Roots, and Anatomy of a Short Story. Past faculty and speakers included Dorothy Allison, Mark Childress, Janet Fitch, Richard Ford, Karen Joy Fowler, Lynn Freed, Dagoberto Gilb, Molly Giles, Glen David Gold, Sands Hall, James D. Houston, Louis B. Jones, Alice Sebold, Amy Tan, Al Young.
Costs Tuition is $695, which includes 6 dinners.
Accommodations The Community of Writers rents houses and condominiums in the Valley for participants to live in during the week of the conference. Single room (one participant): $550/week. Double room (twin beds, room shared by conference participant of the same sex): $350/week. Multiple room (bunk beds, room shared with 2 or more participants of the same sex): $200/week. All rooms subject to availability; early requests are recommended. Can arrange airport shuttle pick-ups for a fee.
Additional Information Admissions are based on submitted ms (unpublished fiction, a couple of stories or novel chapters); requries $25 reading fee. Submit ms to Brett Hall Jones, Squaw Valley Community of Writers, P.O. Box 1416, Nevada City, CA 95959. Deadline: May 10. Notification: June 10. Brochure/guidelines available February by phone, e-mail or visit Web site. Accepts inquiries by SASE, e-mail, phone. Agents and editors attend/participate in conferences.

◎ DESERT DREAMS CONFERENCE: REALIZING THE DREAM

P.O. Box 27407, Tempe AZ 85285. (623)910-0524. E-mail: desertdreams@desertroserwa.org. Web site: www.desertroserwa.org. **Contact:** Conference coordinator. Estab. 1986. Biennial. Last conference held April 21-23, 2006. Next conference Spring 2008. Average attendance: 250. Conference focuses on romance fiction. Site: Phoenix, AZ. Past panels included: Plotting, Dialogue, Manuscript Preparation, Web site Design, Synopsis, Help for the Sagging Middle. Keynote speakers in 2006 included Debbie Macomber, Lisa Gardner, Jennifer Cruise and Debra Dixon. Guest editors/agents from St. Martin's Press, Harlequin, Irene Goodman Literary Agency, Borders Group, Ellora's Cave, Spectrum Literary Agency and more.

Costs Vary each year; approximately $175-225 for full conference.

Accommodations Hotels may vary for each conference; it is always a resort location in the Phoenix area.

Additional Information Sponsors contest as part of conference, open to conference attendees only. For brochure, inquiries, contact by e-mail, phone, fax, mail or visit Web site. Agents and editors participate in conference.

N ◎ INTERNATIONAL COMIC-CON

Comic-Con International, P.O. Box 128458, San Diego CA 92112-8458.(619)491-2475. Fax: (619)414-1022. E-mail: cci-info@comic-con.org. Web site: www.comic-con.org/cci/. **Contact:** Gary Sassaman, director of programming. Annual. Last conference held July 20-23, 2006. Conference duration: 4 days. Average attendance: 104,000. "The comics industry's largest expo, hosting writers, artists, editors, agents, publishers, buyers and sellers of comics and graphic novels." Site: San Diego Convention Center. "Nearly 300 programming events, including panels, seminars and previews, on the world of comics, movies, television, animation, art, and much more." 2006 special guests included Ray Bradbury, Forrest J. Ackerman, Sergio Aragones, John Romita Sr., J. Michael Straczynski, Daniel Clowes, George Perez.

Costs $50 by April 19, $55 by June 7, $65 at the door. Special discounts for children and seniors.

Accommodations Does not offer overnight accommodations. Provides list of area hotels or lodging options. Special conference hotel and airfare discounts available. See Web site for details.

Additional Information For brochure, visit Web site. Agents and editors participate in conference.

◎ IWWG EARLY SPRING IN CALIFORNIA CONFERENCE

International Women's Writing Guild, P.O. Box 810, Gracie Station NY 10028-0082. (212)737-7536. Fax: (212)737-7536. E-mail: iwwg@iwwg.com. Web site: www.iwwg.com. **Contact:** Hannelore Hahn, executive editor. Estab. 1982. Annual. Conference held second week in March. Average attendance: 60. Conference to promote "creative writing, personal growth and networking." Site: Bosch Bahai School, a redwood forest mountain retreat in Santa Cruz, CA.

Costs $350 for weekend program with room and board ($330 for members); $100 per day for commuters ($80 for members).

Accommodations Accommodations are all at conference site.

Additional Information Conference information is available after August. For brochures/guidelines, send SASE. Accepts inquiries by e-mail, fax.

MENDOCINO COAST WRITERS CONFERENCE

College of the Redwoods, 1211 Del Mar Drive, Fort Bragg CA 95437. (707)964-6810. E-mail: info@mcwc.org. Web site: http://mcwc.org. **Contact:** Barbara Lee, registrar. Estab. 1989. Annual. Last conference held August 10-12, 2006. Average attendance: 100. "We hope to encourage the developing writer by inviting presenters who are both fine writers and excellent teachers." Site: College of the Redwoods is a small community college located on the gorgeous northern California coast. Focuses are fiction, poetry, creative nonfiction—special areas have included children's (2003), mystery (2002), social awareness. In 2006 faculty included David Skibbins, Jody Gehrman, Paul Levine, Gerald Haslam.

Costs Before June 9, 2006: $300 (2 days); $375 (3 days). After June 9, 2006: $375 (2 days); $410 (3 days).

Additional Information Brochures for the conference will be available in March by SASE, phone, e-mail or on the Web site. Agents and editors participate in the conference. "The conference is small, friendly and fills up fast with many returnees."

◎ MORMON WRITERS' CONFERENCE

Association for Mormon Letters, P.O. Box 13150, Salt Lake City UT 84110-1315. (801)582-2090. E-mail: aml@aml-online.org. Web site: www.aml-online.org. **Contact:** Conference Chair. Estab. 1999. Annual. Conference held November. Conference duration: one day, on a Saturday in late fall. Average attendance: 100. The conference usually covers anything to do with writing by, for or about Mormons, including fiction, nonfiction, theater, film, children's literature. Site: Last few years it has been in Salt Lake City, UT. "Plenary speeches, panels and instructional presentations by prominent authors and artists in the LDS artistic community."

Costs $55, includes catered lunch with pre-registration. AML member and student discounts available.
Additional Information For brochures/guidelines send SASE, e-mail, visit Web site. Accepts inquiries by SASE, e-mail.

PIMA WRITERS' WORKSHOP

Pima Community College, 2202 W. Anklam Road, Tucson AZ 85709-0170. (520)206-6084. Fax: (520)206-6020. E-mail: mfiles@pima.edu. **Contact:** Meg Files, director. Estab. 1988. Annual. Conference held in May. Average attendance: 300. "For anyone interested in writing—beginning or experienced writer. The workshop offers sessions on writing short stories, novels, nonfiction articles and books, children's and juvenile stories, poetry, screenplays." Site: Sessions are held in the Center for the Arts on Pima Community College's West campus. Past speakers include Michael Blake, Ron Carlson, Gregg Levoy, Nancy Mairs, Linda McCarriston, Jerome Stern, Connie Willis, Larry McMurtry, Barbara Kingsolver and Robert Morgan.
Costs $75 (can include ms critique). Participants may attend for college credit, in which case fees are $104 for Arizona residents and $164 for out-of-state residents. Meals and accommodations not included.
Accommodations Information on local accommodations is made available and special workshop rates are available at a specified motel close to the workshop site (about $70/night).
Additional Information Participants may have up to 20 pages critiqued by the author of their choice. Manuscripts must be submitted 3 weeks before the workshop. Conference brochure/guidelines available for SASE. Accepts inquiries by e-mail. "The workshop atmosphere is casual, friendly and supportive, and guest authors are very accessible. Readings, films and panel discussions are offered as well as talks and manuscript sessions."

Ⓝ SAN DIEGO STATE UNIVERSITY WRITERS' CONFERENCE

SDSU College of Extended Studies, 5250 Campanile Drive, San Diego CA 92182-1920. (619)594-2517. Web site: www.ces.sdsu.edu. **Contact:** Becky Ryan, coordinator. Estab. 1984. Annual. Conference held on 3rd weekend in January. Conference duration: 2 days. Average attendance: 375. "This conference is held in San Diego, California, at the Doubletree Hotel, Mission Valley. Each year the SDSU Writers Conference offers a variety of workshops for the beginner and the advanced writer. This conference allows the individual writer to choose which workshop best suits his/her needs. In addition to the workshops, editor/agent appointments and office hours are provided so attendees may meet with speakers, editors and agents in small, personal groups to discuss specific questions. A reception is offered Saturday immediately following the workshops where attendees may socialize with the faculty in a relaxed atmosphere. Keynote speaker is to be determined."
Costs Approximately $365 (2006). This includes all conference workshops and office hours, coffee and pastries in the morning, lunch and reception Saturday evening. Editor/agent appointment extra fee.
Accommodations Doubletree, Mission Valley, (800)222-TREE. Conference rate available for SDSU Writers Conference attendees. Attendees must make their own travel arrangements.
Additional Information Editor/Agent sessions are private, one-on-one opportunities to meet with editors and agents to discuss your submission. For more information fax, call or send a postcard to the above address. No SASE required.

◎ SCBWI/SUMMER CONFERENCE ON WRITING & ILLUSTRATING FOR CHILDREN

(formerly SCBWI/International Conference on Writing & Illustrating for Children), 8271 Beverly Blvd., Los Angeles CA 90048. (323)782-1010. Fax: (323)782-1892. E-mail: conference@scbwi.org. Web site: www.scbwi.org. **Contact:** Lin Oliver, executive director. Estab. 1972. Annual. Conference held in August. Conference duration: 4 days. Average attendance: 800. Writer and illustrator workshops geared toward all levels. Covers all aspects of children's magazine and book publishing.
Costs Approximately $400; includes all 4 days and one banquet meal. Does not include hotel room.
Accommodations Information on overnight accommodations made available.
Additional Information Ms and illustration consultations are available. Brochure/guidelines available on Web site.

UCLA EXTENSION WRITERS' PROGRAM

10995 Le Conte Avenue, #440, Los Angeles CA 90024-2883. (310)825-9415 or (800)388-UCLA. Fax: (310)206-7382. E-mail: writers@UCLAextension.edu. Web site: www.uclaextension.edu/writers. **Contact:** Cindy Lieberman, program manager. Courses held year-round with one-day or intensive weekend workshops to 12-week courses. Writers Studio held in February. A 9-month master class is also offered every fall. "The diverse offerings span introductory seminars to professional novel and script completion workshops. The annual Writers Studio and a number of 1-, 2- and 4-day intensive workshops are popular with out-of-town students due to their specific focus and the chance to work with industry professionals. The most comprehensive and diverse continuing education writing program in the country, offering over 500 courses a year, including screenwriting, fiction, writing for young people, poetry, nonfiction, playwriting and publishing. Adult learners in the UCLA Extension

Writers' Program study with professional screenwriters, fiction writers, playwrights, poets and nonfiction writers, who bring practical experience, theoretical knowledge and a wide variety of teaching styles and philosophies to their classes." Site: Courses are offered in Los Angeles on the UCLA campus and in the 1010 Westwood Center in Westwood Village, as well as online.

Costs Vary from $90 for one-day workshops to $3,000 for the 9-month master class.

Accommodations Students make own arrangements. The program can provide assistance in locating local accommodations.

Additional Information Writers Studio information available October. For brochures/guidelines/guide to course offerings, visit Web site, e-mail, fax or call. Accepts inquiries by e-mail, fax, phone. "Some advanced level classes have manuscript submittal requirements; instructions are always detailed in the quarterly UCLA Extension course catalog. An annual fiction prize, The James Kirkwood Prize in Creative Writing, has been established and is given annually to one fiction writer who has produced outstanding work in a Writers' Program course."

WILD WRITING WOMEN WRITING WORKSHOP

5034 Bell St. Port Townsend, WA 98368. (360)379-1324. E-mail: writing@lisaalpine.com. Web site: www.wildwritingwomen.com. **Contact:** Lisa Alpine. Estab. 2003. Annual. January 2007. Conference duration: 2 days. Average attendance: 50. Designed for serious and would-be serious writers, the conference includes classes on travel writing, chronicling your family legacy, the writer's voice, personal essay, real-time travelogues, food writing, understanding contracts, self-publishing and more. Site: Historic Fort Mason on San Francisco Bay, featuring breathtaking views of the Golden Gate Bridge. "We've arranged a panel discussion with magazine and book editors, a panel with the WWW on how to run a successful writing group, a travel photography discussion and slide show presentation, creativity exercises and more." Classes will be taught by members of Wild Writing Women, LCC, the acclaimed San Francisco writing group and authors of *Wild Writing Women: Stories of World Travel*, an award-winning anthology of travelogues and the 2004 winners of Natja's Best Travel Ezine.

Costs $350 by Dec. 15; $400 after that date. Includes all classes and panels, lunch and a wine mixer.

Accommodations Provides list of hotels and lodging options.

Additional Information Brochures for the 2007 conference will be available in November 2006 by phone, e-mail and on Web site. Accepts inquiries by e-mail and phone.

🅽 🄪 WONDERCON

Comic-Con International, P.O. Box 128458, San Diego CA 92112-8458 .(619)491-2475. Fax: (619)414-1022. E-mail: cci-info@comic-con.org. Web site: www.comic-con.org/wc/. **Contact:** Greg Sassaman, director of programming. Estab. 1986. Annual. Last conference held February 10-12, 2006, in San Francisco. Conference duration: 3 days. Average attendance: 14,500. "In addition to comics publisher panels, you can count on special spotlights on all of our guests. We're currently talking to many major Hollywood studios to once again present exclusive material and appearances at WonderCon. WonderCon offers a giant exhibit hall filled to the brim with the finest in old and new comics, books, original art, anime, manga, movie memorabilia, action figures and toys, DVDs, and much more. WonderCon also presents one of the best Artists' Alley sections in the country with some of the most popular artists in comics—past, present and future." Site: 2006 was held at Moscone West conference center in San Francisco. 2006 included DC Comics panels; special guests Frank Miller, Mark Waid, Grant Morrison and Peter David; and Bryan Singer's *Superman Returns* panel, with a surprise appearance by star Brandon Routh. Check Web site for 2007 guests and programming schedule.

Accommodations Does not offer overnight accommodations. Provides list of area hotels or lodging options. Special hotel rates available for WonderCon attendees. Check Web site for details.

Additional Information For brochure, visit Web site. Editors participate in conference.

WRITERS STUDIO AT UCLA EXTENTION

(formerly Los Angeles Writer's Conference), 1010 Westwood Blvd., Los Angeles CA 90024. (310)825-9415. E-mail: writers@uclaextension.edu. Web site: www.uclaextension.edu/writers. **Contact:** Corey Campbell. Estab. 1997. Annual in February. Conference duration: 4 days; 10 a.m. to 6 p.m. Average attendance: 150-200. Intensive writing workshops in the areas of creative writing, screenwriting and memoir writing. Site: Conducted at UCLA Extension's 1010 Westwood Center.

Accommodations Information on overnight accommodations is available.

Additional Information For more information, call number (310)825-9415 or send an e-mail to writers@uclaextension.edu.

WRITING AND ILLUSTRATING FOR YOUNG READERS WORKSHOP

BYU, conferences and workshops, 348 HCEB, BYU, Provo UT 84602-1532. (801)422-2568. Fax: (801)422-0745. E-mail: cw348@byu.edu. Web site: http://wifyr.byu.edu. **Contact:** Conferences & Workshops. Estab. 2000.

Annual. 5-day workshop held in June of each year. The workshop is designed for people who want to write for children or teenagers. Participants focus on a single market during daily four-hour morning writing workshops led by published authors. Afternoon workshops sessions include a mingle with the authors, editors and agents. Workshop focuses on fiction for young readers: picture books, book-length fiction, fantasy/science fiction, nonfiction, mystery, illustration and general writing. Site: Conference Center at Brigham Young University in the foothills of the Wasatch Mountain range.

Costs $439, full registration includes all workshops and breakout sessions plus a banquet on Thursday evening. $109, afternoon only registration includes all afternoon workshop sessions plus the banquet on Thursday evening.

Accommodations Local lodging, airport shuttle. Lodging rates: $49-95/night.

NORTHWEST (AK, ID, MT, OR, WA, WY)

◎ BOUCHERCON

507 S. 8th Street, Philadelphia PA 19147. (215)923-0211. Fax: (215)923-1789. E-mail: registration@bouchercon2 007. Web site: www.bouchercon.com; www.bouchercon2007.com. Conference held September 27-30, 2007, in Anchorage, AK. The Bouchercon is "the world mystery and detective fiction event." Site: Anchorage Hilton Hotel. See Web site for details. Special guests include Ann Rule, Alexander McCall Smith.

Costs $200 (prior to July 1, 2007), $250 (after July 1) registration fee covers writing workshops, panels, reception, etc.

Additional Information Sponsors Anthony Award for published mystery novel; ballots due prior to conference. Information available on Web site.

CENTRUM'S PORT TOWNSEND WRITERS' CONFERENCE

P.O. Box 1158, Port Townsend WA 98368-0958. (360)385-3102. Fax: (360)385-2470. E-mail: info@centrum.org. Web site: www.centrum.org. **Contact:** Rebecca Brown, creative director. Estab. 1974. Annual. Conference held mid-July. Average attendance: 180. Conference to promote poetry, fiction, creative nonfiction "featuring many of the nation's leading writers." Two different workshop options: critiqued (limit 16 participants) and open enrollment. Site: The conference is held at Fort Worden State Park on the Strait of Juan de Fuca. "The site is a Victorian-era military fort with miles of beaches, wooded trails and recreation facilities. The park is within the limits of Port Townsend, a historic seaport and arts community, approximately 80 miles northwest of Seattle, on the Olympic Peninsula." Guest speakers participate in addition to full-time faculty.

Costs Tuition for critiqued workshop is $575, for open-enrollment workshops $495, for events pass (no workshops) $120. Room and board ranges from $285-$540, depending on the option you choose.

Accommodations "Modest room and board facilities on site." Also list of hotels/motels/inns/bed & breakfasts/private rentals available.

Additional Information Brochures/guidelines available for SASE or on Web site. "The conference focus is on the craft of writing and the writing life, not on marketing."

◎ CLARION WEST WRITERS' WORKSHOP

340 15th Avenue E, Suite 350, Seattle WA 98112-5156. (206)322-9083. E-mail: info@clarionwest.org. Web site: www.clarionwest.org. **Contact:** Leslie Howle, executive director. Estab. 1983. Annual. Workshop usually held in late June through July. Average attendance: 18. "Conference to prepare students for professional careers in science fiction and fantasy writing." Deadline for applications: April 1. Site: Conference held in Seattle's University district, an urban site close to restaurants and cafes, but not too far from downtown. Faculty: 6 teachers (professional writers and editors established in the field). "Every week a new instructor—each a well-known writer chosen for the quality of his or her work and for professional stature—teaches the class, bringing a unique perspective on speculative fiction. During the fifth week, the workshop is taught by a professional editor."

Costs Workshop tuition: $1,700 ($100 discount if application received by March 1). Dormitory housing: $1,200, some meals included.

Accommodations Students stay on site in workshop housing at one of the University of Washington's sorority houses.

Additional Information "Students write their own stories every week while preparing critiques of all the other students' work for classroom sessions. This gives participants a more focused, professional approach to their writing. The core of the workshop remains science fiction, and short stories (not novels) are the focus." Conference information available in Fall 2006. For brochure/guidelines send SASE, visit Web site, e-mail or call. Accepts inquiries by e-mail, phone, SASE. Limited scholarships are available, based on financial need. Students must submit 20-30 pages of ms with $25 application fee by mail to qualify for admission.

⊞ ◎ EMERALD CITY COMICON

3333 184th St. SW, Suite G, Lynnwood WA 98037. E-mail: info@emeraldcitycomicon.com. Web site: www.emer aldcitycomicon.com. Estab. 2002. Annual. Last conference held April 1-2, 2006. Conference duration: 2 days. "The premiere comic book convention of the Pacific Northwest. Includes various creative and publishing panels, artists alley." Site: 2006 ComiCon was held at the Qwest Field (Seahawks Stadium) Event Center in Seattle. 2006 guests included Adam Hughes, Roman Dirge, Brom, Tony Harris, Steve Niles, Sean Phillips, as well as Image Comics, Oni Press, Fantagraphics, Dark Horse, Top Shelf.

Costs $12/day or $18/weekend

Accommodations Offers overnight accommodations. Discounted rate at Marriott SpringHill Suites in Seattle.

Additional Information For brochure, visit Web site. Editors participate in conference.

FLATHEAD RIVER WRITERS CONFERENCE

P.O. Box 7711, Kalispell MT 59904. E-mail: hows@centurytel.net. **Contact:** Jake How, director. Estab. 1990. Annual. Last conference: October 7-9, 2006. Conference duration: 3 days. Average attendance: 100 (max). Deals with all aspects of writing, including short and long fiction and nonfiction. Site: Grouse Mountain Lodge in Whitefish, MT. Recent speakers: Bill Brooks (fiction), Bharti Kirchner (fiction/nonfiction), Jacky Sach (agent), Linda McFall (editor), Gary Ferguson (nonfiction), Gordon Kirkland (humor).

Costs $150 general weekend conference; includes breakfast and lunch, not lodging. $460 for both 3-day work- shop preceeding general conference and general conference.

Accommodations Lodging at Grouse Mountain Lodge. Approximately 50% discount (around $100 a night).

Additional Information "We limit attendance to 100 in order to assure friendly, easy access to presentations."

HAYSTACK WRITING PROGRAM

Portland State University, P.O. Box 1491, Portland OR 97207-1491. (503)725-4186. Fax: (503)725-4840. E-mail: snydere@pdx.edu. Web site: www.haystack.pdx.edu. **Contact:** Elizabeth Snyder, director. Estab. 1968. Annual. Program runs July 14 through August 4. Average attendance: 10-15/workshop; total program 200. Offers week- end and weeklong workshops in fiction, nonfiction, nature writing, memoir, dangerous writing, poetry and essay. Site: Classes are held at the Cannon Beach Elementary School in Cannon Beach, OR, a small coastal community. Instructors include Marvin Bell, Judith Barrington, Sandra Scofield and Whitney Otto among others.

Costs Non-credit. Approximately $415/course (weeklong); $225 (weekend). 2 quarter credits: $505. Does not include lodging.

Accommodations Various accommodations available including B&B, motel, hotel, private rooms, camping, private homes.

Additional Information Free brochure available after March. Accepts inquiries by e-mail and fax. University credit (graduate or undergraduate) is available. Classes are held in the local school with supplemental activities at the beach, community lecture hall, galleries and other areas of the resort town.

◎ HEART TALK

Women's Center for Ministry, Western Seminary, 5511 SE Hawthorne Blvd., Portland OR 97215-3367. (503)517- 1931 or (877)517-1800, ext. 1931. Fax: (503)517-1889. E-mail: wcm@westernseminary.edu. Web site: www.we sternseminary.edu/women/. **Contact:** Kenine Stein, administrative assistant. Estab. 1998. Every other year (alternates with speaker's conferences). Conference held in March. (2005 date was March 12.) Conference duration: writing, 1 day; speaking, 3-4 days. Average attendance: 100+. "Heart Talk provides inspirational training for women desiring to write for publication and/or speak publicly." Site: "Western Seminary has a chapel plus classrooms to accommodate various size groups. The campus has a peaceful park-like atmosphere with beautiful lawns, trees and flowers." Topics in 2005 ranged from writing fiction, nonfiction, gift books, book proposals, and greeting cards to editing, steps to getting published, ministering to people in pain, writing for children and more. 2005 keynote speaker was Patricia Rushford. 14 workshops by Marion Duckworth, Kimberly Schumate, Jeannie St. John Taylor, Karla Dornacher, Liz Heaney, Doris Sanford and Patricia Rushford.

Costs $55 in 2005; box lunch can be ordered.

Additional Information Conference information available in January by e-mail, phone, fax and on Web site. For inquiries, contact by mail, e-mail, phone. Conference "is open to Christian women who desire to begin to write for publication. Please view our Web site for Heart Talk 2007 Writer's Conference details. They will be posted as they become available. E-mail us to be added to our Heart Talk mailing list."

◎ NATURE WRITERS RETREAT WITH NORTH CASCADES INSTITUTE

North Cascades Institute, 810 Highway 20, Sedro-Wooley WA 98284-9394. (360)856-5700 ext. 209. Fax: (360)856-1934. E-mail: nci@ncascades.org. Web site: www.ncascades.org. **Contact:** Deb Martin, registrar. Es- tab. 1999. Annual. 2006 conference was held October 10-14. Conference duration: 4 days. Average attendance: 32. Led by three outstanding authors and poets, the NCI Nature Writing Retreat engages amateur and professional writers alike—lectures, discussions, readings and writing exercises centered on the natural world. "Nature writing, at its simplest, strives to explore basic principles at work in nature and to convey these in language that introduces readers to the facility and wonder of their own place in the world." Site: North Cascades Enviromental learning center in North Cascades National Park. Faculty: Gary Ferguson, Kathleen Dean Moore, and Anna Maria Spagna.

Costs 2006 costs were $575 (double occupancy), $495 (commuter), $725 (single). All options include meals.

Additional Information For conference information, visit Web Site, e-mail or call.

PACIFIC NORTHWEST WRITERS CONFERENCE

P.O. Box 2016, Edmonds WA 98020-9516. (425)673-2665. Fax: (425)771-9588. E-mail: pnwa@pnwa.org. Web site: www.pnwa.org. **Contact:** Brenda Stav, association executive. Annual. 2006 conference held July 13-16. Average attendance: 450.

Accommodations Hotel shuttle to and from airport available. Offers discounted rate for overnight lodging; $129/night in 2005.

Additional Information Offers contest with 11 fiction categories: young writers, romance genre, screenwriting, adult genre novel, Jean M. Auel Mainstream Novel, Judine and Terry Brooks Juvenile/YA Novel, adult short story, juvenile short story/picture book, poetry, nonfiction book/memoir, adult article/essay/short memoir. Entry requirements vary with category. Guidelines for contest available on Web site; brochure for conference available on Web site in late February. Accepts inquiries by e-mail, phone, fax. Agents and editors participate in conference.

N SITKA CENTER FOR ART AND ECOLOGY

P.O. Box 65, Otis OR 97368. (541)994-5485. Fax: (541)994-8024. E-mail: info@sitkacenter.org. Web site: www.sitkacenter.org. **Contact:** Dee Moore, workshop program coordinator. Estab. 1970. "Our workshop program is open to all levels and is held annually from late May until late November. We also have a residency program from September through May." Average attendance: 10-16/workshop. A variety of workshops in creative process, including book arts and other media. Site: The Center borders a Nature Conservatory Preserve, the Siuslaw National Experimental Forest and the Salmon River Estuary, located just north of Lincoln City, OR.

Costs "Workshops are generally $50-300; they do not include meals or lodging."

Accommodations Does not offer overnight accommodations. Provides a list of area hotels or lodging options.

Additional Information Brochure available in February of each year by SASE, phone, e-mail, fax or visit Web site. Accepts inquiries by SASE, e-mail, phone, fax.

SITKA SYMPOSIUM

P.O. Box 2420, Sitka AK 99835-2420. (907)747-3794. Fax: (907)747-6554. E-mail: island@ak.net. Web site: www.islandinstitutealaska.org. **Contact:** Carolyn Servid, director. Estab. 1984. Annual. Conference held in July. Conference duration: 1 week. Average attendance: 60. Conference "to consider the relationship between writing and the ideas of selected theme focusing on social and cultural issues." Site: The Symposium is held in downtown Sitka. Many points of visitor interest are within walking distance. The town looks out over surrounding water and mountains. Guest speakers have included Alison Deming, Scott Russell Sanders, Rina Swentzell, Barry Lopez, William Kittredge, Gary Synder, Margaret Atwood, Terry Tempest Williams, Robert Hass, Richard Nelson and Linda Hogan.

Costs $365.

Accommodations Accommodation info is listed on Symposium brochure and Web site.

Additional Information Conference brochures/guidelines are available for SASE or online. Accepts inquiries by e-mail and fax.

SOUTH COAST WRITERS CONFERENCE

P.O. Box 590, 29392 Ellensburg Avenue, Gold Beach OR 97444. (541)247-2741. Fax: (541)247-6247. E-mail: scwc@socc.edu. Web site: www.socc.edu/scwriters. **Contact:** Janet Pretti, coordinator. Estab. 1996. Annual. Conference held President's Day weekend. Workshops held Friday and Saturday. Average attendance: 100. "We try to cover a broad spectrum: fiction, historical, poetry, children's, nature." Site: "Friday workshops are held at The Event Center on the Beach. Saturday workshops are held at the high school." 2006 keynote speaker was Molly Gloss. Other presenters Jayel Gibson, Leigh Anne Jasheway-Bryant, Karen Karbo, Joe Kurmaske, E. Sandy Powell, Heidi Ratner-Connolly, Joanna Rose, Tim Schell, Clemens Starck, Linda Swanson-Davies and Carol Wissmann.

Costs $50 before January 31; $60 after. Friday workshops are an additional $35. No meals or lodging included.

Accommodations Provides list of area hotels.

Additional Information Sponsors contest. "Southwestern scholarship open to anyone. This year's scholarship topic is 'Breaking Rules.' Contact SCWC for details."

TIN HOUSE SUMMER WRITERS WORKSHOP

P.O. Box 10500, Portland OR 97296. (503)219-0622. Fax: (503)222-1154. E-mail: emily@tinhouse.com. Web site: www.tinhouse.com. **Contact:** Lee Montgomery, conference coordinator. Estab. 2003. Annual in July. Conference duration: 1 week. Average attendance: 100. A weeklong intensive of panels, seminars, workshops and readings led by the editors of *Tin House* magazine and Tin House Books, and their guests—prominent contemporary writers of fiction, nonfiction, poetry and film. Site: The workshop will be held at Reed College in scenic Portland, OR, just minutes from downtown and the airport. Facilities include bookstore, library, mail service, an art gallery, print shop and athletic facilities. Each afternoon agents, editors, writers and filmmakers will discuss ideas and offer a range of discussions on topics and issues concerning the craft and business of riting. See Web site for specifics. 2006 faculty included Lorrie Moore, Michael Ondaatje, Aimee Bender, Dorothy Allison, Steve Almond, Antonya Nelson and Elissa Schappell.
Costs 2006 tuition was $950; food and lodging $550. Application fee $35. Scholarships available.
Additional Information Attendees must submit writing sample and attend by invitation. Deadline: April 1, then rolling while space allows. Admission is based on the strength and promise of the writing sample—up to 15 pages of fiction. Brochures available in February for SASE, by fax, phone, e-mail and on Web site. Accepts inquiries by SASE, e-mail, phone, fax. Agents and editors attend conference.

WRITE ON THE SOUND WRITERS' CONFERENCE

Edmonds Arts Commission, 700 Main Street, Edmonds WA 98020. (425)771-0228. Fax: (425)771-0253. E-mail: wots@ci.edmonds.wa.us. **Contact:** Kris Gillespie, conference coordinator. Estab. 1986. Annual. Last conference held October 7-8, 2006. Conference duration: 2 days. Average attendance: 180. "Conference is small—good for networking—and focuses on the craft of writing." Site: "Edmonds is a beautiful community on the shores of Puget Sound, just north of Seattle. View brochure at www.ci.edmonds.wa.us/artscommission/index.stm."
Costs $104 by Sept. 21, $125 after Sept. 21 for 2 days, $68 for 1 day (2005); includes registration, morning refreshments and 1 ticket to keynote lecture.
Additional Information Brochures available August 1. Accepts inquiries by e-mail, fax.

WRITERS STUDIO

P.O. Box 820141, Portland OR 97282-1141. E-mail: jesswrites@juno.com or jessica@inspirationnotebook.com. Web site: www.writing-life.com or www.inspirationnotebook.com. **Contact:** Jessica P. Morrell. Estab. 1991. "Every year I teach a variety of one-day and weekend workshops in Portland and Eugene, OR; Seattle, WA; Vancouver, B.C., and at the Oregon Coast. Subjects include Deep Fiction; Fiction Middles; The First 50 Pages; Show, Don't Tell; Secondary Characters; Narrative Nonfiction; Between the Lines: the Subtler Aspects of Fiction. Please contact me for details about my schedule. I generally teach two workshops each month except December." *Between The Lines* and *Writing Out the Storm* author Jessica Morrell is scheduled to participate as faculty.
Costs Price ranges from $70-225. Accomodations and meals sometimes included.
Accommodations Provides a list of area hotels or lodging options.
Additional Information Available via e-mail or mail inquiries.

WRITING IT REAL IN PORT TOWNSEND

(formerly the Colorado Mt. Writer's Workshop), 394 Colman Drive, Port Townsend, WA 98368. (360)385-7839. Web site: http://writingitreal.com/wirconference2007.htm. Established 1999. Annual. Last conference held June 22-26, 2006. Conference duration: 4 days. Average Attendance: 35. Named one of the top retreats by *Personal Journaling Magazine*, this conference focuses on fiction, poetry and personal essay. The conference is designed to lift writers, novice or experienced, to the next level. Site: Held at a hotel (housing there or around town) in Port Townsend, WA. Features personal writing. Faculty includes Sheila Bender, Meg Files, Jack Heffron.
Costs $400. Accommodations and meals separate. Daily activities include craft talks, small group manuscript workshop, hands-on exercises for creating new work, instructor and group responses, readings.

CANADA

♻ ◎ BLOODY WORDS MYSTERY CONFERENCE

Phone/fax: (416)497-5293. E-mail: soles@sff.net. Web site: www.bloodywords.com. **Contact:** Caro Soles, chair. Estab. 1999. Annual. Last conference held June 9-11, 2006. Average attendance: 300. Focus: Mystery/true crime/forensics, with Canadian slant. Purpose: To bring readers and writers of the mystery genre together in a Canadian setting. Site: Victoria, British Columbia. Hotel TBA. Conference includes two workshops and two tracks of panels, one on factual information such as forensics, agents, scene of the crime procedures, etc. and one on fiction, such as "Death in a Cold Climate," "Murder on the Menu," "Elementary, My Dear Watson," and a First Novelists Panel. Guests of honor in 2006 were Mary Jane Maffini and Stuart Kaminsky.

Costs 2006 fee: $175 (Canadian)/$165 (US), included the banquet and all panels, readings, dealers' room and workshop.

Accommodations Offers block of rooms in hotel; list of optional lodging available. Check Web site for details.

Additional Information Sponsors short mystery story contest—5,000 word limit; judges are experienced editors of anthologies; fee is $5 (entrants must be registered). Conference information is available now. For brochure visit Web site. Accepts inquiries by e-mail and phone. Agents and editors participate in conference. "This is a conference for both readers and writers of mysteries, the only one of its kind in Canada. We also run 'The Mystery Cafe,' a chance to get to know 15 authors, hear them read and ask questions (half hour each)."

▨ BOOMING GROUND

Buch E-462, 1866 Main Mall, Creative Writing Program, UBC, Vancouver BC V6T 121 Canada. (604)822-2469. Fax: (604)822-3616. E-mail: bg@arts.ubc.ca. Web site: bg.arts.ubc.ca. **Contact:** Andrew Gray, director. Estab. 1998. Average attendance: 30 per session. Conference on "fiction, poetry, nonfiction, children's writing. We offer three sessions of online-only mentorships each year in January, May and September. Online mentorships offer 16 weeks of work with an instructor, allowing up to 120 pages of material to be created. Site: Online and by e-mail.

Costs $780 (Canadian) for online-only mentorships; Some scholarships available.

Accommodations Not available.

Additional Information Workshops are based on works-in-progress. Writers must submit ms with application for jury selection. For brochures/guidelines visit Web site, e-mail, fax or call. Accepts inquiries by phone, fax, e-mail. "Classes are offered for writers at all levels—from early career to mid-career. All student work is evaluated by a jury. Our mentorships are ideal for long-form work such as novels, collections of poetry and short fiction."

▨ HUMBER SCHOOL FOR WRITERS SUMMER WORKSHOP

Humber Institute of Technology and Advanced Learning, 3199 Lake Shore Blvd. West, Toronto ON M8V 1K8 Canada. (416)675-6622 ext. 3448. Fax: (416)251-7167. E-mail: antanas.sileika@humber.ca. Web site: www.humber.ca/creativeandperformingarts. **Contact:** Antanas Sileika, director. Annual. Workshop held July. Conference duration: 1 week. Average attendance: 100. Focuses on fiction, poetry, creative nonfiction. Site: Humber College's Lakeshore campus in Toronto. Panels cover success stories, small presses, large presses, agents. Faculty: Changes annually. 2006 includes Francine Prose, Alistair Macleod, David Bezmozgis, Joseph Boyden, Wayson Choy, Bruce Jay Friedman, Isabel Huggan, Kim Moritsugu, Olive Senior and others.

Costs Workshop fee is $950 Canadian ($800 US).

Accommodations Provides lodging. Residence fee is $350 Canadian ($280 US).

Additional Information Participants "must submit sample writing no longer than 15 pages approximately 4 weeks before workshop begins." Brochures available mid-February for e-mail, phone, fax. Accepts inquiries by e-mail, phone, fax. Agents and editors participate in conference.

▨ MARITIME WRITERS' WORKSHOP

UNB Arts Centre, P.O. Box 4400, Fredericton NB E3B 5A3 Canada. Phone/fax: (506)453-4623. E-mail: atitus@unb.ca. Web site: www.unb.ca/extend/writers/. **Contact:** Andrew Titus, coordinator. Estab. 1976. Workshop held annually in July. Average attendance: 50. "We offer small groups of 10, practical manuscript focus. Novice writers welcome. Workshops in four areas: fiction, poetry, nonfiction, writing for children. The annual Maritime Writers' Workshop is a practical, wide-ranging program designed to help writers develop and refine their creative writing skills. This weeklong program will involve you in small group workshops, lectures and discussions, public readings and special events, all in a supportive community of writers who share a commitment to excellence. Workshop groups consist of a maximum of 10 writers each. Instructors are established Canadian authors and experienced teachers with a genuine interest in facilitating the writing process of others. For over a quarter century, Maritime Writers' Workshop has provided counsel, encouragement and direction for hundreds of developing writers." Site: University of New Brunswick, Fredericton campus.

Costs 2006: $395 tuition.

Accommodations On-campus accommodations and meals.

Additional Information "Participants must submit 10-20 manuscript pages which form a focus for workshop discussions." Brochures available after March. No SASE necessary. Accepts inquiries by e-mail and fax.

▨ SAGE HILL WRITING EXPERIENCE

Box 1731, Saskatoon SK S7K 3S1 Canada. Phone/fax: (306)652-7395. E-mail: sage.hill@sasktel.net. Web site: www.sagehillwriting.ca. **Contact:** Steven Ross Smith. Annual. Workshops held in July and November. Conference duration: 10-14 days. Average attendance: Summer, 30-40; Fall, 6-8. "Sage Hill Writing Experience offers a special working and learning opportunity to writers at different stages of development. Top quality instruction, low instructor-student ratio and the beautiful Sage Hill setting offer conditions ideal for the pursuit of excellence in the arts of fiction, nonfiction, poetry and playwriting." Site: The Sage Hill location features "individual accommodation, in-room writing area, lounges, meeting rooms, healthy meals, walking woods and vistas in several directions." Various classes are held: Introduction to Writing Fiction & Poetry; Fiction Workshop; Fiction Colloquium, Nonfiction Workshop; Writing Young Adult Fiction Workshop; Poetry Workshop; Poetry Colloquium; Playwriting Lab.

Costs Summer program, $895 (Canadian) includes instruction, accommodation, meals and all facilities. Fall Fiction Colloquium: $1,195 (Canadian).

Accommodations On-site individual accommodations for Summer and Fall programs located at Lumsden, 45 kilometers outside Regina.

Additional Information Application requirements for Introduction to Creative Writing: A 5-page sample of your writing or a statement of your interest in creative writing; list of courses taken required. For workshop and colloquium programs: A résumé of your writing career and a 12-page sample of your work-in-progress, plus 5 pages of published work required. Application deadline for the Summer Program is in April. Fall Program deadline in August. Guidelines are available after January for SASE, e-mail, fax, phone or on Web site. Scholarships and bursaries are available.

THE VICTORIA SCHOOL OF WRITING

Suite 306-620 View St., Victoria BC V8W 1J6 Canada. (250)595-3000. E-mail: info@victoriaschoolofwriting.org. Web site: www.victoriaschoolofwriting.org. **Contact:** Jill Margo, director. Conference held the third week in July annually. "Five-day intensive workshop on beautiful Vancouver Island with outstanding author-instructors in fiction, poetry, nonfiction, work-in-progress and other genres."

Costs $595 (Canadian).

Accommodations On site.

Additional Information Workshop brochures available. Accepts inquiries by e-mail, phone or Web site.

THE WRITERS' RETREAT

15 Canusa St., Stanstead QC J0B 3E5 Canada. (819) 876-2065. E-mail: info@writersretreat.com. Web site: www.writersretreat.com. **Contact:** Anthony Lanza, program director. Estab. 1998. Year-round. Conference duration: 2-5 days. Any length of stay for residency. The Writers Retreat workshops feature instruction in fiction writing, nonfiction writing and screenwriting. "Our sole purpose is to provide an ambiance conducive to creativity for career and emerging writers. Residency includes a private studio and breakfast, a library with reference books, wireless Internet, critique, on-site editor. The Writers Retreat is a full literary service retreat including residency, private mentoring, workshops, editing (exclusively for residents). Site: Quebec headquarters are located on the Vermont/Quebec border with a satellite facility in Ouray, Colorado and Zihuatanejo, Mexico. Workshops include Self-Editing for Publication, Story Realization, Dynamics of Dramatic Structure, Screenwriting Dynamics and more.

Costs Most workshops are conducted at the retreat in Quebec and Mexico and in the USA. Residency starts at $525/week. Private mentoring starts at $1,495. Workshop tuition varies from $150-$1,120, depending on the format.

Additional Information Accepts inquiries by SASE, e-mail and phone.

INTERNATIONAL

CREATIVITY AND THE JOURNEY INWARD: A WRITING RETREAT IN THE SACRED VALLEY OF PERU

995 Chapman Rd., Yorktown NY 10598. (914)962-4432. E-mail: emily@emilyhanlon.com. Web site: www.thefictionwritersjourney.com. **Contact:** Emily Hanlon. Estab. 1997. Annual. Last conference held July 6-18, 2003. Average attendance: 20-25. Conference focuses on "Using all forms of writing, including fiction, poetry and journaling to explore the writer's journey as our passion, our teacher and guide to our deeper truths. We combine this with a journey into the authentic spiritual heart of the Andes, land of the Inca and the Quechuan people of Pachamama, Mother Earth." Site: "Wilka T'ika (sacred flower) is a retreat center in the heart of the Sacred Valley of the Inca. Situated between Cusco and Machu Picchu, the guest house offers grace and comfort enhanced by the aura of the Andes." Panels include "fiction writing techniques, among others, to open to a deeper creativity and explore the imaginative possibilities inherent in such an ancient place." Workshops led by Emily Hanlon, novelist, and Carol Cumes, author/anthropologist.

Costs "The final fee is not yet set, although it will be around $3,300. This includes all workshops, hotels, transport in Peru, specially selected guides, all entrance tickets, workshops with healers and many but not all meals."

Accommodations "We suggest travel agents to help with all the bookings and provide transportation once participant arrives in Cusco." Offers overnight accommodations. "The guest cottages are newly-built in traditional 16th century Spanish colonial style." Single and double rooms available, all with private baths.

Additional Information "Participants need to speak to Emily Hanlon on the telephone and write a letter (or e-mail) as to why they want to come to the retreat, what draws them to it and what they desire to experience in terms of their writing." Brochures available on Web site, by e-mail, by phone. Accepts inquiries by e-mail, phone. "It is important for all participants to know that we are at very high altitudes. Cusco is 12,000 feet, Wilka T'ika is 9,000 feet and Machu Picchu is 7,000 feet. Time and concern are given to acclimating everyone to high altitudes, however people with special health concerns should contact their physician. There is moderate climbing at times. All in all, this is a most unique, once in a lifetime experience for anyone seeking to explore the relationship between their writing, creativity and the spiritual journey."

🌐 PARIS WRITERS WORKSHOP/WICE

20, Bd. du Montparnasse, Paris 75015 France. (331)45.66.75.50. Fax: (331)40.65.96.53. E-mail: pww@wice-paris.org. Web site: www.wice-paris.org. **Contact:** Marcia Lebre, director. Estab. 1987. Annual. Conference held June-July. Average attendance: 50. "Conference concentrates on fiction, nonfiction and poetry. Visiting lecturers speak on a variety of issues important to beginning and advanced writers. 2006 writers in residence were Lynne Sharon Schwartz (novel), Ellen Sussman (short fiction), Jason Shinder (poetry), Vivian Gornick (creative nonfiction), Katharine Weber (writing intensive tutorial). Located in the heart of Paris on the Bd. du Montparnasse, the stomping grounds of such famous American writers as Ernest Hemingway, Henry Miller and F. Scott Fitzgerald. The site consists of four classrooms, a resource center/library and private terrace."

Costs 600 Euros (500 Euros for early bird registration by May 17)—tuition only.

Additional Information "Students submit 1 copy of complete manuscript or work-in-progress which is sent in advance to writer-in-residence. Each student has a one-on-one consultation with writer-in-residence." Conference information available late fall. For brochures/guidelines visit Web site, e-mail, call or fax. Accepts inquiries by SASE, phone, e-mail, fax. "Workshop attracts many expatriate Americans and other English-language writers from all over Europe and North America. We are an intimate workshop with an exciting mix of more experienced, published writers and enthusiastic beginners."

◎ WRITING, CREATIVITY AND RITUAL: A WOMAN'S RETREAT

995 Chapman Road, Yorktown Heights NY 10598. (914)926-4432. E-mail: emily@emilyhanlon.com. Web site: www.awritersretreat.com. **Contact:** Emily Hanlon. Estab. 1998. Annual. Last retreat held in Costa Rica Sept. 24-Oct. 6, 2006. "In 2007, we have tentative plans to hold the retreat in Ireland." Average attendance: 20 is the limit. Women only. Retreat for all kinds of creative writing and anyone interested in creativity and spirituality. Site: (In 2006) Samasati Retreat Center was an ideal setting for a gathering of women passionate about their writing and eager to connect with others of like mind and heart. Called by one writer who has been to Samasati "as close to heaven as you can get." Samasait is situated on 250 acres of virgin tropical forest overlooking the Caribbean Sea. "Here we will open doorways to new stories, characters, techniques and a deeper creativity." The Samasati Retreat Center is in a primary and secondary rain forest that is natural habitat to hundreds of species of birds, butterflies and wildlife; at an elevation of 650 feet, the climate is delightfully cool even on hot days. The retreat includes days to explore the rain forest, walk the magnificent beaches and swim in Carribean waters. There are Yoga classes, bird watching, river and sea kayaking, scuba diving, coral reefs, horseback riding on the beach, hiking at Samasati Biological Reserve, Dolphin Connections, as well as Indian Reserves and National Parks and a Wildlife Refuge.

Costs Range from $3,150 to $4,100 depending on choice of room and payment schedule. 12 days, includes room, workshop materials, all meals, and some sightseeing adventures. See Web Site.

Additional Information Conference information free and available online. Accepts inquiries by e-mail, phone. "More than just a writing workshop or conference, the retreat is an exploration of the creative process through writing, 3-hour writing workshops daily, plus creativity workshops and time to write and explore." Please e-mail or call if you would like to be put on the Ireland mailing list.

Publishers and Their Imprints

The publishing world is constantly changing and evolving. With all of the buying, selling, reorganizing, consolidating and dissolving, it's hard to keep publishers and their imprints straight. To help you make sense of these changes, we offer this breakdown of major publishers (and their divisions)—who owns whom and which imprints are under each company umbrella. Keep in mind that this information is constantly changing. We have provided the Web sites of each of the publishers so you can continue to keep an eye on this ever-evolving business.

HARPERCOLLINS

www.harpercollins.com

HarperCollins Australia/New Zealand
Angus & Robertson
Collins
Fourth Estate
HarperCollins
Harper Perennial
HarperSports
Voyager

HarperCollins Canada
HarperCollins Publishers
HarperPerennialCanada
HarperTrophyCanada
Phyllis Bruce Books

HarperCollins Children's Books Group
Amistad
Julie Andrews Collection
Avon
Joanna Cotler books
Eos
Laura Geringer Books
Greenwillow Books
HarperCollins Children's Books
HarperFestival
HarperKidsEntertainment
HarperTempest
HarperTrophy
Rayo
Katherine Tegen Books

HarperCollins General Books Group
Amistad
Avon
Caedmon
Collins
Dark Alley
Ecco
Eos
Fourth Estate
Harper paperbacks
Harper Perennial
Harper Perennial Modern Classics
HarperAudio
HarperCollins
HarperEntertainment
HarperLargePrint
HarperSanFrancisco

HarperTorch
Morrow Cookbooks
PerfectBound
Rayo
ReganBooks
William Morrow

HarperCollins UK
Collins
General Books
- HarperFiction
  — Voyager
- Harper Entertainment
  — HarperSport
  — Tolkien and Estates
  — HarperCollins Audio

- HarperThorsons HarperElement
- HarperCollins Children's Books

Press Books
- Fourth Estate
- HarperPress
- HarperPerennial

Zondervan
Inspirio
Vida
Zonderkidz
Zondervan

HOLTZBRINCK PUBLISHERS

www.holtzbrinck.com

Farrar, Straus & Giroux
FSG
FSG Books for Young Readers
Faber & Faber, Inc.
Hill & Wang
North Point Press

Henry Holt and Co. LLC
Books for Young Readers
Metropolitan Books
Owl Books
Times Books

The MacMillan Group
MacMillan Education
Nature Publishing Group
Palgrave MacMillan
Roaring Brook Press
St. Martin's Press
Griffin Books
Let's Go

Minotaur
St. Martin's Paperbacks
St. Martin's Press
Thomas Dunne Books
Truman Tolley Books

Tom Doherty Associates
Forge
Tor Books

Pan MacMillan
Boxtree
Campbell Books
MacMillan
MacMillan Children's
Pan
Picador
Priddy Books
Sidgwick & Jackson

PENGUIN GROUP (USA), INC.

www.penguingroup.com

Penguin Adult Division
Ace Books
Alpha Books
Avery
Berkley Books
Chamberlain Bros.
Dutton

Gotham Books
HPBooks
Hudson Street Press
Jove
New American Library
Penguin
Penguin Press

Perigree
Plume
Portfolio
Putnam
Riverhead Books
Sentinel
Jeremy P. Tarcher
Viking
Fredrick Warne

Penguin Children's Division
Dial Books for Young Readers
Dutton Children's Books

Firebird
Grosset & Dunlap
Philomel
Price Stern Sloan
Puffin Books
Putnam
Razorbill
Speak
Viking Children's Books
Frederick Warne

RANDOM HOUSE, INC.

www.randomhouse.com

Ballantine Publishing Group
Ballantine Books
Ballantine Reader's Circle
Del Rey
Del Rey/Lucas Books
Fawcett
Ivy
One World
Wellspring

Bantam Dell Publishing Group
Bantam Hardcover
Bantam Mass Market
Bantam Trade Paperback
Crimeline
Delacorte Press
Dell
Delta
The Dial Press
Domain
DTP
Fanfare
Island
Spectra

Crown Publishing Group
Shaye Arehart Books
Bell Tower
Clarkson Potter
Crown Business
Crown Publishers, Inc.
Harmony Books
Prima
Three Rivers Press

Doubleday Broadway Publishing Group
Black Ink/Harlem Moon
Broadway Books
Currency
Doubleday
Doubleday Image
Doubleday Religious Publishing
Main Street Books
Morgan Road Books
Nan A. Talese

Knopf Publishing Group
Anchor Books
Alfred A. Knopf
Everyman's Library
Pantheon Books
Schocken Books
Vintage Anchor Publishing
Vintage Books

Random House Adult Trade Group
Random House Trade Group
Random House Trade Paperbacks
Strivers Row Books
The Modern Library
Villard Books

Random House Audio Publishing Group
Listening Library
Random House Audio
Random House Audio Assets
Random House Audio Dimensions

Random House Audio Roads
Random House Audio Voices
Random House Audio Price-less

Random House Children's Books

BooksReportsNow.com
GoldenBooks.com
Junie B. Jones
Kids@Random

Knopf/Delacorte/Dell Young Readers Group

Alfred A. Knopf
Bantam
Crown
David Fickling Books
Delacorte Press
Dell Dragonfly
Dell Laurel-Leaf
Dell Yearling Books
Doubleday
Wendy Lamb Books
Magic Tree House
Parents@Random

Random House Young Readers Group

Akiko
Arthur
Barbie
Beginner Books
The Berenstain Bears
Bob the Builder
Disney
Dragon Tales
First Time Books
Golden Books
Landmark Books
Little Golden Books
Lucas Books
Mercer Mayer
Nickelodeon
Nick, Jr.
pat the bunny
Picturebacks
Precious Moments
Richard Scarry
Sesame Street Books
Step Into Reading

Stepping Stones
Star Wars
Thomas the Tank Engine and Friends
Seussville
Teachers@Random
Teens@Random

Random House Information Group

Fodor's Travel Publications
House of Collectibles
Living Language
Prima Games
The Princeton Review
Random House Español
Random House Puzzles & Games
Random House Reference Publishing

Random House International

Arete
McClelland & Stewart Ltd.
Plaza & Janes
Random House Australia
Random House of Canada Ltd.
Random House of Mondadori
Random House South Africa
Random House South America
Random House United Kingdom
Transworld UK
Verlagsgruppe Random House

Random House Value Publishing

Children's Classics
Crescent
Derrydale
Gramercy
Testament
Wings

Waterbrook Press

Fisherman Bible Study Guides
Shaw Books
Waterbrook Press

Resources

SIMON & SCHUSTER

www.simonsays.com

Simon & Schuster Adult Publishing
Atria Books
The Free Press
Kaplan
Pocket Books
Scribner
Simon & Schuster
Strebor
The Touchstone & Fireside Group

Simon & Schuster Audio
Pimsleur
Simon & Schuster Audioworks
Simon & Schuster Sound Ideas

Simon & Schuster Children's Publishing
Aladdin Paperbacks
Atheneum Books for Young Readers
Libros Para Niños
Little Simon®
Little Simon Inspirations
Margaret K. McElderry Books
Simon & Schuster Books for Young Readers
Simon Pulse
Simon Spotlight®
Simon Spotlight Entertainment

Simon & Schuster International
Simon & Schuster Australia
Simon & Schuster Canada
Simon & Schuster UK

HACHETTE BOOK GROUP USA

(formerly Time Warner Book Group)

www.twbookmark.com

Warner Books
5Spot
Aspect
Back Bay Books
Mysterious Press
Springboard
Thor
Time Warner Audio Books
Warner Business Books
Warner Faith
Warner Forever
Warner Vision

Little, Brown & Company
Bulfinch Press
Little, Brown Adult Trade
Little, Brown Books for Young Readers
Megan Tingley Books

Canadian Writers Take Note

While much of the information contained in this section applies to all writers, here are some specifics of interest to Canadian writers:

Postage: When sending an SASE from Canada, you will need an International Reply Coupon ($3.50). Also be aware, a GST tax is required on postage in Canada and for mail with postage under $5 going to destinations outside the country. Since Canadian postage rates are voted on in January of each year (after we go to press), contact a Canada Post Corporation Customer Service Division (located in most cities in Canada) or visit www.canad apost.ca for the most current rates.

Copyright: For information on copyrighting your work and to obtain forms, write Canadian Intellectual Property Office, Industry Canada, Place du Portage I, 50 Victoria St., Room C-114, Gatineau, Quebec K1A 0C9 or call (819)997-1936. Web site: www.cipo.gc.ca.

The public lending right: The Public Lending Right Commission has established that eligible Canadian authors are entitled to payments when a book is available through a library. Payments are determined by a sampling of the holdings of a representative number of libraries. To find out more about the program and to learn if you are eligible, write to the Public Lending Right Commission at 350 Albert St., P.O. Box 1047, Ottawa, Ontario K1P 5V8 or call (613)566-4378 or (800)521-5721 for information. Web site: www.plr-dpp.ca/. The Commission, which is part of The Canada Council, produces a helpful pamphlet, *How the PLR System Works,* on the program.

Grants available to Canadian writers: Most province art councils or departments of culture provide grants to resident writers. Some of these, as well as contests for Canadian writers, are listed in our Contests and Awards section. For national programs, contact The Canada Council, Writing and Publishing Section, 350 Alberta St., P.O. Box 1047, Ottawa, Ontario K1P 5V8 or call (613)566-4414 or (800)263-5588 for information. Fax: (613)566-4410. Web site: www.canadacouncil.ca.

For more information: Contact The Writer's Union of Canada, 90 Richmond St. E, Suite 200, Toronto, Ontario M5C 1P1; call them at (416)703-8982 or fax them at (416)504-9090. E-mail: info@writersunion.ca. Web site: www.writersunion.ca. This organization provides a wealth of information (as well as strong support) for Canadian writers, including specialized publications on publishing contracts; contract negotiations; the author/editor relationship; author awards, competitions and grants; agents; taxes for writers, libel issues and access to archives in Canada.

Printing & Production

Terms Defined

I n most of the magazine listings in this book, you will find a brief physical description of each publication. This material usually includes the number of pages, type of paper, type of binding and whether or not the magazine uses photographs and/or illustrations.

Although it is important to look at a copy of the magazine to which you are submitting, these descriptions can give you a general idea of what the publication looks like. This material can provide you with a feel for the magazine's financial resources and prestige. Do not, however, rule out small, simply produced publications, as these may be the most receptive to new writers. Watch for publications that have increased their page count or improved their production from year to year. This is a sign the publication is doing well and may be accepting more fiction.

You will notice a wide variety of printing terms used within these descriptions. We explain here some of the more common terms used in our listing descriptions. We do not include explanations of terms such as Mohawk and Karma which are brand names and refer to the paper manufacturer.

PAPER

A5: An international paper standard; 148×210 mm or 5.8×8.3 in.

acid-free: Paper that has low or no acid content. This type of paper resists deterioration from exposure to the elements. More expensive than many other types of paper, publications done on acid-free paper can last a long time.

bond: Bond paper is often used for stationery and is more transparent than text paper. It can be made of either sulphite (wood) or cotton fiber. Some bonds have a mixture of both wood and cotton (such as "25 percent cotton" paper). This is the type of paper most often used in photocopying or as standard typing paper.

coated/uncoated stock: Coated and uncoated are terms usually used when referring to book or text paper. More opaque than bond, it is the paper most used for offset printing. As the name implies, uncoated paper has no coating. Coated paper is coated with a layer of clay, varnish or other chemicals. It comes in various sheens and surfaces depending on the type of coating, but the most common are dull, matte and gloss.

cover stock: Cover stock is heavier book or text paper used to cover a publication. It comes in a variety of colors and textures and can be coated on one or both sides.

CS1/CS2: Most often used when referring to cover stock, CS1 means paper that is coated only on one side; CS2 is paper coated on both sides.

newsprint: Inexpensive absorbent pulp wood paper often used in newspapers and tabloids.

text: Text paper is similar to book paper (a smooth paper used in offset printing), but it has been given some texture by using rollers or other methods to apply a pattern to the paper.

vellum: Vellum is a text paper that is fairly porous and soft.

Some notes about paper weight and thickness: Often you will see paper thickness described in terms of pounds such as 80 lb. or 60 lb. paper. The weight is determined by figuring how many pounds in a ream of a particular paper (a ream is 500 sheets). This can be confusing, however, because this figure is based on a standard sheet size and standard sheet sizes vary depending on the type of paper used. This information is most helpful when comparing papers of the same type. For example, 80 lb. book paper versus 60 lb. book paper. Since the size of the paper is the same it would follow that 80 lb. paper is the thicker, heavier paper.

Some paper, especially cover stock, is described by the actual thickness of the paper. This is expressed in a system of points. Typical paper thicknesses range from 8 points to 14 points thick.

PRINTING

There are many other printing methods but these are the ones most commonly referred to in our listings.

letterpress: Letterpress printing is printing that uses a raised surface such as type. The type is inked and then pressed against the paper. Unlike offset printing, only a limited number of impressions can be made, as the surface of the type can wear down.

offset: Offset is a printing method in which ink is transferred from an image-bearing plate to a "blanket" and from the blanket to the paper.

sheet-fed offset: Offset printing in which the paper is fed one piece at a time.

web offset: Offset printing in which a roll of paper is printed and then cut apart to make individual sheets.

BINDING

case binding: In case binding, signatures (groups of pages) are stitched together with thread rather than glued together. The stitched pages are then trimmed on three sides and glued into a hardcover or board "case" or cover. Most hardcover books and thicker magazines are done this way.

comb binding: A comb is a plastic spine used to hold pages together with bent tabs that are fed through punched holes in the edge of the paper.

perfect binding: Used for paperback books and heavier magazines, perfect binding involves gathering signatures (groups of pages) into a stack, trimming off the folds so the edge is flat and gluing a cover to that edge.

saddle stitched: Publications in which the pages are stitched together using metal staples. This fairly inexpensive type of binding is usually used with books or magazines that are under 80 pages.

Smythe-sewn: Binding in which the pages are sewn together with thread. Smythe is the name of the most common machine used for this purpose.

spiral binding: A wire spiral that is wound through holes punched in pages is a spiral bind. This is the binding used in spiral notebooks.

Glossary

Advance. Payment by a publisher to an author prior to the publication of a book, to be deducted from the author's future royalties.

Adventure story. A genre of fiction in which action is the key element, overshadowing characters, theme and setting. The conflict in an adventure story is often man against nature. A secondary plot that reinforces this kind of conflict is sometimes included. In Allistair MacLean's *Night Without End*, for example, the hero, while investigating a mysterious Arctic air crash, also finds himself dealing with espionage, sabotage and murder.

All rights. The rights contracted to a publisher permitting a manuscript's use anywhere and in any form, including movie and book club sales, without additional payment to the writer.

Amateur sleuth. The character in a mystery, usually the protagonist, who does the detection but is not a professional private investigator or police detective.

Anthology. A collection of selected writings by various authors.

Association of Authors' Representatives (AAR). An organization for literary agents committed to maintaining excellence in literary representation.

Auction. Publishers sometimes bid against each other for the acquisition of a manuscript that has excellent sales prospects.

Backlist. A publisher's books not published during the current season but still in print.

Biographical novel. A life story documented in history and transformed into fiction through the insight and imagination of the writer. This type of novel melds the elements of biographical research and historical truth into the framework of a novel, complete with dialogue, drama and mood. A biographical novel resembles historical fiction, save for one aspect: Characters in a historical novel may be fabricated and then placed into an authentic setting; characters in a biographical novel have actually lived.

Book producer/packager. An organization that may develop a book for a publisher based upon the publisher's idea or may plan all elements of a book, from its initial concept to writing and marketing strategies, and then sell the package to a book publisher and/or movie producer.

Cliffhanger. Fictional event in which the reader is left in suspense at the end of a chapter or episode, so that interest in the story's outcome will be sustained.

Clip. Sample, usually from a newspaper or magazine, of a writer's published work.

Cloak-and-dagger. A melodramatic, romantic type of fiction dealing with espionage and intrigue.

Commercial. Publishers whose concern is salability, profit and success with a large readership.

Contemporary. Material dealing with popular current trends, themes or topics.

Contributor's copy. Copy of an issue of a magazine or published book sent to an author whose work is included.

Copublishing. An arrangement in which the author and publisher share costs and profits.

Copyediting. Editing a manuscript for writing style, grammar, punctuation and factual accuracy.

Copyright. The legal right to exclusive publication, sale or distribution of a literary work.

Cover letter. A brief letter sent with a complete manuscript submitted to an editor.

"Cozy" (or "teacup") mystery. Mystery usually set in a small British town, in a bygone era, featuring a somewhat genteel, intellectual protagonist.

Cyberpunk. Type of science fiction, usually concerned with computer networks and human-computer combinations, involving young, sophisticated protagonists.

Electronic rights. The right to publish material electronically, either in book or short story form.

E-zine. A magazine that is published electronically.

Electronic submission. A submission of material by e-mail or on computer disk.

Ethnic fiction. Stories and novels whose central characters are black, Native American, Italian-American, Jewish, Appalachian or members of some other specific cultural group. Ethnic fiction usually deals with a protagonist caught between two conflicting ways of life: mainstream American culture and his ethnic heritage.

Experimental fiction. Fiction that is innovative in subject matter and style; avant-garde, non-formulaic, usually literary material.

Exposition. The portion of the storyline, usually the beginning, where background information about character and setting is related.

Fair use. A provision in the copyright law that says short passages from copyrighted material may be used without infringing on the owner's rights.

Fanzine. A noncommercial, small-circulation magazine usually dealing with fantasy, horror or science-fiction literature and art.

Fictional biography. The biography of a real person that goes beyond the events of a person's life by being fleshed out with imagined scenes and dialogue. The writer of fictional biographies strives to make it clear that the story is, indeed, fiction and not history.

First North American serial rights. The right to publish material in a periodical before it appears in book form, for the first time, in the United States or Canada.

Flash fiction. See short short stories.

Galleys. The first typeset version of a manuscript that has not yet been divided into pages.

Genre. A formulaic type of fiction such as romance, western or horror.

Gothic. This type of category fiction dates back to the late 18th and early 19th centuries. Contemporary gothic novels are characterized by atmospheric, historical settings and feature young, beautiful women who win the favor of handsome, brooding heroes—simultaneously dealing successfully with some life-threatening menace, either natural or supernatural. Gothics rely on mystery, peril, romantic relationships and a sense of foreboding for their strong, emotional effect on the reader. A classic early gothic novel is Emily Bronte's *Wuthering Heights*. The gothic writer builds a series of credible, emotional crises for his ultimately triumphant heroine. Sex between the woman and her lover is implied rather than graphically detailed; the writer's descriptive talents are used instead to paint rich, desolate, gloomy settings in stark mansions and awesome castles. He composes slow-paced, intricate sketches that create a sense of impending evil on every page.

Graphic novel. A book (original or adapted) that takes the form of a long comic strip or heavily illustrated story of 40 pages or more, produced in paperback. Though called a novel, these can also be works of nonfiction.

Hard science fiction. Science fiction with an emphasis on science and technology.

Hard-boiled detective novel. Mystery novel featuring a private eye or police detective as the protagonist; usually involves a murder. The emphasis is on the details of the crime and the tough, unsentimental protagonist usually takes a matter-of-fact attitude towards violence.

High fantasy. Fantasy with a medieval setting and a heavy emphasis on chivalry and the quest.

Historical fiction. A fictional story set in a recognizable period of history. As well as telling the stories of ordinary people's lives, historical fiction may involve political or social events of the time.

Horror. Howard Phillips (H.P.) Lovecraft, generally acknowledged to be the master of the horror tale in the 20th century and the most important American writer of this genre since Edgar Allan Poe, maintained that "The oldest and strongest emotion of mankind is fear, and the oldest and strongest kind of fear is fear of the unknown. These facts few psychologists will dispute, and their admitted truth must establish for all time the genuineness and dignity of the weirdly horrible tale as a literary form." Lovecraft distinguishes horror literature from fiction based entirely on physical fear and the merely gruesome. "The true weird tale has something more than secret murder, bloody bones or a sheeted form clanking chains according to rule. A certain atmosphere of breathless and unexplainable dread of outer, unknown forces must be present; there must be a hint, expressed with a seriousness and portentousness becoming its subject, of that most terrible concept of the human brain—a malign and particular suspension or defeat of the fixed laws of Nature which are our only safeguards against the assaults of chaos and the daemons of unplumbed space." It is that atmosphere—the creation of a particular sensation or emotional level—that, according to Lovecraft, is the most important element in the creation of horror literature. Contemporary writers enjoying considerable success in horror fiction include Stephen King, Robert Bloch, Peter Straub and Dean Koontz.

Hypertext fiction. A fictional form, read electronically, which incorporates traditional elements of storytelling with a nonlinear plot line, in which the reader determines the direction of the story by opting for one of many author-supplied links.

Imprint. Name applied to a publisher's specific line (e.g. Owl, an imprint of Henry Holt).

Interactive fiction. Fiction in book or computer-software format where the reader determines the path the story will take by choosing from several alternatives at the end of each chapter or episode.

International Reply Coupon (IRC). A form purchased at a post office and enclosed with a letter or manuscript to a international publisher, to cover return postage costs.

Juveniles, Writing for. This includes works intended for an audience usually between the ages of two and 18. Categories of children's books are usually divided in this way: (1) picture and storybooks (ages two to nine); (2) easy-to-read books (ages seven to nine); (3) middle-age [also called "middle grade"] children's books (ages eight to 12); (4) young adult books (ages 12 to 18).

Libel. Written or printed words that defame, malign or damagingly misrepresent a living person.

Literary fiction. The general category of fiction which employs more sophisticated technique, driven as much or more by character evolution than action in the plot.

Literary fiction vs. commercial fiction. To the writer of literary, or serious, fiction, style and technique are often as important as subject matter. Commercial fiction, however, is written with the intent of reaching as wide an audience as possible. Commercial fiction is sometimes called genre fiction because books of this type often fall into categories, such as western, gothic, romance, historical, mystery and horror.

Literary agent. A person who acts for an author in finding a publisher or arranging contract terms on a literary project.

Mainstream fiction. Fiction which appeals to a more general reading audience, versus literary or genre fiction. Mainstream is more plot-driven than literary fiction and less formulaic than genre fiction.

Malice domestic novel. A mystery featuring a murder among family members, such as the murder of a spouse or a parent.

Manuscript. The author's unpublished copy of a work, usually typewritten, used as the basis for typesetting.

Mass market paperback. Softcover book on a popular subject, usually around 4×7, directed to a general audience and sold in drugstores and groceries as well as in bookstores.

Middle reader. Juvenile fiction for readers aged 8-13, featuring heavier text than picture books and some light illustration.

Ms(s). Abbreviation for manuscript(s).

Multiple submission. Submission of more than one short story at a time to the same editor. Do not make a multiple submission unless requested.

Mystery. A form of narration in which one or more elements remain unknown or unexplained until the end of the story. The modern mystery story contains elements of the serious novel: a convincing account of a character's struggle with various physical and psychological obstacles in an effort to achieve his goal, good characterization and sound motivation.

Narration. The account of events in a story's plot as related by the speaker or the voice of the author.

Narrator. The person who tells the story, either someone involved in the action or the voice of an observer.

New Age. A term including categories such as astrology, psychic phenomena, spiritual healing, UFOs, mysticism and other aspects of the occult.

Noir. A style of mystery involving hard-boiled detectives and bleak settings.

Nom de plume. French for "pen name"; a pseudonym.

Nonfiction novel. A work in which real events and people are written [about] in novel form, but are not camouflaged, as they are in the roman à clef. In the nonfiction novel, reality is presented imaginatively; the writer imposes a novelistic structure on the actual events, keying sections of narrative around moments that are seen (in retrospect) as symbolic. In this way, he creates a coherence that the actual story might not have had. *The Executioner's Song*, by Norman Mailer, and *In Cold Blood*, by Truman Capote, are notable examples of the nonfiction novel.

Novella (also novelette). A short novel or long story, approximately 20,000-50,000 words.

#10 envelope. 4×9½ envelope, used for queries and other business letters.

Offprint. Copy of a story taken from a magazine before it is bound.

One-time rights. Permission to publish a story in periodical or book form one time only.

Outline. A summary of a book's contents, often in the form of chapter headings with a few sentences outlining the action of the story under each one; sometimes part of a book proposal.

Over the transom. A phrase referring to unsolicited manuscripts, or those that come in "over the transom."

Payment on acceptance. Payment from the magazine or publishing house as soon as the decision to print a manuscript is made.

Payment on publication. Payment from the publisher after a manuscript is printed.

Pen name. A pseudonym used to conceal a writer's real name.

Periodical. A magazine or journal published at regular intervals.

Plot. The carefully devised series of events through which the characters progress in a work of fiction.

Police procedural. A mystery featuring a police detective or officer who uses standard professional police practices to solve a crime.

Popular fiction. Generally, a synonym for category or genre fiction; i.e., fiction intended to appeal to audiences for certain kinds of novels. Popular, or category, fiction is defined as such primarily for the convenience of publishers, editors, reviewers and booksellers who must identify novels of different areas of interest for potential readers.

Print on demand (POD). Novels produced digitally one at a time, as ordered. Self-publishing through print on demand technology typically involves some fees for the author. Some authors use POD to create a manuscript in book form to send to prospective traditional publishers.

Proofreading. Close reading and correction of a manuscript's typographical errors.

Proofs. A typeset version of a manuscript used for correcting errors and making changes, often a photocopy of the galleys.

Proposal. An offer to write a specific work, usually consisting of an outline of the work and one or two completed chapters.

Protagonist. The principal or leading character in a literary work.

Psychological novel. A narrative that emphasizes the mental and emotional aspects of its characters, focusing on motivations and mental activities rather than on exterior events. The psychological novelist is less concerned about relating what happened than about exploring why it happened. The term is most often used to describe 20th-century works that employ techniques such as interior monologue and stream of consciousness. Two examples of contemporary psychological novels are Judith Guest's *Ordinary People* and Mary Gordon's *The Company of Women*.

Public domain. Material that either was never copyrighted or whose copyright term has expired.

Pulp magazine. A periodical printed on inexpensive paper, usually containing lurid, sensational stories or articles.

Query. A letter written to an editor to elicit interest in a story the writer wants to submit.

Reader. A person hired by a publisher to read unsolicited manuscripts.

Reading fee. An arbitrary amount of money charged by some agents and publishers to read a submitted manuscript.

Regency romance. A subgenre of romance, usually set in England between 1811-1820.

Remainders. Leftover copies of an out-of-print book, sold by the publisher at a reduced price.

Reporting time. The number of weeks or months it takes an editor to report back on an author's query or manuscript.

Reprint rights. Permission to print an already published work whose rights have been sold to another magazine or book publisher.

Roman à clef. French "novel with a key." A novel that represents actual living or historical characters and events in fictionalized form.

Romance novel. A type of category fiction in which the love relationship between a man and a woman pervades the plot. The story is often told from the viewpoint of the heroine, who meets a man (the hero), falls in love with him, encounters a conflict that hinders their relationship, then resolves the conflict. Romance is the overriding element in this kind of story: The couple's relationship determines the plot and tone of the book. The theme of the novel is the woman's sexual awakening. Although she may not be a virgin, she has never before been so emotionally aroused. Despite all this emotion, however, characters and plot both must be well developed and realistic. Throughout a romance novel, the reader senses the sexual and emotional attraction between the heroine and hero. Lovemaking scenes, though sometimes detailed, are not generally too graphic, because more emphasis is placed on the sensual element than on physical action.

Royalties. A percentage of the retail price paid to an author for each copy of the book that is sold.

SAE. Self-addressed envelope.

SASE. Self-addressed stamped envelope.

Science fiction [vs. fantasy]. It is generally accepted that, to be science fiction, a story must have elements of science in either the conflict or setting (usually both). Fantasy, on the other hand, rarely utilizes science, relying instead on magic, mythological and neo-mythological beings and devices and outright invention for conflict and setting.

Second serial (reprint) rights. Permission for the reprinting of a work in another periodical after its first publication in book or magazine form.

Self-publishing. In this arrangement, the author keeps all income derived from the book, but he pays for its manufacturing, production and marketing.

Sequel. A literary work that continues the narrative of a previous, related story or novel.

Serial rights. The rights given by an author to a publisher to print a piece in one or more periodicals.

Serialized novel. A book-length work of fiction published in sequential issues of a periodical.

Setting. The environment and time period during which the action of a story takes place.

Short short story. A condensed piece of fiction, usually under 1,000 words.

Simultaneous submission. The practice of sending copies of the same manuscript to several editors or publishers at the same time. Some editors refuse to consider such submissions.

Slant. A story's particular approach or style, designed to appeal to the readers of a specific magazine.

Slice of life. A presentation of characters in a seemingly mundane situation which offers the reader a flash of illumination about the characters or their situation.

Slush pile. A stack of unsolicited manuscripts in the editorial offices of a publisher.

Social fiction. Fiction written with the purpose of bringing about positive changes in society.

Soft/sociological science fiction. Science fiction with an emphasis on society and culture versus scientific accuracy.

Space opera. Epic science fiction with an emphasis on good guys versus bad guys.

Speculation (or Spec). An editor's agreement to look at an author's manuscript with no promise to purchase.

Speculative fiction (SpecFic). The all-inclusive term for science fiction, fantasy and horror.

Splatterpunk. Type of horror fiction known for its very violent and graphic content.

Subsidiary. An incorporated branch of a company or conglomerate (e.g. Alfred Knopf, Inc., a subsidiary of Random House, Inc.).

Subsidiary rights. All rights other than book publishing rights included in a book contract, such as paperback, book club and movie rights.

Subsidy publisher. A book publisher who charges the author for the cost of typesetting, printing and promoting a book. Also called a vanity publisher.

Subterficial fiction. Innovative, challenging, nonconventional fiction in which what seems to be happening is the result of things not so easily perceived.

Suspense. A genre of fiction where the plot's primary function is to build a feeling of anticipation and fear in the reader over its possible outcome.

Synopsis. A brief summary of a story, novel or play. As part of a book proposal, it is a comprehensive summary condensed in a page or page and a half.

Tabloid. Publication printed on paper about half the size of a regular newspaper page (e.g. *The National Enquirer*).

Tearsheet. Page from a magazine containing a published story.

Techno-Thriller. This genre utilizes many of the same elements as the thriller, with one major difference. In techno-thrillers, technology becomes a major character. In Tom Clancy's *The Hunt for Red October* for example, specific functions of the submarine become crucial to plot development.

Theme. The dominant or central idea in a literary work; its message, moral or main thread.

Thriller. A novel intended to arouse feelings of excitement or suspense. Works in this genre are highly sensational, usually focusing on illegal activities, international espionage, sex and violence. A thriller is often a detective story in which the forces of good are pitted against the forces of evil in a kill-or-be-killed situation.

Trade paperback. A softbound volume, usually around 5×8, published and designed for the general public, available mainly in bookstores.

Traditional fantasy. Fantasy with an emphasis on magic, using characters with the ability to practice magic, such as wizards, witches, dragons, elves and unicorns.

Unsolicited manuscript. A story or novel manuscript that an editor did not specifically ask to see.

Urban fantasy. Fantasy that takes magical characters such as elves, fairies, vampires or wizards and places them in modern-day settings, often in the inner city.

Vanity publisher. See subsidy publisher.

Viewpoint. The position or attitude of the first- or third-person narrator or multiple narrators, which determines how a story's action is seen and evaluated.

Western. Genre with a setting in the West, usually between 1860-1890, with a formula plot about cowboys or other aspects of frontier life.

Whodunit. Genre dealing with murder, suspense and the detection of criminals.

Work-for-hire. Work that another party commissions you to do, generally for a flat fee. The creator does not own the copyright and therefore cannot sell any rights.

Young adult. The general classification of books written for readers 12-18.

Zine. Often one- or two-person operations run from the home of the publisher/editor. Themes tend to be specialized, personal, experimental and often controversial.

Genre Glossary

Definitions of Fiction Subcategories

The following were provided courtesy of The Extended Novel Writing Workshop, created by the staff of Writers Online Workshops (www.writersonlineworkshops .com).

MYSTERY SUBCATEGORIES

The major mystery subcategories are listed below, each followed by a brief description and the names of representative authors, so you can sample each type of work. Note that we have loosely classified "suspense/thriller" as a mystery category. While these stories do not necessarily follow a traditional "whodunit" plot pattern, they share many elements with other mystery categories. In addition, many traditional mysteries are marketed as suspense/ thriller because of this category's current appeal in the marketplace. Since the lines between categories are frequently blurred, it seems practical to include them all here.

Classic Mystery (Whodunit). A crime (almost always a murder or series of murders) is solved. The detective is the viewpoint character; the reader never knows any more or less about the crime than the detective, and all the clues to solving the crime are available to the reader.

Amateur detective. As the name implies, the detective is not a professional detective (private or otherwise), but is almost always a professional something. This professional association routinely involves the protagonist in criminal cases (in a support capacity), gives him or her a special advantage in a specific case, or provides the contacts and skills necessary to solve a particular crime. (Jonathan Kellerman, Patricia Cornwell, Jan Burke)

Courtroom Drama. The action takes place primarily in the courtroom; the protagonist is generally a defense attorney out to prove the innocence of his or her client by finding the real culprit. (Scott Turow, Steve Martini, Richard North Patterson, John Grisham)

Cozy. A special class of the amateur detective category that frequently features a female protagonist. (Agatha Christie's Miss Marple stories are the classic example.) There is less on-stage violence than in other categories and the plot is often wrapped up in a final scene where the detective identifies the murderer and explains how the crime was solved. In contemporary stories, the protagonist can be anyone from a chronically curious housewife to a mystery-buff clergyman to a college professor, but he or she is usually quirky, even eccentric. (Susan Isaacs, Andrew Greeley, Lillian Jackson Braun)

Espionage. The international spy novel is less popular since the end of the cold war, but stories can still revolve around political intrigue in unstable regions. (John le Carré, Ken Follett)

Heists and Capers. The crime itself is the focus. Its planning and execution are seen in detail and the participants are fully-drawn characters that may even be portrayed sympathetically. One character is the obvious leader of the group (the "brains"); the other members are often brought together by the leader specifically for this job and may or may not have a previous association. In a heist, no matter how clever or daring the characters are, they are still portrayed as criminals and the expectation is that they will be caught and punished (but not always). A caper is more light hearted, even comedic. The participants may have a noble goal (something other than personal gain) and often get away with the crime. (Eric Ambler, Tony Kenrick, Leslie Hollander)

Historical. May be any category or subcategory of mystery, but with an emphasis on setting, the details of which must be diligently researched. But beyond the historical details (which must never overshadow the story), the plot develops along the lines of its contemporary counterpart. (Candace Robb, Caleb Carr, Anne Perry)

Juvenile/Young adult. Written for the 8-12 age group (Middle Grade) or the 12 and up age group (Young Adult), the crime in these stories may or may not be murder, but it is serious. The protagonist is a kid (or group of kids) in the same age range as the targeted reader. There is no graphic violence depicted, but the stories are scary and the villains are realistic. (Mary Downing Hahn, Wendy Corsi Staub, Cameron Dokey, Norma Fox Mazer)

Medical thriller. The plot can involve a legitimate medical threat (such as the outbreak of a virulent plague) or the illegal or immoral use of medical technology. In the former scenario, the protagonist is likely to be the doctor (or team) who identifies the virus and procures the antidote; in the latter he or she could be a patient (or the relative of a victim) who uncovers the plot and brings down the villain. (Robin Cook, Michael Palmer, Michael Crichton, Stanley Pottinger)

Police procedurals. The most realistic category, these stories require the most meticulous research. A police procedural may have more than one protagonist since cops rarely work alone. Conflict between partners, or between the detective and his or her superiors is a common theme. But cops are portrayed positively as a group, even though there may be a couple of bad or ineffective law enforcement characters for contrast and conflict. Jurisdictional disputes are still popular sources of conflict as well. (Lawrence Treat, Joseph Wambaugh, Ridley Pearson, Julie Smith)

Private detective. When described as "hard-boiled," this category takes a tough stance. Violence is more prominent, characters are darker, the detective—while almost always licensed by the state—operates on the fringes of the law, and there is often open resentment between the detective and law enforcement. More "enlightened" male detectives and a crop of contemporary females have brought about new trends in this category. (For female P.I.s—Sue Grafton, Sara Paretsky; for male P.I.s—John D. MacDonald, Lawrence Sanders, Robert Parker)

Suspense/Thriller. Where a classic mystery is always a whodunit, a suspense/thriller novel may deal more with the intricacies of the crime, what motivated it, and how the villain (whose identity may be revealed to the reader early on) is caught and brought to justice. Novels in this category frequently employ multiple points of view and have a broader scope than a more traditional murder mystery. The crime may not even involve murder—it may be a threat to global economy or regional ecology; it may be technology run amok or abused at the hands of an unscrupulous scientist; it may involve innocent citizens victimized for personal or corporate gain. Its perpetrators are kidnappers, stalkers, serial killers, rapists, pedophiles, computer hackers, or just about anyone with an evil intention and the means to carry it out. The protagonist may be a private detective or law enforcement official, but is just as likely to be a doctor, lawyer, military officer or other individual in a unique position to identify the villain and bring him or her to justice. (James Patterson, John J. Nance, Michael Connelly)

Technothriller. These are replacing the traditional espionage novel, and feature technology as an integral part of not just the setting, but the plot as well. (Tom Clancy, Stephen Coonts)

Woman in Jeopardy. A murder or other crime may be committed, but the focus is on the woman (and/or her children) currently at risk, her struggle to understand the nature of the danger, and her eventual victory over her tormentor. The protagonist makes up for her lack of physical prowess with intellect or special skills, and solves the problem on her own or with the help of her family (but she runs the show). Closely related to this category is the Romantic Suspense. But, while the heroine in a romantic suspense is certainly a ''woman in jeopardy,'' the mystery or suspense element is subordinate to the romance. (Mary Higgins Clark, Mary Stewart, Jessica Mann)

ROMANCE SUBCATEGORIES

These categories and subcategories of romance fiction have been culled from the *Romance Writer's Sourcebook* (Writer's Digest Books) and Phyllis Taylor Pianka's *How to Write Romances* (Writer's Digest Books). We've arranged the ''major'' categories below with the subcategories beneath them, each followed by a brief description and the names of authors who write in each category, so you can sample representative works.

Category or Series. These are published in ''lines'' by individual publishing houses (such as Harlequin and Silhouette); each line has its own requirements as to word length, story content and amount of sex. (Debbie Macomber, Nora Roberts, Glenda Sanders)

Christian. With an inspirational, Christian message centering on the spiritual dynamic of the romantic relationship and faith in God as the foundation for that relationship; sensuality is played down. (Janelle Burnham, Ann Bell, Linda Chaikin, Catherine Palmer, Dee Henderson, Lisa Tawn Bergen)

Glitz. So called because they feature (generally wealthy) characters with high-powered positions in careers that are considered to be glamorous—high finance, modeling/acting, publishing, fashion—and are set in exciting or exotic (often metropolitan) locales such as Monte Carlo, Hollywood, London or New York. (Jackie Collins, Judith Krantz)

Historical. Can cover just about any historical (or even prehistorical) period. Setting in the historical is especially significant, and details must be thoroughly researched and accurately presented. For a sampling of a variety of historical styles try Laura Kinsell (*Flowers from the Storm*), Mary Jo Putney (*The Rake and the Reformer*) and Judy Cuevas (*Bliss*). Some currently popular periods/themes in historicals are:

Gothic: historical with a strong element of suspense and a feeling of supernatural events, although these events frequently have a natural explanation. Setting plays an important role in establishing a dark, moody, suspenseful atmosphere. (Phyllis Whitney, Victoria Holt)

Historical fantasy: with traditional fantasy elements of magic and magical beings, frequently set in a medieval society. (Amanda Glass, Jayne Ann Krentz, Kathleen Morgan, Jessica Bryan, Taylor Quinn Evans, Carla Simpson, Karyn Monk)

Early American: usually Revolution to Civil War, set in New England or the South, but ''frontier'' stories set in the American West are quite popular as well. (Robin Lee Hatcher, Elizabeth Lowell, Heather Graham)

Native American: where one or both of the characters are Native Americans; the conflict between cultures is a popular theme. (Carol Finch, Elizabeth Grayson, Karen Kay, Kathleen Harrington, Genell Dellim, Candace McCarthy)

Regency: set in England during the Regency period from 1811-1820. (Carol Finch, Elizabeth Elliott, Georgette Heyer, Joan Johnston, Lynn Collum)

Multicultural. Most currently feature African-American or Hispanic couples, but editors are looking for other ethnic stories as well. Multiculturals can be contemporary or historical, and fall into any sub-category. (Rochelle Alers, Monica Jackson, Bette Ford, Sandra Kitt, Brenda Jackson)

Paranormal. Containing elements of the supernatural or science fiction/fantasy. There are numerous subcategories (many stories combine elements of more than one) including:

Time travel: One or more of the characters travels to another time—usually the past—to find love. (Jude Devereaux, Linda Lael Miller, Diana Gabaldon, Constance O'Day Flannery)

Science fiction/Futuristic: S/F elements are used for the story's setting: imaginary worlds, parallel universes, Earth in the near or distant future. (Marilyn Campbell, Jayne Ann Krentz, J.D. Robb [Nora Roberts], Anne Avery)

Contemporary fantasy: From modern ghost and vampire stories to ''New Age'' themes such as extraterrestrials and reincarnation. (Linda Lael Miller, Anne Stuart, Antoinette Stockenberg, Christine Feehan)

Romantic Comedy. Has a fairly strong comic premise and/or a comic perspective in the author's voice or the voices of the characters (especially the heroine). (Jennifer Crusie, Susan Elizabeth Phillips)

Romantic Suspense. With a mystery or psychological thriller subplot in addition to the romance plot. (Mary Stewart, Barbara Michaels, Tami Hoag, Nora Roberts, Linda Howard, Catherine Coulter)

Single title. Longer contemporaries that do not necessarily conform to the requirements of a specific romance line and therefore feature more complex plots and nontraditional characters. (Mary Ruth Myers, Nora Roberts, Kathleen Gilles Seidel, Kathleen Korbel)

Young Adult. Focus is on first love with very little, if any, sex. These can have bittersweet endings, as opposed to the traditional romance happy ending, since first loves are often lost loves. (YA historical—Nancy Covert Smith, Louise Vernon; YA contemporary—Mary Downing Hahn, Kathryn Makris)

SCIENCE FICTION SUBCATEGORIES

Peter Heck, in his article ''Doors to Other Worlds: Trends in Science Fiction and Fantasy,'' which appears in the 1996 edition of *Science Fiction and Fantasy Writer's Sourcebook* (Writer's Digest Books), identifies some science fiction trends that have distinct enough characteristics to be defined as categories. These distinctions are frequently the result of marketing decisions as much as literary ones, so understanding them is important in deciding where your novel idea belongs. We've supplied a brief description and the names of authors who write in each category. In those instances where the author writes in more than one category, we've included titles of appropriate representative works.

Hard science fiction. Based on the logical extrapolation of real science to the future. In these stories the scientific background (setting) may be as, or more, important than the characters. (Larry Niven)

Social science fiction. The focus is on how the characters react to their environments. This category includes social satire. (George Orwell's *1984* is a classic example.) (Margaret Atwood, *The Handmaid's Tale*; Ursula K. Le Guin, *The Left Hand of Darkness*; Marge Piercy, *Woman on the Edge of Time*)

Military science fiction. Stories about war that feature traditional military organization and tactics extrapolated into the future. (Jerry Pournelle, David Drake, Elizabeth Moon)

Cyberpunk. Characters in these stories are tough outsiders in a high-tech, generally near-future society where computers have produced major changes in the way that society functions. (William Gibson, Bruce Sterling, Pat Cadigan, Wilhelmina Baird)

Space opera. From the term "horse opera," describing a traditional good-guys-vs-bad-guys western, these stories put the emphasis on sweeping action and larger-than-life characters. The focus on action makes these stories especially appealing for film treatment. (The Star Wars series is one of the best examples, also Samuel R. Delany.)

Alternate history. Fantasy, sometimes with science fiction elements, that changes the accepted account of actual historical events or people to suggest an alternate view of history. (Ted Mooney, *Traffic and Laughter*; Ward Moore, *Bring the Jubilee*; Philip K. Dick, *The Man in the High Castle*)

Steampunk. A specific type of alternate history science fiction set in Victorian England in which characters have access to 20th-century technology. (William Gibson; Bruce Sterling, *The Difference Engine*)

New Age. A category of speculative fiction that deals with subjects such as astrology, psychic phenomena, spiritual healing, UFOs, mysticism and other aspects of the occult. (Walter Mosley, *Blue Light*; Neil Gaiman)

Science fantasy. Blend of traditional fantasy elements with scientific or pseudo-scientific support (genetic engineering, for example, to "explain" a traditional fantasy creature like the dragon). These stories are traditionally more character driven than hard science fiction. (Anne McCaffrey, Mercedes Lackey, Marion Zimmer Bradley)

Science fiction mystery. A cross-genre blending that can either be a more-or-less traditional science fiction story with a mystery as a key plot element, or a more-or-less traditional whodunit with science fiction elements. (Philip K. Dick, Lynn S. Hightower)

Science fiction romance. Another genre blend that may be a romance with science fiction elements (in which case it is more accurately placed as a subcategory within the romance genre) or a science fiction story with a strong romantic subplot. (Anne McCaffrey, Melanie Rawn, Kate Elliot)

Young Adult. Any subcategory of science fiction geared to a YA audience (12-18), but these are usually shorter novels with characters in the central roles who are the same age as (or slightly older than) the targeted reader. (Jane Yolen, Andre Norton)

FANTASY SUBCATEGORIES

Before we take a look at the individual fantasy categories, it should be noted that, for purposes of these supplements, we've treated fantasy as a genre distinct from science fiction. While these two are closely related, there are significant enough differences to warrant their separation for study purposes. We have included here those science fiction categories that have strong fantasy elements, or that have a significant amount of crossover (these categories appear in both the science fiction and the fantasy supplements), but "pure" science fiction categories are not included below. If you're not sure whether your novel is fantasy or science fiction, consider this definition by Orson Scott Card in *How to Write Science Fiction and Fantasy* (Writer's Digest Books):

> "Here's a good, simple, semi-accurate rule of thumb: If the story is set in a universe that follows the same rules as ours, it's science fiction. If it's set in a universe that doesn't follow our rules, it's fantasy.
>
> Or in other words, science fiction is about what could be but isn't; fantasy is about what couldn't be."

But even Card admits this rule is only "semi-accurate." He goes on to say that the real boundary between science fiction and fantasy is defined by how the impossible is achieved: "If you have people do some magic, impossible thing [like time travel] by stroking a talisman or praying to a tree, it's fantasy; if they do the same thing by pressing a button or climbing inside a machine, it's science fiction."

Peter Heck, in his article "Doors to Other Worlds: Trends in Science Fiction and Fantasy," which appears in the 1996 edition of the *Science Fiction and Fantasy Writer's Sourcebook* (Writer's Digest Books), does note some trends that have distinct enough characteristics to be defined as separate categories. These categories are frequently the result of marketing decisions as much as literary ones, so understanding them is important in deciding where your novel idea belongs. We've supplied a brief description and the names of authors who write in each category, so you can sample representative works.

Arthurian. Re-working of the legend of King Arthur and the Knights of the Round Table. (T.H. White, *The Once and Future King*; Marion Zimmer Bradley, *The Mists of Avalon*)

Contemporary (also called "urban") fantasy. Traditional fantasy elements (such as elves and magic) are incorporated into an otherwise recognizable modern setting. (Emma Bull, *War for the Oaks*; Mercedes Lackey, *The SERRAted Edge*; Terry Brooks, the Knight of the Word series)

Dark fantasy. Closely related to horror, but generally not as graphic. Characters in these stories are the "darker" fantasy types: vampires, witches, werewolves, demons, etc. (Anne Rice; Clive Barker, *Weaveworld, Imajica*; Fred Chappell)

Fantastic alternate history. Set in an alternate historical period (in which magic would not have been a common belief) where magic works, these stories frequently feature actual historical figures. (Orson Scott Card, *Alvin Maker*)

Game-related fantasy. Plots and characters are similar to high fantasy, but are based on a particular role-playing game. (Dungeons and Dragons; Magic: The Gathering; Dragonlance Chronicles; Forgotten Realms; Dark Sun)

Heroic fantasy. The fantasy equivalent to military science fiction, these are stories of war and its heroes and heroines. (Robert E. Howard, the Conan the Barbarian series; Elizabeth Moon, *Deed of Paksenarion*; Michael Moorcock, the Elric series)

High fantasy. Emphasis is on the fate of an entire race or nation, threatened by an ultimate evil. J. R. R. Tolkien's Lord of the Rings trilogy is a classic example. (Terry Brooks, David Eddings, Margaret Weis, Tracy Hickman)

Historical fantasy. The setting can be almost any era in which the belief in magic was strong; these are essentially historical novels where magic is a key element of the plot and/or setting. (Susan Schwartz, *Silk Road and Shadow*; Margaret Ball, *No Earthly Sunne*; Tim Powers, *The Anubis Gates*)

Juvenile/Young adult. Can be any type of fantasy, but geared to a juvenile (8-12) or YA audience (12-18); these are shorter novels with younger characters in central roles. (J.K. Rowling, C.S. Lewis)

Science fantasy. A blend of traditional fantasy elements with scientific or pseudo-scientific support (genetic engineering, for example, to "explain" a traditional fantasy creature like the dragon). These stories are traditionally more character driven than hard science fiction. (Anne McCaffrey, Mercedes Lackey, Marion Zimmer Bradley)

HORROR SUBCATEGORIES

Subcategories in horror are less well defined than in other genres and are frequently the result of marketing decisions as much as literary ones. But being familiar with the terms used to describe different horror styles can be important in understanding how your own novel might be best presented to an agent or editor. What follows is a brief description of the most commonly used terms, along with names of authors and, where necessary, representative works.

Dark Fantasy. Sometimes used as a euphemistic term for horror in general, but also refers to a specific type of fantasy, usually less graphic than other horror subcategories, that features more "traditional" supernatural or mythical beings (vampires, werewolves, zombies, etc.) in either contemporary or historical settings. (Contemporary: Stephen King, *Salem's Lot*; Thomas Tessier, *The Nightwalker*. Historical: Brian Stableford, *The Empire of Fear*; Chelsea Quinn Yarbro, *Werewolves of London*.)

Hauntings. "Classic" stories of ghosts, poltergeists and spiritual possessions. The level of violence portrayed varies, but many writers in this category exploit the reader's natural fear of the unknown by hinting at the horror and letting the reader's imagination supply the details. (Peter Straub, *Ghost Story*; Richard Matheson, *Hell House*)

Juvenile/Young Adult. Can be any horror style, but with a protagonist who is the same age as, or slightly older than, the targeted reader. Stories for middle grades (eight to 12 years old) are scary, with monsters and violent acts that might best be described as "gross," but stories for young adults (12-18) may be more graphic. (R.L. Stine, Christopher Pike, Carol Gorman)

Psychological horror. Features a human monster with horrific, but not necessarily supernatural, aspects. (Thomas Harris, *The Silence of the Lambs*, *Hannibal*; Dean Koontz, *Whispers*)

Splatterpunk. Very graphic depiction of violence—often gratuitous—popularized in the 1980s, especially in film. (*Friday the 13th*, *Halloween*, *Nightmare on Elm Street*, etc.)

Supernatural/Occult. Similar to the dark fantasy, but may be more graphic in its depiction of violence. Stories feature satanic worship, demonic possession, or ultimate evil incarnate in an entity or supernatural being that may or may not have its roots in traditional mythology or folklore. (Ramsey Campbell; Robert McCammon; Ira Levin, *Rosemary's Baby*; William Peter Blatty, *The Exorcist*; Stephen King, *Pet Sematary*)

Technological horror. "Monsters" in these stories are the result of science run amok or technology turned to purposes of evil. (Dean Koontz, *Watchers*; Michael Crichton, *Jurassic Park*)

Literary Agents Category Index

Agents listed in this edition of *Novel & Short Story Writer's Market* are indexed below according to the categories of fiction they represent. Use this index to find agents who handle the specific kind of fiction you write. Then turn to those listings in the alphabetical Literary Agents section for complete contact and submission information.

Action/Adventure

Erotica

Ethnic

Experimental

Family Saga

Agents Category Index

Horror

Humor/Satire

Mainstream/Contemporary

Occult

Picture Books

Plays

Poetry in Translation

Poetry

Agents Category Index

Thriller

Translation

Westerns/Frontier

Women's

Young Adult

Conference Index by Date

Our conference index organizes all conferences listed in this edition by the month in which they are held. If a conference bridges two months, you will find its name and page number under both monthly headings. If a conference occurs multiple times during the year (seasonally, for example), it will appear under each appropriate monthly heading. Turn to the listing's page number for exact dates and more detailed information.

Category Index

Our category index makes it easy for you to identify magazines and book publishers who are looking for a specific type of fiction. Publishers who are not listed under a fiction category either accept all types of fiction or have not indicated specific subject preferences. Also not appearing here are listings that need very specific types of fiction, e.g., "fiction about fly fishing only."

To use this index to find markets for your work, go to the category title that best describes the type of fiction you write and look under either Magazines or Book Publishers (depending on whom you're targeting). Finally, read individual listings *carefully* to determine the publishers best suited to your work.

For a listing of agents and the types of fiction they represent, see the Literary Agents Category Index beginning on page 558.

ADVENTURE

Magazines

Book Publishers

EROTICA
Magazines

Book Publishers

ETHNIC/MULTICULTURAL
Magazines

Book Publishers

EXPERIMENTAL

Magazines

Book Publishers

Book Publishers

FEMINIST

Magazines

Book Publishers

GAY

Magazines

HISTORICAL

Book Publishers

HORROR

Magazines

HUMOR/SATIRE

Magazines

Book Publishers

LESBIAN

Magazines

Book Publishers

LITERARY

Magazines

Book Publishers

MAINSTREAM/ CONTEMPORARY

Magazines

Book Publishers

Zahir 341

Book Publishers

Artemis Press 393
CrossTIME 406
Dan River Press 407
Diskus Publishing 409
Harbor House 420
Llewellyn Publications 432
New Concepts Publishing 440
Outrider Press, Inc. 443
Silhouette Nocturne 456
Spice 459
Triumvirate Publications 463

REGIONAL

Magazines

Advocate, PKA'S Publication 224
Anti Muse 344
Apple Valley Review 344
Arkansas Review 229
Axe Factory Review 230
Barbaric Yawp 231
Bellingham Review 232
Bibliophilos 233
Big Country Peacock Chronicle 346
Big Muddy: A Journal of the Mississippi
    River Valley 234
Black Mountain Review, The 235
Blackbird 346
Blue Mesa Review 236
Boston Review 370
Briar Cliff Review, The 237
Broken Bridge Review 238
Bryant Literary Review 238
Callaloo 239
Chaffin Journal 241
Concho River Review 244
Confrontation 245
Convergence 349
Cream City Review, The 247
Creative With Words Publications 324
Crucible 247
Dan River Anthology 325
Desert Voices 248
Downstate Story 248
Eureka Literary Magazine 250
First Line, The 326

Flint Hills Review 253
Gambara 256
Gettysburg Review, The 257
Grasslimb 259
Green Hills Literary Lantern, The 259
Gulf Coast 261
Hawai'i Pacific Review 263
Hayden's Ferry Review 263
Heartlands Today, The 263
Illya's Honey 265
Indiana Review 266
Jabberwock Review, The 268
Karamu 269
Kelsey Review 328
Left Curve 329
Louisiana Literature 273
Louisiana Review, The 273
MudRock: Stories & Tales 331
New Millennium Writings 280
New York Stories 281
North Carolina Literary Review 283
North Central Review, YOUR
    Undergraduate Literary Journal 283
Northwoods Journal 284
Ohio Teachers Write 285
Palo Alto Review 287
Passages North 289
Pikeville Review 290
Pleiades 292
Pointed Circle 293
Portland Review 294
Prairie Journal, The 294
Raven Chronicles, The 298
Riverwind 300
Roanoke Review 301
Rockford Review, The 301
Rose & Thorn Literary E-Zine, The 360
So to Speak 305
Southern California Anthology 305
Southern Humanities Review 305
Southwestern American Literature 306
storySouth 361
Straylight 309
Struggle 309
Sycamore Review 310
Talking River Review 311
Thema 312

RELIGIOUS/INSPIRATIONAL
Magazines

Book Publishers

Writer's Digest

WRITE BETTER
GET PUBLISHED

DISCOVER A WORLD OF WRITING SUCCESS!

Are you ready to be praised, published, and paid for your writing? It's time to invest in your future with *Writer's Digest!* Beginners and experienced writers alike have been relying on *Writer's Digest*, the world's leading magazine for writers, for more than 80 years — and it keeps getting better! Each issue is brimming with:

Get a FREE ISSUE of *Writer's Digest!*

- Technique articles geared toward specific genres, including fiction, nonfiction, business writing and more

- Business information specifically for writers, such as organizational advice, tax tips, and setting fees

- Tips and tricks for rekindling your creative fire

- The latest and greatest markets for print, online and e-publishing

- And much more!

Get a FREE TRIAL ISSUE of

Writer's Digest
WRITE BETTER GET PUBLISHED

Packed with creative inspiration, advice, and tips to guide you on the road to success, *Writer's Digest* offers everything you need to take your writing to the next level! You'll discover how to:

- Create dynamic characters and page-turning plots
- Submit query letters that publishers won't be able to refuse
- Find the right agent or editor
- Make it out of the slush-pile and into the hands of publishers
- Write award-winning contest entries
- And more!

See for yourself — order your FREE trial issue today!

ROMANCE

Magazines

Book Publishers

SCIENCE FICTION

Magazines

Book Publishers

SHORT STORY COLLECTIONS
Book Publishers

THRILLER/ESPIONAGE
Magazines

Book Publishers

TRANSLATIONS
Magazines

Book Publishers

WESTERN

Magazines

YOUNG ADULT/TEEN
Magazines

General Index

Markets that appeared in the 2006 edition of *Novel & Short Story Writer's Market* but are not included in this edition are identified by a two-letter code explaining why the market was omitted: **(ED)**—Editorial Decision, **(NS)**—Not Accepting Submissions, **(NR)**—No (or late) Response to Listing Request, **(OB)**—Out of Business, **(RR)**—Removed by Market's Request, **(RS)**—Restructuring, **(TS)**—Temporarily Suspended, **(UC)**—Unable to Contact, **(UF)**—Uncertain Future.

X

More great resources
from Writer's Digest Books!

Between the Lines: Master the Subtle Elements of Fiction Writing—Plot, character, scene. Any seasoned writer knows how to handle them. But what about the finer aspects of the craft that transform a novel, short story, or memoir into a timeless masterpiece? Author and writing instructor Jessica Page Morrell offers step-by-step instructions focusing on the most difficult elements of fiction, including transitions, prologues, subtext, revelations, misdirection, and balance, and presents strategies for blending these unique components seamlessly throughout a work.
ISBN-13: 978-1-58297-392-0
ISBN-10: 1-58297-392-X, paperback, 304 pages, $14.99, #11016

Rules of Thumb: 73 Authors Reveal Their Fiction Writing Fixations—Whether it's the simplest of prohibitions (don't use too many adjectives) or a cherished writing maxim (show, don't tell), all writers have a rule of thumb that guides their work. In this book, contemporary fiction writers share their favorites. Insight and revelations from a range of writers, including John Barth, Rick Moody, Melanie Rae Thon, Bret Lott, Thisbe Nissen, and more, are packed into 73 original essays detailing the one secret each writer swears by.
ISBN-13: 978-1-58297-391-3
ISBN-10: 1-58297-391-1, hardcover, 256 pages, $19.95, #11015

The Writer's Little Helper: Everything You Need to Know to Write Better and Get Published—This book gives you everything you need to create great characters, maintain a compelling pace, craft believable dialogue, attract the attention of agents and editors, and much more. With big ideas, time-saving tips and revision-made-easy charts, author James V. Smith, Jr. offers effective guidance with short checklists, Q&As and practical tools. Plus, the unique format allows you to read from start to finish or to focus only on the areas in which your fiction needs work.
ISBN-13: 978-1-58297-422-4
ISBN-10: 1-58297-422-5, hardcover, 256 pages, $19.99, #11038

Take Joy: A Writer's Guide to Loving the Craft—Author Jane Yolen combats the perception that writing is a strenuous, solitary craft in this sweet, insightful book. She reveals the silver lining of the writing life through 15 easy-to-digest essays on plot, beginnings and endings, voice, point of view, writing poetry, and more. This optimistic guide urges writers to re-experience the joy of doing what matters most to them.
ISBN-13: 978-1-58297-385-2
ISBN-10: 1-58297-385-7, paperback, 208 pages, $14.99, #11008

**These and other fine Writer's Digest Books are available
at your local bookstore or online supplier.**